INTERNATIONAL MILITARY AND DEFENSE ENCYCLOPEDIA

INTERNATIONAL MILITARY AND DEFENSE ENCYCLOPEDIA

Volume 4

M–O

Editor-in-Chief
Col. Trevor N. Dupuy, USA (Ret.)

Executive Editor
Col. Franklin D. Margiotta, USAF (Ret.), Ph.D.

Managing Editors
Mr. Curt Johnson
Col. James B. Motley, USA (Ret.), Ph.D.

Associate Managing Editor
Mr. David L. Bongard

Brassey's (US), Inc.
A Division of Maxwell Macmillan, Inc.
Washington · New York

Brassey's (US), Inc.

Editorial Offices
Brassey's (US), Inc.
8000 Westpark Drive
First Floor
McLean, Virginia 22102

Order Department
Brassey's Book Orders
% Macmillan Publishing Co.
100 Front Street, Box 500
Riverside, New Jersey 08075

LIBRARY OF CONGRESS CATALOGING-IN-PUBLICATION DATA

International military and defense encyclopedia / editor-in-chief,
Trevor N. Dupuy . . . [et al.].
p. cm.
Includes index.
ISBN 0-02-881011-2 (set)
1. Military art and science—Encyclopedias. I. Dupuy, Trevor Nevitt, 1916–
U24.I58 1993
355'.003—dc20

92-33750
CIP

ISBN 0-02-881064-3 (vol. 4)

10 9 8 7 6 5 4 3 2 1

PRINTED IN THE UNITED STATES OF AMERICA

INTERNATIONAL HONORARY ADVISORY BOARD

EDITORIAL BOARD AND SUBJECT EDITORS

ASSOCIATE EDITORS

CONTENTS

ABBREVIATIONS AND ACRONYMS

AA antiaircraft
AAA antiaircraft artillery
AASR advanced airborne surveillance radar
AAM air-to-air missile
AAW antiair warfare
AB airborne
ABD airborne division (Sov)
ABM antiballistic missile(s)
about the total could be higher
ac aircraft
ACDA Arms Control and Disarmament Agency
ACE Allied Command, Europe
ACM advanced cruise missile
ACV air cushion vehicle/vessel
AD air defense
adj adjusted
AE auxiliary(ies), ammunition carrier
AEF auxiliary(ies), explosives and stores
AEW airborne early warning
AF stores ship(s) with RAS capability
AFB air force base
AFV armored fighting vehicle
AFR Air Force Reserve (US)
AGHS hydrographic survey vessel(s)
AGI intelligence collection vessel(s)
AGM air-to-ground missile
AGOR oceanographic research vessel(s)
AGOS ocean surveillance vessel(s)
AH hospital ship(s)
AI artificial intelligence
AIFV armored infantry fighting vehicle
AIP air-independent propulsion
AK cargo ship(s)
ALCM air-launched cruise missile(s)
amph amphibious/amphibian(s)
AMRAAM advanced medium-range air-to-air missile
ANG Air National Guard (US)
AO tanker(s) with RAS capability; area of operations
AOE auxiliary(ies), fuel and ammunition, RAS capability
AOT tanker(s) without RAS capability
AP passenger ship(s); armor piercing
APC armored personnel carrier(s)
APDS armor piercing, discarding sabot missile
API armor piercing, incendiary
APO army post office
AR Army Reserve (US)
AR repair ship(s)
Arg Argentina
ARM antiradiation (antiradar) missile
armd armored
ARNG Army National Guard (US)
arty artillery
AS submarine depot-ship(s)
ASAT antisatellite weapon
aslt assault
ASM air-to-surface missile(s)
ASRAAM advanced short-range air-to-air missile
ASROC antisubmarine rocket
ASTT antisubmarine TT
ASUW antisurface-unit warfare
ASW antisubmarine warfare
AT tug(s)
ATBM antitactical ballistic missile
ATF advanced tactical fighter
ATGW antitank guided weapon(s)
ATK antitank
ATTU Atlantic to the Urals
Aust Australia
avn aviation
AVT aviation training ship
AWACS airborne warning and control system
BA Budget Authority
BB battleship
bbr bomber(s)
bde brigade(s)
bdgt budget(s)
Be Belgium
BMD ballistic missile defense
BMEWS ballistic missile early warning system
bn battalion(s)/billion(s)
BSAG battleship surface attack group
bty battery(ies)
Bu Bulgaria
BVR beyond visual range
CAD computer-aided design
CAP combat air patrol; civil air patrol
CAS close air support
Cat Category
cav cavalry
cbt combat

CBW chemical and biological warfare
CC cruiser(s)
CCM counter-countermeasures
Cdn Canada
CCP Chinese Communist Party
CD civil defense
cdo commando
CEP circular error probable
CG SAM cruiser(s)
CGF Central Group of Forces (Sov)
CGH CG with helicopters
CGN nuclear-fueled CG
cgo freight aircraft
Ch China (PRC)
C^3I command, control, communications, and intelligence
CINC commander in chief
CLOS command line-of-sight
COIN counterinsurgency
comb combined/combination
comd command
COMINT communications intelligence
comms communications
CONUS Continental United States
coy company(ies)
CP command post
CPSU Communist Party of the Soviet Union
CV aircraft carrier(s)
CVBG carrier battle group
CVN nuclear-fueled CV
CVV V/STOL and hel CV
CW chemical warfare
CY current year
Cz Czechoslovakia
DD destroyer(s)
D Day day operation begins
DDG destroyer(s) with area SAM; destroyer(s) with hel
def defense
defn definition
det detachment(s)
DEW directed-energy weapon; distant early warning
div division(s)
Dk Denmark
ECM electronic countermeasures
ECR Electronic combat and reconnaissance
ELINT electronic intelligence
elm element(s)
EMP electromagnetic pulse
engr engineer(s)
EOD explosive ordnance disposal
eqpt equipment
ESM electronic support measures
est estimate(d)
EW electronic warfare
excl excludes/excluding
exp expenditure
FAC forward air control
FAE fuel-air explosive
fd field
FEBA forward edge of the battle area
FF frigate(s)
FFG frigate(s) with area SAM
FGA fighter(s), ground-attack
FH frigate(s) with helicopter
FLIR forward-looking infrared radar
flt flight(s)
FMA foreign military assistance
Fr France
ftr fighter(s) (aircraft)
FW fixed-wing
FY fiscal year
GA Chinese Integrated Group Army
GB Sarin (chemical agent)
GBU guided bomb unit
GCI ground control intercept
GD Soman (chemical agent)
GDP gross domestic product
Ge Germany
GLCM ground-launched cruise missile
GNP gross national product
gp group(s)
GP general purpose
GPS global positioning system
Gr Greece
GW guided weapon(s)
hel helicopter(s)
HARM high-speed antiradiation missile
HQ headquarters
Hu Hungary
HWT heavy-weight torpedo(es)
hy heavy
ICBM intercontinental ballistic missile(s)
IFF identification friend or foe
IFS International Financial Statistics
IG inspector general
IMF International Monetary Fund
imp improved
incl includes/including
indep independent
Indon Indonesia
inf infantry
INF intermediate-range nuclear forces
IR infrared
IRBM intermediate-range ballistic missile(s)
Is Israel
It Italy
k kilobyte
KE kinetic energy
kg kilogram(s)
kHz kilohertz

km	kilometer(s)
KT	kiloton(s)
LAMPS	Light airborne multipurpose system
LAW	light antitank weapon
LCA	landing craft, assault
LCAC	landing craft, air cushion
LCM	landing craft, mechanized
LCT	landing craft, tank
LCU	landing craft, utility
LCVP	landing craft, vehicles and personnel
LHA	landing ship(s), assault
LHX	light helicopter, experimental
LKA	assault cargo ship(s)
log	logistic
LORAN	long-range air navigation system
LPD	landing platform(s), dock
LPH	landing platform(s), helicopter
LSD	landing ship(s), dock
LSM	landing ship(s), medium
LST	landing ship(s), tank
lt	light
LWT	light-weight torpedo(es)
m	million(s)
MAC	Military Airlift Command (US)
MAAG	military assistance and advisory group
MAD	mutual assured destruction; magnetic anomaly detection
maint	maintenance
MBT	main battle tank(s)
MC&G	mapping, charting, and geodesy
MCC/I/O	mine countermeasures vessel(s), coastal/inshore, offshore
MCMV	mine countermeasures vessel(s)
MCR	Marine Corps Reserve (US)
MD	Military District(s)
M Day	mobilization day
mech	mechanized
med	medium
medevac	casualty transport/air ambulance
MEF/B/U	Marine Expeditionary Force(s)/Brigade(s)/Unit(s) (US)
MFO	Multinational Force and Observers
MG	machine gun
MHC/I/O	minehunter(s), coastal/inshore/offshore
MHz	megahertz
MICV	mechanized infantry combat vehicle(s)
mil	military
MINURSO	UN Mission for the Referendum in Western Sahara
MIRV	multiple independently targetable re-entry vehicle(s)
misc	miscellaneous
Mk	mark (model number)
ML	minelayer
MLRS	multiple-launch rocket system
MMW	millimeter-wave radar
mob	mobilization
mod	modified/modification
mor	mortar(s)
mot	motorized
MPS	marine pre-positioning squadron(s)
MR	maritime reconnaissance/motor rifle
MRASM	medium-range air-to-surface missile(s)
MRBM	medium-range ballistic missile(s)
PSC	principal surface combatants
psi	pounds per square inch
PSYOPS	psychological operations
R&D	research and development
RAS	replenishment at sea
RCL	recoilless launcher(s)
RCS	radar cross-section
RDF	rapid deployment force
recce	reconnaissance
regt	regiment(s)
RF	radio frequency
RL	rocket launchers
Ro	Romania
ROM	read-only memory
ro-ro	roll-on, roll-off
RPG	rocket-propelled grenade
RPV	remotely piloted vehicle(s)
RV	re-entry vehicle(s)
SAC	Strategic Air Command (US)
SACEUR	Supreme Allied Commander, Europe
SACLANT	Supreme Allied Commander, Atlantic
SAH	semi-active homing
SALT	Strategic Arms Limitation Treaty
SAM	surface-to-air missile(s)
SAR	search and rescue; synthetic aperture radar
SDI	Strategic Defense Initiative
SES	surface-effect ship(s)
SF	Special Forces
SGF	Southern Group of Forces (Sov)
SHAPE	Supreme Headquarters Allied Powers, Europe
SIGINT	signals intelligence
sigs	signals
SLAR	side-looking airborne radar
SLBM	sea- or submarine-launched ballistic missile(s)
SLCM	sea- or submarine-launched cruise missile(s)
SLEP	service life extension program
SLOC	sea line of communication
some	up to
SOP	standard operating procedure
Sov	Soviet
Sp	Spain
SP	self-propelled
spt	support
SQ	superquick fuze

sqn	squadron
SRAM	short-range attack missile(s)
SRBM	short-range ballistic missile(s)
SS(C/I)	submarine(s) (coastal/inshore)
SSB	ballistic-missile submarine(s)
SSBN	nuclear-fueled SSB
SSGN	SSN with dedicated nonballistic missile launchers
SSM	surface-to-surface missile(s)
SSN	nuclear-fueled submarine(s)
START	Strategic Arms Reduction Talks
STOL	short take-off and landing
STOVL	short takeoff, vertical landing
SUGW	surface-to-underwater GW
Sw	Sweden
Switz	Switzerland
sy	security
t	tons
TA	Territorial Army (UK)
tac	tactical
TAC	Tactical Air Command (US)
TADS	target acquisition and designation system
TASM	tactical air-to-surface missile
TD	tank division
T&E	test and evaluation
TERCOM	terrain contour-matching guidance
tk	tank(s)
tkr	tanker(s)
TLE	treaty-limited equipment
TOE	table of organization and equipment
TOW	tube-launched, optically tracked, wire-guided antitank missile
tps	troop(s)
tpt	transport(s)
trg	training
TT	torpedo tube(s)
Tu	Turkey
UHF	ultra high frequency
UN	United Nations
UNAVEM	UN Angolan Verification Mission
UNDOF	UN Disengagement Observer Force
UNFICYP	UN Force in Cyprus
UNIFIL	UN Interim Force in Lebanon
UNIKOM	UN Iraq/Kuwait Observer Mission
UNMOGIP	UN Military Observer Group in India and Pakistan
UNTSO	UN Truce Supervisory Organization
URG	underway replenishment group(s)
USGW	underwater-to-surface GW
USMC	US Marine Corps
UUGW	underwater-to-underwater GW
UV	ultraviolet
veh	vehicle(s)
VERTREP	vertical replenishment
VHF	very high frequency
VIP	very important person(s)
VLS	vertical launch system(s)
V(/S)TOL	vertical(/short) takeoff and landing
WGF	Western Group of Force (Sov)
WP	Warsaw Pact
wpn	weapon
Yug	Yugoslavia

Designations of Aircraft and Helicopters listed in Country Articles

Type	Name/designation	Origin	Maker
AIRCRAFT			
A-3	Skywarrior	U.S.	Douglas
A-4	Skyhawk	U.S.	MD
A-5	Fantan	China	Nanchang
A-6	Intruder	U.S.	Grumman
A-7	Corsair II	U.S.	LTV
A-10	Thunderbolt	U.S.	Fairchild
A-36	Halcón (C-101)		
A-37	Dragonfly	U.S.	Cessna
AC-130	(C-130)		
AC-47	(C-47)		
Airtourer		NZ	Victa
AJ-37	(J-37)		
Ajeet	(Folland Gnat)	India/U.K.	HAL
Alizé		France	Breguet
AlphaJet		France/Ge	Dassault/ Breguet/ Dornier
AM-3	Bosbok (C-4M)	Italy	Aermacchi
An-2	"Colt"	USSR	Antonov
An-12	"Cub"	USSR	Antonov
An-14	"Clod"	USSR	Antonov
An-22	"Cock"	USSR	Antonov
An-24	"Coke"	USSR	Antonov
An-26	"Curl"	USSR	Antonov
An-30	"Clank"	USSR	Antonov
An-32	"Cline"	USSR	Antonov
An-124	"Condor" (Ruslan)	USSR	Antonov
Andover	[HS-748]		
Atlantic	(Atlantique)	France	Dassault/ Breguet
AS-202	Bravo	Switz	FFA
AT-3		Taiwan	AIDC
AT-6	(T-6)		
AT-11		U.S.	Beech
AT-26	EMB-326		
AT-33	(T-33)		
AU-23	Peacemaker [PC-6B)	U.S.	Fairchild
AV-8	Harrier II	U.S./U.K.	MD/BAe
Aztec	PA-23	U.S.	Piper
B-1		U.S.	Rockwell
B-52	Stratofortress	U.S.	Boeing
BAC-111		U.K.	BAe
BAC-167	Strikemaster	U.K.	BAe

Type	Name/designation	Origin	Maker
BAe-146		U.K.	BAe
BAe-748	(HS-748)		
Baron	(T-42)		
Be-6	"Madge"	USSR	Beriev
Be-12	"Mail' (Tchaika)	USSR	Beriev
Beech 50	Twin Bonanza	U.S.	Beech
Beech 95	Travel Air	U.S.	Beech
BN-2	Islander, Defender, Trislander	U.K.	Britten-Norman
Boeing 707		U.S.	Boeing
Boeing 727		U.S.	Boeing
Boeing 737		U.S.	Boeing
Boeing 747		U.S.	Boeing
Bonanza		U.S.	Beech
Bronco	(OV-10)		
Buccaneer		U.K.	BAe
Bulldog		U.K.	BAe
C-1		Japan	Kawasaki
C-2	Greyhound	U.S.	Grumman
C-4M	Kudu (AM-3)	S. Africa	Atlas
C-5	Galaxy	U.S.	Lockheed
C-7	DHC-7		
C-9	Nightingale (DC-9)		
C-12	Super King Air (Huron)	U.S.	Beech
C-18	[Boeing 707]		
C-20	(Gulfstream III)		
C-21	(Learjet)		
C-22	(Boeing 727)		
C-23	(Sherpa)	U.K.	Short
C-42	(Neiva Regente)	Brazil	Embraer
C-45	Expeditor	U.S.	Beech
C-46	Commando	U.S.	Curtis
C-47	DC-3 (Dakota) (C-117 Skytrain)	U.S.	Douglas
C-54	Skymaster (DC-4)	U.S.	Douglas
C-91	HS-748		
C-93	HS-125		
C-95	EMB-110		
C-97	EMB-121		
C-101	Aviojet	Spain	CASA
C-115	DHC-5	Canada	De Havilland
C-117	(C-47)		
C-118	Liftmaster (DC-6)		
C-119	Packet	U.S.	Fairchild
C-123	Provider	U.S.	Fairchild
C-127	(Do-27)	Spain	CASA
C-130	Hercules (L-100)	U.S.	Lockheed
C-131	Convair 440	U.S.	Convair
C-135	[Boeing 707]		
C-137	[Boeing 707]		
C-140	(Jetstar)	U.S.	Lockheed
C-141	Starlifter	U.S.	Douglas
C-160		Fr/Ge	Transall
C-212	Aviocar	Spain	CASA
C-235		Spain	CASA
CA-25	Winjeel	Aust	Commonwealth
Canberra	(B-57)	U.K.	BAe

Type	Name/designation	Origin	Maker
CAP-10		France	Mudry
CAP-20		France	Mudry
CAP-230		France	Mudry
Caravelle	SE-210	France	Aérospatiale
CC-109	(Convair 440)	U.S.	Convair
CC-115	DHC-15		
CC-117	(Falcon 20)		
CC-132	(DHC-7)		
CC-137	(Boeing 707)		
CC-138	(DHC-6)		
CC-144	CL-600/-601	Canada	Canadair
CC-18	F/A-18		
CF-116	F-5		
Cheetah	[Mirage III]	S. Africa	Atlas
Cherokee	PA-28	U.S.	Piper
Cheyenne	PA-31T [Navajo]	U.S.	Piper
Chieftain	PA-31-350 [Navajo]	U.S.	Piper
Chipmunk	DHC-1		
Citabria		U.S.	Champion
Citation	(T-47)	U.S.	Cessna
CJ-5	[Yak-18]	China	
CL-215		Canada	Canadair
CL-44		Canada	Canadair
CL-601	Challenger	Canada	Canadair
CM-170	Magister [Tzukit]	France	Aérospatiale
CM-175	Zéphyr	France	Aérospatiale
CN-235		Sp/Indon	CASA/IPTN
Cochise	T-42		
Comanche	PA-24	U.S.	Piper
Commander	Aero-/Turbo-Commander	U.S.	Rockwell
Commodore	MS-893	France	Aérospatiale
Corvette	SN-601	France	Aérospatiale
CP-3	P-3 Orion		
CP-121	S-2		
CP-140	Aurora (P-3 Orion)	U.S.	Lockheed
CT-4	Airtrainer	NZ	Victa
CT-39	Sabreliner	U.S.	Rockwell
CT-114	CL-41 Tutor	Canada	Canadair
CT-133	Silver Star [T-33]	Canada	Canadair
CT-134	Musketeer		
Dagger	(Nesher)		
Dakota		U.S.	Piper
Dakota	(C-47)		
DC-3	(C-47)	U.S.	Douglas
DC-4	(C-54)	U.S.	Douglas
DC-6	(C-118)	U.S.	Douglas
DC-7		U.S.	Douglas
DC-8		U.S.	Douglas
DC-9		U.S.	MD
Deepak	(HT-32)		
Defender	BN-2		
DH-100	Vampire	U.K.	De Havilland
DHC-1	Chipmunk	Canada	DHC
DHC-2	Beaver	Canada	DHC
DHC-3	Otter	Canada	DHC
DHC-4	Caribou	Canada	DHC
DHC-5	Buffalo	Canada	DHC
DHC-6	Twin Otter	Canada	DHC
DHC-7	Dash-7 (Ranger, CC-132)	Canada	DHC
DHC-8		Canada	DHC

TYPE	NAME/DESIGNATION	ORIGIN	MAKER
Dimona	H-36	Ge	Hoffman
Do-27	(C-127)	Ge	Dornier
Do-28	Skyservant	Ge	Dornier
Do-128		Ge	Dornier
Do-228		Ge	Dornier
E-2	Hawkeye	U.S.	Grumman
E-3	Sentry	U.S.	Boeing
E-4	[Boeing 747]	U.S.	Boeing
E-6	[Boeing 707]		
EA-3	[A-3]		
EA-6	Prowler [A-6]		
Electra	(L-188)		
EC-130	[C-130]		
EC-135	[Boeing 707]		
EMB-110	Bandeirante	Brazil	Embraer
EMB-111	Maritime Bandeirante	Brazil	Embraer
EMB-120	Brasilia	Brazil	Embraer
EMB-121	Xingu	Brazil	Embraer
EMB-312	Tucano	Brazil	Embraer
EMB-326	Xavante (MB-326)	Brazil	Embraer
EMB-810	[Seneca]	Brazil	Embraer
EP-3	(P-3 Orion)		
Etendard		France	Dassault
EV-1	(OV-1)		
F-1	[T-2]	Japan	Mitsubishi
F-4	Phantom	U.S.	MD
F-5	-A/-B: Freedom Fighter; -E/-F: Tiger II	U.S.	Northrop
F-6	J-6		
F-7	J-7		
F-8	J-8		
F-8	Crusader	U.S.	Republic
F-14	Tomcat	U.S.	Grumman
F-15	Eagle	U.S.	MD
F-16	Fighting Falcon	U.S.	GD
F-18	[F/A-18]		
F-21	Kfir	Israel	IAI
F-27	Friendship	Nl	Fokker
F-28	Fellowship	Nl	Fokker
F-35	Draken	Sweden	SAAB
F-84	Thunderstreak	U.S.	Lockheed
F-86	Sabre	U.S.	N. American
F-100	Super Sabre	U.S.	N. American
F-104	Starfighter	U.S.	Lockheed
F-106	Delta Dart	U.S.	Convair
F-111		U.S.	GD
F-172	(Cessna 172)	France/ U.S.	Reims-Cessna
F/A-18	Hornet	U.S.	MD
Falcon	Mystère-Falcon		
FB-111	(F-111)		
FH-227	(F-27)	U.S.	Fairchild/ Hiller
Flamingo	MBB-233	Ge	MBB
FT-5	JJ-5	China	CAC
FT-6	JJ-6		
FTB-337	[Cessna 337]		
G-91		Italy	Aeritalia
G-222		Italy	Aeritalia
Galaxy	C-5		

TYPE	NAME/DESIGNATION	ORIGIN	MAKER
Galeb		Yug	SOKO
Gardian	(Falcon 20)		
Genet	SF-260W		
GU-25	(Falcon 20)		
Guerrier	R-235		
Gulstream		U.S.	Gulfstream Aviation
Gumhuria	(Bücker 181)	Egypt	Heliopolis Ac
H-5	[Il-28]	China	Harbin
H-6	[Tu-16]	China	Xian
H-36	Dimona		
Halcón	[C-101]		
Harrier	(AV-8)	U.K.	BAe
Harvard	(T-6)		
Hawk		U.K.	BAe
HC-130	(C-130)		
HF-24	Marut	India	HAL
HFB-320	Hansajet	Ge	Hamburger FB
HJ-5	(H-5)		
HJT-16	Kiran	India	HAL
HPT-32	Deepak	India	HAL
HS-125	(Dominie)	U.K.	BAe
HS-748	[Andover]	U.K.	BAe
HT-2		India	HAL
HU-16	Albatross	U.S.	Grumman
HU-25	(Falcon 20)		
Hunter		U.K.	BAe
HZ-5	(H-5)		
IA-35	Huanquero	Arg	FMA
IA-50	Guaraní	Arg	FMA
IA-58	Pucará	Arg	FMA
IA-63	Pampa	Arg	FMA
IAI-201/-202	Arava	Israel	IAI
IAI-1124	Westwind, Seascan	Israel	IAI
IAR-28		Ro	IAR
IAR-93	Orao	Yug/Ro	SOKO/ IAR
Il-14	"Crate"	USSR	Ilyushin
Il-18	"Coot"	USSR	Ilyushin
Il-20	(Il-18)		
Il-28	"Beagle"	USSR	Ilyushin
Il-38	"May"	USSR	Ilyushin
Il-62	"Classic"	USSR	Ilyushin
Il-76	"Candid" (tpt) "Mainstay" (AEW) "Midas" (tkr)	USSR	Ilyushin
Impala	[MB-326]	S. Africa	Atlas
Islander	BN-2		
J-2	[MiG-15]	China	
J-5	[MiG-17F]	China	Shenyang
J-6	[MiG-19]	China	Shenyang
J-7	[MiG-21]	China	Xian
J-8	[Sov Ye-142]	China	Shenyang
J-32	Lansen	Sweden	SAAB
J-35	Draken	Sweden	SAAB
J-37	Viggen	Sweden	SAAB
JA-37	(J-37)		
Jaguar		Fr/U.K.	SEPECAT
JAS-39	Gripen	Sweden	SAAB
Jastreb		Yug	SOKO
Jet Provost		U.K.	BAe

Type	Name/designation	Origin	Maker
Jetstream		U.K.	BAe
JJ-6	(J-6)		
JZ-6	(J-6)		
KA-3	[A-3]		
KA-6	[A-6]		
KC-10	Extender [DC-10]	U.S.	MD
KC-130	[C-130]		
KC-135	[Boeing 707]		
KE-3	[E-3]		
Kfir		Israel	IAI
King Air		U.S.	Beech
Kiran	HJT-16		
Kraguj		Yug	SOKO
Kudu	C-4M		
LIM-6	[MiG-17]	Poland	
L-4	Cub		
L-18	Super Cub	U.S.	Piper
L-19	O-1		
L-21	Super Cub	U.S.	Piper
L-29	Delfin	Cz	Aero
L-39	Albatros	Cz	Aero
L-70	Vinka	Finland	Valmet
L-100	C-130 (civil version)		
L-188	Electra (P-3 Orion)	U.S.	Lockheed
L-410	Turbolet	Cz	LET
L-1011	Tristar	U.S.	Lockheed
Learjet	(C-21)	U.S.	Gates
Li-2	[DC-3]	USSR	Lisunov
LR-1	(MU-2)		
Magister	CM-170		
Marut	HF-24		
Mashshaq	MFI-17	Pakistan/ Sweden	PAC/ SAAB
Matador	(AV-8)		
MB-326		Italy	Aermacchi
MB-339	(Veltro)	Italy	Aermacchi
MBB-233	Flamingo		
MC-130	(C-130)		
Mercurius	(HS-125)		
Merlin		U.S.	Fairchild
Mescalero	T-41		
Metro		U.S.	Fairchild
MFI-15	Safari	Sweden	SAAB
MFI-17	Supporter (T-17)	Sweden	SAAB
MH-1521	Broussard	France	Max Holste
MiG-15	"Midget" trg	USSR	MiG
MiG-17	"Fresco"	USSR	MiG
MiG-19	"Farmer"	USSR	MiG
MiG-21	"Fishbed"	USSR	MiG
MiG-23	"Flogger"	USSR	MiG
MiG-25	"Foxbat"	USSR	MiG
MiG-27	"Flogger D"	USSR	MiG
MiG-29	"Fulcrum"	USSR	MiG
MiG-31	"Foxhound"	USSR	MiG
Mirage		France	Dassault
Mission-master	N-22		
Mohawk	OV-1		
MS-760	Paris	France	Aérospatiale
MS-893	Commodore		
MU-2		Japan	Mitsubishi
Musketeer	Beech 24	U.S.	Beech
Mya-4	"Bison"	USSR	Myasishchev

Type	Name/designation	Origin	Maker
Mystère-Falcon		France	Dassault
N-22	Floatmaster, Missionmaster	Aust	GAF
N-24	Searchmaster B/L	Aust	GAF
N-262	Frégate	France	Aérospatiale
N-2501	Noratlas	France	Aérospatiale
Navajo	PA-31	U.S.	Piper
NC-212	C-212	Sp/Indon	CASA/ Nurtanio
NC-235	C-235	Sp/Indon	CASA/ Nurtanio
Nesher	[Mirage III]	Israel	IAI
NF-5	(F-5)		
Nightingale	(DC-9)		
Nimrod		U.K.	BAe
O-1	Bird Dog	U.S.	Cessna
O-2	(Cessna 337, Skymaster)	U.S.	Cessna
OA-4	(A-4)		
OA-37	Dragonfly		
Orao	IAR-93		
Ouragan		France	Dassault
OV-1	Mohawk	U.S.	Rockwell
OV-10	Bronco	U.S.	Rockwell
P-2J	[SP-2]	Japan	Kawasaki
P-3		Switz	Pilatus
P-3	Orion	U.S.	Lockheed
P-95	EMB-110		
P-149		Italy	Piaggio
P-166		Italy	Piaggio
PA-18	Super Cub	U.S.	Piper
PA-23	Aztec		
PA-24	Comanche	U.S.	Piper
PA-28	Cherokee	U.S.	Piper
PA-31	Navajo	U.S.	Piper
PA-34	Seneca	U.S.	Piper
PA-44	Seminole	U.S.	Piper
PBY-5	Catalina	U.S.	Consolidated
PC-6	Porter	Switz	Pilatus
PC-6A/B	Turbo Porter	Switz	Pilatus
PC-7	Turbo Trainer	Switz	Pilatus
PC-9		Switz	Pilatus
PD-808		Italy	Piaggio
Pembroke		U.K.	BAe
Pillán	T-35		
PL-1	Chien Shou	Taiwan	AIDC
Porter	PC-6		
PZL-104	Wilga	Poland	PZL
PZL-130	Orlik	Poland	PZL
Q-5	"Fantan" [MiG-19]	China	Nanchang
Queen Air	(U-8)		
R-160		France	Socata
R-235	Guerrier	France	Socata
RC-21	(C-21)		
RC-47	(C-47)		
RC-95	(EMB-110)		
RC-135	[Boeing 707]		
RF-4	(F-4)		
RF-5	(F-5)		
RF-35	(F-35)		
RF-84	(F-84)		
RF-104	(F-104)		
RF-172	(Cessna 172)	France	Reims-Cessna

Type	Name/designation	Origin	Maker
RT-26	(EMB-326)		
RT-33	(T-33)		
RU-21	(King Air)		
RV-1	(OV-1)		
S-2	Tracker	U.S.	Grumman
S-3	Viking	U.S.	Lockheed
S-208		Italy	SIAI
S-211		Italy	SIAI
Sabreliner	(CT-39)	U.S.	Rockwell
Safari	MFI-15		
Safir	SAAB-91 (SK-50)	Sweden	SAAB
SC-7	Skyvan	U.K.	Short
SE-210	Caravelle		
Sea Harrier	(Harrier)		
Seascan	IAI-1124		
Searchmaster B/L	N-24		
Seneca	PA-34 (EMB-810)	U.S.	Piper
Sentry	(O-2)	U.S.	Summit
SF-37	(J-37)		
SF-260	(SF-260W Warrior)	Italy	SIAI
SH-37	(J-37)		
Shackleton		U.K.	BAe
Sherpa	Short 330, C-23		
Short 330		U.K.	Short
Sierra 200	(Musketeer)		
SK-35	(J-35)	Sweden	SAAB
SK-37	(J-37)		
SK-50	(Safir)		
SK-60	(SAAB-105)	Sweden	SAAB
SK-61	(Bulldog)		
Skyvan		U.K.	Short
SM-1019		Italy	SIAI
SM-601	Corvette		
SNJ	T-6 (Navy)		
SP-2H	Neptune	U.S.	Lockheed
SR-71	Blackbird	U.S.	Lockheed
Su-7	"Fitter A"	USSR	Sukhoi
Su-15	"Flagon"	USSR	Sukhoi
Su-17/-20/-22	"Fitter"	USSR	Sukhoi
Su-24	"Fencer"	USSR	Sukhoi
Su-25	"Frogfoot"	USSR	Sukhoi
Su-27	"Flanker"	USSR	Sukhoi
Super Etendard		France	Dassault
Super Galeb		Yug	SOKO
Super Mystère		France	Dassault
T-1		Japan	Fuji
T-2	Buckeye	U.S.	Rockwell
T-2		Japan	Mitsubishi
T-3		Japan	Fuji
T-6	Texan	U.S.	N. American
T-17	(Supporter, MFI-17)	Sweden	SAAB
T-23	Uirapurú	Brazil	Aerotec
T-25	Neiva Universal	Brazil	Embraer
T-26	EMB-326		
T-27	Tucano	Brazil	Embraer
T-28	Trojan	U.S.	N. American
T-33	Shooting Star	U.S.	Lockheed
T-34	Mentor	U.S.	Beech
T-35	Pillán [PA-28]	Chile	Enaer
T-36	(C-101)		
T-37	(A-37)		
T-38	Talon	U.S.	Northrop
T-39	(Sabreliner)	U.S.	Rockwell
T-41	Mescalero (Cessna 172)	U.S.	Cessna
T-42	Cochise (Baron)	U.S.	Beech
T-43	(Boeing 737)		
T-44	(King Air)		
T-47	(Citation)		
TB-20	Trinidad	France	Aérospatiale
TB-30	Epsilon	France	Aérospatiale
TC-45	(C-45, trg)		
T-CH-1		Taiwan	AIDC
Texan	T-6		
TL-1	(KM-2)	Japan	Fuji
Tornado		U.K./Ge/Italy	Panavia
TR-1	[U-2]	U.S.	Lockheed
Travel Air	Beech 95		
Trident		U.K.	BAe
Trislander	BN-2		
Tristar	L-1011		
TS-8	Bies	Poland	PZL
TS-11	Iskra	Poland	PZL
Tu-16	"Badger"	USSR	Tupolev
Tu-22	"Blinder"	USSR	Tupolev
Tu-26 (Tu-22M)	"Backfire"	USSR	Tupolev
Tu-28	"Fiddler"	USSR	Tupolev
Tu-95	"Bear"	USSR	Tupolev
Tu-126	"Moss"	USSR	Tupolev
Tu-134	"Crusty"	USSR	Tupolev
Tu-142	"Bear F"	USSR	Tupolev
Tu-154	"Careless"	USSR	Tupolev
Tu-160	"Blackjack"	USSR	Tupolev
Turbo Porter	PC-6A/B		
Twin Bonanza	Beech 50		
Twin Otter	DHC-6		
Tzukit	[CM-170]	Israel	IAI
U-2		U.S.	Lockheed
U-3	(Cessna 310)	U.S.	Cessna
U-7	(L-18)		
U-8	(Twin Bonanza/ Queen Air)	U.S.	Beech
U-9	(EMB-121)		
U-10	Super Courier	U.S.	Helio
U-17	(Cessna 180, 185)	U.S.	Cessna
U-21	(King Air)		
U-36	(Learjet)		
U-42	(C-42)		
U-93	(HS-125)		
UC-12	(King Air)		
UP-2J	(P-2J)		
US-1		Japan	Shin Meiwa
US-2A	(S-2A, tpt)		
US-3	(S-3, tpt)		

Type	Name/designation	Origin	Maker
UTVA-66		Yug	UTVA
UTVA-75		Yug	UTVA
UV-18	(DHC-6)		
V-400	Fantrainer 400	Ge	VFW
V-600	Fantrainer 600	Ge	VFW
Vampire	DH-100		
VC-4	Gulfstream I		
VC-10		U.K.	BAe
VC-11	Gulfstream II		
VC-91	(HS-748)		
VC-93	(HS-125)		
VC-97	(EMB-120)		
VC-130	(C-130)		
VFW-614		Ge	VFW
Victor		U.K.	BAe
Vinka	L-70		
Viscount		U.K.	BAe
VU-9	(EMB-121)		
VU-93	(HS-125)		
WC-130	[C-130]		
WC-135	[Boeing 707]	U.S.	Boeing
Westwind	IAI-1124		
Winjeel	CA-25		
Xavante	EMB-326		
Xingu	EMB-121		
Y-5	[An-2]	China	Hua Bei
Y-7	[An-24]	China	Xian
Y-8	[An-12]	China	Shaanxi
Y-12		China	Harbin
Yak-11	"Moose"	USSR	Yakovlev
Yak-18	"Max"	USSR	Yakovlev
Yak-28	"Firebar" ("Brewer")	USSR	Yakovlev
Yak-38	"Forger"	USSR	Yakovlev
Yak-40	"Codling"	USSR	Yakovlev
YS-11		Japan	Nihon
Z-43		Cz	Zlin
Z-226		Cz	Zlin
Z-326		Cz	Zlin
Z-526		Cz	Zlin
Zéphyr	CM-175		

HELICOPTERS

Type	Name/designation	Origin	Maker
A-109	Hirundo	Italy	Agusta
A-129	Mangusta	Italy	Agusta
AB-. . .	(Bell 204/205/206/212/214/etc.)	Italy/U.S.	Agusta/Bell
AH-1	Cobra/Sea Cobra	U.S.	Bell
AH-6	(Hughes 500/530)	U.S.	MD
AH-64	Apache	U.S.	Hughes
Alouette II	SE-3130, SA-318	France	Aéro-spatiale
Alouette III	SA-316, SA-319	France	Aéro-spatiale
AS-61	(SH-3)	U.S./Italy	Sikorsky/Agusta
AS-332	SuperPuma	France	Aéro-spatiale
AS-350	Ecureuil	France	Aérospatiale
AS-355	Ecureuil II		
ASH-3	(Sea King)	Italy/U.S.	Agusta/Sikorsky
AUH-76	(S-76)		
Bell 47		U.S.	Bell
Bell 204		U.S.	Bell
Bell 205		U.S.	Bell
Bell 206		U.S.	Bell
Bell 212		U.S.	Bell
Bell 214		U.S.	Bell
Bell 406		U.S.	Bell
Bell 412		U.S.	Bell
Bo-105	(NBo-105)	Ge	MBB
CH-3	(SH-3)		
CH-34	Choctaw	U.S.	Sikorsky
CH-46	Sea Knight	U.S.	Boeing-Vertol
CH-47	Chinook	U.S.	Boeing-Vertol
CH-53	Stallion (Sea Stallion)	U.S.	Sikorsky
CH-54	Tarhe	U.S.	Sikorsky
CH-113	(CH-46)		
CH-118	Bell 205		
CH-124	SH-3		
CH-135	Bell 212		
CH-136	OH-58		
CH-139	Bell 206		
CH-147	CH-47		
Cheetah	[SA-315]	India	HAL
Chetak	[SA-319]	India	HAL
Commando	(SH-3)	U.K./U.S.	Westland/Sikorsky
EH-60	(UH-60)		
EH-101		U.K./Italy	Westland/Agusta
FH-1100	(OH-5)	U.S.	Fairchild-Hiller
Gazela	(SA-342)	France/Yug	Aérospatiale/SOKO
Gazelle	SA-341/-342		
H-34	(S-58)		
H-76	S-76		
HA-15	Bo-105		
HB-315	Gavião (SA-315)	Brazil/France	Helibras/Aérospatiale
HB-350	Esquilo (AS-350)	Brazil/France	Helibras/Aérospatiale
HD-16	SA-319		
HH-3	(SH-3)		
HH-34	(CH-34)		
HH-53	(CH-53)		
Hkp-2	Alouette II/SE-3130		
Hkp-3	AB-204		
Hkp-4	KV-107		
Hkp-5	Hughes 300		
Hkp-6	AB-206		
Hkp-9	Bo-105		
Hkp-10	AS-332		
HR-12	OH-58		
HSS-1	(S-58)		
HSS-2	(SH-3)		
HT-17	CH-47		
HT-21	AS-332		
HU-1	(UH-1)	Japan/U.S.	Fuji/Bell
HU-8	UH-1B		
HU-10	UH-1H		
HU-18	AB-212		
Hughes 269		U.S.	MD
Hughes 300		U.S.	MD
Hughes 369		U.S.	MD

Type	Name/designation	Origin	Maker
IAR-316/-330	(SA-316/-330)	Ro/France	IAR/ Aérospatiale
Ka-25	"Hormone"	USSR	Kamov
Ka-27	"Helix"	USSR	Kamov
KH-4	(Bell 47)	Japan/U.S.	Kawasaki/ Bell
KH-300	(Hughes 269)	Japan/U.S.	Kawasaki/ MD
KH-500	(Hughes 369)	Japan/U.S.	Kawasaki/ MD
Kiowa	OH-58		
KV-107	[CH-46]	Japan/U.S.	Kawasaki/ Vertol
Lynx		U.K.	Westland
MH-6	(AH-6)		
MH-53	(CH-53)		
Mi-1	"Hare"	USSR	Mil
Mi-2	"Hoplite"	USSR	Mil
Mi-4	"Hound"	USSR	Mil
Mi-6	"Hook"	USSR	Mil
Mi-8	"Hip"	USSR	Mil
Mi-14	"Haze"	USSR	Mil
Mi-17	"Hip"	USSR	Mil
Mi-24	"Hind"	USSR	Mil
Mi-25	"Hind"	USSR	Mil
Mi-26	"Halo"	USSR	Mil
Mi-28	"Havoc"	USSR	Mil
Mi-35	(Mi-25)		
NAS-332	AS-332	Indon/ France	Nurtanio/ Aérospatiale
NB-412	Bell 412	Indon/ U.S.	Nurtanio/ Bell
NBo-105	Bo-105	Indon/Ge	Nurtanio/ MBB
NH-300	(Hughes-300)	Italy/U.S.	Nardi/MD
NSA-330	(SA-330)	Indon/ France	Nurtanio/ Aérospatiale
OH-6	Cayuse (Hughes 369)	U.S.	MD
OH-13	(Bell 47G)		
OH-23	Raven	U.S.	Hiller
OH-58	Kiowa (Bell 206)		
OH-58D	(Bell 406)		
PAH-1	(Bo-105)		
Partizan	(Gazela, armed)		
RH-53	(CH-53)		
S-55	(Whirlwind)	U.S.	Sikorsky
S-58	(Wessex)	U.S.	Sikorsky
S-61	SH-3		
S-65	CH-53		
S-70	UH-60		
S-76		U.S.	Sikorsky
S-80	CH-53		
SA-315	Lama [Alouette II]	France	Aérospatiale
SA-316	Alouette III (SA-319)	France	Aérospatiale
SA-318	Alouette II (SE-3130)	France	Aérospatiale
SA-319	Alouette III (SA-316)	France	Aérospatiale
SA-321	Super Frelon	France	Aérospatiale
SA-330	Puma	France	Aérospatiale
SA-341/-342	Gazelle	France	Aérospatiale
SA-360	Dauphin	France	Aérospatiale
SA-365	Dauphin II (SA-360)		
Scout	(Wasp)	U.K.	Westland
SE-3130	(SA-318)		
SE-316	(SA-316)		
Sea King	[SH-3]	U.K.	Westland
SH-2	Sea Sprite	U.S.	Kaman
SH-3	(Sea King)	U.S.	Sikorsky
SH-34	(S-58)		
SH-57	Bell 206		
SH-60	Sea Hawk (UH-60)		
Sioux	(Bell 47)	U.K.	Westland
TH-55	Hughes 269		
TH-57	SeaRanger (Bell 206)		
UH-1	Iroquois (Bell 204/ 205)		
UH-12	(OH-23)	U.S.	Hiller
UH-13	(Bell 47J)		
UH-19	(S-55)		
UH-34T	(S-58T)		
UH-46	(CH-46)		
UH-60	Black Hawk (SH-60)	U.S.	Sikorsky
VH-4	(Bell 206)		
Wasp	(Scout)	U.K.	Westland
Wessex	(S-58)	U.S./U.K.	Sikorsky/ Westland
Whirlwind	(S-55)	U.S./U.K.	Sikorsky/ Westland
Z-5	[Mi-4]	China	Harbin
Z-6	[Z-5]	China	Harbin
Z-8	[SA-321]	China	Changhe
Z-9	[SA-365]	China	Harbin

Source: International Institute for Strategic Studies. 1991. *The Military Balance, 1991–1992*. London: Brassey's.

Note: The use of [square brackets] shows the type from which a variant was derived. "Q-5 . . . [MiG-19]" indicates that the design of the Q-5 was based on that of the MiG-19.

(Parentheses) indicate an alternative name by which an aircraft is known—sometimes in another version. "L-188 . . . Electra (P-3 Orion)" shows that in another version the Lockheed Type 188 Electra is known as the P-3 Orion.

Names given in "quotation marks" are NATO reporting names (e.g., "Su-27 . . . "Flanker").

When no information is listed under "Origin" or "Maker," take the primary reference given under "Name/designation" and look it up under "Type."

M

MACARTHUR, DOUGLAS [1880–1964]

Douglas MacArthur was born on 26 January 1880 in Little Rock, Arkansas, the son of Arthur MacArthur and Mary Pinkney Hardy. MacArthur's father was an army officer who had had a distinguished career as a commander during the Civil War, the Spanish-American War, and the Philippine Insurrection. Determined on an army career, MacArthur, with the help of his mother, won an appointment to the U.S. Military Academy at West Point. He graduated first in his class in 1903 and was commissioned a second lieutenant of engineers.

MacArthur's first assignment was as a junior construction engineer officer in the Philippines. Promoted to first lieutenant, he was then sent with an engineer party detailed to survey the Bataan Peninsula. In October 1904, MacArthur was transferred back to the United States. He was then assigned to the Golden Gate harbor defenses in San Francisco. In October 1904 he was sent to Tokyo as an aide to his father, now a major general assigned as an observer of the Russo-Japanese War. After the war he accompanied his father on an inspection tour of the Orient.

In late 1906, MacArthur returned to the United States to attend the Army Engineer School at Fort Belvoir, Virginia. During the winter while classes were not in session he served as a special aide to President Theodore Roosevelt. Graduating in August 1907, MacArthur was assigned to river and harbor duty in Wisconsin. In 1908 he was transferred to Fort Leavenworth, Kansas, and appointed a company commander in the 3d Battalion of Engineers. In 1909, MacArthur also became an instructor at the General Service, and later, the Cavalry School at Fort Riley, Kansas. On 27 February 1911 he was promoted to captain of engineers and appointed adjutant of the 3d Battalion.

From March to July 1911, MacArthur served in San Antonio, Texas, with the Maneuver Division, which had been raised in response to tension along the Mexican-American border. After the death of his father in September 1912, MacArthur requested a transfer in order to take care of his mother. In early 1913 he was sent to Washington, D.C., and assigned as a member of the Engineer Board. In May he was appointed superintendent of the State, War, and Navy Building. In September, MacArthur was named a member of the General Staff. From May to November 1914 he took part in the Vera Cruz expedition and gathered intelligence on Mexico. In December he was promoted to major.

On 30 June 1916, MacArthur was assigned as military assistant to Secretary of War Newton D. Baker and appointed head of the Bureau of Information of the War Department. Secretary Baker and MacArthur developed a great respect for one another and worked closely together in developing the army. A champion of the new National Guard units, MacArthur was responsible for convincing the secretary that guard units could fight alongside regular army units in Europe if the United States became involved in World War I.

World War I

On 6 April 1917 the United States declared war on Germany. MacArthur was instrumental in organizing a multistate National Guard division, the 42d "Rainbow" Division, for service in France. On 5 August 1917 he was promoted to colonel of infantry in the National Army and was appointed the 42d's chief of staff. Sent to France with the division in October 1917, MacArthur fought in the Aisne-Marne operation from 25 July to 2 August 1918. With the brevet rank of brigadier general, he commanded the 84th Brigade at St. Mihiel on 12–17 September. During the Meuse-Argonne campaign (4 October–11 November), MacArthur became the youngest division commander of the war when he was appointed to lead the 42d in the "race to Sedan" (6–11 November). After the armistice, MacArthur remained in Germany as part of the occupation force until April 1919, when he was recalled to the United States.

Interwar Years

MacArthur was appointed superintendent of West Point in June 1919, and was promoted to brigadier general in the regular army in January 1920. He held the post of superintendent until late in 1922, when he was ordered to the Philippines. Before leaving on his new assignment, he married Louise Cromwell Brooks on 14 February.

MacArthur was promoted to major general on 17 January 1925. Shortly after, he returned to the United States and took command of the IV Corps Area in Atlanta. Later that year he was transferred to command the III Corps Area with headquarters in Baltimore. In October of that year, he was assigned the distasteful duty of sitting on the court-martial board of his childhood friend, Col. William "Billy" Mitchell. In September 1927, MacArthur accepted the post of president of the American Olympic Committee while still commanding the III Corps Area. In 1928 he returned to Manila as commander of the Department of the Philippines.

MacArthur was recalled to the United States in August 1930, and in November was appointed Chief of Staff of the Army with the temporary rank of general. Because the Great Depression imposed great fiscal constraints, MacArthur devoted his energies as chief of staff to preserving the meager strength of the army. He reorganized the tactical forces of the army by merging the corps areas into four armies, giving each a regional as well as a field responsibility. He backed the development of both a tank force and a modern air force, but the uncertainty of the national budget consistently thwarted his efforts.

In the summer of 1932, MacArthur was ordered by President Herbert Hoover to disperse some 11,000 unemployed protesters, nicknamed the "Bonus Army," who had camped in the Anacostia area of Washington. A large number of these men were World War I veterans who had been promised bonuses at the end of the war and had been given insurance policies instead. With the Depression in full swing, they had marched to Washington to demand cash for their policies, and threatened to wipe out a nearly empty treasury. Following orders, MacArthur led some 600 infantry and cavalry with six tanks against the hostile mobs and dispersed them in what the press cynically referred to as the "Battle of Anacostia Flats."

In late 1932, Franklin D. Roosevelt was elected president. When MacArthur's term as chief of staff expired in 1934, Roosevelt extended it for another year. In October 1935, MacArthur reverted to the permanent rank of major general and was sent to the Philippines to organize its defenses prior to its projected independence. In August 1936, MacArthur received a unique honor when he was appointed a field marshal in the Philippine Army by the Philippine government. Having divorced his first wife in 1929, MacArthur married Jean Marie Faircloth on 30 April 1937. This union produced a son, Arthur MacArthur IV. On 31 December, MacArthur retired from the U.S. Army and remained in the Philippines to help the government prepare for independence.

With the Japanese war of conquest in China threatening to break out into the rest of Asia, and the German conquests in Poland and France, U.S. strategists began to prepare for America's possible entry into the war. On 26 July 1941, MacArthur was recalled to active duty with the rank of lieutenant general and appointed commander of U.S. Army Forces in the Far East (USAFFE). He immediately set about trying to bolster the Philippine defenses against a possible Japanese invasion.

World War II

Following the Japanese attack at Pearl Harbor (7 December 1941), the United States entered World War II. Although informed of the attack on Pearl Harbor, MacArthur was still surprised when the Japanese launched air attacks against Clark and Iba airfields in the Philippines the following day. On 10 December the Japanese began their invasion of the Philippines, making small landings in northern Luzon. MacArthur realized these were only preliminary moves, and held back his forces for the main landings that he expected would come at Lingayen Gulf. When the Japanese landed in the gulf on 22 December, MacArthur's troops put up a desperate resistance. Since the Japanese possessed both sea and air superiority, however, MacArthur was soon forced to fall back. From 23 December 1941 until 1 January 1942, MacArthur surprised the Japanese by conducting a brilliant fighting withdrawal and side-slipping his army into partially prepared defensive positions on the Bataan peninsula. Forced from Bataan, MacArthur finally fell back to the fortified island of Corregidor in Manila Bay where, under heavy bombardment, he hoped to receive supplies and reinforcements. The situation was hopeless, however, and MacArthur was ordered by President Roosevelt in February 1942 to leave the Philippines. Against his will MacArthur, several members of his staff, and his family slipped out of the Philippines on 11 March and made their way to Australia. In a speech made on his arrival MacArthur gave his solemn pledge, "I came through and I shall return!"

On 28 March, MacArthur was awarded the Medal of Honor. In April he was appointed Supreme Commander, Allied Forces, Southwest Pacific Area, effectively splitting command in the Pacific with Adm. Chester W. Nimitz, Commander-in-Chief, Pacific Ocean Area. In command of one Australian and two U.S. divisions, MacArthur began planning a counteroffensive against the Japanese in New Guinea. From July to September 1942, his forces successfully repulsed a Japanese offensive against Port Moresby. MacArthur then launched his counteroffensive. From September 1942 to January 1943 his forces pushed across the Owen Stanley Range and captured the fortified Buna-Gona complex, driving the Japanese out of southeastern New Guinea.

During September and August 1943, MacArthur directed the U.S. Sixth Army in a series of amphibious leap-frog assaults, capturing the rest of New Guinea's strategic coastal points. In December he invaded New Britain to cut off and isolate the Japanese from their base at Rabaul. In February 1944, MacArthur personally led the attack that seized the Admiralties Islands. His brilliant victories at Hollandia and Aitape in April surrounded the Japanese Eighteenth Army and left it isolated and ineffective. MacArthur then resumed his leap-frog campaign west along the northern coast of New

Guinea. On 30 July he captured Cape Sansapor, ending the campaign and effectively destroying Japanese power in New Guinea.

MacArthur then converged his offensive with that of Admiral Nimitz in the Central Pacific. In September, MacArthur took Molotai in the Molucca Islands while Nimitz took Pelelieu in the Palau Islands. When Nimitz encountered only light resistance along the Philippine coast, he recommended that proposed landings on Mindanao and Yap be canceled and an assault launched against Leyte in the central Philippines. MacArthur quickly agreed and, despite tremendous logistical difficulties, boldly moved up the scheduled invasion of the Philippines by two months. On 20 October, MacArthur landed with his troops on Leyte and spoke the words the Philippine people had waited two long years to hear, "I have returned."

Supported by Admiral Kincaid's Seventh Fleet, MacArthur expanded operations in the Philippines to Mindoro on 15 December. That month MacArthur was promoted to General of the Army (Fig. 1). On 9 January 1945 he invaded Luzon, retaking most of the island and completing the liberation of the Philippines in a bitter campaign that ended with the Japanese surrender on 15 August. In April, MacArthur was appointed Commanding General of U.S. Army Forces in the Pacific. In August he was also appointed Supreme Commander for the Allied Powers in Japan in order to take the Japanese surrender in Tokyo Bay (2 September 1945).

Figure 1. Douglas MacArthur, General of the Army, in Manila. (SOURCE: Robert F. Dorr Archives)

Postwar Years

After the Japanese surrender, MacArthur was appointed Supreme Commander of Allied Occupation Forces in Japan. For the next six years MacArthur—as virtual viceroy of Japan—directed the reorganization and reconstruction of the governmental, social, and economic systems of Japan. He saw to the elimination of Japan's ultranationalist, militarist, and feudal beliefs and traditions, replacing them with more liberal and democratic ideologies. He reformed Japan's political system, introducing a liberal constitution, and reformed the economy and improved rural life by introducing land reform. He changed outdated social norms by instituting women's rights. He modernized the health and welfare programs and the educational system and was responsible for improving relations between the United States and Japan. In January 1947, MacArthur was also appointed Commander of the Far East Command, which comprised all U.S. forces in Japan, Korea, the Ryukyus, the Philippines, the Marianas, and the Bonin Islands.

Korean War

Shortly after the outbreak of the Korean War on 25 June 1950, MacArthur was ordered by President Harry S. Truman to provide assistance to South Korea. The United Nations (UN) quickly passed a resolution calling for concerted military assistance to Korea, and on 8 July, MacArthur was appointed Supreme Commander of UN Forces in Korea.

The speed of the initial North Korean attack had overwhelmed the weaker South Korean Army and overrun most of the peninsula before U.S. forces could arrive. The UN forces—composed mostly of the U.S. Eighth Army, which had been on peacetime occupation duty in Japan—were virtually surrounded and reduced to holding a small perimeter around Pusan in southeast Korea. MacArthur managed to stop the North Korean offensive along the Naktong River and then directed the defense of the Pusan Perimeter. Over the objections of the Joint Chiefs of Staff, MacArthur created the X Corps and launched a daring amphibious landing at Inchon in the North Korean rear area on 15 September. This brilliant strategic envelopment resulted in the destruction of the North Korean forces in South Korea and led to the recapture of Seoul, the South Korean capital, on 26 September.

After receiving approval from the UN and the U.S. government, MacArthur invaded North Korea on 1 October. As his troops approached the Yalu River they were attacked by overwhelming Chinese forces on 25–26 November and forced to retreat south of the 38th Parallel. MacArthur conducted a skillful fighting withdrawal and managed to stabilize the front south of Seoul. Having received conflicting intelligence reports concerning Chinese intentions, MacArthur had chosen to discount the probability of Chinese troops engaging in the war and was taken by surprise. With China's entry into the conflict MacArthur was convinced that the UN was facing a "new war," and he advocated the use of airpower against targets in China. UN troops resumed the offensive in early 1951, taking Seoul on 14 March and again driving into North Korea.

MacArthur's public disagreement with U.S. policy and differences over civil-military relations and strategic direction of the war led to increasing tension with President Truman. Truman, without the consideration of forewarning MacArthur, publicly announced the general's dismissal on 11 April 1951. MacArthur learned of his dismissal from a friend who had heard the news on the radio and then reported it to the general. Shortly after, MacArthur received the official order.

Twilight Years

MacArthur had not been back to the United States since 1937; he returned to a hero's welcome, his parade resulting in the largest popular turnout in the history of New York City. On 19 April he delivered a farewell speech to Congress in which he uttered the unforgettable line, "Old soldiers never die, they just fade away." In 1952 he accepted the position of Chairman of the Board of the Remington Rand (later Sperry Rand) Corporation. MacArthur took up residence in the Waldorf Astoria Hotel in New York City and, with the exception of occasional speeches and his board duties, lived in relative seclusion. In 1961 he returned to the Philippines to help celebrate the fiftieth anniversary of that nation's independence. Invited to give the commencement address at West Point in 1962, he delivered the most memorable and moving of all his speeches. His memoirs, *Reminiscences*, were published in 1964. MacArthur died on 5 April 1964 at Walter Reed Army Medical Center in Washington, D.C.

MacArthur was one of America's greatest and, equally, most controversial generals. Reflecting a superb military mind, his amphibious campaigns in the Pacific and at Inchon were masterpieces of strategy, efficiency, and boldness. His knowledge and understanding of the culture and mentality of the Orient made possible the reconstruction of Japan as a modern democratic state. His love of the Philippine people was surpassed only by his devotion to his own country, and he is acclaimed as a Philippine hero even today. MacArthur's extraordinary life is best described by the three tenets he lived by—duty, honor, country.

VINCENT B. HAWKINS

SEE ALSO: Amphibious Warfare; Envelopment; Korean War; Nimitz, Chester William; World War I; World War II; Yamashita, Tomoyuki.

Bibliography

Hunt, F. 1954. *The untold story of Douglas MacArthur*. New York: Devin-Adair.
MacArthur, D. 1964. *Reminiscences*. New York: McGraw-Hill.
Manchester, W. 1978. *American Caesar*. Boston: Little, Brown.
Mayer, S. 1971. *MacArthur*. New York: Ballantine Books.
———. 1971. *MacArthur in Japan*. New York: Ballantine Books.
Pfannes, C. E., and V. A. Salamone. 1981. *The great commanders of World War II*. Vol. 2: *The Americans*. New York: Kensington.

MACHINE GUN

In today's modern armies, machine guns constitute the main direct firepower of infantry troops against dismounted forces, lightly armored vehicles, and aircraft. Their use, however, is not restricted to infantry formations, and they appear in other combat units, in aircraft, aboard ships and patrol boats, as well as in combat support and combat service support units. They are classified by mission and physical characteristics into four general categories: light, general purpose, medium, and heavy.

Historical Background

Rapid-firing and multiple-firing weapons, precursors to the modern, fully-automatic machine gun, were considered as early as the fifteenth century, when nations sought ways to increase their military's ability to inflict losses upon an enemy without increasing the overall number of gunpowder weapons.

Among the first successful designers of rapid-fire weapons was London lawyer James Puckel (1667–1724), who invented a single-barrel gun with manually operated revolving cylinders; this gun was reportedly capable of firing "63 times in seven minutes." Although the British Board of Ordnance declined to accept the weapon into service after a demonstration in 1717, Puckel was issued a patent (1718). The only record of service of the weapon comes from an account of an abortive expedition against the French in Saint Lucia and Saint Vincent in 1727.

In 1851, Belgian captain T. H. J. Fafchamps invented the *mitrailleuse*, a multiple-firing weapon with 37 rifled barrels encased in a wrought-iron tube. An iron plate with matching holes was used for loading and sealing the chambers, and a hand crank fired the weapon. In one minute, a practiced team could fire as many as 12 bursts, or 444 rounds. The *mitrailleuse* was accepted for French service in 1867 but lasted only a year because of repeated mechanical failures and because it was used in batteries—its proper tactical use among infantry was never exploited. The name continues in French use to describe a machine gun regardless of type.

The most successful rapid-fire weapon of the mid-nineteenth century was the handiwork of Dr. Richard Jordan Gatling (1818–1903), a South Carolina inventor less remembered for his agricultural inventions than his 200-shots-per-minute Gatling Gun. Patented in November 1862, the gun fired cartridges sequentially from six musket-caliber barrels that were rotated by a hand crank, which also fired the weapon. Feeding ammunition was accomplished by gravity-feed mechanisms developed by James G. Accles in 1865 and by L. F. Bruce in 1881, and by a positive-feed magazine developed by Accles in 1893.

After numerous modifications, the United States Army ordered 100 of the weapons in 1866, and within twenty years, Gatling's "labor-saving device for warfare" saw service in nearly all the militaries that could afford it, and in most regions of the world. The concept of the Gatling Gun survives today in the form of electric-powered, multibarreled "miniguns"—machine guns used on aircraft and also for air defense.

Gatling's rapid-fire gun, however, did not meet the definition of fully-automatic fire, which may be stated as: that process of feeding, firing, and ejecting carried out by the mechanism of the weapon, after a primary manual, electrical, or pneumatic cocking, as long as the trigger is held to the rear and there is still ammunition in the belt, feedstrip, or magazine. The same process describes semiautomatic fire, except that the trigger is pulled only once per shot and must be released between shots.

Hiram Maxim: Father of the Machine Gun

Intrigued by the challenge of designing a fully-automatic gun, Hiram Stevens Maxim (1840–1916), an American who later became a naturalized British citizen, set about designing such a weapon in England in 1881. Between 1883 and 1885, Maxim patented most of the processes that would be used to deliver automatic fire on the battlefield. These processes relate to the method by which the energy developed from the expanding gases of exploding gunpowder is used in the operating cycle, either (1) the backward thrust of the recoiling mass, which is called recoil activation, or (2) the pressure generated by progressively burning powder in the barrel, called gas operation.

Maxim used the principle of the short recoil system, in which the barrel and breechblock return together a short distance until residual chamber pressure is low enough and the bolt can be opened without fracturing the cartridge case. The barrel then stops and the breechblock continues to the rear, its hooked lugs extracting and ejecting the spent case, then returning forward by the action of a recoil-compressed spiral spring. On its return, the firing mechanism cocks, the next cartridge is seated into the chamber, the barrel is shoved forward, and firing reoccurs. This cycle continues as long as the machine gun's trigger remains depressed.

The London press described Maxim's machine gun in 1884. A report read: "Hiram Maxim . . . has made an automatic machine-gun with a single barrel, using the standard calibre .45 rifle cartridge, that will load and fire itself by energy derived from recoil at a rate of over 600 rounds a minute." Maxim's name became synonymous with the machine gun he created, and by the time of his death in 1916 every major power had adopted the weapon, although some would replace it with other systems.

The tactical advantage offered by the Maxim was that it could be fired from the prone position, and the gun was small enough to be concealed. This increased the survival of crews and also led to more varied employment possibilities.

Developments in Ammunition

The success of the machine guns developed by Maxim and his contemporaries (Hotchkiss, Browning, and Lewis are three) would not have been possible without technological advances in metallurgy and chemistry. These combined to create the percussion ignition, center-fire metallic cartridge (developed by Col. Edward M. Boxer in 1866), and smokeless gunpowder (developed by Paul Vieille in 1886 and by Alfred Nobel in 1891). The fixed, or metallic, cartridge combined primer, propellant, and bullet in a stable case that was weatherproof and strong enough to withstand rugged, rapid handling by machine guns, as well as other weapons.

Before the advent of smokeless powder, firing positions could easily be identified as weapons discharged, enveloping the firer in a cloud of smoke. As battles continued, the smoke could be so dense as to obscure the battlefield, increasing the confusion of attacker and defender alike. Smokeless powder also had to be relatively slow burning, so as not to damage or destroy the weapon by blowing up in the firing chamber before expanding gases forced the bullet from the barrel.

With certain refinements, the ammunition used by machine guns today retain these characteristics.

Contemporary Description, Operation, and Use.

Light Machine Guns

Light machine guns are found primarily in infantry squads and are served by a crew of two. These weapons are supported by a sturdy bipod to aid in accurate firing and usually weigh about twice as much as a rifle of the same caliber. As opposed to rifles, light machine guns have heavier, removable barrels that permit replacement when one becomes too hot from firing. Another distinguishing feature of light machine guns is that they are usually designed to use the same ammunition as the rifles in the squad.

Although capable of operating independently, light machine gun teams are usually protected by other squad members. When engaging a target, as the gunner fires, the assistant gunner will call corrections to the strike of the rounds and also assist with feeding or reloading ammunition.

The Finnish M78 Valmet, based on Finland's M76 assault rifle, is a good example of a light machine gun that is ideal for use by infantry squads in areas where they must operate dismounted. The M78 fires a 7.62mm cartridge, the length of which can vary from 39 to 51 millimeters (1.6 to 2 in.), from either a 15- or 30-round box, or a 75-round drum, making it a quite flexible weapon. The gun has a heavier and longer barrel than the M76 rifle and is fitted with a bipod and a carrying handle. It weighs 4.7 kilograms (10.3 lb.) empty, and 5.9 kilograms (13 lb.) with a loaded 30-round box. It is gas operated, has a selective fire switch, and a cyclic rate of fire of 650 rounds per minute. A version of the Valmet light machine gun fires a lighter, 5.56mm × 45mm cartridge.

General-Purpose Machine Guns

The general-purpose machine gun is a classification that came out of World War II as a development of the medium machine gun that had been in use since World War I. Combat experience showed that more effective fire could be produced by a lighter and handier machine gun. Such a weapon can be carried in a squad or section and used in the same way as a light machine gun, or it can be mounted on a tripod, fitted with an optical sight, and used as a medium support gun. It can also be mounted in tanks, armored cars, armored personnel carriers, aircraft, and patrol boats.

General-purpose machine guns are gas operated, featuring an adjustable gas intake from a point in the barrel. The gas regulator provides firing reliability independent of ambient conditions. Barrels are highly wear-resistant, air cooled, and capable of being changed in a few seconds. The front sight consists of a blade or cylinder fitted near the muzzle of the barrel, and the rear sight is a light, folding frame with spring-loaded thumb catches for setting the range slide.

Ammunition used in general-purpose machine guns varies in caliber and length, a typical round being 7.62mm × 51mm of the type used in the U.S. Army's M60 machine gun. Cartridges are contained in disintegrating link belts or articulated belts, with 50 to 250 rounds per box container. Many types of ammunition are used, including ball, tracer, armor piercing, incendiary, and armor-piercing incendiary. There are also blank, star, and drill cartridges.

General-purpose machine guns are available in an infantry model designed for use in mobile action, fired from the hip or using a bipod. They can also be mounted on tripods for defensive operations, on external cradles, and in swivel antiaircraft mounts. There are turret and coaxial models for use in armored vehicles, and twin mountings for helicopter and armed aircraft employment.

The weight of the general-purpose machine gun with butt and bipod can be as much as 11 kilograms (24 lb.), and can increase to 24 kilograms (52 lb.) with the addition of tripod and heavier barrel. The effective range of these weapons varies from 500 meters (1,650 ft.) to over 2,000 meters (6,600 ft.) depending on the means used to stabilize the weapon during firing. Rates of fire depend on the design of the particular machine gun and can vary from 550 to over 1,000 rounds a minute.

There has been some criticism of the concept of arming the infantry squad with the general-purpose machine gun in lieu of the light machine gun because of the added weight and the lesser effect compared with that of medium machine guns. In the future, the trend may be to have a light machine gun at the squad level, with the general-purpose gun being retained as a support weapon.

The most effective tactical use is made of general-purpose machine guns when they are used in pairs or more, their fires integrated with other weapons of a rifle platoon or company. This is done on the defense by planning interlocking, primary-direction-of-fire of machine guns and rifles, while covering dead (unobserved) space to the front with fragmentation grenades, claymore antipersonnel command detonated mines, grenade launchers, and indirect-fire mortars and artillery. Because of the value of the weapon in area denial and inflicting casualties, defensive operations also require that the machine gun be manned continuously for security, and be used only when the defenses are seriously threatened and not against enemy reconnaissance probes.

In offensive tactics, general-purpose machine guns will often be used to provide supporting fire for assaulting troops as part of a platoon or company attack. Selection of terrain for the supporting position is critical since at some point in the attack the assault elements will advance beyond the location selected for supporting machine guns. A typical support-fire technique is to fire from a position behind and to one side of the line of advance, walking the strike of the rounds ahead of the assault force. Similarly, if terrain permits, supporting fire may be directed over the heads of troops as they advance toward an objective on higher ground. An alternative offensive tactic is to have teams of general-purpose machine guns accompany the assault force to the objective, employing the weapon as a light machine gun. In this way, each squad may retain control over the firepower of the weapon.

In addition to direct involvement in ground combat actions, general-purpose machine guns are also used as air defense weapons. An example of such use is the German 7.62mm MG3, a successor to the well-regarded 7.92mm MG42 used in World War II, mounted in pairs on a twin pedestal.

The M60 machine gun previously cited, which came into service in the U.S. Army during the late 1950s, is typical of many general-purpose machine guns. The primary squad weapon of U.S. and allied forces in the Vietnam War, the M60 is gas-operated, the barrel drilled radially downward 20 centimeters (8 in.) from the muzzle. After a bullet has passed this point, a small amount of propellant gas is forced through the vent where it enters the gas cylinder and forces an enclosed piston to drive back the operating rod. This short-stroke action carries the bolt back and imparts enough energy to complete the cycle of operation.

The M60 is a full automatic weapon only and has a cyclic rate of fire of 550 rounds a minute, which is slow enough for an accomplished firer to squeeze off a single round (Fig. 1). Its feed system is designed for the disintegrating link–type ammunition and was originally based on the German MG42 feed system used during World War II and subsequently modified. The M60 features a removable barrel assembly that also contains the gas cylinder plug and attached bipod legs, which makes for an awkward, two-man effort to remove a hot barrel.

Another type of machine gun that fits the general-purpose classification is the multibarrel machine gun, or minigun, of the type specifically designed for U.S. forces in Vietnam. The 7.62mm M134 Minigun uses a Gatling-type action and is based on the 20mm Vulcan air defense weapon. The M134 uses Gatling's concept with six rotating barrels fitted to a gun housing that contains a rotor assembly and bolt assembly. Six bolts are matched to the barrels and, when loaded, the weapon fires through the bolt-barrel match at the twelve-o'clock position. Fully-automatic firing is provided by a 28-volt electric motor, and the M134 can fire at a rate of 6,000 rounds a minute.

When mounted in an aircraft, such as the AH1-Series Cobra helicopter, the M134 has proven effective as a close-air support weapon against dismounted infantry, lightly armored vehicles, and patrol boats. Subsequent models have been designed for use on ground vehicles and watercraft and can be employed in both a ground support and air defense role.

Medium Machine Guns

Medium machine guns were first used in World War I, in pairs or larger numbers, as a support weapon to provide a heavy volume of fire for long periods. Most of the early medium machine guns were variants of Maxim's design or the similar Browning, the exception being the Hotchkiss. These water-cooled, belt-fed weapons were usually manned by a crew of three to four and used the same ammunition as that fired from rifles, although some cartridges were specially made for longer-range fires. The use of medium machine guns declined after the Korean War, as it was felt that more effective fire could be provided by guns mounted on light armored vehicles and by general-purpose machine guns.

Figure 1. Two combat-ready Marines, an M60A1 machine gunner and his assistant, practice firing their weapon. (Source: U.S. Marine Corps)

Heavy Machine Guns

The heavy machine gun is one that fires a round of ammunition larger than the standard rifle cartridge and less than 20mm in caliber. The most popular caliber for many years has been the 12.7mm in service since World War I. Subsequently, 14.5mm machine guns were developed to provide a gun with greater hitting power. Most heavy machine guns are mounted in armored vehicles, although there are still some fitted to ground mounts. Others are retained in a variety of mounts as light antiaircraft weapons.

12.7mm Heavy Machine Guns

The 12.7mm heavy machine gun is gas operated and fully locked, with an adjustable gas intake from a point in the barrel. The barrel is highly wear-resistant, air cooled, and equipped with a quick-change barrel, although some models have a fixed barrel. The feed mechanism differs from type to type; some models use a large circular drum and feed from the left, while others have a flat rectangular feed cover and can be readily adapted to feed from either side.

There are a variety of two-wheeled mounts that can be moved by manpower, pack animals, or motor. A shield is sometimes provided when the configuration is for use against ground targets, and the mount can be converted for antiaircraft use.

Typical weights are about 36 kilograms (79.2 lb.) for the gun and something under 13 kilograms (28.6 lb.) for the barrel. Rates of fire are about 575 rounds per minute with an effective range of about 2,000 meters (6,600 ft.).

14.5mm Heavy Machine Guns

The 14.5mm guns are short-recoil operated with gas assistance from a muzzle booster. This type of gun was designed after World War II with a view to simplicity of manufacture. The body consists of a simple metal cylinder to which the various attachments are riveted or welded. The gun is solid in construction and all components are robust. Apart from the ejection opening, it is well sealed against dust and dirt. The barrel can be changed. Designed initially as an antiaircraft gun, the 14.5mm has also been successfully employed as an armored fighting vehicle machine gun.

The 14.5mm heavy machine gun generally weighs about 49 kilograms (107.8 lb.), has a cyclic rate of fire of about 600 rounds a minute, and ranges similar to 12.7mm guns. These weapons can be mounted on towed carriage mountings for combinations of one, two, or four guns. Twin- and four-gun assemblies are in wide use.

The 14.5mm KPV heavy machine gun, produced by the Soviet Union shortly after World War II, is an example of these heavier automatic guns. Designed expressly to fire the high-velocity antitank round used in the PTRD41 antitank rifle in an air defense role, the weapon is simple and easily manufactured. Subsequently, the Soviet military found the weapon suitable for mounting on armored fighting vehicles for use in ground combat. Its total weight approaches 69 kilograms (151.8 lb.), and it can be found in the republics of the former Soviet Union, other Soviet-influenced countries, and China. This heavy machine gun was used extensively by North Vietnam during the Vietnam War.

Summary

The evolution of the machine gun bears witness to the great advances in weapons-related technology, and although today's weapons are mature systems, robust and reliable, the evolutionary process is unlikely to cease. New advances in munitions, propellants, light-weight composite materials, electronics, and machine tooling promise to improve the lethality of machine guns even further.

Light machine guns will see increasing use in infantry squads, providing them with greater firepower than previously and more useful in terrain restrictive to the use of heavier guns. General-purpose machine guns are likely to continue in their diverse roles, providing support for infantry as well as protection against aircraft. Increased use of high-rate-of-fire general-purpose miniguns against air and ground targets will also occur. The distinction between heavy machine guns and machine cannon of over 20mm will blur as high-explosive rounds of less than 20mm are added to the firing capabilities of 12.7mm and 14.5mm guns.

From the ship-defense weapon envisioned by James Puckel in the early eighteenth century, to the thousands-of-rounds-a-minute miniguns used in a general-purpose role today, rapid-fire and fully-automatic guns demonstrate the quest of the world's militaries to improve the lethal effectiveness of their fighting forces. The machine gun, which proved its terrible potential in World War I, forced changes in tactical thought and deployments on the battlefield. Although it may never have a similar impact in another war, the machine gun will remain the infantry's most effective direct-fire weapon against other infantry.

SAMIR H. SHALABY

SEE ALSO: Ammunition; Automatic Weapon; Technology and Warfare.

Bibliography

Dupuy, T. N. 1984. *The evolution of weapons and warfare.* Fairfax, Va.: HERO Books.
Jane's infantry weapons, 1983–84. 1983. New York: Jane's.
Reid, W. 1976. *Arms through the ages.* New York: Harper and Row.

MADAGASCAR, DEMOCRATIC REPUBLIC OF (formerly Malagasy Republic)

Madagascar is a large island off the southeast coast of Africa, and governs several smaller islands nearby. A French colony during the late nineteenth and early twentieth centuries, it is known for the richness and variety of its wildlife.

Power Potential Statistics

Area: 587,040 square kilometers (226,656 sq. mi.)
Population: 12,398,600
Total Active Armed Forces: 21,000 (0.169% of pop.)
Gross Domestic Product: US$2.4 billion (1990 est.)
Annual Defense Expenditure: US$37 million (2.2% of GDP, 1989 est.)
Iron and Steel Production: none
Fuel Production: none; 2.11 million metric tons petroleum products processed in 1986.
Electrical Power Output: 430 million kwh (1989)
Merchant Marine: 14 vessels; 59,416 gross registered tons
Civil Air Fleet: 5 major transport aircraft; 115 usable airfields (30 with permanent-surface runways); none with runways over 3,659 meters (12,000 ft.); 3 with runways 2,440–3,659 meters (8,000–12,000 ft.); 42 with runways 1200–2,440 meters (4,000–8,000 ft.).

For the most recent information, the reader may refer to the following annual publications:
The Military Balance. International Institute for Strategic Studies. London: Brassey's (UK).
The Statesman's Year-Book. New York: St. Martin's Press.
The World Factbook. Central Intelligence Agency. Washington, D.C.: Brassey's (US).

History

Madagascar and its surrounding islands were settled about 2,000 years ago by a mixture of African and Malay voyagers arriving by sea. Beginning about A.D. 800 Arabic-speaking traders arrived and settled on Madagascar, some integrating with the natives but others retaining their "national" identity into modern times. European contact began in earnest in the mid-1600s, when there were several unsuccessful English and French colonization attempts.

Trade with Europeans gradually increased, and the arrival of firearms fostered the development of larger kingdoms, especially the Sakalava in the seventeenth and eighteenth centuries, and the Merina in the nineteenth. With unofficial British aid, the Merina kingdom won half the island by the mid-1830s, but despite early attempts at Westernization the Merina rulers of the nineteenth century tended to adopt policies directly opposing those of their predecessors. The French established a protectorate over the remnants of the Sakalava state in northwest Madagascar in 1840, but this lapsed with the accession of Queen Ranavalona II in 1868.

The French were not content with Merina domination,

and with a show of force compelled Queen Ranavalona III to accept French control of foreign relations. Great Britain recognized the French protectorate in 1890, and on 30 September 1895 a French military expedition occupied the capital of Antananarivo (Tananarive). The French rule of the island was in the hands of Gen. Joseph S. Galliéni from 1896 to 1905. He established French authority throughout the island and on the whole governed justly and fairly. Madagascar had a Vichy government after the fall of France in 1940, but the British occupied the island in 1942 to prevent its use as a Japanese base.

Following World War II, there was increased agitation for independence, and in June 1960 the Malagasy Republic became a fully independent member of the French community. In response to student unrest in 1972, political authority was transferred to Gen. Philibert Ramanantsoa. A referendum in October of that year gave the general power for five years, but he was replaced in 1975 by Commander (now Admiral) Didier Ratsiraka. A new constitution was inaugurated on 21 December 1975 which placed executive power with the Supreme Revolutionary Council and established a Popular National Assembly. Further, the Malagasy Republic was renamed the Democratic Republic of Madagascar.

The only political group allowed was the National Front for Defense of the Revolution. In the 1982 local council elections seven parties (all under the National Front) were allowed to participate, but open politics do not in fact prevail. The real executive authority rests with the president, Adm. Didier Ratsiraka, not with the Supreme Revolutionary Council.

Politico-Military Background and Policy

Since General Ramanantsoa became head of the government in 1972, Malagasy policy has shifted from support of the West to a more independent and neutral stance. There are still strong ties with France, which remains Madagascar's major trading partner. Under the 1975 constitution the size of the armed forces has doubled, but most of the additional personnel are engaged in civic action work.

In theory, all males reaching age 20 are liable for eighteen months of national service, in either the armed forces or for civil purposes. In fact, relatively few men actually perform their military service, and Madagascar's armed forces have remained small.

Strategic Problems

Madagascar has few external strategic problems, aside from claims on nearby islands like Tromelin, Juan de Nova, and Bassas da India which are administered by France. Similarly, no other nation poses a serious security threat to Madagascar.

The nation's relative poverty is a major weakness. There is little domestic industry, and the economy is dependent on foreign earnings from agricultural exports (e.g., coffee, sugar, cloves) to purchase machinery, food, and fuel. Most of the people are subsistence farmers which, coupled with the high population growth rate, offers the prospect of environmental disaster within three decades. The government is aware of this, as evidenced by the armed forces' commitment to civic action.

Military Assistance and Defense Industry

Madagascar has depended on France and the Soviet Union for its military equipment. The army's materiel is mostly Soviet while the navy's is French; the air force has mixed Soviet and Western aircraft.

Alliances

Madagascar is a member of the United Nations, and of the Organization of African Unity (OAU), although it takes little part in continental African affairs.

Defense Structure

Madagascar's armed forces are divided among the Popular Army, the Aeronaval Force, and the Gendarmerie. By statute, power over the armed forces rests with the Supreme Revolutionary Council, but in fact it lies with President Ratsiraka. The Popular Army, by far the largest service, has the leading role in defense planning.

(For an explanation of the abbreviations and symbols used in the following section of military statistics, see the list of Abbreviations and Acronyms in each volume.)

Total Armed Forces

Active: 21,000. Terms of service: conscription (incl for civil purposes), 18 months.

ARMY: some 20,000
2 bn gp.
1 engr regt.
1 sigs regt.
1 service regt.
7 construction regt.
Equipment:
Light tanks: 12 PT-76
Recce: 8 M-8, est. 20 M-3, 10 Ferret, est. 35 BRDM-2.
APC: est. 30 M-3 half-track.
Towed arty: 76mm: 12 ZIS-3; 105mm: some M-101; 122mm: 12 D-30.
Mortars: 82mm: M-37; 120 mm: 8 M-43.
RL: 89mm: LRAC
RCL: 106mm: M-40A1.
AD guns: 14.5mm: 50 ZPU-4; 37mm: 20 Type 55.

NAVY: est. 500 (incl some 100 marines). Bases: Diégo-Suarez, Tamatave, Fort Dauphin, Tuléar, Majunga.
Patrol Craft: 1 Malaika (Fr PR48-m) PCI.
Amphibious: 1 Toky (Fr BATRAM) LSM, with 8 × SS-12 SSM, capacity 30 tps, 4 tk; plus craft; 1 LCT (Fr EDIC), 1 LCA, 3 LCVP.
Support and Miscellaneous: 1 tpt/trg.

AIR FORCE: 500; 12 cbt ac, no armed hel.

FGA: 1 sqn with 4 MiG-17F, 8 MiG-21FL.
Transport: 4 An-26, 3 BN-2, 2C-212, 2 Yak-40 (VIP).
Helicopters: 1 sqn with 6 Mi-8.
Liaison: 1 Cessna 310, 2 -337, 1 PA-23.
Training: 4 Cessna 172.

PARAMILITARY
Gendarmerie: 7,500 strong; operates as a rural police and internal security force, equipped with light infantry weapons. It also includes a marine police force equipped with five small inshore patrol craft, which formerly belonged to the navy.

Future

Madagascar is not likely to face any serious military crises in the near future. The greatest challenge facing the nation is that of economic development, and the armed forces are already making a significant contribution to development through their rural construction and civic action programs. Therefore there is likely to be little change in Madagascar's defense forces in the near future.

DAVID L. BONGARD
TREVOR N. DUPUY

SEE ALSO: Organization of African Unity; Sub-Saharan Africa.

Bibliography

American University. 1973. *Area handbook for the Malagasy Republic.* Washington, D.C.: U.S. Government Printing Office.
Brown, M. 1978. *Madagascar rediscovered: A history from early times to independence.* London: Damien Tunnacliffe.
Hunter, B. ed. 1991. *The statesman's year-book, 1991–92.* New York: St. Martin's Press.
International Institute for Strategic Studies. 1991. *The military balance 1991–1992.* London: Brassey's.
Jolly, A. 1980. *A world like our own: Man and nature in Madagascar.* New Haven, Conn.: Yale Univ. Press.

MAHAN, ALFRED THAYER [1840–1914]

Rear Adm. Alfred Thayer Mahan, U.S. Navy, stands as one of the world's most influential naval strategists (Fig. 1). Writing at a time of U.S. expansion westward and of an increasing U.S. role on the world scene, he had tremendous influence on naval thinking worldwide, on U.S. foreign policy, and on the naval development of many nations, including the United States, Great Britain, Germany, and Japan.

Early Life and Career

Alfred Mahan was born on 27 September 1840 at West Point, New York. His father, Dennis Hart Mahan, taught at the U.S. Military Academy and educated an entire generation of American Civil War leaders in civil and military

Figure 1. Alfred Thayer Mahan, 1887. (SOURCE: U.S. Library of Congress)

engineering. Mahan, however, pursued a different course. After attending Columbia College for two years, he entered the U.S. Naval Academy and graduated second in his class in 1859.

From 1859 until 1885, his career was unremarkable. During the Civil War he served on the screw steamer *Pocahontas* in the Port Royal, South Carolina, expedition of November 1861; on the screw sloop *Seminole* while it conducted blockade duty off Sabine Pass, Texas, in 1863 and 1864; in the South Atlantic Squadron aboard the *Alger* in 1864 and again in 1865; and on the *Philadelphia* as it operated off Charleston, South Carolina, in 1864. After the war, he had various sea and shore billets.

Teacher and Naval Theorist

Mahan's real talents were first revealed in 1883 when he published his first book, an account of U.S. naval operations during the Civil War. The book so impressed Capt. Stephen Luce that he adopted Mahan as his protégé. In 1885, Luce, then president of the newly established Naval War College at Newport, Rhode Island, invited Mahan to lecture on naval tactics and history at the college. Mahan taught there from 1886 to 1889 and also served as president of the college from 1886 to 1888. During this time he fought to ensure that the college was not absorbed into the navy's other training facilities and insisted that its curriculum stress the historical, theoretical, tactical, and strategic principles of naval warfare. His efforts were seminal in making the college the intellectual center of the new navy.

During his first tour at the college, Mahan wrote *The Influence of Sea Power Upon History, 1600–1783*, which was based on his lectures at the college and published in 1890 (this book later brought him to the attention of Theodore Roosevelt). Mahan left the college in 1889 but returned in 1890 to write a sequel to *Influence* entitled *The Influence of Sea Power Upon the French Revolution and Empire, 1793–1812*, published in 1892. He again served as president of the Naval War College in 1892 and 1893. After another tour of duty at sea, he returned to the college briefly before retiring in 1896 to devote full time to writing. His subsequent works included *The Interest of America in Sea Power, Present and Future* in 1897, *Sea Power in Its Relations to the War of 1812* in 1905, and *Naval Strategy* in 1911. He was recalled to active duty during the Spanish-American War, was an American delegate to the first Hague Peace Conference in 1899, and was promoted to rear admiral on the retired list in June 1906. Mahan, who raised the respectability of the field of naval history, was president of the American Historical Association in 1902 and foretold the defeat of the Central Powers and the German Navy in World War I. He died on 1 December 1914 at Quogue, New York.

Essence of Mahan's Theories

Concerning the United States, Mahan warned of the danger of neglecting seapower, a tendency he felt was inherent in democracies. Arguing that America's future lay in the seas, he cautioned against the nation's being distracted by the westward expansion that was then occurring across the continent.

Mahan made several other significant points. First, he placed great emphasis on the use of sea forces to project military power into areas controlled or threatened by enemy forces (sea power projection), arguing that U.S. coastal defense was a garrison function that most appropriately should be assigned to the army. Second, he stressed the great importance of a nation's sea lines of communication, those sea routes or lifelines across which its merchant ships and naval power pass. Third, he believed that while being first on the scene of a crisis was important for a navy, it was even more important to arrive with decisive naval superiority. Finally, in order to assure an adequate U.S. naval projection capability, Mahan said that it was necessary to have naval bases overseas. He recommended acquiring Hawaii and the Philippines in the Pacific and—placing great importance on the Panama Canal—he encouraged acquiring Cuba to assure control of the canal's eastern approaches.

Mahan's writings are more difficult to comprehend than those of Karl von Clausewitz and other military strategists, since they were based on his lectures at the Naval War College rather than being prepared as continuous narrative. For example, one must consult portions from several of his works to truly understand his views on the importance of the Panama Canal. Despite the difficulties, the U.S. Navy has followed Mahan's precepts concerning superior capability for power projection by sea and has also deemed it important to be on the scene of a crisis first with superior naval power. Using the resulting strategy, the navy has conducted its twentieth-century operations so effectively that, in terms of the frequency and success of its use of naval power, America may be viewed as history's preeminent sea power, challenged only by Great Britain's use of seapower in ages past. Additionally, by following Mahan faithfully the navy avoided suffering the great uncertainty and introspection that the U.S. Army endured after the American defeat in Vietnam. Often disparaged by some for the imperialistic aspects of his strategy, Mahan is responsible for the tremendous success of the U.S. Navy in the twentieth century.

Significance of Mahan's Theories

Written at a time of great and rapid technological advancement in navies, and immediately preceding emergence of the United States as a world power after the Spanish-American War (1898), Mahan's works profoundly affected both U.S. and worldwide naval developments before World War I. Because of a concord of interests and a personal relationship, Mahan regularly offered counsel to President Roosevelt and therefore had great influence on U.S. foreign policy and expansion overseas. His writings also considerably influenced battleship construction in the United States, Great Britain, Germany, Japan, and other nations.

BRUCE W. WATSON

SEE ALSO: Civil War, American; Gunboat Diplomacy; Maritime Strategy; Naval Warfare; Strategy.

Bibliography

Bowling, R. A. 1980. *The negative influence of Mahan on the protection of shipping in war.* Orono, Me.: Roland Alfred Bowling.

Hattendorf, J. B. 1986. *A bibliography of the works of Alfred Thayer Mahan.* Newport, R.I.: Naval War College Press.

Livezay, W. E. 1947. *Mahan on sea power.* Norman, Okla.: Univ. of Oklahoma Press.

Reynolds, C. G. 1978. *Famous American admirals.* New York: Van Nostrand Reinhold.

Spiller, R. J. 1989. *American military leaders.* New York: Praeger.

Taylor, C. C. 1920. *The life of Admiral Mahan, naval philosopher.* New York: George H. Doran.

Turk, R. W. 1987. *The ambitious relationship: Theodore Roosevelt and Alfred Thayer Mahan.* New York: Greenwood Press.

MAINTENANCE

The term *maintenance* has three distinctly separate military meanings and applications.

The first describes all supply and repair action taken to keep a force in condition to carry out its mission. In this sense, it has largely been supplanted by the term *logistics*, supply and repair being two principal functions of logistic support in peace and in war.

Maintenance also describes the routine, recurring work required to keep a facility—plant, building, structure, ground facility, utility system, or other property—in such condition that it may be continuously utilized, at its original or designed capacity and efficiency, for its intended purpose.

The third meaning is the subject of this article. Here the term *maintenance* describes all the action taken to retain materiel in, or restore it to, a specified condition. This includes inspection, testing, servicing, classification as to serviceability, modification, repair, recovery, rebuilding, and reclamation. Here attention is confined to the application of this term to land forces. Naval and air forces are covered in other articles in this publication.

A maintenance service, or equivalent military organization, is responsible for ensuring the operational fitness of army equipment. Consideration is given to achieving this aim from an early stage in the development of materiel.

Equipment engineering (maintenance) input is as vital during the design, development, and production phases as is the support provided during the service life of the equipment. Reliability, accessibility, maintainability, durability, and other important characteristics are "designed into" each piece of equipment with full regard to its maintenance as well as its operational performance. Information—much of it technical—is collated so that maintenance specifications, schedules, illustrated parts lists, and publications are prepared prior to an equipment's acceptance and introduction into service. Similar arrangements are made to ensure that initial scales (lists and quantities) of assemblies, components, and spare parts are calculated so that stocks are available immediately when an equipment enters service. These scales will be refined through usage experience during an equipment's service life, quantities will be altered, and supporting stocks will be adjusted.

While in service, equipment is regularly and systematically inspected, tested, and classified as to serviceability. Defects are investigated and rectified through normal repair, the introduction of permanent modifications, or the development of new techniques and tools. Major overhaul and refurbishment may be necessary during service life and undertaken according to a planned program or when otherwise required.

Maintenance capabilities are classified according to the complexity and the amount of time the repair takes, and also the level or echelon at which they are carried out.

The crews of vehicles or weapons may be trained to make minor adjustments and replace certain components. For instance, within the battalion, maintenance tradesmen, artisans, or technicians will undertake what are termed *unit* or *first-line* repairs, because they are carried out within the unit and are the first line of maintenance support. Some armies call this *organic* or *organizational* repair—terms obviously vary and can be difficult to translate from one language to another.

Complex tasks taking more time are generally undertaken by the mobile maintenance workshop that supports battalions, usually close at hand, to which equipment is backloaded. In most armies, the terms *field* and *second-line* repairs are used for these.

Certain more specialized workshop facilities that carry out *intermediate* repairs may be available at a *third line*. The complete rebuilding of equipment or assemblies, called *fourth line*, is classified as a *base* repair and is located even farther to the rear, requiring additional backloading. Some armies term this latter category *depot* repair. Base or depot maintenance workshops are highly specialized technically and are normally located in a rear support area.

When a piece of equipment breaks down or is damaged, the cause is diagnosed and recorded (Fig. 1), and then a condition code is specified. Apart from the code that describes the item as "serviceable," others indicate that:

1. No repair is needed at that time, but the fault should be kept under observation.
2. It can be returned to serviceability by the crew, if applicable.
3. It requires unit repair by maintenance tradesmen, artisans, or technicians immediately available within the battalion.
4. It needs field repair at the supporting workshop.
5. It must have more specialized attention.
6. It is beyond local or economic repair.

A battalion will normally have an integral or organic maintenance platoon, with a nucleus and detached company sections undertaking unit repair as first-line support.

A regiment (brigade) may have its own maintenance company, and a division its own maintenance battalion each capable of deploying mobile workshops that carry out field or second-line repairs and provide recovery and backloading facilities. They support battalions and all other units in the field formations and are located in a forward area of the combat zone.

Quite often field or second-line maintenance resources will be retained at divisional level and not specifically allocated to regiments (brigades). Centralization of effort and control may improve efficiency, economy, flexibility, protection, and survivability, as well as provide a reserve capability for unforeseen needs. The allotment of resources to regiments (brigades) is an alternative and will also have advantages. The structure and procedures vary

Figure 1. Airborne forces—Captain and equipment engineers inspect damaged assembly. (SOURCE: British Army [Royal Electrical and Mechanical Engineers])

among armies, and the solution adopted depends on the operational situation and logistic doctrine.

Another variation may involve the field or second-line maintenance workshop detaching well-equipped, highly mobile, forward repair teams to rectify a breakdown "on site" in battalion operational areas. This capability may be restricted to prioritized, main battle equipments and may be limited to assembly exchange. Repair is carried out as close to the point where the equipment has broken down as is tactically prudent and technically feasible; each forward repair team will have some recovery capacity. The merits of this system are twofold: equipment that is operationally vital is restored to battleworthiness and functional efficiency as speedily as is practicable, and its backloading to the main field workshop is avoided. Forward repair teams, therefore, are a way of providing crucially important second-line maintenance at first-line level.

Yet another variation may be to split the main field workshop—that is, its resources less the forward repair teams—between two separate, operational locations on the battlefield. To do so may position support facilities nearer to customers, further enhancing concealment and survivability and enabling the two elements to "leapfrog" during a major move. On the other hand, this physical separation may unduly dissipate skilled and specialized resources, encumber control, and complicate the supply of assemblies, components, and spare parts. The choice, again, will be a tactical and technical decision.

At third line may be found specialized maintenance facilities that are needed to support fighting formations but which, by their nature, are better deployed farther to the rear; these are often static rather than mobile. Complicated electronic repairs may fall into this category, as well as helicopter maintenance.

The timely, constant, and comprehensive supply of assemblies, components, spare parts, and consumable materials (from welding rods to nuts and bolts) is vital to the maintenance activity. Equipment that is classified beyond repair, or beyond the capabilities of repair and recovery at that time, may be "cannibalized," but this can only supplement and not replace effective supply support. The provision of tools and maintenance equipment is also vital.

Vehicle and weapon crews, like most equipment users, have a ready-to-hand stock of minor components, piece parts, and consumables. The battalion's maintenance platoon, or its equivalent in other units, will carry a mobile holding of supplies needed for unit repair at first line. Forward repair teams will take with them a small quantity and restricted range of major assemblies and the wherewithal to effect assembly exchange. Maintenance battalions or companies providing field repairs in divisions and regiments (brigades) will require a mobile second-line stock of supplies of a wide range and of a substantial quantity. The size or degree of specialization of static stocks will vary at third and fourth lines; a base maintenance workshop, for example, may be supported by its own supply depot.

Stocks on hand at each echelon seldom meet every demand—in fact, scales (lists and quantities) reflect frequency of demand for particular items—and stocks used have to be replenished. The supporting supply system provides operationally urgent or routine requirements based on priority of need and target delivery times.

In some armies, the maintenance service provisions, stores, and supplies its own requirements of assemblies, components, spare parts, consumables, tools, and specialist equipment. In others, a separate supply service meets the needs of the army as a whole as well as the maintenance function. Some organize supply and maintenance on a "user" basis with the artillery, for instance, having its own resources. Yet others work a combination of these systems. There is no standard pattern; the system practiced will generally have grown up by custom and tradition, and each will have advantages and disadvantages.

The maintenance plan aims to ensure the operational fitness of equipment. It forms the basis for providing the maintenance resources required to ensure that equipment operates effectively in peace, during training, and in war.

Maintenance planning depends fundamentally upon estimated equipment casualty rates. These are calculated and established by taking a wide range of usage measurements and the full range of army materiel into account. For example, some rates are based on average daily mileage of tracked and wheeled vehicles, on the flying hours of army fixed-wing aircraft and helicopters, or on the number of rounds fired with specific charges by guns. The aim is to use the rates as an aid to forecasting equipment failure as well as an estimate of expenditure or consumption of supplies in both peace and war. Maintenance planning also depends fundamentally on the estimates of battle attrition in war. This will help to forecast the extent, nature, and frequency of battle damage sustained by individual equipment in combat or support environments.

Estimates of equipment failure and battle attrition rates enable maintenance resources to be forecasted, justified, provided, allocated, and deployed, together with requisite supply stocks. However, the calculation of these rates may well prove to be a difficult process requiring skillful research, sound military judgment, and practical evaluation, as well as computerized assistance. Forecasts necessarily have to be based on the next war, not the last one, and are difficult to apply to the battlefield universally—spatially, temporally, longitudinally, or laterally. Therefore, maintenance planning, like supply and other logistic planning, must retain the ability to revise the rates quickly based on actual combat experience at the particular time fighting occurs so as to allow a margin for error and to keep some maintenance resources in reserve.

Preventive maintenance features prominently and significantly in any maintenance plan: regular inspection, functional testing, and scheduled or unscheduled servicing of a multiplicity of materiel. Detailed records help with the continuous and analytical assessment of workload activities, trends, training needs, development of skills, tools, equipment, techniques and procedures, and assemblies and spares requirements, and with the allocation and control of all resources. Equipment serviceability statements indicate to the tactical, logistical, and maintenance commanders and their staffs the running operational status and readiness of important parts of a force's inventory. If testing is satisfactory, then performance on ranges and field exercises is another indicator of equipment fitness for role. The state of equipment in a given unit is also a measure of supporting maintenance capability and competence.

When a force is committed to operations short of "general" war—that is, to a "limited" war—its composition in terms of combat, combat support, and combat service support elements can vary considerably, even within a single regiment (brigade) or a division. The scale of equipment taken with the force can also vary considerably: troops may be equipped to light, normal, or heavy scales and may rely on specific forms of transport or may move mainly on foot. How the type of combat, terrain, and climate is likely to modify estimated equipment casualty and attrition rates, and whether quiet, normal, or intensive rates of equipment utilization are expected, are other important factors. All these considerations will be taken into account when developing a maintenance plan for supporting the particular force involved.

The requirement for maintenance resources will be tailor-made to the force and to a set of parameters such as those mentioned. Obviously, resources will differ for operations in jungle, desert, mountainous, steppe, tropical, temperate, and very cold environments. Once needs have been assessed and resources decided, maintenance facilities will be phased into the area of operations and deployed to conform with the overall tactical and logistic plans. If, after arrival and during the course of the conflict, some maintenance resources are clearly in excess, they will be returned to base; if deficiencies appear in type or quantity, reinforcements will be dispatched; if attrition demands replacements, these will also be provided.

In a general war, the full panoply of maintenance support is likely to be needed, less those elements strictly geared to peacetime requirements that will probably switch to different operational roles. Repair, recovery, backloading of equipment casualties, and route clearance are the principal maintenance tasks to be undertaken in this scenario.

Before battle is joined, units expect to have time to deploy from their peacetime barracks—either inside or outside the envisaged theater of operations—to their battle positions. During deployment, some equipment will break down, otherwise fail, or be accidentally damaged. Maintenance support has to be positioned in the operational areas of field formations early and in sufficient strength to deal with casualties sustained during deployment so that maximum equipment is held at the appropriate battleworthiness status. Many of these remedial tasks are likely to be outside the capability of unit or first-line repair resources and will require field or second-line maintenance attention.

The fluidity and lethality of conventional conflict—leaving aside the catastrophic effects of nuclear strikes—are likely to take a heavy toll of equipment in general war. High casualty and attrition rates will complement high utilization, expenditure, and consumption rates. This will be the case particularly for main battle equipments: armored fighting vehicles, infantry combat vehicles, attack helicopters, weapon systems of all types, surveillance and detection devices, combat engineer equipment, certain communications systems, and some logistic support vehicles and equipment.

There will have to be strict prioritization of maintenance tasks, well-controlled allocation, and husbandry of maintenance resources so that they are available for critical tasks; also needed are flexible cross-servicing among maintenance elements to enable the timely reallocation and switching of resources to deal with higher priority tasks in adjacent areas of the battlefield. The rapid recovery of equipment casualties, their repair to battleworthiness standards, and their prompt return to their operational roles will have a decisive influence on the conduct and outcome of the battle.

Some contend that in a full-scale general war, there will be insufficient time to repair equipment casualties. They may be right, but recent intensive combat experience has shown that for every tank destroyed, three are damaged and repairable. As far as other main battle equipments are concerned, the contrast is even greater: for each one destroyed, ten are damaged but are repairable. Therefore, maintenance must remain a key part of combat service support, must continue to have the technical resources to respond as effectively and for as long as possible to the needs of forces and their materiel, and must endeavor to help sustain operations in the most difficult circumstances envisaged. Training for this particular role is particularly challenging in peacetime.

Not only will repair and recovery be vital, but also the backloading of equipment casualties to farther rearward, better protected, and more specialized maintenance facilities. In recent conflicts with their Arab neighbors, the Israeli armed forces operated an impressive backloading system and quickly returned a high proportion of fit tanks to combat; in their case, efficient backloading systems and special tank workshops were key factors in their operational success. Tracked or wheeled vehicle casualties may be towed back, drawn on suspended hoist, or carried on other transport. The establishment of equipment collecting and backloading points—strategically and logistically well placed, with good communications and control—will assist with the timely backloading of all useful, repairable, high-priority materiel. Evacuation may well be undertaken mainly during the hours of darkness and by road, though certain armies plan to make much use of railways for as long as this form of transport operates. The importance of the maintenance task to remove "hulks" and keep routes clear of damaged, broken-down equipment for all forces and activities requires no additional emphasis.

Only if equipment casualties are beyond repair should they be abandoned; later, resources may become available to enable their restoration and return to battle. Only if repairable equipment casualties are in danger of being overrun and captured by the enemy should they be destroyed.

The maintenance role, therefore, remains crucial in general war as in other forms of conflict. The magnitude of the task, and the obscurities the fog of war will create, will not make it easy for maintenance troops and their commanders. They will have to draw extensively upon their resources of ingenuity, improvisation, and endurance in conditions difficult to simulate on training exercises.

J. H. SKINNER

SEE ALSO: Attrition: Personnel Casualties; Consumption Rates, Battlefield; Engineering, Constructional; Infrastructure, Military; Logistics: A General Survey; Replacements: Personnel and Materiel.

Bibliography

Berman, M. B. 1988. *Evaluating the combat payoff of alternative logistics structures for high-technology subsystems.* Santa Monica, Calif.: Rand Corporation.

Federal Republic of Germany. 1972. Kommission zur überprufung der Materialerhaltung für Rad- und Kettenfahrzeuge einschliesslich des Ersatzteilwesens. *Rationalisierung der Materialerhaltung für Rad- und Kettenfahrzeuge.* Bonn: Bundesministerium der Verteidigung, Org. 4.

Integrated Logistic Support Symposium. 1969. *Proceedings.* Chambersburg, Pa.: USAMC Maintenance and Engineering Office.

Rybakov, K. V. 1971. *Zapravka qusenichnykh i kolesnykh mashin.* N.p.

Tripp, R. S., M. B. Berman, and C. L. Tsai. 1990. *The concept of operations for a U.S. Army combat-oriented logistics execution system with VISION (Visibility of Support Options).* Santa Monica, Calif.: RAND Corporation.

U.S. Department of the Army. 1958. *PM: Preventive maintenance guide for commanders.* Washington, D.C.: Government Printing Office.

MALAYSIA, FEDERATION OF

The Federation of Malaysia, with its capital at Kuala Lumpur, is located along the strategically significant and commercially advantageous Strait of Malacca and the South China Sea. Malaysia, with a population of about eighteen million, is geographically separated: Western Malaysia is situated on the southern portion of the peninsula that extends from Thailand and Burma. The eastern Malaysian states of Sabah and Sarawak lie 644 kilometers (412 mi.) away on the northern half of Borneo, the world's third largest island, and border Indonesian Kalimantan.

Malaysia's climate is tropical with temperatures averaging 80° Fahrenheit (27°C), and an average annual rainfall of 254 centimeters (100 in.) owing to southwest (April to October) and northeast (October to February) monsoons. In both peninsular and insular Malaysia the terrain is primarily coastal plains rising to hills and mountains; indeed, the highest mountain (4,101 m [13,455 ft.]) in Southeast Asia is in the state of Sabah on Borneo.

Incredibly well endowed with natural resources (tin, petroleum, natural gas, timber, copper, iron ore, bauxite), Malaysia has one of the highest standards of living in Southeast Asia, with a per capita income of about US$2,000. The country is the world's leading producer of natural rubber, palm oil, and tin; it is a net exporter of petroleum and natural gas. Despite this, bitter ethnic tensions within a population that is 59 percent Malay and other indigenous groups, 32 percent Chinese, and 9 percent Indian are a source of government concern, and complex political and personality interplay is a feature of this former British colony.

Power Potential Statistics

Area: 329,750 square kilometers (127,317 sq. mi.)
Population: 17,730,200
Total Active Armed Forces: 127,900 (0.721% of pop.)
Gross Domestic Product: US$43.1 billion (1990 est.)
Annual Defense Expenditure: US$1.7 billion (3.9% of GDP, 1990 est.)
Iron and Steel Production: none
Fuel Production:
  Crude oil: 28 million metric tons (1989)
  Natural gas: 6.2 million tons LNG (1988)
Electrical Power Output: 16,500 million kwh (1990)
Merchant Marine: 157 vessels; 1,530,756 gross registered tons
Civil Air Fleet: 53 major transport aircraft; 119 usable airfields (32 with permanent-surface runways); 1 with runways over 3,659 meters (12,000 ft.); 7 with runways 2,440–3,659 meters (8,000–12,000 ft.); 18 with runways 1,220–2,440 meters (4,000–8,000 ft.).

For the most recent information, the reader may refer to the following annual publications:
The Military Balance. International Institute for Strategic Studies. London: Brassey's (UK).
The Statesman's Year-Book. New York: St. Martin's Press.
The World Factbook. Central Intelligence Agency. Washington, D.C.: Brassey's (US).

History

Similarly to Indonesia, Malaysia was part of the early Buddhist Malay Kingdom of Sriwijaya, based in Sumatra, that dominated the Malaysian peninsula from the ninth to the thirteenth century. This was followed by control from Java as part of the Hindu Kingdom of Majapahit in the fourteenth century. During this period Muslim influence began to spread throughout the region, and conversions to Islam accelerated with the rise of Malacca under Muslim rule.

Malacca was a major center of shipping and commerce; Chinese, Arab, Malay, and Indian merchants traded there. The Portuguese conquered Malacca in 1511; the Dutch gained control by 1641. In 1795 the British won control; by 1826 they had combined their settlements of Malacca, Penang, and Singapore into the Straits Settlements Colony, and then established protectorates over the Malay Sultanates on the peninsula. In 1895, four of these became the Federated Malay States. The British brought public administration, public services, and large-scale rubber and tin production. They also encouraged immigration of Chinese and Indians (until the 1930s) to provide the extra workers needed for economic expansion.

The Japanese invaded and occupied Malaysia from 1942 to 1945. After World War II an increased popular wish for independence asserted itself, and in 1957 the Federation of Malaya was established on peninsular Malaysia. Independence from the United Kingdom was negotiated under the leadership of Tunku Abdul Rahman, who later became prime minister. Former British colonies of Singapore, Sarawak, and Sabah joined the federation on 16 September 1963, and the name Malaya was changed to Malaysia; Singapore withdrew and became independent nearly two years later.

Twelve of Malaysia's post–World War II years (1948–60) were marked by communist-inspired revolution, in which insurgents (mostly Chinese citizens) tried to take over by armed force. British forces were instrumental in successfully resolving the conflict. A small (several thousand) remnant of dissidents relocated in southern Thailand; their survivors continued the struggle until 2 December 1989, when about 1,200 armed members surrendered to Malaysian forces. Only about 100 communist insurgents remain active in North Kalimantan and Sabah.

The communist rebellion was further exacerbated by Indonesia's objection to the formation of Malaysia, and a confrontation (military, economic, political, and diplomatic) continued until the fall of Indonesian president Sukarno in 1966. Cordial relations followed.

Politico-Military Background and Policy

Malaysia is a federated constitutional monarchy, with thirteen component states and two federal territories; it is a member of the British Commonwealth and has a bicameral parliamentary form of government. The elected paramount ruler is also the commander-in-chief of the armed forces and the leader of the Islamic faith in Malaysia. The states have limited powers, which are expressed through an assembly and a chief minister; nine of these have hereditary rulers, most with the title of sultan. Malaysia's judicial system is based on English common law; the Supreme Court reviews legislative acts at the request of the Supreme Head of the Federation. As with most Southeast Asian nations, leaders once in power have tended to stay in power and become increasingly authoritative.

Malaysia, a carefully nonaligned nation-state, has formal diplomatic relations with all sides of the international scene; it is a moderate member of the Non-Aligned Movement of Islamic Countries. A keystone of Malaysian foreign policy is support for regional cooperation, especially within the Association of Southeast Asia Nations (ASEAN), of which it is a member. Also of policy interest is the fact that Malaysia is promoting new initiatives that focus on Japan and South Korea as models for economic development.

The Armed Forces Council, chaired by the Minister of Defence, coordinates the independent services—the Royal Malaysian Army, Air Force, Navy, and Police Force. Military service is voluntary, and modest force reductions are a recent feature.

Strategic Problems

Malaysia is well regarded internationally, due in part to its economic performance and ability to service debt. There are, however, four sources of international disagreement:

a complex dispute with China, the Philippines, Taiwan, and Vietnam over the rights to the Spratly Islands in the South China Sea; a fishing-rights conflict with Thailand, and intrusions of aggressive Thai fishermen into Malaysian waters; the wish of Brunei to purchase the Malaysian salient that divides Brunei into two parts on the north shore of Borneo; and a twenty-year claim by the Philippines to Sabah (a claim which may soon be withdrawn, and Philippine citizens repatriated from Malaysian territory).

Malaysia is part of the key to control of sea lanes through the Strait of Malacca and in the South China Sea. Thus, considerable regional and global significance is attached to its geography. While Malaysia is fully responsible for its own security, membership in the Five-Power Defense Arrangement (FPDA) provides some military ties to Britain, Australia, New Zealand, and Singapore. Cooperation with predominantly Chinese Singapore is at times problematic.

Although Malaysia is of geostrategic interest, exogenous threats appear minimal. The federation's most pressing strategic difficulty lies within its borders—deep-seated racial cleavages and inequal distribution of power. Traditionally, economic power has been in the hands of ethnic Chinese, and Malays have held political power. Various measures have been taken from time to time to reduce, or at least cover over, the ethnic differences. However, the danger of renewed, overt violence remains close to the surface.

Malaysia's economic progress has been essential to helping overcome ethnic tensions; it is difficult to believe that societal stability could be maintained without such progress. Thus the primary strategic focus for Malaysia must be to maintain relative economic prosperity while proactively moving to dispel racial hatreds.

Military Assistance

Far greater significance is placed on economic assistance from major powers than on military aid. U.S. financial commitments from 1970 to 1984 were US$170 million; from other Western nations US$3.8 billion was received from 1970 to 1987. In contrast, the United States provided US$950 thousand in military aid in 1988. Malaysia's military equipment is predominantly of Western origin, much of it coming from the United Kingdom and the United States in the form of armored vehicles, ships, and aircraft.

Defense Industry

Malaysia is the world's third largest manufacturer of semiconductor devices and the world's largest exporter of semiconductors. Thus it makes an indirect but substantial contribution to command and control, guidance, and other electronic-based military systems of nations around the globe. As a part of Malaysia's overall GNP, however, defense-related products and services are quite minimal.

Alliances

Malaysia is a charter member of ASEAN and a member of the defense-aligned FPDA organization. While also a member of the Non-Aligned Movement (NAM), Malaysia has made numerous regional agreements outside the framework of its more formal memberships; some of these are related to mutual defense concerns, but most to economic cooperation. Malaysia is also a member of the United Nations and a wide variety of international economic, trade, and health organizations.

Defense Structure

Malaysia's army of 105,000 was reduced to 97,000 in 1990. It is organized into one corps HQ, four divisions, one counterinsurgency command, and nine independent infantry brigades with an assortment of combat support assets. The Malaysian navy of 12,500 personnel is balanced over two regional commands plus the fleet command. Ships and boats include four frigates with helicopter decks for antisubmarine-warfare Wasp helicopters, 29 patrol craft of offshore and close-in types, eight missile craft, five mine warfare vessels, and an assortment of amphibious landing craft and tender vessels. Key bases are located at Lumut, Tanjang Kuantan, Woodlands (Singapore), Lubuan; and Songei Antu.

Malaysia's 12,000-member air force has 67 combat and reconnaissance aircraft and a complement of transports, liaison planes, and helicopters organized into four commands. The air force maintains a squadron of air field defense troops. Fifteen observers served with United Nations forces in Iran and Iraq. Malaysia's paramilitary force is predominantly the 18,000-member police field forces, organized as four brigades with a total of 21 battalions and complemented by air and marine assets. Australia maintains an army infantry company and an air force detachment in Malaysia.

(For an explanation of the abbreviations and symbols used in the following section of military statistics, see the list of Abbreviations and Acronyms in each volume.)

Total Armed Forces

Active: 127,900
Reserves: 40,600: Army 38,000; Navy 2,000; Air 600.

ARMY: 105,000 (reducing to 97,000).
1 corps, 4 div HQ.
1 area sy comd (COIN).
9 inf bde, consisting of 36 inf bn (1 APC, 1 AB), 4 armd, 5 fd arty, 2 AD arty, 5 engr regt. 1 SF regt (3 bn).
Reserves: 1 div HQ; 1 bde HQ; 12 inf regt; 4 highway sy bn.
Equipment:
Light tanks: 26 Scorpion (90mm).
Recce: 162 SIBMAS, 140 AML-60/-90, 92 Ferret (60 mod).

APC: 184 V-100/-150 Commando, 25 Stormer, 360 Condor.
Towed arty: 105mm: 150 Model 56 pack, 40 M-102A1 († in store); 155mm: 9 FH-70.
Mortars: 81mm: L16.
ATGW: SS-11.
RL: 89mm: M-20.
RCL: 84mm: Carl Gustav; 106mm: 150 M-40; 120mm: 5 Wombat.
AD guns: 35mm: 8 Oerlikon; 40 mm: 36: 24 40/70, 12 L/70.
SAM: 48 Javelin, 12 Rapier.
Assault craft: 165 Damen.

NAVY: 10,500.
Two Regional Commands: plus Fleet.
Area 1: Malayan Peninsula (west of 109°E).
Area 2: Borneo Area (east of 109°E).
Bases: Area 1: Lumut (HQ), Tanjong Gelang, Kuantan; Woodlands (Singapore), trg base. Area 2: Labuan (HQ), Sungei Antu (Sarawak).
Frigates: 4:
2 Kasturi (FS-1500) with 2×2 ASW mor, deck for Wasp hel; plus 2×2 MM-38 Exocet SSM, 1×100mm gun.
1 Hang Tuah (UK Mermaid) with 1×3 Limbo ASW mor, hel deck for Wasp; plus 1×2 102mm gun.
1 Rahmat with 1×3 ASW mor, 1×114mm gun hel deck.
Patrol and Coastal Combatants: 37
Missile Craft: 8: 4 Handalan (Sw Spica) with 4 MM-38 Exocet SSM; 4 Perdana (Fr Combattante II) with 2 Exocet SSM.
Patrol: 29:
Offshore: 2 Musytari with 1×100mm gun, hel deck.
Inshore: 27: 6 Jerong PFI, 3 Kedah, 4 Sabah, 14 Kris PCI.
Mine Warfare: 5: 4 Mahamiru (mod lt Lerici) MCO; 1 diving tender (inshore).
Amphibious: 2 Sri Banggi (US LST-511) LST, capacity 200 tps, 16 tk, (but usually employed as tenders to patrol craft). Plus 33 craft: 5 LCM, 13 LCU, 15 LCP.
Support and Miscellaneous: 3: 2 logistic/fuel spt, 1 survey.

Naval Air: No cbt ac, 6 armed Wasp HAS-1 hel.

AIR FORCE: 12,400; 67 cbt ac, no armed hel; 4 Comd.
FGA: 2 sqn: with 32 A-4 (26 A-4PTM, 6 TA-4);
Fighter: 1 sqn with 13 F-5E, 4-F.
Recce: 1 recce/OCU sqn with 2 RF-5E, 2 F-5F.
MR: 1 sqn with 3 C-130HMP.
Transport:
Aircraft: 4 sqn: 1 with 6 C-130H; 2 with 14 DHC-4; 1 with 2 BAe-125 (VIP), 1 Falcon-900 (VIP), 2 HU-16 (1 tpt, 1 VIP), 12 Cessna 402B ac; 1 NAS-332 hel.
Helicopters: 4 sqn with 31 S-61A, 17 SA-316B (liaison).
Training: 4 trg units:
Aircraft: 10* MB-339; 42 PC-7 (4* wpn trg); 10 Bulldog;
Helicopters: 8 SE-3160, 7 Bell 47, 4 S-61.
AAM: AIM-9 Sidewinder.
Airfield Defense Troops: 1 sqn.

FORCES ABROAD
UN and Peacekeeping:
Angola (UNAVEM II): observers.
Iraq/Kuwait (UNIKOM): 8 observers.

PARAMILITARY
Police Field Force: 18,000; 4 bde HQ: 21 bn (incl 2 Aboriginal); Shorland armd cars, 140 AT-105, SB-301 APC.
Marine Police: 51 Inshore Patrol Craft:
15 Long Hitan (38-m) PFI
9 Sangitan (29-m) PFI
27 PCI ⟨.
Police Air Wing: 4 Cessna 206, 7 PC-6 ac.
Auxiliary Police Field Force: (Area Security Units), 3,500 men in 89 units.
Border Scouts (in Sabah, Sarawak): 1,200.
People's Volunteer Corps (RELA): 180,000.
Customs Service: 38 patrol craft: 8 Perak (Vosper-32m) armed PFI, about 30 craft ⟨.

FOREIGN FORCES
Australia: Army: 1 inf coy. Air Force: det with P-3C ac.

Future

Malaysia's security concerns as well as its economic interests link it to the West in fact, if not in principle. This relationship, in some cases direct and in others indirect (i.e., through ASEAN), is likely to expand with time. Equally likely is that minor difficulties will result from misperceptions of political intent or the domestic agendas of major and regional powers.

Although the West, and the United States in particular, will remain central to overall regional security, Malaysia will have reason for heightened interest in the activities of Japan and a reemerging China. Too, the resolution of conflict in Indochina will remain an important subregional matter, as will continuing developments in Vietnam.

Of primary future concern will be economic growth and internal stability among ethnic groups. In the case of the latter, such antagonisms do not bode well for the country's future; a high political value will be placed on economic performance as an offset. Malaysia's government is committed to growth and has demonstrated that it is prepared to act when required. Although the government's programs have occasionally been ill-advised, the general performance in recent history has been better than that of many other countries. Backed by a great variety of natural resources, Malaysia has the capability to continue its present performance.

CHARLES F. HAWKINS
DONALD S. MARSHALL

SEE ALSO: Association of Southeast Asian Nations; Colonial Empires, European; Indonesia; Indo-Pacific Area; Singapore.

Bibliography

American University. 1985. *Area handbook for Malaysia*. Washington, D.C.: Government Printing Office.
Andaya, L, and W. Barban. 1982. *A history of Malaysia*. New York: St. Martin's Press.
Far Eastern Economic Review. 1988. Malaysia. In *Asia 1988 yearbook*. Hong Kong: Far Eastern Economic Review.
Fisk, E. K., and H. Osmanrani. 1982. *The political economy of Malaysia*. New York: Oxford Univ. Press.
International Institute for Strategic Studies. 1991. *The military balance 1991–1992*. London: Brassey's.
Matahir bin Mohammed, D. S. 1982. *The Malay dilemma*. Kuala Lumpur: Federal Publications.
Nagata, J. 1984. *The reflowering of Malaysian Islam: Muslim religious radicals and their roots*. Vancouver: Univ. of British Columbia Press.

Purcell, V. 1968. *The Chinese in Malaya.* New York: Oxford Univ. Press.
Rafferty, K. 1990. Malaysia. In *The Asia and Pacific review.* 11th ed. Saffron Walden, U.K.: World of Information.
Roff, W. R. 1975. *Origins of Malay nationalism.* New Haven, Conn.: Yale Univ. Press.
Scalapino, R. A., and M. Kosaka, eds. 1988. *Peace, politics and economics in Asia: The challenge to cooperate.* New York: Pergamon-Brassey's.
U.S. Central Intelligence Agency. 1991. *The world factbook 1991–92.* Washington, D.C.: Brassey's.
U.S. Department of State. 1986. Malaysia. *Background Notes.* February. Washington, D.C.: Department of State, Bureau of Public Affairs.

MANAGEMENT

In the broadest sense, management is the process of coordinating all the resources of an organization in order to accomplish organizational objectives. Management is a necessity in all organizations today, and this is certainly true of military organizations. Without some orchestration, these resources—human, capital, and technological—cannot be expected to come together naturally as a finely tuned, well-run organization. Management is the process of establishing organizational goals and objectives, assembling the necessary resources, recruiting and selecting employees who will do the work of the organization, coordinating the efforts of many workers, resolving the inevitable problems that arise in any organized endeavor, and ultimately distributing the outputs produced by the organization.

Prehistoric hunting parties and the huge multinational organizations of the present exhibit a common element. People unite and form an organization when the task is either too great or too difficult to be accomplished by individuals acting independently. Management thus arises out of the functional imperative to organize. Working together, a number of people can accomplish what the same number could never achieve individually.

Evolution of Management

Although the managerial function has certainly changed over time, clearly it has been present from the earliest periods of history. Although little was written about the practice of management in early times, its presence can be inferred from the significant accomplishments of early societies. Consider, for example, the pyramids of Giza that were built around 2500 B.C. These pyramids covered an area of thirteen acres and contained about 2,300,000 blocks of granite and limestone, each weighing up to 5,000 pounds. The logistical problems alone, housing and feeding thousands of workers, required managerial skill that would be admired even today. The existence of these pyramids is evidence of early management approaches: establish a goal, assemble the necessary resources, and coordinate efforts in order to accomplish the goal (Tansik et al. 1980). Similarly, the Greeks, Romans, and Chinese accomplished significant management feats such as the construction of monuments, structures, and aqueducts that further illustrated the existence of management practices in early societies (Wren 1972).

The existence of military organizations also demonstrated the presence of management approaches from the earliest of times. Early military leaders were forced to grapple with management problems resulting from leading large groups of men in order to accomplish tactical and strategic objectives. History is replete with illustrations of military leaders who determined an objective and then led soldiers in an endeavor designed to accomplish it (Clausewitz 1984).

In Exodus 18 we also find some early written evidence of the existence of management considerations. Moses, while leading the Israelites from Egypt to Canaan, found himself overwhelmed with attempting to resolve the problems of his people. Jethro, his father-in-law, offered him the following management advice:

> The thing thou doest is not good. Thou will surely wear away, both thou and this people that is with thee; for this thing is too heavy for thee; thou are not able to perform it thyself alone. Hearken now unto my voice, I will give thee counsel. . . . Thou shalt provide out of the people able men . . . and place such over them to be rulers of thousands, and rulers of hundreds, rulers of fifties, and rulers of tens. . . . If thou shalt do this thing, and God command thee so, then thou shalt be able to endure, and all this people shall also go to their place in peace.

Although it is clear that management has existed since the earliest of times, it was not until the rise of industrialization in the late nineteenth century that scholars began to write in detail about the notion of management. Frederick Taylor, generally acknowledged as the "father of scientific management," began his work in the Midvale Steel Works in Philadelphia in the late 1800s. He sought to develop productivity enhancements through time and motion studies in order to determine the best way to accomplish certain tasks. He believed that the application of scientific methods to the tasks faced by factory workers would result in increased productivity without the expenditure of additional human effort. Taylor saw the following five fundamental principles as underlying a scientific approach to management (Taylor 1947):

1. Replace rules of thumb with science
2. Achieve unity in group action, rather than disharmony
3. Achieve cooperation of human beings, rather than chaotic individualization
4. Work for maximum rather than restricted output
5. Develop all employees to the fullest extent possible

Henri Fayol, a French industrialist, was another significant figure in the evolution of managerial thought. Although Fayol made numerous contributions to the field of management, perhaps the most significant was his statement of fourteen general principles of management. Fayol considered such principles as division of labor (specialization), unity of command (a single superior), and a scalar chain (a "chain of superiors") to be general principles of management, although he acknowledged that their implementation should be dependent upon individual situations (Fayol 1949). These principles remain applicable to most military organizations today.

Max Weber, the noted German sociologist, advocated his notion of bureaucracy around the same time Fayol's ideas were becoming known in the United States. Weber also contributed to the evolution of managerial thought by advocating a "rational" organizational structure with the tasks subdivided into specialized jobs. This notion was similar to Fayol's conception of division of labor. Weber also believed that a definite set of rules must be followed in order to ensure predictability in the work place. Furthermore, he advocated the use of an impersonal attitude when dealing with subordinates to ensure fairness and the maintenance of a clear authority structure (Weber 1947).

In response to management's continuing desire to increase productivity and employee efficiency as well as to the rising influence of psychology on management practices, the human relations school of management emerged in the 1930s. Elton Mayo conducted a series of studies on worker behavior in the Hawthorne Works plant of the Western Electric Company on Chicago's west side. The initial study involved an illumination experiment. Employees were divided into a test group and a control group to study the effects of lighting on productivity. Investigators believed that enhanced lighting would increase productivity; not surprisingly, this proved to be true. To further investigate the hypothesis, however, Mayo decided to decrease the lighting. Productivity again increased. To further confuse the situation, the control group's production improved every time a change was made in the test group. This phenomenon, now known as the "Hawthorne Effect," dramatically illustrated the importance of the role of human behavior in management. The concept of a "social" worker was therefore balanced with the earlier notion of a "rational-economic" worker (Mayo 1953). The work of Mayo and his associates led to an increased emphasis on the behavioral sciences as applied to management and to the recognition that managers operated within a social system consisting of human beings with individual needs.

As management thought continued to evolve, Douglas McGregor presented two theories that emerged from much of the behavioral research following the Hawthorne studies. In 1960, McGregor speculated that managers possessed fundamentally different assumptions about human nature that accounted for differences in the two theories. Theory *X*, based upon rational-economic assumptions tacitly made by earlier scholars, assumed that the average person had an inherent dislike for work. Therefore, the worker must be coerced or threatened with punishment if any meaningful work were to be accomplished. Theory *Y*, derived from much of the behavioral science research, assumed that the expenditure of effort and energy in work was as natural as recreation and relaxation. Therefore, according to Theory *Y*, people would exercise self-direction and self-control to contribute to the accomplishment of organizational goals. McGregor's Theory *X* and Theory *Y* made explicit the differences in underlying assumptions about human nature, which in turn explained some differences in management concepts and techniques (McGregor 1960).

In 1981 William Ouchi extended McGregor's earlier work when he developed Theory Z to explain the implications for management when an industrial society emphasizes values not considered in either Theory *X* or Theory *Y* (Ouchi 1981). The popularity of Theory Z was largely attributable to the success of Japanese management in producing highly competitive products for the world market and the increased productivity of the Japanese worker. Theory Z was also based upon several fundamental assumptions about human nature that applied more directly to Japanese society than to Western societies. Theory Z assumed that industrial workers desired intimate and cooperative work relationships with seniors, peers, and subordinates, and that they had a strong sense of moral obligation, discipline, and order. Furthermore, Theory Z assumed that workers were alienated in a work environment where family ties, traditions, and social institutions were minimized. The essence of Theory Z assumptions was the importance of the group rather than the individual, a consideration particularly relevant to Japanese society.

Functions of Management

Although different writers over the years have used different terms, it is generally agreed that management consists of four major functions: planning, organizing, leading, and controlling.

Planning

Planning is generally considered the primary function of management, since logically it is the first issue to be addressed in most organizations. Planning energizes the process of management. Managers initially determine the goals of the organization. Then they must plan how those goals are to be accomplished. During World War II, after the Allies decided to invade Europe, General Eisenhower assumed the overall management responsibility for planning all aspects of the Operation Overlord invasion. This is an illustration of the planning function of management on an extremely large scale. Eisenhower was responsible for planning the activities of more than three million Allied soldiers who participated in the invasion of Normandy.

Planning is pervasive throughout an organization's life cycle, a necessary function from the time of the organization's inception and continuing throughout all aspects of its subsequent life. The results of planning are blueprints that serve as guides for members of the organization to follow in order to achieve specific goals or, more broadly, the organization's purpose. Some plans are designed for a specific, short-term objective; others become relatively permanent. Depending upon their scope, some plans may become standing policies or procedures in an organization.

Organizing

The second major function of management is organizing. This responsibility concerns dividing the overall organization into units and subunits. For example, armies are divided into corps, corps into divisions, divisions into brigades, brigades into battalions, and so forth. Within each unit and subunit are particular responsibilities and an associated hierarchy of reporting relationships. This organizing function of management dictates the structure of the organization. Organizing also refers to coordinating these units and subunits so that their efforts are synchronized, each contributing to the accomplishment of organizational goals and objectives.

To use again the example of General Eisenhower: as he planned the Normandy invasion he assigned units and subunits of American forces to land at two beaches—Utah and Omaha—and units and subunits of British forces to land at three beaches—Gold, Juno, and Sword. The Overlord invasion plan called for the separate but coordinated invasion of Normandy, which illustrates the organizing function of management.

An important aspect of the organizing function of management is the placement of authority. An organization's structure dictates how authority is transferred within that organization. Senior-subordinate relationships are referred to as the "chain of command" in military organizations; the process of transferring authority from one level in the organization to a subordinate level is known as the delegation of authority. Eisenhower, of course, could not personally command each of his units and subunits during Operation Overlord; therefore he delegated part of his command authority to subordinate commanders.

Leading

The third major function of management, leading, is also referred to as directing. Its primary purpose is to bring about desired forms of behavior on the part of organization members so that their individual efforts contribute to the collective accomplishment of organizational goals and objectives. It is an interpersonal influence process in which managers frequently engage.

Another aspect of leading concerns the broad range of activities by which a manager establishes the climate, values, and personality of the organization. Both aspects of the function of leading are essential to the management process.

Of the four functions of management, leadership is the most integrative; elements of leadership are present whenever a manager plans, organizes, or controls. In the military in particular, leadership plays a vital, integrative role. During the Normandy invasion, three U.S. generals—Matthew B. Ridgway, Maxwell D. Taylor, and James M. Gavin—literally led their soldiers into battle as Operation Overlord began.

Controlling

The fourth function of management is control, which involves the process of monitoring progress against the objectives derived from planning. Controlling closes the loop of the management process by assessing the extent to which the organization has achieved its set goals and purposes. The process of collecting information, comparing it with expectations, and then making subsequent adjustments as necessary are essential to the control function of management.

Control is important in the management of every organization; it is especially crucial in military organizations, particularly during combat operations. Consider the uncertainty facing General Eisenhower when Operation Overlord was launched. An essential part of his preinvasion planning included detailed methods to monitor the progress of the Allied forces as they reached Normandy. Only with such a control apparatus could he assess the success or setback of his forces and order adjustments to the original plan of operation.

Although it may appear that the four functions of management are distinct and may even have a specific sequence, they are in fact highly interrelated (Fig. 1). For

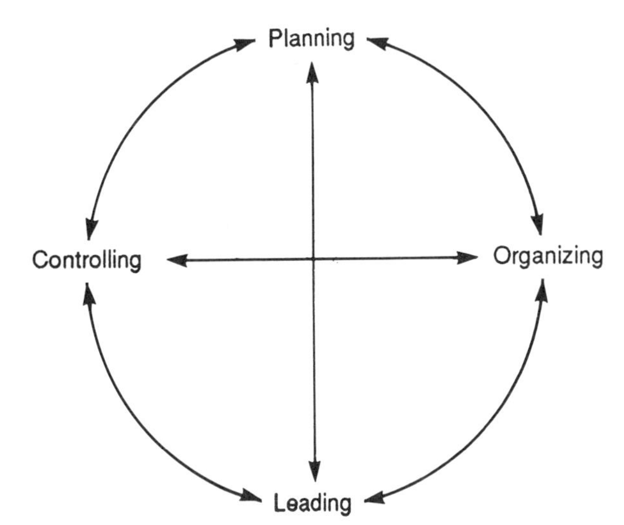

Figure 1. The interrelationship of the four functions of management. (Source: Hersey and Blanchard 1988)

instance, it is difficult to distinguish between Eisenhower's planning and organizing functions when he developed the concepts of Operation Overlord.

Managers at various levels in the organizational hierarchy tend to spend different amounts of their time with each of the functions of management. The traditional view of management posits, for example, that managers at the top of an organization tend to allocate relatively more of their time to planning than do managers at the bottom of the hierarchy. A fleet admiral will likely spend a greater proportion of his time planning long-range, strategic operations than will an ensign assigned to fulfill one small aspect of the overall strategic plan.

A Behavioral Management Approach

The aforementioned four management functions—planning, organizing, leading, and controlling—represent a traditional perspective of management. Some recent researchers have presented a view of management functions that is a considerably less rational model. Henry Mintzberg is the best-known researcher who has devoted considerable attention to what managers actually do in the process of management. From his research he derived the following "facts".

1. Managers work at a hectic, unrelenting pace. They are action-oriented and dislike contemplative activities. Their actions are brief, varied, and discontinuous.
2. Managerial work involves a number of regular activities, which include ritual and ceremonial acts.
3. Managers prefer verbal interactions such as face-to-face and telephone communications.
4. Managers deal with specific rather than general information. They live with the pressures to allocate their time to the most pressing matters of the day.

The implication of Mintzberg's work is that modern managers actually spend their time in a less rational way than is characterized by the traditional perspective on management. Mintzberg saw the modern manager acting as a figurehead in performing ceremonial roles, a crisis manager who must address the immediate pressures of the day, a spokesperson who communicates to groups external to the organization, and a negotiator who steps into the middle of disagreements and problems (Mintzberg 1980).

Future Trends in Management

An important future trend in management—one that does not directly affect the military—is the internationalization of management enterprises and activities. At an increasing rate, management groups from one country have begun to purchase enterprises and conduct ongoing management practices in a foreign country. This has been particularly true with Japanese enterprises purchasing companies in the United States.

It is also likely that in the future there will be increased emphasis on the social responsibility of management and an increase in the extent to which the applications of ever-expanding technologies are assessed and evaluated before they are implemented. Such assessment must consider costs and benefits to the society as a whole and to the interests and concerns of local communities.

Management in the coming decades will be faced with a scarcity of resources, such as petroleum, land, water, and clean air. Since these shortages restrict the potential for unlimited growth, the managerial ramifications will likely be significant.

Relatively recent changes in some aspects of the work force will also affect management in the future. The percentage of white collar employees and the percentage of women in the work force continue to increase, as does the education level of employees. Thus, the expectations of workers for genuine job satisfaction and challenge are likely to increase accordingly.

Jeffrey A. McNally

See Also: Administration, Military; Command; Command, Control, Communications, and Intelligence; Coordination; Generalship; Leadership; Organization, Military; Planning, Military; Span of Control: Military Organizations and Operations; Span of Control: Theories and Concepts.

Bibliography

Clausewitz, C. von. 1984. *On war*. Ed. and trans. M. Howard and P. Paret. Princeton, N.J.: Princeton Univ. Press.
Drucker, P. F. 1973. *Management: Tasks, responsibilities, practices*. New York: Harper and Row.
Fayol, H. 1949. *General and industrial management*. Trans. C. Storrs. London: Pittman and Sons.
Hersey, P., and K. Blanchard. 1988. *Management of organizational behavior*. Englewood Cliffs, N.J.: Prentice-Hall.
Mayo, E. 1953. *The human problems of an industrial civilization*. Cambridge, Mass.: Macmillan.
McGregor, D. 1960. *The human side of enterprise*. New York: McGraw-Hill.
Mintzberg, H. 1980. *The nature of managerial work*. Englewood Cliffs, N.J.: Prentice-Hall.
Ouchi, W. 1981. *Theory Z*. Reading, Mass.: Addison-Wesley.
Tansik, D. A., et al. 1980. *Management: A life cycle approach*. Homewood, Ill.: Richard D. Irwin.
Taylor, F. W. 1911. *Principles of scientific management*. Easton, Pa.: Hive.
Weber, M. 1947. *The theory of social and economic organization*. Trans. A. Henderson and T. Parsons. New York: Free Press.
Wren, D. A. 1972. *The evolution of management thought*. New York: Ronald Press.

MANCHU EMPIRE
(Qing, or Ch'ing Empire)

The Qing dynasty (1644–1911), the last in the 2,000-year-long feudal society in China, marked the transition of China from its early historical period to the modern period. Although some of the Qing dynasty rulers were able to provide periods of peace and prosperity to their nation, the corruption of officials, peasant rebellions, and wars eventually led to the overthrow of the Qing dynasty and the beginning of a new era in Chinese history.

Background

The Manchu, the dominant ruling class of the Qing dynasty, was an ancient nationality in China, previously living in the Heilongjiang River basin in the northeast. For 3,000 years, during the Shang (ca. 16th–11th centuries B.C.) and the Zhou (770–221 B.C.) dynasties, the ancestors of the Manchu were called the Sushen. Later they were called the Yilou (Han dynasty [206 B.C.–A.D. 220]), the Wuji (Southern and Northern dynasties [420–589]), and the Mojie (Sui dynasty [581–618]). When the Tang dynasty (618–907) set up a local authority in the Heilongjiang River valley in the eighth century, the area became Chinese territory.

In the early tenth century, the Mojie came to be called the Nuzhen, and they founded the kingdom of Jin (1115–1234) with Yanjing (present-day Beijing) as the capital. They ruled northern China, but in 1234 they were conquered by the Mongols and driven back to northeast China. In 1616, Nurhachi, chief of the Nuzhen branch in Jianzhou, unified the whole Nuzhen after 30 years of warfare and set up the state of Jin in 1616, making himself the khan. Nurhachi then declared war on the declining Ming dynasty. When he led his 60,000-man army in an attack on the strategic township of Ning Liao (present-day Xingcheng in Liaoning Province) on 2 March 1626, he was defeated by the 10,000-man Ming army, which defended the city with eleven Western cannon. Soon afterward, Nurhachi died of illness and was succeeded by his son, Abahai. In 1636, Abahai proclaimed himself emperor and changed Jin to Qing. He conquered Korea and Mongolia and removed the serious threats from the northeast. Qing troops then began to push south toward the Shanhaiguan Pass garrisoned by Ming soldiers. Abahai died suddenly in September 1643 and was succeeded by his 6-year-old son, Fulin (Emperor Shun Di), with two princes (the late emperor's brothers) acting as regents. On 26 April 1644, a peasant army led by Li Zicheng seized Beijing and put an end to the Ming dynasty. The Manchus took advantage of the situation and marched southward. They defeated Li Zicheng's peasant army at the Shanhaiguan Pass and occupied Beijing on 6 July. Fulin made Beijing his capital in October. This marked the establishment of the central government of the Qing dynasty.

The Qing troops again marched southward to bring the whole country under their control, burning, killing, and looting indiscriminately. Further, the Qing government ordered the Han men to shave their heads or have them cut off, forcing them to shave off their hair on the front part of their crown and wear a pigtail at the back in accordance with the Manchu custom. This aroused great indignation in every stratum of the society. With the support of the masses, the peasant armies and the remnants of the Ming forces jointly waged wars of resistance against the Qing troops. The Qing court had to change its highhanded policy and learn to divide and be conciliatory to win over the rebels. It was only after several years of struggle that they gained control of the situation.

Unification and Expansion

The next emperor, Kangxi (1662–1722), learned from the mistakes of the Qing army in its southward march and formulated new policies in order to win the support of the local Han officials and intellectuals. To eliminate the strong barriers between the two nationalities, he respected the Han people's culture and adopted some of their customs and governmental traditions. He basically adopted the legal and official appointment systems of past dynasties in central China. To bring about economic recovery, he reduced taxes and encouraged land reclamation. He also had the Huanghe (Yellow) River harnessed to lessen the danger of floods. In addition, Kangxi strengthened the central government by removing dissidents from their posts. The peasants were able to enjoy a period of peace and prosperity, and the whole nation was rehabilitated. As a result, the Qing dynasty unified the country and expanded its territories. During the reigns of Emperor Kangxi, Emperor Yong Zheng (1723–35), and Emperor Qian Long (1736–95), Qing forces successively suppressed three revolts led by Han military governors in Yunnan, Guangdong, and Fujian; occupied Taiwan after overthrowing Zheng Chenggong's government; drove off the czarist Russian aggressors stationed in Yakesa on the north bank of the Heilongjiang River; and signed treaties that fixed the eastern portion of the boundary between China and Russia. They also subdued the Dzungars in Xinjiang Uygyr Autonomous Region, fought against Tibetan hereditary headmen in Dajinchuan and Xiaojinchuan in Sichuan Province, and posted high commissioners there to strengthen control over the minority regions in southwest China. Externally, the Manchu launched two expeditions against Burma, brought Annam into submission, and entered Nepal, forcing Kuorke to sue for peace.

By the mid- to late eighteenth century, the Qing territory stretched eastward to the sea, west to Lake Balkhash and the Pamirs, south to the islands in the South China Sea, and north to Gorno-Altay, Sayan Mountains. It reached the Outer Xingan Mountains and Okhotsk Sea in the northeast and Guangxi, Yunan, and Tibet in the southwest. With a population of about 300 million, China was the strongest country in Asia.

Military Strength

The pillar of strength of the Qing dynasty was its armed forces. In 1615 Nurhachi set up the Eight Banner system by which soldiers were also laborers during times of peace.

Before the Manchus entered the Shanhaiguan Pass, the largest registered permanent units were the Gushans; each had a strength of 7,500 and a banner of a special color (called *qi*). In 1601, Manchuria had a small population and formed only four Gushans, which had yellow, white, red, and blue banners. Later, when another four Gushans were added, they hemmed the red banner with white edges and the other three banners with red edges. These were the eight original banners. By the time the Qing forces entered the Pass, there were already 24 banners, but the forces were still called the Eight Banner Troops.

Throughout the Qing dynasty, the main force of the Manchu army defended the capital. Those stationed in and outside Beijing city year-round amounted to over 100,000 men. Garrisons stationed at strategic points around the country and in northeast China and Inner Mongolia amounted to another 100,000 men. The overall strength of the Eight Banners never exceeded 300,000. In addition, there were the Green Battalions of Han origin, made up of Han recruits and some landlords' private armies. They were identified by their green banners. The name came from their unit battalion, which usually had a strength of about 600,000. The Eight Banners were better paid and better equipped than the Green Battalions. The two were the main military forces of the Qing dynasty before the Opium War (1840). Other military forces included some native armies (of minority nationality) and some local armies that were organized in times of emergency and disbanded or reorganized afterward.

A Declining Empire

In the early nineteenth century, because of huge financial expenditures required in protracted warfare and the embezzlement and corruption at all levels of government, social contradictions were sharpened and popular rebellions and uprisings took place in different parts of the country. The Qing dynasty had passed its heyday and was on the road to decline.

In the early 1840s, Britain unleashed a war of aggression against China, claiming that the Qing government had burned its opium; the British forced the Qing government to sign humiliating treaties. Other foreign governments followed suit and gradually turned China into a semicolonial and semifeudal country. Xianggang (Hong Kong), Aomen (Macao), and Taiwan and the Penghu Islands were occupied by Britain, Portugal, and Japan, respectively. The vast lands north of the Heilongjiang River, east of the Wusuli River, and that beyond the present boundary in Xinjiang were taken secretly by czarist Russia, and the Pamirs were divided up between czarist Russia and Britain.

The embryo of capitalism in China, which had germinated before the Opium War in trade and industries such as silk weaving, cotton dyeing, porcelain making, coal and iron mining, and cigarette and sugar production, was stifled. Production came to a standstill and the economy stagnated. The peasant revolution of the Taiping Heavenly Kingdom spread to eighteen provinces, and the Uprising of the Nian Forces in the north, operating in close cooperation with the Taipings, repeatedly defeated the Qing troops. The Qing court was shaken to its very foundations.

Beset with difficulties both at home and abroad, the Qing government staged a movement to make the country strong during the reigns of Emperors Tong Zhi and Guang Xu (1862–1908). Adjustments were made in the closed-door policy; observation groups and students were sent abroad to study or conduct investigations. With the financial aid of Britain, the United States, and France, officials such as Zeng Guofan and Li Hongzhang, who were of Han origin, initiated the Westernization Movement. They built modern munitions industries such as Jiangnan Machinery Manufacturing Bureau and Fuzhou Shipping Bureau, where the technical skills of the Western countries were adapted. They bought foreign warships and established the Northern Sea Fleet. And they set up a naval academy and defense academy to offer modern military education.

Troops of the Eight Banners and the Green Battalions were so corrupt after the Opium War that their combat capabilities had been greatly weakened. To suppress the strong Taipings and Nian Forces, Zeng Guofan and Li Hongzhang were sent to Hunan and Anhui to organize the new landlord army: the Hunan army and Huaihe River army. Marshals and commanders were granted military leadership with full powers by the central government, and foreign instructors and advisers were employed. Meanwhile, the National Guards, which recruited soldiers in the provinces, and the Lian Troops, which consisted of soldiers selected from the Green Battalions, were stationed at strategic points throughout the country. By the end of the nineteenth century, however, these troops also became corrupt and impotent. The government decided to organize a new army with Western military equipment and organization. But the plan was never carried out in full.

The Taiping Rebellion (1850–64), which spread to the greater part of China, and the Uprising of the Nian Forces, the Uprising of the Dagger Society in Shanghai, the Yunnan Hui People's Uprising, the Guizhou Miao People's Uprising, and the Hui People's Uprising in Shannxi and Gansu all dealt heavy blows to the ruling class despite the fact that these uprisings were suppressed by the government and ended in failure. The combined forces of the eight powers (Britain, the United States, Russia, France, Germany, Japan, Italy, and Austria) subsequently sacked Beijing and Tianjin, while czarist Russia also seized the opportunity to feather its own nest. This was the second time China had lost vast territories and her national sovereignty since the period of the Opium War. During the Sino-Japanese War of 1894–95, China's newly organized naval force was destroyed and its land forces suffered disastrous defeats.

The Hundred-Day Reform

The Qing rule was faced with a serious crisis. In 1898, with the support of the intellectuals and the masses, Kang Youwei, Liang Qichao, Tan Sitong, and other representatives of the national bourgeoisie and the enlightened gentry sent notice to the court demanding immediate constitutional reform. Emperor Guang Xu supported the reform and proclaimed new laws. The reform movement, however, was soon put down by the die-hards led by Empress Dowager Ci Xi. Thus ended what is known in Chinese history as the "hundred-day reform." With its failure, the hope to save China through reform vanished. Filled with indignation at the danger of China being divided up among the imperialist powers, revolutionaries in Guangding and other places arose and eventually overthrew the Qing dynasty in 1911, putting an end to the feudal monarchy in China. The revolution of 1911 marked a new beginning in Chinese history.

ZHOU SHI-CHANG

SEE ALSO: China, People's Republic of; Colonial Empires, European; Genghis Khan; Japan, Modernization and Expansion of; Korea, North; Mongol Conquests; Russia, Expansion of; Taiwan.

Bibliography

Cai Meibiao, et al. 1986. *A History of China.* Vol. 9. Ed. Kuo Muoruo. Shanghai: People's Publishing House.
Dai Yizhu, ed. 1980. *A concise history of the Qing dynasty.* Shanghai: People's Publishing House.
The great encyclopaedia of China military. 1988. Shanghai: China Great Encylopaedia Publishing House.
The Qing dynasty. 1980. In *Cihai Dictionary.* Shanghai: Shanghai Dictionary Publishing House.
Xiao Yishan. 1980. *The history of the Qing dynasty.* Rev. ed. Taipei: Taiwan Commercial Press.
Zheng Tianting, ed. 1981. *Documents on the history of the Ming and Qing dynasties,* vol. 2. Tianjin: Tianjin People's Publishing House.

MANEUVER

Maneuver is one of the two basic components of combat, the other is firepower. In some usage, maneuver is simply another word for the movement of forces. More often, it is used to mean relational movement—for example, movement relative to an opponent's position, as in Napoleon's *manoeuvre sur les derrières.* In the term *maneuver warfare,* the word *maneuver* refers to an entire style of war, most often associated in this century with the German army. In modern usage, maneuver warfare theory has come to define maneuver in terms of time rather than position.

Maneuver as Movement

The use of the word *maneuver* as nothing more than a synonym for *movement* is seen in the common American use of the phrase *tactics of fire and maneuver* to describe an open-order advance by alternate rushes. No movement relative to an enemy, such as movement around his flank or into his rear, is implied. The simple movement of the rushing element is the *maneuver.* Such usage is also encountered in discussions or briefings, as in a battalion commander saying, "I maneuvered my unit to this road junction." He means only that he moved the unit; no movement relative to the enemy is to be understood.

This use of the word *maneuver* can be thought of as colloquial. While not incorrect, it is imprecise.

Maneuver as Movement Relative to an Enemy's Position

The sense in which the word *maneuver* is most often used, and is reflected in the definition offered in the U.S. Army's *Field Manual (FM) 100-5: Operations,* is "the movement of forces in relation to the enemy to secure or retain positional advantage." In this sense, *maneuver* means an attack on either or both of an enemy's flanks, movement into his rear to disrupt his supporting elements, or encirclement. Because such action is relational to the enemy, it may involve his movement more than one's own. *FM 100-5* says: "The effects of maneuver (obtaining an advantageous position) may also be achieved without movement by allowing the enemy himself to move into a disadvantageous position, as in an ambush or with stay-behind forces." This suggests that the essence of maneuver—in the classic usage of the term—is not movement per se but the achievement of positional advantage.

In this sense, maneuver has been one of the most powerful tools in warfare since the beginning of recorded history. Because of basic human psychology, a force that is hit where it is weak, where it does not expect to be hit, or in such a manner as to leave it cut off from its supplies, reinforcements, or line of retreat tends to panic and disintegrate. The principal effect of maneuver is thus more mental than physical—and therefore more powerful than simple physical attrition.

Maneuver played a major role in classical warfare, where decisive battles were usually battles of maneuver. At the Battle of Marathon in 490 B.C., the Greeks achieved a decisive victory by maneuvering against both flanks of the Persian force—a double envelopment. While most battles between phalanxes tended to be indecisive, the Thebans won decisively at Leuctra in 371 B.C. by attacking first on their left with the bulk of their force, pushing back the Spartan right, then turning and rolling up the Spartans from the right. This maneuver is often known as the oblique attack. The Theban leader Epaminondas may have been the first commander to employ an unequal distribution of forces to provide a basis for maneuver.

Perhaps the most decisive classical battle, one that influenced much subsequent military thought, was Cannae in 216 B.C. It was a battle of maneuver in which the Carthaginians under Hannibal drew the Roman center forward, then attacked around both flanks to encircle the Roman force. The Roman army was annihilated. Later, the Romans won the Second Punic War with a strategic maneuver in which the Roman commander Scipio Africanus invaded Carthaginian North Africa, forcing Hannibal to evacuate Italy to come to the defense of his homeland.

In Europe, maneuver went into eclipse with the fall of the Roman Empire. Medieval and early modern warfare tended to be straight-on slogging matches at the tactical level, with little or no thought given to the operational level. In contrast, in Asia, the Mongols were masters of strategic maneuver, moving in widely separated columns that concentrated unexpectedly at an enemy's most vulnerable point.

By the end of the seventeenth century, maneuver had again become a major part of European warfare. At the operational level, maneuver was often intended to separate an opposing army from its magazines, on which it depended for its supplies; an army thus cut off usually withdraws. *Tactical* maneuver is illustrated by the battle of Leuthen between the Austrians and the Prussians in 1757. The Prussians attacked in oblique order from the right, breaking the Austrians' line and forcing them to withdraw.

Napoleon placed heavy emphasis on maneuver, at least in his early battles and campaigns. French revolutionary armies were better adapted to rapid operational and tactical maneuver than were the professional armies of the European monarchies. Napoleon's were the first armies to be divided into divisions, which facilitated maintaining control while maneuvering; they freed themselves from dependence on magazines by living off the land; they raised the march step from 70 to 120 paces per minute; and they made extensive tactical use of light infantry operating in loose formations and of fast-moving columns.

Napoleon was famous for the *manoeuvre sur les derrières*, in which he employed a small portion of his force to capture his opponent's attention while swinging his main body behind the enemy, cutting his communications. Alternatively, he would overwhelm the enemy's center, again moving into his rear and cutting him off.

Speed, surprise, and shock were central components of Napoleonic maneuver at both the tactical and operational levels. It may be said that Napoleon introduced *tempo* into modern European warfare, presaging twentieth-century maneuver warfare.

In his later years, as emperor, Napoleon relied less on maneuver and more on brute force at the tactical level; Waterloo provides a good example. The postwar Napoleonic heritage caught more of his later tactics than the earlier, fluid tactics that emphasized maneuver.

But by the middle of the nineteenth century, the introduction of the rifled musket made brute force offensive tactics increasingly costly in casualties. The Prussian general Helmuth von Moltke (the Elder) responded by reemphasizing maneuver in the *Kesselschlacht*, where the object was to encircle the enemy, forcing him to assault into rifle fire in order to break out. A plan by Graf Alfred von Schlieffen early in the twentieth century expanded the *Kesselschlacht* concept to the operational level, calling for a massive encirclement of the French armies by the German right.

The death knell for maneuver on the modern battlefield seemed to sound with the failure of the Schlieffen plan in 1914. The battlefield had become one continuous field with no open flanks around which to maneuver, while the tactical strength of the defense seemed to preclude penetration. Firepower was dominant over maneuver.

Maneuver Warfare

In 1917 and 1918, maneuver reappeared on the western front in the form of new and radically different German tactics. On the defense, instead of densely manning forward trench lines and attempting to hold every inch of ground, the Germans allowed the Allied attacker to penetrate through a thinly held forward outpost line. As the Allied forces penetrated deeper, they encountered a growing density of machine-gun positions, prepared for 360-degree defense, and small groups of riflemen fighting from shell holes. This firepower disorganized the attacker and absorbed his momentum. When the German commander judged that the attack had begun to disintegrate, he launched a powerful counterattack designed to encircle the attacking force and restore the original defensive line. These "elastic defense" tactics relied heavily on maneuver, not only in looking to the encircling counterattack to achieve the decision, but also in using the attacker's momentum against him. In practice, they proved devastatingly effective.

On the offense, the new tactics brought maneuver down to the squad (*Stosstrupp*) level. Instead of attacking in waves, assault troops organized in combined arms squads (light machine gun and trench mortar) attempted to infiltrate through weak points in the Allied defenses. Squads maneuvered independently, with corporals making tactical decisions. The attack had an unlimited objective; forward movement was to be sustained as far as possible. Enemy strong points were bypassed—a use of maneuver—and reserves were funneled in behind the most successful penetrations in order to expand them. Firepower was used to support maneuver by suppressing the defenders while the attackers moved behind them, and wherever possible positions were taken from the flank or rear (*Durchbruch und Aufrollen*).

The 1918 German offensive used these tactics, and they solved the tactical riddle of trench warfare. Massive breakthroughs were attained, and the Germans again advanced to the Marne. The tactical successes, however, could not be converted into victories at the operational level. The most important reason was again a factor of maneuver: a differential in operational mobility. The Germans had to advance on foot, with horse-drawn artillery and supplies, while the Allies shifted operational reserves by rail to build new defenses behind collapsing sectors of their line. Pitting rail against foot mobility, the Allies were able to outmaneuver the Germans on the operational level.

In World War II, the Germans solved the problem of operational mobility. The answer was the Panzer division: mechanized forces that could move forward faster than a rail-mobile defender, such as France in 1940, could shift laterally. The blitzkrieg combined the tactics of 1918—offensive and defensive—with the operational mobility afforded by mechanization. It is important to note, however, that as the German general Hermann Balck stated, blitzkrieg was conceptually complete by 1918, only the operational means were lacking. Similarly, the German tank tactics of World War II were identical to the infantry tactics of 1918.

This revolution in tactics and operations was largely missed by the Western Allies. While German and Soviet tactics were dominated by maneuver, British and American tactics remained refinements of the Allied tactics of World War I, relying primarily on massive firepower and materiel superiority. At the operational level, the Western Allies had some commanders who used maneuver, most prominently Gen. George S. Patton, but most Allied campaigns were frontal, linear, and slow-paced.

In the past decade, however, the German way of war has been discovered in both the United States and the United Kingdom, where it is often referred to as *maneuver warfare*, in contrast to *attrition warfare*. Maneuver warfare is now official doctrine in the U.S. Marine Corps, and its substance (although not the term) is the basis for the current edition of the army's *FM 100-5*.

Used in the term *maneuver warfare*, maneuver means substantially more than seeking positional advantage. It describes a style of warfare, a way of thinking about both tactics and operations. In maneuver warfare, the objective is the enemy's collapse as a cohesive, functioning force, not his incremental destruction through the application of firepower. The larger the force that can be collapsed as a whole, the better. Operational art dominates over tactics, and at the tactical level, the goal is to avoid battle as much as possible while attaining operational objectives. High tempo is itself a weapon.

Maneuver warfare regards both tactics and operations as highly situational. Therefore, it does not define itself in formulas or recipes telling the practitioner what to do. Rather, maneuver warfare is defined in terms of a few central concepts, derived from past German practice, of which five are of main importance at the tactical level:

1. Mission tactics (*Auftragstaktik*). In order to maintain high tempo and to take advantage of fleeting opportunities for decisive maneuver, the authority to make decisions must be decentralized. At the same time, unity of effort must be maintained. These two requirements are reconciled primarily through mission tactics, in which orders tell the subordinate what is to be accomplished while leaving him maximum latitude in deciding how to accomplish it. In effect, he is given a goal, and it is left to him to attain it. This is done at all levels of command. As part of mission orders, the subordinate is expected to show a high level of initiative. In turn, errors resulting from mistaken initiative are treated lightly.

2. Focus of effort (*Schwerpunkt*). In each situation, a commander decides what he will do to achieve a decision and what unit he will do it with. That unit is then designated the focus of effort. It receives all possible support: artillery and other supporting arms, reinforcements, reserves, supplies, and so on. To the greatest extent possible, the available combat power is concentrated to back its effort. This often means risks must be taken elsewhere. The object is to be superior at the point of decision, even if the force as a whole is inferior. As the situation changes, the focus of effort may be shifted, but at all times combat power is concentrated in its support.

3. Throwing strength against weakness, not against strength (*Lücken und Flächentaktik*, or tactics of surfaces and gaps). In the attack, a force practicing maneuver warfare does not attempt to advance a line; maneuver warfare is nonlinear. Rather, the force attempts to penetrate where the enemy is weakest and to avoid his strong points. Once in his rear, the strong points can be attacked from the flank or rear while the advance simultaneously continues into his depth. The logic of strength against weakness is carried over into the defense as well, where the counterattack is launched when the enemy is deemed weakest. At the operational level, the German's advance through the Ardennes in the 1940 campaign is a good example of throwing strength against weakness rather than against strength. Because the French had committed their reserve in Belgium, the German action had the nature of a counterattack.

4. The objective. In maneuver warfare, the objective is defined in terms of the enemy, not terrain. Combined with mission orders, this leaves the subordinate free to use terrain as he sees fit. Generally, maps used in maneuver warfare do not have "goose eggs" symbolizing terrain objectives, nor do they have many, if any, lines. Instead, actions are shown as thrust vectors, indicating what is to be done to the objective (i.e., the enemy force).

5. The reserve. The reserve is given high importance in maneuver warfare and is the unit that often brings the decision. It is generally stronger than in attrition warfare, and it often comprises the best units and commander. The weaker the total force, the larger the percentage of the force that is generally kept in reserve. Strong reserves are as important at the operational level as they are at the tactical level.

These concepts are all intended to produce a force that is highly agile, fluid, and flexible. Maneuver theory sees warfare as dominated by unpredictability, uncertainty, and rapid change. Tactics are highly opportunistic, the operational level somewhat less so; but at both levels, a high premium is placed on doing the unexpected. Fog and friction are seen as normal, and the goal is to operate within them, magnifying them for the opponent. Command and control are replaced by leadership and monitoring, and implicit communication, based on a shared way of thinking, is stressed over explicit communication through "systems."

Maneuver Defined in Terms of Time Rather Than Place

In recent years, maneuver warfare theory has come to place its main emphasis on time rather than place. Traditionally, maneuver was defined as relational movement seen in terms of place; Sir Basil Liddell Hart's "indirect approach" is an example. Recent theoretical work, particularly that of retired air force colonel John Boyd, has instead emphasized relational movement in time or tempo.

Colonel Boyd's work began with the study of air-to-air combat. He noted that in the Korean War, where U.S. aviators achieved a 10:1 kill ratio over their North Korean opponents, the principal U.S. fighter, the F-86, was inferior to the North Korean MiG-15 in several traditionally key respects, including climb, acceleration, and sustained turn rate. The F-86, however, had two advantages that proved decisive: better outward visibility and quicker response to the controls. In other words, the U.S. pilot could see more easily and quickly what was going on and his aircraft could respond more quickly to a change in the situation. To use these superiorities, the Americans developed tactics that stressed a series of different actions. Each time the action changed, the Americans gained a time advantage that they could convert into positional advantage. Further, as the North Korean pilot realized he was losing in each successive action or maneuver, a psychological dimension became a factor: he tended to panic.

Colonel Boyd proceeded to examine the history of ground combat from the perspective gained from his study of air combat. He found that in many decisive battles, something similar had happened. One side took an action or a series of actions to which the other side could not quickly respond, and the side with the slower response was defeated. In effect, the slower side was outmaneuvered in time.

Generalizing, Colonel Boyd developed a theory that lies at the heart of current U.S. understanding of maneuver warfare. The theory states that conflict can be seen as time-competitive cycles of observation, orientation, decision, and action (OODA). Each party begins by observing. On the basis of the observation, each forms a mental picture of the situation—orientation. On the basis of this orientation, each makes a decision, then acts. Assuming the action has changed the situation, each again observes, starting the cycle anew. These cycles are often referred to as "Boyd cycles" or "OODA Loops."

The party that consistently goes through the cycles faster than its opponent gains a large, often a decisive, advantage. By the time the slower side acts, the faster party is already doing something different from what had been observed and the action of the slower side is irrelevant. With each cycle, the slower party falls farther and farther behind—that is, the time margin by which its action is inappropriate grows. Its situation is not just bad, nor is it simply deteriorating; it is deteriorating at an ever-accelerating pace. At some point, the slower party realizes what is happening, and it is then that it tends to panic or grow passive. It may be for the most part physically intact, but it has been defeated. A good example of this process is, again, the German campaign against France in 1940. Many of the actions the French took were correct, but they were always too late.

The Boyd theory defines what is meant by tempo: it is not just speed, it is relational speed. And it in turn defines what is meant by maneuver in modern maneuver warfare theory.

William S. Lind

See Also: Attrition: Personnel Casualties; Auftragstaktik; Blitzkrieg; Envelopment; Frederick the Great; Hannibal Barca; History, Military; Interior and Exterior Lines of Operation; Mobility; Moltke the Elder; Napoleon I; Principles of War; Schlieffen, Alfred, Count von; Schwerpunkt; Scipio Africanus; Tactics.

Bibliography

Liddell Hart, B. H. 1974. *Strategy.* New York: Signet Books.
Lind, W. S. 1985. *Maneuver warfare handbook.* Boulder, Colo.: Westview Press.
Lupfer, T. 1981. *The dynamics of doctrine: The changes in German tactical doctrine during the First World War.* Ft. Leavenworth, Kans.: combat Studies Institute.
Simpkin, R. E. 1985. *Race to the swift.* London: Brassey's.

MAN-MACHINE INTERFACE

The application of technology to warfare has led to engagements that are fast, accurate, and lethal. But while the acceleration and diffusion of technology are being lauded as potential force multipliers, we must remember that weapon systems are controlled by men who, while perhaps better trained and with infinitely better communications, have no greater cognitive capacity than those who took the field at Marathon.

Three factors determine the effectiveness of a modern weapon system: the equipment, the men who operate and support it, and the interface between them—the man-machine interface (MMI). Failure of *any* one of these three will negate the effectiveness of the whole system. The MMI must allow the man to communicate his intentions to the machine quickly, easily, and precisely while receiving from the machine, just as quickly and easily, the information he requires.

Importance of the Man-Machine Interface

Man is included in military systems for his versatility, pattern recognition, reasoning, and intuitive strength; but these are offset by weaknesses, such as limited and serial information processing and performance degradation under stress. Qualitative descriptions of the relative strengths and weaknesses of the man and machine, which can serve as general design guidelines on the man-machine mix, have been with us for some time (Fitts 1951, 1962; McCormick and Sanders 1982).

But irrespective of the eventual man-machine mix, it should be appreciated that the human component is becoming increasingly costly to recruit, train, and retain, and that this problem can be seriously exacerbated by a demographic trough that in the United States will mean a 20 percent to 40 percent drop in the number of 15- to 19-year-old males in the recruitment pool by 1996. When coupled with a general tightening of defense budgets, this means that policymakers must seek the most efficient use of their expensive and limited human resource. Optimization of the man-machine interface is an effective move in this direction.

In the 1980s it was argued that automation and the application of artificial intelligence would materially reduce the military manpower requirement. The evidence so far is controversial (Binkin 1986), but on balance it indicates that automation does not reduce the manpower requirement, it merely moves the position of man in the loop while generally demanding ever-higher levels of skill and competency from operators and maintainers.

The system and the operator are an organic whole that, together, counter the operational threat. Equipment deficiencies can be countered to some extent by operator capability and operator deficiencies by system aiding, both at definable cost either in the quality of required personnel/lowered performance or in development and unit costs.

MMI Requirements

In an ideal world, an effective MMI (military or civil) would have the following characteristics:

- It should be fast, accurate, and sufficiently precise for the task at hand.
- It should present information in a form that is task relevant and easily encoded and retained by the operator.
- Its control elements should be closely and appropriately matched both to the operator's capabilities and to the information displayed by the system.
- Its operation should be natural and easy to learn by the target user population, follow standard control/display stereotypes, and accommodate both "novice" and "expert" users.
- It should be oriented to the operation of tasks and involve a minimum amount of system management.
- It should assist human decision making by presenting data in a clear and integrated context and, where aiding is present, by presenting clear and unambiguous alternatives.
- It should be robust and show minimum degradation in the presence of stress (e.g., noise/vibration, sleep deprivation).
- It should be fault-tolerant and designed to minimize the potential for, and impact of, human error.
- The requirement for the operator to perform multiple tasks simultaneously should be kept to a minimum and, if possible, totally eliminated. Where such simultaneous tasks are unavoidable, and where the tasks are incompatible, they should be moved either to the machine or to another operator.
- Where there is a requirement for the operator to use multiple systems, the MMI philosophy should be consistent, both between different systems and between different generations of equipment.

A consideration of any one of these desirable qualities reveals the inherent difficulties and complexity of the task of MMI design, which requires a multidisciplinary team drawn from system technology, human engineering (ergonomics), psychology, physiology, and design. This team approach is necessary not only because the knowledge base is spread across disciplinary boundaries, but also because the measurement and evaluation techniques required are equally diffuse.

The MMI design team for any system is faced with a variety of problems. First, the exact form of the MMI is task and population dependent, and its design, while obeying general principles, must be refined to meet the specific requirement. The second problem is that the present level of knowledge of the processes underlying different elements of the MMI varies widely. Thus, while anthrometric data on factors such as arm reach, key spacing and pressure, and sitting height are relatively well documented, our knowledge of complex decision making using multiple sources of probabilistic information is much less detailed.

For those areas where knowledge is more complete, there are a number of agreed standards such as MIL-STAN-1472C (U.S. Department of Defense 1981) or DEF STAN-0025 (U.K. Ministry of Defence 1988), as well as MMI reference documents for system designers (e.g., Van Cott and Kincade 1972; Salvendy 1987) and collated volumes on specific topics such as tracking skill (Poulton 1974), man-computer interaction (Smith and Monier

1984), and human perception and performance (Boff and Lincoln 1988).

Where knowledge is less complete, the system designer must be prepared to allow both development time and cost to evolve a good MMI by experimentation and research. The requirement for such time and cost allowances is accepted as essential for the technology component of the system; it seems somewhat perverse, as the MMI is so critical for operational performance, to treat it in a different way than other vital system elements.

MMI Design Process

The form of the MMI is determined by: the task, the means selected to achieve the task, the capacity and capability of both the equipment and the operator, and the environment in which the system will function.

Therefore, the MMI must be defined in the context of the system's capability and concept of operation and should be developed in parallel with the technical aspects of the system, from feasibility to final production stage. Where the human may be a limiting factor on system performance, early consideration of human factors will serve to refine and balance alternative technical solutions.

Unless human factors are considered early in the design process, there is a possibility of developing systems with poor performance, unacceptably high training costs, inadequate safety, or low availability due to difficulty in diagnosing faults and effecting repairs. To reduce this risk, it is essential that the development of training materials and maintenance design and documentation be linked to the equipment design process.

Figure 1 is a schematic of a recommended design process for a weapon system. This proceeds from an initial system definition (based on current capability and the perceived threat) through progressive refinement to a final product. For the MMI, *every* stage from the definition of system function to final production is important, and an effective MMI can be achieved only if it forms an organic part of *all* these stages.

Unfortunately, in the past, the human operator has sometimes been considered only after the detailed design stage, and training design has, in many cases, not commenced until production has been well under way. An early, thoroughgoing task analysis for a variety of man-machine combinations would serve to limit the possible development to options that are effective and supportable. In addition, those charged with assessing the system should be aware of the techniques and tools available to permit such an assessment. A thorough description of these analytical procedures is provided by Meister (1985).

In the past, it has been argued (justifiably) that MMI research and development on a complex system could take place only after the system had been built and trials could be run on a prototype. This approach, however, has

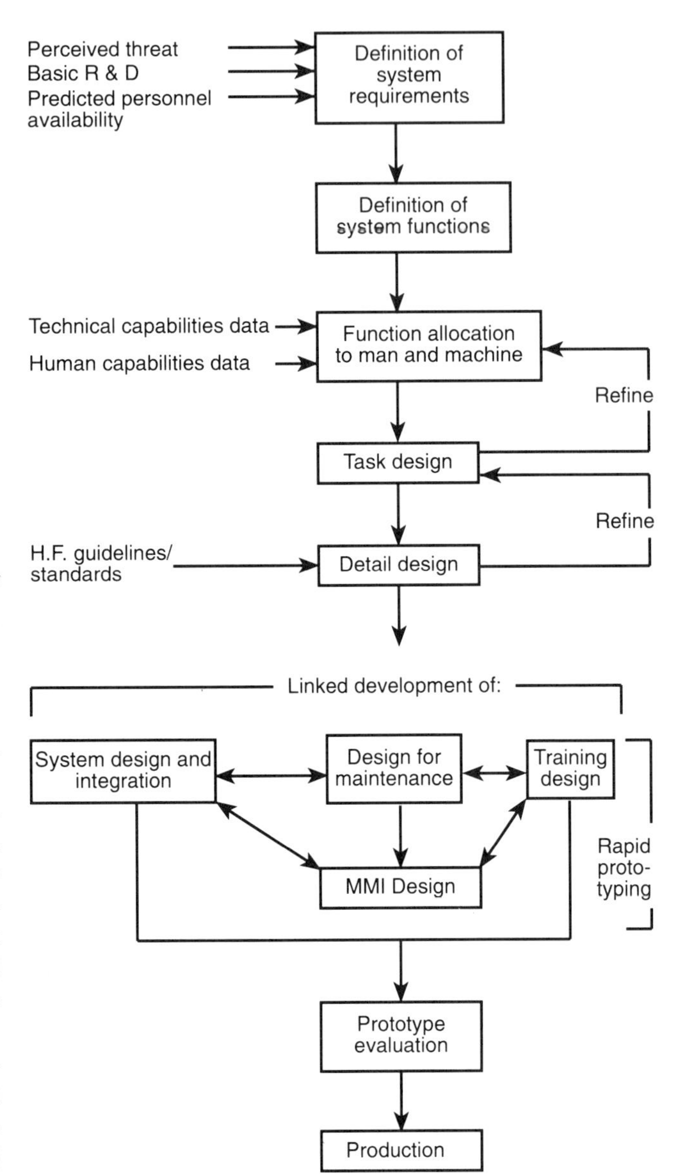

Figure 1. The recommended system design process.

been superseded by the advent of cheap, fast, general-purpose computers that permit "rapid prototyping" of the system's MMI in software. This allows a "spiral" development of MMI wherein an initial MMI design is developed, tested on the user population, and repeatedly revised. The use of such MMI demonstrators has a number of significant advantages:

- It allows potential users to become conversant with the capabilities of novel systems, leading to better-informed deployment and utilization plans by the customer.
- It allows an early assessment of the manning and training requirements for systems under development, giving a better appreciation by the customer of eventual ownership costs.
- It provides advance warning to the customer of any

changes that may be required in his recruitment and selection processes.

- It allows the MMI to be delivered to the detailed design stage of any project as a proven, low-risk element.
- It provides a "kickstart" to consideration of training devices, as the MMI development system (or parts of it) may be suitable as a trainer with little or no modification, leading to savings in both time and money.

MMI Design Principles

Several essential features of any MMI are presented below.

1. The operator must be able to sense the outputs of the system and control its inputs. Are the *outputs* for the sensory modality employed of adequate:

- Persistence (too short-lived)?
- Intensity (too weak to perceive/too great, possible damage)?
- Frequency (too often/too infrequent)?
- Predictability (too predictable/unpredictable)?
- Accuracy (too inaccurate for the operational task)?
- Discriminability (too great a similarity between different elements)?

The outputs should also be assessed as to whether they make demands of the operator that are beyond his capability for:

- Accuracy
- Speed of response
- Information assimilation
- Endurance
- Multiple task performance.

On the *input* side, the system should not demand:

- Too great a physical force
- Too fast a response time
- Too fine a manipulative capability
- Too many control actions to be performed in a sequence (or at once)
- Control without effective feedback
- An impossible biomechanical response.

2. The system should be tolerant of human error and not designed so as to encourage it. It is estimated that between 40 percent and 80 percent of accidents in industrial, aerospace, and military settings have an immediate human cause. In addition, any error or inappropriate action, even if not hazardous, will have an impact on the overall effectiveness of the system by reducing performance, speed of response, or availability, or by increasing the cost of ownership.

A literature is emerging on human error aimed at systematizing its underlying principles. Rasmussen (1981) has proposed three levels of human performance: skill-based, rule-based, and knowledge-based. Each of these has an associated type of error (see Fig. 2), and it is now possible to construct valid models of human error that can assist in the design of reliable error-resistant systems. Such models are already in limited use in the design process, and it can be confidently expected that further development will lead to more flexible and capable design tools in the next decade.

3. The operator must retain a coherent context for his choice of action. Any intelligent and effective action must be related to the conditions that pertain at the time. Therefore, contextual information is necessary to ensure that the operator remains in contact with his tasks and the world about him. Such contextual information must be available on demand to maintain "situational awareness" and be presented in such a way that it can be quickly and accurately assimilated.

Many military systems are related to the tactical deployment of one's own and opposing assets in space and time. When asset numbers increase, or when the situation becomes dynamic, a reference context must be provided to keep the operator in touch with changes. At its minimum, such context can be provided by a marked-up map, although this is labor intensive, may lag behind reality, and is prone to error. To meet the requirement for rapid updating, many current systems incorporate a Tactical Situation Display, where task-related elements and their spatial relationships and characteristics are presented and updated automatically.

The context required will vary rapidly with time and the task at hand. For example, in an air-to-ground attack, differently scaled displays would be appropriate for different parts of the mission:

FACTORS	Skill-based slips	Rule-based mistakes	Knowledge-based mistakes
Type of activity	Routine actions	Problem solving	
Degree of conscious control	Mainly automated processes Action schemata	Rules	Resource-limited conscious processes
Focus of attention	Not on present task	Directed at problem-related issues	
Form of error	Largely predictable "Strong but wrong" Actions	Rules	Variable
Error detection	Usually fairly rapid	Slow and difficult—often only achieved with the help of others	

Figure 2. Levels of performance and error characteristics.

Scale	*Used to Assess*
Large	Terrain-masking approaches/target orientation
Medium	General navigation for ingress/egress
Small	Own forces refueling, landing site locations, safe corridors

Another area where context is important is in establishing system health and current capability; in all complex systems that are likely to be deployed in the next ten years, the operator will retain some system management function. To be able to discharge this function with the minimum impact on his operational task, the operator requires a system context. System status displays should show the effective mission capability the operator still retains with the current system status, rather than maintenance data.

For any given system, the requirements for contextual information are direct consequences of the system tasks and should be available and defined at the task analysis stage of the design process.

4. The system must be easy to learn and operate. The easier the system is to learn, the lower will be the training cost, the investment needed to ensure adequate performance, and the likelihood of a catastrophic decline in operator performance under stress. The easier the system is to operate, the easier it will be to staff, as a wider section of the available population will be capable of operating it.

These are truisms that, unfortunately, are all too often overlooked in the design process. There is a tendency, in the push for technical performance against a limited budget, to disregard any change/improvement that will assist the operator if it increases the cost of the system. There is also the cumulative effect of allocating "small" extra tasks to the operator during development. This has significant ownership costs for the end user because manning, training, and operational performance are likely to suffer. A clear and early specification of machine and operator requirements should make explicit any compromises imposed by the operating environment.

Future Trends

In one sense, the MMI has been improving steadily over the centuries; for example, sail-handling equipment techniques have steadily evolved to be more compatible with the physical attributes of the sailor. But equipment design has always been subject to trade-offs between such competing interests as appearance, functionality, and cost. It was really only in the 1940s that the professional human factors practitioner emerged, and only relatively recently that there has been sufficient knowledge to design consistently satisfactory MMIs. Where an MMI is patently unsatisfactory, and examples are not hard to find, the explanation is usually not that the information was not available but rather that it was not applied. It may have been that a human factors practitioner was not used, or that he was used too late, or that he could not convince other members of the team of the correctness of his approach. Alternatively, the total system may have been an amalgam of equipments, each of which had a perfectly satisfactory MMI but which together made incompatible or excessive demands on the operator.

Three trends are already well established and are likely to have a major effect on MMI design over the next decade.

1. An expansion of, and easier access to, databases.

Data on the success or failure of MMI design in conventional and more esoteric environments will continue to be acquired from research and operational experience. As new technologies reach the demonstrator stage, they will produce new MMI challenges that doubtless will be duly met and reported. But it is vital that the expansion of the MMI knowledge database be complemented by improvements in the collation, storage, and accessibility of data; their availability, in a user-friendly form, at a desktop terminal is the next goal.

2. An increased promulgation of, and adherence to, standards.

Howarth (1987) defines three types of MMI standard:

- Design: These specify some of the physical parameters of the MMI and are sometimes mandatory. MIL-STD-1472C and DEF STAN 0025 are examples.
- Procedural: These reflect a top-down approach and specify where human factor inputs are to be made in the acquisition process. HARDMAN (U.S. Navy) and MANPRINT (U.S. Army) are examples.
- Performance: These specify the standard to which the MMI must perform, for example, the peak work load that a fully trained operator must be able to achieve.

The mandatory use of all three types of standard is likely to increase.

3. A widening of the scope of the MMI.

Our starting premise was that the MMI was *the* critical interface in system design. As measurement of whole system performance becomes both more important and more necessary, this is likely to become ever more obvious. However, while early consideration of the MMI was dominated by the operator's physical characteristics (reach, strength, motion stereotypes, etc.), and current consideration by his cognitive ones (perceptual speed, memory, flexibility, etc.), in the future, the MMI may include his emotional characteristics. Designers and human factors practitioners will be expanding the questions that they currently ask to include others like: Will the operator's role in this system give him professional satisfaction? Will he have the courage to override the machine when appropriate? How must decision-aids be presented so that they are acceptable? Current data on such questions are scarce and soft, but so, at one time, were data on man's physical and cognitive capabilities. These latter are growing steadily, as is their application. So, in the future, our view of what is included in the term *man-machine interface* is likely to expand and encompass the full range of man's physical, cognitive, and emotional capabilities.

M. F. ALLNUTT
V. P. SCHMIT

SEE ALSO: Psychology, Military; Research and Development Establishments and Policies; Social Science Research and Development, Military; Standardization and Interoperability; Technology Acquisition and Development; Technology and Warfare.

Bibliography

MIL-STD-1472C. 1981. *Human engineering design criteria for military systems, equipment and facilities.* Washington, D.C.: Department of Defense.

DEF STAN-0025. 1988. *Human factors for designers of equipment.* London: Ministry of Defence.

Binkin, M. 1986. *Military psychology and defense manpower.* Washington, D.C.: Brookings.

Boff, R. K. R., and J. E. Lincoln, eds. 1988. *Engineering data compendium: Human perception and performance.* Wright-Patterson Air Force Base, Ohio: Aerospace Medical Research Laboratory.

Fitts, P. M., ed. 1951. *Human engineering for an effective air-navigation and traffic-control system.* Washington, D.C.: National Research Council.

———. 1962. Functions of man in complete systems. *Aerospace Engineering* 21:34–39.

Howarth, C. I. 1987. Psychology and information technology. In *Information technology and people: Designing for the future,* ed. F. Blackler and D. Oborne. Leicester: British Psychological Society.

McCormick, E. J., and M. S. Sanders. 1982. *Human factors in engineering and design.* New York: McGraw-Hill.

Meister, D. 1985. *Behavioral analysis and measurement methods.* New York: Wiley.

Poulton, E. C. 1974. *Tracking skill and manual control.* New York: Academic Press.

Rasmussen, J. 1981. Models of mental strategies in process plant diagnosis. In *Human detection and diagnosis of system failures,* eds. J. Rasmussen and W. Rouse. New York: Plenum.

Salvendy, G., ed. 1987. *Handbook of human factors.* New York: Wiley.

Smith, S. L., and J. N. Monier. 1984. *Design guidelines for user-system interface software.* Rept. No. MTR-9420. Bedford, Mass.: Mitre Corp.

Van Cott, H. P., and R. G. Kincade, eds. 1972. *Human engineering guide to equipment design.* Washington, D.C.: Government Printing Office.

MANPOWER, MILITARY

Manpower is one of the most important elements of military power. Men and women do the fighting, transport the supplies, operate the bases, and direct military forces of nations and coalitions in combat. The military manpower process establishes the numbers and kinds of men and women who serve in and support a nation's armed forces. The result of this process is a military manpower program.

This discussion of military manpower addresses: (1) military unit design, which translates work to be accomplished into authorizations for staffing military units; (2) military manpower programming, which allocates authorizations to units and sets targets for the personnel systems within the armed forces; (3) military manpower mobilization, which brings military and civilian strength from peacetime staffing levels to wartime strength and sustains it during protracted combat; and (4) military manpower policy, which defines the way in which a particular nation organizes and staffs its military forces and obtains the necessary personnel.

National military manpower programs are as much a result of national traditions and domestic political considerations as they are of a rational engineering process. The size and composition of a nation's armed force and the way military personnel are obtained (especially in peacetime), are political matters, not always based entirely on national security considerations. The existence of large international military coalitions, such as the North Atlantic Treaty Organization (NATO), means that coalition politics affect national manpower programs, although the impact may be weak.

Manpower versus Personnel

In its broadest sense, the military manpower process covers all aspects of providing people for armed forces. This is accomplished through two systems: manpower and personnel.

The first step in the manpower process is determining the job to be done. The next step is establishing the number of people and types of skills and experience to do the work. The final step is translating these skill and experience requirements into authorizations for workers, which enables a commander to order, requisition, or hire workers from a personnel system. The output of the manpower process is a set of authorizations for people.

Personnel supplies people to the fill the manpower authorizations. The personnel system acquires, tests, trains, assigns, promotes, retires, and categorizes people in the work force. The output of the personnel system is people.

In military terms, manpower authorizations are also called billets and spaces. Manpower deals with spaces; personnel deals with people. Manpower deals with authorized strength; personnel, with assigned or effective strength. The objective of the manpower process is to make the authorizations match the work load. The objective of the personnel system is to fill each authorization with a worker who has the prescribed skill and experience.

THE SCOPE OF MILITARY POWER

Military manpower covers all military units and the military personnel, civilian personnel, and contract personnel who work in these units. All of these kinds of people work in armed forces, depending on national military policy, and the military manpower process must consider them. There are usually separate personnel systems for military personnel, civilian employees, and contractor employees.

The General Manpower Process

The general manpower process is a systematic way to relate work output to labor input. The starting point of the process is an assessment of the work to be done at a basic work center—a group of related job responsibilities and tasks. The work to be done is broken down into tasks and related to the work-center environment, such as the amount, kind, and condition of equipment and the physical layout and condition of facilities. The determination of how much capital and labor is required is of fundamental importance in work-center planning.

Work is translated into labor using management engineering techniques. Data is obtained from documents, interviews with workers, on-site observation, and surveys. Measurement techniques include time and motion studies, work process studies, and statistical analyses of work experience. The process sets standards for each task by specifying the time it takes a worker (or team of workers) to produce a unit of output. Using the time standards for each skill and the desired level of production, the number of workers for each work center can be established. By combining work centers of various types, it is possible to establish staffing tables for larger organizations that correspond to a given amount of production.

The Military Manpower Process

The military manpower process applies the general manpower process to the design of military units. Because of the nature of military work, the military manpower process has certain characteristics not found in the private sector.

For military personnel, the description of a job in terms of skill and experience is converted into a specialty and grade. The military personnel system usually does not permit lateral entry; most new military personnel enter at the lowest enlisted or officer grade and get promoted to higher grades (assuming competitive performance) as length of service increases. Thus, military grade denotes experience. Military personnel acquire skills through schooling and work experience, and this is indicated by specialty designators.

The military manpower process is designed to describe the potential for work rather than actual work. War, the business of armed forces, is not the usual state, and military units spend more of their time preparing for war than actually fighting. American military forces have fought three major wars since 1945—Korea (1950–53), Vietnam (1965–75), and Iraq (1991)—but spent twice as much time preparing as fighting. Except for the troops who fought in Afghanistan (1980–89), the Soviets did not fight a major war from 1945 to 1991. The Chinese army has been involved in border clashes but has not fought a major war since 1949. Although there are exceptions, such as Iran and Iraq in the 1980s, it is not possible for most armed forces to test the effectiveness of the manpower process and make adjustments to it on the basis of ongoing experience.

The military manpower process needs to focus on wartime work loads. The work done by armed forces in peacetime is not the proper criterion for establishing wartime manpower requirements, since peacetime work is primarily training and getting ready for wartime. The military manpower process, therefore, has to specify the correct number and kind of people needed for a future event that differs substantially from current work and that cannot be practiced realistically—and which may even be different from what is expected.

Measurement of work load for some military skills is inherently difficult because many military activities do not have civilian counterparts. Combat, by definition, is not a civilian occupation. Civilian industry does not engage in tank battles or dive-bombing. The manpower demands for these kinds of activities must be derived from military considerations rather than civilian work load measurements. There are some skills in military units similar to those found in civilian organizations, but even these operate differently in a military environment than they do in civilian life. Therefore, standard management engineering techniques need to be adjusted when applied to the military manpower process.

Relationship to Other Aspects of Military Power

The military manpower process is intimately related to other aspects of military power: operational doctrine, organization, and equipment.

Operational doctrine includes techniques for doing work, tactics for fighting on the battlefield, operational art for maneuvering in the theater of operations, and strategy for the regional or global employment of forces. The military manpower process is affected more strongly by technique and tactics—they play major roles in determining what work is necessary, how it will be done, and how many people it will take to do it—than by operational art and strategy, but all of them are important.

The way in which the various elements of combat power are organized is a key element in the military manpower process. Basic organizational concepts, such as the infantry battalion and the aviation squadron, define the work to be done in particular units and have a great impact on how a particular kind of support is to be provided. For example, what kind of maintenance will be performed by the using unit and what kind by the supporting maintenance unit? Will food be prepared and served at the company or battalion level or at a central base messing facility? The combination of units of various kinds into higher level organizations is also a factor. In the United States, for example, the Marine Corps (essentially a land warfare force with organic air support and special capability for amphibious operations) is combined with the navy. In the Soviet Union, the air defense forces for the homeland are organized into a separate service. Canadian forces are integrated into a single service for air, land, and sea operations.

Equipment is another major factor in the manpower process. The arms and equipment to be used are primary considerations in establishing manpower authorizations for a unit. When horse cavalry existed, there was a demand for people who could ride horses. When aircraft began to be used for military purposes, it was necessary to authorize spaces for aviators. When radar and other advanced electronics gear came into use, people who could operate and maintain high-technology equipment were authorized. Throughout the armed forces, as new equipment is introduced, the personnel systems have to produce personnel with greater literacy and ability than the previous equipment required.

The manpower program, therefore, must be compatible with the equipment that is on hand and must anticipate the equipment that will be procured in the future. Since military personnel systems start all new members at the bottom, there is a delay between the creation of an authorization for a skill and the filling of that authorization with a person who has worked his way up in the ranks to the necessary skill level. It is important to plan in advance for the introduction of new equipment so that qualified personnel will arrive at the same time as the equipment. A good manpower program projects its demands sufficiently in advance to accomplish this feat.

The military manpower process is accomplished in stages. The initial stage is the design of units. The next stage is the design of forces in which the number, type, and composition of units to be in the force structure is established. The third stage is the authorization of nonunit individuals. In the final stage, the manpower program is formulated and processed through the requisite legislative and budgetary approvals.

Design of Military Units

There is substantial agreement throughout the armed forces of the world as to how military forces should be organized. Armies are organized in the Napoleonic manner, modified by Wellington's adaptation to linear tactics and updated to take into account the increasing lethality and range of air-land combat weapons. Air forces are organized basically on the model established by the British in World War I and later by the Royal Air Force. Navies are organized on the British model of the nineteenth century. These basic organizational principles have been stable for many years, although there have been modifications necessitated by changes in technology and to allow for national characteristics.

Military organization is based on a hierarchical aggregation of small elements into larger elements, combining similar or dissimilar elements at different levels to provide a structure capable of waging war. At the bottom are small groups of a few people organized into a team, squad, or section under a leader. These are combined with other small groups to form larger organizations. As the aggregations become larger, it is necessary to specify the allowances of personnel, equipment, and supplies the organization may have. The level at which the military organization is formalized by these authorizations is the unit. In this sense, and although there are smaller subelements, the unit is the fundamental building block of military organization, and the starting point for the military manpower process.

The Concept of Military Unit

The military unit is the basic organizational element for all armed forces. A unit is a group of personnel with associated equipment designed to perform a stated amount and kind of work. This work is described in terms of a military role and a military mission. There are two kinds of units: portable and fixed.

Portable units, which usually include only military personnel, are designed to operate successively in different locations as determined by the military situation. They are portable in the sense that they can be moved as needed. They operate as a coherent group, although subelements may be dispersed locally. Portable units include aviation squadrons, naval ships, combat battalions, and combat support and service support battalions and companies. Portable units have distinct roles and missions in the overall military force structure. They are designed to provide a specific amount and kind of output and are authorized a specific number and kind of people and equipment. Portable units are intended for deployment to a theater of war and employment in combat in a flexible manner.

Fixed units, which are staffed with military and civilian personnel, are designed to operate in the same location. These include air bases, naval bases, training centers, depots, military bases, and administrative headquarters. Fixed units have broad roles and missions that may include a variety of different functions. Their workload varies according to the mission, and the number and kind of people and equipment authorized varies according to the workload.

Both kinds of units are characterized by their roles and missions. The role of a unit is a characteristic of the unit, and represents what the unit does in general. The mission of a unit is the result of a specific military situation and represents a set of goals to be accomplished. The role of an infantry battalion is to close with and destroy the enemy; the mission of the battalion may be to attack or defend a particular terrain feature. The role of an attack submarine is to seek out and destroy enemy ships; the mission will specify an area of operations and/or specific targets. The role of a tactical airlift squadron is to move personnel and equipment short distances to forward airfields; the mission will specify the airfields and the time frame for movement. When assigning missions, commanders have to know the roles and capabilities of available units. These are the basic considerations in unit design.

Service Organizational Patterns

Land, air, and sea forces operate in different environments, and each has different patterns for unit design and employment. Each military service organizes according to the environment in which it operates. Although each has portable and fixed units, the mix varies considerably. Land forces rely extensively on portable units, with fixed units only in rear areas. Air and naval forces make more extensive use of fixed unit bases.

Land forces operate dispersed over the terrain in a theater of war and are oriented toward the enemy with combat units in the front and support units behind. The units tend to operate as coherent elements, with space between adjacent units. The base of operations consists of many portable units of different kinds providing logistical and administrative support. Sometimes these units are clustered into operating bases in the theater of war or the national area. Lines of communications are established from the front lines back to operating bases in the theater or in the national area. Although there is no firm rule, operating bases in the theater of war tend to be aggregations of portable units; operating bases in the national area tend to be fixed units. In low-intensity combat, this linear model of disposition of land forces may not be applicable, and there may exist instead a pattern of regional or local bases which support field operations in areas of operations extending outward from the bases. In all situations, however, land forces use portable units flexibly to create their own operating base on the ground.

Air forces operate differently from land forces because aircraft must rely on airfields, which may be fixed, or in the case of an aircraft carrier, portable. The tendency for air forces, other than carrier-based aviation, is to create fixed units for bases and portable units called squadrons for the aircraft and crews. For carrier aviation, there are two kinds of portable units, the carriers providing the support, and the aviation squadrons with the aircraft and crews. Air bases, however, must be tailored to provide support for specific numbers and kinds of aircraft. The composition of these bases in terms of aircraft maintenance and operations will vary considerably according to the squadrons to be supported.

Naval forces also operate from bases. The ships themselves are portable units with crews designed to operate and fight them. Naval bases are fixed units designed to provide logistical and administrative support to a variety of ships. Nuclear-powered ships can cruise for great distances without refueling. Modern logistical techniques make it possible to replenish ships at sea. Some combat ships, therefore, may cruise for extended periods of time without having to visit a naval base. Most ships, however, remain dependent on naval bases, and ultimately even nuclear powered ships have to return to port.

Land Forces Units

Land forces portable units are commonly categorized as combat, combat support, and combat service support. Combat units are designed to engage the enemy with fire and maneuver and close with and destroy the enemy forces. Combat support units provide services that directly facilitate the combat operations. Combat service support units provide logistical and administrative support. Generally, combat and combat support units are battalions; combat service support units (and some combat support units) are companies. A common delineation among these three categories of land forces units is shown in Table 1.

Combat service support units. It is easier to apply the manpower process to combat service support units than to the others because they provide services similar to those provided by nonmilitary organizations and can, therefore, be measured. Combat service support units tend to provide a single kind of service, and the amount of that service may be specified as its design-level output.

A unit's design-level output is the kind and amount of output thc unit is intended to deliver at wartime strength and under wartime conditions.

For example, a transportation truck company may be designed to provide a specific hauling capacity expressed in ton-miles per day. This design-level output will establish the number of trucks required, which, in turn, will establish the number of drivers needed and the number of supervisors (truckmasters). The number of trucks and the desired operating tempo (number of miles per truck per day) provides the basis for estimating the number of mechanics needed. This leads to an estimate of the number of repair parts and tools to be kept on hand in the unit and the number of parts clerks and toolkeepers required. The number of truck miles to be driven daily also provides a basis for establishing the number of dispatchers and schedulers needed to manage the operation. The design-level

Table 1. *Categories of Land Forces' Portable Units*

Combat battalions	Combat support battalions	Combat service support companies
Infantry	Engineer	Supply
Tank	Signal	Transportation
Cavalry	Military police	Maintenance
Artillery	Military intelligence	Administration
Air defense	Chemical	Medical
Combat aviation		
Special forces		

output, therefore, translates directly to the number of people with various skills needed in the truck company.

These personnel are formed into teams with the appropriate span of control. The basic military organizational elements are shown in Table 2.

A transportation truck company could be organized into three squads of ten trucks each, with ten drivers, a squad leader for supervision, and an assistant squad leader for additional supervision and to fill in for an absent driver. Three squads would be formed into a platoon, with a platoon leader and platoon sergeant for supervision. The required number of fifteen mechanics, toolkeepers, and parts clerks would be formed into a maintenance section with a senior sergeant and a warrant officer in charge. Three truck platoons and the maintenance section would be combined into a truck company with the addition of a company headquarters section consisting of a company commander, a first sergeant, an administrative clerk or clerks, a supply team, perhaps some cooks, and other administrative personnel, depending on how that particular army is organized to provide support at different echelons. Three or four truck companies would be formed into a truck battalion, which would also provide a larger maintenance platoon capable of more complicated work and a dispatching and management capability to operate the trucks in an over-the-road operation. The battalion headquarters would include a commander, a battalion sergeant major, and, for the first time, a staff of officers to assist the commander in operating the battalion. The number and kind of truck companies assigned to the truck battalion headquarters would vary according to the military situation.

The design of a truck company or other combat service support unit is relatively simple because it is possible to convert work-load statements into requirements for particular skills and experience on an engineering basis.

The military environment, however, leads to manpower requirements that might not be considered in a civilian organization. For example, it is normal practice in the military to provide a deputy commander or executive officer at the company and battalion levels. This deputy extends the capability of the commander and replaces him if necessary. Another unique feature of military organization is the provision of a senior noncommissioned officer (e.g., platoon sergeant, company first sergeant, battalion sergeant major) to provide a direct link between the commander and the enlisted personnel. These noncommissioned officers see to it that orders are understood and carried out. Some military organizations include a political deputy commander whose function is to ensure the reliability and enthusiasm of the troops.

TABLE 2. *Basic Land Forces' Organizational Elements*

ORGANIZATIONAL ELEMENT	NUMBER OF PERSONNEL	RANK OF COMMANDER
Squad	6–14	Sergeant
Section	5–40	Senior sergeant
Platoon	25–60	Lieutenant
Company	80–300	Captain/major
Battalion	250–1,000	Lieutenant colonel

Combat support units. The design of a combat support unit is more complicated than that of a combat service support unit because combat support units have multiple roles, and their design-level output cannot be measured or even described easily. Combat engineer units, for example, are capable of performing a variety of jobs, depending on the situation. For defense, a combat engineer battalion would lay mines, improve defensive positions, and construct command posts. For offense, the same battalion would breach minefields and other obstacles, build roads and bridges, and assist in the advance of combat units. During a retreat, this same engineer battalion would destroy bridges and create obstacles. Since the unit's tasks cannot be predicted, it is necessary to use input capability as a surrogate measure of output. For combat engineer battalions, the design-level output is the number of equipment-hours and labor-hours the battalion can provide. This may be refined into general functional terms as x meters of minefields placed per day or y meters of bridge built per hour if the entire battalion is assigned to that task. Generally, however, combat engineer battalions and other combat support battalions engage in many different tasks simultaneously, and are designed to do this with a general design level of capability.

Combat units. The design of combat units depends as much on doctrine as on work load. The actual output of these units depends on what the enemy does in a combat situation. Infantry and tank units are designed to deliver firepower and maneuver to close with and destroy the enemy. Both the way this is done and the unit's strength are established by the fighting doctrine of each army. For example, the size and composition of a rifle squad are functions of tactics rather than work load; the composition of a tank crew is a function of the tank; and the composition of an artillery battery depends on the type of guns, the desired rate of fire, and artillery tactics. The design-level output of fire support units can be established by the number of weapons and personnel, but the actual output depends on the availability of targets and ammunition.

Battlefield tactics are the most important function in the design of combat units, followed by weapons. The basic tactics for land forces engaged in high-intensity combat operations come from infiltration tactics that were introduced by the Germans in 1918. These call for a combination of fire and maneuver, in that a "base of fire"—provided by small arms, automatic weapons, and mortars—supports the "maneuver element." There is a base-of-fire element and one or more maneuver, elements at each level of combat organization, and the base-of-fire weapons become larger, more lethal, and longer in range at each successive level. Table 3 shows how this works.

A similar scheme applies to tank battalions, although the tactical practice with armored units is to deploy platoons of four to six tanks as maneuver elements or bases of fire interchangeably as the situation dictates. Some tank battalions have organic mortar support.

Infantry and tank battalions work together—in combined arms teams—with reconnaissance units on security missions and with artillery battalions and combat aviation units to provide fire support from positions in the rear.

The role of air force units is to fly aircraft sorties to deliver munitions on targets, perform reconnaissance, or transport personnel and supplies. The air force scheme of organization focuses on the aircraft to be flown using the weapon system approach. A weapon system is the weapon plus all of the support required to operate the weapon in wartime.

Air forces units. For air forces, the weapon is the aircraft itself, including armament and devices on the aircraft designed to help deliver munitions and/or evade enemy defenses. The aircraft is considered a platform for electronic gear and weapons, such as missiles, bombs, and guns. The aircraft requires maintenance in the form of mechanics, tools, instructions, and parts. Aircraft sorties require fuel and munitions. Combat operations require command and control facilities and air bases. The personnel in the aircraft crew, and those needed to perform maintenance, supply fuel and munitions, and exercise command and control, need places to sleep and food to eat. The manpower process is applied to define the number and kind of workers needed to support the entire weapon system. These weapon system manpower demands may be aggregated for a given number and mix of weapons.

The primary determinants of air force manpower are the number and type of aircraft, the intended operational tempo, and the location of bases. The support requirements for a particular aircraft can be estimated using the general manpower process based on engineering data and experience. These standards, for example, can be used to predict how many mechanics with particular skills are needed to keep a fighter aircraft in a state of good repair at a particular operational tempo (the number of sorties to be flown per day). An increase in the sortie rate would generate additional requirements for maintenance personnel and may even create additional requirements for flight crews if crew fatigue is a factor. The location of bases establishes the space-time factors in resupply and maintenance operations and determines the number of people required to transport people and parts to the aircraft.

TABLE 3. *Organizational Scheme for Infantry Units*

ORGANIZATIONAL ELEMENT	BASE OF FIRE	MANEUVER ELEMENTS
Rifle squad	Automatic weapon team	Rifle team(s)
Rifle platoon	Light machine-gun squad	Rifle squads
Rifle company	Weapons platoon with ATGMs, light mortars, and heavy machine guns	Rifle platoons
Infantry battalion	Weapons company with heavy ATGMS and heavy mortars	Rifle companies

The squadron is the basic unit of air force organization and includes as a minimum the aircraft and the air crews, whose composition depends on the type of aircraft. Fighter or attack aircraft may carry a single pilot or a pilot and weapons officer; bombers, transports, or patrol aircraft may require a crew of several people. A squadron is often organized into flights of several aircraft, and includes commanders, deputies, and staff officers. Depending on national preference, an aviation squadron may also contain some of the mechanics, armaments specialists, supply specialists, communicators, administrators, and cooks needed to support the weapon system.

In the U.S. Air Force, the squadrons tend to include only the aircraft and air crews; all of the other personnel are organized into functional support squadrons assigned to air bases. There are maintenance squadrons, food service squadrons, communications squadrons, and personnel administration squadrons tailored to specific missions in peacetime and in wartime. This form of organization allows the general manpower process to be applied effectively to provide the necessary support with a minimum of waste, but with some redundancy as a safety factor against personnel losses and the "fog of war" in wartime.

NAVAL UNITS

Naval units consist of ships, aviation squadrons (the design of which is similar to that of air force units) and bases (designed as fixed units).

Determining the number and kinds of sailors a ship needs is a complex problem. The basic assumption is that a ship's crew will be large enough to allow it to operate indefinitely under wartime conditions, even if the entire crew is needed during combat. (A ship is on full alert—at "general quarters"—for only short periods of time because naval combat tends to be short and decisive.) On the other hand, the number of people needed to operate a ship in the absence of combat is relatively small, even on a three-shift basis. Authorized crew size, therefore, is a compromise between peacetime operations and general quarters. In the U.S. Navy, authorized crew size is based on operating indefinitely at Steaming Condition 3 (crew at a heightened state of alert), with three watches manning some weapons and fire control stations. Once this basic assumption is stated, the operating and maintenance characteristics of a ship allow the number and kinds of people needed to be determined by the general manpower process.

As modern ships become increasingly crowded with "black boxes," the real constraint on peacetime crew authorizations may be living conditions rather than combat conditions. For nations with volunteer forces, living conditions for long cruises aboard ship are a factor in recruitment and retention. Even for nations with conscription, the desire to retain technical specialists requires consideration of crew morale. The number of bunks sometime determines the maximum peacetime authorization with a provision for wartime augmentation, when a lower standard of shipboard living would be acceptable.

Fixed Units

Fixed-unit design is based on matching manpower to current work load. As work load increases or decreases, manpower authorizations are increased or decreased correspondingly. Fixed units vary according to their specific mission. While many perform a wide variety of functions, there are some that are single function.

Fixed units offer the opportunity to apply the general manpower process in a straightforward manner, since management engineering techniques are applicable to the operations of a base, a depot, or even a headquarters. Even training centers, where the military environment must be considered, produce an easily measureable output.

There are three important considerations in the design of fixed units; labor productivity, nonavailable manpower, and personnel mix.

Labor productivity is the ratio of useful output to unit of input. Workers do not work continually when on the job. The amount of labor produced in an eight-hour day depends on how many job interruptions occur. Time spent on coffee breaks or listening to supervisors giving instructions cannot also be used for doing work. For example, a mechanic may actually produce for only 32 hours a week while being paid for 40. The productive labor for a given worker for a given work period is, therefore, a function of policy, urgency, and supervision. Labor productivity is taken into account when determining how many people are needed to accomplish a certain amount of work. To provide 160 hours of work output based on 32 hours of real work per mechanic, it would be necessary to authorize five mechanics working instead of four.

Nonavailable manpower includes those who are away from their jobs but still in the organization—that is, employees on vacation, on sick leave, at school, or at management conferences. Although these people are not contributing directly to work output, they are still part of the fixed unit, and it is necessary to provide authorizations for them. To compensate for this nonavailable manpower, an estimate is made of the number of employees the unit will continually be short, and the authorization is increased accordingly. This applies fully to civilian personnel and partially to military personnel. If nonavailable manpower is not accounted for, legitimate absences of employees will reduce output below design levels.

Once the number and skills needed have been determined, it is necessary to consider the kind of personnel (military or civilian) to be assigned to each manpower authorization. Most nations do not mix military and civilian personnel in the same unit, others (e.g., the United States) do. Some organizations (e.g., Soviet transport battalions) are staffed with civilians or paramilitary personnel but function during wartime as part of the military force structure. Some nations use contractors to provide support to military forces. Local labor is frequently used in a theater of operations to support foreign military forces in the form of host nation support or labor battalions. The military manpower program must account for all of these kinds of personnel.

Portable units in general, and combat units in particular, are usually staffed entirely by military personnel who are indoctrinated and trained for combat, subject to military law, and can be compelled to fight. Civilian employees or contract personnel, however motivated and loyal, lack the training and the obligation to serve in the same way as military personnel. However, civilian technicians are sometimes used to augment portable units.

U.S. policy is to fill an authorization in a military unit with a civilian employee unless it can be demonstrated that a military person is required. This is obvious in the case of an infantryman, fighter pilot, or submarine commander, but not as clear-cut for jobs with a high content of civilian-related skills. Thus, the trend in the United States has been to substitute civilian employees for military personnel. This policy was useful as military enlistments decreased in response to the introduction of voluntary enlistment; however, it has not worked well when both military and civilian strengths were constrained by budget actions, and the planned substitutions did not occur. The United States relies heavily on civilian employees to staff its fixed military units.

There has been similar pressure in the United States to substitute private contractors for either military personnel or civilian employees. This has been true particularly in base operations. The assumption is that it is cheaper for contractors to perform the work in peacetime than for the government to do it. How this will work out during wartime has yet to be put to a thorough test.

Military Manpower Programming

Manpower programming is the process of translating unit authorizations into an overall, time-phased set of personnel requirements for an armed force or an entire nation.

The unit design process creates an authorization document for each unit; the units, in turn, are assigned to components or echelons in accordance with required readiness. Force-structure changes are projected into the future so that new equipment and units may be introduced in a sensible and efficient manner.

Unit Authorization Documents

The results of the unit design process are recorded in unit authorization documents, which are used by the supply and personnel systems to issue equipment and assign personnel to the unit. The names of the documents vary for each nation, but the principles are the same. In the U.S. Army, the unit authorization documents are called Tables of Organization and Equipment (TO&E) for portable units and Tables of Distribution and Allowance (TDA) for fixed units. One advantage of authorization documents is the standardization of organization, equipping, and staffing of military units of similar type. The standard tables, however, are often modified so that each unit has its own unique authorization document.

Each authorization document lists the type (military or civilian), grade, and skill of each person authorized for the unit. Strengths are specified for both wartime and peacetime. Wartime strength in equipment and personnel will deliver the design capability that is the basis for the size and composition of the unit. In peacetime, portable military units are usually authorized less equipment and fewer personnel. This is done to save money; it is assumed that there will be sufficient time to bring the units to full wartime strength before they are committed to combat.

The total of the unit authorization documents for a military organization or service—that is, the number of people that the personnel system should assign to the units—constitutes the force structure allowance.

Assignment to Components

Units are assigned to components according to unit readiness, which is the time it takes for the unit to transform itself from peacetime conditions to full wartime capability. There are four general classes of units according to readiness: active, reserve, standby, and planning.

Active units are staffed in peacetime by full-time military personnel. Peacetime authorization is typically 80 percent to 100 percent of wartime personnel strength, and active units also have full sets of equipment at or near wartime authorizations.

Reserve units are staffed in peacetime primarily by part-time military personnel (reservists), but they may also have a small number of full-time military personnel as trainers or administrators. The peacetime strength of a reserve unit varies from 80 percent to 100 percent of wartime strength in reservists and up to 25 percent in full-time personnel. Most reserve units have equipment, but this varies in both amount and quality.

Standby units are staffed in peacetime by a cadre—a group of trained and experienced military personnel, primarily officers and noncommissioned officers, who provide the nucleus of a unit. Upon mobilization, individual reservists or new recruits are assigned to fill the unit and bring it to wartime strength. The active-duty cadre ranges from 10 percent to 20 percent of wartime strength. These units usually have a full set of equipment, often older models.

Planning units have no personnel in peacetime and must be activated, staffed, and equipped upon mobilization. However, a cadre of military personnel and existing military equipment may be predesignated for a planning unit.

A wide range of readiness is possible with various combinations of active-duty personnel, reservists, and equipment sets. In general, the greater the number of full-time active-duty military personnel assigned to a unit, the faster it will achieve full wartime capability upon mobilization. Since active-duty personnel are more costly than reservists, there is an inverse relationship between peacetime cost and readiness for wartime missions.

The basis for allocation of units among the components is a function of strategy, military tradition, and budgets. The general tendency is to keep the minimum number of expensive active units. If there is a lack of confidence in reserve units, more active units will be retained. The exact way reserve units are equipped and staffed is a function of national military traditions, of which there is great variety throughout the world.

Nonavailable Manpower

The military manpower program must also provide for military personnel not assigned to military units. These are a special category of nonavailable manpower. As discussed previously, the authorized strength for fixed units is increased to allow for nonavailable manpower. This is not done for portable units, whose design-level output and authorized strengths are held constant. For military personnel, therefore, the practice is to authorize separate accounts for individual military position not assigned to units. Nonunit military personnel categories include transients, trainees, students, patients, prisoners, and holdees. These are typically assigned to "detachments" rather than to force structure units.

Transients are personnel who are en route from one unit to another. Military personnel are reassigned frequently, and they are allowed travel time to make the move and are often authorized leave in connection with the travel. While the transients are in the process of changing units, they are not available for work at either the losing unit or the gaining unit. In order to keep units at authorized strengths, extra authorizations to account for transients are built into the manpower program. This is extremely important in wartime, when a replacement pipeline of transients is established to facilitate timely replacement of military casualties.

Trainees are new recruits who have not yet qualified for full military service. All military services provide initial training for entry-level personnel. In many cases, recruits receive basic combat training and entry-level skill training at training centers. In some cases, initial training is provided by the units themselves. In either case, the recruits cannot be expected to perform useful work until they have been trained. The practice is to provide additional manpower authorizations for trainees. This allows manpower planners to concentrate on overall trained strength, which is the real measure of the capability of an armed force.

Students are trained personnel who are receiving additional training and education, either in their skills or as part of a general career development program. Full-time students are not available to work in units and are assigned to student detachments.

Other nonavailable manpower includes: hospital patients, who are assigned to patient detachments; military individuals convicted of a crime and sentenced to military or civilian prison, who are assigned to prisoner detachments; and military personnel recovered after unauthorized absences or otherwise not available for work in units (holdees), who are assigned to holding detachments pending disposition.

Accounting rules determine when a military person is reassigned from a unit to an individual's account. A military person ill enough to be in the hospital for a long time will be transferred from his unit to a patient holding detachment, and the unit will requisition another person to fill that authorization. A person only slightly ill will remain assigned to the unit, which will have to work around his absence. Military personnel on ordinary leave (vacation) normally remain assigned to their units, but if they take leave in connection with a change of unit assignment, they are put in the transient account. The individual's accounts are intended to allow the effective strength of units to be maintained as close to authorized strength as possible.

Force Structure Changes

A military manpower program changes constantly because the force structure changes constantly. New units are activated; old units are inactivated; and units are reorganized to accommodate new equipment or tactics.

If the military personnel system is to fill future manpower authorizations, it must be aware of these authorizations well in advance. Since military personnel systems are closed, they must create skills and experience from within—a time-consuming process. It takes fifteen years to develop a battalion commander or frigate captain; three years to develop a good tank commander; and four years (or more) to develop a good fighter pilot. Even if the equipment remained the same, this would present a challenge. The manpower program, therefore, must project changes in manpower authorizations, and this is done by forecasting the manpower impact of programmed changes in the number of types of units.

Force structure changes are projected as far ahead as possible, although the dynamics of planning and budgeting make this a difficult task. Existing unit authorization documents are in effect until modified by a force structure change. Decisions to reorganize, inactivate, or activate units are projected to go into effect at specific future dates, and the authorization document change occurs for the unit at that time. Once the force structure is programmed in this manner, it is possible to calculate the equipment and personnel authorized for the units in the future.

If force structure changes to accommodate new technology are predicted, the military personnel system has time to train and assign the proper personnel. If a new tank or aircraft is to be introduced into the force structure in two years, tank crews and pilots must be trained to operate the new equipment. Qualified mechanics and other support personnel (as well as tools and manuals) should also be available when the new equipment is introduced. It is possible simply to issue the new equipment and let the position learn how to use and maintain it afterwards, but that is neither desirable nor efficient. New technology also may necessitate the redesign of units and the revision of the military manpower program. The redesign may be minor if a new model tank is replacing an existing model; but major changes are likely with the introduction of completely new weapons (e.g., an armed helicopter) that modify battlefield tactics and organization.

Allocation of Authorizations

Once the manpower program is compiled for a particular service and/or nation, it must be ratified through the legislative and budget process. Every nation has a procedure for allocating funds to its military forces. Few, if any, military forces receive all they ask for in the way of money, equipment, and manpower. Several drafts of a particular manpower program will usually be required for a particular fiscal year. Once approved, the manpower program may still need adjustment because of an inability of the personnel systems to fill the authorizations. Although care is taken to coordinate demand with supply, the number of personnel available sometimes fails to match authorizations in quantity or quality. It is sometimes prudent, although not easy, to adjust manpower authorizations to the realities of personnel availability.

The final phase of manpower programming is the allocation of the approved manpower authorizations to the units. This is usually accomplished by bulk allocations of military and civilian authorizations to services, major commands, intermediate headquarters, and finally to the units. At each level, the officials allocating the manpower authorizations do so according to how they perceive priorities of that command at that moment. As a result, the unit authorizations from the top-down allocation process may not match the unit authorizations from the bottom-up work-load analysis. This is a source of frustration for unit commanders, who find their manpower authorizations do not match their work load. This manpower–work load mismatch is prevalent in fixed units but is kept to a minimum in portable units. An additional complication is the gap between authorizations and actual strength caused by imperfect coordination between manpower and personnel managers, and the inherent lag between demand and supply in large organizations.

Military Manpower Mobilization

Military manpower mobilization is the process by which military units are brought from peacetime to wartime strengths and maintained at that level. A mobilization capability must be an integral part of the peacetime military manpower program. How to mobilize is a major element of national military manpower policy. The three major tasks for military manpower mobilization are (1) bringing units from peacetime to wartime strength, (2) replacing losses to keep units at wartime strength, and (3) providing personnel to form new units.

Bringing Units to Wartime Strength

The initial stage of manpower mobilization requires bringing all or a portion of the force structure units from peacetime to wartime strength. Personnel used to bring units to wartime strength are called "fillers." Since the fillers are needed right away, they must already be trained and, hopefully, qualified to perform the jobs to which assigned. The demand for fillers is the difference between the peacetime authorized strength and the wartime authorized strength of the force structure and may be computed exactly by comparing the peacetime and wartime authorizations in unit authorization documents. Meeting the total demand for fillers may be and usually is accomplished over a few days or weeks after initiation of mobilization as units are brought to wartime strength in accordance with prearranged schedules.

Fillers are obtained from active-duty individuals' accounts, from pools of individual reservists, and from retired personnel. Fillers usually report to mobilization stations or replacement centers for assignment to the units they are to fill; sometimes they report directly to the force units.

Replacing Personnel Losses

Once the units have been brought to full wartime strength, the goal is to maintain them at that strength. Personnel attrition in peacetime is caused by normal personnel retirements and separations, accidents, and disease. During wartime, the rate of personnel attrition increases greatly due to combat casualties. Losses from accidents and disease also increase during wartime because of the increased tempo of operations and the employment of forces under difficult and often unhealthy conditions.

The ability to replace personnel losses is perhaps *the* key element in maintaining combat power. However, the goal of the wartime personnel system to replace all losses as they occur with the right kinds of persons is seldom achieved because the numbers and kinds of losses are hard to predict and there are delays in reporting losses and acting on the reports. There is a tendency, moreover, to ignore the need for personnel replacements during the initial stages of a mobilization until battlefield performance suffers because of understrength units.

Personnel used to keep military units at wartime strength are called "replacements," and these fall into two general categories: pretrained individuals and posttrained individuals. Pretrained individual replacements have received at least basic combat and initial skill training and are suitable for assignment to military units in the theater of war without additional training. Posttrained individual replacements are new recruits drawn directly from civilian life who must have initial training before being sent into combat.

Pretrained replacements may be obtained from other active and reserve units, the individual accounts, pools of individual reservists, and retired personnel. Taking replacements from other units does not represent an overall increase in capability, but it may be justified by circumstances. Individual reservists and retired personnel may be used as replacements, either to report directly to units or to backfill against replacements taken from units. Effective utilization of retirees, for example, would be to assign them to support units and release younger personnel to serve as replacements in combat units.

Posttrained replacements are new recruits who either volunteer or are conscripted. These individuals should receive basic combat and initial skill training before being assigned to force units, so there is a delay from the time they join the armed forces to the time they can be used in combat. U.S. law mandates that recruits receive twelve weeks of basic training or the equivalent before being assigned to a unit outside the continental United States. The amount of initial training given to recruits depends on the urgency of the situation. In the early days of World War II, the Soviets were pressing new recruits into service with as little as seven days of training. In the latter days of World War II, the Germans were doing the same. Many nations that rely on volunteers to meet peacetime military strength goals have plans to activate standby conscription systems during mobilization for war.

Creating New Units

Manpower may also be necessary to create new force units during mobilization, and this is accomplished with a cadre and fillers. Once the cadre is in place, fillers are assigned to bring the unit to strength. In addition to recruits, fillers for new units may include veterans completing a combat tour or those released from hospitals. The formation of new force units is a lengthy process. During World War

II, it took about two years for the U.S. Army to form, train, and field a new division. The rate at which new military units can be formed depends on the availability of equipment, training facilities, and military personnel.

Overview of Manpower Mobilization

Military manpower mobilization increases the strength of military units above the peacetime strength. The primary goal is to increase the number of trained military personnel. Military reservists and retirees are recalled from civil life. New recruits are taken into military service, either voluntarily or by conscription. The number of civilian employees in military units increases, and the number of contract employees working in support of the armed forces also expands. Although most attention is paid to increasing military personnel strength during mobilization, ways to increase civilian employees and contract support are also important for nations that integrate these three kinds of personnel into their military force structure.

The demands of military manpower mobilization conflict with other demands for labor. The additional military and civilian personnel for military units are taken from the civilian labor force at a time when the demand for civilian labor to manufacture war materiel, provide civilian goods, and expand infrastructure services is also increasing. There may be insufficient labor to meet all demands, and this constrains the ability of a nation to create new military units during wartime, even if equipment for the units could be made available.

Military Manpower Policy

The military manpower policy of a nation determines the way the nation obtains and employs military and civilian personnel to staff its military units. It influences the design of units, the allocation of units to components, the military-civilian personnel mix in units, the manpower mobilization process, and the overall military manpower program. Military manpower policy is a product not only of a rational process but also of the traditions, customs, and viewpoints of nations and of influential groups within nations.

There are as many different military manpower policies as there are nations. The major parameters of national military manpower policy are the methods used to obtain enlisted military personnel in peacetime, the length of the initial active-duty tour, the proportion of the annual cohort of eligible males who go on active duty, the proportion of noncareer personnel in the active forces, and the nature of the reserve components. (Noncareer military personnel are those who are serving on their initial active-duty tour.)

The major choice in national military manpower policy is whether to maintain peacetime military strength by voluntary means or compulsion. A choice for voluntary enlistment leads to long initial periods of active duty, relatively high noncareer content, and a relatively low proportion of the annual cohort of eligible youth serving. A choice for compulsory service (conscription) leads to additional decisions on the size of the annual cohort conscripted, which tends to be in inverse proportion to the initial term of service. In order to conscript a high proportion of the annual cohort, the initial tour of active duty must be short, and this leads to a very high noncareer content in the active forces. Long initial tours are desirable from the standpoint of military efficiency but mean that only a small proportion of the annual cohort would be conscripted, which causes the problem of how to select those who will serve.

An examination of the relevant parameters of the armed forces of the world reveals four basic models of military manpower policy: voluntary military service, universal military service, short-term compulsory service, and long-term military service.

The voluntary military service model relies on voluntary enlistment, to provide new recruits serving a lengthy initial tour of three or more years. New career personnel comprise about 40 percent of the total strength. A small portion of the annual cohort of eligible males is accepted, usually less than 10 percent but in some nations as high as 30 percent. Active forces constitute a small portion (generally less than 5%) of eligible male youth. (Some Middle East nations maintain active forces above 10% of total eligible males.) Reserve forces tend to be organized into complete units with a complete reserve officer chain of command. Approximately 30 nations (including the United States, the United Kingdom, former British colonies, and countries strongly influenced by these, such as Japan) use the voluntary military service model, and all stem from the British tradition.

The universal voluntary service model relies on conscription to provide new recruits who, with some exceptions, serve a very short initial tour of a year or less. A very high proportion of the annual cohort of eligible males, ranging from 80 percent to 92 percent, is taken into military service. Essentially, every young male serves. The noncareer content of the active forces ranges from 70 percent to 90 percent. Reserves are organized into classes by age, with the younger classes organized into complete units. Almost the entire male population of military age is either on active duty or in the reserves. Seven nations follow this military manpower model. Four of these (Austria, Finland, Sweden, and Switzerland) are the traditional European neutral states. The other three (Greece, Israel, and Turkey) are in a state of military tension and maintain large standing forces relative to the number of male youths of military age. Israel requires long-term initial service from four out of five citizens and has 30 percent of its eligible male youth on active duty.

The short-term compulsory service model relies on conscription to provide new recruits, and these serve an initial active-duty period of about one year. This short initial tour of active duty permits conscripting an average of about 40 percent of the annual cohort of eligible males, with a range of 30 percent to 70 percent. Active military strength ranges from 2 percent to 8 percent of eligible males. Reserves are organized into complete units with a limited reserve chain of command. This model is used by about fifteen nations, including the NATO nations in continental Europe and some nations in South America.

The long-term compulsory service model relies on conscription to provide new recruits who serve an initial active-duty tour of about two years, ranging from one and a half to three years. About 30 percent of the annual cohort is conscripted, with a range from 13 percent to 80 percent; the noncareer content of the active force is about 60 percent. Reserves are maintained as individuals in age classes and are used to fill standby units upon mobilization. This model is used by about 50 nations, and was used in the Soviet Union, almost all Warsaw Pact nations, and most other former communist-bloc nations. Following the collapse of communism and the withdrawal of the Soviet Army from Eastern Europe in 1991, many of these nations adopted the voluntary military service model for their armed forces.

The model of military manpower adopted by a particular nation tends to be independent of total active military strength and, to a certain extent, the proportion of that strength to the number of eligible males in the population. The importance of political ideology and tradition in determining military manpower policy is evident.

Overview of Military Manpower

This discussion tends to mask the great complexity and diversity of military manpower. Not only do the weapons, equipment, tactics, and strategy of warfare change continually, but the techniques of manpower analysis and programming continue to be improved. The essential nature of the unit design process, allocation of units among components, and coping with the introduction of new technology is understood better than before. Interaction between demand from the manpower program and supply from the personnel system is accepted as part of the process. Nevertheless, the fundamentals of military organization and tactics tend to remain stable despite new technology, and thus provide a stable base for military manpower programs. Despite ideological and national differences, the armed forces of the world tend to be very similar in their military manpower programs.

John R. Brinkerhoff

See Also: Attrition: Personnel Casualties; Cadre; Civilian Substitution; Enlisted Personnel; Force Structure; Force Structure, Personnel; Host Nation Support; Mobilization; Organization, Army; Personnel; Recruiting and Retention; Reinforcements; Replacements: Personnel and Materiel; Unit, Military.

Bibliography

Binkin, M., and I. Kyriakopoulous. 1979. *Youth or experience? Manning the modern military.* Washington, D.C.: Brookings.

Brown, J., M. J. Collins, and F. D. Margiotta, eds. 1983. *Changing U.S. military manpower realities.* Boulder, Colo.: Westview Press.

Coffey, K. J. 1978. *Manpower for military mobilization.* Washington, D.C.: American Enterprise Institute for Public Policy Research.

Foster, G. D., A. N. Sabrosky, and W. J. Taylor, eds. 1987. *The strategic dimension of military manpower.* Cambridge, Mass.: Ballinger.

Grinold, R. C., and K. T. Marshall. 1977. *Manpower planning models.* New York & Amsterdam: Elsevier North-Holland.

Jessop, W. N., ed. 1966. *Manpower planning, operational research and personnel research.* Proceedings of a NATO Conference. New York: American Elsevier.

Neihaus, R. J., ed. 1985. *Human resource policy analysis.* New York: Praeger.

U.S. Air Force. 1982. *Air force regulation 25-5, Air force management engineering program.* Washington, D.C.: Government Printing Office.

MANPOWER POLICIES IN THE U.S. AND NATO

A number of significant events have occurred recently that affect future U.S. and North Atlantic Treaty Organization (NATO) military manpower policies. These include German unification, the demise of the Warsaw Pact, and the collapse of the Soviet empire. It is too early to predict the full implications of these events. However, because of the diminished Soviet threat, troop reductions underway in Europe, and reassessment of military budgets and weapon programs, it is apparent that the primary challenge to U.S. and NATO policy makers will no longer be that of maintaining the force structure of past years despite a declining youth population. Rather, policy makers must now evaluate alternative recruiting and retention programs in order to maintain significantly smaller forces in the face of a post–cold war environment—an environment where high-quality military personnel must master sophisticated technology inside societies that perceive a much lowered threat of war.

This article presents a historic overview of manpower policies in the following NATO nations: the United States, the Federal Republic of Germany, the United Kingdom, France, the Netherlands, Belgium, and Denmark. The manpower data and policies covered include the levels and composition of active and reserve forces, the impact of demographic trends on the recruiting and retention of qualified personnel, and the options for supplying military personnel.

U.S. and NATO manpower policies are undergoing rapid change in a transition phase to smaller post–cold war forces and reduced military budgets. This historic background provides an important departure point for understanding the future military manpower policies in the United States and NATO.

For annual updates and analyses of these issues, the reader may refer to the following annual publications:
The Military Balance. International Institute for Strategic Studies. London: Brassey's (UK).
The Statesman's Year-Book. New York: St. Martin's Press.
The World Factbook. Central Intelligence Agency. Washington, D.C.: Brassey's (US).

Manpower Overview

The United States

Table 1 provides a profile of active-duty personnel strength for the U.S. Army, Navy, Marine Corps, and Air Force for 1991. Of the nearly 2 million serving during fiscal year 1991, more than 15 percent were commissioned officers or students at one of the military academies. The army had the most personnel, representing nearly 36 percent of the total active forces. The navy, air force, and marines had 29, 26, and 10 percent, respectively. Women represented more than 10 percent of all active-duty personnel, ranging from 5 percent of the marine corps total to about 14 percent of air force personnel. Female participation in the military has been steadily increasing since the end of conscription in the United States. In 1972, just over 45,000, or under 2 percent of all active-duty personnel, were women. In 1980, over 171,000 women were in the military services, representing about 8 percent of the total.

As indicated in Table 2, the United States relies heavily on first-term enlistees who volunteer for two to four years of military service. In order to achieve the active-duty total of almost 2 million, the four military services accepted 185,000 new volunteers in fiscal year 1991. In addition, 213,000 individuals re-enlisted, and just over 20,000 entered active duty after serving in one of the reserve components. For the air force, two-thirds of the accession requirement was met by the retention of experienced personnel. At the other extreme, only one-third of the marine corps accession requirement was achieved via immediate re-enlistments.

Table 1. *U.S. Active-Duty Military Personnel, End FY 1991*

	Army	Navy	Marines	Air Force	Total
Total:					
Officer	103.7	70.8	19.8	96.6	290.9
Enlisted	602.8	495.1	174.3	409.4	1,681.6
Academies	4.3	4.3	—	4.4	13.1
Total active	710.8	570.3	194.0	510.4	1,985.6
Women:					
Officer	12.5	7.9	0.7	13.3	34.5
Enlisted	67.3	81.0	8.3	58.6	185.1
Academies	0.5	0.5	—	0.5	1.4
Total women	80.3	59.4	9.0	72.4	221.1

Source: U.S. Department of Defense, 1991.

Table 2. *U.S. Enlisted Personnel Accessions, FY 1991 (in thousands)*

	Army	Navy	Marines	Air Force	Total
First enlistments	75.1	51.6	29.7	30.2	184.9
Immediate re-enlistments	75.6	59.6	13.6	64.1	212.7
Other re-enlistments	4.2	1.2	0.9	—	6.3
Reserves to active duty	4.8	23.3	0.9	0.3	29.3
Total	159.7	131.7	45.2	94.5	433.1

Source: U.S. Department of Defense, 1991.

The ready reserve is the primary source of additional units and trained individuals that can be activated to augment the active forces in time of war or national emergency. The selected reserve includes both organized and equipped reserve units and individuals preassigned to active units. Selected reservists receive frequent training, for which they are paid. The individual ready reserve includes a large number of trained individuals who can be used to fill active and reserve units to wartime strength and to replace combat losses. Table 3 shows the strength of the U.S. reserve components at the end of FY 1991. The largest component, the Army National Guard, is made up of more than 441,000 reservists, representing nearly 40 percent of the selected reserve. The army reserve contains nearly 305,000 in the selected reserve and 359,000 in the individual ready reserve. Together, the two army reserve components amount to nearly 65 percent of the ready reserve.

Federal Republic of Germany

The Federal Republic of Germany maintains four active force categories: long-term careerists; temporary careerists; conscripts; and reserve duty training soldiers. A fifth category, the standby readiness component, will be intro-

Table 3. *U.S. Ready Reserve Personnel, end FY 1991*[a] *(in thousands)*

	Selected reserve	Individual ready reserve
Army National Guard	446.1	8.1[b]
Army Reserve	309.7	359.1
Naval Reserve	151.5	107.3
Marine Corps Reserve	44.9	50.4
Air National Guard	117.8	—
Air Force Reserve	84.5	78.7
Total	1,154.6	603.6

Source: U.S. Department of Defense, 1991.

[a]Numbers exclude Coast Guard.
[b]Inactive National Guard.

duced into the military structure in the 1990s. Long-term and temporary careerists represent about one-half of all active forces. Typically, long-term careerists serve in the German military forces for a period of 20 years or more. They currently constitute about one-fourth of all careerist personnel. Most long-term careerists enter as temporary careerists and decide later to become professional soldiers. The remaining three-fourths of the career force are temporary careerists, who join for a minimum three-year obligation. Careerists and temporary careerists are subject to reserve duty following their active service period until age 45 in peacetime and 60 in war.

About half of Germany's peacetime active-force requirement is filled by conscripts. Since 1956, all German males between the ages of 18 and 28 (except residents of West Berlin) have been subject to military or civil service. The term of service has varied from twelve to eighteen months. A small number of women volunteer for service in the medical corps, but Germany's constitution does not require their conscription. Conscripts serve on reserve duty following their active-duty commitment. The total conscript reserve commitment is nine months; all conscripts are eligible for recall to active service until age 45 in peacetime and age 60 in war.

Reserve duty training soldiers constitute a small part of the active-force total. The German Ministry of Defense includes the man-years of reservists on temporary duty in its active-force strength total. Reserve duty training soldiers in 1989 were counted as about 7,000 man-years. This represents approximately 200,000 reserve personnel, each serving twelve days of annual duty.

The number of active-force personnel since 1975 has remained at about 495,000, but significant changes are expected in the composition of the active-duty force in the future. The number of careerists is expected to decline from 266,000 to 250,000; the number of conscripts will also fall from 222,000 to 206,000. The Bundeswehr will compensate for these decreases by increasing its total number of active-duty reservists from 7,000 to 39,000 man-years. The new active-duty reservist category, the standby readiness component, will represent on-call reservists and is expected to total 24,000. These standby personnel, who include both former careerist and conscript soldiers, are expected to play key leadership roles in the early stages of a mobilization. The older active-duty reservist category, reserve duty training, will increase from 7,000 to 15,000 man-years. This increase is expected to occur by means of doubling reserve duty training—about 400,000 personnel per year will spend up to twelve days annually in training. Planners expect to counter potential active-force shortfalls by increasing reliance on reserve duty training and the standby readiness component.

There are two reservist categories. Regular reserves include former conscripts and careerists with continuing obligations in wartime and crisis. The standby readiness component (different from the standby readiness component in active force totals) represents a special subcategory. While the active-force standby readiness component represents a twelve-month ready reserve obligation, the reservist standby readiness component represents a twelve-year reserve obligation for key personnel, who engage in regular training. The aggregate of the two reservist categories is about 2.4 million, from which the Bundeswehr expects to fill 900,000 positions during mobilization. The total number of available reservists is expected to fall to about 1.3 million and the reservist requirements are expected to increase to a million in the 1990s. Thus, almost all reservists would have to be mobilized in the future to meet mobilization goals.

United Kingdom

Unlike its Central Region allies, the United Kingdom has relied on volunteers since 1957 (Britain recruits a small number of volunteer servicemen from Nepal and other nations). Male and female volunteers serve a minimum three-year term, and many remain as volunteer careerists. Volunteers have no reserve obligation, although they may be recalled for service in wartime. Many do volunteer for service in the regular or auxiliary reserves.

The 1989 defense program required slightly fewer than 317,000 active-force personnel. The army personnel total of 158,400 represented almost exactly one-half of active personnel. The Royal Air Force (RAF) and the Royal Navy and Marines represented about 30 percent and 20 percent of active-force personnel, respectively. Female regulars totaled 15,900 or 5 percent of regular forces; this proportion has not changed appreciably in the last decade. The female retention rate has increased about 20 percent in the past five years.

The number of active-force personnel has decreased steadily since the early 1970s. Since 1971, for example, the totals of army, RAF, and Royal Navy and Marine personnel have fallen 8 percent, 17 percent, and 20 percent, respectively. This has coincided with roughly equivalent or greater magnitude decreases in the number of frontline fighting units, measured in army regiments, aircraft squadrons, and major surface combatants. There is little doubt, however, that technological improvements have increased the effective fighting power of individual units. The number of army regiments has fallen 5 percent, the number of RAF squadrons has fallen 17 percent, and the number of Royal Navy major combatants has fallen 24 percent.

Future active-force personnel requirements are uncertain; however, two possibilities are immediately apparent. First, aggregate active-force personnel requirements may continue to decrease as they have since 1970 at a rate of 0.65 percent per year. This seems likely only if shrinkage in army regiments, RAF squadrons, and Royal Navy combatants continues. Such a continued decrease would result in an active-personnel level of 295,000 in the year 2000, representing an aggregate 7.4 percent decrease from current levels. Second, frontline force structure and thus active-force personnel requirements may remain at current levels. This seems somewhat unlikely considering the expected introduction of less manpower-intensive equipment, such as the Type 23 frigate, although historical personnel-to-fighting-unit ratios indicate that this is a relatively steady-state condition.

The United Kingdom reserve system includes service auxiliary personnel, including the Territorial Army, and the regular reserves. Volunteers fill out the auxiliary personnel ranks, while recently released active-force personnel account for regular reserve forces. The number of service personnel in the Territorial Army and other auxiliary forces totals 95,000, and the regular reserves total 225,000. Britain's current reserve personnel total represents nearly a tripling of personnel levels in the early 1970s. The British expect to emphasize reserves more in the future, particularly volunteer auxiliary reserves.

France

France relies on both conscripts and volunteers to fulfill its active-force strength requirements. Volunteers constitute approximately 55 percent of active-force strength. Volunteers typically serve a twenty-year period, although they may enlist for as little as three years. Volunteers are obligated to reserve duty to age 40.

Conscripts constitute about 45 percent of all active-service men and women. All males between ages 18 and 27 are required to serve one year of active service. Registration for service is required at age 17. Conscription occurs between ages 18 and 27. Most enter service between ages 18 and 23. Deferments may be obtained for various reasons, including financial, family, and other professional career considerations. These extend a conscript's service report date to a maximum of age 27. Women may volunteer for service (13,500 currently serve), but are not subject to conscription. Conscripts are obligated to reserve service until age 35 and can be recalled in wartime until age 50. Men who do not wish to serve in the military are able to select from a range of other national service options, including technical assistance and police service. Conscientious objectors must complete this alternative 24-month national service duty.

The French defense program for 1989 required 553,000 active-service personnel; this figure includes Gendarmerie, or National Police Force, personnel and active-duty soldiers in civilian or nonready positions, such as central administration. Careerists outnumber conscripts, and the army has by far the largest personnel requirement. The 1989 active-force personnel requirement represents a moderate average annual decrease from 1970 levels of approximately 0.2 percent. However, these decreases have been mitigated by an increase in total active Gendarmerie personnel. The average annual personnel decrease excluding the Gendarmerie is about 0.5 percent.

Long-range active-personnel goals are not spelled out; however, further reductions are planned in the short term. Continued annual decreases of approximately 0.5 percent may be likely and would lead to a requirement of 523,000 by the year 2000.

France's reserve forces depend greatly on reserve conscripts. Conscripts initially serve four years in the active military reserves, during which time they are immediately recallable and receive annual training. Following active military reserve duty, conscripts serve in the regular reserves. During this period they may be called any number of times for service; however, recall is rare. In addition, volunteers' reserve obligations continue to age 40. France's regular reserves total 356,000, representing a slight decrease from nearly 400,000 in the early 1970s.

The Netherlands

The Netherlands maintains volunteer and conscript active forces. Volunteers serve a minimum four-year term and currently constitute 47 percent of active-personnel strength. Eligible volunteers may become career service personnel, usually with a minimum eight-year commitment. In the case of the navy, the minimum commitment is ten years. A volunteer's initial commitment depends on the volunteer's career path. Officers' minimum stays depend on service requirements, including education and other training. Volunteer service personnel have a reserve commitment to age 40.

Male conscripts constitute the remaining 53 percent of active forces and are obligated to a 24-month term of active service. Despite this 24-month obligation, conscripts typically serve only fourteen months in the navy and sixteen months in the army or air force. The initial four to six months are spent in training. In the remaining eight to ten months, conscripts are placed on "short leave," during which they return home and to work but are subject to an immediate mobilization recall to their initial training unit. Women are not subject to conscription, although they may volunteer for service. As in most other European countries, conscientious objectors may select an alternative national service.

The 1989 Dutch defense program required 101,000 active personnel. This includes 66,000, or 65 percent of active personnel, in the army. Air force and navy active personnel account for 18 percent and 17 percent of remaining active personnel, respectively. Nearly 90 percent of all conscripts serve in the army.

The Netherlands does not forecast long-term active-personnel requirements, although historical evidence indicates continued marginal reductions. Between 1970 and 1989, the number of active-service personnel has fallen from 124,000 to 101,200, representing an approximate 1 percent annual decrease. A continuation of this trend would lead to a further decrease in requirements by 2000 to roughly 90,000 active personnel.

Volunteers must serve in the Dutch reserve forces until age 40. Conscripts are also subject to reserve duty, although for a shorter period. For example, following the short-leave service period, conscripts are placed into a third category, *Rechtstreeks Instromenle Mobilisabele Eenheden* (RIM), the Dutch ready-reserve status. Conscripts may be recalled during this period into any unit that requires additional manpower. After a maximum of eighteen months in RIM, conscripts are placed in the regular reserves for six years during which they may be recalled for annual training. Following this, they remain obligated to reserve duty between ages 35 and 45, depending on their rank and service. The number of regular reserves in 1989 was 175,000.

Belgium

Belgium relies on both careerists and conscripts to achieve its active-force personnel requirements; military policy has not consistently emphasized either category. There has recently been an increased emphasis on improving the utilization of conscripts, particularly as noncommissioned and regular officers.

Volunteers currently constitute just over 45 percent of active personnel. They must enlist for a minimum period of two years; many re-enlist as career service personnel. Volunteers are subject to the same reserve duty as conscripts.

All Belgian males register for conscription at age 15 and in most cases begin a term of service of twelve months (ten months if stationed in Germany) at age 19. Conscripts may alternatively choose a reserve officer training path in which they serve actively for thirteen months followed by reserve duty obligation. Conscientious objectors may elect other national service, such as international development aid. These alternative services include up to twenty-month obligations. Women may volunteer for service but may not be conscripted. Conscripts are subject to reserve duty for eight to fifteen years after active service, up to age 45.

The 1989 Belgian defense program required slightly more than 90,000 active personnel. The army accounts for 67 percent of this total; the air force, navy, and medical service account for the remaining 22 percent, 5 percent, and 6 percent, respectively. Nearly 90 percent of all conscripts are in the army.

Belgium does not forecast long-term active-personnel requirements. Moreover, budget uncertainties and potentially large reductions in Belgium's defense effort complicate attempts at long-term forecasting. Between 1970 and 1989, the number of active-service personnel has fallen from 93,500 to 90,000, representing an approximate 0.2 percent annual decrease. A continuation of this trend would lead to a further 9 percent decrease in requirements by the year 2000, to roughly 88,000 active personnel.

Recalled reservists from the most recent conscription classes are assigned to regular units and called "complements." Usually the regular unit to which the conscript is assigned in wartime is the unit in which he carried out his active service. Recalled reservists from less-recent conscript classes are assigned to reserve units, taking into account military specialties. In addition, some reservists are assigned neither to active units nor to reserve units but are designated as reinforcements until the end of their military obligation (this is limited to eight years for some ranks and specialists). The reinforcement pool is filled out by the recruitment reserve, civilians who have not yet carried out their peacetime military service. Conscripts may be reassigned within the foregoing categories during their periods of obligation. Personnel of the Railway and Telegraph Administration with remaining military obligations are mobilized on the job rather than being assigned to the armed forces.

Mobilization exercises are organized according to the level of readiness that a given unit is expected to hold at the beginning of mobilization. Certain units undergo a two-week mobilization exercise with the active forces every four years. Belgian law established limits relating to mobilization exercises, and those limits are further controlled by the Minister of National Defense. Reserve officers may only carry out mobilization exercises up to a maximum of 30 days each year and NCOs up to 27 days per year. Both officers and NCOs, however, may participate beyond those limits at their own request and may perform voluntary or promotion duties. For other personnel—both draftees and volunteers—there is a legal limit of 66 days of mobilization exercises, reduced to 24 days by the Minister of National Defense, which may be spread over one or more exercises.

Denmark

Denmark also relies on volunteers and conscripts to maintain its defense forces. Volunteers constitute approximately 53 percent of active-personnel strength; they enlist for a minimum 24-month obligation and may become careerist service personnel. Denmark is currently attempting to increase the proportion of volunteer service personnel. Volunteers have no reserve obligation.

All males are subject to conscription in Denmark; Denmark's low military personnel requirements result in only about one-third of those eligible being conscripted. Conscripts must serve a minimum of nine months; specialist assignments in some services require service of up to 27 months (noncommissioned officers serve 15 months and volunteer reserve officers serve 18 months). Women may volunteer for service but cannot be conscripted. Conscripts are subject to reserve duty to age 50.

The 1989 Danish defense program required 29,300 active personnel. This includes 17,000 army, 6,900 air force, and 5,400 navy personnel. About 80 percent of all conscripts serve in the army.

Denmark's long-term active-personnel requirements are uncertain. Significant reductions have occurred since 1970. For example, the number of active-service person-

TABLE 4. *Military Manpower Structure Comparisons: Selected NATO Nations (1989)*

	U.S.	U.K.	GERMANY	FRANCE	NETHERLANDS	BELGIUM	DENMARK
Active forces (1,000s)	2,138	317	495	553	101	88	29
Conscripts (%)	0.0	0.0	46.3	45.4	47.0	29.5	28.7
Women (%)	10.5	5.0	<1.0	2.4	1.6	4.0	2.7
Reserve forces (1,000s)	1,642	320	2,400	356	175	180	75
Reserve/active (ratio)	0.8	1.0	4.8	0.6	1.7	2.0	2.6
Personnel budget (% of GNP)	1.2	1.7	0.5	0.7	0.9	0.9	0.9
Active forces (% of population)	0.9	0.6	0.8	1.0	0.7	0.9	0.6

nel has fallen from 45,500 to 29,300, representing an aggregate decrease of 55 percent and an average annual decrease of 2.3 percent. A continuation of this steep downward trend seems unlikely; continued reductions of slightly less magnitude seem more plausible.

Denmark maintains regular reserve forces staffed by conscripts on reserve duty obligation. Conscripts serve eighteen months in Denmark's Augmentation Force (similar to the Netherlands' "short leave" system). Conscripts are obligated to serve five years in the reserve force, but may be recalled for only a 60-day period in the first nine years of duty. This is increased to 70 days for NCOs. The nine-year period includes conscripts' initial training period. Denmark's reserve forces total roughly 75,000 personnel.

SUMMARY OF NATO MANPOWER STRUCTURE

Table 4 summarizes some of the key elements of the manpower structure in the selected NATO countries for 1989. It allows comparisons of the mix of active and reserve forces, reliance on conscription, and percentage of women. To provide a comparable measure of the military personnel burden, the table shows active military strength as a percentage of total population and military personnel budget as a percentage of gross national product.

Future Manpower Challenges in Selected NATO Nations

MEETING U.S. REQUIREMENTS

At the start of the 1990s a combination of factors increased the pressure on manpower planners in the United States. Evolving military technologies have increased the demand for the most highly qualified segments of the youth population. At the same time, unfavorable demographic changes have made it more costly to attract enlistments. Policymakers are faced with a declining youth cohort and subsequent increases in the civilian opportunities available to potential enlistees.

These trends, along with the economic dilemmas associated with the overall budget deficits, have focused renewed attention on recruiting-program alternatives. The United States has relied on several mechanisms to build its all-volunteer armed forces. These mechanisms include recruiting staffs and the incentive programs that motivate them; the level of standard remuneration given all enlisted personnel (pay, housing, and medical care); and supplementary benefits such as educational funds and bonuses. In addition, recruits have been given options in some details of their enlistment, including the term of service, station of choice, or military occupation. Finally, the nation has funded a substantial advertising campaign to induce enlistments. Table 5 provides information on the FY 1989 budget for recruiting active forces; Table 6 provides the same data for the reserve components.

POLICY DILEMMAS AND POSSIBLE SOLUTIONS IN NATO EUROPE

Demographic conditions in many NATO countries over the next several years will not be favorable for military manpower planners. Unless political factors reduce requirements, it may be necessary for the NATO nations to change their manpower policies. Figure 1 illustrates changes in the size of the 18- to 23-year-old male cohort relative to current cohort levels for the next fifteen years.

TABLE 5. *U.S. Armed Forces Active Enlisted Advertising and Recruiting Resources FY 1989 (Current US$ in millions)*

	ARMY	NAVY	MARINE CORPS	AIR FORCE	TOTAL
Educational funds[a]	60.3	0.0	0.0	0.0	60.3
Enlistment bonus	60.5	19.0	5.8	0.4	85.7
Military pay[b]	279.4	189.2	118.8	89.3	676.7
Civilian pay	29.7	14.2	3.8	7.4	55.2
Advertising[c]	58.7	11.9	13.5	8.8	121.4
Recruiting support	100.3	33.7	23.1	19.1	176.2
Other[d]	28.8	11.2	10.3	6.3	149.7
Officer medical totals	33.9	63.8	14.6	29.1	144.2
Totals	651.6	343.0	189.9	160.4	1,469.4

Source: Office of the Secretary of Defense (Force Management and Personnel) from FY 1990–91 Budget of the President.

[a] Accrual charges for Army and Navy College Fund.
[b] Pay for recruiting personnel; includes retirement accrual.
[c] DoD total includes US$28.5 million in joint advertising.
[d] Includes leased facilities that are shared by the services, joint market research, training and communications expenses.

TABLE 6. *U.S. Armed Forces Reserve Components Enlisted Advertising and Recruiting Resources FY 1989 (Current US$ in millions)*

	ARMY NATL. GUARD	ARMY RESERVE	NAVAL RESERVE	MARINE RESERVE	AIR FORCE RESERVE	AIR NATL. GUARD	TOTAL
Education	40.6	23.2	13.3	6.1	10.3	9.9	103.4
Bonuses	40.4	23.7	5.0	0.8	3.0	8.1	81.0
Pay[a]	139.6	94.3	40.8	11.2	16.5	21.7	324.1
Advertising	12.1	19.0	2.8	2.6	3.2	1.7	41.4
Recruiting	31.4	21.7	6.3	3.9	1.3	4.1	68.7
Other[b]	6.1	3.5	4.1	0.0	1.5	0.4	15.6
Officer/med.	5.3	19.1	25.0	0.0	3.6	0.0	53.0
Total	275.5	204.5	97.3	24.6	39.4	45.9	687.2

Source: Office of the Secretary of Defense (Force Management and Personnel) from FY 1990–91 Budget of the President.

[a] Military pay for recruiting staffs only, includes retirement accrual.
[b] Includes civilian pay, communications, and training.

West Germany will experience the most precipitous drop in the 18- to 23-year-old cohort—about 30 percent between 1990 and 1995. Moreover, this decrease is not a temporary aberration even though a slight increase is anticipated in the early 2000s. It reflects the low fertility rates that will likely continue in Germany. The average size of single-year cohorts (the number of 18-year-olds or 19-year-olds, etc.) in this fifteen-year period is about 310,000.

In comparison, the decrease in the male youth cohort in Britain is modest. As illustrated, the number falls slightly in the early 1990s, but returns to 1990 levels in about 2005. The decline in France is also modest—about 10 percent in the mid-1990s; however, France's youth cohort fails to return to current levels. From 1990 to 2005, average single-year cohort sizes for Britain and France are 370,000 and 405,000, respectively.

Belgium, the Netherlands, and Denmark face slightly more serious decreases in male youth cohorts, ranging from about 15 percent to 25 percent. Moreover, in each case the cohort appears unlikely to return to current levels until perhaps after 2005. The average 1990–2005 single-year cohort levels for Belgium, the Netherlands, and Denmark are 54,000, 99,000, and 33,000.

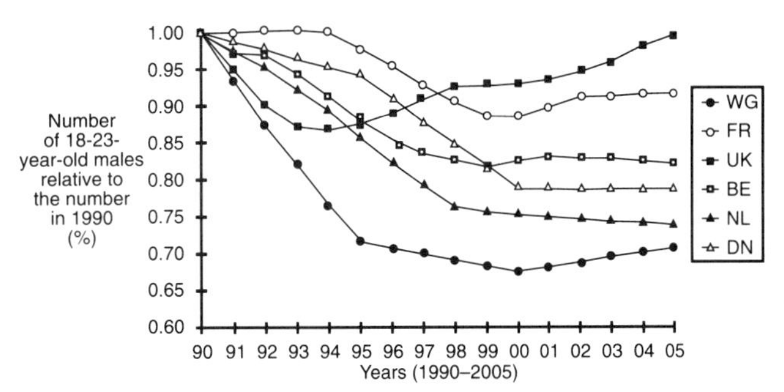

Figure 1. Estimated changes in strength of the 18- to 23-year-old male cohort (1990–2005).

Outlook for Germany. The situation in Germany is in a state of flux. The East German enemy on the border has now become part of a unified Germany, and elements of the East German military are integrated into a smaller unified German military. Most of the once major concerns of West German manpower planners are under review and modification because of the new political circumstances. The final effects of these dramatic changes on NATO and on a united Germany will be worked out over the next decade. For now, the authors have solid information available only on the situation facing the West Germans before East Germany was integrated. The reader should recognize that some of these conditions, plans, and policies will persisit into the future, but that they will be substantially modified by a diminished threat and the availability of (former) East German youth.

The steep decline in the number of West German youths has far-reaching implications for manpower policies. The decline will complicate both careerist and conscript objectives. The annual conscript requirement in the 1990s under Bundeswehr 2000 personnel goals is 225,000. Combined with other national organization requirements, such as the border patrol and police, the aggregate requirement falls only slightly below the average single-year cohort size of 300,000.

Continuation of current policies will lead to a shortage of up to 100,000 conscripts in the 1990s; however, West German MoD planners have lessened the severity of the demographic trough in several ways. First, planners have deferred the drafting of many eligible males until the end of their eligibility period, thus taking advantage of the excess supply just preceding this trough (this measure, of course, is costly to society since many males will be drafted as they reach the steepest part of their income earnings profile). This mitigates the shortfall in the near term, but after about 1997 the excess supply will have been exhausted. Second, planners have lowered medical standards and removed the marriage exemption. They have established new regulations that should greatly reduce the number of conscientious objectors and installed greater incentives for choosing military service rather than alternative service. These changes may permit the Bundeswehr to achieve its conscription goals. However, the room for error is not large, and the Bundeswehr may be forced to consider the politically difficult choice of conscripting foreign nationals and women.

This decrease in the 18- to 23-year-old cohort will also likely complicate careerist recruitment for West Germany. In particular, the Bundeswehr will be forced to recruit a higher percentage of careerists from the youth cohort. The increased recruitment requirement appears modest, but the cost may be high as the Bundeswehr competes with industry for scarce youth labor.

West Germany has responded to retention problems with increased financial incentives. In particular, bonuses and higher pay are in line for Luftwaffe pilots who have since 1958 received only a 29 percent increase in flight pay while living costs have increased severalfold.

West Germany may consider several policy options to help meet its active-force obligations in the 1990s; two commonly occur in public debate. First, although the constitution appears to prohibit military service by women, there has been discussion of permitting up to 20,000 women to serve in noncombat positions. Second, consideration has been given, although it has so far been rejected, to recruiting or conscripting some of West Germany's 4.5 million foreign workers.

The United Kingdom. The demographic situation in the United Kingdom is likely to cause short-term complications in recruiting volunteers, although these will lessen in the long term as Britain's youth cohort returns to 1990 levels. In the 1990s, Britain faces an average 8 percent fall in the male youth cohort. It is questionable whether the nation will similarly decrease its requirements. Britain will likely be forced to recruit a higher proportion of its 18- to 23-year-old cohort. The costs of this increased recruitment requirement, although greatly influenced by other macroeconomic factors, will likely increase.

The United Kingdom has recently experienced difficulty in the retention of pilots and other skilled personnel. The MoD has countered this problem with flight bonuses and has also begun to offer bonuses for other critical personnel. Recently, the MoD has offered pay bonuses for Royal Marines and long-service-at-sea bonuses for seagoers.

France. France's volunteer and conscript requirements will be affected only modestly by adverse demographic conditions. France's aggregate annual conscript and volunteer requirements, based on an average volunteer length of stay of ten years, are 250,000 and 30,000, respectively. This requirement appears to fall below the average single-year youth cohort in the 1990–2005 period. Exemptions for conscripts will probably be tightened, albeit modestly; as in the German and British cases, France will likely be forced to increase military salaries as it recruits a slightly larger share of the cohort as volunteers. However, this share of volunteers will probably increase only slightly in the 1990s, since France appears likely to reduce its manpower requirements at a rate comparable to the decrease in the male youth cohort.

Belgium. Belgium faces slightly more serious demographic developments than Britain or France, but it appears that the average annual cohort pool of 54,000 will be sufficient to meet manpower requirements. Continued modest decreases in requirements, a ten-year average volunteer length of stay, and stable conscript policies indicate annual volunteer and conscript requirements of about 8,500 and 24,000, respectively. On the average, roughly one-half of the 19-year-old cohort must be drafted or volunteer for service. Belgium's need for a larger volunteer share of the youth cohort will likely require an increase in volunteer wages, although the increases will probably be modest.

The Netherlands. Demographic developments in the Netherlands threaten to complicate Dutch military manpower policies, although the effects may be modest. The nation will require an annual conscript accession of roughly 45,000 and a volunteer accession, based on a ten-year volunteer length of stay, of 5,000. This represents a total annual accession of about 50 percent of a single-year cohort. Once again, this may result in a slight tightening of conscript exemption policies. In addition, the need for higher volunteer recruitment shares of the male youth cohort may result in slightly higher volunteer salaries.

Denmark. Denmark's annual volunteer and careerist accession requirements, assuming continued reductions in active personnel and continued conscript policies, are about 1,000 and about 12,500, respectively. This compares favorably with the single-year cohort average of 33,000 from 1990 to 2005. The share of volunteers from the male youth cohort appears likely to increase slightly as Denmark increases the volunteer-to-conscript ratio. This may increase volunteer salaries as the military competes for scarce youth labor; however, the cost will be mitigated by further decreases in aggregate service personnel. By decreasing aggregate personnel and increasing reliance on volunteers, Denmark may be able to maintain its current low draft share of the male youth cohort.

Comparing Policies for Meeting U.S. Requirements

Whether one believes that demographic trends will make it difficult to meet future requirements or, instead, that dramatic political changes will render current manpower levels unnecessary, it is clear that defense policymakers in the United States and NATO Europe must evaluate alternative enlistment programs. In the most pessimistic scenario, personnel managers will have to allocate scarce resources to recruit and retain the requisite numbers of high-quality individuals. On the other hand, if manpower requirements are significantly reduced, budgets will be scrutinized and less effective programs cut. In either case, comparisons of alternative policies for attracting new enlistments should be based on calculations of a complex stream of costs and benefits associated with each policy option. This section examines the United States situation and identifies the categories of information necessary for making definitive choices among resource alternatives.

Calculating Marginal Costs

Ultimately, reallocation of resources must be based on comparing changes in manpower outcome with changes in level of expenditure. Even on the cost side, identifying such changes can be problematic. It is relatively simple to compute current average costs of recruiting by comparing budgetary outlays with total numbers of enlistments, but such an exercise falls short of providing the marginal expenditure figures necessary for evaluating alternative policy options. For example, if the government pays an extra US$3,000 for each new recruit who is attracted by an expanded enlistment bonus program, the marginal expenditure also includes those individuals who qualify for the bonus but would have enlisted without it. Thus, a 20 percent expansion in an eligible group implies that for every new individual receiving a bonus, five others who would have enlisted anyway also earn the extra US$3,000. Thus, the marginal expenditure is US$15,000 for every new recruit.

For enlistment benefits that are delivered at the end of the service tour, calculating marginal expenditures can be controversial. To begin with, the relevant cost can be sensitive to the choice of a rate for discounting the future stream of outlays. In addition, it is hard to predict this future stream *a priori*. This can be particularly important in the case of educational benefit programs, where participants usually use only a fraction of their entitlement. Since utilization rates may depend on external factors, future cost estimates will be uncertain.

Calculating Marginal Benefits

The efficacy of any expenditure should be evaluated according to multiple goals. These policy objectives may be mutually consistent yet involve important tradeoffs. It is difficult to rank alternative programs without first determining the relative importance of alternative policy objectives, such as those discussed in the following paragraphs.

Increasing the quantity and quality of accessions. A primary goal of many recruiting programs is to increase the number of individuals willing to enlist in the military. At the same time personnel managers are concerned with the quality of those actually enlisting. Thus, manpower planners may have to make tradeoffs between volume and quality objectives. Since high-quality individuals have attractive private-sector alternatives, it takes extra effort to induce them to join the military (a "high-quality" enlistee, in the army's definition, is one who has a high school diploma and a score at the 50th percentile or higher on the Armed Forces Qualification Test). Since the time of recruiters is a scarce resource, decision to emphasize the quality of the force necessarily comes at the expense of quantity, if resource expenditures are held constant. Perhaps more importantly, alternative recruiting programs may have different impacts on the volume and quality of enlistments. This may be the direct result of eligibility requirements, as when educational benefits or enlistment bonuses are tied to educational background or test scores. As a result, recruiting programs can be designed to enhance the quality mix at the expense of a more general expansion of enlistments. Even if eligibility requirements are neutral with respect to applicant characteristics, alternative programs may appeal to different segments of the recruiting market. For example, it is likely that educational benefits would have a greater appeal than bonuses to high school graduates. It is also possible for television commercials and newspaper advertising to target different audiences. Ultimately, the evaluation of the effectiveness of any program in expanding enlistments must consider both quality and quantity.

Occupation and term-of-service effects. Although some individuals may enter the military without any prespecified occupation, the enlistment contract often specifies a particular training, job, and term-of-service obligation. As a result, alternative recruiting programs must be evaluated in terms of their ability to channel the aggregate flow of enlistments into the required skill distribution. Enlistment benefits can be tied to particular occupations, such as combat arms, that are traditionally difficult to fill. Such a policy maintains the integrity of the overall wage structure while providing flexibility for responding to critical shortfalls that require some compensating differential if manpower requirements are to be met.

Alternative recruiting programs may appeal to separate groups with different preferences for military training and occupations. For example, advertising may be effective in attracting individuals who view military service as a human capital investment in pragmatic job-related training in fields such as electronics. Educational benefits may be attractive to those who wish to accumulate funds for college; such individuals will not be interested in vocational training and may be more willing to be trained in combat skills. At the same time, college-bound youths would be less likely to sign up for long terms of service. Thus, educational benefits are not likely to be as efficient in drawing individuals to slots that require long and expensive investments in training.

Total force management implications. Given overall strength requirements, recruiting policies should be evaluated in terms of their implications for total force management. Total force implications are often the result of the particular terms of an enlistment contract that specifies the length of the initial enlistment active-duty tour and a requirement for subsequent service in the reserve forces. Incentives for attrition, re-enlistment, and reserve accession can be altered by the nature of the recruiting programs emphasized. For example, educational benefits are payable only if the individual completes the first term of enlistment. On the other hand, the availability of a college fund reduces the incentive to re-enlist. However, students with prior service would be productive members of the military reserve components.

Alternative recruiting programs may selectively attract individuals with different propensities for completing their first term, re-enlisting, or transferring into a reserve unit. These differences may be quite independent of any incentive effects of the enlistment program itself. For example, marginal individuals, barely induced by a supplemental bonus, may be unlikely to re-enlist. On the other hand, a recruit who was inspired by a television theme emphasizing national service and patriotism may be more likely to develop a subsequent taste for military life and, as a result, have a high likelihood of re-enlistment.

Interservice effects of recruiting programs. From a central planning perspective, knowing the enlistment effects of a recruiting program on a particular military service is not sufficient. This is especially true if separate services maintain independent and competitive recruiting management organizations. Ultimately, the effectiveness of any recruiting resource expenditure must be evaluated in terms of its broad effects on all services. Three different outcomes are possible. First, a recruiting program may affect only an individual service. For example, the Army College Fund might draw from a market segment that would otherwise not consider military service. As a result, any expansion of army enlistments because of this program would come directly from the civilian sector. In such a situation, the army and central planning perspectives are identical. In contrast is a scenario in which army educational benefits draw some enlistments away from the other services. (In such a scenario, carried to the extreme, the gains of one military service would come entirely at the expense of the other services. Clearly, this is not a desirable outcome.) Finally, a recruiting program might induce desirable enlistment effects for all services simultaneously. For example, increases in one service's advertising budget or recruiter staff could promote broader awareness of or interest in military service that benefits everyone.

Productivity effects. Although difficult to document, an ideal comparison of recruiting programs should consider potential productivity effects on personnel. Such effects may be the direct result of incentives induced by the program itself. For example, individuals receiving educational benefits realize that their civilian opportunities will be attractive at the end of their first term of service. Thus, they have fewer incentives to perform well. Individuals attracted by alternative programs may have systematic and inherent differences that will affect subsequent productivity. A college-bound youth may be more highly disciplined or motivated than one who was attracted by an enlistment bonus. Also, individuals induced to choose a less-preferred military occupation could end up being less productive than a person signing up for his or her first choice.

Recruiting programs could also have broader effects on the productivity of military personnel. Those who receive no equivalent enlistment benefits might, for example, become resentful and unmotivated. In contrast, an effective advertising campaign that cultivates patriotism, pride, and a positive image of military service could very well raise the morale of all personnel.

Conclusions

Most research in the U.S. military manpower community has focused on the short-term enlistment effects of alternative resource expenditures such as recruiting staffs, military pay, bonuses, educational benefits, and advertising. Although they provide useful information about effects on enlistment supply, none of these studies takes a comprehensive look at the multiple criteria for evaluation. However, some recent research suggests that these criteria are important and can alter significantly the ranking of programs depending upon the policy objective. For example, an econometric analysis of enlistment bonuses found that alternative programs, such as recruiting staffs and advertising expenditures, were significantly more cost effective at attracting enlistments into the U.S. Army (Polich et al. 1986). On the other hand, bonuses proved to be a remarkably effective program for channeling high-quality enlistees into critical military occupations. Another recent study concluded that a particular service's advertising campaign does not draw enlistments from the other military services. Even more significantly, advertising for one service appears to benefit all services simultaneously. Thus, the most significant competition appears to be with the private sector, not among military services (Dertouzos and Polich 1989). Although the interservice effects of alternative expenditures are unknown, it is unlikely that they would have the same magnitude as advertising.

Although these studies document the importance of multiple criteria in evaluating manpower policies, no comprehensive analysis of alternative strategies for achieving personnel goals currently exists. As a result, decisionmaking is based on intuition rather than on rigorous logic and is unduly influenced by political rather than economic factors. Given the sheer magnitude of military personnel expenditures and the likelihood, even under vastly different scenarios, that these budgets will be closely scrutinized in the future, these policy issues merit further analysis.

James N. Dertouzos
Joseph E. Nation

See Also: Accession Standards; Compensation; Force Structure, Personnel; Manpower, Military.

Bibliography

Army Gazette. 1987. West German army officials see forces shrinking in 90s. 20 February.

Borack, J., and B. S. Siegel. 1981. An econometric model of navy enlistment behavior. TN-81-16. Navy Personnel Research and Development Center, January.

Brown, C. 1985. Military enlistments: What can we learn from geographic variation? *American Economic Review* 75 (March).

Central Intelligence Agency. 1992. *The world factbook, 1991.* Washington, D.C.: Brassey's (US).
Clark, S. L. 1988. Who will staff NATO? *Orbis* 32, no. 4 (Fall).
Cralley, W. E. 1981. The impact of youth unemployment rate and the expiration of the GI Bill on Marine Corps enlistments. Memo 81-3020.10, Center for Naval Analyses, October.
Dertouzos, J. N. 1984. *Recruiter incentives and enlistment supply.* Rand Corp., R-3065-MIL, November.
Dertouzous, J. N., and J. M. Polich. 1989. *Recruiting effects of army advertising.* Rand Corp., R-3577-FMP, January.
Der Mittler-Brief. 1987. Die konzeption reservisten (The reservist concept). No. 4, p. 6.
England, J. 1989. "W[est] German pilots morale takes a dive. *Washington Times,* 2 February.
Fernandez, R. L. 1982. *Enlistment effects and policy implications of the educational assistance test program.* Rand Corp., R-2935-MRAL, September.
Gotz, G. 1989. *Balancing manpower costs and capabilities.* Rand Corp., N-2880-RC, March.
Greenston, P., et al. 1983. Analysis of air force enlistment supply for the development of a recruiting policy analysis model. Economic Research Laboratory, Inc. September.
Horne, D. K. 1984. An econometric analysis of army enlistment supply. Manpower and Personnel Policy Research Group, Army Research Institute, MPPRG-84-5, May.
House of Commons Defence Committee (British). 1988. Statement on the Defence Estimates 1988 (Session 87-8). London: Her Majesty's Stationery Office.
Hubatshek, G. 1988. Radical plans for W. German army. *Jane's Defence Weekly,* 26 March.
Hunter, B., ed. 1991. *The statesman's year-book, 1991–92.* New York: St. Martin's Press.
International Institute for Strategic Studies. 1991. *The military balance 1991–92.* London: Brassey's.
Jane's Defence Weekly. 1987. Germans make plans to draft more troops. 26 January.
Lillard, L. A., and D. J. Macunovich. 1988. Why the baby bust cohorts haven't boomed yet: A reconsideration of cohort variables in labor market analyses. Working draft, Rand Corp., October.
Ministre de la Défense (France). 1988. Le service national et vous (National Service and You).
Ministry of Defence (Great Britain). 1989. Statement on the Defence Estimates 1989, Vol. 1 and 2.
Ministry of Defense (Germany). 1988. Die neue "konzeption reservisten" (The new reservist concept). July, pp. 2–3.
———. 1985. *White Paper 1985: The situation and the development of the federal armed forces.* Bonn: Federal Ministry of Defense.
Morey, R. C., and C. A. Knox Lovell. 1987. Improving the allocation of monetary and non-monetary enlistment incentives for the U.S. Army: Analyses of the FY81–FY86 experience. Report for U.S. Army Recruiting Command, February.
Office of the Assistant Secretary of Defense for Manpower, Installations, and Logistics. 1985. *Quality of military enlisted personnel.* Report to the House and Senate Committees on Armed Services. Washington, D.C.: Government Printing Office.
Office of the Secretary of Defense. 1991. *Annual report to the Congress.*
———. 1991. *Population representation in the military services.*
Polich, J. M., J. N. Dertouzos, and S. J. Press. 1986. *The enlistment bonus experiment.* Rand Corp., R-3353-FMP, April.
Presse- und Informationsamt (Germany). 1988. Wehrdienst—Kriegsdienstverweigerung—Zivildienst (Military Service—Avoiding Service—Civil Service). July.
Service d'Information et de Rélations Publiques Des Armées (France). 1988. French Defence and Its Armed Forces.
Tan, H. W., and M. P. Ward. 1985. *Forecasting the wages of young men: The effects of cohort size.* Rand Corp., R-3115-Army. May.
The NATO Report. 1987. Vol. 2 (20 July):41.
The NATO Report. 1988. Bonn Budget Review. 11 January.
The NATO Report. 1988. Vol. 3 (11 January):14
Tuohy, W. 1987. West German forces get top rating. *Los Angeles Times,* 1 January.
U.S. Department of Defense. 1991. *Selected manpower statistics.* Directorate for Information, Operations and Reports. Washington, D.C.: Government Printing Office.
Wehrtechnik. 1988. Die ausbuildung im heer (Army training). April.

MANSTEIN, ERICH VON [1887–1973]

Fritz Erich von Manstein was born von Lewinsky on 24 November 1887 in Baden, Germany, the son of General of Artillery Eduard von Lewinsky. Upon the death of his parents Erich was adopted by Major General von Manstein, whose name he subsequently bore. Following in his father's footsteps, he was accepted into the Prussian Cadet Corps and upon graduation was commissioned an officer cadet in 1906.

World War I and Interwar Years

In 1914 Manstein attended the War Academy but it was closed after the outbreak of World War I. During the war he served on both the western and eastern fronts. In 1919 he was promoted to captain and upon the formation of the Reichswehr, Germany's postwar defensive force, was one of the few officers chosen to remain in service.

From 1919 to 1927, Manstein held a variety of troop and staff appointments before being transferred to the Reichswehr Ministry in 1927. Promoted to major, he remained with the ministry until Hitler's rise to the chancellorship of Germany in 1933. In that year Manstein was promoted to colonel and appointed a departmental chief on the General Staff. By 1935, he was appointed head of the Operational Section of the General Staff. In 1936 Manstein was promoted to *generalmajor* (brigadier general). In 1937 he served as 1st Deputy Chief of the General Staff under Gen. Ludwig Beck. After Beck's dismissal by Hitler in August 1938, Manstein was promoted to *generalleutnant* (major general) and given the command of a division in Silesia.

World War II

Prior to the outbreak of war in 1939, Manstein was appointed chief of the General Staff, Southern Army Group, under Gen. Gerd von Rundstedt. Manstein served well in this post during the Polish campaign, displaying a talent for planning operations.

In late 1939 the General Staff was considering plans for the invasion of France. Manstein submitted a plan that called for a rapid thrust of massed armored forces through the Ardennes Forest in Belgium to seize strategic crossing points on the Meuse River along the center of the French lines. This plan was first rejected, then adopted, by the chief of the General Staff, Franz Halder. Hitler became aware of Manstein's plan, was impressed by its daring nature, and approved it.

In January 1940 Manstein was given command of the XXXVIII Army Corps for the French campaign. On 10 May the operation began; Manstein's corps broke through the French lines and drove for the Meuse River. By 10 June his troops—the first German troops to cross the river—were pushing deep into the enemy's rear lines. Later that month Manstein was promoted to *general der infanterie* (lieutenant general) and in July was awarded the Knight's Cross.

Manstein was then appointed to command the landing forces for Operation Sea Lion, the planned cross-channel invasion of Great Britain. With the cancellation of Sea Lion, he was transferred to East Prussia and appointed commander of the LVI Panzer Corps in preparation for Operation Barbarossa, the invasion of Russia. The LVI Panzer Corps was one of the two corps that constituted the Fourth Panzer Group of Field Marshal Ritter von Leeb's Army Group North. For Manstein, command of a panzer corps was the culmination of a long-standing ambition.

Operation Barbarossa began on 22 June 1941. By 26 June, Manstein's forces had driven more than 320 kilometers (200 mi.) into enemy territory—80 kilometers (50 mi.) on the first day alone—reaching the Dvina River and establishing a bridgehead. The speed of his advance worked against him, however, since he was forced to halt due to the inability of the rest of the panzer group to protect his corps' exposed flanks.

The German advance recommenced on 2 July against stiffening Russian resistance. Manstein, ordered to advance his corps between Moscow and Leningrad, recommended that the Fourth Panzer Group be consolidated for a drive on Leningrad. In August, Hitler ordered the drive on Moscow halted and shifted the focus of his armies north to Leningrad and south to the Ukraine.

The Fourth Panzer Group was ordered to take Leningrad and Manstein's advance proceeded apace. Before he could link up with General Reinhardt's corps, however, Manstein's corps was pulled out of the line and sent toward Lake Ilmen to assist General Busch's Eighteenth Army, which was being severely pressed by Russian counterattacks. Manstein smashed into the flank of the Russian Thirty-fourth Army and rolled it up, relieving Busch's army.

For this victory Manstein was appointed commander of the Eleventh Army, Southern Army Group, on 12 September 1941. Manstein's primary objectives were to take Rostov and the Crimea but, realizing that his forces were not strong enough to do both, he concentrated his efforts on the Crimea. Manstein recognized that in taking the Crimea he could not only eliminate the Russian air threat to Romania's vital oil fields and secure the Eleventh Army's flank, but also provide an excellent staging area for a German offensive across the Kuban Isthmus into the Caucasus.

Realizing the threat, the Russians committed two armies to the Crimea in an offensive that resulted in heavy fighting in September and October. Manstein, hard-pressed and threatened with being cut off with his back to the Black Sea, was reinforced by Kleist's First Panzer Army, which drove down the Dneiper River into the Russian rear. By 5 October the Russians were stopped and Manstein immediately launched a counteroffensive. While Kleist moved against Rostov, Manstein pursued the Russians and cut off their escape from the peninsula by taking Kerch and Sevastopol. Kerch fell on 15 November and, after a long and arduous siege, Sevastopol fell on 4 July 1942. In roughly ten months the Eleventh Army, although greatly outnumbered, had taken the Crimea and captured more than 430,000 prisoners. Hitler, greatly impressed with the victory, awarded a special decoration to the soldiers of the campaign and promoted Manstein to field marshal (Fig. 1).

With the opening of the German summer offensive in June 1942, Manstein was given command of the Leningrad front with orders to take the city. With depleted forces and against his better judgment, Manstein attempted to obey Hitler's directives but failed to capture the city. He did, however, destroy a Russian army counterattacking in the Lake Ladoga sector.

By 20 November, the situation of Gen. Friedrich von Paulus' Sixth Army in Stalingrad had become disastrous. Manstein was given command of Army Group Don and sent to effect Paulus' relief. Realizing that the withdrawal of the Sixth Army would create a breach in the lines, Manstein at first attempted to reinforce Stalingrad. When this proved impossible because of Hitler's refusal to pull the needed forces from other areas of the front, Manstein tried to coordinate a breakout with Paulus. Despite the valiant efforts of Manstein's troops, the breakout was unsuccessful and the Sixth Army capitulated on 2 February 1943.

Due in large part to Manstein's persuasion, Hitler eventually allowed a withdrawal to the Mius River. On 14 February, with his army group redesignated Army Group South, Manstein launched an offensive to retake Kharkov. Setting a brilliant trap, Manstein lured the Russian Sixth Army to attack. Counterattacking against its flanks, he pushed the Russians back to the Donetz River, recapturing Kharkov. Although a great coup for Manstein, Kharkov was the last major German victory in the east.

Figure 1. Field Marshal Erich von Manstein (left) on an inspection tour in Russia. (SOURCE: U.S. Library of Congress)

Manstein had overall direction of the southern jaw of Operation Zitadelle, the German offensive against the heavily fortified Kursk salient, begun on 5 July. Although Manstein's forces breached the Russian defenses, they were too worn to deal with the Russian mobile reserves and the ensuing counteroffense.

After the disastrous defeat at Kursk on 11 July 1943, the initiative passed to the Russians, who began to push the Germans back step by step. Manstein argued persistently for a deliberate delaying strategy, with the German armies husbanding their strength instead of fighting costly defensive actions. Manstein believed that, if the Russians were allowed to penetrate deep into the German lines, he could strike the flanks of the penetrations with his panzers and destroy their spearheads, thus containing the threat and winning a war of attrition in the east. While Hitler sometimes allowed withdrawals to conserve forces, he vetoed Manstein's counteroffensive operations as too risky.

It was primarily due to Manstein's skill in maneuver that his army group was able to stave off disaster and withdraw to the Polish frontier. This success, however, did not save him from Hitler who, tired of constant retreats and arguments over strategy, relieved Manstein of command on 25 March 1944.

Manstein retired to his estates where he remained for the rest of the war. Eventually captured by the British, Manstein was taken to Hamburg to face war crimes charges. Although cleared of two counts of massacring Jews, Manstein was convicted on one count of failing to protect civilian lives and, on 19 December 1949, was sentenced to 18 years of imprisonment. This sentence was later commuted to 12 years, but in August 1952 Manstein was given a medical parole. Released in May 1953, Manstein served briefly as a military advisor to the Federal Republic of Germany. He died at his home in Irschenhausen on 12 June 1973.

Manstein was a brilliant, talented commander whose skill in operational planning was surpassed only by his leadership ability in the field. Manstein's talents contributed to many major German successes on the eastern front. Had Manstein been allowed to execute his concept of delay and counterstroke operations, the war in the east might have taken a different turn.

VINCENT B. HAWKINS

SEE ALSO: Guderian, Heinz; Konev, Ivan Stepanovich; Mechanized Warfare; Rokossovskii, Konstantin Konstantinovich; World War II; Zhukov, Georgi Konstantinovich.

Bibliography

Manstein, F. E. von. 1970. *Lost victories.* New York: Henry Regnery.

Pfannes, C. E., and V. A. Salamone. 1980. *The great commanders of World War II.* Vol. 1, *The Germans.* New York: Kensington.

Wistrich, R. 1982. *Who's who in Nazi Germany.* New York: Bonanza Books.

MAO TSE-TUNG [1893–1976]

No other twentieth-century figure has had as profound an effect on the strategy of modern politico-military conflict as Mao Tse-tung (Fig. 1). In a life that spanned 83 years, this revolutionary, common soldier, battlefield commander, commander in chief of armies, strategic thinker, and absolute ruler of the People's Republic of China left an indelible mark on his era. For good or ill, Mao guided the most populous nation, the largest Communist party, and the most sizable armed forces on earth at a critical time. This article focuses mainly on his influence in the military arena.

Early Education

Mao Tse-tung was born in 1893 in the Hunan Province village of Shaoshan. His father's relative prosperity, derived from ownership of some land and a small shop, afforded Mao the opportunity to study Chinese and Western classical literature. At a young age he had learned about Washington, Napoleon, Peter the Great, and Sun Tzu and their contributions to both the military art and the na-

Figure 1. Mao Tse-tung, chairman of the Central People's Government of the People's Republic of China. (SOURCE: U.S. Library of Congress)

tional development of their countries. Mao's inclination in school toward philosophy, history, and geography rather than the sciences revealed an early interest in abstract theory and the sweep of events on a grand scale.

Mao combined this early instruction with practical experience when, in 1911, he became a soldier with the revolutionary forces that toppled the crumbling Ching dynasty. This brief exposure to conflict was followed by further study toward a teaching career in Hunan and at the University of Peking. During this time, he enthusiastically absorbed the radical ideas of Marx and Engels and the Russian writers Bakunin, Tolstoy, and Kropotkin.

Development of a Communist Revolutionary

After 1919, Mao was increasingly active in revolutionary politics. The 26-year-old teacher wrote, published, and distributed his writings and those of others espousing the radical Marxist approach to the revitalization of China.

On 1 July 1921, Mao Tse-tung joined eleven comrades in Shanghai to found the Chinese Communist party. During the next six years, Mao served the party in various capacities. He moved often between Shanghai, Canton, and Changsha in south-central China to avoid the police.

In this period, Mao was a strong proponent of Communist participation in a united front with the Kuomintang party, led by his later nemesis, Chiang Kai-shek. Mao became a firm believer in using such "marriages of convenience" to achieve ultimate victory.

The rising leader became identified with China's enormous peasant class, with whom he believed the nation's destiny resided. Mao's championing of the Chinese peasant catapulted him into a leading position in the Communist party when the urban workers—the preeminent revolutionaries in conventional Marxist theory—failed in their fight against Chiang in the wake of the united front's dissolution in 1927.

The Battlefield Classroom

Association with the Communist armed forces also fueled Mao's rise to the top. In 1927, with Chu-Teh, Chen-Yi, and Lin-Piao, who would thereafter be among his chief lieutenants, Mao formed the Red Army. Chu-Teh, schooled in traditional military thought, deserves much of the credit for refining Mao's early military ideas.

Mao's experiences in this period convinced him that any successful struggle against the entrenched power of the state would be protracted; victory would come only after a long, arduous politico-military effort to gain the allegiance of the Chinese peasants and through them control of the countryside. Only then could the Kuomintang-controlled urban centers be surrounded, isolated, and eliminated, one by one.

For this "revolutionary war" strategy to succeed, however, especially in the initial stages, the Red Army had to survive. In the early 1930s, Mao was unable to dissuade his comrades from engaging Chiang's stronger forces in open combat. The Communists were beaten at almost every turn. Finally, in October 1934, Chiang's armies closed in on the Communist forces at Juichin in Kiangsi Province for the coup de grace. As they would many times thereafter, the Communists wisely chose to retreat and save their army to fight another day. Strategic or tactical withdrawal in the face of unfavorable battlefield conditions became a primary principle of Mao's form of warfare.

Thus began the Long March. For the next year, the Red Army fought its way west to Siikiang Province and then north to a Communist base in remote Shensi Province—a distance of more than 9,600 kilometers (6,000 mi.). Although tens of thousands perished and the survivors suffered grievously on the rigorous trek, it forged a hardened, disciplined, and ideologically committed Red Army.

The Anti-Japanese War

The war against the Japanese, which broke out in earnest in 1937, provided Mao with another laboratory to test the politico-military concepts he had developed and to discover others for the eventual fight with the Chinese central government. Mao dispatched his forces from their stronghold at Yenan in Shensi Province against Japanese lodgments in northeastern China. Communist guerrilla forces, avoiding the well-defended cities and other strongholds, penetrated far into the Japanese rear. At the same time, Communist cadres worked among the peasants to develop paramilitary forces, establish local political control, and eliminate all opposition. This process was made easier by the hatred of the peasants for the brutal Japanese invaders. As a result of the struggle against the Japanese, Mao Tse-tung and his Communist Party became identified by many of the people as the embodiment of Chinese nationalism.

From a patchwork quilt of "liberated areas" behind enemy lines, the Communists implemented the mobile war phase of Mao's revolutionary war strategy. Main force units carried out lightning strikes on exposed Japanese positions and then withdrew to safety. Guerrillas raided supply depots, ambushed road and rail traffic, and sabotaged lines of communication. The Communists were never strong enough to destroy the Japanese army in northern China, but by September 1945 they had confined it to a few isolated bastions.

Civil War Victory

With the elimination of the Japanese threat in 1945, Mao prepared for the cataclysmic struggle with Chiang Kai-shek's government. The prize would be all of China. As during the Long March and the fight with the Japanese, however, the initial objective was to delay an all-out confrontation with Chiang's stronger Nationalist armies until a favorable balance of power developed.

By late 1946 and the breakdown of an American-arranged ceasefire, the Communist position was improving. In the Communist-controlled areas of China, the party had established a harsh, puritanical but efficient and relatively incorrupt administration. The battle-toughened Red Army was well supplied with Soviet and captured Nationalist arms. Of even greater importance was the fact that the Communists were convinced the national destiny of China was in their hands.

Conversely, the Nationalists were thoroughly disenchanted with Chiang's corrupt, politics-ridden, and paralyzed administration. Economic inflation was rampant; Nationalist forces had adequate materiel but lacked effective leaders, a sound strategy, and the will to win. Finally, the close association of Chiang's regime with the United States sullied its nationalist credentials in the eyes of many Chinese.

In the civil war that ensued on mainland China from 1946 to 1949, Mao put into practice all that he had learned in his long politico-military apprenticeship. In the last stage of revolutionary war, the general offensive, the Red Army's mobile columns outmarched, encircled, and routed one Nationalist unit in the field after another. Chiang's troops were compressed into urban enclaves, which were then reduced in turn. Operating from their heartland position in the north, the Communists overran Manchuria and central China where they destroyed Chiang's strongest armies. The Red Army, against diminishing opposition, then advanced across the Yangtze River and completed the conquest of mainland China. In large part, this victory was achieved by the Chinese Communist adherence to the strategy of revolutionary war developed by Mao Tse-tung.

Post–Civil War Years

In the following years, Mao's revolutionary war concept continued, with good and bad effect, to influence the employment of the Chinese armed forces. In the initial, fluid stages of the Korean War, Chinese units used their mobility and endurance to great advantage against United Nations' forces. In the conventional positional warfare along the 38th Parallel, however, the relatively lightly armed Red Army suffered enormous casualties and failed to defeat its enemies.

Until his death in 1976, Mao remained an ardent proponent of maintaining large, ideologically inspired Chinese land armies, backed by regional militia, to defend the nation. He clashed with other Chinese leaders who called for greater emphasis on smaller, regular air, sea, and ground forces armed with sophisticated modern weapons. He prevailed more often than not.

The International Influence of Revolutionary War

During the post–civil war years, Mao had many disciples abroad. Cuba's Fidel Castro and Che Guevara, Cambodia's Pol Pot, and other revolutionaries throughout Asia, Africa, and Latin America followed his prescriptions for overthrowing governments defended by well-established armed forces and powerful allies. As adapted to the special conditions found in Southeast Asia, the strategy was successfully pursued by Vietnam's leaders in their long, bloody struggle against France, South Vietnam, and the United States. Clearly, the character of many of the modern world's conflicts reflects the revolutionary war concepts developed by China's Mao Tse-tung.

EDWARD J. MAROLDA

SEE ALSO: Chiang Kai-shek; Chu Teh; Korean War; Taiwan; Vietnam and Indochina Wars; World War II.

Bibliography

Archer, J. 1972. *Mao Tse-tung: A biography.* New York: Hawthorne Books.

Bartke, W. 1981. *Who's who in the People's Republic of China.* Armonk, N.Y.: M. E. Sharpe.

Boorman, S. A. 1969. *The protracted game: A Wei-Ch'i interpretation of Maoist revolutionary strategy.* New York: Oxford Univ. Press.

Chao, S. M., ed. 1961. *Chinese communist revolutionary strategy, 1945–1949.* Princeton, N.J.: Center of Public and International Studies, Woodrow Wilson School of Public and International Affairs, Princeton Univ.

Elliot-Bateman, M. 1967. *Defeat in the East: The mark of Mao Tse-Tung on war.* New York: Oxford Univ. Press.

Hook, B., ed. 1982. *The Cambridge encyclopedia of China.* Cambridge: Cambridge Univ. Press.
Mao Tse-tung. 1963. *Selected military writings of Mao Tse-tung.* Peking: Foreign Language Press.
O'Ballance, E. 1962. *The red army of China: A short history.* New York: Frederick A. Praeger.

MAPPING, CHARTING, AND GEODESY

Mapping, charting, and geodesy (MC&G), first used in a 1955 Hoover Commission Report, was officially recognized as a collective term in 1962, when the Defense Intelligence Agency (DIA) was given responsibility for managing the overall Department of Defense (DOD) mapping, charting, and geodetic program. (*Geodesy* is defined as the science of determining the size and shape of the Earth, the precise positions of points on the Earth's surface, and the variations in the pull of gravity.) The program remained with DIA until January 1972, when the newly formed Defense Mapping Agency (DMA) began the complex task of consolidating all MC&G functions under one agency.

MC&G Today

The absence of integrated systems to perform truly automated mapping has led to attempts to automate selected steps of the mapping process through state-of-the-art data gathering, analysis, and display. Contemporary MC&G therefore combines conventional and somewhat less standard techniques.

Conventional Mapping

Virtually all topographic maps in current files were made photogrammetrically; that is, they were compiled from airborne stereoscopic photographs (Fig. 1). These maps are designed to meet the National Map Accuracy Standards, which require that 90 percent of all points tested for elevation be correct to within half the contour interval and that 90 percent of all principal features be plotted to within 1⁄50th of an inch (or 1⁄30th, depending on the map scale). The use of high resolution continuous-tone photographs combined with sophisticated analytical photogrammetric and error adjustment techniques produces maps of the greatest precision possible using the current technology.

Future automated mapping systems may build on the photograph's accurate planimetric data storage capability by carefully scanning aerial photographs (rather than gathering data through stereo compilation) and entering the scanned data directly into an integrated system. Already, orthophotographs (aerial photographs with all relief displacement removed) are commonly used to provide a viewing background for more sophisticated image classification systems.

Figure 1. Aircraft view from 50,000 feet of Washington, D.C. The picture was taken with infrared film during the summer of 1977. (SOURCE: U.S. Department of Defense)

Civilian companies will continue to produce large-scale topographic maps for planning and development purposes, but the use of stereoplotting to map large land masses will be abandoned. This does not imply that the small-scale aerial photograph is becoming obsolete; the capability of the modern aerial photograph to provide information about planimetric features is unrivaled, and the three-dimensional model formed from overlapping stereophotographs is still the best source for accurate elevation data.

Many stereoplotters automatically store elevation data in a digital format during the compilation phase—for example, Digital Topographic Elevation Data (DTED) from DMA, and Digital Elevation Model (DEM) data from the U.S. Geological Survey (USGS). These data are made available to automated mapping and display systems. Digital elevation data compose the most important element in three-dimensional terrain modeling, which provides the cornerstone for line-of-sight, cross-country mobility, flood analysis, land use planning, view shed analysis, and many other applications.

The major obstacle to truly automated mapping is the inability of machines to recognize and correctly identify features (and then automatically label them). Defined as automatic pattern recognition, this problem must be solved before automated mapping will become a reality.

Multispectral Imagery

Special combinations of films and filters in a conventional camera, or a multispectral scanner (MSS), may be used to image particular features of the Earth in different portions of the spectrum, thereby revealing features invisible or unclear to conventional photography. Spectral imaging of simple vegetation is a good example of this application. Vegetation reflects only 15 percent of the electromagnetic energy in the visible range (0.5–0.6 μm, i.e., green), while it reflects 50 percent of the energy in the near-infrared (NIR) range (0.7–1.3 μm). Obviously, a detector operating in the NIR range will identify more vegetation than one operating just in the visible (green) range.

In an attempt to discern previously hidden differences in features, highly sophisticated MSSs are being used to gather data from several slices of the electromagnetic spectrum. Some experimental airborne systems claim to measure energy in over 100 spectral bands as they attempt to capture the unique "spectral signature" of several different types of features. Difficulty in handling the tremendous volume of data that results is the major disadvantage of such systems and, to date, they have not been shown to be cost-effective for routine work.

Thematic Mapper, a satellite-borne MSS with an instantaneous field of view (IFOV), or footprint, of 30 meters, operates in seven bands (3 visible, 1 NIR, 2 mid-IR, and 1 thermal IR). Instruments on board the satellite measure the strength of electromagnetic energy reflected (or emitted, in the case of thermal energy) from features on the Earth in each of the seven bands. At any instant the scanner is viewing an area on the ground 30 meters square—the IFOV. The IFOV is the size of one cell (sometimes called a pixel), and is a measure of the system's resolution or ability to discern detail. Because the amplitude of emitted energy in the thermal range is small, the radiometers measuring in this range can view an area 120 meters square. This lowers the spatial resolution, but increases the radiometric resolution; that is, it allows the device to measure smaller temperature differentials.

Compared with earlier satellite systems, which employed only four bands, Thematic Mapper is able to measure greater detail and to recognize a wider range of features. In the three visible bands, the satellite captures scenes as the human eye would see them. The NIR range emphasizes vegetation, and the two mid-IR (MIR) ranges are used to differentiate snow from clouds and to discriminate among mineral and rock types. The thermal IR (TIR) band is useful for detecting differences in temperature of ocean currents (commercial fishing is conducted at the juncture of two differing currents), the higher temperature of stressed vegetation (due to disease), thermal plumes from nuclear power plants, and many other applications. Thematic Mapper data are available from EOSAT, Lanham, Maryland.

SPOT (Système pour l'Observation de la Terre), the French addition to the satellite data-capture arena, substituted "push-broom" technology for the scanner. Thematic Mapper uses a rapidly rotating mirror to scan a wide swath as the satellite races overhead. In contrast, SPOT has 6,000 individual detectors mounted on a bar. As the satellite passes overhead, its array of panchromatic (0.51–0.73 μm) detectors view a swath 60 kilometers (37 mi.) wide (each viewing 10 meters). The sensors are time-calibrated to record every 10 meters (33 ft.) on the ground, giving SPOT its superior 10-meter resolution in its panchromatic range. SPOT's MSSs view a 20-meter swath and record every 20 meters (66 ft.), rendering an MSS resolution of 20 meters.

SPOT's enhanced technology has pointable optics, which provides for off-nadir viewing. This side-to-side viewing capability affords full-scene stereoscopic imaging from two different satellite tracks, which makes the system available for more conventional mapping. Its output "is a potential source of imagery for 1:50,000 and smaller scale mapping tasks" (Gugan 1988). For map scales larger than 1:50,000, conventional aerial photography is still necessary.

The National Oceanic and Atmospheric Administration's (NOAA's) AVHRR (Advanced Very High Resolution Radiometer) is a meteorological satellite (Metsat) that carries an MSS operating in five bands (red, NIR, MIR, and TIR). With a footprint of 1.1 kilometer (.62 mile), its spatial resolution is very poor, but it has the advantages of excellent temperature differentiation and temporal reliability, making it useful for weather prediction, snowfall estimation, and small-scale land use determination.

Lillesand et al. (1987) list several other Metsats. NOAA's GOES (Geostationary Operational Environmental Satellite) images the entire hemispherical Earth twice an hour in a visible and a TIR band and is used for weather forecasting and snow cover mapping. The U.S. Air Force maintains a meteorological satellite program with scanners on board that measure in the visible, NIR, and TIR ranges. A unique feature of the USAF's satellites is that they can be tuned to record under the reduced lighting of nighttime, to capture unusual images of the aurora borealis, volcanoes, forest fires, and so forth. The Nimbus Metsat series has been instrumental in monitoring the color and temperature of the oceans, the latter being pivotal in forecasting weather on land.

Thermal Infrared

Although the thermal sensor on board Thematic Mapper and other systems was discussed earlier, TIR imagery is sufficiently important to warrant further discussion. Operating in the electromagnetic range of 8.0 to 14.0 μm, these devices may be of varying sophistication, but all measure and record the radiant temperature of objects within their FOV. Airborne radiometers store electromagnetic energy measurements in the 8 to 14 μm range on magnetic tape, which is later converted to a photographic medium. This TIR imagery is useful for analyzing the soil (water content is related to temperature), determining vegetative stress, measuring heat loss in underground steam pipes, identifying buildings with inadequate insulation, or any application where temperature differential will reveal the information desired.

There are several satellite-borne thermal sensors or MSSs with the capability to measure in the thermal range of the electromagnetic spectrum. NASA's Thermal Infrared Multispectral Scanner (TIMS) is an MSS that operates entirely in the TIR range and has been used extensively for geologic mapping (Lillesand et al. 1987).

The ground resolution element (area viewed on the ground as a result of the IFOV) varies with the apparatus and, of course, the flying height. A resolution cell small enough to count seals in the arctic has been used on an experimental basis, while very large footprints of more than a kilometer square are commonplace. Thermal scanners operate equally well in daylight or at nighttime, which enhances their information-gathering capability through a comparative analysis.

The side-to-side motion of the TIR scanner produces severe distortions in the shape and location of objects on the imagery. This reduction in geometric fidelity is sufficiently serious to limit the usefulness of thermal scanner imagery for conventional mapping. However, to a trained TIR image interpreter, the information revealed through temperature differentials is extensive and unique. This unique information, when integrated with other imaging devices, permits TIR imagery to make a substantial contribution to orthodox mapping.

Radar

Radar, a day/night, all-weather remote sensing system operating in the microwave portion of the electromagnetic spectrum, has been used for years for military reconnaissance and is now a standard tool at all airports. It is also a powerful tool for acquiring natural resource data (Lillesand et al. 1987). Its ability to map beneath the clouds and to penetrate (to some extent) vegetation has made radar the only usable mapping device in some parts of the world.

The ground-resolution cell size of Side Looking Airborne Radar (SLAR) is controlled by the pulse length and antenna beam width (Lillesand et al. 1987). To achieve a resolution suitable for either reconnaissance or mapping, early systems needed a very short pulse length (readily interrupted) and a very long antenna (impractically so, i.e., hundreds of feet). The advent of synthetic aperture radar (SAR), which electronically simulates a very long antenna, has greatly increased the resolution of radar systems, making them more applicable to mapping, albeit still for only small scales. Wise and Trinder (1987) found the geometric accuracy of SIR-B (Shuttle Imaging Radar, A version in November 1981, B version in October 1984) to be suitable only for 1:250,000 mapping or smaller. They admit, however, that "the definition of boundaries and textural detail of areal features may . . . be useful for thematic mapping." Ali (1987) is slightly more optimistic, maintaining that a digitally processed SAR image may be suitable for mapping at 1:150,000 or smaller.

Radar, which works by measuring the strength and time of return of electromagnetic pulses, is useful for both image detection and recognition. Angular objects (e.g., bridges, buildings, hedge rows, tree lines) are considered corner reflectors and present a very pronounced return (i.e., a bright spot on the image). Grass, crop lands, and so forth, are diffuse reflectors—only some of the signal is returned, which diminishes the brightness on the image. Specular reflectors like smooth lakes, rivers, roads, and parking lots render no reflection, making them appear distinctively black on the image. Experienced radar image interpreters become very skillful in considering subtle factors such as the moisture content, electrical characteristics, and unique geometric shapes of the reflectors which enables radar imagery to contribute to the overall mapping effort.

It is not surprising that radar imagery has its own distinctive distortions which must be corrected prior to applying the imagery to mapping. Radar systems cause slant-range scale distortion, which means that objects near the flight line appear smaller than they really are with the distortion becoming less at greater ranges. Relief displacement, which is present in all raw imagery, appears in radar imagery also. However, here the tops of mountains or buildings appear closer to the flight line than do the bases (the opposite of what appears on a normal photograph).

Radar imaging from space has become a particularly useful tool. Seasat-1 is a radar imaging satellite that provides important repetitive data on ocean waves, storms, water resources, agricultural assessments, and geologic formations (Lillesand et al. 1987). The radar systems transported in the space shuttle captured data on land and sea features that are still being analyzed. Europe, Canada, and Japan have similar systems.

Global Positioning System

The Global Positioning System (GPS) is a space-based radio positioning navigation system that can provide extremely accurate three-dimensional position and velocity information to suitably equipped users anywhere on Earth. Users with lightweight, small, inexpensive receivers can determine position to accuracies of 10 meters (33 ft.) and velocity to accuracies of 3 centimeters (0.1 ft.) per second when the receivers are permitted to contact at least four satellites (USAF 1976). More than 20 GPS satellites are destined for eventual orbit about the Earth.

GPS has found tremendous application as a navigational device both within and outside of the military. Hajela (1990) maintains that GPS can also provide ground control (both vertical and horizontal) for surveyors when a sufficiently large net is adjusted.

GPS was made possible through the ability to define satellite orbital parameters with great precision. Orbital parameters, in turn, derive from a firm understanding of gravity. Satellites rotate around the gravimetric center of the Earth; their distance from this center point is affected by the density of the Earth. In other words, a satellite passing over a particularly dense region of the Earth will lose altitude, and it will regain altitude when it passes over a less dense area.

The National Geophysical Data Center in Boulder, Colorado, maintains a gravity database providing gravity values gathered from more than 80 percent of the Earth's surface (NGDC 1988). The NGDC offers several different gravity databases for sale. Many were compiled by other agencies, including 860,000 observations from all 50 states provided by DMA.

MC&G Challenges

The greatest technical challenge facing the MC&G community (both military and civilian) today is how to fully automate the mapping process. Systems now in operation automate or partially automate some facet of the mapping process, but truly automated mapping is several years away. The problem can be simply defined. The mapping community has decided upon a fixed number of features (more than 200) that it wishes to display on its maps; automated mapping would mean that a machine (computer) must recognize, either in some real-time system or by scanning images, the required features, determine their position, properly display them, and, finally, label them in the appropriate colors on some acceptable format (either in a printout or on a video screen). The establishment of an integrated system is beyond the reach of current technology.

The specific area that is most troublesome in automating the mapping process is automated feature extraction (pattern recognition). Computers can be programmed under ideal conditions to trace a road from spectral imagery. When the road's surface reflectivity changes because of shadows, changes in surface, or diminished lighting (or when the road simply winds around a hill or is temporarily hidden by a grove of trees) the computer requires human assistance.

A multitude of similar examples exists. Considerable work is needed before knowledge-based or artificial intelligence systems are capable of duplicating what the human mind finds simple (but tedious).

MC&G Tomorrow

The mapping systems of the future will be digital and will be a combination of the many data-gathering/image-forming entities that now exist. The complexity and interdependence of the various data-gathering devices will require the use of expert systems and artificial intelligence to assist in making the many difficult discriminatory decisions required to separate distinct features from within the images (Ripple 1987; Robinson 1987). The computer will be asked to make decisions in the manner of a photointerpreter (i.e., by considering structural, spectral, and contextual knowledge) (Swann 1988).

Geographic Information Systems

The demand for topographic maps and for maps of specific themes of the Earth's surface, such as natural resources, has accelerated greatly in the twentieth century. In addition, the users of such data have demanded the ability to analyze as well as display the data.

Burrough (1986) has summed up the manifold uses of thematic data.

> Urban planners and cadastral agencies need detailed information about the distribution of land and resources in towns and cities. Civil engineers need to plan the routes of roads and canals and to estimate construction costs, including those of cutting away hillsides and filling in valleys. Police departments need to know the spatial distribution of various kinds of crime, medical organizations the distribution of sickness and disease, commercial interests the distribution of sales outlets, and potential markets. The enormous infrastructure of what are collectively known as "utilities" i.e., water, gas, electricity, telephone lines, and sewerage systems all need to be recorded and manipulated in map form.

The military's demand for maps parallels, and in many areas exceeds, that of the civilian community.

The availability of computers for mapping and spatial analysis, the progress experienced in automated data capture (e.g., Landsat in 1972), and improvements in database management provided the tools for developing geographic information systems (GIS). All that remained was for someone to demonstrate the technique. This was done by Ian McHarg (1969).

A GIS may be thought of as "digital geography," a "decision support system," or a combination of hardware and software that permits the encoding, storage, retrieval, manipulation, analysis, and display of geocoded data. It requires digital data, and hence is expediting the transformation of several years of analog data to digital data and is underscoring the need to ensure that new data is gathered digitally. By overlaying several layers of stored data (e.g., elevation, vegetation, water, and land use), GISs can produce maps and conduct analyses that will reveal previously obscured information.

Although expensive and time consuming to implement, GISs have already found a niche in the scientific commercial community. Elevation data may be purchased from the USGS, which accepted the mission in the late 1970s of establishing a digital elevation database for the entire nation. In addition, the USGS offers digital planimetric data (hydrography and transportation), land-use and land-cover data, and geographic names information (Dept. of the Interior 1988).

The Department of Commerce's National Geophysical Data Center markets magnetic, altimetry, gravity, and topographic data. Recently, census data (from the Bureau of the Census) in the form of the new TIGER (Topologically Integrated Geographic Encoding and Referencing System) files have been made available to the general public. Today, several service companies will produce digital data from any analog source on a commercial basis.

LEON G. THOMPSON

SEE ALSO: Air Reconnaissance; Intelligence, Imagery; Reconnaissance and Surveillance; Satellite Technology; Sensor Technology.

Bibliography

Ali, A. E. 1987. Geometric accuracy testing of orbital radar imagery. *Photogrammetric Engineering and Remote Sensing* 53(11):1533–37.

Burrough, P. A. 1986. *Principles of geographic information systems for land resources assessment*, Oxford: Clarendon Press.

Defense Mapping Agency. 1982. *MC&G.* U.S. Naval Observatory. Washington, D.C.

Gugan, D. J., and I. J. Dowman. 1988. Topographic mapping from SPOT imagery. *Photogrammetric Engineering and Remote Sensing* 54(10):1409–14.

Hajela, D. 1990. Obtaining centimeter-precision heights by GPS observations over small areas. *GPS World*, January/February.

Lillesand, T. M., and R. W. Keifer. 1987. *Remote sensing and image interpretation.* 2d ed. New York: Wiley.

McHarg, I. 1969. *Design with nature.* Garden City, N.Y.: Natural History Press.

National Geophysical Data Center. 1988. Gravity data base. Boulder, Colo.

Ripple, W. J., and V. S. Ulshoefer. 1987. Expert systems and spatial data models for efficient geographic data handling. *Photogrammetric Engineering and Remote Sensing* 53(10):1431–33.

Robinson, V. B., and A. U. Frank. 1987. Expert systems for geographic information systems. *Photogrammetric Engineering and Remote Sensing* 53(10):1435–41.

Swann, R., D. Hawkins, A. Westwell-Roper, and W. Johnstone. 1988. The potential for automated mapping from geocoded digital image data. *Photogrammetric Engineering and Remote Sensing* 54(2):187–93.

U.S. Air Force. 1976. NAVSTAR global positioning system, joint program management plan. Los Angeles, Calif.: Space and Missile Systems Organization.

U.S. Department of Defense. 1971. Directive 5105.27, Study of the mapping, charting and geodesy intelligence issue. Washington, D.C.: Government Printing Office.

U.S. Department of the Interior. 1988. U.S. GeoData. Reston, Va.: U.S. Geological Survey, National Cartographic Information Center.

Wise, P. J., and J. C. Trinder. 1987. Assessment of SIR-B for topographic mapping. *Photogrammetric Engineering and Remote Sensing* 53(11):1539–44.

MAPS, CHARTS, AND SYMBOLS, MILITARY

Maps and charts are graphic representations, normally on a plane (flat) surface, that depict natural or artificial features of part or all of the earth. They are prepared at an established scale and map features are positioned relative to a coordinate reference system. Man-made and natural features are represented by symbols, lines, colors, and forms.

To enhance the ability of map users to recognize features portrayed, such features are represented by conventional signs and symbols. Most symbols are exaggerated in size on maps beyond the point of what they actually represent. For example, on a 1:250,000-scale map, the symbol for any building occupies an area of some 500 square feet on the ground, while a road symbol, if in actual scale, would be over 500 feet wide.

Maps provide information on the existence of, location of, and distance between ground features (e.g., populated areas and routes of travel and communication). Maps also indicate variations in terrain; extent of vegetation; presence of streams, lakes, and oceans; and heights of natural terrain features. The proper use of maps by military personnel enables troops and materiel to be transported, stored, and placed into operation at prescribed places and times.

Classes of Maps by Type

Topographic maps portray terrain features as well as the horizontal positions of the features represented. Vertical positions, termed "relief," usually are represented by contour lines.

Photomaps are first-instance or reproductions of aerial or satellite photographs on which grid lines, place names, route numbers, approximate scale, and other data have been superimposed.

Joint operations graphics are a series of 1:250,000-scale military maps designed for joint ground and air operations. These maps are published in air and ground versions with identical topographical data on each. Ground versions have elevations and contours in meters, air versions in feet. The air versions also have symbols that identify aids and obstructions to air navigation.

Photomosaics are assemblies of aerial photographs that are published when time does not permit compilation of a more accurate map. Accuracy of such maps depends on the methods employed in their preparation.

Military city maps are topographic maps, usually with a scale of 1:12,500 or 1:25,000, of cities that show important buildings, streets and their names, and other urban data of military significance.

Special maps are prepared for special purposes, such as trafficability, communications, or assaults. These maps usually are overprints of standard topographic maps with data not normally found on standard maps.

Classes of Maps by Use

Administrative maps are used to graphically record information pertaining to administrative matters, such as supply and evacuation installations, personnel and medical installations, straggler and prisoner-of-war collection points, service and maintenance areas, main supply routes, traffic circulation, and similar data.

Battle maps show ground features in sufficient detail for use by all combat forces, usually on a scale of 1:25,000 or 1:50,000.

Controlled maps have precise, or registered, horizontal and vertical ground control as their basis.

General maps have a small scale and are used for general planning purposes.

Line route maps, or map overlays, are used for signal communications operations and show actual routes and types of construction of wire circuits in the field. They also show the locations of telegraph stations and switchboards.

Map charts are representations of sea-land areas. They have the characteristics of a map to represent the land area and the characteristics of a chart to represent the sea area, with special characteristics added to make the map chart useful in military operations, usually amphibious operations.

Operation maps show locations and strengths of friendly forces involved in a given operation. They also may indicate predicted movements and locations of enemy forces.

Situation maps show the tactical, operational, or administrative situation at a given time.

Strategic maps have a medium or smaller scale, and are used for planning operations such as troop movements, concentrations, and logistics operations.

Tactical maps have a large scale and are used for tactical and administrative purposes.

Traffic circulation maps show traffic routes and measures for traffic regulation. They indicate the roads for specific classes of traffic, the locations of traffic control stations, and the directions in which traffic may move. They are also called circulation maps.

Weather maps show prevailing or predicted weather conditions over a large area. They are usually based on weather observations taken at the same time at a number of stations.

Classes of Maps by Scale

Map scale is expressed as the ratio of representational map distance to true ground distance (Fig. 1). Confusion can arise when the terms *small scale*, *medium scale* and *large scale* are read in conjunction with the quantitative scale. Map scale classes and their general uses are:

Small-scale maps. These are maps of 1:600,000 and smaller scale which are used for general planning and for strategic studies. The standard small scale in the U.S. armed forces is 1:1,000,000.

Medium-scale maps. Maps at scales larger than 1:600,000, but smaller than 1:75,000, are used for planning operations such as troop movements and concentrations and logistics operations. The standard U.S. medium scale is 1:250,000.

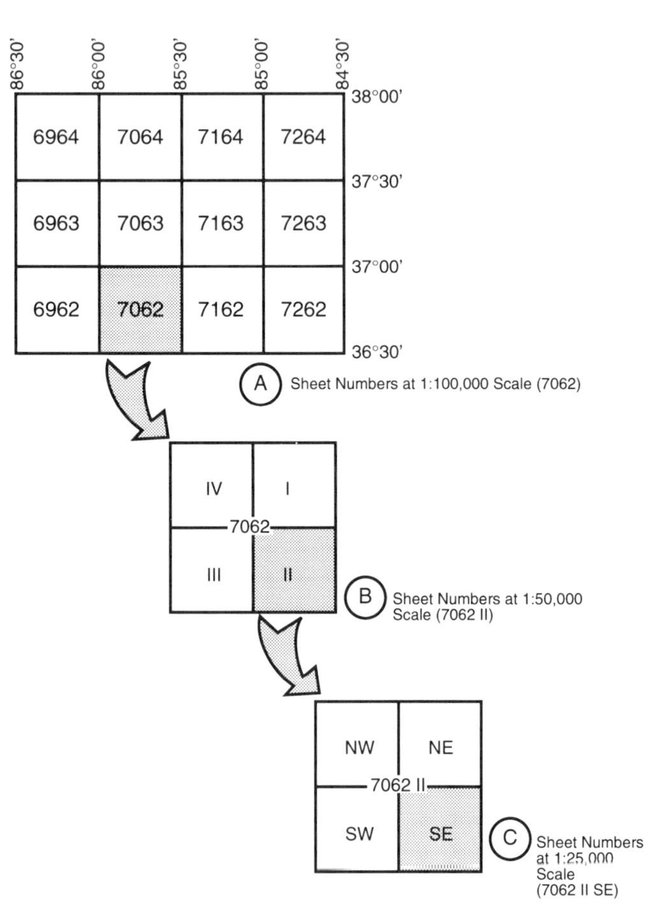

Figure 1. Map identification—1:100,000, 1:50,000, and 1:25,000 scales.

Large-scale maps. Such maps are used to meet the tactical, technical, and administrative requirements of field units. The standard U.S. large scale is 1:50,000.

Topographic Map Colors

Most military maps used in ground operations are topographic maps that differentiate among various types of terrain features through the use of different colors. This also may render the map a more nearly natural representation of the terrain. Colors usually found on North Atlantic Treaty Organization (NATO) maps are:

- Black—the majority of man-made or cultural features.
- Blue—water features such as lakes, rivers, and swamps.
- Green—vegetation such as woods, orchards, and vineyards.
- Brown—all relief features such as contours.
- Red—main roads, built-up areas, and special features.

Other colors are used to show special information on military maps. The meaning of these colors is, as a rule, indicated in the marginal information of the map. An example of such a color is purple, used in aeronautical symbols and related information on joint operations graphics.

Marginal Information

The marginal information found on almost all military maps can be considered a "user's guide" to the map in question. Within NATO most military maps are relatively standardized in their depictions of information, although there are exceptions. These exceptions are pronounced when maps from outside NATO are encountered. Nonetheless, almost all maps, regardless of their country of origin, have marginal information that informs the user of the map's peculiarities; therefore, marginal information on any map should be examined prior to map use. Most Western maps have similar types of marginal information. Some of the more important data elements to be found in marginal information are:

Sheet name. The name of the map sheet is usually found in two places on most military maps: the center of the upper right margin and in the lower right corner. Map sheets are usually named after their most prominent cultural or geographic feature. Usually the name of the largest city or town on the map is used.

Sheet number. The sheet number is usually found in the upper right corner and is used as a reference number for the map sheet. For small-scale maps (1:1,000,000 and larger) sheet numbers are based on an arbitrary system that facilitates the orientation of larger-scale maps.

Series name and scale. These data are normally found in the upper left margin of the map. A margin series usually comprises a group of similar maps with the same scale and format. The series name may also be a group of maps serving a common purpose, such as military city maps. The name of the series is that of the most prominent area.

Series number. This number normally appears in the upper right and lower left margins and is a comprehensive reference expressed either as a four-digit number (e.g., 1215) or as a letter followed by a three- or four-digit number (e.g., M221; R6221).

Edition number. The edition number, usually found in the upper margin and in the lower left margin, gives the age of the map relative to other editions of the same map and the agency responsible for its production. The highest number represents the most recent edition of the map. For example, EDITION 2-DMA indicates the second edition of a map prepared by the United States Defense Mapping Agency. The higher edition number usually supersedes previous editions of the same map.

Bar scales. These scales are usually found in the lower center margin and are used to convert map distance to ground distance. There are usually three or more bar scales, each with a different unit of measure.

Adjoining sheets diagram. Most military maps at standard scales contain a diagram that illustrates the adjoining sheets. On small-scale maps (1:100,000 and larger) the diagram is termed the *Index to Adjoining Sheets* and consists of as many rectangles as required to surround the sheet under consideration. All represented sheets are identified with numbers. Sheets of an adjoining series, which have the same scale, are represented by dashed lines whether they are published or merely planned. On maps of 1:50,000 scale, the sheet number and series number of the 1:250,000 scale map of the area are also shown below the Index to Adjoining Sheets.

Legend. The legend is located in the lower left margin of the map. It identifies and illustrates the topographic symbols used to depict the most common features on the map. Symbols are not always the same, hence the legend is critical to avoid errors in use.

Declination diagram. In large-scale maps, this diagram is located in the lower margin. It indicates the angular relationships of true north, magnetic north, and grid north. This diagram is crucial to using the map, as the map must always be aligned with the earth's surface prior to use by orienting it on the correct north-south ground alignment through the use of a compass. On maps of 1:250,000 scale this information is stated in a note in the lower margin.

Contour interval. This information appears in the center of the lower margin and states the vertical distance between adjacent contour lines on the map. It is an important datum, as it allows the user a ready means of computing his elevation.

The foregoing items of marginal information are only the most important ones; there are many data in the margins of military maps which the user must consider. A more detailed coverage of marginal information may be found in military map reading manuals, such as the U.S. Army's *Field Manual 21–26.*

Map Grids

To use a map to determine one's position, a precise location system is required. Such a system should:

- require no knowledge of the geographic area in question.
- be applicable to large areas.
- require no landmarks.
- be applicable to all map scales.
- be simple to understand and use.

The traditional geographic coordinate system based on meridians of longitude and parallels of latitude has long been used for navigation at sea and in small-scale maps (Fig. 2). Both latitude and longitude represent a circle drawn around the earth; geographic coordinates are expressed in angular measurement. Each circle is divided into 360 degrees, each degree into 60 minutes, and each

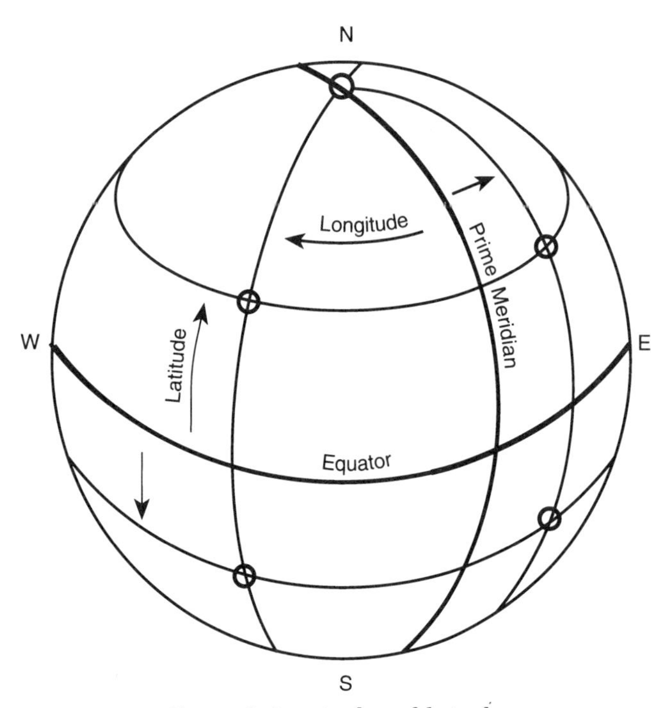

Figure 2. Longitude and latitude.

minute into seconds. Longitude is measured east or west from the prime meridian at Greenwich, England; latitude is measured north or south from the earth's equator. It should be noted that many nations outside NATO do not use the Greenwich meridian as standard. While longitude and latitude are satisfactory for naval operations, there are two disadvantages to using this system for ground operations. First, latitude and longitude are curved lines, and second, the smallest subdivision of either is the second, which is accurate to only 24 meters (75 ft.). The curvature of the lines of longitude and latitude also cause quadrangles formed by the intersection of the parallels to be different sizes and shapes, which complicates measuring directions and locating points. Further, 24-meter (75-ft.) accuracy is not sufficiently precise for all military ground operations. Military grids overcome these problems, although longitude and latitude usually are also indicated on military maps.

Military grids are no more than a rectangular grid superimposed on the transverse Mercator projection normally used in military maps. The universal transverse Mercator (UTM) grid covers the earth between 84 degrees north and 80 degrees south latitude (Fig. 3). As its name implies, it is superimposed over the transverse Mercator projection. The earth has 60 UTM zones and the grid is identical in each. Base values in meters are assigned to the central meridian and to the equator, and the grid lines are fixed in parallel to these base lines. Each grid line is given a value indicating its distance from the origin. Each grid zone between 84 degrees north and 80 degrees south is 6×8 or 6×12 degrees of latitude and longitude in size, is given a designation (Fig. 4), and is further subdivided into 100,000-meter squares. Each

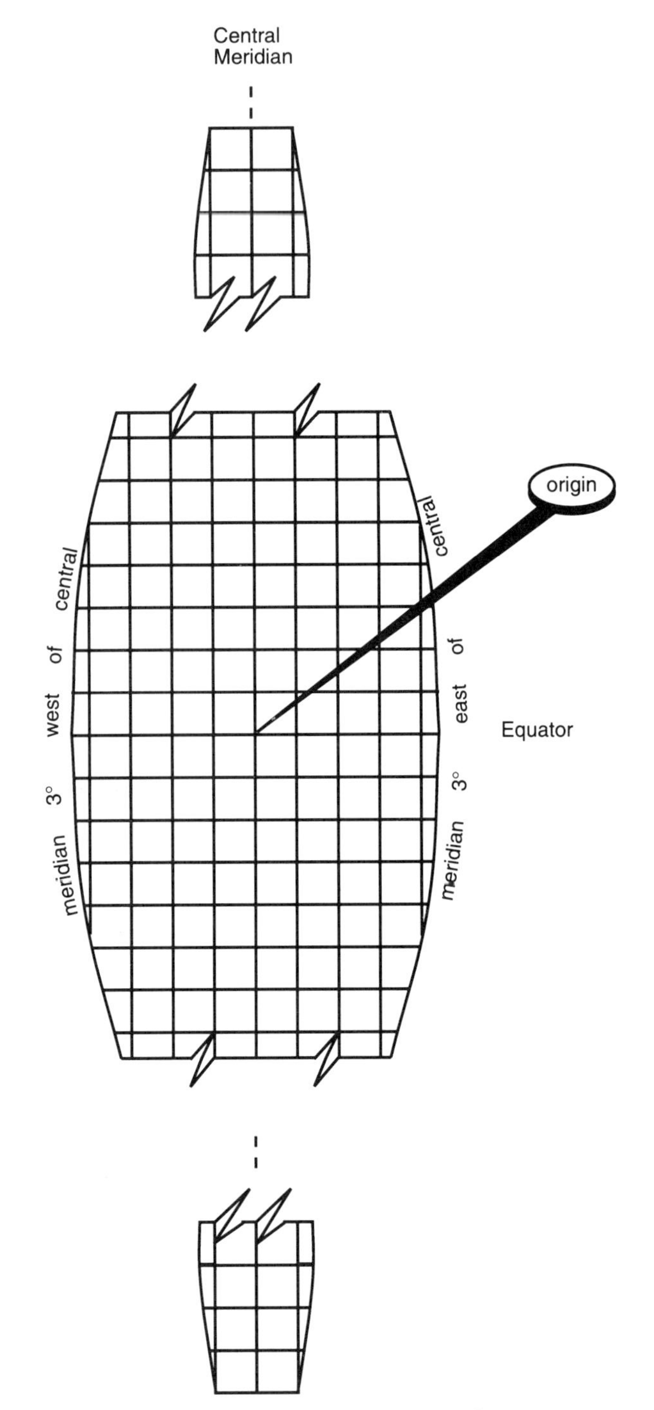

Figure 3. Representative UTM grid zone.

100,000-meter square is identified by a pair of letters that is unique within the area covered by the grid zone designation (Fig. 5). The identification of the 100,000-meter square identification letters usually is shown in the marginal information on most NATO military maps. This system ensures that no two locations can be located at the same point on the earth. Military maps are broken down from 100,000-meter squares through 1:50,000- and 1:25,000-scale sheets (see Fig. 1).

The regularly spaced grid lines that appear on all large-scale military maps are divisions of the 100,000-meter

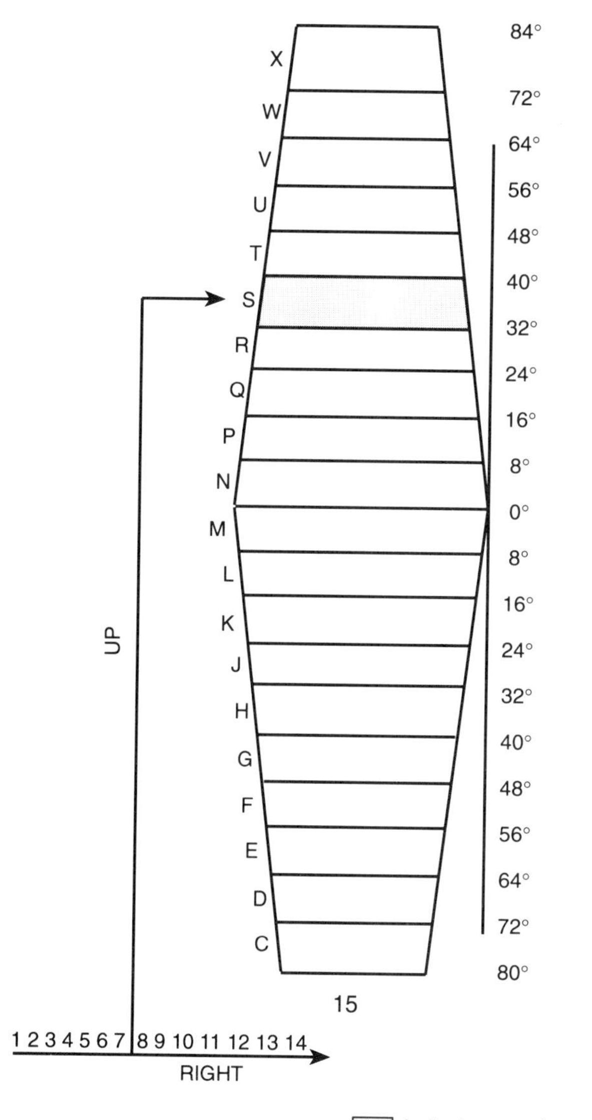

Figure 4. Grid zone designation.

square and are spaced at 1,000- or 10,000-meter intervals. Each grid line has a specific designation that can be used to pinpoint one's location. Most Western grid references are read from left to right, then up.

Military Symbols

Military symbols are graphic aids used on maps to identify items of operational interest. The keys to good military symbols are simplicity, uniformity, and clarity. Symbols are used to depict both friendly and enemy units, weapons, equipment, and activities. Within NATO, military symbols are governed by a standardization agreement (STANAG 2019) that generally defines the usage of symbols throughout the alliance, although there are variations.

Military symbols provide an easily recognizable means to express an operational plan, concept, or situation on a map. Under ideal conditions, colors are used to distinguish among friendly, enemy, and other symbols. The colors used within NATO are:

- Black or Blue—Friendly units, weapons, activities, and ground environment symbols not encompassed by other colors.
- Red—Enemy units, weapons, and activities.
- Yellow—Chemical, radiological, or biological areas, whether friendly or enemy.
- Green—Man-made obstacles, whether friendly or enemy.

Within NATO, fields around the basic symbol are used to display specific data regarding the symbol in question. The use of fields is necessary to clarify the status of the unit, weapon, or equipment depicted by the basic symbol.

Military symbols consist of a basic designator that indicates the type of organization represented, an interservice symbol, a size symbol, a unit role symbol, an equipment indicator, and various fields surrounding the basic symbol to further clarify and specify its identity. Representative NATO/U.S. military symbols are presented in Figures 6 through 10.

CHARLES Q. CUTSHAW

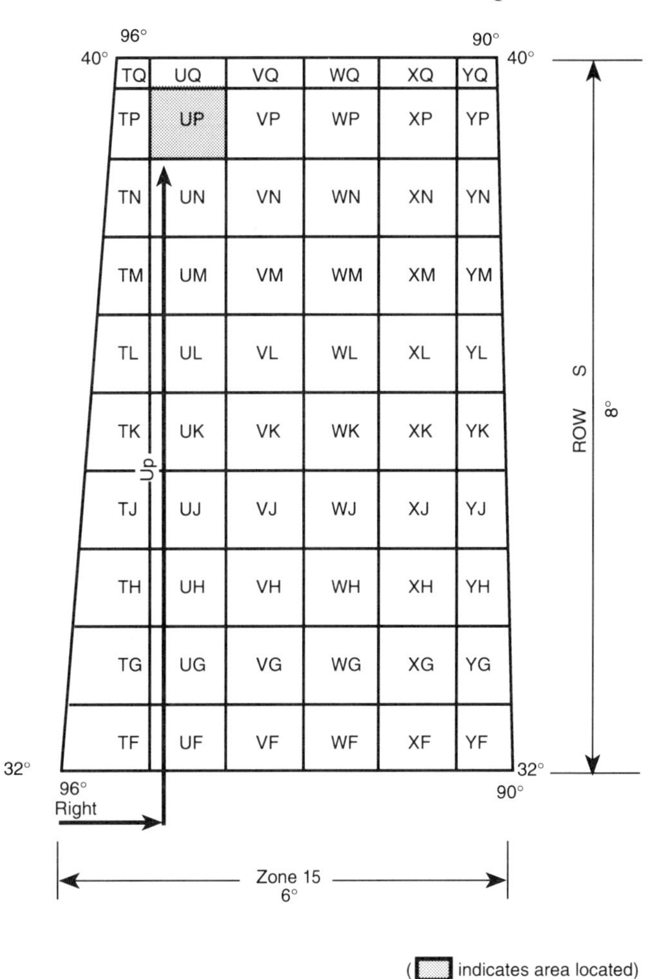

Figure 5. 100,000-meter square representative designation.

Description	Symbol
Unit	
Headquarters	
Logistical, medical, or administrative installation	
Combat service support element of a U.S. combat unit (brigade trains and below)	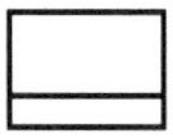
Armor	
Armored cavalry	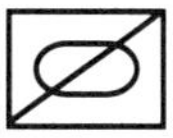
Airborne (normally associated with another brach/functional symbol)	U.S.  NATO 
Air assault (units organic or assigned to air assault divisions and trained in air assault operations but without sufficent aircraft to perform air assault missions	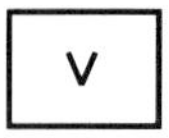  V
Air cavalry	
Air defense	
Amphibious	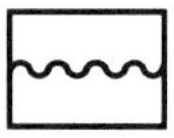
Antiarmor	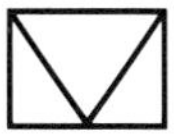

Description	Symbol
Engineer	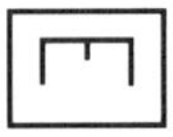
Electronic Warfare	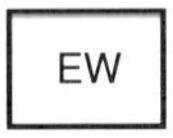 EW
Field Artillery	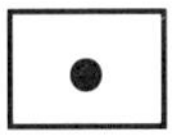
Infantry	
Infantry, Mechanized APC	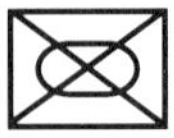
Maintenance	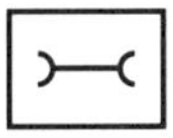
Medical	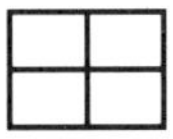
Ordnance	
Psychological operations	
Quartermaster	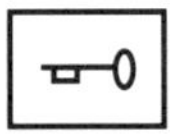
Signal/communications	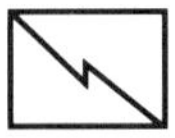
Surface-to-air missile	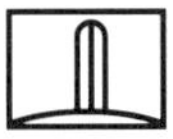

Figure 6. Basic military symbols.

Description	Symbol
Class I—Subsistence	
Class II—Clothing, individual equipment, tentage, organizational tool sets	
Class III–POL Air Force	
Class IV—Construction	
Class V—Ammunition All types (less special)	
Class VI—Personal demand	
Class VII—Major end items	
Class VIII—Medical materiel	
Class IX—Repair parts	
Class X—Material to support nonmilitary programs	CA

Figure 7. Logistics role indicators.

Symbol	Description
XXXX 8	Combat arms regimental system (CARS) Eighth Army
XXX 3	III Corps
XX 10 3/8	10th Infantry Divsion, III Corps, Eighth Army
X 1 10/3	1st Brigade, 10th Infantry Divsion, III Corps
II 2-15 1/10/3	2d Battalion, 15th Infantry, 1st Brigade, 10th Infantry Division, III Corps
I A 2–15/1/10	A company, 2d Battalion, 15th Infantry, 1st Brigade, 10th Infantry Division
●●● 2 XX A/2-15/10	2d Platoon, A Company, 2d Battalion, 15th Infantry, 10th Infantry Division
● 1 2/A/2–15	1st Squad, 2d Platoon, A Company, 2d Battalion, 15th Infantry

Figure 8. Representative fields for military symbols.

Weapons. Symbols are used to indicate the type and location of a weapon or group of weapons. When a weapon symbol appears on a map or overlay, the base of the shaft indicates the location of the weapon. To show the approximate size of a particular weapon, the procedure is as follows:

Select the appropriate weapon symbol.

(light automatic weapon)	(gun)

Add horizontal bars (one for medium or two for heavy) to denote the size.

(medium machine gun)	(heavy gun)

If a weapon has a high trajectory, a ○ is placed at the base of the shaft.
If the weapon has a flat trajectory, a ∧ is placed at the base of the shaft.

(medium mortar)	(light antitank gun)

If the weapon is primarily for air defense, a ⌓ is placed at the base of the shaft.

(air defense missile)	(air defense gun)

If the weapon is rocket launched, a ⩓ is placed at the head of the shaft.
If a weapon is also tracked, self-propelled vehicle, a ⬭ is placed below the weapon symbol.

(rocket launcher)	(a tracked, self-propelled medium howitzer

Figure 9. Representative equipment symbols.

U.S. Description	STANAG 2019 Description	Symbol
Squad/crew	Smallest unit/UK section	●
Section unit larger than a squad but smaller than a platoon	Unit larger than a U.S. squad/UK section but smaller than a platoon equivalent	●●
Platoon or detachment	Platoon/troop equivalent	●●●
Company, battery, or troop	Company/battery/squadron equivalent	I
Battalion or squadron	Battalion equivalent	II
Group or regiment	Regiment/group equivalent	III
Brigade	Brigade equivalent	X
Division	Division	XX
Corps	Corps	XXX
Army	Army	XXXX

Figure 10. Unit size designations.

SEE ALSO: Geography, Military; Meteorology, Military; Theater of War.

Bibliography

Pombrik, I. D., and A. N. Shevchenko. 1985. *Karta ofitsera* (The officer's map). Moscow: Military Publishing House.

U.S. Army. n.d. Field Manual 21–26. *Map reading.* Washington, D.C.: Headquarters, Department of the Army.

U.S. Defense Intelligence Agency (DIA). 1978. DDB-2680-41-78. *Handbook of Soviet armed forces military symbols.* Washington, D.C.: Defense Intelligence Agency.

MARINE

The term *marine* refers to a military person who serves on board warships or operates in close conjunction with naval forces, generally as the land fighting element of a naval force. The term refers to both officers and enlisted personnel, including noncommissioned officers. In French, the equivalent term is *marin fusilier,* which has been shortened simply to *marine* in many countries. The term *naval infantry* is also used for troops that accompany and fight as parts of naval forces.

The first navies were really armies on ships. The sailors ran the ships, and the forebears of the marines did the fighting. In ancient warfare, circa 500 B.C., these were the Greek *epibatae,* or heavily armed sea soldiers. Later Roman warships carried "soldiers of the sea." During the Middle Ages, nations did not maintain organized navies and marine forces, but ordinary soldiers were put aboard ships whenever fighting was expected. In the 1600s, both Great Britain and the Netherlands realized the need for regular troops aboard their men-of-war. The British formed a corps of marines in 1664; the Dutch, in 1665. The American Continental Congress authorized a Marine Corps on 10 November 1775 in the first year of the American Revolutionary War (Fig. 1).

During the days of sailing ships, marines were stationed in the rigging and in the "fighting tops" of the masts, armed with muskets and rifles to snipe at crews in opposing ships. They were expected also to repel boarders. As the combat distance between ships increased in the mid-nineteenth century because of the greater range of naval guns, the use of marines in this manner was no longer needed. Marines were used to serve as a security force to maintain order on ships and to provide each warship with a small landing force for military operations on shore. Several warships operating together could put together a sizable expeditionary force of marines for raids and limited-objective attacks.

Figure 1. Landing at New Providence, 3 March 1776. The Continental Marines (U.S.) in their first amphibious assault, led by Marine Captain Samuel Nicholas. (SOURCE: USMC Historical Section)

During the twentieth century, marines have often been used as relatively small elite forces for combat missions requiring great skill and daring. They have also been specialists in amphibious warfare. The role varies from nation to nation. The Soviets maintained several regiments of naval infantry, primarily in the Baltic Sea, presumably for amphibious operations. The Royal Marines of the United Kingdom are a relatively small force designed to operate with the Royal Navy. The U.S. Marine Corps is a large force with three active and one reserve infantry divisions and a substantial air wing of combat aircraft and helicopters for each division. The role of the U.S. Marine Corps is to provide expeditionary elements of naval forces and carry out major combat missions, including amphibious assault if required.

ROBERT F. LOCKMAN

SEE ALSO: Amphibious Forces; Enlisted Personnel.

MARITIME LOGISTICS

Maritime logistics is that part of the sustainment of a nation at war that is by the seas. Of the four elements of logistics—procurement, distribution, maintenance, and replacement of material and personnel—the emphasis of maritime logistics has been on distribution, or simply transport on the high seas. Transportation by ships at sea and on inland waters and rivers has been and remains prominent in peace and war not only because the oceans cover 70 percent of the earth's surface, but also because ships are by far the most economical means of shipment. Merchant ship transport is even superior to rail or truck for bulk cargoes on coastal routes when ships are an alternative. When rapid delivery is an urgent consideration, compact goods are shipped by air, but in peace or war, air transport will deliver only a small fraction—less than 5 percent—of all materials.

Indeed, naval warfare can profitably be studied and interpreted entirely in the context of the attack, defense, exploitation, and denial of the sea lines of communications. The strategic implications were established a century ago, starting with A. T. Mahan's *The Influence of Sea Power Upon History 1660–1783* (1890). Mahan treated maritime logistics as a central theme because in war the interruption of trade, especially by blockade, has a deep-seated effect on the morale of a nation and its material ability to conduct a war. Sir Julian Corbett's *Some Principles of Maritime Strategy* extended Mahan's historical approach and is the seminal work on maritime theory. "Command of the sea," wrote Corbett, "means nothing but the control of maritime communications, whether for commercial or military purposes. The object of naval warfare is the control of communications." (1988, p. 94). A review of contemporary thought reaffirms Corbett's perspective (see, e.g., Till 1984).

The success of naval strategy has been and still is measured by the extent to which seapower influences the movement of the strategic materials and ground forces of the contending sides. As one author observed regarding the operations analysis of the two great U-boat campaigns against North Atlantic shipping,

> The navy's problem in protecting merchant shipping was not underseas warfare, but overseas transport. This did not diminish the strong emphasis on antisubmarine measures but did effectively set them in a wider context. It suggested studies of methods of decreasing turnaround time in ports, placing valuable cargoes in the least vulnerable positions in a convoy, analysis of unorthodox high-speed merchant ships, and the like. (Whitmore 1961)

This context is still valid, and the essential issue remains efficient maritime logistics.

Since World War II the projection of seapower over land by direct attack has achieved more prominence. Nevertheless, Corbett's sweeping conclusion that the strategic aim of naval warfare is the control of communications still lies at the heart of all strategic planning.

From another perspective, maritime logistics acts as the great and sobering constraint on naval operations, that is, on the execution of strategy and campaign plans. (Operational planning is about 90% logistical planning.) The ability to support distant movement and sustained operations of combat forces delimits their objectives as much as does the fighting power of the enemy. (The sustainment of a navy is termed *naval logistics*.)

WAYNE P. HUGHES, JR.
MARK L. MITCHELL

SEE ALSO: Antisubmarine Warfare; Blockade and Maritime Exclusion; Logistics, Naval; Mahan, Alfred Thayer; Maritime Strategy; Naval Warfare; Sea Control and Denial; Submarine.

Bibliography

Corbett, J. S., [1911] 1988. *Some principles of maritime strategy*. Reprint. Annapolis, Md.: U.S. Naval Institute Press.
Eccles, H. E. 1950. *Operational naval logistics*. Washington, D.C.: Government Printing Office.
Mahan, A. T. 1890. *The influence of sea power upon history 1660–1783*. Boston, Mass.: Little, Brown.
Till, G. 1984. *Maritime strategy and the nuclear age*. New York: St. Martin's Press.
Whitmore, W. F. 1961. Military operations research—A personal retrospect. *Operations Research* 9(2):258–65.

MARITIME STRATEGY

Maritime strategy concerns the use of the sea for support of national or alliance policies in peace and war. Such strategy encompasses the maritime aspects of war as well as security in time of peace. It is true that maritime strategy has its practical expression in the control of seaborne communications. Similarly, as Alfred T. Mahan insisted, there is a strategic value and use for command of the sea which is achieved and enforced by a superior battle fleet.

Maritime strategy uses seapower broadly, and naval forces (and naval strategy) narrowly. But maritime strategy is a more inclusive concept than seapower or naval strategy. With some reservations—for example, the offensive spirit, morale, and fighting power—naval tactics must be unique to the technology of the era in question (see Keegan 1989). The naval tactics of the battles of Cape St. Vincent (1797) and Trafalgar (1805), for example, are as irrelevant to sailors today as the tactics employed at Sluys (1340) or Salamis (480 B.C.). It is indeed interesting to ask how ships were designed, maintained, and fought, both individually and as a fleet. However, maritime strategy concerns the policy behind the use of ships, naval bases, naval engagements, and all other aspects of maritime activity.

National and alliance security today has four areas of concern—land, sea, air, and space. Navies pursue naval objectives but those objectives have value only in terms of their strategic effectiveness for the preservation of peace, the successful prosecution of war, or some other policy objective. Maritime strategy is often used to advance policy goals that far transcend the sea. Although a navy may fight for the right to use the seas at will, maritime passage does not have strategic value in and of itself. The question is how can one use freedom of maritime passage?

After May 1943, when Grand Admiral Doenitz withdrew the U-boat wolfpacks from the North Atlantic, the Allies enjoyed an unusual degree of maritime and maritime-air supremacy. The forces of the Third Reich, however, still had to be driven back from the beaches in Sicily, Italy, and France, and rolled back from the steppes. Thus, although control of the sea in critical areas is a precondition for success in war, it is only a precondition.

The subject was described well by Julian Corbett in his 1911 book, *Some Principles of Maritime Strategy:*

> By maritime strategy we mean the principles which govern a war in which the sea is a substantial factor. Naval strategy is but that part of it which determines the movements of the fleet when maritime strategy has determined what part the fleet must play in relation to the action of the land forces; for it scarcely needs saying that it is almost impossible that a war can be decided by naval action alone.

Scope and Significance

A first-class navy is expensive and difficult to acquire and maintain. Even second-class naval capabilities are not easily obtained. Land-minded, continental powers will not have prominent maritime elements in their national military strategies, but they have often used maritime strategy to supplement their continental strategy. For example, geography has obliged both Germany and the former Soviet Union to attend first to their land-based fighting power. The military fortunes of both these continental nations, however, were strongly influenced in this century by events at sea. It is questionable if Stalin's USSR could have defeated the Third Reich without the distraction of German and other Axis assets to the south and west, and the lend-lease aid by sea from North America. Germany tried twice in this century to win a war by action at sea (1917 and 1942–43) after its failure to secure victory by swift campaigns on land.

Maritime strategy is most prominent in the defense arrangements of traditionally sea-dependent countries or coalitions. Such a strategy, however, does not imply the dominance of maritime over land, air, or space elements in national military strategy. A predominantly continental state or coalition may need maritime strategy to thwart the sea-based military strategy of a maritime enemy. This point has been true for all of the great coalition wars of modern history, from the War of the League of Augsburg (Nine-Years War, 1689–97), through World War II, to the structure of deterrence and counterdeterrence between East and West in the 1980s. Just as sea powers need to be reminded from time to time that continental powers are not readily susceptible to defeat at sea, so continental powers have had to learn and relearn the maxim that—as a general rule—sea powers have to be defeated at sea.

The subject of maritime strategy is best approached by recalling Mahan's characterization of the sea as a "great highway" and "a wide common"; and by J. H. Parry's reminder (1974) that "[a]ll the seas of the world are one." In his turn, Corbett (1911) argued that "[c]ommand of the sea, therefore, means nothing but the control of maritime communications, whether for commercial or military purposes. The object of naval warfare is the control of communications, and not, as in land warfare, the conquest of territory. The difference is fundamental."

Strategically, the sea has value because it connects—or can divide—land areas. The physical geography of the world's oceans and landforms, as Parry notes, means that the ability to use the "great highway" literally can accord a global mobility (modified by technological considerations). The coalitions that defeated the Central (1914–18) and the Axis powers (1939–45) did not succeed simply because their lines of communication were maritime rather than continental. Maritime dependence is always a potentially fatal weakness for a sea-based power—as Imperial Athens discovered in 404 B.C. and Britain almost discovered in 1917, 1941, and 1943. There are reasons why sea-dependent countries are better able to defend their interests at sea than continental powers are able to threaten those interests. But nothing in history—ancient, medieval, or modern—suggests that sea powers must win at sea, any more than land powers must win on land. If that were the case, history would show a series of stalemates between the "tiger" and the "shark."

In practice, maritime strength is complementary to other strengths, just as maritime strategy is complementary to other strategies. It is not the job of the maritime strategist to design schemes for seapower to deter or win a war. Rather, the job of that strategist is to explain how seapower can make the maximum contribution at the least cost to achieve the country's policy goals. In other words, maritime strategy is geographically circumscribed, but its strategic significance transcends geography.

For example, the maritime strategy of the United States and the North Atlantic Treaty Organization (NATO) envisaged the possibility of early offensive operations in the Norwegian Sea and beyond. Such hypothetical operations have only instrumental value: to narrow Soviet strategic choices and to preclude a third battle of the Atlantic; to alter favorably the strategic-nuclear balance; to support Norway, Britain, and Iceland; to press the Soviet military frontier backwards; and to diminish any optimism in Moscow over the likely outcome of a long war. What would be at stake would not be control of the Norwegian Sea, but what the ability to use the Norwegian Sea could mean for the successful prosecution of the war. During a conflict, battles and campaigns should be waged only with reference to policy purposes.

For somewhat similar reasons of geography both Germany and Israel have demonstrated skill in winning battles and campaigns. But, neither has an enviable record in waging and winning wars as a whole. Indeed, there is some truth in the adage that nothing fails like success. The scale of the German military crisis of 1942–43 was multiplied by the very scale of territorial conquest; while the Israeli victory in the Six Days War of 1967 has produced negative long-term consequences for Israel's national security.

The scope and significance of maritime strategy will vary in detail from era to era and conflict to conflict. It is no exaggeration, however, to say that from the sixteenth century to modern times, maritime strategy has repeatedly shaped the "general course and character" of war (Cruttwell, 1936). It is not an accident that great continental states or coalitions have never achieved an outcome better than a draw (1697, War of the League of Augsburg; and 1748, War of Austrian Succession) in armed struggles with maritime-led coalitions. The significance of maritime strategy is not that superior seapower has won wars, but seapower enabled wars to be won.

How Does Maritime Strategy "Work"?

Maritime strategy works by helping shape a course in conflict so that the enemy is systematically disadvantaged. It is not seapower that can accomplish this, but superior—or the superior use of—seapower. For example, although the strategic and operational direction of Germany's High Seas Fleet was very poor in 1914 and 1915, the deficient relative strength of that fleet meant that its guiding concept—quite contrary to service doctrine—had to be restricted to that of a rather passive "fleet in being."

Maritime strategy is about the uses of seapower, not about ships or naval battles. Nonetheless, sound strategy can always be thwarted by tactical impossibilities. The French navy, during the second Hundred Years' War (1689–1815), was superior to Britain's in ship design and construction, and in sophistication of naval tactical thought. However, a lack of qualified personnel forced the French navy to learn that strategically ambitious use of the sea must be founded upon an excellent naval fighting instrument.

Maritime strategy per se is neutral in regard to the combat value of a navy. But, it is self-evident that if a country or coalition has a navy incapable of accepting battle on almost any terms (except perhaps in heavily fortified coastal bastion areas), the "wide common" of the sea can be used only at enormous risk or at the sufferance of the enemy. For example, France could not invade Britain unless the French navy was capable of facing the Royal Navy in battle. There were many official schemes hatched in Paris to evade that point, and some of them had theoretical merit. As Corbett observed, however, invasion over an uncommanded sea is not a practicable operation of war. Adolf Hitler agreed in 1940.

The relative significance of the maritime element in war can range from the insignificant (e.g., the Franco-Prussian War of 1870–71) to the all-embracing (e.g., the Pacific War of 1941–45 and the Falklands/Malvinas War of 1982). The potential for maritime strategy to have specific effects depends upon the geography of the conflict and the policy objectives of the rivals. Similarly, there is no single correct all-purpose maritime strategy. For example, people with an Anglo-American background think of maritime strategy as synonymous with the purposes and methods of the Royal Navy from the Dutch Wars to 1918, and with the plans and ideas of the U.S. Navy since that date. Such a view is not incorrect, but it ignores the maritime perspectives of countries unaccustomed to the exercise of first-class naval power.

Six Contributions of Maritime Strategy

It is useful to isolate six important contributions that maritime strategy can make to the successful prosecution of conflict, or to deterrence. These contributions apply more to countries and coalitions with superior fighting strength at sea than they do to continental powers that are trying to make optimum use of second-class (or lower) naval power.

First, maritime strategy wields time as a weapon of war or as a factor in the deterrence of war. Superior seapower provides the material for a theory of success in a prolonged war. In the classic age of "fighting sail" prior to the

French Revolution, British strategy in wars against France was one of financial attrition. Although France was larger and physically more richly endowed, the British institutions for public credit were greatly superior, success in maritime conflict tended to be self-financing, and the cost of supporting large armies year after year was devastating to the French royal treasury. The American Revolution made an enormous contribution to the genesis of the French Revolution. Aside from the inspiration of the American example, the French conduct of hostilities against Britain from 1778 to 1783 bankrupted the French treasury and set in motion the calling of the States-General and the ensuing upheavals.

Seapower directed by a concept of maritime strategy is effective only on a timescale of years because seapower works slowly upon the will and ability of an enemy to prosecute a war. That is, maritime strategy provides for the gradual debilitation of the foe. It is paradoxical that truly major sea battles (Trafalgar, Jutland, Midway) have occupied only a few hours.

The point here is not to argue that maritime strategy must be a strategy for success in a long war, but rather that superiority in seapower maximizes the prospects for success. More often than not, the state or coalition that is highly dependent upon maritime power lacks plausible options for victory in a short war.

The validity of this argument is not limited to a particular period or periods in history. Maritime strategy worked for Britain in the eighteenth century to effect the financial embarrassment of the French state and in the early twentieth century worked to effect the material embarrassment of a German empire whose industrially and agriculturally based war machine was starved of necessary supplies.

Second, the continuity of the world's oceans and seas lends itself to a geographically inclusive, rather than exclusive, perspective for maritime strategy. The presence of a powerful navy and the subsequent strong representation of maritime points of view in the government do not necessarily mean that a war will be waged in a geographically extensive manner. However, it is by the very nature of the sea (its continuity), of seapower, and of the way sea lines of communication can serve national strategy that maritime strategy will encourage exploitation of the lines of communication, and the extent of those lines will suggest a geographic widening of the conflict.

The country or coalition that can secure working control of the sea lanes is liberated from continental confinement and can work to isolate the military assets of the enemy. Critics of the so-called "blue-water" strategy have noted that maritime strategists, in their preference for geographically extensive conflict, show an unwillingness to face the main strength of an enemy on land. These critics also note that the geographic extension of war that sea superiority permits can lead to a pointless dispersion of scarce national resources. Although these points are occasionally true, they cannot invalidate the argument that maritime strategy for a superior seapower can provide valuable and effective war-widening opportunities. The soundness of a proposal to widen a conflict geographically must be evaluated for each case. Maritime strategy is only one component of national or coalition strategy.

Third, maritime strategy with superior seapower can cause a fatal overextension on land by frustrated continental powers. The maritime element of national strategy so limits the enemy's operational choices (i.e., he may triumph to the water's edge, but what then?) that, in the hope of a war-winning stroke, the continental power may undertake more than it can achieve on land. This was what caused the downfall of Napoleon and Hitler.

Great states and coalitions are never equally competent on land and at sea. Their strategic geography forces them to prioritize their efforts in different military environments. In the early stages of a conflict, continental states will perform well on land and maritime states will perform well at sea. The struggle centers around how each side can use its particular strength (strategic power and effectiveness) to achieve an effective winning quantity and quality. In modern times, maritime powers have recovered better from disasters on land (although sometimes recovery occurred over the course of years; e.g., the events of 1803–1814) than continental powers have recovered from, or found ways to offset, near-exclusion from the high seas.

It has never been the expressed purpose of the maritime element of a national or coalition military strategy to frustrate a continental foe at the water's edge so that he will then overextend himself on land. The continental allies of maritime powers would not be enthusiastic about their role in such a strategy nor would they appreciate the implied pessimism about short-term (i.e., land-based) military prospects. On the other hand, the historical examples of maritime strategy frustrating continental foes, which then proceed to overextend themselves on land, are obvious.

Fourth, maritime strategy can unite materially superior coalitions to their mutual benefit to deter or conduct a war. Their national security can be augmented by the mobilization of friendly states on a global basis. Control of the sea means access to the strategic assets of virtually the entire world. The United States, Britain, and the USSR were enabled by their seapower to wage global war with a global strategy against the Axis powers. As Herbert Rosinski wrote in 1944: "[In] global war, merchant shipping is the ultimate key to strategy" (Rosinski 1977).

In any conflict, extensive or limited, between countries large or small, the ability to use sea lines of communication and the ability to deny such use to the enemy, can shape the course and outcome of the conflict. However, control of the sea lines of communication is not invariably a war-winning asset. For example, the United States had complete control off the coasts of Korea (1950–53) and North and South Vietnam (1965–73), but these countries are not islands, and could not be defeated from the sea alone.

Fifth, maritime strategy provides unique qualities of mobility and flexibility to the national strategy of a maritime power. Mobility lies in the very nature of maritime power and with the extent and interconnections of the world's oceans and seas. The flexibility provided to a maritime power cannot be matched by territorially limited land power, by land-based airpower (restricted by fixed-site airfields), or by space power (limited by the physical laws of orbital motion). Endowed with this mobility and flexibility, naval forces can threaten several objectives, can be switched from one operation to another and back again, and can be hidden from view in the vastness of the oceans. Sensors in space pose a growing threat to the security of surface ships, but a mixture of active and passive countermeasures should prevent any guaranteed-effective wide-area ocean surveillance.

As a result of the flexibility accorded to a superior maritime power, Adolf Hitler was obliged to fortify and garrison the entire shoreline of northern, western, and southern Europe (late 1942, 1943, and early 1944) because he did not know where the maritime assault by the Allies would take place. Thus, while large German garrisons sat idle on the shores of Europe (e.g., Norway and Greece), the eastern front disintegrated for lack of men and equipment—a testament to the potency and flexibility of maritime power.

Sixth, maritime strategy has a unique ability either to connect or isolate territories. Mahan wrote in 1890 that "travel and traffic by water have always been easier and cheaper than by land," a statement that was undermined even as he wrote by the growth of railroads and later by the use of the internal combustion engine for long-haul transportation. However, much of the world's land area remains poorly served by all-weather roads or by ample rail networks, while the transport of bulk cargoes by sea far surpasses transport by air.

The strong maritime element in U.S. national military strategy provides for the interconnectedness of North America with the other continents that is critical for Western security. As with the Anglo-American alliance of 1941–45, the Western alliance today is enabled by its superiority at sea to plan operationally and strategically in global terms. The sea itself is neutral—as is the concept of seapower. It is not the sea or seapower that connects the United States with NATO in Europe, with Israel, with Japan, China, and Australia. If an enemy state or coalition deployed a superior fighting instrument at sea, the sea lines of communication of the Western world would be broken.

Maritime strategy explains how sea lines of communication help shape a structure for deterrence or military conduct in action that will achieve the ends set by policy. In and of themselves, and particularly over a short time period, open sea lines of communication have no particular strategic meaning. The question is how they can be used. As an example, in late May–early June 1940, the Royal Navy (with some French assistance) used its not undisputed, but still real, command of the narrow seas to evacuate the British Expeditionary Force and many French soldiers from an operationally impossible situation in Flanders. That maritime command could have been used to rapidly redeploy large numbers of well-equipped British forces from the home islands (and elsewhere) to join in the Battle of France. Those British forces did not exist, however, and the fact that the Royal Navy could have ensured their safe transit to French Atlantic ports was therefore irrelevant.

The Continuing Utility of Maritime Strategy

While the details of maritime architecture and naval tactics have evolved and changed radically, the relevance and content of maritime strategy have undergone very little change over the millennia. Donald Kagan wrote that the Peloponnesian War "was one of those classic confrontations between a great land power and a great naval power. . . . To win, each had to acquire the capacity to fight and succeed on the other's favorite domain" (1987). Those words could be applied to the Anglo–French contest in the eighteenth century (particularly to the struggle against revolutionary and Napoleonic France), to Anglo–German strategic relations from the early 1900s to the 1940s, and to Soviet–American strategic relations after 1945. The strategic uses of seapower in war for the United States today would—with the exception of truly long-range nuclear bombardment—be entirely comprehensible to Pericles, to Pitt the Elder, to Mahan, or to Fleet Adm. Ernest King.

Briefly, maritime strategy provides for: security in the supply and resupply of the homeland and of allies overseas; the denial of uncontested sea passage to enemies or to neutrals carrying supplies to enemies; the raiding and threatening of accessible enemy coastlines; and the seizure and occupation of coastal targets of opportunity (or the threat of seizure and occupation). Maritime strategy is about the use, and the purposeful denial of use, of the seas in times of peace and war.

Two effectively insular powers at war—the Dutch Republic and England in the first two of their three wars in the seventeenth century—might have had a national military strategy that was nearly synonymous with maritime strategy. But in most historical cases, maritime strategy is subordinate to national military strategy, which in turn is subordinate to a grand strategy guided by policy. Thus, maritime strategy can rarely be concerned with the success of war or deterrence strictly through maritime action. Instead, the subject of maritime strategy is how best to use the sea to deter or to win in crisis or war.

The structure and content of maritime strategies must vary from country to country and from situation to situation, but the nature and purposes of that strategy are generally the same over time and among policies of very different strengths. Everything said here with explicit reference to Britain or the United States about the relationship of maritime strategy to national military strategy and to policy holds true for all other countries, large and small, maritime or continental in orientation. India, Pakistan, Israel, Indonesia, and so forth—all require a maritime dimension to their national strategies. Physical and political geography, and their strategic relations, mandate that maritime strategy will be studied and practiced for as long as there is a need for strategy.

COLIN S. GRAY

SEE ALSO: Amphibious Warfare; Antisubmarine Warfare; Blockade and Maritime Exclusion; Convoy and Protection of Shipping; Gunboat Diplomacy; Naval Forces; Naval Warfare; Sea Control and Denial; Seapower.

Bibliography

Barnett, R. W., and C. S. Gray, eds. 1989. *Seapower and strategy.* Annapolis: U.S. Naval Institute Press.
Baugh, D. A. 1987. British strategy during the First World War in the context of four centuries: Blue-water versus continental commitment. In *Naval history: The sixth symposium of the U.S. Naval Academy,* ed. D. M. Masterson. Wilmington, Del.: Scholarly Resources.
Brewer, J. 1989. *The sinews of power: War, money, and the English state, 1688–1783.* New York: Knopf.
Corbett, J. S. [1911] 1988. *Some principles of maritime strategy.* Annapolis: U.S. Naval Institute Press.
Cruttwell, C. R. M. F. 1936. *The role of British strategy in the Great War.* Cambridge, England: Cambridge Univ. Press.
Kagan, D. 1987. *The fall of the Athenian Empire.* Ithaca, N.Y.: Cornell Univ. Press.
Keegan, J. 1989. *The price of admiralty.* New York: Viking Press.
Mahan, A. T. [1890] 1957. *The influence of sea power upon history, 1660–1783.* New York: Hill and Wang.
Parry, J. H. 1974. *The discovery of the sea.* New York: Dial Press.
Rosinski, H. 1977. *The development of naval thought: Essays,* ed. B. M. Simpson III. Newport, R. I.: Naval War College Press.
Roskill, S. W. 1962. *The strategy of sea power: Its development and application.* London: Collins.
Starr, C. G. 1989. *The influence of sea power on ancient history.* New York: Oxford Univ. Press.

MARLBOROUGH, JOHN CHURCHILL, DUKE OF [1650–1722]

John Churchill, Duke of Marlborough (Fig. 1), was England's most successful military leader; he never lost a major battle, and he exhibited a brilliant grasp of tactics, strategy, and diplomacy. As commander of British forces fighting on the European continent during the War of the Spanish Succession, he was one of the two greatest soldiers of his day, the other being his ally and collaborator in his most famous victories, Prince Eugene of Savoy.

Figure 1. John Churchill, Duke of Marlborough. (SOURCE: U.S. Library of Congress)

Early Years and Rise to Command

John Churchill was born 26 May 1650 into a family suffering from having been on the losing side in the English civil war. Even after the Restoration, the Churchill family possessed only modest means. At the age of 17, Churchill became a page to James, Duke of York, younger brother of King Charles II. Soon after, Churchill entered the Foot Guards as an ensign.

As a junior officer, Churchill first saw combat in 1668 with the English garrison of Tangier, where he took part in the mobile operations that were characteristic of skirmishes with the Moors. In 1670 he served with naval infantry in the Mediterranean. A brief interlude in England followed, during which he continued to develop close ties in the court. In 1672 Churchill served under the duke of Monmouth with English forces allied with France against the Dutch. During 1674 he distinguished himself in several battles and earned the praise of the great French marshal Turenne and King Louis XIV. In these years, Churchill served alongside several French officers against whom he would fight later in his career. He also learned much about the French army and acquired solid military experience.

Churchill became a close confidant of the duke of York and benefited considerably when the latter ascended the throne as James II (1685). Churchill also gained influence through his marriage to Sarah Jennings, a most influential lady-in-waiting to Princess Anne, daughter of James II and the future Queen Anne. Churchill was given several diplomatic assignments. He received a colonelcy in 1677, and was made brigadier of foot in 1678. He defended James II against an attempted coup led by the duke of Monmouth (the illegitimate son of King Charles II), and fought against his old commander in the campaign of Sedgemoor (1685) in which Monmouth was defeated by the Royal Army. However, Churchill did not support James II when William of Orange (James's son-in-law) landed, at the invitation of English Protestants, at Torbay in 1688. Churchill deserted his longtime benefactor, James II, and the defection weighed heavily in the outcome and the accession of William and his wife, Mary (eldest daughter of James II), to the English throne.

Although Churchill was made the duke of Marlborough by the new monarch, his initial relationship with William III was not smooth. Marlborough assumed responsibility for the organization of the army and was promoted to lieutenant general even though William favored his own Dutch officers for senior positions and was not certain of Marlborough's loyalty. In 1690 Marlborough successfully commanded an expedition against Irish Jacobites. He was involved in court intrigues, which were always to plague his career, and was briefly imprisoned in the Tower of London (on accusations that later proved to be false), which kept him from serving in the latter part of the War of the League of Augsburg (1688–97) against the French.

War of the Spanish Succession

At the beginning of the War of the Spanish Succession (1701), Marlborough regained William's favor and was appointed captain-general of the English forces that were deployed to the continent and allied with Dutch forces against France. Marlborough's responsibilities included authority to negotiate the Second Grand Alliance against France. He was also designated allied commander but with considerable limitations on his authority, particularly with regard to his Dutch allies.

Marlborough's reputation was won in the ensuing war. His initial campaigns in the Netherlands and Rhineland (1702–1703) were hindered by the timidity of his Dutch allies, who were still in awe of the French army and unfamiliar with Marlborough's capabilities. From the beginning, Marlborough demonstrated a quick grasp of maneuver and a strong will to act.

Meanwhile, King William died and Queen Anne (to whom Marlborough's wife was still very close) assumed the English throne. From this point on, Marlborough's accomplishments can be summarized by four great battles.

Battle of Blenheim

In 1704 Marlborough executed his famous strategic march from the Spanish Netherlands (Belgium today) to the Danube to relieve his Austrian allies, who were threatened by a Franco-Bavarian army. The move was a masterpiece of logistical planning, deception, and drive. Once in southeastern Germany, Marlborough conducted a difficult assault of the Schellenberg (2 July 1704). Soon after, he joined forces with Eugene of Savoy, who commanded the Imperial army. Together they decisively defeated the French and Bavarians at the Battle of Blenheim (Blindheim, in Bavaria) on 13 August 1704. This victory exposed the relative deterioration of the French army since its preeminence in the earlier years of Louis XIV's reign.

The true significance of his victory was reinforced by the military achievements—often allied with Eugene on the battlefield—that followed.

Battles of Ramillies and Oudenarde

In 1705 Marlborough, again commanding an allied force against the French, breached the fortified lines of Brabant along the eastern border of the Spanish Netherlands. In so doing, he demonstrated his mastery of strategic maneuver. His pattern, to be repeated in subsequent campaigns, consisted of a feint in one direction followed by a rapid movement and concentration of forces at another location to carry out his main thrust.

Marlborough's campaign in the Low Countries continued against Marshal Villeroi and the Elector of Bavaria. For the rest of 1705, Marlborough was on several occasions frustrated when, after successfully maneuvering the enemy into a potentially decisive battle, his Dutch allies refused to cooperate in a conclusive engagement. After a winter of travel to many capitals in Europe to gain support in the alliance, Marlborough returned to the Low Countries in the spring of 1706. He was surprised to find Villeroi ready to engage.

The resulting Battle of Ramillies (23 May 1706) evolved much like that of Blenheim. Following the failure of a major thrust on his right, Marlborough concentrated his cavalry on his left and personally led a series of charges that overwhelmed the French right so quickly that Villeroi was unable to use his reserves. In two hours the allies put the enemy to flight and followed up with a vigorous pursuit. Many cities fell, and all of Brabant and Flanders were won. Besides showing Marlborough's mastery of tactical command, the Battle of Ramillies demonstrated the superiority of the English line infantry of the time.

Marlborough was frustrated in his campaign of 1707 because he was unable to develop a major battle against a large French force under a new commander, Marshal Vendôme. Surprisingly, and for some unexplainable reason, Marlborough did not exhibit his usual dynamic, creative leadership. It was also a year of reverses for the allies on other fronts in Spain and Italy.

The inactivity of 1707 was compensated for when Marlborough confronted Vendôme at the Battle of Oudenarde, Spanish Netherlands (11 July 1708). Initially, Vendôme surprised Marlborough by rapidly placing the much larger French army in a position that threatened the English lines of communication to the North Sea. Prince Eugene, before his own forces could arrive, joined Marlborough and was there to assist in managing a desperate situation. He eventually took command of the allied right wing while Marlborough personally led the decisive flanking movement on the French right.

The allied victory was also helped when almost half of the French force was never committed. This was due to differences between Vendôme and the duke of Burgundy. The latter, as a "prince of the blood," had been given titular command but argued with Vendôme on almost every aspect of his plan. Still, the victorious outcome was another display of Marlborough's mastery of tactical command. His victory at Oudenarde freed the Spanish Netherlands from French control, although the French still held several fortresses. Marlborough undertook a series of successful sieges that further attested to his virtuosity. His aggressiveness and use of deception even made siege warfare appear more a war of maneuver.

Malplaquet and Retirement

In 1709 Marlborough confronted his most able French opponent, Marshal Villars, at the Battle of Malplaquet. Even with Eugene's able assistance and a considerable advantage in numbers going into battle, it was a most costly victory. Marlborough attempted his usual tactical scheme of throwing the opposing forces off balance and then exploiting a weakened sector of the enemy's defense. Villars, however, did not fall for any such ploy, and led his men inspirationally even though he had been seriously wounded. In some respects it was a Pyrrhic victory: the losses of the allies far exceeded those of the French and the disproportionate number of Dutch casualties did not sit well with the public. The battle did not help Marlborough with his political enemies back in England. These were gaining influence with Queen Anne as Marlborough's wife was losing favor with her former patron.

Marlborough had one more chance against Villars in the summer of 1711, in a campaign against the French *Non Plus Ultra* defense lines. At his best in deception and quick marches, Marlborough "out-generaled" his French adversary and successfully penetrated the line to besiege and take the town of Bouchain. Villars was unable to intervene. Unfortunately, Marlborough's political influence had disappeared in Queen Anne's court and he was relieved of command by the end of the year. With Marlborough absent, Marshal Villars prevailed on the battlefield; little of Marlborough's efforts were reflected in the Treaty of Utrecht in 1713.

Later Years

Marlborough retired to his estate in Woodstock, England, and continued supervising the construction of Blenheim Palace, richly decorated with paintings and memorabilia of his victories. For a time he traveled and received honors from many of the courts of Europe. Following the death of Queen Anne and the succession of the Elector of Hanover as George I to the English throne in 1714, Marlborough regained political influence. His health, however, had begun to deteriorate. In 1716, he suffered a stroke that left him partially paralyzed. He died in June 1722 after a second stroke.

Assessment

Marlborough's reputation as a great general is solidly established in military history. He was an excellent strategist, tactician, and battlefield leader. While he had problems in domestic politics, he demonstrated unusual aptitude as a commander. He was able to get the most from ineffective allies, and worked brilliantly with allied commanders.

Albert D. McJoynt

See Also: Eugene, Prince of Savoy-Carignan; France, Military Hegemony of; History, Early Modern Military.

Bibliography

Chandler, D. 1973. *Marlborough as military commander.* New York: Scribner.
———. 1976. *The art of warfare in the age of Marlborough.* New York: Hippocrene Books.
Churchill, W. S. 1968. *Marlborough, his life and times.* New York: Scribner.
Kemp, A. 1980. *Weapons & equipment of the Marlborough wars.* Poole, U.K.: Blandford Press.
Barnett, C. 1974. *The first Churchill: Marlborough, soldier and statesman.* New York: Putnam.

MARSHALL, GEORGE CATLETT, JR. [1880–1959]

Gen. George C. Marshall was a principal architect of American military policy and strategy in World War II and went on to become one of the nation's most renowned statesmen. He did not achieve his military prominence as a field commander, but as the principal army advisor to two presidents of the United States. His civilian career led him to serve in the two most senior positions available to a nonelected American official.

Early Life and Career

George Catlett Marshall, Jr., was born in Pennsylvania on 31 December 1880. He graduated from the Virginia Military Institute (VMI) in the class of 1902, having been First Captain. He was commissioned into the United States Army. He endured the slow promotions of a peacetime army while serving in various assignments to midwestern posts, as well as two tours in the Philippines.

When the United States entered World War I in 1917,

Marshall deployed to France with the 1st U.S. Division. General Pershing, commander of the American Expeditionary Forces, soon realized Marshall's staff skills and assigned him to the General Staff. Thus, Marshall did not realize his ambition of being a regimental commander. However, Pershing vested considerable trust and authority in Marshall's staff position.

Following the Armistice (November 1918) Colonel Marshall became Pershing's aide. Like most other Regular Army officers, he reverted to his peacetime rank (major). In 1921, Pershing became U.S. Army Chief of Staff. Marshall was promoted to lieutenant colonel and followed Pershing to Washington.

In 1924 Marshall received a regimental command, followed by a series of senior post assignments. As assistant commandant of the U.S. Army Infantry School at Fort Benning, he started his famous "little black book," which listed young officers who had impressed him with their leadership abilities. Later, he served as commander of the Illinois National Guard division. In 1936 Marshall was promoted to brigadier general, and was in Washington as Chief of Army War Plans in 1938. Shortly thereafter, he became Deputy Chief of Staff.

World War II

Although Marshall's first meeting with President Roosevelt in 1933 went badly, Marshall's talents prevailed. In 1939 Roosevelt selected Marshall to be Chief of Staff over 32 senior officers. As Marshall put on his second star, war broke out in Europe with the German invasion of Poland.

The new Army Chief of Staff faced and overcame difficult challenges. Marshall persuaded a reluctant Congress to provide funds for preparedness. He contended with various pressure groups: isolationists as well as zealous interventionists. In 1941 passage of the Lend-Lease Act interfered with the goal of readying U.S. forces, since much-needed equipment was diverted to the support of England and Russia. After the Japanese bombed Pearl Harbor in December 1941, America's priorities became clearer.

The American army was vastly enlarged with newly produced arms and with men who needed to be trained—a requirement that strained national mobilization plans. Worldwide operations were planned and directed through newly created allied and multiservice staffs. Senior officers were selected to command in the various theaters of operations. Crucial decisions had to be made in allocating the limited available resources to wage a global war.

Marshall participated in the high-level formulation of U.S. and Allied strategy and policy in the war. His vision was crucial in many fundamental force structure decisions. He recognized that U.S. armored and air forces had to be expanded far beyond envisioned programs. Marshall was daring in his support of a relatively "independent" U.S. Army Air Corps, with considerable leeway to pursue advanced airpower doctrines. He supported the "Europe first" strategy, much to the displeasure of General MacArthur and the U.S. Navy. But even here, he was at odds with the British allies—specifically Churchill. Marshall pushed for an early cross-channel operation as the most direct and quickest route to defeat Germany, rather than approach from the "soft underbelly" of south Europe. Most of Marshall's judgments proved correct. However, his advocacy of going immediately into Western Europe was premature, as events in North Africa proved. The American forces needed more combat experience.

As a "chief" and not a commander, Marshall's "battlefields" were usually conferences. A series of them marked the main decisions that shaped Allied strategy. The first two conferences (Arcadia in December 1941–January 1942 and Casablanca in January 1943) were tremendous tests for senior American military leaders. The British, who had considerable experience in combined and joint planning, dominated the initial conference. The concept of running a war through councils of military chiefs was new to the Americans, but Marshall learned fast. In the conferences that followed, Marshall generally was the dominant influence on matters of military policy and grand strategy.

By 1944 Marshall was directing action on six fronts. He and the other senior U.S. military chiefs were elevated to five-star rank to put them on a par with Allied field marshals. Unlike some other popular U.S. generals of the time, Marshall quickly stopped any pretensions to political ambitions.

Roosevelt died on 12 April 1945, and Marshall started to work with the new president, Harry Truman. He quickly won the highest respect from Truman, and the general's influence was at its peak.

Marshall reluctantly supported the use of the atomic bomb as the lesser of two evils when considering the alternative, the conquest of more Pacific islands and the invasion of Japan itself. Even then, he was not sure that the bomb would eliminate the need for an invasion of the mainland. After Japan surrendered in August 1945, Marshall immediately submitted his resignation and recommended Eisenhower for his job. Upon Truman's request Marshall delayed his retirement until November of that year.

The Statesman

President Truman asked Marshall to go to China ten days after his retirement. Marshall's assignment was to bring about reconciliation between the Nationalist government under Chiang Kai-shek and the Communist Party under Mao Tse-tung. It was a futile mission, an effort marked by American lack of understanding of the Chinese political situation.

In January 1947 Truman appointed Marshall Secretary of State. His first crisis was communist-inspired civil wars in Greece and Turkey. Three months later the "Truman Doctrine" was announced and the U.S. Congress voted to aid Greece in its fight against the communists. Marshall recognized that much of postwar Europe was destitute and vulnerable to communist subversion. On 5 June 1947 he announced a program whereby the United States would finance European economic recovery; this concept became known as the "Marshall Plan." Marshall's reputation contributed greatly to obtaining the necessary financial support for the project from the U.S. Congress. He oversaw the development of a massive foreign military assistance program to supply and train the military forces of democratic countries, so they would be prepared to defend both against communist subversion and possible communist aggression. His health forced him to resign in 1949.

In 1950 North Korea invaded South Korea and Truman appointed Marshall Secretary of Defense. This was a difficult period for the U.S. Army. Many contentious issues had to be faced, such as the racial integration of the military forces and the dismissal of MacArthur when he challenged the authority of the president. Political opportunists tried to rise to power on a tide of anticommunism. Even Marshall was accused of not being anticommunist enough. But his reputation was secure, and he resigned in September 1951 with a remarkable record of distinguished service to his country.

In 1953 Marshall was awarded the Nobel Peace Prize for the Marshall Plan. After a lingering illness, he died on 16 October 1959 and was buried at Arlington Cemetery. A Marshall Foundation was formed in 1953. His papers are at VMI, where there is a museum in his honor. History remembers few military chiefs of staff, but Marshall will be an exception to that rule—not only because of his role as a soldier, but also his accomplishments as a civilian statesman.

ALBERT D. MCJOYNT

SEE ALSO: Chiang Kai-shek; Eisenhower, Dwight David; Korean War; MacArthur, Douglas; Pershing, John Joseph; Mao Tse-tung.

Bibliography

Pogue, F. C. 1965–87. *George C. Marshall.* 4 vols. New York: Viking.

———. 1968. George C. Marshall: Global commander. In *Harmon Memorial Lectures in Military History 1968*, no. 10:1–20.

Bland, L. I., and S. R. Ritenour, eds. 1981–1986. *The papers of George Catlett Marshall.* Baltimore, Md.: Johns Hopkins Univ. Press.

MATERIALS TECHNOLOGY

The separate disciplines of metallurgy, polymer science, and ceramics are now conveniently integrated into the subject of materials science and engineering (MSE), an underlying objective of which is to understand and interpret the relationship between microstructure and macro properties such as the mechanical, chemical, electrical, magnetic, and optical aspects of materials. The use of materials in structural applications, the subject of this section, is concerned with mechanical properties—specifically strength, stiffness, and toughness. These parameters are central in determining the suitability of materials for structural applications. Where the material is to be used in high temperature applications, the melting point is an additional factor in selecting the appropriate material.

The total environment for the operation of military equipment is perhaps the severest of all operating conditions. Equipment must operate at higher (or lower) than normal temperatures under aggressive chemical environments, and frequently under shock loading. Added to this is the ever-present need for greater agility and high mobility in the field, which puts a premium on strong, stiff, lightweight materials.

Stiffness, or the modulus of elasticity, is a measure of the resistance a material has to *elastic* deformation. When elastic stability is important, as in such structures as aircraft, materials with high elastic moduli are required. On the other hand, the stress at which a material yields *plastically*, and remains deformed after the load is removed, is a measure of its strength. In general, as a material's strength increases, the fracture toughness—that is, the material's capacity to tolerate the presence of cracks under tensile loading—decreases.

For a particular element, density is determined by the nuclear structure, while stiffness is related to the interatomic, inter-molecular structure. Strength and toughness of materials, however, are strongly dependent on the microstructure, such as grain or particle size, and also on the size and distribution of discrete hard (or soft) particles introduced into this structure. In most materials, these particles can be controlled to produce the desired properties by alloying with other species from the same family of materials and/or subjecting the material to particular thermal cycles to precipitate the desired phases.

Sections on metals, polymers, and ceramics will be followed by one on composites, which will highlight the advantages of combining and reinforcing materials with fibers or particles. Properties may then be tailored to particular applications. The various combinations are shown schematically in Figure 1.

Polymers

Low strength and stiffness and the low softening temperature of bulk polymers has inhibited their use in structure applications. In the form of fibers, however, polymers have the highest strengths and elastic moduli yet achieved in any material. It was therefore logical for fibers to be incorporated into polymers to improve their mechanical

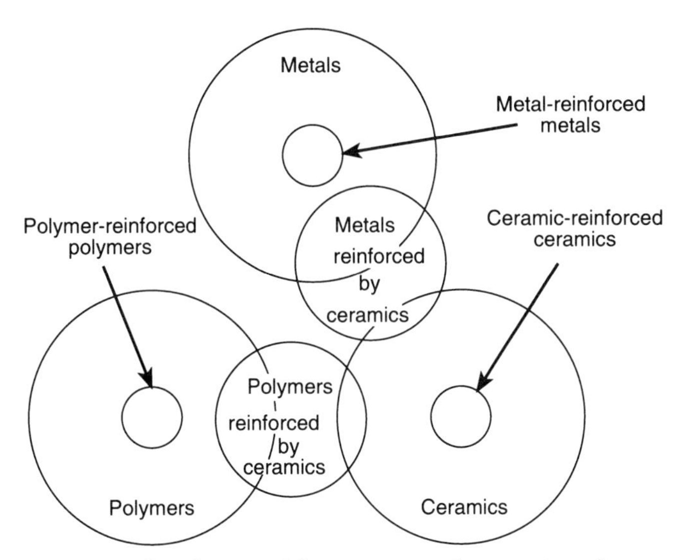

Figure 1. Classification of basic structural materials and composites.

properties. These "composite" materials will be discussed in detail later.

A typical engineering polymer is Nylon 6.6, which has a tensile strength of about 80 megapascals (MPa; one-third that of "mild" steel) and a tensile elastic modulus of 35 gigapascals (GPa; one-sixth that of "mild" steel). In contrast to most metals, polymers "creep" under sustained loads near room temperature; for this reason, properties measured as a function of time and temperature, rather than as static, must be used in designing with polymers. Polymers may also be more sensitive to environmental conditions, particularly moisture, chemical solvents, and ultraviolet light.

A convenient classification of polymers divides them into thermosets and thermoplastics. The former typically have low viscosities prior to curing, a process that involves a chemical reaction to cross-link the polymer chains into rigid, three-dimensional networks. After curing, they cannot be reshaped by heat. Thermosets include polyesters, phenolics, epoxies, bismaleimides, and polyimides. Epoxies are currently the dominant resin used for advanced polymer-based composites. Phenolics are inexpensive and have good fire resistance, but they tend to be more brittle and shrink more than epoxies.

In thermoplastics, the polymer chains are entangled with each other but not interconnected. At processing temperatures, usually in the region of 300°C, the long chain molecules "melt" to produce a viscous liquid that can be readily processed, for example by injection molding. The process is reversible and on cooling may result in an amorphous, semicrystalline or crystalline substance. Stiffness increases with increasing crystallinity. Thermoplastics include polyethylene, nylon, and polycarbonate.

Amorphous polymers such as polystyrene, polyvinyl chloride, polymethyl methacrylate, and acrylic tend to be brittle, although polycarbonate, a tough plastic used for its high impact toughness and ballistic protection, is an exception. To enhance fracture toughness, particles of another rubbery polymer are incorporated into the structure to impart fracture toughness. Semicrystalline polymers are inherently tough because of their duplex microstructure of crystalline regions interspersed with rubbery amorphous material.

Orientation of ordered crystal-like regions, such as occurs in nylon, can be achieved by confining flow conditions during processing, such as by spinning to produce fibers with very high strengths, relatively high softening temperatures, and improved resistance to solvents.

Recent developments in thermoplastic polymers have produced materials with excellent high temperature properties and solvent resistance, such as polyetheretherketone (PEEK), which, as a high-performance composite, has applications in aerospace. Continuous operation at temperatures up to 180°C will ultimately be required for military aircraft. Currently, carbon-reinforced PEEK is used for B-1 bomber wing-reinforcing ribs. A bonus with PEEK is its high resistance to flame penetration and reduced generation of smoke and toxic by-products.

Thermoplastics are more conveniently processed than thermosets, which require time-consuming curing. High melting point thermoplastics may replace epoxies and other thermosets in composites in the 1990s. The application of short-fiber-reinforced thermoplastic composites will also allow the introduction of high-rate process-forming techniques. This is in contrast to the labor-intensive lay-up techniques intrinsic to epoxy-based continuous fiber composites.

Oriented polyethylene (Spectra 1000) currently has the highest specific strength (tensile strength divided by the fiber density) of all fiber materials, including boron fibers and steel. In terms of specific stiffness (elastic modulus divided by the fiber density), this fiber is only outclassed by high-modulus carbon. Polyethylene fibers promise to replace high-performance Kevlar, particularly for woven structures for ballistic protection and advanced composites.

Metals

Almost all metals for structural applications are alloys that contain other elements for strengthening purposes. Elements that are soluble in the host metal in the solid state may impart strength by their very presence in solid solution. In other alloy systems, precipitation of fine hard compounds by appropriate thermal treatments can further harden the alloy. In this instance, maximum strengthening occurs at a critical size and dispersion of the precipitate particles.

Alloys of iron, aluminum, titanium, and nickel are currently the most utilized materials in the production of military hardware, although the use of other nonmetallic materials is increasing rapidly, usually at the expense of metallic alloys. (By volume, the production of plastics overtook the production of iron and steel in 1980.) Overall, the annual tonnage of steel is about 50 times that of aluminum.

The modification of steel by heat treatment, such as quenching from high temperatures followed by reheating to temper the hard structure, allows achievement of a wide range of properties that combine both strength and toughness. High-strength steels generally contain carbon—a most potent alloying element—up to 0.5 percent and, nickel, chromium, molybdenum, silicon, and vanadium in proportions of 2 percent or less. Strengths up to 2000 MPa can be obtained by quenching and tempering. High strengths are also achieved in low-carbon, high-nickel steels. These maraging steels can be conveniently machined to complex shapes and hardened by a low-temperature aging treatment that produces the precipitation of fine particles. In combat aircraft, high-strength steels are used (about 11% of all materials) in critical components such as aircraft landing gear and drive shafts, where resistance to high loads is important. High purity is essential to avoid the initiation and propagation of fatigue cracks from nonmetallic impurities, and it is for this reason that vacuum refining techniques are used in the production of high-strength steels.

Medium-strength steels, with strengths up to about 1000 MPa, are used for gun barrels, ballistic protection, and submarine and ship construction. These steels are also quenched and tempered; contain carbon, nickel, chromium, and molybdenum alloy additions; and have higher fracture toughness to accommodate explosive impact loading conditions. The new generation of high-strength low-alloy steels (HSLA) relies in part on fine grain size, produced during the hot rolling operation, to achieve both strength and high-fracture toughness. In these alloys, the alloy content, particularly carbon, is reduced, making these steels easily weldable and well suited for the more economic construction of ships and submarines.

Low- and medium-strength steels that transform to a body-centered cubic atomic configuration—ferritic steels—undergo a transition from ductile to brittle behavior on cooling, and fracture mechanics is used to assess the safety of structures when cracklike defects are present. Fracture mechanics is also used to predict the risk of failure from fatigue loading or stress corrosion. It is the role of the metallurgist to ensure that these modes of failure do not occur at the operating temperature by controlling the composition and microstructures.

Where lightweight and medium strength (600–1300 MPa) are required, as for example in aircraft and ship superstructure, aluminum and titanium alloys—one-third to one-half the density of steel—are a higher cost substitute. Aluminum may be alloyed with zinc, magnesium, and copper; and titanium with aluminum and vanadium, to achieve these strengths. In marine warfare, these alloys have the added advantage of being nonmagnetic and more corrosion resistant than steel. Titanium has been used by the USSR for the construction of fast, deep-diving—700 meters (2,310 ft.)—submarines (Alfa class) that are more difficult to detect. The cost penalty for the use of titanium is, however, about two to five times that of steel hulls.

A new development in aluminum alloys, particularly for aerospace, is the aluminum-lithium series. By the addition of about 2 percent lithium, which is half the density of water, alloys 10 percent lighter have been produced with a 15 percent increase in stiffness and improved fatigue life performance. Exploitation of these properties in aircraft will realize a 12–15 percent weight savings with concomitant fuel saving.

High-temperature alloys

As the speed of military aircraft increased, so did the requirement for materials to operate at higher temperatures. This is true for both airframe and propulsion systems, and as a result, the development of suitable materials will be the most critical factor in future aerospace developments. Aluminum alloys using various methods for stabilizing the dispersed strengthening phases at higher temperatures have been developed for this purpose. For higher temperatures, titanium and nickel alloys are required. Because the boundaries between grains are a source of creep at high temperatures, their presence is usually kept to a minimum and in extreme cases (e.g., in gas turbine blades) single crystals of the alloy are grown to improve creep performance.

By the critical dispersion of hard stable particles, useful mechanical (creep) properties can be achieved in metal-based alloys up to one-half to three-quarters of their melting point (T_m) in degrees Kelvin. For example, aluminum alloys have been developed for use up to 0.56 T_m (250°C), and nickel alloys have achieved 0.74 T_m (980°C). Titanium alloys are limited to about 0.4 T_m (500°C). For further improvements at high temperatures, particularly for propulsion systems where there is a requirement to double the thrust-to-weight ratio by the end of this century, titanium and nickel aluminides and ceramics are being developed. These materials are brittle and require new codes for designing with brittle materials.

Metallic alloys operating at the highest temperatures require surface protection to avoid hot corrosion, which may be catastrophic with some alloys. Various aluminide and thermal barrier coatings are used for this purpose. By the judicious use of these coatings, the life of components at very high temperatures can be improved quite spectacularly.

Rapidly Solidified Alloys

Metals technology has seen a revolution in the past decade as the quite unique properties of rapidly solidified materials have been exploited. In order to achieve the high cooling rates of about one million degrees per second, small particles or thin foils are required. The structures of rapidly solidified materials vary from the completely disordered liquid state to extremely small crystalline (nanocrystalline) materials. Consolidation of rapidly solidified materials without loss of properties can be achieved by low-temperature sintering or explosive compaction. Unique mechanical, chemical, and magnetic properties are achievable. Fracture strengths of over 1000 percent those of conventional iron-carbon alloys have been obtained, and their use in structural applications will increase.

Wires and Whiskers

By "cold drawing" high-carbon steel (i.e., at temperatures near ambient) through dies into fine wires, extremely high strengths can be obtained—for example, 4.5 GPa. Grains are elongated and fragmented during the wire drawing so that further uniaxial deformation is extremely difficult. Metal whiskers grown from metal vapor, on the other hand, achieve a very high order of crystalline perfection and derive their near theoretical properties from this state. The steel wires, also known as piano wire, are used for their high strength, while both the wires and the whiskers may be incorporated into metal matrix composites.

Ceramics

Because of their high-temperature strength, hardness, and corrosion resistance, ceramics are an important class of advanced materials with great potential for military applications. The bulk of ceramic developments have so far been for the electronic and telecommunications industries. Recent discoveries of superconductivity in ceramic materials at temperatures approaching ambient promise that applications in the electrical/electronic areas will continue to be robust. At the same time, ceramics used in structural, load-bearing applications are continuing to increase as techniques for reducing brittleness are developed. These ceramics fall into two classes, oxide and nonoxide. The two main oxide ceramics are oxides of aluminum (alumina) and zirconium (zirconia), which have applications in wear-resistant parts and cutting tools.

Nonoxide ceramics include carbides and nitrides of silicon, boron, and titanium, as well as borides of titanium. Other structural ceramics combine oxides with nonoxides. Sialon, for example, is an alloy of silica, alumina with aluminum nitride, and silicon nitride. These ceramics have applications in heat-resisting parts for engines, with the added advantage of light weight. Ceramics based on aluminum, silicon, and boron are less than half the density of iron alloys and one-third that of nickel alloys. Perhaps the most outstanding property of ceramics is their potential for extremely high strength at room and elevated temperatures, provided that tensile brittleness can be overcome. In compression, alumina has a yield strength of over 2.5 GPa, whereas in tension the maximum strength before fracture occurs is only 0.15 GPa.

The extremely high melting points of ceramics preclude their production by a conventional melting and casting process. Monolithic ceramics are therefore formed by injection molding or slip casting from fine powders by mixing with organic binding agents, then pressing and sintering at high temperatures. Although time consuming, consolidation from the powder has the advantage that complex shapes can be formed precisely and frequently without need for machining.

The most serious barrier to widespread acceptance of structural ceramics into critical structures is their brittleness, which can usually be traced to the presence of critical-size flaws in sizes ranging from 0.02 to 0.05 millimeters. These defects are inadvertently introduced during manufacture and are difficult to detect. To realize the full strength potential in tension, flaw size must be reduced further or the toughness of the ceramic increased. One technique devised for toughening ceramics is transformation toughening. When a crack forms it generates a high local stress at the crack tip, which in turn transforms this material into a more stable phase. The transformed phase has a greater volume and thus forms compressive stresses to stop the crack. Zirconia, in which the structure is partially stabilized (PSZ), is an example of transformation toughening whereby fracture toughness is increased three- to fourfold and critical flaw size increased by a factor of ten. The introduction of ceramic particles and fibers into ceramics is another technique for improving toughness; silicon carbide whiskers in alumina, for example, increase the flaw size by a factor of ten.

The future applications of ceramics in military diesel engines will exploit their high-temperature strength and low-thermal conductivity, thereby reducing the need for water cooling and effectively recovering the energy from the exhaust gases so as to improve efficiency. Cylinder liners and pistons made from silicon carbide and silicon nitride will improve diesel engines by reducing friction, wear, and component inertia. As an alternative to monolithic ceramics, improvements are being obtained in existing diesel engines, without redesigning, by the application of plasma-sprayed ceramic coatings to critical metallic components such as cylinders and piston heads. Micron-thin hard titanium nitride coatings are also being applied by vapor deposition to extend the life of cutting tools and gears. Applications of ceramics to gas turbines are more demanding and require greater strength reliability and higher operating temperatures. Silicon nitride and silicon carbide are expected to meet these demands in the 1990s.

Specific military applications for structural ceramics include lightweight armor for personnel and aircraft, gun barrel liners, missile radomes, and heat tiles for reentry space vehicles. For ceramic armor, it is essential to back the ceramic tiles with a tough backing material such as aluminum plate or a strong fiber-reinforced resin such as Kevlar-reinforced epoxy. The kinetic energy of fragments of the projectile and the ceramic is thereby absorbed by the backup plate.

Ceramics are also used as aircraft and missile radomes because they can withstand the aerodynamic heating experienced at high Mach numbers and also resist rain and dust erosion. These properties combine with low dielectric and microwave losses. Alumina has been used as a base ceramic for radome development.

Radar and infrared sensor windows in missiles require a good combination of dielectric and mechanical properties. Careful tailoring of ceramics is required to improve thermal shock resistance and to compensate for changes in dielectric constants and self-emittance of infrared with increasing temperature. Toughened zirconia has fulfilled these requirements.

Fibers and Particles

Silicon carbide and alumina are available in the form of whiskers (about a 2μm diameter), fibers (20 μm diameter), and particles for the reinforcement of metals, polymers, or other ceramics. When incorporated into metals and ceramics, they enhance high-temperature strength. Carbon fibers vary in modulus depending on the method of production. Pyrolized rayon fibers have a low modulus, 28 GPa, while higher modulus fibers are polyacrylonitrile (PAN) (340 GPa) or petroleum pitch (up to 800 GPa).

Composites

The technological thrust behind advanced composites is the exploitation of the ultra-high strength and high stiffness available in new fiber (or particulate) materials. This is achieved by encasing the reinforcing materials in a softer and more ductile matrix, which enables the load to be distributed more uniformly between fibers (and particles) and also along the length of the fibers. The matrix also protects the reinforcement from surface damage and adverse environments. Fracture toughness of fiber-reinforced composites is achieved by blunting cracks that intersect fibers and by the pull-out of fibers from the matrix.

Mechanical and physical properties of fiber-reinforced composites are not the same in all directions. They are strongest when loaded along the fiber length and weakest when stressed transversely. Complex loads require fibers to be orientated at various angles.

Composites are classified according to the matrix material—that is, polymers, metals, and ceramics. The first synthetic composites were polymer-based, which are currently the most highly developed and represent the largest volume production. Metal and ceramic composites are currently under intensive research to exploit higher temperature applications.

Polymer Matrix Composites (PMCs)

PMCs significantly extend the range of application of lightweight materials. Polymers, for example, are the lightest family of common materials, but they are too soft or too brittle for structural applications. By reinforcing with strong and stiff fibers such as glass, aramid (Kevlar), boron, or carbon, the strength can be increased by up to a factor of ten; the fracture toughness of brittle polymers can also be enhanced. These composites have revolutionized the capabilities of weapons systems and platforms, particularly in aerospace and guided missiles.

Control of the properties of fiber-reinforced composites depends on the strength of the bond between the fiber and the matrix. If this bond is too strong, load transfer to the fiber will initiate fiber fracture. By controlling the interfacial strength between fiber and matrix, transverse cracks may be diverted along the fiber-matrix interface. Cracks may also be blunted by pulling out broken fibers from the matrix.

PMC evolved during the 1940s and glass-reinforced polyester was first used, in nonstructural areas, in the 1950s. Improved glass fibers were later developed and used for missile bodies (Polaris, Poseidon, and Trident were all filament wound), grenade launchers, helicopter rotor blades, hulls for minehunters, and hulls for lightweight combat vehicles. Stronger and stiffer aramid (Kevlar) and carbon fibers replaced glass for the manufacture of lighter ballistic missile bodies, which significantly increased their range. Lighter weight combat helmets with improved ballistic performance were developed using Kevlar and oriented polyethylene-reinforced resins (mainly phenolics and vinylesters) to replace metallic alloys.

The classification of matrix materials used for PMCs is similar to that used for polymers. Thermosetting polymers (polyesters, vinylesters, epoxies, bismaleimides, and polyimides) tend to be more brittle, more difficult to process, and time limited in application compared with thermoplastic polymers. Examples of the latter are some polyesters, polyetherimide, and polyamide imide, which enables higher operating temperatures of up to 250°C to be achieved.

Metal Matrix Composites (MMCs)

MMCs have been more difficult to develop than PMCs, but the potential for higher temperature applications, up to 800°C, has driven research. Other advantages include higher electrical and thermal conductivity, low-moisture pickup, fire resistance, and better laser survivability. Disadvantages include increased density and high cost.

The most common matrices are aluminum, titanium, and magnesium alloys with continuous reinforcement fibers such as silicon carbide, alumina, boron carbide, boron, and carbon fibers. Reinforcements may also be in a discontinuous form, such as particles or whiskers. All reinforcements enhance the wear resistance of MMCs.

Reactions between the reinforcements and the matrix are much more likely in MMCs because of the high processing and operating temperatures. Fiber coatings are necessary for some systems to curtail deleterious reactions and to promote wetting during processing. Boron-and-carbon-fiber–reinforced aluminum and magnesium alloys have been utilized as struts in space structures. These composites have the high damping characteristics and high thermal conductivity required for space applications.

Heavier alloys have been reinforced by high modulus, high-temperature strength fibers, and wires. For example, tungsten wires have been used to stiffen depleted uranium long-rod kinetic energy penetrators, and also for improving the higher temperature strength of nickel- and iron-based alloys for applications in gas turbine engines.

CERAMIC MATRIX COMPOSITES (CMCs)

Developments in CMCs have been driven by requirements for improved fracture toughness in monolithic ceramics and for materials operating at very high temperatures, as in advanced gas turbine engines. The simplest CMCs are those matrices reinforced by whiskers or fibers from the same material, such as silicon carbide fiber–reinforced silicon carbide. With these simple systems, self-induced cracking from a mismatch in thermal expansion coefficients is avoided. On the other hand, bonding between the fiber and the matrix may be so strong that cracks, once initiated, will continue, as in monolithic ceramics. Fiber coatings are therefore required to weaken the bond interface strength and allow cracks to be stopped by crack deflection at the fiber-matrix interface and/or by fiber pull-out.

Typically, ceramic matrix materials have high melting points and are relatively lightweight, such as alumina, silicon carbide, and silicon nitride. The most significant ceramic fiber used so far in CMCs is silicon carbide in fiber, whisker, or particulate form. As well as higher fracture toughness, CMCs demonstrate less variability in toughness from sample to sample, avoiding an unwanted characteristic found in monolithic ceramics.

Glass can also be markedly toughened by reinforcing with carbon fibers, as in borosilicate glass-graphite composite, which is lighter than aluminum but can be used up to 600°C. Compared with monolithic glass, these composites are four times stronger and toughness is increased by a factor of ten.

For applications above 2000°C, such as rocket nozzles, space vehicle shields, and aircraft brakes, carbon fiber–reinforced carbon-matrix composites are employed. Protection against oxidation of these carbon-carbon composites above 400°C is, however, necessary, and silicon carbide and silicon nitride are used as surface coatings.

Conclusion

It is apparent that the properties of materials have a significant effect on the performance of military equipment. New materials can provide advantages over old materials, and they can allow new designs for equipment that were not possible before. The higher performance, however, must be weighed against the often higher cost of the equipment, the difficulty of manufacture, and the ease of replacement on the battlefield.

MAURICE E. DE MORTON

SEE ALSO: Armor Technology; Technology and Warfare.

Bibliography

Ashby, M. F., and D. R. W. Jones. 1980. *Engineering materials*. Oxford: Pergamon Press.

Cohen, M. 1987. Progress and prospects in metallurgical research. In *Advanced Materials Research*, pp. 51–110. Washington, D.C.: National Academy Press.

Chou Tsu-Wei. Guide to Engineering Materials. 1988. *Advanced materials and processes inc. metal progress*. Metals Park, Ohio: ASM International.

Garden, T. 1989. *The technology trap: Science and the military*. London: Brassey's.

Ichinose, N., ed. 1988. *Introduction to fine ceramics. Applications in engineering*. New York: Wiley.

Kelly, A. 1987. Composites for the 1990s. In Technology in the 1990's. The Promise of Advanced Materials. *Philosophical Transactions of the Royal Society of London* (Series A) 322:409–23.

Suzuki, H. 1987. A perspective on new ceramics and ceramic composites In Technology in the 1990's. The Promise of Advanced Materials. *Philosophical Transactions of the Royal Society of London* (Series A) 322:465–78.

U.S. Congress, Office of Technology Assessment. 1988. *Advanced materials by design*. OTA-E-351. Washington, D.C.: Government Printing Office.

MATHEMATICAL MODELING AND FORECASTING

The terms *modeling* and *forecasting* embrace everything from theoretical physics to economic forecasting. This article addresses only the aspects directly applicable to military affairs: modeling and predicting the outcome of a battle, the consequences of a strategic posture, the cost of an item of military hardware, and so forth.

Because of the enormous national and individual consequences of military engagements men have always wished to predict the outcomes of battles, and they have willingly grasped at even spurious methods of divination. In this respect, mathematical modeling has some common roots with the Roman practice of observing the behavior of sacred chickens to foretell the outcome of a battle. However, it has a much closer affinity with the common (and common-sense) practice of observing the enemy numbers and order of battle to try to guess the probable outcome of an engagement before offering or avoiding battle. Despite the many well-known instances where it has failed catastrophically, from Claudius Pulcher's decision to engage the Carthaginian fleet (in which instance the chickens' prediction proved superior) to the French defeat at Agincourt, the common-sense method has probably worked fairly well on the average.

Another ancient source of modern forecasting methods is the problem of logistics. Historically, armies have lived primarily off the land; the commanders who could estimate the yield of the land and supplement it where necessary usually (but not invariably) had an advantage over those who trusted to the favor of fortune. Some historical strategic policies, such as that of the Roman Empire or the nineteenth century British Empire, appear so nicely calculated as to have been inherently mathematical in outlook; more often, however, the historian finds no coherent national strategy whatsoever. One can only speculate on the consequences had Hannibal been supported by such a strategic policy.

Certain games—notably checkers, chess, and Go—are crude models of battles; they can be thought of as mathematical simulations in that the rules of play form a rigorous mathematical structure. At most, however, these ancient games served as training aids and introductions to a rigorous style of thought appropriate to strategy and tactics. The tradition of training through such games has continued, with ever-increasing realism, through sandbox and tabletop models down to the current interactive computer-implemented war games.

Developing Methods of Forecasting

Early Deterministic and Stochastic Models

The application of rigorous mathematical modeling to military affairs began in World War I, when the British mathematician F. W. Lanchester and the Russian theorist M. Osipov formulated mathematical models for battles. These models became the germ from which most later theories have grown. In deterministic Lanchester-type models, the "state of the system" at any time is determined by the men and/or equipment surviving (and effective) on each side of the battle and their disposition at that time. Rules are proposed, usually in the form of differential or difference equations, for the evolution of the state over time, and by solving the resulting system one predicts the outcome of the battle.

An alternative to the deterministic model is the stochastic model, in which the probabilities of transitions in the state of the system are set forth in terms of a present state, and the probabilities of various end states are then computed. Such stochastic models are often substantially more difficult than deterministic ones. However, a stochastically formulated model may often give rise to a deterministic one by considering the mean value of the state.

As a simple example of the deterministic Lanchester-type model, consider two opposing forces, one side having $N(t)$ and the other $M(t)$ units surviving and effective at time t. If we presume that the rate of destruction of each force by the other is proportional to the remaining units of the opponent, the differential equation governing the evolution of the battle is

$$\frac{dN}{dt} = -k_1 M(t), \quad \frac{dM}{dt} = -k_2 N(t) \qquad (1)$$

where k_1 and k_2 are the constants of proportionality measuring "effectiveness." The solutions then give the size of each force at time t, in terms of the initial forces at $t=0$ and these constants, as

$$M(t) = M(0)\cosh(k^1k^2)^{1/2}t - \left(\frac{k_2}{k_1}\right)^{1/2} N(0)\sinh(k_1k_2)^{1/2}t$$

$$N(t) = N(0)\cosh(k_1k_2)^{1/2}t - \left(\frac{k_1}{k_2}\right)^{1/2} M(0)\sinh(k_1k_2)^{1/2}t \qquad (2)$$

This model can be thought of as roughly representing an engagement with aimed fire on both sides, each unit on one side causing depletion of the other in proportion to the number of effective units remaining on the first side. Note that, except for the special case where both sides are evenly matched, as t becomes large one side goes negative and the other begins to grow! To be more realistic it would be necessary to modify the equations to account for such things as the fact that if one side is larger than the other there will not be enough targets for each unit to aim at, so redundancy of targeting will cause a departure from strict proportionality. Such modifications complicate the model and may sometimes make the solution of the differential equations more difficult, but often they do not change the essential nature of the solutions within some useful region.

A stochastic model for a similar "aimed fire" situation might proceed as follows. Assume that each unit chooses a target independently from among those on the other side. It then has a fixed probability of destroying that chosen target (the probability is independent for each unit). Each unit fires at the same fixed rate. (The probabilities and rates of fire may be different for the two sides.) The probability that any one N unit is picked as a target by one of the M units is just $1/N$. Suppose the probability of the target being destroyed, given that it is targeted, is p_1; the probability that the unit is targeted and destroyed is p_1/N; and the probability that it survives independent attacks by the M units of the opponent is $(1 - p_1/N)^M$. Similarly, the probability that a unit on the other side will survive is $(1 - p_2/M)^N$. (For convenience, we assume that the rates of fire are the same on both sides and that the time between shots is the same. We thus proceed by volleys for purposes of discussion. Converting to processes that are continuous in time or that have differing rates of fire is quite complicated and does not affect the general nature of the results.) The probability that n of the N units and m of the M units survive a volley is then

$$P(n,m|N,M) =$$

$$\left(\frac{N!}{n!(N-n)!}\right)\left(1-\frac{p_1}{N}\right)^{Mn}\left(1-\left(1-\frac{p_1}{N}\right)^{M}\right)^{N-n}$$

$$\left(\frac{M!}{m!(M-m)!}\right)\left(1-\frac{p_2}{M}\right)^{Nm}\left(1-\left(1-\frac{p_2}{M}\right)^{N}\right)^{M-m} \qquad (3)$$

This is the transition probability from state (N,M) before the volley to state (n,m) after the volley. (The probability of transition to a state with n or m greater than N or M, respectively, or negative, is 0.) These transition probabilities are usually arranged in a square matrix of size $N(0)M(0)$ with each position in the matrix representing a combination of an initial state (N,M) and a final state (n,m). The transition probabilities for k volleys are then just the elements of the k'th power of the matrix for one volley, as computed above. This approach permits use of sophisticated techniques of matrix analysis to extract information about the long-term behavior and statistics of the process.

In a more sophisticated stochastic model, the transitions associated with a volley may depend on factors other than the total current number of survivors before the volley—for instance, an ammunition supply may be diminishing, range may be changing, and so on. Often, these variables can be included as part of the description of the state of the system, and transition probabilities can be computed—for instance, from (M,N,X,Y,R) to (m,n,x,y,r), where X,Y and x,y are the stocks of ammunition on each side before and after the volley, and R and r are the range before and after the volley. This approach preserves the basic mathematical structure of the problem as a Markov stochastic process (i.e., one in which the future states of the process depend only on the present state and not on the previous history) and permits the same sophisticated analytical tools to be used.

Although the deterministic and stochastic models formulated above appear to be quite unrelated, this is not the case. The continuous formulation of the deterministic model can be replaced by a stepwise "volley" approach; the differential equation then becomes a difference equation. (This is precisely how the solutions of differential equations are approximated numerically when analytical methods of solution fail.) Or the discrete time could be eliminated from the stochastic model and a continuous "stochastic differential equation" model formulated. The discrete "volley" deterministic model can then be used to provide a useful approximation that is computed more easily than the continuous stochastic model.

Moreover, if one computes the expectations of the surviving forces on each side, the deterministic model, with the values of the "effectiveness" constants k_1 and k_2 chosen appropriately proportional to the "kill probabilities" p_1 and p_2, yields an approximation to these expected values which is valid for small values of (i.e., to the first order in) p_1 and p_2. If the "more realistic" modifications discussed previously are introduced to account for multiple targeting when N and M are unequal, the approximation becomes even better. Specifically, the expected values of n and m after one volley are

$$\bar{n} = N\left(1-\frac{p_1}{N}\right)^{M} = N\left(1-\frac{Mp_1}{N}+\frac{M(M-1)p_1^2}{2N^2}-\ldots\right)$$

$$= N - Mp_1 + \frac{M(M-1)p_1^2}{2N} - \ldots$$

and

$$\bar{m} = M\left(1-\frac{p_2}{M}\right)^{N} = M\left(1-\frac{Np_2}{M}+\frac{N(N-1)p_2^2}{2M^2}-\ldots\right)$$

$$= M - Np_2 + \frac{N(N-1)p_2^2}{2M} - \ldots \qquad (4)$$

Therefore, if we set k_1 and k_2 equal to p_1 and p_2 divided by the time for one "volley" and drop all terms involving their squares, we have the difference equation analogous to our discrete model: the rate at which N decreases (per volley time) is k_1 times M, and the rate at which M decreases is k_2 times N. The terms involving higher powers of the probabilities represent the changes in the number of expected survivors due to multiple targeting. They thus provide a guide to the changes that should be made in the deterministic model to account for such effects. This suggests that the following deterministic model is more "realistic":

$$\frac{dN}{dt} = N\left[\left(1-\frac{k_1}{N}\right)^{M}-1\right],\ \frac{dM}{dt} = M\left[\left(1-\frac{k_2}{M}\right)^{N}-1\right] \qquad (5)$$

The deterministic model is an attempt to formulate our intuitive expectations about the average behavior of our stochastic model, which is based on more carefully considered probabilistic assumptions. This is frequently the case with deterministic models, and they often can be improved by careful consideration of underlying stochastic assumptions. Although not all battle models can be thought of as extensions of Lanchester's pioneering work, the link between deterministic and stochastic models of the type we have illustrated is so strong that it seems appropriate to refer to both as Lanchester-type models. However, differential equation models yield continuous solutions, which will usually involve fractional units; the stochastic model always yields only integers.

Lanchester's work included a second type of model, proposed to represent unaimed fire. In that model, the casualties each side experiences are not only proportional to the remaining strength of the opposition, but also proportional to its own remaining forces—the more survivors, the more likely one is to be hit by unaimed fire. For such a case, the differential equations analogous to (1) take the form:

$$\frac{dN}{dt} = -k_1MN, \frac{dM}{dt} = -k_2MN \quad (6)$$

(Mixed cases, where one side is aiming and the other is laying down a field of fire, can be represented by choosing one differential equation from (1) and the other from (6). Such a model has been proposed to represent an ambush.) Just as with the aimed fire model, this model for unaimed fire can be rationalized as approximating the average behavior in an appropriate stochastic model.

Richardson's Model

The next notable attempt after Lanchester at military-related mathematical modeling was the work of the British meterologist L. F. Richardson, who subscribed to the theory that arms races cause wars and, in particular, had caused World War I. Richardson posited that the armaments maintained by two parties should satisfy a pair of first-order linear differential equations

$$\frac{dQ_1}{dt} = aQ_1 + bQ_2 + c, \frac{dQ_2}{dt} = eQ_1 + fQ_2 + g \quad (7)$$

The coefficients b and e were to represent the stimulus to arm caused by fear of the other side's existing armaments and were assumed to be positive. The coefficients a and f were to represent the natural aversion to the burden of armament and were taken to be negative. The constants c and g were to represent the tendency to maintain some minimal armament in the absence of any external threat, so that if Q_2 were 0, for instance, Q_1 would tend to an equilibrium value of $-c/a$. If the quantity $af - be$ is negative (i.e., if the mutual fear outweighs the mutual aversion to arm), then the solutions tend to infinity. In the opposite case, with $af - be$ positive, then the solutions tend to equilibrium at

$$Q_1 = \frac{gb - cf}{af - be}, \quad Q_2 = \frac{ce - ga}{af - be} \quad (8)$$

Richardson sought to adjust the constants in these equations so that the solutions would fit data he gathered concerning armaments of the parties involved prior to the onset of World War I. He concluded that the appropriate values of the constants to fit the data indicated instability ($af - be$ negative) and that the unstable arms race had resulted in war when the parties perceived that they could not maintain their security in the face of the growing armaments of their opponents. Although Richardson's work has been criticized extensively, there is one sense in which the basic form of his model—as opposed to his conclusions or his treatment of data—must be correct. Regard Q_1 and Q_2 as components of a vector Q. If the process being studied satisfies any (vector) differential equation of the form $Q' = F(Q)$, where F is a smooth vector-valued function of the vector Q, and if Q' (the rate of change of Q) is not independent of very small changes in the components of Q from a fixed $Q(0)$, then a system of the form given by Richardson must approximate the solution of the system for values of Q near the initial point $Q(0)$, that is, to first order in the components of $Q - Q(0)$. From Taylor's theorem,

$$\begin{aligned} F_1(Q_1,Q_2) &= \\ F_1(Q_1(0),Q_2(0)) &+ \left(\frac{\partial F_1}{\partial Q_1}(Q_1(0),Q_2(0))\right)(Q_1 - Q_1(0)) \\ &+ \left(\frac{\partial F_1}{\partial Q_2}(Q_1(0),Q_2(0))\right)(Q_2 - Q_2(0)) + R_1 \end{aligned}$$

and

$$\begin{aligned} F_2(Q_1,Q_2) &= \\ F_2(Q_1(0),Q_2(0)) &+ \left(\frac{\partial F_2}{\partial Q_1}(Q_1(0),Q_2(0))\right)(Q_1 - Q_1(0)) \\ &+ \left(\frac{\partial F_2}{\partial Q_2}(Q_1(0),Q_2(0))\right)(Q_2 - Q_2(0)) + R_2 \end{aligned} \quad (9)$$

where the components of the "remainder" vector R are of second order in $Q - Q(0)$. If we then set

$$\begin{aligned} a &= \frac{\partial F_1}{\partial Q_1}(Q_1(0),Q_2(0)), \; b = \frac{\partial F_1}{\partial Q_2}(Q_1(0),Q_2(0)), \\ c &= F_1(Q_1(0),Q_2(0)) - Q_1(0)\frac{\partial F_1}{\partial Q_1}(Q_1(0),Q_2(0)) \\ &\quad - Q_2(0)\frac{\partial F_1}{\partial Q_2}(Q_1(0),Q_2(0)), \\ e &= \frac{\partial F_2}{\partial Q_1}(Q_1(0),Q_2(0)), \\ f &= \frac{\partial F_2}{\partial Q_2}(Q_1(0),Q_2(0)), \\ g &= F_2(Q_1(0),Q_2(0)) - Q_1(0)\frac{\partial F_2}{\partial Q_1}(Q_1(0),Q_2(0)) \\ &\quad - Q_2(0)\frac{\partial F_2}{\partial Q_2}(Q_1(0),Q_2(0)), \end{aligned} \quad (10)$$

the Richardson model gives an approximation to the arbitrary smooth system, provided a, b, e, f are not all 0. (Richardson's model and this analysis of its applicability as an approximation can be extended to more than two dimensions to treat the case of more parties.) With six constants to adjust, the Richardson model can usually provide an acceptable approximation to empirical data, but sometimes the signs of the constants yielding the best approximation are not those Richardson hypothesized.

Although a linear Richardson-type model may be useful as a local approximation to an inherently nonlinear process, it cannot provide a key to determining the overall instability of the system. When the Richardson model indicates stability, then the system will be stable if it starts not too far away from the long-run equilibrium point indicated by the model (so that the remainder terms in the approximation remain small). However, when the model indicates instability, with the solutions going to infinity, the remainder terms may eventually dominate and lead to stability at some point quite different from that indicated by the model. Thus Richardson's proposed use of the model as a predictor of war resulting from an unlimited arms race is inherently fallacious. A number of authors have suggested modifications of Richardson's model by the addition of nonlinear terms or even the complete replacement by a particular nonlinear system $Q' = F(Q)$. Such modifications have no inherent justification of the type offered above for Richardson's model. Each requires an independent justification based on its inherent reasonableness as a model of the process it is attempting to portray.

World War II Applications

Although Richardson's work was done before World War II, it did not attract widespread attention until it was republished in the 1950s. The serious application of mathematical modeling and prediction to military affairs began with various groups of British and (later) American scientists practicing what came to be known as "operations research." Anecdotes have attributed the beginning of this activity to Winston Churchill's call, during the Dunkirk evacuation, for graphs showing how many planes would be left to defend Britain if he kept losing planes by covering the evacuation. Finding that Britain would soon be left defenseless against the Luftwaffe, he withdrew air cover from the evacuation and thereby maintained the capability to fight the subsequent Battle of Britain.

The use of radar, the structure of naval convoys, antisubmarine warfare, strategic bombing, and numerous other facets of the war quickly became the subjects of mathematical models that were exploited to increase the efficiency and effectiveness of the Allied forces. While many of the models developed were too specialized for detailed discussion here, the general activity generated a body of knowledge and techniques that developed into a number of mathematical subdisciplines now studied independently. Particularly notable among these are linear programming, developed originally to solve logistics problems; the theory of stochastic processes as applied to the study of filtering noisy signals and designing servomechanisms; and queuing theory, which was applied to many diverse problems from control of aircraft gun turrets to unloading convoys. Some of these topics had been studied previously (Erlang developed queuing theory to study the design of telephone switching networks a decade earlier), but the wartime effort gave a tremendous impetus to such studies, which expanded in the postwar era to include the study of civilian operations as well.

Postwar Development

After the war, numerous groups were established to conduct, on a more formal basis, the sorts of analyses that had been done on an ad hoc basis during the conflict. The United States was a leader in this effort. Eventually, the Department of Defense and the various branches of the U.S. armed forces set up a number of quasi-independent think tanks to study problems of interest to them. Contractors to the U.S. Army produced models of land combat, while navy contractors studied submarine warfare questions. As nuclear forces expanded, questions of strategic policy became dominant, and as weapon systems became more complex and expensive, the need to make the most efficient choices among competitive systems and to forecast the costs of the systems became critical. From the 1960s onward, analyses of the costs and benefits attached to various proposed weapons systems—their "cost-effectiveness"—played an ever-increasing role in U.S. military decision making, both in weapons procurement and in formulating the strategic policies the systems were to serve. Modeling and forecasting became major concerns of the U.S. defense establishment and, to a lesser extent, of the defense establishments of other developed nations.

Computer-Based Models

The rapid growth of computing capability has led to the development of extremely detailed models (or simulations) that attempt to represent the probable fate of every individual unit and to account for the targeting of every weapon. Historically, such detailed simulations have suffered from two difficulties. First, the very richness of detail they present has sometimes been a barrier to their effective utilization—it is difficult for a decision maker at the national level to make use of the fact that the post office in Kennebunkport, Maine, has a computed probability of 0.423 of surviving a particular nuclear attack. Second, the level of detail achieved has made the simulations relatively inflexible, because any variation from assumed conditions has required massive recomputation—a slightly different type of nuclear attack, in the example cited, would require recomputation of the survival probabilities of all the post offices in the nation.

The continued development of computer capabilities promises to relieve both of these difficulties by allowing the rapid preparation and graphical presentation of usable summaries rather than raw data, and by easing the massive recomputation necessary to study the effects of varying conditions. As of this writing, however, such efforts can be quite costly. It is often more useful to devise simpler, less detailed models, which can be studied either analytically or with very limited calculations to assess the likely results before embarking on a massive detailed simulation. Despite their verisimilitude, such elaborate simulation efforts still rest, at some level, on intuitively derived assumptions about the processes involved. These assumptions must always be examined carefully in using any model, no matter how detailed, and the results must always be viewed with appropriate skepticism.

Current Mathematical Models

Many recent modeling efforts have not been in the traditions of Lanchester and Richardson, in that they have involved little or no dynamics. Rather than addressing the evolution of a process over time, they are concerned with a single step, such as an attack, or at most two steps, such as an attack and retaliation. Other models make conjectural quantitative estimates intended to guide decisions, but the accuracy of these estimates can only be determined after the decisions are made and the results are known. (Models for estimating costs of weapons systems or the effects of nuclear attack are examples.)

Many of these new models are closely akin to physical, engineering, or econometric models, but it is difficult to discuss them in general because each is tailored to an individual problem. Some examples of generally static models may suffice as illustrations. The first example considers the estimation of the number of survivors of a single attack on a nation by nuclear weapons. A second example is a static model for mutual deterrence between two equal parties. A very simple econometric type of analytical model concerns an attempt to estimate the eventual cost of proposed military systems. In addition to these static models, a number of modern dynamic approaches will be cited.

Static Models

Modeling a Nuclear Attack. Consider first the problem of estimating the number of survivors of an attack on a nation by nuclear explosions. What is meant by survival? One hour? One week? A decade? A nuclear attack could have many devastating and life-threatening effects ranging from immediate vaporization of persons close to nuclear explosions to disruption of the economy and the social order resulting in deaths from starvation, crime, and lack of medical attention. It has even been conjectured that climatic or genetic effects might render agriculture impossible.

For some purposes—calculating deterrent effects, for instance—it suffices to estimate the minimum number of casualties threatened. This can be done by considering only prompt casualties due to the immediate effects of the explosions. Many of the effects of nuclear radiation are long-term and only cause casualties after some days have passed. Those that reliably cause immediate casualties are generally so limited in range that their victims would also be killed by blast effects. (Burns, which depend on the weather, are not reliable.) Thus, if one is concerned only with estimating the absolute minimum number of casualties, only the effect of the blast (overpressure) need be considered. The amount of overpressure resulting from a nuclear explosion is easily calculated from tabulated empirical data, and the probability of various levels of overpressure producing an immediate casualty is also known empirically.

Given the locations of the explosions and of the population, the minimum expected number of casualties can easily be computed. Whatever might be done about the location of the explosions, the location of the population varies over time. If one assumes that the attacker cannot choose the time, it is necessary to consider the time when the (minimum expected number of prompt) casualties will be fewest. (If the attacker *can* choose his time, it will probably be the time at which the casualties will be greatest, but we will assume here the former case.) Determining just this variable with complete accuracy imposes a formidable task on the modeler. Even if the attack comes without warning, one must consider the habitual variations over time of the locations of the entire population of the attacked country and the effects of all possible targetings of the weapons involved in the attack. (If one were really only interested in a true minimum, of course, one might consider the least efficient attack, probably resulting in almost no casualties, but what we are really after is the minimum casualties that the attacker can guarantee, so we assume efficient targeting.) If warning is assumed, one must conjecture how a population threatened with a nuclear attack would relocate.

Gathering accurate data on matters concerning the population of a potentially hostile power is virtually impossible. Only vague and unreliable estimates of average populations of regions are available, and one must "assume away" the difficulties (or switch to concentrating on destroying buildings, which have verifiable locations and do not move.)

Given an assumed population density, one must find the targeting that produces the maximum number of expected prompt casualties. Even this can be a challenging mathematical problem because of the complex variation of the probability of injury with distance from the explosion. To simplify calculations, it is customary to compute the radius at which the probability of prompt destruction by overpressure is 50 percent. Population inside this radius is assumed destroyed, and population outside remains unharmed. Given the sizes and numbers of the bombs to be used, finding the optimal targeting and the minimum number of prompt casualties expected then becomes a relatively straightforward procedure, but one that demands very large amounts of computation. Unfortunately for the modeler, if the bombs are delivered by missiles they cannot be placed precisely at the selected sites, but often can be delivered only with some error, which further complicates matters.

But out of all this uncertainty there comes, finally, a

simplification. It turns out that if one carries out these computations in detail, the results can be approximated by relatively simple formulas. Assume that the population of each city is distributed in a symmetric Gaussian distribution about its center, characterized by the total population N of the city and a radius R that measures the dispersion of the population, so the density at distance r from the center is

$$D(r) = \frac{N}{2\pi R^2} e^{-\frac{r^2}{2R^2}} \qquad (11)$$

Assume further that the weapons, each "destroying" a circular area A, are placed "at random" (i.e., form a Poisson process) with an average density m. The probability that an arbitrary point in the plan will not be covered by one of the areas (and so will not be destroyed) is e^{-mA}. For a constant initial population density D, the expected density remaining is $(1 - e^{-mA})D$. If we consider variable population densities D and variable densities m for placing the centers of the circles of destruction, the formula remains a valid approximation as long as the radius of the circles is small compared with the distances over which the density D varies appreciably. (In the limit as A goes to 0 while m increases to keep the product mA fixed, the approximation becomes exact.)

The assumptions made could be thought of as characterizing an attack by small weapons delivered with random errors that are a substantial fraction of their destruction radius. It may seem absurd to characterize nuclear weapons as "small," but assumption of the above formulas does allow an analytic calculation of the density m that maximizes the destruction when D is given by Equation (11). If the integral of the density m is M (the total number of weapons), the net destruction produced by choosing the m that maximizes the destruction is of the form

$$f(M) = (1 - (1 + B\sqrt{M})e^{-B\sqrt{M}})N, \qquad (12)$$

where $B = (A/\pi R^2)^{1/2}$. Fortunately, there are no empirical data on the destruction of cities by thermonuclear weapons, but if U.S. census data for urban areas are used, the circular areas of destruction are chosen to correspond to one-megaton weapons, and the weapons are placed to maximize the destruction, then the resulting destruction in each urban area can be approximated to reasonable accuracy by an appropriate choice of the constant R for that area. Thus, the relatively complicated computations necessary when using actual circles of destruction and population data can be replaced by a simple formula.

Modeling mutual deterrence. Consider a static model of mutual deterrence between two parties equal in all respects. Each has a land-based force of M missiles in hardened silos, spaced well apart. Each missile bears π independently targeted warheads, and each warhead has an independent probability p of destroying a missile at which it is targeted. Each party demands that Γ of its missiles must be expected to survive an all-out attack by those of the other side. An all-out attack will result in π warheads being targeted at each missile. The probability of surviving this number of independent attacks is $(1 - p)^{\pi}$, and the expected number surviving the attack is $M(1 - p)^{\pi}$, so the required minimum force on each side to achieve the desired goal is $M = \Gamma(1 - p)^{-\pi}$.

As the number of warheads on each missile, π, is increased, however, each warhead becomes less powerful, so p, the probability of destroying its target, decreases. Thus, if one knew the relationship between π and p, it would be possible to determine the increase (or decrease) in the missile forces needed to maintain a minimal deterrent in the face of a bilateral increase in the number of warheads carried by each missile. This model has been greatly simplified by the assumption of equality between parties, but, even so, it has been found that when similar models are constructed without this assumption, the essential behavior does not differ dramatically from that exhibited in the simpler model. Thus, the simpler model forms a useful tool for exploring qualitative behavior without engaging in the very elaborate calculations of a full-scale simulation.

Modeling systems costs. A third type of model, really econometric in nature, is concerned with the attempt to estimate the eventual costs of proposed military systems. Some of these are based on the idea that the cost per unit of manufacturing the system will tend to decrease as more are produced, because the producers will learn by experience to be more efficient. If one postulates an irreducible minimum cost per unit of A and an additional initial cost per unit of B, which is reduced by a fixed factor, λ, for every unit produced, then the total cost for N units is given by

$$C(N) = AN + \frac{B}{1-\lambda}(1-\lambda^N) \qquad (13)$$

One can then attempt to estimate the values that should be attributed to the parameters A, B, and λ, for the particular system being considered. Although this sort of model has had some success in estimating production costs in cases where the problems of production are relatively well understood and substantial research and development is not involved, the feasibility of estimating the parameters for truly new and different systems is extremely questionable.

Dynamic Models

In addition to the sorts of static models that have been illustrated above by very simple examples, there have been many continuations, both deterministic and stochastic, of the Lanchester tradition, trying to capture the dynamics of warfare for particular types of engagements. While some have simply been elaborations and complications of the basic idea, several new strains of thought have been added that lead to quite different sorts of problems. To illustrate the first of these, let us assume that the commander of one side (in a deterministic model) has a choice of tactics, or that some parameters of the battle are under his control—for example, assuming limited ammunition, he might decide the rate and consequently the accuracy of fire. Then one is faced with the problem of choosing the tactics that yield the best outcome. The mathematical discipline of *control theory* treating such problems has developed rapidly in the past few decades, and mathematical techniques for attacking such problems are very well developed.

If the model is stochastic, an even more complex problem is presented. Here it is not enough to decide in advance on the tactics yielding the best expectation, which would be a control theory problem. Instead, it is necessary to have a flexible decision rule that at any stage of the battle will tell which choice, based on the progress of the battle so far (i.e., the present state of the system), can be expected to yield the best outcome, in view of the fact that future tactics will change randomly depending on probabilistic future states of the system. Again, a branch of mathematics, *dynamic programming*, has been developed to treat precisely this sort of problem. Essentially, dynamic programming works backward from the last step of the battle, when there are no more decisions to be made, and computes the optimum decision for each state that might be presented just before the last step. Knowing what the decision will be at the last step for each state, it then becomes possible to compute, for each possible prior state, the decision that yields the best *expected* ultimate result, working backward step by step. The techniques of dynamic programming have been developed relatively recently (compared with control theory, which has roots extending back to the 19th century). Many problems present awkward and tedious computations, but the rapid development of computers has made solutions more and more tractable for a wide variety of problems, so that problems that were once computationally infeasible can now be solved.

Battles, however, are not one-sided affairs. Usually commanders on both sides have choices. The study of the type of problem resulting from this sort of consideration is known as the theory of *differential games*. This theory has been developed even more recently than dynamic programming and presents difficult conceptual problems in mathematics. Although some progress has been made, some basic theorems have been proved, and some enlightening examples have been solved, this field, which attempts to deal with the problem of ultimate military interest, is not yet capable of providing solutions to many problems of practical importance.

The development of dynamic programming and differential games has largely arisen in and been supported by the community concerned with military mathematical modeling. It has sometimes been useful—both mathematically and as a training exercise—to incorporate the mathematical models into simulations with human decision makers (rather than the ideal mathematical optimal decision makers assumed in the theories). This approach yields some insights into both the nature of optimal solutions and the psychology of the competitors. The human commander today may be playing against another human or against a computer program designed to achieve an optimum or near-optimum strategy.

Conclusion

Mathematical modeling in military affairs has roots in ritualistic augury as well as in common sense. The desire to know and to influence the future in matters of such import can be overwhelming, and one of the things sometimes overwhelmed is common sense. It is absolutely essential in applying any mathematical model to examine its assumptions in the most critical fashion. For instance, the model derived above to approximate the minimum guaranteed fatalities that could be threatened by a retaliatory attack might slowly become transformed, through inattention, to "the fatalities expected in a nuclear attack," which might be quite a different matter. But even when the foundations of the model may be questionable, it is necessary to ask whether they are good enough approximations to yield some useful insight into qualitative questions.

ROBERT H. KUPPERMAN
HARVEY A. SMITH

SEE ALSO: Cost Analysis; Lanchester Equations; Mathematics and the Military; Models, Simulations, and War Games; Operations Research, Military; Osipov Equations; Strategic Warfare, Operations Research in; Systems Analysis.

Bibliography

McNichols, G. 1984. *Cost analysis*. Operations Research Society of America Monograph. Washington, D.C.

Richardson, L. F. 1950. *Arms and insecurity*. Pittsburgh: Boxwood.

Taylor, J. G. 1983. *Lanchester models of warfare*. Operations Research Society of America Monograph. Washington, D.C.

MATHEMATICS AND THE MILITARY

Much of mathematics, like the physical sciences, originates with man's attempt to understand the world around him. Physical and engineering problems have always provided continuous impetus to mathematical inquiry. In fact, mathematical sciences play an essential role in the analysis and modeling of a variety of problems that arise in military sciences, engineering, and operations. Today, the interaction of mathematics with other fields such as life sciences, economics, and behavioral sciences has made this discipline even more indispensable as a framework for understanding and providing solutions to a variety of critical problems encountered in national defense.

Most of the contributions of the mathematical sciences tend to be generic and have applicability to a wide range of defense needs. In this paper, however, the primary consideration is the many challenging problems pertaining to armed forces of the future. Such challenges include the design, implementation, and use of robots and autonomous machines; image analysis and the design of multisensor automatic or semiautomatic target recognizers (ATR); near-real-time battle management systems; man-machine interfaces; and weapon system design, including the design of novel armor-antiarmor, smart materials, and structures.

While many contributions of mathematics have resulted in direct practical applications or have provided a natural framework for other disciplines, the motivation of much of mathematics is simply to gain understanding of inherent mathematical structures. Aesthetics and abstraction are essential components of mathematical thinking. The abstraction that is fundamental to the nature of mathematical modeling often complicates access to this field by others. The advent of computers and computing should help to bridge the gap between the so-called pure and applied mathematics.

Some Success Stories

The following paragraphs describe some examples of the successful application of mathematical theory to military use.

Spline Functions. The problem of the representation of a function from sampled data has a long history; it is closely related to the problems of interpolation and approximation of functions, both of which go back to the beginnings of mathematical analysis. The theory of splines was developed in response to a particular problem in filtering methods in signal processing. It has since found applications in an ever-increasing list of areas of interest to the military, such as vulnerability modeling, computer-aided design, and signature analysis and prediction, while also making possible substantial gains in numerical computation, graphic representation, and data analysis for test purposes. In data analysis, further studies have been made of the interpretation and representation of data using splines with variable knots. The current work in this area deals with multivariate splines and their applications.

The Fast Fourier Transform. In 1964 Professor John Tukey (Princeton University) and his associate (at IBM), developed a fast mathematical procedure for performing calculations with discrete Fourier transforms. This fast, economical, and efficient procedure is called the Fast Fourier Transform (FFT). The speed improvements afforded by this procedure made possible real-time control and guidance systems for aircraft and missiles, real-time sensor data analysis, and real-time image analysis. FFT computes the Fourier transform, which extracts the desired information content from the received data in many fewer steps than earlier techniques. Many similar attempts are underway to develop fast algorithms that exploit the special structure of the problems. Related questions of computer implementations and the design of special-purpose processors also constitute an area of considerable interest.

Front Tracking Algorithms. Shock waves occur in the operation of numerous weapon systems, missiles, and aircraft. The prediction of shock, blast, and combustion effects is important, both in system design and the design of defensive measures. Owing to the high cost of experimentation, it is not feasible to obtain adequate predictions of threat or performance by testing a significant number of physically realistic situations. Thus, the ability to predict effects numerically would greatly improve the design processes of important military systems. The elaborate physical phenomena that occur, however, are not easily captured by straightforward computations, even on supercomputers, because of the complexity and number of computations required to achieve accurate numerical representation of such physical events. Algorithmic improvements are needed to permit accurate two- and three-dimensional computations in this important area. Front tracking is a successful algorithmic development of this type. It is an adaptive method that takes advantage of known analytic solutions. It is useful for problems containing singularities and discontinuities concentrated on surfaces, such as occur in a variety of fluid dynamics problems. These include shock waves, contact discontinuities, material interfaces, slip lines, and chemical reaction fonts.

Research Trends

This section presents several examples of research trends that offer considerable promise for the operational capability of future armed forces.

Nonlinear Analysis. Nonlinear equations that model such phenomena as combustion, detonation, transonic flow, nonlinear optics, wave propagation in complex media, VLSI (very large system integration) devices, neural networks, and control systems exhibit a range of behavior for which effective mathematical understanding either is not available or is only now beginning to emerge. Advances in fundamental knowledge of nonlinear systems are, therefore, needed to understand fully the structure of physical phenomena such as bifurcation, phase transition, multistability, and transition to chaos and turbulence. Recent discoveries that nonlinear phenomena from different fields do indeed display common features have rejuvenated activity in this area with a goal of developing common methods of analysis. Still, there is a need for a better understanding of nonlinear waves in two and three space dimensions, both theoretically and computationally, for our ability to predict the performance of materials and both rigid and flexible structures under ultra-high rates of (impulsive) loading, and their vulnerability to high-energy radiation. Propagation of nonlinear waves and beams through perturbed inhomogeneous atmosphere must be made predictable. The numerical computations of these waves and their interactions strain existing computer methodology and hardware in two dimensions, and are totally inadequate in three dimensions.

Composite and novel materials are modeled by large systems of nonlinear partial equations of mixed types. The analysis of such equations is needed to understand phenomena such as delamination, local stability, shock formation, and propagation. Nonlinear theories present the capability to predict and control the large dramatic changes experienced by many substances in the form of phase transitions and the formation of defect structures. Finally, many intractable physical and engineering problems lead to nonlinear systems with a large number of degrees of freedom. Many of these systems (e.g., fluids) consist of a large number of elements interacting in a simple way. This simple microscopic picture can develop more complicated nonlinear macroscopic behavior. A fundamental problem is how collective large-scale behavior evolves from this many-element system.

Computational Geometry. Progress in robotics and autonomous systems will extend available manpower and provide alternatives for the performance of hazardous and high-risk duties. Research in robotics and autonomous systems has posed a number of challenging problems that appear susceptible to mathematical solution. Robot motions planning increasingly requires the development and use of novel algorithmic ideas based on algebraic and differential geometry. Computational geometry is needed to describe and compute the motion of robotic manipulators; it is also a necessary ingredient of navigation of mobile autonomous systems. Geometric approaches also hold promise for solving a variety of other computational problems. For example, there are discrete combinatorial problems for which efficient procedures have been discovered using ideas from geometry. Obstacle avoidance problems involve a large combinatorial search in three dimensions. Also, inverse robotic kinematics, solid modeling, and computer-aided geometric design will benefit considerably from novel algorithmic approaches to nonlinear geometry.

Interactive Data Analysis. Interactive graphic data analysis is an area of statistics that combines all of the techniques and algorithms arising from computational statistics with modern data analysis. It is an area in which a statistician or other data analyst coordinates modern computer graphics and interactive database tools. The thrust of work in this area includes (a) large sample statistics; (b) fast algorithms for data handling, transfer, and display; (c) new algorithms for the realistic display of data of high dimensions; (d) techniques for small data sets; and (e) procedures for sample re-use, which have been found to be extremely computer intensive. Existing statistical procedures do not adequately address these needs. Thus, the goal of current research in modern data analysis is to produce algorithms and procedures that are fast, flexible (in terms of dimensionality of the data and basic assumptions), and accurate (in terms of the statistical inferences produced). The so-called classical approaches to data modeling, such as stepwise regression, are known to be unstable and do not produce credible inferences even though the assumption of normality is satisfied. More modern techniques avoid the normality assumption and take advantage of the enormously successful capability of the human eye-hand combination, along with the speed and accuracy of the computer, in ferreting out structure and reducing data dimensionality. Recent work in this field shows considerable initial promise, but much remains to be accomplished.

Intelligent Control Systems. Intelligent response to the dynamic combat scenario places stringent requirements on the speed and subtlety of analysis of the environment. The battlefield commander is faced with a large volume of information from many diverse sources that is usually imprecise and incomplete, contains errors, changes with time, and may arrive in the wrong time sequence. Yet the commander must use this information to make intelligent decisions in order to remain in control of the evolving battle. Moreover, there is an increasing move toward autonomous data collection, fire control, and computer-aided decision making. The principal goal of research on intelligent control systems is to develop the conceptual and mathematical foundations of intelligent systems, blending the analytical and theoretical insights of control and signal processing with the problems of artificial intelligence. This could be done, perhaps, by incorporating a priori structural and other information in models and representations at different levels of abstraction. Particular attention is being given in this area to information processing corresponding to sensory modalities such as vision, mathematical foundations of learning and machine intelligence, and a theory and associated algorithms for resulting parallel and distributed computations.

Conclusion

Mathematical sciences are at the forefront of today's rapidly progressing scientific and technological fields. This is primarily due to the inescapable significance of modeling and analysis and the advent of modern computers. Computational methods have emerged as indispensable and enabling tools for a broad spectrum of scientific and engineering problems that underlie many critical military applications. High-performance computing is becoming the most pervasive and promising tool for a variety of applications. Interdisciplinary research, in which mathematical sciences will play a pivotal role, is needed to make efficient use of current supercomputers, networks of current computers, special-purpose and experimental systems, and the new generation large-scale parallel architectures. Basic studies in theoretical foundations will be needed, as well as development of new mathematical and computational algorithms for the relevant applications areas.

Other newly emerging areas of research of interest to the military require progress in more foundational subfields of mathematics. These include computational nonlinear algebra and symbolic computations that derive considerable impetus from advances in algebraic geometry and number theory. Furthermore, current research and potential breakthroughs in fields such as integral and stochastic geometry, constructive combinatorics, and spatial statistics hold considerable promise for the much-needed development of efficient algorithms for multisensor automatic target recognizers. Continuing attempts to understand a wide spectrum of nonlinear phenomena such as turbulence, coherent structures, chaos, and order, have drawn upon and greatly stimulated several branches of core mathematics, including global analysis, algebraic geometry, and topological dynamics.

JAGDISH CHANDRA

SEE ALSO: Lanchester Equations; Models, Simulations, and War Games; Osipov Equations.

Bibliography

Chandra, J., ed. 1984. *Chaos in nonlinear dynamical systems.* Philadelphia: Society for Industrial and Applied Mathematics (SIAM).

Chui, C. 1988. *Multivariate splines.* Washington, D.C.: Conference Board of Mathematical Sciences (CBMS) 54.

Cooley, J. M., and J. W. Tukey. 1965. An algorithm for machine calculation of complex Fourier series. *Mathematics of Computation* 19:297–301.

de Boor, C. 1978. *A practical guide to splines.* New York: Springer-Verlag.

Farin, G., ed. 1987. *Geometric modeling: Algorithms and new trends.* Philadelphia: Society for Industrial and Applied Mathmatics.

Glimm, J., E. Isaacson, D. Marchesin, and O. McBryan. 1981. Front tracking for hyperbolic systems. *Advances in Applied Mathematics* 2:91–119.

Launer, R., and A. Siegel, eds. 1982. *Modern data analysis.* New York: Academic Press.

Sastry, S., and M. Bodson. 1989. *Adaptive control.* Englewood Cliffs, N.J.: Prentice-Hall.

Wolfram, S., ed. 1987. Complex Systems, 1, August. Champaign-Urbana, Ill.: Wolfram.

MAURITANIA, ISLAMIC REPUBLIC OF

A northwest African country with a hot, dry climate, the northern four-fifths of Mauritania is desert, but the southern regions are part of the moister Sahel zone. Although generally an agricultural country, there are considerable deposits of high-grade iron ore in the northeast.

Power Potential Statistics

Area: 1,030,700 square kilometers (397,953 sq. mi.)
Population: 1,983,000
Total Active Armed Forces: 11,750 (0.593% of pop.)
Gross Domestic Product: US$942 million (1989 est.)
Annual Defense Expenditure: US$37 million (4.2% of GDP, 1987 est.)
Iron and Steel Production:
Crude steel: 0.004 million metric tons (1986)
Fuel Production: none
Electrical Power Output: 136 million kwh (1989)
Merchant Marine: 1 vessel; 1,290 gross registered tons
Civil Air Fleet: 2 major transport aircraft; 29 usable airfields (9 with permanent-surface runways); none with runways over 3,659 meters (12,000 ft.); 4 with runways 2,440–3,659 meters (8,000–12,000 ft.); 17 with runways 1,220–2,440 meters (4,000–8,000 ft.).

For the most recent information, the reader may refer to the following annual publications:
The Military Balance. International Institute for Strategic Studies. London: Brassey's (UK).
The Statesman's Year-Book. New York: St. Martin's Press.
The World Factbook. Central Intelligence Agency. Washington, D.C.: Brassey's (US).

History

Historically, Mauritania has been an area of interaction between the Berber-Arab cultures to the north, and the sub-Saharan cultures to the south. Mauritania's people were converted to Islam in the eleventh century A.D., when the country was conquered by Muslims from Morocco. French influence began to enter the area in the early twentieth century, but French rule was not fully established until 1934. Mauritania was a member of the post–World War II West African Federation, and became an autonomous but not fully independent state within the French Community following the French constitutional referendum of September 1958.

Mauritania gained full independence in June 1961, and subsequently withdrew from the French Community in 1966. For nearly two decades, the country was governed by the regime of Moktar Ould Daddah and his Mauritanian People's Party (PPM), but he was deposed in a bloodless military coup in July 1978. This coup followed military reverses in campaigns against Polisario guerrillas in Western (or Spanish) Sahara, where Mauritania had allied with Morocco to divide the former Spanish colony. Following several coups in 1978–79, the Military Committee for National Salvation (CMSN) was established, and Col. Mohamed Khouna Ould Haidalla emerged as the leading figure.

Haidalla's regime was troubled by severe drought in the Sahel region, and its support of the Polisario guerrillas drew strong opposition. Another bloodless coup on 12 December 1984 brought Lt. Col. Maayouia Ould

Sid'Ahmed Taya to power. Taya undertook economic reforms, liberalized national political life, and in December 1986 held Mauritania's first-ever municipal elections. Taya's regime has also moderated Mauritania's foreign policy, and moved toward closer ties with the United States.

Mauritania's security situation was complicated by widespread unrest among its southern peoples in summer 1989. Refugees fleeing to Senegal from government suppression sparked several minor border clashes between Mauritanian and Senegalese forces, but by early autumn, following promises of reform in Mauritania, tension had been reduced and calm had returned to both sides of the border.

Politico-Military Background and Policy

The Mauritanian army was formed from French-raised colonial troops in November 1960, and until Mauritania left the French community in 1966, France provided considerable technical support, equipment, and training. When Spain evacuated the Western Sahara in 1976, Morocco and Mauritania concluded an agreement whereby Mauritania gained the southern third of that country while Morocco received the remainder. This brought Mauritanian forces into conflict with the Polisario guerrillas, and despite French and Moroccan aid, they suffered losses and defeats. The Haidalla regime reversed this policy and recognized the Polisario, abandoning claims to the Western Sahara in 1978. The Taya regime has maintained a neutral policy toward both the Polisario and Morocco.

The armed forces are recruited solely from volunteers. The armed forces, which were 18,000 strong during the conflict in the Western Sahara, have since been reduced in size.

Strategic Problems

Mauritania's principal strategic problems are internal. First, the country's poverty decreases its ability to maintain an effective defense, and with Mauritania's dry climate and lack of natural resources, economic development will be difficult. Second, there is a traditional rivalry between the Moorish (Arab-Berber) peoples of the north and the less numerous African peoples of the south. The Taya regime dealt harshly with Toucouleur dissidents in late 1986, sending several dozen to prison for long terms. While ethnic unrest is unlikely to bring down the government, it could prove troublesome, as shown by the events of mid-1989.

Military Assistance

Mauritania receives considerable economic aid from the United States, averaging US$2–3 million annually in development assistance during the 1980s, plus food aid and other assistance. Most military aid comes from France, a total of FFr 68.9 million (US$9.9 million) in 1986. In 1988, Mauritania received a total of US$10.13 million of military aid from the United States and France. This represents a considerable portion of Mauritanian defense spending, since total government expenditure was US$225 million in 1984.

Defense Industry

There is no domestic arms industry and all weapons are imported.

Alliances

Mauritania is a member of the Arab League, the United Nations (UN), and the Organization of African Unity (OAU). Mauritania has close security and economic ties with France, and has grown closer to the United States since the mid-1980s. Mauritania has had good relations with the United States, except for the period from June 1967 to December 1969, when relations were suspended as a result of U.S. support for Israel during the Six-Day War.

(For an explanation of the abbreviations and symbols used in the following section of military statistics, see the list of Abbreviations and Acronyms in each volume.)

Total Armed Forces

Active: 11,750. Terms of service: conscription (2 years) authorized.

ARMY: 11,000. 6 military regions.
7 mot inf bn.
1 para/cdo bn.
1 arty bn.
2 Camel Corps bn.
1 armd recce sqn.
4 AD arty bty.
1 engr coy.
Equipment:
Recce: 39 AML-60, 20-90, 40 Saladin.
Towed arty: 105mm: 10 M-101A1/HM-2; 122mm: 20 D-74, 10 D-30.
Mortars: 81mm: 100; 120mm: 15 AR-51/-EC1A-L/SL.
ATGW: 4 Milan.
RCL: 57mm: M-18; 75mm: M-20; 106mm: M-40A1.
ATK guns: 85mm: 12 D-44.
AD guns: 23mm: 50 ZU-23-2; 37mm: 25 M-1939; 100mm: 12 KS-19.
SAM: SA-7.

NAVY: 500. Bases: Nouadhibou.
Patrol Craft, Inshore: 6:
1 N'Mada (UK Jura) PCO.
3 El Vaiz (Sp Barcelo) PFI.†
1 El Nasr (Fr PATRA) PCI.
1 Z'Bar (Ge Neustadt) PFI.

AIR FORCE: 250: 7 cbt ac, no armed hel.
COIN: 5 BN-2 Defender, 2 FTB-337 Milirole.
MR: 2 Cheyenne II.
Transport: 2 Cessna F-337, 1 DHC-5D, 1 Gulfstream II, 1 Skyvan 3M.

PARAMILITARY
Gendarmerie 1,800; 6 regional coy (Ministry of Interior).
National Guard: (Ministry of Interior) 2,800 plus 1,000 auxiliaries.
Border Guard: 100.

Future

Mauritania's present government is dedicated to a policy of national development, emphasizing progress, education, literacy, and national unity. The government faces no serious internal or external threats, and should be able to retain sufficient popular support to stay in power for the foreseeable future. This leaves economic development and potential ethnic conflict (with possible foreign involvement) as Mauritania's greatest problems.

DAVID L. BONGARD
TREVOR N. DUPUY

SEE ALSO: Morocco; Sub-Saharan Africa.

Bibliography

American University. 1973. *Area handbook for Mauritania* Washington, D.C.: Government Printing Office.
Hunter B., ed. 1991. *The statesman's year-book, 1991–92.* New York: St. Martin's Press.
International Institute for Strategic Studies. 1991. *The military balance, 1991–1992.* London: Brassey's.

MEASURES OF EFFECTIVENESS

In the most general sense, a measure of effectiveness is an indicator of a system or activity's capability to achieve its specified objectives or accomplish its goals. Any selection between alternative means of performing an operation requires either an explicit or an implied measure of effectiveness as a rationale. The selection process generally involves allocating scarce resources (dollars, aircraft, ships, battalions) or selecting between alternative courses of action (strategies, tactics, acquisition strategies).

This definition of measures of effectiveness encompasses selection of such alternatives as strategies to deter nuclear war; tactics to win a battle; weapon systems to defeat a specified enemy; forces to achieve a defined objective; supply systems that provide prescribed logistic support; transportation systems required to deliver troops or supplies over a given distance, to a given destination, or in a given time period; or materiel acquisition strategies.

A measure of effectiveness requires careful definition of the total context: the alternatives that are to be evaluated (tactics, troops, weapon systems, transports); the objective to be achieved; the processes by which the objective can be achieved; and the environmental factors that influence effectiveness (threat parameters and tactics, night or day, climatic conditions, terrain). A measure of performance, in contrast, is defined by technical and measurable specifications in the absence of a context. Performance measurements include, for example, the speed of an aircraft or vehicle, weapons accuracy and hit probability, maximum weapons range, or maximum aircraft range and altitude. These contribute toward achieving a given objective but are not measures of the degree to which an objective is attained.

To understand the context in which measures of effectiveness are evaluated, the concepts of systems analysis (cost-effectiveness analysis) and operations research should be defined. Niskanen (1967), as an economist, states that

> cost-effectiveness analysis is specifically directed to problems in which the output (effectiveness) cannot be measured in market prices, but where inputs are substitutable at exchange relationships developed in the market. It addresses the problem of maximizing effectiveness subject to a *generalized* resource constraint measured in dollars.

In the defense sector, there is no market evaluation of effectiveness, and marginal priorities are determined not by a market system but by the political structure. On the other hand, Niskanen stated that classical operations analysis "can be conducted entirely in physical and other nonmonetary terms. It addresses problems of maximizing effectiveness, subject to a set of *specific* resource constraints, measured in the amount and type of resources available." There is no market evaluation of either input or output.

Measures of effectiveness should have three primary attributes: (1) they must be relevant to the stated objective; (2) they must be a measure of the dominant attributes of the required capability—in other words, if the criteria being measured are met, a high probability must exist that the objective will be achieved; and (3) they should provide some quantifiable relationship (not necessarily scalar) to the achievement of the objective.

Measures of effectiveness can be expressed in many ways. The most common method is the choice of a measurable parameter that can be correlated to a resource level. Common examples used are the number or fraction of casualties inflicted or sustained, the amount of area occupied, and so on. The relationships can be linear or nonlinear. In many cases, nonlinearity results from diminishing returns as a result of adding forces or weapon systems. However, this nonlinearity is usually ignored for ease of analysis.

In a number of analyses, nonparametric statistics or preferential ranking methods may be used to rank alternatives. In other instances, measures of effectiveness can be expressed in yes/no terms. For example, deterrence of nuclear war is either successful or it is not. Or a matrix of attributes defined in yes/no terms is developed, and the collection of answers for each option is used to determine relative rankings. Measures of effectiveness are also commonly expressed in confidence terms: for example, the probability that deterrence will be successful or that a campaign will be won, or, at a lower level, the probability that a submarine transiting a barrier of given dimensions at a given speed will be detected and attacked.

Hierarchy of Objectives

A useful analytical model should be able to assist all decision levels, from the highest national authority to the commander of a small tactical unit or force. The analyst's most difficult choice is the selection of the principal objective that is appropriate for the particular decision level. Selection and definition of the objective are essential to the selection of measures of effectiveness.

A hierarchy of objectives can readily be developed. At the top of the pyramid would be national objectives, such as "keeping the peace" and "maintaining liberty." These are lofty goals, but their achievement is not readily measurable, nor can criteria indicating achievement of these goals be clearly defined. Lower down in the pyramid is the objective of a skirmish by a small force—perhaps the seizure of a hill. The degree to which this objective is achieved can be analyzed.

There are as many levels of analysis between these extremes as there are rational levels of decision making. Unfortunately, the definition of the objective and the relevant measures of effectiveness are frequently subject to suboptimization. For example, the objective of a campaign or a war is usually *not* to kill as many enemies as possible, but to control population, resources, or territory. The might of Persia was measured by the great number of people they had subjugated and the vast amount of territory they controlled. The postwar Soviet Union considered itself a winner because it controlled all of the people of Eastern Europe. The United States provides an exception: its forces did not fight to control Koreans, Vietnamese, or Grenadans; they entered the contest to assure those people the right to control their own destiny. By choosing too low an objective—for example, "killing enemy troops"—the analyst excludes examination of nondestructive courses of action to achieve the true objective, including alternate tactics, strategies, or political means.

The following example illustrates the suboptimal selection of objectives and of measure of effectiveness. It is assumed that an enemy has five bridges over which to send supplies and reinforcements. A friendly airstrike has the potential of destroying three bridges. Consequently, at first glance, the airstrike's expected performance should be 60 percent. However, because the enemy may change the supply routes, marshal additional resources, employ deception, or rely on additional means of crossing the river (air, boat), the impact on the enemy's throughput capability after the strike, a more proper measure of effectiveness, may in fact indicate a much smaller impact.

Analysis at the next-higher decision level should include the contingency that the enemy could anticipate a problem and stockpile sufficient supplies on his side of the river to satisfy his immediate needs. Consequently, the loss of the three bridges may not decrease his forces' combat capability appreciably. Having determined the expected marginal decrease of the enemy's combat capability, it might be decided that other alternatives could provide more reduction in the enemy's combat capability than the air strike.

Analysis of alternative courses of action at the subnational level (insurgency, counterinsurgency, or terrorism) is much more difficult since, as Niskanen (1967) states, insurgents do not have a vulnerable value base. The objective of countering insurgents is therefore limited to defensive actions—that is, defeating actions that would cause a detrimental change to the status quo.

Englund (1984) points out that measures of effectiveness are not directly transferable to different applications. For example, systems analytical techniques may estimate that a future fighter aircraft can shoot down six aircraft during its combat lifetime compared with only two for the current fighter. While many decision makers may not believe the absolute values of these results, they might trust the ratio of relative effectiveness for rank ordering and determining which alternative to buy.

Complexity of Measures of Effectiveness

Of course, the ideal would be a single, quantifiable measure of effectiveness that assesses the single most important attribute of the objective and that can be related, in a proven manner, directly to the resources required. Unfortunately, this situation rarely occurs.

Historically, *simple* measures of effectiveness were used to determine the outcome of a contest. One measure was the fraction of archers killed by each side, or the ratio of archers remaining on each side after the contest. Given a certain ratio of archers surviving on each side, the battle outcome was relatively predictable.

With the advent of more lethal weapons, riflemen and cannons had to receive different values commensurate with their relative ability to inflict damage—*compound* measures of effectiveness. The fraction of weapons of each type remaining in the contest at any time in the battle had to be weighted by the weapons' relative capability to inflict casualties. The result was then combined in some meaningful manner to arrive at a single measure related to the potential of achieving the objective.

Another level of complexity is introduced when two systems are evaluated in terms of accomplishing a number of tasks. For example, navy destroyers can escort merchant ships, defend carrier battle groups against aircraft and submarine attacks, visit foreign ports in peacetime to represent their home country, and serve as a peacekeeping force to deter hostile action. Different classes of destroyers or other navy ships have the potential of performing each of these tasks with a different degree of success. Therefore, the objectives to be achieved must be weighted by their importance before a *complex* measure of effectiveness relative to each vessel can be determined. This problem also occurs when comparing specialized systems with generalized systems. Hughes (1984) mentions the difficulty of comparing an antisubmarine warfare (ASW) frigate, which performs ASW best, with multipurpose destroyers, which can perform many missions, including ASW, but probably do not perform ASW as well as the specialized ship.

The analysis becomes even more complicated when the alternative systems to be evaluated are very different—for example, when comparing the effectiveness of attack aircraft and long-range ground weapons to destroy deep interdiction targets under various circumstances and given various threats. In such circumstances, some analysts have used equal effectiveness domains or multidimensional surfaces for each alternative and examined the intersections. While methodologically elegant, most of these measures are suboptimizations. Frequently, proponents of each alternative engage in contests of "judgmental analysis." The proper analysis is to go to the next-higher decision level and select the objective and measure of effectiveness appropriate to that level. Occasionally, going to the next higher level will uncover additional courses of action, rendering all of the original courses suboptimum.

In an attempt to evaluate the effectiveness of a system in different contingencies, Attaway (1968) suggested the use of three variables in cost-effectiveness analyses. Two fundamental variables are cost and contingencies; using effectiveness as the third variable generates a three-dimensional surface. The view of this surface probably provides more insight than hard data for tradeoff analyses.

Measures of effectiveness (output) at any level must be useful to serve as inputs to the analysis at the next-higher decision level (which is usually more aggregated). In other words, the residual capabilities and posture following many lower-level engagements will serve as input to higher-level analysis. In the optimum, a hierarchy of models results in which the analysis at the highest, most aggregated, level is directly traceable to analyses at each of the more detailed, higher-resolution (lower) levels.

Too frequently, particularly in analysis at higher decision levels, measures of effectiveness are selected because they are quantifiable or their relationship to resource levels can readily be quantified, rather than because the measures are the most relevant or the dominant ones.

Combat Capability Indices

Historically, combat capability indices have been associated with weapon systems or small force units. These indices were used to determine the outcome of an engagement, the amount of casualties suffered by each side, and the movement of the forward edge of the battle area (FEBA). They are even more frequently used as inputs to higher-level analyses and more-aggregated simulations and wargames, in lieu of outputs from higher resolution, lower level analyses.

Such generalized indices are supposed to represent the combat capability (usually a measure of lethality) of a major weapon system or small force under all types of conditions. They have been called firepower potentials (FPP), firepower scores (FPS), weapons effectiveness indices (WEI), combat capability indices, and other names. All of them share the common assumption that it is possible to determine a single index for a weapon system based only on performance parameters, regardless of the mission objective, context, posture, or the nature and vulnerability of the threat. Use of these indices further ignores synergism in the mix of complementary weapons. For example, if one weapon is used in a suppression mode, thus preventing accurate return fire, another weapon may be much more effective than it would be if the enemy fire were not suppressed. In addition, indices do not consider the deterrent value of weapon systems even if they do not hit the target. Analysis showed that guns on the stern of merchant ships in World War II were very inaccurate and may never have shot down an aircraft. However, results also showed that merchant ships equipped with guns were rarely attacked or sunk by aircraft, since they usually had the choice of attacking undefended ships. In other words, the guns, even with little actual capability, had a great deterrent value.

In a related example, Hughes (1984) points out that in the recent Falkland Islands (Islas Malvinas) campaign, a weapon well known to be very effective against aircraft attacking at high altitudes actually kept these planes to low altitudes. This reduced the bombing effectiveness of the attacking aircraft and at the same time brought them into range of other antiaircraft weapons. Although those weapons were "officially" less effective, they ended up shooting down most of the aircraft. Analysis based purely on the number of attacking aircraft destroyed, however, would have reached the wrong conclusion regarding the weapons' relative effectiveness.

Indices further neglect the importance of the other functions of combat. For example, there are no scores for the effects of intelligence and target acquisition. A gun is much more effective if the locations of enemy target densities are known. In addition, combat capability is affected by the mission, the force posture, the terrain, the tactics, or the element of surprise, but the indices are not. Dupuy (1985) has done considerable analysis of historical battles in an attempt to develop quantifiable factors for such parameters. However, there are still no indices to reflect improvements in command, control, and communications or in logistic support. Obviously, long, vulnerable supply lines that result in shortages of ammunition and missiles will affect the capability of the weapons.

Combat capability indices are generally based on historical types of warfare and "balanced" forces. Therefore, they cannot be used to evaluate different tactics optimimzed for new weapon systems, or tradeoffs in force structure resulting in a different force balance. Some years ago, a new tank with shoot-on-the-move and night-fighting capabilities was given a score of 1.05 compared to the incumbent series of tanks. This 5 percent improvement was clearly absurd, since the new system has a high capability for night fighting while the current tank had none. If tactics were optimized to account for the new ability for night combat, the difference in the new system's capability might have been orders of magnitude greater than the 5 percent estimated.

Combat capability indices have generally been added arithmetically to arrive at a score for the force on each side, and the force ratio has been used to determine casualties and FEBA movement rates. Unfortunately, there is little historical evidence to validate correlation between such indices and battle movement, and even if such evidence were found, its application to future wars would be very suspect. There is considerable evidence that future war will depend heavily on intelligence gathered by many new means and by fast-reacting command and control systems, assisted by decision support systems that process and display large amounts of information in fractions of a second. No rules have been found to estimate the impact of new intelligence and modern computer-assisted command and control on weapons capability indices, force ratios, or combat results.

Therefore, responsible analysts have recommended for many years that such indices not be used to determine outcome of combat, or to serve as indicators of the outcome of engagements in more aggregated simulations. Instead of single indices, the output of simulations representing smaller engagements should be directly input into higher level models in a hierarchical manner.

The use of indices is further complicated by the inability to determine consistent criteria for a win or a loss in a tactical engagement. As a result of analyzing 80 battles, McQuie (1987) found no consistent measures of casualty production or casualty loss rates. In other words, criteria to determine whether an engagement has been won or lost based solely on casualty generation have exhibited such a wide variation that such measures should not be used as sole or principal determinant for the outcome of a battle in combat analyses.

Strategic Defense Analysis

In strategic analysis, objectives, measures, and criteria of success are at such a high level of abstraction that most criticism or analytical studies center around semantics and definitions. In addition, common terms used—deterrence, assured destruction, mutually assured destruction, damage limitation, counterforce, countervalue—contain such a high emotional value that they tend to sway political judgment in a democracy, and their use in a purely analytical context may get lost.

In the years immediately after World War II, the United States clearly had strategic superiority with respect to its major prospective opponent, the USSR, and thereby could achieve an assured degree of Soviet destruction. With the rapid development of the Soviet strategic forces, it soon became evident that either country could destroy the other. The major objective then became deterring strategic nuclear war. But deterrence is a very obtuse concept. To start with, two assumptions are required: first, that the enemy will always act rationally; second, that one can estimate how, in the *enemy's* view, our capabilities and intentions would deter them from initiating nuclear war. Therefore, the argument of how much deterrence is enough is really a set of assumptions regarding the enemy's perception and his intentions. Finally, arguments about deterrence are purely intellectual. So far no one has started a nuclear war—on one hand, that may be evidence that deterrence has worked. On the other hand, how can we determine what lesser capability would deter an enemy from starting a nuclear war?

Historically, concepts like assured destruction and mutually assured destruction required a defined fraction of the military (counterforce); otherwise, population and industry (countervalue) must be be destroyed for the concept to be useful. Then one can either measure the expected level of destruction that given forces can achieve, compared with the required level of destruction, or one can perform stochastic analyses to determine the confidence that the required level of destruction can be achieved.

One fallacy with this type of analysis is the lack of analysis regarding credibility of use. In other words, the enemy must believe in our resolve to unleash world-destructive forces, and furthermore, he must guess what threshold he must cross before we would take such a step. The more destructive the retaliatory step becomes, the less credible its use becomes. Such measures also assume that nations are inherently vindictive. In fact, survivors of a mass nuclear strike, who have lost most of their families, are not likely to be consoled by the assurance that an even larger fraction of the enemy's population was destroyed.

With the advent of Reagan's Strategic Defense Initiative, analysis of the number of enemy re-entry vehicles (RV) that would leak through the defense has become a common measure in many supporting studies. This, again, is a bad measure. Not all RVs are the same size, lethality, or sophistication. Furthermore, the purpose of defense is not to kill RVs but to protect population, cities, industry, and military targets. With limited resources, optimal defensive deployments can be developed to blunt the most threatening enemy strikes while letting those that can cause less critical damage pass through. Of course, this type of analysis is iterative and takes into account optimal enemy strategies.

Many analysts have emphasized that analysis of strategic defense alone is meaningless; we must start with national objectives regarding nuclear strategies. The overall national objectives must be to deter nuclear war by denying enemy decision makers the confidence that an attempted attack will meet their goals, and to assure the Soviets that, if an attack occurs, retaliatory destruction will be inevitable. Or as Kent (1988) stated, the correct statement of our broad objectives is not assured destruction of the enemy, certainly not mutual assured destruction, but, rather, assured restraint of enemy behavior in the broadest sense. He then analyzes his strategic concepts in terms of three generic forces: strategic offensive forces, strategic defensive forces, and defense suppression forces. Through analytical steps he reaches the conclusion that, given certain assumptions regarding the behavior on both sides, it would be possible, eventually, to focus on mutually assured survival. This is an objective on which one could reach general agreement. The argument then changes from a definition of illusory, ill-defined national objectives, to the best way to achieve mutual assured survival.

It must also be mentioned that analyses of tradeoffs between offensive and defensive forces in a context less than overall national strategic objectives is not constructive and only serves to generate illusory conclusions to support either of the proponents.

Summary

Measures of effectiveness must estimate a capability in a carefully defined context. The objective must be carefully and clearly defined and must be relevant to the decision to be made. Suboptimization will lead to exclusion of potential alternatives. A generally acceptable success criterion for indicating the accomplishment of the objective is essential.

Measures of effectiveness must indicate the capability of systems or forces to achieve specified objectives that are appropriate to the decision level being supported. The measures must also represent the dominant attributes of the capability. It is preferable, but not essential, that the measures be expressed quantifiably. Relative effectiveness can also be expressed in nonparametric statistical terms or by using preferential ranking techniques. In addition, a series of yes/no criteria, which differentiate between the alternatives, can be used to rank them. Comparisons of very different alternatives must be made at higher objective levels to prevent suboptimization.

The validity of generalized effectiveness indices, to be applied to a variety of situations, is at best questionable. Lower-level analyses should be performed in detail to determine not only expected outcomes and remaining resources on each side but also postures and definition of the environment. Higher-level analyses should build on the output of detailed lower-level analyses, without using simple indices or ratios.

It is essential to remember that the fundamental purpose of military modeling and supporting analyses is communication. Therefore, the choice of the measures of effectiveness used to rank alternatives must be credible and communicate to the decision makers the essence of the differences.

John G. Honig

SEE ALSO: Cold War; Cost Analysis; Defense Decision Making: Analysis and Models; Deterrence; Economics, Defense; Nuclear Employment Policy and Planning; Nuclear Theory and Policy; Planning, Military; Strategic Defense Initiative: Policy Implications.

Bibliography

Attaway, L. D. 1968. Criteria and the measurement of effectiveness. In *Systems analysis and policy planning*, ed. E. S. Quade and W. I. Boucher. Rand Report R-439-PR. Santa Monica, Calif.: Rand Corp.

Bonder, S. 1971. Systems analysis: A purely intellectual activity. *Military Review*, February.

Dupuy, T. N. 1985. *Numbers, predictions and war*. Rev. ed. Dunn Loring, Va.: HERO Books.

Kent, G. 1988. *An overall analytical framework for considering U.S. strategic forces*. Santa Monica, Calif: Rand Corp.

Hughes, W. P., Jr., ed. 1984. *Military modeling*. Alexandria, Va.: Military Operations Research Society.

McQuie, R. 1987. Battle outcomes: Casualty rates as a measure of defeat. *Army*, November, pp. 30–34.

Niskanen, W. A. 1967. Measures of effectiveness. In *Cost effectiveness analysis*, ed. T. A. Goldman. Praeger Special Studies in U.S. Economic and Social Development. New York: Praeger.

Stockfisch, J. A. 1975. *Models, data and war: A critique of the study of conventional forces*. Rand Report, R-1526-PR. Santa Monica, Calif.: Rand Corp.

MECHANIZED WARFARE

According to an authoritative definition, to mechanize a military force is "to equip [it] with armed and armored motor vehicles." While Leonardo da Vinci may have been the first to design an armed and armored vehicle, his was without a motor in the modern sense; therefore, the story of mechanized warfare may be said to begin with the Industrial Revolution. For it was the products of that revolution that first appeared as "armed and armored motor vehicles," tanks, in battle in World War I.

Success in warfare comes from operational concepts—the set of schemes that, at tactical and operational levels, describe how battles are to be fought and campaigns conducted. Technology simply provides the means whereby existing concepts may be executed more effectively, or revised concepts introduced. Such is the case with mechanization. For example, Karl von Clausewitz's doctrine of massing at the decisive point in battle, basically an operational concept, is considerably facilitated by mechanization—a technology that enabled masses of troops and firepower to be brought to bear more quickly than before mechanization. Through mechanization, battles acquired a degree of tactical and operational mobility commanders had never enjoyed before. Later, mobility enabled blitzkrieg and mobile defense to become the dominant operational concepts of World War II, even though the operational utility of those concepts had been more than adequately demonstrated before mechanization—for example, by Napoleon in the Ulm campaign of 1805; and by the "foot cavalry" that marched with Stonewall Jackson in that busy summer of 1862 in the Shenandoah Valley of Virginia. It is important to understand the mechanization story in terms of the operational concepts that underlie the mechanization process in all armies.

Mechanization

The first armed and armored motor vehicle was the tank, which was introduced in World War I for the specific purpose of overcoming obstacles to maneuver by foot infantry—physical obstacles such as trenches, firepower obstacles such as the fires of artillery and machine guns. In that role, the tank moved at an infantry rate of march. In fact, in one very early battle in which the U.S. Army employed tanks, the tank unit commander, Col. George S. Patton, Jr., actually marched along on foot with the tanks as they attacked; he was wounded in that action—a reminder of one reason the tanks were there in the first place. It was possibly the missed opportunity to exploit the tactical breakthrough with tanks at Cambrai on 20 November 1917, and the realization of what might have been had the Allied forces been ready to exploit the breakthrough, that caused some officers to see tank-equipped forces as a modern equivalent of heavy cavalry and not just as protected firepower support for infantry. And so was born the idea of independent mechanized forces as a decisive arm in battle. It is the development of that idea that one inevitably follows in tracing the evolution of mechanized operations.

In the paragraphs that follow, the word *mechanized* will be used as defined—that is, "armed and armored vehicles." The term *armor* will be used to mean the combined arms team of tanks, infantry, artillery, engineers, signal, and other supporting arms, combined in proportions dictated by mission, enemy, terrain, and weather in the operational area but with tanks as the primary combat element. *Armored* and *armor*, at least in regard to organizations, are synonyms.

Armored Forces

The concept of an armored force as the dominant arm of a mixed military force of tanks, infantry, and artillery likely first came to being in both Great Britain and Germany at roughly the same time. In the former, mixed battalions of tanks and motorized (truck-mobile) infantry carried out tactical exercises (trials) in 1921 and 1922 as part of a temporarily assembled Experimental Brigade. Then, in 1923, the Royal Tank Corps was established. An Experimental Mechanized Force conducted tactical exercises in 1927 and 1928. Biases over what had been learned were so deeply rooted that the idea of a mixed armored force built around tanks was set aside; for British forces, it would not become a factor again until World War II. What did survive the trials on Salisbury Plain, however, was the perception and the pen of the British military writer, Capt. Basil H. Liddell Hart. As a young officer in World War I, Liddell Hart was shocked by the waste of massed infantry against massed artillery and machine guns, and he became convinced that if war must be fought, mechanization seemed a much less manpower-intensive way of successfully combining fire and maneuver. So, as his army and his country turned away from large-scale mechanization, Liddell Hart began to write about warfare of the future based on his growing conviction that mechanization could in substantial measure avoid, or at least reduce, the awesome bloodshed of World War I.

The second country, Germany, was prohibited by the Versailles Treaty from having most types of armored vehicles. Nevertheless, officers were studying and experimenting, as best they could, with mechanization, rapid tactical troop movement, and close cooperation between mechanized formations and armed aircraft to facilitate rapid operational-level maneuver.

So, in one country, Great Britain, soldiers were concentrating on the capabilities of tanks, whether they should be "light" or "heavy," and how best to organize and operate combined arms units. In the other, Germany, the Wehrmacht thinkers, largely unencumbered by technical and organizational details, carefully examined how best to combine ground and air mobility at tactical and operational levels to achieve quick decisive victory.

The Germans seized an additional important initiative around 1925 by entering into an agreement with the Soviets to set up and operate a tank factory and a school to teach mechanized warfare in the Soviet Union. Further, they conducted field experiments with Soviet forces to validate their ideas. From this experience, they emerged with a fairly well laid out set of operational concepts—doctrine, tactics and techniques, organization, and equipment needs. Several if not many of the Wehrmacht's most outstanding field commanders reflected the profound intellectual effects of this period of development and growth; noteworthy among them were Heinz Guderian, Hasso von Manteuffel, and Erwin Rommel.

For the Soviets, the major outcome of the German experience in the Soviet Union was the organization of large Soviet army formations known as Motor Mechanized Corps, and the design, production, and fielding of the

T34/76 tank—lineal antecedent of every Soviet tank up to, at least, the T80/125 model.

From the debut of the tank on World War I battlefields to the beginning of German military operations in Europe in World War II, milestones in armor force development were the Spanish Civil War (1936–39) and Soviet-Japanese hostilities along the border of Japanese-occupied Manchuria (1939). Of the latter, very little is known in the West; about the former, a great deal is known.

The armies of several nations drew some mistaken conclusions from events of the war in Spain. These nations concluded that operations in Spain confirmed that tanks—even heavily armored infantry support tanks—would very quickly fall prey to infantry antitank weapons. Therefore, it would not be operationally possible to maneuver major formations at a rate greater than that of advancing (on foot) infantry because to do so would expose the tanks to antitank weapons without infantry support.

The Soviet general staff was persuaded by the campaigns in Spain that they had previously pursued a wrong course. So, virtually on the eve of World War II, they disbanded their Motor Mechanized Corps—then about divisional size. Coincidentally, there was a purge of Soviet officers, which included many of those who were looked on as apostles of mobile warfare. Despite this fact, Gen. Georgi Zhukov, in the Battle of Khalkin Gol (Nomonhan) against the Japanese in Outer Mongolia in mid-August 1939, demonstrated that armor—the combined arms team of tanks, infantry, and artillery—was a powerful battle-winning arm. The influence of this battle on Soviet political leadership, only a few days before the outbreak of World War II in Europe, is still not entirely clear. It does not seem to have affected the Soviet decision, made at that very time, to enter into a nonaggression pact with Germany. It may also have alerted the general staff to the folly of their decision to disband the Motor Mechanized Corps. Certainly the German campaigns in Poland (1939) and France (1940) were manifest evidence of the power of mechanized combined arms forces; so while Khalkin Gol may have been a precursor, it was by no means the only such evidence. In any event, with the successful German campaigns in Europe as evidence, the Soviets, in a dramatic turnabout, quickly re-created large mechanized formations consistent with the concepts they had earlier learned from the Germans.

While German thinking about mechanized warfare had been initially uncluttered by concerns over equipment and organizational design because of Versailles Treaty limitations, once the decision to abrogate the treaty had been taken (1936), equipment design and organization problems came to the fore, and the Germans confronted the first of several persistent problems in mechanization: what should be the proportion of tanks and infantry; what and how much indirect fire support is necessary for battles whose successful outcome hinges on quick maneuver in violent direct fire battles? These are central problems in the mechanization equation. In the armies of many countries, they have not been resolved to this day.

The war establishment organization of circa 1939 Wehrmacht panzer (tank) divisions called for more tank units than infantry units at battalion and company levels, at a ratio of roughly four to three. By contrast, so-called light divisions had a more balanced organization in wartime, even though their nonwar tables of organization called for four infantry battalions and one tank battalion. This was more likely a reflection of the ability to equip tank units, given the state of mechanization at the time, than it was of a clear operational, hence organizational, concept. There were, in addition, independent tank brigades; it was intended that these should be used as necessary to "heavy up" light divisions or pure infantry divisions. After the Polish campaign, most of the tank battalions in these brigades were assigned to the light divisions they had previously supported, thus giving the light divisions relatively balanced ratios of tank and infantry units.

Operationally, it may well be that the failure of Guderian's panzer divisions to completely encircle British forces at Dunkirk was more a function of the imbalance of tanks and infantry than anything else. For by the time the channel coast was within reach, the panzer divisions' infantry had been depleted to the point that the corps was not able to push infantry across the low ground in sufficient numbers to capture Dunkirk. It was a lesson not lost, for the 1941 German panzer divisions featured a much higher proportion of infantry than had their 1939 predecessors.

The second great dilemma with mechanized forces is that of logistics support. All armies, even the most robust, have faced this problem since the beginning of mechanization. To the Germans it came early in the campaigns of Rommel's Afrika Korps in North Africa. Since the Afrika Korps was the nemesis of both British and U.S. forces in North Africa, its operations have been widely studied and analyzed in the West. In perspective, however, it was a relatively small force—no more than 10 percent of the Wehrmacht's armor and mechanized forces. Even so, Rommel nearly ran through the British to the Suez Canal and beyond to the oil-rich Middle East. Had he done so, especially before the Allied landings in Northwest Africa, the war would surely have taken a quite different turn. That he did not do so is a reflection of gross logistical difficulties built up after months of highly mobile operations. To illustrate: when the Afrika Korps went in on its final attacks against the British in the Western Desert, before the British victory at El Alamein (October-November 1942), more than 80 percent of its equipment had been taken from the enemy; yet day after day Afrika Korps vehicle and maintenance crews were able to field sufficient fighting strength to permit the battle to continue. Eventually this makeshift logistics system, and the relatively high replacement equipment losses to British air and naval action against the German Mediterranean convoys, combined to hobble the Afrika Korps. The marvel is that Rommel was able to do as much as he did with so little for so long, and that his forces came close to decisive victory despite their relatively small size and obviously inadequate logistical support.

In the United States, mechanization enjoyed slow beginnings. Perhaps no more than a handful of U.S. Army officers had experience with tanks in World War I, and the dominant persuasion of U.S. Army leadership in the period following World War I was that infantry was still the primary force in battle. Nonetheless, an experimental armored force, the 7th Mechanized Brigade, was assembled at Fort Knox, Kentucky, in the early 1930s and began to explore mechanization. Equipment was scarce. While this was largely a reflection of lean budgets during the Great Depression, it also reflected the infantry mindset of U.S. army leaders and U.S. isolation from the most likely arenas of conflict. Then Army Chief of Staff Douglas MacArthur perhaps best reflected all this when he testified before the U.S. Congress in the early 1930s to the effect that the United States should not buy too many tanks, because they became obsolete so quickly. Inferred, of course, was the notion that mobilization—the systemic product of the Industrial Revolution—would enable training centers (military manpower factories) and tank and aircraft plants (military equipment factories) to spring into being and quickly produce integrated masses of men and equipment. These would then go off to war, fight, and win largely by simply overwhelming the enemy with numbers.

Confronted by this systemic bias, it was difficult, if not impossible, to achieve substantial mechanization of U.S. forces in time of peace. So it was that U.S. Army mechanization languished in the years between the world wars. In the Kentucky hills along the Ohio River valley, U.S. Army cavalrymen, led by Brig. Gen. Daniel Van Voorhies, struggled to bring out of their nominally funded experiments the lessons that would enable sound operational concepts—doctrine, tactics, and techniques for mechanized operations—to be drawn up. However, so strong was the infantry bias, and so limited the mechanization investment in these years, that most of the imaginative cavalrymen who had led U.S. tank units in World War I went back to the cavalry. According to institutional wisdom, tanks and mechanization were only for support of dismounted infantry, anyway; besides, cavalry and horses were more fun. In the years when his peers were struggling through Kentucky brambles with their embryonic mechanized force, Col. George S. Patton, Jr., perhaps the leading U.S. Tank Corps personality in World War I, was enjoying cavalry life in command of the 3d U.S. Cavalry Regiment at Fort Myer, Virginia.

On the eve of World War II, the armored forces of the U.S. Army found themselves with only tentative operational concepts, limited tactical experience in field trials, no operational-level experience at all, even in war games, and a handful of tanks, assigned to general headquarters (GHQ) tank battalions.

Indeed, even the tanks would not have been present had it not been for the persistent efforts of (later) Maj. Gen. Adna R. Chaffee who, as a War Department staff officer, was successful in ensuring modest funding for building tanks. This was accomplished despite the vociferous opposition of the chief of cavalry.

President Franklin D. Roosevelt ordered partial mobilization in 1940, and after the Japanese attack at Pearl Harbor, 7 December 1941, the expanded and intensified mobilization system quickly began to produce soldiers and equipment in numbers. An armored force was organized at Fort Knox under Major General Chaffee, and in great haste the United States set about to make up for lost time. Tactics and techniques were put together in tentative form, subjected to field trials in organizations as large as a corps, changed and amended as appropriate, then committed to battle, first in 1943 in North Africa.

Mechanization in World War II

Blitzkrieg—lightning war—a term made famous by media accounts of German training and early operations in World War II, was the serendipitous combining of considerable thinking by the Germans about mobility in war, tank and motorized forces, and a stable of remarkably talented field commanders. In blitzkrieg, mechanized and motorized formations moving at a rate at least four times that of dismounted infantry were sure guarantors of tactical and operational success. However, throughout the war, whether in Western Europe, North Africa, or Russia, the Panzertruppen almost always were at or beyond the limits of their logistical capabilities. From the German point of view, early and striking blitzkrieg successes in the west must be laid alongside three and a half years of strategic defense—actually offensive defense in the east, and later a somewhat shorter period of similar activity in the west. The role of mechanized forces in these strategic offensive-defensive operations was incomparably tougher than was the case in the blitzkrieg days. This was because, in defensive operations, the initiative was yielded to the enemy, first at the strategic and then the operational level. The single factor that made blitzkrieg so effective was that it seized the initiative at all levels, from highest to lowest. The history of war instructs that more often than not victory in battle goes to the side that, at some point, seizes the initiative and sustains it to the end. Particularly, this is the case if surprise can also be achieved.

It is instructive to examine why, despite considerable numerical superiority, the Soviets were not able to defeat the Wehrmacht in the east much sooner than they did. The answer is most likely in the mix of tanks and infantry, and in the Soviets' inability to take and hold the initiative. For most of the war, the Soviets had no mobile infantry—mechanized or truck mounted. Soviet tanks were, technically at least, as good or better than German tanks, and as the war continued, Soviet tank units came to be fairly well commanded. Yet, whether at tactical or operational levels, tanks alone could not succeed without infantry. Typically, in a corps- or divisional-level battle, Soviet tanks would break through a thin belt of German infantry and penetrate fairly deeply. Without infantry, they quickly fell prey to German antitank guns, reserves, or both. Then the tanks, having become separated from their supporting infantry near the forward line of troops, were helpless. German artillery then immobilized the unprotected infantry. It was a pattern repeated many times. The Soviets were among the first after World War II to field fighting vehicles for infantry; the lessons of World War II were obviously not lost. Soviet tanks improved in quality, the T34/76 being succeeded by the surprisingly effective T34/85, as the mainstay of Soviet tank formations. The Soviet tractor industry produced good-quality, effective, tank cannon—largely derivatives of the Soviets' excellent field artillery—and the two came together to produce large numbers of very effective tanks. It is fair to say that operational mobility—at division and corps level—not only brought the Germans success in blitzkrieg operations but also succeeded in offensive-defensive operations in keeping the Soviet Army out of Germany proper for nearly four years.

In the west, where they saw themselves on a strategic defensive, German forces were also overwhelmed by numbers. The late U.S. start in mechanization was reflected in many ways during the war. Operationally, most U.S. commanders—with a few exceptions, like Patton—had not reflected sufficiently on concepts of mobile action. Early tanks were found to be undergunned. However, tank destroyers—open-turreted gun motor carriages with larger guns—were also fielded and the larger guns—76mm and 90mm—were moved to tanks. Infantry was motorized in some but not all infantry divisions; in armored divisions, infantry was mounted in half-tracks with light, bulletproof armor. Artillery in armored divisions was self-propelled but mounted on open-topped carriages.

Having pioneered in thinking about and experimenting with armor operations, the British entered the war reflecting the relative hiatus in mechanized developments that had set in following the Experimental Force trials on Salisbury Plain. In equipment, organization, and operational concepts, however, they were well ahead of their U.S. allies. British armor unit commanders proved themselves competent in the North African campaigns, although it was not until large amounts of U.S.-made equipment arrived, and British equipment holdings became substantially greater than those of the Afrika Korps, that conclusive successes were achieved. The British, however, suffered from underpowered armored vehicles, especially tanks. Traditionally, British tanks have featured better guns (firepower) but less motor power (mobility), and British operational concepts have concentrated more on battle attrition than on fast-moving mobile operations.

The state of military mechanization to the end of World War II found the world's larger armies each with a mechanized army inside a much larger "dismounted" army. These mechanized armies were not truly mechanized, in that they were not fully armored and armed. Infantry lacked mounted weapons, except for machine guns, and infantry carriers were at best lightly armored and without overhead cover. Artillery was towed or self-propelled but in the latter case lacked overhead cover. All these were grist for postwar developments.

Mechanization After World War II

Mechanization, NATO, and Nuclear Weapons

Following World War II, all surviving armies set to work on doctrinal, organizational, and equipment changes and improvements derived from their experience in and observations of the war just finished. In the West, it is fair to say that for the most part these changes primarily reflected perceptions about operations of the German Wehrmacht. The striking performance of the panzer divisions in the early days in the West and in Russia, and the equally striking effectiveness of German mobile defensive operations, especially in the Soviet Union during the last years of the war, formed the basis for most of what was codified.

The offense remained the dominant form of combat, even for forces in strategic or operational defensive posture. Mobile strike forces arrayed deep in defensive zones would mass quickly to conduct offensive operations against deep penetrating armor formations, which would have been stripped of their supporting infantry as they broke through the infantry-heavy forward defensive zone. The Soviets codified their experience into an offensive operational concept featuring mass, momentum, and continuous land combat—mass meaning numbers concentrated in a small area, momentum meaning the product to be achieved by combining mass and velocity, and continuous land combat meaning the offensive employment of successive echelons at a rate that in the end would simply overwhelm the defender. Other than in the offensive zone, forces would be deployed for defense, in considerable depth, featuring infantry, well dug-in forward and heavy mobile armor reserves. To execute this concept there were, and are, tank divisions with mechanized infantry and motorized rifle divisions—mechanized infantry with tank support. Artillery, at first largely towed, underwent extensive modernization in the 1970s and 1980s. There were two aspects to this modernization. The weapons not only became self-propelled, they also became nuclear capable, able to provide artillery support for mechanized forces under all possible circumstances. The first-line units of Soviet forces were fully mechanized combined arms forces—tanks, infantry, artillery and supporting air defense, engineer, signals, and other organizations. Theirs was a truly mechanized army, embracing in a uniquely Russian way the operational concepts first seized on so long ago by the early advocates of mobile warfare—Mikhail Tukhachevsky, Guderian, J. F. C. Fuller, Liddell Hart, Van Voorhies, and Patton.

In Western Europe and the United States, as this doctrinal evolution unfolded, it quickly became apparent that the growing conventional strength of the Soviet Union was a most vexing problem. For inherent in the changing force balance was the unpleasant truth that no longer could the Allies be guaranteed numerical superiority. So as the North Atlantic Treaty Organization (NATO) was being set up in the early 1950s, Gen. Dwight Eisenhower, as SACEUR, set forth the need for 96 divisions and 9,000 tactical fighters to defend NATO. Rejected by member countries unable or unwilling to provide these staggering resources, Eisenhower, when president, finally settled for 26 divisions—12 of them to be West German—1,400 fighter aircraft, and 15,000 theater and tactical nuclear weapons. Of the latter, about 7,000 were deployed, and 4,000 remained as of early 1990. Technology in the form of nuclear weapons was to make up for the disparity in numbers.

The U.S. Army had disbanded nearly all its armored divisions at the close of World War II. At NATO's inception, the United States re-created its armored forces, deploying several infantry and armored divisions to Western Europe. The remainder were stationed within the continental United States for deployment to reinforce the Europe-deployed force, or elsewhere as required. When the North Koreans invaded South Korea in June 1950, U.S. Army divisions stationed in Japan deployed to Korea. Tank battalions were deployed from the United States to provide tank support for foot or truck-mounted infantry. But no mechanized units larger than tank battalions were employed by U.S. forces in Korea.

In the beginning, and for some time after, the United States, and so NATO, controlled an overwhelming strategic nuclear capability. From the mid-1960s, Soviet nuclear capabilities grew to the point that by the 1970s the United States no longer had the capability to reduce a Soviet counterstrike to reasonably tolerable levels. It was an early perception of this developing reality that led the administration of Pres. John F. Kennedy to abandon the strategy of massive nuclear retaliation and to embrace the flexible response doctrine in its stead.

For a time, the Soviets apparently believed that war between NATO and the Warsaw Pact would be nuclear—it would begin and end that way. With time, the awesome totality of a nuclear conflict at tactical, operational, and strategic levels apparently overwhelmed the Soviets' ability to think logically about the matter. At that point their attention turned once again to operational concepts for the conventional battle—mechanized forces.

From about 1966, when they concluded they had achieved nuclear "parity," the Soviets embraced the notion that they could and should try to win at theater level, avoiding the use of nuclear weapons. Their conventional weapons developments in five-year plans for 25 years clearly focused on development and deployment of impressive capabilities in tanks, infantry fighting vehicles, artillery, air defense, radio-electronic combat, combat helicopters, ballistic missiles, and fixed-wing airpower. All of these means were designed to make mass, momentum, and continuous land combat a viable operational concept for conventional operations at the theater (operational) level of war.

The deployment in the early 1970s of large numbers of antitank guided missiles (ATGM) by NATO forces—weapons designated by acronyms such as TOW, HOT, DRAGON, MILAN—and the adoption in the West of an operational concept called Active Defense in 1976 gave pause to Soviet conventional force development. NATO, recognizing the considerable lack of operational depth in its geography, adopted a theater-level posture called Forward Defense. This concept recognized that in NATO's area, especially in the central region, there was insufficient maneuver room to conduct large-scale mobile defensive operations like those of the Wehrmacht in World War II, and on which the mobile defense doctrine of Western armies was based. Active Defense simply recognized the advantages to be had by employing long-range, high-hit probability, antitank guided missiles in depth in the Forward Defense. In effect, it expanded the close battle space—the space at the forward line of troops—by virtually doubling the effective range of direct-fire systems employed there. To the Soviets, it meant that Soviet ability to break through NATO's antitank defenses without risking substantial loss and possible defeat was uncertain at best, doubtful at worst. NATO was again calling on technology to resolve the difficult problem of how to defend successfully against overwhelming numbers. In response, the Soviets set about to solve the technical riddle of the shaped-charge warheads used on antitank guided missiles.

By the mid-1970s, the Soviets began to field a technological solution to the antitank guided missile problem—composite or laminate armors that were more than a match for early model ATGM warheads. While tank fleets with this advanced level of protection were growing apace—production running 3,000 to 4,000 units per year—Soviet technology provided the means for even better protection in the form of what is popularly called reactive armor. This consists of an array of appliqué boxes covering the tank's armor and containing specially designed explosives that detonate on impact, destroying the integrity of the incoming ATGM shaped-charge jet. Such armor was first fielded by the Israeli Defense Force (IDF) in the late seventies and early eighties. It went to war in the 1982 Operation Peace for Galilee mounted on IDF tanks and other more lightly protected armored vehicles. Some of these boxes fell into Syrian, and so into Soviet, hands. Beginning about 1986, similar, improved boxes began to appear on tank fleets in Group Soviet Forces Germany. Meanwhile, improved models were available in Israel.

Tanks with reactive armor on top of built-in composite or laminate armor would quite likely defeat the warheads of all deployed ATGMs in the world today and are a very attractive solution to what, for the Soviets, had been a most vexing problem—how to get through the deepening belts of antitank guided missile systems deployed forward in NATO without suffering inordinate losses in Soviet tanks.

The Soviets obviously believed that they had the means to achieve quick, decisive victory at the theater level of war with such thoroughness and dispatch that the West would not be able to make the nuclear decision before the Soviets were already consolidating their theater-level gains. With these competing technical developments in being, and as the laboratories set about to resolve the next chapter in the armor-antiarmor saga, NATO's doctrine developers were at work to complete a more robust version of Forward (Active) Defense, one that would truly take on the twin problems of how to cope with numbers—mass in the close-in battle—while at the same time preventing mass and velocity (movement) from building momentum and preventing follow-on echelons from closing in quickly to overwhelm forward defenders. In the U.S. Army, this early 1980s doctrine is known as AirLand Battle. Its most important ideas are: deep attack against the follow-on echelons and the close-in battle are inseparable; seizing and holding the initiative through maneuver of forces and fires is essential to success; the objective of the battle is to win—not just to avoid defeat. Successfully conducted, the AirLand Battle can, with conventional means alone, considerably postpone the time at which the defender must consider the first use of nuclear weapons, thus raising dramatically the nuclear threshold.

Thus stood matters between NATO and the Warsaw Pact in regard to doctrine, forces and organizations, equipment, and the entire panoply of military capabilities at the end of the 1980s. In the Soviet Union, internal reforms started by Mikhail Gorbachev during his years as general secretary of the Communist Party created the dramatic spectrum of government, economic, social, and finally military changes that began the 1990s. The Warsaw Pact is no more; Soviet forces will soon be gone from Eastern Europe, remaining there now only because there is no place for them to go in the former Soviet Union. The Russian republic has become the dominant member of a coalition of republics whose political, economic, social, and military futures have yet to be shaped. In place of the enormous conventional forces threat traditionally posed by Warsaw Pact forces, there remains a residual set of risks and uncertainties reflecting emerging policies of governments long dominated by dictators and Marxist economic centrism. Dominating residual military capabilities in the former Soviet Union's republics is, of course, the intercontinental ballistic missile/nuclear threat. The fairly clearly defined parameters of the long-standing deterrent standoff between the West and the Soviet Union no longer exist.

Meanwhile, as the Soviet threat—primarily the threat to NATO Europe—diffuses, world attention has been captured by events in the Middle East. As will be seen subsequently, doctrine (tactical and operational), organizations and forces, equipment, and training systems, all developed primarily for operations against the Warsaw Pact, have fought and won a substantial and dramatic victory against Iraqi forces armed with Sovieet equipment, trained in Soviet tactics, and deployed in numerically superior force structures against the United States and allied coalition forces in the 1991 Gulf War. That victory is ample demonstration of the battle worthiness of AirLand Battle doctrine—the culmination of mechanization of warfare.

Mechanized Operations in Vietnam

Although large-scale armor and mechanized operations were not characteristic of U.S. Army operations in Vietnam, the story of the Vietnamese experience highlights many recurring dilemmas in mechanization, and some new concepts of mobility.

After World War II, the French returned to Indochina and set up a colonial administration. Accompanying French military forces included armor units—tanks and "mechanized" infantry, although the latter were either truck or half-track mounted mobile infantry rather than truly "armed and armored" infantry. These armored units remained for nearly ten years, departing in 1956 when the last French units left Indochina. French experience, and that of their Vietnamese allies, determined concepts for employment of armor units of the South Vietnamese army. This experience also influenced the thinking of many U.S. military commanders concerning the feasibility of employing armor units in Vietnam.

The U.S. Army of the late 1950s and early 1960s, in fact, had little information regarding the use of armor in Vietnam. What little did exist came from scarce French army battle reports, and from some information regarding the numbers and types of U.S. equipment that had been made available to the French, and which they in turn had deployed to and employed in Vietnam. That equipment was of World War II vintage; it consisted of light tanks, half-tracks, and scout cars. By 1954, the French had deployed to Vietnam a vehicle fleet of about 450 tanks and tank destroyers and nearly 2,000 scout cars, half-tracks, and amphibious tractors. While those numbers seem substantial, the equipment was scattered over an area of nearly 230,000 square miles. By comparison, the U.S. Army deployed to Vietnam, and had in operation at the height of the fighting in 1969, nearly 600 tanks and 2,000 other armored vehicles operating over an area less than a third that size.

Of the U.S.-made equipment used by the French in

Vietnam, all had been manufactured before 1945. Generally, armored vehicles were in poor repair and not fit for fast-moving mobile operations in a country where movement was difficult to begin with. Largely because of the poor mechanical condition of these vehicles, armor operations were a perpetual logistical nightmare. So, armor units were fragmented, set up in many small static positions, and at best used in support of infantry, at whatever marching pace the terrain may have permitted. The mix of armored vehicles and infantry always favored infantry by a substantial margin. All these facts and supporting evidence were duly reported by the French in some very candid after-action reports. Indeed, after the deployment of U.S. advisers following the French departure, observer reports contained the same kinds of information. Heavily classified and largely contained within the files of the U.S. Department of State, these reports were not disseminated in the Department of Defense. Thus there was a dearth of available information on which to base U.S. Army estimates about military operations in Vietnam. Indeed, most of what was known was derived not from military after-action reports, but from material written by civilian observers. Perhaps foremost among these was Bernard B. Fall, whose book *Street Without Joy* devotes one chapter to the six-month history of the destruction of a French mobile force—Groupement Mobile 100. The tragic tale of Groupement Mobile 100's demise seemed to many to symbolize the fate that awaited any armored or mechanized force trying to fight in the jungle. In truth, Groupement Mobile 100 was not really an armor unit. It was a truck-mounted task force of four battalions of infantry. Numbering about 2,600 troops, it was reinforced by one light artillery battalion and ten light tanks. The Groupement moved on roads and deployed to fight on foot. This made it extremely vulnerable to the simplest kind of ambush, and a series of such encounters finally destroyed it. The fate of this unfortunate force became the source of much adverse comment on French armor operations in Vietnam; it completely obscured many French and Vietnamese successes with armored forces. Later, U.S. commanders would repeat many of the mistakes reported on by the French, and learn for themselves many lessons the French had drawn about armor operations in Indochina.

As World War II closed, the U.S. Army included sixteen armored divisions and many smaller battalion-sized armor units, largely tank battalions for support of foot- or truck-mobile infantry divisions. The divisions of this armored force consisted of integrated combined arms teams of tanks, half-track mobile infantry, and armored artillery. In the doctrine for employment of these units, there were no recognized limitations because of terrain, geography, or levels of combat intensity. Under the doctrine, forces were to be tailored for the mission, the threat, terrain and weather, and availability of friendly troops. It was believed that there was sufficient flexibility in the organization itself to permit adjustment to almost any set of circumstances. However, U.S. armored divisions were employed only in the European and North African theaters of operations in World War II. In the Pacific, armored battalions were deployed to support foot-mobile infantry, as was also the case in the later war in Korea. It was widely accepted that in jungle areas especially, but in operations in the Pacific Ocean areas in general, there was no opportunity for large-scale independent mobile combined arms operations such as those of the World War II armored divisions. Force planners for Vietnam therefore concluded there was no place for armor units there—especially tanks. So it was that most U.S. Army divisions deploying to Vietnam initially left behind their organic tank and armored cavalry units.

Meanwhile, the South Vietnamese army armored force was expanding under the tutelage of U.S. Army armor advisers. In the beginning, and for some time thereafter, tactics reflected French employment doctrine, as well as pressures to minimize casualties and equipment losses. Defense in static position, convoy escort, clearing roads, mobile relief force—all were typical missions. With the advent of post–World War II equipment—principally the U.S.-made M113 armored personnel carrier—small-unit mobile operations became possible, and success in several operations, primarily in the Mekong Delta, marked a turning point in U.S. and Vietnamese attitudes toward mobile operations. Now they were considered possible, even desirable, and the equipment held up. Over time, all this led to an increased capability and spirit of aggressiveness on the part of the Vietnamese tank, cavalry, and mounted infantry soldiers. Some of the most remarkable actions of the North Vietnamese 1968 Tet offensive and the North Vietnamese use of tanks in the 1972 offensive were those of the Vietnamese Armor Command. On the U.S. Army side, it was not until 1967, when a task force of officers was appointed to evaluate operations of tank and other armored units, that the extent of U.S. misperceptions about armor operations was finally set forth. It was found that operations by armor units had been conducted in every region of Vietnam; the severest restrictions on mobility were experienced in the Mekong Delta rice-growing areas and in the heavily forested areas of the Central Highlands. In coastal plain, piedmont, and the plateaus of the Central Highlands, armored vehicles were able to move with ease about 80 percent of the time, and indeed these areas had been traversed by French and Vietnamese armor units before the arrival of U.S. forces.

Vietnam's summer or southwest monsoon blows onshore, out of the Indian Ocean, from June through September, bringing the wet season to the Mekong Delta, the piedmont, and most of the highlands and plateaus of central South Vietnam. The northeast part of the country has its monsoon from November through February, when onshore northeast winds shed moisture over the northern third of the country. Even with these conditions further limiting mobility during the peak of the monsoons, the study group concluded that tanks could move about in mobile operations in more than 60 percent of the country during the dry season and more than 45 percent of the country during the wet season. The extremely versatile M113 armored personnel carrier in several configurations—troop carrier, cavalry assault vehicle, mortar carrier—could move in about 65 percent of the country year-round.

By the time these conclusions were made known (1967), the major force decisions had been made, and with some minor changes, the U.S. armor unit troop basis remained—constrained to the end by dependence on foot, truck, armored personnel carrier, or airmobile infantry, the latter being only foot-mobile when dismounted. There were no large-scale, division-level mounted mobile operations. In the Cambodian invasion of May 1970, however, a three-brigade task force led by a U.S. armored cavalry regiment staged the largest and most successful U.S. forces mobile operation of the war. In a fast-moving, hotly contested series of battles against three North Vietnamese divisions reinforced by three antiaircraft regiments, the 11th Armored Cavalry Regiment, in about five critical days, attacked into Cambodia for a distance of nearly 100 kilometers (60 mi.), and reached, along an extensive line, the limits of advance authorized by Pres. Richard Nixon. It was the first, and indeed the only, mobile armored forces operation of large size during the war, until the North Vietnamese army attacked southward with considerable tank strength in the last days of the war.

Recognizing the need for mobility so dramatically demonstrated by tortuous foot-mobile operations in the jungle areas of the central and southwest Pacific in World War II, imaginative U.S. officers developed, in the early 1960s, new concepts in force mobility using the newly developed capability of the helicopter. Following some exciting field trials with heliborne infantry, it was concluded that airmobile infantry answered the needs for mobility so urgently felt in jungle operations of World War II.

While to some extent their perception was correct, it quickly became apparent that heliborne infantry also enjoyed some singular disadvantages. Foremost among these was the need for sure knowledge of the terrain and enemy by troops and leaders who had deployed quickly by helicopter to areas in which they had not operated recently, if at all. In addition, once on the ground, air-mobile infantry is foot-mobile; in all too many cases, the enemy proved to be more mobile tactically simply because he had been there longer and knew the terrain intimately. Availability of firepower—artillery—to support the heliborne infantry is critical. All too often, overzealous heliborne commanders deployed troops near or beyond the limits of immediately available indirect fire, into situations in which the enemy had all his fire support available. Thus disadvantaged, heliborne forces inevitably suffered inordinate losses. Finally, as with all mobile operations, logistical support of deployed heliborne forces presents a problem. Just as the troops themselves were transported by helicopter, so were all their consumables, from rations to ammunition.

The U.S. Army's involvement in Vietnam highlights once again the persistent dilemmas of mechanization: the mix of units necessary for truly mobile warfare; the problem of bringing infantry to battle behind armor protection; and logistics support for armor units whether or not engaged in high-speed mobile operations. These dilemmas were aggravated, in this circumstance, by the mythology about jungle warfare, especially against what was for too long considered to be an "insurgent," "irregular" enemy that all too soon turned out to be a tough, highly motivated, well-led, regular military force—the North Vietnamese army.

Mechanized Operations in the Middle East

By the time the State of Israel was proclaimed, it was quite clear to the leaders of the Jewish underground that as a nation they faced the likelihood of an all-out war against Arab armies that outnumbered them and were well equipped with fairly modern weapons, including armor—tanks, armored cars, half-tracks. Therefore, if the new nation was to survive, let alone grow and flourish, similar weapons in considerable numbers had to be available to the Israeli defenders. Their worst fears were realized when, following independence on 14 May 1948, Arab armies invaded from all sides. Egyptian armor and infantry columns attacked along the coastal road through Gaza, headed for Beersheba and Jerusalem. Syrian tank and infantry columns attacked into Galilee across the Golan Heights. The Iraqis and the Transjordanian Arab Legion attacked west across the Jordan River toward the Mediterranean coast.

The Israeli Defense Force (IDF) entered the 1948 War of Independence with nine underequipped territorial infantry brigades. In equipment, they were in no way ready to cope with modern forces featuring tanks, armored cars, and truck or half-track mobile infantry on equal terms. Nonetheless, with considerable ingenuity—genius in the use of what equipment they did have—and by means of superlative leadership they were able to beat off their attackers and survive. In many battles, the Israelis used mobility as a means of overcoming superior numbers and better equipment in the hands of their foes—a lesson not lost as they looked to the future. The campaign in Galilee and later in the Negev Desert demonstrated the IDF's growing ability to exploit tactical advantage by moving swiftly to achieve operational advantage. In at least one case this led to a strategic advantage—the long outflanking sweep into the northern Sinai that brought the War of Independence to a close.

The Israelis set about after the 1949 armistice to reorganize and refit their forces for other battles surely to follow. Due to the size of the population and the embryonic economy, it was necessary to invoke conscription and establish a reserve army as the mainstay of the military establishment. Twelve brigades existed at war's end. Nine became reserve units; the remaining three were organized into one armored and two infantry brigades. This arrangement largely reflected lack of sufficient equipment to outfit more than the one armored brigade. They then set about in earnest to study armor operations and to procure for their forces sufficient tanks and other armored vehicles to equip more armored units. In the beginning, the French Cavalry School provided doctrinal education for officers; in addition, the French provided a considerable number of armored vehicles. There also began at this time a remarkable system of adapting the equipment of other nations to unique IDF needs. It is a technique of improvisation that has survived to this day, only diminishing as the IDF has acquired its own tank—the Merkava—in sufficient numbers to obviate the need for piecing and patching tanks from other armies.

Equipment unreliability and the difficulties of working out doctrine—tactics and techniques—plagued the Israeli Armored Corps in the years between the War of Independence and the Sinai campaign of 1956. Many, if not most, senior leaders were, by 1956, still convinced that armor in support of infantry was the only feasible operational technique. Then the sudden and unexpected successes of the Armored Corps in the 1956 Sinai campaign converted, among others, chief of staff Moshe Dayan to believe in the potential of high-speed mobile operations with armored forces. Thus it was that, following the Sinai campaign, the IDF set about to remake an infantry army with tank support into a mechanized army. Several new armor brigades were formed, some based around tank units, others around half-track mobile infantry.

In the decade following the Sinai campaign, the Israeli Armored Corps increased in strength, in equipment resources, and in command ability, largely under the remarkable leadership of Maj. Gen. Israel Tal. In the Six-Day War of 1967, it proved its mobile armored mettle against the Egyptians, Jordanians, and Syrians. The experiences of 1956 and 1967 convinced Israel's armor leaders of the superiority of tank forces in lightninglike operations. So impressed was the leadership with the potential for success tanks alone provided, it was concluded that infantry, in an IDF primarily made up of less-well-trained reservists, was not compatible with the requirements of mobile battle. Because of the cost of buying or building armored vehicles for the infantry, and the overriding need for funds to build tanks, mechanization of infantry largely went begging.

There was, however, a larger issue than budget. The IDF's armor leaders recognized the need to mechanize whatever infantry they were to have with armored personnel carriers, if not with mechanized infantry fighting vehicles. The most readily available vehicle was the U.S.-made M113 armored personnel carrier, which, despite the fact that it provided only a modicum of overhead protection for embarked infantry, required that infantry dismount in order to fight and to remount in order to move. In addition, because the carriers were far less armored than even the tanks of that day, there was no way for the infantry to attack along the same axis and in concert with the tanks—they simply could not survive at the same level of protection as the tanks. This meant that infantry had to stand off, just at the time they were needed most. It also meant that enemy gunners, seeking to separate tanks from their supporting infantry, so as to get at the tanks with antitank weapons, would immediately target the infantry with artillery. It is the persistent problem of how to bring infantry to battle under sufficient armor to allow them to survive at the same rate as tanks.

In October 1973, Egypt, Syria, and other Arab states attacked Israel once again. The Israeli Armored Corps at first suffered from lack of infantry with the assaulting tanks, a problem corrected in later battles, and demonstrated once again the value of mobility in battle.

Soon laid out for all to see were the lessons of the October War: the staggering density of the battlefield at critical points; the presence on both sides of large numbers of modern weapon systems, mostly armored or mechanized; the increased criticality of command control; the increased likelihood of interrupted command control due to large numbers of sophisticated electronic warfare means; the inability of any single weapon system to prevail, reaffirming the essentiality of combined arms combat; the outcome of battle reflecting, more often than not, factors other than numbers. In addition, it was starkly obvious that large-scale destruction in a short time was a most likely outcome of first battles in modern war, especially if surprise is an operative factor. Even as this drama was unfolding, the Israelis were hard at work under the scrutiny of Major General Tal, by now in charge of tank design and development, seeking a solution to their twin problems of a tank uniquely designed for the IDF and infantry under armor. The answer was the Merkava—Israel's "native" tank. With a front-mounted power train, a small turret ring, and trunnions mounted high in the turret, Merkava presents a nominal silhouette when hull down in the Sinai dunes or Golan boulders. In addition, doors opening rearward from a large rear stowage compartment leave room for an infantry squad, orders group, or for medical evacuation under fire—all under the same level of protection afforded by the tank itself. By 1990, the Merkava was in its third serial of production, and was probably the most survivable tank in the world. Certainly it was the best designed from a standpoint of the survivability of the crew, vital tank components, and its capability to provide an acceptable way to get infantry to and from battle under armor. It was clearly the best solution any army had found to date.

Mechanization—The Future

The combined arms team of armor tanks, mechanized infantry, artillery, and all supporting arms remains the pivotal force in conventional warfare. This is certainly the case in Korea, where large forces in high states of readiness face one another across international boundaries. Further, it is the case in the Middle East and in other areas of the Third World to which the world's largest arms producers have provided significant amounts of modern military equipment.

A perspective about the Third World is useful. In order to view the Middle East as a theater of operations in perspective, it is instructive to span the 30-odd years from the Sinai campaign of 1956 to the present. In the 1950s, the major armies of the region—Egyptian, Syrian, Iraqi, and Jordanian aligned against the Israelis—had in them combined inventories of about 1,500 first-line tanks and no more than about 500 first-line fighter aircraft. By 1990, those numbers were closer to 15,000 tanks and 5,000 first-line fighter aircraft. In numbers and in the mix of equipment present to be employed in battle, the Middle East is a theater in which armed conflict can be expected to be mobile mechanized warfare with first-line modern equipment, as dramatically demonstrated in the 1991 Gulf War.

Mechanization is also spreading into other parts of the Third World. In the mid-1980s, a study group in the United States, having examined the equipment holdings of several dozen nations of the world, found that in no less than 50 were there significant numbers of fairly modern tanks, infantry fighting vehicles, personnel carriers, artillery, and even combat helicopters. And so the belief, still held by some, especially in the United States, that somehow light infantry—foot, wheeled vehicle, or air mobile—can be inserted, survive, and accomplish a combat mission in the so-called Third World is more and more a myth. If the light infantry is to be the insertion force, then it must be equipped with weapons and protective measures that will enable it to fight successfully and survive against the threat it can expect to find. In no army has this been done—save possibly the Soviet airborne forces with their paradrop-capable armored vehicles and other equipment for operations against NATO rear areas.

Operationally, as well as tactically, conventional force warfare—mechanized battles of the future—will be set in the context of operational concepts that seek to take advantage of increased mobility in offensive and defensive operations to achieve rapid decisive success, bringing to military operations the opportunity for resolution of political conflict quickly and the advantage of the most imaginative, and so successful, of the mobile mechanized combatants. Nowhere is there more dramatic evidence of this than in coalition operations against Iraq's considerable modern mechanized forces in operations in Kuwait and southern Iraq in the early months of 1991 (see Fig. 1).

Donn A. Starry

Figure 1. The U.S. Army's Abrams tank in the Iraqi desert during Operation Desert Storm, February 1991. The Abrams' awesome mobile protected firepower was a principal contributor to the victory achieved by the allied coalition in operations to free Kuwait from its Iraqi invaders. (Source: Courtesy of U.S. Army Armor Center, Fort Knox)

See Also: Air-land Battle; Arab-Israeli Wars; Armor; Armor Technology; Blitzkrieg; Combined Arms; Fire and Movement; Forward Defense; Guderian, Heinz; History, Modern Military; Land Warfare; Manstein, Eric von; Mobility; Patton, George Smith, Jr.; Rommel, Erwin; Tank.

Bibliography

Brownlow, D. G. 1975. *Panzer baron: The military exploits of Baron Hasso von Manteuffel.* North Quincy, Mass.: Christopher Publishing House.

Dayan, M. 1965. *Diary of the Sinai campaign.* New York: Harper and Row.

Eshel, D. 1989. *Chariots of the desert: The story of the Israeli armoured corps.* London: Brassey's.

Guderian, H. 1952. *Panzer leader.* New York: E. P. Dutton.

Harmon, E. N. 1970. *Combat commander: Autobiography of a soldier.* Englewood Cliffs, N.J.: Prentice-Hall.

Herzog, C. 1975. *The war of atonement: October, 1973.* Boston: Little, Brown.

———. 1982. *The Arab-Israeli wars: War and peace in the Middle East. From the war of independence through Lebanon.* New York: Random House.

Horrocks, B. 1977. *Corps commander.* New York: Charles Scribner's.

Kahalani, A. 1984. *The heights of courage: A tank leader's war on the Golan.* Westport, Conn.: Greenwood Press.
Patton, George S., Jr. 1947. *War as I knew it.* Boston: Houghton Mifflin Company.
Pitt, Barrie. 1980. *The crucible of war: Western desert 1941.* London: Jonathan Cape.
———. 1982. *The crucible of war: Year of Alamein, 1942.* London: Jonathan Cape.
Robinett, P. McD. 1958. *Armor command.* Washington, D.C.: McGregor and Werner.
Rommel, E. 1953. *The Rommel papers,* ed. B. H. Liddell Hart. New York: Harcourt, Brace.
Simpkin, R. E. 1979. *Tank warfare: An analysis of Soviet and NATO tank philosophy.* London: Brassey's.
———. 1980. *Mechanized infantry.* New York: Brassey's.
Slim, W. 1956. *Defeat into victory.* London: Cassell.
von Manstein, E. 1955. *Lost victories.* Chicago: Henry Regnery.
von Mellenthin, F. W. 1955. *Panzer battles: A study of the employment of armor in the Second World War.* Norman: Univ. of Oklahoma Press.

MEDICAL RESEARCH AND TECHNOLOGY

Military medical research and related technological developments address health issues that limit a nation's ability to assemble, train, and use a fighting force. The goal of this work is to limit manpower loss and promote rapid return to duty through suitable prevention, protection, and treatment.

Three general challenges are important. First, there are those from biologically active substances: infectious diseases, toxins, and synthetic chemicals. Second are those from trauma and transfer of energy: injuries from missiles, blast, burns, radiation, temperature, and pressure. And third are those from stress: performance overload, sleep loss, demoralization, battle shock, and post-traumatic stress.

This article discusses these problems, current strategies for addressing them, and technological approaches to their solution.

Background

In some countries, including the United States, retired service members and families of active duty members are treated in military hospitals and clinics. "Military medicine," however, commonly includes only those topics directly related to combat or preparation for combat. Military medical research therefore extends only to subjects immediately relevant to the fighting ability of a generally young, previously screened, primarily male population.

Military medicine most narrowly defined is the treatment of combat injury. However, disease, nonbattle injury, and performance deficiency produce all manpower loss in garrison and much combat theater loss as well. During World War II and in Korea and Vietnam, disease and nonbattle injury accounted for over 70 percent of hospital admissions for U.S. ground troops. This assessment is skewed because many casualties died or returned to duty without being admitted, but other measures show the same general pattern. The U.S. Army in Vietnam found that half of all noneffective duty days involving hospital, dispensary, or quarters admission were due to disease or nonbattle injury. A further analysis of combat casualties comes from the 1982 Israeli incursion into Lebanon and resembles the U.S. Army experience in World War II. In those cases, every five combat casualties included approximately one killed, three injured, and one suffering from incapacitating stress.

Illness, noncombat injury, and stress thus account for most military garrison and operational personnel loss. The impact of these casualties on unit effectiveness is magnified by the large manpower and logistical burden their care imposes. As recent Middle East experience suggests, a commander might in some situations prefer a less lethal but severely incapacitating weapon (e.g., a sulfur mustard blister agent) over a highly lethal one (e.g., an organophosphate "nerve gas").

The discussion following is an overview of three broad areas of research and technological development. Several subjects are presented within each area, but a comprehensive account of all programs is not possible in the available space.

For some topics, the military medical community has primary responsibility for identifying the problem, assessing responses, and implementing the solutions that protect deploying personnel. Examples include vaccines to prevent infectious diseases. For other topics, medical responsibility is advisory and secondary to that of troop commanders, trainers, doctrine developers, or nonmedical equipment designers. Examples include the prevention of combat psychiatric casualties, design of a chemical agent protective suit, or promulgation of safety standards for microwave exposure.

Biologically Active Substances

THREATS

Throughout history, major personnel losses have resulted from small amounts of foreign, biologically active materials that kill and incapacitate. Three groups are currently important.

First are infectious diseases: bacteria, viruses, or parasites that reproduce inside the body. The impact of natural illnesses has been reduced greatly during the past century through sanitation, control of insects and other carrier organisms, and development of drugs and vaccines.

But in many parts of the world, military operations still face extremely high risks from endemic infections. U.S. military personnel suffered nearly as many cases of malaria in Vietnam (44,000) as fatalities from all causes. And some recent operations in Central America have seen high attack rates of leishmaniasis, a sandfly-borne parasitic disease for which there is no rapid, satisfactory treatment.

Disease may occur when personnel from a country with relatively little widespread infection, and thus minimal natural immunity in the population, deploy to a country with much disease. Hepatitis A, for example, is a relatively mild childhood illness in many parts of the world and confers long-lasting immunity after one infection. But for adults with no prior exposure, it can be devastating.

Other serious infections create little or no protective immunity, even following repeated episodes of the disease. For example, during May 1989, one-third of a battalion of Royal Thai Army special forces patrolling near the Laotian border were incapacitated by malaria, although many had previously contracted and recovered from it.

The natural diseases of greatest current military interest are respiratory (bacterial and viral); diarrheal (primarily bacterial); parasitic (e.g., malaria, schistosomiasis, leishmaniasis); viral (e.g., acquired immunodeficiency syndrome, hepatitis, dengue and other arthropod-borne diseases); sexually transmitted (e.g., gonorrhea); and others (e.g., meningitis and wound infections).

In addition, particular concern attends other highly infectious organisms that are potential biological weapons threats. Anthrax, Q fever, Rift Valley fever, tularemia, and others with lethal or greatly incapacitating effects have either been put into weapons or considered for such use. As the means to produce these organisms becomes cheaper and more widely available, development of defensive medical strategies is assuming increasingly high priority.

The second group includes biologically produced compounds: nonliving (that is, nonreproducing) chemicals normally generated by a wide variety of simple and complex plants and animals. Most importantly, this group includes the compounds collectively termed *toxins* that are harmful to some other organisms. (The shared label implies no common chemical structures or mechanisms of action.) Principal toxin sources include plants (e.g., ricin); bacteria (e.g., shigella, botulinum, tetanus); or animals (e.g., snake, shellfish, and invertebrate venoms).

Less well studied, but of growing concern, are a diverse group of biological regulator substances called *physiologically active compounds*. Some have been isolated from human or animal cells, others from body fluids. All appear to influence dramatically one or another bodily process when given in extremely small amounts. Although the functions of these chemicals are not fully understood, their potency has raised the concern that they could be employed as weapons were they produced in volume and were suitable delivery systems available.

The third group includes relatively simple synthetic molecules with highly reactive chemical structures. Examples are chemical warfare agents (e.g., organophosphate "nerve" agents, mustard, cyanide); riot control chemicals; behavior-altering compounds (e.g., lysergic acid diethylamide, or LSD); and toxic environmental contaminants found in fuels, fire suppressants, munitions, herbicides, and so on. These substances may be immediately harmful, as are chemical warfare agents. They may also pose long-term carcinogenic and mutagenic risks, as suggested in the case of the Agent Orange defoliant used by the United States in Vietnam.

Strategy

Five features of biologically active threats are central to medical defense: (1) the group is large, diverse, and growing; (2) the agents work through relatively specific interactions with the body's complex molecular structure; (3) they are effective in remarkably small amounts; (4) all animals, including man, have an intrinsic defense, the immune system, that in some cases inactivates foreign materials in the body; and (5) many biologically active challenges have been successfully met by developing drugs and vaccines against them.

Medical defensive strategy rests primarily on understanding the mechanisms of action for these threats well enough to design prophylactics and treatments that work in the exposed individual at the cellular level. In many cases, the most successful approach appears to lie through enhancement of the immune system. This cell-focused plan offers the possibility of protecting personnel in advance of exposure. If successful, it degrades individual performance trivially compared to protective suits, masks, or other passive external defenses. It only modestly burdens the logistics system. The strategy may be limited, however, because the number of threats far exceeds the resources to address them individually.

Drugs and vaccines often have been more successful against infectious diseases than against smaller molecules such as toxins and synthetic chemicals. The generally greater size and complexity of the former agents probably offers more opportunities than the latter for successful attack at the molecular level. Furthermore, the greater complexity of natural infectious agents is often associated with a longer interval between exposure and the onset of illness, time during which a successful intervention can occur. Infectious organisms have latent intervals ranging from hours to years. Small threat molecules, in contrast, generally need only seconds to hours to take effect.

Developing effective diagnostic technologies is the second critical response strategy and reflects several important needs. Timely diagnosis, combined with epidemiology and disease surveillance efforts, gives a commander the choice of avoiding a biologically active threat or of seeking to eliminate it before personnel are exposed. Diagnostic technologies are essential when designing protection such as masks, suits, filters, ventilation systems, environmental decontamination procedures, and so forth. Diagnosis is central to research concerned with creating drugs and vaccines. Finally, diagnosis is required so that appropriate treatment can be given quickly to casualties.

These needs are driven partly by the remarkable potency of the threats. Natural diseases often require only a few bacteria, parasites, or viral particles to produce infection. Toxins and chemical warfare agents may kill or incapacitate in microgram or milligram doses. Biologically active threat material usually enters the body in larger amounts only when accompanying a traumatic injury. In such situations, when the body's complex system of internal compartments is breached, the trauma itself usually becomes the life-threatening event.

Diagnostics additionally are required because the victim's appearance following exposure often provides only limited clues for identifying the causal agent. For example, the diarrhea, vomiting, sweating and tearing, headache, fast pulse, and labored breathing caused by a rapid-onset gastrointestinal infection might easily be mistaken for a moderately severe exposure to nerve gas.

Diagnostic technologies for infectious diseases are almost entirely qualitative, because no threshold quantities are assumed to exist. For self-replicating threats, any exposure is unacceptable. In contrast, diagnostics for materials such as toxins and synthetic chemicals should be both quantitative and qualitative. Safety thresholds may exist in those situations, thereby allowing acceptable, low-level exposures. Safety standards are more fully discussed in the section on Trauma and Energy threats.

Technologies

The central technologies reflect a reductionist view of living systems in which the functions of organisms such as man are seen simply as aggregates of processes taking place in organs, tissues, and ultimately the molecules of individual cells and fluids. The view can be traced to Descartes' *Treatise of Man* (1664), but the expansion of knowledge since World War II is the basis of most current efforts. This mechanistic paradigm has been influenced greatly by engineering principles, of which the feedback circuit and parallel processing are prominent examples. It further includes the central principle of homeostasis, in which living system processes are seen to operate so as to maintain stable internal conditions in the face of unstable external ones.

Technological and conceptual progress in three broad areas is central. The first area concerns the structure and reactivity of molecules in biological systems. This is particularly important for proteins, nucleic acids, and certain foreign chemicals. Proteins are the most important large class of biological molecules and include the enzymes, hormones, antibodies, receptors, membranes, surface coats, and other components essential here. Nucleic acids are responsible for long-term information storage in cells and are the basis for many diagnostic procedures. Critical foreign chemicals include the simpler threats outlined above, plus prophylactic and therapeutic drugs. Detailed understanding of the workings of these molecules is accruing rapidly through methods that include x-ray crystallography, chromatography, spectroscopy, computer modeling, radio labeling, and a variety of other synthesis, cleavage, separation, and sequencing processes.

The second area concerns creating and modifying biologically active molecules. This partly involves using synthetic chemistry processes to design new drugs or to enhance the potency and specificity of existing ones. More recently, the explosion of "biotechnology" methods, many based on recombinant DNA, permits the engineering of molecules too complex to be handled easily by traditional chemical methods. By modifying the normal cellular mechanisms that produce nucleic acids and proteins, techniques such as monoclonal antibody production and the polymerase chain reaction increasingly offer means to generate carefully targeted large molecules—in volume—for prophylaxis, treatment, and diagnosis.

The third area concerns the organization and functions of cells and tissues in biological systems. The important techniques include isolated tissue and organ culture, electron and other forms of microscopy, ion-sensitive electrodes, telemetry, micro-sampling and injection methods, micro-chemical analysis, and computer-supported data collection and processing. The resulting information concerns the membranes defining the body's intricate compartmental structure, the recognition and selective transport of molecules between compartments, the processes underlying cell maintenance and reproduction, and the storage and use of genetic information. Attention has been given particularly to the immune system that in many cases can recognize foreign molecules and direct the production of proteins that encapsulate and inactivate them.

Products

Civilian and military research programs have produced a variety of products with the technologies outlined above and will offer additional ones in the near and more-distant future. Drugs that directly inactivate threat organisms or agents are central. Examples particularly relevant to the military include a series of antiparasitics such as mefloquine and halofantrine. Other compounds, such as pyridostigmine pretreatment for nerve gas exposure, work instead by protecting a critical enzyme during exposure to the threat.

Protective proteins are increasingly important. Vaccines, such as those for adenovirus, meningitis, and hepatitis, induce the immune system to produce such proteins. Additional vaccines against malaria, diarrheal diseases, and wound infections are in various stages of development. Toxoids produced in animals can be administered to provide "passive" protection against toxin exposure. Still other drugs and proteins offer the promise of enhancing immune function generally, rather than in response to specific challenges.

Several protein- and nucleic acid–based methods offer increasingly sensitive and specific diagnostic methods for rapid threat identification. Related possible products include improved insecticides, repellants, filters, decontaminants, and impregnated fabrics.

New technologies such as microencapsulation and liposomes allow drugs and vaccines to be targeted more directly, both spatially and temporally, to increase specificity and decrease side effects.

Finally, increasingly sophisticated threat assessment models, often using small computers, give both doctrine developers and field commanders better information on which to base their decisions.

Trauma and Energy

Threats

Although diverse in origin and immediate means of application, these threats work finally by transferring inordinate amounts of energy into the body. Most dramatic are the blunt and penetrating mechanical traumas directly caused by shells and fragments. Closely related are the impact injuries secondary to blast, acceleration, parachute jumps, vehicle and other accidents, and so forth. Thermal energy injuries include fire- and blast-induced burns as well as military operations conducted in extremely hot or cold environments. Specialized energy weapons produce ionizing (nuclear), laser, microwave, or electromagnetic pulse (EMP) radiation. Finally included are the noise, vibration, and pressures associated with many large weapons platforms.

First attention in this threat group is given to the high-velocity, explosive projectiles upon which virtually all modern land, sea, and air combat are based. The enhanced lethality and accuracy of these weapons pose steadily increasing threats to military personnel and rapidly escalating impediments to all protection or treatment strategies. Approximately two-thirds of the fatal combat casualties suffered by the Israeli Defense Force during the 1982 Lebanese incursion had such massive head or thorax injuries that they probably could not have been saved by medical intervention of any kind.

This threat group additionally includes the problems of using one's own weapons safely, of fighting in inherently dangerous natural conditions, and of minimizing contamination of space in and around military facilities. Some of these concerns, such as blast-induced fire suppression, are immediately relevant to combat performance. Others, such as noise-induced hearing loss, also pose longer-term health and performance risks. Still others, such as high-power microwave sources, may or may not also cause health problems for nearby civilians. Even when such health hazard considerations are thought unrelated to combat, they have a dramatically growing impact on the design, production, testing, deployment, training use, and cost of military hardware systems.

Strategy

The central features of energy-generated injuries are three: (1) the initial harm is inflicted nearly instantly in most cases; (2) the primary damage is not based on molecular-level interactions; and (3) all but the most modest insults involve at least some tissue destruction.

Mammalian evolution has produced only a few primitive and minimally effective reflex responses that protect against this general kind of assault before damage is done. These include the flexor withdrawal reflex, eyeblink, middle-ear muscle contraction, and so forth. The primary military defensive strategies, medical and otherwise, therefore have focused on avoidance, protection external to the individual, and after-the-fact treatment of injury. Treatment is designed primarily to limit the spread of damage and to keep the casualty alive long enough to allow natural healing mechanisms to act.

An increasingly important further approach is directly related to the cellular and molecular strategy previously discussed. This work addresses the secondary cascade of biochemical and physiological events that follow trauma or other energy-induced injury. These subsequent events include not only normal recovery processes, but also others that frequently kill or impair. For example, burns and blunt trauma often kill through overwhelming complications such as infection, acute renal failure, or acute respiratory distress syndrome. And permanent brain damage following blunt head injury appears to be caused by secondary biochemical events. These and other harmful aftereffects appear to contradict the principle of homeostasis, are not fully understood, and are the objects of much current attention.

Diagnostic technology is critical for addressing trauma and energy-related threats. The threats are fewer in number than biologically active ones, and individually rather distinct, so that only modest effort has been spent on qualitative diagnostics. Because the possible existence of safe-exposure thresholds is so important, however, diagnostics that quantify energy threats have been pursued extensively. Blast, temperature, pressure, noise, vibration, laser, microwave, and ionizing radiation all have received much quantitative attention.

Exposure standards pose complex legal and policy questions on which consensus may be difficult to achieve. Personnel risks must be estimated partly to allow protection in training and other garrison situations. They are more prominently needed to provide force developers and commanders with tools for anticipating combat losses. Because of cost, danger to human subjects, and restrictions on animal testing, such estimates are often based on inadequate data.

Risk estimation requires that appropriate endpoints be chosen. Medically certifiable disease and injury are obvious choices and are suitable for some purposes. Coal dust hazards, for example, are judged on the incidence of black lung and other diseases. But the issue is complicated because not all tissue-level biological changes are necessarily harmful. Furthermore, some critical hazards involve little or no intrinsic health risk. Flash blindness, for example, is essentially harmless, yet can produce a catastrophic alteration in pilot or tank commander behavior.

Judging a risk threshold to exist and establishing an exposure standard are a declaration of how safe is safe enough. In civilian environmental assessments, that matter is treated primarily in the context of disease incidence over and above "natural" occurrence rates. Dioxin levels in the United States, for example, probably will be set to allow one "excess" cancer case for approximately every million lifetime exposures. Although applicable in some military situations, this simple approach generally is unsatisfactory, for it fails to balance the risk against the needs of mission accomplishment.

Technologies

The first technology area relevant to trauma and energy-generated casualties is that of the cell- and tissue-based methods discussed previously. Although some specific biochemical and physiological processes involved differ from those pertinent to biologically active threats, the techniques are quite similar. Trauma and energy-injury research differ somewhat in the additional emphasis placed on interactions among major organ systems in a whole-body context.

The second area of technology includes a diverse set of engineering disciplines, most involving electronics. Multichannel data acquisition and computer analysis in real time, for example, play a central role. Large-volume data processing and modeling of complex energy fields are also critical. Miniaturized electronics for telemetry, plus advances in biological and physical sensor technology, are also important. Finally, multiple advances in materials science have been the basis for a variety of personal and collective protective systems.

Products

Efforts to set exposure standards, although incomplete in several areas, have contributed to the evolution of much military equipment. Made possible principally by advances in materials science, these developments have substantially limited personnel loss and ineffectiveness. Examples include: hearing protection, laser and ballistic protective goggles, high acceleration (G) suits, diving suits and equipment, cold weather clothing, boots, helmets, vehicle suspension and seat design, parachutes, vehicle ventilation systems, flame-retardant fabrics, and many more. Closely related efforts have been directed toward developing increasingly sophisticated medical field equipment for forward deployment: portable X-ray, generators for sterile water and oxygen, and so forth.

Biotechnology products in various stages of research and development include blood substitutes, biologically active materials that prevent organ failure (brain, kidney, lung) and promote tissue repair, improved nonblood rehydration fluids, synthetic skin and bone, early biochemical diagnostic indicators of shock, drugs to enhance body heat production, and vaccines to prevent wound infection.

Stress

Threats

Many serious challenges to establishing and maintaining an effective force cannot readily be associated with the threats previously discussed or with any obvious damage to body tissue. Yet the affected individuals' performance may deteriorate sufficiently to render them partly or completely useless to a commander for significant periods of time. A striking example was the large number of "gas hysteria" casualties during World War I. Those soldiers were convincingly incapacitated by the false belief that they had been exposed to chemical warfare agents.

Combat psychiatric casualties generally are reckoned at about 20 percent of total casualties in ground fighting. During extremely heavy fighting, they may be much higher: 50 percent of all U.S. Marine casualties on Iwo Jima in World War II were neuropsychiatric. That figure substantially understates the total, however, for no simple means are available to count the performance shortfalls that generate fatal outcomes or degrade operational efficiency in significant but nonfatal ways.

Established sources of psychiatric and performance incapacity include attentional overload, particularly when multiple decision-making tasks must be executed concurrently. Closely related are deprivation and fragmentation of sleep, especially for commanders and others in critical decision-making assignments. Participation in or proximity to intense fighting, particularly when trauma casualty rates are high, is the classic source of battle shock. Additional contributing sources include lack or destruction of psychological cohesion within units, especially those below battalion size; family turbulence and uncertainty about family welfare during deployment; and inappropriate temporary or long-term demobilization, without suitable psychological support.

Strategy

Stress-related casualties and performance decrements are difficult to analyze because of their complexity and their loose relation to the cellular model of medicine and biology outlined above. That model adequately accommodates many studies of brain function. All but the simplest studies of behavior, however, are based on a largely distinct language that more nearly resembles everyday speech than that of cell science. In spite of this unsatisfactory and long-standing dichotomy, requirements and strategic approaches can be identified and pursued.

The first requirement for preventing stress reactions and performance failures is effective selection, assignment, training, and leadership. These challenges probably exceed all others in difficulty and importance. As the complexity of military equipment and missions increases, so do the demands on personnel and the risks of stress breakdown. The ability of numerically inferior Israeli and British forces to prevail in the Middle East and the Falklands/Malvinas amply illustrates the enormous weight of the issues that concern unit "quality." The pressures on command and control personnel are especially acute, as was well shown when the U.S. warship *Vincennes* misidentified and destroyed a civilian airliner.

The second requirement, as with the preceding threat groups, is for diagnostic techniques to assess stress and performance. General-purpose screening to ensure a reasonably healthy fighting force works well. More demanding test requirements to identify personnel for select assignments as pilots, sonar operators, special forces, and so forth, are often less well met. To the extent that a candidate pool will support a higher rejection rate, more sophisticated assignment-specific selection methods could be useful. Diagnostic criteria for performance breakdown serve purposes similar to those noted earlier. Threat avoidance, doctrine and equipment development, training, prevention, and casualty management all benefit from sensitive and specific performance assessment tools.

The third requirement is for improved treatment of stress casualties. These include full-blown cases of battle shock, post-traumatic stress disorders, and a variety of lesser problems often seen as disciplinary failures.

Technologies

Training and leadership are not primarily medical responsibilities. But the interview and interpretation methods of psychiatry, clinical psychology, and social work provide insights into the interpersonal relations upon which leadership rests. These methods are similarly important to the challenge of developing more uniformly effective means to train leaders.

A variety of cell biology methods similar to those previously discussed are relevant to functions of the nervous and neuromuscular systems. An expanding interest in drugs that affect the brain and behavior, driven largely by the civilian pharmaceutical industry, is directly relevant to several military issues. Drugs that act on the central nervous system are among the most difficult to develop. They require careful evaluation to detect unacceptable side effects such as impaired memory, potential for abuse, or other inappropriate behavior.

Electronic technologies, similar to those noted previously, are also critical. Most important are the computer and graphics-display equipment used in training simulators and a variety of performance assessment tools. A wide variety of sensor technologies, particularly applicable to studies of brain function, are also relevant.

Products

Evaluations of several aspects of military life from the psychiatric perspective are the basis for doctrinal recommendations to multiple audiences. Subjects include morale, cohesion, leadership style, command and military community climate, family and social support systems, and others.

Drugs to induce brief periods of sleep, for limiting jet lag, and possibly for use during sustained operations, have been tested. Drugs to improve the treatment of battle shock casualties and otherwise intervene in the stress process would be similarly welcome. Other drug possibilities include ones to work through the nervous system to enhance immune function and others to limit fatigue.

A variety of computer-based cognitive test batteries are emerging that can greatly increase the capacity to evaluate performance in selected environments. Somewhat related to training simulators, these programmable tools allow rapid assessment of critical decision-making skills. As for the previously discussed threats, such instruments may allow doctrine developers and field commanders to model threats to personnel by entering estimates of local conditions into previously written algorithms.

Finally, neuropsychological exposure standards are evolving. Principal subjects include work-rest cycles, unit rotation policies, and psychological burnout criteria.

C. Fred Tyner

See Also: Attrition: Personnel Casualties; Biological Warfare; Casualties: Evacuation and Treatment; Chemical Warfare; Medical Service; Medicine, Military.

Bibliography

Bancroft, W. H., ed. 1990. Workshop on future products, Division of Communicable Diseases and Immunology. Walter Reed Army Institute of Research. Washington, D.C.

Belenky, G. L., ed. 1987. *Contemporary studies in combat psychiatry.* New York: Greenwood Press.

Good, M. L., ed. 1988. *Biotechnology and materials science.* Washington, D.C.: American Chemical Society.

Walter Reed Army Institute of Research. 1990. *Annual Report.* Washington, D.C.

MEDICAL SERVICE

Until the middle of the nineteenth century, the treatment and care of wounded soldiers often was left to the civilian population. Rarely was there any pity for the wounded enemy; only one's own casualties might be lucky enough to be treated. Moreover, the primitive and onerous treatments were usually ineffective or even lethal (Schadewalt 1972). In fact, the commanders' lack of interest in their wounded was probably motivated by the feeling that they would only burden the campaign, particularly since most had little chance of recovery.

Historically, illness has played a larger role than enemy

weapons in the losses of an army. Rapidly spreading infectious diseases and epidemics sometimes compelled generals to break off a campaign because their troops had been decimated and there were no means of protection or treatment.

Military hospitals originally were established only for standing military forces outside of their home country. The Romans set up their *valetudinaria* in garrisons at the frontiers of the empire, and the Crusaders founded hospitals to treat knights and pilgrims. Military hospitals were first established in connection with permanent garrisons during the eighteenth century. Later, hospitals were established for large training areas; for example, near Krasnoe Selo, Russia, in 1823 and near Châlons sur Marne, France, in 1857 (Heyfelder 1866).

Until the beginning of the nineteenth century, medical treatment was rendered by army "surgeons" who had originally been barbers. A few actual physicians acted as consultants to the generals, and later were found at the regimental level. Until the Napoleonic Wars, there were no medical units on or near the battlefield to render initial treatment or to evacuate casualties. Volunteers were generally not allowed to rescue wounded soldiers before the end of a battle. Dominique-Jean Larrey and Percy, military physicians under Napoleon I, brought primary surgical care to the battlefield with *ambulances volantes* and horse-drawn vehicles for transporting surgeons and assistants. Their experiences led to the establishment of military medical units and mobile hospitals in many areas.

Still, treatment of the multitude of casualties in war was a constant, and seemingly unsolvable, problem for military medical services. It required hours and days to rescue wounded soldiers after the end of combat action, and those who did not die in the interim had only a small chance of successful treatment once they reached the dressing stations. The Russian anatomist and surgeon Nikolaj Iwanowitsch Pirogow (1810–81) addressed this problem with a new military medical organization developed during the Caucasian War (1847) and the Crimean War (1854–55). It connected battlefield dressing stations to hospitals located away from the battle area. To increase the injured soldier's chance of survival, the surgeon at the dressing station confined himself to inspecting the wound, rendering necessary initial treatment, and sorting all casualties according to severity and priority for further treatment. The wounded were then evacuated as soon as possible for definitive treatment in hospitals (Pirogow 1864). Pirogow's policy of the "dispersion of casualties" and his insistence on careful sorting according to the kind of treatment remain the basic rules of war surgery today.

Wounds caused by slashing or thrusting weapons were never unique to the military; moreover, such wounds often healed without complication. Beginning in the fourteenth century, however, shell fragments and bullets changed the face of military medicine. Firearms caused different types of wounds: they were deeper and often inaccessible, they penetrated the body and destroyed limbs, and they were far more likely to be complicated by infection. Sometimes several soldiers were hit by the same projectile. Only the medical experiences gained during the sixteenth century, especially those gained in the field of anatomy by Andreas Vesalius (1514–64), improved the chances of surgical therapy. The French surgeon Ambroise Paré (1510–90) pioneered new methods of treatment and a new operating technique. Moreover, he developed a great variety of operating instruments and made exceptional contributions to the scientific information of other surgeons by publishing his experiences and recommendations (Goerke 1988). Further progress in war surgery, however, was not possible until the introduction of general and local anesthesia, disinfectants, and antiseptics.

The formation of vast national armies at the end of the eighteenth century presented medical officers with the relatively new problem of infectious diseases: venereal diseases, typhoid fever, cholera, dysentery, typhus, diphtheria, and bubonic plague. The concentration of so many men promoted the outbreak of epidemics that frequently took a deadly course. But military order made it easier to enforce essential hygienic procedures and the armies of the nineteenth century became pioneers of modern hygiene and of preventive and environmental medicine (Waldman and Hoffman 1936). Weekly steambaths for all Russian soldiers did much to prevent skin disease, especially scabies, while the careful airing and frequent changes of sickrooms in Prussian hospitals helped prevent infectious diseases and wound fever. Military medical control of brothels curtailed the spread of venereal disease in the French Army (Heyfelder 1866; Kirchner 1872).

Military medicine has been in the forefront of medical research, particularly in the fight against infectious disease. The German medical officer Emil von Behring (1854–1917) was a pioneer in the field of immunization. In 1890, he developed a method of treating diphtheria and tetanus with serum. Before that time, nearly 10 percent of all wounded soldiers developed tetanus, and 80 to 90 percent of those soldiers died.

In addition to improved medical organization, more effective medical treatment, and better training of medical personnel, the development of humanitarian ideas beginning in the nineteenth century was essential to relieving the lot of the wounded. Military physicians had repeatedly sought neutral status for hospitals, but it was not until late in the nineteenth century that any formal agreement was reached. As the result of his observations during the Battle of Solferino in 1859, the Swiss Henry Dunant (1828–1910) was able to persuade several European sovereigns and governments to meet. In the course of the Geneva Conference, on 22 August 1864, sixteen countries accepted the first convention to relieve the lot of wounded soldiers of armies in the field (Unschuld and Locher 1972). The organizations of voluntary nursing founded by virtue of that resolution became indispensable national elements in support of the military medical services. Experiences in modern warfare show that the need for volunteers to care for wounded soldiers will continue to exist in the future.

Table 1 shows the immense progress that has been made in the past century in the treatment of casualties and on their chances of survival. Since the Franco-German war in 1870–71, medical first aid has been given on the battlefield, and followed up by battalion surgeons in advanced dressing stations and by general surgeons in clearing stations. Military surgeons realized very early that the timing and quality of the first surgical treatment is decisive in most cases for the fate of the casualty. An accurate excision of the wound within the first six to twelve hours after the injury, and immobilization of the wounded part of the body can prevent pyrogenic infection, tetanus, or gas edema. On the other hand, casualties with burns or brain and/or facial injuries have better chances of survival and restoration if there is no early surgical treatment after general first aid, and specialized treatment is delayed (Rebentisch 1980).

During the trench warfare of World War I, larger surgical operations were sometimes carried out in clearing stations, if they were well established and if the field hospital was too far away. That included operations for abdominal gunshot wounds—an absolute surgical taboo before the war (Rebentisch 1984). Depending on the need for further treatment, the casualties were then evacuated to the nearest divisional field hospital or directly to a war or home hospital. Later, in the 1930s, military medicine gained some experience in neurosurgery and in bone surgery from the Spanish Civil War (1936–39).

The mobile warfare of World War II forced medical companies to set up quickly relocatable clearing stations and to reinforce them by motorized surgical teams. Some medical units (e.g., in North Africa) equipped buses or trucks for surgical treatment. Such procedures often helped to shorten the interval between the injury and the first treatment. After treatment, however, patients had to remain at the place of surgery to ensure therapeutic success. At this time, air support first became important to the evacuation of casualties. German aircraft saved thousands of wounded soldiers from captivity by flying them out of encircled Stalingrad during the winter of 1942–43 (Wagenbach 1965). The military medical experiences and research activities of World War II established the basis of modern emergency and intensive care medicine. They decisively promoted the vital importance of early and effective treatment of shock. New methods of anesthesia as well as the application of sulfonamides and antibiotics improved the success of surgery and the therapy of infectious diseases. But the time between injury, rescue, and evacuation to the battalion surgeon was first shortened by the U.S. forces in Vietnam, who were able to rescue many casualties by helicopter, often from behind enemy lines, and take them to surgical hospitals within less than 30 minutes.

Modern Military Medicine

Modern military medicine has evolved enormously since World War II. Today it is understood to be fundamental to military preparedness and effectiveness.

Military Medicine and Operational Readiness

Armed forces depend on the physical and psychological fitness of their soldiers, and the medical service is responsible for preserving and restoring that fitness. The more difficult the mission and the greater the responsibility for personnel and materiel, the higher the demands on fitness

TABLE 1. *Soldiers Killed in Action, Dead of Wounds During and After Medical Treatment, and Recovered, Compared with the Total Number of Wounded in Different Wars*

		Killed in Action and Wounded in Action				Wounded Who Were Medically Treated	
War	*Army*	*Total number*	*Killed in action (%)*	*Died of wounds (%)*	*Recovered*	*Died*	*Recovered*
Mexican War (1846–48)	U.S.	4,947	21.2	10.3	68.5	13.0	87.0
Crimean War (1845–55)	British	14,849	18.6	12.4	69.1	15.2	84.8
Crimean War (1845–55)	French	50,108	20.4	19.9	59.6	25.1	74.9
War in Italy (1859)	French	19,590	12.9	15.1	71.9	17.4	82.6
American Civil War (1861–65)	Union	388,182	18.0	11.5	70.4	14.1	85.9
German-Danish War (1864)	Prussian	2,443	17.3	12.9	69.8	15.6	84.4
German-Austrian War (1866)	Prussian	16,284	15.7	8.9	75.4	10.7	89.3
German-French War (1870–71)	German	116,821	14.8	9.4	75.8	11.1	88.9
World War I (1914–18)	German	5,587,244	13.8	5.2	81.0	6.0	94.0
World War I (1914–18)[a]	French	3,675,000	18.4	6.8	75.3	8.3	91.7
World War I (1914–18)[a]	British	2,576,058	16.1	6.5	77.4	7.7	92.3
World War I (1914–18)[a]	U.S.	261,657	14.4	5.2	80.4	6.1	93.9
World War II (1941–45)[b]	U.S.	800,735	21.9	7.4	70.7	9.5	90.5

[a] Casualties include those caused by poison gas.
[b] Casualties include U.S. ground and air forces.

and capability. Decisive factors in determining the overall capability of armed forces are the organization and mission of the army in peace and war, the principles of leadership and action it follows, the available technology of weapons and equipment, the recognized need for education and training, and especially, the physical and psychological endurance of every soldier and of the entire force. Military leaders need physicians to ascertain the fitness of future soldiers for employment and service. Only physicians are trained to make binding decisions on questions regarding health and on injuries or health hazards.

Recruiting is important to maintaining the strength and effectiveness of the military. Medical services play a large role in determining the physical suitability of a recruit for military service.

Recruitment may be the responsibility of military or civilian agencies. Medical examinations are a mandatory part of the mustering procedure and follow national guidelines. Those guidelines ensure that personnel requirements will correspond to the mission of the armed forces and the special demands of a specific branch of service. The medical examination may be performed by military medical officers or civilian physicians.

In some countries (e.g., France) soldiers enter service immediately after mustering. Where there is a delay, a further examination is conducted when the draftee takes up service. That examination is performed by medical officers, usually the battalion surgeons concerned. When time elapses between the mustering and the date of entry into service, about 3 to 5 percent of the recruits originally fit for duty must be dismissed again because of a health injury.

No military commander, except in a critical military situation, is allowed to disregard a well-founded medical statement about the physical or psychological conditions of a soldier. To do so violates common law and risks the confidence of the soldiers in their leaders' judgment.

Cooperation between the military leader and the medical officer depends on the assignment of a medical officer to every level of military command. The medical officer must be able to make decisions from a military medical point of view on all health problems. The medical officer must be involved early in every situation and must have access to information about military intentions, because medical support often must be prepared even before the field units take action.

The importance of this kind of communication became clear during World War II. As the war progressed, medical officers began to take a regular part in briefings and in issuing orders and provided their comments on health problems and medical support. The control of the medical service from a rear command post was given up as a result of experiences that showed that effective medical support during a battle depends on close contact between the senior medical officer and the medical forces on the battlefield.

The functions of a military physician presuppose a broad knowledge of the military service and the daily life of soldiers in garrisons and in the field. A physician must understand the organization, training and equipment, nutrition, clothing and accommodation, military routine, and demands of weapons and technical equipment that a soldier deals with. The tasks of civilian life cannot prepare a physician for military service. Consequently, military medical service tasks cannot effectively be delegated to civilian physicians and auxiliary personnel.

In most armed forces the Surgeon General and staff are part of the top military echelon. In some countries (e.g., Germany, France, and Denmark), the Surgeon General bears the central responsibility for the functioning of all military medical services. In other countries, (e.g., the United States, the United Kingdom, and Italy), the medical services belong to the individual military services.

Experience shows that in war a joint medical service is the most effective form of organization for the best interests of the wounded soldiers and of the military leadership. This holds true all the more when forces must defend the territory of their own country, and the military and civilian medical services must operate in close cooperation with each other.

Medical Support in Peacetime

A broad scope of military medical care and support must be available at all times, regardless of the demand for treatment. That includes preventive, curative, and rehabilitative medicine, in peacetime as well as at war.

Maintaining and enhancing military medical effectiveness requires planning, preparation, and realization of military medical needs concerning organization, personnel, materiel, and infrastructure.

The military medical organization must be based on the principles of the armed services, yet it must also respect the demands of good medicine. Consequently, the medical service must be represented at headquarters to provide medical advice, guidance, and decisions, but must also be able to supervise the medical field units.

To accomplish the tasks of medical care in a peacetime army, medical officers and personnel must be available in all garrisons to operate the dispensaries and to accompany the military units during exercises. They are supported by a net of hospitals and research institutes. Other medical units must maintain operational readiness for wartime. Subordinated to the field army or to the territorial army, they have the mission to educate and train medical personnel of all ranks, to keep the materiel ready for action, and to take part in maneuvers and other exercises.

In contrast to other military formations, the medical service needs a multitude of additional personnel, even during peacetime: nurses, medical technicians, and cadre personnel. The professional qualifications of physicians, dentists, pharmacists, veterinarians, nurses, medical technicians, and other medical specialists are governed by law, but the medical service itself is responsible for educating and training nonprofessional personnel in both medical matters and common military questions.

The operational readiness of the military medical service depends on its ability to provide considerable personnel and materiel reinforcements and on the ability to adapt peacetime medical support to the conditions of war. The medical service of the German armed forces, for instance, is to increase from a peacetime strength of about 23,000 military and 4,000 civilian personnel to 110,000 military and 47,000 civilian personnel in wartime. The mobilization of the military reservists and in particular the recruitment of the civilians poses a problem for the military medical service that is not faced by the forces in general, especially since a settlement with the civilian health service is necessary.

There is no difference between that materiel used by military medical facilities in peacetime and that used by civilian installations. Materiel that is needed in wartime, but which cannot be prestocked in peacetime (e.g., perishables) must be registered and arrangements must be made so that deliveries can be made on short notice.

The infrastructure of the peacetime medical facilities should meet all requirements for accomplishing diagnostics, treatment, and nursing and for storing materiel. Furthermore, the medical service should identify buildings suitable for use as hospitals in wartime, check their suitability and capacity as far as possible, and make initial preparations.

Military Medical Support in Wartime

The fundamental tasks of the medical service in wartime are

- To render medical care to wounded or sick soldiers
- To relieve the combat units of wounded soldiers by providing first aid and evacuating casualties to suitable medical facilities; to rescue and provide medical assistance to casualties injured by nuclear, biological, or chemical agents and to support other branches of the services in identifying such means
- To provide medical advice to political and military leaders and to evaluate general decisions and orders in light of their consequences for the military medical service
- To maintain the medical support capability on the battlefield and in the rear combat zone, especially the availability of adequate transportation for ground, air, or waterway evacuation and the efficiency and capacity of the hospitals
- To collect and analyze current medical experiences, documentation, and statistical data
- To cooperate with allied medical services to ensure first aid or initial treatment by the closest medical aid post and to achieve the earliest possible reintegration of a wounded soldier in the national medical service chain
- To cooperate with the civilian health service, in particular with public health officials, in the interest of mutual assistance in the application of personnel and materiel as well as emergency treatment by both medical services; to act as an interface in balancing allied requirements
- To render military medical assistance in matters concerning prisoners of war and to cooperate with the International Red Cross.

Organization of the Military Medical Service

The development of a great variety of weapons, the introduction of high technology in warfare, and the unavoidable specialization within the armed forces of the late twentieth century make teamwork the basis of leadership. That principle is followed at all levels of combat, combat support, and supply troops. It also applies to the medical service in accordance with its mission, in the following ways:

- The medical service must maintain the lives and restore the health of soldiers and must not be subject to materiel considerations.
- Medical decisions are the exclusive privilege and duty of physicians.
- In carrying out their medical duties, physicians need not obey any order given by nonmedical personnel; they are responsible for deciding what kind of materiel or support they need to accomplish their mission.
- The medical service depends on personnel and materiel support from the rear area, but its net of medical facilities must be interconnected by an independent chain of evacuation, reinforced when necessary by transport provided by the field units.
- The medical service has an internationally agreed upon noncombatant status and, like the civilian health service, functions in wartime under the protection of the Geneva Conventions.

The organizational consequence of these requirements is that medical service elements must be allocated to all military units, as required, and must be subject to the missions and operations of those military units. However, when losses occur, the medical service must care for and evacuate casualties irrespective of the conduct of combat operations. The military side must help to maintain the capability of the medical service and keep medical personnel informed about its intentions. It must not call on members of the medical service to engage in combat.

The network of medical support also must include the many different institutes needed to perform research and documentation.

Medical Service on the Battlefield

To ensure that first aid is rendered to all casualties as early as possible, all soldiers must be trained in first aid to help themselves and their fellow soldiers. Having received first aid, the wounded soldier should leave the battlefield as soon as possible. There will occasionally be situations where the wounded must remain in the field: for example, where enemy fire prevents evacuation, where there are insufficient personnel to evacuate the wounded, or where the commanding officer is compelled to keep every capable soldier in action.

First aid support is assigned to the field units at a ratio of 1:50. They arrange or support the rescue of casualties, render first aid, collect the wounded, and evacuate them to the battalion surgeon. They use cross-country vehicles or armored personnel carriers to transport wounded.

It remains the combat unit's responsibility to transport wounded soldiers to the next aid post. Stretcher-bearer units are found only in a few armies and there is no certainty they will be available on the battlefield. Instead, each military unit must train additional soldiers to support the medical service as required. Unlike the official medical service personnel, these soldiers are protected by the Geneva Conventions only while rendering medical assistance or engaged in the evacuation of casualties.

Carrying a wounded man drains personnel resources and is even more arduous on difficult ground, under bad weather conditions, and under enemy threat. The military leader must consider carefully whether he can afford to weaken the fighting strength of his unit to save or evacuate casualties. He then must consider the risk to the wounded who remain on the battlefield or to whom medical treatment is delayed.

The battalion station. The battalion aid station should be located out of the range of the enemy's infantry weapons but within easy reach of the ambulances. During long-range operations and quick actions of armored or motorized troops, the battalion surgeon must follow his combat force closely. If two medical officers are available, one must accompany the operation while the other sets up a field station to render first aid to casualties of all participating units. This procedure has been proven viable during attacks with a limited objective.

The battalion surgeon renders first aid, concentrating on shock treatment, hemostatic therapy, relief of pain, and immobilization of injured parts of the body. Subsequently, the surgeon arranges the evacuation of the wounded soldiers to the nearest clearing station and then either cares for further casualties or follows his troops.

The clearing station. The clearing station at the brigade level or at a higher command level has the mission of sorting the wounded, rendering initial (mainly surgical) treatment, and making the patients transportable so they can be evacuated. Depending on the military situation, the mission of the combat troops, and the medical efficiency of the clearing station and the evacuation system, the senior medical officer must decide the extent of surgical treatment. In this context, the following considerations apply:

- Military situation: Intensity of combat; stability of the military situation; connection with neighbors; behavior of the enemy; air superiority
- Combat mission: Current and expected type of combat activity, strength, and fighting ability of the troops; possible resistance by the enemy
- Medical efficiency: Surgical and nursing capacity and experience; accommodation of the clearing stations in buildings, tents, or open air; expected time at present location; available supplies
- Casualty evacuation: Number, suitability, and mobility of ambulances; traffic conditions; additional air transport means; makeshift solution of evacuation in case of a mass casualty situation; threat by the enemy

As a rule, clearing stations go beyond strictly emergency surgery to include any treatment measures necessary to maintain the chance of recovery. When there is no military action, when the military situation is stable, or when medical conditions and experiences permit, a clearing station may be allowed to carry out major surgeries as well. In fact, this may be unavoidable in a critical military situation—for example, when the combat troops including their medical elements are encircled and the wounded cannot be evacuated. Moreover, the time lost between the injury and the arrival of a casualty at the clearing station frequently compels the surgeon to start surgery. (This is especially true for abdominal gunshot wounds.)

Hospitals. Field hospitals at division level or army corps level have the mission of treating surgical and internal injuries. Their surgical capability is greater than a clearing station's. Generally, they remain in one location longer, have better nursing capabilities, and therefore can perform more difficult and protracted surgeries. Buildings are the preferred location for field hospitals, but some armies use special inflatable tents, while others use only standard tents. Some medical services do not have field hospitals (e.g., Germany) because the military policy of defending only one's country obviates that requirement.

Station hospitals used in peacetime and wartime are comparable to civilian hospitals. But because station hospitals cannot meet the wartime requirements for casualty treatment, the medical services must plan for reserve hospitals in the rear combat zone. These should be located at suitable places with good traffic connections, and their accommodations should approach peacetime conditions. Schools, military barracks, and larger hotels are suitable, provided that there are good sanitary conditions, kitchens, and water and power supplies. The equipment for wartime use must be stored inside or near the buildings identified for use, to ensure that the hospital can be put into operation in the shortest possible time. The structure of such buildings will determine what kind of medical treatment can be rendered there in wartime; some are better for surgical purposes, while others should be reserved for more conservative therapy.

Military Medical Personnel

In peacetime, medical personnel have the following responsibilities:

- To render medical care in the infirmaries of the garrisons and training areas
- To operate the military hospitals and the medical, pharmaceutical, and veterinary research institutes
- To provide military and military medical education and training
- To manage medical documentation and statistics
- To provide medical guidance

Medical personnel make up between 4 and 6 percent of the total strength of the peacetime military. In addition, civilian specialist and cadre personnel are needed in hospitals, institutes, depots, and headquarters.

Many more medical personnel are required in wartime—a 9 to 10 percent proportion of total military personnel. These medical personnel support mobilized formations, operate stationary hospitals, complete the medical evacuation system, and balance potential losses. During World War II, almost half of all physicians were called up for military medical service in Germany.

Table 2 shows the increase in military medical personnel in the German Army during the first four years of World War II (Wagenbach 1965).

Medical Officers

Medical officers once were exclusively physicians; now, the medical officer career may be open to physicians, dentists, pharmacists, and veterinarians. In some countries, a professional group will have its own career field; in others (e.g., the U.S. Army), the pharmacists are members of a Medical Service Corps.

Members of all four professional groups hold officer ranks in the military organization, but are still subject to the laws and rules of their professions. They must study at public or approved private universities or at corresponding military medical institutions (as in France and some Eastern European countries). Once they have completed their studies, they must be licensed by the government. Their general military training and specialized military medical instruction then takes place at military medical academies or schools. Specialized qualifications that are in the interest of the armed forces or the medical service may be acquired by working in special facilities of the armed forces or by being delegated to civilian institutions.

Military physicians are responsible for the following tasks:

- Health care for military personnel and units, comparable to general practitioners in the civilian arena
- Specialized medical investigation, treatment, and evaluation, mainly in military hospitals and institutes
- Teaching assignments
- Leadership functions and professional tasks at headquarters

The demand for physicians, particularly specialists, increases drastically in wartime.

Few civilian physicians will be conscripted, since the medical support of the civilian population also must be ensured. Most wars of the twentieth century, including civil wars, showed higher civilian losses than military losses. Consequently, governmental agreements mandate that in the event that reservists are mobilized, only a small number of physicians, dentists, and pharmacists will be available for military duty; the rest will remain under civilian control.

For example, dentists execute preventive and therapeutic dentistry in infirmaries and hospitals during peacetime; in wartime, they may support physicians in the treatment of facial injuries. In some armies (e.g., the U.S. Army), there are dental corps; in other armies, dentists are members of the medical corps, have civil servant status, or work under civilian contracts.

Pharmacists are responsible for the wide range of medical materiel support of the medical service—for both the materiel itself and for the logistic organization. In addition, they perform military pharmaceutical research, and, because of their qualification as food chemists, they supervise the quality of some of the food issued to soldiers. In wartime, they play an important role in the detection of toxic agents. If they are not members of the medical corps, they are integrated into a medical service corps (as in the

TABLE 2. *Number of Medical Personnel in the German Field Army and Reserve Army During the First Years of World War II*

	Field Army					Reserve Army			Totals	
	Medical Units		*Hospitals*			*Hospitals*				
Years	Officers	NCOs and Lower Ranks	Officers	NCOs and Lower Ranks	Red Cross	Officers	NCOs and Lower Ranks	Red Cross	Officers	Medical Personnel
1939–40	7,789	92,348	1,314	9,731	1,241	6,380	24,179	17,062	15,492	126,258
1940–41	12,127	115,264	3,258	17,951	3,899	3,776	26,153	22,580	19,161	159,368
1941–42	12,757	150,060	4,427	30,472	9,507	4,484	46,047	45,637	21,668	226,579
1942–43	17,034	164,898	4,689	28,737	8,413	4,818	53,438	55,055	26,541	247,073

U.S. Army). In some armies they serve as civil servants.

Veterinarians, once the most important group of medical specialists, have lost many duties owing to the motorization of the armies. However, they are still indispensable to the modern army because they supervise food of animal origin both for daily consumption and for wartime storage. In addition, they cooperate with physicians in the control of infectious diseases and epidemics. In wartime, under the threat of biological agents, their expertise may be of tremendous importance. If they form a veterinary corps, they may be independent of the medical service. In many armies, they are members of the medical corps.

Line Officers

Line officers conduct many high-level tasks that do not require medical professionals. In peacetime, they serve in military schools or training units and perform normal staff work; they also occupy the regular positions of medical officers as commanders of medical companies and battalions, which do not provide peacetime medical care. In wartime, however, line officers are replaced by medical officers, but continue to function as deputies and as commanders of ambulance units.

In some armies, line officers are members of a medical service corps together with a number of other specialist officers. In other armies, line officers are members of the different branches of the military (e.g., infantry) and are attached to the medical service for limited periods of time.

Enlisted Medical Personnel

Noncommissioned officers and lower ranks are recruited from volunteers or draftees according to the system of military service. They perform a multitude of tasks within the modern medical service system: stretcher-bearers and first-aid support in the field units and medical units, ambulance drivers, nurses, or specialized assistants in surgery, anesthesia, and other medical fields. The higher their qualifications, the higher the military ranks they may reach. The effectiveness of the medical service largely depends on their skills and understanding of medical methods.

Even if there are sufficient enlisted medical personnel in peacetime, the demand for well-trained personnel and qualified reservists in wartime can be ensured only by periodic training in hospitals.

Education and Training of Military Medical Personnel

The two fundamental objectives of the education and training of medical personnel are to convey sufficient knowledge of military medical procedures and to instill the appropriate military behavior. Beyond the medical and administrative knowledge that they need to accomplish their professional tasks, medical officers and officer candidates must acquire a comprehensive understanding of military organization and the principles of command and control. Accompanying the soldiers on their daily routine, particularly during exercises, gives them the necessary insight into military regulations and orders.

Noncommissioned officers and lower ranks of the medical service are educated and trained in medical units or schools of the armed forces. After their military basic training, they take courses on first aid, nursing, and military occupational specialties in the different medical service fields.

In wartime, the medical service is affected more than other branches of the military with regard to the quality and the quantity of required personnel. The medical service should have sufficient qualified personnel as early as possible, because medical support must be operational by the time the combat forces reach their starting position. From the initial deployment, and particularly after the first shot is fired, the medical service must be ready to rescue, evacuate, and treat wounded personnel, both on the battlefield and in the rear combat zone. Thus, the early mobilization of medical personnel and urgently needed medical units and facilities should be a high priority.

Medical Materiel

Medical materiel is subject to the Geneva Conventions. It must be kept separate from other materiel and must not be destroyed to prevent it from falling into the hands of the enemy, but rather must be kept in good condition so that the enemy may use it as well. Consequently, medical materiel must be controlled by the medical service. It is stored, maintained, transported, and delivered by medical personnel under the supervision of pharmacists.

Medical materiel consists of:

- Medical consumable items: drugs; fluids; bandages; syringes; needles; surgical, dental, and laboratory materiel; nursing items; medical gauzes; antiseptics; disinfectants; etc.
- Medical nonconsumable items: surgical and other instruments; equipment for diagnostics and treatment; laboratory equipment; hospital furniture; field medical equipment; stretchers; etc.

The materiel is supplemented by so-called nonmedical materiel that is urgently needed to accomplish the medical service's mission. That materiel is to be selected and provided by the medical service. It includes ground ambulances, aircraft, rail ambulance cars, small arms, and all materiel needed to operate medical facilities, such as kitchen equipment, sanitary installations, and so forth.

Only the materiel that is required in wartime will go into long-term storage. Peacetime materiel is used and supplemented by materiel that comes out of short-term storage from depots or directly from civilian suppliers.

All materiel for peacetime use must be comparable in quality and quantity to that used in the civil sector. Materiel for wartime may be more simple, but must be rugged enough for use under field conditions.

Research and Development

All military medical services collect and analyze military medical experiences to consider their broader significance. Furthermore, they engage in research in the field of prevention, identification, and therapy of injuries typical of military service.

To develop guidelines for treating war injuries, the researchers must observe and study each new weapon and its effects on the human body, which may be of local, general, acute, or long-term importance. Moreover, they must determine methods for lifesaving and early treatment with a view towards improving the efficacy of emergency medicine. The results of these studies should influence the medical procedures used on the battlefield. These studies also lead to standards for the qualification of medical personnel and the quality of medical materiel.

Medical advice from the standpoint of ergonomics is required for the development of new weapons, vehicles, and weapon carriers. Facilities that are too small, lack ventilation, or are too noisy will reduce the ability of the soldier to fight and will accelerate the physical and psychological exhaustion of the soldier in combat.

The Geneva Conventions

The importance of the first three Geneva Conventions protecting wounded or captured soldiers on land or on water has not been reduced by advances in technology and employment of weapons; rather, it has increased. As long as there is no worldwide ban on nuclear, biological, and chemical weapons, some of the protective measures will remain of limited value (e.g., the establishment of zones of refuge and medical care).

On the battlefield, the medical service is only able to help if its members are identifiable by the international symbol of the Red Cross and if the enemy observes the fourth Geneva Convention on the protection of civilians at war. The military medical service may be relieved from additional burdens in the combat area as long as the civilian population is protected from military actions and as long as the efficiency of the civilian health care system is maintained.

Civil-Military Cooperation

Peacetime requires close cooperation between civilian and military health services in every country. The military medical service always depends on the advice and support of civilian specialists. Similarly, the military medical service must be prepared to meet urgent civilian requirements for personnel or materiel in case of disasters or other emergencies.

The requirement for cooperation, however, is of the greatest importance in preparing for war because both groups must establish a functioning medical service by order of the administration or of the armed forces command. Wartime requires intensive cooperation at many different levels. The experiences of World War II show impressively that mutual assistance operates on short-term agreements, often without much notice to the civil or military authorities.

The military medical service may depend on support from civilian hospitals in the initial treatment of wounded soldiers. And the civilian medical service may request local military medical relief in the form of hospital accommodations or medical materiel. However, the national military medical service is responsible for meeting any additional military medical support requirements from allied nations operating on its national territory. At the very least, it can act as an interface with the national civil health service.

A prerequisite to civil-military cooperation in medical matters is the establishment of comparable territorial structures and the appointment of competent professional interlocutors on both sides.

ERNST REBENTISCH

SEE ALSO: Attrition: Personnel Casualties; Branches, Military; Casualties: Evacuation and Treatment; Civil-Military Cooperation; Land Warfare; Medical Research and Technology; Medicine, Military; Territorial Army.

Bibliography

Buchholtz, A. 1911. *Ernst von Bergmann.* Leipzig: Vogel.
Cantlie, N. 1974. *A history of the Army Medical Department.* Edinburgh-London: Churchill Livingstone.
Franz, C. 1936. *Manual of war surgery.* Berlin: Springer.
Goerke, H. 1988. Ambroise Paré—Pioneer of modern surgery. *Wehrmedizin and Wehrpharmazie* 3:14–18.
Heyfelder, O. 1866. *The camp of Krasnoe Selo in comparison with the one at Chalons.* Berlin: Reimer.
Kirchner, C. 1872. *Medical report about the Royal Prussian Field Hospital within the Palace of Versailles.* Erlangen: Enke.
McLaughlin, R. 1972. *The Royal Army Medical Corps.* London: Cooper.
Pirogow, N. J. 1864. *Fundamentals of general war surgery.* Leipzig: Barth.
Rebentisch, E. 1980. *Military medicine.* Munich-Vienna-Baltimore: Urban and Schwarzenberg.
———. 1984. 100 years of military medicine. *Forschritte der Medizin* 102:225–31.
Schadewaldt, H. 1972. Combattants and non-combattants—The influence of war disasters on the civilian population: A historical review. *Wehrmedizinische Monatsschrift* 16:353–59.
Unschuld, P. U., and W. Locher. 1987. *The voluntary medical service during the War of 1870–71: Diary of Franz Clarus.* Munich: Cygnus.
Wagenbach, G. 1965. The organization of the Armed Forces Medical Service in World War II, with special regard to

the year 1943—Part 1. *Wehrwissenschaftliche Rundschau* 15:285–301.
Waldmann, A., and W. Hoffmann. 1936. *Manual of military hygiene*. Berlin: Springer.

MEDICINE, MILITARY

Military medicine is the body of knowledge related to the unique diseases and injuries incurred during military operations. It also includes the specialized forms of organization that have evolved to provide medical support to military forces and to rapidly move and treat patients during combat. Modern military forces require a continuum of medical support from first-aid at the front line of troops to state-of-the-art hospitals in sovereign territory. Within this continuum, care becomes increasingly sophisticated as the wounded or sick patient moves to the rear. By bringing the resources to provide the specific kinds of care needed for combat injuries into close proximity to the fighting, military medicine provides the greatest chance for survival and recovery.

Historical Background

Medical personnel and organizations have been a nearly universal feature of military forces. Military forces and the policymakers who create them have invested significant resources in providing medical support for their troops. Moreover, since military forces usually represent the full capabilities and power of the culture, the medical technology provided to the military typically represents the leading edge of knowledge for that society. Military medicine has been not only beneficiary but the source of the latest in medical knowledge.

Modern Military Medicine

Through the long history of armed conflict by organized forces, military medical systems have developed along remarkably consistent lines. Today, the military medical care systems of even highly disparate nations exhibit a number of common features.

Chief among the common features of modern military medicine is an emphasis on prevention. The main purpose of medical support is to conserve combat power. Avoiding unnecessary losses of manpower to illness and accident preserves the strength of the unit prior to battle. Hence, extensive immunization, sanitation, and safety programs are characteristic of military medical care.

Although military members typically are thoroughly screened before being accepted for the armed forces (see below), no system of physical examination can eliminate all pre-existing conditions or prevent the illnesses that appear after entry into active service. Consequently, military medical systems must be prepared to treat the usual ailments to which any human population is subject. Much of the patient population in military treatment facilities is indistinguishable from that found in any large civilian medical care system.

Common Features of Military Medical Systems

In addition to the usual ailments, military medical systems must also treat a range of unique syndromes and injuries that are rare or unknown in other populations. The effects of modern weapons, the stress of continuous operations, and the noise, toxins, and other hazards of the battlefield environment combine to produce syndromes of injury that are not normally found in civilian or peacetime settings.

Because military operations are by nature unpredictable, extreme variation in workload is a common feature in military medicine. Casualties occur in clusters, both spatial and temporal. Although it may be possible to predict with limited accuracy the casualties to be suffered by attacking forces, it is difficult to make such predictions for defending forces. The opponent seeks to maximize his advantage by inflicting casualties at a time and place of his choosing, often precisely and deliberately at the point in space and time where all kinds of support, including medical care, for the defending forces are at a minimum.

The corollary to this phenomenon of casualty clustering is an inevitable mismatch between the demand for services and the resources to provide them. No conceivable level of medical support could be adequate to the type of mass casualty characteristic of many modern weapons systems. Conversely, during periods of quiet, most military medical systems will appear to have considerable excess capacity. The workload generated by disease and nonbattle injuries will not fully occupy their capabilities.

The types of treatment needed and the specialties required of providers also can vary considerably. Combat operations generate large numbers of casualties requiring surgical and orthopedic care. These specialties are much less in demand during peacetime or periods of inactivity in wartime. Since the demand for primary care, internal medicine, and other medical specialties is largely independent of casualty rates, the requirement for these types of providers is constant, related primarily to the size of the force and the environment in which it is located.

Another common feature of military medical systems is the need to function in close proximity to the supported force. Saving of life, conservation of manpower, and the effect on morale are largely functions of the speed with which wounded and sick personnel can be evacuated, treated, and returned to duty. To achieve this in a timely manner, the medical unit must operate close to and in coordination with the combat unit. The medical unit also faces operational constraints ranging from requirements for cover and concealment to communications security. Such considerations may have a profound impact on the status of a medical unit or its personnel under international humanitarian law (see below).

To operate in such close proximity to combat units, military medical systems also must be both mobile and flexible. They must be capable of rapid displacement to follow supported units in advance or retreat and to respond to changes in demand for care. Many land force medical units achieve this capability by including vehicles in the organization. A concomitant operational flexibility enables medical units to conduct movement by echelons, utilize structures of convenience in urban terrain, and modify their treatment capabilities by adding specialized providers and equipment.

The requirements for mobility and proximity impose significant austerity on military medical systems, especially units deployed near the front lines. Treatment systems in forward areas tend to be less sophisticated and resource-intensive than those found in rear areas. The austerity of forward-deployed military medical systems, combined with the large variations in workload, inevitably require resource-based treatment decisions.

Virtually all medical care for military forces is provided by organizations which are themselves military or have a military-like structure. The need for medical care systems to be fully compatible with supported forces and the necessity to maintain command and control of medical assets generally have produced organizations denoted and organized as military units: companies, squadrons, battalions, and so forth. The personnel serving in these organizations, with few exceptions, wear uniforms, hold military rank, and are subject to military discipline.

Differences Among Military Medical Systems

The principal variations among military medical systems reflect differences in the nations and military forces that the medical care systems support.

Geopolitical situation. The geopolitical situation of the nation greatly influences the size and organization of its military medical systems. Continental powers that can use land transport to rapidly evacuate casualties to sovereign territory may be able to reduce the proportion of medical support that must be deployable. Maritime nations, which project forces outside continental limits, typically must provide a larger proportion of deployable medical assets and devote considerable resources to rapid evacuation, typically by air.

Mission and organization of supported forces. Military medical care systems are tailored to complement and reinforce the function of the supported units. Land forces whose mission is primarily internal security and which are not armed or equipped for large-scale combat operations primarily require medical support for illness and nonbattle injuries. Conversely, strategic air or missile forces may have no deployable medical assets whatever, but require large-scale medical support at their bases in order to deal with casualties from counterforce attacks. Although a few nations have experimented with joint or combined logistical support structures, including medical care systems, the majority still have separate medical care structures for land, sea, and air forces.

Forces that rely on large reserve components and are mobilized only for short periods of time or in a crisis may have medical care systems that provide little more than operational support. The reserve military personnel and their families meet their peacetime health care needs through civilian systems. Forces manned largely by conscription also have reduced needs for peacetime medical care, since conscripts usually serve for brief periods of time and typically do not have dependents. Large standing forces manned by career personnel require extensive peacetime health care systems for both service members and families.

Civilian health care system. A final source of variation in military medical care systems is the capability and organization of that nation's civilian health care system. As developed nations devote increasing proportions of national wealth to health care, there is an understandable desire to avoid duplication. Where the civilian system is well developed and nationalized, it frequently provides military medical care other than that provided by deployable units. In contrast, the dominant position of the military in many developing nations often leads to a disproportionate investment in military health care. While those civilian systems are relatively primitive, the military forces frequently have the best and most capable health care system.

Functions of Military Medicine Systems

Military medical systems perform a series of common functions, including operational care, care during low-intensity conflicts or disasters, and nonoperational care.

Operational Care

Although most military forces spend the majority of their time training for operations rather than performing them, military medical systems are at least partially operational at all times. The operational role of military medical care systems begins with the selection and qualification of personnel. Physical and mental examinations are designed to detect pre-existing diseases and other defects that may make the recruit unable to bear the stresses of training and active service. Recruits are classified by physical and mental condition to identify suitable candidates for training in various special units or activities. As the physical and other demands of the particular military function increase, physical standards are applied more stringently. Many occupations (e.g., aviators, divers, parachutists, etc.) require continuing medical surveillance and reexamination to ensure the continued physical qualification of the incumbent.

The most obvious role for military medical care systems occurs during active combat. The essential function of the health care system is to conserve military manpower so that it may be applied in battle. Much of this kind of activity is preventive in nature; however, no system of preventive medicine is completely effective—particularly against combat casualties.

Treatment of the wounded and sick is vital to conserving manpower, and it is a necessity for any nation with humanitarian aims. The preservation of life, limb, and sight are ethical imperatives of any medical care system. Achieving these goals requires the capability to rapidly assess, evacuate, and treat serious conditions. During operations, the most immediate source of trained manpower is the force already deployed. Thus, the ability of the medical care system to rapidly return lightly wounded or sick personnel to duty is key to maintaining the strength of the force. This imperative works against the operational pressures to keep medical units small and mobile. Much of the work in designing medical forces is an effort to strike a balance between competing needs: to create units that are small enough to move and be supported and yet have sufficient capability to treat and return casualties to duty.

It is difficult to overemphasize the importance of medical care in preserving the morale of troops. Modern warriors intellectually accept the risk of injury as one of the realities of combat. Much of the psychology of combatants, however, consists of defense mechanisms aimed at keeping the realization of this risk at a distance. Medical care systems support these psychic defenses by removing casualties from the battlefield and by giving the combatant a sense of confidence that he will receive care if wounded.

Although some nations overlook this necessity or provide for it through nonmilitary systems, rehabilitation is a key element in medical care for combatants. As the capability to save life has increased, so have the numbers of severely injured survivors. Providing prosthetic limbs, physical and occupational therapy, counseling, and other rehabilitative services to veterans is critical to maintaining morale and fighting spirit in combatants.

Provision for aged and permanently disabled veterans is another essential part of the continuum of care. As with rehabilitation, this need may be met through nonmilitary systems, but nations that totally neglect it have found it increasingly difficult to maintain sizable standing forces.

Low-Intensity Conflicts

In the present era, insurgencies and other forms of low-intensity conflict are the predominant form of armed strife. Military medical systems provide the same functions in such conflicts as in general warfare. In addition, since military medical units are frequently the most capable and flexible health care institutions in developing nations, they can be a useful adjunct to the political and psychological struggle. The provision of preventive, therapeutic, and veterinary services by military medical units can be a very effective demonstration of the dedication and capability of the national government.

Disaster Relief

Because of their flexibility and mobility, military medical units can be extremely useful in responding to a sudden increase in medical demand or a widespread destruction of civilian medical care systems. Natural disasters, in particular—earthquakes, cyclones, floods—frequently produce sudden demands for care of traumatic injuries and infectious diseases. At the same time, they often damage or destroy existing medical care facilities. Military medical systems can move treatment capability into an area, operate without reliance on fixed structures or power sources, and rapidly evacuate large numbers of sick and injured people. Typically, military systems are withdrawn gradually as civilian capability is restored.

Large numbers of refugees, whether from natural disasters, famines, or conflicts, can easily overwhelm the capability of civilian medical care systems. Moreover, refugee populations frequently suffer from conditions that are relatively rare in the usual civilian patient population. Again, the mobility and flexibility of military medical units can be extremely useful. Military health care providers may also be better trained to deal with the typical health problems of refugees, such as malnutrition, infectious diseases, exposure, and psychological stress, since many of these conditions are common in military operations.

Nonoperational Care

Depending on the capabilities and organization of civilian health care systems and other factors, military medical care may perform a variety of functions which are not strictly related to the operational role.

General health care. Like any large employer, military forces provide their members with a range of benefits, including pay and medical care. Although these benefits may vary greatly, most nations find it necessary to provide treatment to military personnel and families.

The need to maintain control of the patients, to ascertain their fitness for further duty, and to maintain the bond between service members and their units, all provide a strong argument for treating military personnel within the military health care system. Care that is beyond the capability of the military medical system may be obtained from civilian providers, usually without charge to the service members. Care to military dependents is usually provided in military hospitals, by purchase of insurance, or by ensuring that family members are eligible for the national health care scheme. In those countries which provide dependent care in military facilities, family members frequently constitute the large majority of patients.

In some developed countries, military pensioners and their families may also be eligible for care in military facilities. Since these populations are typically elderly, their health care requirements are considerably greater than those of the young and highly select population of serving members. Military treatment facilities may also be participants in some national health schemes and treat patients who have no military connection at all.

Training. Military health care systems provide a wide variety of training, from the complete education of physicians, nurses, and other professionals, to the schooling of technicians and the training of units. Many military forces or nations operate professional schools or academies that provide a complete education for health care professionals. Forces that operate large, full-service hospitals frequently incorporate graduate medical education into the facilities. With few exceptions, military medical care systems also provide complete training for medical technicians such as aidmen, ambulance drivers, and so forth—functions sufficiently specialized that civilian training is unlikely to support.

Medical units must practice their functions and tasks to ensure that they are capable of performing during operations. Training for mobility and operation of equipment is relatively straightforward. Training in actual patient care is more difficult, since most units do not treat the kinds of patients in peacetime that are encountered during actual operations. Such training typically involves the use of simulated patients to provide some realism (Fig. 1).

Organization

Military medical systems are virtually always organized as military units or military-like structures. As such, they exhibit a number of common features of organization.

Especially during operations, medical units and organizations are usually functionally aligned with other major support organizations. In most cases, the medical function is included in and subordinated to either the personnel function or the logistic function.

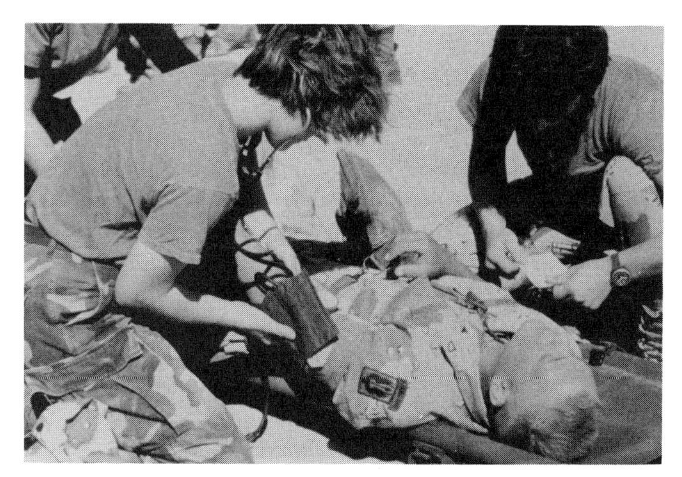

Figure 1. Soldiers perform a mock mass casualty exercise. (SOURCE: U.S. Army)

There is no unanimity regarding the most effective form of organization at the highest level. Some nations have a unified military medical system that is not part of any particular branch. Others rely on a single service (most typically the army) to provide medical support to all services. However, most nations have separate medical departments in each service.

Some nations have military medical systems with fixed facilities such as hospitals, training centers, clinics, and medical depots. Some also operate production facilities for medical materiel including some medications and biologic products. In peacetime, these facilities constitute the largest portion of the medical departments and are primarily engaged in providing medical care as a benefit to service members and others. Such large facilities provide a useful reserve for absorbing large increases of patients in the event of mobilization and active combat.

Among the unique features of military medical systems are mobile medical treatment and evacuation units that may be positioned at the point of need. These range from small dispensaries staffed by a single medical practitioner and a few ancillary personnel to large hospitals capable of providing virtually every service available in a medical center. In addition to treatment facilities, deployable medical units include evacuation units, supply units, medical maintenance units, laboratory units, preventive medicine units, and so on.

Most large combat or operational units include some medical support. For example, most warships have a medical department staffed with one or more physicians or specially trained medical corpsmen. In land forces, maneuver battalions often include a medical platoon to provide care. This pattern of "organic" medical support in land forces is usually maintained up to the level of the division. Organic medical support tends to be directed primarily at care of minor illnesses and immediate stabilization of casualties. More elaborate or definitive care is provided by separate medical units that support the combat forces.

To use more elaborate kinds of medical care efficiently and to preserve the flexibility to respond to changing conditions, most military medical systems place the majority of deployable resources in medical units that are not organic to any particular combat unit. These may be denominated as medical battalions, brigades, and so on, or they may be identified with terms reserved for medical units (e.g., hospitals, ambulance companies, etc.).

International Humanitarian Law

The Geneva Conventions and Additional Protocols contain specific rules about the care and protection of wounded and sick personnel during the conduct of hostilities. Military medical care systems provide the means to comply with the requirements of the Geneva Conventions and Additional Protocols, to which most nations are signatories. The overriding principle in this regard is the requirement to provide medical care to wounded and sick combatants of *both* sides.

International humanitarian law (IHL) places obligations on all parties in an armed conflict. Medical establishments and personnel may under no circumstances be attacked, but shall be respected and protected. The special status of medical establishments and units can only be discontinued when they are used to commit acts outside their humanitarian duties and then only after adequate notification. IHL further requires an occupying power that displaces or otherwise interrupts the operation of civil authority to provide replacement services, including medical care.

Protections

In order to enjoy protected status under IHL, medical establishments, transports, and personnel must be identified with the distinctive sign of the Red Cross or Red Crescent. Alleged or actual misuse of these distinctive signs has been responsible for many controversies over compliance with IHL.

Medical personnel are entitled to protected status under IHL. If they fall into the hands of the enemy, they must be permitted to pursue their duties unless the capturing force is providing all necessary care to wounded and sick personnel. Under IHL, medical personnel may not be made prisoners of war and may be retained by the enemy only if they are needed to provide care to prisoners of war.

Prisoners of war must receive medical care equivalent to that provided for a nation's own troops. In addition, IHL requires that prisoners, including the wounded and sick, be moved away from areas of potential harm.

Limitations

Medical establishments and units are given protected status to permit them to carry out their humanitarian activities. Any act outside the scope of these duties may place that special protection at risk.

There also are some limitations on the activities of protected persons. Under IHL, medical personnel may use weapons in their own defense or to defend the wounded and sick in their charge. They may not, however, fire or otherwise take part in active attacks. Medical personnel are also enjoined from using their skills to harm enemy personnel, perform experiments upon them, or otherwise violate the generally accepted principles of medical ethics.

In addition, protected objects (medical units and transports marked with the distinctive sign) may be used only for humanitarian purposes. Carrying ammunition in ambulances, storing large quantities of weapons in hospitals, and other inappropriate acts can be the basis for discontinuing the protections offered to all activities identified with the distinctive sign.

Obligations

IHL requires the capturing power to provide treatment and evacuation of wounded and sick prisoners of war. As a general principle, care must be provided to the same extent as that available to the capturing power's own personnel. Captured enemy medical personnel (who are "retained" but not made prisoners of war) may be used to provide this treatment.

Military Medicine in Wartime

The three basic functions of military medicine in wartime are evacuation, treatment, and research.

Evacuation

Except for the most lightly wounded or sick patient, the first step in caring for a casualty is to move him away from danger and to a site where treatment is available. This movement has the additional benefit of clearing casualties away from areas of active combat to preserve the morale of the fighting forces and avoid impeding operations.

Principles. The broad principles of evacuation have not changed since they were established by Baron Larrey (surgeon to Napoleon's Grande Armée) and Jonathan Letterman (medical director, Union Army of the Potomac, 1862–64). The patient's condition, especially the risk to life, limb, or sight, determines the priority with which he or she is evacuated. Under both IHL and medical ethics, considerations of nationality, race, religion, political opinions, and so forth may not be factors in determining priority for evacuation or treatment. Current U.S. practice is to classify evacuations into one of the following three categories, according to patient need: immediate, meaning that vehicles or aircraft will be diverted to evacuate the patient in the shortest possible time; priority, meaning that the patient will be moved by the next available vehicle or aircraft; and routine, meaning that the patient will be evacuated by vehicle or aircraft following predetermined schedules.

Since one of the main functions of military medical systems is to return casualties to duty as soon as possible, casualties should not be moved any farther from the battlefield than is necessary for their treatment. This principle also helps conserve treatment and evacuation resources. The decision to evacuate casualties is made by the tactical (not the medical) commander and must be made with consideration for the tactical situation. When evacuation cannot be performed safely or when it may imperil the unit by revealing its location, the commander may decide to retain the wounded and sick. Such a decision would be made only with great reluctance and with full knowledge of the negative impact on the morale and effectiveness of the unit. Under IHL, a commander does not have this option for prisoners of war. If evacuation is not possible, the commander is obligated to release his prisoners.

Evacuation systems work best when the means of evacuation are dedicated to this one purpose. Use of shared means of transport for medical evacuation has two significant risks. One is the practical problem that the means may not be available when a medical necessity appears. A potentially more serious issue is the protected status of medical establishments under IHL. Vehicles that do not display the distinctive sign cannot rely on any protected status while evacuating the wounded and sick. Conversely, use of vehicles with the distinctive sign for improper purposes such as transport of ammunition or fresh troops may forfeit the respect and protection afforded to medical establishments, vehicles, and units.

Means. The chain of evacuation naturally begins at the point where the casualty falls ill or is wounded. Depending on the circumstances, ground, rail, air, or sea evacuation may be used to move the patient.

The simplest means of ground evacuation is litter carriage of an individual. The casualty will frequently move himself, if possible, toward a place of safety and out of sight and range of the enemy. This movement is often assisted by other combatants in the immediate area. Techniques for carrying or dragging the injured are included in the first aid training given to most service members. Once the casualty is sheltered from direct fire and immediate aid is provided, further movement of the casualty typically occurs by litter. At this point in the evacuation sequence the litter usually is carried by combatant troops, not by medical personnel. (In mountainous terrain, some forces continue to use pack animals.) Litters are carried either to a predetermined collection point or directly to a medical treatment facility if one is located close enough. Most military forces train their combat troops to turn over the casualty to medical personnel at this point and resume their combat missions. Further treatment and evacuation of the casualty is the responsibility of the military medical system.

On the modern battlefield, most movement of patients occurs by motorized vehicles. These ground ambulances go forward to collect patients from collection points and return them to forward treatment facilities. They also move patients between echelons of treatment. The U.S. practice is to call vehicles from the rear to come forward and evacuate patients to facilities farther back. When patients must be moved through areas subject to small arms fire and indirect fire (artillery, rockets, etc.), armored vehicles may be used as ambulances. When properly marked with the distinctive sign, armored vehicles are entitled to the same respect and protections afforded to any medical unit under IHL. Most of the vehicles used for transporting casualties are unarmored motor vehicles that are frequently expressly designed for this purpose. Ambulances are designed to include equipment for life support and the comfort of the casualties during transportation.

In theaters where rail transportation systems are well developed, specialized hospital trains have been used to move large numbers of patients over long distances. This means is especially useful for continental powers. Since rail evacuation is relatively slow, this method is most suitable for patients who are well stabilized but who may require lengthy periods of treatment and recuperation in rear areas.

Air evacuation is the most recent and possibly the most significant innovation in casualty evacuation. The speed and flexibility of aircraft have made it possible, under the right circumstances, to transport casualties from the battlefield to the hospital in minutes, with great savings of life, limb, and sight.

The helicopter's ability to land and take off vertically and to hover allows it to pick up patients from many locations where neither conventional aircraft nor land vehicles could operate. Cleared areas just large enough to accommodate the rotor may serve as landing pads. In conditions where landing the helicopter is impossible, techniques have been developed to evacuate patients by winching them up on cables lowered from the aircraft. Life support equipment is frequently installed in helicopters to facilitate the transport of severely injured casualties. Helicopters have several drawbacks, however. They are noisy and subject the casualty to considerable vibration. Also, as the number and sophistication of antiaircraft systems on the modern battlefield has grown, the risk to helicopter air ambulances has increased. Since many of these systems are heat seeking or radar guided, the distinctive sign offers no protection. The Additional Protocols to the Geneva Conventions provide procedures for notifying and obtaining agreements between adversaries to permit free passage of medical aircraft. Such agreements, when practicable, can effectively protect air ambulances.

Fixed-wing air ambulances are less flexible than helicopters but offer the advantage of greater speed, range, and comfort. They are most useful for moving casualties between rear echelons of care and returning them to sovereign territory. Most fixed-wing air ambulances are equipped with sophisticated life support equipment and may be capable of providing limited in-flight treatment.

Ships are useful for transporting large numbers of patients. Sea transports may also be capable of providing fairly extensive treatment during evacuation. The major role of hospital ships, however, is as rapidly deployable medical treatment facilities. Their ability to provide sophisticated care while remaining self-contained and independent of the shore can be very useful in supporting amphibious operations or in circumstances where treatment facilities cannot be established ashore.

Treatment

Military medicine uses the same modalities of treatment as civilian medicine. However, because of the circumstances under which they function and the conditions they must treat, military medical systems operate differently. Given the problems of proximity, austerity, and resource mismatch, efficiency is a much greater factor in military medical care.

Self aid. The continuum of military medical care begins with the injured or sick individual. Most military forces train all personnel to provide self aid and immediate aid to casualties. The injured service member is trained to apply his own dressing, control bleeding, and move to an area of shelter, when possible. Land forces frequently require each soldier to carry some of the medical supplies needed to treat him if he is injured. Soldiers in some forces or special units also carry a unit of fluid for intravenous infusion. The risk of drug abuse has curtailed the practice of issuing injectable analgesics to each service member.

"Buddy" aid. In most military forces, each service member is trained to apply dressings, control bleeding, clear airways, perform cardiopulmonary resuscitation, administer chemical agent antidotes, and carry or drag a casualty to shelter. When necessary, each service member helps to carry the casualty on a litter. Nonmedical personnel usually turn over the management of the casualty to medical personnel and resume their combat mission.

Combat medic. The first individual in the chain of evacuation and treatment who is properly classified as a medical person under IHL is normally a trained technician assigned at the platoon or company level. This individual is a noncombatant who will normally wear the distinctive sign and carry no weapons. His function is to provide more sophisticated first aid for the casualty, including splinting of fractures, infusion of intravenous fluids, and insertion of emergency airways. He also takes charge of patients needing evacuation and may direct teams of nonmedical personnel carrying litters, loading vehicles, and so forth.

Unit aid post. The first point where a casualty typically is treated by a physician or other professional is the unit aid post. These are usually found at the battalion or regimental level and located within a few kilometers of the front. Since they are close to the fighting and within the range of indirect fire, unit aid posts are frequently camouflaged, thus losing some of the protections of the distinctive sign. As a consequence of proximity and other operational factors, these aid posts are very austere and normally provide only stabilization of casualties and preparation for further evacuation. Although the physician at the unit aid post may be adequately trained, the austerity of the post normally precludes performing major surgical procedures. Except for minor illnesses and some psychiatric casualties, patients are not normally held at this level.

Field hospitals. Most forces include a range of hospitals of varying size and sophistication. Those deployed close to areas of active combat tend to be more mobile and to be designed to treat acute injuries. As casualties move farther back, the facilities become larger and more capable of providing definitive care for a broader range of conditions. In a fully developed theater of operations, sufficient field hospitals may be deployed to treat and return to duty patients requiring many days of therapy and recuperation. Patients requiring more lengthy treatment or who are not expected to return to duty would be evacuated to fixed facilities, typically in sovereign territory.

Field hospitals, especially those receiving casualties directly from the front or from unit aid posts, function under conditions of austerity and highly variable workload. Consequently, they are frequently forced to apply the concept of triage (see below). Field hospitals are capable of performing a variety of surgical procedures to repair injuries, fix fractures, treat burns, etc. In addition, they may treat medical conditions requiring hospitalization or specialty evaluation.

Triage. This term, derived from the French word meaning "to divide into three parts," denotes the process that military medical systems use to organize casualties and make the most efficient use of time and resources. The concept of triage is one of the most significant contributions of military medicine, but it often is poorly understood and applied. Properly used, triage only applies when multiple casualties are received or expected. A casualty in the "immediate" category has a wound or other condition that presents an imminent threat to life, limb, or sight. Treatment is provided as soon as possible and ahead of patients in other categories. Casualties in the "delayed" category have conditions which make it possible to delay treatment until patients in the "immediate" category have been treated or at least stabilized. The "expectant" category, typically the smallest one, represents casualties so serious that the time and resources needed to provide treatment cannot be made available. Patients placed in the expectant category are not abandoned; they are attended to, and every effort is made to make them as comfortable as possible.

It should be noted that the patient's prognosis is not the critical issue in triage. Especially shortly after injury, predicting the final outcome for a casualty is extraordinarily difficult. Rather, the critical issue in determining that a patient must be placed in the expectant category is the resource mismatch existing at the time the patient appears. Would the resources—time, personnel, equipment, and supplies— that this patient will consume be of more benefit to patients in the other categories who require treatment or who may be expected to require it? When resources are in excess of the need, no patient should be classified as expectant.

Research

Military medical systems have both the opportunity and the need to conduct research. This research generally focuses on issues and conditions with direct application to caring for military personnel. However, many military physicians and other professionals conduct research of general applicability.

Unique military syndromes. Military medicine must be prepared to treat a variety of conditions and syndromes that are not commonly found in civilian health care settings. Military weapons systems, including shell fragments, high-velocity projectiles, lasers, and incendiaries, inflict characteristic types of injuries. Research into better methods of treatment for these conditions is aimed at improving the survival and recovery of casualties. Military casualties also are subject to combinations of injuries, stress, chemical intoxication, and so forth, which present additional unique challenges for military medical research.

The modern battlefield is one of the most stressful environments possible. The danger, fear, noise, isolation, sleep deprivation, requirement for instantaneous decision making, and other conditions the service member must withstand are without parallel in civilian occupations. Many military medical systems conduct research into methods of alleviating and treating the stress experienced by service members in combat.

Despite the stringent IHL restrictions against chemical weapons, chemical agents continue to be developed, manufactured, and used. Although some chemical warfare agents are related to industrial chemicals and pesticides, most research into improved methods of treatment and prophylaxis is conducted by military scientists.

The syndrome of injury resulting from nuclear weapon detonation may include blast, secondary missile wounds, burns, and radiation. Fallout also may lead to exposure to radiation. Research into treatment of these conditions has application to both military operations and civil defense.

Exotic diseases. A key determinant in conserving military manpower is the prevention of naturally occurring disease. Military deployments frequently expose troops to infections endemic to the area of operations. Research into prophylaxis and treatment of such diseases in the military may also benefit indigenous populations. Contributions by military researchers to the alleviation of suffering from endemic disease include the discovery by Ronald Ross (Major, Royal Army Medical Corps) of the transmission of malaria and by Walter Reed (Major, U.S. Army Medical Corps) of the transmission of yellow fever.

Examples of National Military Medical Systems

Much of the preceding discussion has focused on U.S. systems and doctrine for military medical care. However, the discussion is generally applicable to most systems in place in developed countries. Nevertheless, the details of such systems differ among even closely related nations.

Israel

The Israeli military medical care system is designed to complement the mission, situation, and organization of its forces. Albeit on a small scale, Israel's geopolitical situation is that of a continental power. Thus, the Israeli military is predominately a land force with limited capability for power projection. Israeli forces are manned by a system of nearly universal military service with the large majority of personnel in the reserves. Under normal circumstances, Israel does not maintain large standing forces deployed outside her boundaries. (Granted, there are disagreements regarding Israel's sovereignty over certain territories.)

Since Israel has a highly developed national health care system, the military forces do not operate fixed medical care facilities. Instead, service members and their families are cared for within the national scheme. During active operations, combat casualty care is provided under a system comparable to that of the United States, with perhaps more acute surgical care available in forward areas. Short distances, the terrain, and other factors tend to encourage the Israelis to rely more on armored ground ambulances than on helicopters for forward area evacuation. After initial stabilization, casualties are evacuated from Israeli deployable medical facilities directly to civilian hospitals.

United Kingdom

The British military medical system consists of three service-specific medical establishments, although the control is centralized under a single Director General at the Ministry of Defence. Britain maintains a relatively small professional force, a sizable portion of which is deployed outside sovereign territory. This situation has led to the development of a fairly extensive system of military hospitals that provide care to service members and families. Britain also has a very extensive system of national health care to which all Britons are entitled. In a unique arrangement, British military hospitals treat nonmilitary patients under the national health scheme and receive reimbursement from the civilian system. In this way, some of the apparent excess capacity of the military hospitals is effectively employed in peacetime. In the event of major hostilities, workload in excess of the capacity of the military hospitals is diverted to the national health system.

Soviet Union

The Soviet military operates a very extensive medical system in peacetime that parallels in many respects the civilian health care establishment. The military system includes a large number of *sanatoria* that provide not only specialized treatments but also recreation. Organizationally, the Soviet military medical system is subordinated to the logistics function, known as the "rear services." The

Soviet organization for wartime support is characterized by extensive reliance on physician-extenders called *feldshers* functioning at the battalion level. As they are configured for rapid offensives, Soviet land forces emphasize minimum medical treatment in forward areas and speedy evacuation of casualties to hospitals located at the army (functionally equivalent to a NATO corps) level. Treatment facilities at levels below the army are minimal.

Future Developments

Although the fundamentals of military medicine—triage and evacuation—will not change materially in the future, technological progress will radically change the sophistication of treatment at every level. Miniature electronic components will monitor patients' conditions and alert physicians and other practitioners. Filmless radiography will locate fragments and diagnose fractures. Monoclonal antibody tests will rapidly identify infectious organisms. Fluids for intravenous infusion will be produced on the battlefield. At the same time, the proliferation of man-portable "fire-and-forget" antiaircraft missiles will make evacuation by helicopter air ambulances increasingly hazardous, requiring more treatment to be provided in forward areas. The advent of lasers, directed particle-beam weapons, new chemical agents, and other innovations in weaponry will create new syndromes of combat and military occupational injury that will require new treatments. The future of military medicine will be full of challenge, opportunity, and progress.

JAMES W. KIRKPATRICK

SEE ALSO: Attrition: Personnel Casualties; Casualties: Evacuation and Treatment; Medical Research and Technology; Medical Service; Military Aid to the Civil Power; Morale; Replacements: Personnel and Materiel.

Bibliography

Baird, J. 1986. Army, British: medical services. In *The Oxford companion to medicine*, vol. 1, pp. 80–6, ed. J. Walton, P. B. Beeson, R. B. Scott. Oxford: Oxford Univ. Press.

Joy, R. J. T. 1986. Armed forces of the USA. In *The Oxford companion to medicine*, vol. 1, pp. 73–80, ed. J. Walton, P. B. Beeson, R. B. Scott. Oxford: Oxford Univ. Press.

Rebentisch, E., and H. Dinkloh. 1980. *Wehrmedizin: Ein kurzliches Handbuch mit Beitraegen zur Katastrophenmedizin.* Münich-Vienna-Baltimore: Urban and Schwartzenberg.

U.S. Department of Defense. 1975. *Emergency war surgery: First U.S. revision of the emergency war surgery NATO handbook.* Washington, D.C.: Government Printing Office.

Zajtchuk, R., D. Jenkins, and R. Bellamy, eds. In press. *Textbooks of military medicine series.* 18 vols. Washington, D.C.: Government Printing Office.

Note: Readers seeking further information on military medicine must expect to encounter some frustration. There are no extensive textbooks on this subject published in English and few generally available sources other than official field manuals. Most available works cover historical events and the development of military medical systems.

MERCENARY

The problem of defining the mercenary has confronted nations throughout the centuries and has not yet been resolved. There is no definition of the mercenary fully accepted under international law and the term is often applied inconsistently by individuals and nations under the sway of emotional and political currents.

The traditional definition of the mercenary has emphasized the remunerative benefit of armed service. Like any professional, the mercenary expects to receive compensation for his services. However, to suggest that his profession could be defined as simply "soldiering for pay" is superficial. All members of armed services throughout the world receive compensation for their military services, and a monetary reward is an important factor of motivation for some individuals. But the monetary question is not useful to distinguish the mercenary from other military operatives. For this reason, a broader examination of the observable characteristics of military activity offers a more sound approach to establishing an operational definition of the mercenary. In other words, to understand what the mercenary is, we must first establish what he is not.

In the modern era, the preponderance of mercenary activity has occurred in the developing world, particularly in Africa. It is therefore most appropriate to draw illustrative examples from the African context in order to develop a complete profile of the contemporary mercenary.

Military Operative Profiles

In examining what men have done in the military context in developing nations, we may draw five main functional groupings: standing army, auxiliary, partisan, agent, and mercenary. No single element is sufficient to distinguish any one of these military operatives from the rest. Only through an examination of several observable traits in combination can we draw some useful distinctions to separate the mercenary from other military operatives.

STANDING ARMY

The first grouping consists of the officially constituted armed forces of a sovereign power. Throughout the developing world, these forces are most often organized along the model of the colonial authority. They are composed of indigenous troops although some countries may accept foreign nationals for service. One state that was accused of using mercenaries in this way was Rhodesia (Zimbabwe).

In fact, however, the government emphasized a consistent policy for potential recruits, making it clear that the only way to serve Rhodesia in a military capacity was as a member of the regular armed forces. A similar policy has been pursued by South Africa, which applies very stringent criteria to foreign enlistees and subjects all recruits to the same rigorous training. Similarly, the French Foreign

Legion, although it has often performed military functions in developing nations, cannot, as a duly constituted body of French government forces, be called a mercenary force.

Auxiliary Troops

Auxiliary troops were perhaps best defined by Machiavelli in *The Prince* as "those supplied by a foreign power which has been called upon for assistance." They are therefore the armed forces of a foreign power that operate on the territory and at the request of another nation. It is further characteristic of auxiliary forces that their allegiance remains with their home power, which retains ultimate control of their operations as well as responsibility for their equipment, training, maintenance, and salaries.

Included in this category are those personnel seconded to one nation from another. While relatively unknown in the United States, the policy of seconding was widely practiced by the European colonial powers and continues to the present day. Generally, in this process, an officer in the armed service of a more developed nation is assigned, on a temporary basis, to serve in a similar capacity in the armed forces of a second country. For example, regular Belgian officers were seconded to the postcolonial *Armée Nationale Congolaise* (ANC) to serve as its interim leadership. Similarly, many British officers, of all services, were seconded to Nigeria after independence to strengthen its armed forces. The practice remains common today.

A unique type of auxiliary force should be noted here because they too have at times been called mercenaries—the armed forces of the United Nations (UN). These composite groups, mandated by United Nations resolutions, have been employed as combat troops (Korea, 1950; Congo, 1960) and as truce supervisory and peacekeeping forces (Middle East, 1956, 1973; Cyprus, 1964). These auxiliary forces have operated under their own command, in coordination with host governments. As with other auxiliary forces, the troops of the United Nations commands remain members of their own nations' armed forces.

Partisans

A third category of military operative is the partisan. He is a native of the country in which he operates and his efforts are directed toward the overthrow or replacement of that country's government. This category includes insurgent guerrilla leaders such as Dr. Jonas Savimbi, the head of the Union for the Total Independence of Angola (UNITA), and Shah Ahmad Massoud of the Afghan mujaheddin; and secessionist movement leaders like Moise Tshombe of Katanga and Colonel Ojukwu of Biafra.

Special consideration is necessary in the case of *colons*, individuals of European descent who were born in the developing world or who grew up under a colonial regime. As independence swept the colonial powers out, many fled the country. Others remained under the new government and were integrated into the national forces. Some who opposed the postindependence regimes joined partisan groups or mercenary forces. The *colon* question cannot, therefore, be treated on the basis of a group identity. Again, setting aside the criterion of motivation, the *colon* is to be considered with reference to his actions.

Agents

Agents are sent by one foreign power to support an armed insurgent movement within another country. As with auxiliaries, these individuals are instruments of their countries' foreign policy and are funded and supported by their countries in an attempt to influence the target nation. In this case, they operate outside the framework of the legitimate government and may perform a variety of roles for insurgent movements such as military advisers, political instructors, or logistics coordinators.

Mercenaries

In distinguishing among these military operatives, there are three key factors: citizenship, degree and type of support from their own government, and their level of integration into the national structure.

The characteristics of the mercenary with regard to these factors are: (a) he is not a citizen of the country in which he operates; (b) he has not been sent by, nor does he receive overt support from, his own government; (c) he takes an active role in armed conflict outside the established structure of the standing armed forces. Table 1 summarizes these definitions and distinctions.

If one considered only the traditional profit motive attributed to mercenary forces, Swedish Baron Gustav von Rosen, who flew for Biafra without pay, could not be considered a mercenary. Yet Rosen was instrumental in obtaining aircraft for the secessionists, outfitting the airplanes with military hardware, and carrying out several successful strikes against the federal Nigerian forces. Given these clear military actions, one can not ignore his activity merely on the basis of high motivation. Like many others, he was a foreign national conducting independent military operations in Biafra without the consent or support of his national government.

Types of Mercenary Forces

Mercenary forces in the modern era may be classified as one of three principal types: the operational maneuver group, the coup strike force, and military support personnel.

Table 1 . *Characteristics of Military Operatives*

Operative	Local citizen	Own gov't support	Integrated into forces
Standing army	Yes/no	Yes	Yes
Auxiliary	No	Yes	Yes/no
Partisan	Yes	No	No
Agent	No	Yes	No
Mercenary	No	No	No

Operational Maneuver Group

The most widely recognized mercenary force consists of operational maneuver groups of ground forces, often supported by air and naval components. Such forces operate independently under the command of a single, dominant mercenary leader. Although their organizational plans may differ widely, they most often remain under the direct control of the head of state. These forces may be employed in a spearhead role for indigenous troops or may operate independently as integral units. The Congo campaigns, the Nigerian civil war, the southern Sudan insurgency, and the postindependence fight for Angola are characteristic of this type of mercenary operation.

Coup Strike Force

The coup strike force consists of a single, close-knit group of mercenaries hired for the specific goal of conducting a military coup d'état. Usually well financed, trained, equipped, and directed by an exiled opposition leader, the coup strike force is employed to spearhead a popular rebellion within the target country. Since 1970, there have been mercenary coup strike force attempts in Guinea, Equatorial Guinea, Benin, Togo, the Seychelles, the Maldives, and the Comoro Islands with the latter government changing hands twice. Other substantial plots by mercenary coup strike forces have been directed at the governments of Dominica, Haiti, and Suriname.

Military Operations Support

Military operations support personnel are generally integrated into the structure of the mercenary forces but may not play a direct role in combat operations. Their technical efforts are, however, essential to effective modern warfare and such personnel are to be considered as part of the operational mercenary force that they directly support. Under this heading are classed the experts necessary for modern combat systems such as the aircraft mechanics and avionics experts who have supported mercenary air operations over the Congo, Biafra, and, more recently, Central America. Medical personnel, communications technicians, special operations advisers, navigation specialists, ground mechanics, and munitions experts have all played such central, though often less visible, support roles in mercenary force operations.

Organization and Structure of Mercenary Forces

Operational Maneuver Group

The structure of mercenary operational maneuver groups varies widely. The consistent pattern, however, is to adopt the format of the country of the mercenary leader rather than that of the nation in which the force operates. Because of this trend, mercenary groups tend to resist integration into the national structure and may be readily identified by the characteristics peculiar to the previous training of their leaders. The four basic types are the British export model, the French commando group, settler forces, and the Foreign Legion model.

British export model. The first modern British export model appeared in the Congo at independence in 1960. Known as the International Company or White Legion, this mercenary group was organized under the command of three former British army officers. They brought with them lessons from the Special Air Service (SAS) and operations in Indochina, including the importance of positive interaction with the natives and the necessity of maintaining good order and discipline even in jungle combat conditions.

The International Company was established as a 200-member, all-white, anglophone organization to conduct autonomous operations using independent platoons of 30–40 men serving under one or two officers. Each platoon was formed while under training and worked from separate village bases.

When Michael Hoare returned to the Congo in 1964, he formed the Fifth Commando, known popularly as the Wild Geese, along the same basic lines. The general strength of the Fifth Commando was usually less than 200 men and included a number of nonanglophone mercenaries who were organized into individual subcommando groups by common language to reinforce order and esprit and to facilitate control. In addition, there was a small headquarters group including a medical officer and communications technicians.

Overall, the British model could be characterized as disciplined under a well-defined chain of command. This included separate messes for officers, noncommissioned officers (NCOs), and enlisted men, and required traditional standards of military appearance and courtesy. Emphasis was placed on decisive leadership by officers, clear transmission of orders, and expeditious execution in all operations. Generally operating as an all-white, homogenous force, torture was forbidden and the taking of booty discouraged.

Inasmuch as Hoare's organization represented an effective export of the British system, the failed attempt by British "Colonel" Callan to exercise command in Angola points to another principle of mercenary organization: operational success is directly proportional to the degree to which a proven organizational system can be modified to function in the bush environment. This is particularly true for a mercenary organization typically composed of personnel with uneven backgrounds, strong individualist tendencies, and disparate motivation.

In combat operations, Callan chose to disregard most of his experience with the elite British Parachute Regiment. Instead, he organized his first twenty British recruits into four-man teams and sent them out on hopelessly ineffective hunt-and-destroy missions against Cuban patrols. Eventually, 141 British and six American mercenaries came under Callan's control. But, without any organizational structure or the type of disciplined approach that the ex-military mercenaries understood, the situation quickly led to mutiny and disbandment of the force.

French commando group—guerrilla style. The French commando group organization presents a marked contrast to the disciplined, police-type approach of the British. This guerrilla-style organization traces its origin to the *Organisation de l'armée secrète* in Indochina and Algeria. These groups believed that the only way to contest a revolutionary war was to fight a revolutionary war in return. This prescription included classical combat, psychological warfare, guerrilla warfare, and pacification operations combining political, military, and economic action.

The basic organizational model, developed by the French in Indochina, consisted of small groups (40–80 men) of natives hostile to the targeted armed forces. They were led by French officers and NCOs who were characteristically young and nonconformist by nature.

This type of force was first organized in the Congo in 1961 under disciples of Roger Trinquier, a French expert in guerrilla warfare. Originally established as a special force under the Ministry of the Interior, the white-led, native teams were implicated in several covert operations, including a plot to kidnap high-ranking UN officials.

In late 1961, the scope of operations expanded as Robert Denard, a former French commando with previous service in Indochina and Algeria, replaced Trinquier's hand-picked successor. Denard adopted a more overtly aggressive posture with this force, putting less emphasis on the subtleties of active pacification and more on direct military action.

Denard was recalled to the Congo in 1965 and reestablished the same type of counterinsurgency organization that came to be known as the *Sixième Brigade de Commandos Etrangers* (6 CODO). Under Denard, 6 CODO reached a maximum strength of 550 men and was organized into two major groups designated *Premier Choc* and *Deuxième Choc*. These were further divided into subcommando units, each of which worked in conjunction with an ANC battalion.

The French commando organization is the source of the popular image of the bearded mercenary in camouflage fatigues, bristling with knives, grenades, and cartridge bandoliers. Known as the *affreux* or "terrible ones," these individuals characterize an organization very different from the regimental British approach. The French would hold long conferences and open debates on tactics and operations and had no established procedures or definitive chain of command. Great stock was placed on the political and psychological weight of actions, and operational torture was considered an acceptable tool. Finally, whereas the British preferred to operate in all-white columns, the French were easily integrated and most often combined with native forces to conduct joint operations.

Settler forces—the colonial model. A third type of mercenary organization is the settler plan. Led by European settlers who exercised control over native troops, the force adopted the form of the previous colonial military organization. Sharing a common language, and understanding the cultural attitudes and local customs, these mercenary forces were extremely successful in both direct military operations and in long-term pacification efforts.

The first such group was organized by colonial Belgian plantation owner Jean Schramme as the Leopard Battalion and began operations in the Congo against the ANC and UN in mid-1961. For an organizational model, Schramme adopted the quaternary concept of the colonial armed forces, the *Force Publique*. The basic unit was the *peloton*, which consisted of about 30 natives led by two European officers. These officers, trained as reservists in the colonial Belgian forces, understood the country, the people, their customs and history, as well as the "secrets of the bush," where they conducted nearly autonomous operations for periods of one to two weeks. In consonance with the colonial army on which it was modeled, Schramme's force emphasized training, order, and discipline, developing an effective force of some 1,000 men at its peak.

Forced into exile with the fall of Tshombe in 1963, Schramme retained his organization in neighboring Angola. When recalled in 1964, he was able to return quickly with a ready force of 750 disciplined men. On this base, Schramme built a larger force known as the Tenth Commando (10 CODO). This new Leopard Battalion was given the responsibility for pacification of large areas of rebel-controlled territory. Schramme's knowledge of the Congolese and his innate organizational ability soon enabled him to establish effective political control over areas liberated from rebel domination. This control eventually became autonomous to the degree that President Mobutu felt his central government authority threatened, leading him to expel forcibly Schramme's unit in the fall of 1967.

Foreign Legion model. The Foreign Legion model combines the discipline of the British with the adaptability of the French. The model was developed in Biafra by ex-Legionnaire Rolf Steiner who was called upon by Colonel Ojukwu to form the Fourth Commando Brigade in the late spring of 1968.

In keeping with the international character of the Legion, the German Steiner collected nine mercenaries as the core of the Fourth Commando, including men from Ireland, Wales, France, Belgium, and Rhodesia. Under this leadership, he formed three strike forces of battalion strength (1,000 men) consisting of locally recruited natives. The strike forces were further divided into companies of 200 men each, led by a Biafran junior officer. As Steiner hoped, his group quickly became an elite force of over 3,000 and, in typical Legion style, adopted distinctive berets, scarves, and even the colors, device, and anthem of the continental model.

Opinion of the effectiveness of this organization is mixed. Their lack of great success may be attributed to the fact that there were few field leaders, their orders were often countermanded by the classically trained Biafran headquarters, and they were frequently starved of basic supplies. Nevertheless, the Biafran experience demonstrated the adaptability of the Legion model and its flexible yet firm operational style.

Coup Strike Force

Under certain circumstances, a small, well-armed and trained mercenary coup strike force can pose a credible threat to the government of a small, developing nation. Since 1970, mercenary forces have attempted eight coups in nations that share many common characteristics: Guinea (1970), Equatorial Guinea (1972), Benin (1977), Togo (1977), the Comoro Islands (1975, 1978), the Seychelles (1981), and the Maldives (1988).

Background considerations. The first considerations are the geographical similarities of these countries. All are very small and have open oceanic coastlines where their capitals and principal cities are located. This combination of small size, open coastline, and concentrated authority facilitates the rapid entry and movement of an armed force that could reach the center of power (capital, presidential palace, etc.) in a short time. By the same token, the reaction time for defense forces is cut considerably.

Second, large or powerful opposition elements were operating in exile, most often in a neighboring country where they could form the basis for a new popular government. This outside exile support also provided the substantial amounts of cash, equipment, facilities, and influence necessary to mount a military coup operation.

A third important common factor among these nations is the type and style of government in power. Except for the Maldives, all were one-party systems in which the power was concentrated in one individual and systems for orderly succession had not been instituted. With a single, central leader who also controlled the military, these nations were highly susceptible to any type of plot that targeted this individual.

A final factor is the generally weak state of the military forces in these nations. Most of their forces were small, poorly trained, ill-equipped, and totally unprepared to deal with a surprise assault by well-armed and coordinated foreign troops.

Sea-based assault. The most common tactic for the mercenary-led coup has been the sea-based assault. The first to occur was in Guinea where a two-pronged attack from the sea was aimed at strategic points in the capital.

Coming ashore at night in small boats, the force had well-defined military objectives that included the power and radio stations, the airfield, the presidential palace, and prisons. Failure to capture President Toure and the radio station enabled him to use it to summon the People's Militia. Within a day, the attacking elements were withdrawn and aid poured in via the airfield from sympathetic states.

An unsuccessful coup attempt against the Republic of Maldives in November 1988 followed a similar pattern. Landing by sea, a force of less than 100 Sri Lankan Tamil mercenaries was unable to capture Pres. Maumoon Gayoom or to seize and hold major objectives in and around the capital before Indian government troops could be airlifted to intervene. Within 24 hours, the mercenaries seized a small ship from Male harbor and fled to sea where they were subsequently captured and interned by Indian naval forces.

Another seaborne mercenary coup attempt involved a plot to take over Equatorial Guinea as a new homeland for the defeated Biafrans. Under the plan, a group of thirteen mercenaries were to journey to Africa in a fishing boat, join up with 50 Biafran commandos, and storm ashore in the capital to seize President Nguema and install a new government. The plan was foiled by Spanish authorities in the Canary Islands, who arrested the European team and impounded their arms enroute.

The first successful seaborne assaults were actually two different coups, each carried out by mercenary leader Robert Denard in the Comoro Islands. In 1975, the Comoros unilaterally declared independence, abruptly ending 132 years of French rule. The following month, Denard and seven mercenaries waded ashore by the presidential palace, arrested President Abdullah and installed Ali Solih in his place. Denard remained for three months to train the new, 1,600-man army, and then returned to France.

Shortly thereafter, Solih began to drift toward an erratic form of Chinese revolution, causing France to stop further aid. Former President Abdullah, in exile in Paris, approached Denard with a partnership deal, assuring him of French government nonintervention.

Denard assembled a team of 45 mercenaries for the task. His plan was to repeat his earlier success and he contracted a large trawler and several inflatable assault boats. After two months sailing, with an intermediate stop in the Canaries to pick up the remainder of his force, Denard arrived off the palace at Moroni, captured Solih, and secured victory within two hours. Only light resistance was encountered and the mercenaries were greeted as national heroes. Most remained to set up lucrative businesses or to work with the militia units, including Denard, who remained as army commander-in-chief until forced out by pressure from the Organization of African Unity (OAU).

Denard's effectiveness can be attributed to a combination of several factors not present in the other forces. First, he was obviously well financed, enjoyed at least the tacit complicity of the major power interest, and was backed by native leaders who could reasonably expect popular support. His military objectives were within the capability of the force available and his equipment was composed of common items (shotguns, elephant guns, etc.) that would not arouse the suspicion of other government authorities encountered enroute. Finally, his men were well trained and disciplined and responded with decisiveness and initiative in the field.

Air assault. The three mercenary coup attempts involving air assaults are among the best documented but least successful plans, all of which were apparently compromised. The attempt against President Eyadema of Togo in 1977 involved a small nucleus of mercenaries allied with Togolese insurgents and supported by several serving members of the British SAS. The plot was never executed, probably due to compromise through the involvement of active duty SAS troops. In addition, although some of the mercenaries spent up to two months in Togo, they were never able to rehearse, conduct team training, or train their Togolese support troops.

Compromise was probably also the direct cause of the failure of a mercenary group led by Robert Denard to Benin in 1977. This group of 100 French mercenaries was ferried by air from France to Morocco, where they trained with Moroccan army assistance. They were then flown to Gabon where they were kept isolated until the morning of the attack.

Arriving unannounced at the capital airfield, the mercenaries were so confident of success that they moved on their objectives slowly and deliberately, even taking time to stack their supplies neatly on the tarmac. However, as the force advanced from the airfield, they were counterattacked by the presidential guard and 200 army troops joined by machete-wielding civilians. The mercenaries' hasty retreat took 30 minutes, cost two lives, and left twelve stragglers behind.

Compromise also led Michael Hoare to abort his coup attempt on the Seychelles in 1981 when airport customs agents discovered an automatic weapon in the luggage of one of his mercenaries. A firefight quickly enveloped the airport and continued until Hoare was able to commandeer a jetliner to return to South Africa, where he was charged with air piracy and eventually brought to trial and convicted.

Operational Requirements and Force Structure

Each type of mercenary force is best organized to respond to a particular set of operational requirements. Establishing a correlation between operational requirements and force structure yields a useful analytical tool to assess the likely mercenary force to be introduced and its potential for success in a given situation. Such a correlation is detailed in Table 2.

If a country is perceived to be at the point of engaging mercenary troops, an analysis of its military requirements could give a strong indication of the type of mercenary force likely to be involved. Similarly, once a mercenary force has been identified, its type could be an indicator of its potential effectiveness in the specific military situation. If it is well suited to the military tasks required, the mercenary force could exercise dramatic influence on the outcome of the conflict. If it is not, its influence is likely to be minimal.

TABLE 2. *Operational Requirements and Force Structure*

Requirement	Suitable Model
Guerrilla warfare, harassment, covert action	French commando
Area pacification, paramilitary regional control	Settler
Point control, autonomous strike groups, advisory/training assistance	British export
Core leadership for local forces, cohesive development of diverse local groups	Foreign Legion
Coup against small, lightly defended developing nation	Coup strike force

GERRY S. THOMAS

SEE ALSO: Coup d'état; French Foreign Legion; Morality and War; Paramilitary Forces; Peacekeeping; United Nations.

Bibliography

Dempster, C., and D. Tomkins. 1980. *Firepower*. New York: St. Martin's Press.
Germani, H. 1967. *White soldiers in Black Africa*. Capetown: Nasionale Beekhandel Beperk.
Hempstone, S. 1962. *Katanga report*. London: Faber and Faber.
Hoare, M. 1967. *Congo mercenary*. London: Robert Hale.
Mockler, A. 1969. *The mercenaries*. New York: Macmillan.
———. 1987. *The new mercenaries*. New York: Paragon House.
O'Brien, C. C. 1962. *To Katanga and back*. New York: Simon and Schuster.
St. Jorre, J. de. 1972. *The Nigerian civil war*. London: Hodder and Stoughton.
Schramme, J. 1969. *Le Bataillon Léopard*. Paris: Laffont.
Steiner, R. 1978. *The last adventurer*. Boston: Little, Brown.
Thomas. G. S. 1984. *Mercenary troops in modern Africa*. Boulder, Colo.: Westview Press.

MERCHANT FLEET

The sea has and always will play an essential role in transport and communications around the world. Yesterday it was the only way to move from one landmass to another. Tomorrow, as the skies, airports, and their approach routes grow ever more congested, the seas and the merchant ships that sail them will remain vital.

Origins of Merchant Shipping

Sea travel was already common when Themistocles, Thucydides, Homer's *Odyssey*, and the Laws of Oleron described it. The great voyages of discovery, the merchant adventurers, and mass movements of colonizers followed. This article summarizes developments toward world shipping as it is today.

Ships developed originally as multipurpose vehicles carrying people and goods for trade and for war. With the notable exception of the war galley, until the middle of the sixteenth century size was the main difference in ship design and function. All might carry goods to trade, a crew, and cannon and soldiers to protect them.

Gradually at first and then at an ever-increasing pace that continues to this day, ships became more and more specialized. Perhaps the first split in ship types was into fighting ships and trading ships. Fighting ships developed in western Europe through men-of-war, a single type of warship, splitting into large, heavily armed and armored vessels and the smaller, faster, more maneuverable types and then into the degree of specialization we see in today's fighting navies. Similar specialization took place in merchant shipping.

Types of Merchant Ships

World merchant ships fall into fairly well-defined groups: liners and bulk carriers, ferries, and specialist vessels.

Liners

Liners, which almost invariably involve the use of container-carrying vessels, set out to provide a regular service for customers on the basis of scheduled sailings between advertized ports. Liner service is maintained whether trade is lively or lethargic. Much of liner shipping operates within what is known as the *conference system,* in which companies collaborate to provide continuity of service but compete for the space available. The operation of consortia within the conference system is well established, and in some countries, notably the United States, regulations have long defined the relationship between the operators of conference lines and those liner operators who are not members of a conference. Cargo-sharing arrangements are now defined in the United Nations Liner Code, in force since 1983. It does not, however, apply to cargo sharing within the Organization for European Cooperation and Development (OECD). The code goes a long way toward meeting the aspirations of developing countries and is certainly preferable to unilateral cargo reservation.

Liner cargoes have tended to specialize in manufactured or refrigerated goods, although bulk cargo of various kinds is increasingly being transported by containers. The development of the container has facilitated the intermodal movement of cargo, linking up with overland movements to the port of loading and from the port of discharge, thereby facilitating door-to-door service. In various parts of the world, however, trade is still serviced by the more traditional break-bulk ships. Also relevant in the context of conference operations is the development of shippers' councils, by which customers have a forum for discussion with the providers of shipping services.

Bulk Carriers, Ferries, and Specialist Carriers

The bulk trades ("dry," e.g., grain, iron ore; or "wet," notably crude oil or refined petroleum products) are transported on the basis of contracts for a voyage, a period of time, or a total volume of cargo. Sometimes the cargo is carried for the account of the original producer of the cargo, who requires delivery either to its own premises or to its buyer, but in recent years the traditional vertically integrated structure has been weakening, and traders have emerged who negotiate the sale of cargoes during various stages of the transportation operation, not least when the cargo is on the high seas.

Recent years have seen the growth of the ferry industry, designed to accommodate vehicles or trains on a roll-on/roll-off (RO/RO) basis and normally operating on fixed routes of comparatively short distances. These ferries also carry substantial numbers of passengers with or without cars, as well as in buses.

Air transport has replaced the large passenger ships in the general movement of people; because of a resurgence of interest in cruising as part of the leisure industry, however, large, modern ships have been designed to cope with the increasing opportunities for tourism.

The development of specialist carriers has always been a feature of modern merchant shipping. Recent examples include highly-sophisticated vessels for gas cargoes, specially compartmentalized ships for petroleum products or chemicals, and vessels that can switch from carrying dry bulk cargo to oil, as well as those designed for heavy lifts (including the carriage of ships themselves perhaps requiring major repairs) and vessels specially designed for the excavation of minerals from the seabed. Those concerned with volatile or otherwise dangerous cargo are, of course, subject to strict international operating and safety regulations.

The offshore oil and gas industries have also inspired specialist ships. These range from the mobile drilling rigs, whose function is subsequently handed on to a massive fixed or moored production platform, to a variety of support vessels.

Merchant shipping is thus constantly evolving new ways of anticipating or responding to the requirements of world trade.

Development of Merchant Shipping

The general shape of modern shipping began to form during the nineteenth century. The major maritime nations were already established, and specialist ship-owning or ship-managing companies began to emerge, running, by today's standards, large numbers of comparatively small ships from a multitude of ports. Shipowners tended to specialize in trading with specific areas.

Some generally accepted customs of navigation were respected. International commerce had already established principles as to how business should be conducted (e.g., the charter parties and bills of lading), and in the United Kingdom the Admiralty Court had been adjudicating on maritime matters for more then 500 years. However, the role of governments, both nationally and internationally, in regulating the safe operation of ships and the general responsibilities of owners toward people and cargo did not really begin to take shape until the second half of the nineteenth century. That period saw, in the United Kingdom, for example, the agitation by Samuel Plimsoll and others leading to the introduction of regulations for the safe loading of ships. The growth of the trade union movement in various countries was also highly relevant.

Gradually, international maritime regulations began to emerge as various governments accepted responsibility for conferences aimed at producing and revising international conventions. Inspired by the international legal profession, the Comité Maritime International (CMI) formed in 1897 and based in Brussels, played a vital role in the development of several conventions, especially on subjects concerned with liability. The CMI operated through consultation with shipowner, trade, and maritime law interests in the maritime countries and with governments, such work leading up to a series of what were known as Brussels Diplomatic Conferences. The United Kingdom was responsible for the Safety of Life at Sea Convention, organizing conferences that over the years updated the Safety of Life at Sea Convention.

Following the formation of the United Nations in 1948, the task of reviewing international maritime regulation passed to the Inter-governmental Maritime Consultative Organisation, itself formed in 1958 and renamed the International Maritime Organization (IMO) in 1982. Other branches of the United Nations, such as its Committee on Trade & Development (UNCTAD), have also produced conventions, although these tend to relate to quasi-commercial activity. The formation of IMO led to ongoing reviews of maritime regulatory matters. Today IMO work covers a wide range of conventions, including navigation, safety, construction, and the environment.

World War I ravaged the merchant fleets of all the countries involved, and after some years of recovery the economic slump of the late 1920s and 1930s produced serious overtonnage problems. This led to collaboration between essentially independent-minded shipowners nationally or internationally, in attempts to mitigate the consequences. Schemes were introduced whereby agreed numbers of ships were put into lay-up, with the owners of those ships still trading contributing funds to pay some form of compensation to owners who had withdrawn their ships from trading. These actions were not enough, however, and various governments began to provide direct subsidies or other forms of assistance to keep their merchant fleets intact.

World War II again demonstrated the vulnerability of merchant ships to sea warfare. Official histories commissioned by the governments of the major maritime nations detail merchant ship operations and the tremendous losses of men on ships during that time. The period of rehabilitation and recovery following that war led to comparative prosperity. When economic hardships came again, however, the trend of national legislation against cooperative ventures by the business world seeking to influence supply of a product or service (e.g., U.S. antitrust legislation) gave little scope for collaboration among owners to mitigate their overtonnage problems.

The immediate post–World War II era required massive relief programs for Europe and brought to light the need for assistance to other parts of the world. The major benefactor was the United States, initially through the Marshall Plan, and it may not have seemed unreasonable to require that half of such cargoes should be shipped in American merchant vessels. Warnings that the justifiable requirements in those particular circumstances would create precedents for less justifiable motives were quickly substantiated, and an increasing number of countries—themselves the recipients of aid cargoes—introduced requirements for fixed percentages of trade with their countries being carried in ships of the national flag. Aspirations to encourage a national fleet by countries particularly dependent on international sea communications are understandable, but some were carried to excess instead of relying on the world's ocean traders and turning national attention to the efficiency of port operations and internal communications.

The growth of union power in maritime countries led to a series of international agreements providing the framework of conditions for life at sea. Governments, shipowners, and trade unions met in the ILO for this purpose. In some countries more detailed conditions of service and sometimes rates of pay came to be agreed upon between representatives of owners and seafarers. However, shipping has always been open to the widest international competition; as the standard of living and social conditions rose throughout the traditional maritime countries, owners became prone to competition from those who could employ crews whose standards of living or social expectations were far lower and also from the state trading fleets.

Such conditions led American owners to register their ships in countries such as Panama and Liberia, which were not trading nations in a comparable sense and which permitted owners much greater freedom as to the nationality and conditions of employment for seafarers. These became known as "flag of convenience" countries. Originally they did not require owners registering with them to conform to the then-existing international conventions, but, over the years, acceptable standards have been introduced by a number of them.

The 1960s and 1970s saw an increase in discrimination against the free choice of transportation and in protectionism, by which countries sought to restrict the operations of other flag ships in national trades. The restriction of cabotage is a major feature, but similar restrictions have been applied to long-haul movements. The economic effect of such practices in liner trades is gradually being offset by the UN Liner Code, referred to earlier.

This period also saw an increase in incentive packages provided by governments, principally to sustain interest in their national shipbuilding industries. The result was an overoptimistic view of the development of world trade, and many shipowners were enticed into expansion programs, either by government assistance to shipbuilding industries or the comparatively easy availability of credit from bankers. What may have seemed prudent or acceptably adventurous investment for individual companies gradually contributed to a worldwide overtonnage problem when economic problems arose—especially those created by the oil crisis of 1979 and subsequent related problems.

Competition from countries enjoying cheaper operating costs became more serious as the disparity in social conditions between, for example, European countries and those in the Pacific became wider. Agreements between owners and seafarers in the European countries could not be changed overnight, however, and a prolonged period of transition was necessary to enable owners to move their ships to ports of registry from which they had greater freedom of negotiation on seafaring employment conditions. In the meantime, also growing up was a community of international ship operators who ensured that their assets were afloat in every sense of the word and who could move their operations as best suited them, free from national restrictions. Some governments appeared quite content that their owners should operate on such a basis, assuming, somewhat complacently, that in an emergency, national legislation would enable them to take control of ships registered abroad but ultimately controlled within that state. This begs the question whether they fully appreciated the consequences of the internationality of both ownership and registration that has been emerging. In 1987–88 some of the traditional maritime countries began to attract such ships back to the national flag—the Norwegian International Ship Register is a case in point. Among the most significant features have been the removal of nationality restrictions on crews, the end of collective bargaining, relaxation of tax obligations for crews and of social costs for owners, and assistance with training costs. Some governments have included financial assistance of various kinds.

World Fleet

All these considerations have affected the development of the world fleet, and Tables 1 through 9 demonstrate their effect on the sizes of national fleets over the past 100 years. (The top ten shipping countries in terms of millions of tons are shown in Tables 1 through 8; Table 9 summarizes the rankings of the top shipping countries over the last century. The U.S. figures include its reserve fleet.) The developments mentioned in the preceding paragraph have put the tonnage tables on the move again. In 1886 Lloyd's Register first produced tables showing world tonnage.

Defense

Merchant ships have a major role in the defense strategy of any country dependent on communication by sea. Until recently, consideration of defense implications inevitably focused on the NATO Alliance and the Communist bloc, but the relevance of merchant shipping in the defense context is not the exclusive concern of those nations. It is, however, relevant to reflect on the different attitudes in those two groups. Merchant shipping in the Communist countries, especially the Soviet Union, developed on the basis of a national plan that has taken full account of defense requirements. Various features included in the design of most Soviet merchant ships could not be justified economically but could have a defense application in time of emergency. The cost consequences of such features are, of course, less relevant with ships operating on a state-trading basis. Such operations also provide scope for flexibility in the employment of personnel. The central control of operations also facilitates the quick redeployment of merchant ships during time of emergency. The new spirit prevailing in what was the Soviet Union and

TABLE 1. *Leading Shipping Countries in 1886*

Rank/Country	Millions of tons (gross weight)
1. UK	6.5
2. France	.7
3. Germany	.6
4. USA	.5
5. Spain	.4
6. Italy	.2
7. Netherlands	.2
8. Russia	.1
9. Sweden	.1
10. Denmark	.1
World	10.3

Source: Lloyd's Register of Shipping.

TABLE 2. *Leading Shipping Countries in 1900*

Rank/Country	Millions of tons (gross weight)
1. UK	12.1
2. Germany	2.2
3. USA	1.5
4. France	1.0
5. Norway	.8
6. Spain	.6
7. Italy	.5
8. Japan	.5
9. Russia	.5
10. Netherlands	.5
World	22.4

Source: Lloyd's Register of Shipping.

TABLE 3. *Leading Shipping Countries in 1914*

RANK/COUNTRY	MILLIONS OF TONS (GROSS WEIGHT)
1. UK	20.5
2. Germany	5.1
3. USA	4.3
4. Norway	1.9
5. France	1.9
6. Japan	1.7
7. Netherlands	1.5
8. Italy	1.5
9. Austria/ Hungary	1.0
10. Sweden	1.0
11. USSR	0.8
World	45.4

Source: Lloyd's Register of Shipping.

TABLE 4. *Leading Shipping Countries in 1921*

RANK/COUNTRY	MILLIONS OF TONS (GROSS WEIGHT)
1. UK	20.6
2. USA	16.0
3. France	3.2
4. Japan	3.0
5. Italy	2.2
6. Norway	2.2
7. Netherlands	1.8
8. Sweden	1.1
9. Spain	1.0
10. Denmark	0.8
11. USSR	0.5
World	57.3

Source: Lloyd's Register of Shipping.

TABLE 5. *Leading Shipping Countries in 1939*

RANK/COUNTRY	MILLIONS OF TONS (GROSS WEIGHT)
1. UK	16.9
2. USA	8.7
3. Japan	5.4
4. Norway	4.7
5. Germany	4.1
6. Italy	3.3
7. Netherlands	2.8
8. France	2.7
9. Greece	1.8
10. Sweden	1.4
11. USSR	1.1
World	61.4

Source: Lloyd's Register of Shipping.

TABLE 6. *Leading Shipping Countries in 1950*

RANK/COUNTRY	MILLIONS OF TONS (DEAD-WEIGHT)
1. USA	46.7
2. UK	23.7
3. Norway	8.2
4. Panama	4.8
5. Netherlands	4.2
6. Italy	4.0
7. France	3.8
8. Sweden	3.0
9. Japan	2.1
10. Denmark	1.8
[12. USSR	1.3]
World	120.6

Source: Lloyd's Register of Shipping.

Eastern Europe, which could well include a more commercial approach to the operation of its merchant ships, may eventually change this situation; whatever the prospects, this change would take a considerable time to stabilize and bear fruit. For the present it remains a fact that the size and shape of the merchant fleets of the Communist bloc countries correlated to perceived defense requirements.

Meantime, NATO is known to have plans for pooling merchant ship resources in the event of hostilities in which the NATO Alliance became involved. These plans were made when NATO countries were among the strongest of the traditional maritime countries and when, at least at

TABLE 7. *Leading Shipping Countries in 1975*

RANK/COUNTRY	MILLIONS OF TONS (DEAD-WEIGHT)
1. Liberia	126.0
2. Japan	63.3
3. UK	52.7
4. Norway	45.4
5. Greece	37.5
6. Panama	21.9
7. U.S.	20.3
8. France	17.9
9. USSR	16.2
10. Italy	15.5
World	544.1

Source: Lloyd's Register of Shipping.

TABLE 8. *Leading Shipping Countries in 1988*

RANK/COUNTRY	MILLIONS OF TONS (DEAD-WEIGHT)
1. Liberia	93.6
2. Panama	70.6
3. Japan	47.0
4. Greece	39.6
5. Cyprus	32.8
6. USA	26.4
7. USSR	23.8
8. China	18.9
9. Philippines	15.4
10. Bahamas	14.9
[16. UK	10.3]
World	619.6

Source: Lloyd's Register of Shipping.

TABLE 9. *Summary of Positions in World Tonnage "League"*

COUNTRY	1886	1900	1914	1921	1939	1950	1975	1988
Austria/ Hungary	—	—	9	—	—	—	—	—
Bahamas	—	—	—	—	—	—	—	10
China	—	—	—	—	—	—	—	8
Cyprus	—	—	—	—	—	—	—	5
Denmark	10	—	—	10	—	10	—	—
France	2	4	5	3	8	7	8	—
Greece	—	—	—	—	9	—	5	4
Germany	3	2	2	—	5	—	—	—
Italy	6	7	8	5	6	6	10	—
Japan	—	8	6	4	3	9	2	3
Liberia	—	—	—	—	—	—	1	1
Netherlands	7	10	7	7	7	5	—	—
Norway	—	5	4	6	4	3	4	—
Panama	—	—	—	—	—	4	6	2
Philippines	—	—	—	—	—	—	—	9
USSR/ Russia	8	9	(11)	(11)	(11)	(12)	9	7
Spain	5	6	—	9	—	—	—	—
Sweden	9	—	10	8	10	8	—	—
UK	1	1	1	1	1	1	3	(16)
U.S.	4	3	3	2	2	2	7	6

the outset of an emergency, they would have an adequate supply of merchant ships. Despite acknowledging the importance of merchant shipping to the defense of the individual NATO partners, however, none of the countries (with the possible exception of the United States and its aging reserve fleet) seems prepared to recognize the defense implications of competition from cheaper or otherwise uneconomic competitors by providing meaningful support to their merchant ship owners. The conviction seems to remain that the pool of NATO-owned or

-controlled ships would remain adequate for foreseeable needs. This view appears to ignore what is actually happening to the NATO fleets, in terms both of ships and personnel.

Some of the roles to be undertaken by NATO merchant ships in time of emergency can quite easily be envisaged. Transatlantic reinforcement would need general cargo, RO/RO, and container vessels (the latter also requiring transshipment facilities). European reinforcement would involve ferries, short sea RO/RO, and bulkers. Naval support (ships taken up from trade) would use merchant ships as minelayers, minesweepers, administrative escorts, submarine escorts, rescue vessels, escort oilers, support tankers, tankers for basic oil supplies and water supplies, harbor support, stores carriers, and salvage vessels. More generally, the requirement would involve freighting tankers, ships for general support and ammunition, specialist vehicle transporters, troopships, hospital vessels and even prisoner-of-war ships, ships to carry aircraft and operate helicopters, repair and diving support vessels, offshore support vessels as auxiliary minesweepers as well as evacuation of oil and gas platforms located at sea, and short sea bulkers and coasters for transshipment and cargoes for smaller ports. Finally, the need to sustain civilian life and economic wartime production is no small task in itself.

Such a listing will be obvious to anyone who gives the matter a few moments' thought. It provides a lead to the numbers and wide variety of types of ships likely to be needed and also gives some idea of the conflicting priorities that could well emerge. Who has first choice? What of other requirements? What of attrition?

Shipping has always been an international industry in the sense that it must operate in an international market. It is now becoming increasingly internationalized both in the ownership of vessels and in the provision of crews. Given present trends toward overseas registration, options will become progressively fewer. Local registration or other restrictions, joint ownership, joint ventures, and increasing reliance on foreign crews will also reduce the availability of NATO ships, even if requisitioning powers are used. Owners who have moved away from a national flag may become involved with international partners whose immediate response to a call from NATO might not be as quick as would be necessary. Mixed crews may be reluctant to respond to a call from NATO, not to mention those from former Communist bloc countries who are becoming increasingly available and are establishing a reputation for efficiency.

Traditional shipping companies obviously prefer to own or control the ships they operate. Traditionally, they also preferred to be responsible for the crew as well. Now harsh facts have forced several to hand the basic staffing service to someone else. Similarly, one does not have to "own" the ships to operate an efficient shipping service. The trend to overseas registration and personnel could quite easily extend to mixed overseas ownership, and where then is the national power to control? Owners have warned of these developments for long enough. Moving from the national register even to a closely related country of registry is a big step. The next step to a truly foreign base is much easier. Thereafter, the trend would appear to lead entirely away from ownership and toward chartering. Tension or hostilities can surface in unexpected areas and involve a mixture of national considerations and interests. The different nationalities involved could take time to reach common cause.

Apart from the inevitable effects of attrition, an adequate supply of merchant ships would be vital to sustain civilian populations and essential wartime production. These issues seem not to be addressed with sufficient urgency by the countries of the NATO Alliance, either individually or collectively, at the present time.

Future

After a prolonged slump, leading to major restructuring of companies and disposal of tonnage, some signs of improvement are evident in various shipping markets. The world fleet is growing older, and replacement is a current subject for consideration. Most of the world's fleet will need to be replaced by the end of the century. However, reinvestment debates need to take into account tendencies to prolong, indeed exacerbate, overtonnaging in certain trades, not least in container services, as well as the competitive advantages of others, whether by government subsidy or otherwise.

The continuing development of world trade may encourage countries to remove barriers against economic shipping services. Major interest will focus on the development of the shipping policy of the European Economic Community as well as other similar groups. Governments have a responsibility to endeavor to equalize conditions between their shipowners and others. Protectionism and subsidy distort and reduce the benefits of free trade.

Most countries of the world have access to the sea, and all use merchant shipping to some extent. Issues involving ownership, management, and efficient operation of the shipping industry will continue to be debated, but merchant ships will continue to carry the majority of world trade for a long time to come.

HORACE G. DAVY

SEE ALSO: Blockade and Maritime Exclusion; Convoy and Protection of Shipping; Law of the Sea and Piracy; Logistics, NATO; Maritime Logistics; Naval Auxiliary and Support Ships.

Bibliography

Bauer, K. J. 1988. *A maritime history of the United States: The role of America's seas and waterways.* Columbia, S.C.: Univ. of South Carolina Press.

Corlett, E. 1981. *The revolution in merchant shipping, 1950–1980.* London: HMSO.

Ewart, W. D., and H. Fullard, eds. 1972. *World atlas of shipping*. New York: St. Martin's Press.
Kilmarx, R. A., ed. 1979. *America's maritime legacy: A history of the U.S. merchant marine and shipbuilding industry since colonial times*. Boulder, Colo.: Westview Press.
Lewis, A. R. 1978. *The sea and medieval civilization*. London: Variorium Reprints.

METEOROLOGY, MILITARY

Meteorology, as defined by Webster, is "the science of the atmosphere, especially with respect to weather and climate." It involves the study of phenomena that are not only in the air, but also on the surface of the earth, such as fog, dew, water, ice, wind, pressure, temperature, humidity, sunshine, and the like. Meteorology is especially concerned with the prediction of future weather and climatological studies.

Military meteorology is that meteorological information of particular interest to armed forces. It affects every aspect of military operations, and is tailored to meet the specific needs of military commanders.

History

Meteorology as a discipline began at least as far back as early Greek civilization. In the third century B.C., Aristotle wrote *Meteorologica*, perhaps the best known early attempt to study, organize, and present meteorological data. His pupil, Theophrastus, observed and cataloged more than 200 weather phenomena, which he described in his *Book of Signs* (perhaps the first listing of weather indicators). By the first century B.C., the Greeks in Athens had established a weather observatory called the "Tower of Winds."

Meteorology as science, however, could not occur until observations could be made with precision. Not until the invention of the thermometer and the barometer in the late eighteenth century did this become possible. Even then, progress was slow until the invention of the telegraph in the mid-nineteenth century made it possible to rapidly send weather observations to a central location where they could be collected, analyzed, and plotted on maps to provide a rough picture of the weather over a large area. This made it possible to obtain a general idea of the movement of storms.

In America in 1743, Benjamin Franklin, who had already established the connection between lightning and electricity, correctly observed that storms were moving weather systems. In 1816, the first known weather map was drawn by Heinrich W. Brandes of Germany. He discovered that storms were moving low-pressure systems that were easily identified and tracked on weather maps.

Early efforts to establish weather reporting networks often followed the occurrence of some weather disaster. For example, in 1854, after a violent storm near Balaklava caught the Allied fleet by surprise and caused great damage, the French government decreed that weather reports would be collected and sent to a central location. In America during 1868 and 1869, severe storms on the Great Lakes caused loss of life and extensive damage to shipping. This resulted in the establishment of a weather reporting network by the United States government, principally to warn against storms. This network was a responsibility of the U.S. Army Signal Corps and was the forerunner of the national weather service.

The science of meteorology took a great leap forward in 1922 when the Norwegian, V. Bjerknes, published the Polar-Front theory. This theory, still in use today, permits the scientific analysis of air masses and fronts and the tracking of storms. Later, Petterson developed formulas to mathematically calculate the movement of weather fronts, and Rossby developed diagrams to portray the structure of the upper atmosphere.

Meteorology, as a practice, began with the establishment of national weather services. Since weather affects nearly everything man does (his comings and goings, his work, his play, his health, and his disposition), the practical goal of the science of meteorology is to provide a service (i.e., to make an accurate prediction of the weather as far into the future as possible). A forecast of the weather for a given time and place is not only convenient to man in his everyday life, it is worth millions of dollars to the farmer, the fisherman, and the businessman, and it may be the decisive factor in the success or failure of a military operation.

The ultimate goal of the science of meteorology is to provide a weather service for a large and varied group of consumers. Because each group has different needs, meteorology is subdivided into specialties such as aviation, tropical, and military.

A national weather organization provides weather service to the general public and satisfies the needs of most consumers. Some consumers, however, for whom the weather is critical or whose need is unique, have set up special weather services to cater to their special needs. For example, most television stations and airlines have their own weather advisers, and the military generally has its own weather service.

National weather services throughout the world today use standardized procedures and processes. They are monitored by the World Meteorological Organization of the United Nations and share weather data and information freely, except in time of war.

A weather forecast requires thousands of surface and upper air measurements (mainly pressure, temperature, moisture, wind speed and direction, cloud type and amount, and precipitation) at specified times from around the world. These reports are transmitted to weather centers throughout the world, checked for error, and plotted on weather maps. Lines are drawn (manually or by computer) connecting points of equal pressure (isobars), equal temperatures (isotherms), equal moisture (moist tongues), and wind direction (streamlines) for the surface and for several levels in the upper atmosphere. With these distribution patterns of conditions in the atmosphere for some time in the past, the forecaster attempts (manually or by computer) to determine patterns that will occur in the future and to predict the weather that will occur with those future patterns.

Limitations of the Science of Meteorology

Meteorology is a very complicated science; it involves many other branches of sciences, including higher mathematics, thermodynamics, chemistry, mechanics, radiation theory, physics of fluids, transfer of energy, laws of motion, oceanography, and so forth. It is extremely difficult to write equations that can be solved by computers without making assumptions and ignoring small variables, which may have large effects on the answer.

Further difficulties in producing an accurate forecast are caused by the lack of sufficient weather observations (a minimum of one per square mile is needed), inaccurate observations, the impossibility of having an up-to-the-minute global picture of the "state" of the atmosphere, and the thousands of variations and perturbations in the atmosphere caused by constant movement of the air over geographic features (e.g., mountains, rivers, lakes, oceans, forests, cities, fires, deserts, glaciers, snowpacks, etc.) and by constant variations in clouds, sunshine, water vapor, and carbon dioxide. Small, often unnoticed, changes in the state of the atmosphere can produce major effects. The innumerable changes constantly occurring in the atmosphere approach the randomness of chaos. According to the "Chaos Theory" a butterfly flapping its wings in Peking might cause a snow storm in Washington three weeks later.

Radar and satellites, which can give a continuous picture of cloud cover for large areas of the earth's surface, are a great aid to the forecaster, especially in predicting the movements of large storms, hurricanes, and tornadoes. Despite the research and the modern scientific equipment, meteorology remains an inexact science; and the forecaster is hardpressed to make an accurate "rain" or "no rain," "snow" or "no snow" forecast for a given location for more than 24 hours in advance. Forecasters still rely to some extent on intuition (i.e., on having a "feel" for the weather).

Effects of Weather on Military Operations

Although meteorology is not an exact science, there are two absolutes: (1) it is always present, and (2) it always changes. It is these changes that affect man and everything he does, including warfare.

Every phase of warfare is affected by weather. Military commanders through the ages have recognized this and have tried to pick propitious times for their operations. Before there were meteorologists, commanders consulted the gods, priests, oracles, and astrologers. For example, the Romans sacrificed a goat and had priests read the signs before their assault on Masada.

The weather affects every aspect of military operations, both tactical and strategic. It affects planning, logistics, transportation, communications, equipment, ballistics, and troop efficiency and morale.

Extremes of heat, cold, and humidity create problems with equipment as well as with troop morale and efficiency. Ballistics are affected by wind, temperature, and humidity. High winds, especially those associated with fast-moving cold fronts, thunderstorms, tornadoes, hurricanes, and typhoons, are detrimental to all forms of transportation, notably sea and air, and to paradrop operations. Rain can create mud, which hinders ground transportation of troops and supplies. Snow and ice make all forms of movement more difficult. Clouds, especially low clouds and fog, make air drops and bombing operations more difficult, and practically prohibit strafing of enemy positions and close air support of friendly troops. Fog creates problems for troop movement, reconnaissance, and aircraft and ship operations.

In the nineteenth century, Prussian general Karl von Clausewitz in his classic book, *On War*, recognized that weather injected an element of chance into the best laid military plans. He wrote, "Fog prevents the enemy from being discovered in time, a gun from firing at the right moment, a report from reaching the general," while rain "prevents one battalion from arriving at all, and another from arriving at the right time because it had to march perhaps eight hours instead of three. . . ."

History is replete with examples of the effect of weather on military operations. In some instances, different weather patterns might have changed the course of history. For example, unfavorable winds delayed the launch of William the Conqueror's fleet in the invasion of England in 1066; a storm (typhoon), ever after called the Kamikaze or Divine Wind, resulted in the defeat of Kublai Khan's invasion of Japan in the thirteenth century. Unusually warm weather in Holland in the winter of 1672–73, after the Dutch had flooded much of their land, prevented the ice from getting thick enough to support Louis XIV's cavalry, so the invasion was called off.

Cold, ice, and snow can be a help or a hindrance to the military commander. Hannibal evidently took into account the alpine snows when he planned his march on Rome, but Napoleon failed to allow for the Russian snows when he marched on Moscow, and the Germans failed to allow for the severity of the Russian winter in their siege of Stalingrad. On the other hand, an unusually cold winter allowed the Russians to supply the city of Leningrad by truck over frozen lakes.

A good example of the importance of weather in military operations was Operation Overlord, the allied invasion of France. It was recognized early in the planning that weather might be a critical factor, and the weatherman became a key member of the planning team. The Allied High Command asked their meteorologists to predict the best weather for the invasion compatible with certain tide and moon conditions in the months of June, July, and August. After much study of weather reports, maps, and climatology, the consensus was 5 June. However, the weather was so bad that the invasion was postponed until 6 June. Even then, there were high winds, low visibility, and rough seas that created problems for the invasion; but it caught the Germans, who thought no one would attempt an invasion in such weather, by surprise. The weather became worse later on, and had an invasion been attempted then, it might well have failed.

Weather also played an important part in the Pacific during World War II. For instance, the Japanese were able to take advantage of a fast-moving cold front to shield the advance of their fleet toward Pearl Harbor. They also used cloud cover to hide the movement of their fleet during the battle of Midway. Severe cold fronts, moving south from Japan, greatly hindered the operation of U.S. fighter strikes from Iwo Jima to Japan. After the loss of a number of aircraft in these fronts, the strikes were halted until weather reconnaissance could be established along the fighter routes.

Weather reconnaissance, the gathering of weather information from special aircraft flights, played an important role in military operations during World War II. In the early days of the war this was mostly target reconnaissance to provide information for fighter and bomber strikes. It also provided valuable weather information along the North Atlantic ferry route, but it really proved its greatest value in the Western Pacific. From the beginning of operations in the Pacific, the U.S. Air Force weather experts had argued for the use of special weather reconnaissance aircraft because of the difficulty of making forecasts for such a large area with so few weather reports. It was not until a severe typhoon sank two destroyers and badly damaged an aircraft carrier that the formation of a specially trained and equipped B-24 weather reconnaissance squadron was authorized. This was the first long-range weather reconnaissance squadron to be manned, equipped, and trained for the sole purpose of gathering weather data, and it proved invaluable in providing weather reports over ocean areas and in locating and tracking typhoons and tropical storms. It was also used to provide route and target weather reconnaissance for fighter strikes against the Japanese home islands.

This service proved so valuable that after the war several other weather reconnaissance squadrons were organized and used not only in the Pacific, but also in the Atlantic to track tropical storms and hurricanes.

Another good example of the effect of weather on military operations occurred during the Berlin Airlift, which was probably the greatest air supply operation the world has ever seen. Weather was the greatest single threat to the operation. The book, *A Special Study of Operation Vittles*, has this to say about the effect of weather on the airlift: "Weather, the bane of all aircraft operations, furnishes the greatest single threat to the success of Operation Vittles. For the weather in this area is not only notoriously bad but also subject to rapid changes."

Most of the factors for a successful airlift, such as supply, maintenance, personnel, communications, and flight and control procedures, could be controlled, but not the weather. It soon became apparent that predicting take-off and landing minimums with 60-meter (200-ft.) ceilings and 0.8-kilometer (0.5-mi.) visibility was beyond the state-of-the-art of forecasting. So the Berlin Airlift operated on observed weather and the observations were made constantly at the take-off and landing points (i.e., the runways). This was the birth of runway observations and it triggered the development of special automatic, electronic observing equipment such as the ceilometer (to measure cloud heights continuously) and the transmissometer (to measure visibility continuously). Even so, cloud height and visibility could vary from one end of the runway to the other and could change within minutes. Therefore, with respect to the weather: if the aircraft had take-off minimums at the load bases, they went; if they could not land because of the weather in Berlin, they returned fully loaded. This, of course, was wasteful of manpower, fuel, time, and money, but it ensured that the maximum tonnage was delivered to Berlin. Thus, although the Berlin Airlift was not an economical operation, it was a success and caused the Russians to lift the blockade.

Organization of Military Weather Services

Weather information is so important to military operations that in time of war, weather observations are often transmitted in secret codes to deny them to the enemy.

The military commander needs a wide range of meteorological information for his operations; not only current observations (temperature, wind, precipitation, etc.) and forecasts for short-range planning, but climatological data to give him averages and extremes of weather phenomena for long-range planning. He needs to know the stormy seasons, the dry seasons, and the monsoon seasons, the seasons of heat and cold and rainfall in order to plan for worst case scenarios.

Why would any commander ignore or overlook such vital information? Sometimes due to ignorance, but often due to frustration. It is easier to pin down such details as logistics, troop strength, terrain, and tactics, which remain relatively stable, than to pin down the weather, which changes from day to day, even hour to hour, and which the forecaster cannot predict with certainty. Still, the successful commander must apply this sometimes inaccurate information to his planning and operations.

To provide this important information, the armed forces

of most countries have established special military meteorological organizations to provide weather information and advice to the commander. Much of this advice is based on the same basic weather data available from the national weather services, but it is supplemented by special data available only to the military (e.g., reports from combat zones, enemy territory, remote areas, weather reconnaissance flights, etc.) and it is specially tailored for particular military operations, which are usually highly secret. This special tailoring can best be done by military personnel who are well acquainted with military requirements and operations. Also in time of war, it is necessary that such personnel be in the military service so that they can be ordered into the field with land, sea, and air forces under combat conditions. Often weather personnel are in the vanguard of an operation, going ashore as soon as a beachhead is established or operating behind enemy lines. The first U.S. officer killed by enemy action in World War II was a uniformed weatherman.

In the military services, meteorological information is gathered by extensive networks, processed and presented (usually by a staff weather officer) in the form of weather reports, forecasts, and climatological studies to the commander for his use in planning and operations.

Military weather serivces are generally organized along military lines into wings, groups, squadrons, detachments, or comparable units paralleling the organizations of which they are a part. Nearly all military weather organizations consist of observing stations, forecasting stations, weather centrals (centers), and staff weather units. They provide weather service to military commands from the highest headquarters down to field units. Each major commander usually has a staff weather officer to keep him abreast of weather conditions. Daily command briefings usually contain a weather briefing on current and forecast weather.

The Air Weather Service of the U.S. Air Force, which provides weather service to the U.S. Army and the U.S. Air Force, is perhaps the largest military weather organization in the world. It has a command (administrative) headquarters, a global weather central, two overseas weather centers, and seven wings, to serve major commands, each with subordinate squadrons and many detachments located on air bases and with military units throughout the world. It also has mobile weather units (which can be deployed with troops in the field), weather reconnaissance units, and paradrop units. The U.S. Navy has its own Naval Weather Service to provide weather information to its bases, units, and ships at sea.

Future Developments

It is easy to see why the military commander is impatient with and frustrated by his weather adviser, who often cannot tell if it will be raining or snowing or clear three days from now. It is also easy to see why the meteorologist is frustrated by having to tailor his forecast to operational conditions (e.g., tides, phase of the moon, time of year or month or day, state of readiness, etc.). Most of the time the forecaster is not brought into the planning procedures early enough and his problem is to try to fit the weather into an action which has already been chosen because of other parameters.

Meteorology (weather) has always played a part in military operations, sometimes a critical part. While the still-inexact science of meteorology cannot be fully relied upon by the military commander, neither can it be ignored, except at the risk of failure or perhaps disaster.

Progress has been made since the day when the cave man sniffed the wind. Computers and satellites will further improve, perhaps an exact equation for future weather can be written, but the realm of meteorology is so vast and so changeable that the problem of its best use by the military will probably always be with us.

Today, weather is a critical factor in the launch of space shuttles and satellites, and even if warfare moves into space, there will be meteors and particles and radiation to contend with, and the future commander will probably continue to be frustrated because his meteorological adviser will not be able to give him an exact answer. The ultimate military weapon would be complete control of the weather.

NICHOLAS H. CHAVASSE

SEE ALSO: Arctic Warfare; Desert Warfare; Fog of War; Geography, Military; Radar; Reconnaissance and Surveillance.

Bibliography

Aviation Operations Magazine. 1949. A special study of operation vittles.

Battan, L. 1984. *Fundamentals of meteorology.* Englewood Cliffs, N.J.: Prentice-Hall.

Byers, H. 1974. *General meteorology.* 4th ed. New York: McGraw-Hill.

Cole, F. 1970. *Introduction to meteorology.* New York: Wiley.

Hughes, P. 1970. *A century of weather service.* New York: Gordon and Breach.

Lutgens, F., and E. Tarbuck. 1989. *The atmosphere.* Englewood Cliffs, N.J.: Prentice-Hall.

Thompson, P., and R. O'Brien. 1965. *Weather life science library.* New York: Time.

McGraw-Hill encyclopedia of science and technology. 1982. 5th ed. New York: McGraw-Hill.

Smith, D.G., 1982. *The Cambridge encyclopedia of earth sciences.* New York: Cambridge Univ. Press.

MEXICO (United Mexican States)

During the 1980s, Mexico experienced severe economic and social difficulties: large external debts, rapid population growth, inflation, unemployment, and pressures to emigrate became more acute. To resolve these problems, the Mexican government has established programs to stabilize and deregulate the economy and has implemented political reforms. Challenges, however, continue to hinder Mexico's progress toward establishing a better quality of life for its people.

Power Potential Statistics

Area: 1,972,550 square kilometers (761,602 sq. mi.)
Population: 91,024,000
Total Active Armed Forces: 175,000 (0.192% of pop.)
Gross Domestic Product: US$236 billion (1990 est.)
Annual Defense Expenditure: US$1 billion (0.6% of GDP, 1988 est.)
Iron and Steel Production:
 Crude steel: 7.17 million metric tons (1986)
 Pig iron: 5.373 million metric tons (1989)
Fuel Production:
 Coal: 6.46 million metric tons (1989)
 Crude oil: 144.8 million metric tons (1989)
 Natural gas: 98.48 million cubic meters (1988)
Electrical Power Output: 108,976 million kwh (1990)
Merchant Marine: 64 vessels; 999,423 gross registered tons
Civil Air Fleet: 174 major transport aircraft; 1,537 usable airfields (195 with permanent-surface runways); 2 with runways over 3,659 meters (12,000 ft.); 33 with runways 2,440–3,659 meters (8,000–12,000 ft.); 276 with runways 1,220–2,440 meters (4,000–8,000 ft.).

For the most recent information, the reader may refer to the following annual publications:
The Military Balance. International Institute for Strategic Studies. London: Brassey's (UK).
The Statesman's Year-Book. New York: St. Martin's Press.
The World Factbook. Central Intelligence Agency. Washington, D.C.: Brassey's (US).

History

The history of Mexico can be divided into four periods: (1) the pre–Spanish conquest age before 1519, when the Indian empires such as the Aztecs and the Mayans dominated; (2) the period of Spanish conquest and colonial administration (1519–1810); (3) the nation-building stage of the nineteenth and early twentieth century, which includes the wars of independence from Spain (1810–21), the formation of the federal republic, the war with the United States, a brief civil war, the occupation by the French in the 1860s and their ouster, and the dictatorship of Porfirio Díaz (1876–80, 1884–1910); and (4) the current period, which began with the social revolution of 1910–21 and encompasses the proclamation of the 1917 Constitution; the consolidation of the Revolution under Presidents Obregón, Calles, and Cárdenas, including the formation of the National Revolutionary Party (now the Institutional Revolutionary Party), which has dominated politics since 1929; the institutionalization of the Revolution, 1940–64; and the period of Mexican development and social, political, and economic challenges to the ruling elite from 1964 to the present.

Politico-Military Background

The Revolution gave the armed forces a basis for their popular origins and initiated their role as a defender of the revolutionary creed and the regime. In the 1920s, under Presidents Obregón and Calles, the military was depoliticized and professionalized. President Lázaro Cárdenas continued these efforts in the 1930s by establishing two autonomous defense ministries, national defense and the navy, and by developing a separate sector for the military within the ruling party. The sector was abolished in the 1940s.

Compulsory military training for all 18-year-old males was instituted in 1941 in preparation for Mexico's participation in World War II. The German sinking of two Mexican commercial vessels in the Gulf of Mexico led President Avila Camacho to declare war on the Axis powers in 1942. Six thousand Mexicans served in the U.S. Army under a joint agreement during the war. A Mexican air squadron was also sent to the Pacific combat zone.

Following World War II, U.S. influence on the Mexican military remained strong. The military was reorganized using the U.S. as a model, and equipment was upgraded with U.S. products. In keeping with its principles of nonintervention and self-determination, however, Mexico refused to enter any defense pacts with the United States. No grants of arms or assistance under the U.S. Military Assistance Program were accepted by Mexico after 1950.

Politico-Military Policy

With the discovery and exploitation of major new petroleum reserves during the administration of President López Portillo (1976–82), and as a result of continued industrial growth and political stability, Mexico in the late 1970s and early 1980s began to demand a larger role in regional and world politics. Consequently, the poorly paid and equipped military, which had been assigned the task of guaranteeing domestic political stability and implementing civic action programs, needed to be modernized. The ruling elite set goals to increase the size of the armed forces, upgrade old equipment, improve military training and education, and salaries and nonwage benefits.

Major economic difficulties under Miguel de la Madrid's administration (1982–88) forced the program of military modernization to be scaled down. However, the need to reassess the traditional defense posture became even more apparent as the strategic importance of the Gulf oil reserves increased, as drug interdiction and destruction efforts increased in response to U.S. pressure, and with the fear the guerrilla actions in Guatemala, El Salvador, and Nicaragua could spread to Mexico. As tens of thousands of Central American refugees flooded into southern Mexico in the 1980s, the military increased its patrols along the Guatemalan border, and naval surveillance was increased in territorial waters. For the first time in recent memory high-ranking military officers were included in national security planning. By 1990, over 25 percent of the military was involved full time in antidrug activities.

No major shifts in military planning have taken place under President Carlos Salinas de Gorturi (1988–). The closeness of the July 1988 presidential and congressional elections, which saw Salinas, the PRI candidate, garner only 50.7 percent of the vote; Cuauhtemoc Cárdenas, of the left-of-center National Democratic Front, obtain 31.1 percent of the vote; and Manuel Clouthier of the conservative National Action Party (P.A.N.), take third with 16.8 percent of the total, demonstrates a trend toward democratization. If the ruling party chooses to repress the opposition, the military could be called upon to play an even larger role in quelling domestic disturbances. Such action could move the military into the political arena and upset the post-1940 civilian-military balance in Mexican politics.

Strategic Problems

Since 1910 Mexico's national security concerns have emphasized the avoidance of political or economic domination by other nations, maintenance of internal political stability, and the prevention of social unrest. The last serious challenge to Mexico's sovereignty occurred during World War II. Mexican–U.S. relations have been strong since World War II, although many Mexican political leaders view U.S. domination as the greatest threat to their sovereignty. In the 1980s, the U.S. military policy in Central America, Mexico's debt problem, immigration and drug traffic problems along the northern border, and Mexico's support for the Sandinista government in Nicaragua, the El Salvadoran rebels, and the Contadora and Arias Peace Proposals have strained bilateral relations. Mexican–U.S. relations improved in the 1990s as both governments sought closer economic relations through a free-trade agreement.

In the early 1950s Mexico almost went to war with its southern neighbor, Guatemala, after an attack on Mexican fishing boats in Guatemalan waters. Relations since then have been cordial but tense due to the influx of Guatemalan refugees. In 1984 military personnel relocated 50,000 refugees farther from the southern border. In addition, a new military zone was created in Chiapas, a southern border state.

Mexican geopoliticians have identified the strategic importance of the Isthmus of Tehuantepc since 1950, but particularly since the development of the oil fields in the 1970s. Military exports have been involved in oil security planning and protection, and naval patrols have increased in the area.

The increasing strength of the political opposition as demonstrated by the 1988 elections, external debt of over US$100 billion, larger gaps among regions and between urban and rural areas on economic and social measures, austerity in government (particularly social services spending), and high rates of unemployment and underemployment remain serious threats to political stability; if not addressed, these could pose a problem for Mexico in the 1990s.

Military Assistance

In the fiscal year 1987 Mexico received US$29.974 million for defense articles and services from the United States, and 244 students were trained under the U.S. funded International Military Education and Training Program.

Defense Industry

During the military modernization program of the 1970s, emphasis was placed on the development of a domestic defense industry. As a result, uniforms, related supplies, and small arms and munitions began to be produced internally. Mass production of G-3 automatic rifles started in the 1980s under a co-production agreement with the Federal Republic of Germany. The state-owned Dina Naconal truck factory began manufacturing the DN-III armored car and the military version of the three-quarter ton truck. By the late 1980s Mexico's defense-related production was still rated inferior to Argentina's and Brazil's.

In the López Portillo administration (1976–82), priority was placed on funding scientific and technological developments with possible military applications. It is estimated that between 1978 and 1982, one-third of the funds allocated to the industrial sector were directly tied to military use. Industries involved included: telecommunications, electronics, transport, chemical, engineering and automotive, ferrous and nonferrous metallurgy, instruments and technological innovations, and the computer industry.

Alliances

Historically, Mexico has subscribed to an independent foreign policy based on the principles of nonintervention and self-determination. It is a member of the UN and the OAS and its related committees, and the General Agreement on Tariffs and Trade (GATT) and is the only non–South American member of the Latin American Integration Association. Mexico recognized the revolutionary government of Nicaragua (1979–90) and has never cut diplomatic ties with Cuba. Despite occasional tension, relations with its neighbors, the United States, Guatemala, and Belize, are cordial.

Defense Structure

The president is the commander in chief of the armed forces. He appoints two cabinet-level officials, the Secretary of National Defense, who heads his ministry and is in charge of the army and the air force, and the Secretary of the Navy, who is responsible for his ministry and the navy. Mexico is divided into 9 regions and 36 zones, one zone in each of the 31 states and an additional zone in

Chiapas, Oaxaca, Veracruz, and Guerrero, and one in the Federal District.

(For an explanation of the abbreviations and symbols used in the following section of military statistics, see the list of Abbreviations and Acronyms in each volume.)

Total Armed Forces

Active: 175,000 (60,000 conscripts). Terms of service: 1 year conscription by lottery.
Reserves: 300,000.

ARMY: 130,000 regular (incl est. 60,000 conscripts).
36 Zonal Garrisons: incl 1 armd, 19 mot cav, 1 mech inf, 3 arty regt, 80 inf bn.
1 armd bde (3 armd, 1 mech inf regt).
1 Presidential Guard bde (4 inf, 1 arty bn).
3 inf bde (each 3 inf bn, 1 arty bn).
1 AB bde (3 bn).
AD, engr and spt units.
Equipment:
Recce: 50 M-8, 120 ERC-90F Lynx, 40 M-11 VBL, 70 DN-3/-5 Caballo, 30 MOWAG.
APC: 40 HWK-11, 30 M-3 halftrack, 40 VCR/TT.
Towed arty: 75mm: 18 M-116 pack; 105mm: 100 M-2A1/M-3, M-101.
SP arty: 75mm: 5 M-8.
Mortars: 1,500 incl 81mm.
ATGW: Milan (incl 8 M-11 VBL).
ATK guns: 37mm: 30 M-3.
AD guns: 12.7mm: 40 M-55.

NAVY: 37,000, incl naval air force and marines. 2 Areas: Gulf: 6 Naval Zones. Pacific: 11 Naval Zones. Bases: Gulf: Vera Cruz (HQ), Tampico, Chetumal, Ciudad del Carmen, Yukalpetén. Pacific: Acapulco (HQ), Ensenada, La Paz, San Blas, Guaymas, Mazatlán, Manzanillo, Salina Cruz, Puerto Madero, Lázaro Cárdenas, Puerto Vallarta.
Destroyers: 3:
2 Quetzalcoatl (US Gearing) ASW with 1 × 8 ASROC, 2 × 3 ASTT; plus 2 × 2 127mm guns, hel deck.
1 Cuitlahuac (US Fletcher) with 5 × 533mm TT, 5 × 127mm guns.
Patrol and Coastal Combatants: 97:
Patrol, Offshore: 43:
2 Uxmal (imp Uribe) with Bo-105 hel.
6 Cadete Virgilio Uribe (Sp 'Halcon') with Bo-105 hel.
1 Comodoro Manuel Azueta (US Edsall) (trg).
3 Zacatecas (US Lawrence/Crosley) with 1 × 127mm gun.
1 Durango (trg) with 1 × 102mm gun.
17 Leandro Valle (US Auk MSF).
1 Guanajuato with 1 × 102mm gun.
12 D-01 (US Admirable MSF).
Patrol, Inshore: 34: 31 Quintana Roo (UK Azteca) PCI; 3 ex-US Cape Higgon PCI.
Patrol, River: 20 ⟨ .
Support and Miscellaneous: 14: 1 PCI spt, 3 log spt, 6 ocean tugs, 3 survey, 1 tpt.

Naval Air Force: (500); 9 cbt ac, no armed hel.
MR: 1 sqn with 9 C-212, 11 HU-16 (SAR).
MR HEL: 12 Bo-105 (8 afloat).
Transport: 1 C-212, 2 Cessna 180, 3 -310, 1 DHC-5, 4 FH-227, 1 King Air 90, 1 *Learjet* 24.
Liaison: 3 Cessna 150, 2 -337, 2 -402.
Helicopters: 3 Bell 47, 4 SA-315.

Marines: (8,000). 3 bn (incl 1 Presidential Guard); 15 gp.
Equipment:
Amph Veh: 25 VAP-3550.
Towed arty: 105mm: 8
Mortars: 100 incl 81mm.
RCL: 106mm: M-40A1.

AIR FORCE: 8,000 (incl 1,500 AB bde); 113 cbt ac, 25 armed hel.
Fighter: 1 sqn with 9 F-5E, 2 -F.
COIN: 9 sqn: 6 with 70 PC-7; 1 with 12 AT-33; 1 with 10 IAI-201; 1 hel with 5 Bell 205, 5 -206, 15 -212.
Recce: 1 photo sqn with 10 Commander 500S.
Transport: 5 sqn with 2 BN-2, 12 C-47, 4 C-54, 8 C-117, 2 C-118, 9 C-130A, 1 Citation, 5 Commander 500, 1 -680, 3 Skyvan.
Presidential Transport:
Aircraft: 7 Boeing 727, 2 Boeing 737, 1 L-188, 3 FH-227, 1 Jetstar, 1 Merlin, 5 T-39.
Helicopters: 1 A-109, 2 AS-332, 4 Bell 206, 1 -212, 2 SA-330.
Liaison: 3 Baron, 1 Cessna 310, 1 King Air, 1 Queen Air 80.
Training:
Aircraft: 41 Bonanza, 20 CAP-10, 20 Musketeer, 10 PC-7.
Helicopters: 4 MD 500E.

PARAMILITARY *Rural Defense Militia* (R): 14,000.

Future

In recent years, the Mexican government has moved forward on economic reform but less so on political reform. A key element in Mexico's economic strategy is a free-trade agreement among the United States, Canada, and Mexico. This agreement, however, is viewed by some Americans as detrimental to U.S. interests because it will export U.S. manufacturing jobs to Mexico where labor is cheaper. Such feelings may well undermine future U.S.-Mexican relations.

Politically, the Mexican government is confronted with increasing demands to democratize its political system, deal with drug trafficking and allegations of senior army officers' involvement with traffickers, and acts of civil disobedience, which have become a traditional weapon of Mexico's weak antigovernment parties just as voting fraud has been a tool of the ruling Institution Revolutionary Party (PRI). These problems, for the foreseeable future, may continue to underscore Mexico's unsteady progress toward greater democracy.

ROGER ANDERSON

SEE ALSO: Central America and the Caribbean; Guatemala; Organization of American States; Spanish Empire; United States of America.

Bibliography

Bailey, J. J. 1988. *Governing Mexico: The statecraft of crisis management.* New York: St. Martin's Press.
Camp, R. A. 1992. *Generals in the palacio: The military in modern Mexico.* New York: Oxford Univ. Press.
Hunter, B., ed. 1991. *The statesman's year-book, 1991–92.* New York: St. Martin's Press.

International Institute for Strategic Studies. 1991. *The military balance, 1991–92.* London: Brassey's.
Levy, D., and G. Szekely. 1987. *Mexico: Paradoxes of stability and change.* 2d ed. Boulder, Colo.: Westview Press.
Ronfeldt, D. 1984. *The modern Mexican military: A reassessment.* La Jolla, Calif.: Center for U.S.–Mexican Studies, Univ. of California-San Diego.
Rudolph, J. D., ed. 1984. *Mexico: A country study.* Washington, D.C.: Government Printing Office.
U.S. Central Intelligence Agency. 1991. *The world factbook, 1991–92.* Washington, D.C.: Brassey's.

MIDDLE EAST

The Middle East, also known as the Near East, is usually defined as consisting of the countries of the Arabian peninsula and those immediately adjacent. The countries in the Middle East are Egypt, Israel, Jordan, Lebanon, Syria, Iraq, Iran, Kuwait, Saudi Arabia, Oman, Yemen, Bahrain, Qatar, and the United Arab Emirates (UAE). Most of these nations are both Islamic and Arabic (Israel and Lebanon are the two notable exceptions), and these ties of language and religion have bound the region together even when it was divided by politics. Although other nations in the Mediterranean basin, notably the other North African states besides Egypt, Sudan, Pakistan, and Afghanistan share cultural and historical tradition, those states more properly belong to Africa or to South Asia.

History

The Middle East was the place of origin of two critical developments in human history. First, the development of agriculture, which took place in the hills north and west of the Tigris and Euphrates valleys (modern Iraq, ancient Mesopotamia) around 8000 B.C., enabled people to live in permanent settlements and freed them from following the migrations of game. Second, the first cities were founded, in the alluvial valleys of Mesopotamia and of the Nile in Egypt, about 4,000 years later. The Middle East is therefore the cradle of civilization; although civilized cultures arose separately in Central America, the Andes, and China (the Indus Valley civilizations may have been sparked by Mesopotamian culture), the ancient civilizations of the Middle East were the first.

Although Egypt was politically and culturally stable, Mesopotamia and the Mediterranean coast experienced considerable turbulence, including the rise and fall of Sumerian, Babylonian, Assyrian, and Persian empires, the last conquered by Alexander the Great between 334 and 323 B.C. For nearly a millennium—from 300 B.C. to A.D. 640—Middle Eastern history was dominated by conflict between an empire based in the Mediterranean basin (first Hellenistic, Roman, then Byzantine) and a second empire based in Mesopotamia or Persia (Parthian, then Sassanid) for control of northern Arabia and the broad "Fertile Crescent" from the Mediterranean east to Mesopotamia. No empire held the upper hand for very long, and the last war between Sassanid Persia and the Byzantine Empire (610–628) left both states drained, weakened, and ripe for conquest.

This set the stage for one of the most remarkable events in human history, the explosion of Islam. From a few thousand followers in 628, the religion founded by the prophet Mohammed of Mecca, and spread by the valor and will of his successors and their generals, grew to encompass all of the Middle East and North Africa within 40 years. In the process, Islam's conquests destroyed the Sassanids, reduced Byzantine holdings in Asia to a rump in modern Turkey, and profoundly affected the development of the Middle East, not least by spreading the Arabic language and the Muslim faith across the entire region. The first few centuries of Islamic rule were culturally brilliant, not only preserving much of the knowledge and techniques of the ancient world, but adding new developments as well, such as algebra and much of modern mathematics and geometry. This era ended as the political unity of Islam disintegrated in the late ninth and early tenth centuries.

The end of the universalist Muslim state brought a return to the traditional Mediterranean basin versus inland Persian conflict. This pattern was interrupted by the Crusades, a 200-year series of expeditions and wars by elements of Western Christendom to capture and then hold the Holy Land (essentially Palestine and Lebanon) that ended when the Crusader fortress of Acre fell in 1291. After this interruption, the old conflict resumed and staggered on under various successor states until Sifavid Persia and the Ottoman Empire had become so weak in the mid-nineteenth century that they could barely maintain internal order.

By that time, outside influences from Russia and Western Europe had become more important. The British established a protectorate over Egypt in 1882 (it had been practically independent from Ottoman rule since 1820), and both Russia and Britain carved spheres of influence out of Persia. Britain, drawn by oil fields, became heavily involved in the Persian Gulf basin, and France appointed itself protector of the long-isolated Christian minorities of Syria and Lebanon. To its misfortune, the Ottoman Empire fought against Russia, Britain, and France during World War I (1914–18), and in the aftermath of that war the Ottoman state was dismembered. Palestine, Jordan, and Iraq became British mandates and protectorates, Syria and Lebanon became a French mandate, Persia (now renamed Iran) maintained a precarious independence, and ibn-Saud unified the vast and thinly settled regions of central Arabia as the new kingdom of Saudi Arabia.

This period of political decline and foreign domination matched a growth of Arab nationalism, begun by intellectuals in Egypt and the Levant in the 1830s and 1840s. Although unsuccessful in its efforts to create a nation-state of all Arabs, this movement awakened in the people of the Middle East the desire for their political independence. The situation was further complicated in the Levant by the arrival of Jewish Zionist colonists from Europe, determined to rebuild a Jewish homeland in Palestine, thereby incurring considerable Arab hostility.

Although the British had made some steps toward encouraging self-rule in Egypt and Jordan in the 1920s and 1930s and had allowed Iraq to become virtually independent, neither these states nor any of their neighbors except Saudi Arabia and Iran achieved full independence until after 1945. The French left Lebanon and Syria in 1946, and the British abandoned their Palestine Mandate in 1948, frustrated by the thankless task of trying to satisfy both Arab and Jewish demands at once.

The continuing Arab-Israeli conflict has been marked by five wars (May 1948–February 1949, October–November 1956, June 1967, October 1973, June 1982) and innumerable political crises and has turned the Middle East into a political powder keg. Efforts to bring about some permanent regional security by such measures as the Central Treaty Organization (CENTO), which included Iran, Iraq, Turkey, Pakistan, and Great Britain and was begun in 1955–59, have never been especially active, particularly since Iraq withdrew after the monarchy was overthrown in 1958. The British, who had long provided some stability in the Arabian peninsula, granted independence to South Yemen (later the People's Democratic Republic of Yemen) in 1962, and as part of their "withdrawal from east of Suez" in the late 1960s the British dropped their protectorates of the Persian Gulf states of Qatar, Oman, and the Trucial States (which became the United Arab Emirates on 18 July 1971).

The postwar Middle East also has been disturbed by terrorism, beginning with attacks by radical Jewish resistance groups like the Irgun on British personnel in Palestine in the late 1940s. The establishment of Israel created a dispossessed population of Palestinian Arabs, providing a base of support for dozens of terrorist groups since, most now under the broad umbrella of Yasser Arafat's Palestine Liberation Organization (PLO). Although most of the terrorist acts committed by these groups are aimed at Israel, many are in fact attacks on perceived Israeli allies and associates. The PLO's influence in Lebanon, which had created a state-within-a-state during the early 1970s, is in large part responsible for starting the civil war there in 1975 and for contributing to the spasmodic disintegration of the Lebanese state through 1990.

Finally, the costly eight-year Gulf War between Iran and Iraq had great effects. Sparked to some extent by the revolutionary Shiite enthusiasms of the Islamic republic that replaced the shah's regime in 1978–79, it was precipitated by Iraqi efforts to take advantage of turmoil in Iran by seizing a disputed border region. The war absorbed billions of dollars and thousands of lives, contributed to still more sectarian bloodshed in Lebanon, and eventually drew heavy involvement by the United States and its allies in an ultimately successful effort to safeguard free passage through the Persian Gulf. The war also witnessed a potentially troublesome expansion of both states' military capabilities; Iraq ended the war with a sizable stockpile of chemical agents (which it used on several occasions) and short-range ballistic missiles like the FROG-7 and Scud. These developments provoked Saudi Arabia to purchase Chinese DF-3 missiles, and there are reports of a joint Egyptian-Argentinean project to develop a missile with a 600-kilometer (370-mi.) range.

Thus, despite the Egyptian-Israeli Camp David peace treaty of March 1979, the Middle East remains a region of great potential conflicts, made more dangerous by the increasingly sophisticated weapons available to its relatively large armed forces.

Population

The Middle East is lightly populated, because of the low proportion of arable land, with about 180.26 million inhabitants as of summer 1990. Iran is the most populous with 54,370,000, but of these, 18 percent are of Turkic ancestry, 3 percent are Kurds, and another 3 percent are Arabs; 5 percent are Sunni Muslims (to 93 percent Shiites), and 2 percent are Christians, Jews, and Bahais, although many of those have fled abroad since the revolution. Egypt is next most populous, with some 53,170,000 people, largely Sunni Muslims, but with some 3.15 million Coptic, Greek, and Armenian Christians as well.

None of the other countries has more than 20 million people. Iraq has nearly 17.8 million, of whom 78 percent are Arabs, 17 percent Kurds, 5 percent other minorities; 63 percent are Shiites (but are not generally sympathetic to Iran), 34 percent are Sunni, and 3 percent are Christian. Saudi Arabia's 14.13 million people are almost entirely Sunni Muslim, but 10 percent of the people are Afro-Asians, descended from former slaves; Yemen has a population of 11.56 million with an almost identical ethnic-religious structure. Syria, the only other country with more than 10 million people, has some 12.1 million citizens, including some 925,000 Kurds and Armenians. Nearly three-fourths of all Syrians are Sunnis, but 16 percent are either Alawite Muslims or Druze, and one-tenth are Christians.

The remaining ten Middle Eastern states all have populations of less than five million, and Bahrain and Qatar both have populations of 500,000 or less. Despite their small size, though, several are ethnically diverse. The United Arab Emirates (UAE) is the best case. Barely one-fifth of its 1.88 million people are native citizens; 23 percent are Arabs from other countries, half are from South Asia, and 8 percent are from Europe, Iran, and elsewhere.

In the religious arena, the UAE is more homogeneous, since 80 percent are Sunnis, 16 percent are Shiites, and only 4 percent are non-Muslims. Qatar has a similar ethnic makeup as some 40 percent of its 444,000 people are Arab, 18 percent Indian, 18 percent Pakistani, 10 percent Iranian, and 14 percent of other origins. In Bahrain 63 percent of the country's 503,000 inhabitants are native, 13 percent Asian, 10 percent other Arab, 8 percent Iranian, and 6 percent of other origins; moreover, there is a substantial Shiite community, about 30 percent of the whole (the rest are Sunnis).

Lebanon has relatively little ethnic diversity (93 percent Arab, 6 percent Armenian, 1 percent other), but there are thirteen Christian and five Muslim sects in the country. Some 35 percent of Lebanon's 2,965,000 people are Sunnis, 25 percent are Shiites, 25 percent are Christian, and 10 percent are Druze. Kuwait also is ethnically diverse: 39 percent of the population of 2.14 million are native Kuwaitis, with another 39 percent foreign-born Arabs (including many Palestinians), 9 percent South Asians, 4 percent Iranians, and 9 percent others. The religious situation also is divided, with 45 percent Sunni, 30 percent Shiite, 10 percent other Muslim (Alawites and so forth), and 15 percent Christians, Hindus, and Parsis.

Oman's 1,468,000 people are nearly entirely Arab, but there are small minorities of Baluchis (many in the armed forces), Indians, and Zanzibarians (a former Omani possession). Three-quarters of the people are Ibadhi Muslims, the rest being Sunnis and Shiites, with a sprinkling of Hindus. Jordan has 3,173,000 people, about half of whom are Palestinians. All Jordanians except for a Christian minority of 5 percent are Sunni Muslims. Israel's population of 4.62 million is 83 percent Jewish, 13 percent Muslim and 2 percent Christian Arab, and 2 percent Druze. These figures do not reflect the 905,000 non-Israeli inhabitants of the West Bank, of whom 9 percent are Christian and the rest Muslim.

Military Geography

Modern military geographic consideration of the Middle East is dominated by the three ocean areas that touch its land area: the Persian Gulf, the Red Sea, and the Mediterranean Sea. The Suez Canal provides a vital shortcut from Europe and the Mediterranean to East Africa and Asia. Further, the Arabian peninsula faces the Indian Ocean.

There are few severe geographic obstacles on land, but the deserts of central and eastern Iran and the great deserts of central Arabia form an obstacle to major military operations because of a lack of roads and the harsh desert conditions. The mountains along the Iran-Iraq border are a significant obstacle, but not by any means impassable, as both sides' mountain troops showed in the Gulf War.

Strategic Significance

The strategic importance of the Middle East stems from two geographical factors: its location at the crossroads between Africa, Asia, and Europe, and its great deposits of oil and natural gas. The petroleum deposits in the Middle East contain about five-eighths of the world's proven oil reserves outside the former Eastern bloc. Most of this oil is concentrated along the shores of the Persian Gulf and at some smaller fields in Iraq close to the Iranian border. This wealth has allowed the Gulf states (Saudi Arabia, Kuwait, Bahrain, Qatar, the UAE) to fuel major development efforts and has turned the Gulf into a major financial and trade center. Iran and Iraq, with smaller reserves in proportion to their larger populations, have undertaken less ambitious development efforts, and both spent all their oil revenue (and then some) paying for their war efforts from 1980 to 1988.

The economic power of the Arab oil-producing nations (organized as the Organization of Arab Petroleum-Exporting Countries, or OAPEC) was demonstrated during the famous oil embargo of 1973. Directed against Western Europe and especially the United States for their support of Israel, this embargo brought home to the industrialized nations their dependence on Arab petroleum and produced a price rise of nearly 100 percent within a year of the embargo's start (October 1973). Although the OAPEC cartel is still potentially powerful, political quarrels among its members (especially regarding the Gulf War) have weakened it and made any common decisions difficult to reach and hard to enforce. Despite this, OAPEC will remain potent until the oil runs out (by the middle of the twenty-first century) or until industrialized nations develop effective alternate energy sources.

A major factor in the Middle East "equation," complicating the issues of oil supply and geographic importance, is the seemingly perennial Arab-Israeli conflict. With the exception of Egypt, which is finally gaining some acceptance in the Arab world after its virtual ostracism following the signing of the Camp David treaty with Israel in 1979, Israel is not officially at peace with any of its neighbors. Syria, in particular, has maintained a hostile and uncompromising attitude. The Arab world's hostility to Iran and solidarity behind Iraq led Iran to seek military supplies from Israel, producing a classic justification of the aphorism that "politics make strange bedfellows."

The role of the PLO in the Arab-Israeli conflict is crucial, since no settlement can be reached without the PLO's approval or agreement. The PLO dialogue with the United States, begun only in December 1988 (and later interrupted) held out some hope, but Israel became more intransigent and hard-line under successive center-right Likud governments. As of early 1992, Israel and the Palestinians have begun substantive negotiations toward devising a plan for Palestinian self-rule in the occupied territories.

Regional Alliances

General

The Central Treaty Organization is, as mentioned earlier, essentially a dead letter; it has not really been active since the late 1950s. Several other smaller organizations do have some effect on regional politics. OAPEC, the Arab subgroup of OPEC (Organization of Petroleum-Exporting Countries), has considerable economic importance. The Arab League, an organization more than 40 years old, is often distracted by the quarreling of its members but provides an important forum for Arab unity.

Gulf Cooperation Council (GCC)

The GCC is perhaps the most effective multinational organization in the Middle East. Comprising Saudi Arabia and the five smaller states of Kuwait, Bahrain, Qatar, the UAE, and Oman, the GCC provides both economic coordination and an informal military alliance. The Iranian Revolution and the ensuing Iran-Iraq War provided an important incentive for regional cooperation among the conservative, Western-oriented Gulf states. All six members have distanced themselves somewhat from the United States and Western Europe since 1979–80, but most welcomed the multinational naval presence in the Gulf, which kept this Gulf war from expanding during the spring and summer of 1988. The lessons the GCC learned during the war should serve it well for many years, and the GCC is a modest but important stabilizing factor in the region.

Recent Intra- and Extraregional Conflicts

Since 1945, the Middle East has been a "cockpit of war," with five major international conflicts, several smaller clashes, plus assorted coups and civil wars. The risks posed by these conflicts are made more severe by the vital interests that both the former Soviet Union and the United States have in this area, so that any major conflict brings the possibility of major superpower involvement. The most dramatic incidence of this occurred in 1973 during the October War, when both the United States and the USSR placed their armed forces on limited military alert to indicate to the other that they would not permit the wholesale military defeat of their clients (Israel, and Syria and Egypt, respectively).

18 November 1945–11 December 1946: Revolt in Azerbaijan.

1945–48: Terrorism in Palestine: Radical Zionist and Arab groups attacked each other and the British.

14 May 1948–7 January 1949: Israeli War of Independence/First Arab-Israeli War. This was preceded by several months of violence in Palestine (November 1947–May 1948). There were four phases of fighting, separated by UN truces: 14 May–11 June, 9–18 July, 6 October–5 November, and 20 December 1948–7 January 1949; only Israel and Egypt were involved in the last phase.

30 March 1949–23 November 1951: Four coups d'état in Syria (30 March, 18 August, and 17 December 1949, 28 November 1951).

22 July 1952: Military coup in Egypt deposed King Farouk.

1952–55: Buraimi Oasis dispute between Oman and Saudi Arabia.

December 1953–February 1954: Druze rebellion in Syria.

1953–56: Guerrilla and terrorist raids into Israel led to punitive strikes into neighboring Jordan, Syria, and Egypt by Israeli forces.

21 November 1955: Baghdad Pact signed, which created the Middle East Treaty Organization.

29 October–6 November 1956: Second Arab-Israeli War, with Anglo-French attack on Port Said to secure the Suez Canal.

July–August 1957: Imam of Oman led unsuccessful revolt against Sultan Said bin Taimur, ruler of Muscat and Oman.

1 February 1958: Union of Syria and Egypt as the United Arab Republic.

14 April–21 August 1958: Insurrection and crisis in Lebanon, followed by U.S. intervention (15 July).

14 July 1958: Army revolt in Iraq led to overthrow of government and death of King Faisal II and Premier Nuri es Said.

17 September 1960–71: Kurdish rebellion in Iraq.

28 September 1961: Coup in Syria; Syria left United Arab Republic two days later.

19–27 September 1962: Death of Imam Ahmed, followed by republican uprising and declaration of "Free Yemen Republic."

4 July 1964: Britain promised independence for Aden protectorate.

30 November 1967: Aden protectorate became independent as People's Democratic Republic of Yemen (PDRY).

September 1962–February 1968: Yemeni civil war between republicans with Egyptian support and royalists with Saudi support.

5–10 June 1967: Third Arab-Israeli (Six-Day) War.

November 1967: Britain announced withdrawal from Arabia in 1971.

1968–74: Revolt in Dhofar province of Oman, supported by PDRY.

October 1969: Lebanese army clashed with Palestinian commandos in refugee camp.

10–12 February and 7–11 June 1970: Combat between Jordanian army and Palestinian guerrillas.

23 July 1970: Palace coup replaced Sultan Said bin Taimur with his son, Qabus bin Said, and changed name of country from "Muscat and Oman" to "Sultanate of Oman."

17–26 September 1970: Open warfare between Jordanian

troops and Palestinians, complicated by unsuccessful Syrian invasion (19–23 Sept.).

13 November 1970: Coup in Syria (the eleventh since 1949) brought Gen. Hafez el-Assad to power.

13–19 May 1971: Jordanian army drove out remaining Palestinian guerrillas.

18 July 1971: Establishment of United Arab Emirates.

14 August 1971: Independence of Bahrain.

21 September 1971: Independence of Qatar.

1972–73: Border clashes between Yemen Arab Republic and PDRY.

2–8 May 1973: Lebanese army clashed with Palestinian commandos infiltrating from Syria.

6–24 October 1973: Fourth Arab-Israeli (October) War.

13 April 1975: Outbreak of full-scale civil war in Lebanon.

March 1976: Syria sent troops to Lebanon to try to reestablish order.

May 1976: Renewed Kurdish revolt in Iraq.

12–24 July 1977: Border clashes between Egypt and Libya.

14–21 March 1978: Israeli invasion of southern Lebanon.

16 January 1979: Shah of Iran flees Iran.

February 1979: PDRY–Yemen Arab Republic border clashes.

12 February 1979: Ayatollah Khomeini established Islamic republic in Iran.

26 March 1979: Egyptian-Israeli peace treaty signed at Camp David.

3 November 1979: U.S. Embassy in Teheran seized, and U.S. personnel held hostage until 20 January 1981.

May 1980: PDRY–Yemen Arab Republic border clashes.

24–25 August 1980: Failure of U.S. effort to rescue hostages in Iran.

9 September 1980–September 1988: Gulf (Iran-Iraq) War.

7 June 1981: Israeli air raid destroyed Iraqi nuclear reactor at Osirak.

February 1982: Alawite Muslim revolt in Hamah bloodily suppressed by Syrian army.

6–11 June 1982: Israeli forces invade southern Lebanon to drive out PLO forces; Syrians also resist but are defeated; intermittent fighting continued through the siege of Beirut (26 June–3 September).

27 August–3 September 1982: PLO forces leave Beirut for Tunis.

20–22 September 1982: Franco-Italian-U.S. peacekeeping force to Beirut in aftermath of Shabra and Shatilla refugee camp massacres (16–19 Sept.).

23 October 1984: Suicide attacks on French and U.S. forces in Beirut.

13–24 January 1986: Coup in PDRY, followed by civil war.

March 1987: Riots by Iranian pilgrims to Mecca suppressed by Saudi armed forces.

2 January 1988: Israel struck Palestinian-controlled targets in southern Lebanon with warplanes, helicopters, and gunships, killing 21 and wounding 14.

17 February 1988: U.S. Marine Corps Lt. Col. William R. Higgins, Commander United Nations peacekeeping group in Lebanon, kidnapped while driving near Tyre.

27 February 1988: Iraqi forces bombed Iranian oil refinery near Teheran.

19 March 1988: Saudi Arabia confirmed reports that it purchased an unidentified number of medium-range CSS-2 ballistic missiles from China.

20 August 1988: Cease-fire officially began in Iran-Iraq war.

14 February 1989: Fighting breaks out in East Beirut between Lebanese army troops and Christians.

18 April 1989: Riots broke out in southern Jordan over price increases imposed as part of economic austerity program.

13 August 1989: Syrian forces and Druze and Palestinian militia allies launched assault on Christian stronghold near Beirut.

22 November 1989: Lebanese President Moawad is assassinated.

14 December 1989: About 100 PLO guerrillas attacked Syrian Army outposts in southern Lebanon.

17 May 1990: Vatican-sponsored cease-fire takes effect in Beirut.

22 May 1990: North Yemen (Yemen Arab Republic) and South Yemen (People's Democratic Republic of Yemen) merged into single republic of Yemen.

2 August 1990: Iraqi army invaded and conquered Kuwait.

8 August 1990: Iraq annexed Kuwait as its nineteenth province. U.S. troops and aircraft began arriving in Saudi Arabia the following day.

25 August 1990: UN Security Council Resolution 665 imposed a blockade on Iraq.

29 November 1990: UN Security Council Resolution 678 delivered an ultimatum to Iraq, authorizing any means necessary to compel Iraq's compliance with previous resolutions unless Iraqi forces withdrew from Kuwait by 15 January 1991.

31 December 1990: Israeli fighter-bombers struck PLO base near Sidon, Lebanon, killing 12 guerrillas.

16 January 1991: At 4:00 A.M. local time, with Iraqi forces still in place, UN air forces began military operations against Iraq. The air war continued for more than one month, with 900–1,000 combat sorties per day.

19 January–26 February 1991: In retaliation for allied airstrikes, Saddam Hussein launched Scud SSMs against targets in Saudi Arabia, and tried to widen the war by attacking Israeli cities as well. Under pressure from the U.S., Israel uncharacteristically refrained form retaliating.

23–26 February 1991: The allied ground offensive. Despite pre-war predictions, the Iraqi army failed to put up much resistance, and allied ground forces liberated Kuwait in barely 100 hour of active operations.

March 1991: Disorder in Iraq. Following Iraq's catastrophic defeat at the hands of the allies, dissident Kurds and Shi'ites inside Iraq rose in revolt. Saddam Hussein restored order by brute force, increasing the damage in war-torn southern Iraq and inflicting many civilian casualties.

For the most recent information on this region, the reader may refer to the following annual publications:

The Military Balance. International Institute for Strategic Studies. London: Brassey's (UK).

The Statesman's Year-Book. New York: St. Martin's Press.

The World Factbook. Central Intelligence Agency. Washington, D.C.: Brassey's (US.)

DAVID L. BONGARD
TREVOR N. DUPUY

SEE ALSO: Arab Conquests; Arab-Israeli Wars; Arab League; Crusades; Khalid ibn-al-Walid.

Bibliography

Dupuy, T. N., et al. 1980. *The almanac of world military power.* San Rafael, Calif.: Presidio Press.

Paxton, J., ed. 1988. *The statesman's year-book, 1988–1989.* New York: St. Martin's Press.

MILITARISM

The term *militarism,* meaning, loosely, "an excess of things military," seems to have entered into general usage in the middle of the nineteenth century. Like most emotive terms in the social sciences, it has long been the object of a political tug-of-war, with scholars and statesmen arguing that its "true" meaning denotes the particular form of military excess that he or she believes most deserving of censure. The literature on militarism is consequently muddled by the fact that, irrespective of theoretical or conceptual starting points (e.g., Marxism, liberalism, modernization theory), analysts have all too often been explaining very different things.

Intellectual Roots

Concern over an excess of things military is not new; the intellectual roots of the debate go back to antiquity. By the time the term *militarism* became common in Western literature, however, attention was focused on two forms of "excess": the weight of the military in politics and society, and the prevalence of war. The former was a source of controversy in the English, American, and French revolutions, with each witnessing debate over the right to raise armies, the social and political consequences of standing armies, and the relationship between citizenship and military service. Also of great concern were the causes of war and the question of its inevitability in human affairs; the argument of philosophers of the Enlightenment was that war was an irrational holdover from a barbaric age and thus destined to disappear with the march of progress. Both concerns were reflected in the different meanings that were attached to the term in the late nineteenth century, and as a result, the term suffered from ambiguity from its inception.

Two works of this period are of particular importance. The first is Herbert Spencer's *The Principles of Sociology,* written in 1886. Although Spencer did not use the term *militarism,* preferring instead *militant,* his dichotomization of "militant" and "industrial" societies reflected liberal ideas of his time and later. To Spencer, militant societies were those where the interests of the individual were subordinated to the state, most often in the interest of waging war. Industrial societies, in contrast, were those that devoted social energies to production, commerce, and international trade, and where the interests of the individual predominated over those of the state. Thus, militant societies were reactionary, while industrial societies were progressive and destined to supersede the former.

The second work is Otto Hintze's *Military Organization and the Organization of the State* (1975). In opposition to Spencer, Hintze argued that militarism was not a reactionary phenomenon and was unlikely to disappear with modernization. He identified three great epochs of history, with the final one being that of militarism, which he dated from the Napoleonic wars and the creation of the "citizen army." As he used the term, *militarism* connoted a commitment by the state to militarize society and use military power as the predominant instrument of politics. Thus the "epoch of militarism" began when "the whole state acquired a military caste" and "the institutions of the army insinuated themselves in an important way into the realm of civil administration" (Hintze 1975, pp. 200–202). Hintze felt that war and the need for communal defense and military competitiveness were decisive factors in the evolution of the organization of the state. There was no reason to believe that either the state or militarism would wither away given the continuation of the interstate system and interstate competition.

Despite Hintze's arguments, Spencer's optimistic views were more prevalent in the liberal writing in the period before World War I. The emergence of militaristic attitudes and proclivities to war were held to be legacies of the past. Previously, a "love of things military" had been justified, it was argued, by a need for the heroic warrior to preserve peace and internal order, but these sentiments no longer had a place in the modern world. Instead, they constituted a threat to republicanism. The tenacity of deep-rooted militaristic values, associated with the tradition of the chivalrous knight of European feudalism, was explained in part by the desire of the old aristocratic classes to maintain a functional role in society. As the American political scientist Barrington Moore, Jr., was later to argue, it was the aristocratic classes' disdain for trade and money-making that led them to use militarism to justify their privileges and status (1966).

Marxist and socialist writers of the period were similarly concerned with the likelihood of war and, in particular, with the relationships between war, the systemic imperatives of capitalism, and imperialism. In contrast to nonsocialists, however, they held that the roots of war and international competition were not to be found in the attitudes of the ruling classes but rather in the nature of capitalism and its need for new external markets and raw materials. Thus, Karl Liebknecht in *Militarism and Anti-Militarism* (1968) held that the dynamics of capitalism led to new "techniques of arms," forms of warfare, and means of class domination. Lenin went further, arguing in *Imperialism, the Highest Stage of Capitalism* (1939) than the dynamics of imperialist competition in the age of monopoly finance capital meant that the various alliances of the imperialist powers were "*inevitably* nothing more than a 'truce' in periods between wars." Other socialists, however, stressed the relationship between citizenship and military service and, in a tradition dating back to the citizen army of the French Revolution, attempted to develop formulas for militia systems that would mitigate the authoritarian and exclusivist nature of contemporary militaries and serve the interests of both national defense and political/economic democracy (Jaures 1915).

The Interwar Period

Both the focus of the debate over militarism and the nature of explanation changed with the rise of fascism after World War I. The paramilitarism of the fascist *squadristi* in Italy and Nazi Brown Shirts in Germany made it clear that an excessive love of things military was by no means limited to the upper classes. It also suggested that the liberal hope that militarism would fade away was overly optimistic.

No doubt the most important work on militarism of the interwar period was Alfred Vagts's *A History of Militarism*, published in 1936. Vagts contrasted militarism not with pacifism but with what he called "the military way." He presaged later arguments by the American political scientist Samuel Huntington (1957) on the value of the professionalization of the military in his advocacy of the "military way," or as he defined it, the "primary concentration of men and materials on winning specific objectives of power with utmost efficiency" (Vagts 1973, pp. 13ff). Militarism, in contrast, entailed "a vast array of customs" that "may hamper and defeat the purposes of the military way." As he elaborated, "An army so built that it serves military men, not war, is militaristic; so is everything in an army which is not preparation for fighting, but which merely exists for diversion . . ." The decisive factor in the emergence of what Vagts called "modern militarism" was the abandonment of the rationalism of the Enlightenment for the antirationalism of Romanticism where "the glory of 'romance' was being spread over the drab realities of war." Vagts placed responsibility for the romanticization of war on both the upper and lower classes in Western societies, with the former using romantic demagoguery to drum up support for reactionary policies from below. Vagts's concern, then, was the foolish devotion to military pomp and ceremony that he felt contributed to both the outbreak of war and to the needless waste of lives and resources in the course of war.

In another important work of the period, German sociologist Hans Speier suggested that the "new militarism" of fascism was the latest development in a general trend toward the totalization of war in the modern era. For Speier, "extreme militarism" entailed a centralization of power and esteem, a state monopoly on the raising and equipping of armies, and "a universality of military mores" (Speier 1953, pp. 230ff). This latter criterion was met only in the modern era, beginning with the French Revolution with "the moral participation of the masses in politics and war," but he added that the militarism was reaching its highest form "in contemporary dictatorships under which every civilian, whether or not a potential soldier, is urged to discard nonmilitary patterns of behavior and thought." Speier's arguments about the elimination of barriers between the military caste and society were echoed by another important author of the period, Harold Lasswell, who described the tendencies toward the totalization of war and its social consequences in his 1939 work on the "Garrison State." To Lasswell, the world risked evolving into an antiutopia in which the "specialists on violence" became the new ruling class.

The Postwar Debate Over German and Japanese Militarism

If fascism undermined some traditional liberal notions about the withering away of militarism, it also brought into question socialist arguments about the capitalist roots of the phenomenon. Clearly the Western capitalist countries were not all alike either in the size of their militaries or in the extent of their commitment to war. Nor were the most advanced capitalist nations the most "militaristic." Rather, as Barrington Moore argued in *Social Origins of Dictatorship and Democracy*, militarism was most dramatically manifest in countries where capitalism arrived late and imperfectly. Finally, the example of militaristic idiom and military might of Stalin's Russia also gave reason to question whether socialization of the means of production was likely to mean less belligerent state policies.

To many, then, the challenge was to explain the rise of the new militarism in those countries where fascism had actually taken root. Attention turned to the uniqueness of the societies in question. The focus on societal particularities, as well as the growing influence of psychology in the social sciences, led to research on the cultural dispositions, or as they were then called, the "national characters," of the societies in question. The argument was that certain cultures, in particular the German and Japanese, had long traditions of veneration of military norms and institutions and hence were more militaristically inclined than others. This of course raised the question: Why? Explanations tended to focus on geohistorical factors (including vulnerable strategic location [i.e., for Germany], late national unification, and the consequent need for a cult of the military to rally support to the new state); late economic development and the need for a strong, centralized state that could build the economic and military base to compete in the international arena; and the desire for a place in history as a great power.

New Fronts of Debate

While the debate over German and Japanese militarism has continued, the literature on militarism in general has rapidly expanded in the postwar era along two new fronts. Decolonization brought politics in the developing nations onto the academic agenda, and as the military seized power in numerous developing countries, a vast literature emerged on the nature of civil-military relations in these societies. In this new literature, militarism did not denote international aggression but rather the inordinate influence and domination by the military of the political process. Moreover, because military rule was present in such culturally diverse regions as Latin America, sub-Saharan Africa, the Middle East, and Southeast Asia, analysts were forced to abandon the search for the cultural roots of the love of things military and look elsewhere for persuasive explanations. Decolonization suggested that the causes of the new militarism were not militaristic tradition and a love of the martial way of life but rather more recent political, social, and economic conditions. These included the failure to institutionalize civilian rule, insufficient professionalization of the military, excessively rapid social and economic change, the pressures of international capitalism and economic dependency, and many of the other arguments in the literature on political and socioeconomic "modernization."

While the problems of military rule in the developing countries were manifest, the problem of military influence in the industrialized world was less so. Attention here focused on what President Dwight D. Eisenhower called the "military-industrial complex." His warning about the "unwarranted influence" of an "immense military establishment and a large arms industry" came in the middle of the U.S.-Soviet cold war and echoed similar complaints about an undue political influence of the Soviet military by his Soviet counterpart, Nikita S. Khrushchev. Again the hopes of both liberals and socialists that modernization would result in a more rational and peaceful world gave way to new fears about the nuclear arms race, the militarization of the industrial powers' economies, and the prospects of nuclear war. Nuclear weapons, it was stressed, undermined the traditional distinctions between front and rear, combatants and noncombatants, civil and military. Moreover, the general vilification of the national enemy, the bureaucratization of the military establishment, and the concentration of defense industries were pointed to as manifestations of "postmodern" militarism. As for explanation, neither cultural factors nor arguments based on socioeconomic structure could provide reasons for a phenomenon found in such culturally diverse societies as the United States and the Soviet Union. Instead, analysts focused on the dynamics of international military competition and international relations generally.

What can we conclude from this brief review of the evolution of the militarism debate? In the first place, it is clear that analysts have used the term to denote an ever-growing number of properties as well as referents. If at first the term connoted a propensity to making war or an inordinate esteem for the military way of life, new properties (e.g., the predominance of military influence within the state, militarization of the economy, the presence of large military establishments) have at one time or another been treated as sufficient to label a country militaristic. Partly as a result, where once the term was applied primarily to cases such as Wilhelmine Germany, it is now used to denote an immensely diverse set of societies and phenomena.

A second observation is that the term's meaning has been changed in response to new forms of "an excess of things military" in the real world (e.g., the emergence of the military-industrial complex in advanced industrial societies). As a consequence, the literature on militarism now overlaps with a vast array of other subjects in political science, sociology, and political economy. These include the causes of war, the nature and sources of political culture, civil-military relations, the military-industrial complex, modernization theory, and so on. Given the expansion of what it is that needs explaining, it is not surprising that no consensus has emerged over how to explain.

EDWARD W. WALKER

SEE ALSO: Civil-Military Relations; Coup d'état; Political Control of Armed Forces; Professionalism, Military.

Bibliography

Andreski, S. 1954. *Military organization and society*. New York: Humanities.

Berghahn, V. R. 1981. *Militarism: The history of an international debate*. Cambridge, Mass.: Cambridge Univ. Press.

———, ed. 1975. *Militarismus*. Cologne: Kiepenheuer und Witsch.

Burns, C. D. 1931. Militarism. In *Encyclopedia of the social sciences*, pp. 446–51. New York: Macmillan.

Donovan, J. A. 1970. *Militarism U.S.A.* New York: Scribner's.

Hintze, O. 1975. Military organization and the organization of the state. In *The historical essays of Otto Hintze*, ed. F. Gilbert, pp. 178–215. New York: Oxford Univ. Press.

Huntington, S. P. 1957. *The soldier and the state*. Cambridge: Harvard Univ. Press.

Jaures, J. 1915. *L'armée nouvelle*. Paris.

Lasswell, H. 1941. The garrison state and the specialists on violence. *American Journal of Sociology* 47:446–68.
Lenin, V. I. [1917] 1939. *Imperialism, the highest stage of capitalism.* New York: International Publishers.
Liebknecht, K. [1906] 1968. *Militarism and anti-militarism.* Rev. ed. Cambridge: River Press.
Moore, B., Jr. 1966. *Social origins of dictatorship and democracy.* Boston: Beacon.
Pipes, R. 1981. Militarism and the soviet state. In *U.S.-Soviet relations in the era of detente*, pp. 195–213. Boulder, Colo.: Westview Press.
Radway, L. I. 1968. Militarism. In *The International encyclopedia of the social sciences*, pp. 300–305. New York: Macmillan.
Ritter, G. 1954. Das problem des militarismus in Deutschland. *Historische Zeitschrift* 177:21–48.
Speier, H. 1952. *Social order and the risks of war.* New York: Stewart.
Spencer, H. 1886. *The Principles of sociology*, vol. 2, pp. 473–91, 568–667. New York.
Vagts, A. [1938] 1973. *A history of militarism. Romance and realities of a profession.* Rev. ed. New York: Free Press.
Wolpin, M. D. 1981. *Militarism and social revolution in the Third World.* Totowa, N.J.: Allanheld, Osmun.

MILITARY

The term *military* refers to those institutions of managed lethal violence that are legitimized by state control. The broad definition includes all the organized groups, regular and irregular, national and tribal, that use violence for political or social ends. A more narrow definition may distinguish among armies, navies, air forces, marines, and, in some cases, special forces, missile units, and other branches. Police, internal security forces, and intelligence agencies are usually excluded from the definition, although these may have attributes of military organization.

Military systems have existed at least since classical times, but the modern military is generally traced to the rise of west European nation-states in the sixteenth and seventeenth centuries. But from the beginning a distinction was made between officers, usually members of the nobility, and other ranks, typically drawn from the lower strata of the society. There also appeared early on a midlevel group of noncommissioned officers (NCOs) who directly supervised the lower ranks. This tripartite division of commissioned officers, NCOs, and enlisted personnel still characterizes almost all military organizations. Not only do uniforms separate military members from the civilian population, but insignia distinguish the ranks from each other within the military.

In the nineteenth century, the military became professionalized. Rank and authority derived from ascribed status gradually gave way to that based on competence and education. Military academies and schools arose, ranging from officer commissioning programs to colleges of advanced studies in warfare and strategy for senior officers. This era also saw the formalization of military law with a separate judicial, punishment, and incarceration system. A highly structured and disciplined organization continues to be a defining characteristic of the military.

Many of these military patterns of hierarchy, professionalization, and unique lifestyle spread from the west European heartland to the United States and other parts of Europe. These patterns were then adopted by the newly independent states in Latin America, by Japan and China, and, finally, by the successor states of defunct empires in Asia, Africa, and Oceania. By the mid-twentieth century, a military system was seen as a virtual prerequisite for national independence.

Military recruitment and formal organization vary in several ways. Recruitment depends on either volunteers or conscription. Military forces are usually composed of both active-duty units and reserve or militia components. Some military systems, however, consist solely of active-duty professional officers, NCOs, and lower-rank enlisted volunteers. Others consist of a small professional core with a large militia. Most military systems are mixed, with varying ratios of professional and nonprofessional members and varying components of active and reserve units. Despite these variations, a common imperative in all militaries is to maintain a corporate institutional sense of the membership while seeking to instill a moral commitment from the individual.

Although a longstanding institution, the military confronts special tensions in the contemporary world. For example, in less-developed countries, the tendency for the military to intervene in matters of civil order poses problems for democratic politics. In advanced democratic nations, the role of the military is subject to political influences as basic as budgetary control. In many nations, the very purpose of the military as defender of the homeland from external aggression is brought into question by pacifist groups, as well as by changes in the international strategic picture.

As the twentieth century closes, the military may assume new missions—for example, peacekeeping, multinational interventions, anti-drug trafficking, and environmental protection. In basic respects, however, the military in the foreseeable future will resemble the social organization that initially appeared with the rise of the nation-state.

CHARLES C. MOSKOS

SEE ALSO: Academies, Military; Armed Forces and Society; Branches, Military; Education, Military; Policy, Military; Professionalism, Military.

Bibliography

Andrezejewski, S. 1954. *Military organization and society.* London: Routledge.
Edmonds, M. 1988. *Armed services and society.* Leicester, England: Leicester University Press.
Huntington, S. 1957. *The soldier and the state.* Cambridge, Mass.: Harvard University Press.

Janowitz, M., ed. 1964. *The new military*. New York: Russell Sage Foundation.
Moskos, C., and F. Wood, eds. 1988. *The military*. London: Pergamon-Brassey's.

MILITARY AID TO THE CIVIL POWER—A U.S. MODEL

Soldiers and civilians usually agree that the armed forces should not shoulder the responsibilities of civil government. Both recognize the risks of abuse of power and of impairing the military capability of the armed forces. Modern governments have tried to minimize these risks by placing the armed forces under civilian control and by imposing legal restrictions on civilian use. However, in times of domestic upheaval, sudden widespread calamity, or similar threat to the well-being of a nation, the armed forces may be the resource of last resort. In the United States, the Posse Comitatus Act provides the outline for when civilian authorities may use the military. It declares that "Whoever, except in cases and under circumstances expressly authorized by the Constitution or Act of Congress, willfully uses any part of the Army or the Air Force as a posse comitatus or otherwise to execute the laws shall be fined not more than $10,000 or imprisoned not more than two years, or both."

History

Military intrusions into civilian affairs provided one of the sparks for the American Revolution. The American colonists resented British tax and revenue measures passed in the years following the Seven Years' War. In spite of efforts at reconciliation, their resistance became more violent as time went on. British officials and troops in the colonies were harassed, and an entire cargo of tea was thrown in Boston harbor to frustrate collection of the tax on tea. The British government reacted by sending additional troops to Boston to maintain order and by appointing a soldier, General Thomas Gage, royal governor of Massachusetts. When Gage's troops marched to Concord to seize guns and powder stored there, the colonists met them at Lexington and Concord: the American Revolution had begun.

With obvious reference to events in Massachusetts, the Declaration of Independence listed among the "injuries and usurpation" committed by King George III that he had "kept among us, in times of peace, standing armies without the consent of our legislatures" and had "affected to render the military independent of and superior to the civil power." The Articles of Confederation, and later the Constitution, placed the military under civil control to prevent military involvement in civil matters. The Constitution made the president commander in chief of the militia and of the Army and Navy of the United States, and empowered Congress to raise, support, and regulate them.

The Constitution also authorized Congress to permit the militia to be called out to enforce federal law, suppress insurrections, and repel invasions. The first Congress passed a statute allowing the president to call out the militia to protect settlers on the frontier from Indian attack. In the following Congress, the president gained the power to call upon the militia to respond to foreign invasions, to pleas from the states to put down insurrections, and to requests from U.S. marshals to help enforce federal law when they had been prevented from doing so. Two years later, in 1794, when farmers in western Pennsylvania protesting the federal tax on liquor became violent, President Washington used the authority to put down the so-called Whiskey Rebellion.

During the first half of the nineteenth century, Congress expressly approved use of the military to aid civil authorities in only a few other instances—for example, to protect federal timber rights in Florida or to keep peace on the Indian lands. In the years leading to the Civil War, civilian authorities began to call on the military more frequently, spurred by an opinion on the scope of the *posse comitatus* (literally, the "power of the county") by U.S. Attorney General Caleb Cushing.

In common law, the sheriff might call upon every able-bodied man within his county to repel invaders, pursue felons, and keep the peace. Anyone who ignored his call to the posse comitatus could be fined and imprisoned. Congress had often empowered federal marshals to call upon the posse comitatus to help in the execution of their duties, and the Fugitive Slave Act contained such a provision. In 1851, a federal marshal called for the assistance of the state militia to prevent abolitionists from rescuing a slave he arrested under the Act. Attorney General Cushing was asked whether the state militia had been lawfully employed. He not only approved, but declared in sweeping terms,

> "The posse comitatus comprises every person in the district or county . . . whatever may be their occupation, whether civilians or not; and including the military of all denominations, militia, soldiers, marines, all of whom are alike bound to obey the commands of the sheriff or marshal. The fact that they are organized as military bodies, under the immediate command of their own officers, does not in any wise affect their legal character. They are still the posse comitatus."

Although the validity of Cushing's interpretation can certainly be questioned, as it was at the time, civil authorities cited it often in the troubled years that followed to justify use of military forces to enforce federal and local laws.

When bloodshed erupted in Kansas, partisan use of the army became so common that an amendment was offered to the 1856 army appropriations bill that would have forbidden use of the military as part of the posse comitatus in Kansas. The amendment was defeated, but it laid the foundation for the debate that led to enactment of the Posse Comitatus Act twenty years later.

Enactment of the Posse Comitatus Act

During the Civil War, the Republican party was essentially the party of the Union. It controlled both the White House and a considerable majority in both houses of Congress. After the War, military commanders governed the South until civil government could be restored. The first civil governments were overwhelmingly Republican. Union troops remained to shore up the new governments and keep the peace even after the former Confederate states had been readmitted to the Union. Resentment of the troops' continued presence helped revive the Democratic party. By 1876, the Democrats controlled the House of Representatives as well as the legislatures and governorships of all but three states in the old Confederacy: South Carolina, Florida, and Louisiana. On the eve of the 1876 elections, President Grant provided federal troops for the three states "to secure the better execution of the laws of the United States and to preserve the peace." Whether their presence prevented or ensured voter intimidation and election fraud was a matter of partisan dispute. Democrats felt that the election had been stolen; Republicans felt that free elections had been guaranteed.

When Congress next convened, Democratic members of the House offered amendments to the army appropriations bills which would have precluded use of federal troops as a posse comitatus or otherwise to execute federal law without express statutory authority. Debate on these amendments revealed that federal troops had been used for more than preserving peace at the polls in the three southern states. Federal and state officials, in the south and elsewhere, had employed them to collect federal taxes, to maintain order in the state legislature, to disperse strikers in labor disputes, and to enforce a host of federal and state laws.

Congressional debate, however, revealed another more enduring difficulty. The Republicans argued that, as chief executive and commander in chief, the president enjoyed implied constitutional powers to call upon the armed forces when he felt circumstances demanded. Those powers, they argued, were beyond congressional restriction. The Senate amended the House posse comitatus rider to the army appropriations bill to permit use of the army to execute federal law when authorized by the Constitution. The House and Senate compromised on the final posse comitatus language. The army could not be used as a posse comitatus or otherwise to execute the law except where *expressly* authorized by statute or the Constitution. Since the Constitution contains no *express* authorization for use of the army to execute law, it remains unclear whether the compromise language was intended as a meaningless face saver or to embody the Republican concept of presidential implied powers.

Legacy of the Posse Comitatus Act

Widespread military assistance to local law enforcement officials ended with the passage of the posse comitatus provision. Subsequent attorneys general and military commanders did not hesitate to point to the Posse Comitatus Act when denying requests for military assistance for civilian law enforcement.

There were, of course, a number of instances where the military did provide such assistance. Many of these fall within the statutory exception of the Posse Comitatus Act. The president has long enjoyed the statutory authority to use the armed forces to execute federal law in the face of "unlawful obstructions, combinations or assemblages" that made enforcement by any other means impossible. President Cleveland exercised this authority to ensure the free flow of interstate commerce and delivery of the mail during the railroad strike of 1894; so did President Eisenhower to quell civil disturbances following the desegregation of public schools in Little Rock, Arkansas in 1957, and President Johnson to restore order after riots in Washington, D.C., following the assassination of Martin Luther King in 1968.

Still, even when their actions have been consistent with the Posse Comitatus Act, successive presidents and their attorneys general have continued to claim the implied or inherent constitutional powers of the president to resort to the resources of the armed forces to protect federal property and officials, to respond to the calamities of nature, to deal with civil disorders, and to meet other, comparable sudden emergencies.

Constitutional Framework

The Constitution does not say the armed forces may be used as a police force—nor does it say they may not. It does allow Congress to enact laws so that the militia may be called forth "to execute the laws of the Union, suppress insurrections and repel invasions." This language and the colonial distaste for standing armies can be read to mean that only the militia may be used for those purposes. The men who wrote and ratified the Constitution refuted that view when they assembled in the first Congress. There they permitted the president to employ not only the militia but the land and sea forces of the United States to protect the frontier against hostile Indians and to expel foreign ships that constituted a threat to our neutrality.

While the Constitution is otherwise silent on how the military of the United States may be used, it grants both the president and Congress broad powers over the armed forces. The president is commander in chief of the army and the navy, and he commands the militia while it is in federal service. He is also the chief executive and bears the responsibility to see that the laws are faithfully executed. Congress enjoys complementary powers. It alone may declare war; it raises, maintains, and regulates the armed forces commanded by the president; it makes the laws whose faithful execution he must take care to ensure.

The Bill of Rights limits the scope of these powers. Thus, the president may not permit soldiers to be quartered in private homes contrary to the Third Amendment. Nor may he establish military tribunals to deny civilians the right to jury trial in criminal cases when civilian courts of competent jurisdiction are available to enforce the law. In the absence of constitutional or statutory direction or limitation, however, the president may use the military power of the United States when circumstances demand. He need not await a declaration of war to employ the forces of the United States to repel a sudden invasion, for example.

Congress has augmented the president's powers by enacting laws that permit him or his subordinates to use the armed forces to assist or assume the responsibilities of civil authorities under a variety of circumstances. It has also restricted what otherwise might have been his authority through the Posse Comitatus Act.

Applications of the Act to the Military

Military Departments

The Posse Comitatus Act as enacted applied only to the army. The air force originated as the Army Air Corps and as such it was bound by the Act. That coverage continued when the Air Corps was reestablished as the Air Force.

The Act does not mention the navy and the marine corps. Neither appear to have engaged in the kind of law enforcement assistance that led to the Act's passage. While charges of turning the army into a national constabulary sprung up throughout the debate on the army appropriations bill, discussion of appropriations for the navy and marine corps sparked no such allegations. Had federal marshals and local sheriffs used marines or seamen as they used soldiers, the navy and marine corps presumably would have been made subject to the same restrictions. The navy seems to have agreed, for it has bound the navy and marine corps by instructions comparable to the demands of the Act.

The coast guard is also an armed force and during times of war is part of the navy. Congress formed the coast guard by combining the lifesaving and cutter revenue services. Although the revenue service was called into military service during the Mexican and Civil Wars, Congress never mentioned a posse comitatus restriction in debating its appropriations. Moreover, unlike the other services, the coast guard has always been a law enforcement agency. Neither the Posse Comitatus Act nor the instructions of the secretary of the navy bar the coast guard from performing its law enforcement duties. While it is part of the navy, however, it must observe the secretary's instructions when it considers assistance to civilian authorities unrelated to those duties.

Associated Groups

The status of the national guard, the civil air patrol, members of the various reserve components, and civilian employees of the military departments is less clear. The restrictions of the Posse Comitatus Act and the navy instructions probably reach the activities of these groups when they are part of one of the military departments or are acting under the direction or with the approval of someone who is. But each group is distinct and each provides its own basis to dispute the extent of any hold the Posse Comitatus Act may have over it.

The national guard is the organized militia. It enjoys both a state and federal character. As the militia, it predates the Posse Comitatus Act, and the Act makes no mention of it. Still, the modern national guard in federal service more closely resembles part of the army or air force than its post-Civil War ancestor. The Posse Comitatus Act does not affect the national guard in state service, and the Defense Authorization Act for 1989 encourages the states to use the national guard while in state service to assist civil authorities in drug interdiction and enforcement.

The civil air patrol is a "voluntary civilian auxiliary of the Air Force" which the secretary of the air force may call upon "to fulfill the noncombat mission" of the air force. It should probably be considered part of the air force when being used to fulfill the air force's mission. Congress has called for inclusion of the civil air patrol in federal drug interdiction and eradication activities. When it is used in this way, the civil air patrol is subject to the same posse comitatus limitations as the air force.

The reserve components are part of the services with which they are associated. The Posse Comitatus Act applies to their members while they are on duty or in training. When they are not, the Act does not preclude them from assisting civil authorities except perhaps where the assistance is given under the direction of military authority. Thus, members of a local police force may also be members of a reserve unit without contradicting the demands of the Posse Comitatus Act or the equivalent instructions of the navy.

Reconstruction-era congressmen could not have contemplated the present level of civilian employment by the armed forces. Their discussion focused on the use of "troops," not civilians. On the other hand, it makes little sense to hold military members of a service criminal investigation unit subject to the Posse Comitatus Act but not restrict civilian employees of the same unit. The extent to which a civilian employee's assistance to civil authorities is understood to include assistance of the military should determine the Act's application.

Exceptions

The Posse Comitatus Act does not apply "in cases and under circumstances expressly authorized by the Constitution or Act of Congress." As noted earlier, the Constitution does not expressly authorize use of the armed forces to execute the law except by Act of Congress. It is unclear whether the constitutional exception was intended to embody the president's implied or inherent powers or whether it is meaningless and was included only to avoid embarrassing the president and his party.

The statutory exception has greater vitality. It includes a few general exceptions such as the statutory authority of the military to execute the Uniform Code of Military Justice and the president's statutory authority to use the armed forces to deal with insurrections. It also encompasses narrower exceptions such as the statute that permits the armed forces to assist an FBI investigation of a presidential assassination. Statutes that do not expressly call for military assistance to civil authorities, but whose legislative history clearly indicates such a congressional intent, are part of the exception as well.

Executing the Law

No one may use the armed forces to execute civil law without the approval of Congress. But is the proscription limited to use of the armed forces as policemen, or does it preclude using them to perform other governmental functions as well? And does it reach all types of assistance? Although administrative regulations and the history of the Posse Comitatus Act shed some light on these questions, the state of the law is often unsettled.

The armed forces clearly may not be used as policemen. The Posse Comitatus Act sought to eliminate the prospect of the army as a national constabulary. The post-Reconstruction Congress rebelled against the idea of soldiers arresting civilians for civilian crimes, keeping the peace at the polls and during state legislative sessions, ensuring passage through union picket lines, and seizing property for tax violations. They had no occasion to weigh the propriety of soldiers fighting forests fires or delivering the mail in order to assist civil authorities, or of the military providing civil authorities with information or equipment rather than with troops. Until fairly recently, the Act may have been assumed to apply only to the kind of assistance and for the type of civilian enforcement that had stimulated its enactment. Events on the Pine Ridge Indian Reservation and subsequent judicial interpretations changed that.

For several days in early 1973, an armed mob barricaded themselves in the village of Wounded Knee on the Pine Ridge Indian Reservation in South Dakota. They looted a trading post and took hostages. Members of the FBI, the U.S. Marshals Service, and the Bureau of Indian Affairs besieged the village. The Department of Defense provided the law enforcement officers with arms, ammunition, and armored personnel carriers, and two U.S. Army officers advised them. Members of the national guard repaired and maintained the personnel carriers and flew on one air reconnaissance flight. This was hardly the level of military assumption of civilian law enforcement responsibilities that resulted in the Posse Comitatus Act. Yet, in at least two of the criminal trials that followed, the courts suggested interpretations of the Act under which the assistance at Wounded Knee might be considered a violation of the Posse Comitatus Act.

After the Wounded Knee cases, the Act can be said to apply to any activity where civilians are exposed "to the exercise of military power that is regulatory, proscriptive, or compulsory in nature." Congress acted to foreclose the suggestion that the Act also forbids assistance in the form of information or equipment or indirect support services.

The Wounded Knee cases arose as Congress was considering an expanded use of the armed forces. Drug smuggling had become epidemic, and law enforcement officials hoped that military radar could be used to help curb it. The Wounded Knee cases indicated that this might violate the Posse Comitatus Act unless expressly approved by statute.

In a series of statutes beginning with the Defense Department Authorization for 1982, Congress authorized the Defense Department to disclose information acquired in the performance of their duties to law enforcement authorities and to use military equipment and personnel to support drug enforcement efforts. The statute permits only indirect assistance; it specifically preserves the proscription against military arrests or searches and seizures of civilians without statutory approval.

Neither Congress nor the Wounded Knee cases dealt explicitly with the question of incidental assistance. Congress and the Constitution vest the armed forces with certain responsibilities and the authority to meet them. The military may discharge those responsibilities even where there are incidental benefits to civilian law enforcement officials. Under this so-called military purpose doctrine, the possibility of civilian benefit does not preclude military enforcement of the Uniform Code of Military Justice. It does not bar members of the armed forces from conducting searches and making arrests on military installations nor does it stop them from conducting training exercises. As long as there is an obvious, primary military purpose for the conduct, it is permitted. Where the civilian and military benefits seem at least equal, the conduct will be subject to greater scrutiny. For example, military investigators and local police frequently cooperate in the investigation of alleged drug trafficking believed to involve both military personnel and civilians. The courts have generally accepted military participation as long as civil authorities control any investigations directed against civilians, although they seem uneasy about cases where civil authorities use military investigators as undercover agents, particularly when the investigators take part in the arrest of civilian suspects.

Geographical Application

The Posse Comitatus Act applies only within the United States and its territories and possessions. Before Alaska was admitted to the Union, Congress explicitly permitted the use of the army to execute civil law there. The navy instructions adopting the Act have broader applications. They define "civilian law enforcement agencies" to include the coast guard. In the absence of an applicable waiver or statutory authority, the navy and marine corps may not assist or supplant the coast guard beyond the borders of the United States in any way that would violate the Posse Comitatus Act within the United States. Congress has eased this limitation somewhat by permitting members of the coast guard to be assigned to navy vessels for drug interdiction purposes. Nevertheless, members of the navy and the coast guard are still precluded from taking direct part in an arrest or search and seizure that would otherwise be prohibited. While the Posse Comitatus Act may have limited impact overseas, the Mansfield Amendment controls law enforcement use of American armed forces there. Except as provided in Status of Forces agreements or with the approval of the secretary of state and the attorney general, neither members of the military nor any other officer or employee of the United States may make an arrest in a foreign country in connection with drug enforcement efforts.

Impact

Criminal Liability

The Posse Comitatus Act is a criminal statute, but no one has ever been prosecuted under it. Defendants, rather than prosecutors, have sought refuge under its provisions. The courts have indicated that evidence secured in violation of its provisions might some day be excluded, but have generally not applied an exclusionary rule to the cases before them. At least one tribunal has considered searches conducted in violation of the Act per se unreasonable for purposes of the Fourth Amendment. Should that view persist, the Fourth Amendment exclusionary rule might be applied.

Tokyo Rose and some of the other Americans who made German or Japanese propaganda broadcasts in World War II used the Act to challenge the jurisdication of the court in their criminal trials. They argued unsuccessfully that they had been brought within the jurisdiction of the court unlawfully because they had been returned to the United States by members of the armed forces in violation of the Act.

Some of the Wounded Knee defendants found the Posse Comitatus Act more helpful. Several faced charges of interfering with officers in the lawful performance of their duties. They contended that the officers had not been lawfully performing their duties because they had used the assistance of the military in violation of the Posse Comitatus Act to perform those duties. In two instances, questions raised by the military assistance prevented the government from convincing the court that the officers had been engaged in the lawful performance of their duties.

Civil Liability

At one time, violation of the Posse Comitatus Act barred any claim for damages against the United States under the Federal Tort Claims Act. The Tort Claims Act was subsequently amended to include claims resulting from false arrests or abuses of process by federal law enforcement officials. Since then, an arrest or search and seizure resulting from military assistance to civilian law enforcement officials in violation of the Posse Comitatus Act appears to give rise to a claim under the Federal Tort Claims Act, if the agency assisted is a federal agency. Moreover, the victim of a violation of the Posse Comitatus Act has a cause of action for commission of a constitutional tort if he has thereby been subjected to an unreasonable search and seizure or to the deprivation of life, liberty, or property without due process of law.

Prevention

The Posse Comitatus Act's most profound impact has been preventive. It has discouraged civil authorities from inviting the armed forces to assume the responsibilities of civilian government. It has encouraged military authorities to decline the invitations that have been offered.

Conclusion

Throughout their history, Americans have abhorred the use of the military for civil purposes except under extraordinary circumstances. The Posse Comitatus Act reflects that distaste. On occasion, civil authorities have yielded to the temptation to use the resources of the armed forces to address the emerging problems of civilian government. Yet almost every expansion in military use has been followed by a retreat to the original principle. That ebb and flow is likely to continue.

[Note: The views expressed in this article are those of the author. They do not necessarily reflect the views of the Congressional Research Service.]

Charles Doyle

See Also: Civil Affairs; Civilian Substitution; Civil-Military Cooperation; Internal Security and Armed Forces; National Guard of the United States; National Guards: International Concepts; Political Control of Armed Forces.

Bibliography

Coffey, J. P. 1987. The Navy's role in interdicting narcotics traffic: War on drugs or ambush on the Constitution? *Georgetown Law Journal* 75:1947–66.

Engdahl, D. E. 1971. Soldiers, riots, and revolution: The law and history of military troops in civil disorders. *Iowa Law Review* 57:1–73.
Furman, H. W. C. 1960. Restrictions upon use of the Army imposed by the Posse Comitatus Act. *Military Law Review* 7:85–129.
Gates, J. D. 1982. Don't call out the Marines: An assessment of the Posse Comitatus Act. *Texas Tech Law Review* 13:1467–93.
Keig, L. A. 1988. A proposal for direct use of the United States military in drug enforcement operations abroad. *Texas International Law Journal* 23:291–316.
Lorence, W. E. 1940. The constitutionality of the Posse Comitatus Act. *University of Kansas City Law Review* 8:164–91.
Meeks, C. I., III. 1975. Illegal law enforcement: Aiding civil authorities in violation of the Posse Comitatus Act. *Military Law Review* 70:83–136.
Moore, R. H., Jr. 1987. Posse comitatus revisited: The use of the military in civil law enforcement. *Journal of Criminal Justice* 15:375–86.
Note. 1973. Honored in the breach: Presidential authority to execute the laws with military force. *Yale Law Journal* 83:130–52.
O'Shaughnessy, J. P. 1976. The Posse Comitatus Act: Reconstruction politics reconsidered. *American Criminal Law Review* 13:703–35.
Rice, P. J. 1984. New laws and insights encircle the Posse Comitatus Act. *Military Law Review* 104:109–38.
Rowe, P. J. and C. J. Whelan, eds. 1985. *Military intervention in democratic societies.* London: Croom Helm.
Siemer, D. C., and A. S. Effron. 1979. Military participation in United States enforcement activities overseas: The extraterritorial effect of the Posse Comitatus Act. *St. John's Law Review* 54:1–54.
U.S. Department of the Navy. 1984. Cooperation with civilian law enforcement officials; Posse Comitatus Act. SECNAV Instruction 5820.7A. Washington, D.C.: Government Printing Office.

MILITARY POLICE

Military police are a combat support element of modern armed forces designed to accomplish specialized missions in support of the combined arms team. Military police originated from the need to ensure that stragglers on the battlefield were put under military control and returned to the battle and that prisoners were taken into custody. The German term for military police, *Feldjaeger* (literally, field hunter), expresses the original role of these troops. Before World War I, the U.S. Army relied on officers appointed as provost marshals and troops detailed temporarily to perform as military police (MP). For World War I, the U.S. Army established military police units, but Congress blocked a permanent active military police corps after the war, although MP units were authorized for the Army Reserve. With involvement in World War II imminent, the U.S. Army established the military police corps on a permanent basis on 26 September 1941.

Military Police Missions

In the U.S. Army, the military police are responsible for four major missions: battlefield circulation control, area security, enemy prisoner-of-war (EPW) operations, and law and order. The U.S. Air Force and Navy also have military and civilian personnel for the area security and law and order missions.

Battlefield circulation control facilitates the movement of military units and supplies by performing route reconnaissance, controlling stragglers and refugees, and expediting traffic. Complex movements, such as the flanking maneuver of U.S. and coalition forces for Operation Desert Storm in February 1991, require close coordination of military convoys to ensure that units arrive on time where they are needed. The movement plan is based on route reconnaissance performed by the MP units.

MP detachments operate traffic control points on the main supply routes to direct convoys and individual vehicles to their proper destinations. MP teams patrol the roads, enforce traffic and security regulations, and erect signs marking routes in the theater of operations. Stragglers and military personnel absent without official leave (AWOL) are collected at the traffic control points for return to their units. MPs also assist civil affairs units, preventing civilian refugees from hindering military movements by diverting them to secondary routes and assisting their movement out of the area of operations.

Area security is a major function of military police in the theater of operations. MP tactical support units in the U.S. Army are highly mobile and heavily armed with numerous automatic weapons. They are well suited to provide motorized patrols to protect convoys, act as response forces for counterambush operations, and secure designated critical assets, such as bridges, depots, ammunition supply points, and headquarters. When required, they fight, and they are trained and equipped to deal effectively with light forces and guerrillas. Military police and security police also provide physical security to military installations and other key facilities in the rear areas and within the United States; they protect against unlawful trespass and criminal or terrorist attack by providing guards, mobile patrols, and surveillance of key facilities and gates and other means of exit or entry.

EPW operations are a major responsibility of the Military Police Corps of the U.S. Army. (Prisoners of war [POW] are termed enemy prisoners of war [EPW] by the U.S. Army to distinguish them from U.S. personnel captured by the opposing side.) Most EPW are captured by combat units, who are instructed to turn them over to military police personnel as soon as possible. MP units assigned to the divisions and corps gather prisoners at holding areas where trained EPW units collect them and move them to EPW camps. Upon entry to the EPW camps, prisoners are processed in accordance with the Geneva Convention. They are fed, treated, given a physical examination, provided clothing and a blanket, fingerprinted, issued an ID card, and assigned an Internee Serial Number (ISN). The ISN and identity of each EPW is reported to the International Committee of the Red Cross, which has general oversight of prisoner matters. The United States takes pride in treating its prisoners well and making a careful accounting of each prisoner to the Red Cross to facilitate repatriation or other disposition in accordance with international law. During Operation Desert Storm, the U.S. Army MP units of the 800th MP Brigade, U.S. Army Reserve, processed and secured nearly 70,000 Iraqi prisoners, most of whom were repatriated to Iraq.

The law and order mission of the military police involves law enforcement, criminal investigation, military prison confinement, and counterterrorism. Law enforcement ranges from writing tickets for traffic violations on military bases to apprehending military personnel whose conduct is illegal. Criminal investigation to identify persons who violate military law or civil law on military installations is accomplished by specialized units in the army, navy, air force, and Office of the Defense Inspector General. Military investigators present evidence to the Judge Advocate General staff officers of military commands, who decide whether to recommend a pretrial investigation as a prelude to court-martial. MP units secure prisoners convicted of felonies or held in custody while awaiting court-martial, and also defend against terrorist attacks on military installations or activities; this includes providing protection for key individuals and negotiating the release of hostages.

Military Police Force Structure

Military police exist at every level in modern armies from the division to major commands. In the U.S. Army, each division has an MP company, and each corps, an MP brigade with several battalions. There is usually another MP brigade to support the theater army and another brigade for EPW operations. A separate criminal investigation unit typically operates directly under the theater or theater army commander. Commanders of divisions and larger organizations have a staff provost marshal to advise on military police matters and to exercise staff supervision of MP units assigned to or supporting the organization. The British army also has military police units who perform the entire range of police missions. German *Feldjaeger* units emphasize battlefield circulation control and law and order. The Italian armed forces include the *carabinieri*, which act as a military police and internal security force. The French *gendarmerie* is a paramilitary police force with area security and law and order missions. The Soviet armed forces used tactical military police units (*command troops*) for battlefield circulation control missions; separate state security forces (MVD or KGB) performed the other military police missions. These major nations set the general patterns followed by the other armed forces of the world to accomplish the military police missions.

John R. Brinkerhoff

See Also: Gendarmerie; Geneva Conventions; Internal Security and Armed Forces; Organization, Army; Prisoner of War.

Bibliography

U.S. Department of the Army. 1986. *Military police corps regimental history*. Fort McClellan, Ala.: U.S. Army Military Police School.

———. 1988. *Field manual 19-1: Military police support for the airland battle*. Washington, D.C.: Department of the Army.

MINE

A mine is a type of stationary explosive charge designed to damage or destroy ground vehicles, aircraft (e.g., during takeoff and landing), and naval vessels, or to wound and kill personnel who come into direct contact with or approach the device. The main classes of mines are land mines and naval mines.

The history of mines can be traced back to the late 1600s when siege mining techniques, involving the detonation of explosives under enemy fortifications, were developed. Land mines as we know them today, however, were first widely used during World War I. Naval mines were first used on an extensive scale during the American Civil War. Since World War I, the world's armies and navies have devoted substantial resources to developing the tactics and hardware needed to counter mines.

Contemporary mining operations are only one of several countermobility operations designed to stop or limit the mobility of hostile forces. They are the best method in certain situations and represent a challenge in force composition, task organization, maneuver, and timing that would not otherwise affect operations. Minelaying equipment, as well as personnel to operate it, also imposes a cost to a defending commander in terms of assets and resources that he might prefer to expend in other ways.

Fuzing Mechanisms

Most mines are detonated by direct contact or through a variety of influences capable of detecting objects at a distance. Magnetic, acoustic, pressure, and seismic influence mines are triggered by, respectively:

1. changes in the local magnetic field caused by the passage nearby of large metal objects, such as tanks or ships
2. target noise
3. changes in water pressure caused by the passage of ships and submarines

4. vibration created by moving vehicles

Less commonly, influence mines can also incorporate infrared and radar sensors. Other mines can be detonated by remote control.

Mine Components

A mine has five main components: the fuze, detonator, booster charge, main charge, and case. In addition, there may be added features based on its intended use, such as detonating devices and sensors. Figure 1, picturing a standard antitank mine, shows the various features.

The fuze initiates the explosive charge—in some cases spontaneously, in others after a delay—and is meant to be activated by the target. In the example shown in Figure 1, the fuze is a chemical vial that is activated by crushing. The pressure plate is regulated by a spring to prevent its being triggered by a lesser target.

Detonators are generally highly sensitive explosives that ignite the booster charge or the main charge. The detonator may or may not be stored with the mine, depending on its intended use. In the mine in Figure 1, the detonator will fire the booster charge after being ignited by the chemical fuze.

Booster charges are intermediate charges that ensure full detonation of the main charge; they are especially useful in low-sensitivity charges. Booster charges are less sensitive than detonators but more sensitive than the main charge.

Main charges are the stable explosive engineered to produce the striking power of the mine and are acted upon by the detonator or, if one is present, by the booster. A stable main charge is important because it prevents premature detonation by rifle fire, sympathetic explosion, or handling.

The case, which can be made of almost any material, contains the explosive and wells for fuzing or actuators. The case material has particular significance in relation to the detectability of the mine.

The plug or cap is used to access the fuze or detonator area so that the mine may be shipped separately from the fuze or detonator to ensure safety. Some mines have interchangeable fuze/detonators and use a plug to allow changes based on the intended target. Mines may also have multiple fuze wells so that antilift or booby traps may be set as well as the main fuze.

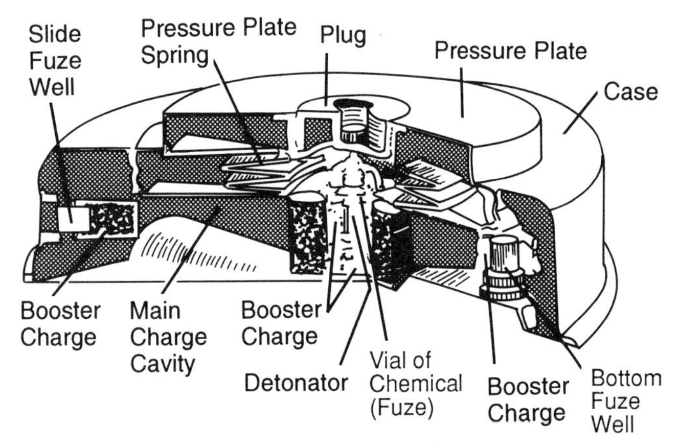

Figure 1. Heavy antitank mine.

Land Mines

Mine warfare on land involves a wide variety of mines, mine countermeasures, and mine counter-countermeasures. Most land mines employ contact or influence fuzes and weigh less than 34 kilograms (75 lbs.); some antipersonnel mines are much smaller.

Three main types of contact fuzes are used in land mines. The most common is the pressure fuze, which triggers detonation when an object of sufficient weight bears down on it, such as a tank track or a man's foot. Another common contact fuzing mechanism is the tripwire. A third mechanism is the tilt-rod fuze, which consists of a thin, upwardly extending rod mounted atop a mine. In this case, detonation is triggered when the rod is bent or broken by, for example, the belly of a passing tank.

The most common influence-fuzed land mines depend on magnetic sensors, others are triggered by acoustic or seismic signals. Some modern influence mines also use infrared or millimeter-band radar sensors. Modern influence mines usually incorporate two or more different sensor types in order to improve their ability to discriminate between targets.

Land mines are generally designed either for use against armored vehicles, especially tanks, or against personnel and may be deployed in fields of one type only or the two may be mixed in a single field.

Antitank mines are effective against both tanks and other vehicles. Pressure-fuzed antitank mines are designed to immobilize the tank by cutting its tread. Tilt-rod mines are designed to detonate beneath the relatively unprotected underside of the tank, and so are capable of causing catastrophic damage. Influence-fuzed mines are designed to be effective against the entire width of the tank. The off-route attack mine is essentially an uncrewed antiarmor rocket launcher that is triggered by a contact fuze, such as a tripwire, or an influence fuze, such as an infrared beam.

Most antipersonnel mines are triggered either by pressure fuzes or tripwires. Bounding antipersonnel mines pop several meters into the air before exploding, substantially increasing their effective casualty radius. Claymore-type mines project their fragments directionally and are usually triggered by tripwires or remote control.

Land mines may be emplaced by hand or mechanically. Mechanical minelayers range from minelaying trailers towed behind trucks to specialized minelaying vehicles. Small scatterable mines can be rapidly emplaced through special launchers on vehicles or dropped from aircraft.

Mines have also been developed that can be laid by artillery.

Land Mine Countermeasures

There are three main ways to counter land mines. The oldest and still perhaps the most reliable method of breaching a minefield is to use trained personnel who use their hands, a bayonet, or a special prod to find the mines.

When enemy fire or time constraints make hand breaching impractical, mechanical measures may be used. The tank flail is a large rotating chain-lined drum extended in front of a tank that attempts to detonate mines in the tank's path. Heavy metal antitank mine rollers set just ahead of the tank's track work on a similar principle. Bulldozer blades or mine plows attached to the front of tanks are the most effective countermeasures for influence mines. A chain strung between the tank's rollers or blades is used to trigger premature detonation of tilt-rod mines.

Another way to clear minefields is through the use of explosives. Special explosive pipes—bangalore torpedoes—can be pushed across a minefield and detonated to clear a path. Alternatively, one can use a flexible explosive hose that is propelled across the minefield by rocket. Fuel air explosives delivered by aircraft or rockets can also be effective in this role.

Mine designers have found a multitude of ways to defeat or degrade the effectiveness of mine countermeasures. For example, mines are designed to detonate if they are tilted or otherwise physically disturbed. Plastic or wood casings are also used in some mines to reduce their detectability by modern electronic mine sensors.

Naval Mines

When Adm. David G. Farragut made his famous command—"Damn the torpedoes, Drayton; full speed ahead!"—to the captain of the steam frigate USS *Hartford* at the Battle of Mobile Bay in August 1864 during the American Civil War, he was actually referring to Confederate naval mines. Naval mines did not account for significant losses until the Russo-Japanese War (1904–1905). The mines used then were the contact and electrically controlled types, which were used in a defensive role until the end of World War I. World War II saw the strategic use of mines. An example of this was the British mining of the English Channel, which, when organized, forced German submarines to take alternate routes, cutting effective patrol time. This had a direct effect on shipping losses. More recent examples of mine warfare can be seen in the U.S. mining of the North Vietnamese harbors. Because of North Vietnam's lack of mine-clearing resources, their logistical shipping was dramatically affected.

Like land mines, naval mines involve a wide variety of types, countermeasures, and counter-countermeasures. Since their targets are much larger than those of land mines, naval mines are likewise larger, averaging 500 to 1,000 kilograms (1,100 to 2,200 lbs.)

Most naval contact mines are moored mines. These are designed to float just below the surface and are kept in place by a cable tether anchored to the ocean floor at depths of up to 600 meters (1,970 ft.). Early moored contact mines detonated only when a ship collided with the mine itself. Modern mines of this type often have "antennas" extending out from the mine that, if touched, will also trigger detonation. Some countries possess unmoored floating contact mines; these may be unintentional, resulting when moored mines become untethered and drift from their mine field.

Most modern mines depend on a combination of magnetic, acoustic, and pressure influence rather than direct contact to trigger detonation. Unlike contact mines, most influence mines are "bottom mines," meaning they rest on the ocean floor rather than being moored and floating near the surface. Bottom mines cause damage by the shock wave and rising gas generated by their explosion. Where the bottom is more than 60 meters (200 ft.) below the surface, bottom mines are ineffective (except perhaps against submarines).

Moored influence mines benefit from both the depth advantage of being moored and from the greater damage possible with influence mines.

A number of countries now possess a variety of more advanced naval mines. Among the most sophisticated is the U.S. CAPTOR (encapsulated torpedo) mine. The CAPTOR, which is moored to the ocean floor, releases an acoustic homing torpedo when approaching ships or submarines are detected. It is apparently effective to a range of some 24 kilometers (15 mi.).

Specialized minelaying ships are in service with several navies. Most navies, however, rely primarily on general purpose surface ships, submarines, and aircraft for minelaying.

Naval Mine Countermeasures

Naval mines can be countered either by "sweeping" or "hunting" them. To enhance survivability of minesweeping and minehunting vessels, every effort is made to reduce their acoustic, magnetic, and pressure signatures. They are therefore typically small, slow vessels made of wood or fiberglass. Since World War II, helicopters have also been adopted for mine countermeasure work.

To counter moored mines, the minesweeper tows a cable that cuts the mine's tether, causing it to float to the surface where it can be destroyed, usually by gunfire. To counter bottom mines, the minesweeper tows special noisemaking devices to trigger acoustic mines or devices that, through the use of electrical currents, create a magnetic signature comparable to that of a ship, thereby triggering magnetic mines. There is no effective way to sweep for pressure mines.

Another way to destroy acoustic and magnetic bottom mines, and the only way to destroy pressure mines, is to hunt for them. In this case, the mine-hunting vessel's high-resolution sonar is used for mine detection and a diver or a small remote-controlled submersible equipped with a television camera and sometimes its own sonar is used to positively identify and destroy the mine. In either case, destruction is accomplished by placing a small explosive charge next to the mine.

Naval mines, like their counterparts on land, have been designed to reduce the effectiveness of mine countermeasures. For example, the incorporation of multiple sensors in influence mines complicates the task of sweeping. The obstruction mine is another type of counter-countermeasure. One such device consists of a moored mine with a serrated mooring cable designed to sever minesweeping cables.

Future Trends in Mines

Because mines have many benefits and are capable of producing wholesale casualties either directly or indirectly by use as obstacles, they should have a bright future. Current deployed antimine technology cannot negate the effects of mine warfare. Synthetic aperture radar technology, not yet fielded in 1990, would allow near real-time area mine-field mapping to be conducted ahead of advancing forces so that entire mine fields could be located and mine locations accurately and completely mapped. When developed and deployed, this countermining technology will divest mine warfare of much of its surprise value.

Both land and naval mines benefit from advancing technology. Sensors that can differentiate between friendly and enemy forces based on system attributes would help in those situations where the threat is a hastily self-placed mine field. Wholesale use of remote neutralization and auto-detection devices would aid in clearing. The increase in off-road antitank mines that fire projectiles at enemy vehicles borders on the robot mine of the future. Will antimine warfare make the mine obsolete or will the future mine make armored vehicles obsolete?

STEVEN M. KOSIAK
DONALD E. BENNETT

SEE ALSO: Fuze; Land Warfare; Mine Warfare, Land; Mine Warfare, Naval.

Bibliography

Crevecoeur, P. 1985. Second-generation AT ground mines. *Armada International* 4:45–51.

Hartman, G. K. 1979. *Weapons that wait: Mine warfare in the U.S. Navy*. Annapolis, Md.: U.S. Naval Institute Press.

Hewish, M. 1986. Land mines: Cheap and effective area denial. *International Defense Review* 8:1085–91.

Manning, H. 1988. Countering the naval mine threat. *International Combat Arms* 11:43–47, 91.

Marriot, J. 1987. A survey of modern mine warfare: Mines and mine counter-measures currently employed. *Armada International* 5:38–44.

Miller, D., and C. Foss. 1987. *Modern land combat*. New York: Portland Books.

Miller, D., and C. Miller. 1986. *Modern naval combat*. New York: Crescent Books.

Sloan, C. F. E. 1986. *Mine warfare on land*. London: Brassey's.

Witt, M. 1985. Sea mines and countermeasures—a survey. *Miltronics* 10:7–21.

MINE WARFARE, LAND

Land mine warfare is an element of military engineering within the scope of land warfare. In its modern sense the term encompasses the planning and laying, the operational use, and the breaching and clearing of minefields. Originally, mine warfare meant the preparation and loading of demolition sites or chambers in the ground, in brickwork or rock, in order to destroy the enemy's military installations.

In terms of etymology, the French word *mine* derived from the Latin *mina* (a vein of ore), which in a figurative sense also meant *tunnel*, *gallery*, or *pit* (to mine = to drive a tunnel). In a military context it meant gunpowder chambers (i.e., demolitions during sieges). The term was later applied to explosive devices that were put on the ground or buried and were designed to block terrain sectors.

Military Mining

Military mining is an offensive form of engineer support against enemy forces defending from field-type or structurally prepared fortifications. The means used to that end is called an "underground mine." It is employed at a particular time against specified targets.

Underground mining has been a facet of siege warfare since ancient times. Before the advent of gunpowder, miners would excavate tunnels under fortifications. The tunnels would terminate in larger cavities with wooden beam supports, and when the supports were burned, the fortification would collapse into the cavity.

Since the invention of gunpowder underground mines with explosive charges have been used, mainly to attack fortresses. They were last employed in World War I trench warfare. Superseded by modern developments in weapons technology, this type of mine warfare has merely historical importance.

DESCRIPTION AND EFFECTS OF UNDERGROUND MINES

Underground mines consisted of a tunnel, which was driven close to or under the perimeter of enemy fortifications, with a demolition chamber at its end, a firing circuit, and the firing point. The location of the mine, the desired effect of the demolition, and the time to fire the demolition were parts of a plan to seize a fortified place. Depending on the effect of the demolition, the mine could make a breach in the lines of fortifications, destroy obstacles and barriers, or even inflict casualties on the enemy and render his weapons useless. Moreover, the demolition often came as a surprise to the defending forces, causing panic and confusion.

Development and Types of Military Mining

At the beginning of the sixteenth century, the Turkish army successfully used underground mines when attacking fortresses, and their method of military mining spread all over Europe. In his famous work on siege warfare (published in 1700) Sebastien Le Prestre de Vauban (French marshal, 1630–1707) laid down principles of military mining that remained valid well into the nineteenth century. Mining was begun as soon as the sappers had completed the last parallel in front of the glacis of a fortress or fortified town. Before starting to work on the trench the glacis was searched for buried *fladderminen* (antipersonnel mines). While working in the tunnels, attention had to be paid at all times to listening tunnels and countermines of the defender. The attackers tried to deceive the listening posts by constructing phony galleries, in which the workers produced a lot of noise (noise gallery); defenders used countermines to collapse mines. The number and locations of demolition chambers were dictated by the type of fortification. According to Vauban's tables, explosive charges for mining could range from a few ounces to 26,690 pounds. The purpose of demolitions was not only to cause destruction, but also—with the rocks and soil ejected and rolling down—to form a breaching ramp that the assault troops could use.

These mining works, which also included the bracing of tunnels and chambers, the calculating and tamping of charges, and the preparing of firing circuits (powder trains) were very time consuming. Military mining during a siege could last 30 days or more. Furthermore, specialists were required for the job. At first, pitmen (coal miners) were hired, and it was not until standing armies were raised in absolutist times that mining units were formed (in France in 1673; in Austria in 1683). Their work demanded courage and special caution. Lack of oxygen and possible flooding made their job difficult. Eighteen miners and 36 unskilled workmen employed in three eight-hour shifts were needed to construct an assault mine.

Vauban's formulas for military mining could no longer be applied to siege operations against fortresses that had been built in accordance with the neo-Prussian method of fortification in the nineteenth century. But it was not until 1860 that the Swiss military theorist Rüstow made a summary of all the efforts up to that time, trying to reform this type of warfare, in his *Doctrine on Modern Siege Warfare*, creating a new theory on mining that was based on the lessons learned in the Turkish Wars (1823) by the Russian army and during the siege of Sevastopol in the Crimean War (1853–56) by the French and English. According to the new method, mine demolitions were used not only to make breaches, but also as an integral part of the approach in front of the glacis. The latest technology in civilian mining, more efficient munitions, galvanic ignition, and ventilators was used in the tunnels. Rüstow paid much attention to the ingenious system of structurally prepared listening galleries and countermines, which were also used against sappers and assault troops. Classical military mining came to an end in the Franco-Prussian War (1870–71).

In World War I, military mining—under different conditions—played a decisive role for the last time in the Dolomites and on the western front. On 7 June 1917 British engineers fired nineteen mines with 430 tons of Ammonal at a depth of 40 meters (44 yd.) at the Wytschaete Salient south of Ypres, destroying three German battalions. On 13 March 1918 Austrian engineers blew up part of Mount Pasubio, which was occupied by the Italians, using 50,000 kilograms (55 tons) of explosive and killing 485 men. Whereas the objective of demolitions in the mountains was mainly to free summits or mountain flanks from enemy forces with a single blow, the demolitions at the western front were designed to destroy large sectors of barriers and trench systems, to inflict high losses of men and materiel on the enemy, and to create wide breaches.

The demolitions on the western front were foreshadowed by the mine exploded by Federal troops under the Confederate earthwork at Elliott's Salient at Petersburg, Virginia, on 30 July 1864. The mine was charged with 8,000 pounds of powder and produced a crater 9 meters (30 ft.) deep, 18 meters (60 ft.) wide, and 52 meters (170 ft.) long. The subsequent Federal assault, however, was unable to exploit the temporary advantage gained by the explosion and the surprise.

Land-mine Operations

By nature, land-mine operations are a defensive type of engineer support against attacking enemy forces. The means used for that purpose is the above-ground land mine. Its effectiveness can be either limited or unlimited in time; it acts against all types of forces and assets without distinguishing between friendly and enemy forces. The purpose of land-mine operations is to block terrain sectors to enhance defensive operations.

Description and Effects of Above-ground Mines

Land mines are transportable, prefabricated explosive devices with fuzes. They are placed in hidden positions in the terrain and actuated by the target, which may be infantrymen or vehicles, with the mines being either "Mobility-kill" or "K-kill" mines.

Development and Types of Mine Operations

In his book *Der vollkommene Deutsche Soldat* (The Perfect German Soldier; 1726) the German military historian H. Frieherr von Flemming described how to use a *fladdermine*. It consisted of one or more pounds of explosive buried at a small depth in the glacis of a fortress and actuated by somebody stepping on it or touching a wire strung out at a low height above the ground. This type of mine evolved into the *tretmine* (step-on-type mine), which went into industrial production before World War I and gained considerable importance in trench warfare during the war. Against infantry, shrapnel mines were used; they were anchored in the ground by a chain and, when activated, were thrown to a height of about 1 meter (1 yd.) and detonated. Toward the end of the war the first antitank mines were developed. These were scattered at random to reinforce wire obstacles and antitank ditches in front of the trench lines.

In World War II, large quantities of antipersonnel and antitank mines (Teller mines) were laid in patterns at all fronts. Laying large minefields with several thousand mines became one of the principal tasks of the engineers of all belligerents (loss rate of armored vehicles to mines was 17%). In the Arab-Israeli Wars, the Vietnam War (loss rate: 70%), the Falklands/Malvinas War, and the (Iran-Iraq) Gulf War, mine operations also played an important role as part of barrier operations.

During the past 80 years a large number of different types of mines have been developed and used in combat (e.g., blast mines, fragmentation mines, shaped-charge mines, mines forming projectiles, and mines with antihandling devices).

Breaching minefields by clearing lanes is possible, although risky. On the other hand, clearing minefields consisting of mines with unlimited laid life is still an unresolved problem. Large areas in North Africa (since World War II), on the Sinai Peninsula, and in the Falklands/Malvinas are still off limits to any type of traffic.

Modern Mine Operations

Conventional mines (first-generation mines) have an unlimited laid life (i.e., they remain effective until rendered useless from wear or decomposition). Modern (second-generation) mines have superseded conventional mines. They have fuzes with a laid life that cannot be changed or that can be preselected; in every case the laid life will be limited, ranging from several hours to several weeks. Upon termination of the laid life the mines will self-destruct or be neutralized automatically. There are some types of state-of-the-art mines that can be switched off prior to laid-life termination.

Regarding their mode of operation, mines are categorized as "antipersonnel mines" and "antitank mines." Antipersonnel mines act by creating a blast wave upon detonation (blast mines) or by propelling pieces of metal in all directions (fragmentation mines). Antitank mines create a blast wave that acts against the wheels and tracks of vehicles, or, when based on the shaped-charge principle, have a full-width attack capability. For activating mines, pressure and tilt-rod fuzes, tripwire-actuated firing devices, and various sensors are used.

Depending on their mode of employment, mines are categorized as "placed," "scatterable," or "off-route" mines. Placed mines are laid by hand or mechanically, either surface-laid (on the ground) or buried. Scatterable mines are dispensed through the air by means of ejection devices; off-route mines are placed manually in hidden positions. The off-route mine's projectile acts only in one predetermined direction. Modern mines may be equipped with an antishock device to prevent their being activated by artillery fire or blast waves. Moreover, they are provided with antihandling devices. They will detonate if someone tries to change their position.

Mines can be placed by hand or by other means. Devices in use in the 1980s included mine chutes hooked up to mine transporters, plowshare-type laying devices (for burying mines), as well as mine launchers, which emplace mines at short distances from magazines by means of ejection charges. Mines can be thrown from helicopters, and artillery rounds can be used to emplace mines at great distances.

With modern mines and methods, a variety of obstacles can be placed in any type of terrain. They can act against armored and nonarmored vehicles, against infantry, or against both vehicles and infantry. They are a suitable means for stopping and containing enemy forces, or for channeling them into particular terrain sectors where they can be destroyed by the fire of friendly forces. Moreover, minefields help defenders hold terrain, gain time, save manpower, and inflict casualties on the enemy. Minefields rarely consist of one or only a few mines. Normally, large minefields up to several kilometers wide and several hundred meters deep are laid in accordance with procedures varying from nation to nation. Minefields consist of several rows of mines laid at predetermined spacings or of mine strips containing clusters of several mines laid at predetermined spacings. The spacing between mines may be measured, determined by means of mine cords provided with markings, or may be programmed in the laying device.

In small minefields the mines are laid in a random pattern. In minefields placed by artillery or aircraft the positions of the individual mines cannot be predetermined. The number of mines to be laid depends on the required obstacle effectiveness, which is expressed by the mine density (number of mines per meter of frontal width). First-generation mines, which act only against wheels and tracks, require a high density (1 to 4 mines per meter), whereas density is low with second-generation mines (about 1 mine every 2 meters). The location and extent of a minefield will depend on the intention of the tactical commander at the front.

It is a responsibility of engineers to plan and employ minefields. Laying minefields with first-generation mines required a lot of manpower (engineer forces at platoon or company strength) and was very time consuming. Minefields consisting of second-generation mines can be emplaced quickly with little manpower required due to modern means of employment. As of the 1980s, minefields could even be laid in a combat environment to increase barrier density, to protect exposed flanks, and to interdict penetrated enemy forces. Minefields consisting of mines whose laid life can be preselected provide the tactical commander with the opportunity to block particular terrain sectors for a limited period of time, and to reuse the mines for the movements of friendly forces (e.g., for counterattacks) after laid life has terminated. Minefields could also be laid during offensive operations, mainly to protect exposed flanks.

The engineer commander advises the tactical commander on barrier planning. Mine operations supplement the main elements of combat: fire and maneuver. They provide engineer forces and assets to lay minefields, reconnoiter and place minefields, provide operational use of minefields, reconnoiter and fight for enemy minefields, and provide information on minefields as well as record minefields.

For special barrier tasks the engineer commander will form barrier reserve forces or mobile barrier detachments for emplacing minefields rapidly and will support combat-effective barrier task forces with engineer forces.

Armies with a defensive organizational structure will always have a strong barrier operations element, as opposed to armies with an offensive structure, which will rely mainly on forces capable of breaching obstacles—and minefields in particular—rapidly and along a wide front.

Mine-clearing assets are engineer equipment suitable for creating passages (lanes and paths) through minefields. Frequently, these assets also can be used to facilitate and expedite the clearing of entire minefields. For detecting mines, mine probes, hand-held detectors, and special engineer vehicles equipped with sensors are used. For breaching, one or several mine-clearing cords (line charges, Giant Vipers) that are towed across a minefield by a rocket are used. Clearing equipment can also be mounted on tanks. Mines are hurled out of the tank's way by steel flails attached to rotating cylinders, are detonated by rollers consisting of steel disks, or dug out of the ground with mine plows. The use of mine-detection parties and mine-clearing assets in a combat environment is made difficult by covering and defending minefields by fire.

Trends and Developments

The new computer-aided technologies will be used for developing new minefield systems. New mines will be developed that act against armored vehicles not only from the bottom but also against the sides and from the top (homing mines). In addition, mines will be developed to attack helicopters and low-flying aircraft. The first step in this direction is the off-route mine. In the future a mine's radius of damage will not correspond with the width of a vehicle, but rather with the size of the area to be blocked. A few "area-covering mines" will suffice to form an "area obstacle system." These third-generation mines will be able to acquire, identify, and destroy targets automatically. For this purpose they will be equipped with "smart" sensor devices (e.g., acoustic, seismic, magnetic, or identification-friend-or-foe sensors). In the future, mine operations will become a third component of battle, equal in importance to the elements of fire and maneuver. Careful coordination of barrier planning with the movements of friendly forces and fire-support plans is required to that end. Apart from the engineers, who plan their minefields as dictated by the terrain and—in a combat environment—by the situation, the artillery will gain importance due to its ability to fire mine rounds at large distances to lay target-oriented minefields deep into enemy terrain. These minefield systems will have a programmed laid life and a remote-control system to be used at will.

Rapidly changing combat situations require immediate collection, transmission, and processing of barrier data. For this purpose computer-aided information systems will be developed and integrated into computerized command post technology. Moreover, theoretical models of remote-control mine detectors and clearing assets have already been developed, which are to be used to breach minefields rapidly and safely.

Ulrich Kreuzfeld

See Also: Engineering Equipment, Combat; Engineering, Military; Fortification; Land Warfare; Mine; Nonattacking Capabilities; Siege; Trench Warfare; Vauban, Sebastien Le Prestre de.

Bibliography

Flemming, H. F. 1726. *Der vollkommene deutsche Soldat.* Leipzig: n.p.

Militärgeschichtliches Institut der DDR, ed. 1983. *Wörterbuch zur deutschen Militärgeschichte.* Berlin: Deutscher Militärvertrag.

Polap, E. 1987. Die Anwendung von Minen im Belagerungskrieg. *Schriftenreihe Festungsforschung* 6:179–205. Marburg: Marbuchverlag GmbH.

Powell, W. H. 1887. The battle of the Petersburg crater. In *Battles & leaders of the civil war,* eds. R. U. Johnson and C. C. Buel. Vol. 4. New York: Century.

Rüstow, W. 1860. *Die Lehre vom neueren Festungskrieg.* Leipzig: Forst'nersche Buchhandlung.

Schaumann, W. 1978. *Schauplätze des Gebirgskrieges.* Cortina d'Ampezzo: Foto Ghedina.

MINE WARFARE, NAVAL

Naval mine warfare is the strategic and tactical use of mines and their countermeasures. It constitutes both *mining operations,* embracing all methods whereby damage may be inflicted or enemy sea operations hindered by the use of mines, and *mine countermeasures* (MCM), which include all measures for countering the mine by reducing or preventing danger or damage to ships and personnel.

Through its history until the present day, the mine has proved to be a most cost-effective weapon that causes physical damage, creates psychological effects, and requires a countermeasures effort far out of proportion to the cost of the mining effort. A naval mine is an explosive device laid in the water with the intention of sinking a ship or submarine or preventing shipping from using an area. Naval mines are relatively small, but they have good hitting power and they can be easily concealed and stored. They require little maintenance, have a long shelf life, and can be laid simply from almost any type of platform—ships, submarines, or aircraft—which need not necessarily be a military platform. Historically, the mine has promised smaller naval powers the possibility of countering the massive investments their enemies make in capital ships. The major naval powers used mines extensively and very successfully in World War I and World War II. Since then the mine has played an important role in the Korean War, the Vietnam War, and, more recently, in the Persian Gulf. The mine has a unique asset of covertness; it provides no visible warning of danger. Mining permits enemy shipping to be attacked without the necessity for minelaying craft to engage or even to locate the target. The primary weakness of a minefield is that it must wait for its target instead of seeking it. The value of the mine, however, lies not only in its potential as an instrument of attrition but also in the deterrent effect upon the enemy's will to use his naval forces and his capability to use shipping to support the national economy and logistics.

History

Underwater mines were used for the first time in naval warfare during the American Revolutionary War (1775–82), when the American David Bushnell devised methods to attack British ships with underwater explosives. Moored mines were used for harbor defense by the Russians in the Crimean War (1854–56). During the American Civil War (1861–65), the Confederates sank various blockading Federal ships by moored and electrically controlled mines. In the Russo-Japanese War of 1904–1905, mines for the first time played a decisive role in naval warfare. The Russians laid around 6,500 moored mines to protect Port Arthur and caused the sinking of six major and four smaller warships of their adversaries. The Japanese laid their mines offensively and succeeded in luring a Russian force over their minefield, resulting in the loss of two major and four smaller Russian ships.

During the First World War about 240,000 mines were laid by the countries involved and by neutrals protecting their own harbors. The British laid about 129,000 mines, of which nearly half were around enemy coasts and in the Mediterranean. In 1918, to block the German submarines's North Sea exit to the Atlantic Ocean, the United States planted 57,000 mines and the British 15,000 in the North Sea Barrage, extending 450 kilometers (250 NM). The major German use of mines, of which they laid about 43,000, was offensive in British coastal waters. The Allies lost an estimated one million tons of shipping in 586 ships; German losses through mines amounted to 150 warships and 40 U-boats.

Nearly 700,000 mines were laid in World War II; they accounted for more ships sunk or damaged than any other weapon. The Allies lost 650 ships, whereas the Axis powers lost around 1,100, with a further 800 damaged. The British in 1942 laid some 96,000 mines from Scotland to Iceland to Greenland to deter U-boats from attacking Atlantic convoys. Nearly the entire surviving Japanese merchant fleet (670 ships) and 65 warships were sunk by the American "starvation campaign," executed in 1945 with more than 12,000 mines.

During the Korean War the landing of United Nations troops at Wonsan had to be delayed for eight days when they discovered that North Korean junks and sampans had laid 3,500 Soviet magnetic mines. In Vietnam, the American mining (May 1972) of Haiphong harbor ultimately stopped the movement of supplies into North Vietnam by sea, thereby contributing to the end of the war. Finally, in the summer of 1984, eighteen merchant vessels belonging to fourteen different nations were slightly damaged in the Red Sea by mines, probably laid by a terrorist organization.

Mining Operations

Minefields are laid for an offensive, defensive, or protective purpose, with an underlying strategic or tactical objective. The choice of minefield type is dependent on the available numbers and types of mines and minelayers, on geographical and environmental circumstances, and on possible enemy reactions and countermeasures.

Strategic mining campaigns have a long-term objective to deny the enemy free access to or use of sea areas considered vital to one's own war effort or to reduce and impede the enemy's warmaking potential. Depending on the importance of the threat, these campaigns can be directed against naval surface forces, submarines, or seaborne communications. Sustained attrition mining is essentially strategic in nature.

Tactical mining supports a limited military objective in time and scope. Historically the mine was not considered an effective tactical weapon because it required too much preparation time for immediate use. Modern mines, however, are more suitable for quick or last-minute deployment in support of a tactical engagement.

Offensive mining is conducted in enemy territorial waters (e.g., harbors or approaches) or waters under enemy control. The purpose of offensive mining may be to destroy or damage enemy ships, to delay or dislocate their movements, or to impose a large mine countermeasures effort on the enemy (Fig. 1).

Figure 1. The Explosive Ordnance Disposal Mobile Unit Six Detachment Eight recovered or destroyed 40 sea mines during its 5-month deployment to the Persian Gulf during Operation Desert Storm and was instrumental in re-opening the major ports of Kuwait. (SOURCE: U.S. Navy)

Defensive minefields are laid in international waters preferably under one's own control, with the declared intention of controlling shipping in defense of sea communications. Their purpose is to inhibit the enemy's freedom of maneuver and to provide protected flanks for friendly shipping.

Protective minefields are laid in waters under one's own control to protect ports, harbors, anchorages, coasts, and coastal routes.

Types of Mines

The mine contains an explosive charge, a primer, a detonator, and a firing system. Modern mines may employ special devices that resist mine countermeasures, that can deactivate the mine, and that can identify the target. The most common devices used to increase the mine's resistance to countermeasures are the arming delay and the ship counter. To render the mine permanently inoperative on expiration of a predetermined time after laying, a device called a *sterilizer* can be included. Mines can be classified according to the method of actuation of the firing system (i.e., sensor), the position underwater, or the purpose.

Classified According to Method of Actuation

The term *actuation* defines the operation of a mine firing mechanism by an influence or a series of influences in such a way that all the requirements of the mechanism for firing (or for registering a ship count) are met. A *ship counter* is a device in the mine that prevents it from detonating until a preset number of actuations has taken place. The two main categories of this type are controlled mines and independent mines.

Controlled mines can be controlled by the user after they have been laid. The mine may be armed or made safe, or it may be fired. The earliest controlled mines consisted simply of a series of large explosive charges on the seabed connected by electrical cables to a position on the shore overlooking the minefield. As the target was observed passing over the position of the mines, they were detonated by electrical signal from ashore. Modern cable-controlled mines may contain detecting mechanisms that signal the presence of a ship or submarine to a remote station, or they may be operated in conjunction with some separate means of detection. Controlled mines are most useful in protective or defensive minefields but may be used in offensive mining. More sophisticated means are being developed to provide for remote activation of cableless controlled mines, for instance, by extreme low-frequency coded radio transmissions.

Independent mines rely on their own sensors for firing. This type of mine can be further divided into contact mines and influence mines.

A contact mine is designed to fire by physical contact between target and the mine case or its appendages (i.e., a contact sensor). A mine can be fired by the force of contact between hull and mine (the so-called plain contact mine); by the hull or propellers catching a buoyant line attached to one of the horns or switches of the mine (the snagline mine); or by the ferrous hull touching a copper or brass antenna fitted to the mine, setting up galvanic action to fire the mine (antenna mine).

Influence mines are actuated by the effect of a target on some physical condition in the vicinity of the mine or on radiations emanating from the mine. Early in World War II, mines were developed that relied for their actuation on the moving target creating a noticeable variation in the environment by disturbing the earth's magnetic field (magnetic mines), producing noise (acoustic mines), or changing the water pressure (pressure mines). Other actuation methods, such as the use of the electrical potential within the water (the underwater electric potential mine), have also been developed. Modern mines normally have a combination of two or more sensor types in their firing circuits (combined influence mine) as a means to thwart countermeasures.

Classification According to Position Underwater

Mines under this heading can broadly be divided into ground or bottom mines, moored mines, and moving mines.

Ground or bottom mines remain on the seabed by their own weight. Their firing mechanism is usually of the influence type, and therefore ground mines cannot be laid effectively in deep water except for use against submerged submarines. Modern ground mines have self-burying casings that make clearing them more difficult.

Moored mines have positive buoyancy and are held

below the surface at a preselected depth by a mooring attached to a sinker on the bottom. A moored mine may contain either an influence or a contact firing mechanism. The moored mine is effective for use in extensive protective and defensive minefields. Modern moored mines may be used for deep-water barriers to depths greater than 1,000 meters (approx. 3,300 ft.) for use against deep-diving submarines.

Moving mines include various mine types such as drifting, oscillating, creeping, mobile, homing, and rising mines.

Classification According to Purpose

Mines can further be defined by the purpose for which they were designed or laid. Examples of this category are the continental shelf mine, which is capable of offensive, defensive, and protective use against surface ships and submarines in water depths up to hundreds of meters; the maritime anti-invasion mine, for use in very shallow water depths; the antisweeper and antihunter mines, specially designed to sink or damage minesweepers and minehunters; and the exercise mine.

Minelayers

Mines can be laid by surface vessels, submarines, aircraft, and even by rocket or by hand. Factors to be considered in the selection of the delivery platform include the type of minefield to be laid, the distance from mine stockpile to target area, the level and type of opposition likely to be encountered, environment limitations, and the need of one's own forces to operate in the mined area.

Surface Vessel Delivery

Surface vessels offer the advantages of being able to carry more mines than either aircraft or submarine minelayers and of delivering them with greater accuracy. A surface vessel, however, does not have the covert capability of the submarine and is more vulnerable to enemy attack. Almost any surface ship or craft can be rigged to lay mines. The conventional minelayer is particularly vulnerable because it is slow and easily recognized. Therefore, those retained in active inventories today are principally to lay defensive minefields within range of friendly covering forces. Modern types of surface vessels, like the surface effect ship, can be built or adapted to carry and lay mines with an increased speed of response capability. The merchant ship has shown in the world wars that it can be a very effective mine laying platform. Roll-on/roll-off ships, ferries, and a host of other craft are suited for clandestine minelaying operations in peacetime or in times of rising tensions before hostilities have commenced.

Submarine Delivery

Submarines have the advantage over other types of minelayers in that they can approach an area, remain there for sufficient time for accurate minelaying, and withdraw in complete secrecy. A submarine, however, is restricted to water areas that are accessible from the open sea, that are deep enough to allow submerged operations, and that are not defensively mined by the enemy. The submarine, therefore, is the most effective platform for laying mines covertly and for laying mines in areas that are too well defended for penetration by air or surface craft. The majority of modern submarine-laid mines, both moored and ground, are designed to be laid through the torpedo tubes, making every type of submarine suitable for this task.

Aircraft Delivery

Aircraft can penetrate quickly into areas denied to surface vessels and submarines. Another advantage enjoyed by aircraft is that they are not themselves endangered by minefields. Major disadvantages associated with aircraft are that their weapon load is relatively small, aerial minelaying is less accurate, and they are vulnerable to antiair warfare. Aircraft can be said to be the most suitable vehicles for a majority of offensive minelaying operations, especially those that have to be executed quickly, and for replenishing existing fields. Generally, all aircraft that can carry bombs can also carry mines of the same nominal weight.

Mine Countermeasures

Antimining operations, or MCM, can be divided into offensive countermeasures and defensive countermeasures. Offensive countermeasures are taken to prevent the enemy from successfully laying mines; defensive countermeasures are taken to reduce the effect of those mines that have been laid successfully either by the enemy or by friendly forces.

Offensive Mine Countermeasures

Offensive MCM include strategic bombing, attacks on enemy minelayers, and the laying of offensive minefields. Strategic bombing entails long-range bombing of the industrial potential, shipyards, storage depots, and other facilities required to support enemy minelaying. Attacks on enemy layers can be carried out on the port or airfield at which the minelayers are based or on the minelayer while in transit. Offensive minefields laid off the enemy's harbors contribute to the destruction of its surface and submarine minelayers.

Defensive Mine Countermeasures

The risk of mines once they have been laid can be reduced by passive and active measures. Passive countermeasures do not physically affect the mines but aim at (1) localizing the threat by routing ships passing through mineable waters so that mine clearance forces can be concentrated, (2) locating the minefield by visual or radar detection of the mines while they are being laid, (3) altering one's own navigational aids to shipping to hamper accurate enemy minelaying, (4) detailed route and area surveying by

MCM vessels to produce bottom contour charts that show in detail the composition of the seabed and all objects on it, and (5) taking ship self-protective measures to reduce magnetic and acoustic influences. Ships' pressure influences are most difficult to suppress other than by special design. The only possible action a ship can take against pressure-influence mines is to proceed very slowly in shallow waters.

Active mine countermeasures are measures to attack the mine after it has been laid. The two basic techniques employed for this purpose are minesweeping and minehunting.

Minesweeping is the technique of countering mines by MCM vehicles using mechanical or influence gear. The former physically cuts the mooring wire; the latter actuates the mine. The mechanical method originally entailed a pair of minesweepers drawing a wire sweep between them through the water like fishing trawlers, with the aim to cut any moored mines free from their sinkers. The mines then could be destroyed as they floated on the water. The standard wire sweep today is deployed astern and on the quarter of a single minesweeper. Ground mines have to be swept by other means. Magnetic mines may be actuated by an artificially induced field created by an energized wide electric loop towed astern of the sweeper. Acoustic mines are triggered by a special acoustic noisemaker representing typical ships' noise signatures towed well astern of the sweeper. An MCM vehicle can tow magnetic and acoustic sweeps at the same time in order to actuate a double-influence mine of those types.

Minehunting is the branch of mine countermeasures based on determining the positions of individual mines and concentrating countermeasures on those positions. Minehunting has been developed over the last decades because it has proved to be a relatively safe and effective method of dealing with modern ground mines. The only way to ensure that an area is free of such mines is to carry out a detailed physical inspection of the seabed. Originally carried out by divers, minehunting can currently be carried out by MCM vehicles using acoustic, optical, or magnetic means. A modern minehunting system generally consists of an MCM vehicle fitted with high-resolution sonars for detection of minelike objects and a remote-controlled underwater vehicle for positive identification and disposal of the mine.

Mine Countermeasures Vehicles

MCM vehicles are divided into surface, subsurface, and airborne vehicles. They may be manned or unmanned, remotely controlled or programmed, and single role or multirole. Surface MCM vessels can be conventional displacement vessels, surface effect ships, or hydrofoils, capable of either single- or multirole sweeping and hunting. Subsurface vehicles may be utilized from submarines, primarily for minehunting. Special MCM helicopters can carry and stream their own gear for sweeping moored influence mines and for minehunting. Remotely controlled vehicles are defined as unmanned airborne, surface, and/or subsurface vehicles that receive their commands from a parent vehicle or a self-contained system. These vehicles can perform MCM tasks without directly endangering personnel.

Future of Naval Mine Warfare

Naval mining continues to be an important part of naval warfare, and it will undoubtedly find future application. Modern technologies in mine development lead to ever-increasing effectiveness in detecting and seeking specific targets and in resistance against mine countermeasures. The emergence of deep-water rising and mobile mines has vastly enlarged the area of the ocean susceptible to offensive and defensive mining against both surface vessels and submarines. To the traditional forms of mining operations has been added use by terrorists, emphasizing the psychological effects of this weapon of stealth. In the face of these developments, the future of mine countermeasures would seem an uphill fight, in which readiness in all respects should be the primary aim.

J. Jan W. van Waning

See Also: Antisubmarine Warfare; Blockade and Maritime Exclusion; Convoy and Protection of Shipping; Mine; Sea Control and Denial; Underwater Management.

Bibliography

Breemer, J. S. 1988. Mine warfare: The historical setting. *Naval Forces* 9:36–43.

Daniel, R. J., E. C. Pitts, et al. 1984. Mine warfare vessels and systems. *Combat Craft* 2(4):126–37.

Dicker, R. J. L. 1986. Mine warfare now and in the 1990's. *International Defense Review* 19(3):293–95.

Griffith, M. 1981. *The hidden menace*. Greenwich, U.K.: Conway Maritime Press.

McDonald, W. 1985. *Mine warfare: A pillar of maritime strategy*. Annapolis, Md.: U.S. Naval Institute Press.

Vego, M. 1986. The Soviet view on mine warfare. *Navy International* 91(March):176–80.

Watts, A. J., et al. 1988. Mine countermeasures. *Navy International*, June, pp. 279–307.

MISSILE, AIR-LAUNCHED CRUISE (ALCM)

A cruise missile is a small pilotless aircraft that may be armed with a nuclear or nonnuclear warhead. The air-launched cruise missile can be carried singly on small fighter-sized aircraft or in larger numbers on bomber-sized aircraft. Typically powered by a turbofan jet engine, the cruise missile has a range over 2,500 kilometers (1,350 mi.) with an approximate speed of 800 kilometers (500 mi.) per hour. Capable of operating at high or low altitudes, most cruise missiles can be expected to fly at low altitudes to avoid enemy defenses.

The cruise missile offers a number of options not found in other weapon systems. Cruise missiles can attack a wide variety of surface targets such as ships, fortifications, troops, airfields, and radar installations. In recent years this weapon has proven to be highly accurate and reliable. It can be used against soft as well as hardened targets and, in some configurations, can strike multiple targets. As a stand-off weapon launched outside enemy defenses, it does not expose the air crew to hostile fire. Cruise missiles can penetrate enemy defenses because the missiles are small, can fly at low altitudes, and can have flexible flight paths and profiles. Their low cost relative to aircraft, and extended shelf life can make them comparatively cost efficient. Small size and ease of transportation enhance carriage and launch from aircraft.

The cruise missile does have certain disadvantages compared with other weapons. After launch, the missile cannot usually be recovered for reuse. Each missile can typically be configured only for one mission (e.g., antiship, nuclear land attack, radar suppression). Compared to some munitions, like gravity bombs, the cruise missile is more expensive and complicated to maintain. Unlike manned aircraft, a cruise missile cannot be recalled from its mission after it has been launched.

Systems Components

The typical air-launched cruise missile has a torpedo-shaped fuselage 4 to 10 meters (13–33 ft.) long (Fig. 1). Some cruise missiles have folded wings and tail surfaces to minimize drag during external carriage, prior to launch. The forward portion of the missile usually carries an inertial guidance unit, a navigation computer, a target sensor (if so equipped), and warhead. In some missiles a submunition dispenser may be substituted for the single warhead. The center section of the missile carries the fuel, with the engine mounted at the rear. Depending upon desired range and type of propulsion, the fuel may be 50 percent of the fuselage volume. High-explosive warheads (unitary or submunitions) may use one-third of the missile volume. The engine and flight control electronics occupy the remaining space.

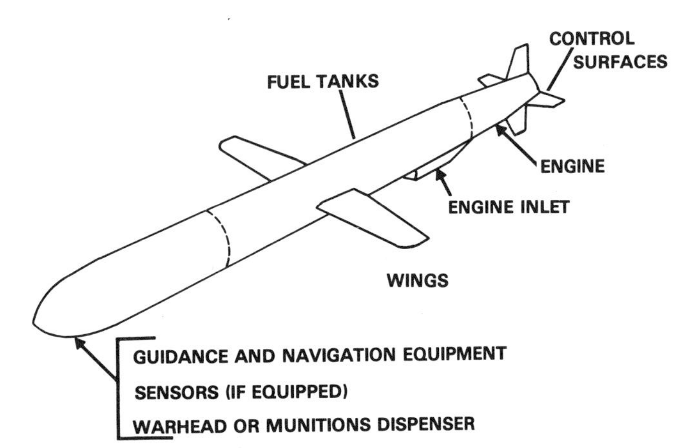

Figure 1. The generic ALCM.

Early Development

Since the advent of heavier-than-air flight, the concept of an unmanned flying bomb has been attractive because of its potentially longer range and the difficulty of defending against it. The cruise missile enhances the early concept of an unmanned flying bomb with an ability to maneuver around known defenses and attack targets from any azimuth. Development of a practical cruise missile during and after World War I was hampered by a limited knowledge of aerodynamics, unreliable engines, and inaccurate guidance systems.

During World War II, Germany developed the V-1 "buzz bomb," the first effective cruise missile used in large numbers in combat. The V-1 was one of the first airborne weapons to have a true all-weather, day/night capability. The V-1 was small (7.7 m/25.5 ft.), powered by a pulsejet engine, had an approximate maximum speed of 740 kilometers (400 mi.) per hour, and an operational range of 275 kilometers (150 mi.). A gyroscopic autopilot, using a magnetic compass and barometric altimeter, provided guidance. Although a ground-launched version was deployed initially, an air-launched version was also used. Typically a German He-111 bomber carried the V-1s to within 110 kilometers (60 mi.) of the English coast before launch. This procedure complicated air defense since a V-1 could approach its target from any direction. Despite this tactical advantage, the air-launched V-1 was less accurate than the ground-launched version. Only half of the V-1s that made it to the target area hit within 45 kilometers (24 mi.) of their intended targets.

Because of the missile's inaccuracy, the V-1 was not a successful weapon, but was significant in the development of cruise missiles. It cost the Germans one-third as much to build and operate as it did the opposing Allies in damages and defenses. Although one-third of the V-1s launched were destroyed before reaching their targets, the V-1 demonstrated the capability of a cruise missile to penetrate a highly concentrated defense. The V-1 also proved the concept of an unmanned, all-weather, day/night weapon. These factors showed post–World War II observers the potential of the cruise missile.

Post–World War II Development

Poor accuracy continued to be the major shortcoming in cruise missile development following World War II. A partial solution to the accuracy problem was the use of a larger warhead. The development of the hydrogen bomb in the late 1950s with its small size and weight (relative to its destructive power) made cruise missiles more effective. Through the 1960s, both the United States (AGM-28 Hound Dog) and the Soviet Union (AS-3 Kangaroo) used nuclear-warhead-equipped cruise missiles to supplement the nuclear bombs carried by their strategic bombers. The inertial navigation systems of these missiles were satisfactory for short flights, but longer range cruise missiles, such as the U.S. Snark and Regulus (I and II), were less successful.

It became apparent that long-range flight would require a means for navigation updates after launch, and a number of different updating techniques were tried in an effort to improve cruise missile accuracy. Radio control was feasible but was abandoned because it could be jammed or deceived, and was limited to line-of-sight operation. Astro navigation held promise but usually required a high-altitude flight profile so the missile could remain clear of clouds. The use of on-board radar proved to be a practical method for improving terminal accuracy. A number of countries developed antiship missiles that used radar to home in on the target. The French AM-39 Exocet, the U.S. AGM-84 Harpoon, and the Soviet AS-6 (Kingfish) are examples of air-launched antiship missiles in service throughout the world. The Exocet and Harpoon cruise missiles have proved to be devastating weapons. In the 1980s, British (Falklands/Malvinas), American (Persian Gulf), Libyan (Gulf of Sidra), and Iranian (Persian Gulf) warships suffered losses to these air-launched, antiship cruise missiles.

Current Systems

The use of terrain contour matching (TERCOM) allows the cruise missile (land-attack variant) navigation system to collect and compare terrain information with stored terrain elevation data. Terrain elevations are divided into cells, gathered to form a "map," and digitized into data usable by a computer. Each cell has distinct elevation data, which is combined in the cruise missile's memory. During flight the missile uses a radar altimeter to compare actual terrain elevations with the stored terrain map data. This comparison identifies the missile's position relative to the map and indicates any necessary corrections to the missile's inertial navigation system (INS). The development of lightweight, high-speed computers and the use of TERCOM updates has enabled cruise missiles to accurately navigate over land, for extended distances, with minimal risk of jamming or deception.

The use of TERCOM navigation coupled with component miniaturization, microelectronics, high-energy fuels, and small, efficient jet engines made possible the development of long-range cruise missiles. The overall size of the cruise missile was reduced while maintaining long range and good accuracy. This decrease in missile size and weight permitted an aircraft to carry more missiles without an unacceptable increase in aerodynamic drag.

In the 1980s the first of the current generation of strategic cruise missiles went into service with the United States Air Force. The nuclear warhead–equipped AGM-86B ALCM (air-launched cruise missile) with a range of over 2,500 kilometers (1,350 mi.) used TERCOM updating as an aid to en-route navigation (Fig. 2). During the 1991 Persian Gulf War, B-52 bombers launched conventionally armed ALCMs of this type (designated AGM-86C) against high priority Iraqi targets including power generation and transmission facilities and communication sites. About three years after the U.S. deployment, the Soviets fielded the AS-15 (Kent) cruise missile. The AS-15 was estimated to have similar performance to the American ALCM but with a range of 3,000 kilometers (1,800 mi.).

Using the American ALCM as an example, the following is a description of a typical launch-to-target mission for a long-range cruise missile. Prior to launch, the carrier aircraft (typically a bomber) transfers navigational and target information to the missile. At launch, the missile falls away from the bomber, the flight control surfaces extend, and the cruise missile begins its programmed flight.

The missile flies at altitudes controlled by barometric or terrain-following sensors. During flight, the cruise missile uses several TERCOM updates to correct navigational errors en route to the target. The first TERCOM maps used by the missile are large, which improves the probability of the missile navigation system finding the next map to update its INS position. The TERCOM maps become progressively smaller, yet contain the same number of cells as the larger maps. That is, the ALCM samples the same number of cells; but the cells are smaller, represent a smaller surface area, and therefore the accuracy is improved. This accuracy-funneling effect continues until the cruise missile reaches the target. The radar altimeter used for TERCOM updates also allows low-altitude flight to avoid enemy defenses by means of terrain masking. By

Figure 2. The U.S. Air Force ALCM. (SOURCE: U.S. Air Force photo)

planning the cruise missile's route of flight so that hills are used to block the signal from threat radars, the missile can thread its way through known enemy defenses to reach the target.

The flexibility of the air-launched cruise missile permits employment in a variety of combat missions. The route of the carrier aircraft or the cruise missiles can be changed prior to missile launch by substituting an alternate mission. It is also possible to change just the target coordinates for any or all the missiles. In this case, the reprogrammed missile flies most of the preplanned route before diverting to the new target. In some systems, to prevent unauthorized missile launch and to ensure proper information insertion, special codes are entered and must be verified before missile launch.

Even though Russian and U.S. strategic cruise missiles are very accurate (estimated to be 33–200 m/100–600 ft.), some military missions require greater accuracy. Antiship cruise missiles have a reported accuracy of less than 10 meters (35 ft.), but the radar required for this accuracy is susceptible to jamming and deception. An optical sensor mounted in the nose of the missile can overcome this limitation. Digital scene matching area correlation (DSMAC), another guidance system, matches a prestored digital image with a real-time picture of the target. Once the optical seeker on the cruise missile spots the target, it compares the prestored DSMAC "picture" with the actual image. This provides steering inputs to the missile to home in on the target. This type of guidance can provide a cruise missile with pinpoint accuracy. Similar systems can use infrared radiation (IR), instead of an optical sensor, to detect targets during darkness.

Attacking dispersed targets, such as individual vehicles in a column of tanks, would require several cruise missiles equipped with unitary high-explosive warheads. In the 1980s, the U.S. Navy developed land-attack cruise missiles that used a cluster of submunitions. The submunitions gave a single cruise missile wide-area, multiple-target capability against personnel, parked aircraft, or vehicles, without resorting to a nuclear warhead.

The cruise missile already fulfills a vital role as a decoy to distract and overload enemy air defenses. When equipped with the appropriate receivers, the missile can detect the presence of air defense radars. When a threat radar signal is detected, the cruise missile can spoof the radar, pass it by, or, if equipped with a warhead, attack it. Not only must air defense be able to detect a cruise missile, it must be able to do so without risking attack by defense suppression versions of the cruise missile. Examples of short-range, antiradar missiles are the French Martell AS.37 and the U.S. Air Force AGM-88 HARM (high-speed antiradiation missile). The USAF AGM-136 (Tacit Rainbow) is an example of a new breed of antiradar cruise missile. Designed to loiter (up to several hours if necessary) over the battlefield, when Tacit Rainbow detects the appropriate air defense radar signals, it homes in on the transmitter and destroys the radar with a high-explosive warhead. The loiter capability over the battlefield separates Tacit Rainbow from early antiradar missiles, which required the launch aircraft to circle over enemy defenses for extended periods.

Future Developments

The air-launched cruise missile has become a cost-effective, accurate long-range weapon. Compared with a manned aircraft, the cruise missile is cheaper to produce, thus allowing more vehicles to be built for a given amount of resources. In addition, a cruise missile does not require expensive (and extensive) aircrew training. Once launched, the cruise missile is difficult to defend against and provides an attractive alternative to a manned, penetrating aircraft. As air defenses continue to improve, however, the cruise missile must evolve to maintain these advantages.

Improved terrain-following capability is one possible enhancement to aid the cruise missile's capability to penetrate enemy defenses. A nonemitting sensor can be added to provide forward-looking obstacle avoidance (such as trees or power lines). Reduced radar and infrared signatures can make the cruise missile less vulnerable to detection by defensive systems. Countermeasures similar to those used on manned aircraft can be another option to confuse enemy defenses. In the 1960s, the U.S. Air Force GAM-72 Quail, an air-launched decoy missile, carried an electronic countermeasures package to deceive defensive radar.

Similar to the advances made in manned aircraft, major cruise missile components will probably continue to improve. Advanced composite airframe materials will save weight and therefore improve missile performance. Smaller, more efficient engines will allow a decrease in fuselage size. Exotic fuels, with high energy-to-weight ratios, promise to increase range, yet reduce fuel volume. Continued advances in computers will permit added capabilities without increases in space or weight. Advanced ramjet technology may permit the development of a long-range, supersonic cruise missile.

Advanced avionics systems promise even better performance and accuracy. Ring-laser gyroscopes, miniaturized doppler sensors, satellite navigation signal receivers, and various terrain-recognition systems all promise near-zero-deviation navigation accuracy. Millimeter-wave or laser forward-looking radars may permit nap-of-the-earth flight trajectories. These radars, when coupled with infrared or optical sensors and automatic target recognition logic, could give a zero-miss distance capability for the cruise missile. With the capability to recognize a specific target signature, the cruise missile may be able to attack imprecisely located, mobile, or camouflaged targets.

Cruise missiles could also carry reconnaissance sensors.

In this role the cruise missile could conduct surveillance in a high-threat environment without risking manned aircraft. When suitable targets were located, their presence and location could be reported via data link to the battle commander or directly to manned aircraft queuing for an attack. In another version of this concept, cruise missiles equipped with a warhead could not only locate suitable targets but attack them as well.

Arms Control Considerations

An area of continuing debate among nations is how to treat cruise missiles during arms control negotiations. Their small size and mobility make them hard to detect during storage and movement, and a wide variety of aircraft can carry air-launched versions. As demonstrated with antiship cruise missiles, the carrier aircraft, in most cases, has no distinguishing characteristics to identify it as a cruise missile carrier. As shown in Russian and U.S. strategic cruise missiles, external missile configuration may not make it possible to determine if the warhead is conventional or nuclear. The cruise missile's relatively low cost compared with manned combat aircraft, and its flexibility will continue to make the cruise missile a useful weapon system. Therefore, the cruise missile will probably remain a defense policy issue between advocates (who value the cruise missile's unique features) and opponents (who see these same features as barriers to arms control verification).

THOMAS D. PHILLIPS
ROBERT A. FRYE
MICHAEL M. ELLER
ALAN P. WILLIAMS

SEE ALSO: Airpower, Strategic; Missile, Air-to-surface; Missile, Cruise; Missile, Guided.

Bibliography

Betts, R. K. 1981. *Cruise missiles*. Washington, D.C.: Brookings.
Broad, W. J. 1984. Cruise missiles: What they are and do. *Current News*, Part 1, p. 6.
Gottenmoeller, R. E. 1987–88. Land-attack cruise missiles. *Adelphi Paper 226*. London: International Institute for Strategic Studies.
Blake, B., ed. 1987. *Jane's weapons systems, 1987–88*. London: Jane's.
Korb, E. L., ed. 1982. *The world's missile systems*. 7th ed. St. Louis, Mo.: General Dynamics.
Longstreth, T. K. 1983. Cruise missiles: The arms control challenge. *Arms Control Today* 13(1).
Simonsen, E. 1986. Winged wizards of deterrence (cruise missiles). *International Combat Arms* 4:36–42.
U.S. Department of Defense. 1984. *Soviet military power*. Washington, D.C.: Government Printing Office.
Werrell, K. P. 1985. *The evolution of the cruise missile*. Maxwell AFB, Ala.: Air Univ. Press.
Young, S. H. H. 1988. Gallery of USAF weapons. *Air Force Magazine* 71(5):187–88.

MISSILE, AIR-TO-AIR

Air-to-air guided missiles (AAMs) include all guided missiles launched from aircraft for the primary purpose of destroying a target in the air or in space.

Defensive aircraft are used mainly to counter aerial attacks, which must be intercepted as early as possible after the threat becomes known. Pertinent details about the attacking aerial target must be learned in order to direct the intercepting aircraft to engage it at a safe distance and use its AAMs effectively.

Air-to-air missiles were first developed in World War II. Early types had command guidance, with steering commands sent to them either along fine wires or via a radio link from the launching aircraft. The first AAMs in World War II were German weapons steered to their targets by signals passed along fine wires unwound from bobbins on the wingtips of the delivery aircraft. By the 1950s, the technology had achieved more advanced guidance enabling the AAM to home on its target by one of two methods of guidance: infrared (IR), or heat, radiation; or semiactive radar homing (SARH).

In recent years, the high speeds and altitudes at which modern bombers and interceptors operate have posed many problems to interception. The speed of combat jet aircraft has increased some 2–2.5 times and now exceeds Mach 2 and even Mach 3, while the ceiling of supersonic aircraft has increased to 30 kilometers (98,000 ft.) and more.

Against these advances are the facts that the ranges of cannon and machine guns are practically limited to a few hundred, or at most a few thousand, feet, and that once a bullet is fired it will trace a path through space that is governed solely by the physical laws of nature. It is these limitations, and the speed and maneuverability of contemporary aircraft, that have led to development of the air-to-air missile. Interceptors armed with AAMs now have the capability of striking at considerably longer ranges and with much greater effect.

Air-to-air Missile Guidance

First-generation interceptor missiles were guided by radio commands from the pilot of the aircraft. It was difficult for the pilot to perform this function while he was involved in aerial combat. Therefore subsequent guidance development concentrated on a self-homing missile that the pilot could release and then forget.

The flight path of the target is first observed by an early warning system. Ground radar picks up the enemy intruder at maximum range and tracks it along its flight path. Interceptor aircraft are scrambled and directed to the attacking aircraft by a control system tied in with the ground radar, thus bringing them into position to observe the target directly. The interceptor must be vectored into position so that the target can be detected by the interceptor's radar. Having searched the assigned sector and located the target, the interceptor must next, in order to employ its weapon, determine the target's range and motion. Once the missile is launched, the interceptor's radar tracks its position and commands for missile guidance are computed and transmitted.

There are three principal types of AAM homing:

- active radar homing, in which the missile tracks the target with its own radar, transmits energy, and homes in on the reflection of that energy from the target. This constitutes a fire-and-forget weapon.
- Semi-active radar homing (SARH), where the missile homes on the energy of the interceptor's radar as reflected by the target. No transmitter in the missile is required. The interceptor's radar also functions as a search radar in the initial phase of weapon system operation. The drawback to SARH is the need for target illumination by the fighter's radar. This makes the launching interceptor aircraft vulnerable to attack in return by a fire-and-forget missile.
- IR homing, in which the missile homes on energy originating at the target, such as the heat of its engine. The heat homer is also a fire-and-forget weapon.

The types of AAMs used and their weight, range, and guidance systems depend on the carrying aircraft, its mission, and the operating conditions. The missiles used to date have about reached their upper limit in size, since space for missile attachment in an interceptor aircraft is limited.

The aircraft and its AAMs should be considered a single weapon system, not as separate items. The interceptor has, practically speaking, become a guided missile platform designed primarily for launching AAMs against enemy aerial targets.

Advanced techniques are continually being developed in an effort to make the AAM interceptor weapon system more efficient and deadly. These techniques are concerned with warheads, fuzing, structural integrity under high-g loading, and guidance.

Infrared Air-to-air Missile

The most common method used for AAM guidance is homing on the infrared energy emitted by the hot engines of enemy aircraft. An IR-guided missile can be attracted by the jet exhaust of enemy bombers, or even by the heat generated by aerodynamic friction. IR missiles have hemispherical noses that are transparent to heat, and radar versions have slightly tapered noses that appear opaque. An IR-target-tracking sensor is housed in the nose of the missile, where it is protected by a nose cone of glass plates. The missile is also fitted with an IR receiver that can search for an IR-emitting target, lock on to it, and home the missile on its target.

The angular error between the homing head axis and the line of sight from the missile to the target is monitored, and a signal is generated to program the missile's gyro to reduce that angular error to zero; or in other words to bring the missile onto the correct line.

In the IR homing system, the missile has a sensitive receiver in its nose (usually cryogenically cooled by liquid nitrogen or some other cold medium to reduce background "noise") that detects the slightest spot of heat anywhere in its cone of surveillance. Some modern missiles have what is called a staring focal plane array in which modified optics focus the radiation onto an array of supersensitive cells that provide virtually 100 percent lock-on to the correct target. Most missiles use a miniature telescope that focuses on the feeble heat located by the detector and physically points toward it. The missile then steers itself so as to cancel the difference between the pointing angle of the telescope and its own axis; thus it keeps flying toward the target. The latest-generation seekers are even capable of detecting an enemy aircraft's cool areas against the slightly colder sky background. They can thus be used for engagement head-on or from any other direction. IR homing works especially well on a clear night, and such systems have been refined to the point where even on a scorching day they no longer try to home on the sun or its reflection; but the received signal is rapidly attenuated by snow, rain, or clouds. Soviet interceptors, for these reasons, usually carry a mix of missiles with different types of guidance.

Earlier AAMs homed on the exhaust gases of an attacking aircraft's engines. Thus they were successful if launched from behind the target. They were, in other words, pursuit missiles. IR missiles, in contrast, are capable of successful interception from any direction, sensing heat either from the jet engine and its exhaust in the rear of the target or from local airframe hot spots, caused by aerodynamic heating, when attacking from the front. This method of operation is intended mainly for high-altitude interception in clear weather or at low levels beneath clouds.

Second-generation missiles using more sensitive IR receivers could home from any angle. However, with the advent of ever higher-speed targets, the missile's homing head had to sweep through a widening arc, which increased both its cost and its complexity. Nevertheless the IR guidance system has developed to such a point that it permits target interception from virtually any direction against both subsonic and supersonic targets at any altitude.

The advent of all-aspect IR missiles changed the tactics of aerial warfare considerably, since it was no longer necessary to maneuver into a cone to the rear of a target to get off an effective shot. Tactics were also changed by the self-contained guidance unit of the IR missile. Once the missile locked onto the target the delivery aircraft could break away, greatly reducing its vulnerability. Earlier versions of the missile required active guidance all the way to the target; current weapons, unless affected by natural phenomena or electronic countermeasures, should be able to guide themselves to the target. All-aspect IR missiles were used to good effect by the British during the Falklands/Malvinas campaign and by the Israelis during fighting in the Bekaa Valley of Lebanon in 1982.

All recent models of the IR missile have had seeker heads of amazing sensitivity that not only lock on at great distances from the target aircraft and from any aspect, but also have improved performance in clouds and rain.

Semiactive Radar Homing (SARH)

With SARH, the fire-control radar of the launch aircraft is used as a target-illumination radar. The missile's homing head derives guidance signals from the missile autopilot, based on reflected radar energy received from the target. During the homing period, the SARH head generates flight control signals for stabilization and guidance of the missile on its way to the target.

SARH requires the launching fighter aircraft to be equipped with a radar that can lock on to the hostile aircraft. When the AAM is fired, its sensitive radar receiver (located in the nose and tuned to the fighter's radar signals) picks up the radiation reflected from the target and causes the missile to steer continuously toward its source. No matter how the hostile aircraft maneuvers in an effort to escape, it is outmaneuvered by the AAM until the missile either strikes the target or its warhead is triggered by a proximity fuze as it flashes past the target.

Many radar missiles feature semiactive homing, although they have the disadvantage that the launching fighter must continue to illuminate the target with its radar until the attack is complete. This restricts the fighter's subsequent maneuvering until the missile has impacted, detonated, or missed the target. Fighter radars are mounted in the nose of the aircraft and, like the aircraft's weapons, they point forward. Thus the only way to keep radar illumination on the target is to fly straight toward it, or at least to keep it within a forward cone of about 65 degrees.

The advantage of radar homing is that it provides reliable head-on attack capability. Radar homing guidance is thus often chosen instead of IR for all-weather capability and a longer target-acquisition range. To offset the somewhat lower accuracy of radar guidance as compared with IR, a much heavier warhead is used, thus increasing the range of lethality due to blast. SARH works better than IR over long ranges in rain and snow. Homing radars, both SARH and IR, also have a major advantage in that the homing signals get stronger as the target approaches.

AAM Active Homing Guidance System

In this system, the missile is launched from an aircraft (either an interceptor or a fighter bomber) against a target, which may be either an aircraft or a missile. In active homing the missile itself emits the radiation that is to be reflected from the target. The advantage of this arrangement is in part a function of the fact that emitted energy, such as radio or heat waves, falls off in proportion not to the distance, but to the square of the distance from the target.

Once the missile guidance system has obtained a target lock-on, the missile system is capable of independently generating a fire-control solution. Thus, as soon as the missile is launched, the interceptor aircraft is free to break contact with the target aircraft.

Combined Systems in AAM Application

Normally an interceptor aircraft is equipped with at least two pylons, and it is usual to load AAMs in pairs, one a heat homer (IR) and the other a radar homer. Thus the pilot has the option of choosing the appropriate version under existing conditions or, to ensure maximum lethality, firing both missiles of a pair in rapid succession.

The IR version has a much shorter range than the SARH missile. When the range is sufficiently close that either missile can be employed, standard practice is to ripple-fire the missiles in pairs, leading with the IR version closely followed by the SARH.

Every known version of Soviet AAMs, for example, is in service with a choice of radar or IR homing. This provides for the greatest lethality under whatever weather and other conditions prevail and also doubles the spread of wavelengths over which the enemy must provide countermeasures. Thus the Soviet AA-6 Acrid, when mounted on the Mig-25 Foxbat A interceptor, consists of four missiles—two IR homers on the inner pylons and two SARH on the outer ones.

Short-range Air-to-air Missile (SRAAM)

The SRAAM is a third-generation AAM designed for high reliability and low cost. It is visually aimed and guided by a passive IR homing system. Thrust vector control enables it to outmaneuver subsonic aircraft. The high-explosive warhead is detonated by proximity or contact fuzes.

The tactical applications of SRAAM are close-in interception and dogfight engagements. SRAAM can be used by heavy aircraft in self-defense as a "bomber defense missile," or by fighter interceptors as offensive weapons for use in attacking enemy bombers. The modern multirole strike aircraft, however, is almost as maneuverable as an interceptor. This has led to a need for a dogfight, or close-combat, missile. Such a missile does not need a particularly long range, but it does need extreme maneuverability to enable it to follow the target's twists and turns.

Close-combat AAMs are therefore designed to be as small and light as possible. An example is the Soviet AA-8 Aphid (IR seeker), one of the smallest guided AAMs, being produced as the air-combat missile of Air Defense (PVO). Carried by the Mig-21 and the Mig-23 on body pylons, the missile may have better maneuverability than any other AAM over ranges up to about eight kilometers (five mi.).

Advanced Short-range Air-to-air Missile (ASRAAM)

The BBG AIM-132 ASRAAM uses a gimballed IR seeker of advanced design and also carries an inertial reference unit, the latter used to fly the weapon close enough to a low-observable target to allow the seeker to carry out an autonomous search.

ASRAAM retains the wingless configuration of SRAAM, but it is steered by small movable tail fins. To date, no modern AIM combines a wingless fuselage with thrust vectoring. The French Matra's MICA combines thrust vectoring with cruciform wings and tail fins. The high maneuverability provided by thrust vectoring, particularly in the period just after launch, makes it ideal for a short-range missile. Its great weakness is that it can be used only as long as the power plant is operating.

Advanced Medium-range Air-to-air Missile (AMRAAM)

The medium-range missiles such as Sparrow, Skyflash, Aspide, and Super 530 all have SARH guidance. The longer wavelengths are certainly better suited to operations over long ranges (on the order of tens of miles), but the fact remains that even the largest and most powerful AAMs, such as the Soviet AA-5 Ash and AA-6 Acrid, are invariably deployed in matched IR/radar pairs.

In the air-to-air regime there has been developed a beyond-visual-range (BVR) missile, called AIM-120 AMRAAM, that is reliable and effective. Rather than homing directly on reflected energy from the target, the AIM-120 determines its own interception course with the help of target position updates provided by the launch aircraft, which increases the launch range (depending on the performance of the launcher's radar). But the crucial tactical difference between the AIM-120 and a semiactive weapon such as the AIM-7 Sparrow is that the latter requires constant target illumination, blinding the launch aircraft radar to other targets and precluding multiple simultaneous attacks.

AMRAAM (AIM-120A) originated in the United States as the result of a joint U.S. Air Force and Navy study and development project dedicated to finding a new BVR air-to-air weapon to replace the AIM-7 Sparrow missile. The AMRAAM program, with the ASRAAM project, forms an important NATO family of weapons covering future AAM requirements. The United States is responsible for development of AMRAAM, while European members of NATO are free to undertake development of a new generation of ASRAAMs.

An AMRAAM has been launched from a U.S. Navy FA-18 at very close range in a look-down nose-on attack. Prior to launch the AMRAAM received target information from the FA-18's fire control system. After launch the AMRAAM went immediately into the active mode, locked onto the target with its on-board active radar, and tracked the target drone to intercept, this despite the presence of heavy radar-return clutter from the ground.

AMRAAM will be compatible with F-14, F-15, F-16, and F-18 aircraft, as well as with Tornado and other air defense and air superiority interceptor aircraft operated by NATO. Its guidance system employs digital techniques based on a microprocessor and other engineering details, including a traveling wave tube transmitter and an integrated RF processor on the seeker gimbal.

The sequence of engagement occurs as follows. In the prelaunch phase the aircraft radar acquires and tracks the target while an on-board computer calculates launch acceptability zones and displays this information to the pilot. During the launch phase, after the pilot makes his decision to launch AMRAAM, inertial reference data on the target and the launch aircraft are fed into the missile computer to provide the necessary initial information. The AMRAAM is then fired and leaves the aircraft. The midcourse phase is carried out using inertial data. The terminal phase begins when the seeker transmitter is turned on at a predetermined point and the target is detected. The seeker then tracks the target and the missile completes the intercept.

AMRAAM maintains its course toward the target on a strap-down inertial system until, near its target, it activates a small active seeker in its nose. This may be a small radar operating on millimetric wavelengths at some 94 GHz. Laser scanning could be required to provide positive target identification, and clever fuzes will be needed to detonate the warhead as the missile flies at Mach 4 in one direction and the target at Mach 2 in another.

AMRAAM is a fire-and-forget missile. This will make a tremendous difference to the West's air combat capability, since it will not require the interceptor to illuminate the target before ignition of the missile's motor.

Long-range Air-to-air Missile

The true long-range AAM has a range of 180 kilometers (112 mi.) or more and a high altitude ceiling. It can be launched at enemy aircraft operating either well above or below the launching aircraft. The U.S. missile Phoenix, carried by the U.S. Navy's F-14 Tomcat interceptor, has a range of about 160 kilometers (100 mi.).

For employment at long ranges, there is no practical alternative to active homing, usually using radar wavelengths. The longer wavelengths are certainly better suited to operations over such long ranges. The AIM-54 Phoenix AAM is the first armament to offer BVR capability with autonomous (launch-and-leave) operation. Using it, the pilot who fires the missile can break away immediately and either make his escape or engage other targets.

Guidance of the F-14's Phoenix begins after it is fired in the direction of the target and is flying on autopilot (which in the new AIM-54C version is a strap-down inertial unit). When the missile nears the target, its own radar is switched on. The planar-array scanner searches and locks on, after which the missile homes on the reflections of its own radar. The AIM-54C model of the Hughes Phoenix was the first production missile to use software control. Analog circuitry used in the original AIM-54A version has been replaced by software-programmed digital designs. These offer stream raid discrimination, improved beam attack, and rear-quarter opening rate capability.

Effects of Stealth Technology on Air-to-air Missiles

Stealth features are designed to reduce radar and IR signatures, and modern avionics packages will incorporate significant stealth-enhancing technologies. Most attention has been focused on the use of RAM (radar absorbent material) coatings that absorb radar microwaves and reduce radar signature. Heat damping can be accomplished through a combination of air circulation and hot-cold air mixing. In addition, exhaust can be dispersed with thrust vectoring techniques.

Future operational versions of AAMs will probably incorporate design refinements to reduce radar cross-section, thereby reducing radar detectability. New aircraft will also incorporate stealth technology, making them less susceptible to detection and tracking by fire-control radars. Thus stealth technology will affect the guidance of AAMs and their homing by means of radar and IR.

Air-to-air Missiles for Helicopters in Aerial Combat

The recent trend is toward use of small self-homing AAMs for defense of relatively small and slow aircraft such as tactical helicopters and close-support aircraft. Such missiles must be able to lock onto their targets with no help from the launching aircraft.

The best counter to the helicopter is an air combat helicopter specifically armed for the task. Since 1981 the U.S. Army has been considering the possibility of offensive air combat operations using helicopters equipped with AAMs. Tactical helicopters are well armed for air-to-air combat, since they are capable of carrying the short-range IR-guided AAM.

Air-to-air Stinger is a lightweight system consisting of a launcher and missile weighing about 45 kg. It is used as a self-defense weapon for helicopters engaged in air-to-air combat. It provides a fire-and-forget defensive capability to army helicopters including gunships such as the AH-64 Apache. Current plans call for four Stinger missiles to be carried on each Apache. Each air-to-air Stinger launcher assembly is a self-contained unit, which includes an AAM that is either fully autonomous (possessing a fire-and-forget capability) or at least has autonomous terminal homing.

A particularly attractive missile now in advanced development is the French Matra Mistral, a close-range IR homer weighing only 17 kg and capable of reaching ranges of 300 to 6,000 meters (980 to 19,700 ft.) at Mach 2.6. The missile can be carried in paired tubes which, with sensor refrigeration, weigh 70 kg. The missile is instantly reactive and is fitted with a modern laser proximity fuze.

Among several novel alternatives is a new class of dual-role missiles with capability against both air and surface targets. Helicopter versus helicopter combat is still theoretical, but it is expected to be similar to tank warfare.

Warheads of Air-to-air Missiles

Most AAMs carry high-explosive warheads fitted with proximity fuzes, usually infrared-actuated. Since it does not take a very large explosion to put an aircraft out of action, the warhead weighs only about 30 kg. SARH missiles, being less accurate than their IR counterparts, tend to have larger warheads. Delivery of the warhead is, of course, the sole purpose of the AAM. The factors taken into account in warhead selection are the launching aircraft, the missile, the guidance system, and the intended target.

AAMs can be equipped with a variety of warheads, each designed for a different purpose. Among these are an isotropic warhead (or unoriented charge) that scatters fragments in all directions, a nonisotropic (or directional) warhead that concentrates its power in a single direction, a blast-type warhead, and a thermal warhead.

From the early days of experimentation with Falcon, Sparrow, and Firestreak missiles, the objective has been to bring a large warhead somewhere within lethal distance of a target aircraft, then use a sophisticated proximity fuze to detonate it at the point of closest approach. As a result, AAMs have generally been large and heavy. Even with the benefits of later electronics and other miniaturization, medium-range AAMs are not found below about 193 kg. The warhead of the AIM-7F Sparrow weighs about 40 kg and that of the AIM-54C Phoenix not less than 60 kg. Russian warheads almost certainly are heavier still.

Air-to-air Missile Fighting Effectiveness

When fighter aircraft were armed with missiles alone, some of their capability was lost. Without guns some fighters, particularly the early U.S. Air Force and late U.S. Navy Phantoms, lost much of their effectiveness. It is a truism a fighter should carry weaponry that is usable at all ranges and in response to all opportunities.

Historically, the ability to obtain kills has always existed. In Vietnam, however, the SARH Sparrow was difficult to use in close air combat and achieved a probability of kill (PK) per launch of only 8 to 10 percent. The heat-seeking Sidewinder did better, achieving a PK of about 15 percent, but it also suffered from a minimum range limitation (Fig. 1). The latest version of Sidewinder (the AIM-9L) scored a PK of nearly 70 percent when employed during the Falklands/Malvinas war, although it should be

Figure 1. A pilot, dressed in a flight suit, stands next to the heat-seeking Sidewinder air-to-air missile, 1956. (SOURCE: U.S. Library of Congress)

acknowledged that there were no major fighter-versus-fighter engagements or dogfights. No firm data are available for performance of the weapon in the Arab-Israeli wars, but it is believed that the PKs achieved were higher than those experienced in Vietnam.

Multimode Air-to-air Missile Operation

Ideally air-to-air missiles should be fire-and-forget weapons that home on their targets without further assistance from the launching aircraft, leaving it free to maneuver as necessary. The AIM-54 Phoenix missile carried by the U.S. Navy's F-14 Tomcat is a good example of this type, although it also has some drawbacks. These include emissions that can be detected by the target, alerting it to take evasive action, and the fact that it is the most costly AAM.

It is possible to construct an IR-homing missile for beyond-visual-distance interception. This would be an ideal system except for problems of target discrimination when flight time exceeds one minute. During this time a friendly aircraft could stray across the missile's path, presenting a larger IR source than the original target, and thus probably causing the missile to switch targets.

Technical trends in future AAMs will include a multiple target capability and multimode operation in the following features:

- long-range interception with inertial guidance, in-flight error correction via data link from the launching aircraft's radar, and homing head terminal guidance;
- medium-range interception using inertial guidance and the homing head for terminal guidance, the missile thereby being fire-and-forget and fully self-contained after launch;
- dogfight and close-range interception with homing-head lock-on achieved before firing and release of the missile from the aircraft. From that point the missile would be fire-and-forget and would require no further assistance from the launch aircraft.

The multimode operation requirement will probably be met by providing interchangeable homing heads so that a missile may be equipped with either an active radar head or a passive IR seeker. Both types would be comprehensively protected against enemy countermeasures and would only switch on a few seconds after commencement of the inertial guidance phase.

France's Matra Mica project is applying AAM multimode operational techniques and is expected to enter service in the 1990s. The missile's operating range capability is designed to cover ranges of from a few hundred meters to more than 50 kilometers (31 mi.), depending on the homing head in use. Weighing 110 kg, it will be provided with alternate patterns of seekers. The IR seeker will probably be used for aerial combat missions and an SAR unit for interception sorties. Both patterns of seeker will be used only in the last few seconds of missile flight, most of the trajectory at medium and long ranges being under the control of a strap-down inertial guidance unit. During long-range engagements the missile will be given in-flight updates by the launching aircraft.

In the past, AAMs have been categorized according to weight. Short-range dogfighting weapons have weighed 50–70 kg, while long-range interception weapons weighed 200–300 kg. Only the superpowers could afford to develop and deploy massive weapons such as the U.S. Phoenix (weighing 450 kg) and the Soviet AA-6 Acrid. In the mid-to-late 1970s, however, the concept of intermediate-weight AAMs appeared, the objective being to meet the conflicting requirements of the short-range dogfight and long-range interception.

The new concept of a single AIM suitable for all missions established an important requirement. It remains to be seen, however, whether the cost of such intermediate-weight weapons can come close enough to that of the lightweight dogfight missile to make it cost effective for that mission. New technology has made it possible to reduce the weight of AIMs of all types without degrading performance, but the effect on dogfight missiles has been minimal because such missiles must carry warheads large enough to destroy their targets.

In the longer term, weight reductions in weapons of this class would involve elimination of a conventional warhead, with the weapon relying instead on destruction by kinetic energy following a direct hit—a technique that would require both pinpoint accuracy and high missile speed. Should these be achieved, reductions in missile size and weight could follow, thus allowing more dogfight rounds to be carried on a single fighter. Even more significant, weight reductions would permit intermediate-weight weapons to match or exceed the range performance traditionally associated with heavyweight designs and thus put an end to the era of such heavy missiles.

Future Technology

Missile sensors, too, will undergo change. In the dogfight missiles, radar-based seekers are unlikely to replace IR designs, but in future short-range AIMs the IR sensor is unlikely to be of the traditional nonimaging type. Nonimaging seekers react to a point source of heat, but the recently developed IIR (imaging infrared) seekers create a thermal image of the target, locking onto a portion of this image by means of signal processing. Such seekers are more complex and expensive, but their future cost is likely to be reduced by new electronic technology.

Radar-equipped aircraft are vulnerable to detection and attack by antiradiation missiles (ARMs). The energy emitted by jamming systems could allow ARMs to home on the source. Passively-guided AIMs could, in theory, also be countered by the simple expedient of shutting down the target radar. Creation of an effective air-to-air ARM would require a passive seeker to be teamed with inertial guidance and a data link for mid-course updating.

Multimode Guidance

Active, semiactive, and passive radar seekers, as well as improved IR seekers, are unlikely to be able to cope with the most significant future threats, such as stealth aircraft and low-flying missiles. If these offer minimal targets to the radar and IR sensors carried by an interceptor aircraft, they will be even more elusive against the much smaller and less sensitive seeker heads fitted to AIMs. A possible solution is dual-mode guidance. An AIM could carry IR and radar seekers in the hope that a target that proves elusive to one might be detectable by the other. The U.S. Navy has studied the feasibility of updating the AAM Sparrow by fitting it with a dual-mode homing head that would combine IR and SAR seekers within the same nose radome.

The use of multimode guidance, coupled to data links for mid-course updating, offers a true solution to the problem of engaging low-observable targets. Using such techniques, the interceptor would be able to fly the AIM round under autopilot-inertial control, getting it close enough to the quarry to give its seeker a good chance of achieving lock-on. This ability to fly close to a target before engaging terminal guidance is already present in the Hughes AIM-54 Phoenix, and by the end of the 1980s it was expected to be available to the U.S. Air Force and other NATO elements as a result of fielding the AIM-120 AMRAAM.

By the mid-to-late 1990s, such a capability will be an essential feature in the AIMs of all nations facing a significant military threat. This type of multimode guidance is incorporated in several emerging missile designs. Matra's Mica will use inertial guidance in the early and middle stages of long- and medium-range engagements, activating an IR or radar seeker in the last few seconds of flight. Short-range firings will involve locking the seeker on prior to launch.

Air-breathing Propulsion

Current AAMs are powered by single- or two-stage solid-propellant rocket motors. The technology is relatively simple, reliable, and combat proven. Since an AAM flies for its entire trajectory in the relatively dense medium and lower atmosphere, it might be feasible to use the latter as a source of oxygen, replacing the conventional rocket motor with an air-breathing power plant such as a ramjet or ducted rocket (basically a solid-propellant ramjet). Such a system could be powered throughout its flight to the target, maintaining velocity and maneuverability, providing long range, and allowing for the use of thrust vectoring as a means of directional control. Until now, however, air-breathing power plants have not been used in an operational AIM weapon.

For short-range missiles, the solid-propellant rocket is likely to remain the best choice. Designers accept the complexity of the air-breathing solution only when long range is required. AAMs of the 1990s will use such propulsion to cruise at very high speed, about Mach 3.5, to ranges of at least 80 kilometers (50 mi.).

Sensors and Aiming Aids

At short range, when IR-guided missiles are being used, the seeker head can be used as a target detector, conducting its own autonomous search. A more reliable technique, given the likely number of aircraft taking part in future battles, would be to cue the seeker head by means of a helmet sight. The former Soviet Union, for example, adopted a helmet sight for use in aiming the short-range missile armament of the Mig-29 Fulcrum.

Performance of electro-optical-based sensors is limited by weather; equipment of this type would need to be linked to the aircraft's radar and fire control systems. To reduce the chances of a radar transmission's being detected, designers of fighter aircraft radars are now placing emphasis on low-probability-of-intercept techniques. Threat data can also be obtained via data links from an electronic warfare aircraft or a ground-based radar network.

The next step in air-to-air missilry will probably be development of a system of laser homing. The trend of development will always be toward the shoot-and-scoot type of missile. Advanced tactical fighter (ATF) armament includes both AMRAAM and ASRAAM.

KHEIDR K. EL DAHRAWY

SEE ALSO: Aircraft, Military; Air Interdiction; Electronic Warfare, Air; Missile, Guided; Missile Technology Applications; Radar Technology Applications; Sensor Technology; Technology and the Military.

Bibliography

Friedman, R. S., et al. 1985. *Advanced technology warfare.* London: Salamander Books.

Gunston, B. 1983. *An illustrated guide to modern airborne missiles.* New York: Arco.

Jane's weapon systems 1987–1988. 1987. London: Jane's.

ADDITIONAL SOURCES: *International Defense Review; Military Technology.*

MISSILE, AIR-TO-SURFACE (ASM)

Air-to-surface guided missiles include all guided missiles launched from aircraft against any target on the surface of the earth. Surface targets vary greatly in size, and may be stationary or mobile. Hence, the accuracy required of the missile guidance systems varies. The motion of the missile launch platform must also be taken into account.

Targets are often difficult to locate and identify. Stationary targets are frequently hidden; mobile targets may be camouflaged. Both types may be painted or covered so as to make them indistinguishable from their background. When observation is made by electronic means, suitable countermeasures may be employed by the intended targets.

The air-to-surface missile (ASM) is typically used against the most difficult targets, such as bridges, rail or road junctions, airfields, and troops on the march. ASM designers have for a number of years sought to create fire-and-forget weapons that, once launched, could find their own way to the target, leaving the launching aircraft free to take protective action or seek another target.

Methods of Guidance Used for ASMs

Television homing is one method of missile guidance. A TV-fitted missile can relay the pictures taken back to an operator in the launching aircraft, who then guides the missile by means of radio commands; alternatively the missile can use the TV picture to guide itself to the target, in which case it is a true homer.

Another method involves visual guidance to a selected target by means of a nose-mounted television camera and a data link over which both video and command signals are passed between aircraft and missile. A camera mounted in the nose of the missile is aligned to the missile axis, while the pilot is equipped with a monitor screen incorporating an aiming graticule. When the target is viewed by the camera and has been correctly aligned, missile release is initiated and the aircraft is free to break off. This method is used in the U.S. Maverick missile, which is guided by a small TV system in the nose of the missile. The aircraft's pilot chooses a target on a TV monitor located in his cockpit, locks the missile's electro-optical tracker onto the target, and fires the missile, which is then automatically guided to the target by the TV tracker.

TV guidance is of no use at night, under conditions of low visibility, or against camouflaged targets. Thus an imaging infrared (IR) guidance system for use with ASMs is being developed. This new system enables daytime missiles to operate at night as well by replacing their TV guidance with imaging infrared guidance.

With an *infrared homing* guidance system, the missile receives the IR emissions given off by a target and homes onto them. It is a useful method against ships, which have strong and distinctive IR emissions, but has more limited use against land targets. It can, however, be used against those land targets that have strong IR emissions, such as tanks, parked aircraft, and vehicles. The Maverick missile has an alternative IR homing head for use against land targets. The advantage of IR homing is that it can be used day or night and can detect targets through camouflage or under partial cover such as woods.

In *antiradiation homing,* the missile is fitted with a radar receiver that searches for enemy radars and, when it locates one, locks onto it and homes. The system was developed originally for homing on ground-missile guidance radars. In Vietnam the enemy managed to confuse U.S. antiradiation missiles by continuously switching from one radar to another; a missile was unable to determine which one to attack and often fell harmlessly between two radars. This problem has been overcome by recent advances in IR detectors.

In an *active radar homing* (ARH) system the missile carries its own radar, which searches for the target, locks on, and guides the missile to it.

Semiactive radar homing (SARH) is a method in which the missile is fitted with a radar receiver and the launch aircraft carries a radar transmitter. The aircraft illuminates the target with its radar and the missile homes on the reflected energy.

Laser guidance is currently considered one of the most accurate methods of homing. The missile is fitted with a laser-seeking receiver that receives reflected energy from a target illuminated by a laser beam. Most targets reflect laser energy. The reflections that the missile picks up are used to guide it to the target. The target can be illuminated by an airborne laser, usually mounted in another aircraft. As soon as the pilot sees from his indicators that the missile has locked onto the laser reflections, he can release it and turn away.

A *combined system* of guidance is sometimes used. The types of guidance employed depend on the intended range of operation of the missile. If it is intended for short-range application, the mid-course and terminal guidance phases may be combined and utilize a single guidance method. Examples of the techniques that might be employed for short-range air-to-surface missiles (SRASMs) include command, active, IR, and semiactive homing guidance.

If the missile is intended for long-range employment, distinct mid-course and terminal guidance phases may be employed, using two or more guidance methods.

Strategic ASM

Long-range stand-off air-to-surface strategic missiles (see Table 1) provide the capability of attacking targets from well outside the range of local defenses. Such missiles have nuclear warheads and are guided to their targets by an automatic and built-in navigational system. The missile carries a guidance computer and instruments or sensors that provide information concerning its own position.

The most common type of navigational guidance for such purposes is called inertial guidance, a system in which missile displacement is measured by the double integration of accelerometer signals. This approach is usually used in missiles following a near-ballistic or cruise trajectory. After the missile is launched, it is the task of the inertial navigator to measure the distance traveled by the missile parallel to its axis of reference. These measurements are fed into the guidance computer, which has been programmed with the information needed to correct any error in the missile's position by passing steering commands to its control system.

Tactical ASM

For supersonic air-to-surface tactical missiles (see Table 2), guidance is provided by radio command link using either of two methods of control by the launching aircraft.

TABLE 1. *Strategic Air-to-surface Missiles*

Missile designation	Nation	Guidance	Range (km)	Launch aircraft and remarks
AGM-23 Hound Dog	U.S.	Inertial	1,260	B-52; missile has 4-MT warhead
AGM-86B ALCM	U.S.	Inertial (CEP 90 meters)	2,700	B-52; missile has 250-KT warhead
Blue Steel	U.K.	Inertial with navigation update	2,500	Valiant, Victor, Vulcan; missile has 3-MT warhead

TABLE 2. *Tactical Air-to-surface Missiles*

Missile designation	Nation	Guidance	Range (km)	Launch aircraft and remarks
Bullpup B, AGM-12D	U.S.	Radio command	16	F-4, A-7, A-10, F-5; for use against hardpoint targets
Maverick AGM-65	U.S.	TV self-guidance, imaging IR, passive laser	22.5	
HARM AGM-88A	U.S.	Antiradiation homing	18	Homes on target even if radar is switched off
CONDOR AGM-53A	U.S.	TV remote guidance	60-80	
AS-2 (Kipper)	USSR	Radio command with active radar homing	180	TU-16
AS-4 (Kitchen)	USSR	Inertial navigation with terminal radar homing	450	TU-22, Backfire bomber
AS-6 (Kingfish)	USSR	Inertial navigation and active terminal homing	200	Fitted in Backfire bomber
AS-7 (Kerry)	USSR	Beam-riding with terminal radar homing	10	Fitted in the SU-19 Fencer fighter-bomber
AS-10	USSR	Electro-optical	10-40	
AS-12	France	Wire-guided with optical tracking	6	Helicopter
AS-20	France	Radio command with optical tracking	7-8	Mirage III, G-91, F-104G
AS-30	France	Radio command with either optical or auto IR tracking	10-12	Can be launched from one aircraft and controlled by another
AS-39 Exocet	France	Active radar homing	50-70	
Martel AS-37	France and U.K.	Passive homing radar	60	Mirage III, Jaguar, Atlantic
Kormoran	Germany	Inertial navigation. Active radar or passive radar homing	37	F-104G
Otomat	Italy	Active radar homing	40	

The simplest involves use of a control stick in the cockpit of the aircraft. The operator controls the flight of the missile to the target through visual observation of its flight path. Flares are fitted to the missile to aid in tracking it. The second method, based on a later development, uses a stabilized sight on the aircraft and infrared flares on the missile to provide a form of automatic guidance. Such missiles carry a conventional high-explosive warhead.

In a medium-range supersonic ASM, such as the U.S. Condor, automatic tracking of the target and manual aimpoint update are provided to the missile by a pod-mounted computer that is used to provide course corrections all the way to the target. The computer also provides a cockpit indication when the missile is within range of the target.

Air-launched Cruise Missile (ALCM)

The ALCM is a subsonic turbofan-powered aerodynamic missile designed to be launched from an aircraft. One of its objectives is to complicate the enemy's defensive problems so as to enhance bomber penetration.

The ALCM uses an inertial guidance platform and a terrain contour-matching system that periodically updates the missile's track to the target by comparing observations of the actual terrain being traversed with mapping data prestored in the missile's computer. This provides the missile with a high level of accuracy.

An ALCM carries a 250-kiloton nuclear warhead. Its maximum range at low altitude is about 2,500 kilometers (1,500 mi.), sufficient, for example, to reach 85 percent of potential Soviet targets from launch points outside Soviet territory. A B-52 bomber can carry as many as twenty ALCMs, twelve mounted on wing pylons and eight in the bomb bay. The ALCM is an excellent stand-off weapon for the B-52 because it allows the aircraft to remain outside air defense range while still striking primary targets. When attacking most targets, the B-52 would release its missiles from launch points 350 kilometers (217 mi.) or more outside a country's border.

Short-range Attack Missile (SRAM)

The air-launched SRAM entered development in 1963 and came into service in 1972. It was developed to assist bombers on penetration routes by directly attacking enemy early warning and air defense sites, thus freeing friendly intercontinental ballistic missiles to undertake other deep-strike missions.

The SRAM is a solid-propellant, Mach 3, inertially guided missile mounting a 170-kiloton warhead. It can be fired from the B-52 or FB-111. The B-52 can carry as many as twenty SRAMs, while the FB-111 can deliver six, although on typical operational missions each type of aircraft would probably be armed with four SRAMs.

As noted, SRAM is designed to attack and neutralize enemy terminal defenses, particularly SAM defenses. It has the capability of penetrating terminal defenses and striking targets while the delivering bombers stand off outside the range of enemy defenses. The missile can be launched from either a high or low attack mode. High-altitude launch provides greater range but also increases the missile's vulnerability to enemy defenses.

The new U.S. Air Force Boeing SRAM II (Fig. 1) is a replacement for the original Boeing AGM-69 SRAM. SRAM II is a nuclear-armed and rocket-propelled missile mounting an inertial guidance system. It can reach speeds up to Mach 2.5 and has a range of 55 kilometers (34 mi.) from a low-level launch and 160 kilometers (100 mi.) from high-altitude release. These capabilities derive from the missile's state-of-the-art Hercules motor. The guidance system, based on a ring-laser gyro inertial platform, is more accurate than that of the predecessor system.

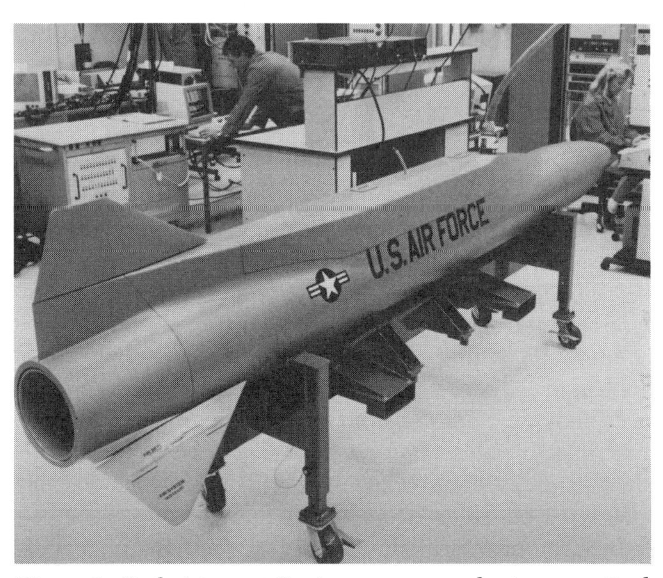

Figure 1. Technicians at Boeing prepare a short-range attack missile for a factory acceptance test. (SOURCE: U.S. Department of Defense)

A B-52H would carry a combination of SRAMs and gravity weapons, using the latter on primary targets and the SRAMs for both defense suppression and attack.

ASM in the Stand-off Missile Attack

A stand-off missile attack is employed to reduce losses to friendly aircraft by attacking enemy targets from stand-off positions, which means staying just outside the target's radius of defensive cover or even farther away, perhaps even in friendly territory behind the forward edge of the battle area (FEBA).

The operational and technical features of stand-off missiles are basically determined by the characteristics of the targets to be attacked, the stand-off ranges required, and missile speed. For attack of targets from different stand-off positions, the targets are classified as follows:

- fixed targets, such as airfields, air defense sites, tunnels and bridges, and railroad yards
- stationary but movable targets such as units in assembly areas; command, control and communications facilities; surface-to-surface missiles; and tactical headquarters
- moving targets such as main battle tanks, infantry combat vehicles, artillery units, air defense weapons, and the like

In the case of long-range missiles employed against fixed targets, especially those such as airfields that can be pretargeted, the key issues are timely availability of attack assets and whether to employ air-launched or ground-launched weapons. The use of stand-off missiles against moving targets depends on the availability of reconnaissance, surveillance, and target-acquisition data in near real time.

STAND-OFF MISSILE (SOM) SYSTEM CONCEPTS

Since the late 1970s, when the North Atlantic Treaty Organization (NATO) first expressed a strong interest in an effective stand-off attack capability for use against land area and point targets, a number of studies have been carried out addressing SOM system concepts, weapon system configurations, guidance and navigation techniques, propulsion and payload issues, technology applications, and feasibility aspects.

Payload characteristics and dimensions are important considerations influencing the shape and overall dimensions of a stand-off missile. The maximum weight of an air-launched SOM is of course determined by the lift capacity and structural limits of the delivery aircraft. When SOMs are intended to be delivered from a wide variety of tactical aircraft, the maximum allowable weight per weapon station is on the order of 1,500 kilograms.

An effective runway attack requires a payload of at least 500 kilograms in combination with high navigational accuracy. While an accuracy level of 50–100 meters (165–328 ft.) might suffice for mid-course navigation, the terminal phase requires accuracies on the order of a few meters.

Another important design factor is missile speed. Studies have concluded that subsonic cruise speeds are preferable for the SOM mission because supersonic speeds impose severe restrictions on shape and design concepts.

SOM attack of enemy armor in assembly areas, and especially on the move, presents two special problems that influence the development of SOM concepts. First, the need for real-time target data requires use of airborne sensors. In the case of a long-range SOM with its subsonic speed and long flight time, along with probable target movement during that time, the actual target position must be relayed to the missile in flight by an external reconnaissance platform providing mid-course updates. This requires coordinated operation of the reconnaissance platform, the SOM launch platform, and the information flow via data links. In the case of a short-range SOM, the sensor system aboard the launch aircraft can be used for target detection, with the missile being launched on the basis of aircraft-derived data. Whether post-launch autonomy can be achieved, or alternatively whether a data link between the missile and aircraft is needed, depends on future technological developments in navigation and terminal guidance systems.

Second, there is a requirement for terminal homing or sensor-fuzed submunitions that can destroy armored targets.

Today the development of an SOM attack capability, especially by long-range SOMs, against moving armor presents a considerably greater technological challenge than similar attacks against fixed targets. Much of the effort in SOM research has gone into development of guidance systems for steering toward a fixed target. Among the methods being used are pure inertial navigation; active mapping by radar or television; terrain comparison, also called terrain-profile matching or terrain-contour matching; imaging infrared; and digital scene-matching area correlation, which is a computerized way of comparing the scene viewed by the missile with "scenes" stored in the computer.

ASM in the Antiradar Role

Antiradiation air-to-surface missiles are used for the destruction of ground defensive radar installations. They were developed originally for homing on ground missile guidance radars. Examples of ARMs (antiradiation missiles) include such early versions as those used in Vietnam.

In the Shrike ASM (AGM-45A) missile the initial warning that the Shrike-carrying aircraft has been illuminated by ground defense radars is probably obtained from electronic countermeasure (ECM) receivers mounted in the aircraft. When within appropriate range, the Shrike sensor heads are switched on. Once target acquisition has been achieved, the missiles are fired. After release, the missile's radar receiver continuously senses the direction of arrival of radar radiation from the target and generates command signals that enable the missile guidance system to home on the enemy radar. Shrike guidance heads have been developed that operate effectively against early warning, ground control intercept, and surface-to-air missile (SAM) guidance radars, each of which covers a different frequency range.

In the standard ARM (AGM-78B), system operation is initiated by reception of hostile radar transmissions by the delivery aircraft. The received signal is processed to extract target location, identification, and threat data. A missile is then launched to home on the source of radar transmission. The missile's dual-thrust motor enables it to follow a variety of pursuit courses to the target where, upon detonation, it activates a visual marker to identify the impact area for follow-up strikes. The target identification and acquisition system installed in the aircraft incorporates sophisticated techniques for countering the various methods used by the opposing force to confuse passive radar-homing missiles by such means as regular or irregular switching off of the ground radar.

The AGM-88-A HARM (high-speed antiradiation missile) has sensitive seekers that can lock onto very weak emissions. It also has longer range, greater accuracy, and less susceptibility to electronic countermeasures than earlier systems.

The advanced lightweight antiradiation missile (ALARM) is a missile that pitches over after release and surveys a wide range of terrain, noting the locations and waveforms of all interesting hostile emissions. It then dives on a selected target, although special software enables it to shift from one target to another if the first should cease to emit or, in certain circumstances, to continue its attack on the original emitter location. ALARM weighs only half as much as HARM, so it can be carried in pairs or triplets on a single pylon.

ASMs Fired by Helicopters

The first combat experience with guided missiles fired by helicopters was gained by France during hostilities in Algeria. The French used their new SS-10 and SS-11 missiles against positions located in rocky terrain and against urban structures. These missiles were also employed in the fighting in Afghanistan in the late 1980s.

By 1960 a second-generation guidance method, known as SACLOS (semiactive command to line-of-sight), had been developed. The operator using this method had to keep his magnifying optical sight on the target. A sensitive IR goniometer (angular detector) in the sight measured the difference in angle between the line of sight to the target and bright flares in the tail of the missile, then automatically generated an error signal to reduce that difference to zero. This so-called TCA (telecommande automatique) guidance has been used on many later helicopter-launched missiles, including the French HOT and the American BGM-71 family of antiarmor missiles.

Almost all current helicopter-launched antiarmor missiles follow the same general principles and employ a hollow- or shaped-charge warhead; penetration of armor depends on warhead diameter, which is made as large as possible. Almost all contemporary missiles are also fired from a storage container, launch tube, or other attachment using the thrust of a booster motor that provides a powerful kick that brings the missile up to cruising speed.

The latest missiles in this category are the former Soviet Union's AT-6 Spiral which has a range of about 10 kilometers (6 mi.), and the U.S. Army's AGM-114A Hellfire. Both systems home on laser light diffused from the target, with the designating laser being mounted in the launch helicopter. The missile has an optical telescope located in the nose that feeds error signals through microelectronic guidance cards so as to operate its control surfaces. Further aft is located a hollow-charge warhead which, upon impact, fires its armor-piercing jet straight through the guidance section.

With missiles of this class it is possible not only to dispense with guidance wires, but also to adopt lock-on after launch as a standard procedure. Having established the presence and rough location of the enemy armor, the attacker can fire a succession of missiles from a helicopter that need not expose itself at all. Each missile is guidance-coded to a particular friendly laser designator, with the lasers being aimed at different targets.

The Hellfire originally followed a rather lofty trajectory that ran the risk of entering low cloud cover and losing the vital guidance lock. As the terrain for each firing cannot be determined in advance, there may even be a case for equipping missiles with some form of ground-proximity or terrain-avoidance system, or alternatively with a programmed memory, so that, should the laser signal be lost, the missile would quickly nose down to bring it back below cloud level. The terminal guidance system of the Hellfire Tactical ASM provides a launch-and-leave capability, thus enabling launching aircraft to reduce significantly their exposure to the target.

The attack helicopter's weapons vary, but they generally consist of antitank guided missiles, either optically or laser guided. Normally the helicopter comes to the hover position in order to aim its missiles.

Most antitank missiles are fired by helicopters or slow airplanes and fly to their targets over substantially horizontal line-of-sight trajectories. The TOW antitank weapon system can also be used as armament for fighting helicopters. Both the gunner's sight and the optical sensor are mounted on a specially developed gyro-stabilizer platform that gives the tracking and control system a constant reference surface. The missile is guided to the target by a joystick operated in the helicopter.

KHEIDR K. EL DAHRAWY

SEE ALSO: Missile, Air-launched Cruise; Missile, Guided; Missile, Intercontinental Ballistic; Munitions, Aerial; Precision-guided Munitions.

Bibliography

Berman, R. 1983. *Rockets and missiles of World War III.* New York: Exeter Books.

Friedman, R., et al. 1985. *Advanced technology warfare.* London: Salamander Books.

Gunston, B. 1983. *An illustrated guide to modern airborne missiles.* London: Salamander Books.

Jane's Weapon Systems 1987–1988. 1987. London: Jane's.

Sorrels, C. A. 1983. *U.S. cruise missile programs: Development, deployment and implications for arms control.* London: Brassey's.

ADDITIONAL SOURCES: *International Defense Review; Military Technology.*

MISSILE, ANTITANK GUIDED

Antitank guided missiles (ATGMs) are a crucially important part of the arsenals of all modern armies and provide infantry troops with an effective, flexible means to defeat opposing armor. The newest class of antitank systems, ATGMs have only been in use for less than three decades. Completely dependent upon electronics technology for guidance, these systems have matured in parallel with technological advances. Substantial improvements in electronics miniaturization, fiber optics, and computational components promise to increase further the battlefield lethality and tactical flexibility of ATGMs.

From the outset of World War II, when the efficacy of modern armor was clearly demonstrated in battle, militaries have sought to improve armor-defeating weapons.

As the quality and capability of armor protection increased, so did the caliber and size of antiarmor guns (which dominated medium and heavy antitank weapons during World War II), until it became apparent that their size and weight would soon become restrictive to efficient and effective use in battle. Weapons manufacturers, scientists, and military procurement officers began turning their attention to rocket-powered munitions that could be guided with the aid of electronics and improved sight devices.

Among the first ATGMs were the ENTAC (France) and the Cobra (Federal Republic of Germany) systems. Designed and fielded in the late 1950s to early 1960s, these wire-guided weapons were manual-control line-of-sight (MCLOS) systems. Effective to ranges of around 2,000 meters (6,600 ft.), MCLOS-type ATGMs were literally small aircraft with fins that more resembled wings, and the gunner controlled their flight much as a pilot would fly an airplane. A joystick apparatus and optical magnification sight permitted the gunner to keep the missile in sight until it reached its target, and to control the missile's direction through wires that played out during flight.

The MCLOS-type antitank guided missiles proved difficult for most soldiers to use—to fire, fly, and accurately strike an intended target. Almost immediately, weapons designers sought to improve ATGMs through automation. This spawned a second-generation ATGM, the semiautomatic-control line-of-sight (SACLOS) system. SACLOS-type weapons used computer technology to bring the missile from the point of firing into the line of sight of the gunner. As long as the gunner holds the center of the sight picture on the target, the ATGM will fly true. SACLOS systems, of which the U.S. Army's TOW (discussed below) is perhaps the archtypical example, were a vast improvement over MCLOS weapons.

Advances in missile guidance technology promise to soon provide a third generation of ATGMs that will be fully, or near-fully, automatic. Through combinations of fiber optics, miniaturized television cameras, lasers, and artificial intelligence programming, ATGMs on tomorrow's battlefield will perform with greater flexibility, survivability, and lethal effect.

In the following, a number of the most significant ATGM systems are described, including some currently under development.

Missiles in Service and Under Development

Red Arrow 8 (HJ-8) Antitank Missile (People's Republic of China)

The Hong Jian (Red Arrow) 8 ATGM, first revealed in the early 1980s, is a second-generation system designed by China's North Industries Corporation to engage tanks and armored cars. In addition, it can be used against fortifications and other battlefield targets.

Red Arrow 8 is a tube-launched, optically tracked, wire command link and semiautomatic infrared guided missile. The operator has only to keep the crosshairs of his sight on the target until the missile impacts. The missile weighs 11.2 kilograms (24.6 lbs.) and is fitted with a 120-millimeter (4.8-in.) HEAT (high-explosive antitank) warhead. It can penetrate 800 millimeters (32 in.) (static) and has a hit probability for a single missile of approximately 90 percent. Rate of fire is two to three rounds a minute. The missile is launched from a circular tube; four wraparound fins unfold as the missile leaves the tube. Its effective range is from 100 to 3,000 meters (330 to 9,900 ft.).

At least four versions of the Red Arrow 8 system have been revealed: mounted in the rear of a cross-country truck, tripod mounted, turret mounted with four missiles in a ready-to-launch position atop a Type YW 531 full-tracked armored personnel carrier (APC), and mounted on a pedestal in a four-by-four cross-country vehicle.

AT-2 Swatter Antitank Missile (USSR)

Swatter is the North Atlantic Treaty Organization (NATO) code name for the missile the Soviets called the PUR-62 Falanga. Of similar size to its predecessor, the AT-1, Snapper, but 29.4 kilograms (64.7 lb.) heavier, this is apparently a more advanced missile (probably in the class of the French SS-11) and certainly one with a different configuration. Control is by means of ailerons on the missile's rear-mounted cruciform wings.

The standard mount on the BRDM-1 armed amphibious vehicle carries four missiles mounted on rails. Radio command to line-of-sight guidance is employed; the command link has three frequencies to protect against electronic countermeasures. It may also have separate terminal homing (probably infrared) along with radio guidance that suits the Swatter for airborne roles such as armament on the Mi-24 Hind attack helicopter.

When deployed on the ground, Swatter does not arm until it is 500 meters (1,650 ft.) from the launch site. The Swatter launcher, as originally deployed on the BRDM-1, has a lateral traverse of 45 degrees. The most common version is that of four missiles in ready-to-launch position on the BRDM-1. In 1983, the improved BRDM-2 four-by-four amphibious armored vehicle was identified mounting the Swatter with a quadruple launcher.

The Swatter uses solid propellant and radio command to line-of-sight guidance, possibly including terminal homing, to reach a range of 500 to 3,000 meters (1,650 to 9,900 ft.). The HEAT warhead can penetrate up to 500 millimeters (20 in.).

AT-3 Sagger Antitank Missile (USSR)

The Soviet PUR-64 Malyutka missile (NATO designation Sagger) is more compact than the AT-1 Snapper or the AT-2 Swatter. The AT-3 (Fig. 1) was first observed mounted on the BRDM-1 four-by-four amphibious scout car in 1965. This version has six missiles under armor protection. When action is imminent, the missiles and

Figure 1. A Soviet AT-3/Sagger antitank guided missile. (SOURCE: U.S. Department of Defense)

their overhead armor protection are raised above the top of the vehicle. This model has been phased out of active service and replaced by the BRDM-2, which has an elevating arm that carries six Sagger missiles, also under armor protection and raised only when required for use. In addition to the six missiles in the ready-to-launch position, an additional eight missiles are carried in reserve. The Sagger has also been used in the air-launched mode from Mi-24 Hind helicopters.

There is also a manpack version known as the "suitcase" Sagger. It is carried in a fiberglass case with the warhead separated from the rest of the missile. The lid of the case incorporates a rail allowing it to be used as a launcher. A separate control unit includes a periscopic sight, control stick, switches for missile selection, and batteries.

Sagger is fired from a remote position, which allows the operator to be 15 meters (49½ ft.) from the launcher. A three-man firing team is normally employed, with a total of four missiles per team. Either one or two men may serve as missile controllers, each with a sight and control unit and two missiles, while the third man deploys ahead, armed with an RPG-7, to provide close-in protection. The Sagger is considered to have an effective engagement range of between 1,000 and 3,000 meters (3,300 and 9,900 ft.). Such a team could be deployed with four missiles checked out and ready to fire in twelve to fifteen minutes.

Client states of the former Soviet Union on occasion devise their own methods of mounting and deploying weapons of Soviet origin. The Yugoslav M-980 mechanized infantry combat vehicle has mounted two Sagger-type ATGMs in the ready-to-launch position, as has the more recent and very similar BVP M80A mechanized infantry combat vehicle. China's North Industries Corporation also produces a missile system similar to the Sagger (Red Arrow 73), which is installed on the Chinese version of the BMP-1, the Wz 501.

The Sagger uses wire-guided command to line-of-sight guidance with optical tracking. It has a two-stage solid-propellant motor and a hollow-charge warhead that can penetrate 400 millimeters (16 in.). The missile has a launch weight of 11.3 kilograms (24.9 lb.) and a range of 500 to 3,000 meters (1,650 to 9,900 ft.)

AT-4 Spigot Antitank Missile (USSR)

This designation was at first provisionally assigned to a man-portable, tripod-mounted version of the AT-5 Spandrel antitank missile, called Fagot by the Soviets. As employed by infantry, a Spigot section comprised three men who carried four rounds plus the sight and mount. Although the Spigot and Spandrel are similar, the AT-5 Spandrel is larger.

The Spigot sight appears to use separate optical paths to track the target (under control of the gunner) and the missile, with corrections to the missile's trajectory being transmitted automatically as a result of the gunner's tracking the target. Along with this semiautomatic command to line-of-sight guidance with optical tracking, the missile has a solid-propellant two-stage rocket motor and a HEAT warhead that can penetrate 500 millimeters (20 in.). The launcher weighs an estimated 10 to 12 kilograms (22 to 26.4 lb.). Range is 2,000 to 2,500 meters (6,600 to 8,250 ft.).

AT-5 Spandrel Antitank Missile (USSR)

The AT-5 Spandrel is deployed on the Soviet BRDM-2 armored fighting vehicle (AFV). It has five tubular launchers mounted on the turret, an arrangement resembling those of the HOT and Milan antitank missiles, and probably carries ten missiles. The BRDM-2 has a hatch in the roof immediately behind the missile launcher, presumably used for reloading. A rotating optical sighting and tracking head is mounted on the roof of the BRDM-2. The shape of the missile launch tubes has led to speculation that a gas generator is used to eject the missile before the propulsion motor ignites. The Spandrel is also fitted as standard on the BMP-2 mechanized infantry fighting vehicle (IFV), which also mounts a 30mm cannon.

The AT-5 uses command to line-of-sight guidance with optical tracking. It has a solid-propellant propulsion system and a HEAT warhead that can penetrate 500 millimeters (20 in.). Its range is an estimated 4,000 meters (13,200 ft.).

AT-6 Spiral Antitank Missile (USSR)

The Spiral was first deployed by the Soviet Union in the early 1980s on the Mi-24 Hind D helicopter, and was also in service with the armed forces of East Germany and Poland. The missile is believed to have a maximum range of about 8,000 meters (26,400 ft.), a HEAT warhead weighing about 10 kilograms (22 lbs.), and radio command guidance system, although some sources suggest it is infrared-guided.

AT-7 Saxhorn Antitank Missile (USSR)

This man-portable system, designated Metis by the Soviets, is believed to be their equivalent of the U.S. Dragon antitank assault weapon. It seems to have a range of about 1,000 meters (3,300 ft.)

AT-8 Songster Antitank Missile (USSR)

The Kobra (Soviet designation) missile is launched from the 125mm gun installed in the T-64B and T-80 main battle tanks. It is believed that there are two versions, one antitank and fitted with a HEAT warhead, the other antihelicopter and carrying a high-explosive fragmentation warhead. Both are loaded through the breech. The missile uses laser- or radio-command guidance and has a maximum range of 4,000 to 5,000 meters (13,200 to 16,500 ft.). It is believed to weigh 25 kilograms (55 lb.).

Swingfire Antitank Missile (United Kingdom)

Swingfire is a British long-range command-controlled antitank weapon system capable of engaging and destroying the heaviest armored and soft-skinned vehicles in service. The missile is wire-commanded by a operator's joystick control; change in heading is achieved through thrust vector control. The system's missile control equipment can be installed either in a vehicle (as in the AFV variant) or on the launcher pallet. The missiles come prepacked in sealed launcher boxes. Propulsion is provided by a two-stage boost and sustainer solid-propellant motor. The warhead uses a hollow charge and is considered powerful enough to defeat all known combinations of armor. Range is from less than 150 meters (495 ft.) at direct fire (300 meters [980 ft.] with maximum separation) to a maximum of 4,000 meters (13,200 ft.). Special features include ease of concealment and immunity to electronic countermeasures (ECM).

Dragon Antitank Assault Weapon (FGM-77 A/FTM-77A) (United States)

Dragon, developed by McDonnell Douglas for the U.S. Army and Marine Corps, employs a command to line-of-sight guidance system and consists of three main parts: a tracker, a recoilless launcher, and the missile. The tracker includes a telescope for use by the gunner in sighting the target, a sensor device, and an electronics package. The tracker is reusable and is temporarily attached to the launcher, which is discarded after firing. The gunner never sees the missile after firing.

The missile is ejected from the firing tube by a gas generator using a recoilless technique. When it emerges, fins flip open and the missile starts to roll. Thereafter, propulsion and control forces are provided by 60 small sustainers that fire in pairs on demand from the tracker. In operation, the gunner sights the target through the telescopic sight, then launches the missile. The tracker senses the missile position relative to the gunner's line of sight to the target and sends command signals over wire to the missile. As commands are continually received, the missile side thrusters apply corrective control forces. The thrusters are fired at appropriate roll angles so that the missile is automatically guided throughout its flight.

The missile has a shaped-charge warhead and, for the Dragon I and Dragon II versions, a range of 60 to 1,000 meters (198 to 3,300 ft.). Dragon III has a maximum range of 1,500 meters (4,950 ft.).

Milan Antitank Missile (French-designed)

Milan is a wire-guided man-portable antitank missile system. The current second-generation system, Milan 2, incorporates a semiautomatic guidance technique. The gunner need only keep the crosshairs of the guidance unit on the target until it is hit. The system consists of a missile in a container and a launcher. The container, which also serves as a launching tube, is mounted on the launch-and-control unit. This in turn can be either mounted on a tripod to be fired from a ground position or mounted on a pivot for firing from a vehicle. Milan also has a night-firing capability with the MIRA thermal-imaging device. Target detection is possible at a range of over 3 kilometers (1.8 mi.), permitting the missile to take full advantage of the system's extreme range. To contend with improved tank armor, the three nations collaborating in Milan and MIRA production (France, West Germany, and the United Kingdom) have evolved an improved warhead (the K115) that has an increased diameter of 115 millimeters (4.6 in.)—as compared with the 103 millimeters (4.1 in.) of the standard item.

Upon launch the missile is ejected from its container by a gas-driven piston, and the launch tube itself is disconnected from the launch unit and discarded to the rear. When the missile emerges from the tube, its wings flick open, imparting a slow spin to the missile, which coasts forward until, at a sufficient distance from the launcher to avoid harm to the gunner, the warhead is armed. An infrared TCA guidance system is built into the launcher/ sight unit.

The Milan uses semiautomatic-command wire guidance (SACLOS) featuring optical tracking of the target only. Infrared tracking of the missile and control by vectoring thrust of the sustainer efflux are automatic. Propulsion is provided by a solid-propellant boost and sustainer motor. The hollow-charge warhead can achieve penetration against a solid target at a maximum lethal range of 850 to 1,000 millimeters (34 to 40 in.). Range is 25 to 2,000 meters (82½ to 6,600 ft.), with a time of flight to maximum range of 12.5 seconds.

SS-11 Battlefield Missile (France)

The SS-11 is a line-of-sight wire-guided battlefield missile intended for firing from land vehicles, naval vessels, and slow-moving aircraft. Normally it is fired from a launching ramp, but it may also be used with a simplified ground launcher. The designation SS-11 applies to the surface-to-surface version; the similar air-to-surface version is known as the AS-11.

The operator acquires the target by means of a magnifying optical device. As soon as the missile enters his field of vision after launch, the operator commands it to his line of sight with a joystick. Tracker flares are installed on the rear of the missile to help the gunner track it. When the missile is installed in a helicopter or ship, the simple sighting device used for land vehicles is replaced by a special stabilized sight.

The missile is driven by a two-stage solid-propellant rocket motor and can be fitted with various warheads. It has a range of 500 to 3,000 meters (1,650 to 9,900 ft.) and a minimum turning radius of one kilometer (0.6 mi.). Using a 140AC warhead, the SS-11 can achieve a minimum armor penetration of 600 millimeters (24 in.).

Since 1962, the SS-11B1 version, using transistorized firing equipment, has been produced with a variety of warheads, including an inert type for practice. Among them are: the Type 140AC antitank warhead; the Type 140AP02 explosive semiperforating antipersonnel warhead carrying 2.6 kilograms (5.7 lb.) of explosives, which is capable of penetrating an armored steel plate one centimeter (0.4 in.) thick at a range of 3,000 meters (9,900 ft.), then exploding some 2 meters (6.6 ft.) beyond the point of impact; and the Type 140AP59 high-fragmentation antipersonnel type equipped with a contact fuze.

A variant of the SS-11 has been produced and supplied to French, West German, and Saudi Arabian forces under the name Harpon.

HOT Antitank Missile (Joint French-German)

HOT (*Haut subsonique Optiquement teleguide Tire d'un tube*) is a heavy antitank weapon developed by Aérospatiale and Messerschmitt-Bölkow-Blohm. The missile is a tube-launched, wire-guided munition using low-speed spin stabilization. Planned as a replacement for the SS-11 missile, it has a mission profile corresponding to a NATO requirement for a missile to operate primarily from vehicles (armored or unarmored) and helicopters. When the missile is launched, infrared radiation from its tracer flares allows a precision goniometer associated with the optical sight to measure the deviation from its reference axis, which is parallel to the optical axis. Any deviation of the missile from the optical axis generates an angular error signal that can be combined with an estimate of range (based on the known flight characteristics of the missile) to provide a measure of the linear departure of the missile from the line of sight. This measurement is then used to generate command correction signals to the missile, whose flight is controlled by means of a jet vane system. Once the target has been visually acquired, all the operator has to do is aim carefully at the target, launch the missile, and steadily maintain his aim during the missile's flight.

The varieties of vehicle types, both land and airborne, to which the HOT system has been adapted is extensive and includes: the M113 services APC with two tubes and eleven rounds stored inside; the AMX 10P APC with four tubes; the Panhard VCR APC with four tubes and fourteen rounds inside; the VAB APC with four tubes and eight rounds inside; and the Rakentejagdpanzer 3 with one tube and eight rounds inside. Among helicopters, the system has been mounted in the B0-105M PAH 1 with six tubes; the Gazelle SA-341/SA 342L with four or six tubes; the Alouette III (in trials only); the Dauphin SA-361H with eight tubes; and the Lynx, also with eight tubes. The HOT has also been fitted to light unarmored vehicles (Land Rover 110 and Peugeot P4) with a single mount.

The HOT thus constitutes a long-range, wire-guided antitank weapon that uses command to line-of-sight guidance incorporating optical aiming with automatic infrared tracking (SACLOS). It uses a solid-propellant booster and sustainer for propulsion and mounts a 136mm hollow-charge warhead (HOT 2 has a 150mm warhead). The system has a range of from 75 meters (247½ ft.) to more than 4 kilometers (2.4 mi.). Time of flight to maximum range is 17.3 seconds. It can penetrate more than 800 millimeters (32 in.) of solid armor in the HOT 1 version (the HOT 2 can penetrate more than 1,300 millimeters [52 in.]) and is also effective against composite armor.

TOW Antitank Missile (BGM-71) (United States)

Fielded in 1972, the TOW (tube-launched, optically tracked, wire-guided) missile is itself contained in a sealed storage and transport container that becomes a launch tube extension when placed in the launcher breech. After the breech locks, all electronic contacts to the missile are automatically closed and the TOW is ready to fire.

The missile contains two solid-propellant motors. The launch motor ejects the missile from the launch tube and is burned out by the time the missile has left the tube. Only after the missile has flown several meters does the flight motor ignite; thus, no protection is necessary for the gunner against hot exhaust gas and propellant particles. The flight motor is mounted in the center of the missile with its two exhaust nozzles mounted on either side, an arrangement that avoids interference with the guidance wires, which are placed at the tail of the fuselage. Steering commands are transmitted by two wires that uncoil from separate spools. Short cruciform wings in the center of the missile and cruciform rudder surfaces all unfold after leaving the launch tube. Missile maneuvering is achieved entirely aerodynamically—that is, without the use of jet vanes—so that TOW maintains good maneuverability throughout its flight. An electronics unit is mounted between the flight motor and the armor-piercing warhead.

After the missile leaves its launch tube, a light source in the tail comes on so that the optical sensor on the launcher, which is bore-sighted with the gunner's telescope, can track the missile along its flight path.

TOW can be installed in most vehicles capable of cross-country travel. Within the U.S. Army it is mounted on jeeps, the high-mobility multipurpose wheeled vehicle (HMMWV), and the AH-1S helicopter. Armored vehicles using TOW include the M901 improved TOW vehicle (ITV), which has an armored weapon station featuring two launchers, a daylight sight, and the AN/TAS-4 night-target acquisition sight. The M-2/M-3 Bradley fighting vehicle also has a twin-tube retractable installation on the side of its turret, the tubes being retracted during loading and traveling. The M-2 infantry fighting vehicle carries five reload rounds; the M-3 cavalry fighting vehicle has ten reloads.

TOW is considered a heavy antitank guided-weapon system. It relies for guidance on automatic missile tracking and command guidance from an optical target tracker, using wire-guidance control of gas-operated aerodynamic surfaces. The warhead is a HEAT shaped charge. The system has a minimum range of 65 meters (214½ ft.) and a maximum range of 3,750 meters (12,375 ft.). Its crew of four can achieve a rate of fire of three launches in 90 seconds.

The first phase of development of an upgraded TOW involved an improved warhead with a diameter of 127 millimeters (5 in.) intended to increase armor penetration. Of the same size and weight as the standard TOW warhead, it features an improved design. This version was called the improved TOW (ITOW) and featured an extensible nose probe to provide optimum stand-off detonation distance so as to gain maximum effect from the hollow-charge warhead.

The second phase of development produced TOW 2, which incorporates a heavier warhead of still greater penetration performance with a diameter of 152 millimeters (6 in.). This occupies the full diameter of the missile body. In this version the missile guidance system has also been improved by use of a subsystem in which the analog computer is replaced by dual digital microprocessors to give greater flexibility in guidance programming as well as higher accuracy. To compensate for this added weight, the missile motor has an improved propellant that provides a 30 percent higher impulse. The TAS-4 sight has also been modified to function as a total independent guidance loop, and a high-intensity thermal beacon has been added to the end of the missile.

An improved version of TOW 2, the TOW 2A, has a tandem warhead designed to defeat reactive armor, a small warhead being added in the missile probe.

Hellfire Modular Missile (United States)

The Hellfire modular antiarmor weapon, originally developed for use from ground attack helicopters in the antitank role, has also been fired in the ground-launched mode during U.S. Army tests. The ground vehicle used was a one-ton pickup truck on which twin Hellfire launcher rails were pedestal mounted together with the fire-control equipment. Modifications to the vehicle were minimal and consisted simply of installing the launcher pedestal, its azimuth and elevation controls, storage racks for six missiles, and a special firing panel.

As originally operated in the air-launched mode, Hellfire used a laser seeker to home onto reflected energy from either an airborne or a ground laser target designator, but combined infrared/radio frequency (IR/RF) and imaging infrared seekers are being developed for the system and will give the missile a wide range of delivery modes, including engagement from defilade. The missile has a range of 7,000 meters (23,100 ft.) and uses tandem twin shaped-charge warheads. The air-launched version is in production and in service with the U.S. Army. An antishipping version has been tested, and the ground-launched version is also available.

KAM-9 (Type 79) Battlefield Missile (Japan)

This system (also known as the Type 79 Jyu-MAT, or heavy missile, antitank) is an extended range SACLOS antitank weapon. It can be used against both armored vehicles on land and armored watercraft. The missile is launched from a tubular container that is also used for transport and storage. A solid-propellant launch motor ejects the missile from the container to a safe distance from the operator, after which the flight motor ignites and accelerates the missile to its cruising speed of 200 meters (660 ft.) per second in a few seconds.

The Type 79 has been designed as a defensive weapon to engage the landing craft of an amphibious assault force, as well as to be employed against tank targets. A special warhead was designed to accommodate this dual role. It is basically a HEAT round incorporating an enhanced fragmentation effect. Two types of fuzes are employed, a contact fuze with a piezo-electric element for the antitank role and a variable delay fuze for the antiship mission.

Prior to firing, the missile container is placed on the launcher, which comprises the firing control device, missile checkout, tracking mechanism, and built-in sight unit. The optical sighting device is designed to be operated by one man. During the missile's flight the operator simply keeps the optical sight trained on the target. Sensors then translate course deviations to electrical signals that are fed into a computer. The computer then calculates necessary course corrections and feeds them into the missile through its guidance cable. Instead of the usual flare for infrared missile tracking, a xenon lamp is used as the infrared source for the Type 79. The lamp is powered by a thermal battery, which also provides electrical power for the missile guidance system. The launching system also features two operational modes, direct and separate firing.

A complete Type 79 firing unit consists of two launcher units, a sight unit, a control/guidance electronics unit, and a connecting cable reel. Each launcher is normally mounted on a tripod and one of them also carries the sight. The second launcher may be sited up to 50 meters (165 ft.) away from the sight; it is remotely operated by a connecting cable. This remote capability, coupled with the use of smokeless rocket motors, offers the operating crew good protection from enemy counterfire and provides enhanced operational flexibility. The missile has a maximum range of 4,000 meters (13,200 ft.)

RBS 56 Bill Antitank Missile (Sweden)

Bofors has developed a light antitank missile, designated RBS 56 and called Bill, for the Swedish army. Development was carried out in close cooperation with the Swedish army.

The RBS 56 is a wire-guided command to line-of-sight weapon with an effective range capability from 150 to 2,000 meters (495 to 6,600 ft.). It is fired from a container/launcher tube that can be either tripod or vehicle mounted. A sight that provides for both day and night operation is carried separately and attached to the container tube before launching. The manufacturer states that preparations for launching can be completed in twenty seconds. Propulsion is provided by a solid-propellant rocket motor that exhausts through nozzles located around the circumference of the missile body to the rear of the sustainer motor, which is housed in the nose section. Cruciform wings and control surfaces, located in the tail section (where there is also a tracking signal transmitter), flip out after launch.

The missile carries a shaped-charge HEAT warhead normally detonated by a delayed proximity fuze. The missile trajectory is automatically maintained at a height of approximately one meter (3.3 ft.) above the gunner's line of sight to the target; this is said to result in a higher kill probability in that the chances of striking the less heavily armored upper surfaces of a tank are increased while the angle of approach of the warhead means that it is less likely to strike a sloping surface at a shallow, glancing angle, thereby enhancing penetration characteristics. The angle of attack also ensures that, even when sloping surfaces are encountered, the thickness of armor to be penetrated is effectively lessened.

The system has a combat range of 150 to 2,000 meters (495 to 6,600 ft.) against stationary targets and 300 to 2,000 meters (990 to 6,600 ft.) against moving targets with a crossing speed of 10 meters (33 ft.) per second. Flight time to maximum range is eleven seconds.

MSS 1.1/MAF Antitank Missile (Italy)

The MSS 1.1 is based on the Italian OTO Melara laser-guided antitank guided weapon. It is a man-portable system that can also be installed on light vehicles such as jeeps. Although its primary role is antitank, it has a secondary role against battlefield fortifications and hovering helicopters.

The complete system consists of the missile in its container, which also acts as the launcher, and a firing post that includes an adjustable tripod, projector, and sighting system. The missile has a two-stage solid-propellant rocket motor. The first stage completes its burn inside the launcher, providing sufficient power to get the missile out of the launcher. Then, at a safe distance from the operator, the second stage ignites and boosts the missile to its maximum speed. In good weather and light conditions an optical sight is employed, while a thermal imaging sight permits night operation.

This 130-millimeter (52-in.) missile weighs 14.5 kilograms (31.9 lbs.). It uses a HEAT warhead and has a maximum all-weather range of 2,000 meters (6,600 ft.), increased in fair weather to 3,000 meters (9,900 ft.); minimum range is 70 meters (231 ft.). Time of flight to the longest range is 16 seconds. At ranges of over 400 meters (1,320 ft.) the missile has a hit probability of 95 percent. Reaction time from initial target acquisition is two seconds.

MAPATS Antitank Missile (Israel)

The systems division of Israel Military Industries, faced with a requirement for a new antitank missile capable of challenging existing and anticipated generations of new armor, developed a weapon system designated MAPATS. The MAPATS employs missile body and control surface arrangements similar to those of the TOW, but it uses an entirely different guidance technique and is thus more than merely an improved version of TOW.

The MAPATS system consists of an infrared beam–riding missile and a launcher/sight unit. It is fired from a crew-transportable launcher. The missile's fiberglass container forms part of the launcher system. Upon launch, the missile follows a laser-generated beam that is pointed at the target by the gunner. The system is said to be immune to jamming and completely automatic. The gunner has only to maintain the crosshairs on the target until the missile hits.

The main components of the launcher unit are the beam generator, a tripod, a traversing unit, the launch tube, and an electronics unit including batteries. The combined weight is less than 70 kilograms (154 lb.). The missile can be installed on a jeep, an M113 APC, or on a variety of other armored vehicles, including tanks.

The missile mounts a hollow-charge warhead weighing 3.6 kilograms (7.9 lb.) that can penetrate 800 millimeters (32 in.). It has a minimum range of 65 meters (214½ ft.)

and a maximum range of 4,500 meters (14,850 ft.). Missile flight time to maximum range is 23.5 seconds.

Antitank Guided Missile Developments

Advanced Antitank Missile System—Medium (AAWS-M) (United States)

This system is intended to be a one-man portable weapon employed at infantry platoon level to defeat existing and anticipated tanks under conditions of day or night, including smoke and dust. It is designed to replace the Dragon and will have superior lethality and range, as well as a shorter time of flight. The operator will also be less vulnerable, and the launch signature will be less than that of the Dragon.

Three guidance technologies are under consideration. Ford's system is a shoulder-mounted missile, called Topkick, in which the operator directs the flight of the missile by sighting directly on the target. The missile is then guided by a low-intensity laser beam emitted by the projectile and the operator's line of sight. The system will engage the target by the top-attack method using two fuzed warheads.

The Hughes system consists of a missile, with a medium-wave infrared staring focal plane array seeker, in a disposable launch tube accompanied by a reusable command and launch unit.

Texas Instruments is proposing a fire-and-forget system using an infrared seeker. The missile would feature two attack modes, top attack for use against armor and direct attack for use against helicopters and fortifications.

Advanced Antitank Missile System—Heavy (AAWS-H) (United States)

The U.S. Army planned to inaugurate in fiscal year 1988 a program for development of the AAWS-H, actually compromising three weapon systems: one, a TOW replacement, another a kinetic-energy kill (KEK) weapon, the third a FOG-M with fiber-optic guidance. The TOW replacement is designated the advanced missile system—heavy (AMS-H). The KEK system is based on the LTV high-velocity missile (HVM); its missile will be a beam rider traveling at 1,500 meters (4,950 ft.) per second. The electro-optical suite would include a thermal imager.

TRIGAT Program (Joint British-French-German)

The British, French, and German governments have decided to collaborate on development of two antitank missiles to meet their national requirements. These are versions of the so-called third-generation antitank (TRIGAT) missile, also known as PARS-3, ATGW3, and AC3G.

Two basic versions of the missile will be developed, a medium-range system (ATGW3-MR) to replace Milan and a long-range system (ATGW3-LR) to replace HOT, Swingfire, and TOW. The ATGW3-MR will be an infantry-portable system weighing about 16 kilograms (35.2 lb.) and designed to attack targets at ranges of up to 2 kilometers (1.2 mi.). It will feature an optical beam–riding missile.

The long-range missile (ATGW3-LR) will be constructed largely of plastic and will involve a conventional cruciform layout with folding wings and fins. It will be a diving attack missile designed to engage targets at ranges of about 5 kilometers (3 mi.) using an as yet unspecified but very advanced warhead reported to be of the forward-facing tandem design. The missile will also feature an imaging infrared homing seeker for automatic target tracking. It will be capable of salvo fire against multiple targets. Both helicopter-launched and ground-launched versions are planned.

Conclusion

ATGMs provide infantry troops their best defense against enemy tanks and armored fighting vehicles. The continuing improvements in range, accuracy, and lethality provide a weapon that can be employed with great flexibility to support a variety of combat missions. Thus, there can be no doubt that active research and development will continue to characterize the field of antitank guided missiles.

Just how effective ATGMs will continue to be against tanks remains to be seen. But their effectiveness has been on the upswing since their inception, and it is likely to continue. As these relatively cost-effective weapons proliferate in the world's militaries, it is well to consider that they may constitute a new "killing power" for the infantry, a capability that could alter the shape of tomorrow's battlefields.

Alaa El Din Abdel Meguid Darwish

See Also: Armor; Armor Technology; Gun, Antitank; Missile, Guided; Missile Propulsion Technology; Rocket, Antiarmor; Tank.

Bibliography

Lee, R. G., et al. 1988. *Guided weapons*. Vol. 1 of *Land warfare: Brassey's new battlefield weapons systems and technology series*. London: Brassey's.

Jane's weapon systems, 1988–1989. 1988. London: Jane's.

Additional sources: *Armada International; Military Technology*.

MISSILE, BALLISTIC

Ballistic missiles are a part of a family of guided missiles classified as "surface-to-surface" missiles. They are commonly subdivided into four classes, based on the range of the missiles.

The four range classes of ballistic missiles are conventionally defined as follows: short-range ballistic missiles (SRBMs)—up to 480 kilometers (300 mi.); medium-range ballistic missiles (MRBMs)—480–965 kilometers (300–600 mi.); intermediate-range ballistic missiles (IRBMs)—965–5,310 kilometers (600–3,300 mi.); and intercontinental ballistic missiles (ICBMs)—more than 5,310 kilometers (3,300 mi.). Ballistic missiles are also classified according to their basing mode: for example, ground-launched ICBMs and submarine-launched ballistic missiles (SLBMs).

The ballistic trajectory includes a boost phase, a mid-course phase, and a terminal phase. In the boost phase the missile is propelled by a rocket motor to the required velocity. In the mid-course phase the missile coasts on a path that is determined by the effects of the earth's gravity. In the terminal phase, also called the re-entry phase for ballistic missiles that ascend above the earth's atmosphere, the missile descends to its target. For multiple, independently targeted re-entry vehicle (MIRV) ballistic missiles, a fourth phase is added, the post-boost phase, during which the multiple re-entry vehicles (RVs) are unloaded from the bus.

Ballistic missiles may be either unguided or guided, but common usage of the term places them in the family of guided missiles. Since the definition of ballistic missiles is based on the missile trajectory, guided and unguided ballistic missiles are generically related; they obey the same Newtonian laws of physics in their flight paths from launch to target impact. Guidance of ballistic missiles generally occurs only in the boost phase, using inertial guidance. An exception is the case of ballistic missiles equipped with terminal guidance to improve their accuracy or to evade antiballistic missiles.

A ballistic missile is propelled to a predetermined velocity and aimed in azimuth and elevation. Figure 1 illustrates four ballistic missile trajectories, in altitude and range, for three different elevation angles and two different velocities. These trajectories neglect the effects of drag caused by the earth's atmosphere.

Under the ideal conditions assumed for the ballistic trajectories in Figure 1, the maximum range attainable for a given velocity is for a 45-degree elevation angle. The figure shows that either a lower angle (30 degrees) or a higher angle (75 degrees) results in a shorter range for the same velocity. Range can be increased by increasing the velocity, as shown by the 45-degree trajectory of a missile with a higher velocity (dotted line). The velocities labeled for these trajectories are maximum velocities achieved during the flight time of the missiles, commonly referred to as end-of-boost, or burnout, velocities.

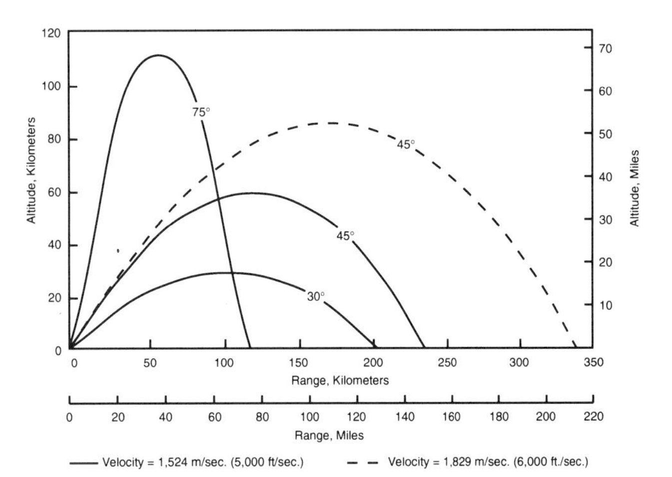

Figure 1. Ballistic missile trajectories.

The accuracy of a ballistic missile is determined by the accuracy of the velocity imparted and the control of direction in the elevation and azimuth planes. It is commonly expressed in circular error probable (CEP), which is a statistical term for the radius of a circle within which 50 percent of the missiles fired will impact. Thus, a CEP of 1 kilometer means that 50 percent of the missiles fired will impact within a circle of 1-kilometer radius and the other 50 percent will impact outside of a circle of this radius. It has been reported in unclassified sources that the CEP of the MX Peacekeeper missile, the latest generation U.S. ICBM, is 120 meters (400 ft.) for its ten nuclear warheads over a range of 9,650 kilometers (6,000 mi.), equivalent to hitting a 1-meter target at a range of 80 kilometers (about a 3-foot-radius target at a range of 50 mi.).

History and Significance

Developments Since World War II

The forerunner of modern ballistic missile weapons was the V-2, developed in Germany during World War II. It was the first long-range ballistic missile, operating at supersonic speed, to be put into operational use against an enemy. The V-2 used a liquid-propellant rocket motor and inertial guidance, and had a range of 240 to 370 kilometers (150 to 230 mi.).

Following World War II, the U.S. Army developed a succession of SRBMs and MRBMs, including the Redstone and the Corporal in the late 1940s, the Sergeant in the 1960s, and the Pershing in the 1970s. The Jupiter and Thor IRBMs were developed in parallel by the U.S. Army and the U.S. Air Force in the late 1950s. Along with the guided ballistic missile developments, the U.S. Army developed two SRBM unguided ballistic missiles (free-flight rockets), the Honest John and the Little John in the 1950s. A derivation of the Redstone missile was used to launch the free world's first satellite into orbit in 1958.

The concept of an intercontinental ballistic missile, long a dream of military planners, received impetus in 1954 from the confluence of two technologies. The first was the development of the thermonuclear bomb, with destructive power measured in megatons (millions of tons of TNT) and of a size compatible with projected rocket propulsion systems. The other was the emergence of inertial guidance systems that had the accuracy and the potential for miniaturization to deliver thermonuclear warheads close to a target at intercontinental ranges.

The first ICBMs were the U.S. Atlas and Titan, developed in parallel, and first tested in 1958 and 1959, respectively. Both Titan and Atlas were liquid-propelled ballistic missiles.

In the 1960s the U.S. Air Force developed and deployed the solid-propelled Minuteman ICBMs in underground silos; the latest of these, Minuteman III, is a MIRV missile. Recently, the MX Peacekeeper ICBM, a larger and more accurate system than Minuteman, was deployed in limited quantity at Warren Air Force Base. A small, single re-entry vehicle ICBM, the Midgetman, is currently under development by the U.S. Air Force.

The first Soviet ICBM was unveiled at the Paris air show in 1967. Using clusters of liquid-propellant engines, the large Soviet vehicle was used for the dual purposes of ICBM and space booster. Soviet ICBM developments proceeded through five generations of development, featuring larger payload carrying capacity than U.S. developments and a wider variety of basing modes (now including road mobile and rail mobile). It is believed that the accuracies of the last generation of Soviet ICBMs, for years less than those of U.S. ICBMs, were comparable to current U.S. systems.

In January 1957 the U.S. Navy began development of the solid-propelled Polaris SLBM, which became operational in 1961. The Polaris was followed by the Poseidon and Trident SLBMs, each bringing substantial increases in payload and accuracy. Soviet SLBM developments lagged behind those of the U.S. by several years, but by 1984 the Soviets possessed the largest fleet of ballistic-missile submarines in the world (U.S. SLBM re-entry vehicles outnumbered those of the Soviets, due to a higher degree of MIRV capability).

Military Significance

The foregoing brief sketch of ballistic missile developments since World War II does not convey the profound implications of these developments to the history of the cold war period. For more than 30 years, both superpowers built up strategic ballistic missile inventories, without moderation from sporadic arms control talks, and at increasing risk to the maintenance of strategic stability through the era of detente.

In the U.S. strategic arsenal that evolved after World War II, two of the three elements of the strategic Triad are ballistic missiles—ICBMs and SLBMs (the third leg of the Triad is manned bombers). The ICBM force is capable of prompt response with a highly accurate delivery system. The primary military advantage of the SLBM force is the survivability afforded by submarine basing. Taken together, the Triad has provided the diversification to ensure deterrence under all conditions of superpower relations since World War II.

The primacy of strategic ballistic missiles in the arsenals of the nuclear powers rests in the speed of delivery, accuracy, and lethality of these weapons. The time required to travel over intercontinental ranges is only about one half hour. Accuracies have reached the point where hardened military point targets can be destroyed. In addition, missile warheads possess destructive powers 10 to 50 times greater than the atomic bomb dropped on Hiroshima during World War II.

With the dissolution of the Soviet Union, the demise of the Warsaw Pact, and the progress achieved in strategic arms control, the threat of ballistic missile attacks has changed dramatically. However, the world leaders continue to modernize their ballistic missile forces, and the proliferation of ballistic missiles into developing nations has introduced a new dimension to the threat. At present, missiles in the developing countries are largely confined to the SRBM and MRBM classes with conventional warheads; they are likely to increase in range over the next several years, and advanced warheads (chemical, biological, and nuclear) may be added.

It has been estimated that twenty nations will possess ballistic missiles by the year 2000, and some of these will develop and produce missiles for their own use and for export. As an example, China has developed the CSS-2 missile, range 2,600 kilometers (1,600 mi.), which has been exported to Saudi Arabia.

The use of ballistic missiles by Iraq and Iran in the "War of the Cities" in 1988, and the Iraqi use of Scud missiles against the coalition forces and Israel in the 1991 Gulf War, marked the first uses of ballistic missiles in combat since the V-2 missiles of World War II. The Iraqi Scud missiles used in these wars, acquired from the Soviet Union, were relatively primitive ballistic missiles, but they had an impact on the damage levels, psychology, and tactics of these conflicts.

Significantly, the U.S. Patriot defense system destroyed a substantial fraction of the Scud missiles fired in the 1991 Gulf War. Patriot, originally developed as an air defense system, was upgraded to give it the capability to shoot down short-range ballistic missiles. The Patriot engagements of Scud missiles marked the first time that hostile ballistic missiles had been destroyed by a defense system, and heralded what will likely become a new era in missile warfare.

Relationship to Arms Control

The Intermediate-Range Nuclear Forces (INF) Treaty, concluded in 1987, eliminated an entire class of missiles (all land-based missiles with ranges of between 500 and 5,000 km, or 310 and 3,105 mi.) from the force structures of both the United States and the Soviet Union. The treaty covered both cruise missiles and ballistic missiles, including the U.S. Pershing and the Soviet SS-20 ballistic missiles. The INF Treaty significantly reduced the levels of U.S. and Soviet missiles, but it did not eliminate all tactical missiles and nuclear weapons. Shorter-range nuclear weapons and nuclear bombs carried on aircraft remained in both force structures, and the treaty did not apply to developing nations in possession of short-range missiles.

The Strategic Arms Reduction Treaty (START), signed in 1991, effects a 50 percent reduction in strategic nuclear delivery vehicles, including substantial reductions in both ICBMs and SLBMs.

Future Development

The ongoing START process provides hope that the threat of strategic ballistic missiles will be further reduced, but the proliferation of shorter-range missiles is likely to continue over the next several years. With the diminution of the former Soviet threat, the scale and pace of the U.S. strategic modernization programs will be curtailed. The MX Rail Garrison program, intended to develop a more survivable, mobile basing mode for the MX ICBM, has already been terminated. The level of effort on Midgetman has been substantially decreased from original planning estimates. Other modernization programs, generally involving technical upgrades at the component and subsystem level, will proceed at a moderate pace. It is reasonable to expect that continued improvements in missile accuracy will be made and that further progress in miniaturization will allow higher levels of fractionization (more reentry vehicles on the same booster and post-boost vehicle).

WILLIAM A. DAVIS, JR.

SEE ALSO: Ballistic Missile Defense; Missile, Guided; Missile, Intercontinental Ballistic; Missile, Strategic Ballistic; Space, Military Aspects of; Space Warfare.

Bibliography

Baker, D. 1978. *The history and development of rocket and missile technology.* New York: Crown.

Dow, R. B. 1958. *Fundamentals of advanced missiles.* New York: Wiley.

U.S. Department of Defense. 1984. *Soviet military power.* Washington, D.C.: Government Printing Office.

MISSILE, CRUISE

A cruise missile is a pilotless jet aircraft equipped with internal navigation capabilities. It has also been defined as a guided missile that uses aerodynamic lift to offset gravity and propulsion to counteract drag. The cruise missile may be armed with either a nuclear warhead or conventional munitions. After launch it is self-guided.

During World War II, the Germans developed the short-range cruise missile V-1, which had a range of 190–250 kilometers (120–155 mi.) but was notably inaccurate. During the 1950s, the United States deployed several cruise missile systems such as Snark, Regulus, Matador, Mace, and Hound Dog. The potential effectiveness of the cruise missile has been revolutionized by the advent of miniaturized electronics, whose performance characteristics provide highly accurate guidance techniques for navigation at very low altitudes and also permit packaging nuclear warheads in small volumes.

The cruise missile, with its flexibility and accuracy over great distances, is an ideal weapon to launch from a moving platform. It effectively extends the range of aircraft, ships, and submarines, also enabling them to fire at long-distance targets without making themselves vulnerable to attack. The United States and the Soviet Union developed air, sea, and ground long-range cruise missiles for deployment in the early 1980s (Table 1).

Sea-Launched Cruise Missile (SLCM)

The SLCM has three variants. One carries a conventional warhead for use in antiship missions. Two variants are used for attacking land troops, one carrying a nuclear warhead and the other a conventional payload.

The SLCM can be launched from the surface by specially converted ships or submarines as either a short-range antiship weapon or a strategic nuclear force missile. The advantage of an SLCM in survivability is important, especially when a submarine is the launch platform. The SLCM would have a high prelaunch survivability against nuclear attack, and this quality is relatively independent of warning.

An SLCM can carry a nuclear warhead to a range of at least 2,400 kilometers (1,500 mi.). The conventionally armed SLCM for land attack missions has a range potential of about 1,280 kilometers (800 mi.). SLCMs also combine high accuracy with the nuclear yield needed to destroy hardened targets.

Air-Launched Cruise Missile (ALCM)

The ALCM is a subsonic turbofan-powered aerodynamic missile, but one whose technology surpasses that of the World War II and postwar cruise missiles. It is designed to be launched from an aircraft, thus complicating the enemy's defensive problems and enhancing bomber penetration.

ALCM program development provides for subsonic flight at low altitude to a range of 2,500 kilometers (1,550 mi.). The range of ALCM-B, launched from a B-52, is at least 2,400 kilometers (1,500 mi.) while that of ALCM-A is 1,120 kilometers (700 mi.). ALCM uses an inertial guidance platform and employs the radar guidance system called TERCOM (terrain contour matching), which provides great accuracy.

The TERCOM system uses an active radar altimeter to measure precisely a profile of the altitude of the terrain over which the missile is flying. The radar's measurement of the contour of the land is compared with a map derived from reconnaissance and stored in digitized form in a computer on board the missile. The system corrects for any deviation in desired track by making a series of fixes on checkpoints along the preplanned mission route. Inertial guidance is used in the intervals between TERCOM fixes. This process of almost continuous measurement and correlation provides a high degree of accuracy, even at the end of extended flights and after performance of evasive maneuvers to avoid defenses and obstacles.

The degree of accuracy is determined by how far the target is from the last TERCOM fix or update. Expected operational accuracy is about 0.08 nautical miles or 150 meters (500 ft.) circular error probable (CEP). With such high accuracy and carrying a nuclear warhead with a yield of 100–200 kilotons, the ALCM provides a major capability for destroying hardened targets such as intercontinental ballistic missile (ICBM) silos and command bunkers.

Initial ALCM systems had limitations in their ability to reach the target from stand-off launch positions due to inadequate range and vulnerability to terminal air defenses. These problems were overcome by the extended range of the ALCM-B, about double that of the ALCM-A. The survivability of penetrating bombers is also expected to be enhanced by the effectiveness of ALCMs in diluting the air defense threat.

The longer-range ALCM greatly increases the bomber "footprint." When the U.S. B-52 became increasingly vulnerable during the 1980s, it was envisaged that long-range ALCMs would be launched primarily or solely from stand-off launch positions, without the launching aircraft's having to penetrate air defenses.

B-52 bombers are being modified to carry twelve ALCMs on external pylons (two wing pylons, each with 6 ALCM-As or ALCM-Bs) and up to eight on internal rotary launchers that are interchangeable with the SRAM (short-range attack missile).

In the early 1990s the U.S. B-1 bomber is expected to replace the B-52G/H and to serve primarily as a cruise missile launch platform in the strategic forces. Deploying ALCMs on the B-1B would require some modification to permit full utilization of the B-1 airframe for internal and external loading of ALCMs. The ALCM loading potential of the B-1B is expected to be 22 (14 mounted externally and 8 internally).

Improvements are also taking place in Russia's long-range strategic bomber force; it is being modified to carry cruise missiles, including at least one new long-range type that can be carried by the Blackjack bomber.

Ground-Launched Cruise Missile (GLCM)

GLCMs can be launched from a ground installation or from such vehicles as a transporter-erector-launcher (TEL). The small size of the GLCM enhances its usefulness as a penetrating weapon by giving it a radar cross section of only 0.05 square meters, making it difficult to detect. The missile is able to fly at extremely low altitudes, less than 50 meters (165 ft.) even over moderately hilly terrain. Taking these two characteristics into account, the GLCM has a high probability of penetration despite the fact that it cruises at subsonic speed.

The GLCM is intended to replace a portion of the theater nuclear aircraft strike force, freeing these aircraft for conventional combat missions. The GLCM's range is about 2,500 kilometers (1,550 mi.). It carries a 10–50-kiloton warhead and is accurate to within a 30-meter (100-ft.) radius of its target. The missile can be launched from beneath camouflage netting and would typically be deployed on trails in wooded areas, relocating frequently to maintain security. GLCMs and their support vehicles are also air-transportable between theaters.

Long-range cruise missiles are expected to have high accuracy that will enable their nuclear warheads to destroy hardened targets. The fixed or stationary targets for theater nuclear missions of the GLCM include airfields, storage facilities for nuclear weapons, ground command posts and communications centers, SAM sites, and ground force staging and assembly areas. Fitting the GLCM with a neutron or enhanced-radiation warhead would make it valuable for long-range use against armor and troop concentrations preparing to attack.

The GLCM achieves its remarkable accuracy with the TERCOM system described above. Portions of the selected flight path to the target are surveyed to determine variations in ground elevation, a task performed by satellites. These surveyed areas are divided into a matrix of squares, with each square given a number representing the average elevation of the ground. The resulting digital contour map is stored in the memory of a small computer installed in the missile. As the missile reaches each survey area, a radar altimeter takes readings that the computer compares with the map in its memory. This allows flight path corrections to be made so that the missile can find the next TERCOM checkpoint and eventually the target. The computer can store contour maps for up to twenty segments of the route to the target. This permits considerable flexibility in plotting the route. The missile can zigzag in a fashion that is unpredictable by the enemy, known defenses can be by-passed, and terrain features such as mountains can either be avoided or exploited to conceal the weapon from enemy radars. Between TERCOM checkpoints, the GLCM is maintained on a set course by an inertial guidance system.

Characteristics, Performance, and Potential

The altitude of the ALCM, SLCM, and GLCM over hostile territory would be quite low, about 30 meters (100 ft.) over flat areas and several hundred meters over rough or mountainous terrain. The speed would be high subsonic, with a typical cruise speed of about 400 kilometers (250 mi.) per hour.

Prelaunch survivability of the launch platform itself may be easier to assure by means of widespread deployment of conventionally armed GLCMs than by concentrating tactical aircraft at a relatively few airfields that constitute high-priority targets for the enemy. Cruise missiles also have the advantage of being less vulnerable than tactical aircraft to the enemy air defense environment.

The principal performance characteristics of a cruise missile such as the ALCM or SLCM are very small radar cross section, low-altitude flight, and high subsonic speed. The missiles use an inertial guidance platform over water or until the first opportunity over land to use the TERCOM system.

Cruise missiles can perform highly accurate strikes using guidance systems that do not require favorable light conditions for terminal guidance. They can improve night adverse-weather attack capability. For conventional land attack SLCMs, their digital, scene-matching area correlator (DSMAC) terminal guidance sensor system does not require bright or clear visibility, but can operate in somewhat dim daylight conditions other than fog or haze and, by illuminating the target, even at night.

A program for an advanced cruise missile weapon is planned that will take advantage of stealth technology, as well as improved propulsion technology, to overcome enemy air defenses.

Potential Roles of Cruise Missiles

Air superiority role. In the case of the air-to-ground task against fixed, heavily defended targets such as airfields, long-range cruise missiles could have a high payoff. Clearly, it is desirable to accomplish an airfield attack mission without exposing air crews and expensive attack aircraft to the air defenses en route to the target and to the heavy terminal defenses near the main operating bases. Even though the cruise missile would itself be vulnerable to low-altitude SAMs that form part of such terminal defenses, concern with its survivability applies with less force than to tactical aircraft.

Close air support mission. Improved guidance achieved since the mid-1980s may enable the cruise missile to dispense terminally guided conventional submunitions against moving targets such as tanks. (The range required of missiles in such a role would obviously be short compared with that required of long-range cruise missiles such as the ALCM and the land attack SLCM.) In the critically important mission of close air support, the cruise missile is inherently less useful than a manned aircraft.

Interdiction. A primary and realistic role for the long-range cruise missile would seem to be undertaking some interdiction missions in order to release tactical-strike aircraft for more immediate support in battlefield interdiction or for close air support. There are important limitations on the combinations of range and payload possible with the long-range cruise missile, however, and these will preclude or greatly hamper their use for some deep-strike interdiction missions, even with the high accuracy of their advanced guidance systems.

The range requirements for cruise missiles performing deep interdiction vary depending on the launch point in the theater of operations, flight path variations required to avoid known air defenses, and the location of the target in enemy territory. Until the late 1980s, cruise missiles on deep-strike interdiction missions requiring a range of 1,280 kilometers (800 mi.) could not be expected to carry substantially more than one 1,000-pound conventional warhead, which for some targets such as bridges would not likely be a large enough payload.

Defense suppression. Defense suppression is a tactical air mission for which cruise missiles seem particularly well suited. A defense suppression version of a cruise missile could take advantage of a guidance subsystem such as a "seeker" that homes in on the emissions of a surface-to-air missile (SAM) radar. SAM sites or complexes, especially their radars, are relatively soft targets and can therefore be destroyed or disabled by area submunitions that are dispersed in large numbers against both equipment and operating personnel.

Defense suppression missions using cruise missiles are thus feasible at long ranges of 800 to 1,100 kilometers (500–700 mi.). Using versions of cruise missiles to degrade or destroy air defense elements, especially during the early phases of a conventional conflict, would be a high-value mission. By softening the air defenses that face aircraft performing close air support and battlefield interdiction, cruise missiles could bring about lower attrition of manned aircraft. Defense suppression with cruise missiles at such long range could thus reduce the losses of tactical aircraft performing those missions for which they remain best suited, such as deep interdiction strikes against targets requiring heavy payloads (2,000–3,000-pound bombs) for destruction.

Soviet Cruise Missiles

The Soviets developed a missile guidance system for their cruise missiles that is similar in technology to the terrain contour matching radar correlator used by the United States in its navy and air force cruise missiles. The guidance system technology employed provides the capability of flying at long ranges and achieving accuracy of nearly 50 meters (150 ft.) CEP. Improvements are also taking place in the Russian long-range bomber force, which is being modified to carry cruise missiles.

The following Russian cruise missiles were scheduled for deployment beginning in 1985.

- AS-X-15 ALCM with a range in excess of 2,400 kilometers (1,500 mi.), to be carried by the Tupolev Backfire bomber or the new intercontinental Blackjack bomber.
- BL-10 ALCM, an extremely large missile with a range of approximately 3,600 kilometers (2,200 mi.). It could be

TABLE 1. *Cruise Missile Programs*

Program	Designation	Range (km)	Payload	Guidance	Launch Platform	Country
SLCM						
Nuclear land attack	BGM-109A	2,500	100–200 kilotons	TERCOM	Nuclear submarines, destroyers, cruisers, battleships	USA
Conventional land attack	BGM-109C	1,300	1000 pounds	TERCOM[a] DSMAC		USA
Antiship conventional	BGM-109B	460	1000 pounds	Active radar seeker		USA
	SS-NX-12	540	not available	not available	not available	USSR
ALCM						
Nuclear	AGM 86B	2,500	200 kilotons	Inertial and TERCOM	B-52G, B-52H, B-1B	USA
Nuclear	AS-X-15	2,400	not available	not available	Blackjack Backfire	USSR
GLCM						
Nuclear	BGM-109G	2,500	100–200 kilotons	Inertial and TERCOM	TELs[b]	USA
Nuclear	BL-10	3,200	not available	not available	not available	USSR
	SS-X-4	not available	not available	not available	not available	USSR

[a] TERCOM accuracy less than 30 ft. using DSMAC terminal guidance.
[b] Ground mobile transporter erector-launchers.
Source: Sorrels 1983.

carried by the Blackjack or by the Tupolev Bear bomber operating as a stand-off carrier aircraft.
- SS-NX-21 SLCM on submarines
- SSC-X-4 GLCM, similar in design and operational capability to the U.S. Air Force's cruise missiles deployed in Europe. The missile can fly at altitudes below the radar horizon, making it difficult to detect.

SALT Constraints

A protocol that expired on 31 December 1981 prohibited deployment of cruise missiles capable of a range in excess of 600 kilometers (375 mi.) on sea-based or land-based launchers. No limits were placed on the development and flight-testing of SLCMs and GLCMs with ranges less than 600 kilometers. The protocol further banned flight testing from sea-based or ground-based launchers of cruise missiles armed with multiple independently targetable reentry vehicles (MIRVs). The protocol, like the treaty, defines cruise missiles—in this case, SLCMs and GLCMs—in a way that includes conventionally armed versions. The treaty defines cruise missiles covered by its terms—ALCMs—in a way that also includes conventionally armed versions as well as nuclear-armed versions.

The range capability of a cruise missile is defined in the SALT II Treaty as follows: The range of which a cruise missile is capable to the maximum distance which can be covered by the missile in its standard design mode flying until fuel exhaustion, determined by projecting its flight path onto the earth's sphere from the point of launch to the point of impact. The Carter administration accepted a range limitation of 2,500 kilometers (1,550 mi.) on the ALCM in the prospective SALT II Treaty.

Future Developments

By the early 1990s, technology being developed may produce terminal guidance systems for cruise missiles that will enable them to detect and strike with high accuracy mobile targets such as convoys of vehicles and tanks, using conventional munitions on interdiction strikes. It may be feasible to replace one of the expensive TERCOM guidance systems on board conventional cruise missiles by using locational update data from navigational satellites, such as the NAVSTAR Global Positioning System, expected to become fully operational by the late 1980s. The use of satellite data from GPS might also obviate the requirement for the digitized maps that support TERCOM. Relying on GPS for target navigation in a conflict may prove risky, however, because some nations have the ability to attack the GPS satellite system itself.

KHEIDR K. EL DAHRAWY

SEE ALSO: Aircraft, Unmanned; Arms Control and Disarmament; Missile, Air-launched Cruise; Missile, Guided; Nuclear Theory and Policy.

Bibliography

Gunston, B. 1983. *An illustrated guide to modern airborne missiles.* London: Salamander Books.

Sorrels, C. 1983. *U.S. cruise missile programs: Development, deployment and implications for arms control.* London: Brassey's.

Stockholm International Peace Research Institute. 1981. *SIPRI yearbook, 1981: World armaments and disarmament.* New York: Crane Russak.

ADDITIONAL SOURCES: *Air Force Magazine, Aviation Week and Space Technology, International Defense Review.*

MISSILE, GUIDED

A guided missile is defined as a space-traversing unmanned vehicle that carries within itself the means of controlling its flight path. A missile guidance system is the group of components that measures the position of a guided missile with respect to its target and causes changes in the flight path as required. Some system elements may be external to the missile at the launching site, en route to the target, or on the target.

Many guided missile research and development programs were initiated during World War II, such as those that produced the German V-1 and V-2 rockets. The V-1 employed a simple guidance system. During the launch and mid-course phases of its flight its azimuth was controlled by a magnetic compass and its altitude by a barometric altimeter. In the V-2 ballistic missile the velocity was also a controllable parameter; the guidance system was designed so as to shut off the propelling motor on command. Early missiles used radio signals to control and shut off the fuel supply, thus controlling missile velocity.

A guided missile system is fundamentally a servo system in which the guidance intelligence is the input and the flight path of the missile is the output (Fig. 1).

Guidance Phases During Missile Flight

There are three phases of missile flight that have characteristics sufficiently different to require the use, in some missiles, of more than one system of guidance during a single flight.

Launch guidance is used during that portion of missile flight between initial firing and the time when the missile has reached a velocity at which it responds to normal control. The missile is launched by use of a booster, which is an auxiliary propulsion system that subsequently separates from the missile; the missile then continues in flight at some preselected velocity under its own internal power. During that portion of the flight when the booster is attached, the control characteristics of the combined missile and booster vary radically from the characteristics of the missile alone, which continues at a higher velocity and with different configuration after separation.

Mid-course guidance is the guidance applied to a missile between the end of the launch phase and the beginning of the terminal phase.

Figure 1. The U.S. Air Force Shrike air-to-ground missile is typical of guided missiles in service today. (SOURCE: U.S. Air Force; Robert F. Dorr Archives)

Terminal guidance is the guidance applied to a missile between the end of the mid-course phase and contact with or detonation in close proximity to the target.

Categories of Guided Missiles

Guided missiles may be classified according to the location of their launch platform and their target. These categories include surface-to-air (SAM), surface-to-surface (SSM), air-to-surface (ASM), and air-to-air (AAM) missiles. Depending on the purpose of the missile, the characteristics of the target, and the potential countermeasures, the guidance system may be varied, or two or more systems may be combined.

Guided missiles used against underwater targets comprise two additional categories of missiles: surface-to-subsurface missiles and air-to-subsurface missiles. The submarine may be used as a launching platform for surface-to-subsurface missiles. The submarine as a target is unique only when it is operating beneath the surface; when it is not submerged, it is merely a mobile surface target.

Homing Guidance Systems

A homing guidance system is a guidance system by which a missile steers itself toward a target by means of a self-contained mechanism that is activated by some distinguishing characteristic of the target. The homing guidance system may be any one of the following types.

Active Homing Guidance Systems

An active homing guidance system is one in which both the source of energy used to illuminate the target and the receiver of the energy reflected by it are carried in the missile itself. It consists of a transmitter and a receiver of energy, which enable the missile to detect the presence of a target; a computer, which predicts from the received energy the future position of the target; and missile control surfaces that respond to computer signals so as to direct the missile to impact on the target. The energy used to illuminate the target may be in the form of radio, light, heat, or sound waves. A missile using active homing guidance is completely independent once homing begins, since thereafter it has no requirement for energy transmitted from an external source or for externally derived guidance intelligence.

Active homing is used to acquire targets at longer range. The missile itself transmits energy and picks up the reflection or echo from the target, then uses that information to steer toward the target. The missile must therefore carry both a transmitter and a receiver; radar is the usual medium. The drawback to the system is the weight of equipment needed and the resultant size of the missile required to carry the radar scanner and power supply. The solution is often a remote high-power transmitter coupled with a small receiver in the missile itself. Active radar homing is used in antiship missiles. It is ideal at sea, where there is generally only one target in the immediate area. On land, the radar would find it difficult to pick out a target from the mass of ground echoes.

A long-range SSM must also employ some other means of guidance (mid-course guidance) to bring it to the point where active homing guidance (terminal guidance) can take over. The acquisition capabilities of the missile's radar must be carefully matched to the accuracy of the mid-course guidance, since it is necessary for the missile radar to lock on the target after launch.

For short-range applications, the radar of the active homing guidance system may be directed by a fire control radar at the launch site, which has initially detected the target. Once the target is located by its active homing system, the missile becomes entirely independent.

In the initial tactical application of the air-to-air active homing guidance system, the missile is launched from an aircraft—either an interceptor or a bomber—against a target that may be an aircraft or a missile. Once the missile guidance system has obtained target lock-on, the missile system is capable of independently generating a fire control solution. Thus as soon as the missile is launched the launching aircraft is free to break contact.

Semiactive Homing Guidance Systems

In these systems, a receiver in the missile receives energy reflected from the target. The system consists of the receiver; a computer, also located in the missile, that predicts from the received energy the future position of the target; missile control surfaces that direct the missile along the correct flight path to achieve impact on the target; and an externally located transmitter that illuminates the target. This transmitter may be located at the missile launching station, or it may be at a surface installation or airborne.

The principal difference between active and semiactive homing is that the semiactive system is not independent of external sources; its guidance intelligence is derived from energy transmitted from a point external to the missile.

In semiactive homing the missile is fitted with a radar receiver and the launch aircraft with a radar transmitter. The aircraft illuminates the target with its radar, then the missile homes on the reflected energy. This does not constitute a true fire-and-forget system, although no actual guidance is required from the air crew. An example is the U.S. Falcon AAM, which is equipped with a semiactive radar homing head operating in conjunction with a target-illuminating radar carried by the launching aircraft.

Passive Homing Guidance Systems

Passive homing is that in which the missile homes on a source of energy radiated by the target. This energy may be in the form of heat, light, sound, or radio frequency waves. Weather conditions, the type of target, aspect, and target background may greatly influence the effectiveness of such systems. These systems operate by picking up radiations from the target, amplifying them, then passing information about their direction and strength to the missile's controls. The missile can then be automatically guided to the source of the energy. Passive homing is usually a relatively short-range technique. The passive system also requires the least amount of equipment to be mounted in the missile proper of any of the several guidance methods, since no transmitter is required.

Command Guidance Systems

Command guidance was the first guidance system to be perfected, being used on the surface for such tasks as remote control of boats, tanks, and cars, and in the air to provide remote control of drone aircraft and glide bombs. Command guidance is defined as a system in which information transmitted to the missile from an outside source causes the missile to traverse a directed path. The typical command system can guide only one missile against one target during a given time interval.

Use of a command guidance system requires that the missile be sufficiently stable to stay within the limits of the equipment (optical or radar) from which command information is generated during the period when the missile has not yet reached control speed.

Applied command guidance systems can be divided into

two general types. Optical tracking command guidance systems are those in which the relative positions of the missile and its target are continuously monitored by a human operator who transmits commands to the missile via a radio link. Such systems are limited in range to optical line of sight, since the operator uses an optical sight to locate and track the target and a manual control to command the missile to his line of sight.

Command-to-line-of-sight wire-guided missiles are designed for firing from land vehicles, naval vessels, slow-moving fixed-wing aircraft, and helicopters. They involve optical tracking and manual wire-guided remote control of the missile by means of the varying thrust of sustainer efflux. The operator acquires the target by a magnifying optical device. As soon as the missile enters his field of vision after being launched, the operator commands it to his line of sight with a joystick. The signals are transmitted over wires trailed by the missile. Tracer elements installed in the rear of the missile assist in visual tracking. When the system is installed in a helicopter or ship, the simple sighting device used with land vehicles is replaced by a special stabilized sight.

Two methods may be used for radar track command when target and missile position and their relative motion are derived from radar tracking information. In single-beam radar track command guidance, the target position and motion are sensed by radar; the position and motion of the missile are not measured, but are rather predicted on the basis of statistical ballistic data. For the ballistic case, the most important factors are velocity, drift (wind), angle of launch in two coordinates, and time. Deviation of the target from the predicted future path can be sensed, and corresponding commands are then signalled to the missile to correct its flight path accordingly.

Two-beam radar track command systems, which are more accurate than the single-beam system, include the missile, target-tracking radar, missile-tracking radar, the computer, and a command link. Missile sensing and tracking means are required to locate the missile and measure its position and motion. Radar tracking of the missile provides integrated range and angle information. Target and missile sensing requirements are analogous. The function of the computer is to generate command signals that ideally result in missile intercept of the target. The computer receives position and rate information, predicts optimum point of impact, and generates steering orders to cause the missile to fly a desired collision course.

All command guidance systems require a communication link between the guidance station and the missile. This link is used to relay remotely generated steering orders and other commands to the missile. Practically speaking, command links are limited to communication by radio or wire.

Beam-Rider Guidance Systems

Beam-rider systems are those that guide missiles by means of a beam directed into space so that the center of the beam axis forms a line along which it is desired to direct the missile. The beam, which may be either fixed or moving in elevation and azimuth, may be a radar beam or a light beam.

The missile carries suitable electronic circuits, servo mechanisms coupled to aerodynamic control surfaces, and other equipment so that the missile will return of its own initiative toward the center of the beam when it has deviated for any reason. The missile launcher is used to point the missile in such a manner that it will initially enter the beam upon launch. Thereafter the beam-riding missile uses an installed mechanism that enables it to measure its position with respect to the center of the beam and move in such a direction as to reduce any measured error to zero.

Self-Homing Guidance

An antiradiation homing missile (ARM) is fitted with a radar receiver that searches for enemy radars and, when it detects one, locks onto it and homes. The approach was developed originally for homing on ground missile guidance radars. Modern electronic counter-countermeasures (ECCM) have made design of an antiradiation homer very difficult. Thus early versions such as the Shrike and the standard ARM, which saw service during the war in Vietnam, are now being replaced by a high-speed antiradiation missile (HARM), which has a longer range, greater accuracy, and less susceptibility to countermeasures. Another approach, exemplified by the German antiship missile Kormoran, has been to fit a missile with two guidance systems—inertial missile guidance and active or passive radar homing.

The U.S. standard ARM (AGM-78B) is an example of a system designed for destruction of SAM battery radars. System operation is initiated by an aircraft's reception of hostile radar transmissions. The received signal is processed to extract target location, identification, and threat data. A missile is then launched and homes on the source of the radar transmission. Another example involves Shrike-carrying aircraft, which probably obtain initial warning of illumination by ground defense radars from electronic countermeasures (ECM) receivers installed in the aircraft. When within appropriate range, the Shrike sensor heads are switched on; when target acquisition has been achieved, the missiles are fired. After release, the missile radar receiver continuously senses the direction of arrival of radar radiation from the target and generates command signals for the missile guidance system, which in turn causes the missile to home on the target radar. Shrike guidance heads have been developed that are effective against enemy early warning, ground intercept control, and SAM guidance radars, each of which operates in a different frequency range.

Television Homing

Television-fitted missiles can be designed either to relay the pictures they take back to an operator in the launch aircraft, who then guides the missile by means of radio commands, or to use the pictures to guide themselves to their target (in which case they constitute true homers). TV is of no use at night, in low visibility, or against camouflaged targets.

Guidance is carried out by a small television system in the nose of the missile. The aircraft pilot chooses a target on a TV monitor in his cockpit, locks the missile's electro-optical tracker onto the target, and fires the missile, which is then automatically guided to the target by the TV tracker. This is the system used by the U.S. Maverick missile. Upon selection of a missile, and prior to engaging a target, gyro run-up is initiated. When this is complete, an indicator lamp signals the pilot that he can uncage the gyro. This action releases a protective dome from the nose of the missile. The aircraft pilot picks up the target on his TV monitor, locks the missile's electro-optical tracker onto the target (either by slewing the missile's nose-mounted TV camera or by changing the aircraft's attitude), then launches the missile, which is automatically guided to the target by the TV controlled tracker.

In the guidance of a medium-range air-to-surface supersonic cruise missile such as the U.S. Condor, a TV remote guidance and control system is used to provide a stand-off capability for use against heavily defended ground targets. After being launched from the parent aircraft, the missile is directed to the target by means of a radio command link. The operator in the launching aircraft has a monitor display unit that shows the scene observed by a TV camera mounted in the nose of the missile. Automatic tracking of the target and manual aim-point update are provided to the missile by a pod computer. Tracking error corrections are sent to the autopilot for terminal control of the missile to the point of impact. The autopilot provides inputs for stabilization in roll, pitch, and azimuth, and in-flight steering commands for the aerodynamically controlled missile in pitch and heading.

This missile can also be programmed for a direct shot to a target from an offset position. Once released from the aircraft, Condor will fly its mid-course path, regardless of weather in the target area. The mid-course guidance system navigates the missile along a preplanned flight path from release over a selected point. Once the missile is in the vicinity of the target, its operator in the aircraft briefly assumes control and acquires the target on a cockpit display while the aircraft is flying away from the target.

Infrared Homing

In this system the missile receives and homes on infrared emissions given off by a target. This approach is useful against ships, whose infrared (IR) emissions are strong and distinctive; it has more limited usefulness against land targets, except those that have strong IR emissions such as tanks, parked aircraft, and other vehicles.

The advantage of IR homing is that it can be used by day or night and can detect targets through camouflage or under partial cover such as in woods. It is said to be capable of successful aircraft intercepts from any aspect, relying either upon heat from the jet engine and its exhaust from the rear sectors or on localized airframe hot spots caused by aerodynamic heating when attacking from the front.

The most common use of IR homing by AAMs is homing on the IR energy emitted by the hot engines of enemy aircraft. The missile is fitted with an IR receiver that can search for an IR-emitting target, lock onto it, and home the missile. One method uses an optical system for focusing the intercepted IR energy on a detector cell. The angular error between the homing head axis and the sight line from the missile to the target is monitored, and a signal is generated to process the missile's gyro so as to bring the missile onto the correct line.

Earlier versions of such AAMs homed on exhaust gases from the engines and were only used for launches from astern of the enemy aircraft; thus they were pursuit missiles. Second-generation systems, using more sensitive IR receivers, were designed to home from any angle, including head-on. With the advent of even higher speed targets, the missile's homing head has had to be modified so as to sweep through widening arcs, thereby increasing its complexity.

Laser Guidance

In laser guidance systems the missile is fitted with a laser seeker (receiver) that receives the laser energy reflected from a target illuminated by a laser beam. Most targets will reflect laser light, and the missile uses these reflections to guide itself to the target. The target can be illuminated by a portable laser operated by an observer on the ground or by an airborne laser, usually located in another aircraft. Once the pilot sees from his indicators that his weapon has locked onto the laser reflections, he can release it and turn away.

In the case of semiactive laser guidance, missiles are equipped with a seeker that picks up a laser beam reflected by the target. The beam originates from a laser designator, which can either be fitted to the platform of the missile (such as a helicopter or a source on the ground) or hand-held by a soldier. Laser guidance is also used for the U.S. helicopter-launched Hellfire missile, which is guided by laser designators using different codes. Two missiles under development, known as Spark and HVM, will also use laser guidance. The HVM will utilize a carbon dioxide laser beam fire control system. The laser will acquire a number of targets and assign missiles to each. By means of synchronous time clocks in the missiles and the aircraft and time coding, each missile will receive only those signals that apply to it and its target. Up to ten targets can thus be attacked simultaneously. The signals are received by an aft-looking optical system in the missile, and thus must be able to penetrate its exhaust gases.

Laser-guided missiles have only limited capability in adverse weather. They also cannot be considered as fire-and-forget weapons, since the target must be continuously illuminated by the laser designator operation until impact.

Inertial Guidance

Guidance for missiles that involve long ballistic flights can be provided by radio command or inertial sensing. Radio was tried in early systems by both the United States and the USSR, but it had the disadvantage of making the missile dependent on external links that were subject to being jammed or otherwise failing. All third- and fourth-generation ballistic missiles thus use inertial sensing in one form or another. Such guidance takes place only during the powered-flight phase.

Inertial sensing use gyroscopes and accelerometers to measure the forces other than gravity that are influencing the motion of the missile. These instruments continuously monitor the location of the missile from launch until thrust termination. On-board computers use this information and an accurate clock to compute the velocity and position of the missile. The computer also directs the autopilot mechanism to steer and control the thrust until actual velocity and preprogrammed velocity coincide. Thrust is terminated at exactly this point.

The guidance system must also be told with as much precision as possible the coordinates of the launch point and of the target. Hence the sensitivity of the geophysical instruments is an important factor. The gravitational effects of the sun and moon must also be included in the guidance calculations.

Guidance of Antitank Missiles

Almost without exception the antitank missiles now in service employ radio command guidance or, more commonly, wire command guidance. Command signals are usually sent in the form of varying voltages through extremely fine wires. In most modern systems two wires, uncoiled from a spool, complete the circuit. The earliest version of radio and wire command guidance was the manual-command-to-line-of-sight (MCLOS) system. Missiles using this guidance mode were referred to as first-generation antitank weapons. The operator launched the missile, then kept the target in his sight while steering the missile on the desired trajectory to the target by means of a joystick. The missile was typically equipped with tracking flares to assist the operator in following its flight.

Command guidance via wire is virtually immune to countermeasures. Another advantage is that the operator is not easily discovered, since he can position himself as much as a hundred meters from the launcher. The drawback is that the flight velocity of missiles using this system must be kept relatively low in order to give the operator sufficient time to correct deviations in the desired trajectory.

Another version of command guidance is the semiautomatic-command-to-line-of-sight (SACLOS) system, developed to avoid some of the drawbacks of MCLOS guidance. Missiles using this system are called second-generation antitank weapons. The operator's task is simplified in that, after firing, he need only keep his sight on the target. A tracker in the launcher senses radiation from the source in the missile and detects any deviation from the line of sight. Computer-generated commands to the missile then bring it back on the line of sight. This form of guidance is also called the angular tracking method, since it is the angular deviation of the actual trajectory from the desired one that is measured.

New guidance modes are now being developed that will further decrease dependence on daylight, fair weather, and visual contact with the enemy. One of these is called the imaging infrared (IIR) guidance mode. Besides increased capability under adverse weather conditions, this approach also provides a fire-and-forget capability. A thermal picture is created by sensing the differences in heat radiated by the objects in view. The operator watches this picture, locates the target, locks on the missile, and fires. After launch, the missile proceeds to the target independent of the operator.

In one application of the IIR mode, the Tank Breaker missile (a shoulder-launched, one-man portable weapon), the picture is miniaturized by using a focal plane array seeker. This mode of guidance will also permit top attack by ground-launched missiles.

Another type of guidance that fulfills the requirements for adverse weather and fire-and-forget capabilities is the millimeter-wave guide, which is able to find targets despite heavy ground clutter and to distinguish tanks and other military targets from nontarget vehicles. During its first stage this guidance system works in an active mode, searching for targets and locking onto one. When the missile approaches its target, in an area where "glints" from multiple reflecting surfaces could cause guidance problems, the seeker switches to a passive mode. It is then guided by natural millimeter wave energy from the sky, which is reflected by the target. The missile then dives to penetrate the top armor of the target tank. This guidance system is currently being developed for the Wasp missile, the only missile with multilaunch capacity. This guidance mode combined with that capacity is expected to provide high accuracy for achieving multiple hits outside visual range. Both Wasp and TOW-3 were expected to become operational before 1990.

Optical command guidance using fiber optics is another approach being studied for TOW (tube-launched, optically tracked, wire-guided antitank missiles). Pictures would be transmitted from the missile in flight via a fiber optic strand to the operator, who would then be able to select a target and send guidance commands back to the missile over the same link. This would provide a mode of transmission considered immune to countermeasures and give the missile an extended range.

Guidance by Satellite

The NAVSTAR Global Positioning System, which consists of 24 satellites grouped equally in three rings situated in circular orbits, was designed particularly so that weapon-delivery systems could navigate intercontinental ballistic missiles (ICBMs) to their targets accurately. With the aid of navigation and geodetic satellites, it is possible to guide a missile to within a few meters of its target anywhere in the world, thereby acquiring unprecedented accuracy. In fact it is possible that satellites are already being used for real-time mid-course guidance of long-range strategic missiles. Such employment will increase the effectiveness of missiles by enhancing accuracy and other capabilities for weapon delivery.

Kheidr K. El Dahrawy

See Also: Missile, Air-launched Cruise; Missile, Air-to-air; Missile, Air-to-surface; Missile, Antitank Guided; Missile, Ballistic; Missile, Cruise; Missile, Intercontinental Ballistic; Missile, Surface-to-air.

Bibliography

Collins, J. 1988. *U.S.-Soviet military balance statistical trends, 1980–87*. Library of Congress, Washington, D.C., 15 April.

Jane's all the world's aircraft 1987–88. 1987. London: Jane's.

Jane's weapon systems 1987–88. 1987. London: Jane's.

Merrill, G., ed. 1955. *Principles of guided missile design*. New York: Van Nostrand.

Stockholm International Peace Research Institute. 1974. *SIPRI yearbook, 1974*.

———. 1978. *Outer space: Battlefield of the future*. London: Taylor and Francis.

———. 1983. *SIPRI yearbook, 1983*.

Additional sources: *Army Magazine; Aviation Week and Space Technology; International Defense Review; Military Review*.

MISSILE, INTERCONTINENTAL BALLISTIC (ICBM)

The intercontinental ballistic missile (ICBM) is an unmanned strategic offensive system permitting rapid surface-to-surface attack of targets beyond the continent of the country from which the system is launched. The North Atlantic Treaty Organization (NATO) definition specifies at least a 5,500-kilometer (3,400-mi.) range. Normally, but not necessarily, armed with a nuclear or thermonuclear warhead, typical features include liquid or solid propellant, two or more booster rocket stages, an inertial guidance system that could be augmented by star, satellite, or terminal guidance, and one or more reentry vehicles, each containing a warhead.

ICBMs have their origins in the pioneering rocket research of the theoretician K. E. Tsiolkovsky (USSR), the experimental scientist Robert H. Goddard (U.S.), and the World War II German program that aimed at developing an intercontinental missile but that was never completed. ICBMs were developed and deployment began in earnest when thermonuclear weapons facilitated a match between attainable warhead size, weight, and yield on the one hand, and missile throwweight, (warhead-carrying capacity), range, and accuracy on the other. Related developments include short-, medium-, and intermediate-range missiles primarily suitable for theater use, and a sea-based variant, the submarine launched ballistic missile (SLBM) which, along with the ICBM, became a key element in both the U.S. and Soviet strategic arsenals. In the United States, the ICBM and SLBM came to share roughly equal status with the long-range bomber, in a strategic deterrent "triad." In the Soviet Union, however, the ICBM became the primary element in the Soviet strategic arsenal. Only recently have SLBMs and long-range bombers noticeably increased in significance in the former Soviet arsenal, which is still dominated by the ICBM.

An increasing number of nations have acquired long-range ballistic missiles—notably the United Kingdom, France, and China, but of these only China has developed a true ICBM. Other nations have developed, or are on the verge of developing, ballistic missiles with a range sufficient to reach targets throughout their regions. Some of these nations are developing space-launch vehicles that could serve as the basis for an ICBM. Given their range, speed, difficulty of intercept, and destructive power, ICBMs have the potential to threaten the security basis of the nation-state system, just as long-range artillery did the security basis of the city-state system. This potential has not been fully realized in the case of the ICBM, however, in part because of the mutual vulnerability and consequent deterrent effect generated by the ICBMs of the United States and the former Soviet Union. Further, work ongoing for nearly three decades by both superpowers to develop at least a partially effective defense against ICBMs points to the potential prospect of altering the ICBM's contribution to the strategic equation.

System Components

The ICBM has several components central to its functions, and others peripheral to them but typical of configurations found in current arsenals. Each component has experienced a distinct but interrelated evolution in the United States and the former Soviet Union, generating a number of variants.

Propulsion

The immediate precursors of the ICBM were single-staged and liquid-fueled—notably the German A-4 (known to the Allies as the V-2) and its spinoff systems in the United States (the Redstone) and the Soviet Union (the SS-3). It was important to get beyond a single stage, however, to be able to carry a useful weight to intercontinental range. In the United States, the first true ICBM, the Atlas, used a so-called "1-½ stage" liquid propulsion system. It actually had two stages or phases of rocket boost, but the two rocket engines in the first phase were discarded in flight. The Soviets' first true ICBM, the SS-6, like the Atlas design, also used a "1-½ stage" liquid design concept, but unlike the U.S. system, it discarded both the first stage engines and propellant tanks in flight. It had twenty main engines, rather than three, making up for thrust per engine with the number of engines. No subsequent ICBM development adopted this design concept. After the Atlas and the SS-6, all ICBMs were designed with two or three major separate booster stages. Large solid-fuel booster stages were first adopted in the United States for the Polaris and Minuteman programs. The Soviets had difficulty with large solid propellant designs at first, with most of their systems being liquid-fueled until they began to field longer-range land mobile systems. Today's Soviet-designed SS-24 and SS-25 systems are solid-fueled, benefiting from work begun with earlier Soviet missiles, most recently the shorter-range SS-20 intermediate range ballistic missile (IRBM).

Guidance

Early ICBMs often used a combination of radio and inertial guidance. This was an unsatisfactory arrangement—especially given the potential vulnerability of radio guidance systems to outside interference or attack. Early in both the U.S. and Soviet ICBM programs, reliance was placed on all-inertial guidance systems of increasing accuracy and reliability. Generally, the Soviets lagged behind the United States in reliability and accuracy, but as of early 1990 had nearly caught up. While the Soviets may not have achieved the accuracy of the U.S. Peacekeeper missile, the circular error probable (CEP) (the circle within which one-half of the reentry vehicles could be expected to fall) of the most recent Soviet ICBM generation at operational range is quite good, and in the future will probably match that of the United States. Regarding reliability, U.S. and Soviet ICBM guidance can be maintained on alert status on a routine basis, facilitating day-to-day readiness.

Postboost Vehicle (PBV)

Also known as a MIRV bus, for the device that deploys reentry vehicles on an ICBM equipped with multiple independently targetable reentry vehicles (MIRVs), the post-boost vehicle (PBV) can also be used to deploy decoys, chaff, and other penetration aids. It can provide additional range before the reentry vehicles are released to continue on unpowered ballistic trajectories to their intended targets. ICBMs today carry up to ten or more reentry vehicles to widely separated targets. The higher the number of reentry vehicles carried, the more targets can be attacked per missile launched. In a missile-against-missile duel, this increases the potential that more missiles can be destroyed than used up in each strike, presuming sufficient combinations of yield and accuracy.

Reentry Vehicle

The container in which the warhead rides in its flight to the intended target is the reentry vehicle. Early reentry vehicles were blunt, had low velocities at impact, and were characterized by limited accuracy. Improvements in heat dissipation technology, beginning with the move away from heat sinks (as in the early Atlas missiles) to ever-improving ablative materials (as in the Titan and the later Atlas and their successor systems in the United States, and similar systems in the Soviet Union), permitted the development of more streamlined reentry vehicles. These had higher terminal speeds and consequently achieved greater accuracy and were less susceptible to uncertainties in weather prediction, and were less vulnerable to enemy countermeasures. The technology exists to produce maneuvering reentry vehicles. This technology has been tested, and at least one such system has been deployed by the United States, namely, the radar image-matching terminally guided system of the Pershing II medium-range missile. The Pershing was developed to enhance accuracy; other maneuvering reentry vehicles could be developed for the primary purpose of evading defenses.

Warhead

The development in the early 1950s of nuclear fusion devices, with the prospect of relatively compact, lightweight, high-yield warheads, spurred the development of ICBMs. Such warheads could be launched on boosters employing then-current technology, with the high yield of the fusion weapons compensating, in some measure, for the inaccuracy of guidance systems. Fusion warheads have been developed further since the inception of the ICBM, permitting greater miniaturization and facilitating the move to employing multiple warheads. They have also been made more resistant to nuclear effects, and can be hardened to withstand ground impact, resulting in the development of earth-penetrating warheads designed to destroy especially hard targets. But ballistic missile warheads need not be thermonuclear or even nuclear. As ICBMs and shorter-range variants proliferate, chemical and biological warheads would seem to be potential alternatives for nations or organizations without access to nuclear warheads. Also possible are ballistic missiles with precision and area conventional munitions, as missile accuracies improve.

Basing Mode

Because of the then-existing state of technology and urgency of proceeding to deployment, early ICBMs were launched from above-ground pads. Given the inaccuracy of the early ICBMs and the slowness of bomber forces to reach the same targets, this was a satisfactory beginning. But as ICBM accuracies and force sizes grew, survivable basing modes became a concern on both the U.S. and Soviet sides. Both moved toward "hardened" fixed silos initially, with the United States passing from semihard "coffins," to hard silos from which missiles had to be raised for launching, to harder silos designed to allow launch from within the silo ("hardening" guards missiles from attack by burying them underground, protected by steel, concrete, and shock-absorbing designs using heavy covers and spring suspensions). As the U.S. Minuteman ICBM was developed, a mobile variant was considered but rejected as undesirable and unnecessary at the time. The Soviets also moved to hardened silos, and to a "cold launch" system permitting rapid reload (only partially achieved in U.S. ICBM force with the more recent Peacekeeper seen in Fig. 1). As the Soviets perceived their silos becoming more vulnerable, they moved on to land-mobile ICBMs (now operational in the former Soviet Union but recently cancelled in the United States; that is, the new small road-mobile missile and/or the larger rail-mobile Peacekeeper). Both the United States and the former Soviets have had sea-mobile ballistic missiles deployed for some time. The British and French have emphasized sea basing as the key to the survivability of their ballistic missile forces, but apparently the Chinese have not. The Chinese appear to rely mainly on land-based ballistic missiles, using concealment and hardness to achieve survivability.

Figure 1. A Peacekeeper missile lifts off from its modified Minuteman silo at Vandenberg AFB, California. (Source: U.S. Air Force)

Command and Control

The ICBM has an advantage among strategic offensive systems because the central authority can be the most certain of controlling authorized launches while assuring against unauthorized execution. The United States, and apparently, the Soviets, British, French, and Chinese, have imposed stringent command, control, and communications (C^3) systems on their ballistic missile forces. In the United States, the national command authority must enable and order a crew to fire, more than one crew must agree to fire, and more than one person per crew is required to agree. In the United States and the former Soviet Union, attention has been paid to assuring that the order to fire will reach launch crews before communications are disrupted and that crews will survive to fire upon receipt of an order to do so. In the United States, one of the key innovations has been the airborne launch control system for the Minuteman and Peacekeeper missiles, allowing launch control from an aircraft if ground control is lost. In the former Soviet Union, hard and mobile command posts and redundant, enduring communication links serve as key elements of a highly reliable and robust nuclear C^3 system.

Developmental History

For both the United States and the former Soviet Union, the development of the ICBM was both driven and constrained by a number of factors, including technology, doctrine, complementary elements of the force structure, elements of the opposing force structure both present and projected, perceptions of opposing doctrine, and organizational and political considerations.

Antecedents to Development

The United States and the Soviet Union emerged from World War II with the potential for ICBM development. Both had their rocket pioneers, notably K. E. Tsiolkovsky in the Soviet Union, and Robert H. Goddard in the United States. They and their contemporaries, students, and successors kept their country's respective technologies moving ahead. In World War II, work on long-range rocketry in both countries took a back seat to immediate needs associated with prosecuting the war. Toward the end of the war, both the United States and the Soviet Union were concerned with the advances the Germans were making in the application of rocket technology to warfare with the V-2 and planned intercontinental missile. As a result, both gave attention to their own exploratory programs before the war ended. When the war was over, both moved to seize German scientists, plans, and facilities to assist in their national programs.

In the United States, German scientists joined an ongoing effort, where they remained key players. Eventually, the German scientists associated with the U.S. Army program and many of their American colleagues were split off to form the nucleus of the National Aeronautics and Space Administration's technical staff, as the army lost its role in the development of long-distance missiles. In the Soviet Union, German missile experts were not integrated with any ongoing effort, but were put to work in a closely watched parallel effort, keeping the Soviet effort secure from prying eyes. Eventually, many of these Germans returned to their country of origin once the Soviets were satisfied that they had learned all they could from World War II experiments.

Development of the First-Generation ICBM

The first Soviet ballistic missile to be operationally significant was the SS-3 MRBM, fielded two years before the first U.S. strategic ballistic missile. This missile was not as technologically demanding as the first U.S. strategic ballistic missile, for the Soviets only had to be able to reach several hundred, rather than several thousand, miles to meet their immediate strategic needs, which was the European theater. But the Soviets found that their early capabilities did not fill all of their ultimate requirements. Thus they rapidly moved toward their first truly intercontinental missile, the SS-6. The SS-6 was an enormous system: 30 by 4.5 meters (100 by 15 ft.) weighing 560,000 pounds, and carrying a payload of some 9,000 pounds, including a multi-megaton warhead. By now the warhead was thermonuclear, accounting for the relatively high yield in the still large payload. The size of the vehicle and its great thrust was made possible by strapping together several smaller boosters and igniting them simultaneously. The SS-6 was not satisfactory as an ICBM, however. Its above-ground vulnerable launch pad would not be easy to remedy given its size, shape, and nonstorable liquid fuel. The emerging U.S. intercontinental threat would have to be met by a follow-on generation of more survivable and producible missiles. Like the SS-3, the SS-6 was quickly phased out and shifted to the Soviet space program.

Both the Soviets and the United States worked on long-range cruise missiles in the early years as well. For the United States, early cruise missiles added to the capability provided by the U.S. bomber force, exploiting proven aircraft technologies, while the rocket, guidance, and reentry technologies needed for a successful ICBM had an opportunity to mature. Certain key technologies that were developed or defined in the process of the U.S. pursuit of cruise missiles carried over directly to the ballistic missile programs. The most significant contributions were inertial navigations systems and rocket engines derived from the V-2. Certain technologies were missing from the equation, however, including one in particular: a relatively small, high-yield thermonuclear warhead. Up to this point, preliminary requirements had called for a missile of great size and thrust to loft the warheads that were projected, and the warheads would have required delivery with then-unachievable accuracies at intercontinental range. Progress was being made in reducing the size of fission weapons, and the detonation of the first fusion bomb in 1951, followed by the first "super" fusion bomb in 1952, led to an intersection of opportunities and requirements that put the ICBM within practical reach.

Now a relatively small and inaccurate missile system could meet operational requirements, given the lighter but more powerful warheads that were becoming available. It was shortly after the first "super" was detonated that Trevor Gardner, Assistant to the U.S. Air Force Secretary, was asked to look into the ICBM program, with a view to its further reduction. He and the Von Neumann group he formed found instead an opportunity for a real breakthrough in the ICBM program. Brig. Gen. Bernard Schriever was put in charge, and a supporting management system was established that gave the effort first call on resources, permission to conduct concurrent development, and direct and immediate access to key decision makers in the air force and the Department of Defense. The air force accelerated the Atlas ICBM to a timely and successful completion.

Three other programs were pursued that might have served to ensure that at least one strategic ballistic missile capability would be produced and deployed at an early date should Atlas fail. These were the Titan ICBM system, and the Thor and Jupiter intermediate-range systems. The president eventually placed top priority on all these projects. Atlas was pushing technology in a new direction, in an attempt to maximize the amount of thrust per pound in order to send a reasonable-sized package to intercontinental range. This was to be done with a thin-skinned metal "balloon," in which the fuel tank did double duty as the body of the missile itself. Rigidity and strength would be achieved by maintaining internal pressure. Titan would provide a more conservative approach—a rigid outer body, which also served as the skin of the fuel tanks.

Both Atlas and Titan worked, but if they had not, Thor and Jupiter missiles, eventually deployed at European bases, would have filled the gap. Jupiter started development before Thor as an army project at Redstone Arsenal under the supervision of the German-American team led by Wehrner von Braun. The army system benefited from a relatively knowledgeable and experienced team at the helm, and it provided at least one critical technological breakthrough that the air force and its contractors had not tried. The Jupiter's ablative reentry vehicle turned out to be a more successful method of dissipating the heat of friction on rapid reentry into the earth's atmosphere. The ability to reenter quickly, in turn, was important to both penetration and accuracy as these characteristics became more important. The army program provided competitive pressure for substantial progress in air force programs, which paid off for the ICBM. It also provided some initial impetus to the navy's Polaris submarine-launched missile program. For a short time, the navy shared in missile development with the army, but when breakthroughs were beginning to be achieved in solid fuels—including stability, ease of manufacture, and specific impulse—the navy moved out on its own very successful program.

Development of the Soviet Second and Third Generations

While these developments were occurring, the Soviets were deferring large-scale strategic missile deployments, looking toward a second generation of long-range missiles while attempting to keep the world thinking that the first was already deployed in large numbers. The second generation included two land-based, theater-range missiles, the SS-4 and SS-5. Going beyond the theater orientation of the SS-4s and SS-5s, and replacing the less than satisfactory SS-6 ICBM, were a pair of ICBMs, the SS-7 and the SS-8. Missile types seemed to appear in pairs by this time. Apparently two competing design bureaus were working on ICBMs, with different design philosophies reflected in their products. Normally those products would both be deployed, but the one that worked best would be deployed in larger numbers. Of these two ICBMs, the SS-7 seems to have received approval. It is believed to have been superior to the SS-8 in terms of reliability, especially because it used storable liquid fuels. As long as both systems were soft or only partially hardened (each had some of each), rapid reaction time became an important hedge for survivability—a feature difficult for any Soviet system of the time to attain given early difficulties experienced in developing and producing reliable, ready inertial guidance systems.

In their third generation, the Soviets deployed three ICBMs, which together resolved many of the problems of the preceding generations. The SS-9 heavy ICBM was a clear spinoff of the large and successful SS-7, and had characteristics similar to some of Titan II's design features. The SS-9 provided significant improvements in a number of areas—alert rate, reaction time, dispersion of launch sites (only one could be destroyed by a single incoming warhead), doctrinal desirability as reflected in the number of systems deployed, communication to and within the force, the availability of a multiple (but not independently targetable) reentry vehicle version, throwweight, yield, and accuracy. These improvements provided the beginning of a significant counterforce capability, and opened up new doctrinal doors, which very likely had been passed through by the time of the SS-9's deployment in 1965.

Joining the SS-9 in the third generation were the SS-11 and SS-13, both candidates to be the Minuteman of the Soviet strategic force structure. Again we see the influence of competing design bureaus—two approaches to the same problem, in this case the need for a producible multipurpose system for eventual widespread deployment. Again the more successful candidate was deployed in larger numbers; in this instance, the liquid-fueled SS-11 seems to have prevailed in the competition with the solid-fueled SS-13, with more than a thousand of the former and fewer than a hundred of the latter eventually deployed.

Each of these missiles would seem to have had unique advantages and disadvantages. The SS-13, because of its solid fuel, might have seemed attractive, but more work apparently needed to be done on solid fuels for them to be relied on for the bulk of the Soviet landbased missile force. The SS-11 is estimated to have greater throwweight, another 1,600 kilometers (1,000 mi.) in range, and a higher degree of reliability, the latter being perhaps the most significant difference between the two. The SS-11's widespread deployment and flexibility, including a low minimum as well as a high maximum range, have made it a potential weapon against the People's Republic of China and Europe as well as the United States. Like the SS-9, the SS-11 has been tested in an MRV mode.

Development of the U.S. Second and Third Generations

The first U.S. ICBM generation ended with the strategic missile program at the beginning of a transitional second generation that spanned several models and years. The Atlas D was followed by the Atlas E and F before this family of systems left inventory; the Titan I was supplemented and eventually supplanted by the Titan II; the navy's Polaris A-1 was joined by the A-2 and then the A-3, with the A-1 and the A-2 eventually phasing out; and an entirely new family of solid-fuel missiles, the Minuteman IA and B models, followed by the Minuteman II, joined the landbased force and came to dominate it. The Polaris A-3 and the Minuteman II formed the transitional link to the third generation of U.S. strategic missile systems, the Poseidon C-3 and the Minuteman III MIRV-equipped systems.

The Titan I had already marked a significant milestone. It was the first strategic missile on either side to be placed in a silo. The Atlas E took a step in this direction by being emplaced in a concrete "coffin" before the Atlas F went into a silo. But none of these were very hard, in that all of the missiles in question had to be fueled and elevated to an exposed position before firing, which took time. The key problem was the cryogenic nonstorable liquid propellants used by the Atlas and Titan I missiles. Once this was replaced in later models by a more stable propellant, the prelaunch fueling operation could be eliminated and the missile could be fired from within a silo, allowing the silo to be hardened to a higher level and the missile to take advantage of the hardness until closer to the moment of launch, important factors once the other side had fielded a significant intercontinental threat.

Other significant improvements incorporated in the Atlas E and F were launch site dispersal so that no more than one could be destroyed by one warhead; adoption of Jupiter and Titan I's ablative reentry vehicle, which became the standard in U.S. strategic missiles (as had been the case from the outset in the Soviet Union), use of all-inertial guidance, seen earlier in the intermediate range Thor and Jupiter missiles, and now another standard feature for future strategic missiles; and a larger, more powerful warhead. But with the new warhead, and despite the improved guidance, accuracy was limited. By the time of the deployment of Atlas E and F, accuracy had become an important factor for operational effectiveness. To improve accuracy, as well as survivability, reliability, and range, another approach to the primary missile force was needed.

A partial answer was the improved Titan—which unlike the improved Atlas, was kept in the force until the mid-1980s. With its storable liquid propellant, Titan II was placed in a launch silo from which it could be fired directly, with better reaction and less exposure time. In addition, improvements in propellant and engine led to a major increase in thrust with only a slightly larger volume, the advantages being throwweight (doubled) permitting a larger yield (doubled), longer range (another 2,400 km [1,500 mi.]), improved accuracy (⅔ of the old CEP), increased probability of successful launch (reliability at the launch site considerably improved), and improved probability of arrival (anticipating the possibility of a Soviet antiballistic missile, provision was made for a package of penetration aids).

Titan II would not, however, provide the answer to the coming proliferation of Soviet hard targets. The Titan was too large and expensive to deploy in the numbers required to ensure target system coverage. Nor could the Polaris program provide the accuracy or yield required even if it had been inexpensive enough to proliferate. The eventual answer would come instead with the deployment of Minuteman, which had been in development since 1957—the year of the first successful Atlas D test. Drawing on the breakthrough in solid fuels that the U.S. Navy was first to exploit with the Polaris, the first model of Minuteman I was deployed beginning in 1962, together with the Polaris A-2 and Titan II. Minuteman was less expensive than these two systems per warhead. It was thus the logical candidate for extensive deployment against the bulk of the opposing target system. After a short examination as a complement to silo basing, a mobile-mode variant was rejected for Minuteman. The Soviets were believed to be far from having sufficiently accurate ICBMs in sufficient numbers to threaten a dispersed, hardened Minuteman force in silos. Minuteman's solid fuel would have facilitated mobility, but security, surety, and public concerns overrode the potential long-term advantages and a mobile force was not developed.

By taking advantage of silo basing and the simplicity of solid rocket motors, the first Minuteman boasted a high alert rate; short reaction time; an increase in hardness, including very little exposure time when firing; good, hardened communications, a degree of on-site retargeting capability; high reliability; and improved accuracy. The only potential drawbacks at the time were range and yield, but against most targets that Minuteman was called upon to attack, its improved accuracy was assessed to adequately compensate for yield. Just a year later, an improved model of Minuteman I continued filling out the force, eventually outstripping the earlier model at maximum deployment by 650 to 130. More of these were deployed than any other U.S. ICBM before or since.

The last member of the second generation of U.S. ICBMs was Minuteman II—which eventually supplanted both models of Minuteman I as the single-warhead member of the Minuteman family. Development of this missile began in 1961, in part to meet the need for improved accuracy and flexibility. Building on the successful Minuteman I lower stages, Minuteman II brought to the force advances in many areas. Accuracy was improved by a factor of two or more, and communications, retargeting, reliability, range, penetration aids, and growth potential through increased throwweight, were also enhanced.

Shortly after Titan II's debut, and two years prior to the fielding of Minuteman II, the Soviets had already deployed their SA-5, thought to have antiballistic missile potential, and had begun to display the Galosh system, identified as an antiballistic missile. Considering how capable these Soviet systems might be, the multiple independently targetable reentry vehicle warhead that had been explored as an option for Minuteman II and Polaris A-3 became more attractive—leading to the third generation of U.S. strategic missiles, Minuteman III and Poseidon C-3. The air force selected an option for the new Minuteman, with fewer reentry vehicles of higher yield, while the navy opted for more warheads of lower yield for Poseidon. The Minuteman choice was influenced by the air force concern to cover the increasing number of hard point targets in the Soviet inventory; the Poseidon choice was influenced by the navy concern not to jeopardize penetration, which could become a weak link in the sea-based deterrent's strong suit of assured retaliation against valued area targets.

The research and development community was enthusiastic about these systems; MIRV technology, deriving from the "bus" concept that had originally been developed for the deployment of multiple satellites, was already available. U.S. Secretary of Defense Robert McNamara was a supporter. Not only was this a way of defeating the Soviet antiballistic missile and of pressing the Soviets to abandon such a system at the bargaining table, it would also provide a way to resolve the air force's demand for more target coverage, without having to deploy more than the 1,000 Minutemans eventually fielded. It was thus an attractive technological opportunity.

MIRV was not the only advance incorporated in Minuteman III or Poseidon C-3. With Minuteman III, other major upgrades were a further hardening of the silo, a rapid retargeting capability, and an improvement in accuracy. But the splitting of the Minuteman III payload into a three-vehicle MIRV came initially at some expense to the yield per vehicle—the air force's hoped-for improvement in hard-target capability was to that degree degraded. The percentage of the total target base that could still be effectively attacked was increased nonetheless, through an increase in number of deliverable warheads, with a high probability of damage against all but the hardest targets. Eventually yield was improved, along with another improvement in accuracy; this would permit a much more effective attack on hardened Soviet missile silos.

Development of the Fourth Generation

The Soviet fourth-generation strategic missiles exhibited some of the same advances as the U.S. third generation, plus some improvements that had not yet been seen in the U.S. force. The Soviets began development and deployment of their MIRVs later than those of the United States. But it does not appear that their new systems made the same sacrifices as the United States in potential counterforce capability in order to achieve assured penetration or target-system coverage. For not only did the number of reentry vehicles per missile increase on MIRV-equipped versions of their fourth-generation missiles—four for the SS-17, ten or more for the SS-18, and six for the SS-19 ICBMs, and three for the SS-20 IRBM—the yield per reentry vehicle remained significant while accuracy was increased, to the point that these systems could threaten nearly any hardened target in the United States or in the territory of U.S. allies. Further, "cold launch" was incorporated into a number of these systems, adapting a technology first used in U.S. and Soviet missile submarines, permitting a more rapid reload of land-based systems.

The fourth U.S. generation could be characterized by a growing capability to put Russian silo-based missiles and other critical hard targets at risk. The most important means to perform this function in the U.S. force structure is the ten-warhead MX, or Peacekeeper, missile, a highly effective system against the proliferation of hard targets in the former Soviet Union. Initially 50 Peacekeepers have been deployed in a silo mode, displacing an equal number of Minuteman III at F.E. Warren Air Force Base in Wyoming. This missile has been in development for many years and has been highly successful, expanding on the MIRV payload and adding to the accuracy afforded by Minuteman III. The silo-based Peacekeeper force represents an increase in U.S. retaliatory capability at risk as Russian ICBM accuracy grows. It also represents an improvement in the deterrent power the Russians would face if the U.S. silo-based missile force were attacked, because each silo that survived holds ten warheads. As with other silo-based ICBMs, all warheads would survive if launched early from under attack or upon first nuclear detonation, a possibility the Russians could not discount.

Development of the Fifth Generation

On the Soviet side, a fifth generation of strategic ballistic missiles was developed and deployed. The Soviets applied their successful experience with the SS-20 intermediate-range missile and earlier mobile systems to long-range mobile follow-ons, the SS-24 rail-based and SS-25 road-based land mobile ICBMs. The SS-25 is a successor to the SS-16 ICBM banned by the Strategic Arms Limitation Talks and its SS-20 intermediate-range derivative. It is a single reentry vehicle, solid-fuel ICBM deployable across thousands of square kilometers of territory on and off the road network of the former Soviet Union. The SS-24 is a completely new solid-fuel ICBM with MIRV and is deployable over thousands of kilometers of trackage. Upgrades are possible for both—the SS-25 could acquire MIRV as the SS-20 did, and both the SS-24 and SS-25 could be given hard-target kill accuracies.

On the U.S. side, a rail-mobile Peacekeeper, and/or a new small road-mobile missile, would take on many of the characteristics of the Soviet fifth generation ICBMs. As Russian accuracies and yields continue to improve, it would be desirable for the U.S. ICBM force to add mobility to the mix. The Scowcroft Commission recommendation of a combination of silo-based and mobile missiles significantly affected the agenda for the alternative being considered by the United States. At the same time, the consensus formed after the report's publication in 1983 has eroded as budgetary pressures, competing priorities, new analyses, a changing world and arms control considerations have continued to shift the focus of the debate.

Prospects for the Future

The ICBM should remain a dominant feature of the former Soviet strategic force for years to come, with mobile ICBMs probably accounting for a more substantial fraction of their ICBM mix in time, with or without strategic arms limits. The future of the U.S. ICBM force is more problematic. While there still appears to be a consensus that a triad of strategic forces ought to be maintained to assure stability and deterrent value, and many see mobility as an appropriate direction for the next ICBM generation, the details remain contested. In the meantime, other nations' ballistic missile forces seem likely to continue to advance. While all such forces, including those of the United Kingdom, France, and China, can be expected to continue to lag behind the forces of the United States and the former Soviet Union in both quality and quantity, even in the event of a new strategic arms agreement, other nations will continue to obtain longer-range ballistic missiles, possibly slowed but probably not stopped by controls on missile technology. It appears, at least for the foreseeable future, that the ICBM and its relatives will continue to be deployed and affect the security dilemma facing all nations.

[The views expressed in this article are those of the author and do not reflect the official policy or position of the U.S. Department of Defense or the Government.]

FRANK B. HORTON III

SEE ALSO: Ballistic Missile Defense; Deterrence; Missile, Guided; Missile Propulsion Technology; Missile Technology Applications.

Bibliography

Armacost, M. H. 1969. *The politics of weapons innovation: The Thor-Jupiter controversy.* New York: Columbia Univ. Press.
Baker, J. C., and R. P. Berman. 1982. *Soviet strategic forces.* Washington, D.C.: Brookings.
Ball, D. 1972. *The strategic missile programs of the Kennedy administration, 1961–1963.* Canberra: Australian National Univ.
Ball, D., and J. Richelson, eds. 1986. *Strategic nuclear targeting.* Ithaca, N.Y.: Cornell Univ. Press.
Beard, E. 1976. *Developing the ICBM: A study in bureaucratic politics.* New York: Columbia Univ. Press.
Bracken, P. 1983. *The command and control of nuclear forces.* New Haven, Conn.: Yale Univ. Press.
Brodie, B. 1959. *Strategy in the missile age.* Santa Monica, Calif.: Rand Corp.
Emme, E. M., ed. 1964. *The history of rocket technology.* Washington, D.C.: Government Printing Office.
Freedman, L. 1983. *The evolution of nuclear strategy.* New York: St. Martin's Press.
Fuhrman, R. A. 1978. *Fleet ballistic missile system: Polaris to Trident.* Washington, D.C.: AIAA.
Gray, C. 1977. *The future of land based missiles.* London: International Institute for Strategic Studies.
Greenwood, T. 1975. *Making the MIRV: A study of defense decision making.* Cambridge: Ballinger.
Gunston, B. 1979. *The illustrated encyclopedia of the world's rockets and missiles.* New York: Crescent Books.
Horton, F. B., III. 1979. *The future of land-based ICBMs: A reappraisal.* Montgomery, Ala.: Air Univ.
International Institute for Strategic Studies. 1989. *The military balance 1988–1989.* London: Brassey's.
Kolkowicz, R., and E. Mickiewicz. 1986. *The Soviet calculus of nuclear war.* Lexington, Ky.: Heath.
Leebaert, D., ed. 1981. *Soviet military thinking.* London: Allen and Irwin.
Sapolsky, H. M. 1972. *The Polaris system development.* Cambridge, Mass.: Harvard Univ. Press.
Schelling, T. C. 1971. *Arms and influence.* New Haven, Conn.: Yale Univ. Press.
Schneider, B. R., C. S. Gray, and K. B. Payne, eds. 1984. *Missiles for the nineties ICBMs and strategic policy.* Boulder, Colo.: Westview Press.
Scott, H. F., and W. F. Scott. 1983. *The Soviet control structure: Capabilities for wartime survival.* Washington, D.C.: National Strategy Information Center.
Scowcroft, B., et al. 1983. *Report of the president's commission on strategic forces.* Washington, D.C.: Government Printing Office.
Snyder, G. 1961. *Deterrence and defense.* Princeton, N.J.: Princeton Univ. Press.
Sokolovskii, V. D. 1963. *Soviet military strategy.* Englewood Cliffs, N.J.: Prentice Hall.

MISSILE PROPULSION TECHNOLOGY

The theoretical principles underlying the design and performance of rocket motors for powered missile flight have been widely understood and practiced for many years. Despite technological limitations that prevent realization of potential performance, advances in materials and propellant technologies enable gains to be achieved over the previous state of the art. Technological innovations are required to meet increasing demands on the rocket plume with respect to stealth and guidance; demand for low-vulnerability or insensitive-munition response to thermomechanical stimuli in service use; and engineering and material innovations for thrust vector control (TVC) guidance devices and ramjets for tactical applications.

The overall emphasis on rocket motor design and technology differs according to whether the application is strategic or tactical and whether liquid- or solid-propellant technology is chosen.

Strategic Versus Tactical

Strategic long-range missiles first appeared in the form of the German V-2 rocket developed under the direction of Werner Von Braun during the Second World War. The range of a missile is a function of the change in velocity induced by operation of its rocket motor. Strategic missiles, designed to carry their payloads over long distances, therefore generally require large velocity increments.

The velocity increment (Dv) produced by a rocket motor in a particular missile depends upon the ratio of the mass of the vehicle before operation of the rocket to the mass of the vehicle following rocket motor firing.

$$\text{Thus: } Dv = I_{sp} \text{ Ln} \left[\frac{M_i}{M_i - M_p} \right]$$

Here M_i is the initial mass and M_p is the mass [in kilograms] of propellant burnt. I_{sp} is the thrust generated per unit mass [in newton seconds/kilogram] of propellant, and is usually referred to as specific impulse. It can be readily shown, using Tsiolkovski's equation above, that the ratio of payload to total vehicle mass decreases exponentially as the velocity increment increases. Strategic rocket motors are therefore large and, together with their propellants, generally represent more than 95 percent of the total vehicle mass. Tactical missiles, with much lower velocity increments, are much more efficient propulsive devices;

the useful mass propelled rarely falls below 40 percent of the total vehicle mass.

Until the mid-1960s, strategic missiles were often powered by liquid-propellant motors despite their complexity and cost. The advent of improved solid rocket-motor propellants has led to the widespread use of solid-propellant motors for both tactical and strategic applications.

Liquid-Propellant Versus Solid-Propellant Rocket Motors

The choice of propellant for a specific rocket application depends upon a number of factors. The majority of military missiles, tactical and strategic, use solid-propellant motors. What liquid engines there are now use packageable hypergolic propellants rather than the older liquid oxygen and kerosene combination in order to reduce reaction time from minutes to seconds.

The specific impulse produced by a liquid-propellant motor is generally greater than that produced by a solid-propellant motor. The density of a solid propellant, however, is normally about one-and-a-half times the density of liquid propellant. Thus, a missile using a solid-propellant motor is generally about 20 to 30 percent smaller than its equivalent liquid-propelled counterpart.

The thrust of a solid-propellant motor has little effect upon its mass. A liquid-propellant engine, on the other hand, has a mass roughly proportional to the thrust. For this reason missiles requiring high initial accelerations almost invariably use solid propellants, whereas large strategic missiles that produce large thrusts, but which leave the pad with low accelerations, often use liquid motors. (The latter, despite their large size, are more efficient than the solid equivalent.)

Tactical missiles, on the other hand, are required to produce a high, usually constant, thrust for a short time. They must withstand rough handling over a wide temperature range and must above all else be cheap. Therefore, almost all are propelled by solid-propellant motors.

Only when extreme reliability is required, with variable and controlled thrust or high specific impulse, are liquid motors overwhelmingly favored. Only in liquid-propellant motors can motor components be tested by actual firing before integration into the final build. Solid-motor reliability must be demonstrated by large numbers of firings and careful statistical analysis.

Only liquid-propellant motors currently possess the ability to be throttled on demand. Numerous attempts have been made to control the thrust of a solid-propellant motor, but none have yet demonstrated a reliable system that could match the flexibility of a liquid counterpart. For less demanding thrust profiles (such as second boost on demand), boost-sustain and pre-determined tailored thrust profiles are all that are yet possible for solid-propellant rocket motors.

For applications in which payload mass is at a premium, the extremely high specific impulse of a liquid system is required. For military geostationary satellites, for example, every point increase in specific impulse represents an extra percentage mass of attitude-control propellant, which translates into more time on station.

In addition, for satellite orbital maneuver and attitude control systems, the flexible on-off variable thrust and small bit impulse requirements are best met with liquid propellants.

In summary, the ability of solid propellants to withstand rough handling and great temperature extremes, together with their relatively low cost and inherent safety (not being subject to spillage hazards, etc.), make them particularly well suited for use in tactical missiles.

Solid Propellants for Rocket Motors

The solid-propellant charge may be cartridge loaded or case bonded. The cartridge-loaded charge is manufactured separately and subsequently loaded into the motor at the final engine assembly stage. In the case-bonded approach, the propellant charge is formed by a casting process in situ within the rocket motor combustion chamber. During the casting process an adhesive bond is formed between the propellant and the inner surface of the lined motor case.

To a first approximation, a solid-propellant charge, when ignited at an exposed surface, burns such that all points on the surface regress linearly at a rate characteristic of that propellant and as a function of the local combustion chamber total pressure.

The propellant charge may take the form of a solid block or have internal perforations of various shapes (Fig. 1). By geometrical design, the burning surface is usually kept constant throughout burn time. The product of the burn-

Figure 1. Charge evolution.

ing surface area and burning rate, in conjunction with the nozzle design, determines the combustion chamber pressure and motor thrust. The propellant charge thickness and burning rate determine the burn time or function time of the motor.

It follows that the ability to adjust or tune the burning rate over a wide range for boost/sustain applications is an important design advantage. The availability of a wide range of burning rates for design selection enables optimization, within the motor envelope, of the charge geometry, and hence the volume loading fraction of propellant in the motor.

The use of a wide range of proprietary burning-rate catalyst modifiers, together with many other minor additives to control the chemical and physical properties of the propellant, provides a large number of formulation permutations for a given generic class of propellants.

Propellants fall into two generic categories: composite and double-base propellants. Composite propellants consist of an inert polymetric binder fuel that is highly filled with a solid particulate oxidizer and other ingredients. The polymetric binder may be plastic (e.g., polyvinyl chloride) or elastomeric (e.g., polyurethane).

The properties of the inert binder are extremely important with respect to stress-strain capability, aging stability, and processing. The most advanced current composite propellants use binders based on a urethane elastomer derived from a hydroxy-terminated polybutadiene (HTPB) precursor.

Practical considerations imposed on thermochemistry studies drive the selection of fillers and have led to the universal use of powdered aluminum metal (AL) as the fuel and particulate ammonium perchlorate (AP) as the oxidizer. These propellants are generically referred to by the acronym AP/AL/HTPB. In terms of process simplicity, low cost, and high energy/density considerations, this class of propellant has unrivaled attractions.

The second category of double-base propellants originates from the nitroglycerine plasticized nitrocellulose binder propellants, such as cordites or extruded double base (EDB). Subsequent derivatives are the base grain cast-double-base (CDB) propellants or the slurry cast-double-base (SCDB). The latter derivatives have advantages over EDB in ease of manufacture of larger sizes of propellant charge/motors, more complex charge geometries, flexibility of formulation, and ability to cast into motors in a case-bonded mode.

The latter double-base propellants have limited low-temperature mechanical properties, in particular strain capability. This limitation is primarily related to the use of nitrocellulose as the binder polymer. More recent advances in technology have led to elastomer modifications in which an elastomer with good low-temperature properties partly or wholly replaces nitrocellulose as the polymer binder. Nitroglycerine is the most common plasticizer, but other less energetic liquid nitric esters can be used. These double-base-derived categories are known as energetic binders and are frequently utilized without fillers. The products of combustion are essentially gaseous and hence are minimum-smoke propellants. The current state of the art has frequent examples of filled versions of these energetic binders. Aluminum/ammonium perchlorate–filled double-base propellants are in service use, but more usually the use of nitramine particulate fillers such as RDX or HMX is preferred for increasing energy/density while retaining minimum-smoke features.

Advances in Solid Propellants for Missiles

In the search for increased performance, the scope for increased energy/density of solid propellants is known in theoretical terms. The realization of further gains requires innovative technology advances to overcome practical limitations of processing, hazards, cost, chemical stability, and mechanical properties in conjunction with the ability to adjust exotic materials to match the utility of a wide range of burning-rate catalytic effects. Such advances are increasingly being driven by the emphasis on missile exhaust plume properties and demands for lower vulnerability or insensitive munitions. (The latter two areas are referred to again in later sections.)

The attractive AP/AL/HTPB class of composite propellants is seriously deficient for missile applications that require low-smoke exhaust plumes or low-signature stealth features in the nonvisible wavelengths.

Some mitigation of the smoke plume density is achieved by omitting aluminum (at the expense of energy/density) from the propellant. However, under typical high-humidity conditions in service deployment, dense acid fume smokes arise from the use of ammonium perchlorate oxidizer. Currently available alternative oxidizers have limitations. Ammonium nitrate is an obvious alternative that gives minimum-smoke performance, but it has serious filler/binder physical incompatibility due to the propensity of ammonium nitrate to undergo several phase (and hence volume) changes over the range of typical service temperatures. Attempts to mitigate or stabilize this phenomenon have been sought for many years.

Minimum-smoke composite propellants are being sought by use of RDX- or HMX-filled HTPB, but significant problems remain. The high RDX filler levels tend to induce detonation in sensitive propellants, which runs counter to the desire for insensitive or low-vulnerability munitions. The high levels of RDX/HMX dominate and limit the available range of burning rates in such propellants and thus their utility to the rocket designer.

Accordingly the trend is to use energetic binders to improve the I_{sp} and thus allow the levels of the nitramine (e.g., RDX/HMX) fillers to be reduced. Two main thrusts can be seen in this trend. First, there are energetic binders based on inert polymers plasticized with energetic plasticizers such as nitroglycerine or alternative nitric ester liquid plasticizers. The immiscibility of butadienes and hence HTPB polymers with liquid nitric esters impels the propellant chemist toward polymers similar to those evolving in the elastomer-modified double-base propellants. Hence the two separate generic categories of propellants are converging in binder, plasticizer, and filler technologies for the future minimum-smoke, stealth, low-vulnerability, insensitive-munitions requirements.

The second major thrust is the replacement of inert polymers in the energetic plasticized binders with energetic polymers. This implies nitrated polymers. Innovative chemical routes must be sought in the laboratories to overcome the formidable problems of processing, hazardous properties, chemical stability, and the effect of nitrate groups in degrading polymer elasticity and low-temperature flexibility/embrittlement threshold.

Rocket Exhaust Plume Properties

There are significant advantages to the missile designer in minimum-smoke rocket exhaust plumes with respect to missile guidance. Transparency of the plume to incident beams in the visible, near, and far infrared is an increasing demand.

Composite propellants of the AP/AL/HTPB class produce copious dense smoke due to condensed-phase suspensions of aluminum oxide and oxidizer-derived hydrochloric acid fumes in the rocket exhaust. So-called reduced-smoke motors using nonaluminized AP/HTPB propellants also produce dense secondary smokes in conditions of modest ambient humidity. Such plumes are essentially totally opaque to wavelength in the visible-to-far infrared.

The double-base propellants and their derivatives, the elastomer modified RDX/HMX versions, are minimum-smoke propellants because the combustion products are virtually entirely gaseous. However, an energy/density penalty is paid vis-à-vis the aluminized composite propellants.

Minimum-smoke propellants per se do not guarantee minimum-smoke rocket motors. The latter require attention to the nonpropellant materials of the motor. Even modest consumption of inert parts, such as combustion chamber insulants, can result in a significant particle count in the exhaust comparable to the incident beam wavelength, and the resultant multiple particle scattering gives rise to significant attenuation of the incident beam transmission.

High-performance rocket motors, including minimum-smoke motors, typically produce powerful exhaust plume flames called secondary flames. These result not only in a visible signature, which is exacerbated in darkness, but also in a hot plume trail that radiates a signature throughout the wavelength spectrum.

Significant advances are foreseen in suppressing such secondary flame in high-performance minimum-smoke rocket motors. This can be accompanied by reductions of several orders of magnitude in signature emission intensity in the range from far infrared through the visible, UV, and microwave frequencies. Furthermore, rocket plumes with secondary flames, including those from minimum-smoke motors, have hot plumes with high electron density and hence high attenuation of incident radar frequency beams. The hot turbulent plumes also result in significant broadening and scattering of incident laser beams. Suppression of the secondary flame can result in virtually zero radar attenuation and laser beam attenuation and avoid laser extinction when the beam traverses a long path length through the flame.

Rocket Motor Hardware and Inert Components

The materials technology involved in rocket propulsion is a wide-ranging science beyond the scope of this article. The insulation liner for the combustion chamber; the refractory materials for the nozzle throat; the insulation liner in the blast pipe, aft closure, and nozzle expansion zone—each of these has a unique technology in properties and processing. The search for improved materials and formulations requires low thermal diffusivity and/or conductivity with large endothermic stages in pyrolysis or protective char formation; high resistance to ablation in hot erosive propellant gas environments; compatibility of properties with propellants and the stress-bearing structures; and low density and, increasingly, demands for low condensed-phase products of the pyrolysis/ablation to minimize effects on rocket exhaust smoke, flame suppression, and condensation on exhaust thrust vector control devices.

The stress-bearing components of the rocket motor case, end closures, blast pipe, and nozzle utilize either metals or fiber-reinforced composites. New high-density aluminum alloys are continually evolving, and these are still popular materials because of low cost and ease of fabrication. For higher performance, high-strength steels and aluminum alloys, often wrapped with kevlar, are the most common choice. Many high-tensile-strength steels are used in missiles today. Moreover, maraging steels with even greater minimum strengths are now available, although fabrication techniques (e.g., flow forming) present some difficulties. Composite steel-laminate resin structures have seen extensive service use in UK missiles, with equivalent minimum ultimate tensile strength (UTS) figures of 290,000 psi.

Increasing research and development attention is being applied to the use of composite structures such as kevlar- and carbon fiber–reinforced resin structures. Cost and performance damage by rough handling in service climatic and mechanical environments and the technology of bonding end closures and attachments are areas where the technology must be demonstrated before their use becomes widespread. The specific strength-to-weight properties of these structures is an obvious attraction. The specific stiffness properties, important for agile missiles, usually require a greater wall thickness and hence have lower volumetric efficiency for propellant compared with that of the high-strength steels.

Thrust Vector Control (TVC) Devices

The concept of a TVC device for steering a missile by deflecting the rocket motor exhaust has wide application in missiles. Examples include low-speed missiles where aerodynamic control is cumbersome in antitank missile launch; vertical launch and rapid turnover of missiles; agile missiles for short-range engagement and high target crossing rates; and mid-course correction in high-altitude space applications. TVC devices fall into three categories: jet exhaust deflection, secondary fluid injection, and movable nozzles.

Jet Exhaust Deflection

One TVC category employs a device to obstruct the jet exhaust on command. This results in an oblique shock wave and side force for steering the missile. Many versions have been demonstrated, including jetavators (gimballed annular ring forming an extension of the nozzle), axial jet deflectors (blades, situated around the nozzle, that move axially into the exhaust), and domed deflectors. The most popular are jet tab spoiler blades or jet vane systems. The jet tab consists of a number of blades that can move into the plane of the nozzle exit to obstruct the exhaust. The jet vanes, on the other hand, are positioned normal to the nozzle exit plane in the undeflected position. The jet vanes operate in an analagous fashion to rudders in rotating and deflecting the exhaust.

Secondary Fluid Injection

In this type of device, fluid is injected unsymmetrically into the nozzle expansion cone through ports. This creates a shock wave in the nozzle supersonic gas flow and an oblique shock wave side force. The fluid may be hot gas from the combustion chamber, but more usually a secondary fluid pressurized by a helium gas bottle or a propellant gas generator is used.

Movable Nozzles

In these devices the entire nozzle and throat—that is, the entire supersonic gas flow—is rotated, thus minimizing thrust losses of the other systems. Two main types are a nozzle with a flexible joint to the motor and a ball-and-socket swivel nozzle concept.

There is no universal TVC device for all applications. Most provide a side force for yaw and pitch control, but full three-axis control (e.g., for roll control) is obtained only with the jet vane or by twin-nozzle TVC systems. The choice of system for any particular application is a trade-off of deflection performance, actuation force and available missile power, complexity, and mass and envelope constraint thrust losses.

Insensitive Munitions Trends

There is an increasing demand for the next generation of missiles, in particular the rocket motor, to manifest low vulnerability to thermo-mechanical attack. Studies of credible attack scenarios are in turn leading to studies of the threats presented by bullets, fragments, sympathetic detonations, and fuel-fire fast and slow cook-offs.

The response of the munition can vary from no reaction or low-order burning to explosion/detonation. The study of response mechanisms and generation of design and technologies for mitigation could lead to significant changes in rocket motor concepts in the next decade.

In the case of a fuel-fire fast cook-off threat, the approach taken is to preempt the cook-off mechanism by arranging for the rocket case to disrupt under the flame, allowing the exposed propellant surface to ignite and burn normally. In the case of bullet and fragment attack, again disruption of the rocket case (e.g., a frangible response to provide rapid venting) can preempt a deflagration-to-detonation mechanism. A reduction in the sensitivity of the propellant to detonation remains the most prominent area for future research and development to meet the new demands.

Solid-Propellant Ramjet Propulsion

In recent years the application of the air-breathing concept to rocket propulsion has gained increasing prominence as a means of obtaining increased fuel efficiency.

Within the secondary combustion chamber (ramcombustor) of a ramrocket (also called a ducted rocket) air from the atmosphere is mixed with hot, partially combusted fuel gas obtained from combustion in a separate primary chamber of a gas generator that contains a solid fuel-rich propellant charge. To decouple the gas generator performance, and hence the fuel supply, from the conditions within the ramcombustor, the fuel supply is choked to sonic velocity on leaving the gas generator. The products of combustion from the ramcombustor are exhausted to the atmosphere at supersonic velocity through a convergent-divergent nozzle to produce motor thrust.

A ramrocket operates efficiently only at a supersonic flight velocity greater than about Mach 2, for it is only at such high velocity that the ram effect of the air is sufficient to produce a combustion chamber pressure high enough to sustain combustion and produce a reasonable propulsive thrust. Often a boost propellant charge, located within the ramcombustor, is used to boost the ramrocket to its operational velocity. Such a system is called an integrated boost ramrocket.

The advantages of ramjet propulsion can be clearly seen in terms of motor specific impulse (I_{sp}) comparisons. Whereas a typical CDB propellant will produce an I_{sp} of

2,200 Ns/kg, a ramrocket can yield an I_{sp} of up to 10,000 Ns/kg, more than a four-fold increase.

Conclusion

The future of missile propulsion technology will be characterized by continued focus on advanced materials research, innovations in propellant design, and applied research in rocket motor engineering. Overcoming problems associated with rocket plume detection, stealth design, and overall system vulnerability will mark the emergence of the next generation of strategic and tactical missiles.

GEOFFREY IAN EVANS
PETER DAVID PENNY

SEE ALSO: Explosives Technology, Conventional; Missile, Ballistic; Missile, Guided; Missile Technology Applications; Munitions and Explosives Technology Applications; Propulsion; Stealth and Counterstealth Technology.

Bibliography

Sutton, G. P. 1986. *Rocket propulsion elements: An introduction to the engineering of rockets.* 5th ed. New York: Wiley.

Williams, F. A., M. Barrere, and N. C. Huang. 1969. *Fundamental aspects of solid propellant rockets.* AGARDograph no. 116. Slough, Eng.: Technivision Services.

Textbook & ballistics & gunnery. 1987. Part I. London: Her Majesty's Stationery Office.

MISSILE, STRATEGIC BALLISTIC

The term *strategic* is interpreted differently by various nations. The former Soviet Union, for example, tended to regard any weapon that could reach its soil as strategic, regardless of its range capability. Existing treaties define strategic weapons as those with a maximum range exceeding 5,500 kilometers (3,300 mi.), and intermediate or theater weapons as those having ranges of 1,000 to 5,500 kilometers (600 to 3,300 mi.). Systems with ranges of less than 1,000 kilometers (600 mi.) are called short-range weapons. The Intermediate Nuclear Forces (INF) Treaty, which applies only to land-based systems, covers both intermediate and short-range weapons systems with ranges of 500 to 5,500 kilometers (300 to 3,300 mi.) In this discussion, we will use those definitions to categorize ballistic missile systems. The SS-20 and SS-4 remain in the strategic weapons systems section. Pershing, GLCM, SS-12, and SS-23 will be found in the battlefield support weapons section.

Fourth-Generation Intercontinental Ballistic Systems

The most important characteristic of the new generation of intercontinental-range ballistic missiles is the introduction of an independent targeting capability for their multiple re-entry vehicles, making them genuine MIRV (multiple independently targetable re-entry vehicle) systems. This capability implies the carrying of guidance computers on the re-entry vehicle platform—the post-boost vehicle (PBV), or "bus."

It is also believed that this generation of missiles utilizes a different guidance procedure, an on-board computer determining deviation from the programmed course and directing corrections in that course or plotting a new course, depending on the attendant circumstances.

Under the SALT treaties, the SS-17 and SS-19 are classed as "light" missiles and the SS-18 as "heavy," the only Soviet heavy missile permitted under the treaty. The SALT treaties also permit a maximum of 820 land-based ICBMs, of which no more than 308 may be of the SS-18 "heavy" type. The full allowance of silos, 820, has been refurbished and hardened for the three new systems since 1972.

Strategic Ballistic Missiles of the United States

PEACEKEEPER (MGM-118) ICBM

Peacekeeper is the name assigned to the weapon formerly known as the Advanced ICBM, or MX. The MGM-118 Peacekeeper missile is a four-stage intercontinental ballistic missile (ICBM) that has been designed to deliver ten MK21 re-entry vehicles to independent targets at ranges usually greater than 8,000 kilometers (4,800 mi.). The missile is 21.6 meters (71.3 ft.) long, 2.34 meters (7.7 ft.) in diameter, and weighs 88,450 kilograms (194,590 lb.). Three of its four stages use solid-propellant materials exhausted through single nozzles. Hydraulically operated thrust vector actuators move the nozzles to guide the missile along its flight path.

The fourth stage, called the deployment stage, uses a liquid propellant to power an axial thrust engine and eight small engines that are used for attitude control. The post-boost vehicle includes a guidance and control system, a deployment module, and re-entry vehicles. The guidance function is performed by a completely self-contained inertial guidance and navigation system. During flight, the missile is completely independent of ground references or commands.

At the time of its assembly each Peacekeeper missile is placed in a support launch canister 23.4 meters (77.2 ft.) long. At launch, a solid propellant in the canister base is ignited and ejects the missile by gas pressure. The first-stage motor ignites automatically after the missile clears the canister. Peacekeeper is the first land-based U.S. ICBM to employ so-called cold-launch techniques.

The first-stage solid-rocket motor weighs approximately 49,000 kilograms (107,800 lb.) and is about 9.1 meters (30 ft.) long. Stage one is equipped with a single movable nozzle that is controlled by signals from the guidance and control system. The second-stage solid-rocket motor weighs approximately 27,000 kilograms (59,400 lb.) and is about 5.5 meters (18.2 ft.) long. Both stages use a synthetic rubber-based solid propellant with aluminum and oxidizer additives.

The third-stage solid-rocket motor weighs about 7,700 kilograms (16,940 lb.) and is approximately 2.4 meters (7.9 ft.) long. This stage uses a synthetic polymer plastic-based solid propellant with aluminum and oxidizer additives. Like stage two, the stage-three single nozzle has an extendable exit cone to improve performance without increasing the length of the missile. The solid propellants in the first three stages are contained in motor cases made of a kevlar epoxy material.

The fourth stage weighs about 850 kilograms (1,870 lb.) and is 1.2 meters (4 ft.) long. Stage four uses a liquid bipropellant rocket propulsion system that provides velocity and attitude corrections for this phase of the missile flight. Following the burnout and separation of stage three, the postboost vehicle maneuvers and each re-entry vehicle is released. The vehicle is then moved by its propulsion systems to new positions where the remaining re-entry vehicles are deployed in sequence. The propulsion system includes the liquid propellants and tanks, an axial engine and its thrust vector actuation system, and attitude control engines that use the same bipropellant as the axial engine.

The missile guidance and control (G&C) system is contained in the postboost vehicle. The G&C system includes the missile guidance and control set containing the inertial measurement unit (IMU) and the missile electronics and computer assembly, ground and flight software, the in-flight cooling subsystem, airborne power supply, missile interconnection cables, the power and the missile umbilical assembly. Inside the IMU is a floated sphere containing gyros, accelerometers, and some associated electronics. The gyros maintain a basic computer-commanded frame of reference with which all missile movements are compared. The accelerometers measure all vehicle velocities with respect to that frame of reference. Utilizing the position and velocity information generated by the gyros and accelerometers, the missile's computer determines all guidance and control functions of the missile. The G&C system also determines the correct release point for re-entry vehicles near the termination of the powered flight path.

The re-entry vehicles, which contain the weapons, are conically shaped and covered with materials that protect the warheads during the flight through the atmosphere to the target. The high-speed re-entry causes extreme heating, thus requiring a surface material to ablate or erode in a controlled manner and thereby protect the weapon throughout its flight.

In addition to the stages and re-entry vehicles, the missile also includes a shroud and the deployment module. The shroud, often called a nose cone, protects the re-entry vehicles during the ascent phases of flight. The shroud is topped by a nose cap made of an alloy called Inconel; it contains a rocket motor to separate it from the missile.

The deployment module provides structural support for the re-entry vehicles and carries the electronics that activate and deploy them. These vehicles are mechanically attached to the deployment module. The mechanical attachment is severed by explosive units that free the re-entry vehicles, allowing them to separate from the deployment module with minimum disturbance. Each re-entry vehicle is deployed at a position that will allow it to follow a ballistic path to its target.

The Peacekeeper missile can carry twelve MK12A warheads or eleven advanced ballistic re-entry vehicles, but it is limited to ten warheads by the SALT provisions. The ten warheads currently baselined on Peacekeeper are of the MK21 type. According to the United States Air Force, Peacekeeper with ten re-entry vehicles has the range to reach the most distant planned hard targets.

In 1972, the U.S. Air Force Strategic Air Command stated a requirement for a new ICBM. This weapon was to be capable of destroying hardened targets and should itself be based in a survivable manner. After the requirement had been validated, the development program was initiated as the MX (Advanced ICBM), renamed the Peacekeeper in November 1982.

The Peacekeeper program, which includes both the missile and a basing system, entered full-scale development in September 1979, about two years later than planned. The basing schemes then proposed to ensure survivability were subsequently found to be unacceptable. When Ronald Reagan took office in January 1981, he initiated a review of American strategic forces and alternative means of modernizing those forces. In October 1981, he proposed, as part of the U.S. deterrent modernization program, continuation of Peacekeeper development with the objective of near-term interim deployment of the missile in Titan and Minuteman silos modified to increase their hardness. He also proposed cancellation of the multiple protective shelter basing system and deactivation of the Titan II ICBM force.

In August 1986, deployment of the first Peacekeeper missiles in modified Minuteman silos got under way. In February 1987, the U.S. Air Force announced that ten sites had been identified as possible rail garrison bases: Barksdale, Louisiana; Blytheville, Arkansas; Dyess, Texas; Fairchild, Washington; Grand Forks, North Dakota; Little Rock, Arkansas; Malmstrom, Montana; Minot, North Dakota; Whiteman, Missouri; and Wurtsmith, Michigan.

The Peacekeeper has a throw weight of 3,580 kilograms (7,876 lb.). Its ten warheads are each 500 kilotons. The circular error probable (CEP) is calculated at 40 meters (132 ft.).

U.S. Air Force Small ICBM

A small intercontinental ballistic missile is being developed by the U.S. Air Force as part of the U.S. strategic modernization program. Proposed as a 16,800 kilogram (36,960 lb.) missile, the small ICBM would have sufficient accuracy to ensure a high probability of damage to hard targets. A single warhead is to be carried to a maximum range of approximately 11,000 kilometers (6,600 mi.). The re-entry vehicle will be the MK21 being developed for the Peacekeeper ICBM with a 500-kiloton warhead. The small ICBM is under consideration for deployment on road mobile radiation-hardened truck launchers so as to enhance system survivability. During peacetime, the launcher would move about at random over large military reservations. During times of imminent hostilities, the launchers would be permitted to travel more extensively so as to further complicate the enemy's targeting task.

The basing mode for the small ICBM has not been fully determined, but the missile will be designed to accommodate silo launching or use of the hardened mobile launcher. The unit's guidance system will be modified advanced inertial reference spheres based on the guidance systems being produced for Peacekeeper. The proposed missile would have a length of just over 14 meters (46.2 ft.), a payload of 453 kilograms (996.6 lb.), and a solid three-stage propulsion system.

Minuteman II ICBM

Minuteman II was introduced as a considerably improved version of Minuteman I. The improvements, however, took the form of an upgrading of the original missile's capabilities rather than a radically new departure such as that represented, in some respects, by Minuteman III. Like Minuteman I, the Minuteman II is a three-stage ICBM carrying a single thermonuclear warhead, but it has increased range and azimuth, providing greater targeting coverage, while carrying a larger payload. A more sophisticated guidance system is capable of pre-storing the locations of a large number of alternative targets, while the overall accuracy of the missile is greater than that of Minuteman I. The increased payload capability enables the missile to carry both a larger thermonuclear warhead and a number of penetration aids. The first- and third-stage motors of Minuteman II are believed to be the same as those on Minuteman I, but the second-stage motor is new.

The Minuteman II is a solid-propellant missile using inertial guidance. Thrust vector control on the first and third stages is provided by four movable nozzles. The second-stage motor has a single nozzle with secondary liquid injection for thrust vector control. The re-entry vehicle is an Avco Type II B and II C with Mk 1 and 1A penetration aids. Its warhead is an MK11C single W-56 thermonuclear warhead with a yield unofficially reported as being about 2 megatons. The missile has a range of 12,500 kilometers (7,500 mi.).

Minuteman III ICBM

The Minuteman III is a three-stage ICBM powered by solid-propellant rocket motors, but it incorporates several features that make it more than a simple product improvement on the two earlier members of the series. Most of the special features relate to the final stage and re-entry system. The most significant in operational terms is the introduction of a MIRV system of three warheads. This MIRV platform is essentially a fourth stage of the missile powered by a 143-kilogram (314.6-lb.) thrust motor and maneuvered by six small pitch and yaw motors and four small roll motors. These are controlled by the fourth-stage guidance package, which also organizes the release of the chaff decoys and the re-entry vehicles.

The third stage of the missile has also been considerably improved by introduction of a new motor using fluid-injection thrust-vector control, which provides finer control of movement than the previous arrangement of four movable nozzles and which, with improved guidance, enables the missile to carry its large payload over a greater range and at the same time reduces the missile's CEP to less than 200 meters (660 ft.)

This missile uses inertial guidance and has a range of greater than 11,000 kilometers (6,600 mi.). Its normal payload is three MIRV warheads plus chaff and decoys. The warheads are MK12s at 170 kilotons each or MK12As with a yield of 335 kilotons each.

Trident C-4 Strategic Weapon System

The UGM-93A Trident (C-4) missile is a three-stage ballistic missile powered by solid-fuel engines and guided by a self-contained inertial guidance system. It has a range approximately twice that of Poseidon, or about 7,000 kilometers (4,200 mi.).

The C-4s guidance system, designated MK5, is smaller and lighter than that for Poseidon, thereby reducing inert weight and providing more space for missile propulsion. The MK5 guidance system is basically a functional equivalent of the all-inertial MK3 Poseidon system. The most significant difference is the addition of a stellar sensor that takes a star sight during the missile's flight. The postboost vehicle corrects its flight path as necessary based on data derived from the stellar sighting. This enables the Trident missile to meet Poseidon accuracy objectives at longer ranges. The function of the guidance system is to generate missile steering commands during powered flight that accurately direct the missile to the correct velocity, position, and attitude for re-entry body deployment on the assigned target. Control information is generated by input from the shipboard fire control subsystem and flight acceleration history.

The postboost vehicle is designed to permit corrections for errors in launch position data and maneuvers to deploy re-entry bodies following third-stage separation. A new MK4 re-entry body was developed for Trident. In addition to the ballistic MK4 re-entry vehicle, the MK500 Evader maneuvering re-entry vehicle was being developed as an option, although work on that system is understood to have been discontinued. Instead, if it is decided to equip with the Trident II (D-5) missile, development of a completely new MK5 re-entry system is more likely.

The launcher subsystem stows and protects the missiles aboard the submarine, pressurizes the launch tube and missile before launch, and launches the missile from the submarine. The launch control system is of a new design providing integrated control and monitoring of 24 missiles and tubes. It will be located in the missile control center to improve weapon system control and reduce the manning needed to operate the equipment.

The fire control subsystem prepares the missile guidance system with targeting and launch position data and coordinates preparation of the launcher and missile test and readiness equipment for the missile launch. Two basic fire control configurations have been developed: the MK88 Mod 2, for retrofitting to Poseidon, and the MK98 Mod 0, for the new Trident submarine. A new fire control computer, the Trident digital control computer (TDCC), was needed to handle the increased computational work involved in providing presettings for the C-4 missile. A digital read-in subsystem will provide a digital guidance interface under control of the TDCC. The navigation data converter will convert analog navigation and optical outputs to digital form. These systems are common to both fire control configurations.

The missile for Trident I weighs 29,500 kilograms (64,900 lb.) and has a range of 7,400 kilometers (4,440 mi.). Payload of the MK4 re-entry vehicle is eight W-76 100-kiloton MIRVs. The missiles have a CEP of 460 meters (1,518 ft.).

Trident II (D-5)

The Trident II (D-5) is in full-scale development. Production of the missile is scheduled to begin with an initial 21 missiles, after which it is planned to produce 72 Trident II missiles per year from 1988 to 1992, inclusive. The first two stages will have cases of graphite-epoxy and a burn time of around 65 seconds each. The third-stage motor then burns for 40 seconds, ending the boost phase. As the total U.S. procurement plans are for 800 missiles, this could result in significant cost reductions.

The missile for this system weighs 59,090 kilograms (129,998 lb.) and has a range of 12,000 kilometers (7,200 mi.). It uses MK6 stellar-inertial guidance providing a CEP of 120 meters (396 ft.). The payload of the MK5 re-entry vehicle is eight to twelve re-entry vehicles, each bearing a 300- to 475-kiloton warhead.

The U.S. Navy launched the first developmental D-5 missile from a flat pad at Cape Canaveral in January 1987. The test program will consist of 25–30 flights, of which 20 will be from flat pads. The first submerged launch was planned for the summer of 1989, using the submarine *Tennessee* as the platform.

U.S. ICBM Modernization Program

The U.S. Congress delayed voting on the recommended program pending a comprehensive review of alternatives, including a new small missile, called Midgetman, in addition to the Peacekeeper. The review of alternatives conducted by the President's Commission on Strategic Forces reaffirmed the need for a new ICBM and recommended that the Peacekeeper missile be deployed in existing silos and that supporting research and development programs be undertaken to provide alternative forces for the 1990s.

The program for ICBM modernization calls for deployment of 100 Peacekeeper missiles in existing silos and development of a small missile suitable for either fixed or mobile deployment.

Minuteman Modernization and Peacekeeper Deployment

The silos of the former system are now having the Minuteman missiles they house replaced by newer Peacekeepers, while at the same time a general effort is under way to improve U.S. ICBM basing facilities.

An integrated command, control, and communications program is designed to improve security, reliability, and data handling capabilities of the National Military Command System. A Minuteman extended survival power system will substantially extend the launch facility survival period by reason of its greater resistance to the effects of nuclear radiation during attack. It consists of high-energy lithium batteries and controls for the application of power. The Minuteman transporter/erector fleet of vehicles is also to be replaced by new transporter/erectors under a major upgrading program.

Most of the electrical equipment at Minuteman silos has been redesigned to support Peacekeeper. The existing Minuteman guidance and control cooler will be replaced by a new guidance and control conditioning unit, and there will also be modifications of the power supply and environmental control systems.

The major facility modification for Peacekeeper deployment involves removing the upper 2 meters (6.6 ft.) of the launch tube liner to allow on-site assembly of the missile stages and re-entry system. The missile and canister will be suspended by a new shock isolation system that will provide protection from nuclear attack and induced ground shock. Hardware modifications will improve visual display and control functions in the launch control console and command message processing group.

Funding for some of these efforts is included in the budget allocations for specific missile programs, such as the Peacekeeper ICBM and the small ICBM.

Strategic Ballistic Missiles of the USSR

SS-4 Sandal (Soviet Designation: R-12)

The SS-4 is an intermediate-range ballistic missile that is a developed version of the SS-3 (Shyster). The Yangel design team completed development in 1957, and the SS-4 was first shown to the public in 1961. It subsequently became a standard IRBM in the Soviet armed forces. It was also the missile that lay at the root of the Cuban crisis in 1962. Depending on the weight of the warhead, the missile has a range of between 1,500 and 2,000 kilometers (900 and 1,200 mi.).

Initially, like the SS-7 Saddler, the SS-4 used nonstorable propellant, which required several hours of preparation before launch. The complete weapon system consists of twelve tractor vehicles with special trailers. Some twenty men are required to erect and launch the missile. Official U.S. sources report that the SS-4 has a reload capacity when fired from soft sites. It is also deployed at hardened sites but without a reload capability. The guidance system employed was originally radio command, operating by means of guidance vanes in the efflux nozzles, but it was observed at the time of the Cuban crisis that a changeover to inertial guidance had been effected. The missile uses a two-stage liquid propellant. It has a launch weight of 27,000 kilograms (59,400 lb.), mounts a 1-megaton nuclear warhead, and achieves a CEP of 2.4 kilometers (1.4 mi.).

Since 1977, according to official U.S. estimates, the proportion of SS-4 and SS-5 missiles in the Soviet arsenal slowly declined as the SS-20 successor system was deployed. Upon signing of the INF treaty in December 1987, the Soviet Union declared 65 deployed SS-4 missiles, with a further 105 such missiles not deployed. There were no SS-5 missiles said to be deployed at that time. The SS-4 missiles were due to be withdrawn within three years under terms of the INF treaty.

SS-11 Sego ICBM

The SS-11 has been reported in four distinct versions—described at one time in official U.S. publications as Mods 1, 2, 3, and 4 and now referred to in three variants only. The basic SS-11 missile is a two-stage storable liquid-propellant rocket with a range of between 10,600 and 13,000 kilometers (6,360 and 7,800 mi.). When it entered service the missile carried a single warhead payload.

In the case of the Mod 2 version, there is still a single warhead, but this is now accompanied by penetration aids. The Mod 3 version, detected soon after the Mod 2 was fielded, was found to have a different re-entry vehicle and warhead arrangement, in particular a MIRV platform equipped with three warheads. No details of the size of these warheads have been revealed, but it has been deduced that they are unlikely to be less than the 200 kilotons of each of the warheads carried by the U.S. Minuteman III, which the SS-11 closely resembles. Many of the modifications to the SS-11 can be attributed to the coincident ABM defense activity in the United States during the late 1960s.

SS-13 Savage ICBM (Soviet Designation: RS-12/SS-12)

First seen in public in 1965, the year of its initial deployment, the SS-13 is a three-stage solid-propellant ICBM comparable to the U.S. Minuteman. It was a product of the little-known ICBM design bureau headed by Aleksandr D. Nadiradze.

The three stages of the missile are separated by truss structures, each with four nozzles. The upper stages are believed to be identical to the two stages of the SS-14 Scapegoat missile, which was abandoned before being deployed. Although the SS-13 has been in service for some time, it has never been deployed statically on a large scale. A total of 60 missiles are based in fields at the Yoshkar Ola base. As far as is known, the SS-13 has never been equipped with more than a single warhead.

A Mod 2 version was deployed in 1972. The Soviets claimed that the SS-25 was a treaty-compliant modification of the SS-13, although U.S. experts calculate that the throw weights of the two missiles differ by considerably more than the 5 percent allowed for modernized missiles. A problem here, however, is the ambiguity of the agreed definition of "throw weight" in the SALT II treaty. The Soviets insisted that no infringement was involved.

The SS-13 is hot launched from a silo and is presumed to use inertial guidance. It has a launch weight of 33,000 kilograms (72,600 lb.), a range of 9,400 kilometers (5,640 ft.), and a CEP of 1,800 meters (5,940 ft.). The nuclear warhead is estimated to have a yield of 750 kilotons.

The Soviets reportedly fired two SS-13s in 1986, the first such launches in two decades, so the United States could judge the validity of Soviet claims that the SS-25 is a modernized version of this missile.

SS-18 Satan Strategic ICBM (Soviet Designation: RS-20)

The SS-18 is the largest of the fourth-generation Soviet intercontinental ballistic missiles and the only "heavy" missile permitted them under terms of the SALT II treaty. It is a two-stage liquid-propelled missile that is the functional successor to the SS-9. By 1983, four different versions of the SS-18 had been identified, each with a different payload/range (see Table 1).

Table 1. *Characteristics of the SS-18 Missile*

	Mod 1	Mod 2	Mod 3	Mod 4
Max range (km)	10,000	11,000	16,000	11,000
Warheads	1	8/10	1	10
Yield	25 MT	500 KT MIRV	20 MT	500 KT MIRV
IOC	1974	1976	Unk	1982

The United States describes the Mod 4 as capable of carrying "10+" re-entry vehicles, implying that it is capable of exceeding the treaty limit for land-based missiles of ten warheads. Some authorities have reported the commencement of flight testing of a follow-on version of the SS-18. Currently carrying the test designator TT-09, this missile appears to be capable of carrying up to ten re-entry vehicles and is probably intended to have greater range and accuracy than earlier versions of the SS-18. Early flight tests of this missile did not, however, prove successful. The first missile launched, in April 1986, exploded soon after clearing the silo. Another launch conducted in September 1986 ended when an explosion occurred during separation of the missile's first and second stages.

U.S. authorities are certain that increased accuracy has been a major consideration in the development program of this new modification, presumably with the intention of improving the missile's hard target capability so as to counter the silo hardness improvement program undertaken by the United States for its Minuteman and Peacekeeper missiles. Some of the more recent tests, moreover, have been carried out using a single re-entry vehicle, from which it is deduced that the former USSR may have a continuing interest in a missile with one very powerful warhead. These single warhead tests may have been part of a comparative test program designed to establish the best way of countering the improved hardness of modern silos, given that single warhead missiles have greater accuracy and hard target capability than MIRV systems.

Like other fourth-generation ICBMs, the SS-18 is deployed in a launch canister within the silo to provide protection to the missile during transportation and silo loading. It uses inertial guidance with a computer-controlled postboost vehicle and achieves, for the Mod 4, a CEP estimated at 250 meters (825 ft.). The missile is cold-launched using a two-stage liquid propellant plus PBV. It weighs some 200,000 kilograms (440,000 lb.).

SS-20 Saber Mobile IRBM (Soviet Designation: RSD-10 Pioneer)

The SS-20, a road-mobile, solid-propellant missile, is the replacement for the SS-4 and SS-5 intermediate-range theater systems. It entered development at the A. D. Nadiradze OKB in Biysk in the mid-1960s. It is believed to comprise the first two stages of the intercontinental SS-16, which was also a road-mobile system, banned under provisions of the SALT II agreement. The SS-20 may, therefore, have been more of an opportunistic system than one with a specific role. SS-4, SS-5, and SS-20 deployment between 1978 and 1983 revealed a steady decrease in quantities of the first two types, matched by comparable increases in SS-20 deployments.

The SS-20 is a two-stage missile with a multiple warhead capability and a maximum range of 5,000 kilometers (3,000 mi.). It employs inertial guidance to achieve a generally accepted CEP of 400 meters (1,320 ft.) for the Mod 2 version of the missile, although it must be observed that the accuracy achieved depends to a significant degree on the accuracy with which the initial launch site has been surveyed and the range to the target. The SS-20 is said to be capable of refiring after launching the first missile, but considerable heat is involved in each launch, which may mean that it is not possible to prepare for a second launch in less than a few hours.

The payload of the SS-20 is another feature that has now been clarified. There may have been an early version with a single re-entry vehicle, but as the three-RV MIRV version entered service in the same year, 1977, and the United States did not designate that version as Mod 2, it must be assumed that the single RV version was not deployed. The Soviets stated that all SS-20s carry three MIRV re-entry vehicles with 150-kiloton warheads. The United States reported flight testing by the Soviets of a genuine Mod 2 version, expected to be more accurate than its predecessor. Provisions of the INF treaty intended to remove this category of missile must call into question its originally envisioned role. Alternatively, its role could be taken over by one of the fifth-generation intercontinental missiles.

SS-24 Scalpel ICBM (Soviet Designation: SS-23)

The U.S. designator SS-24 has been assigned to a new fifth-generation ICBM being developed by the former USSR, possibly as an eventual successor to the existing SS-18 ICBM. The former Soviet Union indicated that the SS-24 was its one new missile permitted under the SALT II agreement. It is in the "light" category, which could give it a size close to that of the U.S. Peacekeeper missile. The SS-24 has an estimated length of 21 to 22 meters (69.3 to 72.6 ft.), a launch weight of 90,000 kilograms (198,000 lb.), and a throw weight of about 3,600 kilograms (7,920 lb.). Its propulsion is provided by multistage solid-fuel engines plus PBV. The payload consists of eight to ten re-entry vehicles with yields of 300 to 500 kilotons. The missile's range is estimated by various sources as being between 8,500 and 10,000 kilometers (5,100 and 6,000 mi.) with a reported CEP of better than 200 meters (660 ft.). The cold-launch technique is used.

Both mobile (transportable) and silo-based versions of the SS-24 are expected to appear. Mobile versions are seen as parallel developments to those carried out by the United States during the 1970s for the purpose of giving its missiles greater survivability through mobility, specifically the early U.S. mobility experiments covering air, sea, and ground launches of the Minuteman missile. All mobile systems will suffer some degradation in accuracy and, presumably, that work led to the preferred options being road or railborne systems, the latter now again being experimented with by the United States for the Peacekeeper system. The rail-mobile version of the SS-24 is carried on a railway vehicle resembling a freight wagon for movement over the nation's rail network. Flight testing of this version has continued. Construction of a series of protective tunnels (as contemplated by the United States for MX or Peacekeeper) is reported to have begun near Kozelsk and Perm. Another mobile model of the SS-24, this one carried on a tracked chassis, is also said to be in development. The rail-mobile version was deployed in 1987, with silo-based deployment, possibly in existing SS-11 bases, expected to follow in the next two or three years.

The first SS-24 flight test reported in the West took place in October 1982 under direction of the Plesetsk Test Center. Testing continued thereafter at a rapid pace so that by September 1983 a tenth flight (ending in failure) was being conducted. In November 1983, an apparently successful launch involving eight re-entry vehicles took place.

SS-25 Sickle ICBM (Soviet Designation: SS-12M)

The designation SS-25 has been assigned to what is believed to be a new fifth-generation ICBM being deployed as a possible successor to the existing SS-11 ICBM. The SS-25 is about the same size as the U.S. Minuteman ICBM, with a length of between 18 and 19 meters (59.4 and 67.7 ft.), a diameter of 1.7 meters (5.6 ft.), a weight of 35,000 kilograms (77,000 lb.), and a range of over 10,000 kilometers (6,000 mi.). The missile uses the cold-launch technique.

Solid propulsion is used for the three-stage missile. A single re-entry vehicle, having an estimated yield of 550 kilotons, is thought to be carried. Like its contemporary, the SS-24, the SS-25 will be capable of either silo deployment or operation in mobile form (road mobile in this case). The United States has stated that 100-plus mobile SS-25 launchers had become operational by early 1987, indicating a rapid rate of deployment as only eighteen had entered service by autumn of 1985, replacing twenty SS-11s. Test flights of the SS-25 reported in the West include a failure in October 1982, a launch of 6,436 kilometers (3,861.6 mi.) from Plesetsk to the Kamchatka Peninsula in February 1983, another failure in early 1983, and a successful flight in May of the same year.

Soviet Submarine-Launched Ballistic Missiles

The Soviet Union never enjoyed the easy access to the world's oceans that the United States has, nor did it have the communications and overseas ports that it would need to confidently commit its primary strategic nuclear force into submarine basing. But the Russian submarine-launched ballistic missiles (SLBMs) are fast approaching those of the United States in throw weight and re-entry vehicle numbers.

One U.S. direction that the Soviets never followed with any confidence was the use of solid propellants for their submarine-based missiles. They did, with the apparently unsuccessful SS-N-17 and with the SS-N-20, venture into solid propellants for SLBMs but evidently with limited confidence, as they also continued to develop liquid-propelled missiles with the SS-N-23. Western navies have always thought that liquid propellants, particularly in the restricted confines of a submarine, represented too great a hazard to compensate for their better performance over solids, but the evidence is that the Soviets had no great problems, the only known liquid propellant–related incident being the loss of an old boat in 1986.

SS-N-5 Serb SLBM

Serb is the code name assigned by the North Atlantic Treaty Organization (NATO) to the successor to the Sark Soviet submarine-launched ballistic missile. Serb has been described as representing the second generation of this class of missiles.

Like its forerunner, Serb is similar in appearance to the Polaris A-2 missile once in service with the U.S. Navy. It is understood to be a two-stage vehicle with inertial guidance. In size it conforms more closely to the dimensions of Polaris than does Sark, which is appreciably larger. According to official U.S. information, the SS-N-5 is approximately 12.9 meters (42.6 ft.) in length and has a maximum diameter of 1.42 meters (4.7 ft.). Launch weight has been estimated at about 18,000 kilograms (39,600 lb.). While there is fairly close agreement among various authorities on these dimensions, there is no comparable agreement on the missile's range capability. Estimates vary from about 1,200 kilometers (720 mi.) to about 2,400 kilometers (1,440 mi.), but the lower figure is considered the more likely. The missile carries a single re-entry vehicle with a one-megaton warhead. Its CEP is estimated at 2,800 meters (9,240 ft.).

SS-N-6 Sawfly SLBM (Soviet Designation: R-21)

All three versions of the SS-N-6 missile are liquid fueled and, based on U.S. information, have a length of 9.65 meters (31.8 ft.) and are 1.65 meters (5.4 ft.) in diameter. The SS-N-6 is a product of the design team headed by Viktor P. Makayev, with work beginning in the mid-1950s.

The Mod 1 is a single 1-megaton version with a reputed range of 2,400 kilometers (1,440 mi.). In October 1972, test flights began of a modified version that became known as the Mod 2, credited with an increased range of about 3,000 kilometers (1,800 mi.) by virtue of an improved propulsion system. According to American authorities, the Mod 2 with a 1-megaton warhead is now capable of reaching any target in the United States from the 100 fathom contour off American coasts.

The SS-N-6 Mod 3 is the latest Sawfly development. It has a range of some 3,000 kilometers (1,800 mi.), carrying a payload of two 500-kiloton re-entry vehicles that are not independently targeted. A U.S. Department of Defense assessment holds that the combination of accuracy and yield of all three SS-N-6 versions is sufficient only for strikes against soft targets. CEP is estimated at 1,300 meters (4,290 ft.).

SS-N-8 SLBM

For some time, the SS-N-8 was thought to be a possible development of the SS-N-6, but U.S. defense authorities have now concluded that there is sufficient evidence regarding this weapon to warrant another designation. According to official U.S. data, the SS-N-8 is about the same length as the SS-N-5 at 12.95 meters (42.7 ft.) but of increased diameter, approximately 1.65 meters (5.4 ft.). This is the same diameter as the SS-N-6, so that its greater length compared to that missile gives the SS-N-8 appreciably larger volume. It employes liquid-fueled propulsion and can carry a single warhead to a range of almost 8,000 kilometers (4,800 mi.). The guidance system is said to incorporate stellar-inertial techniques capable of producing a CEP of 0.4 kilometers (0.24 mi.).

At one point the possibility of three variants of the SS-N-8 was reported, but later information is that two versions entered service. They are a Mod 1 with a single 1-megaton re-entry vehicle and a maximum range of 7,800 kilometers (4,680 mi.) and a Mod 2 with two 800-kiloton re-entry vehicles and an increased range of 9,100 kilometers (5,460 mi.). The SS-N-8 was operational by 1973. It is now deployed in Delta-class submarines. In mid-1983, it was estimated that the USSR had a total of 22 operational Delta-class boats, with the eighteen 12-tube Delta Is and the four 16-tube Delta IIs both armed with the SS-N-8. An official U.S. estimate of a total of 292 SS-N-8s, published in 1987, creates a discrepancy in numbers.

SS-N-18 Stingray SLBM (Soviet Designation: RSM-50)

The two-stage SS-N-18 SLBM is similar in some respects to the SS-N-8, but it is somewhat larger and is believed to be equipped with a more sophisticated guidance system. Liquid propellant is used, and U.S. estimates of the missile's range give figures up to 8,000 kilometers (4,800 mi.).

U.S. sources have identified three models of the SS-N-18. Mod 1 has a payload of three 200-kiloton MIRVs and a range of 6,500 kilometers (3,900 mi.). Mod 2 carries a single 450-kiloton re-entry vehicle and has a range of 8,000 kilometers (4,800 mi.). Mod 3 mounts seven 200-kiloton MIRVs and had a maximum range of 6,500 kilometers (3,900 mi.). The CEPs of Mods 2 and 3 are estimated at 900 meters (2,970 ft.). The missiles are believed to be about 14.1 meters (46.5 ft.) in length and 1.8 meters (5.9 ft.) in diameter.

Before November 1976, the SS-N-18 was tested from land-based launch sites in the USSR. Then, early in that month, the first submarine launch took place in the White Sea. In early 1979, the U.S. Department of Defense revealed that the SS-N-18 had been deployed aboard Delta III–class Soviet submarines. This had been confirmed by 1983, when it was estimated that there were fourteen Delta III–class submarines, each with sixteen missile tubes armed with the SS-N-18 SLBM. There were a total of 224 such missiles operational in 1987.

SS-N-20 Sturgeon SLBM (Soviet Designation: RSM-52)

This missile was first mentioned in 1981–82. According to U.S. intelligence estimates, the solid-propellant SS-N-20 is marginally larger than the SS-N-18 and probably carries a payload that consists of more re-entry vehicles (six to nine 100-kiloton MIRVs, as compared with the seven of the SS-N-18 Mod 3) to a greater range than the SS-N-18 Mod 2's 8,000 kilometers (4,800 mi.); it has an estimated maximum range of 8,300 kilometers (4,980 mi.). The missile's length is estimated at 15 meters (49.5 ft.), its diameter at 2.2 meters (7.3 ft.), and its CEP at 500 meters (1,650 ft.).

In the Typhoon-class submarine, twenty SS-N-20 missiles are stowed in two rows of launch tubes located forward of the boat's sail. The first Typhoon-class submarine was launched in September 1980. Four are now operational, providing a total of 80 missiles, and a fifth is possibly undergoing sea trials. U.S. authorities believe there may also be two or three more of this class under construction, so that by the early 1990s there could be eight of these powerful boats operational.

Soviet ICBM Developments

Both official and unofficial/leaked U.S. sources claimed to have evidence of developmental work on two new Soviet ICBMs in addition to those specifically stated to be already operational, such as the SS-24 and SS-25. There is enough information from these various sources to justify assigning provisional identities to these programs.

The Soviet missile development program was always characterized by continuity of development, with variants of existing missiles appearing even as new generations were being flight tested. These developments were always carried out within the strictures of the SALT treaties, at least as they were construed by the Soviets. Thus there seems every likelihood that further developments will exploit all the freedoms that the existing and any future treaties allow. On this basis, follow-on versions of the new fifth-generation missiles, the SS-24 and SS-25, may be expected, along with further modifications, as noted above, of fourth-generation missiles such as the SS-18.

Given the vulnerability of the fixed-base SS-18 missile, these latter developments are somewhat surprising, particularly as the SS-24 not only reportedly has the same payload and accuracy as the SS-18 but the added survivability that mobile basing provides. In view of the impending missile and throw weight reductions likely under terms of the START treaty, future developments will probably concentrate on improved yield, accuracy, and reliability. These would permit hard-target kill probabilities to be improved, with consequent economies in re-entry vehicle requirements against U.S. silos and command and control facilities.

Chinese Strategic Ballistic Missiles

CSS-2 ICBM (Chinese Designations: DF-3)

This missile is understood to be similar to the first stage of the rocket that launched the first Chinese satellite in April 1970. The missile weighs 27,000 kilograms (59,400 lb.). Its range has been estimated at between 2,500 and 3,000 kilometers (1,500 and 1,800 mi.). According to U.S. sources, the missile entered operational service in 1971. The original version has a single 1- to 3-megaton warhead.

Basing is understood to be at permanent sites from which targets in Central and Eastern Asia can be reached, although estimates suggest a capability for relocation of launch facilities without necessarily implying a mobile system. Production to date is said to total about 50 missiles.

In June 1986, the Chinese began flight tests of a modernized system incorporating a new delivery system, probably of an advanced MIRV type, with some ability to place re-entry vehicles on dispersed targets—according to Chinese sources. This implies that the system now has additional powered stages. The new version is thought to possibly have three re-entry vehicles, each with a 50- to 100-kiloton warhead.

CSS-4 ICBM (Chinese Designation: DF-5)

In May 1980, the People's Republic of China (PRC) launched two test rockets into an impact area in the Pacific Ocean. These constituted what was provisionally understood to be a new strategic ICBM weapon designated CSS-4. According to Chinese reports of that event, no warheads were carried. The similarity of this missile to the Soviet SS-18 implies that the CSS-4 has a payload of 4,000 to 7,000 kilograms (8,800 to 15,400 lb.), enabling it to carry any of the nuclear warheads that have been tested by the PRC. The payload is therefore put in the 1- to 5-megaton range. This missile has liquid propulsion and, for a missile of this size, three stages can be assumed.

U.S. reports claim that CSS-4 missiles were deployed in hardened silos at two sites in central China during 1980–81, and that up to five launchers are now operational with twenty missiles delivered. Chinese sources maintain that the missile only became operational in 1984. A civilian variant of this missile, called Long March 3, carries the Chinese designation CZ-3.

Given the former Soviet Union's concern for the ever-present Chinese threat, deployment of this missile may have been one of the reasons for the Soviet decision to upgrade the Moscow antiballistic missile defense system.

CSS-N-3 SLBM (Chinese Designation: JL-1)

The PRC has been developing a new submarine-launched ballistic missile for use with the new Xia class of nuclear-powered submarine. The Western designation for this missile is CSS-N-3. The naval weapon will have a payload probably consisting of a single 2-megaton nuclear warhead and a maximum range of about 2,700 kilometers (1,620 mi.). It is believed to be operational and deployed aboard the Xia-class boat, with twelve launch tubes in each of two submarines.

Test firings of the missile were carried out in 1982. In 1985, it was estimated that the CSS-NX-3 system was nearing operational status. A number of these weapons were ceremonially paraded in Beijing in October 1984.

CSS-NX-4 SLBM

In late 1985, the *Liberation Army Journal* announced the success of an SLBM underwater test firing of the previous September, a firing that may have been associated with this reported program. Some sources suggest that the CSS-NX-4 missile will carry a single 2-megaton warhead, although a MIRV should not be ruled out. There is also the possibility that future Chinese SSBNs may be modified to carry sixteen missile tubes each.

Strategic Ballistic Missiles of the United Kingdom

Polaris Missile

The United Kingdom's Polaris force of four submarines, each armed with sixteen Polaris A-3 SLBMs, has constituted the British nuclear deterrent since 1969. The plan is to continue them in this role until they are replaced by the U.K. Trident II system in the mid-1990s. Originally, the standard U.K. UGM-27C Polaris A-3 missile, equipped with a U.K.-designed and -built nuclear payload, was used. Subsequently, however, in order to maintain the system's effectiveness, a program code-named Chevaline was instituted to upgrade the missile's payload. Missiles equipped with this system are designated Polaris A-3 TK. All four of the Royal Navy's Polaris submarines are now equipped with this version. Since retirement of Polaris from service with the U.S. Navy, the Royal Navy has been the sole operator of this system.

Each standard missile is capable of carrying a payload comprising three re-entry vehicles with an estimated yield of 200 kilotons each. Under the upgrade program, these were replaced by maneuverable re-entry vehicles with new penetration aids. Other changes brought about included modifications to the fire control system. The missile has a launch weight of 13,600 kilograms (29,920 lb.), a range of approximately 4,630 kilometers (2,778 mi.), and a CEP of 900 meters (2,970 ft.). It uses inertial guidance and a two-stage solid-propellant propulsion system.

Trident SLBM System

A decision by the British government to procure the U.S. Trident SLBM as a replacement for the British nuclear deterrent, then based on the Polaris SLBM system, was revealed in July 1980. At that time, the intention was to acquire the Trident I (C-4) missile from the United States, to outfit with British-built warheads, and to deploy the weapon in submarines of British design and construction. Trident I can be carried in the Poseidon SLBM tube, but the tubes for Trident II missiles are both longer and of greater diameter. Thus, when the U.K. decided to procure the most powerful Trident II (D-5) in the 1990s, and the timing of such acquisition coincided with that envisioned for the British Polaris replacement program, it appeared sensible to adopt the SLBM planned for U.S. service at the same time.

Whereas the original U.K. Trident program was based on building a new class of British SSBN that would use a missile compartment based on that of the U.S. Navy's 640-class SSBN, adoption of the Trident II made this impossible. The solution adopted was that of employing a center section based on that used in the U.S. Navy's Ohio-class SSBN. The British version will have only sixteen missile tubes, however, as compared with the American's 24. In December 1986, the British Defence Secretary disclosed that U.K. Trident missiles would carry "about two and a half times" the number of warheads carried by Polaris—that is, 480.

The Trident II missile is expected to have an in-tube life within the submarine of at least seven years, much longer than Polaris, thereby reducing the on-board maintenance considerably. If the planned fleet of four U.K. SSBNs is deployed, this should be adequate to provide an operational squadron of three vessels continually available, so that with the fourth submarine undergoing refit, there can be one armed Trident submarine on patrol at all times. Refits are planned to take place at intervals of about seven years for each submarine.

It is planned that in the mid-1990s the U.K. Polaris force will be replaced by a fleet of four SSBNs to be built by Vickers at Barrow. Trident II (D-5) missiles to equip this force will be supplied from U.S. sources under an intergovernmental agreement. Warheads will be a British responsibility.

Strategic Ballistic Missiles of France

SSBS IRBM S-3D/TN-61

The SSBS (Sol-Sol-Balistique-Stratégique) is an intermediate-range two-stage solid-propellant missile with a thermonuclear warhead. It is stored in and launched from an underground silo. Launch areas are dispersed and hardened to reduce the effects of an enemy attack. Each area includes the silo, in which the missile is maintained in operational readiness, and an annex housing the automatic launching equipment and support services.

Retaining the same first stage as the earlier S-2, the S-3 has a second stage of higher performance, namely the P-6, originally developed for the SSBS. An advanced re-entry vehicle system is also included. This features a thermonuclear warhead and a re-entry vehicle that is hardened against the effects of high-altitude nuclear explosions from an ABM. There is also a new system of penetration aids designed to counter enemy defenses. The complete system is reported to be hardened against the effects of electromagnetic pulse.

Improvements in the associated ground facilities include both equipment modernization and system modifications to increase reliability and reduce maintenance costs. Development of the S-3 was completed and deployment begun in 1980. The first group of nine S-3 missiles and their associated silo installations on the Plateau d'Albion was officially inaugurated in May 1980. Two groups of nine silos were operational by the end of that year. The missile weighs 25,800 kilograms (56,760 lb.), has a range of 3,000 kilometers (1,800 mi.), and carries a 1.2-megaton thermonuclear warhead.

Reaction time of these systems is reported to be about three and one-half minutes. The French have declared their intention of replacing these increasingly vulnerable fixed-base missiles with a new generation of mobile missiles, both land and seaborne, over the next decade.

SSBS IRBM Type S-4 (SX)

The French Defense Ministry has announced a ten-year program of development for the S-4 land-based IRBM, scheduled to replace the S-3 missile after 1996. The S-4 will be a two-stage, solid-propellant, land-mobile system with a range of 4,500 kilometers (2,700 mi.). Present basing plans call for 33 missiles, each with three targetable and possibly MIRV warheads in the 20-kiloton range, capable of random dispersal around France by air or road during periods of impending hostilities.

MSBS SLBM Family

The MSBS (Mer-Sol Balistique Stratégique) is an intermediate-range, two-stage submarine-launched weapon forming a vital part of the French nuclear deterrent force. In general concept, it is similar to the American Polaris missile family. The M-1 version, which went into service in 1971, was phased out in favor of the M-2 in 1974; that system was in turn supplanted by the M-20 in mid-1977. Now, the M-4 version has entered operational service, and there are plans for an M-5 SLBM to be used to arm the seventh French SSBN in the mid-1990s.

The current MSBS force is based on six nuclear-powered submarines, each able to carry and launch sixteen missiles. The M-4 is operational in *L'Inflexible,* and *Le Tonnant* is undergoing a three-year conversion to this configuration. *L'Indomitable, Le Terrible,* and *Le Foudroyant* are still carrying the M-20 missile, but they will be retrofitted (in that order) with the M-4 version. The fifth and oldest boat, *Le Redoutable,* which was launched in 1967, will not be converted.

Logistical support for the MSBS system is provided by the Ile Longue Naval Base in Brest Bay, which has the assembly and storage facilities needed to keep the missiles in operational readiness. Three SSBNs are intended to be operational at any given time.

M-20 SLBM

The M-20 has an upgraded re-entry vehicle system that includes a thermonuclear charge, hardening against the effects of an ABM explosion at high altitude, and improved penetration aids. The missile weighs 20,000 kilograms (44,000 lb.). It uses inertial guidance and a two-stage solid-fuel propulsion system to attain a range of greater than 3,000 kilometers (1,800 mi.). Its warhead is a TN-60 1.2 megatons with associated penetration aids. A hundred such missiles have been manufactured.

M-4 SLBM

A completely new generation of MSBS, designated the M-4, is now operational aboard *L'Inflexible*. The range has been significantly increased, to over 4,000 kilometers (2,400 mi.), and there are six 150-kiloton thermonuclear warheads, probably in a MIRV-type configuration. The missile weighs 35,000 kilograms (77,000 lb.) and uses a three-stage solid-fuel propulsion system and inertial guidance. M-4 missiles will also be deployed on other existing submarines after certain modifications have been carried out. In addition, the experimental diesel electric submarine *Le Gymnote* has been used for M-4 tests with twin tubes.

M-5 SLBM

The latest development in the French MSBS family of SLBMs is the M-5 version, planned for use in arming the seventh French SSBN, possibly to be laid for service in 1994. This missile will have a range of 11,000 kilometers (6,600 mi.) and the sophisticated penetration aids needed to defeat perceived developments in the Moscow antiballistic missile defenses. The planned payload has been variously reported as either ten or twelve MIRVs.

ALAA EL DIN ABDEL MEGUID DARWISH

SEE ALSO: Ballistic Missile Defense; Missile, Ballistic; Missile, Intercontinental Ballistic; Missile Propulsion Technology; Strategic Defense Initiative.

Bibliography

Chevenement, J. 1989. The French position in a post-INF Europe. *Military Technology* 13/1:317–20.
Cook, N. 1988. Ironies of Saudi's IRBM purchase. *Jane's Defence Weekly* 9(13):627.
Engle, R. 1989. The fourth Soviet ICBM generation on the test stand in Geneva. *Military Technology* 13(1):294–96.
———. 1989. The SS-17 weapon system as an example of the new concept in Soviet ICBM mission doctrine. *Military Technology* 13(1):296–302.
Engle, R., and G. Wolf. 1988. Warhead yield and throw weights. *Military Technology* 12(1):10–21, 347–49.
Jane's weapons systems, 1988–89. 1988. London: Jane's.
U.S. Department of Defense. 1988. *Soviet military power: An assessment of the threat.* Washington, D.C.: Government Printing Office.

MISSILE, SURFACE-TO-AIR (SAM)

The category of surface-to-air missiles (SAMs) includes all guided missiles launched from the surface of the earth whose primary function is to destroy a target in the air. Near the end of World War II the Allies attacked Germany with a great number of bombers flying at such high altitudes that the German antiaircraft guns were unable to engage them. Late in the conflict, in 1945, the Germans began production of antiaircraft missiles such as Wasserfall, Enzian, and Rheintochter, but the war ended before they could complete the project, only a few such missiles having been produced. It was the Allies who got the benefit of that work following the war.

Soon many countries began development of modern air forces through manufacture of jet engines that produced speeds in the supersonic range and highly maneuverable aircraft capable of operation at high altitudes. These developments further complicated the problem for antiaircraft guns because of the long flight time of projectiles aimed at enemy aircraft, consequent loss of velocity, and lack of any means of making corrections to the projectile's flight path subsequent to firing. These deficiencies stimulated development of surface-to-air missiles as the next generation of antiaircraft weaponry.

SAMs are designed to destroy both piloted and pilotless enemy air attack means and to protect a wide variety of targets, from administrative and political centers to naval and air bases, troop concentrations, and rear area installations. The first generation of SAMs appeared during the 1950s in the form of the Nike Ajax in the United States, the SA-1 Guild and SA-2 Guideline in the USSR, and the Thunderbird in the United Kingdom. These missiles were effective against aircraft flying at high speeds and altitudes.

Main Combat Properties

1. Highly effective fire for destroying aerial targets. This capability is achieved in three ways. Controlling the missile during its flight to the target minimizes the chance of a miss due to maneuvers by the enemy aircraft. Because of the high speed and maneuvering capability of air targets, some elements of the missile guidance system must be able to sense the target and measure continuously the position of the missile with respect to the target. Powerful missile warheads, producing thousands of fragments capable of penetrating the target, are another important SAM attribute. And finally the high probability of a hit, due to the accuracy of the missile guidance system, ensures that the missile can be exploded on or very near the target.

2. All-weather capability. SAMs can engage aerial targets under any weather conditions, at any time of the day or night, and in any season of the year.

3. Long range of engagement. The capability for long-

range engagement of the target enables SAMs to effectively defend large target areas such as administrative and political centers and industrial areas. This capability is achieved through use of surveillance and guidance radars, which can detect and track targets at extended ranges, and by the use of powerful boosters in the missiles so that they can reach speeds exceeding those of their targets.

4. Versatility in altitude of engagement. SAMs can engage targets at ranges throughout the target envelope, from high altitude to very low level.

Types of SAMs in Modern Air Defense

Developing technology applicable to air attack systems has led to active research and development programs in SAMs. Designers have emphasized technical capabilities that enable SAMs to engage targets operating at supersonic speeds and from very low level (below 150 meters [500 ft.]) to very high level (above 15,000 meters [50,000 ft.]), targets whose reflecting surface is extremely small, maneuvering targets, targets at short or long ranges, and targets employing electronic countermeasures. To achieve these differing capabilities, air defense planners have developed a variety of SAMs: man-portable antiaircraft missiles, missiles for air defense systems providing close-in protection, missiles for tactical air defense systems, and missiles for long-range air defense systems.

Man-portable and Lightweight Mobile Antiaircraft Missiles

These man-portable air defense systems (MANPADS) are designed to engage enemy aerial targets, including helicopters, flying at low altitudes. They can thus provide immediate close-in protection for combat troops in forward battle areas, for airborne and seaborne troops, and for such sites as airfields, air defense positions, and critical terrain and transportation network points. Such weapons are typically found in infantry, armor, and artillery battalions.

These missiles are characterized by ease of concealment, which enables the firer to gain surprise in engagement with enemy aircraft; light weight, so that they can be carried by individual soldiers and fired from the shoulder; and ease of employment from vehicles and surface ships for immediate protection.

First-generation systems encountered some problems. One of these was the matter of identification friend or foe (IFF). Given the speeds at which target aircraft flew, it was difficult to correctly identify an incoming aircraft as hostile or friendly in time to effectively launch a missile should the aircraft be determined to be hostile. To overcome this problem, launchers are mounted on pedestals or tripods that can also carry an IFF transponder. Other problems include tracking a target flying at high speed, engaging approaching aircraft in a head-on mode, and dealing with an enemy helicopter that pops up from the rear. Most of these difficulties have been overcome to some extent. Portable air defense missiles have been used to some effect in recent campaigns, notably in the Falklands/Malvinas, where the Argentinians used the U.K.-produced Shorts "Blowpipe;" and in Afghanistan, where the mujaheddin guerrillas used the U.S.-manufactured Stinger with devastating efficiency.

U.S. Army Redeye man-portable. The Redeye entered service in 1966, eight years after development began. It is employed in the forward battle area to protect combat troops against low-level attack. Weighing 13 kilograms, it is designed to engage receding air targets flying at subsonic speeds. The system has a range of 2,000–3,500 meters (6,500–11,500 ft.). The target is tracked through an optical sight. After launching, the missile guides itself by homing on the heat energy radiated by the enemy aircraft's engine. This system is still employed in some countries.

U.S. Stinger man-portable. Previously known as Redeye-2, this missile entered service in 1979. It can engage approaching as well as receding targets, and also oblique targets before they reach the crossing point. An IFF feature is incorporated in the aiming unit. The missile, which weighs 15.1 kilograms, is resistant to jamming and is not affected by such heat distractors as flame balls. It can reach a speed of Mach 2.2, thus enabling it to engage high-speed targets, and has a range of 3,000–5,000 meters (9,850–16,400 ft.). Stinger uses a passive infrared homing seeker that makes it a fire-and-forget weapon. A laser guidance system can also be used where the operator tracks the target through a lightweight stabilized sight that aligns the laser beam for target intercept by the missile.

Soviet Strela-2 man-portable (NATO designation: SA-7 Grail). This missile is designed to engage very low–altitude receding air targets whose speeds do not exceed 800 km/hr (500 mph) (a modified type, the Strela-2M, can engage targets moving at speeds up to 950 km/hr [590 mph]). The Strela cannot engage approaching targets. It is a shoulder-launched weapon that can be fired from a variety of stationary positions, as well as from armored fighting vehicles on the move. It employs an infrared homing guidance system.

Soviet SA-9 (Gaskin). This missile is considered an improved version of the SA-7 heat-seeking Strela SAM. It consists of a quadruple launcher and a B-76 Gun Dish fire control radar mounted in front of the missile turret to provide detection and tracking. The method of target acquisition is presumed to be visual with subsequent aiming of the weapon by optical systems. When used as part of a larger air defense system, the SA-9 can be linked to search radars to assist in target acquisition. The system is mounted on a BRDM-2 amphibious reconnaissance vehicle. A full load consists of eight SA-9 missiles, each with a high explosive fragmentation warhead larger than that of the SA-7, thus providing one reload for each of the four launchers. The missile's maximum range is seven kilometers (4.3 mi.). It can engage targets from a minimum altitude of 20 meters (65 ft.) to a maximum of 4,000 meters (13,125 ft.), has a higher missile speed than the SA-7 due to an improved motor, and is capable of employment under conditions of darkness and in all weather. Infrared homing guidance is employed. This missile was first deployed by Soviet forces in 1968 to provide immediate protection for forward formations, especially armored elements, against very low level air attack.

Soviet SA-13 Strela-10 (Gopher). This missile is an improved version of the SA-9 engineered to resist infrared countermeasures. It was introduced into service with Soviet antiaircraft batteries of motorized infantry and tank regiments in the late 1970s. It has a maximum slant range engagement capability of 7.5 kilometers (4.6 mi.) and can intercept targets at 10 meters (30 ft.) altitude and 3.5 kilometers (2.2 mi.). Four ready-to-fire missiles in canisters are mounted on a tracked vehicle, which can then provide protection for mobile armored units. This self-propelled system thus has a mobility advantage over the older wheeled SA-9. The system uses infrared homing guidance.

British Blowpipe. This is a lightweight system characterized by simplicity of operation, instant readiness, and rapid employability from vehicles, small ships, or hovercraft. It is fitted with a fully integrated IFF system to prevent firing against friendly aircraft. The guidance system is based on optical tracking of both missile and target and CLOS (command-to-line-of-sight) radio command. The warhead is a 2.2-kg dual-purpose blast shaped-charge warhead. This missile, which first entered service with the British Army in 1977, is still in production and is used by eleven countries. During the Falklands/Malvinas War it was employed by both sides, and it was also reportedly used in Afghanistan. The missile has a maximum speed of Mach 1.5 and a maximum range of over 3,000 meters (2 mi.). Its maximum effective altitude is 2,000 meters (6,500 ft.). The system's major drawback is excessive weight. At 20.7 kg it is considered too heavy for the task at hand.

British Javelin man-portable. This missile, using a semiautomatic-command-to-line-of-sight (SACLOS) guidance system, is capable of destroying high-speed ground attack aircraft or stand-off helicopters at ranges greater than 4 kilometers (2.5 mi.). It is equally effective against crossing or receding aerial targets, and provides quick reaction defense against the low-level air threat. The system is lightweight and is available in a multiple launcher version consisting of three missiles and an aiming unit for dismounted or vehicle application. Since the Javelin first entered service with the British army and the Royal Marines at the end of 1984 a number of significant improvements have been made, including a higher impulse motor that provides a moderate increase in velocity and 1.5–2 kilometers (0.9–1.2 mi.) additional range; a new blast/fragmentation warhead and a modified fuze; and a guidance system employing SACLOS such that the missile does not have to be directly steered to the target by means of a joystick and radio guidance signals. The effectiveness of the missile will be further enhanced by introduction of the Thorn EMI Air Defense Alerting Device (ADAD), an improved optronic-infrared system.

Swedish RBS-70 low-level system. The RBS-70 is designed to engage helicopters and aircraft flying at very low altitudes. It employs a laser-riding guidance system that cannot be jammed by electronic countermeasures (ECM). The system is simple in terms of training, handling, and employment; is easy to deploy and rapidly prepare for combat action; can effectively be concealed on the terrain and is difficult to locate from the air; and has a high kill probability against both attacking aircraft and helicopters, even on directly approaching courses. The missile's range is about 5,000 meters (3 mi.).

The firing unit is normally operated by one man, although if several missiles are likely to be fired in rapid succession the services of a loader are needed. The weight of the total firing unit, arranged in three manpacks, is 80 kg. The missile body houses a receiver, which senses deviation from the laser line of sight, and a small computer unit that converts the deviation signals into guidance pulses so as to automatically maintain the missile on the laser beam. Both impact and proximity fuzes are fitted in the missile's nose; the proximity fuze employs laser technology. IFF equipment is supported on the mount. The missile is launched by means of a start and booster motor. Once clear of the launch tube, a sustainer motor takes over and powers the missile to its target.

An updated version, designated the RBS-70+, features a new beam receiver that increases the missile's engagement envelope by 30–50 percent. Another version, the RBS-70M Nightrider, is scheduled to enter service with the Swedish army in 1993. It will be fitted with an optronics package that includes a thermal imager for use in bad weather and under poor light conditions. This version will also feature a large fragmentation warhead and a more powerful sustainer motor that will extend the missile's range to 6 kilometers (3.7 mi.). The basic RBS-70 and RBS-70+ systems can be used in conjunction with the Ericsson GIRAFFE G/H band search radar.

French Matra Mistral. This missile weighs 20 kg, has a 3-kg warhead that consists of an explosive charge, impact and proximity fuzes, and a large number of tungsten balls. The proximity fuze has a sharp sensitivity cut-off to avoid premature detonation due to trees or the surface of the sea. The missile's passive IR homing head has a multi-element sensor with a digitized signal processing unit, which offers excellent protection against all known IR countermeasures. The Mistral can be used to engage aircraft flying at up to Mach 1.2 at altitudes of as much as

3,000 meters (10,000 ft.). The so-called "canard" configuration of the missile provides very good maneuverability, enabling it to remain locked onto a target even in an 8-g turn. An IFF system and a thermal imaging sight are available for use with this system.

British Shorts Starstreak. This missile is an evolutionary development of Javelin, which will complement that system. The high-velocity (Mach 4) missile contains three beam-riding darts made of "dense metal" that can be guided individually to their targets. Upon firing, the missile is propelled out of its launch tube by a first-stage motor. At a safe distance a main motor boosts the missile to its maximum velocity in less than 300 meters (980 ft.). When the main motor burns out, the three darts separate from the missile carrier and are guided to their targets. The darts are thought to have a HEAT-type warhead that, with their residual high velocity, combines to produce a kinetic/chemical energy effect when they score a direct hit.

Upgraded MANPADS. There are a number of weapon systems under development that promise improvement in the field of man-portable missile systems. The trend is toward a dual-role capability so as to provide protection for units that may face ground as well as aerial threats. Employing a laser guidance system, the new missile, called Saber, is designed to be shoulder-launched by a single operator.

There is also a trend toward upgrading MANPADS to vehicle-mounted multi-round configurations, and to incorporating night vision devices to provide around-the-clock capability. Examples include the U.S. Army Missile Command's SETTER system, which features a mount with two pods, each containing two Stinger missiles, together with a passive sensing day/night vision system. There are also two self-propelled versions of the Stinger under development in the United States, and Boeing Aerospace has produced the Avenger based on the HMMWV vehicle.

Bofors RBS-90 (formerly the RBS-70M Nightrider). Bofors comprises a fire unit and two all-terrain vehicles. One vehicle contains local surveillance radar, while the other accommodates the mechanically driven two-round launcher incorporating a bore-sighted thermal imager, a laser range finder, and a daylight TV camera. The trend in such systems is toward high- or hyper-velocity missiles so as to counter late-unmasking targets.

Short-range Air Defense Missile Systems

In contemporary warfare, low-level attacks are expected not only in the front but in rear areas as well. The low-level intruder remains one of the most difficult threats to counter. A gap opens between the coverage provided by medium/high altitude systems and the network systems of man-portable antiaircraft missiles and guns. This gap needs to be effectively closed by a specialized SAM system of short-range air defense missiles.

Efficient defense—of troops deployed on the battlefield and of important strategic sites—against the low-level threat requires short-range air defense systems with the following characteristics: rapid reaction time in engaging attacking aircraft that approach at high speed and very low altitude; ground mobility that provides high maneuverability so that troops can be protected during combat operations; air portability so missiles can quickly be moved to restore protection against air attacks from any direction or to reinforce protection in a new direction; ability to produce sufficient firepower to ensure the high kill probability needed to counter multiple and simultaneous attacks at very low altitudes. Achieving a high degree of kill probability involves accurate tracking of the aerial target; efficient guidance to achieve missile accuracy; high missile speed and maneuverability; controlled detonation of the warhead; warhead power; and the ability to fire several missiles simultaneously. To fill the gap in the air defense network, the missile's range must extend out to 5–10 kilometers (3–6 mi.) and provide coverage from very low levels up to medium altitudes. The missile system must also have an all-weather capability, the ability to avoid jamming even when operating under severe ECM conditions, and an integrated configuration in which fire control units and multiple missiles are mounted on one launching platform to facilitate concealment of the deployed system.

Most of the countries producing antiaircraft missiles have concentrated their efforts on developing air defense systems that are capable of dealing with enemy aircraft flying at low and very low altitudes, taking into account the desirable characteristics described above. The new versions of short-range air defense systems (or SHORADS) entering the service of various armed forces, both East and West, and the systems currently under development are designed to be integrated into an air defense system. Among current systems of interest are the following.

Soviet SA-8 Strela-3 (Gecko). This division-level air defense weapon of Soviet ground forces is designed for employment against low and very low level aerial attack. The system consists of a quadruple launcher and associated fire control equipment mounted on a rotating turret carried by a three-axle, six-wheeled amphibious vehicle. The fire control system includes a surveillance radar (with an estimated range of about 29 kilometers [18 mi.]; it can be folded down behind the launcher so the entire weapon system can be airlifted by transport aircraft); a pulse-type tracking radar with an estimated range of 19–24 kilometers (12–15 mi.); an optical target tracker-telescope sight; and a television camera used for optical guidance of the missile, the latter used when the tracking radar and command link are jammed by heavy electronic countermeasures.

The quadruple launching unit includes four missiles on

the launchers and eight reload rounds. In a military parade subsequent to deployment of the Gecko system a new version appeared. It featured two triple launchers instead of the two doubles on the original model, thereby substantially increasing the system's ready-to-fire capability.

The command guidance system operates by proportional navigation and infrared terminal homing. Simultaneous firing of two missiles, with separate guidance for each, can be achieved, thus permitting engagement of two separate targets at the same time.

The system's maximum range is an estimated 12 kilometers (7.5 mi.), with missile speed in the Mach 2 range. The high-explosive warhead weighs some 40 kg.

British Rapier low-level system. This lightweight and highly mobile SAM system has the quick reaction time to be effective against rapidly maneuvering low-flying targets, and also against such slower aerial targets as helicopters, which may suddenly appear at short range over screening terrain. The system is deployed for airfield protection with NATO forces in Britain and Germany. The launch unit is mounted on a specially designed trailer carrying four missiles loaded and ready to fire, the surveillance radar, an automatic IFF system, a computer for target data evaluation, and a command transmitter. When the surveillance radar detects a potential target, the IFF automatically interrogates it to determine whether it is friendly or hostile. If the target is hostile, the tracker operator is alerted and the radar data is used to direct the tracker toward the target so that the operator will be able to pick it up in his optical sight.

The system includes two optical systems: target-tracking optics used by the operator to track the target, and missile-tracking optics used to present the missile's flare image to the television system that monitors missile position. When brought into action the optical tracker is mounted on a tripod and connected to the launcher by cable. A radar tracker is used for night engagement or in conditions of poor visibility; it tracks both target and missile, then feeds displacement data on each to the guidance computer.

Each Rapier missile is treated as a round of ammunition, requiring no test or assembly before use. Two men can quickly and easily load a missile onto the launcher. The missile can attain a velocity of Mach 2 and has a range of 6.5 kilometers (4 mi.). The high-explosive warhead has an impact fuze. Guidance is command-to-line-of-sight.

A self-propelled variant of the Rapier system is mounted on the U.S.-designed M548 tracked carrier so as to provide mobility and an amphibious capability. The system can also be air transported.

The Rapier 2000, an upgraded version due to enter service in the early 1990s, will carry eight rounds. It will mount a new optronic tracker, also used in a scanning mode for surveillance, which is operated from a remote console. This system has been improved in almost every respect in order to meet such threats as heavily armored helicopters flying pop-up maneuvers, high-powered jammers, small targets such as remotely piloted vehicles (RPVs), and cruise missiles.

Rapier 2000 consists of three main elements, each mounted on a trailer: the launcher, surmounted by the optronic tracker; a surveillance and target acquisition radar; and tracking radar. Rapier 2000 will fire the new MK2 missile, which is being developed in two versions: the MK2A, carrying a fragmentation warhead detonated by an "intelligent" proximity fuze for use against small targets such as RPVs; and the MK2B, which carries an impact-fuzed hollow-charge warhead for destruction of armored targets. Both rounds will be powered by a Thermopylae rocket motor burning high-energy propellant, which will extend the system's maximum range to 8 kilometers (5 mi.).

French Crotale System. This is an all-weather low-altitude system designed for protection of fixed and mobile ground forces and ships against multiple and simultaneous attacks from low and very low level high-speed aircraft. It consists of two main units: an acquisition unit and a firing unit. The acquisition unit controls and coordinates up to three firing units. It is equipped with a pulse Doppler surveillance and acquisition radar with moving target indicator, capable of detecting targets flying at speeds up to 1,430 kilometers per hour (890 mph), altitudes up to 3,000 meters (9,800 ft.), and ranges out to 18 kilometers (11 mi.); an IFF system; and a data processing system providing for simultaneous display of 30 targets and tracking of the 12 most menacing.

The firing unit consists of a turret with quadruple missile launchers aligned with and directed by the tracking radar, and a monopulse tracking radar capable of locking onto one target and simultaneous guidance of two missiles to the same target. Its maximum range is 17 kilometers (10.5 mi.). Also included are a television system designed to perform automatic tracking and missile guidance in clear weather or in case of electronic jamming; an infrared localizer to guide the missile on the firing axis after launching; and a digital computer that performs multiple tasks; calculation of possible interception, formulation of remote control orders for guidance, formulation of orders to arm the fuze when the missile nears its target, and ordering the missile to destroy itself in flight when necessary.

The units of this system are mounted on self-propelled cross-country vehicles that can be fitted with sand tires. All vehicles are also equipped with an intervehicle link network for transmitting orders and data by cable and/or through radio communications using VHF radio links. The system is also air transportable, enabling it to continue to provide air defense for troops on the move. It can engage targets at speeds up to Mach 1.2 and altitudes from 50 meters (160 ft.) to 3,000 meters (9,850 ft.). It also features a very short reaction time, six seconds from first detection of a target to missile launch, the result of the highly automated system. Engagement range varies from 500 meters (1,600 ft.) minimum to 8.5 kilometers (5.3 mi.) maximum. Hit probability for a single missile is 0.7. The system has great resistance to electronic countermeasures due to its anti-jamming circuit protection, multiple frequencies, and television target tracking and missile guidance. The high-explosive warhead is detonated by an infrared proximity fuze and has a lethal radius of more than 8 meters (25 ft.). The cable-link communications of the original Crotale have also been replaced with a microwave system for automatic data transmission and interchange of position coordinates among system elements, enhancing the capacity to assign targets to the most suitable launch sites.

Another version, known as Shahine, is an improved Crotale having extended range (over 10 km [6.2 mi.]), a modified guidance system, and a different engine and missile fuze. The Shahine is mounted in a tracked vehicle as opposed to the wheeled-vehicle mount of Crotale. Six ready-to-fire missiles, three on each side of the centrally mounted electronics, are mounted in a separate turret concentric with the radar turret, which provides for independent optical target reconnaissance. With a larger radar dish than available on comparable systems, the Shahine can track up to twelve targets simultaneously and with greater discrimination capability. Target data is displayed on a plan position indicator that identifies the level of threat, number of targets, and bearing of fire units. The fire control radar operates in the K-band on three channels and can engage targets with up to two missiles simultaneously.

U.S. Chaparral system. This is a forward-area missile system developed to meet U.S. Army requirements for low-altitude air defense. The missiles are carried on and fired from a turret mounting four launch rails. Additional missiles (eight reloads) are stored on a pallet for ready access. The operator, located in the turret mount, aims the missile using an optical sight. Once locked onto the target and fired, the missile automatically guides itself to the target's heat source. Guidance is thus initially optical aiming, then IR homing to the target's heat emitter. Maximum range is about 4.8 kilometers (3 mi.) and maximum altitude about 2,500 meters (8,200 ft.). The missile, with a high-explosive warhead, uses a solid-propellant rocket motor to attain a flight speed of about Mach 2.5.

The system is being improved and retained in service. Among the improvements are a thermal imaging sight on the launcher to provide a night and inclement weather capability; a smokeless motor to reduce the battlefield signature; an IFF system; ability to attack aircraft from a head-on aspect or from the side; and an antiglint canopy for the missile launch vehicle to improve battlefield survivability of the overall system.

Euromissile Roland system. This system is the product of a joint Franco-German development program begun in 1964. It is designed for defense of vital objectives against aerial attack by targets flying at low and very low altitudes and supersonic speeds. Roland I is a clear-weather version selected by the French armed forces. It uses optical tracking and infrared missile guidance and can be employed only in daylight and good visibility. Roland II is an all-weather version selected by the German army to provide protection for armored units on the move. To meet this requirement, the equipment has been completely stabilized to permit continuous target acquisition and tracking, thus requiring the missile carrier to halt only at the moment of launch. This version incorporates both optical and radar tracking and guidance systems. It can be employed day or night and in inclement weather. It can be operated in either the optical or radar mode; changeover from one mode to the other is possible at any time, even after the missile has been launched and during the missile guidance phase of an engagement.

All Roland system components are installed in a single vehicle that constitutes an autonomous fire unit, thus permitting a target to be acquired while the missile carrier is on the move. The missile can be adapted, without major redesign, to any type of platform that provides sufficient space; the system lends itself to shipboard installation on most ships, even those of low tonnage. It thus acquires mobility comparable to that of the units it is intended to protect. The German army mounts the Roland system on the chassis of the MARDER armored infantry combat vehicle, while the French mount their system on the hull of an AMX-30 tank. The U.S. Army has mounted its version on a special five-ton 6 × 6 M812A1 truck, for airbase defense.

The Roland missile is designed as a round of ammunition, thus simplifying storage and contributing to the weapon's high rate of fire. There are two launchers, each carrying one missile; in the hull are also two magazines holding four missiles each. Automatic reloading from the magazines takes place in several seconds, also contributing to a high rate of fire. The multiple-effect hollow-charge warhead has a lethal radius of more than 6 meters (20 ft.) and includes safety devices for arming and neutralizing the warhead. Two types of fuzes are used. A radio proximity fuze, specially developed for use against low flying aircraft, initiates detonation of the warhead as the missile approaches its target. When engaging very low-flying targets, the proximity fuze can be disarmed to preclude possible detonation caused by ground effects; in such cases an impact fuze is substituted. The missile's solid-propellant motor enables it to maintain a velocity of about Mach 1.6 for a maximum flight time of thirteen seconds.

The Roland system has a maximum effective range of 6,000 kilometers (3.7 mi.) and a minimum range of 500 meters (1,600 ft.). Targets flying at up to Mach 1.3 can be intercepted. Hit probability is 50–85 percent, depending on the speed and course of the attacking aircraft; it is achieved by the combination of a highly accurate guidance system and use of the multiple-effect hollow-charge warhead initiated by an electromagnetic proximity fuze or an impact fuze. Roland I is guided by a CLOS system using optical aiming and automatic infrared tracking. For Roland II automatic radar aiming is provided. Acquisition of low-flying targets is achieved by a pulse-Doppler radar with elimination of fixed echoes. The system is highly resistant to electronic countermeasures.

A recently introduced version of Roland II features several improvements. The maximum range has been increased to 8,000 meters (5 mi.). The rocket booster motor now gives the missile a maximum velocity of 620 m/s (2,000 ft./s) in approximately two seconds as compared to 500 m/s (1,640 ft./s) achieved by earlier versions. The sustainer motor also keeps the missile at a higher speed so that it requires only fifteen seconds to cover the distance to its maximum range. The higher cruise speed also provides increased maneuverability. The warhead on Roland II is larger (9.1 kg versus 6.5 kg) and the missile is fitted with both a proximity and an impact fuze. The improved missile can be fired from either Roland I or Roland II launchers. To further increase the weapon system's effectiveness in the face of saturation attacks, Euromissile has proposed a "double-banked" Roland turret fitted with four ready-use missiles, two on either side. This would provide four missiles ready for immediate use, enabling the unit to engage a formation of four attacking aircraft.

Tactical Air Defense Missile Systems

These missiles are designed to destroy both piloted and pilotless air attacks. They are employed mainly to provide immediate protection for troop concentrations, both in assembly areas and during the course of operations, as well as for defense of vital objectives, industrial areas, administrative and political centers, and naval and air bases. Some missiles of this type are organized in army-level air defense units to augment divisional air defense capabilities. Other types of longer range are organized in front or theater-level air defense to provide, to the greatest extent possible, unbroken detection and engagement envelopes extending laterally across the entire front or theater and forward of the forward edge of the battle area (FEBA) over enemy territory. The following SAM systems have been developed and are still in service.

HAWK (MIM-23) system. HAWK is an acronym for "home-all-the-way-killer," a missile first developed in the 1950s, which became operational in 1960. The missile has a maximum range of 35 kilometers (22 mi.) and is designed primarily to engage low-level supersonic targets at altitudes ranging from 30 meters (100 ft.) to 11,000 meters (36,000 ft.). It features a two-stage solid-propellant propulsion system; a semi-active homing device; and a conventional high-explosive warhead of the blast fragmentation type. The system is both mobile and transportable, including by airlift.

When a target is detected by the HAWK's acquisition radar, its position is relayed to illuminator radars, which in turn illuminate the target with electromagnetic energy that is reflected back to the missile's radar guidance system. HAWK then tracks the target by following this reflected energy.

The improved HAWK (MIM-23B) has a better guidance system, a larger warhead, an improved motor, and semi-automatic ground systems. The existing improved continuous-wave acquisition radar has been modified to provide single-scan target detection, particularly against maneuvering aircraft. The illumination radar has been fitted with a microcomputer to provide automatic search, discrimination between formation targets, and the capability of controlling missiles in flight so that they home in on the remaining targets during a multiple attack.

A frequency-agile digital continuous-wave acquisition radar with solid-state transmitter has been introduced to improve autonomous detection and provide track information of sufficient accuracy for weapon control. This 3-D radar can detect targets at all altitudes that can be engaged by the HAWK, even during heavy jamming, and also reduces the system's vulnerability to antiradiation missiles.

In a variation called Sparrow HAWK, nine Sparrow missiles are mounted on a modified HAWK.

U.S. MIM-104 Patriot system. This is a surface-to-air medium-range missile system for area and point antiaircraft and antimissile defense. It is designed to counter both high-speed aircraft and missiles. With its improved ECM capability, it was designed as the replacement for HAWK and Nike Hercules in front or theater-level air defense. The first operational units were formed in 1986.

The guidance concept adopted in Patriot is actually a combination of three different principles: preset, command, and TVM (track via missile) proper, the three techniques used in successive phases of the missile's trajectory. Immediately after launch, preset navigation based on a self-contained package stabilizes the missile and steers it into a coarse initial turn. This phase is short in both time and space; it ends when the radar acquires the missile in flight and starts to track both it and the target. A computer correlates the positions of missile and target, computes the most efficient trajectory to interception, and guides the missile onto that trajectory by means of coded signals sent via the same beam by which the main antenna is tracking the missile. In many cases this trajectory will take the shape of a climb to high altitude followed by a final dive onto the target.

With a Patriot system in operation, there may be up to five beams in the air: three beams of the main antenna—surveillance and detection, target track and illumination, and missile track and command uplink; the reflected beam from the target to the missile; and the TVM downlink beam. The missile's very high accuracy is mainly due to an innovative TVM that combines the advantages of command guidance with SARH (semi-active radar homing). The key points of its design and operational concept are enhanced mobility, multiple target acquisition capability, very short reaction time, high single-missile kill probability, flight speed of about Mach 3, range of about 60 kilometers (37 mi.), warhead options of nuclear or conventional blast/fragmentation, and a four-missile load on the launcher. The key element in the system is a phased-array radar, which performs all the functions of surveillance, acquisition, and track/engage and missile guidance.

Soviet SA-2 V75 Dvina (Guideline). This missile (Fig. 1), first introduced into service in 1958, provides area defense against medium- to high-altitude threats. Its maximum altitude of target engagement is 18 kilometers (59,000 ft.), with a maximum slant range of 50 kilometers (31 mi.). The missile has command guidance. It is now reaching obsolescence, but is still in service in some countries that are introducing improvements to the system. Its eventual replacement will probably be the SA-10.

Soviet SA-3 S-125 Pechora (Goa). This missile, designed to complement the SA-2, is used to engage aircraft at low and medium altitudes for front-level air defense. Maximum altitude of target engagement is 15 kilometers (49,000 ft.), with a maximum of 50 meters (165 ft.). Maximum slant range is 22 kilometers (13.6 mi.). Semi-active radar guidance is used. The system is vulnerable to modern countermeasures.

Soviet SA-6 9M9 (Gainful). This mobile three-missile system is designed for the protection of mobile divisions against low- and medium-altitude air attack. It is mounted on a modified PT-76 tank chassis and is also air transportable. Its maximum altitude of target engagement is 12 kilometers (39,400 ft.), with a maximum low-altitude range of 30 kilometers (18.6 mi.), and a minimum effective altitude of 60 meters (200 ft.). Guidance is provided by a combination of command link and semi-active homing. Optical tracking of the missile appears possible for low-level operation or under ECM conditions. A radius of 4 kilometers (2.5 mi.) is assumed for the inner "dead" zone. The missile attains a speed of Mach 2.8 and carries an HE-fragmentation warhead with a total weight of about 80 kg. It normally has both impact and proximity fuzes.

Figure 1. The Soviet SA-2 (Guideline) missile. (SOURCE: U.S. Army)

Soviet SA-10. This missile, introduced in 1980, has a range of 100 kilometers (62 mi.) and altitude coverage of 1,000–30,500 meters (3,280–100,000 ft.). It uses solid propellant and active terminal radar guidance. Maximum speed is Mach 6 and it has a 100-kg proximity-fuzed HE-fragmentation warhead. Its role appears broadly similar to that of the U.S. Patriot.

Soviet SA-11. This system comprises four missiles mounted on a large box-like launcher on a tracked chassis. Its range is estimated at 27 kilometers (16.7 mi.), with a maximum altitude of 13.7 kilometers (45,000 ft.). A large 3-D radar mounted on its own tracked chassis is associated with the SA-11, which uses radar guidance. The SA-11 was introduced to replace the SA-6.

LONG-RANGE AIR DEFENSE MISSILE SYSTEMS

U.S. Nike Hercules (MIM-14B). The Nike Hercules, a second-generation missile, introduced in 1958, features enhanced destructive capability and performance over the MIM-3 Nike Ajax. It has proven successful against high-performance aircraft at a variety of altitudes and has also successfully intercepted short-range ballistic missiles. Propulsion is provided by a two-stage solid-propellant rocket motor that achieves supersonic speeds and a range of more than 140 kilometers (85 mi.). Maximum altitude of engagement is over 45 kilometers (147,000 ft.). The missile uses command guidance and can carry either a nuclear or a high-explosive warhead.

Major improvements were made to this system in 1961, when new radars and modifications were added to extend its operational lifetime. These modernizations were designed to make the missile more maneuverable and to improve its ability to withstand ECM.

Soviet SA-4 (Ganef). This high-altitude, long-range surface-to-air missile is highly mobile; it is mounted in a self-propelled tracked vehicle that carries two missiles mounted on an SP ramp derived from the PT-76 tank. The ramp is also used as the launcher, which permits the missiles to be put into action very quickly. The system is used for the long-range protection of battle zones and important installations. It is considered an area-defense SAM system in service with the army to provide high-altitude protection of its forward elements. The concept of employment calls for the lead SA-4 battery to be deployed some 30 kilometers (18 mi.) behind the forward edge of the battle area, with the other batteries moving up in a belt about 15 kilometers (9 mi.) behind.

The missile has a maximum velocity of Mach 2.5, an effective range of about 70 kilometers (43 mi.), and a maximum altitude of 24 kilometers (78,700 ft.). It has an HE warhead, command guidance, and semi-active homing. The propulsion system is a ramjet sustainer with four solid-fuel boosters to provide initial thrust. This system is still in service, although a likely follow-on is the SA-12A Gladiator high-altitude SAM, which uses a phased-array radar capable of handling multiple targets.

Soviet SA-5 S-200 Volga (Gammon). This missile, previously known as the Griffon and then for a time as the Tallin system, is designed to engage aircraft flying at extremely high altitudes and for the interception of not excessively complex missiles. It is normally transported on a single-axle, semi-trailer towed by a tractor. The missile features a two-stage motor, a warhead that can be either nuclear or conventional high-explosive, and a proximity fuze. It employs active radar guidance.

Most reliable sources feel that the missile should have a range of at least 180 kilometers (110 mi.; perhaps as much as 300 km [186 mi.]) and a ceiling of 29,000 meters (95,000 ft.). This very heavy missile system is still operationally viable against aircraft and missiles. It participates with antiballistic missile ABM-1 Galosh to form part of Moscow's defenses. SA-5 sites are still spread throughout the former Soviet Union for protection of strategically important areas.

British Bloodhound MK2. This system went into service with the RAF in 1964. Bloodhound-equipped RAF units are currently deployed in West Germany as part of the NATO air defense of Western Europe. The missile relies on semi-active homing for guidance; a receiver in its nose detects and follows radiation reflected by the target when it is illuminated by a target-illuminating radar (TIR). Launch control by computer is accomplished using data from the TIR. The missile has a range of more than 80 kilometers (50 mi.) and uses an HE warhead with a proximity fuze. The system is air transportable.

STRATEGIC AIR DEFENSE MISSILES

Both the United States and the former Soviet Union have developed antiballistic missile (ABM) systems that provide a limited defense in depth against incoming ballistic or fractional-orbit bombardment missiles.

U.S. Safeguard system. This consisted of the long-range Spartan interceptor missile with a nuclear warhead (range about 650 km [400 mi.]) and the short-range Sprint interceptor missile with a nuclear warhead designed to destroy warheads that have penetrated the upper layer of defense and reached the atmosphere. The system was sited in North Dakota to protect ICBM fields, but it was dismantled in 1976 because of doubts about its effectiveness.

Soviet ABM-1 (Galosh) system. Russia retains this system, which carries a multi-megaton warhead suitable for exo-atmospheric missile interception (with a range of 300 km [185 mi.]) to provide for the defense of Moscow. Since the early 1980s the system has been expanded to include the full 100 launchers allowed under limits of the 1972 ABM Treaty. The first new silo launchers for the SH-08 endo-atmospheric missiles, armed with a low-yield nuclear warhead, became operational in 1985, complementing the remaining force of Galosh ABM-1B exo-atmospheric missiles. The Galosh missiles may be replaced by a combination of the SH-04 exo-atmospheric and the SH-08 endo-atmospheric missiles. Thus a new Moscow ABM system, with 100 silo-based endo- and exo-atmospheric nuclear-armed interceptors, will be fully operational when the SH-08 enters service. It is believed that the ABM silo launchers will have the capability of one reload and refire per silo, although the reload/refire time is unclear. (The ABM Treaty prohibits automatic or semi-automatic or other similar systems for rapid reload of the permitted launchers.) Some air defense missiles also have an ABM capability, particularly the SA-12, which has been tested against tactical ballistic missile reentry vehicles.

Effect of Stealth Technology

The term *stealth* refers to a number of technologies that have been in development for more than two decades. They involve the use of radar-absorbing materials and of designs that scatter radar waves by contouring aircraft to eliminate the flat planes and sharp corners that reflect radar waves.

It is probable that future air targets, particularly bombers, reconnaissance, and fighter aircraft, will incorporate stealth technology. They will thus be less susceptible to detection and tracking by air defense surveillance and fire control radars, whether airborne or ground-based. Stealth thus constitutes one important aspect of the revolution in aerial warfare.

Effect of Electronic Countermeasures (ECM)

All systems based on radar are susceptible to jamming and deception by electronic countermeasures as well as being vulnerable to attack once their position is known. ECM can involve active jamming by electronic means or passive jamming by the use of chaff, which appears as false targets. Jamming continues to be a complementary means of attack on radios and radars. Deception devices are also used as ECM. Obvious targets for attack by electronic warfare include surveillance, target acquisition and tracking systems, and missile guidance systems.

The most common method of dealing with ECM is to build into the radar itself various forms of anti-interception devices. The best known is termed *frequency agility.* This is a method of continuously varying the emitted radar frequency so that an enemy intercept receiver and its associated jammer would find it extremely difficult to lock onto the transmission. The trend in the design of air defense systems is to seek to improve their resistance to jamming and other forms of ECM.

Future Trends

Dual-role Missile

ADATS (Air Defense Antitank System) was designed to fill a dual antiair and antiarmor role. In the air defense role, targets are assumed to include fixed-wing aircraft operating at very low level and helicopters using nap-of-the-earth tactics, all in conjunction with heavy ECM jamming. The use of a pulse-Doppler radar with a detection range in excess of 20 kilometers (12 mi.), electro-optical tracking, and laser beam–riding guidance in conjunction with a Mach 3+ missile and a guidance loop that is highly ECM-resistant is claimed to provide the short reaction time necessary to meet the mission requirements.

Combining Missiles and Guns

The new threat facing army ground forces is composed primarily of armored helicopter gunships using hovering stand-off fire tactics to employ antitank guided missiles. The effectiveness of these weapons can be further augmented through use of the terrain in nap-of-the-earth flight and pop-up firing tactics. The U.S. field army air defense system based on the Vulcan/Chaparral mix was scheduled to be supplanted by the Sgt. York version of the DIVAD (division air defense) gun system, but the latter was canceled in 1985 when it was judged ineffective in meeting the military threat of the Soviet helicopter M-24 HIND-E armed with the AT-6 Spiral antitank guided missile, a weapon with a range of six kilometers (3.7 mi.) or more. At that time it was stated that the best air defense system would be one consisting of a mix of guns and missiles.

Forward Area Air Defense System (FAADS)

The elements of a new integrated U.S. program for forward air defense are a pedestal-mounted Stinger program designed to build a less sophisticated weapon than the DIVAD, and a fiber-optic guided missile (FOG-M) as the non-line of sight segment of FAADS. This missile carries a TV camera in its nose (to be replaced later by a staring focal-plane array) and transmits a video picture to the operator. FOG-M is launched "blind" vertically and transmits an image of the target to the operator, who then guides the missile to impact. The speed of the missile, which is limited to 150–200 meters per second (500–650 fps) so as to provide acceptable picture clarity, makes it primarily an antihelicopter and antitank device.

Single Dual-role (Antiaircraft/Antimissile)

Current trends are toward merging medium surface-to-air missiles (MSAM) and antitactical missiles (ATM) into a single dual-role system. The future MSAM should be able to engage cruise missiles in addition to its primary antiaircraft role, but its capabilities against ballistic missiles would be restricted to self-defense. The French SA-90 (SAMP) system is a project intended as an antiaircraft system with the added feature of a respectable capability against tactical missiles. France is suggesting the ASTER-30 missile as a possible element for both MSAM and ATM programs.

Conclusion

As the foregoing descriptions of systems make clear, the entire field of surface-to-air missiles is in a state of rapid flux, with both the threat to be countered and the means of dealing with it changing rapidly and often. The illustrative weapon systems discussed in this essay may be viewed as representative of the spectrum of approaches to the problem developed during the 1980s and fielded in the early 1990s. Clearly they will be supplanted by subsequent generations of more capable systems as tactics, technology, and the nature of the threat continue to evolve.

Kheidr K. El Dahrawy

See Also: Ballistic Missile Defense; Missile, Guided; Missile Propulsion Technology; Missile Technology Applications; Radar; Strategic Defense Initiative.

Bibliography

Berman, R. 1983. *Rockets and missiles of World War III.* New York: Exeter Books.

Chant, C. 1989. *Air defense systems and weapons: World AAA and SAM systems in the 1990s.* London: Brassey's.

Friedman, R. S., et al. 1985. *Advanced technology warfare.* New York: Crown.

Jane's weapons systems, 1987–1988. 1987. London: Jane's.

Additional sources: *Aviation Week and Space Technology; International Defense Review; Military Technology; NATO's Sixteen Nations.*

MISSILE TECHNOLOGY APPLICATIONS

Since the advent of guided missile systems in the 1940s, missile performance needs have driven technology; at the same time, missile system designers have seized upon technical innovations to raise the levels of missile performance to new heights.

In this article, recent developments in technologies applicable to tactical guided missiles are discussed in terms of how they are likely to affect future missiles and missile systems. It will be seen that such new developments are, in fact, making possible missile concepts and systems that were not previously considered practicable.

As there is a wide range of technologies applicable to guided missiles, they are treated here primarily in terms of their application, in particular in methods of guidance, control, lethal mechanisms, propulsion, and missile structures. Finally, new system concepts made possible by recent advances in technology are discussed.

Guidance

It is probably in the area of missile guidance that advances in electronic technology are having the greatest impact. This is true both for the missiles themselves and for the countermeasures that they must overcome. The possibilities that now exist and that are currently being developed allow much processing to be carried out in the small volume, including the volume of power supplies, appropriate to a wide range of tactical missiles. This enables far greater sophistication to be employed in the use of the variety of signals available from a range of possible sensors—missile seekers, gyros, accelerometers, and so on. A whole range of guidance algorithms has been developed as a result, enabling more precise guidance to be achieved and giving better terminal accuracy in a wide range of adverse conditions.

Missile Seekers

The term *seeker* covers a wide range of devices. In a missile that homes in on a target, it refers to the device, sometimes called a homing head or homing seeker, that locks onto and tracks the target, providing the data on the sightline angle between missile and target that is essential to successful missile homing. In a "stand-off" missile launched from air or ground, the term is applied to the device used to survey the ground and search for a chosen type of target, such as an airfield runway, armored vehicle formation, or hardened shelter. Both types of seeker benefit from the significant advances that have occurred in a wide range of electronic devices, especially those operating in the infrared and radar wavebands, as well as in electronic data processing.

In the 1950s and 1960s, long-range antiaircraft missiles, ground or air launched, used radar seekers that received the radiation reflected from a target aircraft illuminated by ground-based or aircraft-carried tracking radars operating at centimetric wavelengths. Such systems limited engagement possibilities to one target at a time for each illuminating radar. Multiple targets could only be dealt with sequentially, or by having a number of tracking and illuminating radars. Unfortunately, this requirement for multiple radars had cost, operational, and manning penalties. In the 1970s, the advent of phased-array radar technology provided a means for rapidly switching illuminating and tracking radar beams among a number of targets. Thus, one ground-based or airborne illuminating radar could provide illumination of a number of targets, each of which could be engaged without having to wait for another engagement to be completed. The ground-to-air system, Patriot, which has come into service with U.S. forces, is probably the best-known example of this technique.

In air-to-air missile engagements, the need for the aircraft launching a missile to illuminate one or more targets continually places a restriction on the maneuvers that that aircraft can carry out during the period between launch of the missile and its impact on the target. The desire to avoid this restriction on aircraft maneuverability, together with advances in the design of RF oscillators, led to the development of active radar homing seekers for air-to-air missiles. An example of such a system is the U.S. air-to-air missile Phoenix. In this type of system, the missile contains its own radar transmitter to illuminate the target, allowing the missile radar seeker to act as a fully active tracking radar. This was made possible by research conducted from the mid-1950s to the mid-1970s that resulted in the development of smaller electronic devices that operated at more efficient levels. Once the missile homing head has locked onto its target and the missile has been launched, the launch aircraft is free to turn away and carry out whatever maneuver is required.

The continued development of this type of active radar homing head technology is likely to result in future surface-to-air weapons using the same kind of technique. While ground-based, phased-array radar allows the possibility of a much higher engagement rate than previously, such radar can cover only a limited sector in both azimuth and elevation. Complete coverage of local airspace requires a number of such radars, usually four. The use of ground-launched missiles with active radar homing seekers allows the possibility of complete hemispherical coverage by a single ground-based, multifunction phased-array radar. Such a radar can rotate, providing tracking data on targets and missiles in flight at an update rate on the order of once per second. This is adequate for mid-course guidance of missiles in flight and for providing information from which the active seeker can lock onto the target for terminal engagement; however, such a data rate is nowhere near sufficient for target illumination purposes for semiactive missile homing purposes. The combination of mid-course guidance with terminal active radar homing also allows successful operation when the enemy employs a wide range of radar countermeasures that would cause problems with other types of systems. A system of this kind under development by the French is based on the use of the Aster missile and the Arabel radar.

Technological advances have also resulted in the development of radar seekers operating at much shorter millimetric wavelengths. This allows greater range and angular resolution to be obtained for a given antenna aperture. Such developments make it possible to place an active radar homing seeker in a device as small as an 81mm mortar shell (for use against ground-based targets such as armored fighting vehicles) and provide the possibility for airborne imaging and mapping of terrain from stand-off missiles launched from aircraft or ground launchers. The good quality resolution available from the latter devices enables stand-off missiles, using inertial or terrain following mid-course guidance, to obtain a precise image of a target area and that, in turn, allows precision delivery of submunitions onto a wide variety of targets. Weapon payload is tailored to the type of target being attacked; mission planning software allows the seeker information to be used to ensure that the payload is precisely delivered to the target. Examples of the application of this millimeter wave seeker technology occur in the British Merlin terminally guided antiarmor mortar shell and in the French Apache air-launched stand-off weapon, both under development.

Not all homing missiles make use of radar seekers. A wide range of missiles has been developed that home in on the heat radiated from targets as a result of their exhaust emissions or the kinetic heating to which they are subjected. Such missiles were mainly "hot spot" seeking devices and could be countered by the target's deployment of flares or other hot bodies during the homing missile flight time. Advances in infrared detector technology have resulted in the development of missile homing heads in which an image of the target and the area immediately surrounding it is built up. This is done either by scanning a linear array of detectors or by using a matrix of very small infrared detectors as a focal plane array on which an optical infrared image is formed. These detector systems, together with advances in high-speed electronic processing, enable an image of the target to be recognized and nontargetlike countermeasures to be rejected.

These imaging infrared (I^2R) missile seekers can be used in a variety of missiles for which the earlier infrared hot spot seekers were inadequate. Ground targets, such as armored fighting vehicles, attacked from the air or from ground installations, operate in a battlefield containing many infrared sources, both natural and man-made. I^2R seekers provide data allowing the discrimination of the target to be attacked from this background "clutter." This new technology is under development for antiarmor weapons, such as the European long-range antitank missile Trigat and the U.S. medium-range missile AAWS-M.

Fiber Optics Developments

For some time television cameras or thermal imagers have been carried in the nose of air-launched stand-off missiles, relaying information back to the launch unit. The image information received from the missile was processed in the launch aircraft and radio commands were then sent back to the missile, adjusting its flight to its target. Apart from the weight penalties associated with the transmission of information in both directions, such links were subject to enemy countermeasures. The development of high-grade optical fibers allows for the possibility of a fiber-optic link between a missile in flight and a ground unit, with all the image information gained by the missile being processed in the launcher. This allows for the possibility of combining high-power computer signal processing with the innate recognition skills of the human operator (through the use of suitable launcher-unit displays) to select and designate targets on a battlefield against which the missile in flight will then home in on and impact. This concept has been pursued for some years by MICOM in the United States in the FOG-M program. In this, a series of vertically launched missiles can be fired from a launcher, fly subsonically over a battlefield, relay picture information back to the launcher from which the appropriate targets are designated, and be commanded to home in on specific targets. The technique appears to be particularly suitable for dealing with helicopters and armored ground vehicles, but it is also capable of being used against a wide variety of fixed ground installations. The combination of human operators, a secure signal processing link, and image-enhanced signal processing allows for a weapon with great flexibility of use. The rate of engagement, however, might be somewhat limited by the involvement of the human operator.

Instrument Technology

The use of fiber optics and lasers has led to the development of a new range of gyroscopes that have no moving parts. Such instruments are capable of providing instantaneous read-out of angular motion of missiles in flight in missile-fixed axes. To use this information so that guided missiles could successfully engage their targets required more on-board computing than had previously been needed with the larger conventional gyroscopes. The advent of modern digital electronic technology, however, has made this much less of a problem. The all-solid-state guidance component and processing pack enables the missile to be treated like a conventional round of ammunition requiring no testing in service and likely to operate in a far more reliable manner after years of storage and exposure to a wide variety of conditions. These developments, along with the possibility of fixed-phase-array antenna systems for missile radar seekers (especially at millimeter wavelengths), may well lead to missile designs at the turn of the century in which there are no moving parts other than those needed to exert aerodynamic steering forces directly. This offers the prospect of lower unit cost, lower whole life cost, and higher reliability.

Dual Mode Seekers

With the continuing development of countermeasures to missile homing seekers, together with the continuing miniaturization of electronics and sensing devices, impetus has been given in recent years to the development of dual mode seekers. The idea is to develop seekers for missile applications in which two different wavebands of operation provide data that is combined in the most effective manner to reduce sensitivity to enemy countermeasures. Several modes and combinations are possible.

One group comprises passive infrared and antiradar modes, which are applicable to missiles homing in on aircraft targets where these targets may emit radar transmissions. The antiradar mode can be used during the midcourse guidance phase, and the passive infrared mode in the terminal phase or when the radar emissions from the target are switched off. In the application against ground radars, the normal mode would be to home in on the radar transmission but to have the infrared seeker data available should the radar switch off prior to missile impact; the relative position of heat source from the radar (power supply) and the radar emission from the antenna can be sensed during the period of dual mode operation of the seeker.

Other mode combinations include active millimeter wave and passive infrared modes of operation that can be combined in terminally guided submunitions for the attack of armored targets to overcome the use of certain types of countermeasure. Such countermeasures will be rejected because they do not produce the right response in both wavebands.

A third combination, that of active centimeter wave radar and passive infrared homing against aircraft or ship targets, can be used to reduce significantly the effect of countermeasures and, with the use of imaging infrared terminal homing, can provide better aim points for good terminal accuracy and warhead lethality.

General Comments

In a short survey such as this, it is not possible to be exhaustive. It is, however, worth pointing out that the developments in missile seeker technology referred to above can also be applied to ground-based target and missile trackers for use in command guided systems. Laser technology has also allowed the development of precise beam-pointing systems for beam-riding guidance operation. The Swedish Bofors RB-70 air defense missile is an example of a laser beam rider missile. Lasers have also been used for the illumination of targets in semiactive homing missile systems. The U.S. Hellfire antitank guided missile and the Copperhead guided projectile fired from a 155mm gun are examples of the application of this type of technology.

Methods of Control

Although technological advances relating to missile guidance methods occurred rapidly in the 1980s, developments were also occurring in the means for controlling the motion of the missile body in flight.

Aerodynamic control surfaces are probably the most widely used method of controlling tactical missiles in flight. Whereas many of the early antiaircraft guided missiles used hydraulic control actuators, most modern missiles, and those under development, make use of electric and pneumatic actuation systems made possible by recent advances in materials technology. Electric actuators making use of rare earth materials have provided a revolution in this field. With technological advances, stored gas pneumatic actuation systems are becoming more and more appropriate for missiles with limited flight times.

Aerodynamic control methods have their limitations. Modern aircraft are capable of very high agility, and homing missiles need to be several times more maneuverable to ensure good terminal accuracy against such targets; at high altitudes, the use of aerodynamic control surfaces alone can prove a limiting factor in the lethal performance of a missile. One method of overcoming this problem is to use rocket motor thrust to augment the aerodynamic control mechanism. In short-range, air-to-air missiles, in which high missile maneuverability is a special requirement, the missile propulsion rocket motor is likely to be accelerating the missile for the whole time of flight. This allows for the possibility of thrust vector control of the rocket motor exhaust in order to generate missile body incidence and hence aerodynamic lift—and to do this rapidly and effectively. In some cases, the combination of aerodynamic control and thrust vector control is used. This is done where high maneuverability is needed for short-range engagements where the propulsion unit is operating and yet provides a method of control for engagements at ranges beyond that at which the propulsion unit has burned out. The Soviet AA-11 air-to-air missile is an example of the application of this combined technique. Where high maneuverability is required for only a short period during the terminal engagement, a special thrust generating unit placed close to the center of gravity of the missile can be used. The French Aster missile is an example in which this technique is proposed. The missile is controlled using aerodynamic surfaces until the last second or two of flight. Then, the aerodynamic control method is augmented by a very high level of thrust operating through or close to the center of gravity for the last short period of flight to provide high terminal accuracy. By this means, high terminal maneuverability is available even at high altitudes, thus improving the engagement envelope of the missile. Such systems require the use of a special hot gas thruster unit separate from the main missile propulsion motor.

The use of laterally operating thrust units, or reaction control systems, as the sole means of missile control is currently favored for a number of applications. The technique appears to be particularly applicable for generating missile incidence (when the thrust unit operates well forward of the missile center of gravity) for low missile velocities. Such missiles are capable of responding more quickly to the demand for changes in flight path direction early in the launch phase, before they have reached a speed at which aerodynamic controls are more effective.

Another area in which thrust control offers significant operational advantages is where there is a restriction on launch acceleration. Side thrust control can be used to control the flight of a missile at very low speeds, although, in this case, it is important that the thrust vector passes very close to the center of gravity of the missile. This technique is currently under development by EMDG for the medium-range Trigat antitank missile. In this case, the requirement is to launch the missile from within enclosures, which means that the missile must be controlled in flight at a relatively low velocity; the use of a forward-mounted rocket motor, with thrust deflectors, gives good flight-path control immediately after launch.

Lethal Mechanism

The term *lethal mechanism* is used here to encompass the warhead and fuze combination. Warheads containing explosive materials have been used for many years against a wide variety of targets, including aircraft, missiles, and armored ground vehicles, as well as fixed installations. Against armored vehicles, the development of shaped-charge warhead technology for high penetration has been countered by the development of specialty armors that reduce the effectiveness of this type of warhead. This, in turn, has resulted in the development of special warhead systems, including those employing multiple shaped charges, requiring new methods of fuzing. Here again, lasers and laser technology have provided an answer. A small laser beam is transmitted from the missile during flight and a receiver, also in the missile, detects radiation reflected from the target. The received information is used to trigger the warhead at the time at which it will prove to be the most effective.

Fuze characteristics and the pattern of warhead fragments in antiaircraft and antimissile warheads need to be properly matched. Technological advances have occurred in both active and passive infrared fuzes (the former also of the laser type), as well as in the continued development of radar fuzes. Digital electronics technology now allows the programming of fuze characteristics prior to missile launch, enabling the fuze and warhead to be best matched to the type of target being engaged.

Against some targets, fléchette warheads—warheads carrying clusters of small dart-shaped projectiles—are more appropriate. Much work has been done on the problems of dispensing fléchettes from a missile in flight in such a way as to cause maximum effectiveness. Dispensing a large number of fléchettes from a missile traveling at supersonic speeds gives rise to many problems associated with aerodynamic interactions among the fléchettes following dispensing. The problem is to achieve the right balance between fléchette number, fléchette size and weight, and time of dispensing. Thus, the matching of fuze and warhead characteristics is of great importance.

Propulsion

Tactical missiles must withstand rough handling over wide temperature ranges, and cost is a very important factor in choosing the technology to be used in their design. For this reason, they are almost entirely propelled by solid-propellant rocket motors, although some of the longer-range missile applications have used ramjet engines.

Technological advances in propulsion must take into account the necessity of a minimum amount of exhaust smoke, low infrared signature, and, in many cases, the need for low attenuation of visual, infrared, or radar signals through the motor plume. The last requirement is important for missiles using command-link guidance or beam-riding guidance to achieve their mission.

Another area in which technology is being directed is ensuring that tactical missiles do not cause unnecessary damage if they are subject to impact from enemy warhead fragments or from local fires when in storage or transit. This is leading to the evolution of a new range of propellants with the aim of developing a whole range of "insensitive munitions."

Long-range missiles, in which there is an operational need to travel at supersonic speeds, naturally incur a weight penalty because of the need to carry more rocket motor propellant. For these applications, various forms of ramjet or ramrocket are appropriate, as full use can be made of the oxygen available in the atmosphere to reduce the amount of oxidizer required in the propulsion unit load. Applications for which such methods of propulsion are appropriate include long-range air-to-air missiles, long-range surface-to-air missiles, and, possibly, long-range antiship missiles. The advantage of high speed in the latter case is to reduce the time of warning of approach by operating at low altitude over the sea and at supersonic speed. In this way, the ship's defenses are given little time to react.

Missile Structures

In an attempt to reduce missile weight and cost, increasing attention has been given over the years to the use of composite structures such as those using Kevlar and carbon fiber–reinforced resins. Where high performance requires the use of steel or aluminum alloys, weight can often be saved by overwrapping with these materials.

Where cost of manufacture is important, the idea of injection-molded half shells, or pressed half-shell composite structures, has significant advantage. Research in the 1980s has been productively steered in this direction.

New Concepts

The evolution of technology relevant to missile systems, and that of associated technology, is making new system concepts possible. Much of this stems from the continued miniaturization of electronics and the ability to encapsulate high computing power in very small volumes and using very low power levels. The development of sensors that are entirely solid state makes possible the production of missiles that will withstand very high acceleration forces. Thus, in the eighties, we have seen the advent of various kinds of gun-launched guided projectiles, including artillery shells such as the Copperhead, terminally guided mortar shells such as the Merlin, and so on. It is likely that, in the not too distant future, even a shell fired from a tank gun will guide itself to a target, thereby ensuring a higher probability of first-round kill at longer ranges.

In addition to these concepts, the advent of imaging/mapping infrared and radar seekers for stand-off missiles provides the latter with the capability, once in the general target area, of identifying a specific target and then delivering an appropriate payload. The development of infrared and millimeter wave technology has enabled a range of sensor-fuzed munitions to be developed (for example, the U.S. SADARM submunition) capable of destroying a wide variety of armored vehicles and installations if dispensed within reasonable proximity of the target by such a stand-off missile. Such techniques can be applied to other more specialized submunitions suitable for runway cratering and the destruction of hardened shelters. While not yet available, technology is likely to make such systems possible within the next decade.

R. F. JACKSON

SEE ALSO: Electronic Warfare, Air; Electronic Warfare Technology Applications; Missile, Air-to-surface; Missile, Guided; Missile Propulsion Technology; Radar Technology Applications; Sensor Technology.

Bibliography

Browne, J. P. R. 1989. *Electronic air warfare.* London: Brassey's.
Lee, R. G., et al. 1988. *Guided weapons.* London: Brassey's.
Parson, N. A., Jr. 1962. *Missiles and the revolution in warfare.* Cambridge, Mass.: Harvard Univ. Press.

MOBILITY

When Napoleon wrote in his *Maxims*: "Marches are war . . . [A]ptitude for war is aptitude for movement," he referred to the virtues of mobility in warfare. Mobility is the ability of military units to move as effective formations from place to place, including the ability to support units logistically during and after movement. Mobility, as a capability, is distinct from *movement* (the actual mechanics of going from one place to another) and *maneuver*, which usually requires movement, but for the purpose of placing forces in the most advantageous position to perform their mission. Mobility is meaningful only in terms of the relative movement capacities of opposing forces. Mobility serves to augment the strength of a military force by enabling rapid maneuver, deployment and redeployment, the commitment of reserves, and adequate logistical support. An attacking force with superior mobility can choose when and where to attack. Mobility functions on strategic, operational, and tactical (or battlefield) levels; units that are readily mobile strategically are not necessarily mobile at the operational or tactical levels. Further, the meaning of mobility is quite different for air, naval, and ground units.

Strategic Mobility

Strategic mobility is the capacity a unit possesses to move rapidly over very long distances, beyond the limits of the battlefield or between theaters of operations. Strategic mobility between theaters is provided to ground forces—and the supporting elements of air and naval forces—by the use of sea or air transport. Because movement is more rapid, greater mobility is provided by air than surface transport, but air transport is almost always less abundant and more expensive than surface transport.

Strategic mobility may be enhanced by the use of prepositioned stores of both equipment and supplies. This practice allows only the relatively light personnel of a unit, with only personal equipment, to be moved by air to the theater of operations, where they pick up their heavier equipment for actual operations. Currently, four divisions of the U.S. active force reinforcements for NATO in West Germany employ this method to reduce transit time and minimize the burden on air transport resources in the event of war. The U.S. armed forces, which have named this practice POMCUS (prepositioning of materiel configured to unit sets), have deployed other sets of equipment in Norway and the Pacific and regard this practice as an important component of strategic mobility.

Most naval units bigger than patrol boats (more than 200 metric tons displacement) inherently possess strategic mobility as part of their basic design. Naturally, different navies have different mobility requirements. The strategic mobility of naval forces can be enhanced through at-sea refueling and replenishment, techniques developed in their modern form by the American and British navies during World War II.

Aircraft are usually highly mobile, with the exception of helicopters (their mobility is limited by high fuel consumption and relatively short range) and specially designed short-range fighter-interceptors. Inherent in the strategic mobility of aircraft is the availability of suitable and adequately staffed and equipped landing bases to which they can be deployed. Like naval vessels, however, many aircraft may be refueled in the air by specially built tanker aircraft. In-air refueling was first performed on an experimental basis in the early 1920s and was first employed regularly by the U.S. Air Force during the Korean War. It was recently used during the early stages of the Falklands/Malvinas War to enable British Vulcan bombers based at Ascension Island to strike at Port Stanley airfield.

Operational Mobility

Operational mobility is the capability a unit has for movement within a theater of operations. In the case of land units, for example, long-distance mobility is usually provided by railroads and sometimes by air, but over lesser distances (under 200 km [125 mi.]) mobility is usually provided by the maneuver capabilities of the unit itself. Operational mobility is often facilitated by extra transport from outside the unit, such as trucks for a light infantry unit or tank transporters for an armored force. Operational mobility can be complicated by damage to available routes, the presence of other friendly forces on those same routes, and by enemy activity, especially air and artillery interdiction.

Tactical Mobility

Whereas strategic mobility usually involves movement into a combat zone but not into combat itself, and movement within a combat zone and sometimes into combat is a matter of operational mobility, movement within or on the battlefield or in the presence of an enemy is provided by tactical mobility. Tactical mobility has three distinct aspects: (1) the approach to contact (which often partially overlaps with operational mobility); (2) movement while actively engaged in combat activity; and (3) support of units in combat by commitment of reserves and logistical support. Tactical mobility is often a matter merely of minutes and hours, whereas operational and strategic movement is often a matter of days and sometimes weeks.

Tactical mobility depends on different criteria than does operational or strategic mobility because the degree of tactical mobility a unit possesses is usually a function of its own organic (self-contained) transport assets. Although airborne, parachute, and light infantry units are (or can be) highly mobile strategically, their tactical mobility is dependent upon the availability of additional motor transport. Otherwise, they are generally able to move only at the speed of a person on foot (3 to 5 kph [1.9 to 3.1 mph]). Conversely, heavy mechanized and armored formations, although difficult and costly to transport over long distances, have high tactical mobility because they not only are able to move rapidly in the combat zone but also are able to do so in the relative protection of their own armored vehicles.

The apparent incompatibility between strategic mobility on one hand and tactical and operational mobility on the other has sparked considerable discussion in recent years, particularly since the U.S. Army introduced its light infantry divisions in the early 1980s. These divisions can be highly mobile strategically, requiring only 500 cargo aircraft (C-141B) sorties each to move, as opposed to the 4,000 or more sorties required for a "heavy" division (armored or mechanized infantry). The light divisions are, however, both smaller (nearly 11,000 men versus 17,000 for a heavy division) and less heavily armed (fewer vehicles, no tanks or AFVs, lighter artillery) than their heavy counterparts, and many analysts question their usefulness in a high-intensity conflict.

Components of Mobility

Terrain and Weather

Tactical mobility is frequently affected by weather and especially by terrain. Armored and mechanized units, which are highly mobile either in open country or in an area with a good road network, are much less mobile in rugged, broken, marshy, or forested terrain. In those same areas, ordinary, nonmechanized foot soldiers, at a mobility disadvantage in open country, can move about better than their mechanized counterparts. Put another way, in close terrain light infantry usually enjoys tactical mobility superior to that of mechanized forces in the same situation. Towns, villages, and other built-up or urbanized areas have an effect on mechanized force mobility similar to that of forests and mountains. Deprived of the necessary room to maneuver and suffering from restricted visibility, tanks in particular are at a disadvantage in urban situations. One of the tactical lessons of World War II, reaffirmed in more recent Middle East wars and still true for contemporary warfare, was that armor sent into an urban area without accompanying infantry was likely to suffer severe losses.

Planning, Command, and Doctrine

Strategic mobility is largely concerned with matters of lift capacities and ranges of aircraft and the speeds and capacities of ships. However, tactical and, to a lesser extent, operational mobility are necessarily concerned not only with vehicles' speeds, fuel tank capacities, and armor protection (if any) but also with the types of roads and terrain to be traversed, the local weather conditions, and the ability (or lack thereof) of the vehicles in question to maneuver effectively under those conditions. Operational and tactical mobility are concerned with many of the same matters that influence the planning and execution of an operation, and they usually fall under the direction of operational commanders, rather than under the rear-area commands responsible for planning and executing strategic movement. Tactical mobility has the greatest effect on the immediate outcome of battles and engagements, whereas operational mobility influences preparation for the battle and campaign, and strategic mobility influences the conduct of campaigns and of entire wars.

All three levels of mobility are the result of factors other than simple mechanical ability. A highly mobile weapons system does no good for an army that lacks the organizational ability to employ it properly. In this case, *proper employment* means that the local command authority must not only choose the proper time and place (or times and places) to commit the system concerned but also must be in sufficient control of the situation and of its subordinate units to implement its plans. Mobility, as a capability, is thus to a great extent a matter of command and control. This consideration applies to all levels of mobility (tactical, operational, and strategic); in the strategic and operational levels particularly, the staff work necessary for moving troops is often more complex and demanding than at the battlefield level.

Three examples should suffice to demonstrate the importance of organizational and command factors in achieving superior mobility. First, the Roman legions of the second and third centuries B.C. were normally deployed in a three-line formation, with the first line of four evenly spaced cohorts and the other two of three cohorts each. The troops in the second and third lines covered the intervals of the line to the front. This *quincunx* or checkerboard formation allowed the Roman armies of Scipio Africanus' day a degree of tactical flexibility and mobility that was unavailable to their adversaries in massed formations.

Doctrine can have a great effect on movement, or the use of mobility. During the Franco-Prussian War of 1870–71, both armies employed their cavalry for scouting and reconnaissance. The French, with their long experience in Algeria, had learned to keep their cavalry in large groups close to the main infantry columns so as to avoid costly ambushes. The Prussian and allied German forces, not inhibited by such lessons of colonial warfare, let small patrols of their mounted troops range far ahead of their main advancing columns; as a result, Prussian intelligence of French movements was far better than French knowledge of German movements. As a further consequence, in the first months of war the French often stumbled into battle, deprived of accurate intelligence and unable to employ fully what battlefield and strategic mobility their forces did possess.

A final example of similar problems in the use of mobility, from a more technological age, shows the effect of technologies not directly related to movement upon the mobility of forces. At the time that the Germans invaded the Soviet Union in June 1941, the Soviets had the largest tank force in the world, but they were able to exercise command over their armored units in the field only through hand and flag signals because fewer than one tank in ten had a radio. The Germans, by comparison, had less than an eighth as many tanks as the Soviets, but all had radios. The radios provided the Germans with a crucial advantage in combat; their response time to new situations was much shorter than that of the Soviets, and their performance in the fluid battles characteristic of the Russian campaign was consequently superior. The Soviets eventually closed the "radio gap" and by mid-to-late 1944 had as many radios in their armored and mechanized units as did the Germans. The Germans continued to maintain an edge in mobile combat, but an edge due to superior training, leadership, and organization rather than to any serious failure in Soviet communications.

Effects of Technology

In historical terms, the greater speed of modern motor vehicles and the availability of aircraft would seem to indicate that modern armies enjoy greater mobility than their predecessors. This greater mobility is not by any means a hard-and-fast rule, especially regarding certain aspects of strategic and operational mobility. For instance, the advance rate of armies pursuing defeated opponents has changed very little since the early nineteenth century and holds fairly constant whether the pursuers and their opponents are on foot, on horseback, or in motor vehicles. This phenomenon is due to several considerations, principally those of supply.

In the case of a horsed or horse-supported army, the supply requirements for pursuit are fairly simple, and most of the necessary supplies (food and forage) can be gathered from the countryside passed through. A mechanized army, however, aside from greater ammunition requirements, needs tons of spare parts, as well as many tons of fuel and lubricants; the transport and provision of these materials in return requires yet more vehicles, which also consume supplies, and so on. In addition to considerations of supply, modern armies are larger than their predecessors; moving 200,000 people is simply more difficult and complex than moving 40,000 people over the same distance, especially when the larger force is attended by all the equipment and impedimenta of modern war.

Modern forces nonetheless are more mobile than their predecessors in several respects. On the tactical level, heavy units equipped with tanks or armored vehicles can move about under enemy small-arms fire and amid high-explosive shellbursts with relative impunity because they are shielded from the mayhem outside their vehicles. Natural obstacles present less of a problem because creeks and canals can be bridged in a matter of minutes or hours, without the delay of searching for a ford or assembling boats.

A further mobility advantage of modern forces is in the area of amphibious operations. Premodern amphibious assaults against prepared defenses were difficult and risky. They could be undertaken only under the most favorable environmental conditions because of the difficulty in landing ground troops in a ready-to-fight condition. Modern amphibious operations, although requiring extensive planning and staff work, are quite possible against even well-fortified beaches, as the Allies (especially the United States) showed on numerous occasions during World War II.

Finally, the availability of helicopters and transport aircraft permits very rapid advances to seize specific objectives, in either battlefield or strategic terms. Whereas a premodern army could seize an objective behind enemy lines only by a wide outflanking maneuver or by infiltration, a modern force can do the same thing in a fraction of the time and with a far smaller risk of delays and coordination problems by moving troops by air and landing them right on the objective. So-called light infantry forces (without heavy equipment or armored vehicles) are particularly suited to this sort of tactical or operational movement, as they suffer little loss of combat power when dropped off; virtually all of their weapons may be easily lifted by helicopter.

Indeed, the proliferation of helicopters and other V/STOL aircraft in modern armies has greatly increased the tactical mobility capacities of those forces while complicating their operational and strategic mobility. In the case of amphibious operations, for example, the use of helicopters and of high-speed air-cushioned (or surface-effect) landing craft increases the speed of execution of the most dangerous phase of an amphibious assault: the approach to the beach by the landing forces and the crossing of the beach itself. Further, in the case of pursuit operations, helicopter-borne infantry can, in the pursuit of a ground-bound force, play a role very similar to that of mounted infantry or cavalry chasing an all-infantry force; that is, the more mobile pursuing forces may employ their superior mobility to get to passes, bridges, crossroads, and the like ahead of the slower pursued forces, thereby threatening them with encirclement and destruction, and by the very threat of such developments contributing to the disorganization of the retreating forces.

Conclusion

Tactical mobility allows a force to be many places at once; as such, it can be decisive, especially for a smaller force that would otherwise eventually be overwhelmed. The same holds true, albeit on a larger scale, for operational mobility, substituting the theater of operations for the battlefield. On the strategic level, mobility means the rapid commitment of forces to the theater of combat. Strategic mobility may be employed to reinforce success or to stave off disaster, in much the same manner as mobility is employed on the battlefield but over a greater area. Such mobility—strategic, operational, or tactical—is a product of the mechanical abilities of the systems concerned (range of aircraft, speeds of tanks or ships, and so forth), the organizational framework in which they operate, and especially the ability of the command authority to recognize their units' abilities to move and maneuver and to make use of those abilities to achieve their goals.

DAVID L. BONGARD

See Also: Command, Control, Communications, and Intelligence; Deployment; Logistic Movement; Maneuver; Operational Art; Strategy; Tactics.

Bibliography

Abrams, C. W. 1984. Mobility versus firepower. *Art of War Quarterly* (U.S. Army War College, Carlisle, Pa.; reprint of 1953 article).

Adams, J. A. 1988. Balancing strategic mobility and tactical capability. *Military Review* 68(8):9–23.

Armstead, J. H., Jr. 1988. Viewpoint: Too light to fight? *International Combat Arms*, November, pp. 18–19.

Cimral, T. A. 1988. Moving the heavy corps. *Military Review* 68(7):28–34.

Freedman, L. 1986. Logistics and mobility in modern warfare. *Armed Forces* 5(65):65–70.

Hilmes, R. 1985. Battle tank mobility. *International Defense Review* Supplement 18(9):21–23.

Holder, L. D., and E. J. Arnold. 1988. Moving the heavy division. *Military Review* 68(7):35–49.

Isby, D. C. 1986. Mobility on the battlefield—A way of thinking in strategy, operations, and tactics. *Journal of Defense and Diplomacy* 4:19–20.

Lasser, I. O. 1986. Mobility triad: Airlift, sealift and prepositioning in American strategy. *RUSI Journal of Defense Studies* 131(1): 31–35.

Marapoti, J. A. 1984. Battlefield mobility and the survivability of the marine air-ground task force. *Marine Corps Gazette* 68(3):52–62.

Russo, V. M. 1985. Army perspectives on strategic mobility. *Defense Transportation Journal* 41(8):12.

MOBILIZATION

The term *mobilization* has two separate but very closely connected meanings: one with a national, and the other with a military interpretation.

First, it describes the national act of preparing for war or an emergency that may lead to armed conflict, by assembling, organizing, preparing, and activating the full range of additional resources a nation needs to wage war. In this case, the act of mobilization involves all authorities of state and government, the civilian population, and the armed forces. It normally follows the enactment of special legislation, the proclamation of specific powers, regulations, and conditions to be enforced by the government within the state, the nation, and the armed forces, and the declaration of a state of war or a state of national emergency. These measures are normally taken since there may well be a politico-military choice between overt, public promulgation and covert preparations. An act of mobilization could dissuade an enemy from opportunism, adventurism, or outright aggression. It could also further inflame the situation.

Political and military history contain ample illustrations of the risks of indecision or, at the other extreme, the dangers of certitude, that have beset national leaders in times of crisis. National procrastination or positive affirmation, and the range of options between them, have had their merits and pitfalls, their proponents, dissenters, and compromisers, in tense and critical international situations. Recent examples include Suez and Anthony Eden, and Munich and Neville Chamberlain. Many leaders before them suffered similar traumas.

The military meaning of mobilization is the process by which part or all of a nation's armed forces are brought to a state of readiness in a period of crisis or war. It is likely to include the activation of personnel from reserve forces, the activation of materiel reserves, the augmentation of defense industry output, and the assembly and organization of regular and reserve units with their materiel support ready for active service operations. Military mobilization could be part of the national act or it might be disguised as a large-scale exercise.

Nations and armed forces need strategic warning of incipient threats. Intelligence staffs maintain continuous surveillance of the intentions, capabilities, activities, and aspirations of a potential enemy. They constantly relate the actual circumstances to chosen yardsticks, and provide warnings of likely aggression to their political and military leaders. Using a preplanned system of alert measures a nation prepares for mobilization, and its armed forces increase their operational readiness. Yardsticks, indicators, and alert measures must be carefully coordinated and synchronized. Their selection and application must be part of an interactive, interdependent system; whether they relate to national or military resources, or a combination of both.

This series of actions is even more difficult and complicated in a multinational situation. Soviet influence within the Warsaw Pact and its openly declared doctrine of limited sovereignty within Eastern Europe, until the dissolution of the Warsaw Pact and the disintegration of the Soviet Union (1989–91), made the mechanics and decision making more efficient than in the North Atlantic Treaty Organization (NATO), an alliance of free and sovereign nations. The characteristic pulls and pressures will continue to be pronounced within NATO as individual member states are convinced, some more reluctantly than others, to respond to a heightening crisis by mobilizing their nations and forces. The act and process of allied mobilization, therefore, are more difficult and complicated than they would be for a single, sovereign nation.

The North Atlantic Treaty requires member nations to protect and defend each other's territorial integrity whenever, wherever, and however it is threatened within NATO's operational boundaries. The peacetime deployment of in-place forces and their reinforced posture during the transition to war, in the Central Region of Europe, for example, are aimed to involve the military forces of all allies contributing forces to that region in deterring, resisting, and combating aggression.

NATO's cumulative intelligence resources fuel the preplanned, multinational system of alert measures designed to bring allied governments and their assigned or earmarked forces progressively to a state of readiness when senior NATO commanders would assume operational command of tactical components of these forces. When Mobilization Day (M-Day) is reached, within the agreed system of alert measures, it is hoped that M-Day will be simultaneously declared by NATO member states. The alliance is not a supranational organization, so there is no guarantee that synchronization will actually occur, though procedures do exist and are rehearsed within NATO to coordinate the various national acts and military processes of mobilization. The likelihood of a delay by one or more allies cannot be dismissed. If it occurs, a delay may disrupt more than mobilization. It may disrupt the movement and deployment of forces that comprise so-called integrated operational commands in NATO's regions. A delay, for instance, by any one of the Central Region's host nations—Belgium, the Netherlands, or the Federal Republic of Germany—could be catastrophic in political and military terms.

Thus, efforts are made within NATO to coordinate the scope, content, and timing of the individual alert measures of allies. By the very nature and method of functioning of the alliance, national decisions made in scattered capitals of member states determine not only mobilization, but also the strategic movement and concentration, the tactical and logistic deployment, and ultimately the operational readiness of forces, to face an emergency or go to war. There is no lack of recognition that a comprehensive, cohesive, integrated, synchronized, and multilateral regional alert system is needed within NATO. There has always been, however, a lack of combined resolution—political will—to prevent unilateral delays in mobilization; even though the penalties are recognized. Political delays by one nation, which may breed irresolution in others, and military delays of one nation's forces, may jeopardize the intricate, complex movement plan for a number of national contingents which use common or overlapping lines of communication in a particular operational region. These are penalties which, ostensibly, the Warsaw Pact did not share.

Against this not-too-hypothetical allied backdrop, it is necessary to return to mobilization in the context of a single nation and its armed forces, remembering that many states—sovereign or otherwise—are linked to some politico-military alliance.

A nation may constitute its armed forces in different ways: they may consist of volunteers, with a comparatively small reserve that voluntary forces tend to generate; they may be part volunteer, part conscript, with a larger reserve that conscription tends to produce; or they may be based on a system of universal, part-time service, thus integrating short periods of call-up with long reserve commitments, except for a small, regular cadre of officers and NCOs. National attitudes, customs, traditions, and systems differ. More to the point, the efficacy of mobilization depends on the size and content of the military reserve forces, their state of training, and their readiness for their role.

Most nations maintain some permanent forces in peacetime and these can be categorized as pre–M-Day formations and units. The reserve formations and units, and their individual reservists, may be classified as post–M-Day forces. This does not necessarily mean that pre–M-Day forces are in their assigned area or theater of operations; it does mean that their regular availability and, indeed, their operational readiness, may not be dependent on mobilization unless they require reinforcements from the reserve to bring them up to full war readiness.

The latter proviso is often the case and, should mobilization be delayed, pre–M-Day forces may have to fight without reinforcements from the reserves.

Post–M-Day forces, by definition, have to be mobilized. Once assembled, they have their personal weapons issued and their kits are checked; they have a medical inspection and they either form into units or remain as a pool of individual reservists. They may draw their main operational equipment in the home base or after arrival in the theater or area of operations. They may have time for revisionary or intensive training before and after movement by air, sea, rail, or road. The mobilization process is a combat service support function, part military administration (the personnel aspects) and part logistics (materiel aspects). The mobilization system must mesh with the mounting, movement, and staging systems, the whole being a logistic operation.

Some armed forces maintain formations and units at partial readiness in peace, with integral regular cadres; they are dependent upon mobilizable reserves and are never at full strength in peace except during major exercises. Others keep certain formations and units at optimum peacetime readiness, with comparatively small numbers of reservists needed to bring them to war readiness; in this case mobilizable formations and units are required to complete the war order of battle. A third alternative is a mixture of the two options. Individual nations will have their own priorities and methods for active manning in peace, and these will be largely conditioned by the speed and efficiency of their mobilization process.

As an example, the armed forces of a particular nation are part volunteer and part conscript. After periods of permanent military service or a relatively short period of conscription, both volunteers and conscripts join the reserve. While in the reserve, they attend one two-week session and several weekend training sessions each year; until their reserve commitment ends at a stipulated age. The reserve forces of this nation comprise:

1. complete formations (regiments, brigades, or divisions) and complete units (battalions or equivalent) which fill in the gaps in the order of battle during transition to war;
2. individuals who reinforce headquarters and units during transition to war, thus converting those elements of pre–M-Day forces from peace to war establishment;
3. formed units and individuals assigned as battle replacements to replace units lost in war;
4. other specialists required in war; and
5. materiel stocks earmarked in peacetime for equipping reserve forces.

Four conclusions may be drawn from this example. First, the reserves are trained and equipped, and will have rehearsed their duties prior to mobilization. Second, reinforcement formations, units, and individuals (1 and 2 above) must be mobilized early enough in the alert system for them to join their parent formations and units in their operational areas before hostilities start. Third, replacements (3 above) may be mobilized slightly later, but at a precise stage in the alert system, since their role begins after the fighting starts. Fourth, it still depends on the time it takes to mobilize, mount, move, deploy, and establish reserve forces (no matter how well-organized they are) in their respective battle positions or operational areas. Good time appreciations always work backward. Therefore, having made the operational, tactical, and logistic plans which set the requirements, it should be comparatively simple to fix M-Day seen from a military viewpoint.

A political viewpoint, however, may not be that simple. There may be a number of quite different factors to consider. Declaring M-Day too soon in the specific circumstances that pertain, may have, or may be seen to have, an escalating effect. The act of mobilizing may signify to the enemy or potential enemy that negotiations have ceased. The callup of reserves removes people from their civilian employment. These are some of the considerations that may influence a political decision.

In the event that a decision must be made to mobilize or not to mobilize, there are likely to be conflicting priorities. The military commander, who may be allied or national, seeks mobilization at a time which ensures that his forces are complete and in position before war begins. The politician may sanction mobilization only when all diplomatic efforts to minimize the effects of a crisis or to avoid war have been exhausted. When there is conflict, there is generally compromise. When there is compromise, there is usually a risk of adopting, or being forced to adopt, a solution which meets neither requirement.

Mobilization is a vital operation, but it can easily be disrupted or mismanaged due to the stresses and pressures of crisis situations.

J. H. Skinner

See Also: Administration, Military; Combat Service Support; Host Nation Support; Logistic Movement; Replacements: Personnel and Materiel; Reinforcements; Reserve Components; Stockpiles; Supply; Transportation.

Bibliography

Endress, C. A. 1987. *Mobilization.* U.S. Army Command and General Staff College, Combat Studies Institute. Fort Leavenworth, Kans.

Gough, T. J. 1987. *U.S. Army mobilization and logistics in the Korean War.* Washington, D.C.: U.S. Army Center of Military History.

Simon, J., ed. 1988. *NATO-Warsaw Pact force mobilization.* Washington, D.C.: National Defense Univ. Press.

Turner, C. K. 1989. *A mobilization concept for the future.* USAWC Military Studies Program Paper. Carlisle Barracks, Pa.: U.S. Army War College.

U.S. Department of Defense, Office of Industrial Base Assessment. 1989. *A guide for industrial mobilization.* Falls Church, Va.

MODELS, SIMULATIONS, AND WAR GAMES

The successful resolution of national and international crises is the most demanding and crucial test of any government's senior-level decision makers and their staffs. In the United States, this is especially true of Defense and State Department officials.

Good crisis management, however, requires considerable skill and experience of a type and level possessed by few civilian executive appointees to these departments prior to assuming their new duties and responsibilities. All too frequently they acquire the relevant skills and experience by on-the-job training during an actual crisis. Senior-level military personnel are usually better prepared in this regard. Generally, they have had some exposure to wargaming or simulation activities and crisis management seminars at one of the war colleges, or have acquired related (although typically lower level) experiences in one or more command or staff assignments.

Fortunately, a number of mechanisms and techniques exist that can provide valuable training and insight to potential crisis managers. Of central interest to the Department of Defense (and other national entities) are the concepts and practices known as modeling, gaming or, more specifically, wargaming and simulation. This article will discuss what models, simulations, games, and wargaming are; their origins; their uses and misuses; and their relative value and validity for crisis management, as well as for other defense and national/international activities, such as policy making, planning, and operations.

Explanation of Terms

A definition of these four terms—*model*, *simulation*, *game*, and *wargaming*—is key to a better understanding of the larger context of defense analysis and decision making.

Models

A *model* is an objective representation of some portion or aspect of the real world. It may be a representation of an object or structure; it may be an explanation or description of a system, a process, or a series of related events. Models provide a means for structuring and simplifying complex problems.

Models are easier to manipulate than the real world. They serve to accumulate and relate the knowledge we have about different aspects of reality. See Figure 1 for an overview of types of models. A globe is a model of the earth; a network diagram is a model of a communications system or an organization; a set of equations may be derived to represent the dynamics of a sector of an economy. Some models are iconic and look like what they represent, such as a model airplane, a sand table topographical map, or equipment models used for teaching tactics. Others are analog in nature; for example, a slide rule replaces quantities by distances proportionate to their logarithms. Finally, symbolic models use numerals, letters, or other symbols to represent real-world properties.

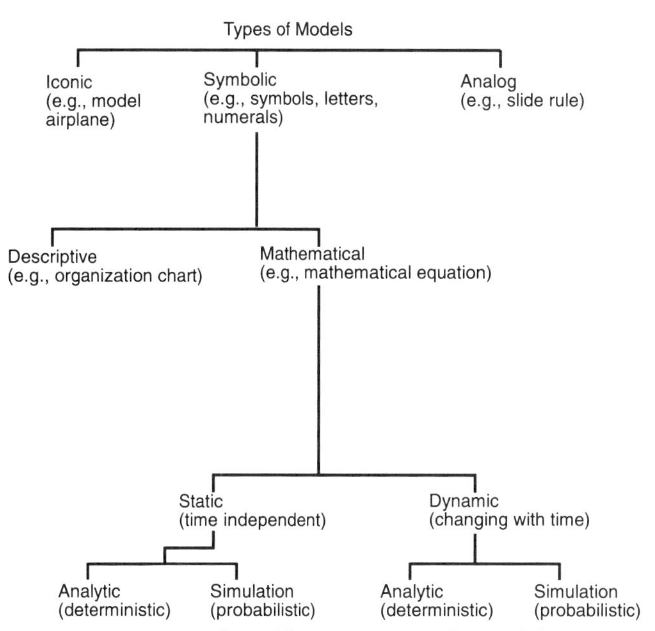

Figure 1. Real-world representation by models.

There are two types of symbolic models. The first is the descriptive model in which properties are expressed in words or diagrams. A typical example is the organization chart. The second type is the mathematical model in which symbols represent logical or quantitative relationships between different entities. Mathematical models can be static (independent of time) or dynamic (changing with time). Math models are further subdivided into analytic math models for which an exact numerical solution can be determined, and simulation math models that may be used to converge on solutions to complex problems involving uncertainty (probabilistic occurrence) and risk.

Models are never intended to be anything more than useful approximations of the real world, or portions of the real world, that they seek to represent. Only the key or salient features are included. Nonessential features are omitted. The specific variables and details incorporated into a model are those considered necessary and feasible given the purpose for which the model has been designed. Representations of broad overall processes, aggregations, or major systems are usually referred to as "macro" models, while highly detailed abstractions of a single subsystem or segment of a process are called "micro" models.

Simulations and Games

The term *simulation* refers to the general process by which certain real-world systems, operations, or phenomena are imitated using representational devices such as models, game boards, computers, or other equipment. The focus of the term is on the process of imitating (or simulating) the reality of concern, rather than on the models or items used or the rules to be followed.

Webster's (3d Intl. Ed.) defines *game* as: "a physical or mental competition conducted according to rules in which the participants play in direct opposition to each other, each side striving to win and to keep the other side from doing so." *Gaming* is simply the process of playing the game itself.

The difference between war games and simulations is generally defined in terms of the realism (degree of abstraction) and human intervention. War games traditionally have evolved from sand-table exercises, in which the territory and the forces were reasonably realistically represented and the human players made all the decisions. The outcome was determined by human referees according to predetermined rules. Such games are costly in terms of both time and personnel involved and are not readily repeatable.

In pure simulations, on the other hand, reality is represented symbolically, by mathematic equations and algorithms, and decisions are made by the computer according to predetermined rules. Games can readily be repeated many times, either to change inputs or to determine the impact of probabilistic events.

In one of the oldest war games known to man—chess—the pawns (foot soldiers) and pieces (bishops, knights, etc.) are really models and serve to represent each opponent's armed forces and capabilities. The chessboard is a highly abstracted model of the battlefield or battle area.

Modern wargaming as we know it is the offspring of military and political science and operations research. These areas are quite broad in scope and contain issues and techniques that have been topics of intensive and expanding study for the past several years. The definition of wargaming is actually a result of an evolutionary drift of the words *game*, *gaming*, and *wargaming* into the military, operations research, and political science vocabularies. *Webster's* defines *war game* in two major ways: (1) "a simulated battle or campaign designed to test concepts rather than the skill of forces or fitness of troops or equipment and usually conducted in conferences by officers acting as the opposing staffs"; or (2) "two-sided umpired training maneuver with actual elements of the armed forces participating." Wargaming then is the process of playing (or executing) a war game to its natural conclusion.

Types and Uses of War Games

War games can be classified in many ways. One approach (see Fig. 2) is to differentiate among them on the basis of their application or purpose, their scope, and the method or technique employed. Typical uses for war games include training and education; operations planning and evaluation; management and evaluation; and force planning. The scope of such games ranges from the one-on-one engagement and the larger skirmish to the battle and thence to the full-blown theater or global-level conflict.

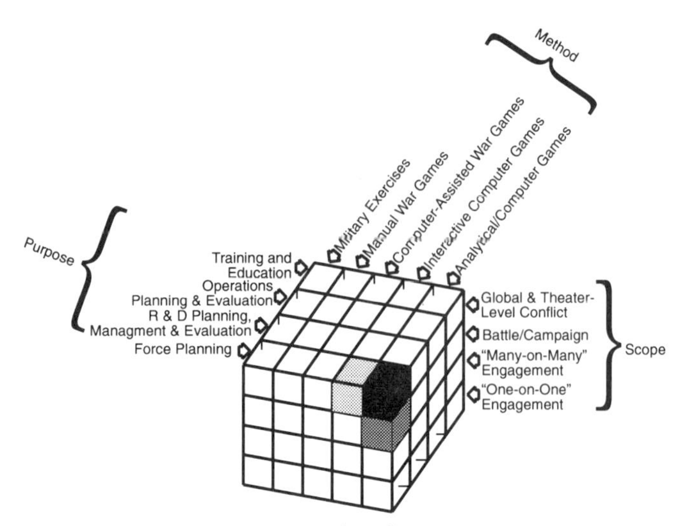

Figure 2. Gaming classification matrix.

Wargaming methods or techniques vary as do a war game's purpose and scope. Techniques range from the familiar military field and command-post exercises or maneuvers to manual war games such as those published by civilian/commercial wargaming companies.

Simulations are particularly useful if the number of quantifiable parameters is large, many probabilistic elements are involved, or a number of varied scenarios are to be examined. Such analyses can be repeated many times to gain insight on the processes involved and the interaction of different parameters. For example, an engagement of tanks can be simulated using different types of tanks and antitank weapons, different tactics and strategies, and different terrains and conditions.

Simulations are used at different levels of analysis, from detailed analyses to determine weapons parameters, tactics, and so on, to aggregated simulations for high-level strategy decisions. For example, nuclear exchanges can only be simulated but some insight regarding relative effects or force ratios can be gained by this technique. In their simplest form, simulations can be a set of equations, such as the Lanchester equations, that describe engagements in simple terms.

The type of technique selected in wargaming directly affects operational realism and the impact of human decision making on the outcome of the war game. For example, as we proceed from military exercises to the partially computer-assisted game, and thence to the interactive, computer, and analytic simulation, we lose the realistic experience so crucial in the training of tactical combat commanders, who need to experience the operational impact of their decisions. The different techniques vary greatly in their relative degree of abstraction, convenience, accessibility and outcome reproducibility. In moving along the spectrum from military exercises to computer analytic games, the set of variables that can affect the simulation becomes ever more limited and simplified. While this results in greater ease of use and reproducibility, it moves from the realism of the field toward a significantly higher degree of analysis and abstraction.

The "unit cost" of each type of war game or simulation can vary considerably. Large-scale field exercises are typically the most costly. The initial cost to design, develop, and fully test a single computer model to play analytic games may also be millions of dollars. Once developed, however, these games can be played (or run) at little cost and in relatively short time.

Appropriate Use

Each technique has its own relative strengths and weaknesses, and is appropriate or useful for different purposes or applications. For instance, field exercises are excellent devices for training and conditioning troops and commanders. They are, however, poor tools to use for force planning since it is not possible to repeat the exercise many times under different circumstances nor to control all parameters. On the other hand, analytic computer games are of little use in conditioning or training troops, because of the lack of realism in portraying the impact of decisions; but they can be of great value in answering or illuminating force-planning questions and issues and in analyzing alternative strategies and tactics.

The most appropriate and valid objectives for using war games and simulations (within the Department of Defense context) are to better understand complex phenomena, identify problems, evaluate alternatives, gain new insights, or broaden one's perspectives. The least valid or appropriate objectives for using war games and simulations are to predict outcomes of specific combat or crisis situations that are affected by leadership, morale, training, and similar factors that are not normally simulated.

War games and simulations play a crucial role in the many studies and analyses done for senior Department of Defense decision makers. Kept in proper perspective, the games are extremely valuable. They are, however, only one type of input and only one key factor of the many that influence the policy and the decision. Among these other influential factors are national strategies; objectives and priorities; budgetary constraints and time considerations; current intelligence and projected trends (e.g., regarding a potential adversary's capabilities and intentions); politico-military judgment; and the individual decision maker's past experience, sense of history, and personal value system. If this larger context is kept in mind, the role of war games and simulations will be seen in a realistic view (See Fig. 3.)

Problems and Misuses

War games and simulations are subject to some problems and misuses. The major potential problems involve communication, data, variabilities, the models themselves, and theory.

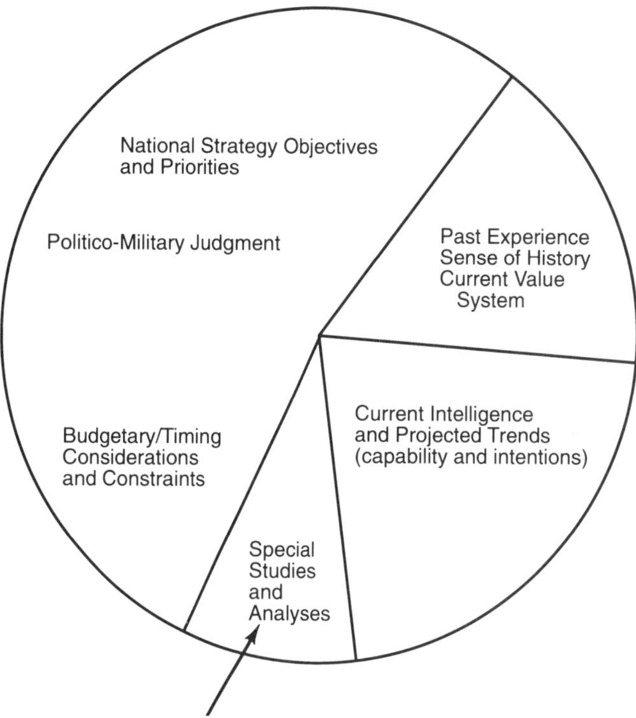

Figure 3. Key factors influencing the policy/decision maker.

A basic problem is the frequent discontinuity or lack of communication or mutual understanding between the analysts who build a war game or simulation and the decision maker who uses its output. As a result, analysts may design models to analyze things that are readily analyzed but fail to address the most critical factors that the decision maker must consider.

Models and war games require specific data for calibration as well as to run the models. However, the "right" data are not always available; they may come from diverse and not comparable sources, or not be in the proper degree of detail. Worse yet, data may not be valid or reliable. It is generally difficult to maintain and update data.

The models themselves can cause problems. They must not only be appropriate for the use intended; they must also have inherent validity, and the results must be sensitive to the key variables being examined. Models must also be updated to be of continuing value.

Another problem is the lack of a proven or universally accepted theory of combat or war. There are only general principles, such as those stated by Sun Tzu, Jomini, Clausewitz, and many others. Furthermore, few instances exist in which the validity of a model can actually be checked against reality. The use of historical data is limited to unique situations, and there are generally insufficient historical data available to provide statistical significance. T. N. Dupuy's quantified judgment method has attempted to extract data from sufficient numbers of battles to gain some insight on the parameters involved.

The principal misuses or abuses of war games and simulations include the areas of prediction and control. The most blatant abuse is advocacy. This involves the use of war games or simulation-backed studies and analyses to "sell" plans, programs, and budgets; it usually requires the analysis to support a predetermined "solution" or position. Analyses may also be misused in a counteradvocacy role to purposely confuse, detract from contrary positions, or otherwise mislead the analytically unsophisticated decision maker or public.

Politico-Military Simulations

Given the potential problems and the periodic abuses cited above, wisdom dictates that use of and dependence upon war games and simulations for any purpose must be kept in proper perspective. Decision makers must become knowledgeable and discerning users of these powerful analytic tools, aided by experienced in-house reviewers and critics. There is no practical, timely, cost-effective, or reasonable alternative to war games and simulations for analyzing certain aspects of a nation's defense or future actions, and no practical substitute for the intelligent and experienced use of these valuable tools and techniques.

One of the most useful techniques for training future and current-day crisis managers is the politico-military (PM) game. This type of simulation is routinely used in the United States by the Organization of the Joint Chiefs of Staff to plan, prepare, and conduct politico-military simulations on an interagency basis within the Executive Branch of the U.S. government.

The typical PM simulation focuses on how to assess and subsequently manage a major crisis. Strict nonattribution is the rule; PM games generally discourage role playing in the belief that it detracts from the crisis resolution and interplay between participants that should be the prime focus of the game. The subjects chosen are timely and of a classified or sensitive nature. Creating the game's hypothetical crisis or "scenario" is a full-time, lengthy process, taking up to six months of intense research and involving numerous discussions with high-echelon government and defense officials, as well as regional and technical experts.

The typical PM game has three "moves," or major segments. In the first move, the two (or more) separate teams address the same crisis scenario. Each team must satisfy the same basic requirement during the course of each move. For example, it must perform an assessment of the crisis situation's impact upon its own national/vital interests, as well as the impact upon the interests of the other nations involved in the crisis. In particular, the team must look at short-term and long-term implications and domestic reactions. Each team must also establish immediate and long-range objectives; identify the political, diplomatic, military, economic, public affairs, and other actions that must be taken to resolve (or contain) the crisis. Finally, the team must identify and plan for the unexpected contingencies that are always a part of the real world.

The second and third moves involve control team "adjustments/contingencies." During the entire PM game the control team simultaneously monitors the flow of events, actions, and so forth, of all teams. This permits it to be an "all-knowing" controller, speeding up or slowing down the game as needed, making one team's task easier or more difficult in order to balance certain initiatives, and so on. The game concludes with individual team and all-teams critiques attended by all participants. Game attendees almost universally speak highly of their gaming experience.

The primary value of such games is that PM simulations permit the examination of hypothetical situations involving the interaction of real-world factors (political, military, social, economic, cultural, religious, psychological, etc.) in order to:

- identify potential world trouble spots,
- identify major national-security issues, problems, and opportunities,
- encourage and stimulate original and creative thinking and exchange of ideas,
- develop new or innovative solutions for the problems identified,
- devise new approaches and concepts, and
- aid in the development of contingency plans.

Summary

Models are representations of the real world and to that extent lack complete realism of a specific situation. Some unquantifiables (leadership, morale, training) are difficult to model.

War games, simulations, and models represent a continuous spectrum. War games provide the most realism and most involvement by human decision makers. On the other hand, they are expensive to conduct, take most time, can generally not be readily replicated, and consequently provide little insight on the process involved.

Simulations can be simple or complex. They are abstractions of the real process, are highly automated, and can be readily replicated with changing parameters, conditions, and scenarios. They are expensive to develop initially, but are relatively easy to run, once developed. Although they may omit key parameters that are unquantifiable, they do provide insight since they can be repeated with variations.

Models can be very simplified representations of the real world, such as the Lanchester equations of combat and simple logistic support models.

High-level war games and models can be useful in analyzing the essence of contingencies in crisis management. In most cases real data and real historical analogs are not present (e.g. nuclear war), and models must rely on logical assumptions, frequently controversial, as a basis of judging the model's validity.

FRANCIS B. KAPPER

SEE ALSO: Crisis Management; Defense Decision Making: Analysis and Models; Lanchester Equations; Mathematical Modeling and Forecasting; Measures of Effectiveness; Simulator; Training Technology.

Bibliography

Ardant Du Picq, C. 1921. *Battle studies: Ancient and modern battle.* New York: Macmillan.
Bonder, S. 1971. Systems analysis: A purely intellectual activity. *Military Review,* February, pp. 14–23.
Dupuy, T. N. 1985. *Numbers, prediction and war: Using history to evaluate combat factors and predict outcome of battles.* McLean, Va.: Hero Books.
Honig, J., et al. 1971. Review of selected army models. Washington, D.C.: U.S. Department of the Army.
Huber, R. K., K. Niemeyer, and H. S. Hofman, eds. 1979. *Operational research games for defense.* Munich: R. Oldenbourg Verlag GmbH.
Lanchester, F. W. 1916. *Aircraft in warfare: The dawn of the fourth arm.* London: Constable.
Organization of the Joint Chiefs of Staff (OJCS). 1991. Catalog of war gaming and military simulation models. 12th ed. Force Structure, Resource, and Assessment Directorate (J-8). Washington, D.C.
Shubik, M., and G. D. Brewer. 1972. Models, simulations, and games: A survey. Report R-1060-ARPA/RC. Santa Monica, Calif.: Rand Corp.
Stockfisch, J. A. 1975. Models, data and war: A critique of the study of conventional forces. R-1526-PR. Santa Monica, Calif.: Rand Corp.
Taylor, J. G. 1978. Attrition Modeling. Presentation at Third Systems Science Seminar, Hochschule der Bundeswehr, Munchen. Monterey, Calif.: Naval Postgraduate School.
Weiss, H. K. 1957. Lanchester-type models of warfare. *Proceedings of the First International Conference on Operational Research,* ed. M. Davies, R. T. Eddison, and T. Page. Baltimore, Md.: Operational Research Society of America.

MOGHUL EMPIRE

The Moghul Empire ruled northern India from 1526 to 1858. Founded by a descendant of both Genghis Khan and Tamerlane, the Moghuls were the last of the Turko-Mongolian dynasties that periodically dominated the urban civilizations of the Eurasian littoral.

Zahir-ad-Din Mohammad "Babur" (1483–1530)

Zahir-ad-Din Mohammad, better known in history as Babur, was born in 1483. His father, Omar Shaikh, the youngest son of Sultan Abu Sa'id, was king of Farghana. Through his father, Babur traced his ancestry back to Timur-i-lang (Tamerlane). Babur's mother was a daughter of Yunus Khan, king of the Chagatai Ulus. Through his mother, therefore, Babur traced his ancestry back to Genghis Khan.

The 78 years between the death of Tamerlane and the birth of Babur witnessed the decline of the Timurids. The cause of their decline was the internecine struggles for power among the Timurids themselves. Babur's own father, for example, faced an almost constant threat from his brothers and his cousins.

While the Timurids fought among themselves, the Uzbeks—an offshoot of the Golden (Kipchak) Horde—under Muhammed Shaibani (1451–1510), another descendant of Genghis Khan, encroached upon the Timurid patrimony. One by one, Babur's cousins and uncles fell before the Uzbeks. For a short time, Babur, king of Farghana since the age of 12, held Samarkand and sat on the throne of Tamerlane. By 1500, however, Muhammed Shaibani was master of both Bukhara and Samarkand and was poised to take Farghana and Tashkent. In June 1503, at the Battle of Akhsi, Babur lost Farghana forever. With a handful of followers, including his half-brothers Jahangir and Nasr—both of questionable loyalty—Babur sought refuge in the mountains of Afghanistan.

CONQUEST OF AFGHANISTAN

Ten years of warfare had taught Babur much. His defeats had resulted not only from his own inexperience but also from the machinations of allies and supporters to whom he had been no more than a pawn. The loss of Farghana freed Babur to follow his destiny.

Now a king without a kingdom, Babur had an army of less than 300 men. As he moved through the mountains, however, he attracted fighters from the local tribes, including the Mongol Hazaras. With this motley force, Babur conquered Badakhshan in 1503, and Ghazni and Kabul, which he made his capital, in 1504. Three years later, in 1507, he occupied Kandahar. Possession of Kabul gave Babur a route into northern India, but he was distracted from India by events in Central Asia. In 1505, and again in 1511–12, Babur attempted to regain his Timurid patrimony. After the Uzbek victory at Ghajdivan (1512), Babur confined his energies to strengthening his control of the kingdom of Kabul. By 1519 he was secure enough to begin raiding Hindustan (northern India).

CONQUEST OF THE SULTANATE OF DELHI

In 1524, Babur invaded the Punjab. As other Muslim conquerors had done before him, including Mahmud of Ghazni, Babur entered the Punjab by way of the Khyber Pass. After leaving a garrison to hold Lahore, Babur retired to Kabul. He returned to Hindustan in 1525. At Panipat, on 20 April 1526, Babur defeated Ibrahim Shah Lodi Afghan, Sultan of Delhi and Agra. Victories over the Rajputs at Khanua (1527) and Gogra (1529), completed Babur's conquest of the Sultanate of Delhi and placed the fledgling Moghul Empire on a firm foundation.

The Moghul Army

Babur conquered the Sultanate of Delhi with 12,000 troops. Cavalrymen, both armored and unarmored, predominated in the early Moghul army. Their armor ranged from the leather armor of the Kalmuks to Indo-Persian–style chainmail reinforced with iron plates. Weapons included the traditional weapons of the steppe: the sabre and bow.

Babur made an important addition to the traditional weapons of his people: firearms. He equipped a select number of infantrymen with matchlocks. Protected from enemy arrows by leather mantlets, these Moghul matchlockmen provided protective fire during siege operations; on the battlefield, they served as both a screen for the cavalry and a pivot for cavalry maneuvers.

Babur also used cannon. These weapons, manufactured and manned by Othmanli (Ottoman) Turkish gunners, along with the matchlockmen, gave Babur an important advantage over his Muslim and Hindu enemies in Hindustan.

Moghul Organization

In general, the organization of the Moghul army followed that of the Mongol army of Genghis Khan, as had the army of Tamerlane. Some organizational flexibility was needed, however, given the mix of forces commanded by the Moghul emperor. Besides his own Turks, the emperor commanded contingents of Afghan tribesmen, Mongol freebooters, Persian mercenaries, and Indianized Turks from Delhi, as well as Rajput and other Hindu levees. There is evidence that the native contingents maintained their own battle order, while those from the Turkic and Mongol homelands adhered to the order mandated by the Yassa of Genghis Khan.

Moghul Tactics

Moghul tactics were a mixture of the traditional and the modern. Babur used many of the same tactics successfully employed by both Genghis Khan and Tamerlane. These he wedded to the evolving tactics of the age of gunpowder. At the First Battle of Panipat (1526), Babur deployed his matchlockmen and gunners behind a defensive line formed by baggage wagons. The wagons, connected by lengths of rope and chain, left gaps in the line to allow cavalry sorties. After Moghul arrow and gunfire had driven the enemy wings in upon their own center, the Moghul cavalry—the right and left wings of Babur's own army—executed the famous and dreaded *tulughma*, the Banner Sweep.

At Khanua, 13 March 1527, Babur again deployed his infantry and artillery as he had at Panipat. At a critical point in the fighting, he abandoned the defensive and ordered the infantry and artillery to advance on the Rajput center. The Rajputs, re-forming to meet a frontal attack, broke off contact with the Moghul wings, which immediately executed the *tulughma*, and the slaughter of the Rajput army began. What his distant cousins, the Ottoman Turks, had done against the Persians at Chaldiran twelve years earlier, Babur did at Panipat and Khanua: combined the traditional tactics of the Turko-Mongolian steppe warrior with those of the dawning age of modern warfare.

Under Babur's successors, the Moghul Empire continued to expand despite occasional reverses of fortune. For a short time, the Moghul domain included virtually all of India.

Moghul Expansion under Babur's Successors, 1530–1707

Humayun (1530–56)

Humayun, Babur's son and successor, had a checkered career. Although he added Mandu and Champanir to the empire in 1535, Humayun was driven out of India by the Afghan, Sher Shah (1539–45), founder of the short-lived Sur Dynasty. Humayun spent sixteen years in exile, mostly in Persia, and was only able to return to Delhi in 1555, a year before his death.

Akbar (1556–1605)

Akbar was the greatest of the Moghul emperors. Like his grandfather Babur, Akbar became king at an early age. Also like his grandfather, he learned to survive the court intrigues, jealousies, and conspiracies of relatives. With the help of Bairam Khan, his guardian, Akbar defeated both the court intriguers and, at the Second Battle of Panipat (1556), the Afghans. In 1561, he conquered Malwa and three years later, in 1564, the Chandels (Gonds) submitted. Chitor was occupied in 1568. The Kingdom of Gujarat submitted in 1573, Bengal in 1576, and Khandesh in 1577.

Akbar the conqueror was also Akbar the conciliator and administrative reformer. In 1562, the year he assumed full control of the government, he married a Hindu Rajput princess. The emperor wished to create a unified state in which both Muslim and Hindu could live together in safety and harmony. Akbar therefore abolished the *jizya*, the tax on nonbelievers. He also reformed the bureaucracy and recruited Hindus to staff its middle and lower echelons. By the end of Akbar's reign, Hindus made up 30 percent of the administrative staff.

Akbar also streamlined the administration by instituting the *mansabdari* system of civil service. *Mansabdars* (officials) were given military rank and were able to recruit and maintain troops appropriate to that rank. Therefore, although their primary duties were civil and fiscal, when occasion demanded, they could perform military duties.

To stimulate the economy and provide needed revenue, Akbar assumed control of all agricultural land in the realm. He abolished the traditional taxes and replaced them with a single tax: one-third of all agricultural and manufactured products.

Jahangir (1605–27)

During the reign of Jahangir, Moghul expansion stagnated. Jahangir, an indolent drunkard, was content to enjoy the wealth of the realm and the fermented juice of the grape.

Shah Jahan (1628–57)

Shah Jahan resumed Moghul expansion. Ahmadnagar was added to the empire in 1632, Golconda in 1635, and Bijapur in 1636.

Shah Jahan also initiated the last Moghul attempts to regain their Timurid legacy in Central Asia. Under the operational command of Aurangzib, the emperor's son, unsuccessful attempts were made to capture both Balkh and Badakhshan in 1647. From 1649 to 1653, the Moghuls tried to reconquer Kandahar, again without success. Shah Jahan was successful, however, in extending Moghul control over parts of the Deccan (central India).

The emperor's wars and the construction of the Taj Mahal nearly bankrupted the empire, and led to the revolt by Aurangzib. Deposed by his own son, Shah Jahan remained a prisoner until his death in 1666.

Aurangzib (1658–1707)

Aurangzib expanded the Moghul Empire into central and southern India. In 1666, Chittagong was occupied. In 1679, the Moghuls won Marwar from the Rajputs. In 1685, Surat was seized. Between 1681 and 1692, Aurangzib personally led his army in the conquest of the Deccan and southern India. By 1692, he ruled virtually all of India. Shortly thereafter, however, rebellion broke out in the newly conquered territories, and Aurangzib spent the last fifteen years of his reign attempting to pacify the realm—in vain.

Aurangzib was also unsuccessful in his attempts to neutralize the growing power of the Marathas under their king, Sivaji. By 1674, the Marathas were the most dangerous rivals of the Moghuls.

The greatest danger to the Moghul Empire, however, proved to be Aurangzib's own domestic policy. Reversing the policy of Akbar, Aurangzib ended toleration of the Hindu religion, destroyed Hindu temples, and reimposed the *jizya*. The emperor expelled experienced Hindu bureaucrats from the administrative apparatus and replaced them with devout Muslims. By restoring Muslim purity, Aurangzib hoped to return the empire to the strict monotheism of Islam. The end result, however, was the rapid decline of the empire following his death.

Moghul Decline

During the reign of Bahadur Shah (1707–12), the Moghul Empire disintegrated. Territorial governors and local magnates became, in reality, independent rulers. The empire therefore repeated the pattern of dissolution followed by its Turkic and Mongol antecedents. Insubordinate governors, rebellious Hindu rajas, and British and French interlopers gradually reduced the Moghul realm to the Sultanate of Delhi. In the aftermath of the Indian mutiny, Bahadur Shah II (1837–57), the last of the Moghuls, was deposed, tried, and exiled to Rangoon, where he died in 1862.

Lawrence D. Higgins

See Also: Genghis Khan; Mongol Conquests; Ottoman Empire; Turkic Empire.

Bibliography

Beveridge, A. S., trans. 1922. *Babur, emperor of Hindustan: The Babur-nama*. 2 vols. London: Luzac.
Burn, R. 1937. *The Cambridge history of India*. Vol. 4, *The Mughal period*. Cambridge: Cambridge Univ. Press.
Gascoigne, B. 1971. *The great Moghuls*. New York: Harper and Row.
Habib, I. 1982. *An atlas of the Mughal empire*. New Delhi: Oxford Univ. Press.
Habibullah, A. B. M. 1945. *The foundation of Moslem rule in India*. Lahore: S. Muhammed Ashraf.
Lamb, H. 1964. *Babur the tiger: First of the great Moghuls*. New York: Bantam Books.
Lane-Poole, S. 1903. *Medieval India under Mohammedan rule, 712–1764*. New York: Putnam's Sons.
Moreland, W. H. 1920. *India at the death of Akbar*. London: Macmillan.
Sarkar, J. 1920. *Mughal administration*. Calcutta: Sarkar and Son.
Spear, T. G. P. 1951. *Twilight of the Mughals: Studies in late Mughal Delhi*. Cambridge: Cambridge Univ. Press.

MOLDOVA (formerly Moldavia)

Moldova, one of the fifteen former republics in the Union of Soviet Socialist Republics (USSR), joined ten other Soviet republics in dissolving the Union on 21 December 1991 when they agreed to form the new Commonwealth of Independent States. This dramatic end to the Soviet and Communist state followed several years of dynamic and unprecedented change. For several more years, relations among the members of the new Commonwealth and with the rest of the world are likely to continue to change. Over time, new structures and patterns will emerge in economics, trade and commerce, politics and government, finance, manufacturing, religion, and virtually all aspects of human life. New arrangements must be devised for dealing separately as sovereign states and as a Commonwealth with the world outside the boundaries of the former Soviet state. If the history of the Soviet Union since 1985 is any guide, we can expect dramatic surprises and dynamic change.

An important question for the world is how the new states and the Commonwealth will organize and provide for their security. The Soviet Union's armed forces, formerly the largest in the world, are likely to be withdrawn from foreign territory, reduced in size, and divided up among the former republics. Also of great concern is the disposition of the largest arsenal of nuclear weapons, the security of these weapons, the command and control of their potential use, and compliance with arms control agreements entered into by the former Soviet government. The world can only hope these issues are settled amicably.

It will be years before all of these issues are resolved for Moldova and some time before events settle down into more routine and measurable patterns. No accurate description of this new country's policies, defense structure, and military forces was available to be included in this encyclopedia. Only time will reveal the future of Moldova as a separate sovereign state. The reader is thus referred to the historic information contained in the article "Soviet Union," and to the latest annual editions of the *Military Balance*, published by Brassey's (UK) for the International Institute for Strategic Studies; the *Statesman's Year-Book*, published by the Macmillan Press Ltd and St. Martin's Press; and the *World Factbook*, developed by the U.S. Central Intelligence Agency and published commercially by Brassey's (US).

F. D. MARGIOTTA
Executive Editor

MOLTKE THE ELDER (Helmuth Karl Bernard, Graf Von) [1800–91]

Helmuth Karl von Moltke served as chief of the General Staff of the Prussian army from 1857 until 1888, playing a central role in Prussia's planning and preparation for its highly successful wars against Austria in 1866 and France in 1870–71. He is frequently referred to as Moltke the Elder to separate his identity from that of a nephew of the same name (Moltke the Younger) who was chief of the General Staff at the time Germany entered World War I. During the elder Moltke's tenure as chief of the General Staff, the Prussian army's General Staff acquired an unmatched reputation for excellence, and the Prussian army served as Prussian chancellor Otto von Bismarck's primary instrument for achieving Prussia's goal of a unified German state.

Early Years

Moltke was born in the northern German state of Mecklenburg on 26 October 1800. His family was part of the old Prussian nobility, but financially it was not well off. Moltke's father served as an officer in the Prussian army and later joined the Danish army. Moltke began his own military experience as a cadet in the Danish army. In 1821, Moltke transferred to the Prussian army to increase his prospects for advancement. He served briefly with troops before attending the Prussian army's war college, where he studied from 1823 to 1826. After two more years with a regiment, Moltke gained an assignment to the Prussian General Staff, where he stayed for the remainder of his career.

Moltke's early career was heavily influenced by the relative poverty of his family, and he turned to writing to supplement his meager income. Moltke's only direct experience with warfare began in 1835, when he received an assignment to Turkey as an observer and adviser to the Turkish army. In 1839, he accompanied the commander of a Turkish army that sought to drive an Egyptian army out of Syria. Here Moltke provided astute tactical and operational advice but saw his advice ignored. The Turkish army subsequently suffered a decisive defeat, and shortly thereafter Moltke returned to Prussia.

Moltke's Rise to Prominence

In 1842, Moltke married his sister's stepdaughter. This union, although a happy one, produced no children. Moltke continued to serve on a variety of staff assignments, while simultaneously publishing accounts of his experiences in Turkey.

At about this time, Moltke also began to receive assignments that brought him to the attention of the Prussian aristocracy. In 1845, he was appointed adjutant to Prussia's Prince Frederick. This brought him into frequent contact with both the current and future kings of Prussia. Moltke impressed both with his quiet diligence and brilliance as a staff officer and adviser. His unqualified support for the crown in its efforts to suppress the revolution of 1848 gained him favor as well.

In 1857, Moltke's loyalty and competence were rewarded with his appointment as chief of the General Staff of the Prussian army. Inheriting a position that had undergone a period of decline under his predecessors, Moltke played a major role in the restructuring of the Prussian approach to warfare.

Moltke as Chief of the General Staff

One of Moltke's most immediate and lasting achievements as chief of the Prussian General Staff was his success in implementing a military mobilization system within Prussia that capitalized on the tremendous strategic mobility potential of the newly invented railroads. Moltke demonstrated a clear understanding of how Prussia could use superior organization and speedy mobilization to help offset its vulnerable geographic location in central Europe and to gain strategic and operational advantages over its potential opponents.

Moltke also introduced into the Prussian army field telegraph units to speed the transmission of orders to subordinate unit staffs and commanders. Under Moltke, the German General Staff underwent a resurgence in the quality of its officer training and the efficiency of its organization that would produce stunning results in its subsequent wars against Austria and France.

War broke out first against Denmark in 1864. At this point, Moltke was still relatively unknown within Prussia; at the beginning of this war he was little more than an adviser to the Prussian war minister, who had the real responsibility for executing the king's directives and supervising the armies in the field. When the chief of staff of the army in the field was removed, however, Moltke temporarily assumed the post and helped direct the Prussian armies to victory.

Moltke intended to retire at this point, but he was persuaded by the war minister, Albrecht von Roon, to remain. Moltke was brought into the inner councils of policy making shortly afterward, a seemingly innocuous appointment at the time, but one that proved to be an important first step in the increasing importance of the chief of the General Staff's role in matters of state policy.

In 1866, war broke out with Austria. Here the fruits of Moltke's organizational and mobilization reforms were seen, as was his superb grasp of large-scale operations. Three Prussian armies rapidly mobilized, concentrated on the battlefield near Königgrätz under Moltke's direction on 3 July, and decisively defeated the main Austrian force in a great battle of encirclement. The Prussian victory permitted Bismarck to conclude a favorable peace with Austria (the Peace of Nikolsburg), which brought several smaller German states into a North German Confederation under Prussia's dominance.

Moltke remained chief of staff through the Franco-Prussian War of 1870–71. Again demonstrating a marked superiority in speed of mobilization, the Prussian armies struck into France. Despite a number of potentially serious mistakes by subordinate army commanders that undermined Moltke's concept for another battle of encirclement like that at Königgrätz, Prussian armies succeeded in surrounding one French army at Metz and, later, another at Sedan. Although the war continued for several months beyond the French defeat at Sedan, these two victories and the subsequent siege of Paris resulted in another set of favorable peace terms that brought about a final, successful chapter to Prussia's long-term efforts to establish a unified German state.

Final Years

Moltke's wife had died in 1868. With her death, he no longer had any desire to retire and so he continued to serve as chief of the General Staff until 1888, when a new kaiser, Wilhelm II, assumed the throne. In retirement, the officer who had done so much to create the Prussian army that crushed two rival powers in relatively short campaigns warned of the end of the era of short, decisive campaigns. He died peacefully on 24 April 1891, having seen the reputation of the Prussian army and its General Staff reach unparalleled heights during his long stewardship as chief. He remains today one of the great military figures of modern times.

DAVID A. NIEDRINGHAUS

SEE ALSO: Envelopment; Franco-Prussian War; Mobility; Prussia and Germany, Rise of.

Bibliography

Addington, L. 1971. *The blitzkrieg era and the German general staff, 1865–1941.* New Brunswick, N.J.: Rutgers Univ. Press.

Craig, G. A. 1955. *The politics of the Prussian army, 1640–1945.* London: Oxford Univ. Press.

Dupuy, T. N. 1977. *A genius for war: The German army and general staff, 1807–1945.* Englewood Cliffs, N.J.: Prentice-Hall.

Gorlitz, W. 1953. *History of the German general staff, 1657–1945.* New York: Praeger.

Holborn, H. 1986. The Prusso-German school: Moltke and the rise of the general staff. In *Makers of Modern Strategy,* ed. P. Paret. Princeton, N.J.: Princeton Univ. Pres.

Kitchen, M. 1975. *A military history of Germany.* London: Weidenfeld and Nicholson.

Pflanze, O. 1973. *Bismarck and the development of Germany: The period of unification, 1815–1871.* Princeton, N.J.: Princeton Univ. Press.

Ritter, G. 1969. *The sword and the scepter: The problem of militarism in Germany,* vol. 1. Coral Gables, Fla.: Univ. of Miami.

Von Sybel, H. 1968. *The founding of the German empire.* New York: Greenwich.

MONGOL CONQUESTS

Under Genghis Khan and his successors the Mongols conquered the largest land empire in world history, an empire that extended over 90 degrees of longitude and included most of the Eurasian landmass. At its height (1206–94), the Mongol Empire encompassed many different nations and religions, all subject to the will of the Great Khan (Kha Khan) and to Mongol law (the Yassa). The Mongol army was the principal instrument used for the expansion and maintenance of the empire.

The Mongol Army

The Mongol army was one of the most efficient military machines in history. Well organized and well trained, the army was a professional fighting force, from its highest-ranking general to its lowest-ranking cavalryman.

COMPOSITION

The basic unit of the army was the *arban* (squad), composed of ten men. Ten *arban* formed a *jagun* (company), with a strength of 100 men. Ten *jagun* formed a *minghan* (regiment) of 1,000 men. Ten *minghan* formed a *tumen* (division), with a total strength of 10,000 men. Two or more *tumen* formed a field army, commanded by an *Or-Khan.*

The Mongol army was composed of light and heavy cavalry. Both the heavy cavalryman and his mount were armored. His weapons included a lance and a saber or mace. Some heavy cavalrymen also carried bows and arrows.

The light cavalrymen, the horse archers, were the core of the Mongol forces. They wore little or no armor, and carried a saber or two to three javelins, but their primary weapon was the bow and arrow. With their powerful, recurved bows, the light cavalry was able to deliver a devastating, almost continuous, suppressive fire at long range, and a deadly rain of armor-piercing arrows at short range.

With the subjugation of the northern portion of the Kin Empire, the Mongols drafted Chinese siege specialists into the army. These specialists played a significant role in the campaigns in China, the Middle East, and Eastern Europe.

Battlefield Deployment

The army normally deployed in five ranks. The first two ranks were formed by the heavy cavalry; the remaining three ranks by the light cavalry. Units deployed so that the light cavalry *jagun* could advance and withdraw between the heavy cavalry formations.

The light cavalry initiated battle by delivering volleys of arrows. When the deluge of arrows had sufficiently disrupted the enemy ranks, the heavy cavalrymen charged. So devastating was the work of the horse-archers, that the enemy usually broke after one charge. The fleeing enemy was ruthlessly pursued and slain.

Discipline

Mongol discipline was harsh. The most common punishments were beatings and death. Death was the penalty for those who failed to obey orders in the field, broke ranks without orders, or looted without permission. To fail the commander of your *arban*, or your comrades, were the most serious offenses.

The disciplinary code applied to officers as well as enlisted men. An officer was required to look after his men, ensure that they had the necessary equipment in good order, and that they received their share of the loot. Failure on the officer's part was punishable by flogging or death. Needlessly wasting the lives of his men was among the most serious offenses an officer could commit.

Size of the Mongol Army

Estimates of the size of the Mongol army vary. The Mongol core of the army may not have exceeded 130,000, but, as the empire expanded, the army added recruits from conquered territories. During his campaign against the Khwaresmian Empire, for example, Genghis Khan marshaled 150,000 troops, including contingents from allied and subject kingdoms. The Khwaresmian Army numbered at least 200,000. However, it was the Mongol organization, operational planning, firepower, mobility, and tactics that accounted for Mongol victories, not numbers.

Mongol Tactics

The Mongols used a number of tactics to gain victory, usually over much larger enemy forces. Their favorite tactic was wide envelopment of the enemy's force. This tactic, the *tulughma* or "Banner Sweep," had two variations: single envelopment and double envelopment. The Mongols also used the single envelopment and the double envelopment—the pincer movement—on the strategic level, as illustrated by the campaigns in North China, Transoxiana, and Eastern Europe.

Another tactic often employed was the feigned retreat, followed by counterattack. The Mongols would retreat before an enemy advance, often for days, and when the pursuing enemy had become sufficiently disorganized, the Mongols would turn and attack, usually from a prepared ambush.

The Mongols would sometimes leave an apparent avenue of escape open for a surrounded enemy. As the enemy troops fled through the gap in the Mongol lines, the horse-archers hunted them down.

Mongol Conquests

The Mongol Empire expanded during the reigns of Genghis Khan, Ogadai Khan, Mangu Khan, and Kublai Khan. The conquests followed a pattern of eastward—later southward—thrusts into China alternating with westward thrusts into Central Asia, Eastern Europe, and the Middle East. A brief chronology of the conquests is given below:

Genghis Khan, 1206–27

1. Hsihsia, 1209; rebellion suppressed, 1227
2. Kara-Khitai, 1211
3. Inner Mongolia, western Manchuria, 1211–13
4. Peking, southern Manchuria, 1215
5. Khwaresmian Empire, 1219–22

Ogadai Khan, 1227–41

1. Conquest of the Kin Empire completed, 1234
2. Russia, Poland, Hungary, Wallachia, 1237–41

Mangu Khan, 1251–59

1. Yunnan Province (China), 1252
2. Tibet, 1252
3. Nan-chao, 1253
4. Persia, Iraq, Syria, 1252–58

Kublai Khan, 1260–94

1. Korea, 1259
2. Sung Dynasty (South China), 1267–79
3. Annam, 1288
4. Burma, 1297

Campaigns in North China and Eastern Europe

The manner in which the Mongols conquered their empire is best illustrated by the campaigns in North China and Eastern Europe.

Initial Campaigns Against the Kin Empire, 1211–15

In 1211 Genghis Khan initiated a series of campaigns against the Kin that did not end until 1234, with the final defeat of these hereditary enemies of the Mongols. The campaign of 1211 was confined to western Manchuria and eastern Inner Mongolia, but in 1213, the Mongols attacked in force. Jebe, one of Genghis Khan's subordinates, feigned a retreat and lured the defenders of Nankou Pass into a prepared ambush, where they were annihilated by the main Mongol army under Genghis Khan.

The Mongol forces then divided into three columns. The left (eastern) column, under Genghis Khan and his youngest son Tuli, moved south towards Shantung Province. The center column, under Jebe, moved through eastern Hopei Province. The right (western) column, under Juchi, Chagatai, and Ogadai, made a wide enveloping sweep around the Kin's left flank, and entered western Shansi Province from the southwest, behind the Kin defenses. Advancing along roughly parallel axes, the three columns moved south toward the Yellow River. Upon reaching the river, the columns reversed direction and converged on Peking, leaving devastation in their wake. Unable to take Peking, the Kin capital, after a long siege, Genghis Khan allowed the Kin emperor to ransom his city. The Mongols then returned to Mongolia with their loot.

In May 1215, the Mongols returned and captured Peking, but the Kin government had already moved to Kaifeng on the Yellow River. Mongol successes, especially in Peking and southern Manchuria, were aided by the revolt of the Khitans—distant cousins of the Mongols—whose own empire, the Liao, had been overthrown by the Kin a century earlier.

Realizing that the war against the Kin would be a protracted struggle, Genghis Khan named Mukhali viceroy, and charged him with the conquest of North China.

Campaigns in Eastern Europe, 1237–41

Ogadai Khan, in consultation with his generals, decided on the conquest of Eastern Europe during the grand council meeting in 1234. The emperor named his nephew Batu, son of Juchi, expedition commander, and the veteran general Subotai, deputy commander. In reality, Subotai was in operational command.

The Mongol attack on Russia was launched in the winter of 1237. The Khanate of Great Bulgary was smashed, and subsequently, the Turkic tribes along the Volga River submitted to the Mongols. The Russian city of Riazan was sacked in December 1237; Moscow, Suzdal, and Vladimir fell in February 1238; and Tver and Yaroslav were taken in March 1238. After regrouping, the Mongols moved into the Ukraine. On 6 December 1240, Mangu, eldest son of Tuli, captured and burned Kiev.

The Mongols paused after the sack of Kiev to rest and regroup. In the winter of 1241 they resumed their westward march. At Przemysl, the army was divided into three columns. Batu and Subotai, with the main army of 40,000, advanced toward Budapest, the Hungarian capital. The northern column, less than 30,000 strong, under the command of Ogadai's son Kaidu, swept into Poland and Silesia. At Liegnitz, 9 April 1241, Kaidu's army overwhelmed a joint German-Polish force of equal size, led by Prince Henry the Pious, Duke of Silesia. Turning southward, Kaidu rode through Moravia and on to Hungary. The southern column, under Kaidu's brother Kadan, about 20,000 strong, rode south through Galicia, then west through Moldavia, Wallachia, and Transylvania, before heading northwest toward Hungary.

King Bela IV of Hungary, with an army of Hungarians, Slovenes, Croatians, Germans, and French Templars (probably more than 80,000 men), set out to meet the Mongols. After a brief skirmish, the Mongols began to slowly withdraw, pursued by the allied army. At Mohi, on the Sajo River, the Mongols turned and attacked at dawn, 11 April 1241. Subotai, with a column of two or three *tumen*, crossed the river above the town, turned the enemy right flank, and attacked. The panic-stricken Europeans were allowed to escape through a gap in the Mongol lines, only to be hunted down and slain. At least 70,000 Europeans died at Mohi.

With Hungary secured, the Mongols began using it as a forward base. Columns raided Germany, Austria, and Dalmatia, and Europe stood open to a Mongol onslaught. Only the death of Ogadai, and the recall of the generals and princes of the empire, saved Europe from the Mongols.

End of the Conquests

The reign of Kublai Khan marked the zenith of Mongol expansion. Kublai's growing identification with China and Chinese civilization, however, was symptomatic of the growing divisions within the empire and the imperial family. In Persia, the Il-Khans (Vassal Kings) converted to Islam and adopted Persian customs. In Transoxiana (Russian Turkestan), the Chagatai Khans also converted to Islam and adopted Turkic customs. Only in the Mongolian Homeland and the Khanate of the Golden Horde did Mongols maintain their original customs. After the death of Kublai Khan, the empire split into five independent kingdoms, with only nominal allegiance to the Great Khan (Kha Khan).

Lawrence D. Higgins

See Also: Ghengis Khan.

Bibliography

Juvayni, A. 1958. *The history of the world-conqueror*. Tr. and ed. J. A. Boyle. 2 vols. Manchester: Manchester Univ. Press.
———. 1977. *The Mongol world empire*. London: Variorum.
Chambers, J. 1979. *The devil's horsemen: The Mongol invasion of Europe*. New York: Atheneum.
Grousset, R. 1952. *L'Empire des steppes*. Paris: Payot.

———. 1966. *Conqueror of the world.* New York: Orion Press.
Halperin, C. 1985. *Russia and the golden horde: The Mongol impact on medieval Russian history.* Bloomington, Ind.: Indiana Univ. Press.
Lamb, H. 1940. *The march of the barbarians.* New York: Literary Guild of America.
———. 1953. *Genghis Khan: Emperor of all men.* New York: Bantam Books.
Legg, S. 1970. *The heartland.* New York: Farrar, Straus and Giroux.
Liddell Hart, B. H. 1927. *Great captains unveiled.* London: Blackwood and Sons.
Martin, H. D. 1977. *The rise of Chingis Khan and his conquest of north China.* New York: Octagon Books.
McNeill, W. H. 1964. *Europe's steppe frontier, 1500–1800.* Chicago: Univ. of Chicago Press.
Prawdin, M. 1967. *The Mongol empire: Its rise and legacy.* New York: Free Press.
Saunders, J. J. 1972. *The history of the Mongol conquests.* New York: Harper and Row.

MONGOLIA
(Mongolian People's Republic)

The Mongolian People's Republic (MPR) is a land-locked communist state in central Asia; its capital is Ulan Bator. Slightly larger than Alaska, this oldest satellite of the former USSR has the lowest population density of any country in the world and a relatively decent standard of living compared with other Asian nations.

A harsh, rugged country with sharp seasonal variation in its cold, dry continental desert environment, Mongolia features mountains in the west and southwest, the Gobi Desert in the southeast; much of the remainder of the country includes desert and semidesert plains. Traditionally, Mongolian economy has been based on agriculture and livestock—Mongolia has the highest number of livestock-per-person in the world. Recent years have evidenced extensive focus on developing mineral resources, and the mining and processing of coal, copper, molybdenum, tin, tungsten, and gold account for a large part of industrial production.

Mongolians, whose ancestors once conquered and dominated much of the known world, are evolving from their previous nomadic way of life and freedom to a more controlled urban existence. Strong proponents of the socialist way of life, they have been willing hosts to substantial Soviet military forces in the past, and have provided a buffer state between Russia (and previously the USSR) and China.

Power Potential Statistics

Area: 1,565,000 square kilometers (604,247 sq. mi.)
Population: 2,209,600
Total Active Armed Forces: 14,500 (0.656% of pop.)
Gross Domestic Product: US$2.2 billion (1990 est.)
Annual Defense Expenditure: not available
Iron and Steel Production: none
Fuel Production:
Coal: 8 million metric tons (1989)
Electrical Power Output: 2,950 million kwh (1990)
Merchant Marine: none
Civil Air Fleet: 25 major transport aircraft; 31 usable airfields (11 with permanent-surface runways); fewer than 5 with runways over 3,659 meters (12,000 ft.); fewer than 20 with runways 2,440–3,659 meters (8,000–12,000 ft.); 12 with runways 1,220–2,440 meters (4,000–8,000 ft.).

For the most recent information, the reader may refer to the following annual publications:
The Military Balance. International Institute for Strategic Studies. London: Brassey's (UK).
The Statesman's Year-Book. New York: St. Martin's Press.
The World Factbook. Central Intelligence Agency. Washington, D.C.: Brassey's (US).

History

Ancient Mongolia is known to the outside world primarily in terms of the impact of conquering Mongolian hordes (A.D. 1209–1291). First organized in 1203 under Genghis Khan, they rapidly dominated China and Persia; their influence extended well into Eastern Europe and Southeast Asia. This conquest has been frequently described (for a simplified version, see Gibson 1980).

Somewhat less known is the significant long-term impact of the Mongol's conquest of Russia: the Golden Horde ruled for over two centuries, with a lasting impact on Russian attitudes, national character, and behavior. After the Manchus conquered China in 1644, they succeeded in bringing Outer Mongolia under their rule in 1691—this provides the basis for modern Chinese claims to Mongolia. However, the present border between China and Mongolia was arranged between Russia and Manchu China in 1727.

Modern Mongolia (formerly Outer Mongolia) became independent of Russia and China—which had passed the region back and forth in the early twentieth century—in 1921. In turn, it was significantly influenced by entry of Soviet troops in 1923 to help put down a counterrevolutionary movement. The Soviets stayed until 1956, helping Mongolia withstand the Japanese threat and maintain internal security. Soviet forces returned in 1960 following the Sino-Soviet split. Although there was a Pan-Mongol movement in the 1920s and 1930s, and some Mongols asserted a preference for China over the USSR, these dissidents met with repression and purges.

Politico-Military Background and Policy

Warriors from before the time of their great conquests, Mongol males were familiar with military service, which was organized under a kind of territorial militia that also served as the basis for national administration. Chinese suzerainty and Tibetan Buddhism purportedly moved Mongols to a passive state from the late sixteenth to early twentieth centuries. Communist fervor and the threats of

Japanese and subsequent Chinese imperialism brought a reawakening of martial and national spirit. Mongolia sent troops to assist North Korea in the Korean War and provided aid to North Vietnam in the Vietnam War.

Mongolia's government is modeled on the Soviet system. The ruling political party is the Mongolian People's Revolutionary Party (MPRP), a communist organization headed by General Secretary Jambyun Batmonh since 1984, and who is also the head of the other significant state apparatus—the People's Great Hural, the Council of Ministers, and the Mongolian People's Revolutionary Army (MPRA). Service in the MPRA is a fundamental duty of all citizens; two years' active duty is compulsory.

In recent years, Mongolia has provided forward basing for Soviet surface-to-air and medium-range ballistic missiles. It also has hosted up to five Soviet army divisions: one was withdrawn in 1987, the remaining were withdrawn by 1991, and the army headquarters of about 3,000 troops is due to leave by the end of 1992. Recently, Mongolians have reflected the policy of openness or *glastnost* with their own version, *il tod*. Relations with China and the United States improved in the late 1980s; the United States established diplomatic relations in 1987, and opened an embassy in Ulan Bator in 1988.

Strategic Problems

Mongolia's strategic location as a buffer state between Russia and China will continue to be an important aspect of the region. Defining relations with the new Russia, and with other former Soviet states will present some challenges to Mongolia. Of perhaps greater interest, however, will be Mongolia's continuing relationship with China. Mongolia rejects Chinese claims to Mongolia despite the one-time suzerainty of the Manchu dynasty. The Chinese use so-called cousins of the Mongols from Inner Mongolia to reconnoiter, harass, and subvert Outer Mongolians along the Sino-Russian border.

Mongolia also faces economic challenges as former communist trading partners change to free market economies. A search for new markets for its products is likely, and expanded relationships with Western powers with a view to economic development will be of strategic importance.

Military Assistance, Alliances, and Defense Industry

Mongolia has been closely linked to the former Soviet Union in terms of military assistance, alliances, and aid. Nearly all of Mongolia's trade has been with communist countries (80% with the USSR). Mongolia may seek to align itself with Russia, particularly in view of the Soviet, now Russian, free trade zone established on Sakhalin Island. Mongolia has no defense industry to speak of.

Defense Structure

The MPRA is relatively small—about 14,000 army members and fewer than 500 serving in the air force—and has become significantly smaller in recent times. The army consists of four understrength motorized rifle divisions with 1950s- and 1960s-vintage equipment. The military is controlled by the MPRP through a dual membership in government and party positions. The Ministry of Defense handles defense matters, and also serves as Commander of the MPRA, as well as a member of the Party's Central Committee.

(For an explanation of the abbreviations and symbols used in the following section of military statistics, see the list of Abbreviations and Acronyms in each volume.)

Total Armed Forces

Active: 14,500 (perhaps 11,000 conscripts). Terms of service: Conscription: males 18–28 years; 2 years.
Reserves: Army 200,000.

ARMY: 14,000 (perhaps 11,000 conscripts). 4 MRD (understrength).
Equipment:
MBT: 650 T-54/-55/-62.
Recce: 135 BRDM-2.
AIFV: 420 BMP-1.
APC: 300 BTR-40/-60/-152.
Towed arty: 300: 122mm: M-1938/D-30; 130mm: M-46; 152mm: M-1937.
MRL: 135+: 122mm: BM-21; 132mm: BM-13-16; 140mm: BM-14-16, BM-14-17.
Mortars: 140: 82mm, 120mm, 160mm.
ATK guns: 100mm: T-12.
AD guns: 100: 14.5mm: ZPU-4; 37mm: M-1939; 57mm: S-60.
SAM: 300 SA-7.

AIR FORCE: 500 plus Soviet technicians; 15 cbt ac; 10 armed hel.
Fighter: 1 sqn with 12 MiG-21.
Attack Helicopters: 10 Mi-24.
Transport: at least 2 sqn: 15 An-2, 18 An-24, 3 An-26, 1 An-32, 1 Tu-154.
Helicopters: 1 sqn with 10 Mi-4, 4 Mi-8.
Training: 2 MiG-15U, 3* MiG-21U, 3 PZL-104, 6 Yak-11, Yak-18.

PARAMILITARY
Militia (Ministry of Public Security): 10,000: internal security troops, frontier guards; BTR-60/-152 APC.

FOREIGN FORCES
USSR: 3,000: Army: 1 army HQ, no cbt unit, withdrawal complete by end 1992.

Future

Mongolia will probably remain a dedicated socialist state, if not a communist one. It will continue to be committed to modernization, decentralization, and alignment with trading partners advantageous to its needs and future economic growth. There is little likelihood of internal unrest or of insurgency; neither will Mongolia be a significant threat to either of its major neighbors of Russia and China.

CHARLES F. HAWKINS
DONALD S. MARSHALL

SEE ALSO: Attila the Hun; Central and East Asia; China; Genghis Khan; Mongol Conquests; Soviet Union.

Bibliography

Dupuy, T. N., G. P. Hayes, J. A. C. Andrews, and G. Hammerman. 1980. Mongolia. In *The almanac of world military power,* 4th ed. San Rafael, Calif.: Presidio Press.
Dupuy, T. N., et al. 1970. *Area handbook for Mongolia,* DA PAM 550-76. Washington, D.C.: Government Printing Office.
Far Eastern Economic Review. 1988. *Asia 1988 yearbook.* Hong Kong: Far Eastern Economic Review.
Gibson, M. 1980. *Genghis Khan and the Mongols.* A Wayland Sentinel Book. Sussex, England: Wayland.
International Institute for Strategic Studies. 1991. *The military balance 1991–1992.* London: Brassey's.
Jagchid, S., and P. Hyer (with foreword by J. Fletcher). 1979. *Mongolia's culture and society,* Boulder, Colo. and Folkstone, England: Westview Press and Dawson.
Lattimore, O., and U. Onon, 1955. *Nationalism and revolution in Mongolia—With a translation from the Mongol of Sh. Nachukdorji's "Life of Sukebatur."* For the Institute of Pacific Relations. New York: Oxford Univ. Press.
Murphy, G. G. S. 1966. *Soviet Mongolia—A study of the oldest political satellite.* Berkeley: Univ. of California Press.
Rupen, R. 1979. *How Mongolia is really ruled—A political history of the Mongolia People's Republic, 1900–1978. History of ruling communist parties* series, R. F. Staar, gen. ed. Stanford, Calif.: Hoover Institute Press.
Sanders, A. 1987. *Mongolia—Politics, economics and society. Marxist regimes* series. London, Eng., and Boulder, Colo.: Frances Pinter and Lynne Reinner.
———. 1988. Mongolia. In *The Asia & Pacific Review.* Saffron-Waldron, England: World of Information.
U.S. Central Intelligence Agency. 1991. *The world factbook, 1991–92.* Washington, D.C.: Brassey's.
U.S. Department of State, Bureau of Public Affairs. 1987. *Mongolia, background notes,* May. Washington, D.C.: Government Printing Office.

MONTGOMERY, BERNARD LAW [1887–1976]

British Field Marshal Viscount (Bernard Law) Montgomery was one of the most controversial and colorful senior Allied commanders of World War II (Fig. 1). His army career spanned half a century and culminated in service as Chief of the Imperial General Staff, but he is best known for his victory over the "Desert Fox," German Field Marshal Erwin Rommel, at the Second Battle of El Alamein, 23 October–3 November 1942.

Early Life and Career

Bernard Law Montgomery, the fourth of nine children of the Rev. Henry and Maude (Farrar) Montgomery, was born on 17 November 1887 in a London suburb. In 1889 the elder Montgomery was consecrated Bishop of Tasmania, and the entire family migrated to Hobart later that year.

Montgomery spent his early years in Tasmania, later noting, "Certainly I can say that my own childhood was unhappy," which he attributed to his tyrannical mother. The Montgomerys returned to England in October 1901. Bernard's elder brother Harold was granted a commission in the Imperial Yeomanry, and served in the final months of the Boer War. This perhaps influenced Bernard, who joined the army class at St. Paul's in 1902. During his four years at St. Paul's, Bernard excelled at cricket and rugby, but was considered "backward" academically, although he later felt ashamed of his "idleness."

Figure 1. Bernard Law Montgomery at a press conference in France, 1944. (SOURCE: U.S. Library of Congress)

After passing the competitive entrance examination in 1906, Montgomery entered Sandhurst in January 1907. Prior to his commissioning, however, he was involved in a "prank" which almost resulted in his expulsion. Apparently at the intervention of his mother, he was readmitted as a Gentleman Cadet, although his commissioning was delayed from January until the summer of 1908.

Montgomery was gazetted into the Royal Warwickshire Regiment on 19 September 1908 and served with its 1st Battalion in India (1908–12). In January 1913, shortly after the unit's return to England, he was appointed assistant adjutant.

World War I

England declared war on Germany on 4 August 1914. Montgomery's battalion arrived in France on 23 August 1914, and three days later he led his platoon into battle at Le Cateau. In the ensuing confusion Montgomery was listed as missing, and he never forgot the absence of proper planning which characterized the commitment of the British Expeditionary Force (BEF) in 1914.

On 13 October 1914, Montgomery was severely wounded while leading an assault during the first Battle of Ypres. For his conspicuous gallantry he was awarded the Distinguished Service Order and promoted to captain. After recuperating, Montgomery served as a brigade-major in England, and deployed with his unit (which later suffered severe losses on the Somme) to France in January 1916.

Montgomery's indefatigable diligence was recognized by his appointment as General Staff Officer 2 (GSO2), 33d Division, in January 1917, followed by selection as GSO2, IX Corps, six months later. He was promoted brevet major on 3 June 1918, and became, two weeks later, a temporary lieutenant-colonel and GSO1 (Chief of Staff) of the 47th Division. He ended the war in that position, having earned an outstanding reputation as an exceptional and ambitious staff officer.

Interwar Years

Montgomery attended the Staff College at Camberley in 1920, followed by service as a brigade-major in Ireland during the "troubles." He served with equal efficiency on the staff of a Territorial Army division (1922–25), as a company commander (1925–26), and as an instructor at the Staff College (1926–28). After a short stint on a War Office committee revising the *Infantry Training Manual*, Montgomery returned to his regiment in 1930 as second-in-command.

In 1931, he commanded the 1st Battalion, Royal Warwicks in Palestine. The battalion went to India in 1934, and Montgomery became chief instructor at the Staff College, Quetta, in June. He then commanded the 9th Infantry Brigade at Portsmouth (1937–38), and continued his quest for high command. As a major general, he briefly commanded the 8th Division in Palestine in 1938, but became quite ill and was sent home to England. After recuperating, he assumed command of the 3d Division on 28 August 1939, less than one week from the start of World War II.

World War II

Montgomery commanded his division as part of II Corps (commanded by Lt. Gen. Sir Alan Brooke, the future Chief of the Imperial General Staff) of the British Expeditionary Force, which landed in France on 30 September 1939. Montgomery incessantly trained his division during the interlude of the "phoney war." After the German onslaught of 10 May 1940, the 3d Division defended the city of Louvain, Belgium, and after the Allied forces disintegrated, his division participated in the retreat to Dunkirk. On 27 May 1940, the 3d Division conducted a night maneuver in the middle of a battle, which prevented the enemy from outflanking II Corps and the BEF. During the last few days of the Dunkirk evacuation, the imperturbable Montgomery commanded II Corps.

After his return to England, Montgomery resumed command of the 3d Division, was promoted to lieutenant general, and selected to command V Corps in July 1940. This was during the crucial period when a German invasion of England seemed imminent; nine months later Montgomery was transferred to command XII Corps. On 17 November 1940 Montgomery became General Officer Commander-in-Chief South-Eastern Command.

Throughout 1942, the military situation in North Africa deteriorated, resulting in the relief, in August 1942, of Gen. Sir Claude Auchinleck and replacement by Gen. Sir Harold Alexander as Commander-in-Chief, Middle East. Montgomery, near the apex of his career, was selected to command the Eighth Army defending the approaches to Cairo. Montgomery restored cohesion and confidence throughout his command. Within a month, adopting Auchinleck's plan, Montgomery stopped Rommel's forces at the Battle of Alam Halfa (31 August–2 September 1942).

Montgomery then turned his attention to the logistical problems of operating in the desert, and planned the Second Battle of El Alamein. Starting on 23 October 1942, this rather unimaginative battle did not go as planned, but Montgomery responded to the changing situations and tenaciously continued the offensive. By 3 November, the Germans had literally run out of tanks.

Montgomery was very slow to exploit the victory at Alamein. He was out-generaled by Rommel, but the tide of war had changed. Rommel's forces were eventually trapped by a giant pincer movement of the Eighth Army attacking from the east, and Allied forces (which had landed in North Africa in Operation "Torch" in November 1941) pushing from the west. Organized resistance in North Africa ceased on 12 May 1943.

Montgomery was involved in the planning for, and commanded the Eighth Army in, Operation Husky, the invasion of Sicily, 10 July 1943. He no longer had complete control, but had to work together with Americans, who were frequently annoyed and insulted by Montgomery's often condescending and boorish behavior.

After commanding the Eighth Army in Italy, Montgomery returned to England in December 1943 to command the 21st Army Group in the invasion of Europe. His Operation Goodwood (18–20 July 1944), an attempt to break out of the Normandy beachhead, was decisively repulsed. Subsequently, he was roundly criticized for the dilatory nature of his attempts to close the "Falaise gap"; however, the blame for the escape of thousands of retreating Germans must be shared by the American commander, Gen. Omar Bradley.

Montgomery's tenure as ground force commander came to an end in August 1944, when Supreme Commander Dwight D. Eisenhower took over direct control of ground force operations. Soon afterward Montgomery was promoted to field marshal.

Differing philosophies on how best to defeat Germany then divided the Allied High Command. Montgomery (like Bradley and Patton) favored a single, knife-like thrust—under his own command—to the Ruhr. (Bradley and Patton believed this should be an American offensive.) But Eisenhower's strategy was to attack Germany on a broad front. Despite the dismal failure of Operation Market Garden in September, the subsequent performance of 21st Army Group was typically efficient, but unimaginative. Montgomery responded well militarily to the German counteroffensive in the Ardennes, but his imprudent claims of having "saved" the Americans resulted in further alienation between himself and the senior American commanders. The Allied advance continued, and on 4 May 1945, Montgomery accepted the unconditional surrender of German forces in northern Europe, having reached the Baltic Sea, near Lübeck.

Aftermath

Montgomery was ennobled as Viscount Montgomery of Alamein on 1 January 1946, and served as chief of the Imperial General Staff from June 1946 to November 1948. He served as chairman of the Western Union Commanders-in-Chief Committee (1948–51), and then as Deputy Supreme Allied Commander Europe (1951–58), under Generals Eisenhower, Ridgway, and Gruenther. Montgomery retired in 1958 after a half-century as a serving officer.

The publication of Montgomery's *Memoirs* in 1958 caused a furor. He was accused of being grossly unfair to many people, especially Auchinleck. In retirement, Montgomery traveled extensively and wrote books and articles. While bearing the Sword of State at the 1968 opening of Parliament, Montgomery collapsed, and afterward faded from the public eye. After being bedridden for three years, Montgomery died at his home at Isington Mill, on 24 March 1976.

Field Marshal The Viscount Montgomery of Alamein, K.G., G.C.B., D.S.O., remains a controversial figure. Ruthlessly efficient, he was vain and at times a showman, and a rather unimaginative but highly charismatic commander. A German field marshal said that generals were like race horses. They were supposed to win and Montgomery won most of the time. That is how "Monty" will be remembered by many.

HAROLD E. RAUGH, JR.

SEE ALSO: Eisenhower, Dwight David; Rommel, Erwin; World War II.

Bibliography

Barnett, C. 1960. *The desert generals.* London: Kimber.

Carver, M. 1962. *El Alamein.* London: Batsford.

Chalfont, A. 1976. *Montgomery of Alamein.* New York: Atheneum.

Hamilton, N. 1981. *Monty: The making of a general, 1887–1942.* New York: McGraw-Hill.

———. 1987. *Monty: The final years of the field-marshal, 1944–1976.* New York: McGraw-Hill.

Lewin, R. 1971. *Montgomery as military commander.* New York: Stein and Day.

Montgomery, B. 1974. *A field-marshal in the family.* New York: Taplinger.

Montgomery, F-M. 1958. *Memoirs.* London: Collins.

———. 1968. *A history of warfare.* London: Collins.

Moorehead, A. 1946. *Montgomery.* London: Hamish.

MORAL GUIDANCE

The term *moral guidance* has been used almost exclusively in Islamic countries, but the concept and measures it entails can be found in some form in all armed forces. Some military in certain countries have "political commissars," citizenship or ideology discussion groups and meetings, internal information programs, leadership schools and seminars.

In Islamic countries, moral guidance may be defined as all measures aimed at building and preserving the morale and the fighting will of individuals in armed forces so as to motivate them to do their utmost to achieve the highest degree of combat efficiency and success in battle with few or no casualties and a minimum loss in materiel and time.

Since men, not arms, win wars, and since morale is the mental attitude of individuals at a particular time and under a particular set of conditions, the main object of moral guidance is to create in a positive manner that mental attitude and to maintain it under all conditions. To accomplish this, armies resort to a variety of measures that will raise morale while, at the same time, eliminating the suppressive forces that work against it.

Fighting Ideology

To obtain the best results in building morale, armies must impart to soldiers a fighting ideology that clearly states the principles for which the soldier is fighting. This ideology answers the question, "Why do I fight?" and motivates the soldier to willingly perform his or her duties, overcome obstacles, face death and discomfort, and defeat the enemy. There are two types of fighting ideology.

SPECIFIC FIGHTING IDEOLOGY

A specific fighting ideology can be religious or ideological. It focuses the soldiers' attitudes on their efforts to defend it. Thus, the triumph of this ideology becomes the object of fighting. An example of this type is Egypt. As an Islamic country, Egypt derives its fighting ideology from Islamic teachings, which can be summed up in the doctrine of a Jihad for God, meaning a struggle for God. According to the Koran, God Almighty said, "And strive for Allah with the endeavor which is his right."

NONSPECIFIC FIGHTING IDEOLOGY

This type of fighting ideology is adopted by those nations that focus on political and strategic objectives. They develop the positive attitudes of the individuals toward the assigned objective in each case.

Its Missions

Moral guidance serves a variety of missions in contemporary armed forces, all of which intend to enhance morale and effectiveness within individual fighting units. Some of these are:

- to plant and promote the fighting ideology in the hearts and minds of the soldiers and to develop their loyalty to their country, its constitution, and its domestic and international policy;
- to develop a sense of responsibility, devotion, enthusiasm, initiative, and wholehearted cooperation among these individuals in order to achieve the highest degree of combat efficiency and combat readiness;
- to build up confidence that their training is adequate, that it permits them to perform their duty with a maximum efficiency and effort, and that they can defend themselves, exist on the battlefield, and defeat the enemy;
- to build confidence in their weapons and to develop their sense of responsibility for maintaining them under all conditions;
- to build confidence in their commanders, that they are capable of leading them to victory over the enemy;
- to make soldiers understand the reasons for the policies and practices in general and the policies of their unit commanders in particular;
- to build pride in one's unit as well as in the armed forces as a whole;
- to build esprit de corps among individuals and to encourage them to put group welfare above individual welfare or desires;
- to organize appropriate ceremonies, particularly traditional ceremonies and those commemorating great events in the history of the unit, the armed forces, and the country;
- to take a sincere interest in another's welfare and to make him comfortable, well-cared for, and as contented as circumstances will permit;
- to explain the nature and objectives of war and the missions and the radius of action of the armed forces;
- to convince combatants that the cause for which they fight is just, reasonable, and that it conforms to the interests and goals of their country;
- to explain the intentions and objectives of the enemy and to develop a feeling of hatred toward him in the hearts of the combatants and to promote their determination to defend their homes and country against enemy aggression;
- to study the contents and methods of the enemy's propaganda and psychological warfare, to make individuals aware of their objectives, to take all necessary measures to protect individuals against it, and to remove its effects;
- to plant and develop offensive spirit, courage, and ability to bear the difficulties of the battle.

Military Leadership

A proficient, well-disciplined unit possessing high morale and esprit de corps can be created with the proper application of the principles of leadership. The commander has the power to make the morale of his men good or bad. The organizational structure of many armies encompasses a moral guidance organization that may be a directorate within the general headquarters that is responsible for planning, supervising, and evaluating all the missions and activities of moral guidance throughout the army. It may comprise branches of planning, research, political affairs, religious affairs, social affairs, information, administration, and a school of moral guidance. The organizational structure may also include branches and sections of moral guidance down to brigade or battalion level.

Moral guidance officers at all levels act as counselors and assistants to their commanders and are responsible for executing all missions of moral guidance.

Qualities of Moral Guidance Officers

Moral guidance officers should possess a good knowledge of the principles of the behavioral sciences—psychology, sociology, anthropology—in order to be able to interpret and anticipate the behavior of individuals under various circumstances. They should also possess traits of both leaders and instructors so as to be able to convince, influence, and direct individuals to the assigned goal in such a way as to command their confidence, obedience, respect, and loyal cooperation.

Moral Guidance in Combat Operations

In addition to the missions mentioned above, moral guidance officers also:

- submit reports to their commanders about the men's morale and their plans of moral guidance before, during, and after combat;
- help the men understand the commander's decisions, instructions, and the assigned missions;
- inform the men about the lessons learned from previous operations in order to make use of them in the battle;
- inform the men and the information media of the outstanding and heroic achievements accomplished by individuals or by units.

The importance of motivating individuals and units concerns all commanders, in times of peace as well as war. While modern communication techniques and extensive psychological research have, over time, somewhat changed the ways in which officers encourage their forces, officers' concern about ideology, missions, and personal qualities have been constants of military operations since the dawn of history. Although the term *moral guidance* has been used more frequently in Islamic countries than in other parts of the world, the measures it entails can be found in all armed forces.

MOHAMMED GAMAL ALDIN MAHFOUZ

SEE ALSO: Land Forces, Effectiveness and Efficiency of; Leadership; Morale; Psychology, Military; Sociology, Military; Unit Cohesion.

Bibliography

Ali, M. N.d. *The religion of Islam*. Cairo: Arab Writer Publishers.

Mahfouz, M. G. 1958. *Fan Al-Qiadah Al-Askariah Matba'at al-kuwat al-mussalaha Al-Qahirah*. Cairo: Armed Forces Press.

———. 1969. *Al-Maadhal illa Al-tawjih Al-ma'anawi al-Najeh matba'at al-kuwat al-mussalaha al-Qahirah*. Cairo: Armed Forces Press.

———. 1977. *Al-Madhlal illa Al-Akida wa Al-Istiratijiah Al-Askariah Al-Islamiah Dar Al-'Ittissam Al-Qahirah*. Cairo: Armed Forces Press.

MORALE

Morale is a widely used term referring to the enthusiasm and persistence with which soldiers, sailors, or airmen engage in the assigned missions of their unit. Often used as if it were an attribute characteristic of a group rather than an individual because of the central role of the unit's mission and goals, it has been called by some the most important single factor in war.

A military unit with high morale performs consistently at high efficiency, carrying out its assigned tasks promptly and effectively, each member contributing his share willingly and assuming that his fellows will do their part as well. Mutual help and encouragement is routine, and success is expected. Exemplary work is singled out for praise, and slackers are scorned. Members are proud of themselves and their unit, develop a strong identification with the unit and its reputation, and take great pleasure in displaying symbols of their affiliation (Shibutani 1978).

Related Concepts

The importance of group solidarity for effective military performance has been recognized for centuries, and military writers have often used the terms *cohesion* or *esprit de corps* as synonyms for morale. In the twentieth century the term *morale* has been drafted for use in nonmilitary contexts, where it has often been used to mean job satisfaction. Consultants to other industrial and commercial organizations have relied on the terms *job satisfaction* and *organizational commitment* to serve morale-like roles.

Cohesion is the bonding of soldiers to each other and their leaders in such a way as to sustain their will and commitment to each other and their unit despite the stress of combat. This personal loyalty, very close to what mental health professionals now call "social support," is often supplemented by a more impersonal bond between the soldier and a secondary group or institution (like a regiment or a large ship) larger than the face-to-face work group but smaller than the nation or even the service. This soldier-institution bond we call esprit de corps.

Job satisfaction is often a major constituent of morale when the term is applied to civilian industry or business, although it applies only in a very limited way to men in combat. In fact what many civilian organizations refer to as "organizational commitment" (Mowday, Porter, and Steers 1982) is probably closer to what military organizations mean by morale. It is more global than job satisfaction, more stable in the face of day-to-day work experiences, and develops and dissipates more slowly. Like morale, organizational commitment has personal, work group, and organizational determinants.

Determinants of Morale

The founder of the U.S. Army's Morale Branch began his task with the assumption that everything in the environment of the soldier, and the state of mind of every person with whom he comes in contact, affects his morale. Although this daunting assessment is probably correct, it is also true that the most important factors in morale fall under three headings: personal, unit, and institutional.

PERSONAL FACTORS

Personal factors include both biological and psychological needs. Good health, good food, adequate rest and sleep, clean dry clothes, washing facilities, and protection from the elements are examples of the former, and are regularly cited as causes of high morale (Manning 1991). The basis for these assertions is the very obvious rise in spirits produced by an occasional hot meal, warm bath, or undisturbed sleep. Most firsthand accounts of combat (Holmes 1985) make it clear that, almost by definition, these needs can be met only sporadically. The answer to this seeming paradox is not simply that all combat soldiers suffer from chronically low morale but what Stouffer and his colleagues (1949) called the concept of "relative deprivation." Servicemen expect to work hard in uncomfortable, hazardous environments where amenities are few. It is not so much the absolute level of physical discomfort that controls their morale as the relation of their discomfort to that of those around them, or that which they have been led to expect is reasonable under the circumstances. Morale soars when the serviceman is provided with physical comforts that exceed his expectations, and plunge when he gets less than he feels is his fair share of whatever is available or possible.

Still at the personal level, there are a number of psychological needs whose fulfillment plays a major role in morale, above and beyond physical factors. Post–World War II, pre-Vietnam social science was nearly unanimous in denigrating patriotism, or equally grand and glorious causes, as sources of motivation for the combat soldier. Disillusioned soldier-writers like Robert Graves and Siegfried Sassoon, as well as social scientists, thought ideology much overrated as an incentive to actual fighting (although not denying its effectiveness at inducing young men to join the armed forces). America's Vietnam experience and Iran's apparently enthusiastic persistence in its devastating war against Iraq suggest that this rejection of "Grand Causes" as important determinants of morale may have been premature or overstated. It would instead seem that at least a general acceptance of the worth of the social system for which the serviceman is fighting, and a clear goal, whether abstract like religion or nationalism or concrete like Berlin or Tokyo or even taking the next ridgeline, is an essential component of high morale.

Just as important as a goal is a role: seeing oneself as a valued member of the fighting force with an important role to play in the unit's mission. Holmes (1985) provides an apt quote from a fellow Briton: "Many a man behaves as a hero or coward, according as how [sic] he is expected to behave." In civilian life suggested cures for low worker commitment include increasing job "scope," or eliminating "role conflict," or "role ambiguity."

Naturally the service member must see his or her goals as attainable, and the roles as ones that can be carried out, requirements that emphasize the importance of both solid training (the service member must be given the appropriate skills to make a valuable contribution) and self-confidence (the service member must be provided evidence that his skills are in fact adequate—through successful training exercises).

Unit Factors

By far the most important single determinant of a soldier's morale—of his willingness to close with and fight the enemy—is his relationship with those around him in his primary face-to-face work group (Glass 1973). A sense of mutual trust, confidence, and esteem among the servicemen and between them and their leaders serves as an effective buffer against the morale-sapping stresses of combat. These feelings, which are called "unit cohesion" in military settings and "social support" by mental health professionals, arise from shared experiences. In past generations, armed forces took advantage of preservice shared experiences by manning units (army regiments most prominently) with men of similar ethnic class and regional origins (and perhaps schooling in the case of the officer corps). Shifting demographics, increased mobility in the general population, and deliberate attempts to avoid inequities in risk and suffering have seriously weakened this cohesion-building strategy and made shared experiences while in the service the real glue which holds the fighting unit together.

Combat experience itself has long been recognized as the primary bonding force in the unit. Stephen Crane's *Red Badge of Courage*, for example, refers to the "mysterious fraternity born out of smoke and the danger of death." The vastly increased accuracy and lethality of today's weapons have made modern forces wary of leaving the task of creating cohesion entirely to the enemy. The U.S. Army, for example, has begun to change its industrial-model individual replacement system to one that focuses on keeping groups of soldiers together for extended periods of time. This in fact is the first requirement for building cohesion—the more time people are together the greater the chance they will discover, invent, and experience commonalities. The more people involved, the more varied the settings, and the longer the group remains stable, the more its members will have in common and the higher the unit's cohesion will be. Three other requirements for high cohesion put some limits on this sweeping generalization. First, the effectiveness of a shared experience is generally proportional to the extent to which it is unique to the unit. That is, being in the army is common to all soldiers, but it is nowhere near as effective in bonding the soldiers of 2d platoon of Alpha Company, 33d Infantry, as their unique experience of, for example, holding a mountain pass in the bitter cold during Exercise Bold Stroke, or even winning the battalion basketball championship. Both of these examples also illustrate two additional requirements for high cohesion: the unit must derive some feeling of success or accomplishment from its shared experiences; and, the greater the requirement for interdependent activity, the greater the resulting cohesion (a successful basketball team requires considerable interdependence among its members; a good track and field team, little, if any).

The net result in a highly cohesive unit is that its individual members feel they are firmly embedded in a network of mutual obligation. They are confident that, in times of difficulty, they have others available who *can* help (i.e., have the ability and training) and *will* help them to stay alive and do their jobs.

Organizational Factors

Leaders, even more than peers, must generate this confidence that they can and will help each unit member survive and succeed. Their subordinates must see not only that their leaders will not expend their lives through incompetence, but also that they will not waste them through indifference. Leaders of high-morale units do this in a variety of ways, including medals and other explicit acknowledgments of abilities and accomplishments, which reassure the soldier, sailor, or airman that he is a valued individual whose life will not be thoughtlessly expended. Paradoxically, firm discipline also provides this assurance, as long as it is seen as evenhanded, for we do not generally impose rules and standards on those about whom we care little. A third way in which leaders bolster morale by demonstrating that they care is by providing clear and meaningful unit missions—by seeing that the efforts of the unit and the risks they incur are for something undeniably worthwhile. For this reason, time spent explaining the *why* of a mission as well as the *what* often pays off in higher morale and stronger determination to succeed.

Leaders are also the links integrating their units into the larger organization and inculcating the values and goals of that parent organization into the small unit. The degree to which they succeed in this determines the extent to which their small units display esprit de corps. High levels of esprit mean that soldiers' loyalties go beyond their fellow unit members and immediate leaders—an important step if morale is to be maintained in combat, where casualties will inevitably undo a will to fight that is based on purely personal loyalties. Large military forces have often attempted to help their leaders in this task of establishing institutional bonding by providing a secondary group that is large enough to survive a bitter fight but not so large that the service member feels he or she is just another number. For navies this is most often a ship, or a formation of ships. For the combat arms soldier it is most often a regiment. Significant features of such secondary groups are distinctive names, colors, dress, territorial affiliation and recruitment, museums, bands, honorary ranks, veterans associations, and publications. Replacements for casualties in the small units (e.g., the rifle companies) of such a system come from within the secondary group (the regiment), which assures that they arrive already sharing a significant body of distinctive experiences with those they are joining. An additional effect is, ultimately, to link each soldier, sailor, or airman's self-esteem to the reputation and expectations of the secondary group.

Consequences of Morale Level

Military leaders have long seen high morale not only as a characteristic of successful fighting troops, but as a major cause of that success. Indeed it might be said that the concept of morale was invented precisely because of the consistent inability to predict military victory purely on the basis of the relative size and composition of opposing forces. Xenophon had discovered and recorded in 400 B.C. that "not numbers or strength bring victory in war; but whichever army goes into battle stronger in soul, their enemies generally cannot withstand them" (Richardson 1978). Napoleon said much the same in opining that "in the end the spirit will always conquer the sword"; Tolstoy, in *War and Peace*, offered that "in warfare the force of armies is the product of the mass multiplied by something else, an unknown X . . . [which] is the spirit of the army, the greater or less desire to fight and to face dangers. . . ." Historians of the twentieth century, psychiatrists struggling with "shell shock," "battle fatigue," and "posttraumatic stress syndrome," and social scientists struggling to measure the "unmeasurable" in the midst of World War II have all provided ample testimony to the essential truth of these assertions as well as helping to codify the variables of which morale is a function. Modern technology has, if anything, given a greater role to morale factors, for greater lethality, range, and accuracy have put devastating firepower within the reach of the most backward of combatants, and made dispersion on the battlefield a necessity for mighty powers as well as for insurgents in developing countries.

FREDERICK J. MANNING

SEE ALSO: Medical Research and Technology; Reinforcements; Replacements: Personnel and Materiel; Unit Cohesion.

Bibliography

Baynes, J. C. 1967. *Morale*. New York: Praeger.

George, A. L. 1971. Primary groups, organization, and military performance. In *Handbook of military institutions*, ed. R. W. Little, pp. 293–318. Beverly Hills, Calif.: Sage.

Glass, A. J. 1973. Lessons learned. In *Neuropsychiatry in World War II, zone of the interior*, ed. R. L. Bernucci and A. J. Glass, pp. 735–59. Washington, D.C.: Office of the Surgeon General, Department of the Army.

Holmes, R. 1985. *Acts of war*. New York: Free Press.

Kellett, N. A. 1982. *Combat motivation*. Boston: Kluwer Nijhoff.

Manning, F. J. 1991. Morale, cohesion & esprit. In *Handbook of military psychology*, ed. R. Gal and A. D. Mangelsdorff. New York: Wiley.

Mowday, R. T., L. W. Porter, and R. M. Steers. 1982. *Employee-organization linkages*. New York: Academic Press.

Richardson, F. M. 1978. *Fighting spirit*. London: Leo Cooper.

Shibutani, T. I. 1978. *The derelicts of Company K: A sociological study of demoralization*. Berkeley, Calif.: Univ. of California Press.

Stouffer, S. A., A. A. Lumsdaine, M. H. Lumsdaine, R. M. Williams, M. B. Smith, I. L. Janis, S. A. Star, and L. S. Cottrell. 1949. *The American soldier*. Princeton, N.J.: Princeton Univ. Press.

MORALITY AND WAR

Most people acknowledge a strong presumption against the moral permissibility of killing others, but nevertheless believe that in some circumstances this presumption is overridden by other moral considerations. This article will survey a range of positions that have been taken on the question of whether, and if so how, warfare can be justified as one of the exceptions to the presumption against killing.

There are two fundamental questions which must be answered by any adequate account of morality and war: (1) is it ever morally permissible to go to war?, and (2) what is it morally permissible to do in war? The answers to these two questions have received the names *ius ad bellum* and *ius in bello*, respectively.

The best-developed and most widely held theory of morality and war is the "just-war" theory; the majority of this article will be devoted to that view. But it is not the only view, so the article begins with a discussion of alternative theorys.

Alternatives to the Just-War Theory

One insightful way of looking at the just-war theory is to first analyze two contrasting theories: pacifism and permissivism.

Pacifism—The Restrictive Option

The term *pacifism* has been used to refer to a variety of views adopted for a variety of reasons. Two are of particular interest here: absolute pacifism and modern-war pacifism.

Absolute pacifism is grounded in the moral principle that some kinds of killing (whether all homicides or only wars) are *never* morally permissible. The absolute pacifist's answer to the two fundamental questions is clear. Under what circumstances does one have a right to go to war? None. That answer, of course, makes the second question moot.

The rejection of this first form of pacifism is usually based on the claim that homicide is permissible when, but only when, the use of force is made necessary by the wrongful acts of others. It is justified insofar as it is the only practical or expeditious way of avoiding or righting those wrongs. It is justified because there is nothing unjust about making it the case that the one who suffers harm in an unjust attack is the aggressor himself rather than the intended victim. After all, were it not for the actions of the aggressor, no one would need to suffer any harm at all, and, if he cared that much about not being harmed himself, he could always avoid the harm by breaking off his attack.

The second form of pacifism, which might be called modern-war pacifism, claims only that the current historical situation is such that no war could in fact meet the criteria which a defensible just-war theory would have to set. This view will be discussed in more detail below.

Permissivism

The question is sometimes raised whether moral principles can even be applied to war. The Roman proverb *inter arma silent leges* (in time of war, the law falls silent) and its English counterpart "All's fair in love and war" both suggest that they cannot. Wasserstrom (1970, pp. 78–85) calls this view moral nihilism with respect to war. Such a view might be defended on the grounds that morality is concerned with evaluating choices whereas war is a matter not of choice, but of necessity. But, as Walzer (1977, pp. 3–20) points out, any particular decision to go to war is necessary only in the sense of being indispensable to previously chosen ends. And the question of whether it was permissible to choose those ends in a given context *is* an appropriate subject of moral inquiry.

But moral nihilism with respect to war is not the only view which is more permissive than the just-war theory. What might be called the permissivist account of the *ius ad bellum* holds that a state has a right to go to war whenever it chooses to do so. This is the doctrine of *Staatsraison* (or, *raison d'état*). A permissivist account of the *ius in bello* would grant belligerent powers (or individual combatants) the right to do whatever is required to win a war. This doctrine has been called the doctrine of *Kriegsraison* (or, *raison de guerre*). These doctrines are logically independent. That produces three possible positions:

1. A state may go to war whenever it wants and is entitled to do anything that would help it win the war.
2. There are only certain conditions that would justify going to war, but once those conditions are met, a nation is entitled to do anything that would help it win the war.
3. A nation may go to war whenever it wants to do so, but there are moral limits on what it may do to win the war.

Hobbesian-Clausewitzian (or Complete) permissivism. The first version of permissivism might be drawn from the writings of Karl von Clausewitz or Thomas Hobbes. Since neither author addressed himself directly to the questions asked here, the attributions are conjectural.

In the opening chapter of *On War*, Clausewitz (1832) presents his understanding of the nature of war. The argument that he accepts the doctrine of *Staatsraison* is an argument from silence. In one famous passage, he says: "War is therefore a continuation of policy by other means. It is not merely a political act but a real political instrument. . . . What still remains peculiar to war relates merely to the peculiar character of the means it employs." If the peculiar character of the means employed had anything to do with moral limitations on the right to go to war, this would surely be the place to say so, but Clausewitz does not. His support of the doctrine of *Kriegsraison* is more explicit: "Philanthropic souls may imagine that there is a way to disarm or overthrow our adversary without much bloodshed. . . . Agreeable as it may sound, this is a false idea which must be demolished. . . . We can never introduce a modifying principle into the philosophy of war without committing an absurdity."

Hobbes (1651) offers what might serve as a theoretical ground for these views. He declares that nations are in a State of Nature relative to one another. In this condition: (1) "There is . . . no mine and thine distinct; but only that to be every man's that he can get; and for so long as he can keep it," and (2) "Force and fraud are . . . the two cardinal virtues" (chaps. 13–14). The first branch of Hobbes's Fundamental Law of Nature requires that those in a State of Nature "seek peace, and follow it," which would seem to require efforts to set up a world government, rather than to permit waging war at will. But Hobbes concedes that sometimes peace will be unattainable. In those cases, the other branch of the same Fundamental Law says that the person (or ruler) in the State of Nature "may seek, and use, all helps, and advantages of war."

Such a view of war will stand or fall with the soundness of Hobbes's general moral theory. For an application of Hobbes's views to a contemporary problem in military ethics, see Morris's *A Contractarian Defense of Nuclear Deterrence* (Hardin 1985).

MacArthurian (or Military) permissivism. The second version of permissivism accepts the doctrine of *Kriegsraison* but not that of *Staatsraison.* It is thus permissive with respect to military means, but not with respect to political ends. This is, perhaps, the view held by Gen. Douglas MacArthur, whose 19 April 1951 speech to Congress includes the following remarks: "I know war as few other men now living know it, and nothing to me is more revolting. I have long advocated its complete abolition. . . . But once war is forced upon us, there is no other alternative than to apply every available means to bring it to a swift end. . . . In war, indeed, there can be no substitute for victory."

In this view, war is hell. Waging war at all thus requires strong moral justification. Thus the doctrine of *Staatsraison* is rejected. Those who force another nation to go to war by treating it unjustly are to be condemned. But from the fact that war is hell, it also follows that justice should be done and peace reestablished as quickly as possible. If certain means (say, the burning of Atlanta or the destruction of Hiroshima by the atomic bomb) contribute to victory, then they are permissible (if not required). Refusal to use means that would hasten victory is irresponsible since it leaves everyone in the hell of war longer than necessary.

Accepting this view presupposes two things. First, it presupposes the dubious factual claim that the awfulness of war is more closely tied to the length of the war than to the nature of the means used. Second, it presupposes the controversial moral claim that worthy ends (whether in the sense of objectives or consequences) sometimes justify morally abhorrent means.

Political permissivism. The final version of permissivism accepts war as a morally unproblematic means of achieving political ends, but does insist that war is a rule-governed activity. War, in this view, is like a duel or a jousting tournament. It is not like a brawl, where there are no rules; and it is not like law enforcement, where one side (the police) claims an exclusive right to the use of force. Perhaps this is the view of war that would have been taken by a Renaissance *condottiere.*

This view is plausible only when wars are fought by soldiers who enlist, not because they feel obligated to defend their country, but either because they enjoy war for its own sake or have made an unconstrained choice of it as a means to some other end. Otherwise, wars initiated at the whim of the attacking nation will involve unjust killing (either of conscripts who do not want to fight at all or of volunteers who are merely acting on their obligation to protect their community against harm). Even when all the soldiers on both sides are people who have freely chosen to be soldiers, political permissivism is only plausible if consent of the victim makes homicide permissible. The maxim *scienti et volenti nulla fit iniuria* (no injustice is done to a willing victim) to the contrary notwithstanding, neither the law nor common morality accepts consent as exculpating homicide. Political permissivism cannot, in the final analysis, be justified.

The Just-War Theory

The most common alternative to the two points of view discussed above is the just-war theory, with origins at least as early as the Middle Ages (Russell 1975; Johnson 1975, 1981). This theory holds that:

1. Going to war is not always wrong in principle,
2. *Staatsraison* is not a sufficient reason to go to war, and
3. *Kriegsraison* is not an adequate criterion of what one may do in war.

War, according to this view, could be justified, but only under certain circumstances.

Since the just-war theory is a *moral* theory, it does not commit itself on the factual question of whether these conditions are sometimes met. Many just-war theorists believe that they are, and hence believe that some historical wars have been justified and that war continues to be a morally acceptable response to certain kinds of injustice. Other people believe that no modern war could meet all of the criteria of a just war. Since such people differ from the absolute pacifist with respect to moral principles, they are often called modern-war (or practical) pacifists. Since they arrive at their position, not by rejecting the just-war theory, but by applying it, they are also sometimes called just-war pacifists. They differ from the mainstream just-war theorists, not over the three points mentioned above, on which both agree, but over the truth of the following:

4. The just-war criteria are sometimes met.

This is not a moral principle, but a factual claim about the modern world.

The moral foundation of the just-war theory varies from author to author. Walzer (1977) relies on a theory of rights; Childress, in his *Just-War Theories* (Wakin 1986), relies on a theory of *prima facie* duties; and other authors appeal to Thomistic natural law. But surely most would agree with Potter (1969, pp. 49–50) that, "rightly perceived, the criteria of 'just war doctrine' pertain to all situations in which the use of force must be contemplated as an immediate or remote possibility. . . . Whenever men think about the morally responsible . . . use of force, some analogue of the just war doctrine emerges."

Despite disagreements over the question of moral foundations, there is fairly general agreement among just-war theorists about the necessary conditions of a just war. Nearly all authors offer the following list—legitimate authority, just cause, last resort, proportionality, prospect of success, right intention, and just conduct. Some authors add other criteria (e.g., declaration of war, comparative justice) but it is doubtful that such variation in the lists reflects anything more than different ways of formulating the same basic position. There are differences among various just-war theorists, but these differences are in their interpretation of the criteria rather than in their enumeration of them. Although this list of seven criteria has become nearly universal among contemporary just-war theorists, there are a number of ways in which it is conceptually inelegant (Kemp 1988). The theory will be presented here in a way that, by following more closely the presentation of St. Thomas Aquinas, avoids those problems.

THE *IUS AD BELLUM*

The first question which must be asked is about the moral permissibility of going to war. This question takes two forms: (1) is it morally permissible to initiate a war, or (2) is it morally permissible to get involved in a war that is already underway. Each of these questions must be faced by public officials and private citizens.

A public official would confront the first question when he asked himself whether war would be a morally permissible response to some problem his country faced (e.g., the occupation of its territory by a foreign power, seizure of its citizens as hostages, predatory raids on its commerce, or negligence of a debtor nation in meeting financial obligations). Although war is, by definition, a community act, and not an individual one, private citizens might also face the same question. The Hearst press, for example, is sometimes accused of having started the war fever which led to the Spanish-American War. If such a thing is possible, then private individuals have, in the morally relevant sense, the power to initiate a war.

A public official would face the second question when he asked, for example, whether he should come to the aid of a victim of aggression, as Britain and France (nominally) did on behalf of Poland in 1939. A private individual would face the same question when he asked, for example, whether his country's war effort was just, and hence whether he was permitted (or required) to enlist.

Legitimate authority. The medieval founders of the just-war theory believed that government authorities were entitled to do certain things that were forbidden to private individuals. Among those special entitlements was the right to kill malefactors when necessary. Since war involves such killing, it could only be waged by those who had that right. Modern theorists tend to recognize a stronger individual right of self-defense (one which extends to a right to intend to kill the aggressor if necessary) and to place more emphasis on the right of revolution than it earlier received. But that cannot be allowed to diminish the importance of this criterion, for the point of the criterion is to insist that the decision to commit a country to a war may be made only by those whom the community has authorized.

The criterion would be violated, for example, by a U.S. president who initiated a war without the permission of Congress or by a military officer who committed his soldiers to war without the permission of his civilian superiors. But there is no reason why the principle must be inseparably tied to an existing political structure. So the criterion would not be violated by a revolutionary leader who could show some good reason why he should be leading a revolution. Whether one held that that good reason would have to be popular support, dynastic right, sincere concern for the common good, or some other reason would vary with one's general theory of political authority.

Just cause. The criterion of just cause forms the substantive core of the just-war theory, and is the criterion from which the theory's name is derived. The point of the theory is to insist that war is only permissible in the service of justice (i.e., in response to some past or impending wrong committed by others). No other reasons for waging war (e.g., promotion of the national interest, or the salvation of those to be conquered in a crusade) are acceptable. To advance such reasons would be to put forward yet another alternative to just-war theory. Most recent defenders of the theory have placed last resort, proportionality, and prospect of success on the same level of generality as just cause. It might be better to say that a nation has a just cause for war only when: (1) a serious wrong has been committed by the nation to be attacked, (2) there is no other way to right the wrong, (3) resort to war will not be more destructive than righting the wrong is morally worth, and (4) there is some prospect of righting the wrong by going to war.

1. *Precedent wrong.* The question of what counts as a sufficient wrong is as central to an understanding of the criterion of just cause as is the discussion of just cause as a whole to the full theory. The traditional answer cites three types of action as justified: repulsion of attack, recuperation of captured things (or persons), and punishment of wrongdoers. Modern international law is more restrictive, allowing only self-defense. This need not, however, be seen as a difference at the level of principle. The problem with the more inclusive list is that in wars to recapture things or punish malefactors the aggrieved na-

tion acts as plaintiff, sheriff, and judge. And the restrictions of the Kellogg-Briand Treaty and the United Nations Charter could be read as an acknowledgment of the dangers of making a nation a judge in its own case. Although modern practice may still be closer to the classical triad than to positive international law on this point, at least the abuses have been less egregious than they were in the last century.

Walzer (1977, pp. 51–127) provides the best recent treatment of this criterion. His discussion of preventive and preemptive wars and the right to intervene in foreign wars raises important issues neglected by most earlier writers. O'Brien (1981, pp. 19–27) also offers a helpful discussion, but there is a need for continued work on these questions.

2. *Proportionality.* The second part of asking what counts as a sufficient wrong focuses on the particular historical situation. Sometimes waging war will cause more destruction than righting the wrong is worth. That may, in part, explain why the U.S. government used military force to rescue the *Mayagüez* from Cambodia in 1975, but not the *Pueblo* from North Korea in 1968.

3. *Last resort.* This criterion requires that all attempts to resolve a dispute by negotiation and arbitration be exhausted before any resort to armed force is made. It does not require that every conceivable alternative, however dim its prospects of success, be tried, but it does require a sincere exploration of every reasonable option. To the extent to which the criterion of precedent wrong is limited to defense against actual armed attack, this criterion may seem less prominent, since there is not much opportunity for exploration of peaceful alternatives to military defense once an invasion has been launched. But even with such a restrictive interpretation of precedent wrong, this need not be the case.

First, the criterion hints at an obligation not only to see that avoidable wars are avoided, but also to see that peaceful alternatives are available. Each nation must do its part in establishing and strengthening such institutions as the International Court of Justice. Second, even once a war has begun, the attacked nation has an obligation to be attentive to ways in which the war could be brought to an end. Though a counterattack may be the only resort in immediate response to an invasion, continuing the counterattack is not permissible once the original invader is sincerely willing to negotiate an end to hostilities along lines fair to all parties involved. For under those revised conditions, waging war would no longer be a last resort.

4. *Prospect of success.* This criterion is closely related to proportionality. Obviously the stringency of attempting to fulfill a positive duty (e.g., to protect one's community) decreases as it becomes less likely that the attempt will succeed. But, when applying this criterion, one must distinguish among the nation's various objectives. Although Finland may have had little prospect of winning its Winter War with the Soviet Union in 1939–40, its war effort may well have succeeded in discouraging the Soviet Union from making similar demands in the future.

Right intention. The criterion of right intention concerns not so much the external act as the internal disposition with which the action is performed. This emphasis on internal, and hence essentially private, features of the action has led some political theorists to ignore the criterion. But its point is valid. Anyone who wages war, not out of a concern that peace return and justice prevail, but out of hatred and revenge, is doing wrong. The proper corrective in such a situation is, of course, not to refrain from performing the external action, for its performance may be an objective moral requirement of the situation, but to purge the bad intention. While that may not be important to the political analysis of a situation, it is relevant to a full moral appraisal of the agents involved.

The *Ius in Bello*

The principles of the *ius in bello* have traditionally received less systematic attention than those of the *ius ad bellum.* The typical analysis concentrates on only two principles, discrimination and proportionality. But more careful analysis reveals that all three of the principles of the *ius ad bellum* apply to individual actions in war as well as to the act of going to war.

Legitimate authority. This criterion might at first seem irrelevant to the *ius in bello.* If the war has been launched by legitimate authority, what more does the soldier need? The question overlooks the existence and significance of rules of engagement, truces, and the like. One example of a case in which the *ius ad bellum* criterion of legitimate authority is met, while the *ius in bello* criterion of legitimate authority is not, might be the bombing of North Viet Nam by Gen. John D. Lavelle's Seventh Air Force despite explicit orders from the Pentagon not to do so.

Just conduct. This criterion, the analogue of the just-cause criterion of the *ius ad bellum,* is concerned with evaluating the acts of war themselves. Explication of the criterion can follow either the moral principles involved (discrimination, proportionality, military necessity or last resort, and right intention) or the kinds of restrictions which the principles impose. Three different kinds of restrictions can be distinguished: on targets, on weapons, and on tactics.

To a certain extent, the moral principles governing the conduct of war can be investigated by looking at the positive international law of war. There are three limitations to this approach. First, as the Martens clause acknowledges, the codification is not exhaustive: "in cases not included in the Regulations [i.e., the Hague Conventions] . . . populations and belligerents remain under the protection and empire of the principles of international law, as they result from the usages established between civilized nations, from the laws of humanity, and the requirements of the public conscience" (Preamble to 1899 Hague Convention II). Second, there are often good reasons for prohibiting targets, weapons, and tactics that are not immoral *per se*. And third, there is no guarantee that the international lawyers are not simply mistaken in some of their permissions and prohibitions. But the Hague and Geneva conventions do nevertheless form a good starting point for the inquiry.

Target restrictions underlie the principle of noncombatant immunity, and the protection afforded to excombatants, medics and chaplains, certain kinds of natural resources (e.g., the water supply), and cultural property (e.g., art museums and architectural monuments). Prohibited weapons include biological weapons, certain kinds of small arms ammunition, and (for first use, at least) chemical weapons. Prohibited tactics focus on the concept of perfidy. This prohibits the use of "moral camouflage" (e.g., the white flag or the Red Cross) and wearing the enemy's uniform. The medieval Truce of God, which forbade private warfare on certain days, would be another example of such a prohibition.

These prohibitions can be grounded either intrinsically (i.e., as a direct violation of some moral principle) or extrinsically (i.e., as a generally useful prohibition of something not immoral *per se*). The prohibition on biological weapons (which is based on their uncontrollability) is a clear example of an intrinsically grounded prohibition. The prohibition on chemical weapons (possibly) and the Truce of God (more clearly) are examples of the latter.

1. *Discrimination*. The principle of discrimination is concerned exclusively with targeting issues, though not all targeting restrictions are derived from the principle of discrimination. It is the *ius in bello* analogue of precedent wrong.

The clearest and most familiar application of the principle is that of noncombatant immunity, which asserts that the deliberate killing of noncombatants is immoral (Ford and Wasserstrom in Wasserstrom 1970; Walzer 1977; O'Brien 1981; Mavrodes in Beitz 1985; Nagel and Murphy in Wakin 1986). The principle is a natural consequence of the antipacifist argument, which justifies killing only the person who is making an attack and hence is in a position to break it off. It does not justify harm to those near and dear to the attacker, however effective making them suffer might be in discouraging the malefactor from continuing his misdeeds. In war, combatants are the ones who are carrying out the attack; thus they are the only legitimate objects of attack. Much of the controversy is focused on three questions: (a) determining whether the principle is best grounded in rights (Walzer 1977; Murphy in Wakin 1986), consequences (Wasserstrom 1970), or convention (Mavrodes in Beitz 1985); (b) determining whether the principle admits of exceptions (Walzer 1977; O'Brien 1981) or is absolute (Nagel and Murphy in Wakin 1986; Ford in Wasserstrom 1970); and (c) sorting out middle cases (e.g., farmers, industrial workers, political leaders, and warmongering private citizens). The first two points of difference, while unresolved, depend for their solution on more general questions of moral theory. The last point, in particular, is less dependent on theoretical issues and needs more attention.

But noncombatant immunity, as important as it is, does not exhaust the scope of the principle of discrimination. The disabled and the shipwrecked, being incapable of further resistance, also gain a moral right not to be subject to direct attack. This immunity is reflected in international law. Prisoners form a slightly more complicated case, but a prisoner who genuinely surrenders must, by law and morality, be given quarter. There is no need, and hence, no right, to kill those who are no longer fighting.

Other cases of immunity under the principle of discrimination include protected persons (e.g., chaplains and medics) and cultural property. Both have received explicit recognition in international law.

2. *Proportionality*. Failing to discriminate between legitimate and illegitimate targets is not the only way of going wrong in military operations. It would also be wrong to permit harmful side effects out of proportion to the good one expects to gain. This criterion, which focuses on a direct comparison of the cost (to all parties) of a given attack and its potential benefit, corresponds to the *ius ad bellum* criterion of proportionality.

This and the following criterion should be able to account for any remaining restrictions on targeting and all restrictions on weapons and tactics. Unfortunately, little work has been done in this area. Consequently, anything more than suggestions about the exact moral bases for various actual and proposed restrictions would be premature.

The criterion of proportionality probably underlies the prohibition of biological weapons. The uncontrollable character of these weapons might be said to create a harm out of proportion to any conceivable political gain.

3. *Military necessity* (*last resort*). Another way of going wrong in military operations would be by failing to choose the least destructive way of accomplishing one's objectives. This would violate the principle of military necessity, which is the principle without which there would be no justification for any destruction. It is a necessary, though not a sufficient, condition for an act of destruction that it have some military utility. Or put differently, all unnecessary military operations are morally wrong, but not all useful military operations are morally permitted. This principle, which focuses attention on alternative means of achieving the same end, corresponds to the *ius ad bellum* criterion of last resort, since a destructive military operation is not the only remaining option (or last resort) in situations in which less destructive alternatives are available.

The criterion of military necessity may underlie the prohibition on the use of dumdum bullets. If an ordinary bullet effectively puts an enemy soldier out of action, and a dumdum bullet adds to the suffering of the wounded without making any real contribution to victory, its use would constitute resort to more costly means when less costly means are available and its prohibition would respond to a moral imperative.

Right Intention. Right intention can also be applied to individual acts in war, quite independently of its application to the war as a whole. An individual soldier can be evaluated both with respect to why he enlisted to fight a given war and with respect to why he performed any particular action. It is possible for his intention with respect to enlistment to be fully correct and his intention with respect to a particular action in the war to be wrong. Perhaps a soldier who enlisted in order to protect democracy from totalitarian aggression later comes to hate the enemy and to kill them, even when necessary, not *out of* necessity but out of hatred. Or perhaps he kills just one enemy soldier out of hatred or a desire for revenge. Then we might say that, even if his killings are objectively justified, he has done (or in one action did) wrong.

Conclusion

Although it has become fashionable in some circles to assert that the just-war theory is not applicable to the modern world, in fact the criteria it lists seem to be exactly the terms in which questions of morality and war continue to be discussed by all parties. Those who believe that no modern war can be justified usually cite one or another of the just-war criteria in defense of their views; political leaders defend the military operations they initiate in terms of these criteria, and the critics of these same operations argue, not that the criteria are insufficient, but that they have not, in fact, all been met.

K. W. KEMP

SEE ALSO: Clausewitz, Karl von; Ethics, Professional Military; Pacifism; Preventive War; Rules of Engagement; Ruses and Stratagems; War Crimes.

Bibliography

Bainton, R. 1960. *Christian attitudes toward war and peace.* Nashville, Tenn.: Abingdon.

Beitz, C. R., *et al.*, eds. 1985. *International ethics.* Princeton, N.J.: Princeton Univ. Press.

Childress, J. F. 1978. Just-war theories. *Theological Studies* 39:427–45.

Clausewitz, C. von. 1832. *Vom Kriege.* Berlin: Ferdinand Dimmler.

Cohen, M., T. Nagel, and T. Scanlon, eds. 1974. *War and moral responsibility.* Princeton, N.J.: Princeton Univ. Press.

Hardin, R., ed. 1985. Special issue on ethics and nuclear deterrence. *Ethics* 95:3.

Hobbes, T. 1986. *Leviathan.* Rev. ed. New York: Collier Books.

Johnson, J. T. 1975. *Ideology, reason, and the limitation of war.* Princeton, N.J.: Princeton Univ. Press.

———. 1981. *The just war tradition and the restraint of war.* Princeton, N.J.: Princeton Univ. Press.

Kemp, K. W. 1988. Just-war theory: A reconceptualization. *Public Affairs Quarterly* 2:121–41.

O'Brien, W. V. 1981. *The conduct of just and limited war.* New York: Praeger.

Potter, R. B. 1969. *War and moral discourse.* Richmond, Va.: John Knox.

Ramsey, P. 1961. *War and the Christian conscience.* Durham, N.C.: Duke Univ. Press.

———. 1968. *The just war.* New York: Scribner's.

Russell, F. H. 1975. *The just war in the Middle Ages.* Cambridge, U.K.: Cambridge Univ. Press.

Sterba, J., ed. 1987. The ethics of nuclear warfare. *Monist* 70:3.

Wakin, M. M., ed. 1986. *War, morality and the military profession.* Boulder, Colo.: Westview.

Walzer, M. 1977. *Just and unjust wars.* New York: Basic Books.

Wasserstrom, R. A., ed. 1970. *War and morality.* Belmont, Calif.: Wadsworth.

MOROCCO, KINGDOM OF

Morocco, located in the northwest corner of Africa, opposite Spain, has long served as a meeting ground for Arabic, African, and European cultures. Its geography is dominated by the rugged Atlas Mountains in the country's center, and the old cities of Fez and Marrakech both lie in the northern foothills of the Atlas.

Power Potential Statistics

Area: 446,550 square kilometers (172,413 sq. mi.)
Population: 25,444,400
Total Active Armed Forces: 195,500 (0.768% of pop.)
Gross Domestic Product: US$25.4 billion (1990 est.)
Annual Defense Expenditure: US$1.4 billion (5.2% of GDP)
Iron and Steel Production: figures unavailable
Fuel Production:
 Coal: 0.838 million metric tons (1984)
 Crude oil: 0.018 million metric tons (1981)
Electrical Power Output: 8,140 million kwh (1990)
Merchant Marine: 51 vessels; 315,169 gross registered tons
Civil Air Fleet: 23 major transport aircraft; 67 usable airfields (26 with permanent-surface runways); 2 with runways over 3,659 meters (12,000 ft.); 13 with runways 2,440–3,659 meters (8,000–12,000 ft.); 27 with runways 1,220–2,440 meters (4,000–8,000 ft.).

For the most recent information, the reader may refer to the following annual publications:

The Military Balance. International Institute for Strategic Studies. London: Brassey's (UK).

The Statesman's Year-Book. New York: St. Martin's Press.

The World Factbook. Central Intelligence Agency. Washington, D.C.: Brassey's (US.)

History

The modern history of what is now called the Kingdom of Morocco begins with the ascension to the throne of the House of Alawi (the present ruling house) in the wake of the collapse of Saadian rule in 1668. As with the Saadians, the Alawite dynasty came to power on a wave of Islamic fervor (as well as opposition to foreign incursions by the Spanish and Portuguese), which originated among the Saharan Berbers. Rashid II (1664–72) and Mulai Ismail (1672–1772) firmly established the regime and saw Morocco more pacified and united than it was ever to be again up to the time of the French occupation.

Although French penetration began as early as 1830 with the conquest of Algiers and subsequent colonization of Algeria, it was not until 1904 that French interests were recognized as "preeminent" in Morocco. In that year, a convention was signed between France and Spain that assigned the Spanish to two zones of influence, one in the north and another in the south. In 1912, Morocco formally became a French protectorate with a French resident-general empowered to direct foreign affairs, control defense, and introduce internal reforms. A new convention was signed with Spain in the same year; this one limited Spanish influence to two less-extensive areas. Most important in this arrangement was the fact that it was the French (not the sultan), as the protecting power, who extended these rights.

The 1930s witnessed a growing nationalist sentiment throughout Morocco. During World War II, the Party of Independence, Istiqlal, demanded full freedom for Morocco with a constitutional form of government under the sultan, Mohammed Ibn Youssuf, who supported the nationalist movement. There was considerable opposition, however, to Istiqlal and the sultan, especially in the countryside and among the great Berber houses of the southern and central regions of the Atlas Mountains. Among the most prominent houses to oppose any break with France was that of Thami al-Glawi, the Pasha of Marrakech. Berber influence led to the voluntary exile (but not abdication) of the sultan in favor of his aging relative, Mohammed Ibn Arafa. But the nationalist fervor continued to increase until, in 1955, Arafa retired and Youssuf returned from exile in France to be recognized once more as the legitimate sultan. On 2 March 1956, France formally recognized the obsolescence of the 1912 protectorate (and, in extenso, the abrogation of the Franco-Spanish agreements on zones of influence). Morocco had gained its independence. In November of that year, Morocco became a member of the United Nations.

Politico-Military Background

In 1957, the sultan was declared king and his son, Moulai Hassan, heir apparent. Upon his father's death in February 1961, Hassan ascended the throne as King Hassan II. In December 1962, a new constitution was approved by referendum, establishing a constitutional (*de jure* if not *de facto*) monarchy with guaranteed personal and political freedoms (this constitution was replaced in March 1972 by the present constitution). The 1960s and 1970s were marked by considerable internal unrest and political instability of governments. The king himself, however, managed to increase his popularity with a policy of nationalization ("Moroccanization"), land redistribution, and, most important, continued efforts to recover the Western Sahara.

From March 1972 to November 1975, tensions increased between Morocco and Spain over the future disposition of the Spanish Sahara. Hassan's attempts to forge an agreement leading to outright annexation of the region—extremely popular among all major political groups within Morocco—were thwarted by Spanish preference for a referendum to be held under UN supervision in order to permit the inhabitants themselves to decide their political future. The formation of the Polisario Front, a local liberation movement supported by Algeria, and the increased tensions between Spain and Morocco in the fall of 1975 led to the Green March in which 350,000 unarmed Moroccan civilians formally "took possession" of the Western Sahara by invading it. These events were quickly followed by a Spanish agreement to hand over governance of the region to a joint Moroccan-Mauritanian administration (a decision vociferously opposed by Algeria). After Spanish departure, Morocco and Mauritania agreed to a division of the territory. By 1979, in the face of increased guerrilla warfare by the Polisario, Mauritania formally withdrew its territorial claims to the region, and Morocco immediately declared the Mauritanian zone a Moroccan province. Moroccan attempts to incorporate the Western Sahara began in earnest at this time.

Politico-Military Policy and Strategic Problems

Moroccan military policy has been shaped by a number of factors, not least among them the war in the Western Sahara and relations with various Arab states and neighbors. Morocco's relations with its immediate neighbors, particularly with Algeria, have often been tense. In July 1962, Moroccan troops entered the region south of Colomb-Bechar in Algeria, a region never officially demarcated. At the same time, Morocco launched a major diplomatic effort in support of the view that the Tindouff area in the extreme southwest corner of Algeria belonged to Morocco. The area contains large deposits of high-grade iron ore and considerable resources of oil and natural gas. For a time, after the agreement between the two countries in 1964 declaring the area a "demilitarized" zone, relations improved. After 1976, however, with Morocco asserting its claims in the Western Sahara, relations rapidly deteriorated. Algerian support of the Polisario movement has been the primary cause of the Moroccan-Algerian tension. In November 1977, after a Polisario raid on a Mauritanian mining town in which Moroccan and French nationals were killed and captured, Hassan warned Algeria that Moroccan troops would pursue Polisario forces into Algerian territory if necessary. The Algerians retorted that any such action would lead to war. In the meantime, the French increased tensions in the area with three air attacks on the Polisario in the Western Sahara. Until the late 1980s Moroccan-Algerian relations remained tense. The Treaty of Union with Libya in August 1984 was largely a result of the politico-military impasse with Algeria. The treaty not only provided Morocco with an ally, but also persuaded Col. Muammar Qaddafi to cut off Libyan aid to the Polisario. Furthermore, it broke the diplomatic isolation of Morocco from its closest neighbors and several other African countries over the issue of the Western Sahara.

The chief preoccupation of Morocco's military policy-makers is the Western Sahara. The initial attempt to control the Polisario insurgency faltered; indeed, by January 1979, the Polisario were making raids in Morocco proper (e.g., a raid on Tan Tan) causing considerable economic disruption as well as casualties. In an attempt to deal with the problem, the government launched Operation Ouhoud in November of that year, adopting Polisario tactics of swift-moving armored columns to seek out and confront the enemy. By 1980, however, emphasis was switched again to defensive tactics with the creation of the sandwall. The "Wall"—an electronically equipped barrier designed to act as a trip wire when breached—originally extended some 600 kilometers (372 mi.) and connected the major towns of Layoun, Bou Craa, and Es-Smara to form a strategic perimeter (*triangle utile*) around an area containing most of the population and the chief phosphate mines. In 1984, the sandwall was extended to the Mauritanian border. In 1986–87, the sandwall was further extended and fortified.

Military Assistance

Since independence was achieved in 1956, France has played a key role in organizing and training the Moroccan armed forces and assisting in Morocco's reassertion of control over the Spanish zones of influence. Another major source of assistance has been the United States. In October 1981, when Moroccan aircraft were shot down near Guelta Zemmour by what Morocco claimed were sophisticated Soviet-built SAM-6 surface-to-air missiles, the king turned to the United States which had already been assisting Morocco in light of its moderate, pro-Western regime. Military aid was increased by large amounts, and U.S. transit bases in Morocco were even discussed. With the signing of the Treaty of Union with Libya in August 1984, Morocco was forced to retreat from its close relations with the United States, but it gained very little in return from Libya. Indeed, by the end of 1985, Morocco appeared to be increasingly isolated as 64 countries granted diplomatic recognition to the Polisario government in exile, SADR. Hassan's talks with Shimon Peres, the Israeli prime minister, at Ifrane in July 1986 further increased his country's isolation from other Arab countries. Libya's intentions of signing a treaty with Iran, and other incidents, led, finally, to the abrogation of the Treaty of Oujda providing for union of the two nations (August 1986). There followed an immediate improvement in U.S.-Moroccan relations. In November 1986, the two countries held joint military exercises, and in July 1987 the United States offered to sell Morocco F-16 fighter aircraft.

To date, Morocco has received some US$70 million in grants and loans from the United States for military training and arms, as well as grants and loans from Saudi Arabia, Kuwait, Qatar, the United Arab Emirates, France, and Spain. Arms transfers have come from Austria (recovery vehicles, tanks), Brazil (armored personnel carriers [APCs]), Egypt (mortars), France (antitank guided missiles [ATGMs], combat aircraft, naval surface-to-surface missiles [SSMs], naval vessels, tank transports, trucks), FRG (light transport aircraft), Italy (helicopters, land mines, shipborne surface-to-air missiles [SAMs]), Japan (trucks), Spain (armored fighting vehicles [AFVs], mortars, multiple rocket launchers [MRLs], naval vessels, electronic equipment), Switzerland (trainer aircraft), and the United States (ATGMs, combat aircraft, SAMs, tanks, tank transporters, trucks). Morocco has also received more than US$20 million in military assistance from former Eastern bloc countries.

Defense Industry

Morocco's defense production consists, primarily, of small-arms ammunition, truck assembly, and aircraft ammunition.

Alliances

Although officially Morocco practices a nonaligned foreign policy, it is sympathetic toward the West, especially since the August 1986 break with Libya. Morocco has played a constructive role in Arab councils on the problems of peace in the Middle East as well. The kingdom remains a member of the United Nations and the Arab League, but in 1984 left the Organization of African Unity over a dispute concerning the seating of SADR. In July 1987, Morocco formally applied for membership in the European Economic Community.

Defense Structure

The constitution of March 1972 provides the king with the power to declare a state of emergency; he is also the commander in chief of the armed forces, making all appointments to military posts. The administration of defense policy is carried out directly from the king through the National Defense Administration (NDA; this has been the case since the second attempt on his life in 1972). NDA concerns itself exclusively with logistics and procurement. Headed by a military officer (the general secretary for national defense), NDA is completely divorced from operational control of the armed forces, which has been vested exclusively with the king. In addition, FAR (*Forces*

Armées Royales) has been restructured with the 1972 dissolution of military regions and reorganization of the military into battalion-sized units only. The king has also instituted a policy of constantly shifting forces around the country in order to avoid concentrations of troops in any one place. A number of units have been assigned to civic action projects, and artillery units have been deployed a great distance from Rabat, the capital. FAR personnel policies were overhauled and many top-ranking officers retired in 1972. The Forward Headquarters (*Etat-Major Avance*) was established in the mid-1970s and has included only officers of unquestionable loyalty. Forward Headquarters is designed to provide the palace with intelligence on troop movements and officers' political sympathies. The war in the Sahara strained the centralized nature of NDA, forcing the king to decentralize in 1980 with the creation of the Southern Zone of military operations under the command of one of the king's closest confidantes, Ahmed Dlimi (now deceased).

(For an explanation of the abbreviations and symbols used in the following section of military statistics, see the list of Abbreviations and Acronyms in each volume.)

Total Armed Forces

Active: 195,500. Terms of service: conscription 18 months authorized; most enlisted personnel are volunteers.
Reserves: 100,000: obligation to age 50.

ARMY: 175,000
3 Comd (South, Northwest Atlas, Border).
3 mech inf bde HQ.
2 para bde.
11 mech inf regt
Independent units:
10 arty gp.
1 AD gp.
9 armed sqn gp.
37 inf bn.
3 mot (camel corps) bn.
3 cav bn.
1 mtn bn.
4 engr bn.
Royal Guard: 1,500: 1 bn, 1 cav sqn.
Deployment:
Northwest Atlas: 1 Royal Guard, 1 mtn bn; 1 armd sqn, 1 mech sqn, 1 cav sqn, 1 arty gp.
South (incl West Sahara): 3 mech inf bde; 9 mech inf regt; 25 inf, 2 para, 2 Camel Corps bn; 4 armd sqn, 1 mech sqn gp; 4 mech sqn gp (UR-416 APC); 7 arty gp.
Border: 2 mech inf regt; 3 inf, 1 Camel Corps bn; 2 armd sqn, 1 arty gp.
Equipment:
MBT: 224 M-48A5, 60 M-60A1.
Light tanks: 58 AMX-13, 100 SK-105 Kuerassier.
Recce: 16 EBR-75, 80 AMX-10RC, 190 AML-90, 38 AML-60-7.
AIFV: 30 Ratel 20, some 30 -90, 45 VAB-VCI.
APC: 420 M-113, 320 VAB-VTT, some 45 OT-62/-64 may be operational.
Towed arty: 105mm: 30 lt (L-118), 40 M-101, 36 HM2 (Fr M-101A1); 130mm: 18 M-46; 155mm: 20 M-114.
SP arty: 155mm: 98 AMX Mk F-3, 44 M-109.
MRL: 122mm: 40 BM-21.
Mortars: 81mm: 1,100; 120mm: 600 (incl 20 VAB SP).
ATGW: 440 Dragon, 80 Milan, 150 TOW (incl 42 SP), HOT.
RL: 66mm: LAW; 88mm: M-20 3.5-in.
RCL: 106mm: 350 M-40A1.
ATK guns: 90mm: 28 M-56; 100mm: 8 SU-100 SP.
AD guns: 14.5mm: 180 ZPU-2, 20 ZPU-4; 20mm: 40 towed, 60 M-163 Vulcan SP; 23mm: 90 ZU-23-2; 37mm: 25 M-38/-39; 100mm: 12 KS-19 towed.
SAM: 37 M-54 SP Chaparral, SA-7.

NAVY: 7,000 incl 1,500 marines. Bases: Casablanca, Agadir, Al Hoceima, Dakhla.
Frigate: 1 Lt Col. Errhamani (Sp Descubierta) with 2 x 3 ASTT (Mk 46 LWT), 1 x 2 375mm AS mor; plus 4 x MM-40 Exocet SSM.
Patrol and Coastal Combatants: 27:
Missile Craft: 4 Cdt El Khattabi (Sp Lazaga 58-m) PFM with 4 x MM-38 Exocet SSM.
Patrol, Coastal: 13:
2 Okba (Fr PR-72) PFC.
6 LV Rabhi (Sp 58-m B-200D) PCC.
1 Lt Riffi PCC.
4 El Lahik (Dk Osprey 55) PCC. (includes 2 with customs).
Patrol, Inshore: 10 El Wacil (Fr P-32) PFI (. (includes 4 with customs).
Amphibious: 3 Ben Aicha (Fr Champlain BATRAL) LSM, capacity 140 tps, 7 tk; plus craft; 1 LCT
Support: 3: 2 log spt, 1 tpt.

Marines: (1,500). 1 naval inf bn.

AIR FORCE: 13,500; 90 cbt ac, 24 armed hel.
FGA: 2 sqn: 1 with 15 F-5E, 3 F-5F; 1 with 14 Mirage F-1EH.
Fighter: 1 sqn with 15 Mirage F-1CH.
COIN: 2 sqn: 1 with 23 Alpha Jet; 1 with 23 CM-170.
Recce: 1 sqn with 4 OV-10, 2 C-130H (with side-looking radar).
EW: 1 C-130 (ELINT), 1 Falcon 20 (ELINT).
Tanker: 1 Boeing 707; 3 KC-130H (tpt/tanker).
Transport: 11 C-130H, 7 CN-235, 3 Do-28, 1 Falcon 20, 1 Falcon 50 (VIP), 1 Gulfstream II (VIP), 5 King Air 100, 3 King Air 200.
Helicopters:
Attack: 24 SA-342 (12 with HOT, 12 with cannon).
Transport: hy: 7 CH-47; med: 27 SA-330, 27 AB-205A; lt: 20 AB-206, 3 AB-212.
Training: 10 AS-202, 2 CAP-10, 4 CAP-230, 12 T-34C.
Liaison: 2 King Air 200.
AAM: AIM-9B/D/J Sidewinder, R-530, R-550 Magic.
ASM: AGM-65B Maverick (for F-5E), HOT.

FORCES ABROAD
Equatorial Guinea: 360: 1 bn.
UAE: some 5,000 (incl 1 para bn (700)).
UN and Peacekeeping:
Angola: (UNAVEM II): observers.

PARAMILITARY: 40,000.
Gendarmerie Royale: 10,000:
1 bde, 2 mobile gp, air sqn, coast guard unit; 18 boats, 2 Rallye ac; 3 SA-315, 3 SA-316, 2 SA-318, 6 Gazelle, 6 SA-330, 2 SA-360 hel.
Force Auxiliaire: 30,000 incl Mobile Intervention Corps (5,000).

OPPOSITION

Polisario: Military Wing: Sahrawi People's Liberation Army: 10–15,000 (perhaps 4,000 active) org in bn.

Equipment: T-55, T-62 tk; BMP-1, 20–30 EE-9 Cascavel MICV; M-1931/37 122mm how; BM-21 122mm MRL; 120mm, 160mm mor; AT-4 Spigot ATGW; ZSU-23-2 23mm SP AA guns; SA-6/-7/-9 SAM.

Future

Morocco's primary security concern will continue to be the Polisario insurgency in the Western Sahara. Although Moroccan forces have enjoyed a large measure of success in limiting Polisario attacks, they have been unable completely to subjugate the area, in part because of continuing, if modest, Algerian support for the guerrillas. The advent of more conciliatory Algerian policies toward its neighbors may, in addition to easing tensions in the Maghreb generally, allow for a permanent solution to the Western Sahara problem. In the event that the proposed UN-administered referendum on the future of the Western Sahara takes place (Morocco officially supports this endeavor), the results are likely to support the continued administration, if not outright annexation, of that region of Morocco. In any event, Morocco is unlikely to alter the basically moderate and pro-Western orientations that have served it so well for four decades.

BARRY O'CONNOR

SEE ALSO: Algeria; Arab League; North Africa; Tunisia.

Bibliography

American University. 1986. *Morocco, a country study.* Washington, D.C.: Government Printing Office.

Hunter, B., ed. 1991. *The statesman's year-book, 1991–92.* New York: St. Martin's Press.

International Institute for Strategic Studies. 1991. *The military balance, 1991–1992.* London: Brassey's.

Levran, A., ed. 1987. *The Middle East military balance.* Tel Aviv: Tel Aviv Univ. Jaffa Center for Strategic Studies.

Middle East and North Africa yearbook. 1988. London: Europa.

U.S. Central Intelligence Agency. 1991. *The world factbook 1991–92.* Washington, D.C.: Government Printing Office.

MORTAR

Mortars are short-range, high-trajectory weapons—usually muzzleloaders and ordinarily small, easily transportable infantry weapons—that are used to lob shells in support of frontline troops, usually by means of indirect-fire techniques. Available on short notice to answer the urgent and varied needs of units, they are indispensable for the attack of point targets, as well as for distributing fire over wide areas.

For many years mortars have been primarily ground-emplaced weapons, but the increasing mechanization of armies, along with the appearance of tactical nuclear weapons, has made it necessary to mount mortars on vehicles so that they can keep up with the fighting troops to which they are attached. Both the U.S. and German armies mounted mortars on half-track armored carriers during World War II.

Mortars have significant advantages in comparison with other artillery weapons, including simplicity and cheapness; high trajectory; high rates of fire; mobility, particularly in difficult terrain; low chamber pressure; negligible barrel wear; small dimensions, leading to ease of concealment; ammunition with excellent antipersonnel characteristics; and a low equipment-to-shell weight ratio. Mortars have been in use since at least the fifteenth century. They may be either rifled or smooth-bored, and either muzzle- or breech-loaded.

General Characteristics

Mortars are usually divided into three classes—light, medium, and heavy. The general characteristics of conventional mortars are as shown in Table 1; but special adaptations, such as the use of rocket-assisted rounds, can have dramatic impact on such things as maximum range.

Mortar Construction

The great majority of mortars have only four main parts: the barrel, the base plate, the mounting, and the sight.

The *barrel* consists of a steel tube with one end closed by a breech piece, which is screwed on or into the barrel. To prevent the escape of gases, a copper washer is inserted as an obturating ring to produce a seal. With few exceptions, the interior of the bore is smooth. The exterior surface is also generally plain, although a few mortars incorporate radial fins to assist in cooling. The firing mechanism is located in the breech piece. In many mortars a safety device allows for retraction of the firing pin, a highly desirable feature. In most light and medium mortars, the misfire drill necessitates lifting the base end of the barrel to cause the shell to drop out of the muzzle into the hands of a waiting crew member.

When a mortar is fired the downward force of the explosion is distributed over an optimum flotation area by means of the *base plate.* This reduces ground pressure, so that the mortar does not sink into the earth when fired. There are square and rectangular base plates, but the most popular today are circular plates that, if properly bedded in, facilitate 360-degree traverse of the mortar. All

TABLE 1. *Characteristics of Conventional Mortars*

Mortar Type	*Caliber*	*Total Weight*	*Shell Weight*	*Max. Range*
Light	60mm or less	15–24 kg	0.4–1.5 kg	500–2,000 m
Medium	60–100mm	25–90 kg	1.6–6.8 kg	2,000–6,000 m
Heavy	>100mm	>91 kg	>6.8 kg	5,000–9,000 m

base plates are ribbed to provide strength, prevent buckling, and ensure against slipping.

The mortar *mounting* normally consists of a bipod, although a few tripods are in service. The mounting supports the upper portion of the barrel and carries the elevating and traversing gears. The latter consists of one or two cylinders, usually containing springs; in some heavier mortars a hydraulic system may be employed. The bipod also contains the cross-leveling gear, which allows the sights to be placed upright regardless of the slope of the ground on which the mortar is emplaced.

To produce the indirect fire that is the mortar's main function, the *sight* must be laid on some selected aiming point. The aiming point can be some prominent and easily recognized feature, or it can be an aiming post put out for that purpose. When the correct angle between the line to the target and the line to the aiming post has been established and then set on the sight, the barrel of the mortar will be pointing in the direction of the target. This permits fire to be placed close to the target; and any subsequent corrections are then made in the line of fire. Target data may be recorded with reference either to aiming point deflection or to the zero line established by a special sight mechanism. It should be noted, however, that since meteorological data are not available at the mortar position, and since true north thus can never be deduced or stored, data are never recorded in terms of azimuth. The actual sighting device that is aligned on the aiming post may be a collimator or a telescope.

Light Mortar

Mortars with a caliber of 50 to 60mm are part of the panoply of weapons at platoon or company level but, at least in large modern armies, usually only for specific tasks such as battlefield illumination and the support of commando-type units. Nevertheless many countries are producing light mortars of different types and characteristics to meet the varying requirements of modern military forces (Table 2). The following paragraph describes the three main types.

The standard light mortar has a circular base, a bipod mounting, a barrel clamp fitted with a recoil absorber, and an optical dial sight. The long-range version, similar to the standard mortar, has a longer barrel that permits the shell to gain velocity in the tube, thus extending the range. The commando-type light mortar has a lightweight barrel and a very small base plate. It is intended to be carried and fired by one man. There is no bipod, the barrel being supported at the requisite angle of fire by the firer's hand. This mortar typically has both a carrying handle and a sling. The table below shows the varying characteristics of these three types of light mortars.

TABLE 2. *Characteristics of Light Mortars*

Characteristic	*Standard*	*Long-Range*	*Commando*
Caliber	60mm	60mm	60mm
Barrel length	740mm	1,000mm	650mm
Base plate diameter	350mm	350mm	150mm
Firing weight	15.2 kg	16.1 kg	5.4 kg
Barrel weight	3.5 kg	4.6 kg	3.2 kg
Base plate weight	4.0 kg	4.0 kg	0.8 kg
Maximum range	3,400 m	4,300 m	1,600 m
Rate of fire (rds/min)	30	25	25

Medium Mortar

Most medium mortars now in service at company level are of 81mm and 82mm caliber (Fig. 1); the only major exception is the U.S. 107mm weapon. Because of their light weight and flexibility, these mortars are considered one of the most important means available to an infantry company for applying indirect fire on short notice. Mortars are able to move with the supported unit and still be ready to respond promptly to any fire mission in support of advanced infantry echelons.

The medium mortar can be transported by land vehicle, helicopter, pack animal, or man-pack. When man-packed it is carried by three soldiers, and it is robust enough to be dropped by parachute. Many efforts have been made to reduce the weight of medium mortars through the use of such lightweight metals as titanium, while at the same time increasing the range and lethality of their projectiles. Table 3 shows the principal characteristics of the various medium mortars.

Heavy Mortar

Heavy mortars of 120mm caliber are now in service in many armies at battalion and regimental level. Mortars of larger size, such as the 160mm weapon, are used as divisional mortars. The 120mm mortar is distinguished by its

Figure 1. An 81mm mortar. (SOURCE: U.S. Army photograph)

TABLE 3. *Characteristics of Medium Mortars*

Characteristic	*81mm*	*82mm*	*107mm*
Weight	Up to 61.5 kg	56 kg	Up to 87.4 kg
Barrel length	1,310 mm	1,220 mm	1,524 mm
Maximum range	4,100 m	3,000 m	6,800 m
Minimum range	85 m	100 m	770 m
Rate of fire (rds/min)	20	15–20	18
Crew	5	5	5

range and firepower. On the debit side, it is much heavier than the medium mortar and has proven very vulnerable to counterbattery fire.

The 160mm mortar is the heaviest used by infantry divisions. Because of its long barrel, the 160mm is a breech-loading weapon. The barrel is pivoted for loading about trunnions placed near the center point. The weapon is towed by the muzzle, using either an armored personnel carrier or a heavy truck. Table 4 shows the characteristics of two types of heavy mortar.

Mounting Mortars on Vehicles

Medium and heavy mortars are mounted on tracked or wheeled light armored vehicles, along with the fire-control equipment needed to employ these weapons. Such an arrangement enables the mortars to keep up with the infantry troops to which they are attached, and to go into action quickly when needed.

To mount medium and heavy mortars without structural modification to the carrier vehicle, a hydropneumatic recoil mechanism is fitted above the mortar's barrel. This device has a long travel, which reduces the force that the firing of each round transmits to the vehicle's structure. The consequent large reduction in recoil eliminates the need for firing a preliminary series of bedding-in rounds that are necessary when the mortar is fired from the ground. Laying of the mortar is thus made easier and the time needed to go into action reduced.

A balance mechanism is also incorporated in the mortar's mounting; this is used by the crew to adjust the pivot to a fixed vertical position. The mortar can therefore be fired normally, regardless of the terrain and without regard to whether the carrier vehicle is on a forward, rear, or side slope. At the rear, the vehicle's floor forms the mortar's base plate. The mortar is simply suspended from the carrier vehicle by cable shock absorbers.

The crew can place the mortar in traveling position by tilting it forward toward the vehicle's floor, then closing the cradle's protective shutters. This also reduces the silhouette of the vehicle and lowers its center of gravity. The carrier vehicle can carry 60 or more rounds, giving the mounted weapon system the firepower required by troops operating far from their bases. These carrier vehicles can be transported by helicopters over short distances by use of a sling, or by transport aircraft over longer distances. The standard mortar crew for mortars mounted in carriers may be reduced to four men instead of the six or seven required by dismounted weapons.

TABLE 4. *Characteristics of Heavy Mortars*

Characteristic	*120mm*	*160mm*
Weight (in firing position)	274.8 kg	1,300 kg
Barrel length	1,854mm	4,500mm
Rate of fire (rds/min)	12–15	2–3
Maximum range	5,700 m	Up to 9,000 m
Minimum range	640 m	750 m
Crew	6	7

Ammunition

Mortar shells are classified in three main categories: explosive, smoke screening, and illuminating rounds. The shell consists of three main parts: the fuze, the steel shell body (incorporating a charge that varies according to the kind of shell), and the fin assembly. The primary characteristics of the various types of 60mm, 81mm, and 120mm mortar rounds are presented in Table 5. The 160mm mortar fragmentation shell weighs 40 kilograms, has a bursting charge of 7.36 kilograms of TNT, and uses a point-detonating fuze.

Future Mortars

Any dramatic change in mortars in the foreseeable future is unlikely. Progress will probably be made, however, in terms of lighter and handier equipment employing new metals and materials. Other areas of potential development are improvement in the aerodynamic properties of mortar projectiles; functioning of the ejection fuze and the ejection process; dispersion and stabilization of submunitions and operation of their fuzes; and optimization of antiarmor and antipersonnel effects. Fire control will be developed by using electronics on a wide scale, which will

TABLE 5. *Characteristics of Common Mortar Rounds*

60mm rounds	*Explosive*	*Smoke*	*Illuminating*
Total weight	1.37 kg	1.83 kg	1.88 kg
Weight of TNT	150 g	—	—
Weight of WP	—	350 g	—
Lethal radius of burst	13.5 m	—	—
Maximum range	1,800 m	1,470 m	1,000 m
Illuminating time	—	—	25–30 sec
81mm rounds			
Total weight	3.25 kg	5.8 kg	4.6 kg
Weight of TNT	500 g	—	—
Weight of WP	—	1.86 kg	—
Lethal radius of burst	21 m	—	—
Maximum range	3,200 m	2,130 m	2,100 m
Illuminating time	—	—	50–60 sec
120mm rounds			
Total weight	16.4 kg	12.6–13.3 kg	12.8–13.3 kg
Maximum range	6,010 m	6,000 m	6,300 m

enable mortars to engage a variety of targets with the need for few, if any, ranging rounds.

SAMIR HASSAN SHALABY

SEE ALSO: Ammunition; Artillery; Artillery, Tube; Firepower; Indirect Fire.

Bibliography

Bidwell, S., ed. 1981. *Brassey's artillery of the world.* 2d ed. London: Brassey's.

Jane's Infantry Weapons 1987–88. 1987. London: Jane's.

Miller, D., and C. J. Foss. 1987. *Modern land combat.* New York: Portland House.

MOUNTAIN WARFARE

Mountain warfare today seems old-fashioned and out-of-date, a romantic memory of skillful men skiing or climbing in remote mountains, conducting a heroic war of their own. In the nuclear age, with its complex weapons systems, the last chapter of mountain warfare seems to be near. And yet one event in December 1979 focused renewed attention on mountain warfare: the Soviet invasion of the mountainous country of Afghanistan. In the beginning, the terrain led to heavy Soviet casualties, as they had problems adapting their routine Eastern-bloc maneuver tactics to mountain-style warfare. A new weapons system was introduced into that war as well: the helicopter. Within weeks of appearing in the skies over Afghanistan, these ungainly-looking machines, massively armed with Gatling-type cannon, rockets, and 225-kilogram (500-lb.) bombs, had become as symbolic of the Soviet presence in Afghanistan as Hueys and Chinooks once were of the American presence in Vietnam. Paratroopers and frontline infantry units were flown directly into battle against enemy positions in the mountains, their task to hold the heights while armored columns and trucks worked their way forward on the ground.

Basic Factors of Mountain Warfare

Mountain warfare is influenced by the environment—terrain, climate, and weather—which has special effects on personnel and equipment.

TERRAIN

It is difficult to classify mountain environments because each major mountain range has specific characteristics that are determined by its soil composition, configuration, altitude, and so on. But, in general, mountainous terrain is characterized by marked differences in elevation, with steep slopes and valleys over an extended area; it may also include built-up areas and plains between mountain ridges, plateaus, passes, and the mountain sides themselves. Such terrain can be found widely distributed around the world (Fig. 1).

When general characteristics of mountainous terrain are reviewed, some important military calculations must be considered: sharp differences in elevation can provide excellent observation points or may mask from view large areas of the ground. These areas present serious problems to vehicle movement and to movement of dismounted troops. The structure of the terrain is normally such that it follows a distinctive pattern or "grain." Road and track networks predominantly follow the drainage pattern, which has a major impact on operations and logistics, channeling the bulk of the forces into operating with the grain of the country. Road networks are generally limited and cross-country movement in higher regions ranges from difficult to impossible. Built-up areas are concentrated in the valleys. Higher elevations often consist of exposed rock, and digging is difficult or impossible. Firepower is less effective in mountainous areas than in lower-lying terrain because rocks and cliffs provide much natural cover. Occupying heights in order to fire down on the enemy is advantageous even though slopes limit grazing fire and create large dead spaces. Thus, weapons with a high angle of fire—such as some artillery guns, mortars, and grenade launchers—take on added importance in mountains. Rugged mountain terrain makes movement so difficult that all equipment should be as light as possible, preferably air-transportable.

CLIMATE

A wide variety of climates exists in mountain regions. Conditions change markedly with altitude, latitude, and exposure to atmospheric winds and air masses. Valleys or plateaus enclosed by major ranges differ climatically from the surrounding exposed peaks. At higher altitudes, sharp differences in temperature exist between sunny and shady areas and also between those areas that are exposed to wind and those that are protected from it.

Figure 1. Croatian legionnaires fighting against Marshal Tito's forces in the mountains of Bosnia, Yugoslavia. (SOURCE: Presse-Hoffmann, U.S. Library of Congress)

Weather

Mountain weather can be erratic, varying from strong to calm winds, and from extreme cold to relative warmth within a short span of time or with minor shifts in location. The severity and variance of mountain weather has a particularly significant impact on military operations. But personnel who are properly trained, clothed, equipped, and supplied may often convert mountain weather into an ally.

Air temperature drops about one degree Celsius for every 200 meters (660 ft.) of increase in altitude. Winds are accelerated when they are forced over ridges and peaks or when they funnel through mountain passes and canyons. Wind effect can result in blowing snow, sand, or debris that impair movement and observation. Rain presents the same challenges as in lower regions, but snow has a significant influence on all operations. An avalanche can cause more casualties than an enemy. Thunderstorms can handicap operations in the mountains and can be hazardous to the soldiers as well. Exposure to sun, snow, and wind may lead to sunburn, snow blindness, frostbite, and windchill.

The effects of mountain geography on military equipment are numerous. Snow-covered roads can make driving extremely hazardous or impossible. Because atmospheric pressure decreases with altitude, air-breathing engines have slower acceleration, reduced gradability, lower maximum speed, and a power loss of 20 to 22 percent at an altitude of 2,000 meters (6,600 ft.) with an increase in fuel consumption of 30 to 35 percent. Altitude and the lower atmospheric pressure also affect the range of weapons, which tends to increase. Cold weather affects engines, batteries, metal and rubber parts, steering, brakes, cooling, and so on. Mountain operations require equipment and clothing not only suitable for movement in rugged terrain but also for cold weather and movement over snow. Radios, microphones, guidance-system components of missiles, as well as rifles may malfunction due to freezing, moisture, and cold.

Theory of Mountain Warfare

Karl von Clausewitz

The German military theorist Karl von Clausewitz (1780–1831) was one of the most prominent military authors to write on mountain warfare. In his book, *On War,* he dedicated four chapters to this specific topic. It seems now that his ideas, dating back to the beginning of the last century, have lost none of their validity. He considered the tactical aspects of mountain warfare from which he proceeded to its links with strategy. He discussed the different aspects of offensive and defensive mountain warfare and placed the main emphasis on defense.

Clausewitz noted that a marching column toils at a snail's pace up a mountain through narrow gorges; gunners and teamsters yell and swear as they flog their weary beasts along the rocky tracks; each broken-down wagon has to be removed at the cost of great effort, while behind it the rest of the column stops, grumbles, and curses. At such a moment, each man secretly thinks that in this situation a few hundred of the enemy would suffice to cause a complete rout. An attack in the mountains could lead troops to conclude that a defender would only need small forces in good positions to stop the enemy. Undeniably, in a mountainous area, a small post in a favorable position acquires exceptional strength. A unit that on open ground can be dispersed by a couple of cavalry squadrons—and will think itself lucky if it can escape capture or annihilation by rapid retreat—can successfully face an army in the mountains. It was only natural to assume that a series of strongpoints of this sort would result in a strong, almost impenetrable front. One only had to guard against being outflanked by extending the position to right and left until it reached adequate points of support. Because these positions seemed firmly linked by inaccessible terrain (columns not being able to march across broken country), one appeared to confront the enemy with an impenetrable wall. For extra safety, one retained a couple of infantry battalions, some horse artillery, and cavalry squadrons in reserve in case the enemy by some fluke succeeded in breaking through.

In Clausewitz's view, mountainous terrain favors the defender but leads to a loss of mobility. If a defender concentrates on strongpoints, there is the danger of being outflanked by the enemy; if a defender, fearful of being outflanked, responds by extending his positions, thus making his front proportionately weaker, an attacker might mass his forces against a single point and pierce the line. In Clausewitz's opinion, the only way out of this dilemma was a higher degree of mobility for the defender. As mobility is inhibited by mountains and no technical means—for example, helicopters—existed in Clausewitz's time, he concluded that defensive mountain warfare would inevitably lead to defeat.

Clausewitz then turned to the central question: whether resistance in defensive mountain warfare is intended to be relative or absolute, and if it is meant to last only a certain time or to end in definite victory. Mountains are eminently suited to defense of the first type. For the second type, they are, except for a few special cases, generally not suited at all. From a tactical point of view, defensive mountain warfare is generally effective only when limited forces are engaged and able to make maximum use of mountain terrain to increase their relative power.

From a strategic point of view, Clausewitz evaluated the mountain area as a battlefield, considering the effect that its possession has on other areas, its effectiveness as a strategic barrier, and the problems of supply to which it gives rise. He came to the conclusion that mountains can offer lasting advantage if absolute resistance is not needed (e.g., to gain time, to secure a flank, etc.), but defense of a decisive kind, which determines the question of possession of the country, must be avoided. Mountains reduce one's control and impede movement in all directions; they impose passivity; and they almost always lead to some degree of cordon warfare. Whenever possible, one should therefore keep one's main force out of the mountains, keeping the mountains to one side or taking up a position in front of or behind them. Acceptance of a major battle in the plains, however, does not necessarily imply that there can be no preliminary defensive action by minor units in the mountains.

After having pointed out that mountains generally favor the defender if he does not seek a decisive battle, and that they favor the attacker in the alternative case, Clausewitz outlines some general ideas about offensive mountain warfare. The latter, Clausewitz avers, is mostly a tactical and not a strategic question. When attacking a widely extended line of defense in mountains, one should concentrate one's forces and try to punch through at one or a few points. When attacking more concentrated mountain positions, the attacker should outflank the defender or attack his rear to cut off the line of retreat of the defender so as to destroy him or make him surrender.

Even if the problem of mobility in mountain warfare is partly solved today by the use of helicopters, the problem of impeded movement generally remains, because it is not feasible to lift whole brigades or divisions by helicopters. The per-machine capacity of helicopters is small, and helicopters cannot maintain altitude and flightway well above 2,400 to 3,000 meters (about 8,000 to 10,000 ft.). Yet the introduction of helicopters into mountain warfare has created a new incentive.

World War I and II

The validity of Clausewitz's theory of mountain warfare can be examined and reviewed through the events of World War I and World War II. During World War I, major forces of Austria and Germany were concentrated against Italy's forces in the Alps, which led to the abovementioned cordon warfare with little movement and tough battles for a few meters of rocky or icy terrain. By the end of that war, in June 1918, along the 500-kilometer (300-mi.) Tyrolean border, 642 battalions and seven cavalry divisions were facing 56 Italian divisions, each side being unable to conduct decisive operations.

World War II reflected a different kind of mountain warfare. Flank operations were fought in mountainous terrain for limited periods of time. Major battles fought in the plains—for example, the German attack against the Soviet Union in the Stalingrad area conducted by the Heeresgruppe Süd—were accompanied by an attack of two mountain divisions in the Caucasus Mountains south of Stalingrad to secure the southern flank of the army group. This might be considered the classic strategic case in Clausewitz's theory, whereas the defense of Norway against the German attack might be considered the exception to the rule from the Norwegian point of view inasmuch as Norway is 70 percent mountainous terrain and therefore has to commit nearly all of its land forces to defensive mountain warfare.

Development of Technology: The Helicopter

In the tactical sense, no major changes in mountain warfare theory have taken place recently. What has changed since Clausewitz's time is the development of technology—the introduction of helicopters to mountain warfare. With this technical means, problems of military movement in mountains seem surmounted. Helicopters can greatly assist in overcoming the difficulties associated with the movement and support of ground forces in mountain regions. However, the employment of helicopters here have notable restrictions.

Darkness, whiteouts, snowfall, heavy precipitation, wind, and fog impede or deny use of helicopters. One still must rely on ground vehicles, pack animals, or the backs of the soldiers to transport weapons, ammunition, food, and so on. The helicopters used in mountain warfare include fighting helicopters and transport helicopters. Their tasks are:

- reconnaissance
- liaison
- transport of troops, weapons, supplies
- attack of enemy troops and positions
- fire support
- deployment of land mines
- shifting reserves
- evacuation

If one considers that whole platoons or companies can be transported within minutes to threatened places, arriving combat-ready, whereas it would have taken hours by foot (not to mention the exhaustion and the rest they would need after such a march), it becomes obvious how technology has fundamentally influenced mountain warfare by creating flying platforms, so that the impediments to movement are overcome. The change is caused by combat and transport helicopters supported by the air force. They guarantee a dual mobility: the mobility of combat units and artillery. They multiply the possibilities of operations and increase their tempo. The era of slow combat movements has probably ended; for the first time mobility in mountain warfare has become a decisive factor.

Organization and Training

Based on the strategic aspect of a country covered by mountains or a country that has mountains along its borders, the question arises: to what extent shall mountain troops be formed and how should they be used and organized?

Kinds of Mountain Troops

Two different solutions can be used. First, a country largely covered with mountains could build up a major force of specialized troops whose only purpose is to fight the war in the mountainous area and seek the decision in that area. The second solution is for a country only partly covered with mountains along its borders to build up only a small force of mountain troops that would have dual missions. The second solution means that mountain troops should be able not only to fight in mountainous areas but also in other areas because it might well happen that no fighting would occur in the mountains, that all the battles would be fought on the plains. Some of the mountain troops would then have to participate in these battles, which means that they must be equipped as mechanized infantry with antitank weapons and also be trained accordingly.

An example of the latter is found in the Federal Republic of Germany. The army has one mountain division of three brigades: one tank brigade, one mechanized infantry brigade, and one mountain infantry brigade, plus the usual combat-service and combat-service support elements of a mechanized infantry division at division level. The special terrain features and the climate in the area where the mountain division is located in peacetime and where it may have to fight during a war require dual capability: it must be able to conduct the battle of combined arms under normal conditions like other divisions of the army and, in addition, it must also be able to fight under extreme terrain and weather conditions.

These factors determine organization, equipment, and training. Therefore, the mountain division does not represent a pure special force but is organized and equipped like the other mechanized infantry divisions of the army. For its special mission, it has been issued the corresponding special equipment. So the German mountain division might be considered a dual-purpose division whereas, for example, a Swiss mountain division with its three mountain infantry regiments, including grenade launchers, antitank weapons, and mountain howitzers, does not include heavy mechanized infantry and armor elements and so can be considered a single-purpose division without other missions.

The Soviet ground forces and their Warsaw Pact allies did not have mountain troops (except Romania, which had 4 mountain cadre regiments). The Warsaw Pact trained its ordinary tank, mechanized infantry, and airborne divisions in mountain warfare and re-equipped them accordingly, just in case they had been called on to fight in mountains. Even so, the equipment issued to Soviet divisions located in the Transcaucasus and Turkestan military districts reflected their mountain environment and missions. *Herald of Combat,* the periodical of the Soviet ground forces, regularly contained information on mountain warfare training.

Training

Mountainous areas present three different kinds of terrain: the first, and lowest level, consists of valleys, where tanks and mechanized infantry can move; the second, intermediate level, is the terrace-zone with minor roads and trails that allow only restricted movement of vehicles; the third and highest level is the summit-zone, where movement by vehicle is practically impossible.

Combat in the low zone can be conducted by mechanized means. Combat on the plateaus and heights permits deployment of light armor and motorized forces. Combat on the summits is limited to the deployment of observation posts, wireless relay stations, and the securing of strongpoints.

These different areas and levels require different training for the soldiers who will have to fight there. Fighting in valleys does not require necessarily special training in mountain warfare techniques. Mountain troops as the infantry of the mountains are specially suited for combat in difficult and wooded terrain and they possess a high combat value in every preplanned deployment area, especially in middle mountains. For deployment in extreme terrain, mountain guides and high-mountain platoons are absolutely necessary.

Specialists

Mountain guides and high-mountain platoons are the specialists in the mountains. Their special training gives them a capability that makes them useful as advisers and teachers, as well as for search-and-rescue operations. France, Italy, Switzerland, and Germany (then, the FRG), for example, have special mountain and winter-warfare schools where they train specialists for difficult missions in the use of special mountain and cold weather equipment. The German mountain and winter-warfare school in Mittenwald, for example, trains 1,250 soldiers every year with 60 percent of the participants coming from the German mountain division, 25 percent from other army divisions or the air force and navy, and 15 percent from other members of the North Atlantic Treaty Organization (NATO). The same school trains officers and noncommissioned officers (NCOs) for mountain duty as guides (17 weeks in summer and 15 weeks in winter) in military mountaineering, mountain search and rescue, mountain combat, military skiing, combat on skis, survival in winter under extreme conditions, comprehensive first aid, and engineer techniques such as construction of field positions in mountains and blowing up snowfields. These specially trained personnel are then qualified to:

1. Advise commanders in planning and executing operations in mountains with respect to:

   - evaluation of terrain and weather, especially of dangers in the mountains;
   - security measures and prevention of accidents;
   - search and rescue;
   - equipping troops with special mountain gear;
   - logistical measures in difficult terrain.

2. Train soldiers of mountain divisions in:
   - military mountaineering including skiing;
   - search and rescue in mountains;
   - combat in mountains.
3. Execute military operations in difficult mountainous terrain;
4. Organize and execute search-and-rescue operations in mountains;
5. Advise and monitor soldiers for off-duty mountain and ski-tours.

Outlook

Mountain warfare seems to play a rather insignificant role in the overall picture of a conventional or nuclear war. Yet there are many mountainous areas in the world that may be the scene of future warfare (as evidenced by events in Afghanistan).

Most likely, a future war will not be fought in mountains, as unfavorable climate and weather conditions generally create too many problems. However, mountains favor the defender and enable him to make use of natural obstacles with relatively small forces, thus increasing his relative power vis-à-vis an attacker. Germany, Greece, Italy, Norway, and Turkey have significant mountain ranges along their borders, although these countries generally lack sufficient depth across their territories. If Warsaw Pact forces had attacked, they would have had to cross these mountains and would have had tc fight in them during outflanking operations. The strategic purpose of the defender would not be to defeat the attacker in the mountains but to show him the will of resistance right from the beginning, cause him the first losses, slow him down, and gain time for other defense measures.

GERHARD SCHEPE
ALEXANDER HARTINGER

SEE ALSO: Arctic Warfare; Defense; Desert Warfare; Geography, Military; Jungle Warfare; Land Warfare; Meteorology, Military; Ordnance Corps.

Bibliography

Bucher, A. 1957. *Kampf im Gebirge: Erfahrungen und Erkenntnisse des Gebirgskrieges.* München-Lochhausen: Schild-Verlag.

Burdick, C. B. 1988. *Hubert Lanz: General der Gebirgstruppe (1896–1982).* Osnabrück: Biblio Verlag.

Lichem, H. von. 1980–82. *Gebirgskrieg, 1915–1918.* Bozen: Athesia.

Lucas, J. S. 1980. *Alpine elite: German mountain troops of World War II.* London/New York: Jane's.

Richmond, M. E. 1987. *Combat operations in mountainous terrain: Are United States Army light infantry divisions preparing properly?* Fort Leavenworth, Kans.: U.S. Army Command and General Staff College.

Schepe, G. 1983. *Mountain warfare in Europe.* Kingston, Ont.: Centre for International Relations, Queen's Univ.

MOZAMBIQUE, REPUBLIC OF

Mozambique lies on the east coast of Africa facing Madagascar. Most of its population are subsistence farmers, and further economic development has been hampered by endemic warfare since the early 1960s.

Power Potential Statistics

Area: 801,590 square kilometers (309,494 sq. mi.)
Population: 16,386,000
Total Active Armed Forces: 58,000 (0.354% of pop.)
Gross Domestic Product: US$1.6 billion (1989 est.)
Annual Defense Expenditure: US$ not available (8.4% of GDP, 1987 est.)
Iron and Steel Production: small-scale domestic production
Fuel Production:
Coal: 0.38 million metric tons (1986)
Electrical Power Output: 1,740 million kwh (1989)
Merchant Marine: 5 vessels; 7,806 gross registered tons
Civil Air Fleet: 5 major transport aircraft; 145 usable airfields (27 with permanent-surface runways); 1 with runways over 3,659 meters (12,000 ft.); 5 with runways 2,440–3,659 meters (8,000–12,000 ft.); 27 with runways 1,220–2,440 meters (4,000–8,000 ft.).

For the most recent information, the reader may refer to the following annual publications:
The Military Balance. International Institute for Strategic Studies. London: Brassey's (UK).
The Statesman's Year-Book. New York: St. Martin's Press.
The World Factbook. Central Intelligence Agency. Washington, D.C.: Brassey's (US.)

History

The earliest written records of the area now called Mozambique are from Arab traders venturing down the East African coast in the eighth century A.D. Arab trade and settlement centered on the southern portion of the Zambezi River. During the eleventh through early fifteenth centuries, the Shona people of southwestern Mozambique and Zimbabwe created a loosely federated empire of client-kingdoms governed from their administrative and cultural center of Great Zimbabwe. Civil war, and the strain imposed on local resources by the 20,000 inhabitants of Great Zimbabwe, led to its abandonment and the partial disintegration of the Shona empire in the late fifteenth century.

European contact began with the Portuguese in the 1490s. Traders rather than colonists, the Portuguese traded with the natives for gold, ivory, and slaves, often competing with Arab merchants. The building of a stone fortress at São Sebastian (near Moçambique on the north coast) in the 1550s showed that the Portuguese intended to maintain a permanent presence. Over the next three centuries, the colony developed unevenly, and much of the country was left in native hands. In the late 1880s, foreign investment allowed large-scale exploitation of natural resources and the origins of a modern economy.

World War I brought serious conflict: Mozambique was

invaded by the German general Paul von Lettow-Vorbeck's native army in 1917, resulting in a serious rebellion along the Zambezi that spring. The rebellion was ruthlessly suppressed by government forces, although guerrilla activity continued until 1930. These crises led the Portuguese colonial government to raise over 100,000 African troops (12 times Lettow-Vorbeck's forces).

By the late 1950s, the wave of nationalism sweeping Africa at last affected Mozambique. Led by westernized Africans and people of mixed race, FRELIMO (*Frente de Libertaçao de Moçambique*, the Mozambique Liberation Front) was founded in June 1962, merging several earlier groups. An armed guerrilla struggle against Portugal began in 1964, and although FRELIMO could not win major victories the cost incurred in fighting it convinced the Portuguese to grant the colony independence. On 25 June 1975 Mozambique became an independent nation.

Independence did not end Mozambique's conflicts. Between 1975 and 1979, it provided sanctuary and armed support to Robert Mugabe's ZANU (Zimbabwean African National Union) guerrillas fighting Ian Smith's white minority government in what was then Rhodesia. This effort, and related support for the African National Congress (ANC), led to South African support for the anti-Marxist *Resistència Nacional Moçambicana* (RENAMO), the Mozambican National Resistance, and produced virtual civil war within Mozambique. A sober appraisal of Mozambique's difficulties led to adoption of more pragmatic policies. This was most visible in the N'komati Accord signed with South Africa in October 1984, which ended Mozambican support for the ANC in exchange for South African abandonment of RENAMO. Although negotiations between the government and RENAMO began in November 1990, as of this writing, the civil war continues in the countryside with undiminished cruelty and ferocity, unaffected by diplomatic developments.

Politico-Military Background and Policy

During the twelve-year struggle against the Portuguese, FRELIMO was merely anticolonialist, but once in power, it implemented Marxist economic development policies. Similarly, after independence Mozambique spurned most offers of aid from the West, accepting assistance from the Soviet bloc and China. President Samora Machel adopted a more moderate and pragmatic program in 1982–85, and sought aid from the United States and other Western nations, as well as South Africa. His successor Joaquim Alberto Chissano continued that policy.

The armed forces are strongly affected by their origins as a guerrilla national resistance movement, and are often involved in rural development projects. Despite their guerrilla origins, however, the army has not been able to gain the upper hand against RENAMO. The armed forces are staffed by selective conscription; males and females over the age of 18 must serve two years. Most of those selected are male, but females serve in medical, communications, combat support, and administrative units.

Strategic Problems

Mozambique's main strategic problems are twofold, and closely related. The poor state of the economy, nearly ruined by a combination of guerrilla action and government mismanagement, is too shaky to support a significant military effort against the RENAMO guerrillas; and until the guerrillas can be checked, the country lacks the internal stability to permit real economic recovery. Still, the four-year-old shift in policy may yet produce improvement.

Military Assistance and Defense Industry

Mozambique received nearly all its military supplies from the Soviet Union and the Eastern bloc. Although most of the equipment is older, the value is considerable. The aid was crucial because Mozambique has no domestic armaments industry. There are also 3,000–8,000 Zimbabwean and 600 Malawi troops in Mozambique, helping to fight against RENAMO.

Alliances

Mozambique's principal alliance was with the former Soviet Union; a twenty-year treaty of friendship and cooperation was signed in 1977. Mozambique also has close ties to Tanzania, but despite significant economic aid has gained little military support from the West. In the late 1980s there were 650 Soviet, 600 Cuban (including some military pilots), 10 North Korean, and 200 Zimbabwean military and security advisers in Mozambique. The North Koreans and Zimbabweans remain. Mozambique is a member of the UN and the OAU.

Defense Structure

Under the constitution the direction of the state is entrusted to FRELIMO, which in February 1977 was reconstituted as the sole political party. The president is commander in chief of the armed forces, and is assisted by a Deputy Minister of Defense (who is also Chief of Staff of the Armed Forces).

(For an explanation of the abbreviations and symbols used in the following section of military statistics, see the list of Abbreviations and Acronyms in each volume.)

Total Armed Forces

Active: 58,000 (incl Border Guard). Terms of service: conscription (selective, blacks only), 2 years (incl women), extended during emergency.

ARMY: est. 45,000 (perhaps 85% conscripts; all units well under strength.)
10 Provincial Commands.
1 tk bde.

7 inf bde.
1 lt inf bde (forming).
Many indep cbt and cbt spt bn and sy units.
6 AA arty bn.
Equipment:†
MBT: some 80 T-54/-55.
Recce: 30 BRDM-1/-2.
AIFV: 40 BMP-1.
APC: 100 + BTR-60, 100 BTR-152.
Towed arty: 200: 76mm: M-1942; 85mm: D-44; 100mm: 24 M-1944; 105mm: M-101; 122mm: M-1938, D-30; 130mm: 24 M-46; 152mm: 20 D-1.
MRL: 122mm: 30 BM-21.
Mortars: 82mm: M-43; 120mm: M-43.
RCL: 75mm; 82mm: B-10; 107mm: B-11.
AD guns: 400: 20mm: M-55; 23mm: ZU-23-2; 37mm: M-1939; 57mm: S-60 towed, ZSU-57-2-SP.
SAM: SA-7.

NAVY†: est. 1,000. Bases: Maputo (HQ), Beira, Nacala, Pemba, Inhambane, Quelimane (ocean); Metangula (Lake Nyasa) where 2 PCI ⟨ are based.
Patrol and Coastal Combatants: 12 Inshore: 2 Sov SO-1, 3 *Zhuk* PFI ⟨; 7 PCI ⟨.
Mine Warfare: 2 Sov Yevgenya MSI.
Amphibious: craft only; 2 LCU†.

AIR FORCE: 7,000 (incl AD units); 43 cbt ac, 6 armed hel.†
FGA: 5 sqn with 43 MiG-21.
Transport: 1 sqn with 5 An-26, 2 C-212, 2 Cessna 152, 1 -172.
Helicopters:
Attack: 6 Mi-24.
Transport: 5 Mi-8.
Training: 4 Cessna 182, 4 PA-32.
AD SAM:† SA-2, 10 SA-3.

PARAMILITARY
Border Guard: 5,000 personnel; 1 bde.
Provincial Militia (organized on a provincial basis): 9 bn; 1 bn (excl Nyasa) per province. The militias often bear the brunt of small-scale actions with RENAMO guerrillas.

OPPOSITION
Mozambique National Resistance (RENAMO or MNR): about 20,000 total fighters, of whom 10,000 are effectively armed and trained. There are 8 active battalions (4 battalions operating in Mozambique, generally in groups of 30 to 200) and 1 200-man special forces group. Equipment includes B-10 82mm recoilless rifles; RPG-7 rocket launchers; 60mm, 82mm, and 120mm mortars; and 12.7mm and 14.5mm anti-aircraft machine guns.
RENAMO forces have attacked government installations and communal settlements, and have repeatedly disrupted internal transportation. They have employed terror tactics to frighten people away from supporting the government, including both selective killing and wholesale massacre. RENAMO has thereby created a serious refugee problem. Worse still, the official end of South African aid has thrown RENAMO onto its own resources, and many of the RENAMO personnel in Mozambique are essentially armed bandits, operating without directions. These groups have been responsible for considerable depredations in rural areas, and are able to operate freely in the chaotic countryside.

Future

Mozambique contains considerable natural resources, and does not face a significant overpopulation problem. It should be able to build a balanced and prosperous economy, but this will happen only if the government can bring order to the countryside and gain the foreign investment it needs to begin economic development. Unfortunately, the economy has waned to such an extent that military operations are often hamstrung by supply and transport shortfalls.

DAVID L. BONGARD
TREVOR N. DUPUY

SEE ALSO: Organization of African Unity; South Africa; Sub-Saharan Africa; Zimbabwe.

Bibliography

American University. 1984. *Mozambique: A country study.* Washington, D.C.: Government Printing Office.
Hanlon, J. 1984. *Mozambique: The revolution under fire.* Atlantic Highlands, N.J.: Humanities Press International.
Herniksen, T. H. 1979. *Mozambique: A history.* London: Rex Collings.
Hunter B., ed. 1991. *The statesman's year-book, 1991–92.* New York: St. Martin's Press.
International Institute for Strategic Studies. 1991. *The military balance, 1991–1992.* London: Brassey's.

MUNITIONS, AERIAL

Aerial munitions are weapons carried on aircraft and delivered against ground and airborne targets. These weapons include a wide variety of guns, bombs, rockets, and missiles. The operational employment of aerial munitions depends on the capability of the delivering aircraft and the characteristics of the target such as location (ground, water, or airborne), defenses, construction, size, and vulnerability.

The choice of aerial munition is dependent upon the mission to be performed and the design of the delivery aircraft. As aircraft have become more sophisticated, a broad range of munitions has evolved to exploit aircraft technology and rapidly advancing weapon system improvements. Consequently, an enormous international catalog of weapons is available for adaptation to any mission.

Munitions Categories

Aerial munitions are identified by categories. These include bombs dropped from aircraft, guided missiles and rockets launched from aircraft against targets on the ground and in the air, and guns used to shoot at other aircraft and strafe targets on the ground.

BOMBS

There is a wide range of munitions that can be dropped from a variety of aircraft. These weapons are generally called bombs or mines and are characterized as having an aerodynamic shape, stabilizing fins, an explosive charge, and a detonating device. There are several types of conventional bombs: fragmentation (high-explosive and antipersonnel), incendiary, cluster, antiarmor, and area interdiction weapons.

Conventional bombs (such as the U.S. Mk-117 750-lb. general-purpose bomb or the British Mk-10 1,000-lb. bomb) are dropped from aircraft, fall ballistically to a target, and are detonated by a fuze either on contact or after a time delay. Mines dropped from aircraft can be detonated on time delay or by fuzes sensitive to other stimuli such as vibration, proximity, or radio transmission. The British Sea Urchin seabed mine can be programmed to detonate on acoustic signatures and magnetic or pressure influences.

Conventional bombs have a variety of delivery configurations and explosive warhead packages. The U.S. Mk-82 500-pound bomb can be fitted with a fuze extender to achieve a surface air-burst or adapted with a Snakeye high-drag tail retarder for use during low-altitude, lay-down delivery in marginal weather.

Cluster bombs made up of canisters of antipersonnel bomblets, incendiary bombs, chemical bombs, leaflet bombs, and napalm can be used effectively against a number of wide-area targets. The CBU-24/B cluster bomb containing several spin-to-arm, antipersonnel fragmentation bomblets proved to be effective in neutralizing antiaircraft artillery (AAA) and surface-to-air missile (SAM) sites in Southeast Asia.

The French BLG-66 Belouga cluster bomb and the German MW-1 multipurpose pod dispenser are versatile weapons that can be employed against area interdiction targets such as vehicle convoys, equipment, fuel storage, parked aircraft, and armored vehicles. The Spanish Expal BME 330-kilogram cluster bomb contains 180 bomblets that are individually parachute retarded and can uniformly cover an area as large as 10,000 square meters when released from an altitude of 45 meters (150 ft.). The U.S. Rockeye II Mk-20 cluster bomb containing 247 dual-purpose armor-piercing shaped-charge bomblets was designed for use against armored vehicles and personnel.

The U.S. BLU-73 fuel/air explosive (FAE) bomb is a special-purpose weapon that can be dropped in clusters of three. During detonation, FAEs take most of the oxygen in the atmosphere and produce a very high impulse that is the product of over-pressure, making them particularly effective against soft targets over a wide area.

Recent emphasis on the need for airfield denial weapons has yielded a number of runway cratering bombs. These include the British JP-233 airfield attack weapon (cratering bomblets) carried aboard Tornado GR1 aircraft; the direct airfield attack combined munition (DAACM) developed by the United States and delivered in BLU-106/B bombs containing 24 kinetic energy penetration weapons; and the French Durandal runway penetration bomb designed specifically for airfield denial.

Precision-guided "smart" bombs were developed to improve the accuracy and effectiveness of conventional high-explosive bombs. Guidance techniques using laser designation and television optical tracking were adapted to bombs to achieve the pinpoint accuracy required for difficult targets such as armored vehicles, hardened aircraft shelters, bridges, and sensitive military targets located in urban areas. The U.S. GBU-15 modular 2,000-pound glide bomb and its rocket-powered counterpart, the AGM-130A, use a TV seeker for daylight attacks or an imaging infrared seeker at night. Both were used successfully in the 1991 Gulf War, as was a series of Paveway laser-guided bombs.

The GBU-28/B hardened target-penetrating munition was developed for use in Operation Desert Storm against deeply buried, hardened command and control facilities. This weapon demonstrated a capability to penetrate more than 30 meters (100 ft.) of dirt or 6 meters (20 ft.) of concrete.

A variety of torpedoes can be launched from helicopters and fixed-wing aircraft against surface ships and submarines. The British Stingray multimode torpedo is in service with the Royal Navy, the Royal Air Force, and the Thai and Egyptian navies.

Various other bombs are armed with nuclear warheads. Nuclear bombs can be carried aboard bomber and fighter aircraft and employed against a range of targets requiring high-yield, devastating explosive power. The U.S. B28 and B41 bombs are thermonuclear free-fall bombs with yields ranging from 1.45 to 9 megatons. Lower-yield tactical nuclear weapons can be delivered in support of theater battle by a host of U.S., NATO, and Soviet fighter aircraft.

Missiles and Rockets

Guided missiles and ballistic rockets are launched from aircraft against ground and airborne targets. Rockets are employed almost exclusively against ground or surface targets while missiles fall into two categories according to their use: air-to-air and air-to-surface.

Air-to-air missiles. Today's family of air-to-air missiles was developed to extend the kill capability of fighter aircraft and is as varied as the situations encountered in air-to-air combat. Missile variables include: speed, detection range, target identification and aspect angle, launch range, maneuverability, warhead size, and fuzing. Radar-guided missiles generally require initial target detection and tracking by the launching aircraft coupled with their own inertial, semiactive or active radar guidance to the terminal phase of the target intercept. The terminal phase can be guided by semiactive radar, self-contained pulse Doppler radar, or infrared (IR) homing with varying fuze devices: impact, proximity, or active laser fuzes. The U.S. AIM-7 Sparrow, the long-range AIM-54 Phoenix, the Soviet AA-9 Amos, and the British Sky Flash missiles represent a broad spectrum of air-to-air, radar-guided missile capabilities.

Advanced fire-and-forget radar-guided missiles that enable a pilot to aim and fire several missiles at multiple targets while maneuvering are in production with ongoing plans for improvements and international co-production. Replacing the AIM-7 Sparrow, the U.S. advanced medium-range air-to-air missile AIM-120 (AMRAAM) will be compatible with the British Tornado F Mk-2, the Royal Navy Sea Harrier, and the German F-4F aircraft, and will be co-produced in Europe.

Infrared guided missiles form a second characteristic group of air-to-air missiles. Technologically, most of these missiles sprang from the U.S. AIM-9 Sidewinder and have grown into a multinational catalog of weapons that use a sensitive IR seeker to locate and home on airborne targets. The improved AIM-9M, the Soviet AA-8 Aphid and AA-11 Archer, the French Matra R550 Magic, and the Israeli Shafir 2 are only a few of the infrared missiles in operational use today.

Advanced IR imaging techniques could provide the capability to aim a missile at a particular point on the target aircraft in order to achieve a high probability of kill. An imaging IR seeker could also provide for an all-aspect attack capability even in severe IR countermeasure environments.

Air-to-surface missiles. Air-to-surface missiles were developed to improve the accuracy of delivering weapons against hardened or heavily defended ground targets and to reduce the vulnerability of pilots in the process. A wide variety of these missiles is available; the type selected for use depends on the nature of the target in terms of its range, mobility, location, defenses, physical characteristics, and inherent signature.

An extension of guided bombs, air-to-surface missiles are self-propelled and generally use inertial guidance systems coupled with active radar, electro-optical, or radiation sensors for terminal guidance and homing. Variations depend on the operational requirement (e.g., tactical interdiction, close-air support of troops, naval surface targets, or strategic nuclear strikes), target characteristics, and capabilities of the delivering aircraft.

The French AM-39 Exocet missile is a medium-range, radar-guided air-to-surface missile that was designed to attack large warships. The Exocet uses inertial guidance coupled with active radar for position updates and terminal fuzing. The Israeli Gabriel Mk-III and the U.S. AGM-84A Harpoon are similar air-to-surface antiship missiles available in operational inventories today.

The U.S. AGM-65 Maverick is a versatile, precision-guided missile that employs a combination of TV electro-optical, laser, or infrared sensors to deliver a high-explosive warhead against point targets at ranges from 8 to 25 kilometers (5 to 16 mi.). The USAF AGM-142A Have Nap program will adapt a version of the Israeli-built Popeye medium-range, inertial/TV-guided standoff missile to provide long-range bombers with a conventional precision strike capability that can be used in support of theater warfare.

The French laser-guided AS.30 missile can deliver a 240-kilogram warhead against targets out to 10 kilometers (6 mi.). The Apache medium-range air-to-surface missile is being developed by the French for carriage on a number of NATO aircraft. The Soviets had an extensive inventory of air-to-surface missiles including the electro-optical guided Kedge and Karen missiles carried aboard the Su-24 Fencer-C aircraft.

Missiles designed to home on electronic radiation form their own distinct class of air-to-surface guided weapons. With the advent of radar-guided SAM defenses, air-launched missiles that seek out and home on radiated energy became an operational necessity. The U.S. AGM-45 Shrike antiradiation missile was used extensively by USAF Wild Weasel aircraft to neutralize or destroy Soviet-built SA-2 sites during strikes over North Vietnam.

The short-range (12 km., or 7.4 mi.) Shrike led the way to the development of the longer-range (56 km or 35 mi.) AGM-78B Standard antiradiation missile (ARM). The need for fast reaction led to the development of the AGM-88A HARM (high-speed antiradiation missile). Subsequent versions of the HARM cover a wide range of the frequency spectra through programmable digital processors installed in the missile and in the aircraft avionics equipment.

Antiradiation missiles are carried aboard fighter aircraft especially fitted with electronic equipment designed to locate and destroy ground radar and electronic guidance emitters. As many as seven British Alarm antiradiation missiles can be carried aboard the Panavia Tornado aircraft.

In a strategic role, the supersonic U.S. AGM-69A short-range attack missile (SRAM) is carried aboard the B-52 and FB-111 aircraft. The SRAM was designed to attack and neutralize terminal defenses deep in enemy territory. Using inertial guidance, the SRAM can deliver a 170-kiloton nuclear warhead at ranges exceeding 200 kilometers (124 mi.).

Air-to-surface missiles are also carried aboard helicopters. These missiles are designed primarily to destroy armored vehicles and hardened point targets. The U.S. BGM-71 TOW (tube launched, optically tracked and wire guided) antitank missile can deliver a high-explosive (HE) shaped charge or an HE charge against tanks and fortifications out to 4 kilometers (2.5 mi.). The follow-on AGM-114A Hellfire antitank missile carried aboard the AH-64 Apache helicopter can be tailored to perform various missions using interchangeable guidance modules.

Later improvements in helicopter-launched missiles include forward-looking infrared (FLIR) line-of-sight tracking and laser-designated guidance. The Norwegian Penguin Mk-2 Mod 7 is a fire-and-forget missile that can be launched from a helicopter against surface ships from ranges of 12 to 16 kilometers (7.4–10 mi.) and uses inertial navigation with IR terminal guidance.

Longer-range missiles launched from fixed-wing aircraft are characterized as cruise missiles. They use sophisticated guidance systems for navigation and folding wings for sustaining lift and are usually propelled by jet engines. The U.S. AGM-86B air-launched cruise missile (ALCM) is carried aboard the B-52 and B-1 bombers. The ALCM can deliver a 200-kiloton nuclear warhead against multiple strategic targets at a 2,400-kilometer (1,490-mi.) range. The Soviet AS-6 Kingfish and AS-15 Kent cruise missiles are similar weapons that can deliver a 200-kiloton weapon to targets ranging from 400 to 3,000 kilometers (250–1,860 mi.).

Similarly, the ship-launched Tomahawk cruise missile was used effectively in the Gulf War to deliver conventional warheads against long-range targets with precise accuracy.

Rockets. While aerial-launched unguided rockets have been employed against both air and ground targets, they are used almost exclusively in the air-to-ground role today. Most rockets are powered by high-impulse, short-burning (less than two seconds), solid-propellant engines and stabilized in flight by folding fins or spin stabilized for use with low-speed aircraft and helicopters. Air-launched rockets are produced in a wide variety of sizes and equipped with a number of target-specialized warheads. Most rockets can be fired individually or in ripples from a family of rocket launcher pods.

The 2.75-inch (approx. 7-cm) folding fin aerial rocket (FFAR) was used during the Korean war as an air-to-surface weapon but later became the mainstay of the USAF's early all-weather fighter-interceptors as an air-to-air weapon adapted to shoot down enemy strategic bombers. A decade later, the 2.75-inch rocket was used extensively by U.S. and Vietnamese aircraft against ground targets in Southeast Asia and is still in use today by air forces around the world as a multiuse, high-explosive air-to-ground weapon. The Brazilian SBAT-70 is similar to the 2.75-inch rocket and can be loaded in a number of reusable launchers as well as a disposable 19-round launcher.

The Spanish Casa-type rocket pod system can be carried on NATO aircraft and can launch as many as 54 37mm or 70mm rockets employing a variety of warheads. To provide increased range and accuracy, the Canadian CRV7 70mm rocket uses a rapid-deploying wraparound fin system and a high-impulse motor. The CRV7 rocket can be fitted with a number of warheads including HE incendiary, fléchette antitank, and HE incendiary semi–armor piercing. This versatile rocket can be loaded in a wide range of launchers, can be carried aboard both fixed-wing aircraft and helicopters, and is in service with air forces throughout NATO. The Belgian 130mm Zuni rocket is also in service with several NATO and other air forces worldwide.

Guns

Machine guns were first employed as aerial weapons during World War I. Although crudely mounted, those early machine guns had a dramatic impact on aerial warfare and introduced a totally new concept of air-to-air combat. A rapid succession of weapon system developments such as firing synchronization (gun and propeller), multiple gun locations, improved gun sights, and increased firing rates led to the awesome firepower of the 20mm M61A Vulcan Gatling gun installed in many modern fighters today.

Using electrical power to rotate the six barrels of the cannon, the Vulcan can achieve firing rates of 6,000 rounds per minute. Combined with a muzzle velocity of 1,036 meters (3,400 ft.) per second, the firepower of the M61A provides an effective close-in kill weapon against maneuvering fighters in air-to-air combat where positive visual identification of the target is required. The M61A cannon is equally effective against ground targets when used as a strafing weapon.

The GAU-8A 30mm gun is a follow-on to the M61A and was designed to engage the full array of ground targets encountered in the close air support role. The GAU-8A weighs 1,723 kilograms when fully loaded. Mounted in the chin of the A-10 fighter bomber, the GAU-8A proved an effective weapon in the recent Gulf War.

The lightweight (81 kg) 30mm DEFA-553 cannon is a French development of the German Mauser revolver gun. It is electrically powered to sustain firing rates of 1,300 rounds per minute. The improved DEFA-554 30mm cannon installed in the Mirage 2000 fighter can reach fire rates of 1,800 rounds per minute at a muzzle velocity of 820 meters (2,690 ft.) per second. Weighing only 85 kilograms, the DEFA-554 can be pod mounted and is well suited for both air and ground targets.

The Swiss Oerlikon 30mm gun Type KCA is also a four-chamber revolver design. Heavier than the French DEFA-553/554, the Type KCA weighs 136 kilograms and can sustain a firing rate of 1,350 rounds per minute at a muzzle velocity of 1,030 meters (3,379 ft.) per second—comparable to the M61A.

Many of the guns and cannons in the rapidly expanding family of aerial weapons can be internally mounted in most modern fighter aircraft or packaged in pods for application to trainer aircraft, missile-equipped fighters, helicopters, and gunships.

Conclusion

Literally thousands of aerial munitions are available today for application to a wide array of complex and demanding missions. As aircraft technology advances and weapon systems continue to evolve, that number will continue to grow in terms of variety and sophistication.

Automated targeting techniques, improved accuracy, and increased warhead effectiveness should reduce the number of sorties required to destroy a target as well as the need for or reliance on tactical nuclear weapons.

As pilot/aircraft interactive displays (such as the helmet-mounted sight and artificial intelligence systems) become an operational reality, the speed and agility of target acquisition and weapons delivery will become an even more dominant factor in the design of aerial munitions. Spurred by these requirements, technology will combine with industry to produce a next generation of missiles, both air-to-air and air-to-ground, that will be faster, more agile, and more discriminating than any system we can imagine today.

Weapons development coupled with force-multiplying systems such as the airborne warning and control system (AWACS) will continue to have a profound impact on aerial combat and doctrine. In the 1991 Gulf War the early detection, identification, and control capability of the AWACS coupled with the formidable capability of the F-15 weapon system proved to be a decisive advantage in maintaining total air superiority.

Space is no longer a technological sanctuary, and as aerial warfare moves into space the development of munitions and weapons will follow within the limits of changing international treaties. Consequently, the challenge will be to recognize the differences between the characteristics of air-breathing and space weapons and react coherently in terms of development and employment doctrine.

KENNETH H. BELL

SEE ALSO: Gun, Aerial; Missile, Air-launched Cruise; Missile, Air-to-air; Missile, Air to-surface.

Bibliography

Air Force Magazine. 1991. USAF almanac. May, pp. 175–79.

Air Force Magazine. 1991. USAF armament and ordnance checklist. October, pp. 68–71.

Bonds, R., ed. 1986. *The international directory of modern American weapons.* An Arco Military Book. New York: Prentice Hall.

Chant, C. 1988. *Encyclopedia of modern aircraft armament,* pp. 15–265. Wellingborough, Northamptonshire, England: Patrick Stephens.

Drendel, L. 1986. *THUD, Modern military aircraft.* Carrollton, Tex.: Squadron/Signal.

International Institute for Strategic Studies. 1991. *The military balance 1991–1992.* London: Brassey's.

Jane's air-launched weapons. 1990. London: Jane's.

Jane's weapon systems, 1988–89. 1988. London: Jane's.

R.U.S.I. 1980. *International weapons developments.* 4th ed. Oxford and New York: R.U.S.I. and Brassey's.

MUNITIONS AND EXPLOSIVES: ENGINEERING AND HANDLING

The word *munition* originally referred only to powder and shot. Now it describes the many items in the military inventory that contain explosives, biological or chemical warfare agents, and nuclear fission or fusion materials; are inert solid shot, like most rifle bullets, but fired by explosive means; or are otherwise innocuous such as drill rounds.

The word *explosive* describes specially manufactured chemical compounds held in bulk quantities ready for use as they are or after loading into munitions.

The term *conventional* munitions and explosives is common, and signifies the absence of nuclear constituents or devices. It is also convenient to include both ammunition and missiles under the collective heading of munitions, and a representative selection is shown in Figure 1. Furthermore, weapons and their munitions are known as *armaments*; together they form part of a military *equipment.*

The military purpose of munitions and explosives is to achieve the required and, to an extent, predetermined effect on selected targets. They are propelled to or placed on a target, then activated to have the optimum desired effect. They are designed and employed to have specified fragmentation, blast, heat, penetration, or disruption ef-

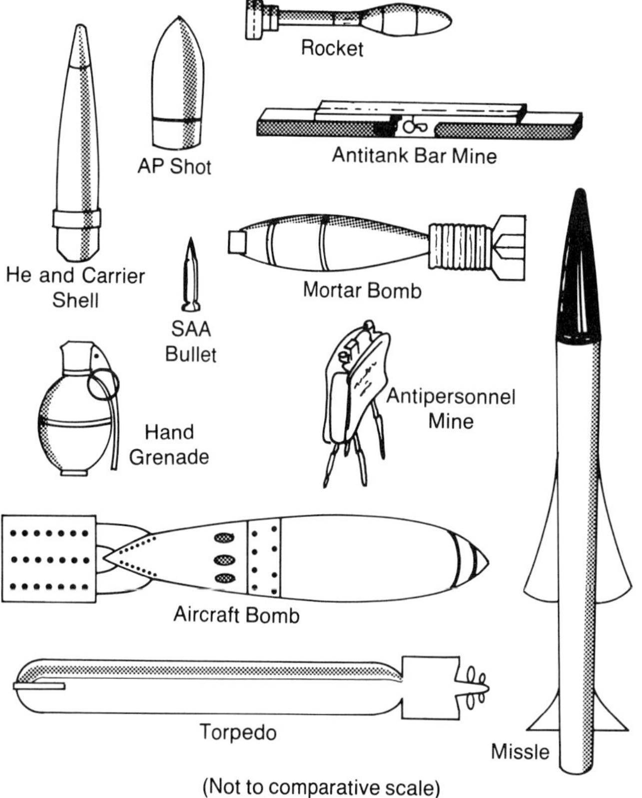

Figure 1. Munitions.

fects against soft targets (troops in the open) or hard targets (armored vehicles). They cause physical, psychological, or physiological damage to troops or people, and they disable or destroy military equipment and facilities, operational positions, or populated areas. They are employed tactically to create artificial obstacles to movement, to demolish obstacles impeding progress, fields of fire or observation, and to destroy abandoned materiel. A small quantity of explosives may be used to render safe or dispose of an unexploded munition or an improvised explosive device. Bulk explosives may also be held for filling munitions at some time in the future.

Nonexplosive munitions such as small-arms bullets and kinetic energy projectiles penetrate and disrupt targets. Other munitions penetrate before exploding or detonating inside the target.

Properties of Explosives

A *low* explosive, once appropriately ignited, burns at a very rapid rate. By exploding, the substance *deflagrates*, producing, for example, the propulsive gases from propellants used in mortars and guns, rockets and missile systems, to fire and launch their projectiles.

A *high* explosive differs from a low explosive in chemical composition and has greater sensitivity. When suitably confined and initiated, it *detonates*, exerting a sudden and intense pressure on its surroundings, which in turn produces a variety of effects at the target end. Examples of high-explosive munitions are hand grenades, mines and demolition charges, mortar bombs and shells, rockets and torpedoes, aircraft bombs, missiles, and improvised explosive devices.

In both cases, low and high explosive substances decompose to produce heat and gas. Power relates to the quantity of heat and volume of gas rapidly released per unit of weight for a given substance. Another important property is sensitivity. Each explosive substance has a sensitivity denoted by a figure of *in*sensitivity: initiators have low and shell fillings have high figures of insensitivity. Thus a munition has a small amount of shielded initiatory substance of relatively high sensitivity to take up and sustain the detonating train, once the munition reaches the target and the fuze activates. This detonating train initiates the main high-explosive filling of the munition, which is composed of a substance of relatively lower sensitivity, adequate for its purpose and safer in manufacture, storage, and transportation.

Velocity of detonation is the rate at which a high explosive releases energy and determines the speed at which the detonating train travels. Brisance is another important property. It is the product of both power and velocity of detonation, and can be described as the *snap* quality of a high explosive. The chemical compatibility of all explosives is also an important property, relating to: internal contact of substances and materials within munitions; and external contact between munitions, packaging, or other materiel stored nearby.

Explosives Engineers

The properties of explosives are vital to the designer of munitions, the explosives engineer in the production industry, and the in-service explosives engineer (ordnance engineer). The designer must also be aware of the military requirement, the characteristics of the target to be defeated, any preferences as to the method of functioning, desired target effects, and many in-service factors. The production explosives engineer must also take these properties and factors into account when deciding upon and supervising the manufacturing processes, quality assurance methods, health and safety precautions, and product handling.

In-service considerations include storage conditions, handling methods, transportation modes, and user environments; the degree and standard of protection to be provided by packaging and shelter; the frequency and means of checking serviceability and safety; the expected shelf life; and the criteria for assessing reliability when the munition or explosive is to be used.

The in-service explosives engineer—the ordnance engineer in the army, navy, or air force—is the technical linkman between the military authorities that specify the requirement, the designer, the producer, and the eventual user. The ordnance explosives engineer may have a comparatively long period of academic education, often including a master's degree and followed by practical training. At the most senior level, he technically manages the complete range of munitions and explosives within a single service or joint service inventory. At the more junior level, he may have responsibility for the "cradle-to-grave" technical management of a particular family of munitions or explosives; the drafting of technical policies, regulations, and procedures; in-service quality assurance and reliability engineering; inspection of storage maintenance and other facilities; and dealing with emergencies.

The ordnance explosives engineer assists the military weapons staff with preparing documents that formally state the military requirements for new or improved munitions and explosives. These documents cover the operational, tactical, logistic, and technical in-service specifications. They include the program for design, development, production, trials, acceptance, and in-service quality assurance. They also specify the target date for introduction into service and outline the estimated life cycle of each munition and critical component.

The ordnance explosives engineer's responsibilities also include: modification of existing munitions and explosives already in the military inventory; design and construction of depots, magazines, permanent or field storage sites, support areas and unit stores; supervision of handling and transportation; and monitoring all safety features and measures.

Policies, Regulations, and Procedures

There are technical policies, regulations, and procedures that govern all aspects of in-service storage and stock maintenance, transportation and handling, use, and disposal of munitions and explosives. The ordnance explosives engineer plays a prominent part in their drafting, in close cooperation with operational staffs, tactical users, and logistic support representatives. When the documents are completed and promulgated, he implements the policies, regulations, and procedures, again in close conjunction with all others involved. He continues with detailed monitoring, inspection, and evaluation processes by which he ensures that safety, efficiency, and other requisite standards are achieved in-service.

Policies and regulations similar to those governing in-service procedures apply to civilian research, development, and production. Government legislation regulates all these processes and has partial or total force with respect to military or military-related activities at home and overseas. Explosives engineers may very well draw up supplementary or additional provisions that apply to their own processes. These specific provisions can be substantial in coverage and detail as the military normally deploys, moves, and uses explosives on a larger scale than civilian industry. Most provisions apply internationally, as well as nationally, and many continue to be enforced in war.

Some examples follow to illustrate circumstances when special military provisions are necessary. If technical policies require specific munitions or explosives to be stored in controlled humidity conditions to achieve a stated shelf life, then regulations specify the parameters for controlled humidity storage that apply to specific items. The regulations are enforced by technical procedures describing the working practices appropriate to these special storage conditions.

Other provisions may relate to munitions or explosives that are incompatible with others, or are of a particularly hazardous or potentially dangerous nature. They may have to be stored, handled, transported, and used separately from other items. Regulated safety distances and protective measures may apply. In certain circumstances, munitions or explosives may be handled only by ordnance explosives engineers, their civilian counterparts, or other suitably qualified personnel. There may be strict limits placed on the quantities stored, transported or used together, and on the disposal of items.

Quality Assurance and Reliability Engineering

Policies, regulations, and procedures also relate to in-service quality assurance and reliability engineering. The manufacture of munitions and explosives, and the assembly of munitions, involve the grouping and identification of a particular production run by lots, batches, or other designated quantities. Each group is then presumed to give uniformity of quality characteristics, serviceability, and end-performance. This system of identification also assists stock control and accounting, supply management, maintenance, and disposal of stocks during the in-service life of each munition type and item.

Manufacturing and assembly processes have become increasingly automated and many have integral inspection and quality control capabilities. Thus, arguments have been advanced, particularly by producers, that the need for in-service acceptance inspections and checks has been correspondingly reduced. With so much at stake, however, at the start of a munition's long service life, military judgment may favor caution and enforce acceptance inspection for safety and reliability reasons. This may entail quantitative, qualitative, and functional tests of a representative statistical example from each production group. The tests provide data with which to compare the characteristics, quality standards, and performance with the stated requirements. The military ordnance explosives engineer or civilian counterpart will plan and supervise acceptance tests, and similar inspections and tests throughout the service life of munitions, with the assistance of a qualified military, civilian, or mixed team of qualified engineers and technicians.

One in-service quality assurance and reliability engineering technique involves component, complete round, or missile *proof*. Having decided upon the sampling criteria, a set quantity of items are selected and proved under physical conditions that represent, naturally or artificially, the operational environment in which they may be required to function. The proof is undertaken by explosives engineers or by the operational user with technical guidance. Military proof teams are usually mobile, operating to an agreed program at home and overseas. Results are recorded and evaluated, thus providing indicators for assessing safety, serviceability, and performance. These and other similar tests help to establish quality and reliability trends which, in turn, assist with the evaluation of storage, stock maintenance, and shelf life criteria. They also provide valuable feedback data for operational users and for explosives engineers engaged in design, development and production, as well as in-service management.

Regular inspection of service support and user storage, handling, and transportation facilities are other important responsibilities of ordnance explosives engineers. Operational staffs and logistic advisers, suppliers, and users must have complete confidence that the munition or explosive is safe and will remain safe, and that its serviceability and performance are assured provided that the prescribed technical regulations and procedures are followed. Regular quality and reliability tests will determine if the munition or explosive has become unsafe or unserviceable during what can be a long shelf life. If either occur and maintenance does not resolve the problem, then disposal becomes necessary.

Emergencies and Disposal

Despite the rigorous precautions, munition and explosives emergencies may arise during peace and war. Incidents or accidents can occur during production, storage, stock maintenance, handling, transportation, or use; malfunctions can happen on operations and training; unexploded items may have to be dealt with effectively; and, in war, enemy destruction or attack may cause major disasters. Trained and qualified military or civilian explosives engineers must investigate and report on incidents, accidents, malfunctions, defects, and failures. The routine action that must be taken to dispose of unexploded items during training and operations is usually a matter for the user. When complications arise, or when the unexploded item is identified in a civilian environment, disposal action is taken by military ordnance explosives engineers, or, in some cases, by other trained and qualified military personnel and civilian police officers.

Most armed forces use the term *explosive ordnance disposal* (EOD) to describe the action taken when a potentially dangerous unexploded munition, improvised explosive device, or quantity of suspicious explosives that constitute a hazard to military operations, personnel, materiel, or facilities, or to the civilian community and property, is believed to exist or is detected. EOD officers, warrant officers, and NCO technicians deal with such incidents, supported by reconnaissance, search and communications personnel, and possibly sniffer dogs. They normally work as EOD teams, and use their skill, mobility, and practiced procedures to locate, gain access to, identify, diagnose, render safe, and dispose of the object or objects. The lead organization in most armed forces is the army's ordnance corps, with naval, air force, other army elements, and some police forces also providing EOD teams. Should the threat justify the commitment of special resources, then centralized EOD tasking, development, intelligence, and forensic agencies may be added.

The term *improvised explosive device* has been mentioned. Such devices can be fabricated in an improvised way and placed in a clandestine manner to destroy, kill, maim, disable, distract, or harass. They normally incorporate nonmilitary components but sometimes use military materiel as well. Terrorist or dissident factions may employ these devices to commit atrocities or disturbances; enemy agents or saboteurs may utilize them during transition-to-war or during war itself to disrupt operations in rear and base areas and to demoralize military forces and civilian populations. In addition, some military munitions scatter unexploded ordnance that requires EOD clearance.

Technology

The armaments industries in those developed countries that have them benefit from new scientific discoveries and rapidly advancing technology just as much as other enterprises. There is, indeed, a wide and lucrative scope for designers, researchers, and developers to use advanced techniques and comprehensive data to conceive all manner of deadly explosive devices for military employment—and this facility is likely to continue to grow unabated.

Developing armaments technology, however, has to be concentrated on precisely stated military requirements for economic, financial, technical, logistic, and operational reasons. Military requirements have to take the wealth of experimental data into account, but they must also reflect operational needs, military experience, and military judgment. Areas for concentration of effort include updated statements of: enemy intentions and capabilities as far as munitions, explosives, and potential targets are concerned, as well as one's own; the types of target, desired effects, and chances of hit/kill; a wide variety of in-service considerations; and the state of the art (or science).

One of the most testing problems concerns the technical and technological relationship between the military requirements stated today and those that may pertain in however many years it takes to design, develop, produce, and introduce into service the new munitions and explosives currently ordered. Gestation time is a difficult and challenging problem common to all military materiel, materiel that is being improved all the time.

There have been significant increases in the lethality, range, and accuracy of conventional and other munitions. From 1970 to 1990, enhancements to the military armory include a specific range of improved conventional munitions (ICMs), extended range projectiles (ERPs), and terminally guided munitions (TGMs). Ever more sophisticated guided missiles are being introduced in an effort to defeat ever more robust, complex, armor-encased fighting vehicles, and for use against softer targets such as ships and aircraft. There are more powerful explosive substances that meet more flexibly, in concept and kind, developing military requirements; other substances, being very difficult to detect, have assisted terrorist purposes.

Research, development, production, technical in-service support, training, and user costs tend to rise in proportion to the degree of technological sophistication. Military judgment has to be applied to maintain the correct mix and balance between, on the one hand, relatively low-cost munitions of the so-called old-fashioned variety and, on the other, comparatively expensive, technologically advanced munitions. Cost penalties are overridden, however, if the target effects and the chances of a one-shot hit/kill are notably improved by advanced sophistication and technology. In the case of munitions, however, these enhancements may be brought about by more effective means of target acquisition and selection, as well as guidance for the weapon system.

Intricate munitions, and particularly such components as fuzes, are not new. The trend toward increasing sophistication does, however, emphasize the risks of faulty manufacture and assembly, onerous and costly quality assurance and reliability engineering practices, and, above all, guaranteed shelf-life, serviceability, and end-performance. It is argued that the old-fashioned variety of munitions are inherently more reliable, maintainable, and durable in storage; they remain serviceable and fit for their eventual role for longer than their more sophisticated counterparts. Countering this is the argument that fewer sophisticated munitions are needed to perform the role, and provided they are produced, packaged, stored, and maintained according to the higher standards required, the costs balance out.

Safety, continued serviceability, and end-performance are the crucial factors whatever the munition characteristics and requirements. The in-service means of verifying these crucial factors is to apply such quality assurance and reliability engineering techniques as component, complete round, and missile *proof* described earlier. These techniques are costly, too, in terms of effort, expertise, and the necessary expenditure of representative samples of munitions. Just how much proof is required, how frequently and how dependable sampling criteria can be made, for both the relatively low-cost and the relatively high-tech munitions, remains a matter of sound military and technical experience and judgment.

J. H. SKINNER

SEE ALSO: Ammunition; Explosives Technology, Conventional; Fuze; Munitions and Explosives Technology Applications; Ordnance Corps.

Bibliography

Baily, A., and S. G. Murray. 1989. *Explosives, propellants and pyrotechnics*. London and Washington, D.C.: Brassey's.

Bebie, J. 1943. *Manual of explosives, military pyrotechnics, and chemical warfare agents: Composition, properties, uses*. New York: Macmillan.

Goad, K. J. W., and D. H. J. Halsey. 1982. *Battlefield weapons systems and technology*. Vol. 3, *Ammunition: Including grenades and mines*. Oxford: Pergamon Press.

Green, C. 1955. *The ordnance department: Planning munitions for war*. Department of the Army Washington, D.C.: Government Printing Office.

Hiller, J. R. 1980. *Production for defense*. Washington, D.C.: National Defense Univ. Press.

Hornby, W. 1958. *Factories and plant*. London: Her Majesty's Stationery Office.

Yinon, J. 1981. *The analysis of explosives*. Oxford and New York: Pergamon Press.

U.S. Strategic Bombing Survey. 1947. *Powder, explosives, special rockets and jet propellants, war gases and smoke acid*. Washington, D.C.: Government Printing Office.

MUNITIONS AND EXPLOSIVES TECHNOLOGY APPLICATIONS

How conventional high explosives function, and the principles relating to their operation, are important considerations for militaries everywhere. This article presents definitions of a range of high-explosive charges used in various munitions, and examines their relative effectiveness against targets. While the effect of different charge types on a target may vary in terms of penetration, when they are compared by caliber of munition, their efficiencies, in terms of crater volume, are quite similar. This is somewhat surprising and shows that, regardless of the way a charge is shaped, similar energies per unit mass are dissipated on detonation.

There are a large variety of designs for munitions that comprise projectiles and missile warheads. Thus, it is helpful to group these into a few basic types with respect to their particular design and application of explosives technology (see Fig. 1). This facilitates study of their principles of operation and examination of typical applications against targets. In practice, however, a mix of these different operational mechanisms will usually be employed.

Energy Carriers

The term *charge* is important and conveys the idea of the explosive as a "carrier of energy." The energy content of a high-explosive charge—the gas volume generated by the chemical reaction per unit of mass—is equivalent to that of a corresponding propellant charge. The significant difference between detonation at a target and combustion in a weapon's firing chamber is that the explosive charge releases energy much faster (by a factor of 10^6). This results in far higher kilo-Joules per second, or generation of gas volume in liters per second, respectively. This quick release of energy by conventional high-explosive charges is the reason for their specific characteristics.

As detonation occurs, the unreacted material in the explosive charge has an initial density ρ_0, an initial temperature T_0, and an initial ambient pressure p_0, within the detonation zone L (see Fig. 2). As detonation progresses, the detonation zone is rapidly subjected to increased density ρ_n, elevated temperature T_n, and significantly elevated pressure p_n. During this process, the detonation front travels with a detonation velocity D, and the explo-

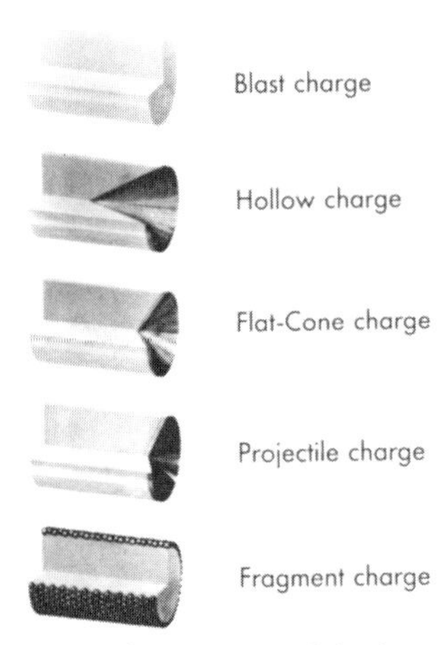

Figure 1. Basic types of conventional high-explosive charges. (SOURCE: Messerschmitt-Bölkow-Blohm GmbH)

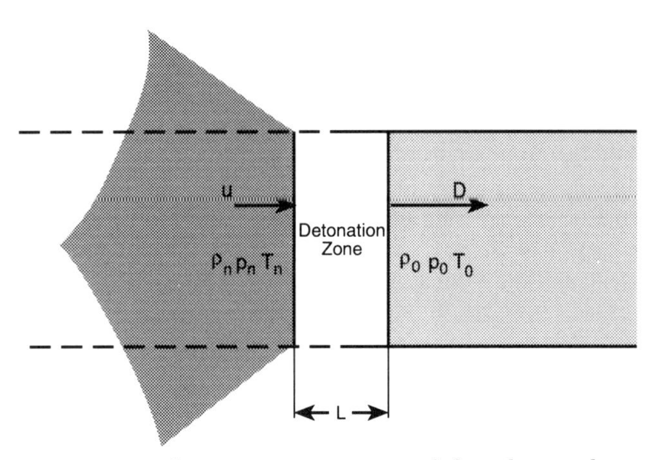

Figure 2. A schematic representation of the relations during detonation. At the shock front, the pressure p, density ρ, and temperature T have initial undisturbed values p_o, ρ_o and T_o, respectively. The detonation zone is of constant thickness. Beyond this zone, p, ρ, and T are significantly increased. (SOURCE: Messerschmitt-Bölkow-Blohm GmbH)

sive products move with their material velocity u, both in the direction of shock waves produced by detonation. The energy released in the detonation zone determines detonation velocity, and occurs between 0.01 μs and 1 μs (μs = microsecond = 0.000001 second).

Considering the high pressure and temperatures of a high-explosive detonation, and the submicrosecond speed in which they are generated, the precise reaction process is unknown.

BLAST CHARGE

Blast charges are cylindrical, designed to fill evenly the space designed for them in warheads and projectiles. The blast that can be produced against a target is extremely powerful. For example, 1 kilogram of high explosive yields about 1,000 liters of gas (at standard temperature and pressure, STP) in 10 μs, and reaches a temperature of several thousand degrees Kelvin. When this gas volume is restricted to the confined space of the casing of the undetonated explosive, an initial pressure of approximately 30,000 bars occurs. The gas then immediately expands, rupturing or disintegrating the casing, and pushes the surrounding air (or other medium) like a piston. This causes a shock wave to form with a very rapid risetime and a period of overpressure. The overpressure is followed by a partial vacuum period, and results in a positive impulse of blast wave, followed by a negative impulse.

The destructive power of the blast wave is caused either by the pressure amplitude or the impulses, depending on the type of target and configuration. If the resonant period of the target is much longer than the interaction time of the positive shock wave, only the impulse causes damage. If the target resonant period is shorter than the pulse, the pressure amplitude is important. Figure 3a shows typical response curves as the blast wave characteristics vary between high peak pressure, low impulse and low peak pres-

Blast Effect

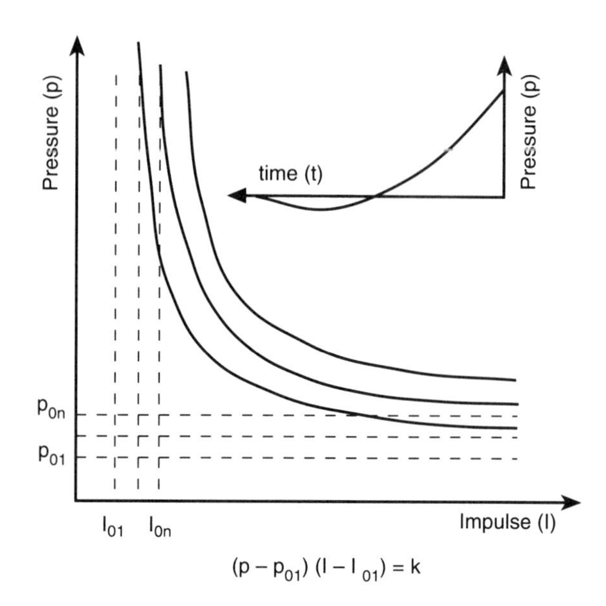

a.

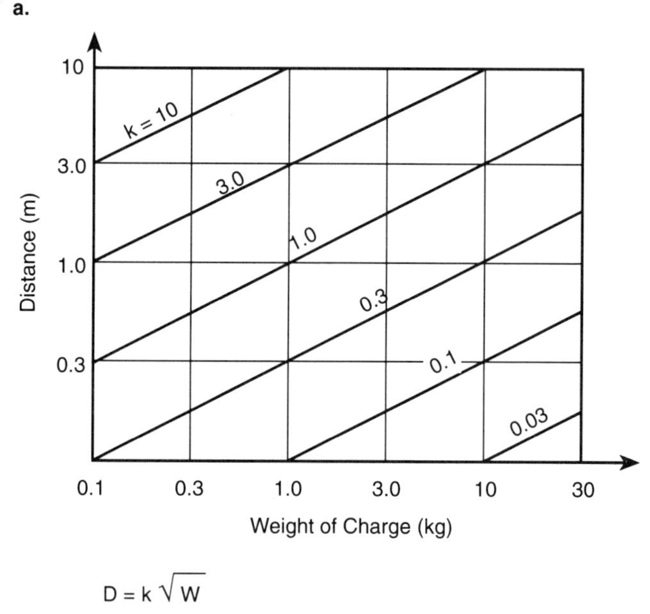

b.

Figure 3. Part a. is a schematic representation of the pressure and impulse load of a target structure caused by the blast wave of a conventional high-explosive charge. Part b. is a representation of the "square root law for high-explosive charges" with different K-factors as a parameter. (SOURCE: Messerschmitt-Bölkow-Blohm GmbH)

sure, and high impulse. The three individual hyperbolas correspond to particular levels of target damage.

With the amount of high explosive usually used in missiles and warheads, the true situation is commonly midway between the extremes. In practice, the distance-to-charge relation (Fig. 3b) follows the "square root law for charges" (i.e., with a ten-fold increase in distance a hundred-fold increase in charge is required to obtain the same destructive effect). In the case of relatively small distances to a target with large dimensions, the distance cannot be measured to the center of mass, but to a suitable reference line or area.

Greater destructive effect can be obtained from the shock wave if there is direct contact with the target, although it is primarily in the localized area of impact. This is because there is no attenuation of the effect of the shock wave by an air gap. In other words, considerable destruction can be obtained with a relatively small amount of high explosive if the charge is placed in direct contact with the target.

Shaped Charge

Sometimes called a hollow charge, shaped charges are hollowed out conically at the front; some are lined with conically shaped metal (e.g., 2-mm-thick copper sheets). Upon impact and detonation of an unlined shaped charge, the conical cavity focuses part of the blast against the target, resulting in greater penetration effect than a comparable blast charge despite the lower weight and somewhat greater distance from center of mass to the target. Figure 4 shows a decreasing hole diameter and increasing penetration when the charge is concentrated by use of a liner along the charge axis.

Another interesting comparison is the length of time that a shaped charge interacts with a target, which is about 40 times longer than that of a blast charge. A shaped charge 100 millimeters in diameter placed against armor plate will penetrate 600 millimeters in 400 μs. In contrast, a blast charge of the same diameter will interact with the target for only 10 μs, and achieve far less penetration.

The "concentration" effect and the increase of the "charge-target interaction time" are the two main phenomena that increase the efficiency of a shaped charge.

If there is some spacing, or standoff, of the shaped charge from the target, the penetration depth can increase up to seven calibers (Fig. 5). This additional, initially unexpected phenomenon shows that an "energy carrier" is generated during detonation, and that it can affect the target in an optimal way.

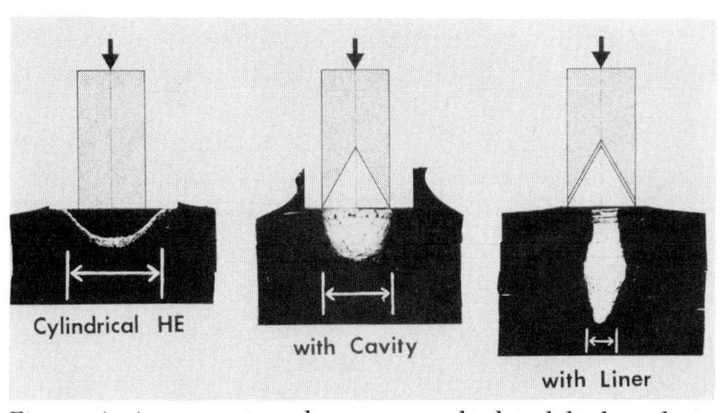

Figure 4. A comparison between a cylindrical high-explosive charge, a high-explosive charge with a cone-shaped cavity without a liner, and a high-explosive charge with a 2-mm-thick, 60° cone-shaped copper liner in the cavity. (Source: Messerschmitt-Bölkow-Blohm GmbH)

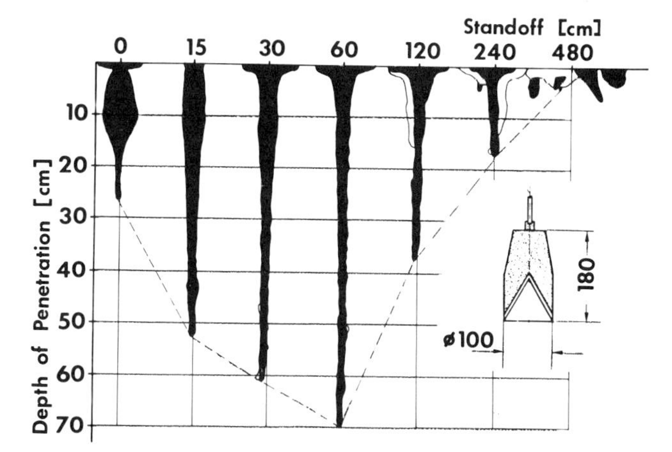

Figure 5. The typical standoff curve of a hollow charge. Initially the depth of the hole increases between the hollow charge and the target up to seven calibers because of the jet elongation effect. For greater standoff the depth of the hole decreases because of the deviation of the jet particles from the axis. (Source: Messerschmitt-Bölkow-Blohm GmbH)

This energy carrier, the jet of the shaped charge, is formed from the liner during the initial stage of detonation. Not to be confused with plasma jets, the jet of a shaped charge is in fact a very high speed extruded length of metal with a very high velocity at temperatures no greater than a few hundred degrees Celsius. Acceleration of the liner and formation of the jet and the metal slug along the line of collapse can best be recorded with a flash radiograph (Fig. 6).

These radiographs reveal the features of the specific efficiency of a hollow charge as:

- Concentration of action along the charge axis through the jet
- Long interaction time through the long jet
- Increased effect at a greater distance, since a longer jet is only formed at a greater distance

The continuous elongation of the jet is limited. After about 150 μs, a jet from a 100-millimeter shaped charge

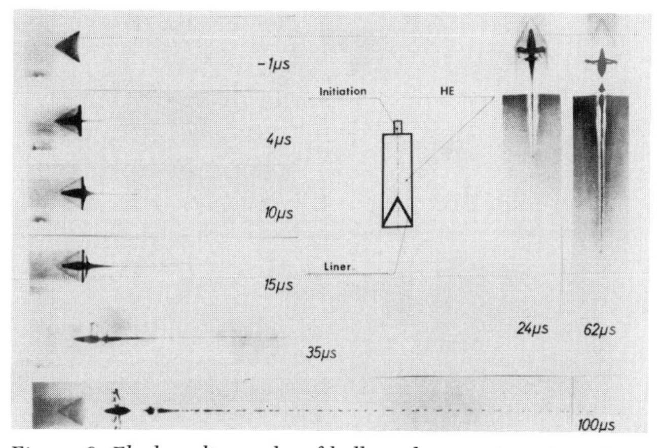

Figure 6. Flash radiographs of hollow charges at various times after detonation showing the jet formation of the liner, the jet elongation up to the particulated jet, and their capacity to penetrate targets. (Source: Messerschmitt-Bölkow-Blohm GmbH)

breaks up axially into particles; thus a so-called particulated jet is formed. The initial homogeneous jet, as well as the particulated jet, exhibit highly efficient penetration and perforation capabilities because of the enormously high pressure applied to any kind of target material. As a first approximation in computing penetration, the material strengths of the target can be neglected and hydrodynamic equations used to compute results that agree very well with practical experience.

Mechanical inertial forces dominate the penetration process, and not thermally driven mechanisms similar to welding and flame cutting. The higher temperatures around the crater after shaped-charge penetration are consequences of deformation. The penetration process depends on purely mechanical displacement due to the high pressure generated during the interaction.

Flat-Cone Charge

Similar in design appearance to shaped charges, flat-cone charges have a larger angle at the cone tip, about 140°, and operate on different physical principles. Whereas the liner in a shaped charge is accelerated along the line of collapse and forms a high-velocity jet and a relatively low-velocity slug, the liner in a flat-cone charge becomes inverted as a whole with a lower velocity, but with a higher mass and larger diameter. Accordingly, the holes created in a target by the shorter, but thicker, jets are not as deep; instead they have larger diameters.

Flash radiographs show the formation of the jet from a copper liner (Fig. 7). Mathematical expressions to explain flat-cone charge principles cannot be based on the well-known hydrodynamic equations of Birkhoff, MacDougall, Pugh, and Taylor (1948), and Pugh, Eichelberger, and Rostoker (1952). Rather, the liner must be sectioned into toroidal zones, and the accelerations, velocities, and directions of each of these toroidal zones must be calculated, taking into account the material flow strength if high accuracy is desired.

Projectile Charge

The jets of shaped and flat-cone charges have an optimum penetrating effect when there is at least some, although relatively small, standoff from a target upon detonation. At greater standoff ranges the jets, while retaining some penetrating capability, tend to break up or particulate axially. Projectile charges, on the other hand, are designed to keep the resulting explosive-formed projectile (EFP) intact after detonation. By adjusting the impulses acting on the toroidal zones created by the explosion so that the tensile elongation of the liner does not exceed its rupture point, an integral mass, called earlier a self-forging fragment (SFF), now an EFP, is formed.

If the impulses acting on the toroidal zones are more elaborately controlled, fin-stabilized flying projectiles can be formed. These EFPs can be accurately aimed over a considerable distance between charge and target (Fig. 8).

The initial conditions and subsequent processes necessary for the proper formation of an EFP can be described quickly and easily, but among all of the charges discussed, this type is the most difficult to realize in practice.

Fragment Charge

During the detonation of any metal-encased explosive charge the casing is distended by the expanding gases and is accelerated to high velocities. Although numerous natural fragments are formed by radial expansion, the fragments can be determined beforehand by special treatment of the casing. For example, grooves or zones of embrittlement in the casing will produce more uniform fragmentation, which can be controlled within certain limits. Depending on the target properties and the design of the warhead, the number, distribution, and size of fragments can be adjusted for optimal effect.

Comparison

In summary, the five fundamental charge types for munitions, and their specific energy transfer mechanisms against targets are:

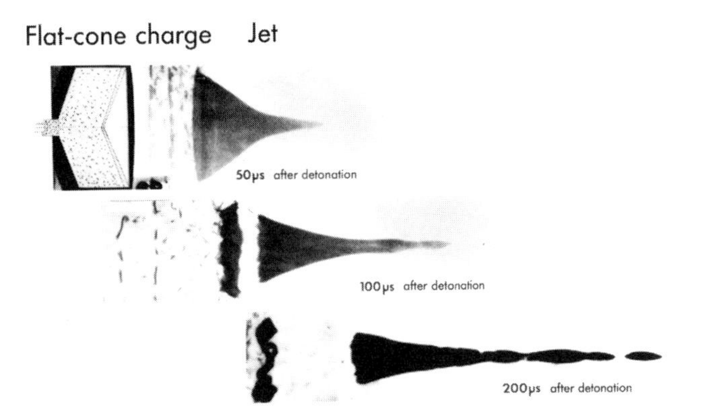

Figure 7. Flash radiographs show the jet formed by the inversion of the flat liner of a flat-cone charge. (Source: Messerschmitt-Bölkow-Blohm GmbH)

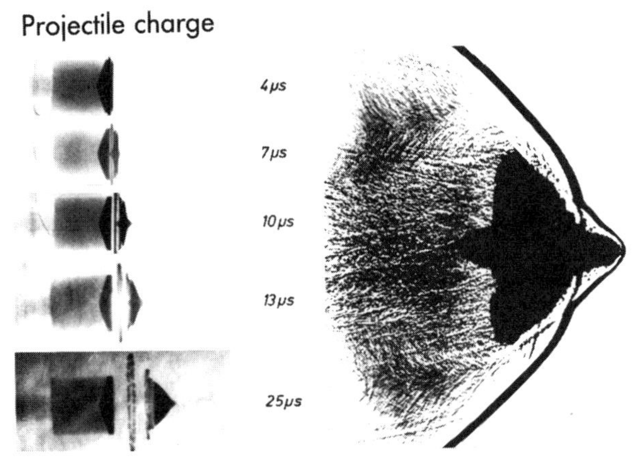

Figure 8. Flash radiographs of the formation of EFPs and a shadowgraph of a flying projectile. (Source: Messerschmitt-Bölkow-Blohm GmbH)

- Blast charge with shockwave
- Shaped charge with very long, but thin, jet
- Flat-cone charge with a shorter, but thicker, jet
- Projectile charge with the explosive-formed projectile over very long standoff range
- Fragment charge with radial expansion to high velocities

Shaped, flat-cone, and projectile charges exhibit their own specific penetration and perforation power with respect to standoff. The shaped charge, especially in close contact with the target, exhibits very high penetration depth. While their optimum standoff distance is somewhat greater than for shaped charges, flat-cone charges show less penetration and larger hole diameters. Projectile charges can deliver concentrated energy at great distances between charge and target. This also applies to fragment and blast charges, which cover a larger area than shaped, flat-cone, and projectile charges, which usually only produce an effect in one direction.

When the penetration depth and corresponding diameter of holes is compared for the different charges (Fig. 9) it is evident that damage to a target increases approximately as a square function of the hole diameter. When this operation efficiency is correlated to the hole volume, it shows that all types of charges generate about the same hole volume—0.19 cubic charge calibers, or D_c^3—including fragment charges (in which case the separate hole volumes are summed). While this is somewhat surprising, it is in no way a new energy constant. Rather, it indicates that from a definite supply of energy in the high-explosive charge, only a certain fraction—the deformation energy in the target—can be realized.

This seemingly trivial physical statement is not always obvious in practice. This observation clearly indicates, however, that the desire of militaries to double the diameter of the crater with the same charge weight and charge diameter in the course of further research and development cannot be achieved, since this would imply a fourfold increase in the energy content of the explosive.

Types	Distance (in D_{Ch})	Crater		$\sum_1^n$ Volume (in D_{Ch}^3)
		Depth (in D_{Ch})	Width (in D_{Ch})	
Blast charge	0	0.2 – 0.4	0.8 – 1.0	$\frac{0.9^2 \times \pi}{4} \times 0.3 \approx 0.19$
Shaped charge	1.5 – 6	5 – 8	0.1 – 0.3	$\frac{0.2^2 \times \pi}{4} \times 6.0 \approx 0.19$
Flat-cone charge	3 – 8	2 – 3	0.25 – 0.40	$\frac{0.3^2 \times \pi}{4} \times 2.7 \approx 0.19$
Projectile charge	1 – 10^3	0.6 – 1.2	0.4 – 0.6	$\frac{0.5^2 \times \pi}{4} \times 1.0 \approx 0.19$
Fragment charge	1 – 10^3	0.05 – 0.10	0.05 – 0.15	$\frac{0.10^2 \times \pi}{4} \times 0.08 \times 300 \approx 0.19$

Figure 9. A comparison of the conventional high-explosive charges with respect to standoffs, charge diameter, penetration depths, and crater diameter (width), and the volumes of the holes computed from depth and diameter values. All values are expressed in charge diameters. (SOURCE: Messerschmitt-Bölkow-Blohm GmbH)

MANFRED HELD

SEE ALSO: Armor Technology; Missile, Antitank Guided; Munitions, Aerial; Munitions and Explosives: Engineering and Handling; Precision-guided Munitions; Ship Protective Systems.

Bibliography

Birkhoff, G., D. P. MacDougall, E. M. Pugh, and G. Taylor. 1948. Explosives with lined cavities. *Journal of Applied Physics* 19:565–82.

Pugh, E. M., R. J. Eichelberger, and N. Rostoker. 1952. Theory of jet formation by charges with lined conical cavities. *Journal of Applied Physics* 23:532–36.

MUSASHI, MIYAMOTO [1584–1645]

Miyamoto Musashi, formally Shinmen Musashi No Kami Fujiwara No Ginshin, more familiarly Niten (his artistic name) or Kensei, "Sword Saint," is Japan's equivalent in strategic thought to China's Sun Tzu or Germany's Clausewitz. His philosophy of military strategy lies midway between that of Sun Tzu and Clausewitz. Musashi's *A Book of Five Rings*, like Sun Tzu's *The Art of War*, has become a source for developing corporate business strategy—first by Japanese businessmen, now internationally. Musashi's book is not specifically *on* strategy, but is rather a guide for those who want to learn strategy. At first reading, the book may seem to be a manual on how to kill an opponent in a duel, but it incorporates ideas of potential military significance at several abstract levels of tactics and strategy.

Musashi the Individual

Exemplifying the *kendo* scholar's goal of "pen and sword in accord," Musashi was a Japanese martial equivalent of Europe's "Renaissance man"—although he was not unique in this (Lowry 1985, pp. 149–50). He devoted his life to the study of fighting and the development of a philosophy of fighting, killing every dueling opponent in the process (his first at age 13, more than 60 by age 29) and participating in six wars. But Musashi was also an accomplished painter, sculptor, poet, designer, and artisan. An orphaned but elite samurai of noble ancestry by inheritance and profession, he was in fact a *Rōnin* ("wave person"—an unemployed wandering warrior) for much of his life, as a result of the Battle of Sekigahara (15 September 1600).

Humble and serious when not actually mastering a foe in combat, in his lifetime Musashi became one of Japan's most renowned warriors. Today he is still a folk hero, more widely known to Japan's general populace than Sun

Tzu to the Chinese or Clausewitz to the Germans. In World War II, Japan named a battleship *Musashi.* This vessel, and its sister ship, *Yamato,* were the largest battleships ever built.

Accomplishments

In combat, Musashi could only be termed invincible: he never lost. He became an expert with all manner of weapons, developing the two-sword way of fencing, *nitoryu.* Later in his career, however, he took to killing his opponents with wooden swords or even cruder weapons made on the spot, even when fighting against experienced and ambitious warriors armed with fine swords. Although his life was devoted to searching for and developing the "way of the sword," he is also noted for his artistic endeavors. His paintings are valued more highly than those of many artists in Japan, and his calligraphy, sculpture, and metalwork are treasured.

Musashi wrote down his final philosophic understanding of fighting while living in a cave in Kyushu, a few weeks before his death. Written as guidance for his pupil—and influenced by Zen, Shinto, and Confucianism— *A Book of Five Rings* is basic to any martial arts bibliography, as well as a guide for businessmen planning sales campaigns.

Musashi's first message, based upon his lifetime of combat experience and study, is that the warrior must recognize, accept, and be guided by the deadliness of his craft. He insists that strategy (in its broadest sense) is inherent in the individual duel. He stresses the overriding significance of understanding and benefiting from knowledge of what is involved in personal combat: Individual minds and movements can change and then be acted upon more swiftly than can those of an army or of any size unit of warriors. "Winning," with its attendant achievement of power and fame through the use of force (his clearly stated goal)—and possible subsequent employment by a lord—is achieved by overcoming other individuals or groups, using three elements of successful combat:

- resolute acceptance of the possibility of one's own death,
- intimate knowledge of the tools of one's trade, and
- a basic overall plan for the end result of one's work.

Musashi's translator uses the English term *strategy* as an equivalent to the anglicized Japanese *heiho.* Derived from the Chinese term for *military strategy,* the Japanese characters reveal a somewhat more complex set of concepts: *heiho,* translated as *hei* (soldier), and *ho* (method or form), should be considered relative to several field concepts of its written characters. These include strategy (the approach of a nation, corps, or division), tactics (small unit), and individual capabilities (in combat)—as well as mastery of such abilities as painting and poetry.

For Musashi, strategy encompasses all of the above. It must be employed by individual warriors and field commanders alike, whether in man-to-man or 10,000-on-a-side fights. Implicit in the above (made more explicit as Musashi treats—still metaphorically—his expanded views) is the significance of such items as

- considering *all* ("10,000") facts and factors involved;
- having intimate knowledge of *all* the weapons one may employ, and knowing just when and how to employ them;
- knowing other traditions and paths to knowledge;
- using, above all, rhythm and timing in execution.

Musashi's treatment of his "five books" (rings) stresses the significance of training and timing, as well as

- interrelating *all* the factors involved;
- using intuitive judgment;
- paying attention, even to trifles; and
- doing nothing that is of no use.

Future

Musashi's *Book of Five Rings* will become an increasingly significant text for military persons of East and West if users develop sufficient vision to sense the strategic and tactical implications of his empirically developed but philosophical metaphor.

DONALD S. MARSHALL

SEE ALSO: Art of War; Clausewitz, Karl von; Doctrine; Strategy; Sun Tzu; Tactics.

Bibliography

Kodansha. 1983. Musashi. In *Encyclopedia of Japan.* Tokyo: Kodansha.
Lowry, D. 1985. *Autumn lightning.* Boston: Shambala.
Musashi, M. 1982. *A book of five rings.* Trans. V. Harris. Woodstock, N.Y.: Overlook Press.
Yoshikawa, E. 1981. *Musashi.* Trans. C. S. Terry. Foreword by E. O. Reischauer. New York: Harper and Row/Kodansha.

MUSIC, MILITARY

From earliest times the military has used musical instruments to rally and lead troops. Bas-relief sculptures and mosaics depict Roman Legionnaires playing serpent-headed wind instruments. Many centuries later, Gen. George Washington ordered that the musicians of the American colonial army—drummers, fifers, and buglers—wear red coats, rather than the Continental Army's blue coats, so that they could be seen through the smoke created by the black powder of the day. By being so attired, they would become an easy rallying point for the troops.

Early History and Development

Drums were probably the first instruments to be used; they provided a cadence for marching and also were used to signal troop movements and to pass orders. Through the mid-nineteenth century, drummers used a complex set of rhythms or "beats" to signal everything from "wake up" to "fix bayonets."

The drum is the only instrument preserved in its oldest form. Many military bands still use drums on which the heads are tuned by old-fashioned rope tautening devices. The drum still provides the cadence for marching troops and, in a few instances, still signals commands. The 3d United States Infantry (The Old Guard) headquartered in Washington, D.C., is the U.S. Army's ceremonial unit. During ceremonial functions they fix bayonets using drum signals for the execution of the movements.

As musical instruments developed through history, many signals became the duty of the bugler. Although electronic communications have greatly reduced its role, the bugle call still regulates and paces life on most military posts throughout the world. The earliest bugle was simply a flared tube through which, by the vibrating or "buzzing" of the player's lips, various pitches were sounded.

Flutes and fifes also provided music for the early military. Flute- or fife-like woodwinds were known in classical Greece, where the Spartans marched into battle to their music. From these three primitive instruments—drum, bugle, and fife—has grown the military band of today.

Later Additions and Refinements

The reed family was the next group of instruments to join the primitive military band. Brass instruments did not develop as rapidly as the woodwinds. The early trombone, known as the sackbut, was the first brass instrument capable of playing a complete scale. These were integrated, along with the fifes, oboes, bassoons, and drums, into the European bands of the seventeenth and eighteenth century.

The bands of Louis XIV (1638–1715) were made up of both double-reed instruments (oboes and bassoons) and drums. Frederick II (1712–86) added clarinets and hunting horns to that instrumentation. Not to be outdone, Napoleon's bands consisted of one piccolo, one high (E-flat) clarinet, sixteen B-flat clarinets, four bassoons, two serpents, two trumpets, one bass trumpet, three trombones, two side (snare) drums, one bass drum, one triangle, two pairs of cymbals, and two Turkish crescents (the forerunner of the "Jingling Johnny" or *glockenspiel*). An exotic import, the glockenspiel represents the Turkish influence in German military music. During wars in the Balkans from the fifteenth to eighteenth centuries, German musicians borrowed melodies and instrumentation from the bands of the Ottoman Janissaries, who had a rich musical tradition of their own.

The keyed bugle and the serpent represent the earliest attempts at making the louder, and more martial, brass instruments capable of playing the chromatic scale, which enabled them to play melodies as well as simply "calls." The serpent was a bass instrument with holes that were covered with the fingers and keys like those found on a modern clarinet. It employed a cupped mouthpiece similar to that used on a trombone or tuba. The keyed bugle was of the same design, but pitched higher.

Wilhelm Wieprecht, the Prussian bandmaster, is generally credited with inventing the valve (ca. 1835), which allowed brass instruments to play the entire chromatic scale. In 1850, the French musician-inventor Adolph Sax, who invented the saxophone, also devised a valve for brass instruments and began producing a family of instruments, called "saxhorns," for the French military. Saxhorn-style instruments are still used by eastern and central European bands and contribute to the darker, more mellow sound of those ensembles.

The Modern Military Band

The instrumentation of the military band was fairly well formalized by the 1860s. It remained for the nations of the world to develop their own nationalistic styles of playing. Bands of the British Commonwealth and the United States are of similar instrumentation; however, many British bands, mainly the Scottish regiments, use bagpipes. The military bands of France and its former colonies often include a corps of bugles, which imparts a different quality of sound to their ensembles. With the exception of the French, the bands of continental Europe use brass instruments that have a darker sound. One of the most distinguishing characteristics of American bands is the use of the brighter-sounding trumpet rather than the cornet.

The military bands of Europe and its former colonies do not as a rule use the American sousaphone. Pitched and played identically to the tuba, the sousaphone is specifically designed for ease of carrying while on the march. Its most notable characteristic is the large, round bell, which projects giraffe-like above the head of the performer. Like the trumpet, the sousaphone possesses a brighter timbre of sound and tends to make the overall sound of the band brighter.

Composition and Duties

Today's military band includes piccolos, flutes, E-flat clarinets, B-flat clarinets, alto and bass clarinets, oboes, bassoons, alto saxophones, a tenor saxophone, a baritone saxophone, trumpets or cornets, French horns, trombones, euphoniums, tubas, and percussion. Numbers of performers vary from nation to nation and band to band. Large bands may have additional performers for harp, piano, bass violin, and electric bass. In addition, a selected bandsman will perform as drum major on marching engagements, performing on his instrument in concert situations. The size of a band usually depends upon the individual band's mission. Support of a small post normally will require a band of 30 to 35 musicians who perform for parades, formations, and public concerts and may in addition provide dance music for official functions. (In addition to their musical duties, post bands and some larger regimental bands may also function in the field as litter bearers, field medical aid personnel, and headquarters and prisoner guards.) Larger bands, such as a regimental or division band, normally have 60 to 70 performers who perform the duties of the smaller post band and in addition support more important occasions and often simultaneous engagements. Bands at large military bases are frequently required in two places at the same time and must have sufficient personnel to respond accordingly.

Because of the additional ceremonial functions, military music in national capitals can be quite complex. For example, in Washington, D.C., there are four major bands to represent the army, navy, air force, and marines. These bands also have string sections forming strolling and chamber orchestras. These string ensembles perform regularly at the White House and at state occasions and are often combined with the band into a symphony orchestra for special events. In addition to the string ensembles, these premier bands also have choruses that perform at official functions and at public concerts. The U.S. Army Band also features a section of heraldic trumpets (adopted from their British cousins) that announce the arrival of dignitaries to the White House.

Administration and Organization

The means of support or funding of bands varies from nation to nation. U.S. military bands are supported by funds appropriated from the Department of Defense and their respective branches.

The regimental bands of the Guards Division and throughout the British military are the financial responsibility of each regiment. Much of this financial burden is carried by the bands themselves, who produce recordings and other items which are sold to defray expenses. By and large, nations either fully fund their military music programs or follow the regimental funding concept.

Most military bands in the field are commanded by a Chief Warrant Officer or equivalent, although many are commanded by a company-grade officer. The premier bands in world capitals are most likely to be commanded by a field grade officer, normally no less than a major and usually a lieutenant colonel, colonel, or equivalent.

Noncommissioned officer structure normally consists of a Band Sergeant Major with others of lower grades commanding and performing within their respective sections, often as solo performers.

Conclusion

Over the centuries, the size, complexity, and responsibilities of the military band have grown along with the rest of the military. Today's military band is a relatively complicated and diverse organization. Like the earliest fife-and-drum duo, the modern band still leads troops into battle and rallies them in the midst of the fighting. But it also sells bonds and raises funds; entertains families and foreign dignitaries; and serves as a symbol of the nation's prestige and power.

JOHN M. TAYLOR

SEE ALSO: Ceremonies and Displays; Uniforms and Accouterments.

Bibliography

Hinds, H. C., and A. C. Baines. 1985. *Groves dictionary of music*. London: Macmillan.
Kappey, J. A. Ca. 1910. *Short history of military music*. London: Boosey.
Apel, W. 1970. *Harvard dictionary of music*. Cambridge, Mass.: Harvard Univ. Press.
Adkins, H. E. 1973. *Treatise on the military band*. London: Boosey.
Wright, A. G., and S. Newcomb. 1970. *Bands of the world*. Evanston, Ill.: The Instrumentalist.

N

NAPOLEON I [1769–1821]

Napoleon Bonaparte, one of history's greatest soldiers, was trained as an artillery officer under Louis XVI. Rising to prominence during the French Revolution, he overthrew the Directory government and seized power, becoming first consul and later emperor of the French. He capitalized on the military accomplishments of the Old Regime and the revolution, conquering most of Europe at the peak of his career (Fig. 1).

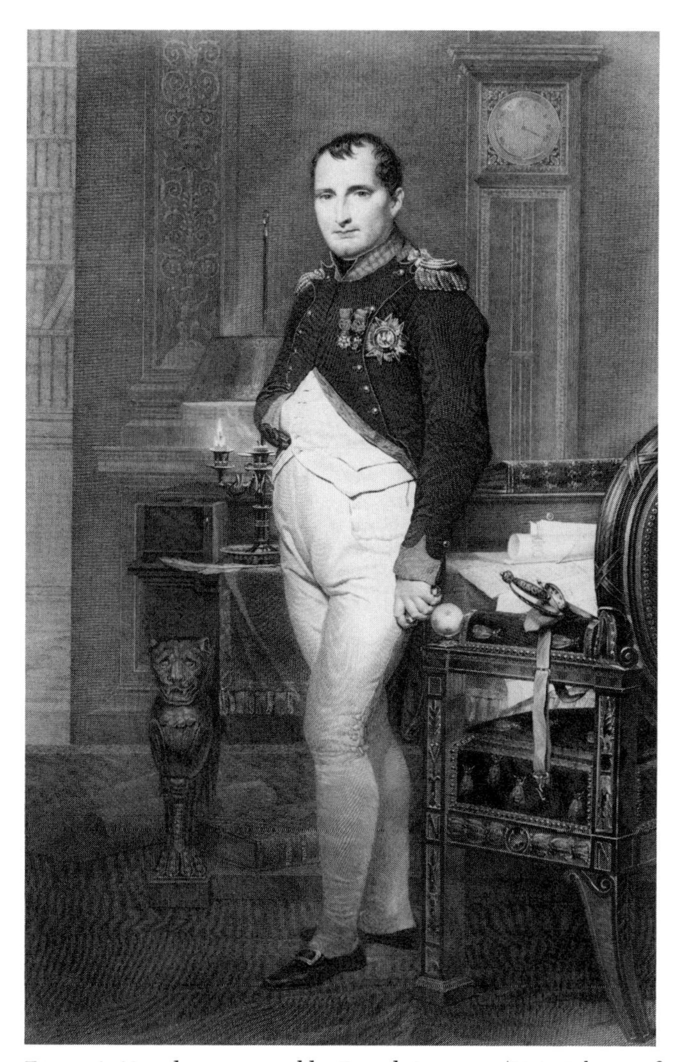

Figure 1. Napoleon, painted by David. SOURCE: (U.S. Library of Congress)

Education and Early Career

Napoleon was born 15 August 1769 at Ajaccio, Corsica. In 1778 he was sent to the *collège* at Autun and in 1779 to the academy at Brienne. In 1784 he matriculated at the Ecole Militaire in Paris and was commissioned an artillery sublieutenant in 1785. Early influences on Napoleon included the theoretical writings of Marshal Maurice de Saxe and the tactical ideas and innovations of Pierre de Bourcet, Joseph du Teil, and Jacques de Guibert. The army Napoleon entered had adopted the artillery reforms of Jean Baptiste Gribeauval, giving it the finest artillery in Europe, and it soon employed the combined-arms division and mixed order of lines, columns, and skirmishers. This force, enhanced by revolutionary changes such as conscription, was ultimately inherited by Napoleon and provided the basis for his conquests.

Napoleon first gained fame commanding the artillery at the siege of Toulon in 1793. The recapture of the city (19 December), due largely to Napoleon's guns, earned him promotion to brigadier general. But in 1794–95, his Jacobin connections and friendship with Augustin Robespierre led to disgrace and unemployment. He regained favor by his role in suppressing a royalist uprising in Paris (5 October 1795) with his famous "whiff of grapeshot." He was rewarded with the Army of Italy, his first independent field command.

Italian and Egyptian Campaigns

Napoleon led the Army of Italy to a series of victories, including Lodi (10 May 1796), Castiglione (5 August 1796), Arcola (15–17 November 1796), and Rivoli (14–15 January 1797). It also provided him with the opportunity to develop further his skills as a commander, and the peace he imposed on Austria in 1797 enhanced his fame in France. Returning to Paris, he discarded as impractical an invasion of England itself, instead embarking on an Egyptian campaign as a means of striking at Britain. After capturing Malta (12 June 1798), he landed in Egypt (1 July), but Lord Horatio Nelson's naval victory at Aboukir Bay (1–2 August) stranded him there. The easy conquest of Egypt led in 1799 to a campaign in Syria, possibly an effort to return overland to France. Stopped at Acre (March–May 1799), Napoleon returned to Egypt, where he learned things were going badly for the French armies in Europe. Napoleon abandoned his army in Egypt and returned to France (9 October) to assume the leading role in the overthrow of the Directory government and to make himself first consul (9–10 November 1799).

Campaigns and Reforms of the Consulate

Needing a victory to enhance his position, in 1800 Napoleon launched a second campaign in Italy, culminating in the victory—actually a near defeat salvaged by the arrival of Louis Desaix—at Marengo (14 June) and a peace with Austria (9 February 1801). Peace with Britain followed in March 1802, but it lasted only until the spring of 1803, although major hostilities did not resume in Europe until 1805.

In the meantime, Napoleon instituted several basic reforms. In 1801 he ordered a change in the artillery (the System of the Year IX). A 6-pounder was to replace the 4- and 8-pounders of the Gribeauval system, the 12-pounder being retained. An army to invade England was established around Boulogne and carefully drilled until, as the Grand Army, it marched to victory at Ulm and Austerlitz. Napoleon had acquired enough popularity to be proclaimed emperor in May 1804; by this time his tactics and strategy had matured.

Tactics and Strategy

Napoleon capitalized on the idea of divisions operating independently of each other but capable of mutual support. In 1803 he adopted the army corps—typically, two to four infantry divisions, plus cavalry, artillery, and other services—as the largest field formation throughout the French army. Thus, the concept of mutual support, which he had previously applied to divisions, he now applied to army corps and even among various war theaters. Although Napoleon acknowledged no fixed principles of war, he gave great attention to such things as mobility, dispersal, concentration, and envelopment. Speed and mobility were critical, because they permitted Napoleon to keep his units dispersed and then concentrate them at the last moment to achieve local superiority over part of the enemy force. Interior lines of communication enhanced Napoleon's mobility, whether on the battlefield proper or throughout a theater. Mobility also permitted surprise and envelopment, both of which contributed to Napoleon's ability to maneuver the enemy out of position.

Napoleon always exercised direct tactical command in a battle, after laying careful plans in advance. He usually met with his major unit commanders very early on the morning of a battle, giving them last-minute instructions based on reconnaissance and then sending them out to implement his plans. He rarely interfered with their implementation, however, except in instances of failure, or an unexpected change in the situation. Although his initial plans frequently went awry, he was quite adept at minimizing the effects of his own errors, seizing unforeseen opportunities, and capitalizing on enemy mistakes. With an army thus organized and led, well trained and rested, Napoleon embarked on perhaps his greatest campaign, the 1805 Ulm-Austerlitz campaign.

Campaigns of 1805–1807

When Austria and Russia attacked France in the fall of 1805, Napoleon moved the Grand Army into Central Europe, capturing one Austrian army at Ulm (20 October) and defeating the combined Austro-Russian armies at Austerlitz (2 December). This campaign serves as an excellent example of Napoleon's war-making concepts. In 1806 Napoleon determinedly pressed for the political reorganization of Europe through military action, establishing the Confederation of the Rhine (12 July) and abolishing the Holy Roman Empire (1 August). This disruption of Germany angered Prussia, which, allied with Russia, declared war on France in 1806. This resulted in an overwhelming Prussian defeat at Jena and Auerstädt (14 October), the French occupation of Berlin, and the establishment of the Continental System (Napoleon's effort to break Britain by closing Europe's ports to British trade while stimulating French industry to fill the void). Prussia and Russia, however, continued the war, leading to a drawn-out winter battle at Eylau (8 February 1807) and another overwhelming French victory at Friedland (14 June). Napoleon's meeting with Czar Alexander I and the Treaties of Tilsit (7 and 9 July) ended this series of campaigns, temporarily brought Russia into the French system, and reestablished a Polish state: the satellite Grand Duchy of Warsaw.

Spanish and Portuguese Campaigns

The Iberian Peninsula, however, remained a breach in the Continental System. Therefore, Napoleon sent Marshal Andoche Junot into Portugal in late 1807. In 1808 Napoleon attempted to force the Spanish to accept Joseph Bonaparte as their king, but the people resorted to guerrilla warfare. Napoleon, having reassured himself of Central European loyalties at Erfurt (27 September–14 October 1808), then led an army into Spain. He defeated the Spanish army, restored Joseph to the throne of Spain, and achieved some success in driving the British out of the peninsula. In Paris, intrigues proliferated, and Austria grew restive. Napoleon returned to France in January 1809, never again setting foot in Spain, although the conflict there lasted until the French were finally driven out in late 1813.

1809 Campaign and the Austrian Marriage

While Napoleon was in Spain, Austria allied with England and in April 1809 invaded Bavaria, a French ally. Napoleon responded quickly, defeating Archduke Charles of Austria in a series of battles and occupying Vienna (13

May). However, during an attempted crossing of the Danube, Napoleon was defeated at Aspern and Essling (21–22 May). He then regrouped, defeated Archduke Charles at Wagram (5–6 July), and forced a peace on Austria.

In late 1809, Napoleon divorced his wife, Josephine Beauharnais, because she could not bear him an heir. He negotiated with both Austria and Russia for a new wife. He settled on Archduchess Marie Louise of Austria, rejecting Grand Duchess Catherine of Russia. Thus he contrived a marriage alliance with Austria, which France had defeated repeatedly, and angered Russia, which Napoleon had never been able to crush completely. Relations with Russia grew steadily worse.

The 1812 Russian Campaign

On 24 June 1812, Napoleon invaded Russia. The principal causes of the conflict were Russian humiliation over the marriage negotiations, Russian withdrawal from the Continental System, and disputes over Poland. The size of Napoleon's army, over 600,000 men, curtailed its speed and mobility. The Russians successfully withdrew (although one army was almost trapped at Smolensk), scorching the earth and making their first real stand at Borodino (7 September). This was a bloody, but indecisive, French success. Napoleon then marched to occupy Moscow, which the Russians had largely destroyed by fire. Napoleon, hoping to force the czar to make peace, waited in Moscow and disregarded warnings about the Russian winter. The French finally abandoned Moscow (19 October), but the weather grew extremely bitter, and the French retreat turned into disaster. Napoleon nonetheless outmaneuvered his Russian adversaries and fought his way out of an encirclement by forcing a costly crossing of the Beresina River (26–28 November). When he learned of a plot in Paris to overthrow him, the unsuccessful Malet Conspiracy (23 October), he abandoned his army at Smogorni (5 December) and returned to Paris. The pitiful remnants of the army continued the retreat to Germany.

Campaigns of 1813 and 1814

As the Russians advanced westward, Prussia allied with them, breaking its alliance with France. Napoleon built a new army of ill-equipped, half-trained recruits. He defeated the allies at Lützen (2 May 1813) and Bautzen (20–21 May). He then accepted an armistice (2 June–13 August) that worked to his disadvantage because, in the interim, Austria joined the allies. Napoleon defeated the Austrians at Dresden (26–27 August), but the numerically superior allies defeated him in a great battle at Leipzig (16–19 October), ending French power in Germany and resulting in French withdrawal west of the Rhine. The allies pursued.

For the 1814 campaign in France, Napoleon carried out a brilliantly conducted war of maneuvers, winning a series of minor victories, despite overwhelming allied strength. But the allies finally drove for Paris, which they entered on 31 March. With his army in disarray, his marshals disillusioned, and the people anxious for peace, Napoleon abdicated unconditionally (6 April). He was given the Mediterranean island of Elba to rule in exile.

The Hundred Days

Disgruntled over the failure of Marie Louise to join him, fearful of being deported elsewhere, and aware of widespread dissatisfaction with the reestablished Bourbon monarchy in France, especially among his former soldiers, Napoleon escaped from Elba and returned to France (1 March 1815). The allies quickly moved against Napoleon, who sought to defeat them before they could unite. He defeated the Prussians under Blücher at Ligny (16 June). The same day he defeated the British under the duke of Wellington at Quatre Bras. The main French force under Napoleon pursued Wellington's army toward Brussels. Wellington held Napoleon at Waterloo until the arrival of Blücher's Prussians, who had eluded the pursuit of Marshal Grouchy's detachment. The Anglo-Prussian allies then decisively defeated Napoleon (18 June). The French army disintegrated. Napoleon was exiled to the island of St. Helena, where, according to recent forensic discoveries, he likely died of arsenic poisoning on 5 May 1821.

Assessment

Napoleon's conquests, which had briefly given France dominion over most of Europe, had exhausted France. But the political and other changes that Napoleon had instituted did not vanish after Waterloo. The consolidation of German states remained, and the sense of German nationalism he had stimulated flourished anew a few decades later. Likewise, the nationalism his conquests had generated in Italy helped lead to that country's later unification. And while military technology soon changed, "Napoleonic" tactics and strategy and organizational innovations continued to affect warfare in many ways. Napoleon's military genius immediately earned him a permanent place among the great commanders of history.

JAMES K. KIESWETTER

SEE ALSO: Art of War; Coalition Warfare; Envelopment; France; French Revolutionary–Napoleonic Wars; History, Modern Military; Interior and Exterior Lines of Operation; Jomini, Antoine Henri.

Bibliography

Chandler, D. G. 1966. *The campaigns of Napoleon.* New York: Macmillan.

Connelly, O. 1987. *Blundering to glory.* Wilmington, Del.: Scholarly Resources.

Dodge, T. A. 1904–1907. *Napoleon: A history of the art of war.* 4 vols. Boston: Houghton Mifflin.

Lachouque, H. 1961. *The anatomy of glory: Napoleon and his guard.* Providence, R.I.: Brown Univ. Press.

Quimby, R. S. 1957. *The background of Napoleonic warfare.* New York: Columbia Univ. Press.
Rothenberg, G. E. 1978. *The art of warfare in the age of Napoleon.* Bloomington, Ind.: Indiana Univ. Press.
Yorck van Wartenberg, M. 1902. *Napoleon as a general.* 2 vols. London: Wolsey Series.

NATIONAL GUARD OF THE UNITED STATES

The National Guard of the United States is the formal title of two of the seven reserve components in the armed forces of the United States. These two are the Army National Guard of the United States (ARNGUS) and the Air National Guard of the United States (ANGUS); together they include the army and air national guard units of all 50 states and four territories (the District of Columbia, Puerto Rico, the U.S. Virgin Islands, and Guam). The other five reserve components are the U.S. Army Reserve, U.S. Naval Reserve, U.S. Air Force Reserve, U.S. Marine Corps Reserve, and the U.S. Coast Guard Reserve.

The national guard differs from the other federal reserve components both in composition and mission. The Army National Guard (ARNG) is organized predominantly into combat units and is the primary combat arms reserve of the United States Army. The U.S. Army Reserve (USAR) consists primarily of combat support, combat service support, and training units. The Air National Guard (ANG) maintains the majority of reserve airframes, providing tactical reconnaissance, tactical air support, support aircraft, a majority of the reserve tactical fighters, and all of the reserve Continental United States (CONUS) Strategic Interceptor Forces. The ANG and the U.S. Air Force Reserve (USAFR) both have airlift capabilities, with the USAFR providing reserve crews for active component aircraft. While the two national guard components consist almost entirely of organized units, the USAR and the USAFR both contain numerous individual ready reservists in addition to organized units.

The concurrent state and federal status of the national guard provides the basis for its dual mission: as federal reserve forces of the U.S. Army and Air Force, and, as state troops, to preserve peace, order, and public safety during emergencies in their respective states. The national guards of the several states essentially serve as the organized militia of each state as provided for in the U.S. Constitution, while the National Guard of the United States is the organization of the states' militias into a federal reserve component.

The National Guard Bureau (NGB) is a joint activity of the Departments of the Army and Air Force and provides administration, organization, and training guidance for the national guard at the federal level. The NGB evolved from the Bureau of Militia Affairs (created in 1908) and serves as the primary channel of communication between the states and the Department of Defense. The chief of the NGB is a lieutenant general appointed from the national guard. U.S. law provides that the composition of personnel serving on active duty with the NGB will be a mix of active component and national guard personnel on active guard reserve (AGR) tours.

Each state or territorial headquarters provides administration and control for state-related missions and peacetime training. The governor of each state and territory appoints a national guard officer as the adjutant general (TAG) for the state or territory. This person serves in a full-time state capacity as commander of the state national guard and as the military adviser to the governor. The adjutants general are also federally recognized general officers (normally major general) in the national guard of the United States. In 1992, 16 of the adjutants general were appointed from the ANG and 38 from the ARNG.

The term *national guard* in reference to the militia was not formally codified in law until the National Defense Act of 1916 mandated its use. The term was first used in America in 1824 by members of the New York militia who formed an honor guard for the Marquis de Lafayette, a famous veteran of the American Revolutionary War and commander of the Paris militia Garde Nationale. The term was in common use by the end of the nineteenth century.

Army National Guard

All Army National Guard (ARNG) tactical units are organized and equipped under the same tables of organization and equipment (TO&E) used for active component units. Nontactical units such as state headquarters units are organized under tables of distribution and allowances (TDA), which reflect the specific needs of a particular command. Most of the TDA units exist for the peacetime administration of the national guard and will not deploy as units even if full mobilization occurs.

With over 2,600 tactical units, the ARNG is the largest of the United States's seven organized reserve components. Its personnel strength accounted in 1991 for about 30 percent of the total army structure (active army, army guard, and army reserve) in organized units; however, it provided almost 50 percent of the total army's organized combat units and 37 percent of the combat support units.

The land combat capability of the guard in 1992 consisted of ten divisions, thirteen separate combat brigades, seven roundout or roundup brigades to augment active divisions, two armored cavalry regiments, two special forces groups, and one Alaskan Scout group. The guard had 70 separate combat battalions, 47 engineer combat battalions, and hundreds of combat support and combat service support battalions, companies, detachments, and headquarters.

All of the major combat units include organic combat support and combat service support units designed for self-sustainment. The guard also contains a large number of separate combat support and combat service support headquarters and units. Major units of the ARNG in August 1991 and the states that provide the major elements are shown below.

Unit	State(s)
Divisions (10)	
26th Infantry	Massachusetts, Vermont, Connecticut
28th Infantry	Pennsylvania
29th Infantry (Light)	Virginia, Maryland
34th Infantry	Minnesota, Illinois, Iowa
35th Infantry (Mechanized)	Nebraska, Kansas, Kentucky
38th Infantry	Indiana, Michigan
40th Infantry (Mechanized)	California
42d Infantry	New York
49th Armor	Texas
50th Armor	New Jersey, Texas
Separate Brigades (13)	
29th Infantry	Hawaii
30th Infantry (Mechanized)	North Carolina
32d Infantry (Mechanized)	Wisconsin
33d Infantry	Illinois
39th Infantry	Arkansas
41st Infantry	Oregon
45th Infantry	Oklahoma
53d Infantry	Florida
73d Infantry	Ohio
92d Infantry	Puerto Rico
30th Armor	Tennessee
31st Armor	Alabama
163d Armor	Montana, Wyoming
Roundout/Roundup Brigades (7)	
27th Infantry (Light)	New York (10th Mountain Division)
48th Infantry (Mechanized)	Georgia (24th Infantry Division)
81st Infantry (Mechanized)	Washington
218th Infantry (Mechanized)	South Carolina
256th Infantry (Mechanized)	Louisiana (5th Infantry Division)
116th Armor	Idaho, Oregon, Nevada (4th Infantry Division)
155th Armor	Mississippi (1st Cavalry Division)
Armored Cavalry Regiments	
107th	Ohio, West Virginia
278th	Tennessee

Air National Guard

The ANG is organized into wings, groups, and units with the same unit composition as comparable active air force units. With over 1,600 aircraft assigned to flying units, it is continuously integrating the newest generation of fighter and airlift aircraft into its inventories. With slightly under 118,000 personnel, the ANG in 1991 contributed about 15 percent of total air force personnel strength.

The air national guard was organized in 1991 into 12 fighter interceptor wings and groups, 19 tactical airlift wings and groups, 14 air refueling wings and groups, 32 tactical fighter wings and groups, 17 wings and groups with other missions, 92 flying units, and 283 mission support units. Each state headquarters unit for the ARNG also contains the state headquarters elements of the ANG. The air national guard contributed 26 percent of the U.S. Air Force Combat Command tactical fighter aircraft and 78 percent of the continental United States interceptor fleet. Major units of the ANG in 1991 are shown below.

Unit	State(s)
Fighter Interceptor Wings and Groups	
102d FIW	Massachusetts
107th FIG	New York
119th FIG	North Dakota
120th FIG	Montana
125th FIG	Florida
142d FIG	Oregon
144th FIW	California
147th FIG	Texas
148th FIG	Minnesota
158th FIG	Vermont
177th FIG	New Jersey
191st FIG	Michigan
Tactical Fighter Wings and Groups	
103d TFG	Connecticut
104th TFG	Massachusetts
110th TFG	Michigan
113th TFW, 175th TFG	Maryland
114th TFG	South Dakota
116th TFW	Georgia
187th TFG	Alabama
121st TFW, 178th TFG, 180th TFG	Ohio
122d TFW, 181st TFG	Indiana
124th TFG	Idaho
127th TFW	Michigan
128th TFW	Wisconsin
131st TFW	Missouri
132d TFW, 185th TFG	Iowa
138th TFG	Oklahoma
140th TFW	Colorado
149th TFG	Texas
150th TFG	New Mexico
152d TFG	Nevada

154th TFG	Hawaii
155th TFG	Nebraska
156th TFG	Puerto Rico
159th TFG	Louisiana
162d TFG	Arizona
169th TFG	South Carolina
174th TFW	New York
183d TFG	Illinois
184th TFG	Kansas
188th TFG	Arkansas
192d TFG	Virginia

Tactical Airlift Wings and Groups (19)

109th TAG	New York
118th TAW, 164th TAG	Tennessee
123d TAW	Kentucky
130th TAG, 167th TAG	West Virginia
133d TAW	Minnesota
135th TAG	Maryland
136th TAW	Texas
137th TAW	Oklahoma
139th TAG	Missouri
143d TAG	Rhode Island
145th TAG	North Carolina
146th TAW	California
153d TAG	Wyoming
165th TAG	Georgia
166th TAG	Delaware
179th TAG	Ohio
189th TAG	Arkansas

Air Refueling Wings and Groups (14)

101st ARFW	Maine
108th ARFW	New Jersey
112th ARFW	Pennsylvania
126th ARFW	Illinois
128th ARFG	Wisconsin
134th ARFG	Tennessee
141st ARFW	Washington
151st ARFG	Utah
157th ARFG	New Hampshire
160th ARFG	Ohio
161st ARFG	Arizona
170th ARFG	New Jersey
171st ARFW	Pennsylvania
190th ARFG	Kansas

Other Units by Type

2 Aerospace Rescue and Recovery Groups
1 Combat Information Systems Flight
8 Combat Information Groups
2 Composite Groups
2 Military Airlift Groups
3 Tactical Air Support Groups
2 Tactical Reconnaissance Wings
4 Tactical Reconnaissance Groups
1 Special Operations Group

History

The origins of the national guard can be found in the military traditions of sixteenth-century England, brought to America by the first English colonists. As early as 1607, the colonists at Jamestown had organized a militia for the defense of the colony. Plymouth followed suit in 1620 when Miles Standish organized four companies of militia. Although these colonies predate the Massachusetts Bay Colony (1629), the birth of the American militia system is reckoned from the formation of the North, South, and East regiments of Massachusetts Bay on 13 December 1636. These regiments—continuing their lineage as the 181st and 182d Infantry, the 101st Field Artillery, and the 101st Engineer Battalion—are among the oldest military units in continuous service in the world.

With the exception of Pennsylvania, other colonies formed mandatory militia units following the example of the Massachusetts Bay Colony. From 1636 through 1754, these militia forces defended the colonies against Indian uprisings, evolving into a training base for new recruits as the colonies matured.

While these militia units were organized and drilled regularly, they were still part-time units composed of citizen soldiers. Sustained operations resulted in economic hardship for both individuals and communities. To alleviate these problems, detachments of paid, full-time volunteers were maintained to patrol the frontiers and give early warning of Indian attack. There is some indication that during this period the majority of the fighting was done by soldiers recruited outside the communities among vagrants, Indians, free blacks, white servants, and apprentices.

The first major test of the American militia system came during the French and Indian War (1754–63). The English colonial authorities recruited provincial units from the colonial militia to augment regular British regiments in their campaigns against the French. One of these units, formed by Maj. Robert Rogers in New Hampshire, gained renown for its irregular tactics and long-range raids. "Rogers's Rangers" was the forerunner of the current U.S. Army Rangers.

During the decade following the end of the French and Indian War, relations between the colonists and the British government began to deteriorate as colonists perceived abuses of their rights by the king and Parliament. By 1774, colonists had established voluntary military companies to supplement the militia. In 1774, Boston established an elite militia force capable of mobilizing on a "minute's" notice. These "Minutemen" have been immortalized as a symbol of the national guard and the American Revolutionary War.

The militia played a significant role in the American Revolutionary War. Militiamen opened the war with a confrontation at Lexington on 19 April 1775; later that day an encounter between the Massachusetts militia and a

British column resulted in the "shot heard round the world." At several major battles—Bunker (Breed's) Hill, King's Mountain, Cowpens, and Guilford Courthouse—the majority of the American forces were militia. Militia units not only augmented the Continental Army during major engagements, but supported the army by harassing British supply lines and confining British units to cities.

During the course of the war, approximately 164,000 militiamen from all thirteen colonies served. A great number of the officers and men of the regular Continental Army, including Gen. George Washington, a former Virginia militia colonel, were recruited from the ranks of the colonial militia. Washington, the first president of the United States, began a long tradition of militia service by future presidents. Eighteen presidents have served in the militia, including such notables as Thomas Jefferson, Andrew Jackson, Abraham Lincoln, Theodore Roosevelt, and Harry S Truman.

Following the American Revolutionary War, the militia remained strictly under the control of the former colonies, now loosely organized as a confederacy, until the ratification of the U.S. Constitution (1787), which provided the basis for organizing the militia of the various states into a federal reserve force when called to active service.

With the Constitution as a base, Congress passed the Militia Act of 1792, which divided the militia into the common and the organized militia. The common militia closely resembled the former colonial militia. The organized militia, consisting of volunteers, was the primary, or "ready," reserve of the army. The Militia Act of 1792 remained the controlling law for the militia for 111 years.

For most of the next 150 years, the United States maintained a relatively small regular army, relying on the proper mobilization and employment of the militia to augment the regular army in times of need. It should be noted that between these times of need, fiscal support for the militia tended to dry up, often resulting in undertrained and poorly equipped units. A few states maintained their militia at their own expense, resulting in a wide disparity in the readiness of units.

During the nineteenth century, the militia was called into federal service four times, each time responding in a manner that validated this unique American military system, but also exposed its many weaknesses. The first call came in 1812, during the second war with Great Britain. At the outbreak of hostilities, the regular army consisted of approximately 10,000 men. The militia answered the call, providing almost 490,000 men by the end of the war, although few of these served in combat. By the conclusion of the war at New Orleans in early 1815, much of the regular army leadership, including such men as Maj. Gen. Andrew Jackson, had been appointed from the ranks of the militia.

In 1845, the admission of Texas into the United States resulted in a border dispute with Mexico. War was declared in April 1846. More than 73,000 members of the militia were called to federal service, comprising some 70 percent of the army that entered Mexico. Questions regarding the legal authority for the militias to serve outside their own states was resolved by the expedient of having all officers and men resign, and then be reenlisted as volunteers. Although at first there was friction between the regular officers and the militia, by the end of the war there were few complaints about the skill and bravery of the militia units. The war with Mexico developed a pattern of militia service that would be repeated until the mid-twentieth century: the regular army would provide a trained cadre of leadership and know-how, the militia (usually serving as volunteers rather than as militia units) would provide the manpower.

The American Civil War started (after South Carolina seceded from the Union in December 1860) when Southern militia troops fired on Union gunboats and Fort Sumter in Charleston Harbor in early 1861. Neither the Union nor the Confederacy expected a long war. Initially, only 75,000 Union militiamen were called to federal service for a period of 90 days (15 April 1861). Less than a month later, President Abraham Lincoln authorized the enlistment of 42,000 men for three-year terms. After the first large battle at Manassas (Bull Run, 21 July), Lincoln called for 400,000 more volunteers.

The Confederacy relied almost totally on the militia to form its armies, having no regular forces at the outbreak of the war. Many West Point–trained officers, such as Robert E. Lee and Thomas "Stonewall" Jackson, resigned from the Union Army and provided the core leadership for the Confederacy.

The length and scope of the American Civil War, considered by many historians to be the first "modern war," resulted in the complete mobilization of the militia. Once the militia had been called into active service—but again serving as volunteers—both sides resorted to conscription for replacements and new units. In all, some 2.8 million men served with the Union forces, and about 1.5 million served with the Confederacy. Due to the small size of the regular army at the outbreak of the war, the majority of units with Civil War campaign credit are national guard units, which served during the war as volunteer units.

From the end of the American Civil War in 1865 until the end of the century, the militia was used extensively in its state status to enforce the "Black Codes" of the South and to quell strikes and labor unrest in the North and the West. The national guard continued to grow in strength and mission during this period. Summer training for units was adopted by most states, and the regular army began assigning advisers to each state. An interesting historical footnote was the organization of a naval militia in several states. Although most of these units were short-lived, they were the ancestors of the U.S. Naval and Marine Corps Reserves.

In 1898, the United States declared war on Spain. Approximately 165,000 national guardsmen answered the call, and again served as volunteers. A few of these units were deployed to the Caribbean, the most famous of which was commanded by Col. Leonard Wood and had as its lieutenant colonel a future president of the United States, Theodore Roosevelt. That unit, the 1st U.S. Volunteer Cavalry, nicknamed the "Rough Riders," was composed of troops recruited from the Texas and New Mexico national guards.

The majority of volunteer units serving in the Spanish-American War were deployed to the Philippines. National guardsmen–volunteers bore the brunt of the first year of combat here, including a rapid adaptation to the unconventional tactics employed by Filipino guerrillas. As demobilization occurred after the capitulation of the Spanish in 1899, the original national guard–volunteer units in the Philippines were replaced by newly raised volunteer units commanded by regular officers, some appointed directly from volunteer units already in the Philippines. Many of these new enlisted volunteers came directly from the ranks of the national guard–volunteer units that had been serving in the Philippines.

The national guard underwent major changes in 1903 with the passage of the Dick Act, which replaced the Militia Act of 1792. For the first time, militia units were subject to inspection by the regular army. The Act mandated 24 drill periods per year and five days of paid annual training. The Dick Act confirmed the militia as the primary organized reserve of the army; it was supplemented by the Militia Act of 1908, which increased the availability of federal funds and created the staff Division of Militia Affairs within the War Department. This division, although staffed by regular army officers, would become the Militia Bureau in 1911, and later the National Guard Bureau. The 1908 act also created the army reserve, although throughout the first half of the twentieth century this new force would remain little more than a collection of individuals.

In 1915, the first of two New York air units received federal recognition. These units, the 1st and 2d Aero Companies, along with several nonfederally recognized air units from other states, were the predecessors of the U.S. Air National Guard. These units were called to active service during the Mexican Border Crisis but were disbanded in 1917 when the units' members were called to active duty on an individual basis and integrated into the fledgling army air corps for service in World War I.

The National Defense Act of 1916 finally ended the long debate over the organization and training standards of the militia. A landmark in U.S. military legislation, the 1916 Act provided that the militia would remain the primary reserve component of the army, and formally titled the combined militia as the national guard. The Act raised the required number of annual drills from 24 to 48, authorized drill pay for national guardsmen, and extended annual training from five to fifteen days per year. The Act required that national guard units be organized in the same manner as regular army units, that national guard officers be subject to federal qualifications, and that units meet specific standards to receive federal recognition.

In 1916, heightened tensions between Mexico and the United States as a result of Pancho Villa's incursions into U.S. territory, and the subsequent punitive expedition into Mexican territory by the U.S. Army, caused President Woodrow Wilson to activate the entire national guard. Eventually, 112,000 guardsmen saw duty along the Mexican-U.S. border. Although there were no battles fought on the border, the incident provided valuable mobilization and field exercise experience for the national guard.

The following year, 1917, saw the entry of the United States into World War I. The national guard provided 40 percent of the American Expeditionary Force (AEF) in the form of seventeen combat divisions. However, a substantial proportion of the men in these units were conscripts, who had been added to bring the units up to full strength. Of the eight American divisions rated as most efficient by the German General Staff, six were national guard divisions (the 26th, 28th, 32d, 33d, 37th, and 42d). Eleven of the national guard divisions acquired more actual combat time than any (except two) of the 8 regular or 17 national army divisions.

After World War I the national guard was reorganized into four cavalry divisions and eighteen infantry divisions. The National Defense Act of 1920 provided for an army that would include the regular army, the national guard, and the organized reserve corps. While the national guard was to remain a state force, the Act provided for increased federal assistance to national guard units. The post–World War I organization also called for each division to form an air observation and reconnaissance squadron. Twenty-nine squadrons were organized between World War I and World War II, forming the initial base of units that would become the U.S. Air National Guard.

In 1933, to provide the federal government with more authority over the national guard, Congress passed a law creating the National Guard of the United States. This new component was identical to the national guards of the states and territories, but was a component of the federal army at all times. For the first time, the national guard could be ordered into federal service without waiting for the consent of state governors.

In 1940, with Europe once again embroiled in a major war, President Franklin D. Roosevelt mobilized the entire national guard for one year of training. The one-year period was extended to eighteen months in September 1941. By December 1941, when the United States finally declared war on the Axis powers, over 300,000 guardsmen in 18 combat divisions, 28 separate regiments, and numerous nondivisional units were already in federal service. Activation of the national guard in 1940 doubled the size of the army.

The overseas service of the eighteen national guard divisions in World War II was divided evenly between the European and Pacific theaters. National guard units participated in every theater of the war, including 34 separate campaigns and seven assault landings.

The conclusion of World War II created a massive demobilization problem for the United States. To facilitate the reduction in force, national guard units were demobilized and the personnel were discharged along with draftees and volunteers through army separation centers. As a result, the national guard existed only on paper until October 1946, when reorganization plans were approved and implemented.

The lessons of World War II showed the need for large, well-trained, well-equipped reserve forces. The reorganization recognized the national guard's dual status and mission. The National Guard of the United States became an "M-Day" (mobilization day) force that was to be organized, equipped, and trained for immediate action in the event of a national security emergency. The national guard of the several states would form the basis of the National Guard of the United States and, in their state capacity, maintain peace within the states. State service also included riot control and disaster relief. Under the new plan, the federal government provided equipment, standardized training, and a majority of the funding for the national guard.

In September 1947, the army air forces became the United States Air Force, and the air national guard was formed. In 1948, a new law established another component, the air force reserve, and authorized drill pay for both the army and air force reserves, placing them on a par with the national guard. The national guard still remained the primary reserve force as the army and air force reserves were composed at that time primarily of officers.

During the Korean War, more than 183,000 army and air guardsmen were activated. The majority saw service in the United States and Europe, releasing regular army units for service in the first limited war in which the United States would participate after World War II. Two national guard divisions (40th and 45th), two national guard air wings (116th and 136th), and several battalion-sized units (primarily artillery and engineer) saw combat in Korea. Many other guardsmen volunteered for active service on an individual basis and served in Korea with active army units.

The Armed Forces Reserve Act of 1952 and the subsequent Reserve Forces Act of 1955 made sweeping revisions to the reserve components of the United States. The army reserve was organized into troop units, primarily combat support, combat service support, and training units. The national guard, which had always been primarily combat units, retained this distinction, and today it remains the primary combat arms reserve of the army.

The national guard placed 40 air squadrons, two divisions, and 104 nondivisional units on active duty in 1961 during the Berlin Crisis. Twenty-two of the squadrons were deployed to Europe.

Eight ARNG units and some 4,300 guardsmen were mobilized and deployed to Vietnam after the Tet offensive in early 1968. The majority of army national guard service during the Vietnam era consisted of riot control and disaster relief in state status. Four ANG TAC fighter squadrons were deployed to Vietnam with 85 percent of a fifth squadron composed of air guard volunteers. Air guard pilots flew 30,000 combat sorties in their year of service. The immense unpopularity of the Vietnam War and the draft resulted in a dramatic shift in the evolution of U.S. military policy leading to the all-volunteer force and the total force policy.

The National Guard in the Total Force

The total force policy of the United States was initiated in 1970 and implemented in 1973. In part, the policy was a response to the all-volunteer force adopted near the end of the Vietnam War. The loss of readily available, inexpensive manpower from conscription made it necessary to reduce the size of the active components without a parallel reduction in overall combat strength and readiness by increasing reliance on the reserve components. The total army consists of the active army, the ARNG, and the army reserve. The total air force consists of the active air force, the ANG, and the air force reserve.

The primary goal of the total force policy is complete integration of the active components with their respective reserve components. By 1974, combat units of the ARNG were affiliated with and training with regular army units. By 1976, national guard units were assigned to "round out" regular army units. Roundout units are assigned to and train with the units with which they will fight when mobilized.

The total army concept resulted in significant improvements in the ARNG. Equipment was upgraded, training was intensified, and missions were expanded. Roundout units were structured and equipped identically to their active army counterparts. Training standards for roundout units are established by the host organization to ensure that the entire unit, both active and guard components, are at an equivalent level of combat readiness.

Increased reliance on the reserve components by the United States has funneled massive support in the form of new equipment and training funds into the national guard, vastly increasing the levels of training and readiness. The majority of national guard units will mobilize immediately and deploy with the active army and air force in the event of a national security emergency. Even the rapid deployment force, the United States's first line of defense for areas where the army is not already forward deployed (Europe and Korea), contains a significant percentage of national guard units.

Training opportunities for national guard units have increased substantially in the past fifteen years. Guard units have been deployed to Europe, Korea, Panama, and Honduras to participate in major training exercises. Mechanized infantry and armor units of the national guard participate routinely in exercises at the National Training Center at Fort Irwin, California.

Air guard units are performing active air force missions at an ever-increasing rate. The air guard supports U.S. Air Force missions in the United States, Europe, the Middle East, the Caribbean Basin, and Central America. The air guard is assigned to active air force training commands for mobilization, training standards, and evaluations.

Individual readiness has also increased. National guard officers, noncommissioned officers, and enlisted men must meet the same standards of professional military education as their regular counterparts. The majority of this education, including initial entry training, noncommissioned officer courses, officer basic and officer advanced courses, is conducted in residence at active component service schools.

The national guard has evolved into a truly professional military force. No longer considered a social organization, nor ridiculed for a lack of military standards, it has emerged as one of the most effective, best equipped reserve fighting forces in the world. This evolution, though, has not been without its costs.

One interesting effect of the total force concept is the priority of force modernization. Many national guard units with priority missions have received new equipment, such as the M1 Abrams tank and the M2 Bradley Fighting Vehicle, ahead of lower priority active component units. This is in sharp contrast to pre-1970 policies for modernizing the active components and transferring the older equipment to the national guard and reserve.

Equipment

Currently, the weapons system inventory of the ARNG still includes some 1960-vintage equipment—for example, the M60 series tanks, M113 series tracked vehicles, UH-1 and AH-1 series helicopters, and several series of tactical light wheeled vehicles. Extensive force modernization for ARNG combat units began with the deployment of the M198 series 155mm towed howitzer. Major modernization programs for the ARNG are shown below.

Weapons System	*Year Assigned*
M1/M1A1 Abrams Main Battle Tank	1985
M60A3 TTS Tank	1985
M2 Bradley Infantry Fighting Vehicle	1985
Improved TOW Vehicles	1985
UH-60A Black Hawk Helicopter	1983
AH-64 Apache Attack Helicopter	1987
HMMWV Tactical Wheeled Vehicles	1985

In 1991 the ANG was still flying some 1960-vintage aircraft, such as the F-4, the C-130, and the KC-135. However, most F-4s were to be phased out by the end of 1992, and extensive modernization programs for the C-130 and the KC-135 will allow these aircraft to be used well into the twenty-first century. Procurement of new generation aircraft began in the 1980s and will continue until the entire force is modernized. Modern aircraft and the years they were introduced into the ANG are presented below.

Aircraft	*Year*
F-15 Eagle	1987
F-16 Fighting Falcon	1987
C-5A/B Galaxy	1985
C-141B Starlifter	1986

Personnel

In 1991 the national guard maintained a personnel strength in excess of 564,000, with over 446,000 in the ARNG and 118,000 in the ANG. Personnel fall into one of three categories with regard to participation and training: active guard reserves (AGR), military technicians (MT), or drilling reservists.

The AGR program consists of national guard and reserve officers, warrant officers, and noncommissioned officers serving in a full-time status for the administration and training of their components. AGR personnel are on active duty and receive the same pay and benefits as their regular army counterparts. ARNG AGR strength was about 26,000 personnel in 1991, ANG AGR strength about 8,500 personnel.

Military technicians (MT) are another class of full-time national guard employees. Technicians hold a dual status, performing full-time administrative, training, and maintenance duties as Department of the Army or Department of the Air Force civilian employees and drilling as unit members during scheduled training assemblies. Technicians must be drilling members of a national guard unit as a condition of employment. ARNG MT strength exceeded 29,000 personnel in 1991, while ANG MT strength approached 24,500. Full-time members of the national guard (AGR and MT) account for almost 13 percent of the ARNG and over 30 percent of the ANG.

The backbone of the national guard is the drilling reservist. Current law requires drilling reservists to perform a minimum of 48 drills and fifteen days annual training per year. Under current training guidelines, this represents a minimum of 39 days of training per year. The average "part-time" officer trains in excess of 81 days per year, with certain specialties (aviators for example) averaging well in excess of 100 days per year.

In addition to training days, drilling reservists are required to continue their professional military education by taking courses from military schools. These courses may be completed in an active duty status or through correspondence courses, either of which requires the devotion of additional time to the national guard. Between 25 and 40 percent of the time devoted to training by M-Day members is unpaid, indicating a high level of dedication by members who also maintain full-time civilian employment.

National guard officers typically have several years active duty service prior to transferring to the national guard, often bringing immensely valuable experience with them. Prime examples of this are national guard pilots, who are normally trained on active duty. By the time many of these pilots transfer to the national guard, they have often accumulated thousands of flying hours. For this reason, national guard pilots are, on the average, slightly older and more experienced than their regular counterparts.

Current Issues

Several major concerns for the national guard have surfaced in recent years. Most involve the current economic debate over defense spending in the United States, but one is unique to the national guard and is tied closely to the increased reliance on the national guard by the total force.

Integration of the national guard into the total force has resulted in many national guard units deploying for overseas training, sometimes under controversial circumstances. The deployment of national guard units for training in Honduras in 1986 provoked several state governors, led by Gov. Michael Dukakis of Massachusetts, to challenge the authority of the federal government to deploy the national guard outside the United States without a mobilization. Congress responded in 1987 with legislation (the Montgomery Amendment) that withdrew from governors the right to cancel guard training. Two lawsuits, one in Minnesota and one in Massachusetts, challenged the constitutionality of the Montgomery Amendment. Courts in both states upheld the amendment, indicating that it falls within the authority granted the federal government in the militia clause of the Constitution. The Supreme Court has refused to review the case, leaving the lower court rulings intact.

Another area of concern for the national guard is the effects of increased training requirements and commitments on drilling reservists. Recent surveys of reserve component personnel indicate that many drilling reservists are at the limits of their available training time. The combination of full-time civilian employment and an average national guard commitment of 81 days per year for officers does not leave these individuals with many days for recreation or family. The challenge is to use the available time more effectively.

Operation Desert Storm

The first test of the total force policy for the U.S. National Guard was Operation Desert Shield/Desert Storm—the U.S. and coalition operation to liberate Kuwait after the Iraqi invasion of 2 August 1990. Both the Army National Guard (ARNG) and the Air National Guard (ANG) participated heavily in this operation. A total of 75,398 national guardsmen were called to active duty for Operation Desert Storm: 63,398 from the ARNG and 12,000 from the ANG.

The ARNG supplied 297 units and about 37,500 personnel to the force in the Persian Gulf. Two ARNG field atillery brigade headquarters and 5 field artillery battalions supported the combat operations of XVIII Airborne Corps and VII Corps. Combat engineer units included three engineer group headquarters, two engineer combat heavy battalions, a battalion headquarters, six separate companies, and five fire fighting detachments. The ARNG provided 65 military police, 39 composite support, 36 medical, 25 quartermaster, and 74 transportation units, as well as 2 postal, 1 personnel services, 5 military intelligence, 6 air traffic control, 9 ordnance, 5 public affairs, and 3 military history units. The overall contribution of the ARNG to total army strength in the Persian Gulf was about 13 percent, and it provided 3 percent of the combat strength, almost 13 percent of the combat support, and about 23 percent of the combat service support troops. In addition, sixteen units with about 3,400 ARNG personnel were deployed to Europe, and 71 units with 22,500 personnel were called up and used in the United States, including three combat brigades.

The most controversial aspect of ARNG participation in Operation Desert Storm concerned three combat brigades that had been assigned as roundout brigades to augment active component divisions in the event of a mobilization. The 48th Infantry Brigade (Mechanized) of the Georgia National Guard was to round out the 24th Infantry Division (Mechanized); the 155th Armor Brigade from Mississippi, the 1st Cavalry Division; and the 256th Infantry Brigade from Louisiana, the 5th Infantry Division (Mechanized). Although the 24th Infantry and 1st Cavalry divisions were deployed to the Persian Gulf in August and September of 1990, their roundout brigades (the 48th and 155th) were not called up until November and December and then only under heavy pressure by Congress to use the ARNG combat brigades. Although the 5th Infantry Division did not deploy, its roundout brigade (the 256th) was also called up in November 1990. The army said that it did not call up these roundout brigades because of uncertainty initially over the availability and length of service of the guardsmen and because General Schwarzkopf wanted combat-ready units—and it would take the ARNG brigades several weeks to get ready. The army therefore substituted active brigades for the 48th and 155th roundout brigades. The three roundout brigades were eventually called up, however, and were given three to five months of training, which for some units included exercises at the U.S. Army's National Training Center. With few exceptions, the ARNG units performed well in the training, and the 48th Brigade was validated as ready for deployment. The other two bridgades did not complete their training before the war was over.

Critics of the performance of the roundout brigades tend to ignore the fact that these units were not expected to be as ready as active units and were supposed to undergo several weeks of post-mobilization training before being sent into battle. They performed much better than in any previous mobilization of national guard combat units of brigade of division size. Ironically, if the 48th and 155th brigades had been called up and deployed with their parent divisions, they would have been able to train for four months in the desert and have been combat ready when the five-day ground war started on 24 February 1991.

Air National Guardsmen responded to the emergency within 24 hours after the Iraqi invasion of Kuwait, as KC-135 aerial tankers, tactical airlift C-130s, and strategic airlift C-5As and C141s volunteered to support the deployment of U.S. forces to the Persian Gulf. After the president authorized the mobilization of reserve units on 22 August 1990, ANG tactical fighter, reconnaissance, and support units were called up and deployed to the theater. After the air war started on 16 January 1991, ANG F-16 aircraft participated in the first daylight bombing raids against Iraq, and ANG RF-4 aircraft flew 367 reconnaissance missions over Iraq. ANG strategic airlift aircraft hauled about 67,000 passengers and 133,500 tons of cargo to the theater, and ANG tactical airlift aircraft hauled 40,000 passengers and 21,000 tons of cargo within the theater. ANG tankers flew 3,500 missions to refuel over 14,000 aircraft en route to their destinations. Just over 2,000 ANG personnel were deployed to the Persian Gulf; another 3,000 were deployed to other overseas locations—primarily Europe—and 7,000 were employed in the United States to provide support for the forces in the Persian Gulf.

Outlook for the National Guard

Under the pressure of reductions in the defense budget brought about by the end of the cold war, it is certain that the strength and force structure of the U.S. National Guard will be reduced. The ANG is likely to remain at about the same strength and receive additional missions from the air force as the active component is reduced, but the ARNG is likely to undergo major reductions. Some of the major ARNG organizations that existed in 1991 were already scheduled for inactivation in 1992 and later years. The ARNG has been programmed in the DOD budget to be reduced by 1995 to a force of 400,000 personnel with eight divisions and fewer than twenty combat brigades. Whether these programmed reductions will actually occur is uncertain because the National Guard has strong support in Congress and many units are justified on the basis of state missions as well as the federal mission.

Whatever the outcome of current and future deliberations regarding its size, the U.S. National Guard has repeatedly demonstrated its worth to the nation since colonial times, most recently by its contribution to the overwhelming victory achieved in Operation Desert Storm. It is certain to continue to be a major element of the military power of the United States.

W. Thralls

SEE ALSO: Cadre; Conscription; Military Aid to the Civil Power; Manpower, Military; National Guards: International Concepts; Reserve Components; Territorial Army.

Bibliography

Creso, L. D. 1982. *Citizens in arms: The army and the militia in American society to the War of 1812.* Chapel Hill, N.C.: Univ. of North Carolina Press.

Dupuy, R. E. 1971. *The national guard: A compact history.* New York: Hawthorne Books.

Galvin, J. R. 1989. *The minutemen.* McLean, Va.: Brassey's.

Gross, C. J. 1985. *Prelude to the total force: The air national guard, 1943–1969.* Washington, D.C.: Office of Air Force History.

Hylton-Green, R., and R. K. Wright, Jr. 1986. *A brief history of the militia and the national guard.* Washington, D.C.: National Guard Bureau.

Mahon, J. K. 1983. *History of the militia and the national guard.* New York: Macmillan.

Prewitt, D. M. 1987. *Citizen soldiers: A history of the army national guard.* Fort Leavenworth, Kans.: Combat Studies Institute, U.S. Army Command and General Staff College.

Wilson, B. J., III, ed. 1985. *The guard and reserve in the total force: The first decade 1973–1983.* Washington, D.C.: National Defense Univ. Press.

NATIONAL GUARDS: INTERNATIONAL CONCEPTS

National Guard is widely recognized as the name of the militia—the organized units of citizen-soldiers available for service in time of emergency. In some countries, however, the national guard is not the militia but all or part of the full-time armed forces, and many countries use other names for their organized militia, frequently incorporating the word *guard* in the name.

By whatever name, these militia forces of almost all countries constitute an important element of the armed forces reserve for wartime use or serve as paramilitary forces available for a variety of missions.

The National Guard of the United States is the most fully organized such force, with more than 500,000 personnel in units of the army and the air force. All these units hold 48 training sessions at their home stations plus at least two weeks of active-duty training each year. The national guard is under the command of state governors for service in local or state emergencies of any kind but also constitutes a major element of the U.S. reserve components available for federal service in a full or partial mobilization for a national emergency or in peacetime under many different circumstances.

Historical Background

From earliest recorded history, communities organized to defend themselves against invaders. By the sixteenth century in England, the militia was separated into two categories: those who would serve only in case of a crisis and those who were members of organized and trained groups.

In later years in the United States as well as in other countries of the world, the public feared large "standing armies" and relied on the militia, which had the added advantage of being cheaper than full-time forces.

All of this presumed that every citizen had the obligation to serve if and when required to defend the country. That presumption still exists in most countries of the world and is reflected in the current organization of national guards and similar military organizations. Many nations today still maintain citizen-soldiers in both categories of a personnel pool and in fully staffed and equipped units.

National Guards as the Militia

In addition to the United States, many other countries use the name *national guard* for the organized militia and place great reliance on those units and personnel as all or part of the armed forces reserve and/or as paramilitary forces available for a variety of missions.

Within the North Atlantic Treaty Organization (NATO) countries, Greece maintains a national guard of 110,000 as a major element of its reserves with 22 infantry brigades, 6 mountain brigades, and 16 independent infantry battalions. The Greek National Guard is responsible for coastal and island defense and for rear area security. In addition, 15,000 national guard personnel serve as cadre for the active-duty territorial army.

In neighboring Turkey, also a NATO nation, the national guard is a paramilitary force with a strength of 50,000 in 45 home-defense battalions. Turkey maintains a separate reserve force of 951,000 personnel with an obligation to age 46.

The national guard in Saudi Arabia is also the principal paramilitary force under the Ministry of the Interior, consisting of 56,000 troops in two mechanized infantry brigades and a ceremonial cavalry squadron. In addition, 10,000 members of the national guard are on active duty with the armed forces.

The Argentine national guard, totaling 200,000 troops, comprises more than 50 percent of the total armed forces reserve. The remaining armed forces are made up of a territorial guard of 50,000 (as a second element of the reserve) and an active force of 95,000.

The El Salvador national guard, one of several paramilitary forces in that country, has a strength of 4,200. The other paramilitary forces have a combined strength of about 20,000, and organized opposition forces in El Salvador consist of a coalition of five groups with strength up to 7,000.

The national guard in Egypt has a strength of 60,000 and is one of several paramilitary forces in the country. Egypt maintains a separate armed forces reserve of 600,000.

Kuwait's palace guard and border guards comprise the national guard.

The Mauritanian national guard is the largest of several paramilitary forces in Mauritania. It has a strength of 2,800 compared with the active force of 11,000.

The Mujahid Force, Janbaz Force, National Cadet Corps, and Women Guards are the elements that make up the Pakistani National Guard's paramilitary force of 75,000.

Sudan's national guard is a small paramilitary force with a strength of only 500. The active armed forces have a strength of 57,700.

Also a paramilitary force, the Tunisia National Guard consists of 7,000 members, including a coastal patrol with thirteen watercraft.

National Guards as Active Forces

In at least three countries the national guard is all or part of the active armed forces.

Panama's armed forces were referred to as the *national guard*. This force with a strength of about 12,000 was both the army and the police. This factor was part of the conflict within Panama and between Panama and the United States, which led to U.S. intervention in 1989.

In Venezuela the national guard, with troop numbers totaling 20,000, is part of the active armed forces, which have a total of about 69,000. The national guard is well equipped with weapons and aircraft, and its missions include internal security and customs.

The national guard in the Republic of Cyprus is the active armed force. It has a strength of 13,000 in two division headquarters, one mechanized infantry brigade, one infantry brigade and eighteen infantry battalions, six artillery battalions, and other support units. Cyprus has a separate militia as its reserve, with 36 light infantry battalions.

National Guards Under Other Names

Most other countries of the world maintain militia organizations like national guards under a variety of names. Exceptions are those countries that rely on a reserve staffed by conscripts who have a remaining obligation after their active service. These countries are in the minority.

Other NATO Countries

Most of the NATO countries (other than the United States, Greece, and Turkey, as already mentioned) maintain organized militias in addition to their reserves of recallable conscripts or volunteers. In most cases the militia troops are important elements of the reserve forces.

In Belgium eleven motorized infantry regiments and four infantry battalions constitute the territorial defense force, part of the reserves.

Canada's militia is the primary army reserve, with a strength of 17,200 that is to be increased. It consists of 52 infantry, eight armored, eighteen artillery, eleven engineer, and twenty support units at the battalion level.

The Home Guard of Denmark is an important element of national defense, with strengths of 58,400 army, 7,600 navy, and 11,700 air force, all constituting part of the reserve structure.

France maintains a territorial defense army organized in six military regions, each having a defense zone brigade.

The Federal Republic of Germany's territorial army consisted of a peacetime cadre of 41,700 in a fully organized command structure, including home defense brigades and regiments.

In the Netherlands, the Home Guard of 5,100 personnel is part of the reserves, which consist of recallable conscripts who have completed their terms of service.

The Home Guard in Norway can mobilize as many as 85,000 troops. Officers and NCOs receive one to four weeks of refresher training to age 44 and may volunteer for extension.

Spain has a Guardia Civil as a paramilitary force of 72,700 in twenty infantry regiments and other specialized units.

The United Kingdom has a fully organized territorial army of 75,000 in units and a home service force of 43 companies, soon to be increased, which are important elements of the reserves.

Warsaw Pact Nations

For its reserve forces the former Soviet Union relied on conscription with extended reserve obligations to age 50 for all males and did not have a separate militia as such. However, this conscription system produced a reserve of 6,217,000 with service in the past five years and totaled over 50,000,000 with remaining obligations to age 50.

Other Warsaw Pact nations maintained organized militias. Bulgaria had 150,000 in the People's Territorial Militia, a paramilitary force.

There were 120,000 troops in Czechoslovakia's militia, an armed paramilitary force.

Three thousand regular troops and a potential strength of 500,000 in 15,000 armed combat groups made up the German Democratic Republic's Workers' Militia paramilitary force.

Hungary also had a paramilitary Workers' Militia of 60,000 troops.

In Poland the paramilitary Citizens' Militia comprised 350,000 troops.

Romania had the Patriotic Guard as a local defense force of 250,000, with about 12,000 on full-time status.

Other European Nations

Other European nations not aligned with NATO or the former Warsaw Pact have similar structures. Sweden has 550,000 in its local defense and home guard army units. In addition, it has about 35,000 volunteers for army units from voluntary auxiliary organizations including the Motorcycle Corps, Radio Organization, and Women's Motor Transport Corps.

Switzerland has compulsory universal service. Its *Landwehr* (militia) gets regular annual refresher training up to age 42, and its *Landsturm* (home guard) gets 13 days' training over each two-year period to age 50.

The militia in Yugoslavia was the territorial defense force with a wartime strength of 860,000 in mobile infantry, artillery, and antiaircraft units.

Middle East and North Africa

Most countries of this area maintain forces with the words *militia* or *guard* in the names.

In Iran the home guard is reported to have a strength of 2,500,000 controlled by the Revolutionary Guard Corps. These forces are loosely organized and separate from the national organized reserves.

Iraq's militia is known as the People's Army, a paramilitary force of 650,000 (before the 1991 Gulf War) that served as the armed forces reserve.

Conscription in Israel includes both males and females and obligates males for reserve unit service to age 54. After that, males may volunteer for civil guard or civil defense service.

The Civil Militia People's Army in Jordan is a paramilitary force of about 15,000.

Libya's People's Militia of 40,000 is the armed forces reserve for an active force of 71,500.

Oman has a Tribal Home Guard paramilitary force of 3,500.

In Somalia the People's Militia is a paramilitary force of 20,000.

Sub-Saharan Africa

In this region the militia of most nations is referred to as *people's militia*. These nations and their militias follow:

Angola: People's Defense Organization, 50,000 in eleven brigades with 10,000 normally serving with the regular army

Benin: People's Militia of 2,000 paramilitary

Burkina Faso: People's Militia, 45,000 trained

Cape Verde: People's Militia, about 650 paramilitary

Congo: People's Militia, 4,700 paramilitary

Equatorial Guinea: Guardia Civil, two companies of trained paramilitary

Ethiopia: People's Militia is the reserve. All citizens 18 to 50 do six months' training before assignment to duties.

Ghana: People's Militia, 5,000 paramilitary

Guinea: People's Militia, 7,000 paramilitary

Ivory Coast: Militia of 1,500 paramilitary

Mali: Militia of 3,000 paramilitary

Mozambique: People's Militias are provincial troops, and Local Militias are village self-defense forces, all with total strength of about 50,000.

Seychelles: People's Militia, 5,000 paramilitary
South Africa: The Citizen Force consists of personnel who continue to serve part-time after their active conscription service. After twelve years it is voluntary.
Tanzania: Citizens Militia, 100,000 paramilitary
Zaire: Civil Guard, 25,000 paramilitary
Zimbabwe: National Militia, 20,000 paramilitary

ASIA AND AUSTRALASIA

In this region various names are applied to national guard types of forces, as follows:

China: The reserve structure has been under reorganization to merge the militia with other reserve forces. The strength of these forces is unknown but is probably more than 1 million.
Burma: People's Militia, 35,000 paramilitary
Indonesia: Militia, 300,000 a year get three weeks' basic training
North Korea: Worker/Peasant Red Militia (WPRM) of up to 3,000,000 in a command structure up to corps level with small arms and some supporting weapons.
South Korea: Civilian Defense Corps, 3,500,000
Malaysia: People's Volunteer Corps, 173,000 paramilitary
Mongolia: Militia of 15,000 under Ministry of Public Security serves as internal security troops and frontier guards.
New Zealand: Territorial Army of 6,700 constitutes part of the reserves, along with a regular reserve force.
Philippines: Citizens Armed Forces Geographical Units of about 45,000 replaced a civil home defense force.
Singapore: People's Defense Force of about 30,000 is part of the reserves.
Thailand: National Security Volunteer Corps of 33,000 is a paramilitary force.
Vietnam: People's Militia is the rural element of the People's Self-Defense Force, which has a strength of about 1 million.

CARIBBEAN AND LATIN AMERICA

The term *militia* is widely used in this region to identify these organizations, which generally are available for service as paramilitary forces.

Belize: A militia of about 350 constitutes the reserve for an active force of 700.
Brazil: State militias with strength of 243,000 are public security forces under army control and considered an army reserve.
Cuba: A territorial militia of 1,300,000 is identified as a paramilitary force separate from the reserves.
Guatemala: A territorial militia of about 725,000 is a paramilitary force but only about 15,000 are armed.
Guyana: A people's militia of 2,000 constitutes the reserve for an active force of 5,450.
Mexico: The Rural Defense Militia of 120,000 is a paramilitary force.
Nicaragua: The Sandinista Popular Militia constitutes a reserve for the army. It has about 50,000 personnel in 37 brigades.
Peru: The Rondas Campesinas is a people's militia, but its strength and organization are not available.
Suriname: The National Militia of 900 is a paramilitary force.

Future

With worldwide pressure to reduce military expenditures, most nations are likely to increase their reliance on national guard types of forces because they are less expensive to maintain than full-time active forces.

For these nations lessons can be learned from the experience of the United States and a few other nations that have invested heavily in personnel, equipment, and training to ensure that such forces can fulfill the missions assigned to them. Only in this way can the cost savings from part-time forces also be cost-effective in terms of national security.

STANFORD SMITH

SEE ALSO: Internal Security Forces; National Guard of the United States; Paramilitary Forces; Reserve Components; Reserves.

Bibliography

Andrade, J. 1985. *World police and paramilitary forces.* New York: Stockton Press.
Association of the U.S. Army. 1988. *Change and challenge: The search for peace in 1988, a global assessment.* Arlington, Va.: AUSA.
Heisbourg, F., comp. 1988. *The military balance, 1988–89.* London: International Institute for Strategic Studies.
Paxton, J., ed. 1989. *Statesman's yearbook, 1988–89.* New York: St. Martin's Press.
U.S. Department of Defense. 1988. *Reserve components of the United States armed forces.* Washington, D.C.: Office of the Assistant Secretary of Defense (Reserve Affairs).
Wright, R. K. 1986. *A brief history of the militia and the national guard.* Washington, D.C.: National Guard Bureau.

NATO (NORTH ATLANTIC TREATY ORGANIZATION)

The North Atlantic Treaty Organization (NATO) is an international organization of indefinite duration for the collective defense and security of sixteen sovereign states in Europe and North America. It provides the framework for a political and military alliance tasked to prevent aggression or to repel it, and is a basis for cooperation and consultation among the sixteen members in political, economic, and other nonmilitary fields. The political headquarters of NATO is in Brussels, Belgium; the three major military headquarters are in Mons, Belgium (for Europe); Norfolk, Virginia (for the Atlantic); and Northwood, United Kingdom (for the English Channel). In addition, there is a Regional Planning Group for the North American Area. The treaty was signed on 4 April 1949 in Washington, D.C., and the member states are Belgium, Canada, Denmark, Federal Republic of Germany (since 5 May 1955), France, Greece (since 18 February 1952), Iceland, Italy, Luxembourg, Netherlands, Norway, Portugal, Spain (since 30 May 1982), Turkey (since 18 February 1952), the United Kingdom, and the United States.

Origin of NATO

The situation in post–World War II Europe was marked by the gradually emerging, conflicting objectives of the United States, the United Kingdom, and France on one side and the Soviet Union on the other. In 1945, the Western Allies proceeded quickly with the demobilization of their forces, thus reducing the armed strength of the allied forces in Europe from 4.7 million at the end of the war to about 0.9 million in 1946. Nations in Europe addressed themselves to the complex task of reconstruction, which at the time meant not only elementary physical survival for millions of people, but in some cases the building of completely new social and political structures. The Soviet Union, on the other hand, maintained its armed forces at a wartime level, with 4 million men still under arms in Europe in 1946.

Soviet territorial expansion had begun during the war with the annexation of the Baltic states of Estonia, Latvia, and Lithuania, and with parts of Finland, northeastern Germany, Poland, eastern Czechoslovakia, and Romania. This territorial expansion was supplemented by a consolidation of control over central and southeastern Europe through the presence of Soviet troops. Together with Communist infiltration under left-wing coalition governments, this led Bulgaria, Romania, eastern Germany, Poland, Hungary, and Czechoslovakia to fall within the Soviet sphere of domination between 1945 and 1948. In addition, the Soviet Union exercised pressure on Turkey by means of territorial demands (northeastern Anatolia) and claimed the right to establish military bases in the Dardanelles. Furthermore, Greece came under Soviet pressure through a guerrilla campaign that received reinforcements from bases in Albania, Bulgaria, and Yugoslavia. This only confirmed the declared Soviet intentions to spread communism worldwide, by military power if necessary. In this way it constituted a threat to the security of the West.

In 1947, the United Kingdom and France had concluded the Treaty of Dunkirk, which was intended to provide a basis for mutual defense against Germany. It was soon to be expanded to the Brussels Treaty, signed on 17 March 1948 by Belgium, France, Luxembourg, the Netherlands, and the United Kingdom. However, in the context of what was perceived as an increasingly threatening Soviet stance in Europe, the treaty came to have a new significance. The five nations pledged themselves to build a common defense system and assured each other of "all the military aid and assistance in their power" should any of the signatories become the object of an "armed aggression in Europe." Because of the relative weakness of the five nations party to the treaty—that is, the power vacuum that left Europe exposed to Soviet pressure even without a threat of direct military attack—the treaty itself was bound to have only a limited effect as long as these countries were not joined by the United States. Already in March 1947 the U.S. government had assured "all free peoples" of its support against internal and external threats. This pledge was substantiated economically by Marshall Plan aid and politico-militarily by American (and Canadian) representatives participating in the meetings of the organs provided for by the Brussels Treaty. By responding favorably to European efforts to create an institutional basis for collective defense, the United States showed that it realized the future of Western Europe was of vital interest to it. To be of lasting impact, however, it was essential for the United States to be constitutionally able to join a defense system superseding the Brussels Treaty.

In consultation with the State Department, Senator Vandenberg drew up a resolution that recommended, in particular, "the association of the U.S. by constitutional process with such regional and other collective arrangements as are based on continuous and effective self-help and mutual aid." It also recommended that the U.S. government contribute to the maintenance of peace by making clear "its determination to exercise the right of individual or collective self-defense under Article 51 (of the United Nations Charter) should any armed attack occur affecting its national security." The five signatories of the Brussels Treaty together with Canada and the United States officially invited Denmark, Iceland, Italy, Norway, and Portugal to accede to the treaty.

The North Atlantic Treaty

On 4 April 1949 the North Atlantic Treaty was signed in Washington. It consists of fourteen articles preceded by a preamble in which the parties to the treaty, among other things, "reaffirm their faith in the purposes and principles of the charter of the United Nations"; express their determination "to safeguard the freedom, common heritage and civilization of their peoples, founded on the principles of democracy, individual liberty and the rule of law"; and declare their resolve "to unite their efforts for collective defense and for the preservation of peace and security."

Articles 1 and 2 define the basic principles to be applied by member countries in conducting their international relations and commit them to the further development of peaceful and friendly international relations, in particular by promoting conditions in the social and economic field.

The key provisions of the treaty are contained in the following articles:

> Article 3:
>
> In order more effectively to achieve the objectives of this Treaty, the Parties, separately and jointly, by means of continuous and effective self-help and mutual aid, will maintain and develop their individual and collective capacity to resist armed attack.
>
> Article 4:
>
> The Parties will consult together whenever, in the opinion of any of them, the territorial integrity, political independence or security of any of the Parties is threatened.
>
> Article 5:
>
> The Parties agree that an armed attack against one or more of them in Europe or North America shall be

> considered an attack against them all and consequently they agree that, if such an armed attack occurs, each of them, in exercise of the right of individual or collective self-defense recognized by Article 51 of the Charter of the United Nations, will assist the Party or Parties so attacked by taking forthwith, individually and in concert with the other Parties, such action as it deems necessary, including the use of armed force, to restore and maintain the security of the North Atlantic area.

Furthermore, in Article 5, member states agree that measures taken under the terms of this article shall be terminated when the UN Security Council has acted as necessary to restore and maintain international peace and security.

> Article 6:
>
> For the purpose of Article 5 an armed attack on one or more of the Parties is deemed to include an armed attack on the territory of any of the Parties in Europe or North America, on the Algerian Department of France, on the occupation forces of any Party in Europe, on the islands under the jurisdiction of any Party in the North Atlantic area north of the Tropic of Cancer or on the vessels or aircraft in this area of any of the Parties.

(The definition of the territories to which Article 5 applies was later revised by Article 2 of the Protocol to the North Atlantic Treaty of the accession of Greece and Turkey. Insofar as the former Algerian departments of France were concerned, the relevant clauses of the treaty became inapplicable 3 July 1962, the date of French recognition of Algerian independence.)

Articles 7 to 14 deal mainly with organizational and procedural matters, including the possibility of denunciation of the treaty after twenty years.

Structure of NATO

The member countries of the alliance regularly consult and exchange information and views, not only on issues involving the alliance as a whole and on matters touching on the interests of the individual member countries, but also on developments in other areas of the world.

The highest authority for political consultation and decision making is the North Atlantic Council, which on occasion meets at the level of heads of government and states of the sixteen member countries. The Council meets generally twice a year at the level of foreign ministers, once in Brussels and once in the capital of a member state. It also meets at least once a week at the level of permanent representatives, who have ambassadorial rank, at NATO headquarters in Brussels.

The primary role of the alliance is to safeguard the security of member states by deterring aggression. Matters specifically related to defense are dealt with by the Defense Planning Committee (DPC), which is composed of the thirteen member countries participating in NATO's integrated defense structure plus Iceland and Spain (i.e., all member states except France). The DPC meets twice a year at the level of defense ministers and regularly at the level of permanent representatives in Brussels.

Nuclear defense policy is developed in the Nuclear Planning Group (NPG), which has the same composition as the DPC. The NPG also meets twice a year, but not necessarily at NATO headquarters.

The chairman of the Council/DPC at both the ministerial and permanent representative level is the secretary general of NATO. Much of the work of the North Atlantic Council/DPC is carried out under his aegis through permanent and temporary committees composed of the international staff and members of national delegations; they give advice and make recommendations. Decisions are taken unanimously by the Council/DPC.

In addition to these political arrangements, the alliance also has a military structure; the Military Committee (MC) is its highest military authority. It is composed of the chiefs of defense of all member states, except France and Iceland. (France is represented by the chief of the French Military Mission to the MC; Iceland can be represented by a civilian.)

The chiefs of defense meet at least three times a year or whenever it is deemed necessary. However, to enable the MC to function on a continual basis with effective powers of decision, each chief of defense appoints a permanent military representative. On this level, the MC meets at least once a week. The chairman of the MC is elected by the chiefs of defense, usually for a three-year period.

The MC gives advice to the Council, DPC, and NPG on those matters necessary for the common defense of the NATO area, and gives guidance on military matters to the Major NATO Commanders (MNC). It is also responsible for a number of NATO military agencies and for the NATO Defense College in Rome. The MC is assisted by an integrated international military staff.

Under the general guidance of the MC, the three MNCs are responsible for planning the defense of their areas and for conducting NATO's land, sea, and air exercises; they assume command and control over allied forces in war. In peacetime, the forces of member countries remain under national command; however, some are placed under operational command or control of NATO (e.g., air defense forces in Europe to the operational command of the Supreme Allied Commander Europe [SACEUR]), some are already assigned to NATO commands, and others are earmarked for these commands. The Federal Republic of Germany is the only NATO country to assign all combat units of its armed forces and two major formations of its territorial army to NATO in peacetime.

There is also a structure of allied headquarters at lower levels.

Evolution of NATO

Immediately after NATO's founding, the North Atlantic Council and the DPC were created. Then, in 1949, the Military Committee (MC), with a Standing Group composed of representatives of France, the United Kingdom, and the United States as its executive body, was established in Washington. A structure for collective defense was initiated by five regional planning groups for Northern, Western, and Southern Europe and one each for the North Atlantic area and North America. Furthermore, a Defense Financial and Economic Committee and—as a subcommittee to the MC—a Defense Production Board were set up.

In 1950, it was decided that ongoing work in the Council and in the MC should be coordinated by deputies to the foreign ministers meeting in continuous session in London. In 1951, however, the Defense Financial and Economic Committee and the Defense Committee were dissolved, as their tasks were given to the Council.

The first major military command, called the Supreme Headquarters Allied Powers in Europe (SHAPE), was installed in 1951 in Rocquencourt near Paris; the three European planning groups became NATO commands Europe North, Center, and South under the authority of SACEUR. In addition to SHAPE, the two other major NATO commands—Supreme Allied Commander Atlantic (SACLANT) and Commander-in-Chief Channel (CINCHAN)—were formed. Also in 1951, an Agreement between the Parties to the North Atlantic Treaty Regarding the Status of Their Forces was signed. This agreement determined the legal status of military personnel of one member country called to serve under NATO command in another country (later expanded by supplementary agreements).

In 1952, the post of secretary general was created to head a permanent international secretariat. To facilitate communication and cooperation among military authorities in Europe, the political headquarters of NATO was moved to Paris. Each member state appointed a permanent representative (i.e., ambassador to NATO), supported by a national delegation of advisers and experts, in order to allow the North Atlantic Council to function in permanent session. This basic organizational structure—a Council of permanent representatives that is chaired by the secretary general, who is assisted by the international staff (IS), and a Military Committee, which is composed of military representatives of member states and is presided over by the chairman of the MC, who is assisted by the international military staff (IMS)—has been maintained ever since.

Greece and Turkey acceded to NATO on 18 February 1952. After negotiations for a European Defense Community (EDC) had been going on for about two years among Belgium, France, the Federal Republic of Germany, Italy, Luxembourg, and the Netherlands, the treaty was signed in Paris on 27 May 1952. The North Atlantic Council agreed to work closely with the EDC. In case of a military conflict, EDC forces were intended to be placed under NATO command. However, as a result of the French National Assembly's rejection of the EDC treaty in August 1954, other ways to integrate the Federal Republic of Germany in a Western defense framework were considered. Results of these deliberations at the London Conference in September–October 1954 were approved at subsequent meetings in Paris in October 1954 and embodied in the Paris Agreements. Essentially, it was agreed that

- France, the United Kingdom, and the United States would terminate the occupation regime in the Federal Republic of Germany and recognize it as a sovereign state.
- The Federal Republic of Germany would undertake to authorize the maintenance of foreign forces on its territory.
- The Federal Republic of Germany and Italy would accede to the Brussels Treaty, the seven European countries thus creating the Western European Union (WEU).
- The Federal Republic of Germany would be invited to become a member of NATO with armed forces to be integrated into the forces of the alliance.
- The United States and the United Kingdom would undertake to maintain their forces on the European continent for as long as necessary.
- A unified military formation would be established by assigning to SACEUR all member countries' forces (with certain exceptions) stationed within the area of his command.

The Federal Republic of Germany's accession to NATO became effective 5 May 1955.

In May 1956, the North Atlantic Council decided to have a committee of three foreign ministers (Pearson from Canada; Martino from Italy; Lange from Norway) examine ways and means to improve and extend NATO cooperation in nonmilitary fields and develop greater unity within the Atlantic Community. "The Report of the Committee of the Three on Non-military Cooperation" was adopted by the Council in December 1956. It recommended full and timely consultation between NATO member governments on issues of common concern. Foreign ministers were called to make an assessment of the political progress of the alliance in each of their spring sessions, based on a statement by the secretary general. It was recommended that NATO member states submit any dispute they had not been able to solve among themselves to "good offices" procedures under NATO before turning to any other international institution or organization. Furthermore, in directing attention to science and technology as an area of special importance to the Atlantic Community, the report was the origin of the subsequently established NATO Science Committee.

In 1952, NATO adopted a strategy of massive retaliation as serving best the goal to deter any potential aggressor. It implied that any aggression would be stopped as close to the border as possible (forward defense), if necessary by threatening the use of U.S. strategic nuclear systems. By the mid to late fifties, with the Soviet Union also developing strategic nuclear capabilities, the United States became vulnerable to a Soviet threat; this strategy thus began to lose much of its credibility as a deterrent and the United States moved toward graduated deterrence as a strategy more suited to match the qualitatively enhanced Soviet posture. During the transatlantic strategy discussions that followed, questions were raised as to whether and under what circumstances the United States might be willing to defend non-American treaty areas by making use of, if necessary, strategic nuclear forces.

The nonnuclear members, such as the Federal Republic of Germany and Italy, became increasingly interested in matters concerning nuclear defense and in taking part in the process by which the strategy governing nuclear weapons was developed and implemented. Some physical sharing of nuclear forces had been adopted by cooperative arrangements with dual key systems (i.e., nuclear warheads under U.S. control, delivery vehicles under control of allies). Proposals for a nuclear Multilateral Force (MLF) in 1962, and in 1964 an Atlantic Nuclear Force (ANF), designed to establish a mode of multilateral ownership for nuclear systems, were discussed but rejected. In the end, NATO opted for improvements in allied consultation on the possible use of nuclear weapons and for an enhanced role of interested allies in the process of nuclear planning. As a result, the Nuclear Planning Group (NPG), made up of ministers of defense, was created in 1967. Membership to this group was limited until 1970 to seven—the United States, the United Kingdom, Italy, and the Federal Republic of Germany as permanent members and three other members serving in rotation. In the 1970s, the membership formula was modified to accommodate the desire of other countries to be included in the NPG work. The differentiation between permanent and rotating membership therefore was given up. In the 1980s, membership increased to fourteen countries—all except Iceland (which since December 1987 has observer status) and France.

During 1967 there was also a change in NATO's strategy from Massive Retaliation to Flexible Response. According to this concept, NATO should be able to deter, and if necessary counter, military aggression of varying scales in any region of the NATO area through a wide range of forces equipped with a well-balanced mixture of conventional theater nuclear and strategic nuclear weapons.

In the sixties, NATO underwent one of its most testing phases with France redefining its membership. At the end of almost a decade of intensive discussions, France's allies had agreed to a change of strategy, but France continued to adhere to massive retaliation. At the same time, France increased its efforts to become, after the United States and the United Kingdom, the third Western nuclear power. Primarily for reasons of strategy, France finally withdrew from NATO's integrated military structure, yet remained a member of the alliance. The Standing Group was disestablished and its authority was transferred to the Military Committee.

As a consequence of France's withdrawal, SHAPE, the allied military headquarters, was moved to Mons, Belgium, in March 1967. In October 1967, NATO's political headquarters was transferred to Brussels.

The strategy discussions in the alliance had reinforced the importance of conventional forces to deterrence and defense. From the outset it was clear that only by combining efforts, pooling resources, and sharing responsibilities could sufficient force capabilities be provided. An elaborate system of dividing roles and tasks in a common force posture was adopted. Since then, more than ever before, every member country depends for its security on the forces of its allies and no country can guarantee its security on its own.

A detailed procedure for common force planning has evolved to ensure an adequate overall force posture and a rational division of effort among member states. Over the years this has resulted in an increasing interdependence of national force contributions that progressively subordinate purely individual considerations to the overall NATO requirements.

The unique collective consideration of an overall allied defense posture and of member countries' contributions to it is being increasingly supported by joint planning in logistics, infrastructure, and civil emergency matters.

On the political side, by the end of 1966, the NATO Council had set up a committee under the chairmanship of the then Belgian foreign minister Pierre Harmel to "study the future tasks which face the Alliance and its procedures for fulfilling them in order to strengthen the Alliance as a factor for durable peace." In December 1967, the Council adopted the text emerging from this examination, which was to be called the Harmel Report. The document described NATO as having two main functions: maintaining "adequate military strength and political solidarity to deter aggression and other forms of pressure and to defend the territory of member countries if aggression should occur" and, in this climate, as the second function, pursuing "the search for progress towards a more stable relationship in which the underlying political issues can be solved." The gist of NATO's philosophy was contained in the sentence, "Military security and a policy of detente are not contradictory but complementary." The Harmel Report stated, furthermore, that "the ultimate political purpose of the Alliance is to achieve a just and lasting peaceful order in Europe accompanied by appropriate security guarantees," and that "any such settlement must end the unnatural barriers between Eastern and Western Europe which are most clearly and cruelly manifested in the division of Germany."

The Harmel Report has been the basis for NATO's policy in the decades since 1967. It has given additional impetus to political consultation on a broad range of intra- and extra-alliance matters. In the field of some arms control negotiations and related issues, NATO has even assumed a management role, as NATO-agreed positions are being elaborated in Brussels on the basis of instructions from capitals.

Since 1968, a Committee on the Challenges of Modern Society has had interested member states carry out a number of pilot studies that cover a wide range of activities dealing with aspects of environmental protection and the quality of life.

In 1968, EUROGROUP, an informal group now comprising all the European members of NATO except France and Iceland, was established. It ensures that the European contribution to common defense is as strong and cohesive as possible.

NATO's two-track decision in December 1979 was a reflection of the Harmel approach. It provided for the modernization of the alliance's land-based longer range theater nuclear forces and proposed U.S.-Soviet arms control negotiations with the objective of establishing agreed limitations on these systems. Standing by this decision by beginning to deploy, despite veiled and open Soviet pressure on selected allies and the Soviets' leaving the negotiation table in 1983, NATO demonstrated a firmness that was instrumental in leading to Soviet acceptance of the Western proposal for a global zero-solution for U.S. and Soviet land-based intermediate-range nuclear forces. The treaty between the United States and the Soviet Union on the elimination of their intermediate-range and shorter-range missiles, which took effect 1 June 1988, accomplished the long-standing alliance objective of eliminating a class of Soviet nuclear weapons and establishing unprecedented standards in verification procedures and in achieving asymmetric reductions. Although contested by some on strategic grounds, it represented a political success for the alliance.

Meanwhile, in 1982, Spain also acceded to NATO and had membership confirmed by the Spanish people in a 1986 referendum.

Intra-Alliance Problems and Contradictions

Although the list of NATO accomplishments is long (e.g., securing peace through deterrence, fostering political consultation, and working together in a variety of military and nonmilitary fields), NATO has not been without its share of internal problems and contradictions.

For instance, there were temporary situations where the political structures in some member states were in conflict with the alliance's purposes and principles as expressed in the preamble to the treaty; Portugal, until its revolution in 1974, was a case in point. NATO's position was generally that of a benevolent admonisher preferring patience and political persuasion over a strict insistence on compatibility of political structures with the alliance's basic democratic principles. However, it should be noted that moves to invite Franco's Spain to accede to NATO were opposed because of the undemocratic nature of the regime.

Furthermore, NATO's role in solving bilateral conflicts between member states did not always live up to expectations. Indeed, NATO's efforts to help in disputes between Greece and Turkey (over rights in the Aegean Sea and over Cyprus) and between the United Kingdom and Iceland (over fishing rights) met with rather limited success, although it was largely NATO's influence that prevented the conflicts from deteriorating further.

As might be expected in an alliance of sixteen sovereign states, internal issues have often arisen resulting from different historic developments and varying definitions of national interest. Some of these issues were or are of considerable political importance—for example, those over Suez in 1956, the Nuclear Test Ban Treaty in 1963, strategy discussions, arms control initiatives, and regional conflicts outside NATO.

The global interests and commitments of the United States often differ from the regionally more confined outlooks of other member states, a fact that tends to cause friction within the alliance. There is a discrepancy between, on the one hand, the undiminished dependence of Western Europe on U.S. military power and, on the other, the evolution brought about by Europe's economic development changing the transatlantic relationship from that of dependents to competitors and in many ways challenging the U.S.'s erstwhile political dominance. In this context, periodic efforts in the United States to have European members accept a greater share of the defense burden have at times led to an atmosphere of recrimination.

Efforts to get NATO involved in out-of-area activities have sometimes resulted in tensions, especially between the United States and its European allies. In the early years of the alliance, the United States was determined not to allow its allies to use NATO for the preservation of their empires in decline. Later, it was the United States that sought NATO support in crises in other regions of the world.

Outlook

Taking into account the high degree of political and military interaction based on the free will of sixteen member states, the North Atlantic Treaty Organization has been, by standards of traditional alliances, an impressive and successful undertaking. Its concept of deterrence has worked. NATO has been able to transgress the narrow limits of a purely military grouping by expanding cooperation into nonmilitary fields and thus increasing solidarity and cohesion among its members. Obviously, each member state derived enough benefits from the alliance so as not to invoke the denunciation clause of the treaty. Spain's accession 33 years after the founding of the alliance is testimony to its undiminished strength and attraction. The adoption and application of policies promoting cooperation, detente, and arms control on the basis of strength and solidarity have improved prospects for a more stable relationship with the East.

As long as NATO's ultimate political purpose, as laid down in the Harmel Report, remains unachieved, the alliance is likely to remain a necessity for its members. NATO's future is linked to the role the United States will play in dealing with threats to Western security, and to the extent to which the European member states will be willing to accept their share of roles, risks, and responsibilities within the alliance. The debate on the equitable sharing of the defense burden will continue, because distribution of the burden may need to be adjusted continuously in light of political, economic, and social developments occurring in member countries. All of this will be influenced by the development of the future threat to Western security and the perception of that threat by the public. There is a danger that NATO might fall victim to its very success. Public support may tend to decline the more peace is perceived as a permanent achievement. Governments will have to make clear to their publics that stability, security, and peace are the result of a politico-military balance that requires a continual effort if it is to be safeguarded.

For the most recent information on this organization, the reader may refer to the following annual publications:

The Military Balance. International Institute for Strategic Studies. London: Brassey's (UK).

The Statesman's Year-Book. New York: St. Martin's Press.

The World Factbook. Central Intelligence Agency. Washington, D.C.: Brassey's (US.)

ROLF SCHUMACHER
ROLF BRABAND

SEE ALSO: Arms Control; Cold War; Escalation; Exercises; Flexible Response; Forward Defense; NATO Policy and Strategy; Nuclear Powers; Policy, Defense; United Nations; Warsaw Pact; Warsaw Pact Policy and Strategy.

Bibliography

Buchan, A. 1963. *NATO in the 1960s*. New York: Praeger.
Cleveland, H. 1970. *NATO: The transatlantic bargain*. New York: Harper and Row.
Ismay, H. L. *NATO: The first five years 1949–1954*. Paris: NATO.
Jackson, H. M., ed. 1967. *The Atlantic alliance*. New York: Praeger.
Kissinger, H. A. 1965. *The troubled partnership*. New York: McGraw-Hill.
Myers, K. A., ed. 1980. *NATO: The next thirty years*. Boulder, Colo.: Westview Press.
NATO. 1981. *NATO basic documents*. Brussels: NATO Information Service.
———. 1984. *The North Atlantic Treaty Organisation. Facts and figures*. Brussels: NATO Information Service.
Neustadt, R. E. 1970. *Alliance politics*. New York: Columbia Univ. Press.
Spaak, P. H. 1959. *Why NATO?* Baltimore, Md.: Penguin Books.
Stikker, D. U. 1966. *Men of responsibility*. New York: Harper and Row.

NATO POLICY AND STRATEGY

Founding the North Atlantic Treaty Organization (NATO) in 1949 was the military and political answer of the free Western democracies to the growing threat from the Soviet Union that developed in the years following the end of World War II. It was the consequence of the unsuccessful attempts of the victorious powers of World War II to come up with a workable, peaceful political order based on the territorial delimitation of Europe between East and West as agreed on at Yalta in 1945. NATO also represents the historic unlimited commitment of the United States to ensure the security and peaceful development of the free nations of Western Europe.

Established as a defense system based on mutual assistance, NATO is primarily a political alliance. Its member countries retain full sovereignty, and the goals laid down in the North Atlantic Treaty emphasize the priority of peaceful settlement of conflicts in accordance with the provisions of the UN Charter. In the absence of automatic military assistance, NATO provides military security to its member states on the basis of voluntarily integrated and committed military capabilities. Based on the political, economic, and military concentration of power of the initial twelve founding nations under the leadership of and protected by the might of the United States, NATO has gradually developed its might and influence in designing the post-World War II order by means of political-organizational procedures. Solidarity and collectivity are the most decisive characteristics of the Atlantic Alliance.

The U.S.'s nuclear weapons arsenal played an outstanding role in this process. In the years of nuclear monopoly it lightened the burden of U.S. security commitments to European countries and was the cornerstone for the American policy of engaging in an alliance. Militarily, it gave the United States the assurance of being invincible. For the non-nuclear NATO member countries, the U.S. nuclear arsenal assured the military superiority of the treaty organization they participated in, despite the overwhelming conventional military potential of the Soviet Union directly at their borders. For these countries, the nuclear potential of the United States was viewed as the only guarantee of the security and survival of their national existence.

In line with its political goals and ideological values, NATO has tailored its military strategy exclusively to deter any use of military force directed against its member countries. Nuclear weapons constitute the ultimate means to prevent war by deterrence. In view of their enormous destructive power, the principle of deterrence provides for the ethical and moral justification for planning the employment of nuclear weapons in case of aggression.

The decades of the postwar era have been characterized by the inexorable antagonism between the humanitarian values, the social orders, and the political systems of West and East and by the potential for military confrontation between the United States with its allies and the Soviet Union with the countries aligned in the Warsaw Treaty Organization since 1955. NATO has successfully adapted its organization, procedures, and strategies to changing boundaries and national policies of its member countries. The historically incomparable contribution made by the North Atlantic Alliance in preserving the peace and freedom of the peoples of the West during these 45 years, surmounting all internal crises and any conflicting interests between Europe and North America, is a result of both the solidarity shown by the member countries and the coupling of the military power of the United States to the security and freedom of Europe.

Shaping the North Atlantic Alliance

In the North Atlantic Treaty signed in Washington on 4 April 1949, twelve North American and European countries (Belgium, Canada, Denmark, France, Iceland, Italy, Luxembourg, the Netherlands, Norway, Portugal, United Kingdom, United States; 1952 accession of Greece and Turkey; 1955 accession of the Federal Republic of Germany; 1982 accession of Spain) pledged to provide mutual military assistance in order to stand up against the rigorous policy of expansion and oppression pursued by the Soviet Union in the post-World War II years and to help bring about the economic and social formation of a free Europe. With the historic decision to permanently link its future to that of Europe on a treaty basis, the United States established its claim as a world power to comprehensively protect freedom and democracy. Neither the United Nations (charter signed in San Francisco on 26 June 1945), nor the early association of European states (Western Union, the Brussels treaty of 1948, the Western European Union as of 1954) afforded sufficient protection in Europe against the threat from the East. To preserve peace and freedom as well as to uphold democracy and human rights in the face of communism, political oppression, and the use of military power as a political means by the Soviet Union required alliance with the United States.

Without the aggressive power policy pursued by Stalin between 1946 and 1948, there would have been no North Atlantic Treaty. The one-year blockade of the access routes to Berlin by Soviet forces, which began in June 1948, was of contributory significance. Following the end of World War II the United States intended to largely withdraw from Europe. The United States expected the United Nations Organization, established in 1945 to be the new custodian of order worldwide. But after Canada supported the idea of a single transatlantic defense system in April 1948, to include the Brussels Treaty and based on mutual assistance, the United States gave up its initial hesitation. The Vandenberg Resolution of June 1948 provided for the constitutional requirements necessary for U.S. participation in the Atlantic Alliance. For the United States the 1949 treaty establishing NATO was a logically consistent follow-up to the policy of containing Soviet expansionist efforts.

The Soviet Union had emerged from World War II as the new Eastern world power. It rejected the Marshall Plan for the collective reconstruction of the whole of Europe, and it forced the governments of its satellite states in East and Southeast Europe to make the same decision. In response to the Marshall Plan, the Soviet Union brought all European Communist parties into line by reestablishing the Cominform (Communist Information Bureau). In light of the Canadian trailblazing and the forceful expansionist policy pursued by the Soviet Union, the United States eased its restraint and became more heavily involved in the security of Europe.

U.S. policy of the early postwar years avoided any "alliance automatism" in the European-American defense alliance based on its monopoly on nuclear weapons. The NATO member countries agreed in Article 5 of the treaty, which has not yet been amended, that an "armed attack against one or more of them in Europe or North America shall be considered an attack against them all," but each ally decides for itself in unrestricted sovereignty what action to take, "including the use of armed force," to render assistance following mutual consultations.

The political and military power of the North Atlantic Alliance therefore has developed not from treaty commitments but from the political solidarity shown by the Alliance members. This was instrumentalized by an extensive treaty organization and by setting up an integrated command and control system in conjunction with a multinational force structure. The effective adhesive used by the Alliance to link its nations to each other is the power of free choice rather than force.

The common values and goals of the member countries are brought together in NATO to form a strong bridge across the Atlantic. In geostrategic terms, NATO is an alliance of maritime orientation; its main theater of operations, Western Europe, is separated from the strategic reserves of its leading power, the United States, by some 6,000 kilometers (3,700 mi.) of Atlantic Ocean. This resulted in significant military strategic disadvantages for NATO vis-à-vis the Warsaw Pact, an alliance of continental orientation, with the Soviet Union being a Eurasian land power. Necessarily this disparity was reflected in considerable asymmetries between the military strategic concepts of NATO and those of the Warsaw Pact. (The Warsaw Pact was subsequently dissolved 1 April 1991.) Stability between East and West as well as NATO's security could not be achieved merely through weapon systems parity but required a balance in military capabilities of quite different characteristics. This at the same time limited the possibilities of quantitative arms control and disarmament designed to achieve parity in numbers of weapon systems.

For the European NATO countries, the alliance with the United States is an indispensable security pact against threats posed by the East (with the events that have occurred in the Soviet Union and Eastern Europe since 1989, this threat has been substantially reduced), and a structure to firmly anchor American military presence on the European mainland. It extends the protective might of the U.S. nuclear power to Europe, and especially to the non-nuclear NATO states. At the same time it allows for joint naval control over the North Atlantic and the European marginal seas, particularly the Mediterranean. In terms of geopolitics, NATO establishes for the West Europeans a common space across the Atlantic with common interests, goals, and values to serve as a stabilizing factor for their national existence and future. For Western Europe—indeed for all European nations—NATO's political significance lies in the linkage of America's future with the fate of Europe.

The geography of the Atlantic Alliance also gives rise to areas of interest and threat situations that are perceived differently in terms of Alliance policy and military strategy by North Americans and Europeans. Above all, Western Europe alone was directly militarily threatened by the Soviet Union's conventional posture. The Soviet Union enjoyed a multiple numerical superiority over NATO from the time of the establishment of the Alliance. The presence of substantial American ground and air forces in Europe as well as a large-scale organization designed to rapidly bring up reinforcements from overseas were therefore absolutely essential to maintain effective conventional defense.

Given the technical possibilities available to East and West in the 1950s, only Europe was at first exposed to the nuclear threat posed by Soviet tactical nuclear weapons, nuclear armed bombers, and intermediate-range nuclear missiles. Before the introduction of intercontinental strategic weapons at the end of the 1950s, this threat could be met only by stationing corresponding American short- and intermediate-range nuclear weapons in Europe. As a result, Western Europe became the strategic bridgehead of the United States in the western outermost part of the Eurasian continent. American policy toward containing the Soviet Union in the 1950s depended to a large extent on the existence of the Atlantic Alliance, for technical and military reasons resulting primarily from the limited range of weapons.

The military-strategic rationale of U.S. Alliance policy was initially based on the realization that the American nuclear weapons monopoly combined with a strong bomber force would not be sufficient to defeat the Soviet Union militarily or to repulse a large-scale Soviet attack launched against Europe or the Middle East. Moreover, the limited range of bombers that were the only nuclear delivery vehicles available at the time required bases located in suitable proximity to the Soviet Union. Furthermore, when the Soviets detonated their first atomic bomb on 29 August 1949, a predominantly nuclear strategy had become worthless. Plans drawn up by the newly established Alliance to militarily contain the Soviet Union were therefore tailored from the outset to have nuclear and conventional means side-by-side, making full use of the capabilities of the European Allies.

The military situation changed rapidly over time. By the late 1960s and early 1970s, both the United States and the Soviet Union had large intercontinental strategic stockpiles at their disposal, enabling them to threaten each other directly from their respective territories. This development reduced the military relevance of the Alliance for the national-security policy of the United States and altered NATO's role in the American policy of containment. Consequently, in American-Soviet relationships, the direct strategic competition between the two superpowers became predominant. At the same time the European Allies had to take greater responsibility for their own security. The linkage between Europe and North America assumed a predominantly political dimension.

The limitation of U.S. freedom of action vis-à-vis the Soviet Union brought about by strategic nuclear parity led the Alliance into a period of reexamination in the 1960s. It emerged from this internal crisis as an alliance with primarily political objectives based on a common, consistent concept. The credibility of Alliance policy is founded on collective military capabilities and backed by the strategic nuclear stockpile of the United States. As to both risk and burden sharing within NATO, the European member countries today also look after American political and military interests in Europe.

The dimension of responsibility, burden, and risks to be assumed collectively finds its structural expression in alliance-wide political consultations, collective conventional and nuclear defense planning, and common instruments for crisis management. Based on recommendations made by the Committee of Three (the foreign ministers of Canada, Italy, and Norway) in 1956, an effective network of bodies was established in the next three decades to formulate and flesh out NATO policy and strategy, with all member countries enjoying full equality.

NATO's political command structure takes into account the unrestricted sovereignty of the member countries. Policy is coordinated through consultations held in the

North Atlantic Council (NAC), the supreme political body of the Alliance chaired by the secretary general of NATO, as well as in the Defense Planning Committee (DPC) and the Nuclear Planning Group (NPG). The member countries are provided counsel by the Military Committee (MC), a body made up of the Chiefs of Staff of the NATO countries.

Military Containment Policy

On the basis of its military capabilities and protected by the umbrella of U.S. strategic nuclear capability, NATO put its stamp on the political profile of East-West confrontation. During the first two decades of its existence, between 1949 and 1969, NATO was viewed primarily as a military alliance. Military capabilities and technologies significantly determined the scope of and requirement for action by NATO as a political factor of control and management in postwar Europe.

Important lessons on how to establish protection for and security in Europe were learned from the Korean War (1950–53), which proved to be the first test for the policy and strategy of containment. The Korean experience showed in a compelling way that without organized military defense, including strong conventional forces under a unified supreme command, Western Europe could not be successfully defended against a comparable attack launched by Soviet armed forces. The forces of the West available in Europe in 1950 could only muster about 14 divisions, compared with 22 Soviet divisions in Germany's Soviet Zone of Occupation alone and approximately 170 to 200 Soviet divisions in Europe altogether.

During the years 1950–54, these realizations were used to develop the basic military and organizational NATO structures that remain valid today, that is a forward strategy designed to meet any attack as far east as possible; setting up integrated defense forces under the command of an American Supreme Allied Commander (SACEUR); and extensive burden-sharing among the Allies. (Given the events of recent years, NATO's military doctrine, strategy, and force structure are undergoing reassessment.)

With the given objectives of convincing the USSR that war does not pay and, should war occur, of ensuring a successful defense of the North Atlantic Treaty area, the NATO Defense Committee as early as 1950 called for the development of an adequate military strength and for close coordination of political, economic, and psychological efforts of all member nations to achieve these goals. At the same time it formulated the fundamental principles of the common defense policy, which to a large extent are the same today: to oppose any attempt of the USSR to increase the threat, to develop a balanced military force, to compensate for numerical inferiority by maintaining technical superiority, to standardize the equipment and procedures of the Allies, and to sustain the unity of the treaty area.

In view of its conventional weakness, the Alliance from its beginning had to rely heavily on the preparedness of the United States to employ strategic weapons if it perceived a nuclear threat posed by another power or if conventional forces were not sufficient to accomplish their mission. The first strategic concept of NATO, dated 9 December 1952 (Military Committee document MC 14/1), the concept of Massive Retaliation, was developed along these lines. It set as the overall strategic aim to ensure the defense of the NATO area by destroying the will and the capability of the USSR and its satellites to wage war, initially by means of air offensive while at the same time conducting air, ground, and sea operations. This was to be accomplished by major offensive operations by allies, appropriately supported by nonconventional means.

This NATO strategy could rely on the U.S. national strategy (the so-called "New Look" provided in the National Security Council Document 162, commonly referred to as NSC-162) of 1953: (1) to neutralize USSR nuclear weapons capability by extensive nuclear armament and strive for clear nuclear supremacy, and (2) to immediately employ tactical nuclear weapons in the event of a Soviet attack launched in Europe or Asia.

The efforts of the NATO allies to substantially increase their conventional forces vis-à-vis the Soviet Union's greatly superior conventional capability, taking into account the lessons of the Korean War, led to the 1952 Lisbon resolution of the NATO Council: to increase Alliance forces in Europe to 50 divisions, to build up air forces comprising 4,000 aircraft, and to provide strong naval forces for the protection of the Atlantic sea lines of communication. But from the outset the Alliance shied away from the costs of realizing these goals and instead continued to rely on the nuclear supremacy of the United States. Moreover, the principles NATO had established for its defense posture were imbued with the conviction (which in the long run contributed significantly to the development of the NATO force posture) that the technological superiority of the West could compensate for the numerical superiority of the East.

Western technological superiority in the 1950s was considered to rest primarily on nuclear technology, appropriate air forces, and promising progress in the development of missile technology. It was against this background that the first Soviet *Sputnik*, launched in October 1957, gave the United States and the whole Western world a profound shock, since it signaled the loss of its technological edge and cast serious doubts on a determining principle of Western defense policy.

Along with designing and fleshing out its military strategy in the 1950s, NATO was at the same time seeking a credible operational concept that would give more effective protection to the territories of the European allies through its forward strategy doctrine. There was no doubt that a credible defense of Western Europe with only the forces of the twelve NATO countries and an American expeditionary force was not possible. There was also no doubt that West German capabilities would have to be incorporated to accomplish the above. Moreover, it appeared to be essential to use the territory of the Federal Republic of Germany (FRG) as a marshaling area for forward defense, which was to be conducted initially as far east as possible in order to protect the territory and population of all NATO member countries. These strategic and military geographic arguments for Germany's integration into NATO were supplemented by economic and political interests; to have the FRG, with its striving economy, share the burden of collective defense would ease the burden of the other allies. In addition, integrating Germany into NATO was considered an effective measure to keep it under control and at the same time to anchor it firmly in the Western camp.

The process of discussions and negotiations necessary to bring Germany—this former "enemy state"—into NATO was politically difficult. It had a determining influence on Alliance policy between 1950 and 1954 and was finally crowned with success in the Paris Agreements signed in October 1954. The FRG was placed under the obligation to bring a military contribution of up to 495,000 men into NATO and to permit on its territory the stationing of Allied forces whose strength would correspond at least to that given on the effective date of the treaty of accession. While the FRG did not attain that manpower strength until the early 1970s, it was from the beginning the only NATO member country to place all of its units (with the exception of two Territorial Army brigades in the case of employment) under the NATO integrated command structure. With Germany as a member state, the buildup of the Atlantic Alliance in Europe continued with Germany as its focal point, the key area for NATO's military posture. As a consequence, Germany over the decades maintained on its soil the world's highest density of conventional and nuclear forces.

The political basis for the normalization of relations between the NATO countries and the FRG was the commitment of the three Western powers (France, UK, U.S.) set forth in the Bonn Convention of 1952 to work toward establishing "a reunified Germany enjoying a liberal-democratic constitution, like that of the Federal Republic, and integrated within the European Community." Following a 1967 study to identify NATO's future tasks (the Harmel report), overcoming the unnatural division of Europe, and that of Germany in particular, was made the top political objective of Alliance policy.

A treaty signed in Paris in October 1954 provided the basis for a more effective West European security structure with West German participation and was, in effect, an extension of the North Atlantic Alliance. In response, on 14 May 1955, the Soviet Union concluded the Warsaw Treaty Organization with its seven satellite states located in the western and southwestern glacis. The Warsaw Pact claimed to guarantee peace in Europe in view of NATO's strengthening, perceived by the East as a threat. According to Article 11 the treaty limited its duration as reaching until the point in time when there would be an "establishment of a system of collective security in Europe and the conclusion for that purpose of a General European Treaty concerning collective security." The Warsaw Pact thus created the political fiction of subordinating the Soviet Union's hegemonial interests as a world power to the goal of European security and integration. The military crushing of the uprisings in both Hungary in 1956 and Czechoslovakia in 1968, with nearly all Pact countries participating, proved the falsity of the declared objective of peaceful coexistence. The reality was a brutal power policy controlled by the ideological-social dominance exercised by Moscow over the Communist state parties of Eastern Europe. With the foundation of the Warsaw Pact, Europe had ultimately been split, both politically and militarily, into two blocs confronting each other in a seemingly irreconcilable manner.

The hardening of the political and military East-West confrontation demonstrated the impossibility of settling this overwhelming problem solely by military means. The strong points of integrated military power under the leadership of the United States had become apparent during the buildup phase of the Alliance, successfully containing the Soviet Union, but its limitations with respect to overcoming the division of Europe were increasingly clear toward the end of the 1950s.

Although the strategic dominance of American power was indeed an indispensable backing and umbrella for European security, the United States was not in a position to resolve or decide militarily the East-West conflict, which had rigidified since 1948 and had been aggravated in the mid-1950s. Neither of the nuclear superpowers would have been willing to risk global nuclear war, and thus its own existence, to settle a potential crisis that was limited to Europe. At the same time it was increasingly questionable if even a regionally limited conflict between East and West could be resolved by nuclear means, which threatened to destroy everything that should be defended. This reality of the limited benefit of military power in the nuclear age—which, however, also included a stabilizing effect on Europe and thus the foundation of European security in a state of imperfect peace—became fully evident in the crises of Hungary (1956), Cuba (1958–61), and finally Czechoslovakia (1968).

Dual-Track Policy: Deterrence and Detente

NATO began to implement a dual-track policy as early as 1956. Militarily, in view of a continual increase in Soviet combat efficiency and the association of East European countries in the Warsaw Pact, NATO decided on a modified form of the strategy of massive retaliation (MC 14/2) in May 1957. As a pertinent basis, SACEUR had prepared a concept for the nuclear defense of Western Europe (Sword and Shield doctrine, also called Tripwire Strategy). It featured conventional forces of limited strength (30 divisions), relying on tactical nuclear weapons stationed in Europe—to include intermediate-range nuclear forces—and backed by the powerful second-strike capability of U.S. and U.K. strategic nuclear weapons. The strategy was designed to demonstrate that in no case is there a NATO concept of limited war with the Soviet Union. It demanded that NATO prepare to take the initiative in the use of nuclear weapons, since NATO would be unable to prevent the rapid overrunning of Europe unless it immediately employed nuclear weapons both tactically and strategically. Today, NATO still considers this concept of nuclear first use, developed back in 1957 under the sign of U.S. nuclear supremacy, a decisive means to deter any use of military force directed against any member country of the Alliance.

Politically, the NATO Council began to implement the conceptual approaches to the nonmilitary goals of Article 2 of the NATO Treaty. In this context NATO began to seek ways to achieve détente and bring about a better understanding among all nations and to take initial steps regarding a general, complete, and controlled disarmament. On the basis of these guidelines, the Committee of Three, established by the NATO Council in 1956, prepared comprehensive proposals for the enhancement of cooperation within the Alliance, for foreign policy consultation procedures, as well as for common efforts to be made in the fields of economy, science, technology, and culture. Since that time, the efforts to bring about arms control and disarmament have, above all, been permanent topics addressed at the meetings of NATO bodies.

On the basis on this dual-track policy, NATO responded to Soviet propaganda against the strengthening and modernization of NATO forces, counteracting in August 1957 with a comprehensive disarmament concept: reduction of all types of armament and military forces, a production stop for fissionable material to be used for military purposes, reduction of existing stockpiles of nuclear weapons, cessation of nuclear weapons tests, and measures to be agreed against the possibility of any surprise attacks. While a large majority of the UN General Assembly welcomed these proposals, they were rejected by the Soviet Union who in 1957 began to pursue a systematic power policy of exercising political and military pressure against the United States and Europe.

In view of its growing strategic nuclear missile capability, the Soviet Union considered itself a nuclear superpower on an equal with the United States and thus also a world power with equal rights. In the late 1950s and early 1960s, in the context of this Soviet policy, the United States and its NATO allies perceived a "missile gap" coming into being. This cast considerable doubt on the credibility of the existing deterrent and defense policies of the Alliance. Even though this missile gap later turned out to have been partly clever propaganda spread by the Soviet Union, the mere perception of such deficit contributed substantially to a rethinking of strategic concepts within both the United States and the Alliance.

Both the 1958–59 Berlin Crisis and the 1962 Cuban Missile Crisis underlined the importance of the military resolve of the United States and the solidarity of NATO. They also showed the necessity for a fundamental revision of Alliance policy and strategy. With the Soviet Union now in a position to directly threaten the U.S. mainland (also from Cuba) with long-range missiles, the United States had lost its invulnerability. This in turn limited the military and political freedom of action of the United States to make full use of its military capability to attain political objectives in crises that did not affect its own territory. This same limitation was demonstrated during the Berlin Crisis when the United States and NATO could not make the Soviet Union yield and when the East German government began construction of the Berlin Wall in August 1961.

The rise of a Soviet intercontinental nuclear-strategic capability called NATO's strategy of massive retaliation basically into question. As early as 1956, when this development became foreseeable, prominent military and political leaders in the United States started to call for a renunciation of the doctrine of massive retaliation, urging adoption of a more flexible policy. But it was not until 1961–62 under the late President Kennedy that this policy was accepted. At the May 1962 meeting of the NATO Council, the U.S. secretary of defense Robert McNamara outlined the essentials of a new strategy of flexible response, under which the United States was prepared to continue shouldering part of the responsibility for Alliance protection and security, but urging the Europeans to assume a substantially more active role. The new policy called for a balance between conventional and nuclear forces; deterrent capabilities below the strategic level using a strategy of controlled response; and maintaining U.S. nuclear strength as a backing for the Alliance.

Given these conditions, the United States together with the United Kingdom (which had become a strategic nuclear power) assured their fellow Allies in the 1962 Athens Guidelines that they would continue their commitments regarding both protection and security of Western Europe. The decision was reached to establish a NATO Nuclear Committee. The attempt to set up a NATO multinational nuclear force (MLF) to implement the new strategic policy failed. Greater participation by the NATO allies in the nuclear aspect of the Alliance was realized beginning in 1968 only by taking part in the planning process for European employment options and through consultation procedures. To this end the Nuclear Planning Group (NPG) was established.

Arguing that the United States would reduce its commitment to safeguard the security of Europe to an unacceptable level, the French Government in 1966 used the change in strategy as a welcome opportunity to withdraw from NATO's military integration. (This withdrawal had been in the making for a long time, in view of France's policy of sovereignty.) Unlike France, the British government formed the basis for a special relationship with the United States and a strengthening of European participation in the concept of nuclear deterrence under British leadership. The 1962 Nassau Agreement between the United Kingdom and the United States arranged for the sale of American Poseidon missiles to Great Britain, thus strengthening European responsibility for the common concept of nuclear deterrence.

Parallel to a greater integration of the NATO allies into military Alliance tasks, the United States took the initiative in disarmament policy in the form of bilateral talks with the Soviet Union. In September 1961 the two chief negotiators Mr. McCloy for the United States and Mr. Sorin for the USSR, submitted a Joint Declaration on Agreed Principles for Disarmament Negotiations to the UN General Assembly. Despite unresolved differences between the two nations concerning verification procedures, this declaration became the basis for Alliance arms control policy in the 1970s and 1980s. The American-Soviet SALT I Treaty and the ABM Treaty of 1972, which served to codify strategic nuclear parity between the United States and the Soviet Union and in which the United States granted the Soviet Union "equality and equal security," were results of that common declaration, as was the "Reykjavik Signal" given by the NATO Council in June 1968 to propose negotiations with the Warsaw Pact on "Mutual and Balanced Force Reductions (MBFR)" in conventional forces stationed in Central Europe.

In view of the political and military changes in East-West relations and the simultaneously changing policy of the United States, NATO's political crisis of the 1960s was overcome in an effort lasting several years. The new Alliance strategy of flexible response emerged in 1967, and the comprehensive politico-military Harmel concept was approved by the NATO Council in December 1967. This concept was first presented in a report, "The Future Tasks of the Alliance," prepared under the Belgian foreign minister Harmel and it has since become the basis for all military and political planning of the Alliance.

The Harmel report assigns first priority to deterrence and collective defense and considers the balance between the military forces of East and West to be the deciding factor for stability, security, and confidence. Complementing that priority is the Alliance's second task: to pursue a policy of détente on the basis of which Europe's political problems are to be resolved. The ultimate political goal of the Alliance, with which all member countries could fully identify, was set as follows: ". . . to achieve a just and lasting peaceful order in Europe accompanied by appropriate security guarantees." As a pertinent prerequisite for this, the Harmel study concluded that "no final and stable settlement in Europe is possible without a solution of the German question. . . ."

Dialogue and Conciliation with the East

Based on the Harmel concept and the military strategy of flexible response, the Alliance attained a dominant political significance with regard to the East-West relationship and the relations between North America and Europe in the two decades from 1969 to 1989. During that second phase of Alliance policy, the military substance of the Alliance was preserved and, even in some cases, strengthened. With a number of special programs intended to augment the conventional forces in particular, the United States pressed its European allies to increase their contributions. Many European NATO countries instead chose to rely on disarmament and détente, although the Soviet Union, and the Warsaw Pact along with it, continued to strengthen their military power and their capability of invading Western Europe by steady armament and improvement of their armed forces during the Brezhnev era from 1965 onward.

These contrasting developments caused increasing clashes of interests among the transatlantic partners. The United States required NATO to maintain an essential equivalence to the USSR with regard to all elements of the NATO triad—strategic, substrategic, and conventional weapons. It was recognized that military power and the arms race could be used as a lever under conditions of strategic nuclear parity in the political struggle of antagonistic U.S. and Soviet systems and interests. But a war between the leading powers would jeopardize their own existence and therefore could not resolve any crisis between East and West. Consequently, the European NATO countries increasingly doubted the U.S. commitment to employ nuclear weapons early enough to defend NATO Europe against the Warsaw Pact with its ever increasing military strength, although this very threat remained the backbone of NATO's policy. While the United States attempted to overcome the political-strategic neutralization of its strategic nuclear potential via the Schlesinger doctrine of limited employment, it did not succeed in fully restoring the strategic link between Europe and America.

Within this political context and in line with NATO's military-strategic concept of flexible response, NATO's Euro-strategic and conventional assets gained an ever greater relevance for the security of the European allies. NATO's extensive tactical nuclear arsenal in Europe, which increased to some 7,000 nuclear warheads in the 1970s, was required for a strategic concept that, in the event of war, provided for the restoration of deterrence through deliberate escalation. If this political aim were to fail, the concept called for the employment of nuclear assets at any given time to prevent conventional breakthrough operations by the Warsaw Pact forces. While the overall aim of this deliberate escalation was political—namely to restore deterrence and to convince the aggressor to halt his attack and to withdraw—tactical nuclear strikes (according to NATO's "General Political Guidelines for the Employment of Nuclear Weapons") would be carried out to achieve the political goal.

While the European NATO countries officially subscribed to this concept, they raised growing concerns in the following years. They argued that the concept of establishing substrategic nuclear capabilities to undercut Soviet strategic options stemmed from the philosophy established in the 1950s, during the era of American nuclear supremacy, and that this concept could no longer be valid in the 1970s under conditions of nuclear parity. In addition, they questioned the military effectiveness of tactical nuclear weapons relative to the collateral damage to the area of employment. They therefore urged that nuclear weapons be assigned a political function only.

A series of NATO studies prepared in the early 1970s confirmed the European NATO countries in their scepticism about the military effectiveness of tactical employment of nuclear weapons. These studies revealed that a nation inferior in the conventional field cannot offset this inferiority by employing nuclear weapons, if the opponent responds at the same or at a higher nuclear level. Conviction also gained ground throughout the Alliance that for an initial use of nuclear weapons NATO would require an even greater preparedness to take risks than the Warsaw Pact would require for its conventional aggression, for NATO could not exclude the possibility of a nuclear response by the Warsaw Pact followed by an escalation to the strategic level, especially if targets on Soviet territory were attacked in an early phase of a conflict. From this perspective, NATO's nuclear arsenal in Europe was of ambivalent significance: While the United States was trying to limit the threat to its own territory by restricting or even excluding strikes against Soviet targets during the initial use of nuclear weapons, Europeans feared that a nuclear war might be regionalized and demanded that the USSR not be considered a sanctuary.

To date, North Americans and Europeans have succeeded in covering up the ambivalence of the divergent opinions with their stated doctrine that nuclear weapons have a political function only and that nuclear weapons hold incalculable risk for an aggressor. Whenever a decision on basing U.S. nuclear weapons in Europe is to be made, however, there is the threat of a crisis within the Alliance regarding the credibility and acceptance of this formula. (This occurred when the introduction of the neutron weapon was planned in 1977–78, as well as after NATO's double-track decision in 1979 to base Pershing missiles and cruise missiles in Europe.)

At the end of the 1980s, also in the United States, the mainstream thinking among military-policy experts tended not to attribute a comprehensive deterrent role to nuclear weapons. Many military strategic experts considered nuclear weapons credible only in terms of "discriminate deterrence," for deterring the Soviet Union from a major conflict.

Already in the 1970s, numerous governments had begun to advocate disarmament on the part of the Soviet Union. The SALT I Agreement of 1972, the promising start of the Mutual Balanced Forces Reduction (MBFR) negotiations during that same year, and the Conference on Security and Cooperation in Europe (CSCE) from 1973 onward with its Final Act of Helsinki agreed on in 1975 have entailed promising approaches to and results for a constructive "security partnership" between East and West.

Despite extensive efforts during the 1970s, no substantial reduction of Soviet military capabilities had yet been achieved by arms control policy, nor was the East-West confrontation in Europe resolved. The initial successes of the policy of détente in the 1970s only led the two alliances to slow down, restrict, and restrain crises and conflicts, despite being disturbed several times by conflicts outside Europe in which both leading powers were reciprocally involved. The Soviet invasion of Afghanistan in 1979 put an end, for the time being, to the policy of détente and raised the question of whether the Soviet Union was prepared to engage in any form of cooperative policy.

In 1983, when the political differences about NATO's double-track decision had reached their critical point, U.S. president Ronald Reagan raised further doubts about the strategic Alliance concept with his Strategic Defense Initiative (SDI) proposal. It was a departure from the principle of counterforces. By turning toward complete defense mainly at the strategic level, SDI created the perspective of a potential European nuclear battlefield and an invulnerable Fortress America. Assuming that a 100-percent-perfect missile defense system cannot be realized technically and financially, the concept of SDI nevertheless was in line with the strategy of the Alliance. Most important in this respect was the maintenance of the U.S. strategic second-strike capability despite the ever growing strategic arsenal of the Soviet Union. At the same time an effective defense system would deny the Soviet Union any first-strike option (which, in the light of Soviet efforts in missile defense and their programs for heavy intercontinental ballistic missiles couldn't be excluded). The public, political, and scientific debate mostly neglected these well founded rationales, focusing rather on assertions of a U.S. attempt to achieve strategic superiority with unsuitable means and to strive for military and technological solutions rather than seeking political arrangements with the opponent to end the arms race. The progressive U.S. arms control policy from 1985 onward, aimed at achieving a balanced ratio of offensive and defensive strategic assets vis-à-vis the Soviet Union, basically terminated this debate.

Along with the deployment of medium-range missiles,

the SDI program without doubt was instrumental in prompting the Soviet Union to show itself conciliatory and in reactivating the dialogue between the world powers in 1985. A series of U.S./Soviet summit conferences were held on the initiative of President Reagan. Besides discussion of approaches to solve the East-West confrontation, these dealt with a wide range of world political issues, and the United States acknowledged the Soviet Union as a politically equal world power. The first substantive result of this rapprochement between the world powers was the intermediate-range nuclear forces (INF) Treaty of 1987, which provided for the destruction of all U.S. and Soviet ground-based, longer-range INF. The United States and the Soviet Union also reached fundamental agreement on how to reduce their strategic nuclear arsenals by approximately 50 percent in a START agreement.

Under these conditions the new Soviet secretary-general Gorbachev, drawing conclusions from the failures of his predecessors' political concepts, initiated a fundamental revision of Soviet foreign policy. He based his policy in part on the realistic assumption that the Soviets could no longer keep pace in the arms race with the West. The starting-point of this change in Soviet policy from spring 1986 onward was the Western policy of political and military self-assertion, which gave rise to an irresistible urge in the Soviet Union to change its political strategy toward the Alliance and the United States. This urge coincided with internal pressure for change in the Communist bloc, pressure characterized by the imminent breakdown of the Soviet Union's national economy under the excessive armaments burden, the growing desire of the people in the East to bring about changes in social policy, and their increasing demands for living conditions more like those of the free West.

The beginning of the crisis in the Soviet Union coincided with a phase of political unity and stability within the Atlantic Alliance under U.S. leadership in the 1980s. The Soviet policy of confrontation in the 1970s finally had convinced most Europeans that only a strong Atlantic Alliance with the United States firmly anchored in Western Europe would secure peaceful development in Europe. The success of the Conference on Security and Cooperation in Europe (CSCE) follow-up meeting in Vienna from 1987–89 with the mandate to enter into negotiations on conventional forces in Europe (CFE), based on the Soviet Union's admission of its conventional superiority in Europe, confirmed the policy of the Alliance. It emphasized at the same time the principle that disarmament cannot have a trailblazing function in political détente, but can be successful only if the negotiating parties have common political goals, including respect for mutual security interests.

The decided policy of common self-assertion based on purely defensive military posture established the prerequisites for a new era of mutual opening, rapprochement and understanding along the lines of common security and the acknowledgement of the mutual security requirements as being of equal rank and value. By conceding this not only to the United States but to Western Europe as well, Gorbachev no longer treated Europe as a theater of conflict and an object of Soviet policy, as his predecessors did. A truly historic change—from the policy of confrontation during the 45-year postwar period to a policy of cooperation for the purpose of common security—can nevertheless only be successful in the long run if the nations formerly under Soviet domination are finally given complete freedom and self-determination.

East-West Cooperation

In 1989, NATO celebrated the fortieth anniversary of its foundation having provided to its sixteen member countries one of the longest periods in their history of peace in freedom and growing prosperity.

The changes in Soviet policy under the leadership of President Gorbachev initiated a period of unprecedented changes and chances. The successful conclusion of the CFE negotiations in Vienna signifies the solution of the main problem of European security. The invasion capability of the several-times-superior forces of the Warsaw Pact has been removed, but the former Soviet Union remains the strongest military power in Europe and will continue to be a nuclear world power. Consequently, NATO must continue to guarantee the security of its member countries on the basis of an assured defense capability.

Based on the acknowledgment of the European security interests by the Soviet Union while fully acknowledging the principles of the CSCE Final Act of Helsinki, the vision of overcoming the postwar confrontation between East and West and initiating a policy of cooperation with all East European nations can perhaps begin to be realized. In his speech before the United Nations in December 1988, President Gorbachev confirmed this hope. He endorsed the goals and values that have guided Western policy since World War II.

During the NATO summit conference in May 1989, NATO formulated its future policy and adopted the "Overall Arms Control and Disarmament Concept." This policy is based on the proven, complementary approaches of the Harmel concept: adequate military strength and political solidarity form the basis for the search for a constructive dialogue and cooperation, including arms control, as a means to establish a just and lasting order of peace in Europe. Militarily, the Alliance does not see any alternative to the concept of flexible response.

To deal with these future tasks, the transatlantic partnership has to rely on a strong European pillar. The presence of North American conventional and nuclear forces in Europe continues to be of vital importance to European security. At the same time European security continues to be of vital importance to the security of North America.

As far as the policy of cooperation with the nations of Eastern Europe is concerned, the NATO countries will, complementary to their alliance policy, initiate a comprehensive program of cooperation in the political, economic, scientific, technological, and human sectors within the framework of the CSCE. Based on the secure foundation of the Atlantic Alliance as the cornerstone of security, peace, and freedom, NATO is holding out its hand to those who side with it in the service to the nations on East and West for the creation of a stable and peaceful world.

1990–1992: A New World Order

Between fall 1989 and summer 1992, the world fundamentally changed; in a peaceful revolution the people of Eastern Europe overcame the Communist regimes and began to build democratic states. On 3 October 1990 Germany was united and regained its full sovereignty; on 1 April 1991 the Warsaw Treaty Organization was dissolved; and on 31 December 1991 the Soviet Union ceased to exist and was replaced by a Commonwealth of Independent States (CIS). This historically unsurpassed success of democracy and the values of the free West was possible only on the basis of the security and stability guaranteed by the Atlantic Alliance during the 45 years of the postwar era. The new democracies in the East also seek security and stability in NATO for their future and ask for a substantial U.S. presence in Europe to assure it.

NATO responded to these developments by adopting a new strategic concept at the summit conference in Rome (7–8 November 1991). It reduced the role of military power in a new security architecture for Europe in which NATO, CSCE, and the soon-to-be-created European Union (EU) and its military instrument, the WEU, form a complementary set of institutions. The new democracies in Europe are directly incorporated into the process of forming a new, just, and lasting peace order for the whole of Europe. NATO has institutionalized its cooperation with the former member states of the Warsaw Treaty Organization in the NATO Cooperation Council (NACC).

However, with the end of the East-West confrontation, new instabilities and risks inside and outside Europe arose. In August 1990 Iraq invaded Kuwait. Based on a mandate of the United Nations, a coalition of forces led by the United States defeated the aggressor and freed Kuwait. NATO, although not directly involved, proved its value for the states participating by supporting the campaign substantially through its organizational capabilities, especially its logistical system. In the light of new risks and regional conflicts emerging in various parts of the European continent, NATO, at least for the time being, is the only organization that warrants stability for all European nations.

HANS HEINRICH WEISE

SEE ALSO: Logistics, NATO; NATO; Western Europe.

Bibliography

Aaron, R. 1966. *Peace and war: A theory of international relations.* New York: Doubleday.

Brodie, B. 1959. *Strategy in the missile age.* Princeton, N.J.: Princeton Univ. Press.

Davis, J. K., et al. 1989. *The INF controversy: Lessons for NATO modernization and transatlantic relations.* Washington, D.C.: Pergamon-Brassey's, Institute for Foreign Policy Analysis.

Freedmann, L. 1987. *The evolution of nuclear strategy.* London: Macmillan Press.

Goodpaster, A., ed. 1985. *Strengthening conventional deterrence in Europe.* ESECS Study Report. Boulder, Colo.: Westview Press

Hoffman, F. S., A. Wohlstetter, and D. S. Yost. 1987. *Swords and shields: NATO, the USSR, and new choices for long-range offense and defense.* Lexington, Mass.: Lexington Books.

Huntington, S. P. 1961. *The common defense: Strategic programs in national politics.* New York: Columbia Univ. Press.

International Institute for Strategic Studies. 1986. *Power and policy: Doctrine, the alliance and arms control.* London: Adelphi Papers.

Jervis, R. 1976. *Perception and misperception in international politics.* Princeton, N.J.: Princeton Univ. Press.

Kissinger, H. 1957. *Nuclear weapons and foreign policy.* New York: Harper.

McNamara, R. S. 1968. *The essence of security: Reflections in office.* London: Hodder and Stoughton.

Osgood, R. E. 1957. *Limited war: The challenge to American strategy.* Chicago: Univ. of Chicago Press.

NAVAL AUXILIARY AND SUPPORT SHIPS

Most naval analysts define "deep-water," or so-called "blue-water," navies as those capable of operating far from coastal waters (i.e., navies that possess battleships, aircraft carriers, cruisers, and large destroyers). These ships usually carry large quantities of fuel and supplies, but for sustained operations, especially in wartime, they must be constantly resupplied with "beans, bullets and black oil," as one author put it; and that requires auxiliary and support ships. Thus, in many respects, it is the auxiliary and support ships that make a blue-water navy blue. Without adequate support, no fleet can remain at sea for long. One reason many naval analysts did not consider the Soviet Navy a true blue-water fleet, despite its large aircraft carriers, cruisers, "battle cruisers," and destroyers, was the short reach of Soviet naval logistics.

Auxiliary and support ships are diverse and numerous. The U.S. Navy has the most complex force, with about 30 different types. Some are used for underway replenishment (UNREP); others for maintenance and repair. Most fall into other miscellaneous, yet important, categories: towing, oceanography, cargo carrying, hospital ships, and so forth. In most navies, the auxiliary and support forces are part of the regular naval forces. In others, for example the Royal Navy, support ships are a separate "auxiliary" force manned by civilian crews, but under navy control. The United States and the former Soviet navies have a combination of the two: integral naval support forces plus civilian-manned, but navy-controlled, forces.

Background/History

Historically, the limiting factor for a ship has been supplies. While armies could "live off the land," navies could not. One of the greatest limitations was fresh water. Very early ships put into port almost every night for supplies and fresh water (and also because of crude or nonexistent navigation devices). Even when ships became larger, cruises were short and the ships often hugged the shore. During the Age of Discovery, ships could carry six months of supplies but only about a three-month supply of fresh water. There were still problems such as disease, especially scurvy caused by lack of fresh provisions.

The major modern problems developed when ships converted from sail to steam. During the American Civil War, for example, the fast, large paddle steamers *Connecticut* and *Rhode Island* would fill up in Federal (Northern) ports with fresh food, beef, vegetables, and other supplies, then set sail south to Texas, replenishing the blockading ships as they went. However, for coal the ships normally went into port. Coaling ships called "colliers" were built, but resupply at sea was a tedious, dangerous business since ships had to be lashed alongside one another.

It should be recalled that part of the "race" in the latter part of the nineteenth century during the Age of Imperialism was for support bases, then called "coaling stations." Great Britain had a magnificent system from Gibraltar and Malta in the Mediterranean to Aden, ports in India, and Singapore and Hong Kong in the Far East. Other countries such as Russia were not so fortunate. This was one reason most historians of the day marveled at the 18,000-mile passage of the Russian fleet during the Russo-Japanese War of 1904–1905, from the Baltic all the way to the tragedy at the Strait of Tsushima. The logistics of this feat was considered a marvel of its time. According to many historians, one factor in the defeat of the Russians was their exhaustion from the logistical strains of their passage. During this same period in 1907–1909, the United States' Great White Fleet made its celebrated passage around the world to show the flag. American strategists of the period, however, were disturbed that nearly three-quarters of the coal was obtained from foreign sources, thus illustrating the potential weakness of the U.S. logistical train. In 1911, the Royal Navy established the Royal Fleet Auxiliary of civilian ships under naval control. Thus, despite its great worldwide coaling station system, the Royal Navy recognized early its need for support ships.

In World War II, the German High Seas Fleet and the British Grand Fleet were, in some respects, the greatest fleets the world had ever known. They were generally kept in reserve, however, and made only occasional forays out to sea. They were never at sea for sustained operations, which would have required massive supply trains.

There were some interwar developments in naval auxiliary and support ships, but the greatest development and growth occurred during World War II in the U.S. Navy's Pacific Ocean fleets. In the Atlantic, the auxiliary and support train was less important because most ships could make an Atlantic crossing without resupply. This was not the case in the vast Pacific Ocean area. The size of the auxiliary and support force grew from 77 in 1940 to over 2,000 in 1945. The U.S. Navy developed many procedures, including the innovative alongside, "abeam," replenishment technique. The Royal and German navies used the "astern" method of refueling, which was simpler but considerably slower and could only be used for refueling. The abeam method was faster and allowed the transfer of stores and ammunition as well as fuel.

Since World War II, underway replenishment (UNREP) has become the standard for most modern large navies with one exception—the navy of the former Soviet Union. Although this navy does have a few modern UNREP ships (described below), it still uses the old, slow astern method and the even more inefficient nineteenth-century practice of tying up alongside for replenishment. Normally, Soviet ships went into an anchorage and had supply ships, usually merchant ships, come alongside.

Auxiliary and supply ships are still important today. The U.S. Navy needed them for sustained operations in both the Korean and Vietnam wars, and more recently for Indian Ocean patrols, where bases are scarce. The Royal Navy required almost the entire Royal Auxiliary Force during the Falklands/Malvinas operations when some ships were at sea for months. Current trends indicate that overseas bases may become more scarce, and their loss will increase the importance of auxiliary and support ships.

Definitions

The terms *auxiliary* and *support* ships do not do justice to the complexity of the categories. While there are different classes of destroyers—large ones close to cruiser category and small ones nearer frigate size—all look similar and fall into the general category of destroyer. This is not the case for auxiliary and support ships.

The U.S. Navy, which has the most sophisticated systems, lists about 30 different types. This does not, however, include service craft such as yard oilers or floating dry docks, which are also important for support. Floating dry docks, for example, proved vital in the Pacific during World War II. Below is a list of the designations or types of support ships in the U.S. Navy.

Designation	*Definition*
AD	Destroyer Tender
AE	Ammunition Ship (single-product ship)
AF	Store Ship
AFS	Combat Store Ship
AG	Miscellaneous Auxiliary
AGDS	Deep Submergence Support Ship
AGF	Miscellaneous Flag
AGM	Missile Range Instrumentation Ship
AGOR	Oceanographic Research Ship
AGOS	Ocean Surveillance Ship
AGS	Survey Ship
AH	Hospital Ship
AK	Cargo Ship
AK	Maritime Pre-positioning Ship
AKR	Vehicle Cargo Ship
AO	Fleet Oiler (single-product ship)
AOE	Fast Combat Support Ship (multi-product or "station" ship)
AOG	Gasoline Tanker (single-product ship)
AOR	Replenishment Oiler (multiproduct or "station" ship)
AOT	Transport Oiler
AP	Transport
AR	Repair Ship
ARC	Cable Repair Ship
ARL	Small Repair Ship
ARS	Salvage Ship
AS	Submarine Tender
ASR	Submarine Rescue Ship
ATA	Auxiliary Tug
ATF	Fleet Tug
ATS	Salvage and Rescue Ship
AVB	Aviation Logistic Ship

Source: Norman Polmar, *Ships and Aircraft of the U.S. Fleet,* 14th ed. (Annapolis, Md.: U.S. Naval Institute Press, 1987).

In the U.S. Navy, there are two broad categories of auxiliary and support ships: mobile logistics ships and support ships. The mobile logistic ships include not only ships that provide underway replenishment to fleet units, but also material support ships—repair ships, often called *tenders*—that act in direct support of units deployed far from their home port. In contrast to the mobile logistics ships, the support ships provide general support to combatant forces or shore establishments. An outline of these categories follows:

1. Mobile logistic ships
   a. underway replenishment—AE, AF, AFS, AO, AOE, AOR
   b. material support (tenders)—AD, AR, AS
2. Support ships
   a. fleet support—ARS, ASR, ATA, ATF, ATS
   b. other—AG, AGDS, AGF, AGM, AGOR, AGOS, AGS, AH, AK, AKR, AOG, AOT, AP, ARC, ARL, AVB

Although these are U.S. Navy terms, many, especially those for mobile logistics ships, are generally accepted designations in international naval circles and journals.

The U.S. Navy has developed a complex, three-step, wartime replenishment process shown in Figure 1. In the first step, merchant ships transport supplies from the United States to forward bases—ports or naval bases as close as possible to the fighting battle groups.

In the second step, supplies are transferred to "shuttle" ships, which are "single-product" oilers, ammunition, and dry goods and food store ships. The shuttle ships, usually escorted by frigates and destroyers, then steam to the battle group where each single-product shuttle ship transfers its supplies to a "multiproduct" "station" ship.

In the third step, supplies are transferred from the station ships to the combatants. A station ship can operate either as a "gas station" with the combat ships steaming to a rendezvous point, or as a "delivery truck" with the station ship steaming to the combatants. Multiproduct station ships, equipped with fuel and cargo transfer stations on each side, can transfer supplies to two combatants simultaneously. Most of these ships also use helicopters for "vertical replenishment" (VERTREP).

There are distinct advantages to this complex system. One advantage results from the use of multiproduct ships for the final step. Ships are very vulnerable during the resupply operation, and instead of requiring alongside time with three single-product ships—one each for fuel, supplies, and munitions—only one multiproduct ship is required. Reduced alongside time means more time for battle and less vulnerability. This system also increases the staying time of the battle group.

Auxiliary Fleets

Until the early 1960s, replenishment fleets and tactics varied little from those developed in World War II. Re-

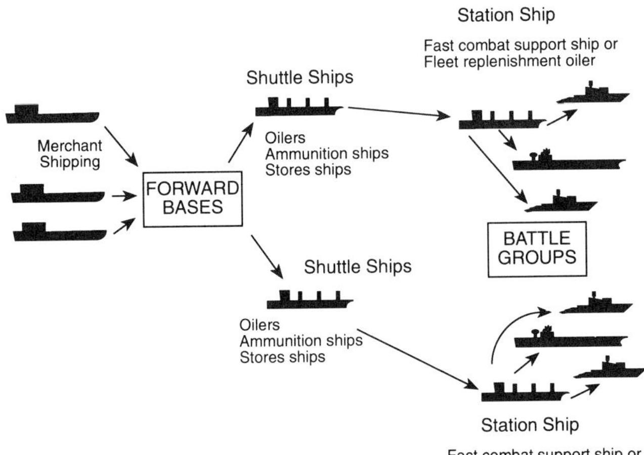

Figure 1. Underway replenishment operations. (SOURCE: Congressional Budget Office, *Issues and Options for the Navy's Combat Logistics Force,* Washington, D.C.: Government Printing Office, 1988)

plenishment ships were single-product ships: AO, AE, or stores ships. Underway replenishment groups and their escorts followed the combatant task force or unit by a few hundred miles. Every few days, there was a "replenishment day" which could, in fact, take almost all day.

That changed in the early 1960s with the deployment of the U.S. Navy's Sacramento-class fast combat support ships. These large, multiproduct ships were fast enough (26 knots) to keep up with the fleet and, at 54,000 tons, are still the world's largest support ships. They can carry 194,000 barrels of fuel, 2,100 tons of munitions, 250 tons of dry stores, and 250 tons of refrigerated stores. The Wichita-class AOR was deployed shortly after the AOEs. Although slightly smaller and slower than the AOEs, they are still considered large, multiproduct vessels. The U.S. Navy currently has four AOEs, seven AORs, and is planning to build four AOEs of a new class for a total of fifteen station ships to support fifteen carrier battle groups.

The "one-stop," AOR replenishment vessel has now become the norm in most navies. The Royal Navy is starting construction of a new, large one-stop multiproduct AOR class. The French navy now has five Durance-class ships in their fleet, a design also used by other countries such as Australia. The Italian navy has a smaller AOR, the Stromboli class, that has been exported to smaller countries. Most of the larger NATO countries now have at least a few AORs in their inventory, or have converted oilers to carry some supplies. There are still some older single-product ships in navies, especially AOs and AEs, but virtually all new support ships are multiproduct ships.

In 1977, the Soviet Navy completed the large replenishment oiler *Berezina*. Analysts assumed this was the forerunner of a large class because its launch coincided with the construction of new classes of Soviet aircraft carriers, cruisers, and large destroyers. However, it turned out to be one of a kind. Second only in size to the American Sacramento class, it has the capacity to support a far-flung Soviet fleet. The Soviets also built some smaller AOR-type ships. There are four replenishment oilers of the Dubna class and six smaller replenishment ships of the Boris Chilkin class. In addition, the Soviet navy often used its merchant marine ships for resupply—so often, in fact, that it was unclear where Soviet naval auxiliaries ended and the merchant marine began.

Most medium-size navies have at least a few UNREP ships. The larger South American navies usually have an older AO or two, some modified to an AOR designation. Japan has two AOEs; India, three AORs; China, four fairly large AORs; and the South African navy is building a new replenishment ship, the SAS *Drakenburg*.

There are even smaller multipurpose vessels for small nations. The Royal Malaysian Navy is building a small replenishment ship with transfer stations fore and aft. Developing nations have used very small landing ship logistics (LSL) as replenishment ships although that is not their prime function. Even these smaller ships have helicopter flight decks that provide VERTREP capabilities.

Although the UNREP ships are often considered the most important because they give navies long-range capabilities, there are many other types. As mentioned above, most navies have "repair" ships called tenders, and larger navies have specialized tenders for destroyers and frigates (AD), submarines (AS), and general repair (AR). Any navy that deploys abroad for extended periods of time must have these ships. The U.S. Navy, for example, has tenders deployed in its forward fleets. The navy of the former Soviet Union, with its large submarine force, has a sophisticated submarine tender fleet. Few modern ships can operate longer than two months without access to a tender.

In addition to tenders, virtually every navy has small harbor tugs and large ocean tugs, yard or harbor oilers, and oceanographic ships. Hospital ships are also important, and the U.S. Navy recently converted two tankers into hospital ships.

Merchant Marine

A nation's merchant marine represents a potential resource for naval support. Most analysts considered the Soviet merchant marine an integral part of the Soviet navy's support system. The United States often charters commercial vessels, and, as shown in Figure 1 above, the merchant marine fleet carries supplies to forward areas (Step 1).

Merchant marine forces are included in most navies' war plans. The Royal Navy has a special program called STUFT (ships taken up from trade) using commercial ships for wartime use. During the Falklands/Malvinas campaign of 1982, the Royal Navy had 50 STUFT merchant ships. The United States keeps track of shipping for Strategic Sealift Assets, listing U.S. flag, NATO assets, and EUSC (effective U.S.-controlled—usually flags of convenience shipping) ships that might be available in an emergency.

However, there are problems with using merchant ships. First, although they might be appropriate for "first-stage" operations to secure forward bases, they are very vulnerable in combat zones. Second, most are not suitable for direct "fleet support," although there are programs to convert these ships. The United States, for example, has a program to provide replenishment equipment, but the ships would still have limited capabilities. Third, and perhaps the greatest problem, is the rapidly dwindling size of the merchant marine fleet. The United States launched its last commercial vessel in 1987. None is currently being built in the United States, and most other NATO countries have similarly declining merchant fleets. Thus, while merchant ships would surely be used in an emergency, their usefulness is clearly limited.

Conclusion

Virtually everyone agrees on the importance of auxiliary and support ships and logistics in general. Naval strategists, as well as operational commanders, consider logistics one of the key elements in overall strategy. During World War II, Fleet Adm. Ernest J. King said, "I don't know what the hell this 'logistics' is that Marshall is always talking about, but I want some of it." And a recent American Chief of Naval Operations, Adm. Thomas B. Hayward, said, "Without adequate and reliable sealift, none of the military plans is executable."

Until World War II, the U.S. Navy Service Force was called the Base Force, a most appropriate name. Without an adequate auxiliary and support fleet infrastructure, no fleet can be considered a "blue-water navy."

JAMES L. GEORGE

SEE ALSO: King, Ernest J.; Logistics, Naval; Naval Propulsion Technology; Naval Warfare; Navy; Organization, Naval; Seapower.

Bibliography

Ballantine, D. S. 1949. *U.S. naval logistics in the Second World War.* Princeton: Princeton Univ. Press.
Carter, W. R. 1953. *Beans, bullets, and black oil: The story of fleet logistics afloat in the Pacific during World War II.* Washington, D.C.: Department of the Navy.
———. 1954. *Ships, salvage, and sinews of war: The story of fleet logistics afloat in Atlantic and Mediterranean waters during World War II.* Washington, D.C.: Department of the Navy.
Commission on Merchant Marine and Defense. 1987. *First report of the Commission on Merchant Marine and Defense.* Washington, D.C.: Government Printing Office.
Congressional Budget Office. 1988. *Issues and options for the navy's combat logistics force.* Washington, D.C.: Government Printing Office.
Eccles, H. E. 1959. *Logistics in the national defense.* Harrisburg, Pa.: Stackpole.
Dyer, G. C. 1962. *Naval logistics.* Annapolis, Md.: U.S. Naval Institute Press.
George, J. L., ed. *The U.S. Navy: The view from the mid-1980s.* Boulder, Colo.: Westview Press.
Jane's Fighting Ships, 1988–89. 1988. London: Jane's.
Polmar, N. 1987. *Ships and aircraft of the U.S. fleet.* Annapolis, Md.: U.S. Naval Institute Press.

NAVAL FORCES

Naval forces are distinguished from other military forces, land and air, by their disposition at sea and the use of the sea for concealment (especially in the case of submarines). The well-known concept of a fleet and "fleet action" by a formation of vessels remains true, as do concepts of different areas or subgroups of maritime operations such as amphibious operations and operations such as mine warfare that are carried out by specialized naval forces. The idea of "an action" by naval forces has now evolved, however, to a point where individual vessels or groups of vessels can be said to be linked *worldwide* and have the potential to act globally, in concert with one another in several different oceanic theaters, to achieve a single strategic aim.

The utility of naval forces is not subject to debate so much as recognized as an element of statecraft and diplomacy, especially at lower levels of conflict between states. In the revised volume of his classic text *Gunboat Diplomacy,* Sir James Cable cites some 40 different instances between 1960 and 1980 when naval surface vessels were used to provide force. There remain, however, differences between "continental" and "maritime" schools as to the potential contribution of naval ships (and submarines) and aircraft to *naval* and *maritime* strategy and national defense policy as a whole.

Caspar Weinberger, former U.S. Secretary of Defense, in his Annual Report to Congress for Fiscal Year 1987, summarized the roles, tasks, and utility of naval forces when he wrote:

> In times of crisis, naval forces are often dispatched to trouble spots, both to support friends and allies and to deter aggression against them. Should deterrence fail, these forces would serve among the lead elements in our forward defense strategy. . . . In their wartime role, naval forces would be called upon to protect friendly shipping from air or sea attacks, to deprive enemy forces of access to strategic areas and to project power against targets at sea or land.

In 1984, the then Chief of Naval Operations in the U.S. Navy, Adm. James D. Watkins, said:

> Naval forces can be sent to the scene with small political costs compared to other military forces. Additionally, seaborne forces arrive ready to carry out all tasks which might be assigned. They need no major logistic support from overseas bases; they do not require access or overflight rights. . . . Their inherent mobility and flexibility make them an ideal instrument to blend in varying amounts with other foreign policy tools. . . . they can be withdrawn easily when the job is done, leaving behind no physical, but strong symbolic reminders of their presence.

Recent demonstrations of the application of naval force include the Royal Navy's crucial role in the Falklands/Malvinas Conflict, the U.S. Navy's role in the invasion of Grenada, and the use of naval force against Libya to prevent further Libyan violations of international law and warn against terrorist attacks. The Iran-Iraq war (1980–88) demonstrated the full range of types of application of naval forces, from escorting trade to the carrying out of surgical strikes against the shore to enforcing an embargo.

The 1991 Gulf War against Iraq provides a classic example of the use of modern naval forces (from several nations) to enforce an embargo (against Iraq) and to combine with air and land forces to defeat an enemy (Iraqi forces that had invaded Kuwait).

Mobile and flexible naval forces can be conveniently categorized into surface, subsurface, air, and space forces, but this would ignore the vital elements of command and control, and of command, control, communications, and intelligence, which bind these assets together, forming what British historian S. W. Roskill has described as the "strength element" of naval force, or "seapower." Nor should we forget what Roskill has described as the "security element," the network of bases supporting the fleet, and the "transport element," the merchant navy.

Major Naval Forces

It is important to compare the navies of the United States and the former Soviet Union. Although it is arguable that the nuclear-powered attack submarine has assumed the role of the "capital ship" from the large flat-deck aircraft carrier, U.S. naval forces have for a long time operated as part of a blue-water navy centered on the carrier battle group, at home on all the world's oceans with a developed logistics train to support it wherever it goes. The United States is an "island nation" dependent on trade and must therefore be able to deploy its fleet wherever it requires. The former Soviet Union was essentially a continental power although it aspired to great navy status and achieved it, but not to the extent of the American presence on the world's oceans.

Whereas U.S. naval forces can project power ashore wherever their political leaders choose, the USSR did not have this capability. Although the new Russian state may continue building large aircraft carriers, its navy remains essentially a coastal defense navy in its philosophy, albeit a very impressive one. Only the U.S. Navy possesses naval force of sufficient strength in all its guises to a be truly a blue-water force, although U.S. mine countermeasures forces remain woefully inadequate. Requests from the former Soviet Union for naval arms control to be included on the East-West agenda probably resulted from a real perception of a need to reduce pressures on the Soviet defense budget, but they also undoubtedly reflected concern in the USSR at the disparity between U.S. and Soviet force levels—particularly numbers of aircraft carriers. In the United States, the main concern is with Russian submarine force levels.

Smaller Naval Forces

If the world's navies can be divided into blue-water forces with truly global reach, regional navies with some means to project power, and coast defense forces, the navies of most of the developing nations would fall into the third category. Since the end of World War II in 1945, it is in this third category that the most change has occurred, with the number of recognized navies (mostly very small) increasing threefold. The creation of these small seaborne military structures, some of which hardly justify the term "navy," has happened as more and more sovereign states were formed from the vestiges of old European-based empires. Thus, the trend of naval proliferation has been closely related to the increase in the number of states in the international system. In most of these small states, naval forces rank third behind armies and air forces in the competition for resources. Armies, and to some extent air forces, are political organizations in a way that navies are not. Although conflict in and between these small states appears relatively more likely to break out than between the major powers of Europe, navies rarely have a role to play and are rarely (if ever) involved in coup attempts or the overthrow of one government by another.

Analysts have attempted to create a hierarchy of levels of naval powers ranging from regional force projection navies through offshore territorial defense forces to token navies equipped with little more than one or two patrol craft and no ability to operate in the 200-mile exclusive economic zone (EEZ).

There are also differences in the ways and means employed by states to maintain law and order at sea and to enforce national jurisdiction within the EEZ. For some larger states, these are tasks traditionally allocated not to naval forces but to coast guard and other forces. For many smaller states, though, it is in these coastal waters that their naval forces are most in demand, for fishery regulation, the prevention of terrorism and piracy, and control of smuggling and immigration.

Comparison of Naval, Land, and Air Forces

As nuclear tensions between the superpowers eased in recent years, and as the use of military force at lower levels of violence has increased relative to its use at higher levels, we can say that for large (superpower) and medium navies, naval forces are likely to be employed more and more in limited actions. Smaller navies still establishing themselves—not on the high seas but in their own much more limited areas of direct military interest—are likely to be employed more and more in constabulary roles policing their interests and resources.

Due to the legal regime of the world's oceans, naval forces routinely confront one another, sailing in close proximity to one another and observing one another's maneuvers and tactics. For this reason, naval forces must be subject to well-defined and strict rules of engagement.

Whereas land forces are in the public eye because of the troops stationed at bases, military exercises, and low-level flights by military jets, naval forces are essentially "out-of-sight" and "out-of-mind." This may be good in one way—naval forces are not subject to as much critical attention—but bad in another; in many countries navies are rarely uppermost in the public's or legislators' minds when it comes to allocating defense funds.

Likewise, ground forces easily bring to mind the image of land fought over and sustained by opposing forces, whereas the notions of "control of the sea," "sea denial," and "power projection" by naval forces do not enjoy the same currency amongst the public.

Even so, these naval forces, which are out-of-sight and

out-of-mind, are not themselves safe in any ocean area from nuclear-propelled vessels, which do not need to refuel, or units equipped with antiship weapons that have ranges measured in hundreds of kilometers. Unlike on land, where there is a geographically well-defined front or theater or battle space, naval forces are subject to attack anywhere. Moreover, how a land campaign is faring may reasonably be judged by the outcome of individual engagements and battles or land lost or gained. The absence of battle lines at sea means that the success of operations by naval forces cannot be judged according to these accustomed means, but only by how much influence engagements at sea have had on the land battle, which may not be apparent until after the crisis is over and the situation has passed.

Evolving Roles of Naval Forces

Naval forces perform both *tactical* and *strategic* operations and there is a difference between their peacetime roles and their wartime roles.

Strategic Roles

The single most important strategic role of naval forces is strategic nuclear deterrence by ballistic-missile-equipped nuclear-powered submarines that use the oceans to conceal themselves from preemptive strike, forming the most secure element of the strategic nuclear triad, which also includes intercontinental missiles and bombers. These missile-equipped submarines remain the least vulnerable leg of the triad, and more than any other naval force they can influence the outcome of a global conflict. The submarine-launched ballistic missile (SLBM) constitutes a secure second-strike capability, although recent improvements in the accuracy and hard target kill capability of the new U.S. *Trident* II weapon have led to criticism that this secure strategic reserve has the potential to be used in a first-strike role as well.

There are threats to the inviolability of the SLBM force, but none of them is critical at this moment. If there are more nuclear accidents of the kind at Chernobyl, or more serious reactor accidents on submarines, there could be more backlash against all forms of nuclear power including nuclear propulsion. There might be a great technological breakthrough in antisubmarine warfare that would "render the seas transparent"; but such is the sheer volume of ocean to be searched by anti-SSBN forces that a widening of SSBN operational practices, made possible by very long-range missiles, could well compensate. Furthermore, submarines become quieter and less easily detected as active and passive control of noise sources in submarines improves.

It has been suggested that applications of naval force against certain types of targets (e.g., nuclear-powered ballistic-missile submarines) should be avoided because it would be destabilizing. Proponents of this view state that if the U.S. Navy should adopt its stated policy of attacking Russian SSBNs then Russia might be forced into a position where it had to use them or lose them. Other proposals to stabilize the pressures applied to the SSBN force were also proposed by the former Soviet Union for many years and were given fresh impetus by the advent of *perestroika* and *glasnost*. These include proposals to restrict deployments of those naval antisubmarine warfare (ASW) forces designed to counter SSBNs and others including restrictions on developing ASW technologies.

Indeed, the scope of naval arms control proposals articulated by the Soviet Union in the late 1980s and early 1990s was very broad. As Capt. Richard Sharpe, Royal Navy (Rtd), wrote in the Foreword to the 1989–90 edition of *Jane's Fighting Ships*, however, "It is devoutly to be hoped that the West will not once again be wrong-footed in the propaganda battle, and that initiatives will be taken early to head off the inevitable attack on the integrity of the West's naval forces, upon which the whole defensive strategy depends."

The defense of reinforcement and resupply shipping throughout the course of a conflict is another strategic task of naval forces. The ability of the West's naval forces to control the sea lines of communication across the Atlantic and Pacific and to reinforce and resupply will determine how long land forces can fight conventionally, and this in turn might well have a determining effect on the nuclear threshold.

A classic strategic concept of naval force at sea is sea control, that is, the ability reliably to use a defined area of the ocean for one's own purpose and deny its use to the enemy. It is questionable, in the light of modern naval weapons such as the antiship cruise missile, whether sea control over a large area is possible to maintain—even by the most well-defended naval forces. We should perhaps acknowledge some ocean areas such as the Norwegian Sea as having such a concentration of naval force that no navy can expect to control the area in a classic sense. These are areas that strategists concede would be areas of "sea dispute."

Tactical Roles

Tactical naval operations by naval forces comprise a range of operations on a more localized scale, often involving a technological battle between radar- and sonar-equipped units. Tactical operations by individual ships and submarines for the purposes of self-defense and for defense of ships in consort with them include antisubmarine warfare (ASW) and antiair warfare (AAW), and operations against enemy surface units (antisurface vessel warfare, ASUW).

Detecting and *attacking* a naval force involves considerable technological sophistication. The main methods are acoustic and electromagnetic (radar). Antisubmarine warfare forces use active and passive sonar and complex signal-processing techniques to hunt submarines. Sonar systems may be fixed (as in the seabed-mounted sound-surveillance, or SOSUS arrays) or fitted in individual naval units comprising a naval force. The acoustic process may be broken down into detection and localization, classification, and identification of submarines. Submarines may also be detected with magnetic anomaly detection (MAD) devices and other nonacoustic devices, the development of which is being addressed with the utmost urgency by naval powers. Once detected and classified, submarines are then attacked with torpedoes (heavyweight and lightweight) delivered directly from ships and other submarines or via air flight weapons (torpedo-carrying missiles) from these platforms, and by depth charges and air-launched bombs.

Naval surface forces are subject to detection by radar and electro-optical means and more recently by satellite surveillance systems. The principal threat to a surface unit is no longer the naval gun, but the sea-skimming antiship missile. These have revolutionized naval tactics since their introduction by the Soviet Union and the first sinking of a naval vessel—the Israeli *Eilat*—by the Egyptian navy. The antiship missile, fast, difficult to counter, and particularly deadly, is the essential modern naval weapon with which even very small navies have been equipped. These and other sea-launched cruise missiles (SLCMs) are the most potent applications of naval force available.

Long-range conventional land-attack and nuclear-armed cruise missiles are presently adding a new dimension to naval actions against land targets many miles from the sea. These stand-off weapons are also taxing the minds of arms control experts seeking a means of verifying agreements limiting numbers of nuclear SLCMs, which are externally indistinguishable from their conventionally-armed counterparts. While reduction in nuclear SLCMs is probably a laudable objective, meaningful arms control would limit the number of nuclear SLCMs but retain the military usefulness and utility of conventional SLCMs.

Unlike their land-based counterparts, naval forces may be subject to attack from any direction and any azimuth. A naval surface unit is subject to missile attack from other surface units, from submarines, from aircraft, and even from shore batteries of antiship missiles.

Conclusion

Naval forces are necessarily high technology forces, for they depend on technology even to exist. Their functions span the spectrum of conflict from peaceful policing operations to participation in all-out war. Naval forces use all dimensions—space, air, sea surface, and subsurface—to accomplish their missions; they are liable to surveillance and attack from those dimensions as well. Their growth, spectacular over the past two decades, has paralleled the increase in the number of sovereign states. Their importance may well increase in the future as states increase their commercial and security interests and their dependence on commercial trade in the maritime areas of the world.

DAVID FOXWELL

SEE ALSO: Battleship; Blockade and Maritime Exclusion; Convoy and Protection of Shipping; Cuban Missile Crisis; Lines of Communication; Maritime Strategy; Naval Warfare; Navy; Sea Control and Denial; Seapower; Submarine.

Bibliography

Couhat, J. L., and A. D. Baker. 1987. *Combat fleets of the world.* Annapolis, Md.: U.S. Naval Institute Press.
Gretton, P. 1965. *Maritime strategy.* New York: Praeger.
Hughes, W. P. 1986. *Fleet tactics.* Annapolis, Md.: U.S. Naval Institute Press.

NAVAL PROPULSION TECHNOLOGY

A warship's propulsion system is composed of three primary subsystems:

- Prime movers
- Transmissions
- Propulsors

The selection of the propulsion system for a given ship concept is influenced by many factors, primary of which are the ship's operating profile and the hull form selection, which in turn are related to the mission. There is almost an infinite number of possible propulsion system concepts when one considers the potential for combining various prime movers into a single system with alternate transmissions and propulsors. Therefore, the technologies in each subsystem have been addressed separately as to their potential for enhancing future surface vehicle operational capability. Reference is made to combined plants only where special emphasis is required.

Prime Movers

The principal types of prime movers applicable to future surface vessels are (1) gas turbines (both simple and regenerative); (2) diesels; and (3) steam turbines (both nuclear and conventional).

Since the design of the U.S. Spruance-class (DD 963) destroyers in 1970, only gas turbine propulsion plants have been selected for new classes of non-nuclear surface combatants. As a result, the number of gas turbine–driven warships in the U.S. Navy's fleet will continue to climb dramatically, even if no new class ship designs are committed to this type of power plant. The gas turbine's greatest virtue is that it can produce a relatively large amount of power for its size and weight. Simple-cycle gas turbine propulsion plants have proven to be reliable, lightweight, compact, and relatively quiet; they also have low manning requirements. Simple-cycle gas turbines cannot achieve the same specific fuel consumption rates as a diesel, but there continues to be a steady improvement in efficiency, financed in large measure by research and development (R&D) funding for aircraft applications.

The development of the intercooled-regeneration gas turbine cycle offers the potential for significant reductions in both full-load and part-load fuel rates of the basic gas turbine, albeit at a cost in increased size and complexity. Fuel rates approaching those of a diesel engine are projected and, if achievable, could enhance the operational capability of future ships. The pursuit and prototype testing of this concept must be continued to validate the technology involved and to ensure timely integration into new surface vehicle construction programs.

A variant of the basic gas turbine propulsion system is the application of the Rankin Cycle Energy Recovery (RACER) system. Steam generated by waste heat from the gas turbine is utilized in a steam turbine to provide additional power for achieving full speed of the vessel. Unfortunately, development and prototype testing of the concept have produced less than satisfactory results, primarily in the steam-generation module. While additional efforts may provide technical solutions to these problems, the development of the intercooled-generative gas turbine previously noted appears to offer a more attractive approach to improving overall propulsion efficiency.

Diesel prime movers have become the standard means of propulsion for merchant vessels, with other prime movers used for very special applications only. However, diesels have generally not found favor with U.S. Navy combatants for a variety of reasons. These include

- Lack of a significant U.S. industrial base
- Noise-reduction problems
- Potentially higher manning level than gas turbines
- Added logistic requirements

In addition, the ability of diesel engines to use lower grade fuels, which provides a significant cost savings to a commercial operator, is not an advantage to the U.S. Navy because of its standardization on a higher grade fuel that can be used with aircraft-derivative gas turbines. The weight of diesel plants also has been a negative factor. Based on a given ship operating profile, however, the combined weight of diesel engine and endurance fuel may be attractive.

Plants combining diesels for cruise propulsion and gas turbines for high-speed boost have found favor with various foreign navies as a compromise that makes use of the best features of both types of power plant. The application of high power-to-weight diesel engines and combined plants should be considered in specialized applications, such as in advanced hull forms.

The predominant type of propulsion in the U.S. Navy's warship fleet today is steam. Over several decades, the conventional steam plant's pressure and temperature have been raised, greatly increasing the amount of energy that can be carried by a given amount of steam. This increase correspondingly decreased the physical size of the propulsion plant needed to produce the required amount of horsepower. Another effect was the improved efficiency with which fuel could be converted into power. However, this pattern of decreased size effecting greater efficiency is not likely to continue, since each increase in pressure and temperature brings more complexity and places greater demands on the materials composing the plant. Even though the higher temperature and pressure result in a more efficient power plant, a point of diminishing returns will be reached that will prevent further increase beyond today's 1,200 pound per square inch (psi) pressure, 950°F steam conditions. In spite of the fact that the steam plant is expected to be useful for a variety of applications in future warships, conventional fuel-fired steam turbine power plants have generally been displaced by gas turbines for the reasons discussed above.

Nuclear-powered steam turbine propulsion plants are heavy and expensive to purchase and maintain. They also require many people to operate them. These disadvantages become less important as ship size and required horsepower increase. The advantages of unlimited endurance and no main propulsion fuel tankage, allowing more space for aircraft fuel and other consumables, have resulted in the standardization of nuclear propulsion for carriers. Future surface vessels between the size of current gas turbine–powered cruisers and carriers could be viable candidates for nuclear propulsion. One further problem is that the cruiser-sized nuclear plants available at this time will probably not be capable of meeting the power requirements for top speed on such vessels if the payload requirement dictates larger-size ships. They may require further development and/or the inclusion of a boost capability (gas turbine boost, for example) to meet this requirement.

Advanced lightweight nuclear plants could be developed to overcome many of the problems discussed in the preceding paragraph. They could be developed to meet the power requirements for a vessel in the midsize range (10,000–20,000 tons), be considerably smaller, and require less manning. However, a significant R&D program would be required for the development of such plants.

A ship propelled by a combination of a nuclear reactor, steam turbines, and gas turbines (CONAG) could operate with far less fuel replenishment than current escort vessels require. This would significantly increase their value to the battle group and their ability to perform other tasks where operations without available fuel replenishment are required. The CONAG concept is appealing because a ship with a single reactor plant of existing design would be less expensive than current two-reactor surface ships, and a single reactor plant with gas turbine boost requires less manning than a two-reactor ship. This lowers crew-related costs and significantly reduces life-cycle costs.

Since existing escort vessels operate at less than 25 knots about 90 percent of the time, the CONAG ship would rarely require gas turbine boost and would thus have low fuel oil requirements. Gas turbine maintenance also would be reduced compared with an all-gas turbine-powered ship. Dependence on replenishment at sea would consequently be reduced significantly.

Two types of well-dispersed propulsion machinery provide redundant power sources that enhance ship survivability. A program for testing the combined main engine complex in a land-based test facility is a necessary step that should be pursued in the development of a CONAG-powered ship. Unfortunately, nonfossil fuel, nonnuclear solutions to warship propulsion must be dismissed, at least for the moment. All indications are that other sources, such as solar energy, ocean thermal energy converters, or the wind will not be practical for warship propulsion even by the early part of the twenty-first century. For example, to collect 50 kilowatts of energy for a warship from solar energy, the entire topside of the ship would have to be devoted to solar energy collection; yet 50 kilowatts represent only a fraction of 1 percent of the power needed for such a ship.

One form of direct energy conversion that offers potential for future applications aboard combatant ships, at least for auxiliary power generation, is the fuel cell. Fuel cells offer the potential for quiet electric power generation in modular form and are capable of power-to-weight ratios competitive with high-density diesel engines. Fuel cells, however, have a limited life expectancy and a continuing reputation of being in the development stage. Their use thus probably will be restricted to unique applications where more conventional sources of power may not be practical.

Transmissions

The two principal types of transmissions to be considered for future surface combatant vehicles are mechanical (gears and shafts) and electrical (including superconducting).

There are a number of choices within each of these categories. In considering which type of transmission is appropriate for a given installation, it is necessary to consider many factors, including

- Type of prime mover
- Type of propulsor
- Weight
- Efficiency
- Reliability
- Quietness
- Flexibility
- Survivability
- Cost
- Reversing ability
- Cross-connecting ability
- Means of generating ship service electrical power

Geared transmissions are the most common choice for combatants because of their lower cost and weight and high reliability. Their disadvantages are a result of limited flexibility in both arrangements and operations. Conventional gear/shafting systems do not have any provisions for reversing, which must therefore be handled by the propulsor or prime mover, and they do not allow the shafts on a twin-screw vessel to be driven by a single prime mover (cross-connected). If reversing gear and cross-connected shafting are required, the advantages of gearing are reduced or eliminated. Nevertheless, gearing will probably remain the choice for most U.S. combatants.

The electric transmission has been widely used in ships with special operating requirements (e.g., icebreakers, survey vessels, surveillance ships). Ease of control, low noise, and flexibility of arrangements have been the primary reasons for its use. Lower weight and improved efficiency electric transmissions continue to be developed (water-cooled and superconducting transmissions, for example). Survivability could be improved because of the arrangement flexibility resulting from use of electric transmissions, while certain hull form types (such as SWATH) may favor electric transmission because of space availability. Any advantages resulting from integrated electric power generation also must be considered.

It is possible to combine electric transmission and geared transmission in a single vessel. Electric transmission is then used for the lower speeds, principally because it is quieter, and shafting and gears for the boost propulsion.

Some dramatic advances are in store in transmission systems. These will be brought about by the availability of superconducting electrical machinery (generators and motors) having weight and volume characteristics only 50 percent as large as those currently available.

The development of electric drive propulsion machinery will not only affect the propulsion system, but also will produce major changes in warship configuration. For example, the reduction gear, most of the propeller shafting, the need for controllable and reversible pitch propellers, and a significant portion of the air-intake and uptake ductwork will be eliminated. The main propulsion prime mover will no longer have to be in line with the propeller, thus introducing a degree of flexibility for high-powered warships. Flexibility of power distribution from one prime mover to more than one propeller will be another benefit, leading to improved gas turbine performance at cruise speeds and cutting fuel consumption. The total gains from these changes will promote reduction in ship size for the same payload, speed, and endurance.

These benefits can be achieved only if recent developments in raising the temperature at which materials achieve zero resistance can be successfully translated to power equipment.

Propulsors

The primary propulsor choices for future surface combatant vessels will be water propellers, waterjets, and pumpjets. Existing pumpjets for surface ships, unlike those for torpedoes, have been relatively conventional propellers in decelerating nozzles. Airscrews and turbojets may be considered for high-speed surface craft, but are inappropriate for large combatants.

Magnetohydrodynamic propulsion has not been developed beyond the research stage, despite many years of work. If such propulsion is found to be attractive, it will most likely be applied to submarines rather than surface ships.

Conventional, fully wetted, or subcavitating propellers can be used in many forms, including open or with a nozzle, with or without vanes or stators, in single or multiple stages, contrarotating, and so on. These propellers have been, and will continue to be, the propulsors for all but a very few high-speed naval ships, such as the surface effect ship (SES). Other types of propellers, such as supercavitating and transcavitating propellers, are appropriate for maximum ship speeds of more than 35 knots. Most conventional single-hull warships have maximum speeds of less than 35 knots.

Recent R&D efforts have led to significant increases in attainable propeller efficiency; reductions in propeller cavitation damage and noise; and propeller-induced hull vibrations. These improvements have been primarily achieved for more heavily loaded propellers, however, such as those on commercial vessels. Thus, many of these new propeller technologies are not appropriate for high-speed combatant vessel use. The primary problem with conventional propellers is that increasing ship speed and associated increases in propeller cavitation-induced noise, damage, and vibrations reduce propeller efficiency. Noise problems associated with propeller cavitation may be reduced or eliminated through the use of special nozzles or vanes, or an air-delivery system (Prairie) that pumps small bubbles of air through the propeller surface.

Waterjets are best suited for high-speed (speeds greater than 35 knots) or shallow-water operations. Their efficiency tends, unlike that of propellers, to remain constant with increasing ship speed. They are typically less noisy, or have a smaller acoustic signature, than propellers at equal, relatively high speeds. High-speed or high-impeller revolutions per minute (rpm) waterjets, which typically use inducer pumps to avoid main pump stage cavitation, are relatively light, but have relatively low (0.55 or less) propulsive coefficients. They also have potential reliability problems because of cavitation, which typically cannot be avoided in the inducer stage. Low-speed or low-impeller rpm waterjets typically can avoid all cavitation and maintain high efficiency (propulsive coefficient of up to 0.65) for ship speed at 40 knots or more. These waterjets are rather heavy, however, due to the large volumes of on-board water. Such waterjets should be very reliable and should have small acoustic signatures.

Waterjets offer several advantages over propellers. They can be used for reversing thrust and for maneuvering, thus eliminating the need for reversing propellers, engines or gears, and rudders. They are less vulnerable to damage than propellers and are probably more easily repaired than propellers. On the other hand, they will probably be significantly more expensive than propellers.

REUVEN LEOPOLD

SEE ALSO: Nuclear Propulsion; Propulsion; Ship and Naval Technology Applications; Warship.

Bibliography

Friedman, N. 1987. *Modern warship design and development*. New York: Mayflower Books.

Lautenschlager, K. 1984. *Technology and the evolution of naval warfare, 1851–2001*. Washington, D.C.: National Academy Press.

NAVAL WARFARE

Naval warfare presupposes an organized state whose geography and national interests allow or impel the construction of organized sea-based forces to defend or advance the security, political position, and deterrent or compellent power of the state. Shaped by political purpose and organization, naval warfare is distinguished from piratical activities serving essentially private ends.

The Scope of Naval Warfare

The concept of naval warfare has traditionally referred to those military operations conducted in sea or ocean areas and in immediately adjacent land areas, control of which either contributes to or depends on the exercise of power on the seas. Naval warfare in modern times must necessarily be concerned with combat not only on the surface of the sea but also both under and over the sea, as well as in the air and on the ground in critical adjacent land areas. In a narrow sense, naval warfare concentrates on military instruments—such as surface vessels, submarines, naval aircraft, and amphibious troops—that are based in a navy and oriented toward specific naval missions, (e.g., control or denial of the sea, projection and support of forces ashore, or land bombardment from the sea).

Although naval forces may act autonomously, most commentators agree that naval forces generally serve political purposes that can be achieved only by a combination of land, sea, and air forces. Writing in 1918, the British naval strategist Julian S. Corbett wrote:

> By maritime strategy we mean the principles which govern a war in which the sea is a substantial factor. Naval strategy is but that part of it which determines the movements of the fleet when maritime strategy has determined what part the fleet must play in relation to the action of the land forces; for it scarcely needs saying that it is almost impossible that a war can be decided by naval action alone.

Moreover, in contemporary times, the general range, accuracy, transparency, and destructiveness of weapons in all environments have further limited the autonomy of naval warfare. Although the special characteristics of weapons systems and missions that directly concern the sea can be distinguished, their contribution must be evaluated within a broader political, geographical, and technological context.

In general, three elements define the importance and meaning of naval warfare: geopolitics, political economy, and technology. On the specific end of the spectrum, one obvious factor—whose impact, however, is not self-evident—stands out: the sea—the medium that is transited, controlled, and contested and that gives rise in the first place to the specialized field of naval warfare.

Geopolitics and Naval Warfare

Crucial to the military posture of a state is the geographical position and location of its principal interests and potential allies and adversaries. The shape and strategy of a state's forces will differ depending on the society's degree of self-sufficiency, the security provided by geographical and topographical features, the existence of common borders with other states as well as the character of those states, and the requirements for moving forces to points distant from the state.

For example, a central continental state that is subject to direct invasion across its borders and that can secure its interests or extend its power by moving its forces across land will probably produce a different strategic perspective from that of an island state with no internal or external threats on the territory of the island and with interests across the sea, perhaps on the periphery of the continental state. The former state is likely to see naval warfare as an *adjunct* to land warfare—protecting the flanks from seaborne attacks and denying the secure use of the sea to any would-be enemy that might project power ashore or support land adversaries of the continental state. Conversely, the island state is apt to see naval warfare as the *foundation* of its territorial immunity and the *precondition* of its ability to protect its interests, secure its friends, and extend its power and influence.

A great continental state may ultimately seek to extend its control over the seas once it has secured itself on land, and an island state may establish and sustain a great land force on a distant continent. Statesmen from both countries, however, are likely to understand that the continental power's land force is central to the protection of the homeland and that the island state's naval force is equally crucial.

These examples represent ideal types, but they point to an important factor in the development of the concept of naval warfare: the meaning, dimensions, and centrality of naval warfare depend on the asymmetrical disposition of the states on the globe's surface. Most treatises on strategy and conflict have concerned land warfare. There is a scarcity of literature on seapower and naval warfare because few states have been dependent on or conceived their national identity in terms of control of the sea and the seaborne projection of major military force. At times, such concerns have animated many states, but consistent attention to these issues has engaged few historical powers—ancient Athens, the United Kingdom, Japan, and the United States among them.

Even in these states, the systematic examination of seapower and naval warfare came quite late despite the fact that commerce and war at sea occurred as far back as the ancient world and were crucial to the Athenians, the Phoenicians, a number of the Italian city-states, the Dutch, and the British. The late-nineteenth-century rise to prominence of studies of seapower and naval force may be attributed to two interrelated factors: the increasingly global basis of economic power, and changes in technology.

Political Economy and Naval Warfare

The eighteenth-century industrial revolution—essentially substituting machine power for human and animal power with all of the subsequent developments—not only generated an enormous increase in economic power but also led to a progressive interdependence of the national economies far beyond the international commerce of ancient times. The late twentieth century is heir to a revolution unleashed more than 200 years ago.

The expansion and diversification of production opened the possibility and desirability of expanded markets and the need for a whole range of mineral and fuel resources as well as raw materials generally. As the state in which the industrial revolution first took hold, Great Britain was impelled by the market-expansion dynamics unleashed by the industrial process to act on—and be dependent on—a broader global stage. Moreover, the preeminent power conferred by the wealth and technology produced catapulted Britain to a position of political preeminence. In some respects, the dynamics of Japanese developments in the late nineteenth and early twentieth centuries mirrored the British experience.

In addition to the broader global stage dictated by the economic developments following the industrial revolution, those same developments increased the complexity and costs associated with building and maintaining naval forces. Construction and outfitting of seagoing vessels have always been enormously expensive and required in the long term a thriving commercial base. If the sea were not central to a state's survival, vital interests, and political economy, then investment in naval forces could always be defined as a luxury that could be radically scaled back in times of economic stringency. That the ancient Athenians and the Dutch and British in early modern times did make such an investment is understandable, given the foundations of their wealth and security. If such forces have historically been costly, the period since the onset of the industrial revolution has seen an increase not only in the power and efficiency but also in the expense of naval forces, especially capital investments. Such costs are not limited to sea-related forces; land-based forces have also experienced cost increases. Nonetheless, so complex is the use and control of the sea—above, below, upon—as well as the projection of power ashore, that naval forces still require impressive geopolitical and economic arguments to justify the demands on the public purse. Ultimately such demands are related to technology.

Technology and Naval Warfare

Archer Jones, the eminent American military historian, has made the distinction between shock warfare and missile or artillery warfare. He states that naval warfare was fundamentally shock warfare until the sixteenth century, when advances in technology and mariners' skills gradually transformed such warfare into artillery warfare. *Shock* action or warfare refers to the direct contact of military platforms, personnel, and weapons—variations of hand-to-hand combat or ramming. *Missile* or *artillery* action involves the launching of projectiles at some distance and may precede, accompany, or substitute for shock action.

Naval warfare from ancient times until well into the age of sail was characterized either by hand combat of troops that had boarded another's ships or by ramming the ships themselves. As long as shock action dominated naval combat, warships were constructed to balance high speed, maneuverability, and a reinforced bow with a strong ram. This meant that vessels on attack were manned by many oarsmen to provide speed and independence from the wind, but the light weight of the ships (dictated by the desire for increased speed) meant that the sides of the ships were particularly vulnerable.

Clearly such narrow, long, light, oar-driven ships had an advantage over the broad, sturdy, sail-driven merchant ships, as the former could overtake and maneuver to ram the side of or board the merchant vessel. In combat with other warships, however, tactical and operational skills were crucial in maneuvering to ram the opposing ships' flanks or alternatively to bring the ships close enough together to lock on to each other and permit the embarked soldiers to engage in pitched battle.

Given the fragility, small carrying capacity, and large complement of oarsmen and soldiers, such naval combatants were tied much more closely to the shore than either the limited merchant ships of the day or, even more dramatically, later sailing or steam vessels. Logistic requirements made base support or shore raids critical to the maintenance of the warships, and the dangers of the open seas to the fragile vessels tethered them closely to the shoreline.

These ship characteristics ensured that sea control was always contested and that blockades could be only intermittent. Ships did not have the staying power to achieve complete dominance at sea or to prolong blockades. At the same time, these ships could convoy troop transports and attack merchant vessels. Command of the sea, blockade, power projection, convoying, commerce raiding—these naval roles were as evident in ancient as in modern times, but their conditions and effectiveness differed.

As the center of political gravity began to shift from the Mediterranean to northern Europe in the late Middle Ages, the large, turbulent Atlantic became more important. At the same time, improved ship design, enhanced mariners' skills in sailing their ships closer to the direction from which the wind blew, and the burdensome cost of supporting a fleet of galleys figured in the greater prominence of the sailing warship, which was not substantially different in design from the merchant ship. For a time, the oar-driven galley and the sailing ship coexisted, but in time the sailing ship supplanted the galley everywhere.

Sailing ships could no longer employ ramming as the dominant warfare tool but instead depended on independent ship action to close and grapple at close quarters with an opposing ship. Elaborate rope nets to forestall boarding and high structures called *castles*, from which the bowman could send his missiles, provided the basis for combat at sea. All this changed with the advent of the cannon, which transformed naval warfare from shock to artillery or missile combat and finally doomed the galley.

The larger size of the warship, increased maneuverability associated with improved ship design and sailing skills, and the "stand-off" attack allowed—and required—by cannon gave the warship in the late medieval and early modern period greater independence from the shore and increased range and staying power. In a fundamental sense, developments in the last 400 years have been but an extension of these capabilities.

Although the transition from sail to steam made reliance on coaling stations and later on oil depots—and therefore on increased base support—more pressing, the general trend has been toward less reliance on large numbers of bases, but critical dependence on the few far-flung bases that remain. This evolution is particularly evident with nuclear-powered craft. Ship repair, aircraft and weapons system maintenance, and personnel needs still tie ships to the shore. Nonetheless, the notion of a blue-water (i.e., open-ocean) fleet with tremendous reach and endurance is a product of the industrial revolution and the technological advances that flowed from it. At the same time, the ability to engage enemy vessels and to attack targets ashore from a very great distance confirms artillery or missile action flexibly deployed over wide areas as the hallmark of contemporary naval warfare. Modern technology also complicates and renders more expensive this expanded capability.

Five major technological developments have shaped the problems and prospects of contemporary naval warfare: (1) the advent of weapons of mass destruction, most particularly atomic, biological, and chemical weapons; (2) long-range, accurately guided aircraft and missiles; (3) powerful sensors that can locate and identify targets over a considerable range; (4) automation extending human control with great accuracy and speed over dispersed and varied forces; and (5) techniques of masking forces to escape the very detection inherent in the above-mentioned sensors. This cluster of advances adds up to an enormously extended battlefield over which contending forces can accurately deliver devastating destruction once the targets are located. Moreover, the line between the sea and the shore blurs under these conditions, and advantages accrue to the side that can bring to bear combined air, land, and sea forces. At the same time, the dimensions of the battlefield extend outside the earth's atmosphere.

If the contending parties to a conflict are equipped with comparable sea-based or other capabilities, the tendency is either toward preemption or, if both sides' forces are configured to be highly survivable, toward stalemate. Therefore, military doctrines generally have tended either toward concentration on the initiation and early stages of conflict or toward deterrence. Much of the literature on naval warfare has shared similar characteristics, although developments during the 1980s in U.S. maritime strategy gave more emphasis to protracted conflict and war termination.

U.S. maritime strategy was built on the premise that general nuclear war was not only not inevitable, but also increasingly unlikely; that is to say, even during conflict, given the strategic second-strike capability of the superpowers, the nuclear threshold would remain at a high level. If a relatively stable nuclear deterrence persists between superpowers and their alliances, some inhibition might also exist against the use of other weapons of mass destruction such as chemical and biological weapons. If comparable capabilities do not exist on these levels as well, however, this inhibition is far less certain. In any case, the possibility of protracted conventional conflict and the issue of finding ways to terminate conflict short of nuclear Armageddon become more salient. Moreover, in less than general war circumstances, conventional forces are likely to be dominant, if not exclusive. Nuclear arms agreements may only further the general trend toward increased development of conventional forces, strategies, and operational concepts. The nuclear umbrella remains as the foundation of the deterrence both of general war and of nuclear use itself, but many commentators now assume that, as long as the sides concerned maintain secure nuclear forces, the nuclear threshold will remain high and conventional action the typical form of armed conflict.

Two cautionary notes are in order. First, whether or not nuclear weapons are used in armed conflict, and leaving aside their deterrent function even during war, all sides to a violent contest must deal with the possibility that they might be used—with the consequent political, strategic, and operational implications. Therefore, a campaign plan that promises success through conventional operations must have mechanisms built into it for keeping the conflict conventional or, alternatively, for responding should the enemy decide to alter the course of battle through the use of nuclear—or chemical or biological—weapons. Second, even with exclusively conventional combat, the complexity and cost of operations are very high as a result of technological developments and of the dispersion of relatively sophisticated weapons among many potential combatants. This is readily apparent in naval warfare.

The irony of contemporary naval warfare is that technology has extended the range and power of naval forces but at the same time increased their vulnerability. The range and accuracy of sensors and of weapons, as well as the ability to control forces with speed and accuracy, give the contemporary naval force great power but also dictate that they be combined in order to defend against precisely the same kind of threats from an adversary. Moreover, as naval forces move in close to land, additional land-based air support is integral to fleet defense and offense. This dilemma holds true not only for armed conflict between major adversaries with comparable capabilities but even in actions where the contestants are unequal. So devastatingly accurate are many modern weapons and so widespread could be the political effects of a successful attack on the naval combatant of an adversary, especially if that enemy were a superior power, that a complex—and expensive—combination of sea, air, and land forces is required in order to both defend and threaten. Moreover, the cost of modern technology has driven all military establishments toward fewer, if more capable, military platforms, with their consequent heightened value. This trend is clearly visible in naval forces, where an enormous extension of power has been purchased at the cost of fewer vessels. This approach is reasonable, but it dictates strategies for joining forces to capitalize on strengths while reducing the vulnerabilities inherent in the spread of sophisticated weapons.

Advances in technology have both extended the capabilities and particularly complicated the problem of those states whose survival or interests depend on maintaining relative dominance at sea. If, for instance, the issue is sustaining by sea and the airspace over the sea interests or allies that lie directly on the periphery of a great land power, then sustained sea control is the absolute precondition. The issue facing the land power with internal land lines of communication is of a different order. It need but *deny* the effective use of the sea to the maritime adversary in order to prevail. A relatively small force of attack submarines might seriously complicate—if not make impossible in a timely fashion—the defense of the sea lines of communication. The notion from land warfare that a 2–3:1 force ratio is required to overwhelm a well-constructed defense might be misleading when applied to defense of the sea lines of communications (SLOCs). Given modern sensors, mining capabilities, submarine "quieting," stealth weapons, and precision-guided munitions, attacks on the SLOCs might be easier and their defense more demanding. For a sea-dependent state, however, mutual sea denial is not stalemate; it is victory for the land power.

Concepts of naval warfare developed by strategists of major maritime powers, therefore, tend to put heavy emphasis on early offensive action in the event of conflict in order to defeat or neutralize the potential threat to the SLOCs. At the same time, sea control, once achieved, can be used to project power ashore and threaten militarily significant targets deep inside the enemy state. Returning to an earlier point, therefore, a maritime power views naval warfare not simply as an adjunct to land combat but also as the foundation of its security and the precondition of its ability to sustain conflict across the seas.

The Sea and Naval Warfare

Discussions of naval warfare are often prefaced by a sharp distinction between land and naval warfare—a distinction that ultimately arises from the environment in which navies operate. The environment associated with the sea is distinct, but the differences can be overdrawn.

Both land and sea warfare may involve temporary intervention in hostile areas, and both may be relatively fixed in place in a restrictive maritime or land theater. Moreover, both land and sea warfare may engage in shock or artillery actions. Both can be aimed at the essentially logistical outcome of securing or denying lines of communication and of threatening or defending industrial and base infrastructure. Both can be used to achieve the neutralization or destruction of opposing forces. At the same time, although differences of scale exist between land and sea warfare, joint fleet action, as well as the combination of air, land, and sea forces, within maritime theaters of operation tend to narrow the differences. Finally, in practice, doctrines of land warfare have more flexibility and strategies of sea warfare have more rigidity than those who seek differences might allow. Nonetheless, important differences remain in the roles and missions of naval and land forces, and these differences are very much associated with the distinct environments.

Naval forces have the dominant role in sea control and power projection. The mission of sea control can connote either positive control of designated sea areas for specified times and purposes or generalized dominance on the world's oceans. It can also imply a negative role—denial of sea control to the other side in either a specific or general sense. The purposes to which naval force will be put depend on the geopolitical posture, resources, and strategic requirements of the states concerned, as well as their general foreign policy objectives.

The mission of power projection includes a broad spectrum of offensive naval operations aimed at carrying military power from the sea to the shore. It could include nuclear strikes from the fleet ballistic missile force, strikes from carrier-based aircraft, amphibious assault forces, and naval bombardment with guns or missiles. As with sea control, this mission can be defined negatively—that is, preventing the adversary from exercising power projection. Maintaining sea control includes securing the sea lines of communication and is an essential precondition of power projection. Both sea control and power projection include the task of sustaining overseas deployed forces.

Sometimes strategic nuclear deterrence is listed among naval missions, but in a real sense a deterrent posture is the outcome of both sea control and power projection capabilities—that is, the ability under a variety of conditions to target and destroy the enemy's forces; industrial and logistical bases; command, control, and communications; or populations. Although ballistic missile submarines are among the least vulnerable strategic nuclear forces and thus at present undergird a stable nuclear balance, the general point remains: to deter or to fight depends on the capabilities and general functions of one's forces.

The same argument holds true for other types of missions, including presence, diplomatic persuasion, and response to crisis: unless the action is purely symbolic, success in these areas depends on the degree to which a state's ability to control the sea and project power is perceived as *credible* and *decisive*. In effect, therefore, the naval warfare missions of sea control and power projection can without distortion generally encompass the many roles that might be undertaken.

If naval warfare concerns combat on the surface of the sea, under the sea, and in the air, then navies can reasonably be organized in three areas—surface, subsurface, and air—and basic warfare tasks—antiair, antisubmarine, antisurface ship, strikes ashore, amphibious assault, mining, and mine countermeasures—can be related to these areas. Surveillance, intelligence, command and control and communications, control of the electromagnetic spectrum, logistics, and nonconventional and clandestine special warfare may be designated as supportive of the warfare areas as well. However, the missions as divided into combat areas and tasks represent elements of naval warfare and not naval warfare itself.

Naval warfare strives to control the environment on, in, under, and around the sea, including critical adjacent land areas, in order to move forces and materiel, to sustain forces ashore, and to attack targets strategically significant to realizing objectives determined by political authority. The sea shapes the problems or the opportunities a nation faces. Naval warfare is a response to these problems and opportunities, but its ultimate significance depends both on the importance of the sea to the nation and the coordination of naval forces with the entire spectrum of military power.

ROBERT S. WOOD

SEE ALSO: Amphibious Warfare; Antisubmarine Warfare; Blockade; Convoy and Protection of Shipping; Maritime Strategy; Naval Forces; Seapower.

Bibliography

Corbett, J. S. 1911. *Some principles of maritime strategy.* London: Longmans, Green.
Gorshkov, S. G. 1975. The development of the art of naval warfare. Trans. T. A. Neely, Jr. *U.S. Naval Institute Proceedings* 101 (6/868):54–63.
Hughes, W. P. 1986. *Fleet tactics: Theory and practice.* Annapolis, Md.: U.S. Naval Institute Press.
Jones, A. 1987. *The art of war in the western world.* Urbana and Chicago: Univ. of Illinois Press.
Landersman, S. 1982. *Principles of naval warfare.* Newport, R. I.: Naval War College Press.
Lautenschlager, K. 1984. *Technology and the evolution of naval warfare, 1851–2001.* Washington, D.C.: National Academy Press.
Levert, L. J. 1947. *Fundamentals of naval warfare.* New York: Macmillan.
Mahan, A. T. 1911. *Naval strategy: Compared and contrasted with the principles and practices of military operations on land.* London: Sampson, Low, Marston.
Moineville, H. 1983. *Naval warfare today and tomorrow.* Oxford, U.K.: Basil Blackwell.
Mordal, J. 1965. *Twenty-five centuries of sea warfare.* London: Souvenir Press.
Pemsel, H. 1975. *A history of war at sea: An atlas and chronology of conflict at sea from earlier times to the present.* Annapolis, Md.: U.S. Naval Institute Press.
Potter, E. B. 1981. *Sea power: A naval history.* 2d ed. Annapolis, Md.: U.S. Naval Institute Press.
Reynolds, C. G. 1974. *Command of the sea: The history and strategy of maritime empires.* New York: William Morrow.
Sanderson, M. 1975. *Sea battles: A reference guide.* Middletown, Conn.: Wesleyan Univ. Press.
Till, G. 1982. *Maritime strategy in the nuclear age.* London: Macmillan.

NAVY

A navy is a military organization created by a sovereign state to conduct operations of national importance in the maritime arena. States have built or acquired navies for: conducting combat in time of war, patrolling the waters adjacent to their borders, protecting merchants ships and convoys, conveying diplomatic messages to foreign countries, transporting combatant troops and equipment abroad, suppressing piracy, enforcing embargoes and blockading adversary shipping, laying and sweeping maritime mines, taking strategic missiles to sea, and a variety of other functions. The range of tasks to be accomplished by a navy requires a multiplicity of ship types and sizes in order to accomplish all of them. In fact, navy ships range from very small craft capable of operating only in well-protected harbors to the largest vehicle ever built by man—the modern aircraft carrier.

The primary advantage of possessing a navy is that its ships can carry and deliver larger payloads over longer distances than can any other weapon systems. Because the earth's surface is approximately 70 percent water, and because the water areas of the world are not politically controlled in the same way as land areas of the world, ships have broad and unencumbered access to the majority of the countries of the world. The primary disadvantage of a navy is that it is highly dependent on technology and the skills of its builders and its operators, and as a consequence navies tend to be expensive both to own and to operate.

Overview

Navies constitute one of the world's growth industries. In 1959, for example, only 67 states maintained a navy. In 1992, the number is 150, and 110 of those have been organized for duties beyond coastal patrol, policing, and general coast guard work. States desire navies for many reasons, and as a consequence the navies they possess range from the very large, diverse, complex navies of the United States (with over 500 ships and nearly 600,000 personnel) to those with greatly more limited interests and capabilities, such as Gabon (with four ships and a total of about 500 personnel).

Two naval strategists, U.S. admiral Alfred T. Mahan and Admiral of the Fleet of the Soviet Union Sergei G. Gorshkov, contributed considerably to the general understanding of navies. Mahan stands as the world's greatest advocate of the projection of a nation's power by means of the sea. Writing in the late nineteenth century, Mahan warned France and the United States that, while developing their land territory appeared enticing, their destinies were ultimately linked to the seas and naval development should be their highest priority. The United States took his advice, and today remains a world power.

Mahan discussed the concept of sea lines of communication, those vital arteries or sea routes that link a nation to its strategic overseas sources of supply. These must be protected, and an enemy's sea lines must be attacked. The most reliable way to accomplish this objective in time of war would be to engage and to defeat the enemy's battle fleet. According to Mahan, shore protection is not a naval function; rather, that is a garrison function better fulfilled by the army. Navies should project a state's power outward and engage enemy power on the seas and in its homeland so that an enemy can never threaten one's own shores. This concept of force projection provided the theoretical basis for U.S. naval development, producing the strongest navy in history.

Soviet admiral Gorshkov divided naval operations into three general realms: "fleet against the fleet," "fleet against the shore," and employment as "the most active instrument of state policy in time of peace." The first, involving the use of seapower against opposing navies at sea, consists of battles among opposing navies and accounts for much of naval history. "Fleet against the shore" involves applying seapower against another's land territory. This was the most important of the three themes, in Gorshkov's view, because operations under this concept struck at the enemy's political heartland and therefore constituted a strategic mission that elevated a navy to the position of a strategic service.

While "fleet against the shore" developed along with the first concept, for centuries it was generally of lesser importance. Its earliest major use was in transporting armies to enemy shores, where they would disembark from their ships, regroup, and conduct land campaigns. The operations of the Greeks against Sicily in the fifth century B.C., for example, and the Viking raids centuries later were early examples. In the twentieth century the notion of "fleet against the shore" has become paramount. Developments in naval gunnery first made possible a significant naval bombardment mission. Amphibious operations progressed and were perfected in World War II. These allowed for much deeper penetration of naval power into enemy territory. Sea-based airpower was also developed, and it played a significant role in the Pacific theater in World War II. With postwar developments, jet aircraft were adapted to carriers. Thus, naval airpower played a major role in the Korean War. The application of nuclear power—nuclear propulsion systems for carriers and nuclear weapons for aircraft—completed the transformation of the navy into a powerful sea projection instrument capable of launching aircraft to strike targets deep inside enemy territory. Finally, the combined application of nuclear power in weapons—particularly missiles—and in propulsion made the submarine a formidable strategic weapon system.

Gorshkov mirrored Mahan in his recognition of the importance of a navy to the overall well-being of a state, and he argued forcefully that the Soviet Union could not be a great country unless it maintained a powerful navy to protect its maritime commerce and its interests in peacetime on a global scale. He wrote that "With the emergence of the Navy onto the ocean expanses, the Soviet Union acquired new and more widespread opportunities to utilize it in peacetime in support of her own state interests."

For major seagoing states, these three functions will remain primary for their navies. For the others—the majority of the states of the world—navies will continue to perform missions that center narrowly on the defense of the maritime approaches to the homeland and the maintenance of order in the waters contiguous to the state. The latter include actions dealing with the conservation and protection of fisheries, antismuggling, safety of maritime operations, search and rescue, pollution control, and in some areas antipiracy and maritime traffic control.

This article will review the environment in which a navy operates, the origins of national navies, and how navies have been composed; it will close with a classification scheme and prospectus for navies in the future.

The Maritime Environment

Of major importance to a state are the physical and political environments in which its navy must operate. The physical environment is characterized by the fact that military forces operate there in a true three-dimensional manner. Forces with very different characteristics are required in order to be able to operate on, under, and above the surface of the water. Likewise, specialized sensors and specialized weapons are necessary if one is to conduct military operations effectively in each of the three strata. Unlike the land, the sea is hostile to supporting and prolonging human life. It requires the continual application of technology in order to support human life at sea, and if the "life support system" fails (the ship sinks), the results are catastrophic for human life. Furthermore, man does not live at sea, and as a consequence tends to be generally unfamiliar with it. Because naval operations are frequently conducted beyond the sight of land, moreover, they tend to be unknown and even mysterious to most people of the world. These are some physical consideration a state should understand when it contemplates acquiring or operating a navy.

The political environment in which a navy operates differs greatly from that on land as well, and the differences are not widely appreciated. Whereas the natural condition of the land today is to be under political control, the natural condition of the seas is to be uncontrolled. Virtually all land areas of the world are under an individual state's sovereign control. Those that are not are either disputed or covered by an international agreement to maintain their status. The reverse is true for oceanic areas: most of the world's oceanic areas are not under the political control of any state. For a navy, this means that there are special regimes of law that apply to the open seas, and there are also special regimes that apply as a ship approaches the land. It is not important, for the purposes of this article, either to detail or to describe the differences, only to recognize that there are significant differences between the political and legal regimes under which ships operate, and that they have singular importance for navies.

Origins of National Navies

Early civilizations built ships to use for migration, for trade, and to accompany and provide logistic support to land armies following coastal routes. Roads were universally poor; land vehicles had low carrying capacity and were slow in comparison to ships. The first ships specifically constructed to conduct warfare were galleys, which differed from "round-bottom" merchant ships because they were narrower, typically had low freeboard, and were comparatively fast and maneuverable because in battle mode they were powered by oarsmen. Galleys could cruise at about three nautical miles per hour (knots) for about six hours. Maximum speed for combat purposes was about seven knots, but that speed could not be sustained for very long without exhausting the oarsmen.

Based on technology from the Cretans, by 1100 B.C. the Phoenicians had built combatant galleys fitted with rams that were used to engage enemy ships in battle. The Greeks were the next generation of Mediterranean seafarers, using ships for transporting troops to foreign shores and for conducting military engagements at sea.

The Romans, essentially land warriors, developed the *corvus*, a hinged gangplank and grappling hook that served to hold an enemy galley alongside so legionaires could board and bring their army combatant skills to bear. The Carthaginians, Rome's primary enemy, were superior in seapower and seamanship at the time, and Rome used the *corvus* to offset the Carthaginian advantage. Subsequently, when the Romans had built and operated galleys for sufficiently long to obtain expertise in sea warfare, they became the dominant seapower in the Mediterranean.

Navies with galleys as the primary combatant ship were not maintained on a permanent basis, but were constructed to meet the requirements of a state at war or preparing for war. Most often, ships, experienced crews, leadership, and training were lacking at the onset of war. This stands as a historical constant with regard to navies: even if a permanent naval structure is maintained, navies are very capital-intensive organizations and they require large investments and long periods of time to construct and make ready to perform their tasks.

When Rome declined, naval development passed to Byzantium. For more than fifteen centuries—from the Battle of Actium in 31 B.C. to the Battle of Lepanto in 1571—there was only minor progress for navies. The reason for this was that except for the suppression of piracy, which has been an incessant task for navies, there were no major wars with maritime dimensions during that period.

True national navies did not appear on the world scene until sailing fleets came into widespread use. Three justifications accompanied the appearance of permanent navies. First, a state might have concluded that its commercial or colonial interests were widely enough dispersed and vulnerable to justify full-time shepherding by maritime military forces. Or, a state might find a navy useful for obtaining and maintaining far-flung colonies and naval bases. Or, third, a state might feel that its vulnerability to attack from seaward axes was considerable and permanent enough to warrant the expense and trouble of maintaining a navy. Some states were probably compelled by more than one of the three motives.

The first organized national navy belonged to Great Britain. For that country the interest in a national navy can be traced back to King Henry VII, near the end of the fifteenth century. King Henry VIII and then Queen Elizabeth used the navy to defend commerce, to defend the home islands, and to "take trade" from their adversaries. It was not until the reign of King Charles I in the middle of the seventeenth century, however, that the issue of a national navy paid for by the citizenry was joined. Charles I's "Ship Money Fleet" was the first true national navy—large, permanent, national, paid for by the Parliament, and controlled by the government. Other navies were organized soon after—the French and Russian in the latter part of the seventeenth century, under the guidance of Jean Baptiste Colbert and Peter the Great, respectively.

The organization of the United States Navy was not to occur until a century later. The Navy Act of 1794 was enacted to protect American merchantmen from capture by North African raiders, but the immediate justification was outbreak of war between Britain and France and the concern within the United States about the free movement of trade on the oceans in time of war.

Even when the clear need for a navy arose, statesmen found that such a course was not particularly easy to pursue. The reason was primarily one of economics. For the most part, navies had to compete with alternatives that were easier for statesmen to rationalize. In order to prosper, navies have historically required a strong champion in a power government position. As a consequence of these factors, few states acquired large seagoing navies. That fact remains true to this day. While many states have large armies, and the number of air forces in the world is impressive, the number of states that maintain large, competent navies is fewer than—and has rarely exceeded—ten.

Yet, many states maintain small navies, since there are significantly more functions today for full-time navies to perform than when navies were in their infancy. The major issues confronting states revolve around what kind of naval forces should be acquired, to accomplish what functions, and in what numbers.

Composition of Navies

Navies consist of ships and craft, sea-based and land-based aircraft of different kinds, support and headquarters bases and facilities, and personnel to perform all required functions. Some states include amphibious forces, or marines, or other special-purpose forces (naval infantry, "frogmen," or ordnance disposal experts, for example) as part of their navies. What sets a navy apart from other armed forces, however, is its ships.

Since antiquity, specialization has been the order of the day in ships. Light *liburnians* were used in the earliest times to hunt down corsairs. For combat there were medium galleys such as *quinqueremes*, and heavy combatants. Sailing navies were composed of ships of the line of battle (battleships), accompanied by frigates and corvettes assigned to scouting and escort duties. In the mid-to-late nineteenth century—the beginning of the steamship era—diversification became even more marked. The capital ships were the battleships, heavily armed and protected, designed for combat against the battleships of an adversary. Battle cruisers, faster and less protected, preceded the main battlefleet. Cruisers acted as antisurface warfare scouts, as commerce raiders, and as combatants against smaller ships. Destroyers and torpedo boats protected the capital ships and provided close escort for merchant shipping.

The explosion of technologies for warfare that took place in the late nineteenth and early twentieth centuries added the third dimension to seapower. Submarines and aircraft brought significantly increased complexity to what had been a strictly two-dimensional field of battle. They also sounded the death knell for battleships as the world's capital ship, but it took Japan's attack on Pearl Harbor in 1941 to demonstrate that fact clearly. Subsequently, aircraft carriers became the preeminent surface ships, and major navies were organized around them.

Differeing philosophies and strategies, conditioned by geopolitical perspectives, resulted in varying, specialized force structures for the world's navies. Generally speaking, the Europeans produced smaller, heavily armored carriers in the interest of providing relatively short-range defense of national territory. European carriers typically had short cruising ranges, and their small size restricted them to carrying less capable aircraft than large carriers could operate. Spanish, French, Italian, and Russian carriers reflected this influence. In contrast, the United States opted to construct large aircraft carriers to embark and employ high-performance fixed-wing aircraft because it envisioned its role as the projection of maritime power well beyond the shores of the North American continent.

Owing to this difference in approach—an anticipation that its aircraft carriers would operate in "high threat" areas—the United States accompanied its carriers with other capable ships: cruisers, destroyers, frigates, and submarines. While the range of a battleship's guns was a respectable 40 kilometers (25 mi.), the range of carrier-based aircraft is measured in hundreds of miles and they can carry nuclear weapons. Cruise missiles integral to many ships of a carrier battle group can reach inland at least as far as attack aircraft. Modern command, control, communications, computing, and intelligence make it possible to organize integrated offensive and defensive battle group operations. These changes have had a major impact on naval warfare, for they forced a consolidation of what had been separate land and sea theaters of warfare. Nevertheless, no state other than the United States possesses and operates battle groups centered on large aircraft carriers.

The majority of the world's navies do not have ships larger than destroyers in their inventories. Typically, those navies consist of fewer than twenty surface ships of 500 gross tons or larger displacement. These ships normally operate in close proximity to the state's coastline, rarely cruising into the open oceans, venturing far from the homeland, or conducting visits to foreign ports.

Surface ships form the centerpiece for navies of the world. Aircraft—including sea- and land-based fixed-wing varieties and helicopters—extend the sensor and weapon capability of ships. They move the horizons of the surface force outward.

Submarines have been built or acquired by more than 40 of the world's navies. Most of these are diesel-electric powered ships, which means that there are important limitations on their operations. Nuclear-powered submarines are operated today only by China, France, Russia, the United Kindom, and the United States. The great advantages of nuclear-powered submarines are sustained speed and endurance while submerged. The states that operate diesel-electric submarines use them essentially for the same mission as their surface ships and maritime aircraft: territorial defense against attacks from the sea. Those that maintain nuclear-powered submarines in their orders of battle, however, find that they are effective for a wider range of tasks, including strategic ballistic missile patrols, antisurface and antisubmarine warfare, covert surveillance and reconnaissance, minelaying, escort of surface ships, land-attack by means of cruise missiles, and covert insertion of agents and raiding parties.

In addition to seagoing forces, modern-day navies require a shore infrastructure to support them. The dependence of navies on shore support has fluctuated over the years. Galleys were almost totally dependent on shoreward services, for they could not carry many provisions or even much fresh water for their labor-intensive operations. By way of contrast, sailing ships were very independent. They could spend months at sea totally free of contact with other ships or land bases. When ships began to rely on means of propulsion other than the wind, the importance of landward sources of supply, repair, and support became prominent once again.

In the 1990s, sophisticated technical equipment in ships and sea-based aircraft demands close attention by highly qualified personnel, and schools are needed ashore to train them. Operating fleets must replenish stores as often as every three days, which requires both highly mobile and stationary logistic infrastructures. Command headquarters for ships at sea continue to be centralized on land. Finally, ships rely upon—or conversely can be attacked by—land-based forces. Ships today are clearly less isolated from, and consequently less independent of, activities taking place on land. Moreover, the historical supremacy of navies has been mirrored in the size and quality of their land-based infrastructure.

Prospectus

Because the geographies and perceived requirements for naval services differ so greatly among states of the world, each state has constituted its maritime forces in a different way. It is useful to offer a general scheme of classification for them, however, for it will demonstrate the range of need and choice, and at the same time indicate the scope of possibilities for the future. A hierarchy of navies composed of six ranks can be suggested for these purposes:

First-rank navies are global navies capable of accomplishing deterrence missions and rapid deployment on a global scale. As of the early 1990s, there were two navies that could be described in this way: those of the United States and Russia. Of the two, the navy of the United States is by far the stronger and diversely more capable. There is very little by way of encouragement to present-day states to invest in a globe-spanning fleet of naval ships.

Second-rank navies are also global navies, but their strategic oceangoing capabilties are more modest. They, too, have limited presence on a global basis, and they maintain the ability to deploy forces rapidly for occasional intervention beyond their home regions. The British and French navies are second-rank under this description.

Third-rank navies are regional navies. They do not have strategic deterrent forces, but do maintain a power projection capability within their oceanic theater of operations. Argentina, Brazil, India, Japan, and Spain maintain such navies. Except for Japan, each of these possesses aircraft carriers in the early 1990s, although the carriers of Argentina and Brazil are obsolete. While Japan has the strongest of these navies, it views itself as constrained by its constitution from having aircraft carriers.

The Chinese navy (the People's Liberation Army Navy, or PLAN) maintains a large inventory of a variety of ships and it also counts ballistic missile submarines in its order of battle. It constitutes a special case, however, because its overseas presence is virtually nonexistent, and its sea-projection capability and ability to operate far from its home bases are poor. Accordingly, the PLAN must be classified a third-rank navy.

Fourth-rank navies are subregional navies. They do not possess carriers, and they have manifestly lesser capabilities than third-rank navies. They are still capable, however, of operations on the high seas. Some are modern and homogeneous, such as those of Australia, Canada, Germany, Greece, and the Netherlands. Others—such as those of Chile, Indonesia, Peru, Taiwan, and Turkey—have outdated ships that are kept primarily for prestige and economic reasons.

Fifth-rank navies are coastal navies with good military potential. Belgium, Israel, and Sweden have such navies. They are tailored to a specific theater to perform specialized tasks. These navies rely heavily on missile-equipped, fast patrol craft, which represent half the developing world's naval capability.

Sixth-rank navies are constabulary forces devoid of significant military potential. Most African navies are sixth-rank navies.

Because of its load-bearing characteristics, the sea will continue in the future to offer a cost-effective avenue for transporting goods—and weapons—in ships. Since the world is politically organized into nation-states, the need will arise to use the seas not only for commerce but also for purposes of state policy. For as long as the use of force remains as a possible instrument of national policy, states of the world with access to the sea will be interested in maintaining a navy. Like all military forces, navies of the future will be obliged to compete for scarce budget dollars and for a priority position in the scheme of national defenses.

SEE ALSO: Fleet; Naval Forces; Organization, Navy; Seapower; Warship.

Bibliography

Brodie, B. [1943] 1988. *Sea power in the machine age.* Reprint. New York: Greenwood Press.
Coletta, P. E. 1980. *The American Naval Heritage in brief.* 2d. ed. Washington, D.C.: University Press of America.
George, J. L., ed. 1986. *The Soviet and other communist navies.* Annapolis, Md.: U.S. Naval Institute Press.
———. 1985. *The U.S. Navy: The view from the mid-1980s.* Boulder, Colo.: Westview Press.
Gorshkov, S. G. 1979. *The seapower of the state.* Oxford: Pergamon.
Lacoste, P. 1985. *Stratégies navales du present.* Paris: Lattes.
Morris, M. A. 1987. *Expansion of third-world navies.* New York: St. Martin's Press.
Rogers, W. L. [1940] 1967. *Naval warfare under oars 4th to 16th centuries: A study of strategy, tactics, and ship design.* Annapolis, Md.: U.S. Naval Institute Press.
Watson, B. 1991. *The changing face of the world's navies: 1945 to the present.* London: Arms and Armour Press.

NELSON, HORATIO [1758–1805]

Horatio Nelson remains Great Britain's greatest naval officer. His expert seamanship, courage, intelligence, and his willingness to fight on in apparently hopeless situations enabled him to achieve a series of victories, culminating at Trafalgar in 1805, that provided Great Britain with undisputed mastery of the seas for over a century. Additionally, his standards of conduct and seamanship set a standard that is still emulated by officers in the Royal Navy.

Early Life and Career

Nelson was born 29 September 1758 at Burnham Thorpe, in Norfolk, England. The son of a clergyman, he went to sea as a midshipman at the age of 12. At the age of 18, he was promoted to lieutenant, and, because of his exceptional ability and devotion, he received an appointment as the captain of a sloop-of-war in 1779, and was then made captain of a frigate. Thus, at the age of 20, Nelson was the youngest captain in the history of the Royal Navy.

Nelson subsequently saw active service in the Americas, the Baltic, and the North Atlantic. From 1793 to

1796, he served three years of arduous service in the Mediterranean Sea. As captain of the 75-gun ship HMS *Agamemnon* in 1794, he was wounded during the occupation of Corsica and lost the sight of an eye. In 1797, as captain of the 75-gun ship HMS *Captain*, Nelson participated in the Battle of Cape St. Vincent on 14 February. During the battle, he engaged the largest ship in the world, the 130-gun Spanish flagship, *Santissima Trinidad*, plus two 112-gun ships, and a 74-gun ship. His bravery and performance in this battle won him promotion to rear admiral and a knighthood. Later in the year, he was sent to capture Santa Cruz de Tenerife. He was repulsed and wounded in this engagement and his right arm was amputated.

Nelson returned to duty and commanded a squadron during the blockade of Cádiz. From there he was sent to seek out the French fleet in the Mediterranean. After several weeks of searching the central and eastern Mediterranean, he found the French fleet anchored at Aboukir Bay, near Alexandria, Egypt, on 1 August 1798. The speed and vigor of Nelson's attack and his tactics allowed him to bring greatly superior firepower to bear on selected portions of the French line, and victory in the ensuing night battle. The 120-gun *Orient*, the French flagship, was destroyed, and nine French ships were captured, while three ships and two frigates were able to escape. Although there were 900 British casualties, including another wound for Nelson, not a single British ship was damaged seriously. The French had lost ten of thirteen ships and had more than 5,000 casualties. This was one of the most overwhelming victories in naval history and sealed the fate of Bonaparte's army in Egypt.

Baron Nelson of the Nile spent the next year-and-a-half involved in operations off the coast of Italy, in which he successfully eliminated the French influence from that portion of the peninsula. He returned to England in late 1800 and was promoted to vice admiral on 1 January 1801.

In February 1801 he became second in command, under Admiral Sir Hyde Parker, of a new fleet being prepared for operations in the Baltic. The objective of this fleet was to display a show of force or to use force, if necessary, to discourage an alliance of the neutral Baltic powers—Russia, Prussia, Denmark, and Sweden—from providing support to France in the ongoing war. The first major problem was that Denmark would not allow the British fleet to enter the Baltic. In late March, the British fleet approached Copenhagen, which was strongly defended by sixteen Danish ships and powerful shore batteries. On 1 April Nelson convinced Parker to allow him to take half of the fleet to attack the Danish fleet and coastal batteries. On 2 April Nelson took the twelve ships with the shallowest drafts and closed in, while Parker stood off to observe.

The resulting battle was one of the most bitterly contested in naval history. At one point, the situation looked so bad for Nelson that Parker signaled him by flag to discontinue the action. Knowing that the unfavorable winds would not allow him to withdraw without losing all of his ships, Nelson ignored the signal and ordered his captains to redouble their efforts. When his flag captain finally brought the signal to his attention, Nelson put his glass to his blind eye and responded, "You know, Foley, . . . I really do not see the signal." Nelson persevered, the Danes surrendered, and Denmark was forced to make peace and leave the alliance. Nelson, who expected to be court-martialed and possibly hung for disobeying orders, replaced Parker, who was relieved of his command.

In part because of Nelson's victory at Copenhagen, Great Britain and France signed a peace treaty in 1802. Hostilities were renewed in May 1803, however, and Nelson was sent to command again in the Mediterranean.

Prelude to the Battle of Trafalgar

For a year-and-a-half the principal duty of the British Mediterranean fleet was to blockade the French fleet at Toulon. On 30 March 1805, however, French admiral Pierre Villeneuve was able to take advantage of bad weather to elude Nelson's blockade. Without being detected by the British, the French fleet sailed out of the Mediterranean and across the Atlantic to the West Indies.

After vainly searching throughout the Mediterranean for the French, Nelson also sailed for the West Indies. Upon learning that Nelson was approaching, Villeneuve set sail immediately for Europe. Nelson searched in vain for the French in the West Indies, and then he, too, sailed for Europe, about a month behind the French.

Villeneuve arrived at Cádiz on 20 August 1805, where he was joined by French and Spanish reinforcements, which brought his fleet strength to 39 ships of the line. He was promptly blockaded by a much smaller British squadron. Nelson joined the squadron on 28 September and took command of a combined force of 34 ships of the line.

Because of the initiation of intensive land campaigning in central Europe (the beginning of the Ulm and Austerlitz campaigns), Nelson expected that Villeneuve would be ordered by Napoleon to proceed into the Mediterranean. He also correctly believed that Villeneuve did not know that Nelson had arrived and that the blockading force was so strong. Thus, he expected the allied Franco-Spanish fleet to soon set sail for the Strait of Gibraltar.

Unable to talk at length personally with all of his captains, Nelson wrote them a lengthy memorandum explaining his concept of the battle that he expected to occur. He intended to concentrate part of his fleet under his second in command, Admiral Cuthbert Collingwood, against the enemy rear. Meanwhile, Nelson and the remainder of the fleet would threaten the leading ships of the enemy line, breaking through its center, and joining Collingwood in bringing overwhelming strength against the rear. "I look with confidence," he wrote, "to a victory before the van of the enemy could succour their rear." He concluded, "But in case signals can neither be seen or perfectly understood, no captain can do very wrong if he places his ship alongside that of the enemy."

The Battle of Trafalgar

On 19 October Villeneuve sailed from Cádiz with 33 ships of the line, heading for the Strait of Gibraltar. Nelson, with only 27 ships of the line, promptly moved to intercept him before he could reach the strait. As the British approached early on 21 October, Villeneuve changed course to the north in order to keep a line of escape to Cádiz open in case the coming battle did not go well. He formed his fleet in a line of battle.

During the morning, the British fleet converged on Villeneuve. The British were in two columns: Nelson was in the north and led eleven other ships from his flagship, HMS *Victory* (Fig. 1). Collingwood had fifteen ships in the southern column and approached the rear of the allied French-Spanish fleet. Just before noon, as the fleets were almost within gunshot of each other, Nelson hoisted the flag signal: "England expects every man to do his duty." Collingwood opened the battle a few minutes later.

Although in his memorandum Nelson had written that "nothing is sure in a sea fight," the Battle of Trafalgar went exactly as he had planned. After threatening the lead allied ships, Nelson led his column to break the line between the thirteenth and fourteenth ships. Thus the British concentrated 27 ships against 20 enemy ships. The battle was over by 5:00 P.M., an overwhelming British victory. Nineteen French and Spanish ships were captured, without the loss of a single British ship.

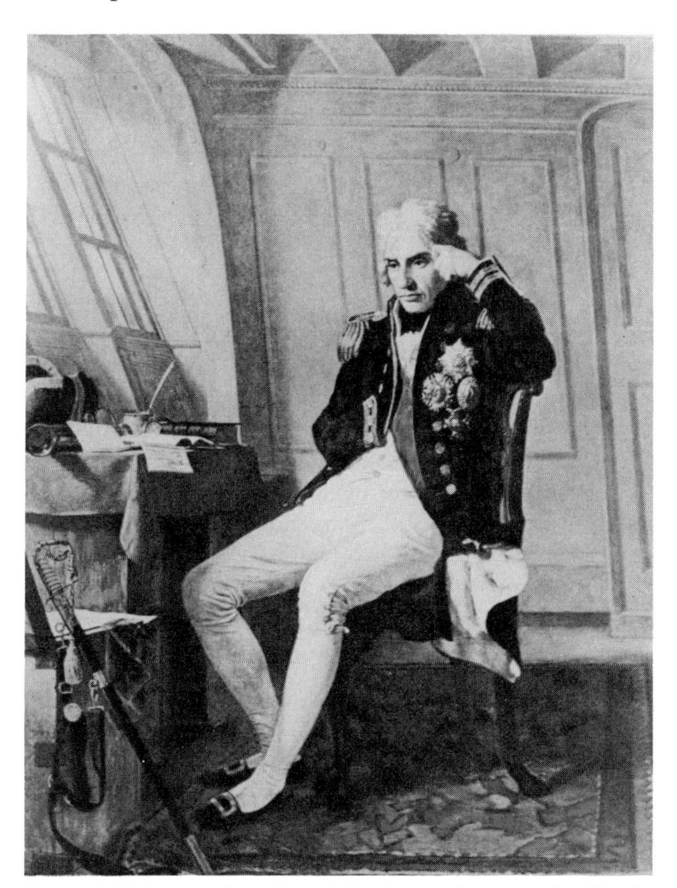

Figure 1. Nelson in the cabin of the Victory *(painting by Charles Lucy).* (SOURCE: U.S. Library of Congress)

The British had, however, suffered a loss far greater than one or more ships. Barely an hour after the battle had started, and as his *Victory* was alongside the French *Redoubtable*, Nelson was mortally wounded by a musket shot from a sniper positioned high on the mast of the French ship. He lived long enough to be told that his fleet had been victorious and replied, "Now I am satisfied. Thank God, I have done my duty."

Lord Nelson's Significance

Like Alexander the Great, Nelson died at the height of his career. Unlike Alexander, however, Nelson's crowning achievement endured for more than a century, as Great Britain exercised undisputed control of the oceans and seas of the world.

BRUCE W. WATSON

SEE ALSO: Seapower, British; United Kingdom of Great Britain and Northern Ireland.

Bibliography

Mahan, A. T. [1887] 1984. *The life of Nelson: The embodiment of British sea power.* 4 vols. Reprint. New York: Found Class Reprints.

NETHERLANDS, KINGDOM OF THE

A small European nation that has long depended on trade and commerce for its livelihood, the Netherlands is the most densely populated nation in Europe. Further, a substantial portion of its land area lies below sea level and has been reclaimed through the use of dikes and drainage canals.

Power Potential Statistics

Area: 37,290 square kilometers (14,398 sq. mi.)
Population: 14,810,800
Total Active Armed Forces: 101,400 (0.685% of pop.)
Gross Domestic Product: US$218.0 billion (1990 est.)
Annual Defense Expenditure: US$6.8 billion (2.7% of GDP, 1990 est.)
Iron and Steel Production:
  Crude steel: 4.346 million metric tons (1986)
  Pig iron: 3.617 million metric tons (1986)
Fuel Production:
  Coal: All Dutch coal mines were closed on 1 January 1975.
  Crude oil: 4.142 million metric tons (1990)
  Natural gas: 71,715 million cubic meters (1989)
Electrical Power Output: 63,570 million kwh (1989)
Merchant Marine: 344 vessels; 2,722,838 gross registered tons

Civil Air Fleet: 98 major transport aircraft; 28 usable airfields (18 with permanent-surface runways); none with runways over 3,659 meters (12,000 ft.); 12 with runways 2,440–3,659 meters (8,000–12,000 ft.) 3 with runways 1,220–2,440 meters (4,000–8,000 ft.).

For the most recent information, the reader may refer to the following annual publications:

The Military Balance. International Institute for Strategic Studies. London: Brassey's (UK).

The Statesman's Year-Book. New York: St. Martin's Press.

The World Factbook. Central Intelligence Agency. Washington, D.C.: Brassey's (US).

History

The history of the Netherlands as an independent state began with the long struggle for independence from Hapsburg Spain, which lasted from 1568 to 1648. In its early stages, this was led by Prince William of Orange (William the Silent), and the government of the Netherlands was a republic. The successful end of the struggle for independence marked the start of a brief era of colonial expansion and power. Although Dutch naval and commercial power was checked by the English in a series of naval wars (1652–54, 1665–67, 1672–74), the Netherlands remained heavily involved in overseas trade. By 1700, it had lost its North American colony but retained colonies in the Caribbean, Guiana, South Africa, Ceylon, and the East Indies.

The Netherlands was closely involved in European affairs in the seventeenth and eighteenth centuries, but its small size and modest resources compelled increasingly minor roles as time went on. The country was occupied by the French during the French Revolutionary and Napoleonic Wars and, after the Congress of Vienna, was merged with Belgium and Luxembourg to form a new Kingdom of the Netherlands (1815). Belgium revolted against Dutch rule in 1830, and the union was officially dissolved in 1839, with Belgium becoming an independent kingdom and Luxembourg an independent duchy.

Over the next century, the Dutch were neutral, avoiding involvement in World War I. They were invaded by the Germans in spring 1940 as part of the attack on France, and although they fought well they were overwhelmed by the Germans' superior numbers and air power. After the war, the Dutch were compelled to grant independence to their East Indian possessions (captured by the Japanese in March-May 1942), which became the nation of Indonesia. The Netherlands joined NATO as a charter member in 1949. In 1964, under pressure from Indonesia, the Dutch turned over Western New Guinea (Irian Jaya) to Indonesia to avoid an armed clash.

Politico-Military Background and Policy

The Dutch have a long and often illustrious military and naval tradition, much of it from the sixteenth century. Dutch policy since 1949 has been directed to support NATO, and the Dutch armed forces are fully integrated into the NATO command structure.

The Netherlands armed forces are staffed through conscription, which applies to all able-bodied males over age 20. Service is for a period of 22 to 24 months, with liability for refresher training through age 35. There is also a draftee's union, which has produced relaxation of some elements of traditional military discipline. Recruits are allowed to wear long hair, omit salutes, and so on; they also receive high pay and overtime compensation. Despite these seemingly lax regulations, the Dutch army performs well in exercises conducted alongside its allies' forces.

Strategic Problems

The Netherlands' main strategic problem is the country's small size and lack of air space. Consequently, they depend closely on NATO for their national security.

Military Assistance

The Netherlands receives no military assistance from abroad in the usual sense. They have participated in several NATO-sponsored technical development projects, however, and Dutch military personnel attend courses in other NATO countries.

Defense Industry

Although most of its military equipment is purchased abroad, the Dutch produce their own armored personnel carriers (YPR-765 and -408) and build nearly all their own naval vessels. The Dutch Fokker aircraft company produces the F-27 and F-28 light transports, widely exported to developing nations.

Alliances

The Netherlands has been a member of NATO since 1949 and is also a member of the European Community, the Common Market, the United Nations (UN), and the WEU. It also maintains especially close ties with Belgium and Luxembourg, which together form the Benelux nations. As part of its NATO commitments, the United States has a tactical fighter squadron of 2,000 men and 24 F-15C/D, and 930 army personnel in the Netherlands.

Defense Structure

Queen Beatrix is the nominal commander in chief of the Netherlands armed forces (*Krijgsmacht*). The Council of Ministers is responsible to the prime minister for preparation and implementation of defense policy. The minister of defense (a member of the council), assisted by three service secretaries, is responsible for military preparedness and armed forces organization. A Military Committee of the three services' chiefs of staff, and chaired by a general or admiral, advises the civilian authorities. Command authority is vested with the chiefs of staff, who are directly accountable to the government.

(For an explanation of the abbreviations and symbols used in the following section of military statistics, see the list of Abbreviations and Acronyms in each volume.)

Total Armed Forces

Active: 101,400 (incl 3,900 Royal Military Constabulary, 800 Inter-Service Organization); 1,750 women; 45,400 conscripts. Terms of service: Army and Air Force 12–14 months, Navy, 12–15 months.
Reserves: 152,400 (men to age 35, NCO to 40, officers to 45). Army 132,200 (some—at the end of their conscription period—on short leave, immediate recall), Navy some 9,000 (7,000 on immediate recall); Air Force 11,200 (immediate recall).

ARMY: 64,100 (40,500 conscripts).
1 Corps HQ, 3 mech div HQ.
3 armed bde (incl 1 cadre).
6 mech inf bde (incl 2 cadre).
1 indep inf bde (cadre).
Summary Combat Arm Units:
17 mech inf. bn.
2 inf bn.
12 tk bn.
4 recce bn.
17 arty bn.
1 Lance SSM bn.
5 AD bn.
3 hel sqn (Air Force-manned).
Reserves: cadre bde and corps tps completed by call-up of reservists.
Territorial Command (41,600 on mob): 2 inf bde, 4 bn, spt units, could be mob for territorial defense.
Home Guard: 3 sectors; inf weapons.
Equipment:
MBT: 913 (incl 163 in store): 468 Leopard 1A4, 445 Leopard 2.
AIFV: 984 (incl 142 in store) (CFE: 718): 718 YPR-765, 266 M-113C/-R all with 25mm.
APC: 2,232 (CFE: 749): 476 M-113, 1,120 YPR-765, 636 YP-408 (in store).
Total arty: 824.
Towed arty: 165: 105mm: 42 M-101; 155mm: 123 M-114.
SP arty: 298: 155mm: 222 M-109A3; 203mm: 76 M-110.
MRL: 227mm: 22 MLRS.
Mortars: 107mm: 141 M-30, 53 M-106 SP; 120mm: 145 (incl 10 in store).
SSM: 7 Lance launchers (incl 1 in store).
ATGW: 753 (incl 135 in store): 427 Dragon, 326 (incl 302 YPR-765) TOW.
RCL: 106mm: 185.
AD guns: 35mm: 95 Gepard SP; 40mm: 131 L/70 towed.
SAM: 474 Stinger.
Helicopters: 62 SA-316 (to be replaced), 29 Bo-105. (Air Force-manned).
Marine: 1 tk tpt, 3 coastal, 15 river patrol boats.

NAVY: 16,600 incl naval air arm (1,600) and marines (2,800) (1,400 conscripts). Bases: Netherlands: Den Helder (HQ); Vlissingen. Overseas: Willemstad (Curaçao), Oranjestad (Aruba).
Submarines: 5: 1 Zeeleeuw with Mk 48 HWT; plus Harpoon USGW; 2 Zwaardvis with Mk 37 HWT; 2 Dolfijn with Mk 37 HWT.
Principal Surface Combatants: 15:
Destroyers: 4 DDG (NL desig = FFG):
2 Tromp with 1 SM-1 MR SAM; plus 2 × 4 Harpoon SSM, 1 × 2 120mm guns, 1 Lynx hel (ASW/OTHT), 2 × 3 ASTT (Mk 46 LWT).
2 Van Heemskerck with 1 SM-1 MR SAM; plus 2 × 4 Harpoon, 2 × 2 ASTT.
Frigates: 11 FF: 1 Karel Doorman with 2 × 4 Harpoon SSM, plus 2 × 2 ASTT; 1 Lynx (ASW/OTHT) hel; 10 Kortenaer with 2 Lynx (ASW/OTHT) hel, 2 × 2 ASTT; plus 2 × 4 Harpoon.
Mine Warfare: 26:
Minelayers: none, but Mercuur, listed under spt and misc, has capability.
Mine Countermeasures: 26: 15 Alkmaar (tripartite) MHC; 11 Dokkum MSC.
Amphibious: craft only; about 17 LCA: 12 (.
Support and Miscellaneous: 9: 2 Poolster AOR (1–3 Lynx hel), 3 survey, 1 Mercuur torpedo tender, 2 trg, 1 aux.

Naval Air Arm: (1,600):
MR: 1 sqn with F-27M (see Air Force).
MR/ASW: 2 sqn (1 trg) with P-3C.
ASW/SAR: 2 sqn with Lynx hel.
Equipment: 13 cbt ac, 22 armed hel.
Aircraft: P-3C: 13 (MR).
Helicopters: Lynx: 22 (ASW, SAR).

Marines: (2,800): 2 cdo gp; 1 mtn/arctic warfare coy.
Reserve: 1 cdo gp.

AIR FORCE: 16,000 (3,500 conscripts).
FGA: 4 sqn with F-16A/B;
Fighter: 4 sqn with F-16A/B (3 ftr/FGA, 1 ftr).
Recce: 1 sqn with F-16A.
MR: 2 F-27M (assigned to Navy).
Transport: 1 sqn with F-27.
OCU: 1 sqn with F-16B (temporarily integrated with 1 F-16A ftr sqn).
SAR: 1 flt with SA-319.
AD: 8 bty with HAWK SAM (4 in Ge).
4 bty with Patriot SAM (in Ge).
Equipment: 181 cbt ac (plus 23 in store), no armed hel.
Aircraft:
F-16: 181: -A: 146 (54 FGA, 64 ftr, 20 recce, 8* trg); -B: 35 (12 FGA, 14 ftr, 9* trg).
F-27: 16 (14 tpt, 2 MR).
Helicopters: SA-316: 4 (SAR).
Missiles:
AAM: AIM-9/L/N Sidewinder.
SAM: 48 HAWK, 20 Patriot, 100 Stinger.
AD: guns: 25 VL 4/41 Flycatcher radar, 75 L/70 40mm systems.

FORCES ABROAD
Germany: 5,700. 1 armd bde (2 armd inf, 1 tk bn), 1 recce bn, 1 engr bn, spt elm (122 MBT, 18 155mm SP, 30 ATGW), 4 HAWK, 4 Patriot bty.
Netherlands Antilles: 1 frigate, 1 amph cbt det, 1 MR det with 2 F-27MPA ac.
Iceland: 30: 1 P-3C (at Keflavik).
UN and Peacekeeping:
Angola (UNAVEM II): observers.
Egypt (MFO): 105: 5 sigs det.
Middle East (UNTSO): 15 observers.

PARAMILITARY
Royal Military Constabulary: (Koninklijke Marechaussee): 3,900 (400 conscripts); 3 'div' comprising 10 districts with 72 'bde'.
Civil Defense: (Corps Mobiele Colonnes): 270 (130 conscripts): 18,500 on mob; disaster relief under Army comd.

FOREIGN FORCES
NATO: HQ Allied Forces Central Europe (AFCENT).
U.S.: 2,750. Army 750; Air 2,000; 1 tac ftr sqn.

Future

The Netherlands has no major national security concerns outside of NATO and will almost certainly continue its strong support of the alliance. Dutch forces are modern, well equipped, and well trained, although their deployment in northern Germany (in the expected path of two Soviet armies) would mean hard fighting in the event of war.

DAVID L. BONGARD
TREVOR N. DUPUY

SEE ALSO: Belgium; European Communities; Military History, Early Modern; NATO; Western Europe.

Bibliography

Everts, P., ed. 1985. *Controversies at home: Domestic factors in the foreign policy of the Netherlands.* Boston and Dordrecht: M. Nijhoff.
Hunter, B., ed. 1991. *The statesman's year-book, 1991–92.* New York: St. Martin's Press.
International Institute for Strategic Studies. 1991. *The military balance, 1991–1992.* London: Brassey's.
Newton, G. 1978. *The Netherlands: A historical and cultural survey, 1795–1977.* Boulder, Colo.: Westview Press.
Snellen, I. T. M., ed. 1985. *Limits of government: Dutch experiences.* Amsterdam: Kobra Publishers.

NEW ZEALAND

A South Pacific nation with abundant natural resources and unique wildlife, New Zealand is also renowned for its natural beauty.

Power Potential Statistics

Area: 268,680 square kilometers (103,737 sq. mi.)
Population: 3,376,400
Total Active Armed Forces: 11,300 (0.335% of pop.)
Gross Domestic Product: US$40.2 billion (1990 est.)
Annual Defense Expenditure: US$832 million (2.07% of GDP, 1990 est.)
Iron and Steel Production:
Crude steel: 0.287 million metric tons (1986)
Pig iron: 0.200 million metric tons (1986)
Fuel Production:
Coal: 2.401 million metric tons (1988)
Coke: 0.008 million metric tons (1986)
Crude oil: 1.657 million metric tons (1990)
Natural gas: 5.36 million cubic meters (1986)
Electrical Power Output: 28,000 million kwh (1990)
Merchant Marine: 21 vessels; 204,269 gross registered tons
Civil Air Fleet: 40 major transport aircraft; 157 usable airfields (33 with permanent-surface runways); none with runways over 3,659 meters (12,000 ft.); 2 with runways 2,440–3,659 meters (8,000–12,000 ft.); 46 with runways 1,220–2,440 meters (4,000–8,000 ft.).

For the most recent information, the reader may refer to the following annual publications:
The Military Balance. International Institute for Strategic Studies. London: Brassey's (UK).
The Statesman's Year-Book. New York: St. Martin's Press.
The World Factbook. Central Intelligence Agency. Washington D.C.: Brassey's (US).

History

New Zealand was unsettled by humans until the arrival of Polynesian voyagers, who reached the North Island between A.D. 952 and A.D. 1150, and settled mostly on the North Island. The islands were discovered and named by the Dutch explorer Abel Tasman in 1642, and limited European settlement began late in the eighteenth century, drawn by lumbering, sealing, and whaling. Great Britain annexed New Zealand over a period of three years from 1838 to 1841 in a process centered around the Treaty of Waitangi (2 February 1840). The native Maoris, whose traditional socio-political structure had been disturbed by the introduction of firearms some 50 years before, were alarmed by European expansion. Scattered fighting began about 1842, and the First Maori War broke out in 1845. It was ended by treaty in 1847.

Over the next decade, European settlement continued to expand, as did the colony's capacity for self-government. In the 1860s, there was a renewed outbreak of conflict between whites and Maoris in the Second Maori War (1860–71). This conflict lasted over ten years largely because of the fighting abilities of the Maoris who proved to be skillful guerrilla fighters. Between 1860 and 1920, the Maoris lost most of their remaining lands, but the communities survived and by the mid-twentieth century had begun to expand once more.

By the 1890s, New Zealand had become largely self-governing, and it was proclaimed a dominion on 26 September 1907. New Zealand provided soldiers during World War I, where they fought as part of the Australian-New Zealand Army Corps (ANZAC) at Gallipoli and in Palestine. New Zealand fought in World War II, sending an infantry division to Egypt (it ended the war in Italy), and later contributing naval and air units to the war against Japan. Following World War II, New Zealand joined in a close defense relationship with Australia and the United States, continuing the close cooperation of World War II.

New Zealand joined Australia, Malaysia, Singapore, and Great Britain in 1971 for joint security arrangements in Southeast Asia, the same year it withdrew its forces from South Vietnam. Political life since the early 1900s has been dominated by the socialist-oriented Labour Party and the centrist National Party, although developments in the late 1980s have blurred the policy distinctions between the two parties.

Politico-Military Background and Policy

New Zealand's foreign and defense policies have been traditionally tied to those of Great Britain, but with the decline of British global power after 1945, and in consideration of close wartime cooperation with the United States and Australia, New Zealand has maintained a close security relationship with the latter two countries in an arrangement known as ANZUS, dating from 1952. New Zealand also made a strong postwar commitment to collective security, playing an important role in both the Southeast Asia Treaty Organization (SEATO) and, since the British withdrawal from Asia in 1971, in the Five Power Pact/ANZUK (Australia, New Zealand, the United Kingdom, Malaysia, and Singapore). New Zealand has also played a major role in South Pacific security, with close ties to Fiji, Tonga, and Western Samoa.

Since the mid-1980s, New Zealand's security policies have undergone considerable revision. A growing domestic antinuclear movement led the Labour government (elected in July 1984) to ban visits by nuclear-powered or nuclear-armed ships to New Zealand ports. Since such conditions comprised the U.S. policy to "neither confirm nor deny" the presence or absence of such weapons on its ships, the U.S. government, after efforts to resolve the impasse, announced that it was suspending some of its security obligations to New Zealand under ANZUS on 11 August 1986. A reassessment of defense needs in 1985–86 led to a Defence White Paper in 1988. Noting a small probability of large-scale conventional warfare in the near future, the new policy foresaw increased need for forces to combat infiltration, terrorism, and other low-level threats. This will lead to greater emphasis on maritime and airborne patrol and reconnaissance, intelligence, and rapid reaction forces.

All of New Zealand's armed forces personnel are volunteers. The active contingents are backed by substantial reserves, and in the army's case, by Territorial Forces as well.

Strategic Problems

New Zealand, as an island nation, faces few immediate threats from abroad. On the other hand, traditionally close ties to Australia coupled with a very high per capita volume of trade, would make it difficult for New Zealand to avoid involvement in a general or regional conflict. Current government policy emphasizes the greater likelihood of irregular conflict as opposed to conventional war. The passage of Nuclear Free New Zealand Law (June 1987) led to the withholding of intelligence material by the United States.

Military Assistance

New Zealand receives no military assistance from abroad, aside from cooperative and reciprocal training arrangements with Australia, Great Britain, and the United States. New Zealand does provide security assistance, partly in the form of military missions, to several small Pacific states, including Fiji, Papua New Guinea, Western Samoa, and Vanuatu.

Defense Industry

New Zealand relies on British or U.S. imports for most of its heavy equipment, but does build some smaller naval vessels. Small arms and ammunition, light vehicles, and light aircraft (built by Victa) are produced domestically, some under license.

Alliances

New Zealand is a founding member of the United Nations (UN) and SEATO. New Zealand is also a member of the Commonwealth, the Five Power Pact (dating from 1971), and the South Pacific Forum (founded in 1947). The country has close defense ties to Australia, and despite some recent policy differences, still maintains cordial relations with the United States.

Defense Structure

Nominally, the commander in chief of New Zealand forces is the Governor-General, representing the sovereign of Great Britain. In the parliamentary government, though, executive power (including authority over the armed forces) is vested in the prime minister and the cabinet, who are responsible to parliament. The minister of defense exercises responsibility for the administration and control of the armed forces, advised by the Chief of the Defence Staff, who is also chairman of the Chiefs of Staff Committee, with members from the General (Army), Navy, and Air Staffs.

(For an explanation of the abbreviations and symbols used in the following section of military statistics, see the list of Abbreviations and Acronyms in each volume.)

Total Armed Forces

Active: 11,300.
Reserves: 9,624. Regular 2,928: Army 1,640, Navy 1,060, Air 228. Territorial 6,696: Army 5,722, Navy 519, Air 455.

ARMY: 4,900.
2 inf bn.
1 lt armd sqn.
1 fd arty bty.
1 SF sqn.
Reserves: Territorial Army: 6 inf bn, 4 fd, 1 med arty bty, 2 armd sqn (1 APC, 1 lt recce).
Equipment:
Light tanks: 26 Scorpion.
APC: 76 M-113 (incl variants).

Towed arty: 105mm: 20 M-101A1 (8 in store), 24 Hamel.
Mortars: 81mm: 72.
RL: LAW.
RCL: 84mm: 61 Carl Gustav.

NAVY: 2,500. Base: Auckland (Fleet HQ).
Frigates: 4 Waikato (UK Leander) with 1 Wasp hel, 3 with 2 × 3 ASTT and 2 × 114mm guns, 1 with Ikara SUGW.
Patrol and Coastal Combatants: 4 Moa PCI (reserve trg).
Support and Miscellaneous: 4: 1 Endeavour AO, 1 AGHS, 1 AGOR, 1 diving spt.
In Store: 4 Pukaki PCI (to be sold).

Naval Air: No cbt ac; 7 armed hel. (Wasp).

AIR FORCE: 3,900; 41 cbt ac, no armed hel.
Operational Group:
FGA: 2 sqn with 16 A-4K, 5 TA-4K.
MR: 1 sqn with 6 P-3K Orion.
Light attack/trg: 1 sqn for ab initio and ftr lead-in trg with 14 BAC-167.
ASW: 7 Wasp HAS-1 (Navy-assigned).
Transport: 3 sqn:
Aircraft: 2 sqn: 1 with 5 C-130H, 2 Boeing 727; 1 with 9 Andover.
Helicopters: 1 with 14 UH-1H.
Communications: 1 flight with 3 Cessna 421C.
Support Group, Training: 1 wing with 4 Airtourer, 18 CT-4, 3 F-27 ac; 4 Bell 47 hel.
Missiles:
ASM: AGM-65 Maverick.
AAM: AIM-9H Sidewinder.

FORCES ABROAD
Singapore: 20 spt unit.
UN and Peacekeeping:
Angola (UNAVEM II): observers.
Egypt (MFO): 25.
Middle East (UNTSO): 4 observers.

Future

New Zealand's defense reorientation follows the pattern of Australia's, with the important exception that Australia did not ban nuclear weapons. It is entirely possible that the United States and New Zealand could reach an understanding and thereby bring New Zealand once more into the ANZUS arrangement, but this is unlikely anytime soon. In light of the small likelihood of New Zealand's involvement in a major war, the security risks posed by the antinuclear stance, while a matter of some concern, are not really vital. The only other potential national security problem is the situation in Fiji, where ethnic disputes between native Fijian and Indian citizens have placed New Zealand (with its security assistance to the Fijian government) in an awkward position.

DAVID L. BONGARD
TREVOR N. DUPUY

SEE ALSO: Australia; Commonwealth of Nations; Indo-Pacific Area; South and Southwest Pacific.

Bibliography

Alley, R. 1984. *New Zealand and the Pacific*. Boulder, Colo.: Westview Press.
Belich, J. 1986. *The New Zealand wars*. Auckland: Auckland Univ. Press.
Henderson, J., K. Jackson, and R. Kenneway. 1980. *Beyond New Zealand: The foreign policy of a small state*. Auckland: Methuen.
Hunter, B., ed. 1991. *The statesman's year-book, 1991–92*. New York: St. Martin's Press.
International Institute for Strategic Studies. 1991. *The military balance, 1991–1992*. London: Brassey's.
Mentiplay, C. 1979. *A fighting quality: New Zealanders at war*. Wellington: A. H. and A. W. Reed.
Merge, J. 1976. *The Maoris of New Zealand: Rautahi*. London: Routledge.

NICARAGUA, REPUBLIC OF

Lying between Costa Rica and Honduras, Nicaragua has become the most heavily armed Central American nation. By 1990, its armed forces were equal to those of the other five nations combined.

This situation may change, as newly elected President Violeta Barios de Chamorro and her administration seek to achieve consensus with the followers of former Communist ruler Daniel Ortega Saavedra. In 1991, for example, the Nicaraguan armed forces reduced their number by 30,000 and abolished conscript service.

Power Potential Statistics

Area: 129,494 square kilometers (49,998 sq. mi.)
Population: 3,923,600
Total Active Armed Forces: 30,500 (0.777% of pop.)
Gross Domestic Product: US$1.7 billion (1990 est.)
Annual Defense Expenditure: US$70 million (3.8% of GDP, 1991 est.)
Electrical Power Output: 1,342 million kwh (1990)
Merchant Marine: 2 vessels; 2,161 gross registered tons
Civil Air Fleet: 12 major transport aircraft; 162 usable airfields (10 with permanent-surface runways); none with runways over 3,659 meters (12,000 ft.); 2 with runways 2,440–3,659 meters (8,000–12,000 ft.); 12 with runways 1,220–2,440 meters (4,000–8,000 ft.).

For the most recent information, the reader may refer to the following annual publications:
The Military Balance. International Institute for Strategic Studies. London: Brassey's (UK).
The Statesman's Year-Book. New York: St. Martin's Press.
The World Factbook. Central Intelligence Agency. Washington, D.C.: Brassey's (US).

History

The history of Nicaragua, whose territory was outside the influence of Mayan civilization to the north, began only with the country's exploration by Spanish conquistadors in the 1520s, and with the founding of León and Granada in 1524. For the next 250 years, Nicaragua was a peaceful, slow-growing agricultural colony, governed from the *audiencia* of Guatemala. The Caribbean coast had a different heritage, settled by black refugees from the British West

Indies (hence town names like Bluefields), and from 1740 to 1786 the "Mosquito Coast" was considered a British dependency.

The movement toward independence in the 1820s and 1830s was complicated by the rivalry between León and Granada, which were usually on opposite sides of any dispute. In 1826, Nicaragua joined the Central American Federation but left twelve years later. Along the east coast the León-Granada conflicts had brought a renewed British protectorate, which was ended by treaty only in 1860. León became the stronghold of the "Liberals"; the "Conservatives," of course, made their headquarters at Granada. In 1855, the Liberals invited American freebooter William Walker to help them against their rivals, and although Walker made himself president in 1856, he was overthrown in 1857 with aid from Nicaragua's neighbors. The country was at peace for most of the next 50 years, enjoying relative prosperity and economic development.

Nicaragua fought a brief and victorious war with Honduras in 1907, occupying Tegucigalpa in December. A prolonged political crisis and intermittent civil war from 1909 to 1912 brought about a virtual U.S. protectorate. U.S. Marines were stationed at the capital from 1912 to 1925, thereby ensuring internal peace. The departure of the marines brought on renewed civil war, so the marines returned in 1926, and for the next seven years they conducted a campaign against the charismatic, ardently nationalist, and anti-Marxist César Augusto Sandino. The marines departed in 1933, following the inauguration of Pres. Juan Bautista Sacasa, and left behind a well-trained national guard under Gen. Anastasio Somoza.

Somoza arranged Sandino's assassination in 1936 and deposed Sacasa later that year. For the next 47 years, Somoza and his son Luis Somoza Debayle ruled Nicaragua as a personal fief. Beginning in 1962, though, the Frente Sandinista de Liberacíon Nacional (FSLN) waged a guerrilla war against the Somozas. By the late 1970s, they were gaining the upper hand, and after seven months of bloody civil war, Somoza resigned the presidency on 17 June 1979. Managua fell to the Sandinistas, led by Daniel Ortega, two days later, ending the civil war. The hard-line Marxist policies soon adopted by the Sandinista government lost them the support of the U.S. government, which began funding anti-Sandinista guerrillas, the Contras, in 1982. The Contras, dependent on U.S. backing, lacked the popular support to overthrow the government, which was hampered by an appalling economic situation (largely self-inflicted) from crushing the insurgents. Lack of support for the Contras in the U.S. Congress reduced their impact after 1986; by late 1988 there were some signs that a compromise solution might be possible. In mid-1989, the increasingly desperate Sandinista regime promised free and open elections in 1990, and most internal opposition groups took part.

Trying to manage an economy running out of control in 1989–90, the Sandinista government held free elections on 25 February 1990 wherein Sandinista president Ortega lost resoundingly to National Opposition Union candidate Violetta Barrios de Chamorro. Ortega retained a position as chief of the armed forces.

Politico-Military Background and Policy

As repulsive and rapacious as the Somoza regime was, it is worth noting that at its largest the national guard numbered perhaps 8,000 men, compared with the 80,000 man army controlled by President Ortega during the height of the Contra threat. This large force, fueled by mandatory conscription since 1983, was greater than warranted by the civil conflict; Ortega claimed it was necessary, however, to defeat a U.S. invasion, an objectively unlikely event that nevertheless loomed large in the Sandinista popular mythos.

Under President Chamorro, the Nicaraguan army has been reduced to 27,000 and ongoing reorganization may trim further the military strength. Mandatory conscription, a highly unpopular policy under the Sandinistas, is now abolished. Future government policy seems likely to seek continued balance among the large number of local political groups, while focusing on longer-term economic recovery. In this regard, the strong central control of government over the economy seems likely to lessen, providing a decentralized opportunity for growth.

Strategic Problems

Nicaragua's main problem during the 1980s was the Contra insurgency, which was largely confined to areas along the Honduran border. Recovering from a decade of resource-draining conflict, which sapped manpower badly needed by a moribund economy, is the prime strategic problem facing Nicaragua today. The manner in which the new democratic institutions address this strategic issue is equally important. Satisfying the majority of Nicaraguans while working carefully with the large Sandinista minority will prove key to future successes.

Defense Industry

Nicaragua has no domestic arms industry, and has, until recently, depended entirely on supplies from abroad, mainly from the Soviet Union and Cuba. Military assistance by the disbanded Soviet Union is no longer a feature, as is likely to be the case with Cuba. Further, the perceived need for a large standing force is greatly lessened, and this diminishes the possibility for military alliances and assistance.

Alliances

Nicaragua is a member of the Organization of American States (OAS) and the United Nations. As noted above, it has close ties with both Cuba and the USSR. There is also considerable trade with Western Europe and Japan, and some with the United States.

Defense Structure

Constitutionally, the commander in chief of the armed forces is the president of the republic, but, in the post-election compromise, President Violetta Chamorro allowed Daniel Ortega Saavedra to remain commander in chief. Despite the new constitution of 9 January 1987, real power rested with the FSLN *commandantes* who directed the war against Somoza, and the official, legal government had little control over policy until after the 1990 elections.

(For an explanation of the abbreviations and symbols used in the following section of military statistics, see the list of Abbreviations and Acronyms in each volume.)

Total Armed Forces

Active: 30,500. Terms of service: voluntary, 18–36 months.
Reserves: numbers/details not yet known.

ARMY: est. 27,000.
Reorganization in progress.
7 Military Regions.
2 armd bde, each 2 tk, 2 mech inf bn.
2 mot inf bde, each 3 motor inf, 1 tk bn.
2 frontier bde.
1 arty bde (4 gp: 1 MRL, 3 152mm how).
8 regional arty gp.
20 inf bn.
4 engr bn.
Equipment:
MBT: some 130 T-54/-55.
Light tanks: 27 PT-76.
Recce: 90 BRDM-2.
APC: 19 BTR-60, 120 BTR-152.
Towed arty: 122mm: 36 D-30; 152mm: 60 D-20.
MRL: 107mm: 16 Type-63; 122mm: 35 BM-21.
Mortars: 82mm: 625; 120mm: 42 M-43.
ATGW: AT-3 Sagger (12 on BRDM-2).
ATK guns: 57mm: 354 ZIS-2; 76mm: 84 ZIS-3; 100mm: 24 M-1944 (BS-3).
SAM: 500+ SA-7/-14/-16.

NAVY: 1,500.
Patrol and Coastal Combatants: 26:
Patrol, Inshore: 26: 8 Sov Zhuk PFI, 10 North Korea Sin Hung PFI ⟨, 8 PCI ⟨.
Mine Countermeasures: 8: 4 Sov Yevgenya, 4 K-8 MSI ⟨.

AIR FORCE: 2,000; 16 cbt ac, 9 armed hel.
COIN: 1 sqn with 6 Cessna 337†, 6 L-39ZO†, 4 SF-260 WL†.
Attack Helicopters: 9 Mi-25.
Transport: 1 sqn with 5 An-26, 1 C-212.
Helicopters: 1 sqn with 38 Mi-8/-17.
Liaison:
Ac: 8 AN-2, 1 Twin Bonanza, 4 Commander; plus 1 Cessna 172, 5 -185†.
Hel: 5 Mi-2, 2 SA-316.
Training: 17 L-39C.
ASM: AT-2 Swatter ATGW.
AD guns: 700+ reported: 14.5mm: ZPU-1/-2/-4; 23mm: ZU-23; 37mm: M-1939; 57mm: S-60; 100mm: KS-19.

FOREIGN FORCES
United Nations (ONUCA): Elm.

Future

The combined problems of the Contra insurgency and the Ortega government's near-catastrophic mismanagement of the economy made Nicaragua's future bleak at the end of the 1980s. The free elections in 1990 and subsequent efforts at reform, reconciliation, and rapprochement among former antagonists open a tentative door to a brighter future. Tensions between the U.S. and the Nicaraguan government have lessened, and continuing democratic elections will help to diminish these further.

It should be noted, however, that the historic perceptions of the Nicaraguan people have tended to support nationalist leaders that have opposed U.S. policy as a matter of pride, regardless of other facts or principles. Moreover, the Sandinistas remain Nicaragua's single largest political party. The fourteen-party alliance that forms the ruling National Opposition Coalition may find it difficult to progress along lines of state reorganization and to rebuild a failed economy along egalitarian terms.

DAVID L. BONGARD
TREVOR N. DUPUY

SEE ALSO: Central America and the Caribbean.

Bibliography

American University. 1982. *Area handbook for Nicaragua.* Washington, D.C.: Government Printing Office.
Christian, S. 1985. *Nicaragua: Revolution in the family.* New York: Random House.
Hunter, B., ed. 1991. *The statesman's year-book, 1991–92.* New York: St. Martin's Press.
International Institute for Strategic Studies. 1991. *The military balance, 1991–1992.* London: Brassey's.
Macauley, N. 1967. *The Sandino affair.* Chicago: Quadrangle Books.
May, R. E. 1973. *The southern dream of a Caribbean empire, 1854–1861.* Baton Rouge: Louisiana Univ. Press.
Nolan, D. 1984. *The ideology of the Sandinistas and the Nicaraguan revolution.* Coral Gables, Fla.: Univ. of Miami Institute of Interamerican Studies.
U.S. Central Intelligence Agency. 1991. *The world factbook, 1991–92.* Washington, D.C.: Brassey's.

NIGERIA, FEDERAL REPUBLIC OF

Nigeria is Africa's most populous country. The climate ranges from the coastal marshes and forests of the south, north through savanna to the near-desert of the far north.

Power Potential Statistics

Area: 923,770 square kilometers (356,668 sq. mi.)
Population: 122,519,000
Total Active Armed Forces: 94,500 (0.077% of pop.)
Gross National Product: US$30 billion (1990 est.)
Annual Defense Expenditure: US$300 million (1% of GNP, 1990 est.)
Iron and Steel Production:

Crude steel: 0.200 million metric tons (1986)
Fuel Production:
Coal: 0.115 million metric tons (1981)
Crude oil: 90.81 million metric tons (1990)
Natural gas: 2,044 million cubic meters (1986)
Electrical Power Output: 11,270 million kwh (1989)
Merchant Marine: 28 vessels; 420,658 gross registered tons
Civil Air Fleet: 76 major transport aircraft; 68 usable airfields (32 with permanent-surface runways); 1 with runways over 3,659 meters (12,000 ft.); 14 with runways 2,440–3,659 meters (8,000–12,000 ft.); 21 with runways 1,220–2,440 meters (4,000–8,000 ft.).

For the most recent information, the reader may refer to the following annual publications:
The Military Balance. International Institute for Strategic Studies. London: Brassey's (UK).
The Statesman's Year-Book. New York: St. Martin's Press.
The World Factbook. Central Intelligence Agency. Washington, D.C.: Brassey's (US.)

History

Nigeria has a long and rich historical tradition. The Nok culture of the central plateau flourished over 2,000 years ago, producing fine ironware and sophisticated pottery. Recorded history in the northern trading cities of Kano and Katsina dates to about A.D. 1000. These cities, famous as trading entrepôts and marketplaces because they were the southern end of trans-Sahara caravan routes, were centers of the Hausa and Bornu kingdoms. In the southwest, the Yoruba kingdom of Oyo was founded about 1400, and between 1600 and 1810 attained a peak of sophisticated political organization. In the early 1800s the Fulani leader Usman dan Fidio subdued the Hausa peoples of the north and founded a caliphate-empire, centered in the city of Sokoto in northwest Nigeria. This Sokoto caliphate lasted until 1903, when it was suppressed by British troops.

European influence arrived in the late fifteenth century when Portuguese explorers and merchants found the Niger delta. They soon began a busy trade in slaves and commodities, but by the late eighteenth century had been supplanted by the British. The British established protectorates over the coastal areas in the late 1800s, beginning with Lagos Colony (1861) and continuing through the Oil Rivers (1887) and Niger Coast (1894) protectorates. The British set up a protectorate over northern Nigeria in 1900 (thereby ending the 15-year charter of the Royal Niger Company), and unified the north and south under one government in 1914. The British abolished slavery and eventually provided Nigeria with a single (if unofficial) language and a nontribal legal system.

By the late 1950s the British had granted a wide degree of self-government (this process had begun in 1922 with legislative councils in the south) in preparation for independence, partly in response to a native independence movement. Nigeria became an independent state and a member of the Commonwealth on 1 October 1960. The new state faced the problem of ethnic rivalry between the pastoralist and Muslim Hausa and Fulani tribes of the north, and the agricultural Christian-animist tribes of the south, like the Ibo and the Yoruba (who were half Christian and half Muslim). Although the federal constitution allowed considerable autonomy for the regional governments (Northern, Eastern, and Western), civil unrest was a major problem in the Western Region.

The Federal government created the Mid-Western Region in July 1963 in an effort to ease tensions, and on 1 October 1963 Nigeria became a republic. The civilian government, unable to deal effectively with Nigeria's problems, was deposed on 15 January 1966 by an army coup which killed the Federal prime minister and the premiers of the Northern and Western regions. The coup, led by Ibo army officers, instituted the Federal Military Government (FMG), led by Gen. J. T. U. Aguiyi-Ironsi. The FMG was no more able to resolve ethnic tensions and unrest than its civilian predecessor, and its efforts to abolish the federal system produced new waves of unrest, including the massacre of Ibos in the north. General Aguiyi-Ironsi was deposed and killed in a coup which brought Lt. Col. (later General) Yakubu Gowon to control of the FMG on 29 July 1966.

The violence against Ibos drove many of them to shelter in their homeland in the southeast, and many Ibos supported secession, a movement led by Lt. Col. Emeka Ojukwu. Efforts by the Gowon-led FMG to provide constitutional guarantees went unheeded by the secessionists, and on 26 May 1967 Ojukwu declared the independence of the Eastern Region as the "Republic of Biafra." Civil war broke out in July and raged until a cease-fire on 12 January 1970. Government troops, poorly disciplined and badly led, made scant progress against determined Biafran troops, but infusions of Soviet arms (Biafra gained limited foreign support) and superior numbers brought FMG forces success.

After the end of the civil war, Nigeria turned to the tasks of reconciliation and reconstruction, efforts aided by increased oil revenues after 1973–74. General Gowon's regime was overthrown in a bloodless coup on 29 July 1975 by army officers who accused him of delaying the promised return to civilian rule. Civilian rule returned in 1979, but widespread corruption and inefficiency in the government led to another coup after the August 1983 elections, on 31 December. The new military government, the Supreme Military Council (SMC), has been headed by Maj. Gen. Ibrahim Babangida since the bloodless coup of 27 August 1985. General Babangida has promised a return to civilian government, and elections are scheduled for October 1991.

Politico-Military Background and Policy

The armed forces, especially the army, have played a major role in modern Nigeria. They have governed the country in one form or another for 14 of 28 years since independence. The armed forces have proved an important institution for fostering nationalism and lessening ethnic rivalry. The SMC came to power with a program to eliminate corruption and restore honesty to government, and has been able to fulfill a substantial portion of its promises.

In international terms, Nigerian policy has been to support the Organization of African Unity (OAU) and oppose foreign intervention (whether by African or extracontinental powers) in the affairs of African states. Following this policy, Nigeria condemned Tanzania's 1976 invasion of Uganda, despite the excesses of the Idi Amin regime, and sent forces to Chad to support the government there against Libyan aggression and intrigue. This policy also reflects Nigerian unease over the continued presence of French troops and French military missions in several nearby states.

The Nigerian armed forces are manned solely by volunteers, for six- or seven-year periods. The armed forces, especially the army, are smaller now than at any time since the end of the Biafran War (1970), when forces numbered some 250,000 men. A major demobilization took place in 1975–77, reducing the forces to about 140,000, and forces currently total about 95,000. This represents only a small part of the 14.72 million estimated males aged 15 to 49 fit for military service.

Strategic Problems

Nigeria faces several strategic problems of moderate importance. First, while Nigeria was a net food exporter when it gained independence, the influx of oil revenue and the lingering effects of ethnic unrest and civil war now require it to import food; and its exports of cocoa, groundnuts (peanuts), and palm oil have fallen. Oil revenue has fueled considerable economic development, but most of this has gone into the federal government rather than to the nineteen state governments. Finally, the patchwork ethnic structure and the traditional rivalry between north and south ensure that local considerations will continue to play a role in national and foreign policy.

Military Assistance

Nigeria receives military aid from a variety of sources, including Great Britain, the United States, France, West Germany, and from the former Soviet Union. In light of difficulties associated with Soviet aid to the Nigerian Air Force in the mid-1970s, most military assistance comes from Western sources.

Defense Industry

Nigeria depends on foreign sources for its armored vehicles, heavy weapons, aircraft, and naval vessels. Little specialty military equipment is produced domestically.

Alliances

Nigeria is a member of the OAU, the United Nations (UN), the Commonwealth, the OAU, and OPEC (Organization of Petroleum-Exporting Countries). Nigeria has no major formal bilateral defense ties, but there are training and advisory missions from the United States and Great Britain in the country.

Defense Structure

Under the SMC government, the president is commander in chief of the armed forces. He exercises administrative control through the minister of defense (currently a major general). The minister works through the Chief of the General Staff (currently a rear admiral), who directs the activities of the three individual service staffs.

(For an explanation of the abbreviations and symbols used in the following section of military statistics, see the list of Abbreviations and Acronyms in each volume.)

Total Armed Forces

Active: 94,500 (reducing).
Reserves: planned; none organized.

ARMY: 80,000.
1 armd div (2 armd, 1 mech bde).
1 composite div (incl 1 AB, 1 air portable, 1 amph bde).
2 mech div (each 3 mech bde).
1 AD bde.
Div tps: each div 1 arty, 1 engr bde, 1 recce bn.
Equipment:
MBT: 157: 60 T-55, 97 Vickers Mk 3.
Light tanks: 100 Scorpion.
Recce: 20 Saladin, est. 120 AML-60, 60 AML-90, 55 Fox.
APC: 10 Saracen, 300 4K-7FA.
Towed arty: 105mm: 200 M-56; 122mm: 200 D-30/-74; 155mm: 24 FH-77B.
SP arty: 155mm: 25 Palmaria.
Mortars: 81mm: 200.
RCL: 84mm: Carl Gustav; 106mm: M-40A1.
AD guns: 20mm: some 60; 23mm: ZU-23, 30 ZSU-23-4 SP; 40mm: L/60.
SAM: 48 Blowpipe, 16 Roland.

NAVY: 5,000. Bases: Apapa (Lagos; HQ Western Command), Calabar (HQ Eastern Command), Warri, Port Harcourt.
Frigates: 2: 1†Aradu (Ge Meko-360) with 1 Lynx hel, 2×3 ASTT, plus 8×Otomat SSM, 1×127mm gun; 1†Obuma (trg) with hel deck, plus 1×2 102mm guns.
Patrol and Coastal Combatants: 54:
Corvettes: 3: 2† Erinomi (UK Vosper Mk 9) with 1×2 ASW mor; 1 Otobo (UK Vosper Mk 3) (in Italy, refitting to PCO).
Missile Craft: 6: 3 Ekpe (Ge Lürssen-57) PFM with 4×Otomat SSM; 3 Siri (Fr Combattante) with 2×2 MM-38 Exocet SSM (in France refitting).
Patrol, Inshore: 45: 4 Makurdi (UK Brooke Marine 33-m), some 41 PCI ⟨.
Mine Warfare: 2 Ohue (mod It Lerici) MCC.
Amphibious: 2 Ambe (Ge) LST, capacity 220 tps, 5 tk.
Support and Miscellaneous: 7: 1 survey, 5 tugs, 1 nav trg.
Naval Aviation: 2 Lynx Mk 89 MR/SAR helicopters.

AIR FORCE: 9,500; 95 cbt ac, 15 armed hel.
FGA/Fighter: 3 sqn: 1 with 21 Alpha Jet (FGA/trg); 1 with †6 MiG-21MF, †4 MiG-21U, †12 × MiG-21B/FR; 1 with †15 Jaguar (12 -SN, 3 -BN).
COIN/Training: 23 L-39MS, 12MB-339AN.
Attack Helicopters:† 15 Bo-105D.
MR/SAR: 1 sqn with:
Aircraft:† 2 F-27MR (armed);
Helicopters: 4 Bo-105D.
Transport: 2 sqn with 6 C-130H, 3 -H-30, 3 Do-228 (VIP), 5 G-222.
Presidential Flt: 1 Boeing 727, 1 Falcon, 1 BAe 125-700, 2 Gulfstream.
Light TPT: 3 sqn with 18 Do-28D, 18 Do-128-6.
Helicopters: incl 4 AS-322, 4 Bo-105CB, 2 SA-330.
Training:
Aircraft:† 25 Bulldog;
Helicopters: 14 Hughes 300.
Missiles: AAM: AA-2 Atoll.

FORCES ABROAD
Liberia: some 5,000; contingent forms major part of ECOWAS force.
Sierra Leone: 800.
UN and Peacekeeping:
Angola (UNAVEM II): observers.
Iraq/Kuwait (UNIKOM): 7 observers.

PARAMILITARY
Coast Guard: operates 10 inshore patrol craft and some 60 boats, performing maritime police and customs duties.
Port Security Police: some 12,000 men, charged with maintaining order in seaports.
Security and Civil Defence Corps (Ministry of Internal Affairs): the main police organization, numbering some 80,000 (including women). It has several paramilitary/riot control units, equipped with West German UR-416 APCs; 1 Cessna 500, 3 Piper (2 Navajo, 1 Chieftain) ac; 4 Bell helicopters; 68 small craft (mostly on inland waterways), and seven hovercraft (including 5 AV Tiger).

Future

Nigeria's earnings from petroleum exports, coupled with its potentially abundant agricultural production, could mark the return to civilian rule as the start of a period of prosperity. These prospects depend on continued domestic peace. Although the constitution provides considerable local authority to the state governments, the state boundaries do not reflect traditional or ethnic divisions, and in fact the main radio station in Bendel State (around Koko) broadcasts its news in six languages and popular programming in eight more, all in a state with barely 4 million people. Even the widespread use of English as a *linqua franca* has not reduced ethnic rivalries, and the issue of national unity will be a major concern for years to come.

DAVID L. BONGARD
TREVOR N. DUPUY

SEE ALSO: Organization of African Unity; Sub-Saharan Africa.

Bibliography

Adamolekun, L. 1986. *Politics and administration in Nigeria.* Ibadan: Heineman.
American University. 1982. *Nigeria: A country study.* Washington, D.C.: Government Printing Office.
de St. Jorre, J. 1972. *The brother's war.* Boston: Houghton Mifflin.
———. *The Nigerian civil war.* 1972 . London: Hodder and Stoughton.
Hunter, B., ed. 1991. *The statesman's year-book, 1991–92.* New York: St. Martin's Press.
International Institute for Strategic Studies. 1991. *The military balance, 1991–1992.* London: Brassey's.
Isichei, E. 1983. *A history of Nigeria.* New York: Longman.
Obasanjo, O. 1980. *My command: An account of the Nigerian civil war.* Ibadan: Heineman.
Zartman, I. W., ed. 1983. *The political economy of Nigeria.* New York: Praeger.

NIGHT VISION TECHNOLOGY APPLICATIONS

Today's technology allows all elements of armed forces to operate effectively at night—so much so that a well-equipped and well-trained force, using modern night vision equipment, has the potential to overwhelm an enemy force not so prepared.

Night vision equipment does not, however, present visual information of the same type or in the same form as that gathered in the daytime by the human eye. For this reason, a well-equipped but poorly trained force, venturing forth at night in the false security of modern technology, is courting disaster.

This article outlines the types and uses of equipment in the field today and speculates on what may come in the future.

The Discipline of Night Fighting Equipment

In general, night vision equipment gathers radiant energy (photons) from the electromagnetic (EM) spectrum, converts it into an electrical signal, inadvertently destroys some of the information, and presents what remains to a human observer or to the evolving "intelligent" machines. The equipment must be sufficiently inexpensive to be issued in high volume, rugged enough to withstand the abuse of the battlefield, able to function without repair for a reasonable time, and be reparable by military support systems.

Imaging systems perform well when they sense the observable characteristics of objects of military significance with sufficient resolution and field of view to make accurate situation assessments possible and allow an effective course of action to be pursued. Practical limitations are met in resolution, since the sensing medium cannot be made continuously finer, and in field of view, since the extent of the sensing medium cannot increase without limit. In addition, the ability to gather photons and convert them into electrons has limits in conversion efficiencies, EM spectral sensitivity, and the inability to collect photons in ever increasing numbers due to atmospheric effects and the physical size and weight of optics and antennae.

Finally, the system must work in real time so that photon collection, conversion, processing, and subsequent presentation are accomplished over the entire field of view no less than about 30 times per second.

Technology

Human capability to operate at night can be augmented by providing hardware that performs the generic function shown in Figure 1. The transducer converts photons into electrons, which can be more readily manipulated. The processor runs the gamut from simple electron acceleration to the more complex process of encoding the position and time of entry and using this inferred information to inaugurate other processes. The latter process allows the information to be preserved and presented in a more useful form than is possible by merely "energizing" the information-bearing electron and passing it through the system in real time. The presentation medium, in turn, varies from a phosphor, which receives the accelerated electron and glows more brightly (emits many more photons) than the incident photon, to an ergonomic display, which presents the essential information in a preprocessed manner designed to allow the user to enhance mission effectiveness.

The information necessary to operate at night can be inferred from the relative position of reflected and emitted photons and their spectral and temporal properties. Figure 1 encompasses the human eye/brain combination, which is highly effective in the functions for which it evolved, but is limited in angular resolution and in spectral and temporal response when functioning at very low light levels.

The military hardware that augments human capability falls into two major categories, active and passive, and is further characterized by the spectral region addressed by the photo/electron transducer.

Active Systems

Active systems generate the photons reflected from the scene, which are sensed by the transducer. This class includes the use of visible light (fires, flares, and searchlights) and of radiation from other spectral regions, which run the gamut of the electromagnetic spectrum from infrared filtered searchlights through radars (including millimeter wave and laser radars). The effective utility of an active system is strongly dependent on the intervening atmosphere between system and scene.

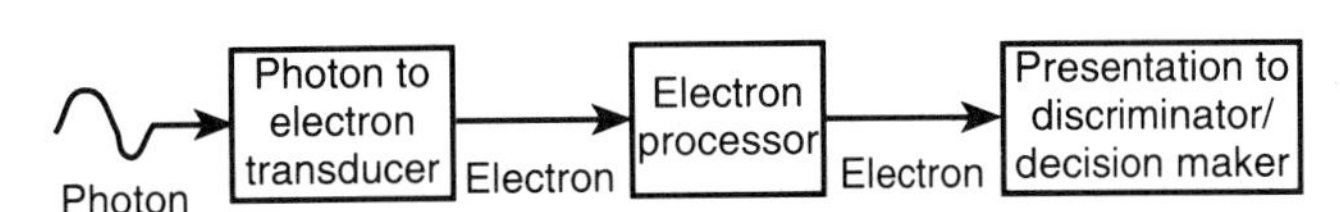

Figure 1. Function of night vision equipment.

The natural atmosphere allows only limited "atmospheric windows"—spectral regions of opportunity that allow EM radiation to penetrate without being scattered or absorbed. Even in these windows there can be heavy signal losses such as, for example, the glare associated with car headlights in even slightly inclement weather. Also, man-made obscurants are more effective against active systems, since they must make a double pass between the observing position and the target. High-energy photons (moving in the blue direction away from the visible) have little practical application because of their inability to penetrate the atmosphere.

World War II witnessed the first use of radar and filtered searchlights, which were highly effective, in part because they were new. The disadvantage of active systems is the vulnerability attendant to generation of the signal. Receiving sensors, of the type used by an active system to interrogate the returning signal, can be employed by the enemy to track the radiation back to its source. This places a premium on passive systems.

Passive Systems

Fielded passive systems are of two types: image intensifiers and thermal imagers.

Image intensifiers. An image intensifier uses the available radiation from the night sky generated by the moon, when present, and by the stars. The transducer is a photo cathode made by evaporating metals to form a thin film.

An objective lens forms an image of the scene on the photo cathode. Electrons are emitted into an evacuated area at the position where the photons strike and at a rate proportional to the intensity of the picture elements in the scene. The current electron processor is a microchannel plate (MCP). This electro-optical amplifier, composed of several million fused glass tubes, has the capacity to emit 10^5 to 10^8 electrons from each tube per single entering electron. This bundle of electrons is then accelerated by an applied field to an energy sufficient to light the phosphor.

Because an objective lens presents an inverted image, and since the electro-optics do not right the image, a fiber optic twist is required behind the phosphor to restore the image to an upright position. The phosphor and fiber optic twist represent the presentation element of Figure 1. The discriminator/decision maker is the human observer.

The first generation of image intensifiers, fielded by the United States in the late 1960s, did not have an MCP but used three stages of tubes coupled together by fiber optics. The initial development of fiber optics was carried out for this purpose.

A third generation of image intensifiers has been developed and deployed. It is similar to second generation but has an improved photo cathode, which collects more of the photons in the near infrared region.

Thermal imagers. Thermal imagers sense emitted photons from objects in the scene. The atmospheric windows available are from 3 to 5 microns and from 8 to 14 microns. The latter region has proved more useful, since the objects of greatest interest emit more photons in this region. The transducer used is a solid-state material that changes an internal electrical property (voltage or conductance) with the incidence of signal photons.

The thermal imager differs from the intensifier in that signal photons are not emitted into a vacuum and guided with electron optics into the electron processor, but rather each discrete sensing element is connected to its dedicated amplifier, which in turn feeds a display element.

It is difficult to build a transducer with a very large number of very small elements and connect each to its individual amplifier. The approach that led to a practical device is shown in Figure 2.

A linear array of detector elements is scanned across the scene, creating two-dimensional coverage by allowing each element to time-share across a line of the scene. If the scanning mirror is used on both sides, synchronizing with the display elements is simplified. Each display element is connected to its sensing elements through an amplifier and glows with an intensity proportional to the amount of converted scene radiation. The display elements can be viewed directly by the eye or remotely by a video system.

The resolution of such a system is determined by the angle subtended by a single detector element. The smaller the element, the higher the potential resolution, but since system sensitivity is dependent on the total amount of detector material in the focal plane, the smaller the element the less sensitive is the system for the same number of elements. An ideal system would have a very large number of very small detectors. The practicality of building such a system decreases with detector size and with an increase in the number of elements. Current fielded technology has detectors in the hundreds, and the obvious course of future development is toward focal planes with thousands or tens of thousands of detectors.

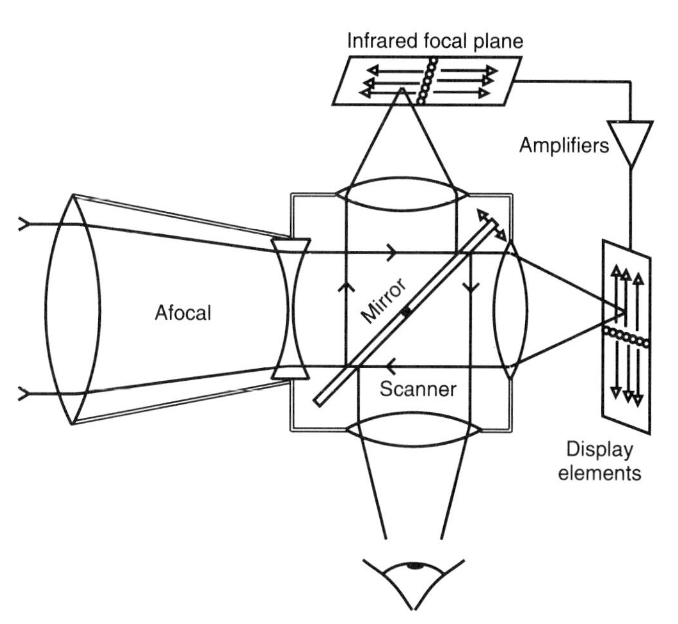

Figure 2. Thermal imager transducer.

System Performance and Utility

Image Intensifier Capability

Image intensifier technology is based on a photo cathode with very low emission of electrons resulting from thermal energy. World War II near-infrared technology required the use of a filtered searchlight in order to raise the photo current signal level of incoming photons above the level of those electrons being generated by heat energy.

Since the generation of filtered light represents a serious breach of security when opposing forces possess the ability to convert infrared radiation into visible energy, the need for passive operation required either cooling the photo cathode, which was logistically too difficult, or developing a better photo cathode. When developed, this photo cathode permitted operation under starlight conditions (hence its name, "Starlight Scope").

It was introduced by U.S. forces into Vietnam in the mid-1960s and was widely copied by other countries. This first-generation technology was composed of three stages, but without an MCP electro-optical amplifier and without the fiber optic twist. These stages were coupled with fiber optic faceplates, the first application of fiber optic technology, which had been developed for this purpose. The intensifier sights were mounted on rifles and crew-served weapons. The range of the devices was well suited to the range of the weapons.

The performance of image-intensifying devices is determined at high light levels (full moon) by the resolution limit imposed by the optical system, but at low light levels (starlight and lower) by the sensitivity of the photo cathode. No increase in light amplification can overcome the lack of signal photons at low light levels, since a single captured photon contains only one piece of information, no matter how bright it can be made. For this reason the practical limitation on the range performance of image intensifiers is about that of the effective range of a rifle.

The impetus for the second generation was the need to develop a smaller tube for head-mounted applications. The night vision goggle was thus developed and fielded in large quantities. This head-mounted device allows general navigation and maintenance functions to be performed at night. It should not be assumed that equivalent performance to day vision is achieved, however, since the field of view is restricted to about one-third of human vision and the amount of available information, because of a paucity of photons, is noticeably limited. In addition, the spectral response of the photo cathode makes foliage take on a "cotton candy" appearance. There is no color vision, and the darker areas are unfathomable, containing shadows, holes, or possibly a hostile tank.

The application of this technology is mainly for relatively short-range operations of infantry forces, including night navigation, maintenance, and fire control for small arms and crew-served weapons. An interesting exception is the use of night vision goggles to conduct night navigation of fixed-wing aircraft and nighttime nap-of-the-earth helicopter flight.

Capabilities of Thermal Imagers

Self-emitted EM radiation from objects is a function of their temperature. Humans have a temperature of about 300 degrees Kelvin and emit radiation that peaks in the middle of an available atmospheric window at a wavelength of about 10 microns. Other living organisms also peak in this region, as do vehicles that transport humans. Thus, far-infrared devices (known as FLIRs, for forward-looking infrared, or thermal imagers) that operate in this window constitute the majority of fielded thermal systems.

The resolution of thermal imagers is inherently less than that of image intensifiers, owing to a smaller number of available sensing elements and the optical diffraction limit. Nevertheless, the improved signal strength coming from the target and the lack of dependence on available light level allow the thermal imager to be more dependable and provide an extension of range performance over the image intensifiers by about two or three times. Also, since targets are brighter than their backgrounds, the thermal imager is better for finding targets, because targets are more conspicuous in the thermal image. Of great military significance is the thermal imager's use of radiation in a spectrum that inherently penetrates atmospheric conditions that defeat the visible spectrum. The result is that thermal imaging systems are the choice for armor and anti-armor weapon sights for night operations and for the majority of other long-range applications.

Capabilities of Other Technologies

It is always possible to make improvements in the performance of fielded systems; the question is whether the resource allocation is worth the improvement. The changes are of two types: evolutionary, in which the fielded technology is upgraded in incremental steps, and revolutionary, in which a new approach is embraced, with consequent large perturbations in the weapon platform and large additional expense.

The discipline of research and development programs must both generate technologies worthy of revolutionary change and determine at what point sufficient progress has been made to warrant expenditures for integration of a new technology approach. In the context of this article there are two other technology approaches that may be incorporated into weapon systems in the coming years: laser radars and millimeter wave radars.

Laser radars. Laser radars are simply thermal imagers with a laser illuminator, gated to take in only a narrow portion of the downrange scene. They have been in development for more than ten years and have proved more difficult to integrate and more expensive than thermal imaging devices.

They have the advantage of greater range performance because of the added signal due to the generated radiation and tend to eliminate the back scatter through gating. Also they are more covert than other illuminators because of the focusing of the beam and the relatively short time the beam is on. To date, however, their added improvement in performance has not been considered adequate to warrant the additional expense.

Millimeter wave radars. Currently fielded radars do not image. This is because diffraction phenomena dictate that resolution possibilities are determined by the ratio of aperture size (antenna) to wavelength. At the wavelengths used for World War II radars, antennas would have to be thousands of feet in diameter to make a usable image.

The impetus for millimeter wave radar is the possibility of obtaining usable resolution with antennas in the one-foot range. This technology is evolving quite rapidly and has the appeal of greater weather penetration than those working in the near and far infrared, while still retaining reasonably high resolution.

While active, these systems are more covert than microwave radars, because they use special beam-forming techniques. It remains to be seen whether they can stand alone and whether their complexity is offset by improved performance over current systems. This technology is a leading candidate as an element in a multisensor system. That would entail, however, still greater complexity and cost.

Training and Doctrine

Technology is of no use unless properly employed. The history of war holds many examples of winners who better understood how to exploit technology advantages than did their opponents.

Night vision technology has special disciplines, since society is intolerant of night training; the equipment is fundamentally disorienting in that it provides sensory information in a different and less satisfying form than human vision; and the concepts of exploiting the advantages of increased night mobility and effectiveness are inherently foreign to our military tacticians. Without well-thought-out doctrine and effective training, the advantages of night operations are not evident and the motivation to think and train for them are thus lacking.

There must first be a commitment on the part of a military force to operate at night. Then an iterative process must take place to train troops and assess their effectiveness. The arrived-at assessment must next be reviewed on the basis of interoperability of the combined arms team, then doctrine must be based on the relative capability of forces operating at night and in the daylight.

There is no point in investing in the hardware if it is not to be effectively employed.

It is essential to grasp the concept that, if forces are more effective at night than are opposing enemy forces, then these forces should choose to fight exclusively at night, if possible. If that condition is expected, then it follows that the majority of training for such forces should take place at night; that military bases should operate at night and sleep in the day; and that the needs of the night forces should dominate those of the day forces. That this is nowhere true today does not mean that an analysis and conscious decision have been made to abandon a night operations initiative. Rather it means that awareness of the potential has not been adequately achieved, that the implications are too bothersome, or that the proper conclusions have not been drawn.

Future Trends in Application of Night Vision Technology

Diminishing Returns for Photon Counters

The history of night vision technology has been dominated by photon counters. Devices that could better convert photons to electrons, those more efficient in regions where information was greatest, were superior to their predecessors and were exploited to develop and field improved equipment. The photon counters have become so good that improvement in collecting signal photons has reached a point of strongly diminished returns. This has come about for two reasons. The first is that fielded equipment has met a large majority of the necessary applications, and further possibilities to improve mission effectiveness by generating devices that see better and farther at night are limited. Second, and more significant, the opportunity to see better and farther at night is limited by the extinction coefficient of the atmosphere. The amount of signal that can pass through the atmosphere falls off exponentially with range. This means that exponential improvements in sensitivity are required to improve range performance. Performance improvements in range are thus not worth the contortions necessary to get them.

Derived Exploitable Technology

Beginning in the late 1960s, when it was noticed that targets were brighter in the FLIR image than were the backgrounds, and that a thresholding technique might allow an alarm to sound upon the entry of a target, there have been continually intensifying efforts to process the signal from night vision devices to allow some form of machine autonomy. That activity is beyond the scope of this article.

It is safe to assume, however, that future advances in the applications of night vision technology will come from the use of multiple sensors whose signal is preprocessed and combined by computers. The potential application for this technology is enormous. The areas of use will run the gamut from assistance for manned systems to totally autonomous operation.

The sensor/processor combination will lead to automated systems that assist in or control the assessment of the battlefield and that assign resources to manage the battle. Weapons platforms will become autonomous, with the ability to navigate to target areas, decide what and when to fight, determine alternate courses of action, and be recoverable so that they can fight again another day.

Weapons will be able to determine points of attack in flight and kill with unerring accuracy.

The ultimate procurement and application question will be not performance but cost, and whether men are more expendable than electronics.

Lawrence J. Acchione

See Also: Air Reconnaissance; Artillery; Electronic Warfare, Air; Surveillance and Target Acquisition Equipment; Technology Acquisition and Development.

Bibliography

Bergmann, R. J., and L. P. Obert. 1980. *Propagation modeling and applications for electro-optical systems.* Fort Belvoir, Va.: Night Vision and Electro-Optics Laboratory. October.

Daly, J., F. Shields, et al. 1977. *Report of the ad hoc study group on commonality of thermal-imaging systems.* Fort Belvoir, Va.: U.S. Army Night Vision Laboratory. June.

Lloyd, J. M. 1975. *Thermal imaging systems.* New York: Plenum Press.

Milham, M. 1976. *A catalog of optical extinction data for various aerosols/smokes.* Aberdeen Proving Ground, Md.: Edgewood Arsenal. June.

Ratches, J. A., et al. 1975. *Night vision laboratory static performance model for thermal viewing systems.* Fort Monmouth, N.J.: ECOM.

NIMITZ, CHESTER WILLIAM [1885–1966]

Chester William Nimitz was born on 24 February 1885 in Fredericksburg, Texas. His father, Chester Bernard, died before Nimitz was born and his grandfather, Charles Henry, helped raise Nimitz until his mother remarried. The Nimitz family was of German descent and claimed ancestry from an order of Teutonic Knights. Charles Henry immigrated to Texas in 1840, where he built and ran a well-known inn.

Nimitz applied for admission to the U.S. Military Academy at West Point in 1900, but was informed by his congressman that all appointments had been filled for the next several years. Informed of an opening at the U.S. Naval Academy in Annapolis, he took and passed the entrance exams in April 1901 and was sworn in as a naval cadet on 7 September. Due to the rapid expansion of the navy and the need for junior officers, Nimitz was graduated a midshipman five months ahead of schedule on 30 January 1905.

Nimitz's first assignment was on the battleship *Ohio*, which was ordered to the Orient as flagship of the U.S. Asiatic Fleet. When the *Ohio* was ordered home Nimitz, opting to stay in the Far East, transferred to the cruiser *Baltimore*. He was commissioned an ensign on 31 January 1907, and shortly after was given command of the gunboat *Panay* in the Philippines. He later took command of the destroyer *Decatur*, which he ran aground on 7 July 1908. Court-martialed and charged with neglect of duty, he received only a public reprimand.

Transferred back to the United States in 1909, Nimitz was assigned to the First Submarine Flotilla and given command of the submarine *Plunger*. In early 1910 he was promoted to lieutenant, and in November of that year he took command of the submarine *Narwhal*. In October 1911 Nimitz was appointed commander of the Third Submarine Division, Atlantic Fleet, and in 1912 he was appointed Commander, Atlantic Submarine Flotilla. Nimitz married Catherine Freeman in April 1913, and the following month he was ordered to Europe to study diesel engines in Germany and Belgium.

On his return to the United States, Nimitz was assigned to the Brooklyn Navy Yard to supervise construction and installation of diesel engines on the oiler *Maumee*. After completion of the *Maumee* in 1916, he was assigned as its executive officer and chief engineer.

World War I

On the outbreak of war with Germany on 6 April 1917, the *Maumee* was ordered to the Atlantic to refuel destroyers. In August, Nimitz was promoted to lieutenant commander and assigned as an aide to Adm. Samuel S. Robison, the commander of Submarine Forces, Atlantic Fleet. Nimitz spent the remainder of the war accompanying Admiral Robison on inspection tours of British naval bases.

Interwar Years

In 1918, Nimitz served as senior member of the Board of Submarine Design at the Navy Department in Washington, D.C. In 1919 he was appointed executive officer on the battleship *South Carolina*. In June 1920, Nimitz was ordered to Pearl Harbor in Hawaii to construct a submarine base. He was promoted to commander in 1922, and from 1922 to 1923 he attended the Naval War College. After completing his tour at the war college, Nimitz was posted to San Pedro, California, and assigned to the battleship *California*, the flagship of the Pacific Fleet. Once again he was working under Admiral Robison, serving as aide, assistant chief of staff, and tactical officer. As Robison's assistant chief of staff, Nimitz was one of the six officers assigned to establish the Naval Reserve Officer's Training Corps (NROTC) in American universities. For three years Nimitz commanded the NROTC at the University of California, Berkeley. In September 1927 he was promoted to captain. In June 1929, Nimitz was appointed to command the Battle Fleet's Submarine Divisions; at the same time he also became Commander, Submarine Division 20, at San Diego. In 1931 he was appointed commander of destroyers at San Diego.

In 1933, Nimitz was appointed captain of the cruiser *Augusta*, which was later designated the flagship of the Asiatic Fleet and ordered to Shanghai. After serving two years in the Far East, Nimitz was transferred to Washington in 1935 as assistant to the chief of the Bureau of Navigation (later designated the Bureau of Personnel). Nimitz was promoted to rear admiral in July 1938. Appointed commander of Cruiser Division Two, San Diego, he was unable to take command due to a hernia operation. When he recovered, Nimitz was instead appointed commander of Battleship Division One, with the battleship *Arizona* as his flagship.

In January 1939, Nimitz was appointed commander of Task Force Seven, which consisted of the *Arizona*, a cruiser, a carrier, seven destroyers and auxiliaries, and one tanker. An enjoyable command for Nimitz, it was also a brief one, as he was transferred to Washington in June of that year and appointed chief of the Bureau of Navigation.

World War II

On 7 December 1941, the Japanese attacked Pearl Harbor and the United States entered World War II. Serving as Chief of Naval Personnel, Nimitz was faced with the enormous task of manning a wartime navy. On 31 December 1941, on the recommendation of Secretary of the Navy Frank Knox, President Franklin D. Roosevelt appointed Nimitz Commander-in-Chief, Pacific Fleet (CINCPAC), with the rank of full admiral. In April 1942, Nimitz was also appointed Commander-in-Chief, Pacific Ocean Areas (CINCPOA), effectively splitting the command of the Pacific with Gen. Douglas MacArthur, who was appointed Supreme Commander, Allied Forces Southwest Pacific Area.

Nimitz's first priority in the Pacific was to defend the Hawaiian Islands and Midway and to protect the lines of communication from the United States to Hawaii and Australia. His second priority was to launch offensive operations against the Japanese in the Central Pacific in an attempt to divert their attention from Singapore and the Dutch East Indies. Facing superior Japanese naval strength, Nimitz resolved to carry out a series of naval and air hit-and-run actions designed to deplete the enemy's strength. While these operations inflicted only minor losses, they did raise American morale.

Nimitz was greatly aided in his operations by Naval Intelligence which, due to U.S. code-breaking success, was able to give him accurate information of Japanese locations and movements. Using this information, Nimitz was able to anticipate and check Japanese naval operations against Port Moresby, New Guinea, at the Battle of the Coral Sea on 3–9 May 1942.

Nimitz was convinced that the Japanese target would be Midway Island. Again, his intelligence service proved invaluable. By way of a ruse, it discovered that Nimitz's hunch was correct and that the Japanese were planning to attack Midway and the Aleutian Islands. Nimitz knew he would face a superior force; he knew also that if he were defeated Hawaii and the United States' west coast would be left open to attack. Nevertheless, he decided to gamble on defeating the Japanese carrier force at Midway. The gamble paid off; on 3–6 June the smaller U.S. force mauled the Japanese, sinking four of their carriers and a heavy cruiser and downing 322 aircraft, against American losses of one carrier, one destroyer, and 132 aircraft. Midway was the turning point in the Pacific War. The Japanese offensive was stopped, and the initiative passed to the Allies.

Nimitz now turned to the offensive. Together with MacArthur he planned the overall strategy for the Pacific Theater as well as providing strategic direction for the major Allied offensive operations in the Central Pacific. Nimitz brilliantly directed the limited offensive against the Solomon Islands from August 1942 to February 1943. He followed this with successful campaigns in the Gilbert Islands on 20–23 November 1943, and in the Marshall Islands from 31 January to 23 February 1944. Nimitz then turned to the Marianas and directed the offensive against these islands from 14 June to 10 August. While directing operations in the Palau Islands from 15 September to 25 November, Nimitz also joined forces with General MacArthur in New Guinea to launch an invasion at Leyte Gulf in the Philippines on 20 October. On 15 December, Nimitz was promoted to the newly created rank of fleet admiral.

In January 1945, Nimitz moved his headquarters to Guam. From there he directed the operations on Iwo Jima from 19 February to 24 March, and then the invasion of Okinawa from 1 April to 21 June. Nimitz continued to direct naval operations against Japan until its capitulation on 14 August. On 29 August, Nimitz sailed into Tokyo Bay on board his flagship, the battleship *South Dakota*. On 2 September he boarded the battleship *Missouri* and, as the representative of the United States, signed the instrument of surrender.

In recognition of his wartime service, 5 October was designated Nimitz Day in Washington, and a grateful nation turned out to welcome its hero.

The Postwar Years

Nimitz's desire to succeed Adm. Ernest King as Chief of Naval Operations (CNO) was granted, and on 15 December 1945 he was sworn in as the first postwar CNO. The job facing Nimitz was both difficult and trying, and he worked constantly and diligently at its success.

During his term as CNO, Nimitz was responsible for demobilizing the wartime navy and helping to determine the future status of America's armed forces. (The end result was the retention of the Joint Chiefs of Staff and the establishment of separate departments for the Army, Navy, and Air Force. Heading these departments would be a Secretary of Defense who would be a permanent member of the President's Cabinet.) Nimitz also played a role in the development of the first nuclear-powered submarine.

On 15 December 1947, Nimitz stepped down as CNO and retired to California with his wife and family. In 1948, he made himself available as a special assistant to the Secretary of the Navy. In March 1949 he was asked to come out of retirement to serve as good-will ambassador to the United Nations. Later that same year he became the UN commissioner for Kashmir, a post he held until 1951 when he returned to retirement.

Nimitz spent his remaining years in quiet, taking time to coauthor *Sea Power: A Naval History*, with E. B. Potter, which was published in 1960. In November 1965, Nimitz underwent surgery, and while in the hospital he contracted pneumonia. His health took a turn for the worse and late in January 1966, he went into a coma from which he never recovered. He died on Sunday, 20 February 1966; in accordance with his wishes, he was buried in Golden Gate National Cemetery.

Nimitz was one of America's greatest naval officers. An experienced commander of great foresight and ability, Nimitz performed arduous tasks skillfully and proficiently. Hard-working but with an easy manner, Nimitz was able to get the most from his subordinates and colleagues without antagonizing them. He was greatly admired and respected by both his sailors and his country. He provided the strategic direction and much of the impetus behind America's victory in the Central Pacific. Edwin Hoyt in his history of the Pacific War (1970) said of him, "The qualities of Nimitz's character were apparent in his face, in his career, and in his heritage; combined, these factors made him precisely the man he was and placed him in this particular situation at this moment in history."

VINCENT B. HAWKINS

SEE ALSO: King, Ernest J.; MacArthur, Douglas; World War II; Yamamoto, Isoroku.

Bibliography

Hoyt, E. F. 1970. *How they won the war in the Pacific*. New York: Weybright and Talley.

Morrison, S. E. 1947–62. *History of United States naval operations in World War II*. 15 vols. Boston: Little, Brown.

Nimitz, C. W., and E. B. Potter, 1960. *Sea power: A naval history*. Annapolis, Md.: U.S. Naval Institute Press.

Pfannes, C. E., and V. A. Salamone. 1983. *The great admirals of World War II*. Vol. 1, *The Americans*. New York: Kensington.

Potter, E. B. 1976. *Nimitz*. Annapolis, Md.: U.S. Naval Institute Press.

Reynolds, C. G. 1978. *Famous American admirals*. New York: Van Nostrand Rheinhold.

NONATTACKING CAPABILITIES

In the early 1980s the concept of nonattacking capabilities gained prominence in the intense controversy generated by the deployment of new U.S. intermediate-range nuclear missiles in Western Europe. The dual-track decision of 12 December 1979 led to insistent questioning of the then-existing North Atlantic Treaty Organization (NATO) defense posture and its dependence on nuclear weapons. Heightened by the deadlock that had been reached in the arms control process in 1983, when INF negotiations collapsed and long-term talks on Mutual and Balanced Force Reduction (MBFR) and Strategic Arms Reduction (START) seemed to be stalling, fundamental criticism of NATO strategies resulted in the development of many proposals to structure Western defense in new ways, including on a nonnuclear basis.

The debate was most intense in the Federal Republic of Germany where the bulk of NATO ground forces confronted the Warsaw Pact forward-standing armies and where opposition to nuclear missile modernization was most prominent. The controversy had two themes: one concerned basing future NATO defense strategy on strengthened and advanced conventional armaments, thereby allowing a drastic cutback in short- and intermediate-range nuclear weapons. The other contrasted the merits of static defense, which relies on emergent military high technologies (e.g., precision-guided munitions and mines, multispectral sensor techniques, and fiber-optic communications systems), with the merits of mobile defense, which is based on tanks and other armored fire platforms.

From a semantic point of view, the concept of nonattacking capabilities is a misnomer: what really is meant is a noncapability or inability to attack because of not being armed to launch a premeditated attack or offensive. This is part of a larger set of coterminous concepts centering on the idea of nonprovocative defense. This idea envisages that the size, structure, weapons, logistics, training, maneuvers, war games, strategic doctrines, and tactical concepts of a country's military forces can be shaped and designed in such a way that they are perceived to provide, in their totality, an effective nonnuclear defense while denoting no offensive capability. Nonprovocative defense does not rely on tactical nuclear weapons; the sole military-political purpose of nuclear arms is to deter their first use by either side. In other words, nonprovocative defense is seen as a self-defensive military posture shaped in such a way that neighboring countries or power blocs reasonably cannot feel threatened by it.

Principles and Precedents

Regarding the present-day set of proposals for the restructuring of NATO forces, many of the labels used to describe the large variety of such projects connote similar impressions of purpose (e.g., defensive defense, nonoffensive defense, defense-only defense, defensive deterrence, reactive defense, nonprovocative defense, structural incapacity for attack, structural inability to launch an attack, area defense, static defense, territorial defense, militia defense, defense by techno-commandos, network defense, autonomous defense, nonnuclear defense, transarmament). However, the common concept can be expressed simply by reference to traditional deterrence theory: dissuasion of attack through effective denial of one's own territory, rather than deterrence of an attack by threat of (nuclear) retaliation.

Within this context two distinct modes of thinking compete: one presses the principle of substantial forward-based static or line defenses that would exact a huge price in manpower and materiel losses from any adversarial move to cross the defense line. The other stresses the principle of the network or "chessboard" defense, which would subject an adversary to ubiquitous war of attrition enhanced by civil noncooperation. In both cases, the hoped-for deterrent hinges on a cost versus benefit analysis supposedly undertaken by a prospective attacker. This calculation is expected to demonstrate that the cost of invasion and occupation surpasses any gains that might derive from an attack. Strategies then stem from ways to drive up the costs of attacking or invading under force of arms.

Common Characteristics

All the many alternative defense proposals of Western European antinuclear and peace movements share the common characteristic of replacing the present NATO strategy of flexible response with a no-first-use policy. Restructured defensive forces are built and trained to operate without actually employing nuclear weapons. By forgoing vulnerable force concentrations in favor of small, dispersed, concealed fighting units, enemy use of nuclear weapons would be made less likely because of a paucity of worthwhile targets such as large NATO troop groupings. In keeping with their nonprovocative character, defensive ground forces would be limited in range and would not be capable of deep counterattacks on enemy territory. Above all, they should systematically exploit the known advantages of the defense.

This strategic theme was developed by Basil Liddell Hart in the 1930s when he explained how the defense is superior to the offense in modern land warfare and how modern weapons developments increase this superiority (Bond 1977). Liddell Hart also, in the early 1960s, expanded an idea developed in 1954 by Bogislaw von Bonin (cf. Brill 1988): reformation of the Federal German Army to concentrate on antitank defense units (*Sperrverbände*) deployed as a continuous screen within 50 kilometers (31 mi.) of the zonal border. Liddell Hart promoted that idea of a semistatic matrix of local defenses and envisaged a deep network of defense posts in the forward zone manned on short notice by a citizen militia of the Swiss type (Liddell Hart 1960).

Thus, salient characteristics of alternative defense postures can be reduced to five principles:

1. *Superiority of Defense over Offense.* While an aggressor may be able to concentrate for a breakthrough of defense lines by exploiting the mobility of his armored forces, this advantage can be offset by the defender's use of natural and man-made obstacles; reinforced positions like shelters, barriers, and fortifications either carefully prepared in peacetime or swiftly assembled from prefabricated parts in a crisis; pre-installed hardened communication systems; preplanned mine fields; and the like. In this, the defender is greatly favored by his intimate knowledge of the terrain to be defended; by the psychological morale and awareness that he is fighting on his ground for its "sacred" defense; and by the fact that most of the small fighting units bearing the brunt of the attack will have been raised and trained in the vicinity of the locations they are to protect.

2. *Specialization in Defense.* If it is a golden rule of economics that specialization begets excellence while reducing cost, applying this rule to military doctrine might produce beneficial outcomes. Renunciation of offensive capabilities relieves defenders of providing "jack-of-all-trades" forces that, because of the multifarious roles they have to fulfill, would not be able to serve all their purposes equally effectively.

3. *Application of the "David versus Goliath" Principle.* This implies a breach of the pattern of answering an aggressor's actions in kind (e.g., of pitching armor against armor, aircraft against aircraft, warships against warships). Rather, offensive options can be matched by defensive options: tanks with antitank weapons, aircraft with ground-to-air missiles, and warships with surface-to-surface or air-to-surface missiles. A successful defense does not depend on numerical or material equality with an aggressor's forces; rather, it relies on the ability to inflict maximum losses on an adversary with minimum outlay (Hannig 1984).

4. *Development of a "No-Target Philosophy."* This entails a tactical double-back: the invalidation of massive conventional or nuclear firepower concentrations by not providing an opponent with suitable targets against which he can gainfully direct fire.

5. *Strategy of Defensive Entanglement.* This may be interpreted as a reformulation of a time-honored military principle: that of avoiding decisive battle and instead subjecting attackers to maximum attrition.

Historical Precedents

Two general historical principles are manifested in the alternative strategic modes described above. One dates from the formation of the early modern territorial state. The other traces its lineage to the Napoleonic period.

In the first case, allusion may be made to that hard shell of fortifications and border defenses, seen as the expression not only of the early modern states' territoriality, but also of their function to accord their citizens protection from outside attack. One can speculate on the degree to which latter-day alternative defense strategists draw inspiration from the history of siege and fortress warfare. If one views fortresses as the centers of a complex deterrence system predicated on prearranged obstacles that enable a weaker power to withstand a stronger one by forcing it to fight at a disadvantage or else to desist (Duffy 1979; 1985), many of our more recent nonattacking capability concepts assume a familiar historical ring.

In the second case, allusion may be made to the practice of territorial defense first encountered by Napoleon I in his wars in Russia and Spain in the early nineteenth century. A practice based neither on deterrence by retaliation nor necessarily on conventional military defense along a front, but rather on struggle in depth using various means of harassment and combat, including guerrilla warfare that consistently defies the aggressor and makes one's own territory and people hard to conquer (Roberts 1986). In other words, as of the late 1980s, much of what forms the defense postures of countries such as Sweden, Switzerland, and Yugoslavia may be rediscovered in one variation or another of defense concepts, as covered by Roberts's definition of territorial defense as a system of defense in depth:

> The governmentally-organized defence of a state's own territory, conducted on its own territory. It is aimed at creating a situation in which an invader, even though he may at least for a time gain geographical possession of part or all of the territory, is constantly harassed and attacked from all sides. It is a form of defence strategy which has important organizational implications, being liable to involve substantial reliance on a citizen army, including local units of a militia type. Characteristically, a territorial defence system is based on weapons systems, strategies and methods of military organization which are better suited to their defensive role than to engagement in major military actions abroad.

Criticisms of Flexible Response

The above historical observations must be qualified by an important rider: the present-day debate of alternative defense concepts is, to a large extent, a belated reaction to the profound qualitative changes in the art of warfare brought about by the development and deployment of thermonuclear weapons of mass destruction. In these terms, prenuclear history may offer insightful analogies rather than applicable blueprints for contemporary action.

Within the overall province of thermonuclear warfare, it is not so much the ICBM-based policy of Mutual Assured Destruction—stabilizing strategic relationships among the great powers now for more than a quarter century—that draws criticism; rather, it is an inherent weakness in NATO's flexible-response posture that comes under close scrutiny.

In theory, flexible response should provide NATO with the ability to respond to any aggression at a level commensurate with an attack. Furthermore, by the threat of controlled triadic escalation, it should persuade an adversary of the immense risks and costs of resorting to violence. Critics claim that in reality, NATO's failure to raise its conventional forces to the level necessary to achieve true flexibility of defensive military options leads to a heavy reliance on tactical, theater, and strategic nuclear weapons to offset the conventional East-West imbalance (Stromseth 1988). The resultant policy of substituting nuclear weapons for conventional inadequacy gives rise to a number of pertinent objections:

1. The "use-them-or-lose them" argument, particularly hinging on the forward deployment of tactical nuclear weapons that would force NATO commanders to apply for their use within the span of a few days after the start of the fighting;
2. The "lack-of-credibility" argument, which assumes that the threat to initiate an escalation process (which would almost certainly trigger an all-out nuclear exchange in defense of Western Europe) rests on an element of bluff, an element perhaps so perceived by the enemy;
3. The "escalation-running-out-of-control" argument, which is predicated on Thomas Schelling's view of deterrence as a strategy with a random ingredient, a threat that leaves something to chance (Schelling 1960), and points toward the difficulty of rationally calculating and controlling escalation sequences in the traumatic and confusing circumstances of war; and
4. The "overrated altruism" argument, according to which it is doubtful that, given superpower nuclear parity, the United States would, in the last resort, commit nuclear suicide in order to defend Western Europe.

All this is enhanced by the critique of considerations supposedly turning nuclear weapons from their politico-strategic role (i.e., deterring a first use by enemy forces) back to their warfighting role in which they may be used to fight and win a nuclear war confined to the Western European theater. Flexible response, to its West European critics, conjures up that drastically vivid description of NATO strategy formulated by Morton Halperin when he was U.S. deputy assistant secretary of defense: "We will fight with conventional forces until we are losing, then we will fight with tactical nuclear weapons until we are losing, and then we will blow up the world . . ." (Barnaby 1986, p. 157).

The real dilemma flexible response poses to West Europeans is that the defense of their half-continent against aggression seems well-nigh impossible without involving widespread, if not universal, nuclear destruction of precisely that which is to be defended—Western Europe's territory, population, societies, and political systems. The only way out of this dilemma lies in turning defense in war into defense against war: the avoidance of war thus becomes the paramount, overriding political objective of security policy. If this critique is valid, alternative defense strategies need to strike a balance among five criteria:

1. *War avoidance*: guaranteeing the territorial integrity and the political self-determination of countries;
2. *Deterrence by denial*: dissuading a prospective opponent from military action by demonstrating credibly that the costs of such an action would outweigh any gains;
3. *Crisis stability*: reducing or removing incentives to preemptive, first-strike military behavior in the short run, as well as relaxing and resolving interbloc conflicts provoking military threats in the medium term;
4. *Damage limitation*: if deterrence should fail, keeping the danger resulting from conventional military action as well as the incentives to escalate to nuclear warfare levels as low as possible;
5. *Social acceptability*: adopting defense concepts that are feasible from the point of view of financial and manpower resources required; that can be borne and supported by a consensus of the population to be defended; and that are compatible with the basic values of the society they are meant to protect.

It is one of the central arguments of alternative defense advocates that these criteria are best met by a policy that aims at a systematic reduction not only of tactical and theater nuclear weapons, but also of conventional offensive and invasion capabilities on both sides of the East-West divide. The inability to launch an attack will become a structural property of the respective military deployment dispositions only if and when both opponents agree to selectively reduce the major weapon systems that have been war-decisive (tanks, armored vehicles, artillery, bridge-building equipment, etc.) while at the same time strengthening their forward-based holding and denial capabilities. It is conceivable that flexible response could then be replaced by a reciprocal disposition of forces marked by enhancing both sides' robust defensive capabilities while diminishing their powers of offense: a situation of mutual defensive superiority or mutual defender dominance. In the period 1987–90, these notions were beginning to take concrete, quantitative form in European defense postures.

Supplementary Motives: Changes in Threat Perceptions

Conducive to the debate of alternative defense concepts in the 1980s was the fact that many segments of West European public opinion no longer supported the alliance consensus that the Soviet Union, in general, must be viewed as an expansionist power (albeit one realistic enough to suspend its ambitions temporarily where so required by adverse circumstances). Rather, in the European military context, the USSR was perceived as a status-quo power. While the USSR remained prepared to support use of military force in developing countries, no gains were to be had offsetting the cost of an attack on Western Europe. Such Soviet action would not only run the risk of both worldwide conflict and nuclear war, but it would also not serve any rationally defined economic purpose, as an attempt to gain control of European productive resources might well be frustrated by the immense destruction being wrought already by large-scale conventional warfare, let alone tactical nuclear warfare. Thus, although the USSR would defend itself if attacked, it would not launch a deliberate, premeditated attack to conquer and hold Western Europe (Dean 1987).

While this train of argument rules out the likelihood of an unprovoked attack on the 1939 model, it leaves open the possibility that conflicting superpower interests elsewhere will spill over onto the European security system. Enhanced by misperceptions and communication breakdowns between U.S. and enemy decision-making centers, this spillover might lead to a 1914-like situation: two alliance systems in a communication crisis, both fearing for the worst from the other side while rapidly mobilizing. In such a situation, military pre-emption would be at a premium; the temptation to destroy the adversary's military resources by a first strike would rise. To avoid this, continuance of interbloc communication would have to be guaranteed on a number of different levels: diplomatic, economic, arms control, and confidence-building. Pre-emption premiums would have to be discounted by dissolving force concentrations and weapon systems that not only threaten the other side but also offer a target for first-strike attacks. This politico-strategic consideration explains the emphasis on a no-target philosophy as well as that on signaling one's opponent of the defensive character of force structures and force deployments to be found in many alternative defense proposals.

Supplementary Motives: Changes in the Art of Warfare

Superiority of the defense over the offense, which represents one of the cardinal assumptions of alternative defense models, hinges to a large extent on the military geography of Europe (with notable exceptions in the North German plain), which favors antitank warfare to the detriment of large-scale concentrations of mobile armored firepower. This geographical constant can be enhanced by a static defense in depth, making use of advantageous terrain as well as of third-generation mines, guided antitank missiles fired from prepared full-cover positions, and short- and medium-range rocket artillery staggered in echelons within fire zones some 50 to 100 kilometers (31 to 62 mi.) deep next to the border (Gerber 1985; Bülow, Funk, and Müller 1988). While an enemy advance can be slowed and worn down by forward-based barriers and minefields, and while it can be delayed and contained by small mobile infantry units operating from numerous covered positions (such as the former British 5th Mobile Group), the brunt of defensive action would have to be borne by rocket artillery units concentrating their fire under orders of an integrated sector or overall battlefield command. Their task would be to wear down an opponent over medium and long distances so that he reaches the defenders' forward positions weakened. Mobile armored reserves would have to be kept ready in rear areas to be moved up to strengthen resistance at threatened points, mop up enemy breakthroughs, or engage in limited counterattacks.

The large number of mainly tactical variations on a common strategic theme developed by most alternative defense projects (cf. Alternative Defence Commission 1983; Bülow, Funk, and Müller 1988; Hannig 1984; Löser 1982; SAS 1984; Gates 1987; Dean 1988) can be grouped under the following three headings:

1. Linear-zonal defense projects as described above;
2. Area, in-depth network, or "chessboard" defense projects, which would cover the whole terrain of the Federal Republic of Germany with a network of techno-commando units of about twenty men each armed with antitank, antiaircraft, and light infantry weapons, defending a small area of familiar territory (Afheldt 1976; 1983);
3. Any variation of these two basic dislocation principles, particularly ones that superimpose a mobile, armored element on linear defense zones or area defense networks.

Whatever their individual characteristics, all of these possibilities have three common premises: superiority of mainly static firepower over mainly armored mobility; intelligent use of limited human resources for fighting purposes rather than for command-control-communications (C^3), logistics, and administrative purposes; and replacement of extensive armored and mechanized warfare options by in-depth staggered economical antitank options making full use of appropriate emergent technologies.

In sum, these prospects connote a single, cardinal premise: that of replacing the traditional demand for parity of military means by the new demand for balancing military options. This principle may be seen at work in the claim that the force of armored thrust can be contained by the stopping capabilities of precise fire enjoying the advantage of surprise and the support of sensor-guided highly active barriers. This principle also may be seen at work in the recommendation to the defender to stay put or operate from covered positions. Tactical battlefield mobility requires an amount of personnel resources three to four times larger (drivers, supply, command, communication, losses suffered from offering openly visible targets) than that needed for effective, conventional static defense. Finally, this principle may be seen at work in new technologies, which seem to make defense much more cost-effective than offense (e.g., new surveillance and target-acquisition systems; increasingly intelligent, fire-and-forget missiles; the development of very destructive conventional warheads; and the automation of C^3/ intelligence [C^3I] operations). All of these drive home the conclusion that it could be cheaper to destroy the weapons of invasion—heavy tanks, long-range aircraft, large warships—than to procure them.

REINHARD MEYERS

SEE ALSO: Army; Defense; Delaying Action; Deterrence; Escalation; Flexible Response; Fortification; Land Forces, Effectiveness and Efficiency of; Land Warfare; NATO Policy and Strategy; Siege; Strategy; Strategy, National Security; Territorial Army.

Bibliography

Afheldt, H. 1976. *Verteidigung und Frieden. Politik mit militärischen Mitteln.* Munich: Carl Hanser.
———. 1983. *Defensive Verteidigung.* Reinbek: Rowohlt.
Alternative Defence Commission. 1983. *Defence without the bomb.* London: Taylor & Francis.
Bahr, E., and D. S. Lutz, eds. 1986. *Gemeinsame Sicherheit. Idee und Konzept.* Vol. 1, *Zu den Ausgangsüberlegungen, Grundlagen und Strukturmerkmalen Gemeinsamer Sicherheit.* Baden-Baden: Nomos.
———, eds. 1987. *Gemeinsame Sicherheit. Dimensionen und Disziplinen.* Vol. 2, *Zu rechtlichen, ökonomischen, psychologischen und militärischen Aspekten Gemeinsamer Sicherheit.* Baden-Baden: Nomos.
———, eds. 1988. *Gemeinsame Sicherheit. Konventionelle Stabilität.* Vol. 3, *Zu den militärischen Aspekten Struktureller Nichtangriffsfähigkeit im Rahmen Gemeinsamer Sicherheit.* Baden-Baden: Nomos.
Barnaby, F. 1986. *The automated battlefield.* London: Sidgwick & Jackson.
Barnaby, F., and M. Ter Borg, eds. 1986. *Emerging technologies and military doctrine: A political assessment.* London: Macmillan.
Bond, B. 1977. *Liddell Hart: A study of his military thought.* London: Cassell.
Brill, H. 1988. *Bogislaw von Bonin im Spannungsfeld zwischen Wiederbewaffnung—Westintegration—Wiedervereinigung.* Baden-Baden: Nomos.
Bülow, A. von., H. Funk, and A. von Müller. 1988. *Sicherheit für Europa.* Koblenz: Bernard & Graefe.
Dean, J. 1987. *Watershed in Europe. Dismantling the East-West military confrontation.* Lexington, Mass.: Lexington Books.
———. 1988. Alternative defence: Answer to NATO's central front problems. *International Affairs* 64:61–82.
Duffy, C. 1979. *Siege warfare. The fortress in the early modern world 1494–1660.* London: Routledge and Kegan Paul.
———. 1985. *The fortress in the age of Vauban and Frederick the Great, 1660–1789.* Vol. 2, *Siege Warfare.* London: Routledge & Kegan Paul.
Gates, D. 1987. Area defence concepts: The West German debate. *Survival* 29:301–17.
Gerber, J. 1985. *Die Bundeswehr im Nordatlantischen Bündnis.* Regensburg: Walhalla und Praetoria Verlag.
Hannig, N. 1984. *Abschreckung durch konventionelle Waffen. Das David-Goliath-Prinzip.* Berlin: Berlin-Verlag.
Hopmann, P. T., and F. Barnaby, eds. 1988. *Rethinking the nuclear weapons dilemma in Europe.* London: Macmillan.
Liddell Hart, B. 1960. *Deterrent or defence.* London: Stevens & Sons.
Löser, J. 1982. *Weder rot noch tot. Überleben ohne Atomkrieg. Eine sicherheitspolitische Alternative.* 2d ed. Munich: Günter Olzog.
Roberts, A. 1986. *Nations in arms. The theory and practice of territorial defence.* 2d rev. ed. London: Macmillan.
Studiengruppe Alternative Sicherheit (SAS), eds. 1984. *Strukturwandel der Verteidigung. Entwürfe für eine konsequente Defensive.* Opladen: Westdeutscher Verlag.
Schelling, T. C. 1960. *The strategy of conflict.* Cambridge, Mass.: Harvard Univ. Press.
Stromseth, J. E. 1988. *The origins of flexible response: NATO's debate over strategy in the 1960s.* London: Macmillan.

NONCOMMISSIONED OFFICER

Noncommissioned officers are enlisted personnel designated as leaders or, particularly in this century, senior technicians. In armies and air forces, the principal noncommissioned officer rank is sergeant. There are a variety of sergeants, such as staff sergeant, gunnery sergeant, technical sergeant, first sergeant, and master sergeant. Junior or apprentice noncommissioned officers may be called corporals, or lance corporals. In the United States, noncommissioned officers form the top six of the nine enlisted pay grades. The two highest noncommissioned officer grades were added after the Korean War and form a distinct senior level of enlisted leaders. No more than three percent of the enlisted members of a U.S. armed force may be serving in these two top grades at any time. Among the ranks in these top two grades are the sergeant majors, chief master sergeants and master chief petty officers. In navies, noncommissioned officers are called petty officers. The lowest grade noncommissioned officer in a navy is a petty officer third class. After promotion to second class and then to first class petty officer, the next higher rank is chief petty officer. Chief petty officers are the highest ranking noncommissioned officers in navies. The most senior chief petty officers, equivalent to command sergeant majors, are the command master chief petty officer and the master chief petty officer.

The authors of the classic study of members of the United States Army conducted during World War II described the function of the noncommissioned officer as being "to bridge the gap between officers and men" (Stouffer et al. 1949). This critical—and often undervalued—role of first-line supervision has also been recognized in the study of the management of large civilian organizations (De Man 1929). Just as concern with the role and effectiveness of first-line supervision was a product of the industrial revolution, the importance of the noncommissioned officer stems from the historical transition from permanent warriors and temporary armies to permanent standing armies (Vagts 1959). Similarly in the naval service, the time passed in the early nineteenth century when adequate wartime manning in the enlisted ranks could be assured through the combination of impressment and the utilization of merchant seamen. A system of long-term enlisted service was required. This system, augmented in England by the Royal Naval Reserve, began to provide a way of ensuring competence at sea in wartime (Lewis 1959).

Despite the importance of noncommissioned officers in the modern military organization, students of military organization—who have devoted extensive research to the recruitment, attitudes, and performance of commissioned officers—have paid surprisingly little attention to noncommissioned officers as a group. For example, a bibliography of some 1,500 studies of military organization includes two complete categories of references to military officers, with not a single reference to a study focused primarily on noncommissioned officers (Lang 1972). In part this may be because noncommissioned officers have not been regarded as military professionals. Professionalism is associated with lifetime pursuit; noncommissioned officers remain enlisted members whose service has generally been limited by the length of an enlistment, with no commitment to lifetime service. Variations on this practice are emerging. In the Federal Republic of Germany's *Bundeswehr*, one who makes the rank of sergeant may apply to become a professional. This involves an entitlement to stay until age 53 and receive retirement pay. It is more typical in contemporary Western military organizations for those members who reenlist for a second term of service to become career members in fact if not in regulation.

In some historical periods and nations, it was the warrant officer who served as the "man-in-the-middle" between commissioned officers and men. In modern military organizations, however, the role of the warrant officer has become increasingly that of the technical expert whose specialty is not conducive to promotion to the highest officer ranks. Thus the bridge between officers and enlisted members has been increasingly that of the noncommissioned officer.

With the further mechanization and specialization of military tasks, similar forces have affected the role of the noncommissioned officer. Over the last century, noncommissioned officers have expanded as a percentage of the enlisted force (Lang 1972, 92ff.). From comprising a small percentage of the total enlisted force at the end of the nineteenth century, the requirement for noncommissioned officers has expanded until they comprise well over half of the enlisted force. This was also the case in the sea service. In the U.S. Navy, there was no insignia to distinguish petty officers from the rest of the crew until the late 1840s, and it was not until the 1880s that a clear military (as opposed to technical) authority began to appear (Downs 1986).

In large part this expansion was due to the increasing specialization and complexity of military organizations. As early as the seventeenth century, obstacles to the movement of lance corporals and sergeants into the commissioned ranks were in place. Today, these obstacles have generally been reduced for junior noncommissioned officers who are able to obtain the necessary credentials for commissioning. In the case of senior noncommissioned officers, however, there remains only a slight opportunity for a commission.

The requirement for enlisted members who are specialists in such occupations as communications, air traffic control, finance, personnel administration, supply, medical technology, and so on, has spawned proposals for dual-track systems that differentiate between technicians on the one hand and combat leaders and military trainers on the other. This will probably continue to be an issue.

As with the warrant officer, the noncommissioned officer often fills a position that is primarily technical as contrasted with line supervision. In some military organizations, enlisted members may have two tracks for promotion—one for technical specialties and one for direct-line supervision. Whatever adjustments are made to accommodate these two requirements, the role of the noncommissioned officer will continue to be central to military efficiency and effectiveness.

FRANCIS M. RUSH, JR.

SEE ALSO: Officer; Professionalism, Military; Promotion; Warrant Officer.

Bibliography

De Man, H. 1929. *Joy in work*. London: Eden and Cedar Paul.
Downs, J. 1986. Prime hand to petty officer: The evolution of the navy noncommissioned officer. In *Life in the rank and file*, ed. D. Segal and H. Sinako. Washington, D.C.: Pergamon-Brassey's.
Lang, K. 1972. *Military institutions and the sociology of war*. Beverly Hills: Sage.
Lewis, M. 1959. *The history of the British navy*. Fair Lawn: Essential Books.
Moskos, C. 1970. *The American enlisted man*. New York: Russell Sage Foundation.
Stouffer, S., et al. 1949. *The American soldier*. Vol. 1. Princeton, N.J.: Princeton Univ. Press.
Teitler, G. 1977. *The genesis of the professional officers' corps*. Beverly Hills: Sage.
Vagts, A. 1937. *A history of militarism*. New York: W. W. Norton.

NORMANS

The Normans were direct descendants ofthe Vikings, or Norsemen, fierce Scandinavian warriors who terriorized much of coastal and riverine continental Europe and the British Isles in the ninth and tenth centuries. In the early 900s, a Norse group seized and colonized Frankish territory at the mouth of the Seine River, a region known since as Normandy. Within a brief time, the Norse conquerors married local women, abandoned their pagan ways for Christianity, and many of them became civil administrators, church leaders, and crusaders in the Frankish kingdom. they ahd become Normans. A Norman force under William the Conqueror invaded and took England in 1066. This historic incursion marked the beginning of Norman rule inEngland and changed the course of Western history. Other Norman groups conquered southern Italy and Sicily, though their rule there did not last.

The Norman Conquest

Duke William of Normandy, a strong and respected leader, inherited his title at age 8. He soon became a noted warrior and put down a major revolt when he was twenty. He was related to the King of England, Edward the Confessor, who had granted him successjion to the English crown. The Earl of Wessex, Harold Godwinsson, was the other principal contender. But Duke William claimed that Harold, who had earlier been shipwrecked on the coast of Normandy, had sworn to support Williams claim.

In 1066 Edward died. Harold was quickly named king by the Anglo-Saxon Grand Council (Witan). Duke William of Normandy also declared his right to the throne, obtained the Pope's support, and began assembling an army. His forces made the channel crossing after a weather-induced wait of several weeks, landing without opposition at Pevensey Bay, near Hastings, on the Sussex coast. Harold was aware of William's preparations and was ready to oppose the invasion. However, an unexpected Norwegian invasion of northern England caused Harold to rush north to deal with that threat. Disposing of the Norwegians in a hard-fought battle, Harold backtracked south, after learning that William and his army had landed at Pevensey.

The Battle of Hastings

Harold and his army moved to Hastings by forced marches. He augmented his depleted force along the way from poorly armed and trained local militia. He and his Anglo-Saxon army met the Norman invaders on 14 October 1066 at the Battle of Hastings. The battle was joined at the hill of Senlac, near Hastings. Each side had approximately 7,000 men, though accounts differ on the exact numbers. Harold's forces, mostly dismounted, deployed on the hilltop as an infantry phalanx. The Norman army consisted of feudal cavalry supported by archers. Harold's forces were charged repeatedly by the Norman knights and showered by flights of arrows. Although the Norman charges failed to secure the heights, the Anglo-Saxons were gradually worn down. Harold was killed late in the afternoon by a Norman arrow. According to one account, the Normans defeated the defenders with another charge after Harold's death. Another account states that the Anglo-Saxons were tricked into rushing down the hill after a fake retreat by the Normans, who then turned and charged and overwhelmed the Anglo-Saxons. In any case, the Anglo-Saxon force was swept from the field that October day, leaving England open to invaders.

The Norman Subjugation of England

Hastings was really a battle between two would-be kings, both of whom had a claim to the throne. When William won he became, in fact, England's ruler and had to face no other major military confrontations. After their victory, the Normans moved quickly to London, where their leader was crowned William I on Christmas Day, 1066. Following his coronation, William spent several years trying to subdue the native Anglo-Saxons, but they resisted him stubbornly. William confiscated the land of most of the old English nobility and gave it to his loyal Norman followers. However, he let members of the old nobility keep their lands and titles if they swore allegiance to him. To consolidate his power through control of the feudal lords, William I ordered preparation of the Domesday Book in 1085. This was an inventory of the land holders in England and showed how their holdings were peopled. To accomplish this survey, the country was divided into districts, each surveyed by census takers familiar with the region. When the Domesday Book was completed in 1086, it became final and authoritative and formed the basis for the Norman administration of England.

The Normans as Warriors and Rulers

The Normans inherited their warlike tendencies and skills from their Norse ancestors. Their adoption of aggressive Frankish military tactics added to their prowess, and enabled them to overwhelm the basically defensive Anglo-Saxon posture.

But the real victory of the Normans in England lay in their ability as rulers and administrators. Their rule of England was capable and evenhanded. They installed an improved legal system and provided good government and security. Under their rule, England was largely free from internal strife and became a more cohesive nation.

Within a few centuries, a new England emerged, melded into one nation, with a common English tongue. The Norman conquest helped bring national unity to England and, eventually, status as a world power.

WALTER P. WHITE

SEE ALSO: Feudalism; History, Medieval Military.

Bibliography

Beeler, J. 1966. *Warfare in England, 1066–1189.* Ithaca, N.Y.: Cornell Univ. Press.

Douglas, D. C. 1977. *William the Conqueror: The Norman impact upon England.* London: Eyre Methuen.

Le Patourel, J. 1976. *The Norman Empire.* Oxford: Clarendon Press.

———. 1971. *Normandy and England, 1066–1144.* Reading, England: Univ. of Reading.

Oman, Sir C. 1978. *A history of the art of war in the Middle Ages*. Vol I: *A.D. 378–1272*. London: Methuen.
Sawyer, P. H. 1978. *From Roman Britain to Norman England*. New York: St. Martin's Press.

NORTH AFRICA

North Africa is located on the southern rim of the Mediterranean basin. It is overwhelmingly Islamic in culture and Arabic and Berber in language. Despite being located on the African continent, the region is bound culturally, ethnically, and politically to the Middle East. It is a distinct geographical region separated from Egypt by about 1,600 kilometers (1,000 mi.) of desert.

History

The indigenous inhabitants of North Africa were the Berbers, who are Caucasian and may have come from the eastern Mediterranean. North African history begins in the ninth century B.C. with exploration and settlements by the Phoenicians. They founded Carthage (near present-day Tunis) in the same century, and established trading posts along the Mediterranean and south along the Atlantic coast for several hundred kilometers. It was from Carthage, which remained their most important southern Mediterranean base, that Hannibal (247–183 B.C.) led his army in a flanking maneuver over the Alps in an attempt to conquer Rome. His invasion failed, and when Rome finally conquered Carthage (146 B.C.) in the last of the Punic Wars, legend says they destroyed the city and sowed salt over its site to prevent further inhabitation.

The Romans went on to establish a far-reaching and well-governed empire in North Africa. After their defeat of the Carthaginians (Phoenicians), the Romans displaced the Greeks who had built outposts in various locations there. Rome governed North Africa for almost eight centuries, building towns and a network of roads, and enhancing cultivation. In the fifth century A.D. the Vandals invaded from Europe, conquered Morocco, and moved eastward, but they were defeated in the east by the forces of Byzantium in the following century.

Late in the seventh century A.D. the Arabs, after the establishment of Islam some years earlier, began their sweep across North Africa. Within a century the Muslim forces had reached the Atlantic, and *El Maghreb* (the West, composed of what is now Algeria, Morocco, and Tunisia) came into being. It took another century for the Muslims to consolidate their North African territory.

During the eighth century a Muslim force from Morocco crossed the Straits of Gibraltar to invade and conquer southern Spain. This force of Berbers and Arabs was called the Moors (from the Roman name for the inhabitants of northwest Africa) by Europeans. Their remarkable civilization flourished for seven centuries in Spain, and their principal cities—Seville, Córdoba, and Granada—were centers of culture and language during Europe's Dark Ages. The Moors were finally defeated and driven from Spain by the forces of King Ferdinand and Queen Isabella, after which most of them settled in North Africa.

After the Muslim conquest of North Africa and its consolidation, the region became a province of the Islamic empire ruled by the Caliph in Baghdad. Soon, however, it was divided into autonomous districts that were ruled by a number of dynasties. The most important dynasty was the Almohade, a Berber group from the High Atlas mountains that invaded Morocco and Spain in the thirteenth century. The Almohades then moved eastward into Algeria and Tunisia, bringing the whole of North Africa (except Libya) under their control—the only Islamic regime since the original Arab seventh-century invaders to do so. Libya, meanwhile, was successively dominated by the Vandals, Turks, and Egyptians during the twelfth and thirteenth centuries.

The Turkish Ottoman Empire annexed North Africa, up to the Moroccan border, in the sixteenth century. The Turkish rule, however, was loose, and various beys, or rulers, governed coastal enclaves until the eighteenth century. This was the time of the Barbary pirates, who wreaked havoc with European and American shipping until early in the nineteenth century.

Decadence and anarchy increasingly gripped North Africa from the mid-1600s onward, abetted by piracy from its shores and incursions by European powers. The United States, in 1795, bought peace from Tunis and Algeria with payment of US$800,000 and a frigate, as well as the promise of a US$25,000 annual subsidy. The United States and Tripoli went to war in 1801 over the U.S. refusal to pay additional tribute. An American naval and land campaign forced Tripoli to conclude peace in 1805—the inspiration for the first lines of the Marine Hymn. In 1830, France invaded Algeria with the announced aim of suppressing piracy. The French did not finally subdue and occupy all of Algeria until 1857. Tunisia acceded to French protection in 1882 and Morocco in 1912. The Italians took Libya from the Turks in 1911, and then spent several decades subduing that sparsely populated country. Libya was under United Nations (UN) mandate after the defeat of Italy in World War II and was given its independence in 1951.

France governed Algeria as a part of France, and large numbers of French citizens settled there and became involved in all walks of life—civil service, commerce, and agriculture. These so-called *pied noirs* (black feet) considered themselves the ruling class in Algeria, and there was deep resentment among the Muslim masses, who thought of themselves as second-class citizens, without a say in the affairs of their country. Although the French presence was also heavy in Tunisia and Morocco, there was less resentment of the colonial power because both countries were "protectorates," and the French ruled from behind a facade of native institutions.

A revolt against the French broke out in Algeria in 1954, and this conflict, which continued for eight years, was marked by brutality on both sides. In 1962, when General DeGaulle was President of France, the Algerian revolt was settled with the granting of self-rule to the Algerians.

The Algerian war was very unsettling for France. The large European population in Algeria, the blow to national pride (especially after France's defeat in World War II), and the brutality combined to make this period extremely traumatic. This led to establishment of the Secret Army Organization (OAS) to oppose Algerian independence, and a brief revolt by French settlers in Algeria. In the end, President DeGaulle quelled the revolt, and a number of French army officers (many of them high ranking) were dismissed from the service or imprisoned.

The upper Saharan countries of Mauritania, Chad, and the Sudan form the southern border of the North African countries and have also had an impact upon them. There have been troubles between Libya and the Sudan and Chad in the past. Morocco's annexation of the Western Sahara has been accepted by Mauritania. Except for the Sudan (with a population of 21.5 million) the other northern Saharan countries are impoverished, with few natural resources and small populations.

POPULATION

Much of North Africa is desert, extending into the northern Sahara, and the population is concentrated within several hundred miles of the coastline. The total population is small—about 50 million in 1988. Morocco and Algeria have almost equal populations of 20 million each, Tunisia has approximately 6.6 million, and Libya's population is about 2.6 million. In area, Algeria is the largest of the four nations, with 1.76 million square kilometers (679,536 sq. mi.), about one-third the size of the continental United States, although most of this is desert.

The major ethnic groups in North Africa are Berber (about 10 million, of Caucasian origin), Arab, and Arab-Berber mixture. These groups are Muslim, predominantly of the Sunni sect. The previously sizable Jewish minority has been greatly reduced by immigration to Israel. Substantial numbers of French still live in North Africa, especially in Tunisia and Morocco, as teachers, businessmen, and professionals. In the postcolonial period, "Arabization" is the order in Morocco and Algeria, and, to a lesser extent, in Tunisia. Libya, under Qaddafi, has been completely Arabized under force of law. Most educated elites in Algeria, Morocco, and Tunisia were educated in France, but the new generation will be expected to think and conduct business in Arabic, not French.

Military Geography

All four North African states have Mediterranean coastlines; Morocco also has a long shoreline on the Atlantic southward from the Mediterranean outlet. There are significant mountain ranges in Algeria and Morocco (and to a lesser extent in Tunisia), which gave the French trouble in subduing those countries. Additionally, there are large desert areas to the south, but neither mountains nor desert are impassable. Morocco controls the south side of the narrow Straits of Gibraltar, the so-called Pillar of Hercules, unfortified. The British dismantled their Gibraltar coast artillery in 1961, and geographic features of this type no longer seem so important in a military sense.

Strategic Significance

Oil and natural gas—found in considerable quantities in Algeria and Libya, in limited amounts in Tunisia, and not at all in Morocco—are the primary strategic considerations of the region. The Algerian and Libyan petroleum reserves, however, are much less than those in the Persian Gulf countries.

Aside from oil, North Africa has considerable geographic importance because it is close to southern Europe and has a generally temperate climate.

Regional Alliances

All of the North African countries belong to the Arab League and the Organization of African Unity (OAU, founded in 1963), although Morocco has had difficulties with the latter over its occupation of the Western Sahara. Morocco also had a short-lived union with Libya in 1985–86, apparently to aid the Moroccans in their struggle against the Algerian-supported *Polisario* guerrillas in the Western Sahara conflict.

Algeria and Libya are also members of the Organization of Arab Oil Exporting Countries (OAPEC).

Recent Intra- and Extraregional Conflicts

In World War II, American troops landed in North Africa (Algeria and Morocco) in November 1942. The German Afrika Korps and the Italian First Army surrendered, 275,000 strong, to the Allies in Tunisia 13 May 1943.

All four North African countries achieved independence in the 1950s and 1960s, but not all as a result of a bitter struggle such as that in Algeria. Since independence, there have been only relatively minor conflicts in the region, although Libya has been erratic. The United States maintained air bases in Libya and Morocco, and a naval facility in the latter country, until nationalist sentiment in the 1960s forced their closing. A partial chronology of conflicts in the region follows.

- 1951: Libya granted independence by the United Nations; Idriss I becomes king.
- 1952: Nasser and the Free Officers Movement depose

King Farouk of Egypt, an event that inspires nationalist moves in North Africa and elsewhere in the Arab world.

- 1954–62: Algerian war for independence; Ahmed Ben Bella becomes first President of Algeria in July 1962. He is succeeded by Boumedienne in 1965 and Bendjedid in 1978.
- March 1956: Morocco gains independence from France; Mohammed V becomes king; Tunisia gains independence from France; Habib Bourguiba becomes president; succeeded by Zine Ben Ali in 1987.
- 1961: Mohammed V of Morocco dies; succeeded by Hassan II.
- September 1969: King Idris I of Libya deposed by Col. Muammar Qaddafi.
- 1975: Morocco occupies former Spanish colony of Western Sahara in peaceful "green march."
- 1975———. Polisario contests Morocco for control of Western Sahara, with little action in recent years.
- 1981–86: U.S.-Libya problems occur: U.S. Navy aircraft down two Libyan SU-22s in 1981; U.S. President Reagan condemns Libyan-inspired terrorist airport attacks in Europe and warns Americans to leave Libya in 1985; in March, 1986, U.S. task force near Libya sinks two patrol craft, attacks mainland radar installations.
- 1983–87: Libya is involved with rebel movement in Chad but finally suffers defeat.
- April 1986: U.S. air strike on Libya in retaliation for Berlin disco bombing in which two U.S. servicemen were killed.
- 1987: Bicentennial anniversary of U.S.-Moroccan relations.
- 1988: Renewal of agreement for U.S. rapid deployment forcers to use Moroccan bases.

For the most recent information on this region, the reader may refer to the following annual publications:

The Military Balance. International Institute for Strategic Studies. London: Brassey's (UK).

The Statesman's Year-Book. New York: St. Martin's Press.

The World Factbook. Central Intelligence Agency. Washington, D.C.: Brassey's (US.)

WALTER P. WHITE

SEE ALSO: Arab Conquests; Arab League; Organization of African Unity; World War II.

Bibliography

Dupuy, T. N. 1980. *The almanac of world military power.* San Rafael, Calif.: Presidio Press.

Fage, J. D. 1978. *A history of Africa.* New York: Knopf.

Cambridge Encyclopedia of Africa. 1981. Cambridge: Cambridge Univ. Press.

Dosert, P. E. 1989. *Africa 1989.* Washington, D.C.: Stryker-Post.

Parker, R. B. 1984. *North Africa: Regional tensions and strategic conclusions.* New York: Praeger.

Paxton, J., ed. 1988. *The statesman's year-book, 1988–1989.* New York: St. Martin's Press.

NORTH AMERICA

North America occupies the northern part of the Western Hemisphere. Overall, North America is thinly populated, with the central and northern sections particularly sparsely settled. It is richly endowed with natural resources, including coal, oil, iron, gold, and uranium. Mexico, while geographically part of North America, is socially and culturally part of Latin America; notwithstanding, it will be covered in this regional survey.

History

Evidence seems to indicate that both North and South America remained uninhabited until migrating peoples from northeast Asia crossed to Alaska, perhaps on a land bridge, during the last ice age—about 25,000 years ago. These people had spread throughout the hemisphere by the end of the first millennium A.D. Their most advanced cultures were located in what is now the southwest United States, central Mexico, Guatemala, and Peru. The arrival of European explorers, led by the Spanish who made their first mainland settlement on the isthmus of Panama about 1513, soon disrupted the native populations, who were ravaged by European diseases, slaughtered by European weapons, and sometimes worked to death in mines and on plantations owned by Europeans. The next 350 years of North American history include a grim and dreary tale of the hardships and depredations inflicted on the native peoples by European settlers and their descendants, hungry for land and natural resources.

Early Spanish settlement was concentrated in Mexico, with some outposts in Florida and a rather isolated series of settlements around Santa Fe in what is now the state of New Mexico. English settlement began nearly a century later, with the first successful efforts in Virginia at Jamestown and in Massachusetts at Plymouth. While the Spanish settlers often interbred with the remaining native population (producing the *mestizos,* or people of mixed ancestry, common to Mexico and Latin America), the English settlers in eastern North America generally drove the Indians out or killed them, interacting with the natives only in trade or war. The English, particularly those in the south along the east coast, began importing African slaves to work on their farms as early as the 1630s, although the practice did not become institutionalized until the end of the century.

Meanwhile, the French had made one unsuccessful settlement attempt in what is now Georgia and had concentrated most of their effort in the valley of the St. Lawrence River (discovered by Jacques Cartier in 1534) and the basin of the Great Lakes. This colony was thinly settled and operated largely as a series of trading centers for furs and timber. Still further north, around Hudson's Bay, the

English Hudson's Bay Company operated its own fur trade in competition with the French.

Mexico in the seventeenth and eighteenth centuries was comparatively peaceful, but the English and French colonies were locked in conflict; even when war was not raging between the home countries, their American colonies were often plagued by border raids and Indian problems. In the end, superior seapower and the greater resources and population of British colonies along the eastern seaboard gave Great Britain control of the former French colony after 1763. Within twenty years, however, the richest and most prosperous colonies had broken with Great Britain, fought free of the mother country in a sometimes bitter war between 1775 and 1783, and created the United States of America.

The American Revolution was certainly a turning point in the history of both North and South America. The United States, ever hungry for land, spread westward rapidly and within 70 years had gained a vast swath of territory extending to the Pacific Ocean. The Revolution also served as an example to many liberally minded Latin Americans, especially the Creoles, American-born people of European ancestry, who generally were barred from high government office but who had usually achieved great economic success. The era of the American Revolution (the 1770s and 1780s) also saw the first Spanish settlement in California.

Great Britain was not reconciled to the loss of its former colonies and during the War of 1812 made some effort to reacquire them. This conflict was occasioned by British refusal to accord the United States the full rights of a sovereign state and fueled by American overland expansion. The war confirmed the independence and sovereignty of the United States and led eventually (by the 1870s) to the creation of the longest unarmed border in the world. The War of 1812 also saw the beginnings of a Canadian national spirit, determinedly different from the mother country but equally determined not to join the United States.

Mexico began its struggle for independence in 1810, but did not become free of Spain until 1821. For most of the next century Mexico was racked by internal disorder, revolution, and civil war. Much of this was caused by social tensions and a failure to create a stable system of government, but much was also due to foreign interference, especially by the French in the 1860s and by the United States in the 1830s, 1840s, and again in the early 1900s.

Although Canada and the United States were at peace after 1815, the United States fought a war with Mexico (1846–48) that ended with U.S. possession of what is now Arizona, California, Nevada, New Mexico, and parts of nearby states. This struggle was provoked by Mexican resentment of the U.S. annexation in 1845 of Texas, a former Mexican possession, largely settled by immigrants from the United States, which had won independence from Mexico in 1836. Mexican political unrest in the decade after 1910 (when longtime ruler Porfirio Díaz was deposed) led to several border clashes and a major U.S. punitive expedition under Gen. John J. Pershing (1916–17).

The United States underwent a series of political crises in the first half of the nineteenth century, provoked by sectionalism, clashes over slavery, and a major divergence of view between northern and southern states over whether states could voluntarily leave the union. The election of 1860, which saw antislavery northern Republican Abraham Lincoln gain the presidency, provoked the secession of most southern states, and led to the Civil War. This struggle raged for four years (April 1861–April 1865), and at great cost in both men and money the secessionist states, which had formed the Confederate States of America, were defeated and brought back into the union. Although the United States recovered swiftly from the physical damage of the Civil War, the political and social effects have persisted.

The years immediately following the Civil War saw several major political changes in North America. The French intervention in Mexico, begun in 1862 when the United States was fully occupied with the Civil War, resulted in the installment of Austrian Prince Maximilian as emperor of Mexico, supported by French troops. The French withdrew in early 1867 under U.S. pressure, ending the last major European military intervention in the Western Hemisphere and leaving Maximilian to abdication, capture, and execution (19 June 1867). That year also saw the purchase of Alaska by the United States from Russia (30 March), and Canada became a fully self-governing federal union on 1 July 1867.

The rest of the nineteenth century saw continued economic expansion in both the United States and Canada. Both countries completed transcontinental railroads and began to export their grain and raw materials to Europe. The United States continued to industrialize and by 1900 was behind only Great Britain and Germany as a steel producer. Mexico lagged behind, hampered by a poorly educated populace and by leaders who tended to regard public office as a means to personal enrichment. The United States took its first steps into the ranks of the great powers when it went to war with Spain in 1898. The United States emerged victorious and in possession of Cuba, the Philippines, Guam, and Puerto Rico. The United States also annexed Hawaii the same year, formally accepting what had been nearly a fact of life for twenty years. Cuba was granted independence in 1902 and the Philippines in 1946, but Puerto Rico and Guam are still part of the United States.

The twentieth century has seen North America play an increasing role in world affairs, especially since the United States assumed a dominant economic and political position after 1945. North America has avoided serious conflict, although the United States and, to a lesser extent,

Canada have been involved in military undertakings overseas, including the Korean War, the NATO alliance, and Vietnam. Canada and the United States are both heavily industrialized and wealthy and have well-educated populations.

Mexico has enjoyed political stability since the early 1920s. However, even with the wealth from petroleum exports since the mid-1970s, the country is still relatively poor and has an unevenly developed economy. Mexico's proximity to the United States has given Mexico's farms and factories a ready market for their goods. Export to the United States and Canada can be particularly rewarding, because Mexican labor costs are so much less that Mexican finished products are considerably cheaper than comparable American, Canadian, or other foreign products. Further, the long-term dominance of Mexican politics by the PRI (Institutional Revolutionary Party) seems to be coming to an end. The margin of victory for PRI candidates in the 1988 elections was surprisingly narrow, and the 1994 presidential contest may see election of the first non-PRI president in more than 70 years.

Population

North America is relatively thinly populated, with most people concentrated along the Atlantic, Pacific, and Gulf coasts; most Mexicans live in the central-south highlands, especially in and near Mexico City. The continent's total population is 355,778,000, including the populations of Bermuda (58,000), St. Pierre and Miquelon (6,300), and Greenland (55,000), as of summer 1988. The United States (including Alaska and Hawaii) is home to 246,043,000 people, or just over 69 percent of the total. About three-quarters of U.S. residents are white; most descended from immigrants from Germany or the British Isles, but others came originally from eastern or southern Europe, Scandinavia, or the Middle East. About 12 percent of the U.S. population is black, 10 percent is Hispanic, and some 3 percent belong to other ethnic groups, including Asians and Amerindians.

Mexico is next most populous, with 83,528,000 people, about 23.5 percent of the continental total. Many of these, some 18 million or 21.5 percent of the total, live in or near Mexico City. Most Mexicans, about 60 percent, are *mestizos,* or people of mixed European and Amerindian ancestry; another 30 percent have wholly or largely Amerindian ancestry. Only 9 percent of Mexicans are descended largely or entirely from Europeans; another 1 percent belong to other ethnic groups, including Asian immigrants.

Canada is the most thinly populated North American state, with 26,088,000 people, or less than one-ninth of the U.S. population, spread over an area 5 percent larger than the United States. Some 40 percent of Canadians are descended from immigrants from the British Isles, but 27 percent—just under 7.0 million—are French-speaking, concentrated in the province of Quebec. Most other Canadians are descended from non-English and non-French European immigrants, but there are small minorities of Asians and blacks. Finally, there are over 400,000 Eskimos and Amerindians in Canada, mainly in the northern and western provinces and territories.

Politico-Economic Relations

The three main nations of North America have what most observers consider stable political and economic systems, although all of them are undergoing significant changes. The recent trade treaty between the United States and Canada will eventually create a free-trade market within those two nations that will nearly match the much-discussed European free market due to appear in 1992. Mexico's political system is under considerable stress, as the voting public, especially in urban areas, is losing patience with the ruling apparatus of the PRI, which has run Mexican politics since the 1920s. It is still too early to assess the long-term effects of these changes, particularly as they relate to regional and national security.

The United States and Mexico enjoy generally good relations, and the United States is an important market for Mexican agricultural and industrial products. Canada and the United States also have close ties, even though the Canadians are sometimes a little nervous about their larger neighbor; as one former Canadian prime minister commented, being Canada next to the United States is "a little like being in bed with an elephant, for no matter how gentle and considerate the elephant, there is always the risk that it will roll over and inadvertently crush its companion." This feeling is enhanced for some Canadians by the intrusion of U.S. goods, especially radio, television, film, and printed materials, into Canadian markets.

Military Geography

The North American continent is crossed by two major north-south mountain chains, dividing it into a relatively narrow eastern coastal plain; an eastern mountain region comprising the Laurentian Plateau and the Appalachian Mountains; the great central plains; and the rugged Cordilleran highlands, which comprise the Rockies, the Cascades, and the Pacific coast ranges, and stretch from Alaska through Mexico. Mexico falls almost entirely within the Cordillera zone, with only a small eastern plain along the Gulf of Mexico. The Great Lakes and the St. Lawrence River form the major inland waterway, but the Mississippi-Missouri-Ohio system is also important, reaching much of the central United States. It is perhaps worth noting that the distance from Paris to Moscow—nearly 3,500 kilometers (2,200 mi.)—is less than the distance from Seattle, Washington, to Washington, D.C.—about 3,650 kilometers (2,300 mi.).

Strategic Significance

North America is dominated, although not controlled, by the economic, political, and military power of the United States. Eastern North America, including the eastern United States and southeastern Canada, is one of the four leading economic power regions of the world, together with western Europe, eastern Europe, and Japan. This power is derived in large part from generally literate, technically skilled populations, wealth in a variety of natural resources, and highly developed methods of economic management. This economic power forms the base for the military power of the United States.

Military invasion from outside the continent has not occurred for more than a century (the tiny Japanese effort in the Aleutian Islands in 1942–43 may be dismissed as small scale and ultimately pointless). The central fact of North American military geography for at least 200 years has been the isolation of this landmass, separated from other world powers by the world's two largest oceans; the threat of invasion is as remote now as it ever was. The new significant fact is the revolution in vulnerability that occurred with the development of thermonuclear weapons and ICBM (intercontinental ballistic missile) delivery systems. The United States has no reliable defense against these weapons and so is terribly vulnerable to a nuclear attack from its principal adversary, the Soviet Union. The Soviets are similarly vulnerable to such an attack from the United States, and both parties in a nuclear war would face devastation of their populations and economies on an apocalyptic scale.

Regional Alliances

The United States, Canada, and Mexico are all members of the Organization of American States (OAS), and both the United States and Mexico are also signatories of the multilateral Rio Pact, part of the treaty structure of the OAS. The United States and Canada are both members of NATO.

The United States has no formal bilateral security treaties with either Canada or Mexico, but bilateral planning agencies exist with both nations, allowing direct military planning for defense of the continent. The U.S.–Canadian defense relationship goes back to the early 1940s and includes arrangements for continental radar warning systems on Canadian soil and joint continental air defense.

Recent Intra- and Extraregional Conflicts

- 22 June 1948–30 September 1949: Berlin blockade (United States involved)
- 25 June 1950–27 July 1953: Korean War (United States and Canada involved)
- 20 January 1955–February 1965: U.S. military aid to Republic of Vietnam (South), including military adviser groups
- 1954–65: U.S. involvement in a series of crises in the Taiwan Straits between the People's Republic of China and the Republic of China (Taiwan)
- 15 July–25 October 1958: U.S. intervention in Lebanon to prevent civil war
- 15–20 April 1961: U.S. involvement in the "Bay of Pigs" operation by Cuban exiles trying to overthrow the Castro regime
- 8 July–11 September 1961: Renewed Berlin crisis, centered on construction of the Berlin Wall (12–13 August)
- 22 October–2 November 1962: Cuban Missile Crisis, bringing United States and USSR to the brink of nuclear war
- 8 March 1965–29 March 1973: U.S. ground forces in South Vietnam: The Vietnam War
- 28 April 1965–28 June 1966: U.S. intervention in the Dominican Republic, assisted by OAS forces after 6 May 1965
- 1 March 1981: Creation of the Rapid Deployment Force (RDF), a new strategic force designed for swift deployment overseas, with forces drawn from the U.S. Army and the U.S. Marine Corps. The RDF has since become CENTCOM (Central Command)
- 1981–88: U.S. support for the anti-Sandinista rebels ("Contras") in Nicaragua, including largely public "covert" actions by the CIA against Nicaragua (1982–83)
- 25–30 October 1983: U.S. invasion of Grenada to end civil unrest and rescue American medical students there

For the most recent information on this region, the reader may refer to the following annual publications:
The Military Balance. International Institute for Strategic Studies. London: Brassey's (UK).
The Statesman's Year-Book. New York: St. Martin's Press.
The World Factbook. Central Intelligence Agency. Washington, D.C.: Brassey's (US).

DAVID L. BONGARD

SEE ALSO: Canada; Mexico; Organization of American States; United States.

Bibliography

Dupuy, T. N., et al. 1980. *The almanac of world military power*. San Rafael, Calif.: Presidio Press.
Paxton, J., ed. 1989. *The statesman's year-book, 1989–1990*. New York: St. Martin's Press.

NORWAY, KINGDOM OF

Norway is the westernmost of the Scandinavian nations. Ruggedly mountainous, with a deeply indented coastline sprinkled with islands, Norway traditionally has been a sea-oriented nation.

Power Potential Statistics

Area: 324,220 square kilometers (125,181 sq. mi.)
Population: 4,207,800
Total Active Armed Forces: 32,700 (0.777% of pop.)
Gross Domestic Product: US$74.2 billion (1990 est.)
Annual Defense Expenditure: US$3.3 billion (3.3% of GDP, 1990 est.)
Iron and Steel Production:
  Crude steel: 0.836 million metric tons (1986)
  Pig iron: 0.391 million metric tons (1988)
Fuel Production:
  Coal: 0.580 million metric tons (1986)
  Coke: 0.313 million metric tons (1986)
  Crude oil. 81.0 million metric tons (1990)
  Natural gas: 3,634 million cubic meters (1989)
Electrical Power Output: 121,685 million kwh (1989)
Merchant Marine: 867 vessels; 23,270,845 gross registered tons
Civil Air Fleet: 76 major transport aircraft; 103 usable airfields (64 with permanent-surface runways); none with runways over 3,659 meters (12,000 ft.); 12 with runways 2,440–3,659 meters (8,000–12,000 ft.); 16 with runways 1,220–2,440 meters (4,000–8,000 ft.).

For the most recent information, the reader may refer to the following annual publications:
The Military Balance. International Institute for Strategic Studies. London: Brassey's (UK).
The Statesman's Year-Book. New York: St. Martin's Press.
The World Factbook. Central Intelligence Agency. Washington D.C.: Brassey's (US).

History

Before A.D. 800, little is known of Norwegian history, as archaeological evidence is scanty and there are no written records. The year 800 marks the beginning of the Viking era, when bands of warrior-traders voyaged throughout northern and western Europe. During the ensuing 250 years, Norwegians settled in Iceland, Ireland, northern Scotland, and Normandy. That period was also one of national unification, and although Harald I Haarfager (Fairhair) is often given credit for uniting Norway about 900, the honor more properly goes to Olaf II (r. 1015–30), who also introduced Christianity.

The line of monarchs descended from Harald I (Olaf II was one of them) died out in 1319, and Norway and Sweden were ruled by the same family. This development led to the Union of Kalmar (1397), whereby Denmark, Norway, and Sweden all came under the rule of one man, Eric of Pomerania. Norway remained with the Union after Sweden broke away in 1448, and was governed by Denmark until 1814. Norway came under the Swedish crown in 1814, but the conditions of Swedish control were never clearly delineated (the Norwegians considered it a voluntary association), and in 1905 Norway became fully independent.

Norway remained neutral during World War I, but the country was invaded by Germany on 9 April 1940. Most of Norway was overrun within two weeks, but fighting continued at the northern port of Narvik until early June. Following the Allied withdrawal from Norway after the fall of Dunkirk (8–9 June), the king and his government fled to Britain. Norway was liberated only after the German surrender (May 1945). The experience of occupation induced Norway to abandon neutrality for collective security, and Norway joined the North Atlantic Treaty Organization (NATO) in 1949. Norway has gained important benefits from exploitation of oil and gas deposits in the North Sea, begun in the mid-1970s.

Politico-Military Background and Policy

The experience of World War II led most Norwegians to question the traditional policy of neutrality. Soviet activities in Eastern Europe in the late 1940s, especially the coup in Czechoslovakia, led Norway to become a founding member of NATO on 4 April 1949. Norway has been a wholehearted supporter of NATO, but in order not to offend the Soviet Union (Norway and Turkey are the only NATO states that border the former USSR), Norway did not permit allied troops, bases, or stored nuclear weapons on Norwegian soil, although equipment for a U.S. Marine brigade has been pre-positioned in Norway.

Norway's armed forces are manned through universal compulsory service, for a period of twelve months in the army and fifteen months in the navy and air force. All Norwegian males reaching age 19 may be called up, and obligation for refresher training continues until age 44, although they may volunteer for extended service. Liability for emergency call-up lasts until age 55 for officers and age 60 for enlisted men. Mobilization would yield 285,000 mobile forces and Home Guard, 60,000 second-line reserves, and 115,000 civil defense personnel. The mobile force reserves and Home Guard could be mobilized within three days.

Strategic Problems

Norway's strategic problems are primarily geographical. The rugged and mountainous terrain, the 1,600-kilometer (1,000 mi.) eastern border, and the lack of truly adequate ground transport in the north (the railroad ends at Bodo, and there is only one road beyond) all make effective defense of Norwegian territory difficult. In the event of a general Soviet attack on Western Europe, northern Norway would have been a major objective, since its seizure would have secured the northwestern Soviet Union, and provided bases for Soviet strikes at NATO's seaborne lines of communications from Canada and the United States to Europe.

Thinly settled northern Norway, especially the area closest to the Russian border (Finnmark) was vulnerable to Soviet assault. The Norwegians station three-fourths of their standing army between Narvik and the Russian border, and have designed their forces for arctic and mountain operations in a determined effort to maximize their defensive capabilities.

Military Assistance

Norway currently receives no military assistance from abroad, other than reciprocal arrangements for military education and training, although it received some U.S. aid in the 1950s and 1960s. Norway provides nearly US$500 million per year in foreign aid to developing nations, but nearly all of this is economic and development assistance, not military aid.

Defense Industries

Despite its modest size, Norway has an active domestic arms industry. Norway builds nearly all of its own naval vessels, some of which are sold abroad, and has developed and fielded the widely-used Penguin SSM. The Norwegians have also modified some equipment in their service, upgrading U.S.-built M-24 light tanks, M-113 APCs, and M-109 self-propelled howitzers.

Alliances

Norway is a member of the United Nations (UN), the European Free Trade Association, and NATO. Norway has close but informal ties with the other Scandinavian states of Denmark, Finland, Iceland, and Sweden.

Defense Structure

The king of Norway, Harald V, who succeeded on the death of his father, Olaf V, is commander in chief of the armed forces. He exercises little real control, and actual direction of defense policy and operations is in the hands of the cabinet. The Minister of Defense is responsible to the *Storting* (parliament) for defense matters, and administers the three independent services.

(For an explanation of the abbreviations and symbols used in the following section of military statistics, see the list of Abbreviations and Acronyms in each volume.)

Total Armed Forces

Active: some 32,700 (22,800 conscripts) incl 400 Joint Services org, 500 Home Guard permanent staff. Terms of service: Army, Navy coast arty, Air Force, 12 months plus 4 to 5 refresher trg periods; Navy 15 months.
Reserves: 285,000 mobilizable in 24–72 hours; obligation to 44 (conscripts remain with fd army units to age 35; officers to age 55; regulars: 60). Army: 159,000; Navy: 26,000; Air: 28,000. Home Guard: War some 85,000. Second-line reserves: 60,000 (all services).

ARMY: 15,900 (13,000 conscripts). 2 Commands, 5 district comd, 1 div, 16 subordinate comd.
Standing Forces:
North Norway:
1 reinforced mech bde: 2 inf, 1 tk, 1 SP fd arty, 1 engr bn, 1 AD bty, spt units.
1 border garrison bn.
1 reinforced inf bn task force: inf, tk, coy, fd arty, AD bty.
South Norway:
1 inf bn (Royal Guard).
Indep units.
Reserves: cadre units for mob: 3 div HQ, 3 armd, 4 mech, 6 lt inf bde; 5 mech, 23 inf, 7 arty bn; 60 indep inf coy, tk sqn, arty bty, engr coy, sigs unit, spt.
Land Home Guard: 80,000: 18 districts each divided into 2–6 sub-districts and some 470 sub-units (pl).
Equipment:
MBT: 211: 78 Leopard 1, 55 M-48A5, 78 NM-116 (M-24/90).
AIFV: 53 NM-135 (M-113/20mm) (CFE).
APC: 150 M-113 (CFE: 81).
Total arty: 527.
Towed arty: 105mm: 228 M-101; 155mm: 48 M-114.
SP arty: 155mm: 126 M-109A3GN SP.
Mortars: 107mm: 97 M-30F1, 28 M-106A1 SP. Plus 81mm.
ATGW: TOW-1/-2, 97 NM-142 (M-113/TOW-2).
RCL: 57mm: M-18; 84mm: Carl Gustav; 106mm: M-40A1.
AD guns: 20mm: Rh-202; 40mm: L/60 and L/70.
SAM: 108 RBS-70.

NAVY: 7,300, incl 2,000 coastal artillery (4,500 conscripts). 8 Naval/Coast defense comd. Bases: Horten, Haakonsvern (Bergen), Ramsund, Olavsvern (Tromsø).
Submarines: 11: 3 Ula with Ge Seeaal DM2A3 HWT; 8 Kobben SSC (3 modernized with Swe T-61) others US Mk 37 HWT.
Frigates: 5 Oslo with 2 × 3 ASTT, 1 × 6 Terne ASW RL; plus 6 × Penguin 2 SSM.
Patrol and Coastal Combatants: 35:
Missile Craft: 35: 14 Hauk PFM with 6 × Penguin 2, 2 × 533 mm TT; 15 Storm PFM with 6 × Penguin 2; 6 Snøgg PFM with 4 × Penguin 2, 4 × 533mm TT.
Mine Warfare: 8:
Minelayers: 2 Vidar, coastal (300–400 mines).
Note: Amph craft also fitted for minelaying.
Mine Countermeasures: 6: 3 Sauda MSC, 1 Tana MHC; 2 diver spt.
Amphibious: craft only; 5 LCT
Support and Miscellaneous: 2: 1 MCM/PF depot ship; 1 Royal Yacht.
Additional in Store: 2 Corvettes, 1 MSC.
Naval Home Guard: 7,000. On mob assigned to the 8 naval/coast defense comd.
7 Tjeld PFT, 2 LCT, some 400 fishing craft.
Coast Defense: 32 fortresses: 34 arty bty: 75mm; 105mm; 120mm; 127mm; 150mm guns. Some cable mine and torpedo bty.

AIR FORCE: 9,500 (5,300 conscripts).
FGA: 4 sqn with F-16 (incl 1 OCU).
Fighter: 1 trg sqn with F-5A/B (has AD role).
MR: 1 sqn with P-3C/N Orion (2 assigned to coast guard).
Transport: 3 sqn: 1 with C-130; 1 with Falcon 20 (tpt, EW); 1 with DHC-6.
Training: MFI-15.
SAR: 1 sqn with Sea King Mk 43.
Coast Guard: 1 sqn with Lynx Mk 86.
Tac hel: 2 sqn with Bell 412 SP.
AD: 22 lt AA arty bty. (Being delivered: 6 bty NOAH SAM, 10 bty RB-70).
Equipment: 85 cbt ac (plus 9 in store), no armed hel.
Aircraft:
F-5A/B: 20 (ftr/trg); plus 9 in store.
F-16: 61. -A: 49 (FGA), -B: 12 (FGA).
P-3: -C: 4 (MR); -N: 2 (coast guard).
C-130H: 6 (tpt).
Falcon 20C: 3 (EW/tpt).
DHC-6: 3 (tpt); MFI-15: 18 (trg).

Helicopters:
Bell 412 SP: 18 (tpt).
Lynx Mk 86: 6 (coast guard).
Sea King Mk 43: 9 (SAR).
Missiles:
ASM: Penguin Mk-3.
AAM: AIM-9L/N Sidewinder.
AD:
Guns: 40mm: 32 L/60, 64 L/70.
SAM: NOAH (Norwegian-adapted HAWK).
Antiaircraft Home Guard (on mob under comd of Air Force): 3,000; 2 bn (9 bty) lt AA; some Rh-202 20mm, 72 L/60 40mm guns (being replaced by Rh-202).

FORCES ABROAD
UN and Peacekeeping:
Angola: (UNAVEM II): observers.
Egypt: (MFO): staff officers.
India/Pakistan (UNMOGIP): 5 observers
Iraq/Kuwait (UNIKOM): 8 observers, medical unit (50).
Lebanon (UNIFIL): 896; 1 inf bn, 1 service coy, plus HQ personnel.
Middle East (UNTSO): 18 observers.

PARAMILITARY
Coast Guard: 680:
Patrol Offshore: 13: 3 Nordkapp with 1 × Lynx hel (SAR/recce), 2 × 3 ASTT, fitted for 6 Penguin (Mk 2 SSM; 1 Nornen, 2 Farm, 7 chartered.
Aircraft: 2 P-3N Orion ac, 6 Lynx hel (Air Force-manned).
Civil Defense Force: permanent peacetime staff of 300 military and 190 civilian personnel, but on mobilization would control some 115,000 people. Charged with rear-area security and guarding important installations and facilities, this force includes 33,000 industrial and 2,000 railway guards. The Civil Defense force is organized into 54 districts, with 14 mobile columns and 108 local units.

FOREIGN FORCES
NATO: HQ Allied Forces Northern Europe (HQAFNORTH).
U.S.: Pre-positioned eqpt for 1 MEB.

Future

Norway will probably continue to support NATO. Recently, Norway's main concern has been finding suitable replacements for the Canadian brigade newly committed to reinforcing CENTAG, although these concerns are recognized as superfluous. The Norwegians were uneasy about the prospect of a German *Luftlande* brigade, but there has also been discussion of the French 27th Mountain Division, British forces, or an additional U.S. Marine brigade being substituted for the Canadians. Norway's strategic position has been eased considerably by the dissolution of the Warsaw Pact and the Soviet Union. In any event, Norwegian ground forces will continue to undergo their slow and steady modernization, and the air and naval forces will retain their technically sophisticated professionalism.

DAVID L. BONGARD
TREVOR N. DUPUY

SEE ALSO: Denmark; Military History, Medieval; NATO; Sweden; Vikings; Western Europe.

Bibliography

Bertram C., and J. J. Holst. 1977. *New strategic factors in the North Atlantic*. Oslo: University Forlaget.
Derry, T. K. 1968. *A short history of Norway*. London: Allen and Unwin.
Hunter, B., ed. 1991. *The statesman's year-book, 1991–92*. New York: St. Martin's Press.
International Institute for Strategic Studies. 1991. *The military balance, 1991–1992*. London: Brassey's.
Udgaard, N. M. 1973. *Great power politics and Norwegian foreign policy*. Oslo: University Forlaget.

NUCLEAR EMPLOYMENT POLICY AND PLANNING

A nation's nuclear policies establish credible goals and planning parameters for its nuclear arsenal. This arsenal and declared national policy are intended to convince a potential adversary that military victory or the attainment of certain political goals through military aggression lies beyond his reach. This conviction, the very essence of deterrence, is maintained by policies that lead to the establishment of credible employment plans for nuclear forces.

The increasing accuracy, better mobility, and improved command and control of nuclear weapons have expanded the range of plausible theater and strategic execution scenarios. Consequently, the challenge of nuclear deterrence is the development of policies and plans that continue to make military aggression, with its attendant escalatory risks, irrational options for potential adversaries. Yet the elimination of certain weapons and the reduction of others in current and anticipated arms control regimes reduce the assets of national security planners and managers to deter increasingly sophisticated and diverse challenges and to meet the full range of national political-military objectives.

Herein lies the challenge and importance of nuclear employment policy and planning in an age of arms control. In order to sustain deterrence in the face of increasingly sophisticated challenges, the United States and presumably all nuclear states develop strategic and theater nuclear employment plans with carefully tailored responses that attempt to anticipate plausible execution scenarios. These plans seek to provide national decision makers with flexible options to pursue national and international goals in the event of a political or military crisis. Should deterrence fail, these options are intended to optimize force application to support escalation control, prompt conflict termination, and, thus, limit damage to a state's homeland (and those of its allies). Other postcrisis national political-military objectives, such as discouraging the resumption of hostilities in the postconflict period and reestablishing a stable period of reconstruction, are also supported by the maintenance of such options.

This essay will focus on the development of strategic and theater nuclear policies, plans, and procedures in pursuit of the above-noted objectives. While the United States is often cited to illustrate a particular point, the following observations are germane to all nuclear powers.

Need for Extensive Nuclear Planning

The expanded range of plausible theater and strategic execution scenarios, the increasing complexity of attacking a mobile target base, and the difficulty of maintaining deterrence and achieving political-military objectives if deterrence fails require a nuclear state to develop a range of plans that anticipate potential employment scenarios for its nuclear assets.

First, the development and maintenance of nuclear plans that presumably address plausible execution scenarios help to convince potential adversaries of a state's resolve and capability to defend its national interests. This recognition bolsters deterrence by complicating the decision-making calculus of a potential aggressor and by making the attainment of its political-military objectives highly uncertain and costly.

Second, planning affords a state the most efficient way of employing nuclear assets in the event of hostilities. Arms control agreements, which reduce force structures or attach operational constraints to specific forces, place a premium upon the optimized application of these constrained forces against a more modern, and therefore sophisticated and survivable, target base. Specifically, as we shall see below, numerous targeting damage requirements, attack prohibitions or delays, and timing schedules must be optimized. Yet there is insufficient time to "zero base" or plan anew these myriad factors in the fog of war.

Planning not only allows a state to maintain deterrence with reduced forces in an arms control regime; it also promotes arms control. The ability to achieve certain attack objectives with fewer yet more efficiently applied forces allows those forces to be reduced while maintaining national security.

Also related to efficiency is the consensus building that occurs during the planning process. During this process, the different doctrines and operational perspectives of a country's military services must be reconciled while striving for force application optimization. Furthermore, consensus building must occur between the members of a nuclear alliance. For instance, to support escalation control and prompt war termination objectives, the North Atlantic Treaty Organization's (NATO) doctrine emphasizes the need for broad participation in nuclear operations to signal resolve and solidarity. Alliance planning, such as that which goes into the formulation of Supreme Allied Commander, Europe's (SACEUR) Scheduled Strike Program (SSP) and Selective Employment Plans (SEPs), ensures that NATO's diverse assets, which include dual-capable aircraft (DCA), short- and long-range missiles, and artillery, are efficiently employed to maximize their deterrent and warfighting effectiveness.

Planning Process

The development of U.S. nuclear weapons employment policies and plans involves civilian and military authorities. The former control policy guidance while the latter develop planning guidance and plans that implement civilian direction. Figure 1 depicts the principal actors and documents for strategic nuclear employment policy and planning. Each step in the process incorporates increasing levels of detail.

Nuclear weapons employment guidance originates with the president. Following input and coordination between the Office of the Secretary of Defense (OSD), the Joint Chiefs of Staff, and the National Security Council (NSC) staff, the National Security Decision Directives (NSDDs), Presidential Directives (PDs), or National Security Decision Memoranda (NSDMs) are signed by the president. These documents outline the broadest national objectives, constraints, and application parameters as well as other factors governing the use of nuclear weapons.

National political-military objectives, e.g., might have such generic requirements as developing plans and options that hold the full range or portions of enemy targets at risk throughout the period of conflict, retaining

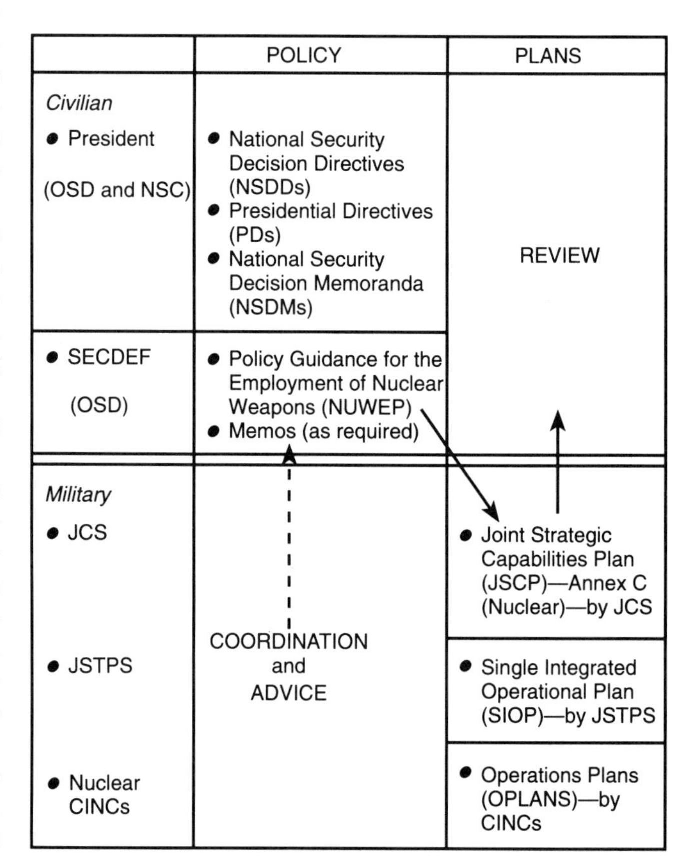

Figure 1. (Strategic) U.S. nuclear weapons policy and planning process.

sufficient reserve forces to encourage prompt conflict termination should deterrence fail, and developing and exercising ad hoc options to deter aggressive behavior and to maximize presidential flexibility in a crisis. Constraints could include particular target categories or locations against which strikes are completely prohibited or execution is constrained to a selected scenario. Finally, application parameters are established by identifying the general order of importance attached to various target categories as well as damage level criteria associated with each.

Presidential guidance is periodically reviewed by the Office of the Secretary of Defense. New presidential guidance may be promulgated to reflect a revised threat or a change in U.S. capabilities. For instance, the deployment of a new weapons system or a new force structure following an arms control agreement may necessitate new guidance. Presidential guidance is periodically elaborated in the secretary of defense's (SECDEF) *Policy Guidance for the Employment of Nuclear Weapons* (NUWEP). NUWEP, most recently published in 1987, further specifies national objectives, constraints, and application parameters and is written with the advice of the uniformed services, the Joint Staff, and the nuclear commanders in chief (CINCs).

Planning Guidance

The NUWEP, along with any additional SECDEF memoranda addressing specific policy requirements or interpretations of presidential guidance, constitute the basis for the military's development of operational planning guidance. Planning guidance is revised biennially (and updated annually) in the *Joint Strategic Capabilities Plan—Annex C (Nuclear)*. The revision is conducted by the Joint Staff and includes representatives from the services, the relevant defense agencies (e.g., Defense Intelligence Agency [DIA] and Defense Nuclear Agency [DNA]), the nuclear CINCs, and others as appropriate. Notably, OSD does not participate formally in JSCP–Annex C development. This separation preserves the military's mandate to optimize military planning within the constraints of existing policy guidance. The JSCP–Annex C consolidates strategic and theater nuclear planning guidance to include rules governing the allocation of forces against various categories of targets; damage criteria; nuclear reserve force requirements, composition, and priorities; reconnaissance responsibilities. It also spells out the responsibilities of the nuclear CINCs and other defense agencies.

Upon being approved by the Joint Chiefs of Staff, an executive summary of the JSCP–Annex C is provided to the secretary of defense to ensure conformance with policy guidance. It is then provided to the Joint Strategic Target Planning Staff (JSTPS) at Offutt Air Force Base in Omaha, Nebraska, as well as to the nuclear CINCs to guide their development of strategic and nonstrategic nuclear operational plans (OPLANS).

Building the Plan

The formal approval of JSCP–Annex C begins an eighteen-month process at JSTPS of building the U.S. strategic war plan: the Single Integrated Operational Plan (SIOP). During this time, critical targets are nominated and assigned priorities. Weapons from a leg or various legs of the strategic triad (e.g., intercontinental ballistic missiles [ICBMs], submarine-launched ballistic missiles [SLBMs], or bomber-delivered weapons—gravity bombs, air-launched cruise missiles [ALCMs], or short-range attack missiles [SRAMs]—are allocated against these targets. Allocation considerations include but are not limited to:

1. The target's time sensitivity. The prompt destruction of some targets is critical to limit damage, disrupt communications, and so on. Other targets might not require prompt destruction. In this instance, a warhead from a more survivable and enduring platform may be used.
2. The target's hardness or resistance to nuclear effects. The hardness of a target drives requirements for a weapon's accuracy, yield, fuzing options (e.g., contact burst, low air burst, or high air burst), and so on.
3. How heavily the target is defended and whether it is more vulnerable to missile- or bomber-delivered weapons. Ballistic missile defenses, such as those surrounding Moscow, may affect the types and number of weapons required as well as their timing in the attack. Other targets with heavy antiaircraft defenses might require an earlier arriving ballistic missile to clear a path for the bomber. Or a cruise missile that flies below the defense's effective engagement envelope may be preferred.
4. Competing requirements for these weapons. There may be more targets than weapons. How and by what criteria are these targets assigned priorities?
5. Footprinting constraints. This parameter addresses the down-range and cross-range dimensions of the ellipse within which the multiple (i.e., multiple independently targetable reentry vehicles—MIRVs) warheads atop a ballistic missile will impact. Is the ellipse sufficiently broad to include a particular set of targets?
6. Cross-targeting. Certain targets are attacked with several weapons from different triad legs. Among other benefits, cross-targeting hedges against failures of a particular weapon or leg.

After weapons are allocated, the application phase is initiated. In this phase, specific weapons (e.g., warhead *X* from SLBM *Y* on submarine *Z*) rather than generic weapons (e.g., an SLBM warhead) are targeted against specific installations. Launch and impact times and operational parameters such as fuzing options are assigned to individual weapons. This "deconfliction," which occurs during the "mission planning" process, minimizes fratricide—the destruction of an incoming warhead by the heat, blast, radioactive pulse, or ejecta (i.e., airborne particulate matter) of a prior detonation.

Extensive computer simulations optimize the efficiency

and effectiveness of the SIOP. Before a SIOP revision becomes operational, the plan is briefed to the JCS and to the SECDEF as a final check on its conformance with policy guidance. During the course of its operational life, the SIOP is war-gamed against a hypothetical enemy war plan as an additional check on its effectiveness. Also, DIA periodically conducts, from an enemy perspective, assessments of the SIOP's ability to deny enemy war aims.

In closing this discussion of the SIOP, two comments are appropriate. First, similar planning and procedures are conducted by each nuclear CINC; the SIOP is used here only for illustrative purposes. Second, and perhaps more important, the myriad factors that must be addressed in the SIOP allocation and application phases substantiate the view expressed earlier that the kinds of weapons (with their respective unique capabilities) eliminated in an arms control regime complicate the nuclear planner's challenge of maintaining deterrence by holding a large and diverse target base at risk.

Plans: Preplanning and Ad Hoc

The SIOP is preplanned. It anticipates plausible scenarios with a range of carefully tailored responses incorporating the many factors discussed above. NATO's nuclear war plans are also preplanned. In general, preplanning allows a particular plan to strike a set or sets of fixed-site targets in a carefully timed manner while avoiding other targets, all in accordance with policy guidance. It also allows the size of the attack to be planned in accordance with the provocation, the degree of military necessity, or in consonance with a state's political-military objectives such as escalation control, damage limitation, conflict termination, or the denial of an enemy's war aims. In addition, the nuclear CINCs develop regional theater and/or functional plans for plausible scenarios.

Neither all scenarios nor the precise locations of all targets can be known in advance of the actual time of force execution. To account for this uncertainty, prudent planners acquire capabilities and develop flexible ad hoc procedures to facilitate rapid replanning in the face of unexpected developments. This second major category of plans generally identifies forces that are well suited to attack emergent targets. These targets include relocatable targets (RTs), such as the SS-24 train-borne and SS-25 truck-borne mobile ICBMs. Since the locations of all targets might not be known at the beginning of hostilities, flexible planning capabilities and procedures must be in place to permit the remaining forces to attack these critical assets as their locations become known.

"Revalued" targets also fall into the ad hoc plans category. These targets may not be sufficiently important to require a weapon at the initial stages of a conflict, but developing events may raise the importance of a target whose initial value was marginal.

Both preplanned and ad hoc nuclear plans must support national or alliance deterrence and warfighting objectives. Therefore, targeteers must possess the capability to respond effectively in the case of immediate and/or protracted operations. This latter requirement, especially valid for emergent and revalued targets, places a premium upon enduring forces (to include reserve forces) as well as the enduring command and control assets to direct them. It should be noted that these nuclear employment plans, their deterrence and warfighting objectives, and the requirements to endure are, in fact, no different from conventional war plans.

Planning and Uncertainty

Planning has been discussed as one means of deterring conflict and achieving other national peacetime and wartime political-military objectives. Planning reduces uncertainty in the eyes of the formulating state, which becomes more confident of its ability to defend its interests. Uncertainty is increased in the eyes of a potential aggressor when a state's declaratory policy and its actual military capabilities make it less certain that the goals of aggression can be achieved at a reasonable cost.

Yet there are numerous factors that either cannot be anticipated by planners or, even if anticipated, cannot be accommodated in existing plans due to political and/or technological shortfalls.

Independent, Uncoordinated National Execution

NATO's nuclear forces are coordinated to minimize fratricide and optimize force application, but the United States and the United Kingdom retain the right of independent force execution outside any NATO context. In short, the right of independent military action to protect national interests is inherent in the concept of national sovereignty. Similarly, before the demise of the Soviet Union, U.S. and Soviet planners who sought to enhance escalation control and prompt conflict termination in the event of nuclear hostilities had to grapple with the uncertainties attending independent nuclear executions. The ability of any nation to identify immediately, for example, an SLBM as originating from any particular nation's submarine is hardly assured—especially in the heat of conflict. Political leaders and military planners can only guess at how others will employ their nuclear forces during actual hostilities.

Relocatable Targets

The challenge posed to preplanning against fixed installations by relocatable targets has already been described. Holding RTs, such as mobile ICBMs, at risk confronts the planner with different force application challenges than would attacks against fixed ICBM silos. The latter require a time-urgent attack with highly accurate, large-yield weapons. By virtue of their survivability, RTs are more likely to be reserved for later attacks so their prompt destruction is less urgent. Also, RTs are not as hardened against nuclear effects as silo-based missiles. Therefore, precise accuracy, time-urgency, and large yields become less critical. The uncertainty about the precise location of RTs, however, the very factor that is said to heighten their stabilizing influence in a crisis, requires the planner to employ more enduring forces (with enduring command and control) against them. This requirement necessitates continuing modernization during and even in spite of progress in arms control.

Besides placing a premium upon the endurance of forces and their command and control, RTs require real-time intelligence to acquire the targets and enduring planning capabilities to develop the most efficient attack. For instance, let us assume that a planner determines that enduring ballistic missiles are best suited to attack RTs when their locations become known. Furthermore, let us imagine that three single-warhead mobile SS-25 ICBMs are discovered within the elliptical footprint of a ballistic missile with ten warheads. Even if the targeteer applies two reentry vehicles (RVs—i.e., warheads) against each RT to increase attack confidence, what is to be done with the other four warheads? Is this an efficient use of weapons? How does one balance warfighting requirements, the attractiveness of ballistic missile endurance, and the cost-effectiveness of placing numerous RVs atop each missile? These are but a few of the questions that bedevil nuclear planners. These questions also must intrude into the deliberations of arms controllers as they balance political objectives with the requirements of deterring an evolving threat.

Political-Military Interaction

Plans are only effective when they are credible. The achievement of deterrence and other national objectives requires plans to be credible in the eyes of potential adversaries. Potential aggressors must recognize that extant forces possess sufficient accuracy, yield, timeliness, endurance, and command and control to deny their aggressive war aims. Equally important is the perception that national or alliance political leaders have sufficient resolve in appropriate instances to use nuclear weapons to defend their interests. In short, the most capable forces with the best plans cannot deter if an adversary perceives that national or alliance leaders are incapable of carrying out their plans (either for political reasons or due to technical command and control deficiencies). For this reason, political decisions to modernize forces and their command and control facilities, the economic commitment to follow through on these upgrades, and regular exercises of war plans are among the many variables that determine whether nuclear plans achieve their ultimate deterrence objective.

Damage Calculation Methodologies

The heavy influences of damage requirements and computer-based war-gaming upon the development of nuclear employment planning were discussed above. It must be noted, however, that damage calculation methodologies are crude and do not begin to measure some of the more fundamental measures of attack effectiveness.

Blast overpressure for a particular nuclear yield is a straightforward calculation. Consequently, it plays a critical role in determining suitable accuracy/yield trade-offs of particular weapons against installations of different hardness levels. It is virtually impossible, however, to quantify numerous physical effects, such as the distribution of ejecta, the distribution of radioactive fallout, the precise effects of the thermal energy released by a nuclear weapon, and how that energy interacts with installations in different geographical settings. The prudent military planner, uncertain of the actual contributions of these physical effects toward damage requirements, is unlikely to incorporate them into war plans. The inability to calculate the full range of these horrific effects substantiates the views of U.S., European, and former Soviet leaders that nuclear war cannot be won and must not be fought. But it also induces planners to err on the side of certainty, thereby increasing perceived weapons requirements and undermining support for arms control.

Even more significant is the inability of damage calculation methodologies to assess the true psychological impact of nuclear destruction. How does one assess, for instance, the deterrent effect of a plan that would lead to a radically new and unpredictable national culture—one that would likely alter popular confidence in national political leadership and national integration? For instance, major economic and military installations of the former Soviet Union were located in areas inhabited by ethnic Russians. Thus, a determined attack against the economic and military installations would coincidentally be an attack against, and pose severe problems for, ethnic Russians, who might have tried to continue their hegemony over the last of the world's great multinational empires. How does one calculate the deterrent impact of such a psychological dimension upon a people whose proportion of the Soviet population is already rapidly decreasing?

Integrating Nuclear and Conventional Operations

The same technological advances that improve the accuracy of nuclear weapons have also contributed to the increasing precision of conventional armaments. Long-range cruise missiles such as the U.S. Navy's Tomahawk Land Attack Missile (TLAM) can deliver conventional submunitions (TLAM-D) with great accuracy against geographically dispersed targets. The accuracy of the Pershing II INF missile can also be incorporated into conventional missiles. These developments raise the obvious questions as to which installations, currently targeted by nuclear weapons, might someday be effectively targeted with conventional munitions. Indeed, influential analysts of theater nuclear war-planning are already debating the extent to which advanced conventional munitions can replace NATO nuclear forces.

From a realpolitik perspective, a state must exploit all its military, diplomatic, and economic strengths in pursuit of its national objectives. Planning that considers nuclear forces as separate from its conventional forces risks sterility and less than optimal effectiveness.

INTEGRATING NUCLEAR OFFENSIVE AND DEFENSIVE OPERATIONS

The debate in the United States about the cost and effectiveness of the Strategic Defense Initiative (SDI) obscures a larger historical perspective. Historically, neither offense nor defense has remained permanently ascendant. It may thus be imprudent to believe that the current ascendancy of offensive nuclear forces will remain unchallenged. In any event, potential breakthroughs in ballistic missile defense and antisubmarine warfare, the high costs of stealth technologies that could limit deployments, and arms control reductions of offensive forces will continue to require careful consideration of enemy defenses in the development of offensive plans. Like the considerations in the preceding two sections, the inability to make precise determinations of the complex relationship between offense and defense will complicate the efforts of nuclear employment planners.

Future

National security and sovereignty requirements guarantee that states and alliances possessing nuclear weapons will continue developing and maintaining employment plans to optimize force application. The development of these complex plans will confront the uncertainties and challenges noted in the preceding section. Arms control will make the development of nuclear employment plans more difficult than ever before: planners will be forced to apply fewer assets against more elusive targets. But the most novel challenge will exist in the West. Military planners and the political leaders whose policies they implement must sustain the support of increasingly politicized publics that sometimes espouse the erroneous view that arms control makes nuclear modernization unnecessary and undesirable. Leaders charged with protecting national interests and deterring nuclear aggression must articulate the need for nuclear planning as well as its benefits to deterrence. The public must be convinced that arms control and nuclear planning are complementary, not mutually exclusive, phenomena that require careful thought and deliberate movement to provide the tangible benefits of the stable deterrence they both seek.

JOHN M. WEINSTEIN

SEE ALSO: Arms Control and Disarmament: Mathematical Models; Conflict Termination; Crisis Management; Deterrence; Escalation; Flexible Response; Force de Frappe; Nuclear Powers; Nuclear Theory and Policy; Strategic Defense Initiative; Strategic Defense Initiative: Policy Implications.

Bibliography

Ball, D. 1981. Can nuclear war be controlled? *Aldelphi Papers 169*. London: International Institute for Strategic Studies.

Carlucci, F. C. 1988. *Annual report to Congress (FY 1989)*, Parts IC and IIIF. Washington, D.C.: Government Printing Office.

Gray, C. S. 1980. Targeting problems for central war. *Naval War College Review* 33, no. 1 (January–February).

Kelleher, C. McA. 1987. NATO nuclear operations. In *Managing nuclear operations*, ed. A. B. Carter, et al., pp. 445–69. Washington, D.C.: Brookings.

Postol, T. 1987. Targeting. In *Managing nuclear operations*, ed. A. B. Carter, et al., pp. 373–406. Washington, D.C.: Brookings.

Slocombe, W. 1987. Preplanned operations. In *Managing nuclear operations*, ed. A. B. Carter, et al., pp. 121–41. Washington, D.C.: Brookings.

Weinstein, J. M. 1984. The strategic implications of civil defense. In *The defense of the West: Strategic and European security issues reappraised*, ed. R. Kennedy and J. M. Weinstein, pp. 39–76. Boulder, Colo.: Westview Press.

NUCLEAR NONPROLIFERATION/ PROLIFERATION

Nuclear proliferation, sometimes labeled "horizontal" nuclear proliferation—the spreading of nuclear weapons into the arsenals of additional countries—is viewed as a threat to the world. If it were a threat in every respect, the problem would be simpler. Nuclear weapons are the most destructive weapon the world has ever known, and thus nuclear proliferation is often viewed as a new and different problem. But nuclear proliferation has varied impacts on the goals and situations of all nations, and this can lead to its being considered just one additional factor of general foreign policy.

Types of Impact

The spread of nuclear weapons will in many cases increase the probability of war because: (1) the rudimentary weapon systems of nuclear weapons states might be very vulnerable to pre-emptive attacks by adversaries, or (2) because the acquisition of such weapons will poison political relations between neighbors. Certainly such weapons can increase the destructiveness in war.

The normal definition of goals for arms control poses three criteria: reducing the probability of war, reducing the destructiveness of war if it occurs, and reducing the economic and other burdens in peacetime of preparations for war. By the first two of these criteria, nuclear proliferation is very much open to criticism. An important problem emerges, however, on the third criterion, because it is indeed possible that nuclear weapons will be cheap in the future, indeed that they might even be a free spin-off from the genuine pursuit of civilian benefits in a growing economy.

The nuclear proliferation issue is therefore different, in a number of important ways, from other issues of international military security. Such differences from the historic positions of East-West confrontation add complexity to the problem. These differences can also offer a useful perspective on the disputes about nuclear and conventional strategy.

Differences from Other Arms Issues

Spin-offs

The first major difference in the area of nuclear proliferation is the spin-off question. In ordinary discussions of military appropriations in the United States and other democratic countries the argument is often made that the defense budget is not as large and burdensome as it seems because there are a great number of useful spin-offs from military to civilian technology. For example, the development of heat shields to allow ballistic missiles to re-enter the earth's atmosphere without burning up provided the technology for Teflon-coated frying pans; and development of radar during World War II provided the means for controlling the flow of civilian airliners.

The taxpayer is well advised to be on guard against such arguments, however, for they are often merely clever salesmanship by public information officers and spokespersons of the military establishment. If Teflon was a byproduct and spin-off of the thermonuclear arms race between the United States and the Soviet Union, it could surely have been developed at a much lower cost, and perhaps at a lower risk of the destruction of all mankind, if it had been pursued directly as a consumer good in a civilian-oriented research project. Spin-offs from military uses to civilian uses may be real, but they will typically be much more expensive than a direct pursuit of any benefits derived.

Much more real, and therefore more worrisome, are the possibilities of a spin-off in reverse, from civilian goods to military weapons. For example, nuclear technology developed and intended solely to produce electrical power for the general economy could also provide an easy way to produce atomic weapons.

In this case, one would not need to worry so much about the duplicities of salesmanship. Rather, concern would center around the risks of "an arms race nobody wanted." In other words, each side would worry about the weapons capabilities of the other side, and each side would increase its capabilities because it would be worried about those of the other side, and so on.

Other examples of such threatening spin-offs from civilian to military uses include options for chemical weapons whenever the chemical industry makes breakthroughs in pesticides, and biological warfare capabilities inherent in all basic research on biology and genetic engineering. In the 1920s, proposals for a ban on bomber aircraft ran head-on into the fact that civilian airliners could be easily converted into military bomber aircraft.

If nuclear power production becomes limited or eliminated because the reactors involved prove to be too accident-prone, or because the problems of storing and treating nuclear waste materials prove unmanageable, then the associated threat of nuclear weapons proliferation would also be substantially reduced. If, however, nuclear power production continues to offer the developing and developed nations of the world an effective source of energy and economic progress, then this linked arms control problem would increase.

Soviet-American Cooperation

A second important way in which the nuclear proliferation problem has been different from other weapons issues is that there was extensive cooperation between the Soviet Union and the United States. Indeed, it is difficult to find another international issue on which the two superpowers were so much in agreement.

One French participant in the international conferences related to nuclear proliferation complained that he could never tell at the meetings in Vienna, Geneva, and New York, who was speaking on the nuclear proliferation issue—the Soviets or the Americans—because representatives from the two superpowers were saying exactly the same things.

American and Soviet representatives to the conferences became well acquainted over the years, and typically were working toward the same end. It was thus not unthinkable for the Soviet and American representatives to ask each other for suggestions on how to vote on a particular resolution.

Power-oriented cynics suggested that this was merely the pursuit of self-interest by both superpowers, as those who had nuclear weapons would naturally want to deny them to those who did not. Such a view ignored some fundamental altruistic features that were involved, by which the Soviet Union and the United States (and many other nations around the world) would regard it as a disaster if nuclear weapons were to come into use in a war between *any* two nations.

Other Americans, more suspicious and hawkish in outlook, claimed that this cooperation in opposing nuclear proliferation was a successful Soviet trick, arguing that all or most of the worrisome possible pursuers of nuclear weapons around the world would be anti-Soviet in their political and military orientation, and that Washington was beguiled into doing the Kremlin's work by supporting the Nuclear Nonproliferation Treaty (NPT) and other portions of the nonproliferation regime. Such a view, however, ignores countries like Iraq and Libya, which have been accused of bomb ambitions and have not been pro-Western in their external orientations. It also ignores how effectively the Kremlin worked to overrule any ambitions for nuclear weapons in Cuba, North Korea, and Romania.

Manifest International Injustice

The nonproliferation effort is also different in the world of international politics because it proffers a double standard on who can possess weapons. The five countries possessing nuclear weapons as of the 1968 final drafting of the Nuclear Nonproliferation Treaty (i.e., the U.S., USSR, Britain, France, and China) are to be allowed to continue to possess such weapons, while all other countries are not. Italian diplomats at an early stage thus denounced the NPT as the "first unequal treaty of the twentieth century."

The logic of the nonproliferation effort (ignoring occasional international propaganda that is mostly window dressing, especially on the alleged importance of Article VI of the NPT, which calls upon the nuclear powers to make progress toward "general and complete disarmament") would be that the ideal number of states possessing nuclear weapons would not be five, but more probably two. If there are two such states, they cancel each other out in terms of either's ability to use nuclear weapons against any other state, or even to threaten such use.

The official national diplomatic positions voiced at the United Nations are often phrased to deny this, arguing that the fewer nations that have nuclear weapons, the better. By this position, five is better than six, and four would be better than five, three better than four, and so on. But, on the next-to-last step in this "logical chain"—the question as to whether or not one nuclear power would be better than two—the answer would have to be in the negative. One would be threatening, while two would be less so, a fact that might well result in a world where nuclear weapons were never totally eliminated. Most of the diplomats at the United Nations, and most of the governments they represent, understand this, even if they do not say so openly or endorse this in General Assembly resolutions. Most of these diplomats and governments joined with Washington and the Kremlin in viewing further horizontal proliferation of nuclear weapons as threatening to the world, threatening in terms of the likelihood of war, and especially threatening in terms of the damage that would occur is such weapons were used in a war.

International Attitudes

The Importance of International Standards

The countries that have not signed and ratified the Nuclear Nonproliferation Treaty feel that they are therefore free, as sovereign nations, to acquire such weapons, whenever they feel it is in their national interest. Argentina, Brazil, India, Israel, Pakistan, and South Africa are the important examples of such nonadherence to the NPT (France and China are two states allowed to have nuclear weapons by the NPT that have also not formally adhered to the treaty, but they say that they will live by its terms; i.e., that they will not give the bomb to other states).

There was a time when nuclear weapons were widely interpreted to be just "weapons like any other weapons," something a nation obtained when the situation warranted and when the necessary technology had been acquired. Yet there is an interesting new tone to international dealings today; even states that have never agreed by any formal international commitment to forego such nuclear proliferation are encountering strong international pressures to do so. It is a distortion of reality to assume that only the nuclear "haves" are supporting the NPT, against the natural interests and desires of all the "have-nots." Rather, the more important pressures come from a number of other nations, ranging from Ireland and Sweden to Sri Lanka and Uruguay, all of which have concluded that the world will be far worse off if more countries (realistically, pairs of countries) insist on acquiring such weapons and joining the "nuclear club." The response that India received from other developing nations and from most of the nonnuclear weapons states, after its 1974 detonation of a "peaceful nuclear explosive," showed how the demonstration of such a capability does not rate very highly, while the damage that is done to the international system is quite high.

Countries like Argentina and Brazil, and Japan and Australia, may thus feel enjoined from ever reaching for such weapons, whether or not they are parties to the NPT. In part, this will be because of the pairings by which no one nation is likely to be able to become the only new nuclear-weapons state in a region. It may be in larger part, however, because the world would be angry at such a move.

In this last decade of the century, it is normal to scoff at the power of formal international law, but it could be a mistake in the opposite direction if the power of world public opinion were underrated. Where other states feel strongly that nuclear weapons are not "just another weapon," the pressures against further proliferation will be greater than predicted two decades ago, and greater than is shown merely by the legal status of formal treaty commitments.

The Nonproliferation "Regime"

Countries that have signed and ratified the NPT have offered two kinds of assurances to the outside world and the public that they will not acquire such nuclear weapons. First, they have agreed, as a matter of formal international treaty commitment, not to acquire such weapons. Nations do violate such treaty commitments, but never without some penalty and trepidation (otherwise, there would never have been any resistance to signing the NPT or any other disarmament treaty). Second, such nations agree to accept the inspection safeguards of the International Atomic Energy Agency (IAEA) over all their sensitive peaceful nuclear activities, reassuring other countries that the materials from such activities are not being diverted into the spin-off of nuclear weapons.

The "regime" phrase can be misleading when it is applied to the NPT (or to any other arrangements whereby NPT nonsignatories also submit to IAEA safeguards, and give pledges and assurances that they are not acquiring atomic bombs) for it suggests that this is being imposed upon the "have-not" nations by the "haves". This has often been the propaganda of Brazilian and Indian diplomats. Yet the reality is that most of the world wants the NPT (or something comparable) to take effect in all the states that could make nuclear weapons, with a combination of promises to forego such proliferation and assurances that the promises are being kept.

Although the attitudes of the superpowers have always been an important ingredient in nonproliferation, the attitudes of nonsuperpowers have also had a restraining effect. The attitudes of Australia thus restrain Japan, and those of Japan restrain Australia, and so forth.

A third important factor has emerged in the changing domestic public opinion attitudes in many of these countries, whereby nuclear weapons are no longer seen as a natural prerogative of sovereignty, but as something qualitatively different, something no longer to be viewed as a great accomplishment, but rather as a great threat and folly.

Public opinion obviously varies: Swedes, Italians, Canadians, and Japanese would probably react strongly against their politicians recommending nuclear weapons as a national option, while Pakistanis or Indians might respond differently. The trend is in the direction of prohibiting such weapons, an encouraging development for anyone seeking support for nonproliferation.

Role of Hypothetical Alternatives

Perhaps nuclear weapons are functional now only as deterrents, for keeping the same weapons in any other nation's arsenal from being used in battle. In any event, all concerned have become aware that these weapons would be enormously more destructive than anything used to date.

If such weapons are thus held back from use, as part of keeping similar weapons from coming into use, the same logical pattern could then explain and predict how in some countries weapons will be held back from production, in exchange for a matching restraint in production on the other side of a border. The knowledge of how to produce nuclear weapons, and the latent capability for producing the necessary materials—simply as a spin-off from civilian projects—will spread. But this does not mean that bombs must spread.

Proliferation: Nuclear Versus Conventional

Nuclear Weapons Are Different

The prospect of proliferation has, as noted, caused a remarkable degree of cooperation between the superpowers, very different from their policies on other arms issues. In addition, the attitudes of many other countries (i.e., electing to pass up nuclear proliferation for themselves, and electing to pressure other potential nations to do the same) have caused them to reach some of the commonsense conclusions on proliferation that are being reached between the superpowers. The world's attitude on nuclear proliferation may now accept some elements of a double standard, by which the larger powers can have these weapons and others cannot. The ways in which nuclear weapons are handled within the command-and-control systems of the United States and Russia may also now square with this outside world attitude that "nuclear weapons are different."

Traditionally, the captain of a ship in any navy is totally in command, any failure to obey his orders amounting to mutiny. In submarines that carry nuclear-tipped missiles in the U.S. Navy, however, the captain cannot by himself order the firing of such missiles; it takes the independent judgment of three officers, the captain and two others, to order such a firing, a judgment by all three of them that they had indeed received a bona fide order from the president of the United States to launch these missiles.

In ships that carry nuclear weapons in the Russian navy, it is similarly reported that there is an officer always on the bridge, again capable of vetoing a decision by the ship's captain that nuclear weapons should be used.

In all the services that we know about in these countries, the officers in charge of nuclear weapons are subjected to more intensive testing on psychological stability, and on general reliability and subordination to duly constituted authority than other officers. What is sufficient for winning a commission in military service in the handling of conventional weapons is thus only the beginning of what is good enough and required for the handling of nuclear weapons.

Nations that cannot be sure that their military services would pass muster on such questions, especially on the subordination of the military to duly constituted authority, have reason to think twice about whether they want to enter the nuclear weapons club, and especially whether they would be so relaxed about having a similar neighbor enter the club.

The idea that "nuclear weapons are just other weapons, like any other," has thus receded from the perceptions in both nuclear-weapons states and in the nonweapons states. Although mankind may be forced to keep nuclear weapons for an indefinite time into the future, they should not be handled or thought of just like other weapons.

Questions of Rationality

As noted, there is great concern about the durability of command-and-control systems where nuclear weapons are involved. Although special psychological tests are applied and checks and balances are instituted to prevent insubordination, there will still be concerns about the rationality of how nuclear weapons are handled, even if rationality is defined as nothing more than a mind-set whereby one does not retaliate when nothing has occurred to retaliate for.

In essence, nuclear deterrence between two adversaries fails when either one of them *could not* retaliate after the other's first strike. It would also fail if one nation retaliated for no reason (e.g., if nation A's cities were destroyed because nation B capriciously or in madness launched a nuclear attack, nation A would have no reason to hold back its nuclear forces).

Thus, if nuclear weapons proliferated, the world would have to worry about a longer and longer list of national leaders and the possibility of such weapons coming under the control of an irresponsible leader. One might posit that, if the world already had to be concerned about the mental health of the leaders of the nuclear weapons states, then limiting the number of such states would be extremely desirable.

At the opposite end of the scale would be the concern that, if nuclear proliferation continued, such weapons might fall into the hands of nonstate actors, into the hands of dissident, secessionist, and terrorist groups. If a group like the Japanese Red Army Faction or the Baader-Meinhof Gang ever gained control over nuclear warheads, it would be much harder to establish deterrence relationships; a clear target for any retaliatory threats would not exist.

The Impact on Pariah States

Nuclear weapons do have some political and military use beyond simply keeping the other side from using them. They have played a major role in reducing the likelihood of a conventional military attack in a number of areas that would otherwise lie exposed to such an attack. This is referred to as "extended nuclear deterrence," or "nuclear umbrellas." Since 1949, this factor has resulted in a considerable saving of money that otherwise might have been spent on conventional military preparations by the Western European NATO countries, South Korea, Taiwan, and Israel.

If such an extension of a superpower's nuclear commitment is no longer credible, however, then it is a powerful argument in favor of nuclear proliferation. This argument would deal a blow to the hope that nuclear weapons and nuclear strategy could be shelved and phased out of political interactions, and that nuclear proliferation was a bad development under all circumstances for all concerned.

Officially, the United States is against the spread of nuclear weapons. But neither does it want Western Europe and South Korea threatened by a tank attack, or Israel "pushed into the sea." Despite the categorical denunciations of nuclear proliferation noted throughout this discussion, the United States might quietly welcome at least the rumors of Israeli, Taiwanese, or South Korean inclinations toward nuclear weapons, for these could also terminate the "fondest dreams" of the opposing regimes that want to wipe out these political entities.

States like Israel and Taiwan have in the past been labeled "pariah states." This means they face neighbors intent on defeating and occupying them through ordinary conventional military combat, while they go unrecognized and have their fate ignored at the United Nations and other international organizations. Nuclear proliferation, or at least the possibility of proliferation, may be the antidote to such a predicament. This possibility is mentioned so late in the discussion not because it is the least important, but because it explains why the other considerations noted do not settle the proliferation question, and why nuclear strategy is so demanding, engrossing, and difficult.

Despite former U.S. Defense Secretary McNamara's sweeping statements, nuclear weapons have had functions other than keeping themselves from coming into use. Their presence may have persuaded Egypt to negotiate with Israel and may have kept Soviet tanks out of Paris.

The Future

The bulk of the argument against nuclear proliferation thus remains correct. But because there are also special cases and complications and some real conflicts of interests and debates about priorities, it will be necessary to consider and monitor the nuclear proliferation situation far into the future: it is very likely that more countries will acquire such weapons.

Predictions of future nuclear proliferation have often been too pessimistic in the past, however, because newspapers often emphasize the negative possibilities and because analysts want to err on the side of caution. For every four or five countries approaching the threshold of acquiring nuclear weapons, perhaps only one will actually do so, with the rest restraining themselves for all the reasons listed above. Most people understand that their own country's actions will affect other countries' actions. And almost no one would assume that a world where everyone possessed nuclear weapons would be safe.

George H. Quester

See Also: Arms Control and Disarmament; Deterrence; Escalation; NATO; Nuclear Powers; Nuclear Theory and Policy; United Nations; Warsaw Pact.

Bibliography

Buchan, A., ed. 1966. *A world of nuclear powers?* Englewood Cliffs, N.J.: Prentice-Hall.

Beaton, J., and J. Maddox. 1962. *The spread of nuclear weapons*. London: Chatto and Windus.
Dunn, L. 1982. *Controlling the bomb*. New Haven, Conn.: Yale Univ. Press.
Jones, R. W., ed. 1984. *Small nuclear forces and U.S. security policy*. Lexington, Mass.: Lexington Books.
Potter, W. C. 1982. *Nuclear power and nonproliferation*. Cambridge, Mass.: Oelgeschlager, Gunn and Hain.
Quester, G. 1973. *The politics of nuclear proliferation*. Baltimore, Md.: Johns Hopkins Univ. Press.
Spector, L. 1987. *Going nuclear*. Cambridge, Mass.: Ballinger.
Waltz, K. 1987. *The spread of nuclear weapons: More may be better*. Adelphi Paper no. 171. London: International Institute for Strategic Studies.
Wohlstetter, A., et al. 1979. *Swords from plowshares*. Chicago: Univ. of Chicago Press.

NUCLEAR POWERS (CHINA, UNITED KINGDOM, FRANCE)

Although the republics of the former Soviet Union and the United States possess the world's largest nuclear arsenals, thereby dominating the global nuclear balance, the nuclear forces of other nations also have a significant impact upon the world balance of power. The People's Republic of China (PRC), France, and the United Kingdom maintain moderately sized strategic nuclear arsenals. In addition, other nations—such as India, Israel, Pakistan, and South Africa—may also have a nuclear capability. Still others are engaged in efforts to become nuclear powers. For some time to come, however, it will be the expanding nuclear forces of other emerging nuclear powers that will have the most significant impact upon the evolving global security environment.

People's Republic of China

The nuclear weapons program of the PRC began in 1953 following collaboration with the Soviet Union in atomic research. In 1957 the Soviet Union agreed to supply China with a sample atomic bomb and technical assistance in the manufacture of nuclear weapons as part of a military aid agreement, in return for which Nikita Khrushchev demanded that Mao Tse-tung acknowledge the leading role of the Soviet Union among socialist states.

This cooperative effort was aborted when the two allies split over ideological differences, which became increasingly serious after 1958. In June 1959 the Soviet Union unilaterally abrogated its military aid agreement with China, thus setting back Mao's plans for a Chinese bomb. In 1964, China exploded its first atomic weapon. Since then, China has slowly but steadily continued to build what has become a large and capable nuclear force.

Nuclear Forces

The modern Chinese nuclear deterrent consists of a relatively small number of intercontinental ballistic missiles (ICBMs), submarine-launched ballistic missiles (SLBMs), and strategic bombers, although China did not deploy its first ICBM until late 1978 or early 1979. By 1989 China had managed to deploy only six obsolete and highly inaccurate ICBMs, all of which used liquid fuel, making them highly unreliable and vulnerable to preemption (due to the time it takes to prepare such missiles for launch). China's intermediate-range ballistic missiles (IRBMs)—the Dong Feng (DF)-3—and medium-range ballistic missiles (MRBMs)—the Dong Feng (DF)-2—are still the mainstay of its strategic nuclear force. The range of these missiles makes them incapable of striking targets in the continental United States, but it does provide sufficient coverage to hit many large urban and industrial centers in the Soviet Union and most Asian nations.

China's ballistic missile forces remain central to Chinese nuclear strategy because China's aging strategic bomber force, made up of approximately 120 H-6 bombers (maximum range 5,000 km [3,100 mi.]), is ill-equipped (lacking modern electronic warfare capabilities) to penetrate the expanding and increasingly effective air defenses of the former Soviet Union. This bomber force remains quite effective, however, against regional powers that do not possess extensive air-defense systems.

China did not deploy its first SLBM-equipped submarine until late 1983 or early 1984. Previously, China's technological backwardness and the nature of Maoist ideology, with its distinct focus upon military affairs on land rather than at sea, virtually precluded any serious effort to develop a sea-based nuclear force. With the rise of Deng Xiaoping following the Third Plenum of the Eleventh Party Congress in 1978 and his eventual consolidation of power at the Party Congress of September 1982, a new emphasis has been placed on building a large naval force. China's acquisition of SLBM-equipped submarines may be part of what some analysts see as a Chinese effort to acquire a blue-water navy. China's ballistic missile–equipped submarine force also serves to diversify, and thereby increase the survivability of, its strategic nuclear arsenal.

China is reportedly developing a mobile ICBM with multiple independently retargetable reentry vehicles (MIRVs). This missile, if deployed, would dramatically improve the survivability of China's ICBM force and further enhance China's nuclear war–fighting capabilities.

China's development of tactical ballistic missiles and a variety of other tactical nuclear weapon systems lead some Western analysts to conclude that the People's Liberation Army (PLA) is seeking a comprehensive nuclear war–fighting capability, based on combined-arms principles (see "Nuclear Doctrine," below). China's first test of an enhanced radiation warhead in September 1988 lent additional credence to this view of Chinese nuclear strategy.

Prior to Deng Xiaoping's military reforms of the 1980s, there existed no organizations within the PLA similar to the Soviet Union's Strategic Rocket Forces (an independent branch of the Soviet armed forces). China's ballistic missiles, before 1983, were commanded by the Second Artillery Corps. In 1983–84, however, as part of Deng's sweeping reforms of the Chinese military, the Strategic Guided Missile Force (SGMF) was created. This new PLA branch was given the task of training its own officers, performing scientific research, and "conducting live ammunition firing, improving overall results of missile launching, and enhancing troops' ability to cope with emergencies and to fight as one" (Xinhua radio, 3 June 1988). The creation of the SGMF exemplified the importance that Deng Xiaoping and other Chinese leaders have placed on modernizing and expanding China's nuclear forces.

NUCLEAR DOCTRINE

Under Mao, the PRC lacked a coherent nuclear doctrine. Military doctrine under Mao revolved entirely around his defense dogma of a "People's War," a concept that relies upon people rather than weapons and technology and emphasizes a strategy of luring an enemy deep into China's interior, where, in a protracted guerrilla war, a combined force of field armies and local militia would annihilate the enemy through hit-and-run guerrilla tactics and general attrition (including the use of nuclear weapons).

One important ideological cause of the Sino-Soviet split was a mostly rhetorical conflict over the role of nuclear weapons in the world Communist revolution. During the continuing crisis of 1957–58 over the islands of Quemoy and Matsu (in the Formosa Straits), Mao criticized Khrushchev for his unwillingness to use nuclear weapons to fight imperialism. Khrushchev himself had stated that communism would triumph in a nuclear war, but he also believed that such a war was no longer "inevitable," or even desirable. Mao, however, argued that Khrushchev had both overestimated the destructive potential of a nuclear war and had failed to see that the inevitable triumph of world communism could, in fact, be accelerated by a nuclear war with the West.

It was Mao's ideological beliefs and his faith in the power of China's masses to overcome any enemy that decisively influenced his views on the utility and function of nuclear weapons. Mao, like Lenin and Stalin, believed that a world war involving conflict between capitalist and socialist states was inevitable, and that this war would be rooted in the "class struggle." In a future war, according to Maoist thought, the masses (people) rather than technology (including nuclear weapons) would play the decisive role in influencing the outcome of such a "class-based" conflict.

In addition to Khrushchev's reformation of the Soviet doctrine of the inevitability of war, top Soviet officials at the time also began talking of a "revolution in military affairs," which, they said, had taken place as a result of the development of nuclear weapons and ballistic missiles. The primary result of this so-called revolution was an increasing Soviet emphasis on nuclear deterrence after Khrushchev's rise to power (although, in fact, the Soviet military sought to effect a "deterrence through denial" strategy).

China, in contrast, did not officially abandon the doctrine of the inevitability of war until 1980. Since then, deterrence of war has taken on added importance in China's military policy.

CCP (and therefore military) doctrine continues to stress that there is no "fire-break" between conventional and nuclear war. PLA military authors have yet to define a dichotomy between conventional and nuclear operational principles. The PLA has instead moved toward a combined-arms approach to military operations through the integration of nuclear forces into operational strategy and tactics.

Mao stressed the need for flexible strategic and tactical principles, and like him, contemporary Chinese leaders still emphasize the adoption of only those tactics and strategies appropriate to the political, economic, and military conditions of the time. China's military is still deeply influenced by Maoist thought but is prepared to modify certain basic doctrines in light of modern conditions. A column in *Beijing Review* in August 1982 observed that no matter how advanced Chinese military weaponry becomes, the PRC "will persist in [a] People's War . . . and further enrich and develop [it] in light of the new situations and modes of operation."

In early 1986, top PLA leaders stated that the likelihood of a major war in the contemporary era had been drastically reduced by the stalemate in the U.S.-Soviet nuclear balance. The world, they said, faced a "relatively long period of stability and peace." The PLA has therefore made a "strategic change of ideology" from preparing for an "early war, major war, and nuclear war" to constructing a "regularized, modernized, revolutionized army."

In the early 1980s, the People's War doctrine was revised to focus more on positional warfare and the initial defense of China's industrial areas and rear staging areas in preparation for an expected counteroffensive. Nuclear forces in this new strategy can be used in one of two fashions: in a massive strike against Soviet industrial and population centers; or in selected strikes against concentrations of Soviet forces and Soviet industrial and staging areas in Siberia, the Muslim republics, and reserve staging areas located between Moscow and the Urals. Chinese nuclear forces may also be used in a combined-arms fashion supporting PLA ground forces during the counterattack.

In addition, Chinese military authors have recently given increased attention to the importance of surprise and gaining the strategic initiative in war. Chinese nuclear strategists may therefore adhere to the (Soviet) belief that the nuclear preemption of one's enemy and delivering nuclear strikes "to the entire depth" of the enemy's rear will be necessary at the outset of a war.

Western analysts are uncertain, however, as to whether

Chinese nuclear forces are designed solely to deter attack through a minimal deterrence strategy—that is, by building the minimum number of nuclear weapons required to convince a potential enemy that he would suffer unbearable or inordinately high costs should he attack—or whether they have been built in accordance with plans to create an effective nuclear war–fighting capability, one that may ultimately be sufficient to achieve military predominance over potential enemies.

The debate has been complicated by the fact that since 1964 there have been no systematic and definitive statements of China's nuclear doctrine and strategy. Prior to 1964, discussions of Soviet and U.S. nuclear doctrines in Chinese military publications left the impression that China's leaders were concerned about the potential devastation of a strategic nuclear exchange and how they could defeat invading forces in the expected conventional/tactical assault that would follow an initial strategic nuclear exchange. Some discussion in these publications also emphasized that the armed forces must "utilize skillfully the effect of atomic surprise attack." Not since 1963, however, have the Chinese openly expressed the need for achieving and maintaining nuclear superiority.

Analysts who favor the view that China's nuclear doctrine is based on a minimal deterrence approach to nuclear strategy (much as the nuclear forces of Britain and France are) argue their case by pointing to, among other things, the fact that China's nuclear forces are still relatively small in quantity and technologically primitive.

This school of thought sees Chinese nuclear forces as retaliatory in nature, a view made more credible by China's publicly declared policy of "no first-use" of nuclear weapons. Critics of the minimal deterrence view of Chinese nuclear strategy, however, contend that the pronouncement of a "no first-use" policy will have little actual value in the event of war and could be nothing more than deception.

Furthermore, such critics suggest, the fact that China's nuclear forces are at present relatively primitive and small in number does not necessarily mean that the Chinese leadership does not *desire* to expand and improve the capabilities of its nuclear arsenal in order to achieve a comprehensive nuclear war–fighting capability.

Some Western analysts assert that China's modern nuclear deterrent is, in fact, designed to carry a nuclear war to the enemy. They point to the fact that China is actively seeking a robust offensive force posture, with sea- and land-based strategic missiles (including a new mobile ICBM), as well as medium- and short-range ballistic missiles and other tactical nuclear systems. China's new emphasis on nuclear war–fighting, some suggest, was made self-evident by the fact that by 1982, PLA ground forces had begun training in a simulated nuclear environment, including the use of tactical nuclear weapons.

China's large civil defense program, which the Chinese leadership still sees as worthy of large expenditures, in an age of defense budget stringency, is also considered to be indicative of doubt on the part of China's leadership about the efficacy of threatening "massive nuclear retaliation" for deterrence purposes.

China may still have confidence that it can survive a nuclear war because, even though large numbers of Chinese reside in densely populated cities, its population is the world's largest—and growing. In addition, a large number of Chinese still reside in the countryside, and China's industry and economy is more rural-based than that of its potential nuclear opponents, which makes China comparatively less vulnerable to nuclear attack.

China's active defenses, particularly air defenses, are still relatively weak, but the Chinese commitment to such defenses remains. Although highly critical of the U.S. Strategic Defense Initiative (SDI)—for the obvious reason that even a moderately effective U.S. or Soviet ABM defense network would render China's strategic nuclear forces virtually obsolete—the Chinese have spoken of the need to improve defenses against nuclear attack, which could include antiballistic missile defenses. (Some influential PLA analysts endorsed U.S. research, as opposed to testing or deployment, of space-based weapons on the grounds that it was necessary to hedge against possible Soviet breakthroughs.)

Both schools of thought on Chinese nuclear doctrine generally accept that it reflects, in part, the current threat perceptions of the Chinese leadership (which are evolutionary in nature).

Security Environment

China considered the Soviet Union to be a major security threat. Other threats result from ideological conflicts as well as conflicts over irredentist claims with such neighbors as India, Taiwan, Vietnam (Chinese and Vietnamese forces have clashed sporadically since 1979, and on 14 March 1988 Vietnamese and Chinese warships exchanged gunfire in a dispute over the Spratly Islands), and other nations who claim sovereignty over all or part of the Spratly Islands, located in the South China Sea (Malaysia and the Philippines, specifically).

The Soviet Union had been China's most pressing security threat since the 1960s, when ideologico-political differences erupted into border clashes along the Ussuri River (most violently in 1969, when the Soviet leadership apparently gave serious consideration to using nuclear weapons against China). The Soviet threat to China was exacerbated in the 1970s as the Soviet Union gained rough strategic parity with the United States, thereby allowing the Soviets to concentrate greater political and military resources on China.

The nature of the Soviet threat, with large numbers of troops deployed and prepared to launch a combined-arms offensive into China, was, in fact, very similar to the People's War scenario Mao envisioned.

After 1969, the Soviet Union had built up its conventional and nuclear forces in the Far East to the point where, as of 1988, Soviet forces in the Far Eastern Theater of Military Operations (TVD) numbered at least 57 divisions, including approximately 400 nuclear-capable surface-to-surface missiles (SSMs) and 1,300 tactical aircraft (including hundreds of dual-capable aircraft). In the mid-1980s, the Soviets deployed a number of Backfire and Blinder bombers, which were capable of hitting most Chinese targets. The Russian Pacific Ocean fleet, based in Vladivostok (a little more than 100 km [62 mi.] from the Chinese border), includes, among other things, two aircraft carriers and as many as 98 submarines, many with nuclear-tipped cruise and ballistic missiles. In addition, Russia deploys fixed and mobile ICBMs in Siberia (many of which, presumably, are aimed at China). (The several hundred intermediate- and short-range SSMs [SS-12/22s, SS-23s, SS-4s, and SS-20s] previously deployed in Siberia have been destroyed under the terms of the Intermediate-range Nuclear Forces [INF] Treaty, signed in December 1987).

Chinese Military Policy in the 1980s

Since the early 1980s, the PLA has undergone considerable modernization of all facets of its mission, operational doctrines, and equipment. Deng Xiaoping's reform efforts have sought to professionalize China's military and reassert the Party's—and the political leadership's—absolute control over it.

Under Deng Xiaoping the PLA has suffered in terms of its spending priority. The amount of money spent on defense in China fell from 17.5 percent of the national budget in 1979 to 8.2 percent in 1988. The PLA's central task, now, is to assist in the realization of the "four modernizations": agriculture, industry, science and technology, and military.

Under the leadership of Deng Xiaoping, Chinese military policy has followed these basic tenets:

1. accommodate "modern conditions" of warfare
2. reduce the size of one's land armies, since they have become less relevant in the age of nuclear warfare
3. accelerate the development of nuclear forces
4. increase the size of China's naval and merchant fleets to: allow China to become a major maritime power; check Soviet and Indian (as well as possibly Japanese) naval expansion; and possibly "liberate" Taiwan
5. develop Chinese military science and technology.

While China's army and air force have suffered under the new modernization program, its nuclear program and the PLA's naval expansion efforts have not.

By April 1987, Deng had reduced the size of the PLA by around 800,000 (to 1 million men), having decreed in mid-1985 a 25 percent reduction in the number of PLA troops.

China's naval and nuclear force expansion programs, in contrast, saw a number of milestones in the 1980s. China tested its first submarine-launched ballistic missile in 1982. In 1983, Liu Huaquing (commander of the navy and a Deng loyalist) helped to establish three special research committees on naval development. That same year, China built its first nuclear submarine equipped with guided missiles and announced plans to build five aircraft carriers and a dozen submarines carrying nuclear-tipped missiles over the course of a decade. This is an ambitious plan, which to some Western observers looks like a drive to acquire a blue-water navy. In May 1988, the PLA newspaper, *Liberation Army Daily*, reported that since 1979, China's navy had tripled its "long-distance combined-arms" exercises over what were conducted from 1950 to 1979. Nevertheless, China's navy, at least for the near future, will remain very much a coastal defense force.

Other strategic force developmental milestones that have occurred in the 1980s include: the introduction of solid-fuel ballistic missiles into the inventory; research and development into a variety of tactical nuclear weapons systems and a new tactical SSM; and the development of a new mobile ICBM.

United Kingdom

The United Kingdom (U.K.) has sought to balance a need for an independent U.K. nuclear force with a continuing reliance on the U.S. nuclear guarantee for Western Europe. The U.K. nuclear deterrent force (UKNDF) serves as a potential "second center" of North Atlantic Treaty Organization (NATO) decision making with regard to possible Allied nuclear responses to a Soviet attack on NATO. The UKNDF bolsters deterrence at a time when the credibility of the U.S. nuclear commitment to the defense of Europe has come into question. Successive British governments, both Labour and Conservative, have supported the idea of maintaining an independent nuclear deterrent for the United Kingdom. Whether future governments will continue to do so is unclear (the Labour party shifted leftward in the early 1980s to oppose any sort of UKNDF).

Britain has cooperated with the United States and other allies in NATO in the targeting of British nuclear forces. According to the 1980 British Ministry of Defence White Paper on "The Future United Kingdom Nuclear Deterrent Force," final decisions on the operational use of the Polaris force "rest with Her Majesty's Government alone; but it is committed to NATO and targeted in accordance with Alliance policy and strategic concepts under plans made by the Supreme Allied Commander Europe (SACEUR), save where Britain's supreme national interests otherwise require."

Britain conducted its first independent atomic test in 1952. The British government gained an operational atomic weapons delivery capability with its own delivery system in 1955, when the first Vulcan bombers entered service.

The modern UKNDF, built with much assistance from the United States, includes submarines, aircraft, and a variety of tactical nuclear systems. U.S.-British cooperation on nuclear force development, however, has not always been stable. In 1962, Robert McNamara, the U.S. secretary of defense, unilaterally canceled, for reasons of cost, a plan to upgrade British Vulcan bombers with nuclear-armed short-range attack missiles (SRAM). The British government was furious, and President Charles De Gaulle pointed to what he regarded as the untrustworthiness of the United States. The Skybolt affair, as it became known, led President John F. Kennedy to sign the Nassau Agreement in December 1962, with Prime Minister Harold Macmillan. In that agreement, the United States promised to sell Polaris missiles and associated parts to the United Kingdom.

NUCLEAR FORCES

The UKNDF includes SLBM-equipped submarines, nuclear-capable aircraft, and a variety of tactical nuclear weapon systems.

Britain operates Tornado, Sea Harrier, Buccaneer, and Nimrod nuclear-capable aircraft as well as ship-borne antisubmarine warfare (ASW) helicopters. Britain has stockpiled some 200 gravity bombs for use with its aircraft, but relies on the United States to supply the Royal Navy with nuclear depth-bombs.

British tactical nuclear forces play a vital role in NATO theater strategy. The Royal Air Force's (RAF) tactical nuclear weapons are integrated into NATO's joint air and land battle plans. Royal Navy tactical nuclear weapons are integrated into NATO ASW defense plans for the region surrounding the United Kingdom and for the protection of NATO's sea-lines of communication (SLOCs).

The British army also deploys nuclear-equipped Lance tactical ballistic missiles. These missiles are under a "dual-key" arrangement, whereby the United States retains final control over all nuclear warheads, while the U.K. government has control over the missiles themselves.

The United Kingdom possesses indirect control over other U.S. nuclear weapons delivery systems stationed in the United Kingdom, including submarines based at Holy Loch, nuclear-capable FB-111 E/F (in mid-1988, the United States reportedly was considering moving nuclear-dedicated FB-111/A aircraft presently stationed in the United States to Britain) aircraft, and the 96 U.S. cruise missiles deployed in Britain from 1984 to 1990. According to the 1952 U.S.-U.K. agreement (negotiated by Prime Minister Winston Churchill) governing the use of U.S. nuclear forces stationed at bases in Britain, "the use of these bases in an emergency would be a matter for joint decision" by the prime minister and the president. Thus, the United Kingdom has veto power over the deployment of U.S. nuclear forces but does not have "dual-key" control over them. (In 1983, in a controversial decision, the British government rejected a proposal for a "dual-key" arrangement with respect to U.S. cruise missiles stationed in the United Kingdom.)

The core element of the British nuclear deterrent is its force of four Resolution-class nuclear-powered submarines, built in Britain with U.S. assistance. Each submarine carries sixteen American Polaris SLBMs, which are outfitted with the British-designed warhead "bus," called Chevaline (with three multiple reentry vehicles [MRVs]).

In July 1980, the government of Prime Minister Margaret Thatcher decided to purchase Trident I SLBMs from the United States to be installed in four new submarines, each expected to carry sixteen SLBMs. In March 1982, the British government decided to purchase the more advanced Trident II/D5 missile system instead (which is more accurate than its predecessor and carries eight multiple independently retargetable reentry vehicles [MIRVs]). The Trident II missiles will be deployed on British submarines beginning in the mid-1990s. Present projections are for the last of the four Trafalgar-class submarines (fitted with U.S. Ohio-class submarine missile compartments) to be deployed some time in 1997–98.

The modernization of the United Kingdom's sea-based deterrent force has been under debate in Britain. The United Kingdom has been agonizing over a budget crisis in recent years; defense spending has declined in real terms since 1986 and is expected to continue declining in the 1990s.

The primary domestic opposition to the British nuclear program has come from the Labour party, which ran unsuccessfully in 1987 on a platform that included a pledge of unilateral nuclear disarmament. In addition, some members of the Social and Liberal Democrats have opposed further British nuclear modernization, although most support the idea of an independent U.K. nuclear deterrent. Still, many in the United Kingdom, including even some Conservatives, have questioned the expense of purchasing four new submarines. Some have suggested that one way for Britain to deal with the budget problem would be to procure only three, or fewer, submarines.

The modernization of Britain's ballistic-missile submarine force will dramatically expand the number of available warheads in Britain's strategic nuclear arsenal. Currently, Britain's four Resolution-class submarines, each equipped with sixteen Polaris missiles, carry a total of 192 warheads. If Britain proceeds to deploy all four planned Trafalgar-class submarines, each equipped with sixteen Trident missiles, and simultaneously phase out the older Resolution-class submarines, then the number of submarine-launched warheads in the British arsenal will grow to 512.

In 1985, the United Kingdom initiated a study to determine the feasibility of a follow-on to Britain's aging force of air-deliverable gravity bombs. Earlier, in 1980, it had rejected an option to procure long-range air-launched cruise missiles in favor of MIRV Trident SLBMs, which, it was believed, would be more cost-effective because they would not be vulnerable to Soviet air defenses. Some British politicians have suggested (as then Social Democrat party leader David Owen did in the mid-1980s) that the United Kingdom equip its future submarines with cruise missiles instead of Trident missiles.

In late December 1987, Britain agreed to join France in a project to study the possibility of jointly developing an advanced nuclear-armed cruise missile with a range of more than 500 kilometers (310 mi.) for their nuclear-dedicated aircraft. This decision came following the initial signing of the INF Treaty on 8 December 1987. British and French officials were concerned that the withdrawal of U.S. INF missiles from Europe would facilitate the military and political neutralization of the Federal Republic of Germany, in addition to the fact that the United Kingdom was concerned that the treaty requires the elimination of systems considered crucial to NATO's follow-on forces attack (FOFA) strategy, for which a new long-range stand-off attack missile could help compensate. In any case, increasingly effective Soviet air defenses required that Britain's force of Tornado aircraft be equipped with some form of longer-range stand-off attack missile in order to reduce aircraft vulnerability.

Nuclear Doctrine

The government of the United Kingdom has expended great effort to explain the purpose of the UKNDF in terms of its role within NATO. Officially, as a "second center" of alliance nuclear decision making, the UKNDF is meant to complicate enemy war planning. It increases uncertainty in that even if, at some critical point in a conflict, the United States does not resort to nuclear weapons, British nuclear forces might be used instead. The UKNDF also was designed to deter a Soviet attack on British territory. To borrow a concept from French nuclear doctrine, the UKNDF tends to "sanctuarize" British territory from Soviet nuclear, or possibly chemical or conventional, attacks.

The UKNDF also serves to "couple" U.S. strategic nuclear forces (as well as conventional forces) to Europe. In a wartime environment, the enemy war planner might not be able to distinguish an independently launched British nuclear attack from an American one, thus "coupling" the two together in the minds of the enemy leadership and holding the U.S. hostage somewhat to British actions.

Because the Polaris missile is not very accurate, and the UKNDF so small compared with the strategic nuclear capability of the United States, many presume that Britain's nuclear targeting strategy includes planning for attacks on Soviet urban and industrial centers. However, according to the 1980 U.K. Ministry of Defence report on "The Future United Kingdom Nuclear Deterrent Force," in the event of a Soviet attack, British targeting policy would be to pose a potential threat only to "key aspects of Soviet state power." British nuclear targeting strategy was more precise, and more discriminating, than a strategy of massive retaliation against Soviet cities would have been.

British nuclear forces are coordinated with overall NATO theater strategy. British tactical nuclear forces would be employed according to accepted NATO strategy, FOFA strategy being the most important in this regard.

France

Since the early 1950s, France has sought to build and maintain a nuclear force as a "third center" in the European nuclear balance (between NATO and the former Soviet Union). President Charles De Gaulle formally laid out France's plan for an independent nuclear force in his famous speech at the Ecole Militaire on 3 November 1958. France's nuclear program, however, began before De Gaulle's rise to power. On 18 October 1945, the Commissariat a l'Energie Atomique (CEA) was created. And in 1952, the French parliament approved the first five-year plan for French atomic development. France exploded its first atomic weapon at Reggane in the Sahara on 13 February 1960. (French nuclear testing is now conducted in the South Pacific.)

France's decision to build an independent strategic nuclear force came as a result of several factors: French (Gaullist) desires for a greater political role both within Europe and in the global arena; concerns about the dependability of the United States in the defense of Europe (then heightened in the wake of U.S.-French disputes over the Algerian War, the Suez Crisis, and Indochina); and doubts concerning the credibility of the U.S. nuclear commitment to Europe (the U.S. massive retaliation strategy was then being questioned).

France is a signatory to the 1949 North Atlantic Treaty, but it is not a participant in NATO's military structure (having withdrawn gradually from 1959 to 1967) and does not publicly acknowledge any consultation with NATO allies regarding the targeting of French nuclear forces (although many assume that such contacts do take place).

Nuclear Forces

The modern French strategic nuclear force, the *Force de Dissuasion* (popularly known as the *Force de Frappe*) consists of nuclear submarines, aircraft, and intermediate-range ballistic missiles.

The mainstay of France's strategic nuclear deterrent, as in the United Kingdom, is its submarine force, the *Force Oceanique Strategique* (FOST), which consists of five Redoutable-class submarines (the first became operational in 1971; each carries sixteen single-warhead M-20 SLBMs) and one Inflexible-class submarine (which became operational in 1985 and carries sixteen M-4 SLBMs). The deployment of the Inflexible-class submarine roughly doubled the number of available warheads in the submarine fleet from 80 to 176. Current plans call for Redoutable-class submarines to be retrofitted with M-4 missiles during scheduled refits. The number of warheads in the FOST arsenal will increase to around 500 warheads following the deployment of France's seventh submarine in 1996, which will be equipped initially with a new intermediate-generation SLBM, the M-45. This new SLBM will ultimately be replaced by an even more advanced SLBM, the M-5, early in the next century.

France first began deploying long-range nuclear-capable aircraft in 1966—the Mirage IIIE, some of which still remain in the French arsenal. The current generation of French nuclear-capable aircraft, comprising the *Forces Aeriennes Strategiques* (FAS), consists of Mirage IVP long-range aircraft, equipped with Air-Sol Moyenne Portee (ASMP) short-range stand-off attack missiles (all Mirage aircraft are capable of striking the territory of the former Soviet Union, with refueling). The ASMP will also be deployed on the newest generation of Mirage aircraft, the Mirage-2000N, as well as Super Etendard aircraft.

France deploys some eighteen silo-based S-3 intermediate-range ballistic missiles, operated by the First *Groupement de Missiles Strategiques* (GMS), on the Plateau d'Albion. Because of the vulnerability of the silo-based missiles, France, with the support of former prime minister Jacques Chirac, studied the possibility of replacing them with a mobile intermediate-range missile, known as the S-4. Prior to the 1988 French presidential election, Mitterrand was on record as favoring a silo-based deployment scheme for the S-4, and criticized the mobile-deployment scheme as deviating from France's doctrine of massive retaliation. In the 1989 defense budget, funding for the S-4 was reduced because of unexpected research costs associated with the new SSBN, Le Triomphant (scheduled to be operational in 1996). France has made the modernization of its SSBN fleet one of the highest defense priorities.

The French nuclear force has also included tactical, short-range systems. France has planned for some time to replace its existing generation Pluton system with a more advanced capability called the Hades. In the late 1980s, the Hades mobile tactical ballistic missile was criticized by Mitterrand as part of a purported effort by then Prime Minister Jacques Chirac to develop a French nuclear war-fighting capability, thus abandoning traditional French nuclear doctrine. The former defense minister Charles Hernu, who proposed eliminating the Hades, also stressed West German misgivings about the targeting of French "prestrategic," or tactical, nuclear forces, fearing that they would be capable only of striking German territory.

After the surprising failure of the Socialist party to gain a clear majority in parliamentary elections in June 1988, Defense Minister Chevenement indicated that the Hades missile would be developed. Chevenement then came out in favor of a bipartisan defense policy, supporting weapon programs already agreed to in the 1987–91 military program law.

France deploys a variety of tactical nuclear weapons, including air-deliverable gravity bombs, the ASMP stand-off missile, and Pluton tactical ballistic missiles. The French army's First Army is deployed in France and is equipped with Pluton missiles in preparation for France's final action before using strategic nuclear weapons, called the National Deterrent Maneuver (*Manoeuvre Nationale de Dissuasion*), which might involve the use of Pluton missiles in conjunction with a conventional counterattack.

Following the signing of the INF Treaty in December 1987, French (and general alliance) concerns about the ability of NATO to implement its FOFA strategy when the United States withdraws its INF missiles led to an agreement between France and the United Kingdom (in late December 1987) to study the feasibility of developing jointly an advanced stand-off attack missile. (The defense committee of the French National Assembly had first suggested the idea of a jointly developed U.K.-French long-range cruise missile in April 1987.) This newly proposed extended-range stand-off attack missile will probably have a range of only 300–500 kilometers (186–310 mi.), which will make it fall just short of the INF Treaty–designated range for INF systems.

In 1983, France tested its first enhanced radiation warhead, but in 1986 the French government officially decided not to build any "neutron" weapons, in keeping with traditional French nuclear doctrine.

Current French nuclear force modernization plans are unlikely to be changed in any fundamental way, as a broad consensus exists within France on the need for a national nuclear deterrent. Even French Communist and Socialist parties who, having opposed the idea of a national strategic nuclear force prior to the mid-1970s, now support it. As president, Mitterrand, a Socialist, has consistently supported French nuclear modernization, even to the point of making cuts in the size of the French ground forces to help pay for nuclear force modernization (such cuts were, in fact, carried out in the early 1980s).

Nuclear Doctrine

From the time of De Gaulle through the 1972 Defense White Paper and successive French governments, there has been a broad consensus within France on both the need for French strategic nuclear weapons and on the fact that they exist to ensure the sanctuarization of France's national territory, or what De Gaulle called France's "splendid isolation." French strategic nuclear forces will be used only for the defense of French territory against nuclear attack, or possibly other forms of attack (Charles Hernu warned in April 1985 that France would respond to a chemical attack with nuclear weapons).

France seeks to deter an enemy attack by threatening a massive nuclear strike on the adversary's territory in response to an attack on France's "vital interests." Precisely what France's "vital interests" are is left intentionally ambiguous.

De Gaulle's vision of French nuclear doctrine had its roots in the writings of Pierre Gallois in the 1950s. Gallois wrote about the need for a "balance of terror" to deter war. The French nuclear deterrent, he wrote, should be based on the principal of "proportional deterrence"—that is, a potential enemy could be deterred from attacking by the threat of suffering destruction out-of-proportion to any expected gains. "Proportional deterrence" meant that France, even with a relatively small nuclear arsenal, could deter a Soviet attack using either nuclear or conventional forces, or both.

Since the mid-1970s, an increasing number of authoritative voices in both France and Germany—including Giscard d'Estaing, Laurent Fabius, Jean-Pierre Chevenement, and Helmut Schmidt (the former chancellor of the Federal Republic of Germany)—have called for France to extend its nuclear deterrent to cover Germany in a so-called enlarged sanctuary. Such a concept was first used in the 1972 Defense White Paper. In 1985, the Socialist party's executive committee, in line with center-right thinking, came out in support of "adapting [France's] nuclear deterrent and defense strategy to the advantage of Western Europe," above all to the benefit of Germany, the "most vulnerable" country in Western Europe. The unification of Germany, as well as the termination of the Warsaw Pact following the collapse of communist regimes in Eastern Europe and the decision to remove Soviet forces from the former German Democratic Republic, Poland, Hungary, and Czechoslovakia, have all served greatly to diminish the previous vulnerability of Germany.

Mitterrand, however, going against a significant French trend away from Gaullist principles, has reiterated his opposition to a policy of clearly stating French "vital interests to exclude the protection of Germany with the French nuclear force." Former prime minister Jacques Chirac, however, came close to this position in December 1987 when he asked: "Who can henceforth have any doubt, in the event of aggression against the Federal Republic, that France's commitment will be immediate and unqualified? . . . There cannot be a battle of Germany and a battle of France."

Mitterrand has always been reluctant to accept French tactical nuclear weapons. Indeed, it was Mitterrand who first labeled France's tactical nuclear forces "prestrategic" so as to reassert the Gaullist doctrine that French tactical nuclear forces were meant primarily, if not solely, for the purposes of firing warning shots before launching a massive retaliatory nuclear strike. Mitterrand is also on record as having stated that French tactical nuclear weapons were introduced because of a "hesitation to give deterrence its true and full meaning" and that "anything short of global response is a weakening of deterrence."

France has historically been opposed to NATO's strategy of flexible response, and French leaders have usually been highly critical of U.S. and other alliance efforts to develop any sort of a nuclear war–fighting strategy/capability or deploy strategic defenses (France has strongly opposed the U.S. SDI program). "There is no flexible response for France," according to Mitterrand.

While France has so far been reluctant officially to extend its strategic nuclear deterrent to include Germany, France's so-called prestrategic nuclear forces, combined with French forces deployed inside the Federal Republic of Germany (near the Rhine) and the increased emphasis within the French army on mobility (following their reorganization in the early 1980s), have resulted in a faint but perceptible "enlarged sanctuary." Many Germans, however, remain disturbed by the prospect of French tactical nuclear weapons falling on German soil and oppose any French extension of a nuclear guarantee to the Federal Republic of Germany.

To help placate German fears, Mitterrand, in early 1986, agreed that France would "consult" with Bonn before firing a Pluton or Hades missile on German territory. Mitterrand further attempted to soothe West German sensitivities when, during a visit to the FRG in October 1987, he stated that France had no intention of exploding a nuclear device on German soil in wartime. In other words, France would adhere strictly to the Gaullist strategy of a massive nuclear response on *enemy* territory in response to an enemy attack.

The targeting of French nuclear forces places an emphasis on the "neutralization of the adversary's administrative, economic and social structures," a policy that would, it seems, still entail a large number of civilian casualties. French targeting policy appears to be similar to the British strategy of targeting "key aspects of Soviet power."

In all cases short of an all-out attack on France, the most probable French nuclear option was to use prestrategic, and possibly some strategic, nuclear forces to deliver strikes on advancing groups of enemy forces and critical targets in the enemy's rear areas. As the modernization of France's nuclear forces continues, a greater variety of possible attack options will open up. More accurate SLBMs, and a greater number of them, will allow for more French dual-capable aircraft and other prestrategic nuclear forces to be dedicated for tactical and operational-level operations, both nuclear and nonnuclear (a possibility made even more likely if France obtains a new advanced air-launched cruise missile), rather than risk being destroyed preemptively as they are held in reserve.

Greater redundancy and flexibility in the French nuclear force will enhance deterrence. An adversary's war-planning will become more complicated by the fact that France would possess much more plausible and effective nuclear options at the operational—i.e., theaterwide—level of war, rather than just at the tactical and strategic levels. In the post-INF environment, many Western defense analysts consider a larger French nuclear role in the defense of Western Europe to be a vital necessity.

Future Developments

China's nuclear forces are not yet sufficient to change the world nuclear balance, but the ongoing economic reforms and China's continuing effort to modernize and expand its nuclear arsenal may, in time, give the Chinese leadership the power and global influence necessary to translate their efforts into political gains. Indeed, if the United States and the Russian Republic agree to reduce their strategic nuclear forces beyond 50 percent under a Strategic Arms Reduction Treaty (START) regime, China would then quickly become a formidable nuclear power, one that would have to be taken into consideration in future international arms control talks. Sharp cuts in the superpowers' arsenals would also greatly enhance the relative power of the U.K. and French nuclear deterrents.

Although France is unlikely to allow its nuclear forces to become subject to negotation, the British government, as a result of a START Treaty, will probably face severe pressure to "review" the UKNDF. Secretary of State for Defence George Younger stated in May 1988 that if U.S.-Soviet arms reductions went further than the START Treaty regime currently envisioned, then the government would reexamine the U.K. nuclear deterrent force "in light of the reduced threat."

A Russian deployment of even moderately effective antiballistic missile defenses could severely degrade the efficacy of the U.K. and French nuclear deterrents and diminish the effectiveness of China's nuclear forces. Russian strategic defense programs, which a few U.S. analysts believe could lead to a Russian decision to abrogate the ABM Treaty, merely reinforce the need for both UKNDF and French nuclear modernization to continue in the future, with particular emphasis on systems capable of dealing with the emerging threats.

JACQUELYN K. DAVIS
ROBERT L. PFALTZGRAFF, JR.

SEE ALSO: Antitactical Ballistic Missile Policy; Ballistic Missile Defense; Deterrence; Flexible Response; Force de Frappe; Mao Tse-tung; Missile, Cruise; Missile, Intercontinental Ballistic; NATO; NATO Policy and Strategy; Nuclear Nonproliferation; Nuclear Theory and Policy (United States, Soviet Union); Strategic Defense Initiative: Policy Implications; Strategic Stability; Warsaw Pact.

Bibliography

Freedman, L. 1985. British nuclear targeting. *Defense Analysis* 1 (2):81–99.

Godwin, P. H. B. 1988. *The Chinese Communist armed forces.* Maxwell Air Force Base, Ala.: Air Univ. Press, Center for Aerospace Doctrine, Research, and Education. For sale by the U.S. GPO, Washington, D.C.

Healy, D. 1987. A Labour Britain, NATO and the bomb. *Foreign Affairs* 65 (4):716–29.

Homes, M., et al. 1987. *British security policy and the Atlantic alliance: Prospects for the 1990s.* London: Institute for Foreign Policy Analysis and Pergamon-Brassey's.

Howorth, J. 1988. French defense: Disarmament and deterrence. *The World Today* 44, no. 6 (June):103–106.

Lin Chong-Pin. 1988. *China's nuclear weapons strategy: Tradition within evolution.* Lexington, Mass.: Lexington Books, D.C. Heath.

Luttwak, E. N. 1980. The nuclear alternatives. In *NATO the next thirty years,* ed. K. A. Myers. Boulder, Colo.: Westview Press.

Marshall, D. B. 1980. The evolving French strategic debate. *Strategic Review* 8, no. 2 (spring):59–77.

Prados, J., J. S. Wit, and M. J. Zagurek, Jr. 1986. The strategic nuclear forces of Britain and France. *Scientific American* 225, no. 2 (August):33–41.

Rosecrance, R. N. 1968. *Defense of the realm: British strategy in the nuclear epoch.* New York: Columbia Univ. Press.

Schwartz, D. N. 1983. *NATO's nuclear dilemma.* Washington, D.C.: Brookings.

Segal, G., and W. T. Tow, eds. 1984. *Chinese defense policy.* Chicago: Univ. of Illinois Press.

Sloan, S. R. 1985. *NATO's future: Toward a new transatlantic bargain.* Washington, D.C.: National Defense Univ. Press.

Wortzel, L. M., ed. 1988. *China's military modernization: International implications.* Westport, Conn.: Greenwood Press.

Yost, D. S. 1984. France's deterrent posture and security in Europe: Capabilities and doctrine. *Adelphi Papers.* London: International Institute for Strategic Studies.

NUCLEAR PROPULSION

Nuclear power can be derived from either fission or fusion processes, but since the latter remains impractical for wide-scale use, conventional nuclear power plants are fission-based. Because the fuel for a nuclear reactor is longer-lasting and relatively inexpensive compared with fossil fuels, and because of the intense heat generated by the fission process, nuclear power provides a cost effective alternative to coal- and petroleum-based propulsion systems. Due to their size, however, nuclear power plants for propulsion are practically limited to oceangoing vessels—ships and submarines.

In nuclear propulsion for ships, the nuclear reactor heats water under pressure. The water is converted to steam outside the reactor and is used to drive steam turbines. In the majority of current nuclear-propelled ships, the steam turbines are connected to the propeller through gearing. In some of today's ships—and probably more in the future—the steam turbine drives an electric generator, which in turn provides the electric power for the electric propulsion motor that is coupled to the propeller.

Nuclear propulsion of ships gives them a power-generated autonomy practically independent of speed, and it eliminates the need for the combustion agents required to operate conventional thermal engines. Thus, it has drastically and lastingly changed the operational conditions of fleets and the hierarchy of their components since January 1955, when the U.S. Navy *Nautilus* sent the now legendary message, "Underway on nuclear power."

From Origins to Prototypes

The concept of a "nuclear engine suitable for submarine applications, should the neutron chain reaction be sustained and controlled . . ." appears to have been brought up in the United States even before (November 1939) the physical laws of uranium fission were known, but priority was naturally given to the explosive uses of fission, and the absolute secrecy surrounding the Manhattan Project long confined the physical results of research to that sole area.

Not until 1948 was a Nuclear Power Branch made official within the Bureau of Ships, under the orders of the future and famous Admiral Rickover. Rickover was also designated liaison officer with the Atomic Energy Commission, omnipotent at the time and jealous of its prerogatives.

Political frictions between the United States and the USSR surfaced shortly after the end of the hostilities against Germany and its allies. The United States feared that the Soviets would increase the threat of their already large submarine fleet by hardening their submarines against naval air attack, using a technique developed by the Germans toward the end of World War II. This concern doubtless played a decisive role in the initiation of the U.S. nuclear naval program.

Development went forward rapidly and without mishap. The land-based prototype of the submarine reactor (STR MARK ONE) ordered in December 1948 reached criticality 50 months later; in an even more remarkable performance, only eighteen months separated the initial operations of the land-based prototype and of the submarine. At that time, there were no nuclear power plants in operation in the United States. The reactor system chosen (pressurized water reactor recommended by Weinberg as early as 1946) rapidly won out as the system best suited to sea-going applications, and was also the basis of remarkable developments for commercial use.

Other countries were also working on programs to provide their navies with nuclear propulsion systems. The information below is drawn from *Jane's Fighting Ships.*

The USSR followed close on the heels of the United States. Two nuclear submarine types were mentioned in 1958 and the icebreaker *Lenin* was presented at the International Conference on the Peaceful Utilization of Nuclear Energy in that year. It is not known whether these achievements were preceded by demonstrations on land. The reactors of the *Lenin* were of the pressurized water type; there is reason to believe that the same was true for the submarines.

Both the United Kingdom and France launched their first nuclear-powered submarines in the 1960s—the British *Dreadnought* in 1963, the French *Redoutable* in 1969. It should be noted that the British submarine was fitted with a U.S reactor plant. The first French land prototype reached full power in 1964, one year before its British counterpart. To start the French program, the United States provided the enriched uranium necessary for a land-based demonstration, under the terms of a Mutual Defense Agreement concluded in 1958. The agreement, made possible by the amendment to the MacMahon law, excluded any exchange of classified information. The French could not put the *Redoutable* into operation until the Pierrelatte gas diffusion plant had supplied the enriched uranium required for manufacture of its first core.

The People's Republic of China introduced its first nuclear submarine in 1974. Information is not available as to whether the reactor, also of the pressurized water type, was preceded by a representative land prototype.

The club of nations with military nuclear-powered ships is very small, limited so far to those countries that have available enriched uranium in substantial quantities. Other countries attempted in different ways to master the technology of ship nuclear systems during the 1960s and 1970s (see Table 1): The Federal Republic of Germany carried out fully successful sea trials of a cargo ship, the *Otto Hahn,* in 1969. Japan manufactured a demonstration ship, the *Mutsu,* in the 1970s; Japan unfortunately encountered both technical and psychological difficulties and has been able only in 1990 to conclude successful tests. Italy's effort focused on the *E. Fermi,* an auxiliary ship; this project appears to have been abandoned due to the impossibility of obtaining the necessary uranium.

Mass Production in the United States and USSR

The industrial mobilization necessary for rapid production of a large series of nuclear-powered ships proceeded without delay in the United States and the USSR, a consequence of the strong prevailing competition and of the successful demonstration of the operational capacities of the first ships. In the United States, for example, from 1955 to 1961, the number of nuclear ships under construction increased by an average of six units a year, more than 90 percent of them being submarines.

Twenty years after the first trials of the *Nautilus,* some hundred nuclear ships had been commissioned in each of the two countries, which bears witness to the maturity of the techniques and to the priorities given to nuclear programs within the naval programs.

The main effort was devoted to submarines because the nuclear propulsion system, realizing its potential and reg-

TABLE 1. *The Start of Nuclear Propulsion: From the Origins to the Prototypes*

COUNTRY	FIRST LAND-BASED PROTOTYPE	FIRST SHIP AT SEA
United States	1953 (STR1)	1955 *Nautilus*
USSR		1958 (S/M and I.B.)
United Kingdom		1963 *Dreadnought*[a]
United Kingdom	1965	1966 *Valiant*[b]
France	1964 (PAT)	1969 *Redoutable*
Germany		1969 *Otto Hahn*
China		1974 S/M class Han
Japan		1974 *Mutsu*[c]

[a] nuclear power plant supplied by United States
[b] British-designed power plant
[c] sea trials not completed

ularly progressing in power-to-weight ratio and core life duration, thoroughly modified the conceptions of use for this type of ship. Maximum speed practically doubled that of conventional submarines; power-rate autonomy at this speed counted in the hundreds of days, compared with the fraction of an hour available from storage batteries.

In the United States, an extensive series of submarine nuclear power plants belonging to the same class was built; for instance, nearly one hundred units of the S5 W pressurized water reactors were constructed. The USSR appears to have built several types of submarines almost simultaneously, probably fitted with different models of reactors. In the United States, after a disappointing experience with the liquid-metal cooled "intermediate" neutron reactor (Seawolf), the pressurized water reactor system appears to have won out completely. The USSR, according to certain authors, allegedly built at least one series of submarines in the 1970s with reactors using eutectics that were better suited to naval use than sodium, which was chosen at the outset for the U.S. prototype.

In regard to their surface fleets, the two countries followed very different policies. The Soviets early on developed a fleet of nuclear-powered icebreakers. This opened entirely new, remarkable prospects for commercial exploitation of the Great North maritime route, which can now be kept open several months longer each year than before. The reactors that equip the icebreakers must meet rigorous specifications with regard to both speed-change rates and mechanical vibrations to be withstood as compared to what would be required on cargo ships. As in submarines, nuclear power gives icebreakers decisive advantages, making it possible for them to carry out tasks beyond the scope of conventionally powered ships. It was not until the end of the 1970s that the Soviet navy investigated nuclear propulsion for large combat ships (displacement above 25,000 metric tons) and aircraft carriers. The Kirov-class cruisers appear to be equipped with fossil-fueled superheaters, an original formula (Fig. 1).

In the United States, nuclear-powered surface ships more or less came into fashion in the 1950s. It was carried forward in the 1960s by the commissioning of one aircraft carrier and three ships, all different and with relatively modest displacements (approximately 8,000 to 18,000 metric tons). This allowed evaluation of the operational capabilities of a nuclear task force and its advantages compared with those of a fleet using conventional systems.

Figure 1. An aerial view of a Soviet Kirov-class nuclear-powered guided missile cruiser. (SOURCE: U.S. Navy)

Experience demonstrated that nuclear propulsion allowed a substantial increase in average speed at sea. In addition, the overall availability of the ships was somewhat better than that of their conventional counterparts because of the high concern for quality and surveillance in all aspects related to nuclear power, but this advantage was obtained at the cost of an extension of construction time by a factor of nearly two and a large increase in the construction costs, deemed incompatible with program and budgetary requirements. A few cruisers of more than 10,000 metric tons were built in the 1970s, but since the 1980s the U.S. Navy policy appears to be stabilized, reserving nuclear propulsion for the very large aircraft carriers (more than 90,000 metric tons) that are the backbone of the U.S. surface fleet.

United Kingdom and France

The French and British programs are completely independent of each other. Both are characterized by the priority given to submarines and by a standardization effort to achieve the best mass effect. The construction rates are of a smaller order of magnitude than those of the major powers.

France gave priority to the construction of a strategic force of ballistic missile submarines before considering nuclear attack submarines; the United Kingdom carried out the two programs simultaneously.

The strategic submarines of the two countries appear to meet similar specifications. The same is not true for nuclear-powered attack submarines (SSNs): in the United Kingdom, the Royal Navy built submarines whose performance and displacement rival those of the U.S. Navy. France, by contrast, endeavored to build a small nuclear propulsion system to achieve a low cost for the ship. At this writing, a nuclear aircraft carrier is under construction in France.

Nuclear-powered Fleets

Table 2 shows the current situation with respect to nuclear-powered ships in operation or under construction. The following points will augment the information in the table.

The number of naval nuclear reactors in operation or under construction is around 700 (that is, more than the number of existing or planned nuclear-power stations in the world). The reactor power plant ratings are estimated to be between 50 and 500 megawatts (thermal). With the exception of fourteen Soviet plants reported to use liquid-metal cooling, all the others appear to be pressurized water reactors.

For ballistic missile submarines (SSBN), an increase in

TABLE 2. *Nuclear-powered Fleets (includes vessels in operation and under construction)*

COUNTRY	NUCLEAR-POWERED NAVAL VESSELS
France	14 submarines: the future ballistic missile–carrying submarine (SSBN) intended to replace the Redoutable-class with displacement of approximately 15,000 metric tons. Displacement of attack submarines (SSN) is 2,700 metric tons.
	1 aircraft carrier (PAN): anticipated displacement of 36,000 metric tons
China	7 submarines: displacement of SSBN 8,000 metric tons; displacement of SSN 5,200 metric tons
United Kingdom	22 submarines: displacement of the future SSBN 15,000 metric tons; displacement of most recent SSN 5,200 metric tons
United States	180 submarines: the most recent SSBN with displacement of 18,700 metric tons; displacement of SSN 7,000 metric tons
	9 aircraft carriers (CVN): displacement of 91,000 metric tons
	9 cruisers (CGN): the most recent with displacement of 10,000 metric tons
USSR	213 submarines: the most recent SSBN with displacement of 25,000 metric tons; displacement of cruise missile–carrying submarines 16,000 metric tons; displacement of SSN 8,000 metric tons
	2 aircraft carriers: displacement of 75,000 metric tons
	4 cruisers: displacement of 28,000 metric tons; possibly equipped with fossil-fueled superheaters
	8 icebreakers: displacement of 20,000 metric tons

Source: Jane's Fighting Ships, 1990–91. 1990. London: Jane's.

the displacement has been observed during the past decade (approximately doubled in the USSR and the United States, multiplied by approximately 1.5 in France and the United Kingdom), resulting in a large increase of the installed power ratings (probably 1.5 to 4 times higher). The same phenomenon is apparent for the other classes of submarines in the republics of the former USSR and the United States, whose displacements are catching up with those of the first series of nuclear-powered ballistic missile–equipped submarines (SSBN).

The search for increased speed performance for submarines has led to substantially improved power ratings for nuclear propulsion systems, but at a relatively small increase in size and weight. In the United States, this trend is illustrated by the approximate doubling of the power-to-weight ratio for submarines, with a similar evolution in the former USSR.

Improvements in nuclear power plant technology have made possible larger and faster submarines; the enormous increase in submarine size is not the result of nuclear power generation systems. Illustrating this point is the fact that the smallest nuclear-powered submarines have a displacement that does not exceed that of the largest conventional submarines by more than 15 percent. Nuclear reactors have been able to adapt to changing needs; it cannot be said that they have yet reached the limit of their ability to increase performance within the same size and weight balance.

Analysis of nuclear-propelled surface ships is difficult because only a small number of these ships was built. But it can be said that nuclear power certainly does not penalize aircraft carriers in regard to size and performance; this also seems to be true for cruisers or ships with displacements above approximately 10,000 metric tons.

Considerations of Technologies

The techniques of pressurized water reactors are well known because they are used in large numbers of nuclear power stations throughout the world. Seagoing nuclear systems cannot be described in detail here, but their crucial features can be pointed out:

- Reliability and availability: all submarines of the Western world and a few Russian submarines are equipped with a single nuclear steam supply system; even a short interruption in steam generation would jeopardize the ship; the naval reactor must necessarily aim at achieving absolute availability, whereas on land the possibility of unscheduled reactor maintenance is not precluded.
- Power fluctuation rates: the required power variation rates on a ship are greater than what can be tolerated in a commercial plant, and the survival of the ship may depend on them.
- Hardening against attack: the naval reactor must be able to withstand extremely severe stresses in frequency and amplitude without hazard for the personnel and, up to a certain level, without failure.
- Environmental constraints: the crew must live for many weeks in the immediate vicinity of the reactor; the standards for health, shielding, and waste management are therefore extremely exacting; there can be no question of releasing contaminants except by accident.
- Acoustic discretion: this is of prime importance to ensure operational credibility of the submarines.

It is evident that the naval reactor, although it uses enriched uranium and water as do commercial nuclear power stations, is substantially different in regard to the overall design and component specifications. With these differences noted, two questions can be asked: (1) Can all the problems raised by the adoption of nuclear propulsion on ships be considered as definitively and completely solved? and (2) Are there incentives for changing techniques, other than the appetite of scientists and the inclination of engineers toward innovation?

In spite of the strict secrecy surrounding nuclear-powered ship operations, it can be asserted that the global balance expressed in reactor-years without accidents affecting the environment is reassuring. Nuclear submarines have been lost at sea, but they have not allowed atmospheric release of nuclear material and apparently have not spread detectable contamination on the ocean bottoms.

Although it is technically possible to build nuclear-powered surface ships of limited tonnage (less than 5,000 metric tons, for instance) with a conventional nuclear architecture, doubt remains as to their nuclear safety in combat or in case of collision. It therefore appears reasonable to restrict nuclear propulsion of surface ships to large ships of at least 10,000 metric tons.

The future of the techniques and methods used for nuclear propulsion of the numerous fleets on the oceans seems assured. The current reactors are particularly well suited to the tasks of the ships that form the bulk of today's combat fleets, and there is presently no demand, no technical or military reason, to change policies. It would require enormous investments to search for alternate solutions, with no assurance of a decisive step forward or of new prospects. Although the technology is nearly 40 years old, it is still without competition.

The technical file is not closed, however. Many teams are still active throughout the world on the theme of nuclear propulsion, seeking ways to simplify the systems and the man/machine interface, alleviate operational constraints (particularly maintenance), and improve controls. This work is an additional guarantee of the operational safety of present and future systems.

Future

Will nuclear propulsion of military ships be developed throughout the world? Political considerations and nonproliferation doctrines both affect the prospects. Nuclear reactors for ships are not classified among the prohibited nonpeaceful applications of nuclear power, but a major obstacle to the multiplication of military nuclear-powered ships is the supply of freely available fissionable material. Another deterrent is the fact that the construction, fitting out, and operation of nuclear-powered ships represent high long-term investments and a mobilization of manpower that must be weighed against a nation's immediate needs in conventional forces.

It is likely that few additional countries, even if they have the required competence or can obtain external help, will undertake the adventure, continuing the effort beyond a demonstration of prestige up to the accomplishment of real strategic ambitions. Another approach would be possible: nuclear-ship development within a mutual defense alliance, grouping countries with close ties to a nation with a nuclear fleet. So far, neither the United States nor the republics of the former USSR has opened the way to such a prospect, with the recent exception of the loan of a Soviet nuclear-attack submarine to India.

It seems safe to predict that the countries now equipped with nuclear-powered submarines will continue to build such ships and maintain their fleets in keeping with their strategic ambitions. Nuclear power for surface forces will be used only for very large ships, except in special cases.

The application of nuclear propulsion to cargo ships has, until now, run up against problems of economic efficiency and the complexity of the concerns that would be raised by the access of such ships to harbors not prepared to accommodate them. This situation could change; it should be realized that technical files are ready in many countries, while suitable harbor facilities are lacking.

JACQUES CHEVALLIER

SEE ALSO: Aircraft Carrier; Environmental Impact of Armed Forces; Naval Propulsion Technology; Submarine; Submarine and Antisubmarine Technology Applications; Technology and the Military.

Bibliography

Duncan, R. G. 1990. *Rickover and the nuclear navy*. Annapolis, Md.: U.S. Naval Institute Press.

Dukert, J. M. 1973. *Nuclear ships of the world*. New York: Coward, McCann and Geoghegan.

Encyclopedia of science and technology. 1982. 5th ed. New York: McGraw-Hill.

Friedman, N. 1984. *Submarine design and development*. Annapolis, Md.: U.S. Naval Institute Press.

Gimpel, H. J. 1965. *The United States nuclear navy*. New York: Franklin Watts.

Hewlett, R. G., and F. Duncan. 1974. *Nuclear navy 1946–1962*. Chicago: Univ. of Chicago Press.

Jane's fighting ships, 1990–91. 1990. London: Jane's. Note: Nuclear ship propulsion coverage starts as early as the 1953–54 edition.

NUCLEAR THEORY AND POLICY (United States, Soviet Union)

Nuclear war, in which two sides exchange nuclear strikes, has never occurred. Thus, national plans for the use of nuclear weapons cannot be based on experience. As a result, nuclear powers have been forced to develop policies for controlling nuclear forces that are based upon theory about such things as the effects of weapons, what targets should be struck, and how the existence of nuclear arsenals affects international relations. This article is a general examination of how theory and policy have combined over almost 50 years to control the development of nuclear forces and to determine the strategies that the United States and the Soviet Union established to govern the use of nuclear weapons in case of a nuclear war. To comprehend the nuclear policies, military forces, and weapon systems of the United States and the newly independent states of the former Soviet Union, one must understand the long development of nuclear theory and policy that took place before the demise of the Warsaw Pact and the USSR in 1991. This past will shape the future of nuclear weapons in our world.

United States

Since the ending in 1961 of the "massive retaliation" doctrine set forth by Pres. Dwight Eisenhower's Secretary of State John Foster Dulles, U.S. nuclear policy has remained remarkably constant, as has the theory behind that policy. Massive retaliation—"a great capacity to retaliate, instantly, by means and at places of our own choosing" against Soviet aggression—has been widely interpreted, incorrectly, as the automatic firing at the Soviets of a massive city-busting salvo from the then-overwhelming American nuclear arsenal in reply to any attack that warranted nuclear retaliation. This interpretation was not necessarily accurate, for the doctrine of massive retaliation most certainly did not assure nuclear retaliation against *any* Soviet aggression regardless of the character of that aggression. The correct definition stressed the "capacity" to escalate to levels of violence substantially higher than those of the initial aggression. Nonetheless, massive retaliation *was* at least implicitly massive: it included neither weapons nor plans designed for the kinds of "discriminate" nuclear responses that were first planned in the 1960s and have remained central to American nuclear strategy ever since.

By 1962, Robert McNamara, Pres. John Kennedy's secretary of defense, had substituted a variety of options for massive retaliation. In 1967, the flexible response doctrine adopted by NATO explicitly applied that variety of possible American nuclear (as well as conventional) responses to the deterrence of Soviet aggression in Europe, which all along had been second only to deterrence of attack on the United States itself as the objective of U.S. nuclear policy. By 1967, the potential flexible nuclear responses ranged from use of tactical weapons, to be used on the battlefields in Europe and probably fired from Europe, to intercontinental strategic weapons, with some chain of escalation from the smaller to the larger held implicit.

Very little changed subsequently. Indeed, the secretary of defense's *Annual Report to the Congress* for fiscal year 1989 stated U.S. nuclear strategy in virtually the same words that had been used by every secretary of defense since McNamara. Every element of McNamara's strategy has been present: deterrence of attack on the United States and, via flexible response, deterrence of nuclear or conventional attack on our European allies; escalation control; the triad; and discriminating response.

This constancy of U.S. nuclear *policy* has been matched by the constancy of U.S. nuclear *theory*. In 1960, Herman Kahn divided U.S. nuclear deterrence into Type I, "the deterrence of a direct attack," and Type II, "using strategic threats to deter an enemy from engaging in very provocative attacks, other than a direct attack on the United States itself."

The unilateral objective of Type-I deterrence is to prevent nuclear attack by the threat of a second-strike retaliation so terrible that the enemy will never mount a first strike. Type-I deterrence also has a multilateral objective in that it aims at mutual stability—that is, each side deterring the other so that neither side will start a war, and both sides having confidence that this is the case. In the early 1960s, this looked relatively simple. It took more than one warhead to dig out a hardened retaliatory weapon, so there seemed to be a disadvantage to going first. Deterrence thus seemed safe, so many of the Type-I issues revolved around the avoidance of undeterrable accidental nuclear war. Later in the decade, however, the advent of the MIRV (multiple independently targetable re-entry vehicle) reversed the equation—one multiple-warhead missile could kill more than one retaliatory weapon—and the worst theoretical fears of several years earlier seemed to be coming to pass. In particular, MIRV raised questions of "pre-emption," the attempt to mount a nuclear strike against an enemy because of the belief that he is about to strike, so that the issue is not war versus no war, but powerful first strike versus feeble second strike. Pre-emption still governs much of the discussion of Type-I deterrence. MIRV also complicated the discussion of arms control: instead of talking just about missiles, other measures—warheads and megatonnage (explosive power in terms of equivalent tons of TNT)—had to be brought into the discussion.

For the United States, Type-II deterrence, use of the threat of nuclear attack to deter anything other than nuclear attack on the United States, had in practice come to mean deterrence of a Soviet attack against Western Europe. In the years after 1960, it became clear from Vietnam and other wars that nuclear deterrence was too dangerous to use in such developing-country conflicts. It may have been relevant to the Cuban missile crisis, but, in any case, that crisis was between the United States and the Soviet Union, with Cuba being merely the locale.

In the future, oil or other issues in the Middle East may become so crucial to the well-being of the West that it may become desirable to extend Type-II deterrence to this region. At the beginning of the 1990s, and for the previous quarter century, however, Type-II deterrence was effectively limited to Europe. As a result, the central military issue of Type-II deterrence was one of American willingness to mount what under the Type-I/Type-II definitions is a *first* strike, a nuclear attack against Soviet forces and perhaps Soviet territory, without the other side having used nuclear weapons. Since Type-I deterrence is *deterrence of* a first strike—in the context of multilateral stability, a first strike by either side—tension existed between the objective of maintaining such stability and the U.S. objective of deterring Soviet conventional aggression in Europe by threatening such a strike.

Since 1945, this tension had dominated U.S. nuclear policy and theory. The dilemma had been how to maintain overall stability without providing the Soviets with a degree of impunity that allowed them to take advantage of their conventional superiority in Europe.

History

U.S. nuclear history since 1945 can be divided into seven periods. Although the division, particularly the dating of the periods, is somewhat arbitrary, the periodicity helps illustrate the waxing and waning of the two sides of the stability/deterrence dilemma.

1945–57: Confidence in American nuclear power. The period that opened with Alamogordo, Hiroshima, and Nagasaki was one in which the United States believed itself to be far ahead in the nuclear arms race. The speed of Soviet development of first the atomic and then the hydrogen bomb shook this confidence only temporarily. Massive retaliation, or, more precisely, U.S. choice of retaliatory modes with little worry about Soviet counterretaliation, seemed well within U.S. capabilities. Although Kahn had not yet coined the Type-I/Type-II terminology, the ability to control nuclear choices extended to deterrence/response against both Soviet attack on the United States and lesser aggressions, particularly in Europe. Little developed in the way of theories of nuclear strategy, with the stress in debate being much more on the moral, philosophical, and historical implications of nuclear weapons than on their military or political use.

1957–61: Concern over the deterioration of deterrence. The confident postwar years ended abruptly in the fall of 1957, when the Soviets put *Sputnik,* the first man-made satellite, into orbit, thus signaling their technological capability to boost missiles carrying nuclear warheads across intercontinental distances. Although massive retaliation remained the official U.S. strategy through the end of the Eisenhower administration in 1961, the fear of a missile gap that would allow swarms of fast-traveling Soviet missiles to wipe out U.S. retaliatory capabilities, still largely bomber-borne, dominated public discussion. Lacking good intelligence on the weapons the Soviets actually had, the fear also entered the deliberations of experts, who stressed the need to do something about it before it was too late. Two highly influential, then-classified reports (both well in train before *Sputnik*) were: the Gaither Report, so-called after H. Rowan Gaither, chairman of a presidential Security Resources Panel of 1957, which warned against the missile gap and stressed the need for steps to avoid devastating surprise attack; and a 1954 report written by a RAND Corporation team headed by Albert Wohlstetter, which had started out to advise the U.S. Air Force on location of bases, and turned instead to what it identified as the far more central issue of the vulnerability of those bases to Soviet attack. In 1959, Wohlstetter published an unclassified version of the warning, which became very influential. The late 1950s and early 1960s also saw the beginning of theorizing about nuclear deterrence and arms control, which began to enter policy in the next period. The Wohlstetter writings and other RAND contributions, including Kahn's book, were part of this; another major part came from Cambridge, Massachusetts, where the Joint Harvard-MIT Faculty Seminar on Arms Control began discussions that ranged from the technical through the legal, with some emphasis on concepts derived from game theory. In 1960, Thomas Schelling produced a seminal conceptual book based on game theory, and in another work he and Morton Halperin applied the theoretical concepts to arms control.

1961–67: Conceptualization and implementation. In 1961, John Kennedy became president, and Robert McNamara his secretary of defense. They quickly realized that the missile gap—a current or imminent Soviet capability to destroy U.S. retaliatory forces—was a myth, but the underlying concept of potential vulnerability set forth by the Gaither Report and the writings of Wohlstetter was crucial, as were the Schelling and Halperin theories, which set forth a broad concept of arms control that included in the definition mutual Soviet-American stabilizing measures achieved by treaty or by tacit agreement, and unilateral steps on either side. Technologically, this period at the beginning of the missile era required more than one first-strike missile to dig out a retaliatory missile "hardened" by being placed in an underground shelter. As a result, the premium was on waiting to be attacked, and stability against preemption seemed achievable by one arms control mode or another. Such stability, however, brought into focus the other product of deterrence theories, the Type-I/Type-II dilemma: the need to protect NATO Europe without the overwhelming American superiority postulated for massive retaliation.

Neither Kennedy nor McNamara was willing to depend fully on the advice of the uniformed military establishment, so the early 1960s provided an unusual opportunity for deterrence and arms control theories to be translated into policy designs, the more so because many of the theorists from RAND and the Harvard-MIT seminar went to Washington as bureaucrats or advisers. With their aid, McNamara reconstructed U.S. nuclear policy, replacing deterrence by fear of massive retaliation causing massive destruction with the much more selective "counterforce" theory that "our principal military objectives, in the event of a nuclear war stemming from a major attack on the [NATO] Alliance, should be the destruction of the enemy's military forces, not of his civilian population," as he put it in a speech at Ann Arbor, Michigan, in 1962. Not only was counterforce a commonsense humanitarian philosophy as compared with what came to be termed countervalue doctrine, but it was a plausible strategy for using the threat of nuclear attack (or additional echelons of attack after the first exchange) as a bargaining device to terminate the war on acceptable military and political terms. As such, it combined the various concepts: protection of nuclear forces against enemy counterforce so that they could mount a Type-I retaliatory strike; targeting them so that a U.S. first—Type-II—strike would destroy much of the enemy's capability to retaliate, thus making the strike plausible enough to convince the Soviets and NATO of American willingness to strike first on their behalf; and doing all this in a context of stability, because the plausibility of response would convince the Soviets not to attack either the United States or NATO Europe in the first place. McNamara put counterforce at the core of stated U.S. ("declaratory") policy; he also constructed the strategic Single Integrated Operating Plan (SIOP) so that it had enough counterforce and other options to make the policy real. All this could be interpreted as arms control within the broad Schelling/Halperin definition, although arms control agreements between the United States and the Soviet Union in the 1960s were confined to the peripheral atmospheric test ban.

Nevertheless, McNamara's policies could not fully convince the NATO Europeans that the United States would really risk Soviet retaliation against the U.S. homeland for an American first strike in defense of Western Europe. Various devices were considered to give Europe more of a say in nuclear deterrence, the most notable being the Multilateral Force (MLF) in which the Lyndon Johnson administration offered to equip multinationally manned ships with U.S. missiles. The missiles would still be under the control of the president of the United States, however, so the Europeans had their fingers on the safety catch but not the deterrent trigger, and the scheme was not implemented. Closely related, this was the period when the British and French independent nuclear deterrents, which had been planned earlier, came to full implementation. This period ended with NATO's adoption of the "flexible response" doctrine, which papered over the Type-II dilemma by promising a range of appropriate retaliation, including nuclear retaliation, to the range of potential aggressions but not specifying which response would be appropriate for what provocation.

1967–74: Instability and arms control. As the decade of the 1960s wore on, afterthoughts and events came together to initiate substantial changes. The afterthoughts were McNamara's. As more of his attention turned to Vietnam, and as the situation there deteriorated, the certainties of crisply implementable selective counterforce options seemed to fade in parallel. His stress turned from the capability to fight a nuclear war, and deterrence through the plausibility of this capability, back toward deterrence through the threat of devastation. In contrast to his 1962 Ann Arbor counterforce statement, in 1967 he contended, "Now it is imperative to understand that assured destruction is the very essence of the whole deterrence concept. . . . It means the certainty of suicide to the aggressor—not merely to his military forces but to his society as a whole." This moved back toward massive retaliation but by no means all the way. The need to assure retaliation depended on the force protection measures introduced a decade earlier; the SIOP continued to stress counterforce options—the new McNamara statement contained no suggestion that it was better to target populations than military forces. Nonetheless, the emphasis had shifted from the advantages of counterforce toward doubts about its efficacy. This shift was bitterly resented by some of the theorists who had initiated the concept. Wohlstetter, for example, would later accuse McNamara of adopting a strategy of mutual assured destruction (MAD) whereby both sides targeted populations and allowed their populations to be targeted. The accusation was denied, and this exchange continued into the 1980s.

As U.S. policy shifted, technological developments in the late 1960s upset the stability of arms control. This stability had been based on less-than-perfectly-accurate single-warhead missiles trying to dig out sheltered missiles. But the entry of MIRVs into both the U.S. and the Soviet arsenals reversed the ratio; now one missile could carry many, more accurate warheads, and those warheads could wipe out more than one missile in the ground with a high degree of confidence. Now, the premium was on getting in the first strike with a MIRV missile, and stability gave way to instability, particularly during a tense crisis which might encourage both sides to launch a preemptive strike.

During this same period, both sides also began developing ABM systems. It has been argued both that MIRV was a reaction to ABM and that ABM was a reaction to MIRV; the only certainty is that the two development streams interacted. In the U.S. debate, MIRV was taken by the arms controllers as a natural, if unfortunate, development of technology. ABM, however, was seen as a much more controversial new direction, with some viewing it as not only technically questionable but also as an additional destabilizing factor, making more difficult the retaliatory second strike that both sides depended upon for deterrence. That debate too has continued. In any case, in 1967, a dubious McNamara recommended a small ABM system ostensibly as a hedge against Chinese threats.

The McNamara ABM system never came into being. Instead, a combination of the weapons developments and surrounding political events led, in the early 1970s, to the first serious Soviet-American arms control negotiations (aside from the relatively insignificant atmospheric test ban treaty). These culminated in several treaties: SALT (for Strategic Arms Limitation Talks) I and II, and the ABM treaty, sometimes considered part of SALT I. The ABM treaty signed in 1972, along with a 1974 protocol, limited each side to a single ABM site; the Soviets built theirs to defend Moscow, and the United States built one to protect ICBM sites in the upper Midwest but soon abandoned it as being not very useful even though allowed.

The SALT I treaty was supposed to be an interim agreement, limiting offensive missile launchers and missiles on the way to a more comprehensive limitation on missiles and warheads. The latter was supposed to be encompassed in SALT II of 1974, which finessed the warhead issue by assuming a certain number on each missile with multiple warheads. The negotiators took several years to work out the details of SALT II after it had been agreed to in principle, and it was never ratified by the U.S. Senate for a number of reasons including the Soviet aggression in Afghanistan. It was, however, observed by Pres. Jimmy Carter's administration and by the Reagan administration until 1984, and probably by the Soviets as well, although that is not considered certain by all Western authorities.

1974–81: Concern over parity and instability. The period after the initial SALT agreements was not a happy one for Western strategists and for arms controllers. Many strategists believed that the Soviets, while probably staying within the letter of the agreements, used them as cover to build more missiles, at least more land-based missiles, than the United States, with more warheads, and much more megatonnage. By the end of the decade of the 1970s, the Soviets had clearly achieved strategic "parity," defined as the ability, equally with the United States, to retaliate after a first strike. This may have been the case before SALT, but SALT had at least accelerated the movement and inhibited the United States from trying to cope with it. Indeed, the more worried of these strategists felt that the United States was heading toward a "window of vulnerability," when the Soviets would have actual strategic superiority, throwing into doubt America's ability to retaliate.

These developments in turn led many in NATO Europe to worry about the viability of U.S. Type-II deterrence to guard them against Soviet attack. Their fears were reinforced by President Carter when, early in his term, he first convinced Europeans to embrace the enhanced radiation or "neutron" weapon, designed to kill soldiers without destroying territory, and then turned around and opposed it himself. As a result of their worries about the continued dependability of the U.S. deterrent, Western Europeans, led by West German chancellor Helmut Schmidt, embraced a proposal by NATO's Nuclear Planning Group to install an Intermediate-Range Nuclear Force (INF) of missiles to reach Soviet targets from Western Europe, partly as a response to the Soviet Union's force of similar range SS-20 missiles, and made it a political symbol of NATO coherence and will. In order to do this politically, they also tried to appease their own peace movements by offering to negotiate the INF against the Soviet SS-20s, a decision that would eventually become very important.

In partial contradiction to the American and European strategists' worries about the effects of parity, however, another American group believed that the period after the initial SALT agreements was one in which both sides failed to exploit opportunities to follow up and move toward more meaningful stabilization than was possible from the new but partial agreements. This group blamed, among other things, the U.S. extension of the counterforce doctrines beyond the reasonable bounds that had first been put into policy in the 1960s. A decade later, Schelling (1985) wrote retrospectively that "since 1972, the control of strategic nuclear weapons has made little or no progress. . . . Ten years ago, late in the Nixon administration, secretaries of defense began to pronounce a new doctrine for the selection of nuclear weapons. This doctrine entailed a more comprehensive target system than anything compatible with the McNamara Doctrine." By this time, McNamara was in agreement with Schelling's interpretation.

Schelling's reference to "secretaries of defense" was primarily to James Schlesinger, who did, in fact, imbue U.S. strategic plans with a wider variety of options—counterforce variations—than had been contemplated by McNamara, certainly in the later days of his tenure. Schlesinger's rhetoric seemed to imply even more change than he instilled—the change was a continuation in the same direction, perhaps an acceleration. Nonetheless, the "Schlesinger Doctrine" is generally counted as a milestone in the history of U.S. nuclear policy. It was not reversed by President Carter, whose nuclear policy was marked primarily by the beginning of several new responses to the onset of strategic parity: INF; the planned "Stealth" bomber, designed to penetrate to Soviet targets by escaping detection by enemy radar; and also MX, a large missile with multiple warheads, supposed to be dependent on mobility for its protection as a Type-I deterrent. The consequent controversy over where and how MX mobility should be implemented demonstrated at the time and later that such mobility raised political problems among Americans who lived in areas where the missile might be based.

1981–85: Reconstruction of U.S. nuclear forces. Pres. Ronald Reagan came to office in 1981 on the claim that Carter, his predecessor and his opponent in the 1980 election, had allowed U.S. defenses to deteriorate dangerously, allowing, for example, a "window of vulnerability." Reagan's platform stressed renewal of U.S. military power, with some stress on the nuclear aspects. He did, in fact, double the defense budget, and he also increased the strategic forces' share within this greater sum. The fleet of ballistic-missile-carrying nuclear submarines was updated and increased. This was noncontroversial because the untargetable nuclear-powered ballistic missile submarine (SSBN) was generally considered to be the mainstay of Type-I deterrence. More controversial, primarily on budgetary grounds, was the B-1 bomber, which had been turned down by Carter because it seemed unnecessary as a filler between the existing fleet of B-52s (to be augmented with cruise missiles) and the Stealth bomber that was being developed. Reagan reinstated the B-1.

The major controversies, however, involved strategies as well as budgets. The new administration dropped Carter's politically as well as militarily dubious MX mobility plan. But rather than immediately substituting an alternative scheme, the Reagan administration proposed putting the MX in hardened silos. This would give them some protection but less than they would have received with the kind of mobility contemplated by Carter, which would have made them untargetable. In the view of MX opponents, this turned the large missile with its multiple warheads into a dangerous Type-II weapon that was capable of doing great devastation if fired in a first strike, but also dangerous to retain as a Type-I retaliator because its relative lack of protection put a penalty on trying to hold it for a second strike. In 1983 President Reagan appointed retired U.S. Air Force general Brent Scowcroft as head of a bipartisan Commission on Strategic Forces. The Scowcroft Report endorsed the mobile version of MX and stressed the additional need for a smaller, highly mobile single-warhead missile, which could be relied upon for the retaliatory role. Congressional Democrats supported the small missile, known as Midgetman, as a pure Type-I weapon, but the Reagan administration never became enthusiastic about it, and as budgets became tighter toward the end of the administration, they proposed dropping Midgetman.

Even more controversial was President Reagan's Strategic Defense Initiative (SDI), which he proposed in March 1983. This was a research and development program to see if it might be feasible at some point in the near future to deploy an effective missile defense system. Essentially, the president was seeking a substitute for "the threat of instant U.S. retaliation to deter a Soviet attack," a system that "could intercept and destroy strategic ballistic missiles before they reached our soil or that of our allies." Other than the president and Caspar Weinberger, his first secretary of defense, few were willing to take the population-protecting version of SDI seriously. Rather, for most of the proponents both in and out of the administration, the primary focus of the SDI program was a system that would contribute to Type-I deterrence: sufficient protection for U.S. missiles to ensure they would be available to deliver a strong counterattack after an enemy first strike. The difficulty for opponents, however, was that an ABM system that could significantly dent a coordinated enemy first strike was *a fortiori* capable of defeating a ragged second strike, mounted after a U.S. first strike had hit the Soviet force. SDI could thus be viewed as a destabilizing Type-II system.

In addition, the opponents of SDI believed that the system would kill any chance of an arms control agreement with the Soviets, upon which they put great weight. In any case, as the Reagan administration ended, the combination of increasing budgetary pressures and increasing doubts about the technical feasibility of even the partial deterrent scheme, far short of the president's dream, seemed to be cutting SDI down to a hedge against accidental or third-party-caused war.

By that time, however, the role of arms control, and the attitude of the Reagan administration toward such control, had made a complete turnabout, a reversal that set the 1985 boundary between this period and the next one. From 1981 to 1985, the desire for a nuclear arms agreement had been a stated goal of the United States, but in the face of clear Soviet obduracy and manipulativeness, it was not a goal taken seriously. The Reagan administration put on the table an offer to commence Strategic Arms Reduction Talks (START, renamed from SALT), but little expectation existed for more than political symbolism. The Soviet Union refused to talk unless NATO first reversed the decision to install INF; NATO's offer to remove INF in return for removal of the Soviet SS-20s was made only in the full expectation of this Soviet refusal. Until 1985, President Reagan's dominant theme in regard to the Soviets was that they ruled an "evil empire."

1985–91: Arms control and reduction. In 1985, Mikhail Gorbachev came to power as general secretary of the Communist Party of the Soviet Union (CPSU). He soon made clear his intention to institute a broad and radical program of change within the USSR, centered on *perestroika,* internal economic and political restructuring, and *glasnost,* openness of discussion. The change apparently affected Soviet nuclear doctrine (see the discussion below of Soviet nuclear theory and policy); it clearly affected many aspects of Soviet international policy. Major shifts in the Soviet attitude toward nuclear arms agreements changed the feasibility of such agreements, bringing some into being; the Soviet shifts and the new possibilities reversed the Reagan administration's skepticism on arms control, although they had much less effect on unilateral U.S. nuclear doctrine.

In 1985, the Soviets agreed to recommence nuclear arms talks with the United States, without the precondition of INF removal. In November 1985, Reagan and Gorbachev came together in Geneva in the first summit meeting the president had had with any Soviet leader. The product was a friendly atmosphere and an agreement to keep the delegations talking and nothing more—at that time.

In November 1986, the two leaders came together again, in Reykjavík, Iceland, at a hasty summit meeting (which they nonetheless tried not to call a summit). This was a very unusual international event: Reagan arrived without having consulted U.S. allies and with very little consultation with his own staff. At various times during the two-day meeting, he apparently suggested cutting in half the strategic nuclear arsenals of the two superpowers, abolishing all nuclear missiles, and abolishing all nuclear weapons. None of these ideas came to immediate fruition, among other reasons because Gorbachev insisted upon the abandonment of SDI as a precondition; this was unacceptable to Reagan.

Soon after Reykjavík, the Western allies were surprised to find that the Soviets seemed willing to trade their SS-20s for NATO's INF. Not only did the Soviets accept the trade itself, but they even agreed to provisions for intrusive inspection and verification on the soil of the Soviet Union (and the United States) that had been completely unacceptable for the previous 40 years. As the details of the treaty were being worked out, the Western Europeans decided to make a virtue of necessity and came into line. In December 1987, Reagan and Gorbachev met again in Washington to sign the INF agreement and once more in Moscow in May 1988 to exchange ratifications.

In the meantime, negotiations went ahead on the even more radical agreement to cut nuclear arsenals in half. At one time it had been hoped that these would go quickly enough to arrive at general agreement in time for the May 1988 meeting, but because both sides realized that arms control negotiations had become serious, both the outlines and the details went more slowly.

When President Reagan left office in 1989, U.S. nuclear policy contained two quite different strands. One, going back to 1961, based Type-I and Type-II deterrence on confronting "the Soviet leadership with an unfavorable outcome in any contingency" and on "selective, discriminating, and controlled responses to the wide and varied nature of potential Soviet acts of aggression," to use the words of Secretary of Defense Frank Carlucci. The U.S. nuclear arsenal, with its wide range of nuclear munitions, remained consistent with this strategy. The other strand was the search for mutual stability through arms control agreements with the Soviet Union.

Soviet Union: Theory and Background

The Soviets traditionally separated deterrence concepts into two categories, with different words to describe them. *Ustrashnenie* is the Western concept, deterrence through threats of unacceptable damage in a retaliatory strike. It connotes "striking terror." *Sderzhivanie,* which connotes "holding at bay," is the Soviet concept, deterrence through threat of denying the enemy his military objectives. In the Soviet view, the opponent will most likely be deterred if he cannot calculate victory no matter what combination of forces he brings to bear. While criticizing the idea of striking terror, the Soviets concentrated on acquiring the military strength to hold their enemies at bay. Soviet criticism of Kahn, Brodie, and other Western theorists has been harsh. According to Soviet analyst A. Arbatov, "H. Kahn explained the aim of [Western] research [on deterrence] in the cynical manner peculiar to him: 'We want to make nuclear forces and nuclear war itself more rational, in order to make it more useful as an instrument of policy.'"

During the early years of the Strategic Arms Limitation Talks, the view was often heard in the U.S. community that the process could be used to educate the Soviets to Western concepts of nuclear deterrence. The notion was that the Soviets, out of their isolation and into the SALT negotiations, would acquiesce to the idea that deterrence is maintained through the threat of unacceptable damage in a retaliatory strike. In doing this, they would be leaving behind the nuclear warfighting strategy that had underpinned their own deterrence concept: deterrence maintained through threat of denying the enemy his military objectives.

Continued hope for the "civilizing" influence of the SALT process meant that the deployment of Soviet fourth-generation ICBMs in the 1970s came as a shock to many in the U.S. strategic community. The missiles seemed optimized not for assuring retaliation but for disarming the U.S. ground-based ICBM force. Deployed in fixed silos, the Soviet missiles with their multiple warheads were counterforce weapons with a high degree of accuracy. They appeared in sufficient numbers to suggest that the Soviets could strike and strike again at U.S. silos and launch facilities, guaranteeing kills by two- or three-on-one targeting ratios. The Soviets thus seemed far from acquiescing in assured retaliation in any of its variants.

U.S. policymakers and strategic thinkers alike drew a lesson from the deployment of the fourth-generation ICBMs: the Soviet Union had its own strategic culture that could not be easily influenced from outside. If this were the case, their logic continued, could the Soviet leaders be deterred by threat of unacceptable damage? Were they not uniquely suited by the nature of their forces to take advantage of a "window of vulnerability" in the 1980s, created by the preponderance of counterforce weapons in the Soviet strategic arsenal? Would the U.S. president really risk retaliating for the counterforce attack if his cities were so threatened?

Although this discussion oversimplifies the complex developments of the mid-1970s, it nevertheless provides the flavor of the profound impact that Soviet strategic modernization programs had in the United States and other allied countries. But even as their modernization programs continued, Soviet leaders were beginning publicly to question and then to deny the goal of victory in nuclear war. Tentatively begun during the Leonid Brezhnev regime, these public declarations grew to a flood under Gorbachev. They came from every sector of the Soviet leadership: Politburo members, authoritative political spokesmen, and the professional military.

In the beginning, it was unclear whether these statements had any link to the essence of Soviet nuclear policy. Were the Soviets changing their views about the utility of nuclear weapons as warfighting assets? Or, struck by the outcry against their counterforce weapons, were they simply engaging in public diplomacy to soften Western fears?

Following Gorbachev's rise to power in 1985, there were indicators that Soviet views about nuclear weapons might be undergoing—or have undergone—actual change. They included Soviet agreement to eliminate a major class of delivery systems in the INF treaty, agreement on a 50 percent reduction in strategic nuclear systems under START, and startling and explicit debates about the utility of offensive military forces overall.

The possibility thus emerges that the former Soviet Union had abandoned the goal of using nuclear weapons to achieve its national strategic objectives and, ultimately, victory in war. But are remaining nuclear forces now limited to an assured retaliation mission? Or is their mission somewhere between the extremes of assured destruction and nuclear warfighting?

This section reviews the roots of the U.S. perception that the Soviets saw nuclear weapons as a military asset of continuing utility, and then describes views on nuclear weapons that developed within the Soviet military beginning in the 1960s. Finally, it explores the links between these military views and the political leadership statements on nuclear weapons that have emerged since the mid-1970s. An analytical separation of this kind is supported by Soviet military theory, which divided Soviet military doctrine into two aspects, one sociopolitical and the other military-technical.

Evolution of Soviet Military Views on Nuclear Weapons

Despite the atomic explosions at Hiroshima and Nagasaki, Joseph Stalin refused to recognize the potential importance of nuclear weapons, forcing the Soviet military to ignore them. Although military theorists may have considered in private the utility of nuclear weapons, public discussions focused on Stalin's "permanently operating factors" in military affairs, an attempt to codify, even sanctify, the Soviet army's World War II experience.

Freed by Stalin's death in 1953, military theorists began to take up the issue of nuclear weapons. Within the decade, they had incorporated nuclear weapons into strategic concepts that had been the mainstay of Soviet military doctrine since World War II and even earlier. Nuclear weapons thus were grafted to a theory that was built on three constants:

- stress on deep operations, or operations on a strategic scale, whether defensive or offensive in nature;
- success in war through a combined-arms strategy; and
- achievement of strategic objectives that add up to total victory over the enemy.

By the late 1950s, however, the invention of ballistic missiles complicated this grafting process. Before nuclear missiles, it was assumed that a deep operation would be sequential and require weeks or even months. Nuclear missiles, however, could strike the enemy simultaneously through the entire depth of his territory, permitting the attacker to achieve his strategic objectives in hours or even minutes. By the early 1960s, Soviet military and political commentators were claiming that the Soviet Union would be able to use nuclear missiles "to rout the enemy on the very first day of the war." This shift to near-simultaneous achievement of objectives was hailed as the most significant contribution of nuclear firepower.

In a speech to the Supreme Soviet in January 1960, Nikita Khrushchev proposed that nuclear missiles should be the main element in modern war, since the traditional branches of the armed forces were becoming obsolete. He also asserted that though the Soviet Union might be struck first with nuclear weapons, it could always survive and retaliate. Khrushchev's stress on assured retaliation, however, failed to gain acceptance in the Soviet military. Instead, professional military strategists grappled with the problem of determining exactly how strategic nuclear missiles could be integrated with military forces—conventional and nuclear—meant for theater roles. The basic question that confronted Soviet theorists was whether or not the Soviet Union's strategic objectives could be achieved by missile strikes alone, without a defeat of the enemy in ground warfare. The first two editions of Marshal Sokolovskiy's *Military Strategy*, the most complete statement of Soviet military theory to emerge in the 1960s, heavily favored the missile-only school.

But as might be expected, this enthusiasm for nuclear missiles roused the opposition of many who had made their careers in the tank forces. Chief among them was Marshal Rotmistrov, a hero of World War II, who was an eloquent critic of the missile-only school. In 1964 he wrote: "It should be remembered that . . . a scornful attitude toward old types of forces or toward the old weapons is not only impermissible, but even harmful, especially within the framework of tactical operations, where the need for 'old' weapons will continue for a significant time."

As the debate progressed, both schools of thought moderated their stands, eventually achieving a consensus that, although the strategic missile forces were the main and most decisive branch of the armed forces, other types of forces would continue to play an important role in strategy. This consensus was more or less in place as attention began to shift again to conventional weapons and the potential for a long theater campaign.

Re-emphasis of Conventional Warfare

By the mid-1960s, the Soviet military was reassessing the utility of nuclear weapons. Among the reasons for this development was a growing perception that neither side could mount a credible first-strike threat. Another reason was growing skepticism that damage limitation measures would be effective, resulting in the conclusion that it was too risky "to make an easy decision on the immediate employment of nuclear weapons from the very beginning of a war without having used all other means to attain its objectives" (Ivanov 1969).

Most significant for the combined-arms strategy was the growing view that, far from expediting theater operations, rapid and decisive use of nuclear weapons would actually hinder them. Military theorists noted that nuclear strikes would prevent formations from moving into areas for strike exploitation. They would also wreck combat capabilities and disrupt command and control, forcing units to spend time not only decontaminating but also waiting for reductions in radiation. By 1967, at least one military writer had concluded that, "for the side that has achieved the necessary results and is successfully developing the offensive, it will be advantageous to delay the beginning of the use of nuclear weapons as long as possible."

Thus, the trends that were impelling NATO toward a strategy of flexible response were having a similar effect on the Warsaw Pact, at least with regard to the conclusion that there was a greater likelihood of a long conventional campaign preceding any nuclear escalation. At that point, however, the two alliances parted company. While NATO pursued its limited nuclear options under the strategy of flexible response, the Eastern bloc sought to perfect its combined-arms strategy with or without the use of nuclear weapons.

Although they began to state a preference for conventional weapons, the Soviets did not believe they could automatically avoid escalation. Theoretical writings from the late 1960s and 1970s thus continued to be peppered with assertions that nuclear weapons, should they be used, would call forth decisive action—that is, inevitable escalation to a general nuclear war. The writings let it be known that Soviet nuclear use in these circumstances would be governed by standard military principles involving surprise; seizing the initiative; and deep strikes against an unlimited range of targets, including command and control and reserve assets. In other words, the use of nuclear weapons had become part of strategic operations in depth. To the extent that nuclear weapons would permit the Soviet armed forces simultaneously to achieve their objectives, they would be used decisively to do so.

But several factors eventually changed this assessment. First among them was the evolution of strategic nuclear parity. Officially recognized with the signing of the SALT I accords, parity spawned gleeful assessments by Soviet military and political spokesmen that the "correlation of forces" was swinging decisively in favor of the Soviet Union and its allies. On this basis, the Soviets felt they had reached superpower status equivalent to that of the United States, and should therefore be permitted to exercise their influence among developing nations. To their chagrin, they found that nuclear parity confers no particular advantage in the Third World.

Second was the emergence of high-technology conventional weapons. A group gathered around Chief of the General Staff Nikolay Ogarkov began increasingly to argue that these weapons were accurate, powerful, and long-range enough to be considered "comparable to nuclear weapons" on the battlefield, and even against deep targets at strategic range. In 1984, Ogarkov argued that improvements in guidance and conventional warhead technologies, when combined with new reconnaissance systems, would make these weapons "global in nature" and effective in a wide range of missions.

Finally, in the late 1970s and early 1980s the Soviet military first faced up to pressure on the defense budget caused by the economic stagnation of the later Brezhnev years. The Strategic Rocket Forces did experience a slowdown in procurement through this period, which may, however, have represented the natural close of the fourth-generation deployment program rather than a real procurement drop. In any case, this budget pressure forced the Soviet military to grapple with the expense of their warfighting strategy. Nuclear weapons are not as expensive to procure as are the means to make them warfighting assets: hardened and redundant command and control networks, for example, and reconstitution capabilities. Recognition that the resources to acquire these "warfighting assets" would not be available further fed the realization, growing since the 1960s, that the nuclear environment was challenging or even impossible to fight in.

These factors, among others, combined to produce the conclusion that nuclear escalation was becoming less and less likely in a conflict between the superpowers. The Soviet military's move away from a belief in inevitable nuclear escalation was probably the major development in the military-technical aspect of Soviet doctrine since the advent of nuclear missiles. In essence, by the mid-1980s, the Soviets seemed to have perceived that the nuclear threshold was high enough that they could seize the initiative in a theater war and successfully carry out a conventional offensive, as long as they were quick. If they were not, then the decisiveness of the initial period of war would be lost and the enemy would either stalemate the battle or escalate it.

Thus, the Soviet military approached the end of the 1980s with a consensus that the nuclear threshold was higher and that conventional warfare, even against long-range "strategic" targets, represented the most likely course of an East-West conflict. Although the Soviets did not openly discuss strategic conventional attacks on the United States, they clearly expected such attacks on Soviet territory as an outcome of U.S. strategies. Conventional attacks of this kind were consistent with Soviet general discussions of the extent of continental theaters of military operations. Like the earlier nuclear war, this conventional war was "global in nature."

Military and Political Interactions on Doctrinal Issues

The military was not alone in its attempts to address the changing strategic scene. As in the early 1960s, a parallel discussion of doctrinal issues went on in political leadership circles in the 1980s. Proceeding from the same issues—the implications of parity, technological change, budget pressures—the civilians were attempting to reorder internal and external perceptions of Soviet national policy on nuclear war.

The opening shot in this campaign was Brezhnev's 1977 speech at Tula, where he argued that nuclear war was suicidal and pledged the Soviet Union to "no first use" of nuclear weapons. The campaign expanded in scope afterward, and the Soviets ultimately rejected the concept of victory in nuclear war. In the Gorbachev era, participants in this campaign went on to address conventional warfare. By the late 1980s, some civilian analysts claimed that the Soviet Union's defensive military strategy meant just that: the armed forces should be configured so that they are incapable of launching an offensive in response to aggression; both NATO and the Warsaw Pact should be unambiguously deployed in a defensive mode.

The response of the professional military was not uniformly enthusiastic. In the words of one officer: "Your 'new thinking' is fine for international consumption, but don't infect our troops with it" (Oberdorfer 1987). Many Western observers agreed with this officer's conclusion that the civilian initiatives were for show, with little bearing on how the military thinks about fighting wars. They pointed to military statements agreeing with the no-victory line or proclaiming the defensive nature of Soviet military strategy as somewhat cynical efforts at public diplomacy.

But the assessment that the military's participation in the debate was wholly cynical oversimplified both the military's position and its relationship with the civilian leadership on these issues. The parallel paths that the two groups followed since the 1970s led them toward similar skepticism regarding the military utility of nuclear weapons. When a military leader said that there can be no victors in nuclear war, he was probably reflecting a real conviction that the destructive potential of the superpower nuclear arsenals was enough to remove the possibility that he could achieve one of his key strategic objectives: preservation of the Soviet state. The central question for him was whether nuclear escalation, once it occurs, need inevitably continue to its ultimate level, intercontinental exchanges between the U.S. and Soviet homelands.

Through the 1980s, Soviet leadership statements on this point, military and political, remained unequivocal. Nuclear escalation, should it occur, would rapidly proceed to its ultimate level. The inevitability of escalation had been removed but not the inevitability of its course once nuclear use occurred. To Western observers, naturally enough, these assertions appeared to place continued emphasis on seizing the initiative, a long-standing hallmark of Soviet nuclear warfighting strategy.

Soviet policy statements thus hindered efforts to discover whether the old nuclear strategy simply remained intact on the far side of a higher nuclear threshold. As Secretary of Defense Carlucci pointed out in 1988 to students at the Soviet General Staff Academy, the Soviets' emphasis on no first use of nuclear weapons was not consistent with their continuing modernization of fixed, land-based ballistic missiles such as the SS-18 ICBM. These missiles, Carlucci maintained, "are best suited for a first strike against U.S. silo-based systems, a capability more compatible with a military doctrine that emphasizes pre-emptive nuclear strikes."

Clearly, the Soviet military had abandoned neither nuclear weapons nor planning for the possibility of nuclear war. If war were to come, the professional soldiers would presumably have a range of nuclear options to present to the political leadership. Among those options would be a pre-emptive attack if the Soviets received clear strategic warning of an enemy launch decision, and another would be to launch on warning if the Soviets received clear tactical warning that an enemy attack was under way.

These options would represent prudent planning should warning be sufficient to exploit them, but for the Soviet military, loss of sufficient warning was one of the main products of the swing toward conventional warfare in the depth of the theater. They expected strategic targets such as airfields, command and control points, and radar sites would come under attack while the war remained conventional. Some of the weapon systems carrying out these attacks—aircraft, cruise missiles—might be armed with either nuclear or conventional weapons. According to the Soviets, this dual capability was one factor that reduced the probability of receipt of warning, for it would muddy the transition between conventional and nuclear war. Another factor was the destruction by conventional weapons of warning assets such as radars and communication networks.

The effect of these developments on Soviet nuclear options seems to have been that the military would plan for the worst case—denial of warning—as if it were the most likely. Instead of a clean launch on warning, for example, they would consider what assets would be available if warning were so ambiguous that the enemy would be able to strike Soviet ICBMs before they could be launched. ICBM launch under attack would thus be an option; so would retaliation with other weapons such as sea-launched ballistic missiles. Given the extreme uncertainties, probably the best options would involve those in which the components of the Soviet nuclear arsenal could act in concert, each force capable of continuing even if the others were brought to a halt, temporary or permanent.

Thus, the focus shifted to conventional weapons, but the pre-emptive options that were the hallmarks of nuclear warfighting remained in existence. For the Soviet military, however, these options became less realistic as conventional warfare lengthened and blurred the transition to the nuclear phase, removing opportunities to receive unambiguous warning.

The Final Legacy of the Soviet Union

The main implication of this development is that Soviet strategic nuclear forces seem to have been decoupled in an important sense from the combined-arms strategy. Because of deep uncertainties about the availability of any particular element of the force at a particular point in the war—especially the point of escalation—the elements would have been seen as an integrated asset, with stress on employment flexibility and the ability of the elements to compensate for the loss of one or more of the other elements.

Indeed, the redundancy, survivability, and sustainability of that force would have been more than sufficient for the Soviet High Command to be confident that it could designate and even redesignate elements to strike particular target sets in a retaliatory attack. Although it is impossible to know the contents of those target sets, the Soviet nuclear arsenal remained large enough that it need not have been limited to a small number of targets. Moreover, nothing the Soviet military said indicated an interest in placing restraints on targeting. In short, the Soviet military adopted an "assured destruction" concept which to them meant counterforce targeting and countermilitary targeting. In contrast, as of the late 1980s, Soviet civilian analysts for the first time indicated an interest in restraining targeting against critical command and control nodes, in order to permit intrawar bargaining.

Elements of the old and the new thus seemed to coexist in this Soviet nuclear strategy. Military and political leaders alike were confronted with a great deal of change, and their attempts to deal with it produced ambiguities and inconsistencies in their theory. The change was mostly the product of an evolving emphasis on conventional warfare, especially as triggered by parity and new technologies. Other triggers, like the increasingly radical reductions in strategic nuclear weapons, were likely in their turn to produce even more ambiguities, which would have to have been resolved over time. The most significant of these would have involved the possibility that restraints on targeting would become an explicit part of Soviet nuclear strategy.

But doctrinal consistency as Westerners view it was never a Soviet long suit. That the Soviets' concept of assured destruction differed from the West's in no way compromised it in their eyes. Both military men and civilians would probably have argued that their conviction on these three points was clear:

- The Soviet Union would have tried to end a war while fighting remained at the conventional level.
- If nuclear escalation occurred, it would inevitably continue until massive devastation obliterated the Soviet Union, the United States, their allies, and perhaps the other countries of the world.
- National strategic objectives were irrelevant in this latter case, and victory in nuclear war was impossible.

These different views about the outcome of conventional versus nuclear war created a paradox in Soviet military doctrine. Conventional war could be fought and won through decisive military action. That same decisiveness on the nuclear side, by contrast, produced conflagration, not victory. But regardless of this outcome, the military was not relieved of a requirement to act decisively should nuclear escalation occur. Thus, while the Soviets had a means and method of war termination at the conventional level, they had none (short of their own destruction) at the nuclear. This is one reason for the sharp military reaction to civilian proposals regarding "nonprovocative defense": military men feared that removing the offensive from Soviet strategy would also remove the sole Soviet method of war termination.

The Soviets could have eased this contradiction by implementing restraints on targeting or introducing the possibility of intrawar bargaining into their doctrinal discourse on nuclear war. Some civilian analysts suggested that strategic command and control targets should be exempted from attack, but this theme was not widely adopted, either by the military or civilian leadership. That they did not do so is doubtless a result of the fact that rapid, decisive escalation—seizing the initiative—is a long-standing pillar of Soviet deterrence theory. In effect, the Soviets continued to behave as if the threat to deny military objectives (*sderzhivanie*) were their operative nuclear deterrence concept.

Future developments such as the agreed radical reductions in nuclear weapons would have tended to change this behavior. For example, deep reductions beyond the START levels, once implemented, would in the end have forced limits on targeting. Thus, the arms control process might have brought the Soviets to accept, de facto, deterrence by threat of unacceptable retaliation (*ustrashnenie*).

Conclusion

This article has shown how nuclear theory and policy have evolved over almost 50 years in response to changes in international politics, technology, and arms control agreements. The world stands poised on the edge of a new era that promises major reductions in the military forces, nuclear and conventional, of the United States and of the newly independent states of the former Soviet Union. Major arms control agreements will likely be ratified and implemented by the governments of the United States and those new republics. These agreements and the reduction of tension between the former superpowers suggests a future world much less threatened by a nuclear holocaust initiated by one of the former protagonists. On the other hand, many serious issues remain to be resolved among the fifteen separate governments of the former USSR; one of the most important is the denuclearization of Ukraine, Belarus, and Kazakhstan. Moreover, nuclear weapons and ballistic missile technology are proliferating throughout the world. Terrorists with weapons of mass destruction and regional conflicts between smaller nuclear-armed powers may become major threats to the world's security and well being. An important issue for the future will be how to use non-nuclear means to prevent nuclear proliferation.

The spread of these dangerous technologies may provide a major incentive for the United States and the former Soviet republics to shift some emphasis in their strategic programs from offensive systems to defensive systems in an effort to ensure protection of their homelands and provide coverage for expeditionary forces that might be deployed to trouble spots in developing nations. All of this suggests that, as the former adversaries move toward a new plateau of accord and stability, potential problem areas within the former USSR and military developments in other areas of the world will remain and nuclear policy and theory will need to be reexamined and restructured. This redefined nuclear theory and policy will inevitably flow out of, but depart from, the intellectual constructs developed since World War II.

ROBERT A. LEVINE
ROSE E. GOTTEMOELLER

SEE ALSO: Arms Control and Disarmament; Deterrence; Escalation; Flexible Response; NATO Policy and Strategy; Nuclear Employment Policy and Planning; Strategic Defense Initiative: Policy Implications; Strategic Stability.

Bibliography

Allison, G., A. Carnesale, and J. S. Nye, Jr. 1985. *Hawks, doves, and owls.* New York: W. W. Norton.

Ball, D. 1981. *Can nuclear war be controlled?* Adelphi Paper No. 169. London: International Institute for Strategic Studies.

Bundy, M., G. Kennan, R. McNamara, and G. Smith. 1982. Nuclear weapons and the Atlantic Alliance. *Foreign Affairs,* spring.

———. 1984. The president's choice: Star wars or arms control. *Foreign Affairs,* winter.

Carlucci, F. M. 1988. *Annual report to the Congress,* pp. 53–55. Washington, D.C.: Government Printing Office.

Discriminate deterrence: Report of the commission on integrated long-term strategy. 1988. Washington, D.C.: Government Printing Office. January.

Freedman, L. 1981. *The evolution of nuclear strategy.* New York: St. Martin's Press.

Garthoff, R. 1962. *Soviet strategy in the nuclear age.* Rev. ed. New York: Praeger.

Gray, C. 1979. Nuclear strategy: The case for a theory of victory. *International Security,* summer.

Holst, J. J. 1986. Denial and punishment: Straddling the horns of NATO's dilemma. *Power and policy: Doctrine, the alliance and arms control, Part II.* Adelphi Paper No. 206 (spring). London: International Institute for Strategic Studies.

Howard, M. 1981. On fighting a nuclear war. *International Security,* spring.

Ikle, F. 1973. Can nuclear deterrence last out the century? *Foreign Affairs,* January.

Ivanov, S. 1969. Soviet military doctrine and strategy. *Military Thought* 5:28.

Kahn, H. 1960. *On thermonuclear war.* Princeton, N.J.: Princeton Univ. Press.

Kaufmann, W. 1964. *The McNamara strategy.* New York: Harper and Row.

Kissinger, H. A. 1957. *Nuclear weapons and foreign policy.* New York: Harper and Row.

Nitze, P. 1985. The objectives of arms control. *Current Policy,* no. 677. Washington, D.C.: Department of State, Bureau of Public Affairs.

Nye, J. 1986. *Nuclear ethics.* New York: Free Press.

Oberdorfer, D. 1987. With reform in the air, can it really be Moscow? *Washington Post,* April 26, p. D1.

Schelling, T. C. 1960. *The strategy of conflict.* Cambridge, Mass.: Harvard Univ. Press.

Schelling, T. C., and M. Halperin. 1961; 1985. *Strategy and arms control.* Elmsford, N.Y.: Pergamon Press.

Weinberger, C. 1985. *Annual report to Congress, fiscal year 1986.* Washington, D.C.: Department of Defense.

Wohlstetter, A. 1959. The delicate balance of terror. *Foreign Affairs,* January.

Wolfe, T. W. 1965. *Soviet strategy at the crossroads.* Cambridge, Mass.: Harvard Univ. Press.

OCEANIA

No agreed-upon boundaries delimit the South and Southwest Pacific subregion, or Oceania. Despite varied usage, Oceania primarily refers to most of the thousands of islands in the Pacific Ocean, but not to the shore nations of its surrounding continents, or to the Japanese islands. Oceania includes the ethno-linguistic areas of Polynesia (including New Zealand), Micronesia, and Melanesia, plus Australia. In this encyclopedia, Oceania does not include the insular countries of the Indonesian cultural area.

The broader term *Pacific Rim* refers primarily to the larger shoreline nations such as the United States, Canada, USSR, China, Korea, and the island Empire of Japan. Another popular term, the *Pacific Basin*, encompasses much of Oceania plus the Pacific Rim.

Geography

Oceania, however delimited, is distinguished by being the world's largest subregion, covering an area greater than the entire land surface of the earth. It also has the world's smallest population for a subregional area. And it includes the world's largest island, Australia, and is the major part of the world's largest biological province, the Indo-Pacific area.

The Pacific Ocean, which surrounds and links thousands of islands, many uninhabited, is a vast water mass with a complex undersea topography and the related complexities of its currents. The islands range in size and type from small islets on submerged coral reefs to very high, mountainous islands with bays and lagoons, themselves surrounded by reefs. Many of the islands are strung out in archipelagos. Weather and climate in the Pacific are extremely variable; they range from areas that experience tropical hurricanes and monsoonal rainy seasons to arid areas that suffer long periods of drought. The sheer size of the Pacific Ocean, the complexity of its currents and weather patterns, plus the large distances between islands and island groups make navigation and the movement of goods and people both difficult and time consuming.

Historical Aspects

Scholars trace human presence among the Indonesian islands back some 40,000 years to early hunter-gatherers who crossed the open waters between Australia and New Guinea. From there man slowly migrated among island groups and isolated islands in all directions. The most notable voyagers were Austronesians, some of whom reached island areas in both Oceania and in the Indian Ocean, from Madagascar off the coast of Africa, to Taiwan (Republic of China) off the coast of China, to the shores of Vietnam on the Indo-Chinese Peninsula, and out across the Pacific to such diverse places as Hawaii in the North Pacific, New Zealand and the Chatham Islands in the South Pacific, and (the most remote of all) Easter Island in the far Eastern Pacific. The Austronesians sailed large twin-hulled voyaging ships and used careful navigational techniques to find their way long before comparably sized ships and techniques were used by Europeans for their voyages of global exploration.

This long period of exploration and settlement by Austronesians was followed by a much more rapid and publicized period of European exploration and colonization from the fifteenth through the nineteenth centuries. By the time Dutch, Spanish, Portuguese, and English vessels were exploring and exploiting the islands of Oceania, resident Austronesian populations had been through one or more cycles of efflorescence and then decline. As in other parts of the globe, the first European explorers and adventurers were rapidly followed by missionaries, traders, planters, slavers, and soldiers, which led to foreign rule over most of the island clusters of Oceania and decimation of the native population by newly introduced diseases—from the common cold to smallpox and syphilis.

World Wars I and II brought to the Pacific significant military actions between continental and island empire powers, which led to some physical destruction and to increasingly rapid cultural change. This has been followed by various degrees of local independence and sociocultural freedom among many island groups. Although some colonialism still exists in various guises, most Pacific population groups are now experimenting with various forms of self-government. There also are notable experiments in revolutionary development that in some cases veer away from democracy, as in the 1980s coup on Fiji and counterrevolutionary activity on New Caledonia.

Cultural Implications

The European rediscovery and subsequent exploitation of Oceania have had more socio-psychological and cultural impacts on the home countries of European discoverers than economic impact (rather different than that of the larger Pacific Rim nations), even though various individual entrepreneurs from the larger countries have done well for themselves in the islands. In particular, early reports of French and British explorers of the Pacific excited philosophers and artists alike and then affected a much larger popular audience in Europe than had earlier explorations because of the propagation of books through better and cheaper printing capabilities. Libraries and private homes have felt the impact of widespread Western interest in Oceanic art forms, as well as the products of European artists who were stimulated by the colors of the Pacific, from Gauguin and Matisse to Biddle and Leetag. There is a vast literature on the pleasures of travel and life in the Pacific islands dating back to the accounts of explorers from Captain Cook's time to the accounts of Nordhoff and Hall, and today's books by Michener and Heyerdal. Now a major and widening role as vacation playgrounds for tourists of the world is emerging throughout the Pacific, with considerable economic implications for all concerned.

Economic Aspects

Prime resources of the Pacific are implicit in the name Oceania: impelled by newly passed Law of the Sea international agreements, which have magnified the legally owned resources of all island territories, these oceanic areas offer possession of fishing rights, transit control, underwater mineral beds, and offshore oil resources to most Oceania entities—regardless of political status. In some cases, such as Nauru, immediate island resource returns have been fabulous. In others, such as the Tokelaus, returns are barely perceptible. As with the countries of South Central Asia, the Indian Ocean, and Southeast Asia, much of Oceania's economic potential will depend on how the island-states handle their population growth and on the manner in which they exploit their newly found ocean resource control rights.

The land resources of the island-states are finite and predictable, and are related to the size of the land area. For example, the resources of small sea-washed atolls with only a few islets to live and to grow coconuts on are very dissimilar from the resources of high mineral-rich islands that have crop and pasture land and spectacular landscapes to draw tourists. Much of the mass-tourist potential will continue to be tied to air travel routes and ease of accessibility to the islands.

Future economic issues will relate to the degree of dependence (economic and political) of the islands on their one-time colonial rulers and exploiters, as well as on other means of raising investment capital. Some of the smaller and more remote island clusters have few potential local resources on which to base modern lifestyles, in contrast to larger island groups with complex sets of resources. (Compare, for example, the Micronesian islands of Kiribati to the Society Islands and Tahiti of French Polynesia). How long French, New Zealand, and U.S. taxpayers will be willing to continue subsidies for modern life patterns of Pacific islanders living on tiny atolls, which never can have a locally derived income to support those lifestyles, is becoming an increasingly significant issue.

Political Matters

Some issues of island political-economic status continue to relate to the quasi-colonial status of such externally controlled island territories as French Polynesia, New Caledonia, and Wallis-Futuna. Their status contrasts to that of former British colonies, such as Fiji, or the currently benign "free-association" (dependent) status of former New Zealand–controlled Niue, Western Samoa, and the Cook Islands. Virtually all these island groups have, or have had, separatist or other forms of independence movements. France has been the most reluctant European power to release its colonies, and today is faced with increasingly difficult situations in its purported "Metropolitan" island territories. On the other hand, Great Britain, which released its colonies soon after World War II, now is faced with counter-democratic revolutionary activity in freed territories (most notably in Fiji). New Zealand's award of internal freedom to its former island territories has been achieved at the cost of a continuing large economic drain, as democratized island states (notably the Cook Islands) have developed the trappings of independent government and party politics, but remain basically dependent upon their sponsoring power for economic support of their contemporary life-style. And Australia, like Great Britain a sponsor of early independence for Papua-New Guinea, must stand by and watch the reported deterioration into "savagery" of its seemingly democratic ex-territory.

Military Aspects

Despite romanticization of the South Seas peoples by their Western discoverers and subsequent authors and cinema makers, most of the island communities, whether Polynesian, Micronesian, or Melanesian, were indeed warlike. People who preferred combat with clubs rather than bows and arrows (as in Polynesia), or who even today may take heads, eat human flesh, or find ways to dispatch members of rival tribes to satisfy vengeance requirements that their deceased ancestors and relatives might rest easily (as in Melanesia), have left some heritage of potential violence in the islands. This potential for savage violence exists despite reported chivalrous conduct by the islanders toward their European enemies in the nineteenth-century conflicts with colonial powers in New Zealand, Tahiti, and Hawaii. Whether that heritage of violence will be exercised in seeking greater independence, or in realizing the settlement of growing internal differences among islanders, remains to be seen.

With the current global trend toward diffusion of increasingly sophisticated weapons, the education of young islanders abroad, and a press toward democratic activism, it is possible that various forms of violence will continue to spread in the Pacific Islands. In addition to the problems created by ethnic differences in Fiji, New Caledonia, French Polynesia, Australia, and New Zealand, economic issues will also impact on how smaller countries without significant capital resources can organize and equip forces to patrol and to secure their vastly increased present territorial water rights.

Nuclear Weapons

There now is in existence a South Pacific Nuclear Free Zone Treaty (1985) (unlike the situation in South Central Asia and the Indian Ocean). Despite protests by foreign activists and local opposition groups, however, France has continued to test nuclear weapons in the South Pacific (albeit underground), and the United States and USSR have continued to test delivery systems for intercontinental nuclear weapons in the North Pacific. Various Pacific island nations and Australia have protested the South Pacific French nuclear tests to no avail. (Protests against launches of missile delivery systems into the North Pacific by the United States and Soviet Union have been fewer and less strong.) More particularly, New Zealand has denied U.S. naval ships the right to visit its ports because of the U.S. "neither confirm nor deny" policy as to nuclear weapons on their naval vessels. This has in effect, but not formally, broken the ANZUS Treaty unity, a situation that remains unresolved.

Future

With the disintegration of the Soviet Union, the future problems of Oceania appear to be involved more with internal affairs than international conflict. Relations between newly independent Pacific states and their former colonial administrators—other than France—appear to be more a matter of the degree of support that the larger powers will provide rather than the use of military force or colonial repression by the larger powers. Development of greater economic self-sufficiency and better means of internal democratic interaction seem to be the foremost issues that confront the nation-states of Oceania.

Subsidiary to the political matters, but of significant economic and quality-of-life concern, are such issues as U.S. offers to dump trash from the West Coast into certain lagoons of Pacific islands in return for purported local ecological benefits and cash payments. Such issues will add to the other economic and cultural problems such as the islanders' attempts to deal with the results of urbanism in their capital cities, overpopulation, local means of debris disposal, invading plants, alcohol and drug control, and other aspects of life in the latter part of the twentieth century.

For the most recent information on this region, the reader may refer to the following annual publications:

The Military Balance. International Institute for Strategic Studies. London: Brassey's (UK).

The Statesman's Year-Book. New York: St. Martin's Press.

The World Factbook. Central Intelligence Agency. Washington, D.C.: Brassey's (US).

DONALD S. MARSHALL

SEE ALSO: Indo-Pacific Area; South and Southeast Asia.

Bibliography

Bellwood, P. S. 1978. *Man's conquest of the Pacific*. New York: Oxford University Press.
Camilleri, J. A. 1987. *The Australia, New Zealand, US alliance: Regional security in the nuclear age*. Boulder, Colo.: Westview Press.
Campbell, I. C. 1990. *A history of the Pacific islands*. Berkeley, Calif.: Univ. of California Press.
Central Intelligence Agency. 1989. *World fact book 1989*. Washington, D.C.: Government Printing Office.
Crocombe, R. 1987. *The South Pacific—An introduction*. 4th rev. ed. Auckland, N.Z.: Longman Paul.
Morley, J. W., ed. 1986. *The Pacific basin: New challenges for the United States*. New York: Academy of Political Science.
Terrell, J. 1988. *Prehistory in the Pacific islands*. Cambridge, U.K.: Cambridge Univ. Press.

OCEANOGRAPHY, MILITARY

The oceans, covering 70 percent of the earth's surface, are the boundary separating continents and the barrier between many nations. The oceans also serve as the highways of trade among the continents and sea-based nations. Effective use of the oceans has enabled nations to influence events far beyond their borders and, more often than not, has been a key factor in determining the outcome of major power struggles.

Oceanography is the universal science of all the disciplines that encompass knowledge of the sea. The physical sciences of oceanography, such as hydrography, maritime meteorology, and physical oceanography, examine the structure and properties of nonliving features of the ocean environment. The life (or biological) sciences of oceanography examine living organisms and the interaction between the species and their ocean environment.

Oceanographic Disciplines of Naval Concern

For navies, the most significant of the physical sciences of the marine environment are oceanography; meteorology; mapping, charting, and geodesy (MC&G); and, to a lesser extent, astrometry and precise time and time interval (PTTI).

Oceanography

Oceanography is the exploration, scientific study, measurement, and prediction of the ocean and its phenomena. Oceanographic study encompasses physical oceanography (waves and surf, tides, currents, physical properties such as pressure, temperature, and salinity); chemistry (seawater, marine sediments, organisms); geology (bottom features, composition); and marine biology (fouling, biomedicine, bioluminescence, echoes, noise, false targets, and sound scattering). Sea ice features and properties (distribution, concentration, and thickness) are of concern to both the defense and commercial communities. Additionally, an extension of classical engineering (mechanical, electrical, structural) and diving, underwater construction, and submersibles are studied within the topic of ocean engineering.

Underwater acoustics is a central focus of oceanography for naval warfare because of its significant impact on surface ship, submarine sensors and weapon systems. Underwater sound is affected by many geological, physical, chemical, and biological factors. Oceanographic acoustic properties include propagation, absorption, reflection, reverberation, ambient noise, refraction (sound channels), and spreading—all of which have an effect on active and passive ranges of sonar equipment.

Meteorology

Meteorology, the science dealing with the physics and dynamics of the atmosphere and its impact on the ocean and vice versa, results in environmental observation and prediction services to support naval forces around the globe. Weather phenomena of direct concern to aviation and naval operations are pressure, temperature, humidity, clouds, wind, precipitation, and impediments or enhancements to visibility and electromagnetic propagation. The impacts can be measured and accommodated in many ways. For example, forecasts of high seas or winds may force ships or aircraft to be rerouted; high seas may diminish radar and sonar performance so that search rates are greatly reduced and search plans must be changed accordingly.

Mapping, Charting, and Geodesy

Mapping, charting, and geodesy (MC&G) employs the collection, transformation, analysis, and storage of geodetic, hydrographic, cultural, and toponymic data. Surveys in this discipline measure water depth, establish precise geodetic position, measure variations in the earth's magnetic field, determine gravity anomalies, and define the shape and texture of the seafloor. These surveys are necessary for the safe and efficient navigation of ships and submarines, aeronautical and land navigation, and the positioning, targeting, and navigating of weapon systems. Also included in MC&G is the evaluation of topographic, hydrographic, and aeronautical features for their effect on military operations or intelligence. Surveys are also used for amphibious, strike, antisubmarine, mine warfare, and logistic support missions.

Astrometry and Precise Time and Time Interval

Astrometry is a program for determining the fundamental position of the sun, moon, planets, and certain stars. The positions of these celestial bodies play an essential role in determining the positions of fixed and movable objects on the surface of the earth and in space. Geodetic position is required for navigation of ships and aircraft.

Precise time and time interval provide the precise measurement of time required for accurate navigation and communications. Various facilities throughout the world often provide accurate time services to ships and aircraft on, under, and above the world's oceans.

Oceanographic Platforms and Ocean Observation Systems

Tactical and strategic advantage accrues to the naval forces that have accurate knowledge of the changing physical characteristics of the ocean and its marine and terrestrial environment. For these and numerous other reasons, collection of data for study of the ocean environment is being accomplished by increasingly sophisticated instruments from many different types of platforms.

Some of the historical methods for studying the ocean depths are still used today, including the Nansen bottle (developed by the Norwegian explorer Fridtjof Nansen) to collect seawater at different depths as well as nets and dredges to collect specimens in the water column and on the seafloor. Sonic transmitters return echoes showing characteristics of the bottom, and more powerful units can sonically indicate the structure of earth layers below the seafloor. Coring devices or deep-ocean drilling units can bring up small or large samples of the earth below the sea, the study of which provides primary evidence of the earth's climatological and geological history. Elaborate underwater cameras can be towed behind oceanographic ships to inspect the seafloor.

Oceanographic Ships and Aircraft

The former USSR maintained the world's largest oceanographic fleet, with more than 200 ships performing oceanographic-related surveys. Russia and Ukraine continue to operate a substantial portion of this fleet, but the total effort will be reduced and most likely will be concentrated in their littoral waters.

Numerous aircraft also contribute to the Russian program. The former head of the Soviet navy, Admiral Gorshkov, has been quoted as saying that, given two equal navies, the side with superior knowledge of oceanography will be the victor.

The oceanographic and hydrographic fleet of the United States includes 11 vessels currently operated for the Naval

Oceanographic Office (NAVOCEANO), 23 vessels maintained and operated by the National Oceanic and Atmospheric Administration (NOAA), and approximately 25 ships actively employed in the academic fleet coordinated by the University National Oceanographic Laboratory System (UNOLS).

Other countries with notable oceanographic and hydrographic fleet resources include Canada, China, France, Great Britain, and Japan. Most maritime countries have a representative capability for surveying along their coastlines.

The United States also conducts airborne environmental surveys and research. Five large P-3 Orion aircraft are assigned to oceanographic-related surveys, approximately six C-130 Hercules aircraft are flown for hurricane reconnaissance by the U.S. Air Force, and approximately twelve smaller planes and helicopters are specially equipped by NOAA for oceanographic and atmospheric research.

Submersibles

As demonstrated in 1985 and 1986 by the discovery and exploration of the *Titanic,* no instruments on surface oceanographic ships can take the place of direct inspection of the depths by manned or unmanned submersibles.

Diving suits, aqualungs, and scuba equipment are all limited in depth by air supply and/or water pressure. To limited depths, access to underwater habitats (pressured the same as the surrounding water) allows free-swimming divers more time for underwater exploration by eliminating the dangerous and laborious pressure changes required for each dive and return to the surface.

Development of the bathysphere (connected to the surface by cables) and the bathyscaph (free navigating) has allowed scientists to descend more than 10,650 meters (35,000 ft.) to the bottom of the ocean. The present state of the art in deep ocean exploration technology was manifested in the joint Franco-American expedition that discovered and photographed the wreck of the *Titanic* at a depth of 3,800 meters (12,460 ft.) on 1 September 1985. This effort mainly employed deep-towed side-scan sonars and unmanned video camera systems rather than relying on manned systems.

Ship Reports and Cooperative Observation Programs

Ship reports have historically been the backbone of the ocean data observational design. In addition to reports provided by platforms for proprietary purposes, the primary source of marine data is the worldwide voluntary observing ship (VOS) program established by the World Meteorological Organization (WMO).

Approximately 7,500 merchant, navy, government, and university research ships from 47 countries report marine weather through the WMO/VOS program. Marine weather reports contain up to nineteen elements such as sea level pressure, wind velocity, wave height, and sea surface temperature. Additionally, more than 300 ships worldwide make subsurface measurements, such as expendable bathythermograph probes for measuring temperature as a function of depth, and conductivity-temperature-depth profiles to characterize the ocean structure. By "piggybacking" on ships of opportunity, these programs save almost 99 percent of the data-gathering costs.

Moored and Drifting Buoys Observation Systems

Moored buoys provide the most reliable routine ocean surface observations within the ocean data observational system. The buoys provide, in addition to the usual meteorological parameters (sea level pressure, wind velocity, and air temperature), various oceanographic parameters such as sea surface temperature, wave period and height, and wave spectra. Since the mid-1970s, improvements have occurred in many buoy system elements, including sensors, data collection and processing systems, buoy hull configurations, and the methods of data transmission or relay.

Until recently, the use of drifting buoys was largely experimental. Beginning with very simple buoyancy devices that were tracked visually to give estimates of ocean currents, these buoys have evolved into sophisticated electronic devices that are automatically tracked by satellites as they drift with the currents throughout the world's oceans. Drifting buoys measure standard meteorological parameters and, in some cases, temperature versus depth profiles for transmission by satellite in real time. A concerted effort is being made to deploy these buoys in the southern hemisphere and other data-sparse areas. Currently more than 400 drifting buoys are deployed worldwide.

Environmental Satellites

Space satellite technology has provided the quantum leap necessary to observe all the world's oceans and indirectly measure the marine environment on a nearly continuous, real-time basis. Satellite oceanic observations, although usually not as precise as direct traditional measurements, do provide timely information, often not available otherwise, to provide for the safety of defense assets and intelligence for strategic and tactical command decisions. In the longer term, oceanic observations from satellites assist in naval planning activities and support military research and development.

Current environmental satellites of interest to defense forces include the geostationary (over the equator) Meteosat (0 degrees longitude) operated by the European Space Agency; the polar-orbiting Meteor-series satellite operated by Russia; two polar-orbiting and two geostationary satellites operated by the U.S. National Environmental Satellite, Data and Information Service; Japan's geostationary GMS; the U.S. Navy Geosat polar orbiter–series satellite; two defense Meteorological Satellite Program polar-orbiting satellites; and, to a lesser extent, the SPOT satellite operated by France.

The quantity of data from such worldwide coverage is staggering, but supercomputer technology is generally keeping pace to process this information. Great challenges exist within the scientific community to control worldwide data archiving and retrieving in a global information system and to develop oceanographic models to integrate optimally the extent and diversity of data available for accurately representing and predicting ocean parameters for civilian and defense interests.

Major questions about the oceans that military oceanographers aspire to obtain from future oceanographic satellite sensors include: location and movement of eddies and oceanographic features (including ice) that affect naval operations, especially antisubmarine warfare (ASW); all-weather ocean surface wind; global distribution of heat, water, and momentum exchange between the oceans and atmosphere; and implications of subsurface structure and heat exchange between layers, as determined through study of associated surface patterns.

Operational Oceanographic Applications

Similar to many nations, the oceanographic activities in the United States are divided between defense (the U.S. Navy) and civil sector (NOAA).

Operational Oceanography in the Military Forces

The U.S. Navy, with 500 ships and 500,000 uniformed and 170,000 civilian personnel, has approximately 3,000 personnel involved with operational oceanography and several hundred more in related research and development.

Physical oceanographic applications and ocean surveying and research. Bathythermographic (temperature versus depth) and other oceanographic observations are collected by ships, submarines, aircraft, satellites, and various in-water arrays of sensors. These data are processed by computers and combined with historical records of air and sea conditions in operational areas to prepare forecasts for naval operations. Regional oceanographic centers and, in some cases, onboard systems produce tailored profiles of sound velocity, ocean layer depths, ocean currents, and surf and ice conditions.

For specific oceanographic studies, the U.S. Navy employs three oceanographic ships for physical oceanographic surveys in response to operational requirements. Two additional U.S. Navy oceanographic ships perform oceanographic surveys to meet U.S. Navy laboratories' development requirements. Currently, NOAA assigns five ships to oceanographic and atmospheric research in response to national and international requirements for environmental monitoring and global change measurements. In addition, approximately twenty ships of the U.S. academic fleet conduct oceanographic and meteorological research for their own oceanography programs, for the navy, or for the National Science Foundation. Both the navy and NOAA also have a number of specially equipped aircraft to conduct oceanographic, meteorological, and magnetic surveys around the world.

Defense products derived from such oceanographic surveys include: environmental databases, submariners' handbooks and guides, oceanographic and sonar atlases, sound velocity charts, mine warfare pilots, and special area studies.

Meteorology and the prediction of real-time environmental conditions. For the real-time assessment of changing environmental conditions, several world centers such as the U.S. Navy's Fleet Numerical Oceanography Center assimilate thousands of observations each day from ships, aircraft, buoys, and satellites. The real-time data, merged with climatology and earlier forecasts, are processed by numerical models into analysis and forecast fields of oceanographic and meteorological parameters of interest to naval operations, such as wind, wave, and ice forecasts. The analysis and forecast fields also serve as the basis for tactical products, such as ship and aircraft routing, acoustic range prediction, atmosphere refractive effects, and typhoon forecast tracks.

Data and product fields can be distributed by the central processing center to defense and civilian users directly by message or computer links or transmitted to regional centers for local enhancement and further dissemination to ships and stations by message or facsimile and teletype broadcasts. In several locations this information is the basis for forecasts to the general public.

For European nations the European Center for Medium Range Forecasting at Reading, England, provides weather field data that is distributed to national centers. There the data are not only used to support local forecasts but also in some cases tailored for military use.

Mapping, Charting, and Geodesy (MC&G). Coastal survey ships collect geodetic data to orient the survey to fixed-position points on the earth, time-correlated position and depth data to define the bottom, side-scan sonar data to detect underwater hazards, tidal data to determine the effect of tides on depth, and bottom samples and current measurements to help locate suitable anchorages and assess their impact on navigation. Two U.S. Navy coastal survey ships collect hydrographic data for use by the Defense Mapping Agency in the production of nautical charts of ports, harbors, and coastal areas. Most of the coastal hydrographic data collected by eight NOAA vessels are processed into nautical charts by the Charting and Geodetic Services of NOAA's National Ocean Service.

The U.S. Navy, through the Naval Oceanographic Office, sponsors a hydrographic cooperative program to augment coastal data collection by assisting foreign countries in developing their own hydrographic capabilities to meet international standards. Additional data are also obtained through bilateral agreements and the International Hydrographic Organization.

Defense products derived from MC&G survey data include: bottom contour charts, magnetic and magnetic anomaly charts, coastal and area studies, nautical charts, sailing directions, and pilot charts.

Navy Oceanography in the Fleet

In addition to the operational oceanography systems interacting with naval forces from ashore, fleet staffs and capital ships of various navies (carriers, battleships, amphibious ships) often have an oceanography officer and appropriate enlisted personnel assigned to the ship's company. These personnel—using data and products provided from ashore and their ship's own systems (computers; radar; ocean, surface, and upper air measurements; and satellite receiving equipment)—provide tailored, on-scene weather and oceanographic services to ship and battle group commanders. Smaller ships and staffs often have an oceanography officer assigned as a collateral duty.

Navy Ocean Science Programs

In partnership with various navy operational oceanographic systems is ocean science, or basic research and exploratory development in the disciplines of oceanography. Studies are conducted on the ionosphere, upper atmosphere, troposphere, ice variation, and the oceans. Ocean science is primarily conducted by academic centers, research institutes, and government laboratories. Certain multinational institutions, such as the NATO Undersea Research Center located in La Spezia, Italy, are also making significant contributions in the ocean sciences.

Conclusion

Oceans are the medium of naval operations. Study and application of the sciences of oceanography and the many related interdisciplinary fields are essential for the most effective employment of a nation's naval forces.

JOHN RICHARD SEESHOLTZ
JULIAN M. WRIGHT, JR.

SEE ALSO: Antisubmarine Warfare; Mapping, Charting, and Geodesy; Meteorology, Military; Satellite Technology; Sensor Technology; Submarine Warfare; Surveillance, Ocean; Underwater Management.

Bibliography

Ballard, R. 1987. *The discovery of the* Titanic. Toronto: Madison Press Books.

Bates, C., and J. Fuller. 1986. *America's weather warriors, 1814–1985.* College Station: Texas A&M Univ. Press.

Bowditch, N. 1984. *American practical navigator.* Pub. No. 9. Washington, D.C.: Defense Mapping Agency.

Busby, F. 1987. *Undersea vehicles directory.* Arlington, Va.: Busby Associates.

Dunlap, G., and H. Shufeldt. 1972. *Dutton's navigation and piloting.* Annapolis, Md.: U.S. Naval Institute Press.

NASA and NOAA. 1987. *Space-based remote sensing of the earth.* Washington, D.C.: Government Printing Office.

Mahan, A. 1919. *Sea power in relation to the war of 1812.* Boston: Little, Brown.

Nelson, S. 1971. *Oceanographic ships, fore and aft.* Washington, D.C.: Government Printing Office.

Pinsel, M. 1981. *150 years of service on the seas.* Washington, D.C.: Government Printing Office.

Trillo, R., ed. 1979. *Jane's ocean technology.* New York: Franklin Watts.

United Nations. 1983. *United Nations Conference on the Law of the Sea.* New York: United Nations.

Urick, R. 1979. *Sound propagation in the sea.* Defense Advanced Research Projects Office. Washington, D.C.: Government Printing Office.

Viola, H., and C. Margolis. 1985. *Magnificent voyagers: The U.S. exploring expedition, 1838–1842.* Washington, D.C.: Smithsonian Institution Press.

Williams, J., J. Higginson, and J. Rohrbough. 1973. *Sea and air, the marine environment.* Annapolis, Md.: U.S. Naval Institute Press.

OFFENSE

The offensive, or offense, is the decisive military operation. (The terms *offensive*, as it pertains to military operations, and *offense*, a commonly accepted principle of war, are used interchangeably throughout this article.) The offense is designed for the destruction of enemy forces and the seizure of important land areas in order to achieve the political objectives of the conflict. Offense pursues positive goals, the objectives of defense are negative (i.e., to repel the enemy and wait until the objective can become positive). The term *offensive* has a general meaning and specifically refers to strategic and operational activities. At lower levels it is called *attack*, and at the lowest level it is called *assault*. The terms *attack* and *assault* are also applicable to actions where fire is involved (like follow on forces attack (FOFA), and assault breaker). When a defensive phase precedes the offensive, the latter is called a "counteroffensive." A pre-emptive attack is an attack made in anticipation of an enemy attack within the offensive or counteroffensive.

Offensive includes the preparatory maneuvers, the proper attack against the enemy forces that are either defending themselves or undertaking a counteroffensive, and the exploitation of success. These three phases are present at all levels—strategic, tactical, and operational.

The terms *offensive*, *attack*, and *assault*, when referring to air or naval operations independent of land operations, have a different meaning. The counter-air offensive aims to destroy the enemy's air defense capability and to gain air superiority. The naval offensive is designed to destroy the enemy's naval forces, gain sea control, and restore the free use of maritime lines of communication. Maritime offensive operations can also be conducted against enemy maritime traffic (sea denial) or be used to project maritime power ashore by means of amphibious assaults, air raids, or ship weapons. Offensive operations can be conducted in space to destroy satellites (ASAT—i.e., antisatellite operations). The objective of an offensive in electronic warfare, as viewed by the commander, is to jam or prevent the use of enemy electronic means or to locate their positions by the use of electronic countermeasures or signal intelligence.

Finally, offensive operations can be conducted through psychological warfare to sap the enemy's morale.

History of Strategic Thought

The relative superiority of attack versus defense is commonplace in military literature. At tactical and operational levels, this assertion is justified by the fact that the attack seems to assure initiative and decisive victory but this is debatable at the strategic level.

According to Karl von Clausewitz, attack (*angriff*) and defense are two different forms of war, each with specific opportunities and bonds, without any reciprocal "polarity." In principle, defense, starting with denial and delay (*abwarten*) and culminating in counterattack (*ruckstoss*), is superior to attack in that defensive posture enhances the strength of the defender. Clausewitz made clear the positive and negative relationship of attack and defense. Indeed, defense may result in raising the political status of the war, forcing the attacker to exceed the limits he has tried to impose on the war.

Until the eighteenth century, war was intrinsically limited by political, economic, geographic, and technical obstacles. These obstacles were overcome in the nineteenth century, however, thus forcing strategic thought to face the problem of keeping war limited by using only military means.

The doctrine of strategic offense and war of rapid decision was basically a German doctrine. German strategy that aimed at parity in Europe and later at a "world condominium" with the British Empire required maintaining a capability so that a limited, as well as a short, war would be possible and successful for the attacker. Significantly, such a doctrine in the early twentieth century influenced other powers with strategic aims comparable to those of Germany. These included the Soviet Union, Fascist Italy, and Imperial Japan. However, for the Western powers, the chief problem was to defend their empires and prevent war; thus, the influence of German strategic thinking was limited to its operational and tactical aspects.

It is important to note that in both Imperial Japan and the USSR, as in contemporary national liberation and revolution strategies, the militaristic doctrine of rapid and decisive war was counterbalanced and often overcome by the opposite political theory of "long-lasting" war, which advocated a strategy of exhaustion, defensive-offensive posture, and indirect strategies. Such an option was justified by the assumption that Western societies could not be mobilized and would suffer losses to the same degree that socialist or underdeveloped societies might.

In Germany during the post-Napoleonic era, the idea of a short and decisive war was revived after the Prussian victory of Sadowa (1866). Shortly after the 1870–71 Franco-Prussian War, however, the German chief of staff, Gen. Helmuth von Moltke (the Elder), became convinced that the French army's improved capabilities and the possibility of a war on two fronts against both France and Russia would inhibit a strategic offensive in the west. Thus, in 1877, the German strategic concept was to plan a defensive-offensive posture in the west and a combined Austro-German offensive in the east.

The concept of a strategic offensive in the west reappeared, however, in 1888, when Moltke's successor, Gen. Alfred von Waldersee, planned a decisive counteroffensive against France and advocated pre-emptive war. Simultaneously, he unsuccessfully opposed Alfred von Tirpitz's naval program, which he feared might reinforce the British antagonism and divert resources from the army.

Late-nineteenth-century developments in mobilization, firepower, supply, and command and control suggested to Waldersee's successor, Gen. Alfred von Schlieffen, the possibility of defeating France quickly in a unique and decisive offensive battle, a large-scale Cannae. About seven-eighths of Germany's western forces were to be concentrated on the right wing, marching as a Napoleonic *bataillon carré* through Belgium and northern France, enveloping the enemy's flank with a maneuver preplanned in detail (*manoeuvre à priori*) similar to a revolving door anchored at Metz, as described by Sir Basil Liddell Hart (1934, pp. 68–69), thus enveloping and destroying the French army in a great and decisive battle of annihilation or encirclement, the *vernichtungs* or *kesselschlacht*.

In the postwar period, Liddell Hart was the Schlieffen plan's main critic, holding it (because of its failure) responsible for World War I massacres and for what he judged to be the Clausewitzian misinterpretation of Napoleon's predicaments. Other scholars (Ritter 1956; Wallach 1967) considered the Schlieffen plan as the "beginning of the German and European misfortunes," even if they acquitted Clausewitz and Moltke (the Elder) of the later militaristic degeneration of German strategic thought. Liddell Hart and Ritter insisted that underestimation of the logistical and technical difficulties were the principal reasons for the 1914 German failure.

Although Schlieffen was strongly criticized in the 1880s by many German generals—including von Schlichting, von Bernhardi, von Bülow, and von der Goltz—opposing offense at all costs and maneuver a priori, none opposed him in the decisive prewar decade.

The military historian Delbrück, developing the Clausewitzian theory of intrinsic superiority of defense versus offense, restored the relative merits of the strategy of attrition (*ermattungsstrategie*) versus that of annihilation (*niederwerfungsstrategie*), and used Frederick the Great and Pericles as two master examples of the former. On this subject he sustained a twenty-year dispute with a serving officer who considered it an insult to national military tradition. But Delbrück thought that only *niederwerfungsstrategie* was suitable for Germany in existing prewar conditions. But after 1916, Delbrück advocated a defensive-offensive posture in the west, with the possibility of a separate peace in order to allow decisive offense in the east. He also criticized Erich Ludendorff's last offensive in 1918 but never extended his criticism to the 1914 war plan. In 1919 Gen. Wilhelm Groener offered the opinion that the German defeat was caused by the deviation of General Moltke the Younger from the basic concept of Schlieffen's plan.

Between World Wars I and II, military reformers in all countries thought that decisive war and strategic offense might be restored by airpower, mechanization, and industrial mobilization. Small, professional, mobile armies, combat-ready and deployed in peacetime, should replace the obsolete large armies and military mobilization that had led to trench warfare in World War I. However, not only the professional conservatism of military staffs but also innumerable technical and practical difficulties undermined such an attractive picture.

The 1939 Polish campaign differed fundamentally from the 1914 *kesselschlacht* not only by 1918-type penetration and encirclement tactics, but also by the improved supply capability and mobility of the German right wing, although they were still largely based on horse-drawn supply trains and an all-conscript foot infantry. Airpower and motorized forces played a subsidiary role, making it impossible for the enemy to concentrate his forces on the southern flank.

Allied commanders in France were not wrong, in 1940, to expect a German "revolving-door" offensive across the same battlefields of World War I. Initially, this was exactly what the German staff planned to do, concentrate all mobile forces on the right wing. It was only later that Gen. Erich von Manstein, supported in a decisive way by Hitler, caused a change in the staff's approach. He moved the Panzergruppe Kleist (tank army) through the Ardennes, breaking down the Allied front (the Yellow Plan), then encircled the Allied left wing (the Red Plan).

Such a risky strategy succeeded due to Allied mistakes such as the poor disposition of reserves and exaggerated accounts of German air and tank superiority, and to the masterly German operational combination of technical elements in what was called "lightning war" (blitzkrieg), a term that was neither official nor German.

According to some, the blitzkrieg operational principle was derived from the 1918 infiltration tactics of the World War I German assault infantry (*stosstruppen*), not from the 1917 Allied tank raid at Cambrai or from the ideas the British military reformers (such as Fuller and Liddell Hart) maintained. Unlike traditional offensive operations, the lightning attack without artillery preparation should be directed against weaker points, bypassing strongholds. Ground-attack aircraft would provide continual fire support to mobile forces. Deep penetration by separate columns would exploit civilian roads and fuel supplies. Improved command and control systems would allow field commanders to coordinate dispersed units.

It was the continuing British resistance, following the French defeat, that strategically decided the war. As shown by A. Hillgruber, Hitler's 1938–40 "artichoke" strategy collapsed in the summer of 1940, forcing him into a desperate attempt at "world lightning war" (*weltblitzkrieg*) in order to limit war at least in time if not in space and scope (Hillgruber, 1965). Despite the German successes at the operational level, lightning attack operations proved inadequate to conquer the USSR, if not to defeat its first-line army. Thus, Germany was in the same situation as it had been in in September 1914, having to face a siege war it could never win because of superior Allied resources.

The Japanese viewed the offensive differently. According to J. Esmein, Japanese strategic "intents" never considered the offensive as a way to decide war, even if it had been recommended, unsuccessfully, by the chief of staff, Uehara (Esmein 1983). Also, at the operational level, the traditional "offensive" attitude of the army was counterbalanced by a "defensive" navy. The Pearl Harbor surprise and the hazardous attack at Midway were in contrast with the Japanese Imperial Navy traditions. The fundamental choice of Japanese strategy was not between offense and defense, but between continental expansion at the expense of China and the USSR, as Tanaka theorized, or Asiatic liberation, as Ishiwara advocated in vain, preaching a long-term Asiatic crusade against the United States as Japan's ultimate mission.

At the beginning of the nuclear era, it appeared that nuclear weapons would be the principal strategic offensive means to win a war quickly, thus preventing an unlimited war. However, since the 1960s, both Soviet and Western military thinking has investigated conventional opportunities for decisive offensive operations in the nuclear era. Western analysts feared strategic scenarios that allowed the USSR to conquer Western Europe with conventional forces alone or to destroy the U.S. deterrent with a preemptive strike. Decisive technological progress in both nuclear and conventional weapons and command, control, communications and intelligence (C^3I) systems in the 1970s restored the possibility of limited nuclear war.

Unlike Western strategy, which bases deterrence on offensive nuclear and defensive conventional forces, Soviet strategy emphasized offense at both levels, refusing to separate nuclear from conventional warfare. Soviet operational planning was based on a surprise nuclear attack, followed by conventional penetrations on a wide front, with the aim of disrupting and destroying the Western forces, taking key positions, occupying territory, and preventing invasion. This is more like the blitzkrieg than the pincer envelopments of the Great Patriotic War (World War II). Soviet military science never gave up the idea of victory (*pobieda*), which only in recent times has returned to Western military doctrine.

Attrition Offensive and Annihilation Offensive

There are two main types of offensive: attrition and annihilation. Attrition aims to weaken the enemy and is based on superiority of forces and weapons. Its goal is the direct annihilation of the enemy. Annihilation aims to destroy the enemy by hitting him with surprise and maneuver, thus neutralizing the majority of the enemy forces. It is based on attacking sensitive points in the enemy system in order to penetrate his defenses, disrupt unit cohesion, and then annihilate or capture the forces that have been surrounded or bypassed.

The attrition offensive consists of exerting uniform pressure against enemy positions. Its success is the result of the sum of each success achieved at lower levels. Such an offensive is normally frontal and directed against the enemy's main forces. Friendly forces are deployed mostly in width to fully exploit their superiority on the front of the defense system. In this type of offensive, fire across the entire front system is of paramount importance and requires enormously superior forces. It is less risky than other types of military operations but more exacting in terms of time and materiel. The attrition offensive gives the enemy more opportunity to disengage and conduct defensive actions in depth.

On the other hand, the annihilation offensive involves the concentration of the majority of forces at critical points of the enemy's system. It requires that some risks be taken elsewhere, demands speed of progress to prevent the enemy from recovering, and implies that the initial deployment of friendly forces be extended more in depth. The annihilation offensive is aimed at the flanks and the rear of the enemy—if necessary after a quick breakthrough of the front. Maneuver, speed, surprise, and firepower in depth are important. These actions can be conducted with numerically inferior forces because their power is multiplied when forces are concentrated at the critical points of the enemy system. This is obtained by exploiting not only material, but also psychological and morale effects that prevent the enemy from reacting.

A typical example of an attrition offensive is the steamroller offensive such as that at Verdun, while the annihilation offensive is typified by the blitzkrieg, the deep offensive conceived by Mikhail N. Tukhachevsky, such as the German invasion of the West in 1940. The so-called indirect approach theory of Liddell Hart is a special case of annihilation strategy.

Comparing the enemy forces to a system, the attrition offensive is applied to its boundaries, which will be increasingly compressed, while the annihilation offensive seeks to penetrate the interior of this system and destroy its cohesion. Aspects of attrition and annihilation may coexist in the same offensive operation and may be combined. The breakthrough of the enemy front to penetrate in depth and strike the flanks and the rear (and to destroy the enemy forces that have been deployed in depth) can be preceded by pre-emptive fires (air strikes and/or artillery).

The infiltration techniques adopted by the German infantry at the end of World War I were necessitated by the high technical-organizational standard achieved by the defense. Through penetration, the defending enemy forces are surrounded and forced to counterattack in order to break out of the encirclement, thus facilitating their annihilation. Attrition paves the way for fast penetrations in depth and annihilation of the enemy forces. In both cases, offensive operations seek to end the fighting in the shortest period of time and in the least depth, both to maintain initiative and surprise and to destroy the enemy forward forces, thereby preventing them from withdrawing and regrouping to form a defense in depth. Conversely, defense makes use of space and time as factors enhancing the combat power of one's own forces, avoiding their destruction, weakening the enemy, and extending him away from his bases. The defender thus waits for the force balance to turn in his favor, allowing him to take the offensive. The use of time and space in the defense is substantially different from their use in the offensive.

With the development of nuclear missiles, the offensive has acquired a technical superiority over defense. As a consequence, the offensive can be countered only by similar means of operations. This happened, in a less obvious way, in naval and air force combat at the tactical and operational levels where defense is structurally impossible and the occupation of air and sea space is meaningless.

Offensive Phases

Offensive operations include three various phases that partially overlap: preparation, conduct of the attack, and exploitation of success.

Preparation encompasses all those activities and preparatory maneuvers for the attack that are intended to obtain mass and surprise. It includes planning for the attack, air and land reconnaissance of enemy defenses, diversionary attacks to render the main thrust sectors vulnerable, and relocation of friendly forces to assembly areas and attack positions near the line of departure. The preparation phase also includes air and land fire strikes to impair the enemy system, prevent the maneuver of enemy forces, and facilitate the penetration of enemy defenses.

The second phase of offensive operations, the conduct of an attack, requires a combination of fire and movement to make contact with enemy forces and to launch the attack. An attack can be conducted many times along the axis of advance to destroy or disrupt enemy forces in depth. It ends with consolidation of captured positions that can be used against possible enemy counterattacks. Consolidation, a temporary defensive posture, involves, in part, the arrival/commitment of reserve forces with which to continue the penetration and exploit the success in depth.

Finally, exploitation of success involves penetration in increasing depth to objectives coinciding with key points of the enemy system until decisive results are obtained—whether by encirclement or destruction of the enemy forces bypassed. Timely utilization of reserves is essential for the final success and to prevent the enemy from withdrawing or counterattacking the penetration and taking advantage of the vulnerability of its flanks. Commanders must give priority to penetration in depth, which is conducted in successive stages to destroy the enemy units encircled. Dispersion of resources is to be avoided.

The outcome of exploitation of success depends heavily on logistic sustainability of the friendly forces penetrating in depth and on the capability of those forces to disrupt the enemy's logistic system. Exploitation of success ends with the consolidation of final objectives, or of any captured position, before the attacking forces lose their offensive capability and become exposed to risk of destruction by the defender's counterattacks.

Principles of the Offense

The offense is a commonly accepted principle of military doctrine. As such, it is very similar to the principle of initiative and with it the freedom of action. Offensive operations stress the need to prevail over the enemy and to exploit opportunities with aggressiveness. Accordingly, offensive operations are governed by principles.

Prerequisites for an offensive are: initiative and speed of maneuver, penetration, and exploitation of success to deny the enemy time to react. The additional principles that an offensive must follow, discussed in the following paragraphs, are those of mass, and, consequently, economy of force, maneuver, unity of command, surprise, and security.

The principle of mass takes different forms in the attrition and annihilation offensives. In the former, it requires concentration of firepower and forces against the enemy in order to engage him in his forward positions and destroy him to prevent his withdrawal and a further defense in the rear positions. The annihilation offensive, as stated earlier, is not designed to destroy the enemy forces progressively, but rather to strike critical points of the enemy system, disrupt its cohesion, and penetrate in depth, disposing of enemy forces encircled in the forward positions later. In terms of numbers, it is a specialized or concentrated mass rather than a large one. The annihilation offensive must seek to acquire local predominance and is based on surprise, speed, and flexibility to minimize frontal engagements. The annihilation of enemy forces opposing the main thrust is only a means, not an end, as in the attrition offensive. Speed is the decisive factor to prevent the enemy from reacting, from protecting his own vulnerabilities by means of withdrawal. The theoretical value of mass is given by Lanchester's quadratic (square) law, which demonstrates that in a frontal engagement the losses of one of the contenders are in inverse proportion to the square of the quantity of his troops and in direct proportion to the enemy forces. Speed and surprise are multiplying factors of mass since they not only affect the material dimensions of the enemy system but also have mental and psychological consequences on its cohesion.

Linked with the principle of mass are those of economy of force, maneuver, and unity of command.

Economy of force means that to concentrate combat power behind the main effort, a commander must allocate minimum essential power to secondary efforts, even if he has to accept some risks.

Maneuver allows both the concentration of power in those sectors where an attack is to be mounted and realization of the opportunity to conduct a surprise attack, that is, to hit enemy vulnerabilities (which can be caused through diversionary maneuvers and deception) and rapidly penetrate in depth, after the mass has achieved a breakthrough, in order to prevent enemy reactions. Maneuver requires concentration of power not only in space but also in time so as to maintain in depth the power necessary to give an attack progressive momentum. To this end, adequate measures must be taken both to reinforce the forward effort and exploit favorable situations. The attack can proceed while a sufficient mass is maintained. However, once the reserves are expended, the attack is vulnerable to counteroffensive reaction by the defender. Maneuver alone cannot gain success, as it also requires successive allocation of power in order to destroy the opposing enemy forces. Maneuver nevertheless is the basis for success. In a counteroffensive the commander's fundamental decision is when to commence action to prevent the enemy from consolidating.

Unity of command is necessary to coordinate the various actions associated with the main and supporting attacks, to exploit mass and surprise, and to obtain the best results through the synergy of the elements of forces available.

Surprise is a multiplying factor of power and mass. It consists of attacking the enemy at the unexpected moment, place, and in an unexpected way, and before he can effectively react. Concurrent with surprise are: speed, secrecy, deception, concurrent diversionary actions, exploitation of adverse weather and terrain, use of new weapons systems, adoption of unusual tactics, or employment of unexpected strength. For surprise to be completely successful, a speedy progression and strength of forces sufficient to achieve the final objectives are required.

Security is conceptually the opposite of the principle of surprise. This does not mean that it is without risk. The more a successful attack is based on maneuver and surprise, the higher are the risks. Security requires a reasonable appreciation of the enemy's capabilities and above all his reaction time. It requires prearrangement of ad hoc measures that can be implemented with a proper redeployment of reserves designed to reinforce the attack, coupled with effective surveillance and reconnaissance. In this case, the best security lies in a speedy advance so as not to allow the enemy any time for reaction. In general, the more risks that are accepted (within reason), the greater is the success. There are comparatively few risks (assuming the superiority of forces) in an offensive based on the attrition of the enemy; they are enormous in an offensive based on maneuver and surprise. With the progression of penetration, the thrust of the attack slows down, partly due to the need to assign an ever-increasing proportion of forces to security duties. Exhaustion of offensive capability happens when mass cannot be maintained and its forces are assigned to security duties to prevent possible counteroffensives by the defender.

Offensive and Defensive Weapons and Negotiations on Conventional Stability

It has never been possible to clearly define whether a weapon or a weapon system is offensive or defensive. For example, the armor of a fully protected knight gave him both an offensive and defensive capability. The construction of forts along frontiers not only gave protection to the borders but created operational bases suitable for operations into enemy territory. Armor allows tanks to penetrate enemy defenses with a certain degree of protection. Light infantry units equipped with antitank and antihelicopter weapons, although not particularly suitable for offensive actions in open terrain, can replace mechanized and armored units, which in turn can be employed in offensive operations. In some cases, especially in difficult terrain, light infantry can be employed in the attack. Maritime mine warfare can be pursued with either defensive or offensive goals. The appearance of multirole weapons systems in air, maritime, and land operations has made the distinction between an offensive and a defensive weapon more difficult. Tanks are essential for the defense to cut off penetrations. A ship can be used to defend a coastal area or a merchant convoy and to attack enemy warships, merchant ships, or coasts. The point is that "the offensive or defensive nature of a weapon depends on the observer's point of view: if it is in front, it is offensive; if it is behind, it is defensive." In principle, it is impossible to infer the offensive or defensive nature of a weapon from its technical data because offense and defense are a combination of defensive and offensive operations.

The offensive or defensive character of a weapon is determined by its use. Some weapons are better suited for offense, others for defense. This defensive or offensive character, however, is not related to the weapon itself but to the general structures, its possible roles in these structures, and above all the tasks assigned ad hoc. For example, the offensive or defensive nature of a tank depends on its quantity and organic position as well. A reasonably limited quantity of tanks can represent an essential element of a defensive structure as they may be used to launch a counterattack, essential to hold the defense positions. A concentration of a large number of tanks in armored units gives it an offensive character.

Tanks, artillery, attack helicopters, mobile antiaircraft and bridging units are systems more suitable for offensive operations. Less suitable are permanent fortifications, mines, antitank weapons, and fixed or semimobile antiaircraft weapons. The problem is assessing the operational outcome or technical performance of available weapons. The problem is not one of theory. In arms control negotiations, it is essential to identify the force structure that allows the realization of stability.

The problem, in military terms, is difficult not only because of qualitative factors that cannot be assessed in an unequivocal way, but also because of aspects that cannot be quantified such as morale, leadership, and reaction time of the political-military decision-making system.

The distinction between offensive and defensive weapons and force structure—or the preeminence of offense over defense (or vice versa)—and the way to correct it is considered of paramount importance in arms control negotiations where security is viewed as mutual rather than unilateral. The possibility of establishing reasonably stable structures derives not so much from a force balance as from the possible distinction between offensive arms or structures and defensive arms or structures. In other words, mutual security should be assured by the predominance of defense over attack and, failing this, by adoption of measures necessary to redress the imbalance between defense and attack to favor the former. In the absence of these conditions it is impossible to identify intrinsically stable structures and approach the problem of arms control unequivocally.

In sum, the qualification of a weapon or a structure as "offensive" or "defensive" depends on the general context in which they might be employed and implies that the various technical inputs be changed into operational outputs.

General Types of Offensive Operations

Surprise Attack

A surprise attack is one where warning time is so short that it does not allow the enemy time to organize a defense. A surprise attack can never be ruled out, although modern surveillance systems make the likelihood of such an attack low, especially at the strategic level. It exists only if sufficient combat power by one side allows it to obtain established objectives.

The problem of a surprise strategic attack has become a very important factor in arms control negotiations. Ruling out the possibility of a surprise attack involves the adoption of operational measures such as confidence and security building measures (CSBM) and structural measures such as redressing imbalances and the reduction and restructuring of forces or the withdrawal of troops from borders.

Pre-emptive Attack

A pre-emptive attack is an operation, undertaken before an imminent enemy attack. It is designed to disrupt the enemy system, inflict losses, and seize the initiative; it can be launched by a defender when the attacker is preparing an offensive.

Hasty Attack or Attack Against Poorly Organized Positions

A hasty attack is launched when the enemy is unexpectedly met face-to-face or when a favorable opportunity must be exploited. In the phases following an attack, it is typical to maintain the momentum of a penetration so as to deny the enemy the initiative or prevent his residual forces from withdrawing to positions in depth and avoiding encirclement or annihilation, or to prevent him from moving his reserves forward to fill the breach or launch a counterattack.

A hasty attack requires little planning and is launched against an unorganized or moving enemy. This type of attack is normal at the lower tactical levels.

Deliberate Attack or Attack Against Strong Defensive Positions

This is a methodical offensive action that concentrates combat power successively (forces and firepower) to gain local superiority and overcome the enemy. A deliberate attack develops through main and subsidiary efforts. It is preceded by recognition and reconnaissance of the enemy system in order to define the attack plan and to weaken the enemy through firepower. It can also include preliminary combat actions that are designed to destroy advanced enemy positions or to take some of them, both to facilitate successive attacks and to deceive the enemy as to the real intentions of the attacker.

A deliberate attack is normally directed against a strongly organized enemy defense. After the preliminary phases, its planning must be adapted to the new situation. At a higher level, it can generate hasty attacks at the lower tactical levels.

Advance to Contact

This type of operation is designed to seek and maintain contact with the main enemy force and to create the most favorable conditions for an attack. It is based on maximum speed so that the enemy is allowed minimum time to strengthen his defense. Advance to contact includes observation and reconnaissance and, if necessary and deemed appropriate, can also include strikes against the enemy covering forces to destroy them.

The advance to contact formation normally includes, in addition to the main body, the advance guard, flanking guards, and, possibly, a rearguard for protection.

Reconnaissance in Force

This is an offensive action before the attack that is undertaken to obtain information about the enemy's location, capability, and reaction. Normally, it is conducted against a limited objective.

Exploitation of Success

This is an offensive operation that follows the attack. It must take place immediately and is designed to carry success into the depth of the enemy's system once his defensive positions are disrupted.

At the lower tactical level it is aimed at expanding the effects of a successful attack and denying the enemy time for countermaneuver. Exploitation of success requires a timely and firm commitment of reserves.

Pursuit

It is through pursuit, the final stage of an attack, that the enemy forces in the advanced positions that escaped encirclement are prevented from organizing further defenses and launching counterattacks. Pursuit must be conducted with maximum possible momentum, maintaining a sufficient mass through the utilization of all available resources and projecting logistic support, which is what determines its success.

Specific Types of Offensive Operations

Raid

A raid is an offensive operation, usually on a small scale, that is undertaken to destroy installations and elements of the enemy system (especially C^3I), capture prisoners, secure information, inflict damage (in particular to the supporting elements), oblige the enemy to disperse his forces in security tasks, and delay the arrival of reserves or supplies. A raid involves a penetration of hostile territory by land-, air-, or sea-borne groups, and is characterized by surprise, swiftness, and quick withdrawal. A raid can be carried out by forces both in the offensive and the defensive postures.

Assault

An assault is the final phase of an attack, when units in contact with the enemy's advanced defense positions make a decisive effort to destroy them. It requires superior forces and weapons, especially if it is a frontal assault.

Meeting Engagements

Typical meeting engagements are those that occur at the beginning of a war, or between the attacking forces penetrating in depth and the defense forces advancing to counterattack. These are hasty attacks whose success depends largely on the speed of reaction and on the capability to seize the initiative.

Counterattack

This is an attack conducted by a defending force against an enemy attacking force for the specific purpose of regaining lost ground, destroying enemy penetrating forces, or gaining the time necessary to reorganize defensive positions in depth. A counterattack allows the defender to increase the opportunities to use his initiative, reducing those of the attacker and preventing the achievement of the attacker's objective of destroying enemy forces or seizing key terrain.

Diversionary Attack (Feint)

A diversionary attack is designed to draw the enemy's attention away from the main attack. Minimal forces are employed to deceive the enemy. A diversionary attack aims to identify vulnerable points in the enemy system that the main attack can exploit. It is usually conducted by a smaller force than that conducting the main attack, on a wider front, with forces extended in depth, and with few reserves.

Demonstration

When an attacking force makes contact with the enemy system but does not engage the enemy, it is called a demonstration.

Holding Attack (Secondary Attack)

A holding attack is a form of diversionary attack conducted against the front of the enemy forces to facilitate the success of the main effort that takes place in adjoining areas. Its purpose is to divert the enemy's attention from the sector of the principal attack and induce him to commit his reserves prematurely. A holding attack can also be designed to hold the enemy forces in their frontal positions, thus preventing them from disengaging and escaping envelopment. It is the most common type of attack subsidiary to, or in support of, the main effort.

In short, a holding attack is a measure that on the one hand facilitates a concentration of a mass superior to that of the defense at the points where the attack is launched and, on the other, allows surprise and maintenance of the initiative.

Maritime Offensive

The main goal of maritime military power is to achieve navigation of the seas to one's own advantage and to the detriment of the enemy. This means free use of sea lanes, both to maintain one's war effort and to bring the offense to the enemy territory. To achieve this goal, two main strategies have been developed throughout the course of history: one, "battle" strategy, aimed at the annihilation of the enemy forces; two, "blockade" strategy, focused on the paralysis or confinement of enemy forces.

These strategies, however, can be pursued only when the naval force balance is favorable. In reaction to this, the weaker navies have developed and perfected other suitable strategies—for example, *guerre de course,* of which privateering was a major form in the seventeenth and eighteenth centuries, and submarine warfare against maritime traffic, its modern version.

All of the above strategies are offensive because at sea defensive operations, even tactical, seem doomed to failure or are less profitable. The absence of the terrain factor—with the exception of some particular cases—deprives defense at sea of its principal strong point, while the offensive continues to enjoy the advantages of mass, initiative, and surprise. The enormous production of resources and the possible scenarios of a modern war make a survey of maritime operations more complex and less clearly defined.

The distinction between offensive and defensive can be easier—but this is only a simplification—when naval-air operations are specifically linked with land (the defense of one's own and an attack against someone else's territory). In this case, *defensive* operations (although in some cases tactical offensive proceedings are involved) are those designed to protect the national territory and maritime frontiers from sea-launched attacks. *Offensive* operations, on the other hand, are those directed against someone else's territory.

Defensive operations include all those operations that modern terminology defines as "power projection" into enemy territory (e.g., landing of forces by means of amphibious assault, coast bombardment, and air and missile attack). Offensive operations include coastal patrolling, mine barrage of possible lanes of approach to friendly internal or territorial waters, defensive mining, interception and neutralization of forces directed toward friendly territory, and running of a blockade.

Naval-air operations related to an attack against enemy territory or the defense of friendly territory represents only one aspect of maritime warfare. The sea is a large line of communication, and as such, its use is essential in the strategy of maritime nations. In this context, naval-air operations are intended both to keep secure friendly maritime lines of communications and to deny the enemy free use of his own. These goals can be attained both through offensive and defensive operations. Those operations against lines of communication have an offensive connotation even when conducted through static means (barrages, minefields, etc.). Conversely, the defense of lines of communication can be considered, in terms of operations, either defensive or offensive according to the situation.

In general, operations that give direct protection to naval formations or maritime traffic and those that interdict obligatory maritime routes (barrages) are defensive in nature, while those designed for the control of maritime areas of interest (which must indirectly give security to friendly lines of communications), by searching and neutralizing the enemy forces in these areas, are offensive in nature.

With the exception of those cases in which a particular oceanographic situation can be exploited, defensive strategies at sea are rather ineffective and are adopted only when more adequate measures are not practicable. An example is the protection of traffic, especially against the submarine threat, which requires an enormous amount of resources to establish an effective screen. In World War II, the Battle of the Atlantic was won by the Allies when new systems (antisubmarine aircraft) were put into service and where, to improve direct protection of convoys, long-range search-and-destroy offensive operations against Axis submarines became possible.

The range and kill capability of modern weapons have given the attacker additional advantages. The first to attack can gain an advantage that often may be decisive. For this reason, even the most strictly defensive tactics require that defense be conducted with an adequate depth in space in order to oppose the offense as soon and as far as possible from the protected objectives.

Air Force Offensives

Air operations also have both offensive and defensive characteristics and aims. Offensive operations are considered to be those conducted to search for, and attack, the enemy, choosing the right moment and place. The same operations can be defensive in nature when conducted to pre-empt enemy initiatives.

Offensive air operations can be a combination of offensive and defensive air missions. Likewise, defensive air operations can be a part of an operation that is offensive on the whole. Since offensive and defensive air operations often have to rely on the same resources and are often conducted in the same airspace and at the same time, they cannot be considered separately. A "counter–air" offensive is a typical offensive operation designed to attain air superiority, which is often a prerequisite for air support of land, air, and maritime forces. Its goal is the annihilation of enemy air bases, antiaircraft defenses, and the airplanes on the ground.

The mass employment of aircraft during World War I gave birth to the "air dominance" doctrine—that is, a strategically offensive deployment of the air force to destroy the resistance and war support capability of enemy populations—that was promoted by Douhet, Trenchard, and Mitchell. A successful result of that conflict could have been possible with massive air attacks against civil and military objectives. The doctrine of "air dominance" was the basis of the massive bombardments during World War II. However, its implementation was a failure. After the war, the doctrine was viewed by NATO as the "dagger and shield"—where the dagger represented the air forces and the shield the land forces—to exploit the major element of its strength in the 1950s. Nuclear weapons gave the doctrine of "air dominance" the technical power required for success. In NATO's nuclear strategy, this doctrine is still present in the planning of decisive first and second strikes.

Carlo Jean

See Also: Blitzkrieg; Clausewitz, Karl von; Defense; Follow-on Forces Attack; Guderian, Heinz; Initiative in War; Ludendorff, Erich; Manstein, Erich von; Moltke the Elder; Operational Art; Principles of War; Schlieffen, Alfred, Count von; Strategy; Tactics; Tukhachevsky, Mikhail Nikolaevich.

Bibliography

Aron, R. 1976. *Penser la guerre. Clausewitz.* Paris: Gallimard.
Esmein, J. 1983. *Un demi plus.* Paris: Fondation pour les études de défense nationale.
Hillgruber, A. 1982. *Hitler's strategie. Politik und Kriegführung 1940–1941.* München: Bernard und Graefe Verlag.
Leebaert, D., ed. 1981. *Soviet military thinking.* London: Allen and Unwin.
Liddell Hart, B. H. 1934. *A history of the world war 1914–18.* London: Faber and Faber.
Mette, S. 1938. *Vom Geist deutscher Feldherren. Genie und Technik 1888–1918.* Zurich: Scientia.
Paret, P., ed. 1986. *Makers of modern strategy from Machiavelli to the nuclear age.* Princeton, N.J.: Princeton Univ. Press.
Ritter, G. 1956. *Schlieffenplan. Kritik eines Mythos.* München: Oldenburg.
Rusconi, G. E. 1987. *Rischio 1914. Come si decide una guerra.* Bologna: Il Mulino.
Vigor, P. H. 1983. *The Soviet theory of blitzkrieg.* London: Macmillan.
Wallach, J. L. 1967. *Das Dogma der Vernichtungsschlacht. Die Lehren von Clausewitz und Schlieffen und ihre Wirkungen in zwei Weltkriegen.* Frankfurt am Main: Bernard und Graefe.

OFFICER

The term *officer* can be used in many ways. There are two major approaches to understanding its use in the context of military organizations. One approach is functional and focuses primarily on the officer as leader of forces in armed combat. This approach dates from the beginning of recorded history. It relegates the officer's ancillary technical and administrative functions to a minor role. Where officership is viewed in terms of the leadership of military forces in the conduct of military operations, or as the capacities and skills associated with such leadership, the possession of military office such as a commission is not a prerequisite (Keegan 1987).

The second approach is organizational, and focuses on the role of the officer within the bureaucratic authority structure of the modern nation-state. Indeed, the first use of the term *officer* to refer to a person occupying a position of authority in the army, navy, or mercantile marine, particularly a person holding a commission, dates back only to 1565 (*Oxford Universal Dictionary* 1955). The focus on the possession of military office and on the qualifications for such office is, in many respects, complementary to the functional approach. Combat leadership and effective generalship remain important factors. However, the size of modern military organizations, their technological and administrative complexity, and their position within the nation-state form and bound the status of the contemporary military officer (Fig. 1).

Prior to 1800, military office was typically a part-time pursuit rather than a full-time profession, and officership was directly related to social position. By the end of the nineteenth century, however, a corps of full-time professional officers existed in most major countries (Huntington 1957).

The emergence of an organized corps of officers recruited on the basis of education and skill rather than social origins, serving on a full-time basis rather than only during periods of conflict, and regarding military service as a profession rather than a part-time vocation is an outcome of two historical processes. One is the centralization of state authority; the second is the Industrial Revolution and the associated division of labor (Abrahamsson 1972).

Figure 1. An example of an officer: Gen. Colin Powell, chairman of the U.S. Joint Chiefs of Staff. (SOURCE: U.S. Department of Defense)

The centralization of state authority resulted in a military organization recruited nationally rather than internationally. It also led to an officer who was recruited, initially in part and later almost entirely, from middle-class subjects of the state. This replaced an officer corps of nobles who could serve numerous masters sequentially.

Technological and logistical innovations in the art of war associated with the Industrial Revolution brought with them a demand for more complex military skills and techniques, an associated proliferation in the division of labor in military organizations, and an increased requirement for coordination and integration of military activities. Professional military schools, which were started in France, England, and Prussia late in the eighteenth century and exported to the United States (West Point, est. 1802), reflected these changes. They both responded to and furthered the transition from an aristocratic to a professional officer corps.

The problems associated with the capability to lead and direct the equipment and employment of huge armies and navies with increasingly complex and diverse activities were paralleled by similar developments in industrial organization. Subordination and discipline are equally important to the successful operation of both modern economic enterprise and contemporary armed forces.

The Industrial Revolution brought with it the requirement for workers to exercise judgment in the performance of their tasks. As the traditional authority system that was dependent on face-to-face relations became less relevant, methods of harnessing this discretion in support of organizational goals became increasingly important (Bendix 1956). Similarly, in military organizations, "as more and more impact has gone into the hitting power of weapons, necessitating ever-widening deployments in the forces of battle, the quality of the initiative in the individual has become the most praised of the military virtues" (Marshall 1947, p. 22).

Thus, officership in the military profession today differs in many important respects from officership as it existed in the military of the late eighteenth century. The transition from officership based on ascribed status and traditional authority to officership as a full-time profession with selection on the basis of achievement rather than social origin paralleled a similar transition from traditional authority to bureaucratic leadership and management in industry.

The pace and details of this transition varied from nation to nation. For the first three-quarters of the nineteenth century, for example, the purchase system, whereby an individual first bought his commission and then paid for each subsequent step in rank, remained in place in the British Army (Woodham-Smith 1953, pp. 21–25). Even after the institution of new procedures (the purchase system was virtually abolished in 1870), the majority of British officers were amateurs, expecting up to six months of leave a year and oriented primarily to such civil concerns as estate management (Harries-Jenkins 1973).

Garnier's (1977) empirical data on British army officer selection outcomes indicate that particularistic criteria related to social class are still important in the selection of British army officers despite the technological sophistication of that army. The continuation of a strong relationship between social class and officer selection does not, however, minimize the significance of the more general transformation from particularistic to universalistic (ascription to achievement) selection criteria. In part this is a matter of degree. The relatively high proportion of British army officers with upper-class social origins today is not the same as the situation in the 1830s, when more than half of all German, British, and Swedish officers were of noble background.

More important is the fact that the contemporary officer's job remains a full-time pursuit rather than an occasional one. Advancement and continued service are now primarily dependent upon meeting specified standards of performance. Moreover, the officer's authority derives from the office itself and is no longer simply another aspect of the authority associated with the status of the officer in the society at large. The officer's authority over other military members is strictly limited by military law, and the authority to act on behalf of the state is similarly circumscribed by delegated organizational authority in place of personal authority.

Although the extent to which these practices are institutionalized in any country varies, appointment age, the maximum age, and years of service permitted for officers in specified grades are nearly always established. In the United States these rules have been translated into detailed federal law covering nearly every aspect of the appointment, promotion, separation, and retirement of officers, including officers of the national guard and reserve whose service is not full-time. Although the specific authority for such rules varies from nation to nation, the results are similar, and the position and authority of the contemporary officer is dependent upon these rules.

FRANCIS M. RUSH, JR.

SEE ALSO: Enlisted Personnel; Noncommissioned Officer; Professionalism, Military; Rank and Insignia of Rank; Warrant Officer.

Bibliography

Abrahamsson, B. 1972. *Military professionalization and political power.* Beverly Hills, Calif.: Sage.
Bendix, R. 1956. *Work and authority in industry.* New York: Wiley.
Garnier, M. 1977. Technology, organizational culture, and recruitment in the British military academy. In *World perspectives in the sociology of the military,* ed. G. Kourvetaris and B. Dobratz. New Brunswick, N.J.: Transaction Books.
Harries-Jenkins, G. 1973. The Victorian military and the social order. *Journal of Political and Military Sociology* 1:279–89.
Huntington, S. 1957. *The soldier and the state.* Cambridge: Harvard Univ. Press.
Janowitz, M. 1974. *Sociology and the military establishment.* Beverly Hills, Calif.: Sage.
Keegan, J. 1987. *The mask of command.* New York: Viking.
Lang, K. 1972. *Military institutions and the sociology of war.* Beverly Hills, Calif.: Sage.
Lewis, M. 1948. *England's sea-officers.* London: Allen & Unwin.
Marshall, S. 1947. *Men against fire.* New York: William Morrow.
Teitler, G. 1977. *The genesis of the professional officers' corps.* Beverly Hills, Calif.: Sage.
Van Doorn, J. 1969. *Military profession and military regimes.* The Hague: Mouton.
Woodham-Smith, C. 1953. *The reason why.* New York: McGraw-Hill.

OPERATIONAL ART

Sir Michael Howard has pointed out that the leading strategists of the postwar years have tended to focus more on grand strategic issues between East and West and less on the operational matters that interested their prewar predecessors, Maj. Gen. J. F. C. Fuller and Capt. B. H. Liddell Hart (Mackenzie and Reid 1989, p. 3). Extended experience with the problems and challenges of organizing the large international effort for the defense of Western Europe, however, gave rise to a recognition of the need for a better conceptual definition and arrangement of activities at the various levels of military command.

In NATO, tactical matters have been largely the responsibility of the national forces assigned to each sector of the frontier. Defense strategy has been determined in the international arena, principally at ministerial levels, with general instructions issued to the major commands in the field. Between the national commands, pursuing tactical objectives, and the major NATO commands, oriented toward strategic objectives, were the intermediate levels, which pursued objectives that, strictly speaking, were in neither category but were designed to give coherence to tactical events and to support the strategic effort. The principal concern of commanders at these intermediate levels came to be known as *operational art* (a term discussed further in the following paragraphs).

Definition

Operational art, a branch of military art, is a concept of military practice dealing with large, combined arms forces for the accomplishment of strategic goals in a theater of war or a theater of operations. It takes into consideration the strategic aims of the belligerent powers, both hostile and friendly, and the tactical doctrines of the forces involved, but its focus is on a level of affairs between the strategic and tactical. Essentially, it provides context and purpose to battles and engagements. It is the principal activity at the operational level of war and involves the design, organization, and conduct of campaigns and major operations (Carlson 1987, pp. 50 ff.).

Purpose and Scope

Operational art is dependent upon other military fields of endeavor, including intelligence, logistics, personnel management, and training. In tandem with opportunities, and within constraints imposed by limitations in these fields, operational art delineates objectives to be accomplished, task organizations to be followed, risks to be incurred, resources to be committed, and the time frame (measured in days or months) within which the action is to take place. It seeks to take maximum advantage of friendly strengths and to minimize opportunities for the opposition to realize its full operational potential. Operational art is a continuing process over the duration of a series of large, joint operations or a campaign, but it remains flexible and adjusts to changes in strategic goals.

Operational art has a scalar quality that sets it apart from both tactics and strategy, and it differs significantly from tactics in both scope and situational specificity. Whereas tactics are composed of standard practices that may be adapted to various situations, operational art is broader in scope and encompasses the application of a specific force to a specific situation for a specific end. On the other hand, it differs from strategy in its more restricted scope and in its sharper focus on the military aspects of the problem at hand. Typically, it focuses on the accomplishment of campaign objectives rather than on those of a particular battle or an entire war. Operational art is usually associated with levels of command at which substantial estimating and planning takes place and includes more than one type of armed force. While it may involve the manipulation of military units and organizations with prescribed tables of organization and equipment, it is not restricted to these in its application of power. The scope of operational art, however, does not ordinarily encompass the full military potential of the state.

The concept of operational art affects command structures, defining responsibilities and permitting flexibility and a wider reach for higher commanders. Whereas tactical-level commanders normally employ specific types of forces in prescribed patterns to accomplish immediate objectives, operational-level commanders may deploy unique task forces with specialized capabilities for longer-term purposes. The successful practice of operational art implies a flexibility in the application of force not normally found in prescribed regulations or guides for the coordination of forces. Instead, it envisions the active participation of operational-level commanders in the maneuver of large forces, occasionally at the risk of subordinate echelons and lesser objectives, for the successful outcome of a campaign.

This is not to imply that lower-level factors may be neglected in the formulation of objectives at higher levels of military art. Operational commanders must take into consideration the conditions and capabilities of tactical units, and commanders and other officials working at the strategic level must give adequate consideration to the battleworthiness and capabilities of subordinate operational commands. Campaigns and wars have been lost when the objectives established for lower-level operations were too ambitious.

It is generally accepted that operational art applies to all environmental dimensions of military affairs—land, sea, and air. Similarly, special operations of significant size involving forces of more than one service, such as vertical envelopments by airborne forces or amphibious landings, are often recognized as operational-level activities.

Relationship to the Principles of War

Of particular importance to the exercise of operational art are the principles of concentration of combat power (mass) and unity of command. Operational art pertains to the employment of combat power at a high level and in such a way that the impact of the resources against the enemy are maximized through coordinated, massed activity. A 1950 U.S. Military Academy text illustrates the connection:

> [During the 1940 Ardennes campaign] the French carried their violation of the principle of concentration of combat power even down to the organization of subordinate units. They dissipated much of their tank strength in separate battalions . . . [T]he German concentration of combat power [under General von Kleist], especially in armor, at the decisive point gave additional assurance of complete success. (USMA 1950, *The Campaign in the West, 1940*)

When the German armor was committed, it was overwhelming and decisive. No cleverness in French tactics could make up for the brilliance of the German action at the operational level.

Soviet View

The Soviets defined operational art as:

> A component part of military art, dealing with the theory and practice of preparing for and conducting combined and independent operations by major field forces and major formations of the Services. Operational art is the connecting link between strategy and tactics. Stemming from strategic requirements, operational art determines methods of preparing for and conducting operations to achieve strategic goals, and it gives the initial data for tactics, which organizes preparation for and waging of combat in accordance with the goals and missions of

> operations. Besides the general theory of operational art, which investigates the general principles of conducting operations, each Service has its own operational art. (1965, *Soviet Dictionary of Basic Military Terms.*)

Some Soviet writers traced the rise of operational art from the first half of the nineteenth century. One writer, in discussing the revolution in modern warfare brought about through the Napoleonic concept of *levée-en-masse*, argued: "in military art a new category was conceived—the operation as an aggregate of a number of engagements and encounters by one or several groupings [of armies] unified by a single concept and conducted on a broad front for several days." (1983, *Soviet Military Encyclopaedia*).

Other Soviet writers suggested that the operational art gained its modern form during World War I and the Russian civil war. They pointed out, however, that Western writers were slow to recognize the development. As combat increased in scope and complexity, the practice of operational art—the control of successive operations in campaigns—became a reality. The practice was clearly more than the tactical manipulation of military units but substantially less than the broad and multifaceted activities connected with the conduct of war. The Soviets dated the term itself from 1922, and its adoption in official Red Army documents from 1925 to 1926 (Gareyev 1985, p. 154).

The Soviets maintained that operational art grew out of their concept of military art and gained its precise expression in Soviet military science. Whereas military art had previously been treated as a two-part theory composed of only strategy and tactics, it was amended to recognize the intermediate level of activity. In 1924, a chair for the study of operational art was established at the Workers' and Peasants' Red Army (RKKA) Military Academy, under the direction of M. V. Frunze, and operational art appeared in the 1924–25 academy study program (Gareyev 1985, p. 154).

Soviet literature associates operational art with army-level operations. The next-higher echelon of command, the front, was defined in the mid-1960s as a strategic-level formation (1965, *Soviet Dictionary of Basic Military Terms*), but in the late 1970s it was defined as an operational-strategic (*oporativno-strategicheskiy*) formation (1978, *Soviet Military Encyclopedic Dictionary*). In 1982, Marshal of the Soviet Union Nikolai V. Ogarkov, Chief of the General Staff, partially explained the shift.

> Today the command authorities of *fronts* can have at their disposal weapons . . . the combat capabilities of which substantially exceed the framework of *front* operations. . . . And with the establishment of strategic nuclear forces, the top-echelon military leadership has acquired the capability to significantly influence the achievement of strategic and military-political aims and objectives. As a result, the previous forms of employment of combined units and formations of the different armed services have in large measure ceased to correspond to present-day conditions.
>
> In connection with this, one should evidently consider as the principal operation in the war today not the *front* but rather a larger-scale form of military operations—the theater strategic operation [*strategicheskuyu operatsiyu*]. (Ogarkov 1982, pp. 24-25.)

The Soviets considered corps-size units as operational-tactical (*oporativno-takticheskiy*) formations; divisions and smaller units as tactical (Donnelly 1988, p. 214).

U.S. View

U.S. military literature in the 1980s devoted extensive coverage to evolving thought about the operational level of war, which was not necessarily associated with any particular echelon of command. It pointed out, however, that theater commanders and their chief subordinates usually plan and direct campaigns (U.S. Dept. of Army 1986, p. 2-2). The implication was that theater matters are of operational consequence in American eyes, while the Soviets consider them strategic.

The difference was manifest in a contradiction of descriptions between Soviet and American military literature regarding the front. As we have noted, the Soviets referred to the front as an operational-strategic formation; American literature called it operational, along with the field army (U.S. Dept. of Army 1978, pp. 1-2).

The American concept of operational art envisioned the imposition of three questions upon a senior military commander. The essence of the art was contained in their practical fulfillment. These are:

1. What military condition must be produced in the theater of war or operations to achieve the strategic goal?
2. What sequence of actions is not likely to produce that condition?
3. How should the resources of the force be applied to accomplish that sequence of actions? (U.S. Dept. of Army 1986, pp. 2-2).

One American writer pointed out that operational art is more than thinking, it involves *doing* as well. In his words: "Deciding what to do is the easiest part. The difficult part is to get it done—especially to get that 'supereffort' which, if made to take place in the way visualized, will bring the enemy to his knees right there on the battlefield" (Cushman 1984, p. 7-1).

It should be noted that there are significant inhibitions within the NATO structure to such "doing." The forces of the alliance are of different quality, equipment, and readiness, and operate according to their own national operational concepts. Similarly, they are provided with battlefield intelligence of widely differing quality from national sources and have differing capabilities for analysis. In wartime they would be directed at the operational level (army group and above) by international commanders and staffs with little capacity for resolving any of these deficiencies. Until a great deal more developmental work is done to apply the emerging thinking on the art to the practical problems of the alliance, Western military enterprise is unlikely to benefit very much from the new thinking (Atkeson 1988, pp. 201–10).

Other NATO Views

The British army was somewhat slower than others to recognize the distinctive qualities of operational art. This was explained by a senior British analyst as a preoccupation with brushfire emergencies in far corners of the empire, with brief shattering experiences in two world wars for which it was neither materially nor professionally prepared. This analyst argued that the regimental system of the British army, as developed in the nineteenth century, afforded the army many qualities better suited for an imperial police force than for dealing with large land-mass operations on continental Europe. In his view, the army retains many of these qualities today (Mackenzie and Reid 1989, p. vii).

Writers have suggested that even the World War II experience did not provide British or American officers with sufficient opportunities for better understanding. While there was a general recognition—and lively debate—of the strategic alternatives, operational discussions tended to focus on tactical issues. Even the operations of the two army groups that landed in France in 1944 were, for the most part, independently pursued, with logistical factors tending to dominate the operational. As a result, both British and American military leaders have tended to focus on winning battles rather than on developing coherent campaign plans. One prominent writer commented, with respect to the Anglo-American tradition and operational art: "It is not merely that officers do not *speak* the word but rather that they do not *think* or practice war in operational terms, or do so only in vague or ephemeral ways" (Mackenzie and Reid 1989, p. 7). Not until the late 1980s did the British army move to establish a higher command and staff course to provide training for its officers in the complexities and coordination of large, international field forces.

The West German army has tended to hang back from questions of operational art and to defer to its NATO partners in matters pertaining to the alliance. Its own operational manual, *100-100: Command and Control in Battle*, devotes little space to matters above national organizational or tactical interest. The result for NATO has been a prolongation of the rather loose views formed between the British and U.S. forces under General of the Army Eisenhower's "broad front" strategy. The result within NATO has been a tendency to favor the delegation of defensive responsibilities to the component national corps, which they are obliged to deal with in context of their separate, largely tactical, objectives.

It is clear that Soviet thinking about operational art is rather more mature—and somewhat more rigid—than its equivalent thinking in the West. A Western consensus may eventually crystallize around a number of basic, evolving notions, but the immediate prospect is for additional discussion of the issues involved before all of the principles can be generally understood, accepted, and applied. As the process unfolds, one may expect that the NATO Alliance will gain a firmer grasp of the military art in one of its most subtle and sophisticated forms.

EDWARD B. ATKESON

SEE ALSO: Doctrine; Hierarchy of Combat; Strategy; Tactics.

Bibliography

Atkeson, E. B. 1988. *The final argument of kings: Reflections on the art of war.* Fairfax, Va.: HERO Books.

Carlson, K. G. 1987. Operational level or operational art? *Military Review* (Oct. 1987): 50ff.

Cushman, J. H. 1984. *Organization and operational employment of air/land forces.* U. S. Army War College reference text for the Center for Land Warfare.

Donnelly, C. 1988. *Red banner: The Soviet military system in peace and war.* Coulsdon, Eng.: Jane's.

Gareyev, M. A. 1985. *M. V. Frunze: Military theorist.* Trans. Foreign Broadcast Information Service. Moscow: Voyenizdat.

Holder, L. D. 1986. Operational art in the U.S. Army: New vigor. In *Essays on Strategy III.* Washington D.C.: National Defense Univ. Press.

Kozlov, S. N., ed. 1971. *The officer's handbook,* USSR Ministry of Defense, Moscow. Trans. and pub. under the auspices of the U.S. Air Force, Washington, D.C.: Government Printing Office.

Mackenzie, J. J. G., and B. H. Reid, eds. 1989. *The British army and the operational level of war.* London: Tri-Service Press.

Ogarkov, N. V. 1982. *Always in readiness to defend the homeland.* Trans. Foreign Broadcast Information Service, JPRS L/104122, 25 March. Moscow: Voyenizdat.

Scott, H. F. and F. William, eds. 1982. *The Soviet art of war: Doctrine, strategy and tactics.* Boulder, Colo.: Westview Press.

Stolfi, R. H. S. 1989. *Soviet naval operational art.* Monterey, Calif.: U.S. Naval Postgraduate School.

U.S. Department of the Army. 1986. *U.S. Army Field Manual 100-5: Operations.* Washington, D.C.: Government Printing Office.

U.S. Department of the Army. 1978. *Soviet army operations.* Washington, D.C.: Government Printing Office.

OPERATIONAL MANEUVER GROUP

The operational maneuver group (OMG) was an important component of the Warsaw Pact offensive concept. The mission of the OMGs was to pass through gaps found or created by forward echelons in the enemy defense and to advance at high speed far into the enemy hinterland. Their primary purpose was not to defeat enemy troops or capture specific objectives, but to spread confusion, to create chaos in the enemy rear areas, and to prevent any planned, coordinated use of enemy assets. In a war against NATO or China, a high-priority task would be the prevention of nuclear response. On the operational level (army or front), an OMG could have consisted of a tank division, a motorized rifle division, or smaller or larger formations.

Deep penetration has a long tradition in Russian and Soviet doctrine. Czarist Russian armies always had excellent cavalry (in which the Cossacks were an important element) and a large number of czarist cavalry troopers and officers rose to high rank in the Soviet army (e.g., Marshal Zhukov). As early as 1927, V. Triandafillov wrote *The Basic Character of Operations of Modern Armies*, which demanded a strategy of deep, rapid armored thrusts into the enemy hinterland with powerful support by friendly airpower. Thus, it is not surprising that in 1939 the Soviet army had more tanks than the rest of the world (France was second) and was about to start production of the T34 (the best tank of World War II according to many experts).

The concept of achieving decisive victory rapidly by striking primarily not at the enemy forces, but at the political, economic, and military structure, gained additional emphasis in the USSR after the advent of nuclear weapons. If victory in a nuclear war is considered possible, it must be achieved before a strategic nuclear exchange, and this victory is desirable before the enemy responds with tactical or theater nuclear weapons. This could be achieved with a superiority of active peacetime conventional forces, strategic surprise, and special forces plus OMGs for massive strikes in the enemy hinterland. Throughout the decades following World War II, this concept has been important in the Red Army and the Warsaw Pact forces.

In a major offensive, the operational level of command (army or front, according to Soviet doctrine) could organize its second attacking wave in one of three ways:

- as a second echelon, that is, as a force with a predetermined mission (and possibly an alternative mission) that is only feasible when the situation is clear and predictable enough to allow detailed pre-planning,
- as a reserve, that is, a force without a pre-planned mission, which allows more flexibility when facing a new situation but requires more planning time during the battle before the force can be committed, or
- as an OMG, when disruption of the enemy defense system deep in the enemy rear areas is the primary consideration.

In theory, an OMG could even be forced parallel to a second echelon. But under most circumstances such a division of forces would leave either the first echelon, or the second echelon, or the OMG too weak to fulfill its mission.

The nuclear environment, and the stated NATO doctrine of flexible response, required that decisive results be achieved by attacking Warsaw Pact forces before the enemy could complete his nuclear decision-making process. Therefore, the enemy must be denied the time to fully activate his forces, to deploy to planned defensive positions, and to complete his preparations. Stable front lines that NATO would attempt to establish for its forward defense were to be prevented by surprise attack of the first-echelon divisions and armies, with OMG(s) passing through the holes and gaps found or created by the forward troops. If the enemy succeeded in a planned deployment to defensive positions, the first echelon would have had to smash holes for the high-speed advance of the OMG.

In the enemy hinterland, the OMG would deploy into widely dispersed subgroups (often of battalion size) to spread confusion; to conceal the OMG's strength, exact location, and intent; and to seize or destroy important objectives such as headquarters, communication centers, and depots. The flanks of the OMG would not be protected by troops assigned to such a mission, but by continuous movement, by the enemy's confusion, and—should further force committal be necessary—primarily by fixed-wing or rotary-wing air support.

The primary objective of an OMG was psychological. But to achieve this goal, the OMG was also given a final physical objective, such as seizing crossings over a large waterway, a port, or major communications center, a major headquarters, or even the enemy's capital.

The concept of OMG systematized the age-old concept of exploitation of battlefield victory by keeping up relentless pressure on the enemy nerve centers. Historical examples include: the pursuit of the Persian king Darius by Alexander the Great in 330 B.C., the pursuit of Muhammad Ala-ud-Din of Khwarizmia from Samarkand and Buchara through Persia to the shores of the Caspian by troops of Genghis Khan, and the advance of Guderian's and Rommel's panzers through northern France in 1940.

OMG tactics require a high degree of daring and initiative. This was often displayed during World War II by many Soviet officers, despite the tremendous losses suffered by the Soviet officer corps during Stalin's purges and in the first phase of the German-Russian war. Also, despite their rigid system of government, communist armies in Korea and Vietnam have displayed an admirable level of initiative and tactical cunning. Thus, it is probable that a lack of initiative would not have inhibited the use of OMG tactics by Warsaw Pact armies.

Logistics have seldom prevented a daring raid. Ammunition consumption traditionally is low; the chief requirement is fuel. What cannot be found locally can today be supplied by air. NATO's traditional shortage of operational reserves would make it very difficult to destroy OMGs with combat troops, once the OMGs had reached the rear areas. Airpower could be a powerful defense, if air superiority in the area was achieved and if the weather permitted, although confusion and the uncertainty of the situation could inhibit successful employment of airpower. The best defense would be preservation of a battlefield situation that denied the enemy the opportunity to use his OMGs. This would require timely deployment of NATO forces to defensive positions in order to prevent surprise and to establish a coherent defense. It would also require maintaining such a coherent defense, as well as close surveillance and coordinated attack of follow-on forces, of which OMGs are a part. Thus, it may not be incidental that the follow-on forces attack (FOFA) concept was enunciated in the early 1980s shortly after the Soviet army's renewed emphasis on deep penetration and OMGs became known to the West.

FRANZ UHLE-WETTLER

SEE ALSO: Follow-on Forces Attack; Operational Art; Strategy; Tactics; Warsaw Pact Policy and Strategy.

Bibliography

Baxter, W. P. 1986. *Soviet airland battle tactics.* Novato, Calif.: Presidio Press.

OPERATIONS RESEARCH (OR), MILITARY

Operations research has always defied precise definition; initially, it was identified simply as "what an operations analyst does." P. M. Morse and G. E. Kimball (1951) defined it in 1951 as "a scientific method of providing executive departments with a quantitative basis for decisions regarding operations under their control." Key to that definition is the use of the scientific method in support of a decision. Peter Zehna (1971) characterized operations research as "a science devoted to describing, understanding, and predicting the behavior of systems involving men and machines." Since it is an applied science, it can cut across many engineering and scientific fields.

The application of scientific methods to military problems has long historical precedent. Originally, it dealt primarily with the use of new weapons or instruments—from the great mathematician Archimedes' effort in defending Syracuse from the Roman fleet, to Leonardo da Vinci's war machines. Vauban advised Napoleon on the better use of existing weapons, rather than new weapons, one of the first applications of the scientific approach to analysis of operations rather than equipment. In World War I, Thomas Edison applied methodologies similar to today's operations analysis to problems of antisubmarine warfare.

Historically, the number of combatants on each side has been a determinant of the likely outcome of an engagement. In the period following World War I, the Englishman F. W. Lanchester and the Russian Osipov independently developed equations that determine the outcome of an engagement at any time in terms of the number of active participants on each side at that time. Unfortunately, Lanchester's contribution, while important and enlightening, did not find an organizational structure for the employment of his equations until World War II.

Between the wars, the English meteorologist L. F. Richardson developed a system of linear equations to prove that an unstable arms race resulted in World War I when the parties perceived that they could not maintain their security in the face of their opponents' growing armaments. Richardson's work did not receive recognition until it was republished in 1950.

In the early days of World War II, scientists in the United States and in Great Britain convinced their military leaders that the scientific approach to military problems could help in solving immediate problems. In Britain, P. M. S. Blackett assembled a team of experts to study counters to the German submarine threat and developed new tactics for Britain's air defense. In April 1942, the U.S. Navy assembled the Operations Research Group. These eminent scientists advised the forces afloat, the Chief of Naval Operations, and his staff on a variety of matters including the operational use of naval equipment, the operational evaluation of new equipment to meet requirements, the development of tactics to be used, the technical aspects of strategic planning, and statistical analyses of operational wartime data. Early efforts dealt with search patterns against enemy submarines, tactics for laying and fuzing mines, sizing and routing of convoys, and the best tactics and weapons mixes for bombers and antiaircraft units.

A number of causes led to the rapid advance of operations research after the war. For one thing, with the advent of World War II warfare, military tactics had become so complex that operations research began to develop as a formal discipline. It was also recognized that modern warfare consists of many similar operations that can be analyzed as a group, rather than as individual, unique battles. Furthermore, the use of complex machines with human interfaces produces much more statistically predictable operations than older methods. (However, both a unique commander and the use of unusual tactics are still important factors.)

Since World War II, operations research has grown tremendously. Weapons, command and control systems, and countermeasures all have evolved so rapidly in both complexity and expense that it has become impossible to perform sufficient tests and field trials to assess the value of tactics. It has therefore become necessary to rely on analyses to develop robust tactics for employing systems in a variety of scenarios, under a variety of conditions. Furthermore, the area of influence on the battlefield, which in turn influences individual engagements, has become very large. Any number of disparate engagements can be influenced by fire support, logistics, airborne troops, and other support that may originate far from the immediate area of the engagement. And each of these forces is responsible in turn for providing support over a large area. Consequently, the area to be included in analyses has grown enormously.

Since World War II, operations research has developed methods to support decisions of military commanders and departmental chiefs at all levels of command, in support of all the military branches and all types of tasks: combat, combat support, logistics, tactics, strategy, test and evaluation, and so forth. The small scientific groups that assisted the commanders during the war rapidly spawned pseudo-governmental think tanks that expanded the application of operations research approaches. Examples of these early groups include Project RAND, the Operations Research Office, and the Operations Evaluation Group in the United States, and the study group at the Royal Military College of Science, Shrivenham, in the United Kingdom.

Operations research—or rather, the use of the scientific method—also has spawned a number of closely related disciplines. While operations research generally deals with the optimum employment of existing resources to achieve a specified objective, systems analysis applies many of the same methods to analyze the cost and effectiveness (benefit) of alternative systems to perform a specified mission. These analyses generally support material acquisitions in the context of resource constraints. Very closely related to systems analysis is economic analysis, which deals with cost/benefit analyses from an economic point of view. Policy analysis is another related area that uses operations research methods to analyze the potential economic or political effects of various policy alternatives, which may have an impact that transcends pure military or defense considerations.

Operations research is totally user oriented; it must provide him with independent advice about his problems in his terms. Furthermore, operations research is generally applied to real-world problems, and frequently must provide the best possible answers within severe time constraints. Many times a situation demands an "about right" answer delivered on time—a more detailed answer would be too late and useless. Furthermore, answers are often based on incomplete and heterogeneous data that must be normalized to be useful.

In the U.S. Army, as in the other military services, operations research capability carries a special designator for military officers. It describes their duties as the use of "techniques such as statistical inference and decision theory, mathematical programming, probabilistic models, network analysis, and computer science" to solve complex operational and strategic military issues (U.S. Army Pamphlet 600-3). Each of the military services has developed training manuals, and operations research has been a major department at the Naval Post-Graduate School since the early days of the school.

The development of operations research in the Soviet Union differed significantly from that in the West. While Western powers recruited young, aggressive scientists to work on military problems, the Soviets drew on their military officers working in technical fields. Their officers had a much stronger educational background in mathematics than students in the West.

Osipov published his studies in 1915, totally independent of Lanchester's reports in 1914 (Helmbold and Rehm 1991). Osipov's papers were accepted more seriously in the Soviet military structure than Lanchester's were in the West. During World War II, a Soviet General Staff Department for the Utilization of War Experience carried out analyses analogous to operations research in the West.

After the war, the Soviets continued to emphasize assisting commanders with real-time solutions. They focused more on organizational and control problems, while in the West emphasis shifted into the battle planning and system acquisition process. Soviet operations research continued into areas of force ratios and combat potentials. However, while in the West such concepts are primarily used in the planning and studies process, in the Soviet Union these concepts were to be used by the field commanders in assessing their real tactical situation. Furthermore, cybernetics, which originated with Wiener in the West, received considerable emphasis in the Soviet Union in connection with development of control processes. The use of economic models and decision theory was delayed for decades in the Soviet Union because of the potential of deviation from orthodox Marxist doctrine.

The Classical Approach to Operations Research

Definition of the Problem

The classical approach to an operational analysis is to carefully define the problem, the objective and the scope of the analysis, the criteria for selecting the preferred course of action, measures of effectiveness for separating alternatives, and the constraints on the selection (usually resources, the environment, or time). The analyst and the decision maker jointly define the problem in operational terms; this is the single most important step toward solving the problem. The definition must clearly specify the objective to be achieved, without prescribing a solution.

Related to the definition of the scope of the analysis is an understanding of the depth of the analysis. The primary factors affecting scope are the time and resources available. In many cases the availability of a model and the availability of data are critical. A detailed model for which adequate data cannot be found may be a waste of time. The tendency to go too far into detail must be resisted equally by the analyst and by the user. Analysts like to go into detail because of their scientific culture, and users like to go into detail because it frequently adds "realism." Unfortunately, the complexity of the problem and the time required to solve it usually grow exponentially with an increase in resolution.

A good analysis should include all alternatives to achieve the objective, and not rule out any until some analysis is performed. Alternatives can be deleted early if they exceed either the available resources or the available time. Similarly, the null hypothesis—the alternative stating that no action should be taken—frequently is omitted as a viable alternative, although it is not obviously untenable. Furthermore, omission of a key variable, either because it is too difficult to analyze or because no data are available, can seriously bias the results.

Measures of Effectiveness and Constraints

The choice of the best measures of effectiveness, or the standards by which alternatives are compared, is another critical factor in operational analysis. There may be a temptation to select a measure because it is easy to quantify, although it presents only part of the solution. During World War II, merchant ships were armed with antiaircraft guns. The gunners were poorly trained, and the crews downed few enemy aircraft, so the guns were to be removed. However, before the decision to remove the guns was finalized, an operational analysis showed that enemy aircraft avoided attacking ships with antiaircraft crews, and therefore very few ships with guns were sunk, compared with unarmed ships. The proper measure of effectiveness was, therefore, the number of ships crossing safely, rather than the number of aircraft downed.

Next, the constraints on the problem must be identified. These may be the resources available, the forces available, time criteria, space limitations, and so on.

Model Selection

Many considerations should be weighed in a selection of the proper analytical model (see Hughes 1984). First is the nature of the decision to be made and the way a model might help in providing insight. The study objectives, the scope and degree of resolution desired, the criteria for choice, and the measures of effectiveness must be clearly understood by the user and the analyst alike, and all of these elements affect the model selection.

A model must have credibility with the user. This is particularly true of models that represent processes in highly abstract ways not normally understood by many decision makers. One method for achieving credibility is to use a model that has been validated in similar usage. If a new model must be developed, the development and use of a new model must be constrained by the time that is available to develop the model, collect the necessary data, run the model, and analyze the results to arrive at logical, defensible conclusions.

Model selection frequently suffers from a lack of preanalysis to refine the scope and identify the critical issues that affect the decision. Only the essential parameters should enter into the analysis. As Albert Einstein said, everything should be made "as simple as possible, but not simpler." Hughes (1984) has stated that the discernment of what is relevant comes from talent and experience.

Finally, models for use in operational analysis must be: objective; transportable; valid, or verifiable; and acceptable. The need for objectivity is obvious, but it is not unusual for models to be applied to prove a preconceived or client-directed conclusion. To be transportable, people other than the originator should be able to use the model. Transportability implies good documentation of the model and the process. In order for the client to believe and defend the results, the model should be acceptable in the analytical community for its methodological soundness, and in the decision-making community because it appears to represent the real-world process in a sensible manner.

Finally, models are characterized by their degrees of resolution. This covers the whole spectrum from duels of individuals or small units, in which each weapon and target pair are analyzed individually, to battles involving large, heterogeneous forces, to analyses of national policies including not only defense but also economic and other considerations involving national values.

Data Collection

After selection of the best analytical approach, the necessary data requirements are identified, data are collected, and the analysis is performed.

A key item directly related to model selection is data availability. Clearly, a model is not applicable if key data are not available or cannot be deduced. In addition to being accurate, data must be applicable, and they are perishable. To be applicable, data not only must measure the key parameter, but also must be comparable. Data selected from different sources may have to be adjusted, normalized, or modified to be comparable. Data are particularly perishable when dealing with high-technology areas. If the state of the art progresses too fast, data become useful only to analyze trends and tendencies.

In many cases, the needed operational data will not be available. In this case pseudo-data may have to be generated by analytical means. This is particularly true in areas of strategic nuclear warfare and electronic warfare, where limited information is available. In many such cases, particularly when dealing with contentious data, the trends or rates of change may be more important than the absolute magnitudes.

Sensitivity Analysis

All analyses include varying degrees of uncertainties. The cause of these uncertainties may be in the assumptions, the modeling of the process itself, or the availability, reliability, or accuracy of key data. To test the robustness of a solution, sensitivity analyses should be performed that determine the degree of variation in the results as a function of changes in the key variables, indicating uncertainties.

Methodologies

Many different methods are applicable to solve operational problems. All analytical methods are representations of the "real world" with varying degrees of abstraction. Hughes (1984) states that "in operations research the goodness of a model is judged by how well it achieves its purpose."

The types of methods most prevalent in operations analysis form a continuum of abstraction in which mathematical models are the most abstract and war games the most realistic. The following general types of methodologies are discussed here: mathematical models, simulations, war games, field exercises, and gaming.

In addition to the degree of abstraction, a principal distinction of automated models is their reliance on either deterministic or stochastic processes. In a deterministic model, each action is followed by one and only one reaction. Selected parameters fix the state of the system at any one time. In general, parameters achieve average value and the results have no explicitly defined confidence limits.

On the other hand, stochastic models involve random processes. The model describes transition probabilities; the next state of the system is determined by the present state and the probability of various end states occurring. Stochastic models do not provide the same results on each replication but must be repeated until a common result is approached. Stochastic models, after replications, can be used to determine the confidence bounds of the final result. In some complex situations, stochastic processes can be used to determine average values for use in deterministic models. For example, if key values for a parameter cannot be determined through repeated field or operational tests, stochastic models of the process can be used to arrive at an "average" value.

Mathematical Models

Mathematical models are logical constructs representing real-world operational processes. Since they are usually highly abstract and represented by mathematical symbolism, they tend to be opaque to the user. Their credibility rests partly on the reputation of the analyst and partly on the ability of the user to understand and believe the underlying logic.

The key to mathematical models is an understanding of the operational process. The analyst should be able to validate the mathematical model against real occurrences or credible simulations.

Mathematical models normally consist of one or more algorithms or equations. Computational limitations generally limit such models to a few key variables.

The earliest mathematical models determined the likely outcome of a battle simply by counting the opposing forces. In the twentieth century, the Lanchester equations have been used to determine the outcome of an engagement in terms of ratios of the opposing forces. This greatly oversimplifies real-world warfare, but it yields some insight regarding battle in certain limited cases. The Lanchester analysis methodology has been extended to differentiate between aimed fire and mass fire. Deitchman developed the use of Lanchester models for ambush analysis. He determined that the ambusher employed aimed fire (square law), while the ambushee uses area fire (mixed Lanchester laws). Inputs have also been adjusted to represent heterogeneous forces, where different types of weapons systems are weighted differently. An extensive literature has developed to extend the use of Lanchester-type equations (see Taylor 1980 and Taylor 1983).

From the early days of operations research during World War II, the problem of searching for an enemy was one of the chief objectives analyzed (Koopman 1946). Search theory has advanced since the war (Washburn 1980), but a unified presentation of the basic results of search theory emerged only recently (Stone 1987). A Bayesian approach is used with a prior distribution for the target's location and a function relating the conditional probability of detecting a target to the search effort.

Simple algorithms are sometimes incorporated into more complex models. Complex force effectiveness models or simulations include simple algorithms in which the outcome of an engagement and the rate of movement of troops is simply determined by the ratio of the opposing forces.

Lanchester-type calculus has been used to derive the opponent force ratios that are required to attack or defend an objective. For example, it is generally assumed that a force ratio of about 5 to 1 is required to attack an enemy who has fortified himself. In fact, in Operation Desert Storm (1991), the Allied forces and the Iraqi forces were approximately equal in number, and the Iraqi defensive positions were well prepared with obstacles. In spite of the lack of numerical superiority, the Allies won a decisive victory.

Force ratios are used as gross measures, as they completely ignore key factors such as terrain, weather, leadership, technological advantages, command and control, human factors, logistic support, and intelligence. Israel could have never won a war in the Middle East if it were to rely on such ratios.

A further limitation on the use of simple mathematical models is the requirement that the mechanism and the interactions involved in the operation being analyzed be clearly understood. However, even if the so-called constants in the simple equations are not constant and the results represent averages, simple algorithms are still useful in gaining further insight into the process and in simplifying communication with the user.

Simple algorithms are also frequently used at high decision levels for sensitivity analyses, to analyze large changes in assumptions or input data, and to perform "what if" exercises. These simple algorithms have frequently been calibrated against more complicated and thorough simulations.

SIMULATIONS

Simulations are models that emulate the operational process. They range from complex, abstract programs to programs that contain a great deal of real-world symbolism and are more transparent to military commanders. Simulations are generally automated and vary greatly in complexity. Many simulations are used for training purposes as well as for analysis. They may vary from totally automated models to models that stop periodically for human interaction. Simulations are gaining additional sophistication by incorporating artificial intelligence rules in the automated decision processes (Silverman and Hutzler 1986).

Simulations generally model stochastic processes. They proceed in either time steps or event steps. At each step the current status is assessed and transition probabilities are provided. Randomness governs both the occurrence of the event and its outcome. For example, if a tank battle is simulated, each weapon is analyzed at each step, and the random process determines both whether a weapon has fired and whether the outcome (e.g., a destructive hit) has been achieved. Because of the random nature of simulations, many replications may be required before closure on a result is achieved.

In generating a simulation, the mechanisms involved in individual subprocesses should be understood. However, the overall process involving all these interactions is usually hidden in the program; as a result, the simulation often provides insight into the overall process, even if the interaction of the individual subprocesses is not understood.

The potential opacity of the many interactions is a principal limitation of simulations. Since the logic cannot be examined in detail, validation of such models against other models is advised. Another limitation is the fact that simulations are built by expert computer programmers who may not have any understanding of the context or the processes involved and may take computational shortcuts that may affect the results.

Another serious limitation of simulations is their inability to consider synergism adequately. It is very difficult to synergistically integrate the impact of weapon effects, intelligence, service support, and command, control, and communications (C^3) and arrive at quantitative force capabilities or indices. Furthermore, although many actions may actually occur simultaneously, they must be analyzed sequentially because of computer limitations. Future computers, with much increased parallel processing capability, will be able to handle larger simulations or the same simulations much faster than today. The Military Operations Research Society (MORS) recently convened a series of workshops on "Simulation Technology 1997" to assess the appropriate direction for military simulation technology over the next decade (MORS 1988–1989). Four key concerns emerged at the initial session:

- The community's ability to model complex processes
- The implications of improved hardware and software
- The effort required to capitalize on parallel processing
- The need for an analyst's "workbench" that could support the development and maintenance of military simulations

WAR GAMES

War games may be defined as any analysis of warfare that involves humans as either players, referees, or decision makers. War games generally involve human decisions applied to a set of scenarios using pre-established rules. They are usually the models most transparent to the decision maker, since they may represent a significant amount of realism. In classical war games, two opposing teams of individuals determine their strategies and tactics and then perform moves. A referee team ensures that the rules are observed and determines the winner of a given engagement. The referee team also can introduce changes in the scenario or obstacles to gain further insight into the decision-making process of the participants. This is the most resource-intensive method of analysis. War games cannot be replicated readily and therefore are totally dependent on the ingenuity of the participants. Considerable discussion of war games is found in Brewer and Schubick (1979).

It is easy to introduce variables into models for the sake of representing realism. However, these factors may not be relevant to the analysis and only complicate the analytical process.

At a MORS workshop on "Future Wargaming Developments" (1989), it was pointed out that war games are particularly useful for

- Stimulating a better vision of future warfare
- Creating frames of reference
- Building consensus about significant issues such as program need
- Assessing operational concepts
- Stimulating insights missed by other analytical models
- Producing insights and issues (not quantitative results)
- Improving the judgment context underlying decisions
- Communicating across diverse technical, policy, and operational communities
- Devising flexible analysis of problems.

War games are particularly useful for assessing complex interactions, issues, and ideas that still have considerable ambiguity. The workshop provided detail on applying war gaming to technology issues, acquisition questions, and test and evaluation decisions.

Field Exercises

Field exercises lie at the extreme end of the complexity spectrum and are generally not designed with an emphasis on gathering data for analyses. Their limitations for analysis purposes are enormous. They are always resource-limited, and each engagement is one of a kind and probably not repeatable. Conditions are uncontrolled from the scientist's point of view but too controlled from an operations analyst's point of view. Resources are carefully controlled and plans carefully drawn to ensure that the planned events will actually occur. There is no surprise and no real stress during the exercise. Troops are generally well briefed on the expected.

Some limited data useful for operations analyses have been gathered on instrumented ranges that do furnish input valuable to small engagement models. However, these data are of very limited scope—for example, detection and intervisibility data and hit and kill probabilities on selected targets.

Game Theory

Game theory is a mathematical theory in which two or more adversarial parties make decisions that affect each other. The simplest form is a two-party, zero-sum game in which two parties play against each other; a loss by one party equals a gain by the other party, keeping the total value of the game zero (Washburn 1990).

When applied to warfare, or more usually to duels, game theory analyzes the optimum action to take by either side, on the basis of what each side analyzes to be the enemy's best alternative. Game theoretic solutions are generally applied to *when* each side should take an action rather than *what* action each side should take.

The U.S. Air Force has applied gaming to a number of issues, and national strategic studies (nuclear exchanges and deterrence) have been studied using game theory. Unfortunately, real warfare is not a truly zero-sum game, and, furthermore, stable solutions are usually not achievable.

Unquantifiables

Critical decision makers for years have expressed the concern that operations analysis frequently assesses certain parameters unrealistically. In 1986, MORS (1991) convened a workshop to review "More Operational Realism in the Modeling of Combat (MORIMOC)," which was generated from a charge of the U.S. Air Force that (1) the lethality of almost everything is overestimated; (2) the creativity of the opponent in limiting damage, or the effect of damage is underestimated; and (3) analysts do not account for the degree to which smart (or dumb) use of forces can dominate the outcome of conflict. The most important result of the workshop was to identify subjects deserving further and more intensive discussion.

Many critical factors are very difficult to model—human performance in particular. MORS also has sponsored a number of workshops on "Human Behavior and Performance as Essential Ingredients in Realistic Modeling of Combat." The purpose of these workshops is to develop understanding of the extent to which human performance and behavior affect combat and the inputs to military decisions, and to define approaches to including human performance factors in modeling and analysis of combat, in order to account for the influence of humans in assessing the battlefield effectiveness of military forces. Considerable insight was gained in the workshops, partly because of the diversity of disciplines represented by the participating individuals.

All analytical and simulation methods are limited also by other critical factors that cannot be readily quantified: terrain, environmental factors, surprise, readiness, leadership, training, morale, fatigue, and so forth. Historical wars, when analyzed using today's methods, result in a much different outcome than actually occurred. For example, few models using the parameters involved in the Mideast conflicts would award a victory to a much outmanned Israel. Some historians have tried to quantify these qualities. Notably among them is Dupuy (1985) who developed the Quantified Judgment Method. He analyzed a large number of historical battles in many different historical wars and determined factors for those human qualities that modify the purely quantifiable parameters.

Model Validation

The importance of validating a model is receiving increasing emphasis. As models become more complex and more opaque, validation becomes increasingly important in order to maintain the credibility with the user.

Payne (1984) observed that all models are technically invalid. They contain abstractions, omissions of observable details, and approximations in computation. They may also be invalid in their logical structure or invalid for a particular application. He states that the correct question to ask is, "What steps have been taken to corroborate this model, and over what range of application can it be shown to be utilitarian?"

A 1990 MORS minisymposium on simulation validation reviewed the verification and validation process carefully, with a view toward having accredited models acceptable for specific purposes.

Applications

In addition to categorizing models by their characteristics of abstraction, they can be grouped by the types of decisions they are designed to support. The following applications of models are discussed below:

- Wartime operations
- Battle planning
- Weapons procurement
- Force sizing
- Human resource planning

- Logistics planning
- National policy analysis
- Information warfare analysis
- Cost analysis
- Training models

WARTIME OPERATIONS

Operations research was born in support of warfare during World War II. Operations research groups have supported most military operations since then.

During World War II, the analysis of wartime operations involved primarily the analysis of current, very heterogeneous data, to solve short-term problems. Thomas (1984) points out that such analyses frequently are little more than simple hypotheses tested with wartime data. A wartime modeler uses a variety of existing data to look for some logical structure. The coarseness of the data leads to hypotheses that are expected to explain only big changes, what Morse and Kimball refer to as "hemibel" thinking. Thomas (1984) emphasizes that World War II analyses involved digging for "facts," deep thought, and imagination. Quick analysis of wartime data does not account for leadership, morale, courage, or luck.

Staats (1991), based on Desert Storm experience, points out that today's battlefield operations analyst does much more than analyze "dirty" data. The men and women in combat who must implement the operations analysis are frequently not highly technically trained, and may be under great stress and suffering from fatigue. It is therefore essential that military analysis on the battlefield be kept simple. A principal type of analysis deals with the most effective distribution of constrained resources to achieve the objective of the mission. During peacetime, the military develops complex models and simulations of all types of contingencies to produce tables, charts, and heuristics that the analyst or the decision maker at the lowest echelon can use in wartime to select the optimum course of action. The key to using these analyses is to adapt that information to the particular situation, improvise where necessary, and integrate the plan with all the other relevant plans competing for the same set of resources.

The Eighth International Symposium on Military Operational Research was held in September 1991 at Shrivenham on the role of operations research in the Gulf War. Many papers presented at that meeting described quick, limited operational analyses that were performed by ad hoc teams to directly support commanders in the field. In many instances, their analyses were accepted and their recommendations implemented. Professor Sheppard summarized the experience in two conclusions: "Gaining the confidence and respect of operational personnel is as essential today as it ever was. . . . Most OR groups seemed unprepared for the demands made upon them and had to depend on quick and untested modifications and improvisations if they were to have any impact."

Similar results were reported from the American study groups, except for the navy's Center for Naval Analyses, whose professionals rotate from Washington to the deployed fleets in peacetime on a routine basis in order to gain experience in fleet operations analysis.

Military historians perform another type of analysis of wartime operations. Dupuy (1985), for example, reviewed data from a series of wars, preferably employing data gathered by all adversaries, to account for trends in the unquantifiables. His Quantified Judgment Method attempts to shed light on the impact of leadership, morale, training, readiness, and environmental factors on the combat capabilities of each side. Such analysis involves an excruciating collection and sorting of data.

BATTLE PLANNING

Battle planning uses quantitative models to prepare for wartime tactics, strategies, and tactical analyses. Its historical antecedent reaches to the early nineteenth century and before, when battles were planned using maps and sandtables. The purpose of battle planning is to improve the tactics and strategies used in wartime and the employment of weapons, and to assist the weapon systems requirements and acquisition selection process. This process may involve all types of models. Hughes (1984) points out that most of these analyses are used to gain insight by observing rates of change. The absolute numbers resulting from these models have limited credibility, but trends are important.

Battle planning can involve all types of models—mathematical models, simulations, or war games—depending on the decision level at which planning occurs, the problem to be analyzed, and the time and data available. Wise (1991) has reported on the use of Lanchester equations for automated battle planning. Specifically, Lanchester equations were used in the command and control module of a high-level combat simulation.

One limitation of battle planning models is determining when combat has ended and selecting a winner. Victory or defeat is frequently considered to be subject to the perception of the commander, in light of the total knowledge he possesses at that time. Perceptions and knowledge limitations, particularly the inclusion of false or uncertain knowledge, are very difficult to model. Considerable research on termination of a battle has been done by McQuie (1987) and Fain (1988). Fain studied 83 defeats in World War II and found 39 contributing factors. However, she isolated three factors that could reproduce the results of the defeat in 80 percent of the cases. Key findings include

- Defeat cannot be accounted for solely on the basis of casualty *rates*.
- The maneuver by each force and their tactical postures are often decisive influences.
- Attackers forced to quit did so in most cases with casualties lower than 5 percent per day.

A recent symposium was held by MORS on the subject of operational art and analysis, dealing with the importance of the operational level and linking the lower tactical level to the higher strategic level of war. Tactics are designed to win battles, operations are designed to win campaigns, and strategy is designed to win wars. Operations analysts have been concerned with tactical problems and, to a lesser extent, with grand strategy. However, the operational art allows the commander to employ his resources optimally by changing the concept of operations to more effectively accomplish his mission. One of the outcomes of this symposium was an emphasis on the long view and on care in choosing measures of effectiveness.

Systems Procurement

Systems procurement is primarily the domain of systems analysis, using operations research methods. These methods are used in both the cost and effectiveness analyses, which are combined to compare the various alternatives examined. This discipline has become increasingly important as the size and cost of systems has grown to preclude building and testing a full array of prototypes in a variety of combat environments. With the uncertainty of future environments and possible enemy countermeasures and the need to compare multipurpose weapons in different scenarios, the analysis of developmental systems must receive primary emphasis. In addition, analysis now considers weapons that have a major influence, even if they never fire a shot, by constraining the enemy's choice of tactics to avoid them.

The primary purpose of cost-effectiveness models is to describe to the decision maker the boundaries of the problem and the required tradeoff. One of the difficulties in these analyses is to completely model the new capabilities, as well as potential enemy countermeasures. For a long time, common U.S. Army models were not able to fully model a new tank's night vision and shoot-on-the-move capability. Consequently the new capabilities were not given the full effectiveness in the cost-effectiveness ratio, and critics considered the new capability to be too expensive. Furthermore, different concepts for employing the new capability, as well as enemy reactions to the new capability, are rarely fully analyzed. For years the new tank was used in simulations just like the old tank with marginally improved capability, rather than as a whole new concept for conducting tank warfare.

Force Structure and Sizing

Force structure and sizing models can easily become very detailed and complex if the decision maker insists on adding "realism" that does not aid the analysis. If force structure models are to be played out in a wide variety of scenarios, simplicity and consideration of only the essential factors is needed to make the analysis manageable.

Hughes (1984) states that force mix problems are, in general, easier to handle than force sizing problems. In the former, alternatives are compared in similar situations. On the other hand, force sizing problems deal with the issue of "how much is enough," which is heavily weighted toward political and economic, as well as military, considerations. The most credible analyses deal with force changes at the margin, increases or decreases, or effectiveness trends.

There is great uncertainty regarding future environments and scenarios in which forces may be called upon to support national policy. Furthermore, it is difficult to determine how forces will be used under such circumstances. This again emphasizes the need for simple models. Nevertheless, such models cannot be validated against facts, and therefore the only proof lies in the credibility of the logic used in the model.

The recent emphasis of force reductions, resulting from the collapse of the Soviet Union, has led to the generation of very comprehensive computerized effectiveness and force costing models that include all aspects of the force, including all the required support at all echelons within the theater.

Human Resource Planning

Human resource planning involves the use of manpower, personnel, and training models. These models differ from the above applications in that considerations of enemy capabilities do not play a significant role. The principal factors analyzed involve demographics, training requirements, increasing complexities of tasks to be performed, weapon systems to be employed, and the use of automated data processing.

Human resource models must consider the impact of long-term trends, since changes in policy generally take years to be fully effective. These types of models are used extensively to support the normal management process, as well as key policy decisions. Many battle planning models and simulations also have served as primary training models.

Logistics Planning

Logistics planning involves maintenance, supply, and transportation processes and resources. Key in these analyses is the tradeoff between short-term (readiness) and long-term (modernization) goals.

Historically, logistic supplies have always suffered severe insufficiencies in peacetime, with the expectation of instant increase at the commencement of hostilities. This policy had some merit in an era of rifles and bullets and cannon rounds. Unfortunately, with modern sophisticated weapons and reliance on very complex missile systems, such a policy may not have much validity (see Honig 1986).

Military operations analysts perform a great service to logistics support in wartime. Staats (1991) and his colleagues developed a system for improving supply of army units in combat by employing logistic release points in conjunction with forward supply battalions. This change in procedure cut the time required to supply a brigade from six hours to three. Many examples can be cited whereby efficiencies in the logistic train made a significant difference in the outcome of war.

In the past, the system acquisition process has not given full weight to the impact of logistics support. There has been a tendency to buy new systems in the acquisition process and let someone else worry about supporting the system in the field later. Unfortunately, with most new weapon systems, the cost to support the weapons in the field is far greater than the cost of initially acquiring them.

Drezner and Hillestad (1984) indicate that logistics planning models include the use of linear and dynamic programming, network analysis, queuing, inventory analysis, and reliability and decision theory. Logistics models deal largely with optimal allocation of limited resources and are largely used to manage the resources as well as in the policy decision process.

More integration of logistical analysis and other support models into battle planning and force structure and sizing models is essential to fully predict the impact of logistics on force capabilities.

National Policy

In this context, national policy analyses include largely economic analyses of nonmilitary actions having potential military significance—for example, analyses of oil supply constraints, embargoes, or freezes of financial assets. Lieberman (1984) includes in this area principal efforts by the U.S. Arms Control and Disarmament Agency to support arms limitation negotiations, as well as analyses of the Soviet economy to sustain its military forces. Such studies also include methods for terminating war once it starts: for example, past studies of conditions to be required for terminating the U.S. conflict in Vietnam. In general, national policy analyses support decisions that transcend considerations of military goals.

In general, strategic studies do not yield credible absolute values, but generally deal in trends. The greatest utility of these models is their use in structuring debates on very controversial subjects in areas where valid data are not available.

Information Warfare Analysis

This broad subject includes C^3 and intelligence (C^3I), electronic warfare, and countermeasures. New concepts in this area cannot readily be examined and evaluated in field tests. Models in this area must rely on analysis and simulation to determine their effectiveness and robustness to countermeasures.

Unfortunately, this area is also frequently modeled inadequately in simulations. For one thing, it is difficult to write programs emulating command and control. It is said that command is an art and that it is highly personal. Furthermore, countermeasures tend to complicate and slow the progress of a simulation.

On the other hand, information warfare can make a significant difference, particularly in modern warfare where knowledge is a key weapon and time is of the essence for making timely decisions. Furthermore, in strategic nuclear warfare, for example, the reliability of the C^3 system is of national importance, as are the political control and crisis management measures. Tactical decisions regarding the detailed management of the forces during President Kennedy's Cuban Missile Crisis were made in the basement of the White House in Washington. The political decision structure must have faith in the C^3 system in place, rather than having to bypass the existing system in every crisis.

Modern information warfare systems are heavily affected by advances in computers and software technology. There is a constant attempt to improve understanding of human decision rules in order to simulate them using artificial intelligence and systems decision theory. One difficulty with using expert systems is the choice of the right expert for the system. Simulation of C^3I also must allow for human factors, including stress, which are difficult to simulate.

Simulations will be increasingly unrealistic if minimal C^3I processes are not adequately included.

Cost Analysis

Cost analysis includes many operations research procedures in cost models. Most notable are cost estimating relationships (CER), which use simple algorithms to relate cost to some key parameter. For years the cost of an airframe for an aircraft was estimated as a function of its empty weight. With the advent of new, lightweight alloys, those relationships are no longer valid. In the early days of electronics, the cost of radios was approximated by the number of vacuum tubes present (This bore a loose relationship to the complexity of the circuits). Today new relationships are evolving.

The problem with developing new CERs is particularly difficult in rapidly advancing technologies. It is usually not possible to get sufficient comparable data to perform analytical processes. A prime example is in automated data processing, which advances so rapidly that by the time sufficient data are available to perform an estimate, the next-generation processor has already been developed.

There are at least three more applications, related to material acquisition, where operations research modeling has been applied. The first is the area of learning. As the quantity of items produced increases, the unit cost should decrease as the operator learns the process and improves it. There is a maximum quantity, not defined, beyond which learning cannot be expected to occur. The second application has to do with production rate. As fewer items are produced in a given time, the fixed production costs are distributed over a smaller quantity of production items and the unit cost increases. At a sufficiently small rate, production becomes uneconomical. Finally, there is an expectation that competition causes the unit price to decrease. This is a very complicated analysis, involving the cost of competing, the size of the buy, the capitalization involved, and other factors.

One of the major problems facing industrial powers today is the cost overrun involved in buying complex military systems (see McNichols 1984). Recent analysis by the U.S. Office of the Secretary of Defense showed that cost overruns are rarely caused by methodological problems, but generally caused by either changes in requirements or changes in program (quantity, schedule).

TRAINING MODELS

Many simulations that were developed originally for analysis purposes are also used for training models. In some cases simulations or wargames are specifically designed to train commanders and their staffs. Some of these models are very sophisticated. Alexander (1991) reports on a corps-level simulation, EAGLE, that integrates artificial intelligence methods and conventional combat modeling algorithms. The author states that most combat models were developed "from the computer to the user." That is, data structures were developed for the convenience of the programmer, rather than the user. EAGLE incorporates an expert-system paradigm to implement command and control processes.

Another extensive facility is the Warrior Preparation Center (WPC), which is a joint U.S. Air Force and Army training facility at Einsiedlerhof, Germany, for senior European battle commanders. This computer facility, with a staff of about 100, runs major exercises for up to 650 personnel, up to a corps staff. It contains many individual combat models. The facility has been in operation for eight years. The principle has always been to keep it simple, using a top-down approach. Furthermore, at high echelons, trends are more important than detailed results. WPC has generated a large number of computer assisted command exercises (CPX) in a relatively short period of time.

Limitations on the Use of Operations Research

Some problems of large scope cannot be subdivided. Analysis of parts of the problem may lead to suboptimizations. But the human mind views problems in the context of the whole environment; suboptimization may lead to the omission of key factors affecting the result.

Related to this limitation is the fact that some operations analysts tend to examine problems, or portions of problems, that are amenable to solution by known mathematical means. Important parameters that are too complex, too hard to quantify, or too hard to measure are dropped in favor of an elegant solution. In particular, such key unquantifiables as leadership, morale, readiness, and training are ignored in favor of weapons effect and weapons performance, which are readily quantifiable. Such analyses trade accuracy of analysis for precision of analysis.

In some instances, operations analysis tends to be too rigid. It will examine the effectiveness of the use of weapons or forces in a conventional manner. It may not recognize the impact of the unusual employment of new weapons, the impact of new countermeasures, or the application of unusual tactics or strategies. For a long time, complex army simulations of ground warfare were unable to model combat at night or in poor visibility. The model simply drew a curtain at a specified range and no target beyond that range was visible. Only after considerable field experimentation could intervisibility data be incorporated in the models. The impact of this limitation was that new weapons with night vision capability could not be evaluated for their full potential, and tactics for optimum use of this night potential could not be evaluated.

The choice of the objective of the operation and the measure of effectiveness are extremely important. During World War II, the famous convoy sizing analysis determined that, because of economies of scale, larger convoys are favored over smaller convoys. In fact, this solution was without limit. In other words, one huge convoy was preferred over many small convoys. This shortcoming ignored such obvious factors as the delay in the delivery of goods while waiting for a big convoy to form and the bottlenecks and vulnerability at the uploading and offloading terminals servicing such a convoy.

In some cases, the choice of measures of effectiveness is not mathematically determinable but subject to political and value judgments. This is particularly true of strategic nuclear exchange models. The model can try to determine the size of the force necessary to penetrate enemy defenses and cause economic and political damage, or the forces necessary to defend against an enemy attacking the friendly economic and political targets. But the model cannot determine how much damage is enough to defeat the enemy, or how much damage the friendly forces can accept before the political and civilian structure fails.

With respect to the selection of the model, a number of cautions should be advanced. In some cases, a complex, intricate model may become an end unto itself. That is, the analyst will search for problems that fit his model, or he will alter the thrust of the analysis to fit his model, rather than address the question the decision makers would like to have answered. To the man with a hammer every problem looks like a nail.

Models are also used out of the context for which they were developed and where the application of the model has questionable validity. Furthermore, modelers frequently do not search for or adapt existing models before they venture out to build their own. In many cases, existing, already validated models will do the job.

Historically, it has been difficult to find scientists who

are equally well versed in both the intricacies of quantitative methodologies and the operational problems that they are trying to solve. This has led to communication problems between the user and the analyst in defining the goals and the parameters of the problem. The U.S. Navy's operations research groups send analysts to sea or to operational commands periodically to learn the real problems of planning and operating a navy task force. In the last few decades an increasing number of Allied military officers have become proficient in the use of operations analysis methodologies, which also has greatly eased the communications problems. In the Soviet Union the problem was different, since in most cases operations research and its related methods were developed largely by the military officers, who were quite proficient in mathematics.

A final caution must be added about the potential dual role of the operations analyst. His objective is to act as the independent advisor to the decision maker. Unfortunately, in defining the problem and selecting measures of effectiveness, bias may be introduced. The intentional or unintentional addition of bias may lead to results that reinforce the client's viewpoint, rather than providing him with an objective analysis of the alternatives. This has led analysts of a problem to focus not on the differences of the outcome but on the differences of the overt or implied assumptions employed.

Summary

Operations research is an important tool that can assist the decision maker at all levels of responsibility. When the decision maker and the analyst have agreed on the definition of the problem, the scope of the analysis, and the criteria for selecting the preferred course of action, the analyst identifies the key factors bearing on the problem, identifies trends, and provides insight into the process involved. He may also estimate outcomes of engagements, operations, battles, or wars under a variety of circumstances.

The analyst has many tools available to assist in the analysis. His selection of the proper tool involves defining the problem, the time available for solution, and the appropriate model, and ensuring that adequate data are available. The method should be validated for the purpose used. Finally, the analyst should evaluate the impact of those key factors that cannot quantitatively be included in the model analysis.

JOHN G. HONIG

SEE ALSO: Cost Analysis; Force Ratio; Lanchester Equations; Mathematics and the Military; Measures of Effectiveness; Models, Simulations, and War Games; Operations Research, Soviet and Western Military; Osipov Equations; Search Theory and Applications; Strategic Warfare, Operations Research in.

Bibliography

Alexander, R. S. 1991. Intelligent application of artificial intelligence. In *Phalanx* (December 1991). Alexandria, Va.: Military Operations Research Society.

Bracken, J. 1989. *Ground, air, and air defense force concentration model.* CAA RP 89-9. Bethesda, Md.: U.S. Army Concepts Analysis Agency.

Brewer, G. D., and M. Schubick. 1979. *The wargame: A critique of military problem solving.* Boston: Harvard Univ. Press.

Dobbie, J. M. 1968. A survey of search theory. *Operations Research* 16, no. 3.

Drezner, S. M., and R. J. Hillestad. 1984. Logistic models: Evolution and future trends. In *Military modeling,* ed. W. P. Hughes, Jr. Alexandria, Va.: Military Operations Research Society.

Dupuy, T. N. 1985. *Numbers, predictions and war: Using history to evaluate combat factors and predict outcome of battles.* Arlington, Va.: Hero Books.

Fain, J., et al. 1988. *Defeat criteria in battle.* Arlington, Va.: Data Memory Systems.

Helmbold, R. L., and A. S. Rehm. 1991. *The influence of the numerical strength of engaged forces on their casualties.* CAA-TP-91-2. Bethesda, Md.: U.S. Army Concepts Analysis Agency.

Honig, J. G. 1986. *Budgeting for sustainability.* Washington, D.C.: Operations Research Society of America Monograph.

Huber, R. K. 1989. *Parity, stability and operational minima: Observations from the analysis of simple geometric models of military operations.* S-8906, IASFOR. Munich: Universitat der Bundeswehr.

Hughes, W. P., Jr. 1984. *Overview.* In *Military modeling,* ed. W. P. Hughes, Jr. Alexandria, Va.: Military Operations Research Society.

Koopman, B. O. 1946. *Search and screening.* Operations Evaluation Group Report. Washington, D.C.: Office of Chief of Naval Operations.

Lieberman, A. 1984. Models in national policy analysis. In *Military modeling,* ed. W. P. Hughes, Jr. Alexandria, Va.: Military Operations Research Society.

Martin, J. J. 1984. Modeling nuclear warfare. In *Military modeling,* ed. W. P. Hughes, Jr. Alexandria, Va.: Military Operations Research Society.

McNichols, G. 1984. *Cost analysis.* Washington, D.C.: Operations Research Society of America Monograph.

McQuie, R. 1987. Battle outcomes: Casualty rates as a measure of defeat. *Army* (November 1987).

MORS. 1985. *Command and control evaluation workshop.* Alexandria, Va.: Military Operations Research Society.

———. 1988–1989. *Simulation technology 1997 workshop (SIMTECH 97).* Alexandria, Va.: Military Operations Research Society.

———. 1989. *Future wargaming developments workshop proceedings.* Alexandria, Va.: Military Operations Research Society.

———. 1991. *More operational realism in the modeling of combat (MORIMOC) proceedings.* Alexandria, Va.: Military Operations Research Society.

Morse, P. M., and G. E. Kimball. 1951. *Methods of operations research.* Boston: MIT Press.

Payne, W. B. 1984. Validity of models as a basis for military planning. In *Military Modeling,* ed. W. P. Hughes, Jr. Alexandria, Va.: Military Operations Research Society.

Richardson, L. F. 1950. *Arms and insecurity.* Pittsburgh, Pa.: Boxwood.

Silverman, B. B., and W. P. Hutzler. 1986. *Artificial intelli-*

gence for military applications. Washington, D.C.: Operations Research Society of America Monograph.
Staats, R. 1991. Desert Storm. *OR/MS Today* (December 1991).
Stone, L. D. 1987. *Theory of optimal search*. Washington, D.C.: Operations Research Society of America Monograph.
Taylor, J. G. 1983. *Lanchester models of warfare*. Washington, D.C.: Operations Research Society of America Monograph.
Taylor, J. G. 1980. *Force-on-force attrition modelling*. Washington, D.C.: Operations Research Society of America Monograph.
Thomas, C. J. 1984. Models and wartime combat operations research. In *Military Modeling*, ed. W. P. Hughes, Jr. Alexandria, Va.: Military Operations Research Society.
Thomas, C. J., and W. L. Deemer, Jr. 1957. The role of operational gaming in operations research. *ORSA Journal* 5(1).
Washburn, A. R. 1981. *Search and detection*. Washington, D.C.: Operations Research Society of America Monograph.
———. 1990. *Two-person zero-sum games*. Washington, D.C.: Operations Research Society of America Monograph.
Wise, B. 1991. Lanchester equations for automated planning. In *Phalanx* (March 1991). Alexandria, Va.: Military Operations Research Society.
Zehna, P. ed. 1971. *Selected methods and models in military operations research*. Washington, D.C.: Office of Naval Research.

OPERATIONS RESEARCH, SOVIET AND WESTERN MILITARY

Military operations research developed differently in the Soviet Union than in the West, starting as a distinct discipline almost twenty years after the British first used the term *operational research* (OR) in 1937. The Soviets had a number of forerunners of operations research that gave their version of the subject more of an engineering control theory and an economics orientation than in the West, where the early practitioners worked in the natural sciences. While the British and Americans recruited some of the best young civilian scientists into early OR during the war years, the USSR drew more upon established military officers working in technical fields for its early most prominent operations analysts.

Soviet military operations analysts had the advantage of being able to draw upon Western OR literature in the mid-1950s, when the journals *Operational Research Quarterly* (U.K., 1950), *Journal of the Operations Research Society of America* (later simply *Operations Research, U.S.*, 1952), *Naval Logistics Quarterly* (U.S., 1954), and *Management Science* (U.S., 1954) already existed. In addition, French, German, and Japanese operations research journals appeared in 1956–7. The Soviets were also able to draw upon Western books on OR, management science, and cybernetics, which were related to operations research in the early Soviet view of the field.

This article describes early Soviet developments, followed by a comparison of various aspects of Soviet and Western military operations research.

Early Soviet Operations Research

As in the West, the Soviet Union had pioneers who did early research similar to what would today be called operations research. M. Osipov wrote a series of long papers on Lanchester equations in *Military Collection*, June–October 1915, independent of Lanchester's 1914 paper in *Engineering*. The economist Leonid Kantorovich (who was also a lieutenant colonel and head of a department at the Naval Academy until 1947) wrote a book on linear programming in 1939, and articles during the war on the transportation problem and probabilities of defeating minefields. Academician A. N. Kolmogorov, Naval Captain A. A. Sveshnikov, and N. A. Gubler developed a theory that was used for artificially dispersing artillery rounds to optimize lethality of fire that included one equation similar to one developed by Bernard Koopman in the United States in search theory. Both were developed during the war. Also during World War II, U.S. intelligence reported on a Soviet General Staff Department for the Utilization of War Experience that they described as roughly comparable to an operations research department. None of these or other efforts led to a continuing body of literature, professional societies, or the other indicators of a separate and distinct profession in the 1940s.

In the mid-1950s the Soviets translated Morse and Kimball's classic *Methods of Operations Research* into Russian. It was followed shortly afterward by translations of Bernard Koopman's articles on search theory and several early American books on operations research (Merrill, a collection of game theory articles) and cybernetics (Wiener, Ashby, Tsien). In June 1959 N. Alekseyev wrote an article in the General Staff journal *Military Thought* on "Organization of Operations Research in the Armed Forces of the Capitalist Countries." There are references in Soviet literature to a 1959 Soviet Naval Academy book by Colonel I. Ya. Diner entitled *Operations Research*. He wrote *Mathematical Methods of Operations Research* in 1964. These efforts led to a lasting role of operations research in the Soviet military and a substantial military operations research literature written by military officers.

The Soviet navy's journal *Naval Collection* contained articles on operations research nearly every month in the early 1960s, with contributors from the Academy of Sciences, the ground forces, and the air force as well as the navy. These articles covered a wide range of OR topics and touched upon systems analysis to a lesser extent. Soviet civilian operations research also began with much work on mathematical programming and game theory. Many authors during this period argued that operations research was a branch of cybernetics; another group argued that it was an independent discipline. The latter view has prevailed.

The leading authors on operations research in the 1960s and 1970s were Yelena S. Venttsel' (Air Force Academy), General-Major Yu. V. Chuyev (Air Force and Academy of

Sciences), General-Major I. I. Anureyev and General-Major A. Ye. Tatarchenko (Soviet General Staff), General-Major K. V. Tarakanov, General-Major A. Ya. Vayner (Frunze Military Academy), Colonel V. R. Durov (Air Defense), and naval officers Rear Admiral L. A. Yemel'yanov, and Captains V. A. Abchuk, F. A. Matveychuk, V. G. Suzdal', and Yu. S. Solnyshkov. Several hundred military OR books have been cited in Soviet literature on nearly every aspect of military operations research. Many of these books are written by officers on the staffs of military academies, higher military schools, and military research institutes. About half seem to have become available in the West and those abound with military examples. The United States has produced far fewer books specifically on military OR, and United States military officers studying OR usually learn from textbooks written for nonmilitary applications.

During the 1980s, notable Soviet military operations research literature declined in comparison with the previous two decades.

Comparison of Soviet and Western Military Operations Research

Soviet/Russian operations research, as viewed through its open literature, differs in emphasis in several ways from Western operations research. The Military Encyclopedia article on OR defined it: "Methods of studying the basic quantitative indicators of operations, and also the activities of people (collectives) with the goal of selecting the optimal solutions for organization and control of actions or processes." In many ways Russian OR seems to have stayed close to the classes of problems, the approaches, and the emphasis on support of field commanders making real-time decisions during operations that were characteristics of early Western OR during World War II, and which have since been replaced by a focus on procurement and planning questions.

The volume of Soviet literature on systems analysis and procurement questions is rather modest compared with that in the West. Soviet literature places more emphasis on troop control (a term roughly comparable to command and control), network graphs (e.g., PERT), probability, and measures of force effectiveness and comparison based on scores for weapon systems. Soviet literature placed less relative emphasis on statistics, decision theory, and Monte Carlo simulation.

The former Soviet Union produced a much more extensive literature for military officers on OR with military examples than did nations in the West. Soviet military OR books often are organized by application area rather than by mathematical method, and they are aimed at officers in general. In the West the few military-oriented OR books are aimed more at OR specialists than line officers. In general, Western OR is done by specialists while the former Soviet Union directed OR education at more of a mass audience of potential users in the military. This was possible partly because of the more extensive mathematical education of Soviets at the high school level. (In the late 1980s it was reported that 98% of Soviet high school graduates had two years of calculus, whereas only about 5% of U.S. students ever take calculus even in college.)

Correlation of Forces and Means

One Soviet/Russian quantitative model that has caught the attention of Western military analysts is the idea of a correlation of forces and means (COFM). The Russian word translated as *correlation* also means *ratio*. The methodology involves (1) calculating a score for each model weapon system on two opposing sides, (2) adding up the scores of the equipment in a military unit, (3) normalizing the scores to their value relative to a standard military unit, and (4) calculating the ratio of opposing forces as a measure of the adequacy for performing specific missions. If the scores are simply counts of weapons, this leads to a *quantitative* COFM. If the scores take the quality of the weapon system into account, this leads to a *qualitative* COFM.

Quantitative COFM can be found in Soviet literature in the 1930s and earlier. Qualitative COFM were introduced in the 1960s when different models of weapons began to vary so greatly in quality that simple counts became inadequate.

Many systems of scoring individual weapon systems have been proposed in Soviet literature. *Commensurability coefficients*, *combat potentials*, and *combat capabilities* are among the terms used, and these terms have been used with varying meanings since the late 1960s. Debates on this issue continued through the 1980s into the 1990s in the General Staff journal, *Military Thought*.

Western ground force analysts have also used systems of weapon scores. One U.S. system of scores developed for the U.S. Army's ATLAS theater model, which was widely used in the 1970s, was called Weapons Effectiveness Indices (WEI) for the individual weapon system scores, and Weighted Unit Values (WUV) for the corresponding normalized unit scores. WEI/WUV scores were determined through a Delphi process involving military officers. The system was later abandoned in the United States when more detailed models were developed.

T. N. Dupuy in the United States developed a system of scores (lethality indices and the quantified judgment method or QJM) for use in historical analyses. This system has been used for a variety of applications.

The Soviet commensurability coefficient system has been outlined in a book on troop control and referred to in several OR books. It is intended for use by a field commander in assessing the capability of his forces to perform assigned missions. On the other hand, the WEI/WUV system was developed by the U.S. Army and intended for use in analyzing force levels and procurement decisions during planning efforts. It was not intended for the field, although the U.S. Marine Corps uses a variant of WEI/WUVs in one of its wargaming systems for training.

Ideological Barriers

Communist dogma held back several Soviet developments in OR. One reason for a Soviet lag in some areas of operations research was the requirement to stay within the proper, gradually changing bounds of Marxist-Leninist philosophical orthodoxy. Kantorovich had to refrain from publishing his ideas on applying linear programming to the Soviet economy from 1942 until the late 1950s because of possible philosophical implications of the concept of shadow prices obtained from the solution of programs. In effect they assign an intrinsic marginal value to resources dependent upon the problem constraints. This was considered to be in conflict with the Marxist view that only labor value was legitimate in Marxist doctrine. Similarly, decision analysis was delayed for more than ten years because of its use of subjective estimates of probabilities that were considered unacceptable in terms of Marxist emphasis on objective values. In both cases considerable debate and discussion was required before these subjects became "politically" acceptable. In several such cases, the Soviet military personnel were the first to publish on philosophically questionable areas, because military necessity permitted their scientists to have access to Western literature, and to adjust Marxist orthodoxy on the basis of defense requirements. State-supported ideology held back Soviet military operations research in ways for which no Western counterpart exists.

Access to Data

Based on limited evidence it appears that Soviet military operations analysts were sometimes denied access to data required for studies. Such basic information as Soviet casualty data on World War II battles was not made available to their own historians until around 1985 and many Soviet combat histories were being revised to take this new source of data into account in the 1990s. The failure to declassify historical casualty and loss data even decades after the fact is not restricted to the former USSR. As late as 1988 Chinese military analysts stated that they were unable to obtain access to their own casualty data from the Korean War. The West generally makes casualty data available shortly after wars, if not during them, and other loss data is declassified within a few years. Operations analysts have access to the classified data in the West during and after the war, but in the former Soviet Union, apparently, even uniformed serving officers were often long denied access to such data even for classified studies. Soviet concepts of need-to-know prior to *glasnost* were exceedingly strict.

Quantitative Historical Combat Data

Other than their own casualty and equipment loss data, Soviet military operations research books show a strong emphasis on use of historical data to test and validate models of combat. Soviet military histories of combat operations generally include far more quantitative descriptions of tactics, forces, and outcomes than are typically found in their Western counterparts. This historical data was useful in developing combat models and measures of operational performance, a use that was much less in evidence in the West until the 1980s. Prior to that time T. N. Dupuy and his associates were almost alone in the West in their attempts to systematically quantify for the purpose of developing a theory of combat. In the 1980s the U.S. Army Concepts Analysis Agency (particularly Robert Helmbold and Robert McQuie) devoted more resources to collecting and examining quantitative combat data.

Soviet histories normally include correlations of forces and means (ratios of personnel, units, and equipment by category) prior to and occasionally at the termination of battle, tactical densities of troops and equipment per kilometer of front in various zones at the initiation of the operations, advance rates during operations, supply levels and consumption, and often additional quantitative data.

Soviet Analysts

In general, Soviet military operations research relied much less on civilians than did operations research in the West, and nearly every publication was by a military officer, often of the reserves. The organizations conducting OR work were the military academies, scientific research institutes, and staffs. Nearly all of the former Soviet analysts who published military OR books, articles in military journals on OR, tactical calculations and decision aids, and military economic analyses were active duty or reserve officers.

The number of Soviet OR specialists who reached general officer rank numbered in the tens, somewhat more than the number in the U.S. military. Officers who specialized in OR theory were usually appointed to academic positions and remained with the same institution for lengthier periods than their U.S. counterparts, sometimes remaining with an institution for decades. A U.S. officer with an OR assignment of any kind lasting a decade would be a rarity. The United States depends upon civilians for most of the continuity in the military OR field.

Based on some writings in the 1970s and much more since *glasnost*, former Soviet officers who are military analysts were sometimes restricted to working on the technical aspects of OR problems, and constrained from objectively questioning the objectives of studies. Soviet military OR literature frequently cited the importance of "scientific substantiation of results" and the use of mathematical models as a part of this process. But articles appearing since *glasnost* have reported that in practice "scientific substantiation of results" was often a euphemism for results based on party decisions. They were "scientific" in the sense that any party decision was deemed to be scientific in that it had been arrived at by Marxist-Leninist thinking. In fact no scientific methods in the Western sense were involved at all.

Advocacy analyses also have been reported publicly many times in Western literature, most notably in the ABM debate in the early 1970s. That debate led to a code of ethics published in the U.S. journal *Operations Research*. Analysts in the former USSR and in the West alike have all struggled at times to maintain their professional standards and objectivity when pressured by consumers of military analysis who seek "scientific" support for decisions made without or in opposition to it.

The biggest difference between the two sides is that U.S. analysts, despite security restrictions, are frequently involved in public debates in the procurement and funding process. Analysis is exposed in the discussion connected with Western defense budgets. In contrast, the secrecy that surrounded Soviet defense matters meant that few details on Soviet OR studies were available to judge them one way or another. Soviet textbooks said the proper things, but there was not enough Soviet analysis made available publicly to judge the quality of Soviet OR analyses in practice. The work of Soviet military operations analysts did not appear to be subject to as extensive a critical review by as many peers as is common in the West. It is doubtful that opposing factions often had access to the data that was required to make objective assessments of the studies of others. *Glasnost* may eventually change this.

The primary reason that more U.S. operations researchers work for the procurement community than on improving current operations in the field and effective use of existing systems is that procurement organizations by their nature have access to funds with which to hire analysts, whereas field commands usually do not control comparable funds to obtain analysts to work on their problems. Soviet procurement decisions took place in a much less public environment and there has been essentially little or no public debate on such matters, thereby calling for less analysis.

Summary

The strengths of the Soviet system include the extent of the mathematical education of all officers (and the general populace); the emphasis on applying military OR to combat operations and the use of coarse models for real-time decisions by a large number of commanders and their staffs; an effort devoted to understanding the basic processes of combat by collecting and analyzing historical combat data; and involvement of average military officers in applying OR to the point that many models are not even considered to be OR, but rather basic troop control.

Weaknesses of the Soviet system appear to be overly strict need-to-know rules for access to data, often denying officers what is required to do their job because of strict security; seeking a single approved model that may then outlast its usefulness because it is officially approved; and failing to permit operations analysts to analyze the entire problem, rather restricting them to working on the mathematical algorithms and the technical aspects of modeling. Discerning problems and how well they are being resolved is difficult because of security regarding the applications of military analysis.

U.S. strengths include diversity and flexibility to continually broaden the scope of quantitative analysis; superior computer and other technical support; the attacking and eventual solution of evermore complex problems involving very detailed models; freer exchange of classified information within the defense community, cooperative efforts and exchanges of information within NATO; and an extensive open literature (compared with that of the former USSR) including descriptions of many applications.

Historically some U.S. weaknesses have included overemphasis on analysis to solve immediate problems without a proper balance of effort devoted to developing a better underlying understanding of such basic processes as attrition, battle termination and disengagement, effects of qualitative factors on performance in combat, integrating the effects of command and control into models, failure to treat electronic warfare adequately; lack of institutional memory leading to rediscovery of work already done; insufficient validation and testing of models; and lack of much of a common educational basis for OR analysts; and an inadequate general level of mathematical education on the part of decision makers who should be using and demanding better quantitative analyses. Most of these deficiencies have been the subject of communal efforts in recent years in an effort to improve the situation. In the United States, the Military Operations Research Society (MORS) and corresponding organizations in the military departments have developed a series of special forums for attacking such problems.

ALLAN S. REHM

SEE ALSO: Combat Effectiveness; Correlation of Forces; Force Ratio; Lanchester Equations; Models, Simulations, and War Games; Osipov Equations; Search Theory and Applications.

Bibliography

Abchuk, V. A., L. A. Yemel'yanov, F. A. Matveychuk, and V. G. Suzdal'. 1972. *Vvedeniye v Teoriyu Vyrabotki Resheniy* (Introduction to Decision Making Theory). Moscow: Voyenizdat.

Chuyev, Yu. V. 1970. *Issledovaniye Operatsiy v Voyennom Dele* (Operations Research in Military Affairs). Moscow: Voyenizdat.

Druzhinin, V. V., D. S. Kontorov, and M. D. Kontorov. 1989. *Vvedeniye v Teoriyu Konflikta* (Introduction to the Theory of Conflict). Moscow: Radio and Communications.
Fendrikov, I. M., and V. I. Yakovlev. 1971. *Metody Raschetov Boyevoy Effektivnosti Vooryzheniya* (Methods of Calculating Combat Effectiveness of Armament). Moscow: Voyenizdat.
Tarakanov, K. V. 1974. *Matematika i Vooruzhennaya Bor'ba* (Mathematics and Armed Struggle). Moscow: Voyenizdat.
Tkachenko, P. N., L. N. Kutsev, G. A. Meshcheryakov, A. M. Chavkin, and A. D. Chebykin. 1969. *Matematicheskiye Modeli Boyevykh Deystviy* (Mathematical Methods of Modeling Combat Operations). Moscow: Soviet Radio.
Vayner, A. Ya. 1989. *Informatika v Voyennom Dele* (Informatiks in Military Affairs). Moscow: DOSAAF.
Venttsel', Ye. S. 1972. *Issledovaniye Operatsiy* (Operations Research). Moscow: Soviet Radio.

OPERATIONS SECURITY (OPSEC)

The National Security Decision Directive (NSDD) of January 1988 requires establishing an operations security (OPSEC) program for each U.S. government executive department or agency assigned to or supporting national security missions with classified or sensitive activities. According to the NSDD, OPSEC is "a systematic and proven process . . . [to deny] potential adversaries information about capabilities and intentions by identifying, controlling, and protecting *generally unclassified evidence* of the planning and execution of sensitive . . . activities" [italics added]. How and why has the U.S. government come to devise a special program for protecting *unclassified* evidence?

Modern-day OPSEC as such is thought to have begun during the Vietnam War, when U.S. forces noted that an increasing number of reconnaissance drones were being shot down over Vietnam and that many air strikes were ineffective, impairing the U.S. air war. It appeared that hostile intelligence had penetrated U.S. forces and had acquired direct access to U.S. planning. Accordingly, an investigatory team, codenamed Purple Dragon, was organized. Purple Dragon found no spies lurking in the planning headquarters, but the team did find stereotyped operational procedures and pilot chatter in the clear that any intelligence analyst could recognize and use to pinpoint U.S. activities. Purple Dragon plugged the leaks by shuffling operational procedures and limiting "innocent" but revelatory conversations among pilots. Their operation is generally acknowledged in the U.S. military as the beginning of modern-day OPSEC.

The special contribution of the Purple Dragon team members came from their effort to put themselves in the positions of their adversaries, studying the U.S. operations step by step, looking for bits of information—perhaps meaningless by themselves—that when pieced together, provided a reasonably accurate picture of U.S. plans, capabilities, or intentions. In essence, Purple Dragon pioneered a "systems approach" to diagnosing and rectifying a breakdown in security. Essentially they keyed in on indicators of events, actions, and observables that cannot be protected, or are difficult to protect, by a security classification system.

OPSEC as a Way of Thinking

Since the Vietnam period, OPSEC has become an important part of military, governmental, and sensitive civilian security practice. Many security practitioners see OPSEC as a management tool for operational effectiveness to prevent sensitive operations, organizations, or activities from being compromised, wittingly or unwittingly. The key to OPSEC, as it is now understood, is in taking the right precautions: determining what information to protect; determining how a "threat" could compromise that information, and implementing countermeasures to maximize effective performance and thereby minimize risk.

The importance of OPSEC is evidenced in its broad application: to industrial espionage, computer security, and personnel management. Arguably, too, we use something like OPSEC in everyday life—for example in home security planning, when we connect a timer to the lights and cancel the newspaper delivery when we are away on vacation.

The Five-Step OPSEC Process

In its military and governmental applications, OPSEC uses a variety of methodologies. Essentially it follows a risk-management process similar to those used in systems security engineering, communications security, computer security risk assessment, and other security functions. The NSDD has attempted to establish a distinctive approach for OPSEC by suggesting five basic steps as the proven system for determining the what, who, when, where, and how of OPSEC. These are (1) identifying critical information; (2) analyzing threats; (3) analyzing vulnerabilities; (4) assessing risk; and (5) applying appropriate countermeasures.

Identifying Critical Information

The first step in OPSEC is to determine what is critical not only from the perspective of the organization itself but from that of an adversary or potential adversary. To understand how an adversary might piece together critical information, the OPSEC practitioner first must examine the operation, organization, or activity in detail to determine what information may be critical in gaining or maintaining an advantage. For example, for military aircraft, critical information may be its specific capabilities: How far (unrefueled), fast, and at what altitude can it fly? Can it operate day or night? What ordnance can it deliver at what range?

Second, the OPSEC officer must break down critical

information into its component elements. Are there aspects of this information that, taken alone or together with other available information, may reveal the whole? What does wing/tail/body design disclose? What does it weigh? What is its fuel consumption and how much is carried?

Finally, the OPSEC practitioner must determine the perishability of the information. Does an adversary have sufficient time to exploit information after collecting it?

Any analytical system that can lead to the development of countermeasures that might include those of concealment and/or deception has the potential for abuse—in today's parlance, for cover up of improper or illegal activity. Thus, this first step takes on added importance. Critical information must be clearly defined in terms of why it must be protected: that is, its importance to the execution of effective and *legal* operations.

Analyzing Threats

The second OPSEC step is "threat analysis," which seeks to define a particular adversary's capabilities for collecting specific, critical information. In this process, the OPSEC analyst must identify the adversary and what the adversary has to gain from exploiting crucial information. Second, the analyst must determine what sorts of intelligence collection techniques the adversary might bring to bear: human intelligence (HUMINT), signals intelligence (SIGINT), imagery intelligence (IMINT), and so on. Last, the analyst should determine the adversary's current state of knowledge, understanding of the field, and access to open-source information.

Analyzing Vulnerabilities

The goal of the third OPSEC step is to determine the paths to the critical information. To do so, the OPSEC practitioner must evaluate the effectiveness of traditional security measures, such as physical security, information security, signal security, and computer security. Next, patterns and procedures of the operation, organization, or activity must be analyzed for telltale signs. This analysis is usually performed by developing an "adversary collection plan," a plan designed to mimic an adversary's attempt to gain access to critical information. This plan is constructed as follows.

First, the analyst constructs a chronological depiction of all events that occur in the operation, organization, or activity. The chronology may be done by functional areas, such as administration, logistics, communications, or operations. Next, the analyst will identify indicators associated with particular events: for example, arrival of truck convoys at a loading dock; transfer or even travel of personnel; or a sharp change in signals traffic. These indicators, in turn, must be assessed for what they may reveal: Do they disclose preparations for some unusual and discernible activity? If so, can the specific sources or causes of the indicators be identified?

Indicators, singly or in combination, can provide significant insights into determining critical information such as the capabilities of weapons systems. For example, the distribution of targets on a surface-to-surface missile test range and their degree of destruction may provide an indication of a missile's range and lethality. The IMINT threat is capable of providing this type of information to an intelligence analyst. And, if unsecured telemetry is used at the test range and is intercepted by a SIGINT threat, additional corroboration can be obtained.

The essence of this step, therefore, is to compare the threat to those indicators that may disclose critical information. If an indicator can be exploited by a threat it is a vulnerability.

Assessing Risk

The fourth OPSEC step brings the preceding steps together by assigning a degree of value or impact to each factor. The idea is to establish relationships between critical information, threat, and vulnerabilities well enough to order the risk. The goal of the step is to prioritize risk so that OPSEC resources can be applied effectively.

Risk assessment methodologies vary widely in sophistication. At the simplest end of the spectrum might be a categorization of risk into high, medium, or low categories arranged in a matrix against the specific indicators. At the other end might be a mathematical model using scenarios and decision trees. The method selected depends on the specific circumstances and is subjective in that it reflects the analyst's sense of what is important rather than some absolute numerical value. Nonetheless, such prioritizations are necessary because time, money, materiel, and people are finite resources. The key factors of an assessment are that it is convincing and sensible to the responsible decisionmaker and that values are assigned to indicate relative risk in a consistent and objective way. For example, the analyst must consider that a "severe" risk may not be crucial if it loses value ("ages out") before an adversary can use it effectively.

Applying Appropriate Countermeasures

The fifth OPSEC step is the effort to prevent or counteract vulnerabilities in operational security. Toward this end, OPSEC practitioners must devise and recommend countermeasures that are both effective and appropriate. Although recommendations for OPSEC measures are the product of joint operational-intelligence analyses, the final choices of countermeasures, according to the NSDD, should be made by commanders, supervisors, or program managers. It is the decision maker, not the analyst, who must determine what constitutes "success" for an operation; which countermeasures might compromise operational requirements or planning for security; and which countermeasures provide the greatest effectiveness at the least cost.

Integrating OPSEC into Operations, Activities, and Programs

At its best, OPSEC should not be an add-on discipline, mobilized for specific operations or activities or to counteract salient threats only. Rather, it should be an integral part of sensitive operations, organizations, and activities. To attain this goal, OPSEC must be supported by education and organization, an evaluation and review process, a comprehensive survey, and a continuing development of methodologies.

Education and Organization

The five-step OPSEC process is based on the participation of all members of a command, organization, or activity. The broad base of participation requires that personnel are trained in the fundamentals of the OPSEC process and how its concepts apply to the working environment. Optimally, participants in OPSEC should not be merely responsive but should be an active part of the effort to identify, understand, and counteract security threats. Constructing such a network requires the assignment of OPSEC training and coordinating personnel with specific responsibilities and capabilities for making OPSEC work.

Review and Evaluation

OPSEC is essentially a dynamic process; most practitioners view it as a cycle rather than as a linear, five-step process. That is, because information, capabilities, and threats are all subject to change, OPSEC must be alert to evolving risks and newly exposed vulnerabilities. Weaknesses in an original plan must be examined and rectified. Controls to monitor steps in the OPSEC process must be devised.

The OPSEC Survey

In determining or evaluating OPSEC posture, it is not sufficient to accept assurances that OPSEC measures are in place and working effectively. Such assurances can be made only through on-the-ground observation and this requires a multidisciplinary team of professionals. Typically, an OPSEC survey team will gather facts on the scene, record the paths (indicators or evidence) that reveal critical information or vulnerabilities, and compile a list of security weaknesses and recommended countermeasures. The survey is basically a four-phase process.

Planning phase. In the first, or planning, phase, the OPSEC survey team is selected and prepares a plan that defines the scope, time frame, and objectives of the survey. Team members, like those of the Purple Dragon team, will need expertise in communications, logistics, contracts, computers, maintenance, administration, operations, and intelligence.

Research phase. The second, or research, phase involves defining the threat, learning from documents about the organization or operation before going on-site, and becoming familiar with the open-source literature on the operation or organization.

Data collection/field survey phase. The third phase is the first on-site phase—data collection, when the team gathers data in the respective areas of expertise of its members. It is in this phase that the actual interviews are made and stated procedures checked against observed procedures. The team's mission is fact-finding, not fault-finding, an objective that should be made clear to the participants, whose candid contributions are vital.

Analysis and reporting phase. In the fourth phase, the team pulls the previous phases together, identifying the key elements of the first four steps of the OPSEC process and recommending the OPSEC measures that should be employed to complete the fifth, countermeasures, step. In all, the OPSEC survey is the key tool by which the team views an organization or operation as an adversary might.

Future of OPSEC

OPSEC has by no means been perfected. In the U.S. military operation in Panama, for example, it was discovered that Panama Defense Force (PDF) troops heard two U.S. soldiers talking about "H-Hour" some three hours before it occurred; a television correspondent was asking questions over the telephone about the operation 36 hours before it took place; PDF forces went on alert after CNN reported troop movements on the night of the operation; and members of the media pool violated secrecy procedures. These breaches of security did not affect the outcome of the operation, but the operation might have been affected in some particulars by a heightened state of alert in Panama. If there are collectors to collect, analysts to analyze, and decision makers ready to receive and act on operational information, its release is potentially dangerous.

The future will be one of high competition, if not militarily, certainly politically and most certainly economically. Competition is a zero-sum game: what one loses, someone else gains. Keeping competitive requires keeping secrets. The five-step OPSEC process is one important contribution to sustaining the integrity of sensitive activities. Properly employed, OPSEC should enhance the performance and effectiveness of sensitive military, political, and economic operations.

Arion N. Pattakos

See Also: Espionage, Legal Aspects of; Intelligence Collection; Intelligence Cycle; Intelligence, Human; Intelligence, Imagery; Intelligence, Signal; Systems Analysis.

Bibliography

Bamford, J. 1982. *The puzzle palace.* Boston: Houghton Mifflin.
Bottom, N. R., Jr., and R. R. J. Gallati. 1984. *Industrial espionage: Intelligence techniques and countermeasures.* Boston: Butterworth.

Burrows, E. B. 1986. *Deep black.* New York: Berkley.
Fisher, R. A., and D. B. Nickell. 1988. The OPSEC check. *Security Management* 32(7):67–70.
Kelly, J. M. 1987. *How to check out your competition.* New York: Wiley.
Lapin, L. 1986. *How to get anything on anybody: Advanced investigative and surveillance techniques.* New York: Gordon Press.
Pattakos, A. N. 1983. OPSEC: Operations security at DoD. *Security Management* 27(11):102–5.
———. 1984. OPSEC: A Guide to the process. *Security Management* 28(7):116–17.
———. 1987. Sneaky people. *Security Management* 31(6):76–78.
———. 1989. SMARTSECs for the 1990s. *Security Management* 33(11):117–18.
Sammon, W. L., M. A. Kurland, and R. Spitalnic. 1984. *Business competitor intelligence: Methods for collecting, organizing, and using information.* New York: Wiley.

ORDNANCE CORPS

Usage of the term *ordnance* is not uniform. One definition, "great guns such as cannon or artillery," is indicated in the context of its historical background. In later usage, however, ordnance embraces all kinds of military weapons, munitions, missiles, and agents, and the related apparatus necessary to activate or discharge them.

The ordnance corps is the branch of an army that procures, stores, and issues weapons and munitions, in some cases including military vehicles. In accordance with its Anglo-Saxon roots, an ordnance corps is usually established in those armies that in principle can be traced back to the British or U.S. armies. The range of ordnance corps responsibilities differs from army to army. For example, maintenance tasks are included as part of ordnance in the U.S. Army, but not in that of the United Kingdom.

The kinds of duties performed by an army's ordnance corps are principally related to the functional area of logistics. In civilian usage, the term *logistics* originally had a relatively narrow meaning and application, such as production logistics or consumer logistics. Militarily, the meaning of *logistics* has generally been rather broad; it is probably best defined as "the creation and sustained support of weapons and armed forces so that they can be tactically employed in order to attain strategic objectives."

Throughout the history of armies, the influence of logistics on the successful outcome of battles has been significant, but it was only in the nineteenth century that a systematic analysis was made of the problems involved in the setting up of armies. Jomini was one of the first to make a distinction among strategy, tactics, and logistics. However, today's logistic problems distinguish themselves from those of the past because of the far greater technological complexity of weapon systems and the greatly increased consumption rates of supplies of all kinds on the modern battlefield. Fighting a modern battle depends to a large extent on the ability to provide continual logistic support to combat forces.

Royal Army Ordnance Corps

Origins

The English ordnance department antedates the British standing army, of which it has since become a part (1857). "The Master of Ordnance, later known as Master General, dates back to the 15th century, the first officially recorded holder of the appointment being Nicholas Merburg in the year 1414. *His function was the supply of war materiel* which is still the primary duty of the RAOC [Royal Army Ordnance Corps]" (Fernyhough 1980).

The master general of ordnance held an important political post. He was the adviser to king and Parliament on military matters. In the early days selection was not confined to soldiers; masters general of ordnance became cabinet ministers and were independent of the army or navy. In this context it should be noted that only an administrative body directly constituted by the government was able to equip the artillery and the engineers with their task-specific material. Obviously, requirements for cannon and gunpowder could not be satisfied by local resources as could the needs of infantry and cavalry.

Few people, and hardly any soldiers at all, were educated in the technology and economics of this matter. The consequence was that, for many centuries, only the civilian element of the government was qualified to deal with such problems.

The office of ordnance played an important part in the development of the British Empire over nearly three centuries. Its main responsibilities were setting up forts and barracks at every new outpost, providing accommodation for the troops and civil government, and caring for Crown lands. In 1683 the five principal officers (lieutenant general, surveyor general, clerk of the ordnance, storekeeper general, and clerk of delivery) formed a board of management, the Board of Ordnance. Chairman of the board was the master general; decisions were taken by vote.

In those days the army consisted of cavalry and infantry. There was little need for a standing army in Britain, but it was gradually realized that an army at home was needed to maintain British garrisons abroad. The task of the Board of Ordnance was to provide war materiel for garrisons overseas and to supply engineer and artillery units. For a long time, the Corps of Royal Engineers included only officers; the artisans were civilians.

The technical corps continued under the control of the master general of ordnance for many years. The Board of Ordnance saw to their clothing and equipment and therefore they were better cared for than the rest of the army. The officers were separately selected and trained in the Royal Military Academy, Woolwich, while the cavalry and infantry officer cadets went to the Royal Military College at Sandhurst.

The Board of Ordnance clothed and equipped its soldiers by means of centralized contracts. After inspection at the Tower, supplies were distributed through the ordnance corps.

The situation in the army (cavalry and infantry) was very different. Regiments were raised by a form of contract between the king and some nobleman who became colonel. A regiment was treated as the personal property of the colonel, who at first clothed it entirely as he pleased.

At that time several departments dealt with army matters. They were not organized under a coordinating head and had no clearly defined responsibilities. These departments and officials included the secretary of state for war and colonies, the secretary-at-war, the commander-in-chief, and the paymaster general. In addition to these, the board of general officers supervised the clothing and regimental equipment of the cavalry and infantry. The Board of Ordnance, under the master general, commanded and equipped the artillery and engineers and supplied the whole army in the field with arms, ammunition, greatcoats, and camp equipment. The commissariat supplied forage and fuel overseas but not at home. Finally, there was a combined army and ordnance medical service under three masters: the secretary-at-war, commander-in-chief, and board of ordnance. Its staff consisted of doctors and purveyors (hospital quartermasters).

1855 to 1904

The Crimean War in 1854 dramatically demonstrated the inherent problems of the fragmented responsibility. Logistics played a far greater role in the Crimea than it had in the Peninsula War or in Flanders, and the resources and experience to mount a coherent, successful operation were lacking.

The main reforms that followed in 1855 can be summarized as follows. There was no longer a secretary-at-war, nor were "war" and "colonies" mixed in one department. A secretary of state for war was responsible for all civil work connected with the army. The Board of Ordnance became part of the War Office and the office of master general was abolished. All civil duties were switched to the secretary of state; military units were placed under the commander-in-chief. The board of general officers was abolished; soldiers' clothing and appointments were provided by the state. The commissariat was transferred from the treasury to the secretary of state, and a permanent military transport corps was created.

Although the structure of army administration was now simplified, unified control was still lacking. Previously there had been two armies, each supplied and administered separately. Now there was one army with two heads: the secretary of state for war—a civilian and a politician—was responsible for supply and finance; the commander-in-chief was responsible for military efficiency but not for economy.

When the War Office accepted responsibility for equipping the entire army, the amateurish methods of supply used during the Crimean War changed to a carefully worked-out system. Procedures were instituted to control the stocks of equipment; a military store officer had to open an account for every unit he equipped. Next it became accepted that any officer of the military store department could be called upon to accompany troops in time of war. A staff of clerks, artificers, and laborers was to be provided to accompany the force.

In 1865 the military store staff corps was formed; it later became the Army Ordnance Corps (AOC). The original personnel of the corps numbered 200 and increased to nearly 400 by 1869.

Noncombatant status was anomalous. The ordnance officer was considered a highly trained and well-paid specialist, but he was isolated from the rest of the army. The supply of arms and equipment became a more and more important factor in the success or failure of military operations, but this aspect of logistics tended to be overlooked due to the isolation of the service directly responsible for it.

1904 to 1918

The next milestone in the history of the ordnance corps occurred in 1904 when a committee under Lord Esher advocated further reorganization in the structure of army control. Under its proposals, which were accepted, the dual control of the army ceased and the Army Council was formed. It survives today, now known as the Army Board of the Ministry of Defence.

The military members of the Army Council in 1904 were the chief of the imperial staff (CIGS), the adjutant general (AG) for personnel, and the quartermaster general (QMG) for materiel. The ordnance services, now called the Army Ordnance Department (AOD), were placed entirely under the QMG.

The World War of 1914–18 showed the deficiencies of the organization and installations. At the start of the war Britain's army was small, but it was the most highly trained and best equipped in Europe. It was virtually destroyed in the first year of the war, and no attempt was made to keep a portion of this valuable manpower as a cadre for the army which was ultimately to be created.

The need for an adequate supply system was felt almost at once. The fighting at Mons and Le Cateau called for extensive and urgent replenishment, but no adequate system existed. Despite the logistics experiences of the South African War (1899–1902), the true significance of supply was not yet recognized. Practice was that when its equipment or supplies ran short, a division was withdrawn from the line, even during heavy fighting, to be re-equipped. But this did not work. Military leaders realized that an efficient supply system was essential, and that ordnance must participate in the logistic planning for a campaign. The British army that began in 1914 in France with one ammunition train and a few hundred tons of reserve had, in October 1918, eight great depots of 336,000 tons of ammunition and more than 120 ammunition railheads, giving final delivery to the enemy of more than 9,000 tons of shot and shell a day.

1918 to 1945

In November 1918 the AOD and AOC were combined into the Royal Army Ordnance Corps, illustrating the increasing value of the ordnance services and giving recognition of their achievements in the war by the grant of the title "Royal." The Duke of York became the first RAOC colonel-in-chief; he succeeded to the throne as King George VI in 1936.

From then on, the RAOC was recognized as an important element in the efficiency of a modern army. Prior to the world depression in 1929, two important decisions were made: (1) the corps in 1927 was transferred from the QMG to the master general of ordnance (MGO), and branches of the Ordnance Directorate at the War Office were redesignated MGO7, 8, and 9; and (2) in the late 1920s responsibility for the supply, storage, and repair of all vehicles was transferred to the RAOC.

Many efforts at forming an up-to-date army ceased with the 1929 depression. By the end of the depression it was apparent that any British army of the future must be mechanized and that an efficient organization for the supply of vehicles and spares was necessary.

At the outbreak of World War II in September 1939, the RAOC was understaffed and overcivilianized. The small military staff was fully engaged in peacetime duties, and the ordnance services had neither the capacity nor the training for war. The corp's noncombatant status isolated it from the rest of the army (up to 1941), it was not in a position to influence logistic concepts, and it was rarely consulted.

The RAOC started with a few hundred officers and a few thousand men of the regular and territorial armies; during the course of only four years it developed into a highly efficient organization of 8,000 officers and 130,000 men.

The corps provided logistic support that had several main features. It maintained a controlling headquarters at the War Office, the Ordnance Directorate. The corps also created a United Kingdom base for the supply of all items of ordnance concern to all theaters and developed a comprehensive field force organization that provided a reliable and flexible system for the maintenance of a field army. In addition, the corps created a workshop organization for the repair, recovery, and manufacture of equipment at the base and in the field (this was the basis for the creation of REME in 1942). Finally, it formed a highly trained technical ammunition branch that inspected, conditioned, and repaired British ammunition and dealt with captured and unexploded enemy ammunition.

The focal points of all RAOC activity were the Ordnance Directorate at the War Office and the complex of central depots in the United Kingdom from which supplies were sent to all operational locations. Here, also, the war organization was well devised and all technical training planned, first under the supervision of Gen. Sir Basil Hill and then under Gen. Sir Leslie Williams (1941–46).

In the course of the war, the corps did active work in many parts of the world, including France (1939–40), Norway, North Africa, the Middle East, Sicily, Italy, and Northwestern Europe (1944–45).

The Western Desert. Fighting in the Western Desert of North Africa provided the RAOC with the experience necessary to build a highly efficient supply and repair system. The field force organization formed as a result of these campaigns proved ideal for all later operations in the war, notably in Italy and northwestern Europe.

The permanent need of the army was for quick replenishment of food, water, petrol, and ammunition. These stores had to be held centrally at the base, with a quick system for getting demands from and stores forward to a unit. These requirements were met as soon as air freight became available. This supply problem will always be present in modern war.

U.S. Army Ordnance Corps

Origins

The U.S. Army Ordnance Corps followed the historical example set by European countries in the Middle Ages, especially England as described above.

The traditions of U.S. army ordnance began with the first days of the American Revolution. In 1775 the Continental Congress authorized General Washington to appoint an official as commissary general of the artillery stores, responsible for the procurement of arms and ammunition. Mr. E. Cheever was elected for this new position and he worked in close cooperation with Maj. Gen. Henry Knox, Washington's artillery chief. (In this function Knox considered himself comparable with the master general of ordnance in the British army.)

Congress established the Board of War and Ordnance in 1776. Its main responsibility was to arrange for the storage and maintenance of powder, artillery, muskets, and other materiel. The first ordnance depot was set up at Carlisle, Pennsylvania, in 1777.

1812 to 1918

The Ordnance Department was founded by an act of Congress on 14 May 1812. The head of this new organization was the commissary general of ordnance, who was directly responsible to the president of the United States. The commissary general of ordnance was responsible for arms and ammunition procurement, for monitoring government armories and storage depots, and for recruiting and training ordnance artificers to be attached to regiments, corps, and garrisons.

The flaming bomb became the official emblem of U.S. Army ordnance in May 1833—the oldest military insignia of the U.S. Army. Prior to its selection by the Ordnance Department it was the insignia of the British Grenadier Guards, the Royal Engineers, and the Royal Horse Artillery.

Some statistics point out the magnitude of ordnance responsibility at that time. During the Civil War (1861–65), the Ordnance Department had to handle 90 million pounds of lead, 13 million pounds of artillery shells, and 26 million pounds of powder, as well as large quantities of other ordnance materiel, to be provided to the Union Army.

During the war with Spain in 1898, the U.S. Army had to learn one first important lesson, namely, how to equip and sustain a largely volunteer force. When U.S. troops were sent to the Philippines, the Ordnance Department had to solve the problems involved in transporting and sustaining an army thousands of miles from home. Both proved to be valuable experiences in light of the expanding twentieth-century role of ordnance in providing complete support to frontline troops.

During World War I, it was not surprising that the department expanded—from fewer than 100 officers, several enlisted men, and a small number of civilian employees to a force of 5,900 officers, 62,000 enlisted men, and about 75,000 civilians.

At that time commercial industries were not prepared to manufacture the highly technical and noncommercial materiel required by the Army. It was necessary for the department to design and manufacture special machinery and tools for making new types of cannon ammunition, tanks, and other noncommercial articles.

Moreover, existing stocks of machine guns proved unsatisfactory for use in combat. Therefore John M. Browning, an arms maker who developed light and heavy machine guns, was given the opportunity to produce these kinds of weapons in numbers in cooperation with the Ordnance Department.

The production of ordnance items grew to a total of 3,000 artillery pieces, 54 railway guns and howitzers, more than 50,000 trucks, 80 tanks, and more than 125,000 machine guns in the years 1917 and 1918.

1918 to the Present

It is understandable that, as the size of the army decreased between World War I and World War II, so did ordnance responsibilities. The great challenge posed by the unavoidable participation of the United States in World War II placed the Ordnance Department in an awkward position, because it was necessary to boost production capacity to an extraordinary extent. Wartime ordnance procurement increased to a level of US$34 billion, nearly half the total of all previous army procurement.

In 1950 the Ordnance Department became the Ordnance Corps upon the enactment of the Army Organization Act. The office of chief of ordnance ceased to exist following a major army reorganization in 1962, although Ordnance Corps personnel continued to perform their various tasks. In October 1985 the Ordnance Department was re-established, to assist the chief of ordnance/commandant of the U.S. Ordnance Center and School (USAOC&S) at Aberdeen Proving Ground, Maryland, which in 1981 was given authority for military personnel in ordnance.

Organization and Roles of Ordnance Establishments

In modern military understanding the ordnance corps is a main part of the logistic services, unless it is organized as a separate branch in the structure of an army.

The following descriptions of organization and roles, primarily in the British and the U.S. armies, will point out what is in line with that organization and where there are deviations.

Great Britain

Regular Army. The RAOC is responsible for the supply of all items of materiel needed in the army (except engineer supplies, construction materiel, and medical items); for the inspection and repair of certain items of materiel; and for the provision of ancillary services. The items of materiel for which the RAOC is responsible may be classified in four categories: (1) combat supplies, consisting of ammunition (including mines and explosives), rations, and petroleum, oil, and lubricant (POL); (2) ordnance stores, including spares and assemblies for vehicles, equipment, and army aircraft, clothing and items of personal equipment, general stores, and technical and warlike stores; (3) vehicles; and (4) guided weapons, for example, infantry antitank systems, provided through the normal ammunition supply chain.

The RAOC is responsible for the inspection, modification, and repair of ammunition, explosives, clothing, and certain general stores (furniture, tentage, textiles, etc.) and for the quality surveillance of rations and POL. The RAOC is also responsible for certain ancillary services including printing, laundry, bathing, industrial gas supply, fire prevention and protection, local purchase and contracts, and clerks; and for explosive ordnance disposal (EOD), which includes the disposal of all stray land service ammunition and the neutralization of improvised explosive devices (IED). The RAOC is represented at all formation HQs in a theater of operations.

The director general ordnance services (DGOS) is the head of the RAOC in the Logistic Executive (Army). He is assisted by the director of supply operations (Army) (DSupOps[A]), who is responsible for stockholding, central supply, and the central ordnance depots of the United Kingdom Land Forces (UKLF).

Territorial Army (TA). The roles of the TA have evolved into a triad: to complete the order of battle of

British forces committed to NATO, principally with I (BR) Corps; to assist in maintaining a secure UK base; and to provide a framework for any further expansion of the nation's reserves in a time of crisis.

There are three categories of TA. Group A consists of formed independent and specialist TA units (including RAOC). Group B includes the University Officer Training Corps (UOTCs), 4,000 strong, and certain specialist pools. Group C is the Home Service Force (HSF), made up of 4,300 ex-regular and TA soldiers.

The TA may be called up by the government in the following situations: when warlike operations are in preparation or progress (the higher liability); when national danger is imminent or an emergency has arisen (the lower liability); and in defense of the United Kingdom against actual or anticipated attack.

Independent units make up 82 percent of the TA. Each unit is based on its own training center and has its own regular army permanent staff. Another 15 percent of the TA is in specialist units. A specialist unit has no premises or regular permanent staff of its own and draws its volunteers from throughout the entire country.

The established strength of RAOC TA is 27 percent of the corps. Two-thirds of them go to the British Army of the Rhine (BAOR) on mobilization, and the RAOC mobilized order of battle is 30 percent TA. There are 15 RAOC Independent TA units located throughout the country with a total established strength of 1055. The RAOC Specialist TA is commanded in peacetime by HQ RAOC TA.

Ministry of Defense (MOD). The MOD consists of five elements under the political direction of the secretary of state for defense.

Central staffs are responsible for defense policy and overall planning. The three service departments (navy, army, and air force) are responsible for management of their respective services in terms of operational requirements, organization, training, personnel, and logistics. The procurement executive (PE) is responsible for the procurement of equipment for all three services, from research through to production.

The PE, headed by the chief of defense procurement, comprises the central divisions responsible for procurement policy and general management of the PE, and the three systems controllerates that deal with land, sea, and air environments: controller of the navy, for sea system equipment; master general of ordnance, for land system equipment; and controller aircraft, for air system equipment.

Royal Ordnance Factories (ROFs). The ROFs are a manufacturing organization employing more than 20,000 people and comprising eleven factories that produce defense equipment. There are also two agency factories managed by industry. The U.K. armed forces are the major customer, but a substantial proportion of production is generated by overseas sales. The ROFs are mainly concerned with the manufacture of finished products, particularly guns, heavy armored fighting vehicles, engineering support, vehicles and equipment, ammunition, bombs, and guided weapons. They also manufacture subassemblies and components for sale as required.

U.S. Army Ordnance Corps

The ordnance corps is responsible for the supply of repair parts and maintenance of ordnance-type equipment. The area of munitions materiel includes monitoring, inspection, stock control, and security. The area of explosive ordnance disposal (EOD) deals with locating, identifying, rendering safe, handling, removing, salvaging, and disposing of all kinds of munitions.

The items of materiel for which the ordnance corps is responsible may be classified in four major categories: (1) conventional tank and ground mobility equipment (related to Tank/Automotive Materiel Management); (2) guided missiles and free-flight rockets (related to Missile Materiel Management); (3) nuclear, conventional, and chemical munitions and warheads (related to Munitions Materiel Management); and (4) U.S. and foreign unexploded conventional, chemical, and nuclear munitions (related to EOD).

In 1986 the ordnance corps was brought in line with the army's regimental system. Key points were the establishment of the position of chief of ordnance, organization of the corps under the whole-branch concept (one branch, one regiment), and establishment of the office of chief of ordnance as the regimental headquarters for the ordnance corps. Aberdeen Proving Ground, Maryland, was established as the "Home of Ordnance Corps," and enlisted soldiers with ordnance training were assigned to combat arms regiments.

Germany

The British and U.S. armies are the main military organizations that have a separate ordnance corps. Armies of countries that were founded with major assistance from these two states, such as the armies of India and Japan, often created branches that were quite similar. Other countries concentrate all logistic tasks, including ordnance tasks, in one branch only. In most cases the ordnance functions are carried out by a special subbranch called the "Logistic Corps/Troops," or some group with a similar title. The German army is a good example.

Army logistic troops. The logistic troops of the German army ensure the materiel readiness of the army and support the medical service; they provide other users (such as the air force and navy) with materiel, for which the army is responsible; and they support allied forces within the framework of agreements established for a state of defense.

The basis for the accomplishment of this logistic mission is the employment of fully mobile, relocatable logistic troops and fixed logistic installations on the one hand, and utilization of civilian installations and services on the other.

Organization (regular army). The logistic troops are organized into supply support troops and maintenance troops; the medical troops form an organic branch. Supply support troops are responsible for the provision, storage, handling, and transportation of supplies. Maintenance troops have to ensure the evacuation and maintenance of disabled army materiel.

In addition to these logistics and medical troops, the army has so-called "units with a logistic mission" at its disposal. Pipeline engineers and the transportation elements of army aviation units fall into this category.

Every level of command in the regular army has its own logistic troops and organic support services for the accomplishment of its logistic missions. Essentially a corps has the logistic troops required for the support of the corps troops as well as depots for the storage of the corps stocks.

Each division has a supply battalion and a maintenance battalion at its disposal. The supply battalion of the division is organized as follows: headquarters and service company, supply company, supply company for materiel, supply company for bulk supplies, and transportation company. The division maintenance battalion includes the headquarters and service company, the maintenance company, the maintenance company for electronic equipment, and the maintenance and evacuation company. A brigade has one supply company and one maintenance company. Battalions and separate units have their own organic support services, which are organized as supply and maintenance subunits.

The preceding descriptions of the ordnance services of the United States, the United Kingdom, and Germany present the overall historical development and areas of responsibility of ordnance troops generally. The role of ordnance troops in supplying, maintaining, and repairing equipment is vital to military operations. The increasing complexity and sophistication of the modern equipment will undoubtedly place greater burdens on ordnance troops in the future, and they must be prepared to meet the challenge and keep their army's equipment functioning smoothly.

GÜNTER PAULEIT

SEE ALSO: Combat Service Support; Consumption Rates, Battlefield; Engineering, Military; Logistics: A General Survey; Maintenance; Mobilization; Munitions and Explosives: Engineering and Handling; Procurement, Military; Standardization and Interoperability; Stockpiles; Tooth-to-Tail: Land Forces; Transportation Corps.

Bibliography

Crocker, L. P. 1988. *The army officer's guide.* Harrisburg, Pa.: Stackpole Books.

Dijkstra, C. J. 1983. *Logistical support.* Paris: Assembly of Western European Union Collective.

Fernyhough, A. E. 1980. *A short history of the RAOC.* Andover, Mass.

Jomini, Antoine-Henri. 1836. *Précis de l'art de la guerre.* Paris.

———. 1881. *Abriss der Kriegskunst.* Berlin: Richard Wilhelmi.

Quick, J. 1973. *Dictionary of weapons and military terms.* New York: McGraw-Hill.

Sterling, P. D. 1987. *Serving the line with excellence: The development of the U.S. Army Ordnance Corps.* Aberdeen, Md.: U.S. Army Ordnance Center and School, Aberdeen Proving Ground.

ORGANIZATION, AIR FORCE

Not unlike most large businesses, the military is organized to facilitate the flow of communication and control among all levels in the organization. Consequently, military organization charts often resemble a pyramid that rests at the working level and converges on top at the highest decision-making authority.

Because of the size of most military organizations, the critical process of planning, problem resolution, decision making, and policy implementation must be facilitated by levels or echelons of control that narrow toward the top of the organization through a formal chain of command at a number of subordinate headquarters. The structure of a military organization is important and, to a large extent, will ultimately determine the success or failure of assigned missions.

Characteristics of an Air Force

Within any military establishment, the organization of each component arm varies with the nature of its mission. Typically, air forces are charged with the responsibility to project military power quickly over long distances. Using aircraft equipped with complex weapon systems, air crews deliver lethal weapons and concentrate firepower in support of ground, sea, and other air forces. Consequently, air forces must be organized to accomplish such missions.

Due to the speed, range, and sophistication of modern aircraft and intercontinental missiles, the command and control of an air force is a critical factor in determining organizational structure. Most air forces are established as separate services that rely predominantly on a large officer corps to command and exercise control over forces provided to support the coordinated efforts of other services.

Most nations choose to staff their aircraft and missile launch facilities with skilled young officers who are physically fit and intellectually suited to the complexity of the task. As a result, air force officers rather than airmen or soldiers do the majority of fighting and training for combat. Enlisted personnel work mostly in jobs that support the aircraft, ballistic missiles, helicopters, and their crews. Air forces of major world powers are organized and trained to provide this support even when aircraft and units are deployed to distant locations.

Organization of an Air Force

Most armed forces are placed under the civilian control of the head of state of a nation and its governing political body. Typically, air force headquarters function in the chain of command alongside the other services under a ministry or department of defense headed by a minister or secretary who reports directly to the head of state on matters of defense policy and command authority. Politically, defense establishments should be subordinate to the policy of national legislatures on matters concerning their budget, funding, force structure, officer promotions, and procurement.

In the United States, the U.S. Air Force is a separate service organized as the Department of the Air Force under the secretary of the air force and a military chief of staff. The departments of the air force, army, and navy form the Department of Defense and report through the secretary of defense to the president and Congress of the United States. During a military emergency the three military service chiefs and the commandant of the Marine Corps can report directly through the chairman of the Joint Chiefs of Staff to the president as the commander in chief.

In the People's Republic of China the military is organized under the Ministry of National Defense, which reports politically to the Communist Central Committee and militarily to the Central Military Commission. The air force, artillery corps, navy, and People's Armed Police are separate service arms that make up the People's Liberation Army.

As a consequence of World War II, the Japanese military establishment was limited by treaty to provide for self-defense only. Although limited in its mission, Japan's Air Self-Defense Force is a formidable organization ranking as the fifth largest air force in the world with approximately 1,500 aircraft.

Similar to the U.S. Air Force, the Royal Air Force operates as a separate service within the British Ministry of Defence. Reporting to an Air Force Board, the Royal Air Force is split into three operating commands that are further broken down into air groups responsible for the operation of stations, units, and squadrons.

Headquarters Functions

An air force headquarters is the top link in the chain of command between the civilian and political policymakers and the operating commands charged with accomplishing military missions. Headed by a military commander, chief of staff, or commander in chief, the headquarters staff formulates decisions regarding military policy and provides top-level policy guidance for operational planning, training, personnel, financial resources and budgeting, research and development, procurement, and logistic support for the operating commands and supporting elements.

Mission Area Commands

To provide for increased span of control and to streamline the decision-making process, major commands are organized under the air force headquarters, usually by mission area. These commands should have the authority to make or delegate decisions in their specific mission areas so that commanders serving closest to operational problems can be effective and accountable for their actions.

Typical mission areas include aircraft and missile operations, personnel, training, communications, security, system development, procurement, and logistics support. Major commands that are assigned the responsibility for accomplishing these missions are as diverse in size and structure as the missions themselves.

The U.S. Air Force since its founding in 1947 had been organized along strategic and tactical lines. In 1992, after the end of the cold war, it restructured its operational forces into two global commands, the Air Mobility Command and the Air Combat Command. In addition, the Air Force Systems Command and Logistics Command were combined into one major command—the Air Material Command—responsible for research and development, procurement, and support of all air force systems and equipment. To accommodate the rapidly evolving air force mission in space, the U.S. Air Force has also formed a Space Command responsible for all air force space operations including missile launch, satellite control, reconnaissance, and space surveillance.

The Russian air forces are headed by a deputy minister of defense who reports to a general staff under the Ministry of Defense. The Russian air forces have three major components: frontal aviation, long-range aviation, and military transport aviation.

Equipped with fighter aircraft and armed helicopters, Russian frontal aviation is charged with the responsibility of maintaining battlefield air superiority and providing tactical support of ground operations.

Long-range aviation has about 900 long-range and medium-range bombers, which are capable of air-to-air refueling and can carry either nuclear or conventional weapons including air-to-air and air-to-surface missiles.

The responsibility for operation of Russian air defense fighter interceptors and long-range strategic missiles is not assigned to the air forces. Two other services, Troops of Air Defense and the Strategic Rocket Forces, are assigned these important mission areas.

Operating Wings and Squadrons

The organizational structure of an air force below the major command level is dependent upon its size, characteristics, and mission needs. Commands may be further broken down into air forces, divisions, and groups, but the ultimate operating unit is a wing comprising three or four squadrons of people and equipment.

In order to exercise full control of all units serving in the wing, the wing commander should have the authority to make decisions regarding the operation and support of the wing. He should also be accountable for all functions performed by the wing and its staff. Areas such as operations, training, standardization and evaluation, maintenance, supply, logistics support, security, transportation, and communications should also fall within the purview of the wing commander.

Because of its mission, a wing should be a homogeneous organization in its makeup and equipment. Furthermore, it should be a self-contained unit equipped with aircraft designed to perform assigned missions and manned with personnel specifically trained to operate and support those aircraft. The wing commander should have control of all of the resources needed to support the operation and deployment of the organization.

Within the structure of a wing, individual squadrons make up the basic fighting team of an air force. A squadron commander is assigned the personnel and equipment necessary to accomplish the squadron mission and ensure its support. The squadron chain of command usually flows through an operations officer to the flight commanders, typically four. The squadron commander and operations officer depend on the support of an executive officer, supply officer, chief of maintenance, and their staffs to conduct the duties of the squadron.

Squadrons vary in size depending on their mission, the number and type of aircraft assigned, and the extent to which the unit is supported integrally from within its own resources or is dependent on the combined support of outside organizations. Where practical, most flying squadrons perform best when they contain their own dedicated support personnel, mechanics, and technicians. With maintenance and support personnel assigned to a squadron under the direct, day-to-day control of the commander and maintenance officer, squadrons can best remain prepared and responsive to changing mission requirements. Unit deployments are greatly facilitated by the availability of squadron-dedicated maintenance.

Squadrons are the basic fighting teams of an air force; within fighter squadrons, flights form the basic combat elements. A formation of four modern fighters manned by highly skilled, well-trained, disciplined pilots can perform difficult missions with a high probability of success.

Composite Organizations

When rapid deployment and mission flexibility are essential to mission accomplishment, air force organizations can be structured as composite units. For example, a composite wing may operate more than one type of aircraft so that it can deploy rapidly and effectively accomplish a number of missions. A composite fighter wing may be equipped with several different types of fighters (such as air-to-air, air-to-ground, or night attack), tankers, airlift aircraft, and AWACS to form a fast-reaction combat team capable of deploying and operating on a worldwide basis.

Supporting Commands

Commands that play a supporting role in an air force generally conform to the organizational lines and structure of the flying units. In the U.S. Air Force, the organization of both the Material Command and the Training Command closely parallels the other major commands although their mission, day-to-day operations, titles, and unit designations may vary widely. In the supporting commands, emphasis is placed on management, technical expertise, and accountability for their specific contribution to the overall mission.

Interaction with an Army and Navy

Air forces seldom have or control all of the aircraft operated by a national defense force. Carrier-based naval aircraft and an assortment of army attack helicopters and support aircraft are important elements in most modern armed forces. These various air arms are charged with the responsibility to work together effectively and are often called upon to operate as an integrated team under a single commander. The conduct of Operation Desert Storm using the combined forces of several allied nations was a classic example of the success that can be achieved by an integrated task force.

Summary and Conclusion

Air forces vary in size, equipment, and mission but most share several unique characteristics—speed, complexity, and global reach. Organization may be tailored to individual capabilities and needs, but in every case the chain of command between the decision-maker or commander and the air crews performing the mission must be streamlined and responsive. As air forces move into space, their responsiveness to command and control will be increasingly important.

As world tensions change, nations may be forced to reallocate their priorities, budgets, and missions. In the process, military organizations including the air forces will ultimately have to adapt to changing requirements. Furthermore, to maintain a credible force of air power within the constraints of shrinking resources, air forces will likely be forced to reduce the overhead of high-level headquarters by merging commands and staffs, particularly those of the supporting commands.

Kenneth H. Bell

See Also: Aircraft, Military; Airpower; Army Aviation; Education, Military; Organization, Military; Organization, Naval; Span of Control: Military Organizations and Operations; Span of Control: Theories and Concepts.

Bibliography

Air Force Magazine. 1984. Soviet Air Force Almanac Issue, March.

———. 1991. 1991 Almanac, May.

Canan, J. W. 1991. No more SAC, TAC, and MAC. *Air Force Magazine*, October, pp. 13–15.
Central Intelligence Agency, Directorate of Intelligence. 1990. *Military organizations of the People's Republic of China.* Washington, D.C.: Library of Congress.
Katz, S. M. 1991. Israeli airpower on the rise. *Air Force Magazine*, November, pp. 46–51.
Mason, R. A. 1982. *The Royal Air Force: Today and tomorrow.* London: Ian Allan.
McMeiken, F. 1984. *Italian military aviation.* 1st ed. Midland Counties: Leiscester.
North Atlantic Treaty Organization (NATO). 1978. *NATO facts and figures.* Brussels: NATO Information Service.
Sabin, P., ed. 1988. *The future of United Kingdom air power.* London and Washington: Brassey's.
Scott, H. F., and W. F. Scott. 1984. *The armed forces of the USSR.* Boulder, Colo., and London: Westview Press and Arms and Armour Press.
Smith, M. J. 1981. *The Soviet air and strategic rocket forces.* Santa Barbara, Calif.: ABC-Clio.
Tyushkevich, S. A. 1978. *The Soviet armed forces: A history of their organizational development, a Soviet view.* Washington, D.C.: U.S. Air Force.
Watanabe, A. 1985. *Japanese air arms.* Rev. ed. Japan: Saitama Komatsu.
Whiting, K. R. 1986. *Soviet air power.* Boulder, Colo.: Westview Press.
Wolk, H. S. 1984. *Planning and organizing the postwar air force 1943–1947.* Office of Air Force History. Washington, D.C.: U.S. Air Force.

ORGANIZATION, ARMY

All modern armies are organized similarly. All include the same basic functions necessary to conduct land combat with modern weapons. The proportions of these functions vary according to national preference and somewhat according to the weapons and equipment available, but all are present in the large combined arms organizations. Armies are designed to operate and fight on land, and are organized hierarchically in relatively fixed patterns from small units to large organizations. The functions of land combat are repeated at each level in the hierarchy, although smaller organizations may not include a separate unit for each function. Armies also tend to integrate their support units with their combat units at each level of the organizational hierarchy. When operating in the field, armies—unlike navies and air forces, which are tied to specific bases—bring their bases with them.

The evolution of army organization has been a process of creating and differentiating the functions of land combat. In early warfare, armies tended to have a single function—infantry combat. Over the course of history, new functions arose as technology evolved; the modern army is a complex and intricate organization requiring a high degree of management and leadership to do its work.

Basic Functions of Land Combat

The *command* function, sometimes called command and control, includes the decision, planning, direction, and feedback mechanisms that manage an army at each level in the hierarchy. At the lower levels, command is accomplished by an individual, sometimes with a deputy or assistant. At the battalion level and higher, commanders have staffs to help them accomplish the command function.

The *maneuver* function uses movement and firepower to seize or defend terrain features, destroy enemy forces, and weaken the will of the enemy to fight. Maneuver is accomplished by infantry or armored units, which alternately move and fire to accomplish military missions. Infantry usually fights on foot even though the troops may ride to the battlefield on horses, trucks, or armored personnel carriers. Mechanized infantry may fight while mounted in fighting vehicles. The infantry's role is to close with and destroy the enemy. Armor achieves shock power with its tanks and can penetrate enemy positions. Generally, the best results are achieved when infantry and armor work together in a combined arms team. The infantry protects the tanks from close-in fires, and the tanks protect the infantry from longer-range fires. Infantry units include considerable firepower capability at each level, and armor units have the firepower of their tanks as well as other fire support. A primary characteristic of modern armies is the integration of fire and maneuver, in which some elements provide a base of fire to facilitate the maneuver of other elements. Tactical missions are accomplished by a carefully concerted alternation of fire and maneuver by all elements in the hierarchy of army organization.

The *reconnaissance* or scouting function consists of finding the enemy, preventing surprise, and sometimes delaying or harassing enemy attackers. Reconnaissance elements are not intended for sustained combat, although they have the capability to fight. The reconnaissance function formerly was performed by foot skirmishers or light cavalry, but in modern armies it is accomplished by personnel in light tanks, high-speed vehicles, helicopters, or aircraft.

The *fire support* function is to destroy, damage, or deter the enemy by bringing fires to bear on his troops, support, or lines of communications. Fire support is performed by rifles, machine guns, mortars, howitzers, rockets, missiles, armed helicopters, and combat aircraft. It is provided by fire support elements in infantry and armor units, and by field artillery units, combat aviation units, naval guns and missiles, and air forces. Fire support provides protection for the maneuver elements by firing on enemy forces. One specialized part of the fire support function provides antiarmor weapons to destroy or damage opposing tanks and light armored vehicles.

The *air defense* function is to destroy, damage, or deter

enemy helicopters, aircraft, and missiles. Air defense is performed by ground elements or aircraft armed with missiles and automatic guns designed specifically for this function. It is provided at each level of the hierarchy in armies, and is obtained also from naval and air forces.

The *combat engineer*, or pioneer, function is to assist the movement of the friendly forces and impede the movement of the enemy forces. The former is accomplished by building roads, airfields, bridges, and rafts and clearing obstacles; the latter is accomplished by damaging roads and airfields, destroying bridges, and constructing obstacles. Combat engineer elements may also build structures and utilities needed for military or related civil use, although engineer construction units are provided to do most of that kind of work.

The *communications*, or signal, function is to transmit messages among the elements of the army and other supporting services. It is accomplished by special sections within headquarters units and at the higher levels of the hierarchy by signal units.

Administration, or combat service support, includes several subfunctions pertaining to the operations of the army in all aspects other than combat itself. Administration includes supply, maintenance, transportation, medical care, personnel management, and subsistence. There are administration elements at every level in the hierarchy starting with the company.

The *aviation* function includes operation of light aircraft and helicopters in support of the army. The aviation function is characterized by the use of aircraft to accomplish tasks of other functions: moving troops on the battlefield as part of the maneuver function; providing aerial reconnaissance; using armed helicopters for fire support; moving supplies, equipment, and wounded personnel; and allowing commanders to view the battlefield from above. Initially, the aviation function also included aerial combat, bombing, and close air support by high performance aircraft, but most nations now perform these functions in air forces separate from their armies.

All of these functions except aviation are performed at each level in the hierarchy of army organization. As organizations become larger, these basic functions are accomplished by specifically designed and designated elements. The fundamental schema of army organization consists essentially of performing these same functions in an integrated and purposeful manner at each level in the hierarchy.

The historical evolution of army organization was achieved by adding new functional elements as compelled by the introduction of new technology. Initially, armies consisted entirely of two functions, command and maneuver; the maneuver elements were foot infantry, and the commanders led in person and even fought in battle. The introduction of horses and wheeled vehicles added heavy cavalry (armor) to the maneuver function and light cavalry to the reconnaissance function. The introduction of standoff weapons, such as slings, bows, and finally guns, caused the fire support function to be differentiated in the form of a special corps—artillery. During the Middle Ages, the engineer function achieved independent status to build fortifications and manage the sieges to destroy them. The communications function was important from the earliest days but gained specific recognition with the introduction of heliographs, telegraphs, telephones, and radios. The essential function of feeding and paying the troops and providing weapons and munitions has always been a necessary part of an army, but as weapons grew more complicated and armies larger it became necessary to create specialized units to perform the administration function. The aviation function arrived with the introduction in World War I of workable aircraft and has evolved, despite the formation of separate air forces, into an important function for most modern armies. Similarly, the command function has evolved from a single general giving instructions by voice to an elaborate network of commanders at various levels, supported by staffs and numerous components, to achieve successful control of all of the other elements of the modern army.

The Hierarchy of Army Organization

Although the names, strengths, and specific roles vary somewhat, all modern armies include the same basic elements in the hierarchy of army organization. Starting from smallest to largest, these are the squad, section, platoon, company, battalion, brigade, division, and army corps.

A *squad* consists of a squad leader (normally a sergeant) and seven to fourteen other soldiers. The squad is used in all branches of an army and is the smallest military organization. Originally, the size of a squad was determined by the ability of a single leader to command by voice, and it was employed as a single entity. However, the increased dispersion necessary to offset the increased lethality of modern weapons required the squad itself to be organized into teams.

The rifle squad is the basic element of infantry combat. There is great variety among rifle squads, but most modern rifle squads consist of a squad leader and two identical fire teams, each having a light machine gun as its principal weapon. Each fire team includes a leader, a machine gunner, and four to six riflemen, whose principal missions are to carry ammunition and protect the machine gunner. The fire teams alternate as maneuver or base of fire elements; that is, one fire team moves while the other team covers the movement with fire. Flexible interaction of fire and maneuver is the fundamental method of land combat at all levels.

A *section* is an organization larger than a squad and smaller than a platoon used within headquarters and in support organizations. It is led by a noncommissioned officer (NCO) and varies in strength from 10 to 40 personnel. In some armies, a section is also a combat element consisting of two or three squads.

A *platoon* consists of three or four squads and is led by a lieutenant or captain platoon leader assisted by a senior NCO—the platoon sergeant. The platoon is used in all branches of an army and has subelements for the maneuver, fire support, and command functions.

A generic rifle platoon includes three rifle squads as maneuver elements, a weapons squad as a fire support element, and a command section. Each rifle squad is a maneuver element for the platoon, although each contains both fire and maneuver capability internally. The weapons squad provides additional fire support with heavy machine guns to augment the fires of the light machine guns in the rifle squads. The command element consists of the platoon leader, the platoon sergeant, and a radio operator representing the communications function.

A generic tank platoon consists of four or five tanks with their crews and is commanded by a platoon leader in a tank. Each tank is a self-contained mobile fighting vehicle armed with a large flat-trajectory main gun, machine guns, and sometimes missiles. A tank platoon may fight in teams of two tanks, alternating fire and maneuver as directed by the platoon leader.

A *company* is a unit of 100–250 personnel consisting of several platoons and other elements. It is commanded by a captain, usually, although majors command companies in some armies. The functions of administration and air defense are introduced at the company level. Administration is performed by a first sergeant as senior NCO, a company clerk, a supply section, a maintenance section (depending on how much equipment the company has), and sometimes a mess section—all within a headquarters platoon. Command is accomplished by the company commander, the first sergeant, and several communications specialists.

A generic rifle company consists of three rifle platoons as maneuver elements, a weapons platoon to provide fire support, a headquarters platoon for administration, and a headquarters for command. A typical weapons platoon provides two new forms of fire support: high-angle fire using light (60mm or 81mm) mortars; and flat-trajectory light antitank fire with light antitank guns or missiles. The headquarters platoon contains small elements for personnel and supply. In the U.S. Army, the mess and maintenance functions for infantry units have been centralized at the battalion level.

A generic tank company consists of three tank platoons as maneuver elements and a company headquarters, which includes personnel and supply sections. Because of the heavy maintenance load for the tanks, company headquarters may also have a maintenance section.

A *battalion* is a unit of 400 to 1,200 personnel consisting of several companies and other elements. It is commanded by a lieutenant colonel and is the smallest organization with a staff to assist the commander. Most staffs are organized to provide principal staff officers for personnel, intelligence, operations, and logistics, although some nations combine intelligence and operations into a single operations staff element, and personnel and logistics into a single administrative staff element. The battalion is the basic unit for combat and combat support branches.

A generic infantry battalion is shown in Figure 1. It consists of three or four rifle companies as maneuver elements, a combat support company, a headquarters company, and a headquarters. The combat support company provides new weapons and equipment to augment those in the rifle companies, including a mortar platoon with medium mortars (107mm), tactical radar equipment, and an antiarmor platoon with heavy antitank missiles. The reconnaissance function is performed by a scout platoon in the combat support company. The air defense function may be introduced at this level by including in the combat support company a section armed with shoulder-fired air defense missiles. A separate engineer section or platoon is sometimes provided as well. The headquarters and combat support companies may be combined into a single unit. The headquarters company includes mess, maintenance, and signal sections, and sometimes a transportation section as well. The headquarters includes the command, staff, and the personnel in the sections supporting the staff. An infantry battalion is a reasonably self-sufficient unit with explicit representation of six or seven of the nine functions of land combat.

A generic tank battalion is shown in Figure 2. It consists of four tank companies as maneuver elements, a headquarters, and a headquarters company. The headquarters company includes a medium mortar platoon for fire support and a scout platoon for the reconnaissance function, as well as a maintenance platoon and a support platoon to carry the battalion's basic load of ammunition and fuel. The combat engineer function is accomplished by an armored vehicle–launched bridge.

A *brigade* is an organization of units with an aggregate strength of from 2,000 to 8,000 personnel commanded by a brigadier general or colonel. A brigade is used to form combat, combat support, and combat service support units into functional or integrated combinations. Brigade headquarters are used to command engineer, transportation, signal, and artillery battalions in single-function or-

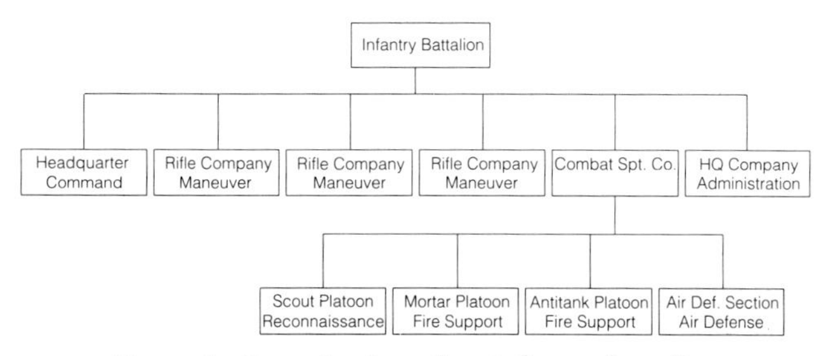

Figure 1. Organization of an infantry battalion.

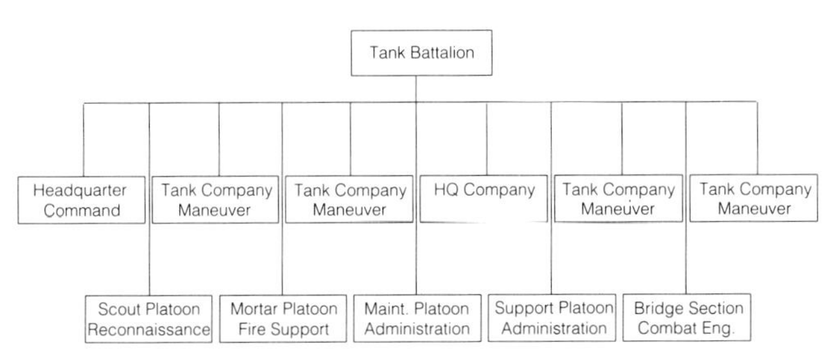

Figure 2. Organization of a tank battalion.

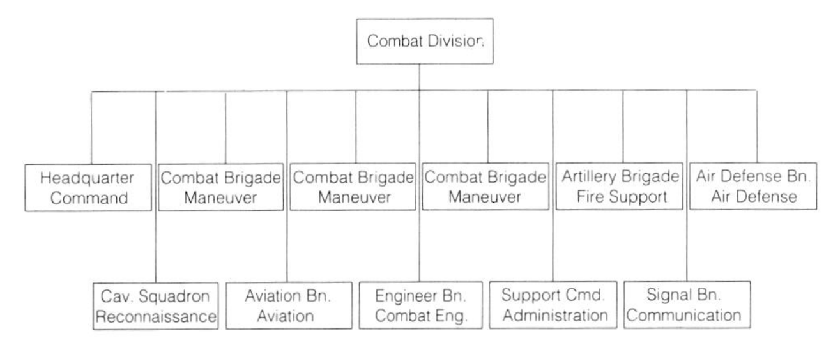

Figure 3. Organization of a combat division.

ganizations. They are also used to command combat service support battalions of different types—supply, maintenance, medical—in multifunction organizations. A group headquarters commanded by a colonel also may be used to command several battalions or companies and may be major subordinate elements of brigades. A regiment has about the same strength as a brigade but is a fixed organization with a definite internal composition, while a brigade is a flexible organization with an internal composition tailored to the specific combat environment. In the U.S. Army, the only regimental organization still in use is an armored cavalry regiment fulfilling the reconnaissance function for army corps. In some armies, the term *regiment* is used for smaller units comparable to battalions in the U.S. and (NATO) armies.

Combat brigades are combined arms organizations, in that they integrate infantry, armor, artillery, and cavalry units under a single commander for combat. A combat brigade may be organic to a combat division or may be a separate organization. An organic combat brigade is a tactical headquarters commanded by a colonel to which combat battalions and combat support units are attached or placed in direct support. Separate combat brigades are usually commanded by a brigadier general and are assigned its subordinate units on a permanent basis.

A generic separate combat brigade includes two to five infantry or tank battalions as maneuver elements, an artillery battalion for fire support, a cavalry troop (company) for reconnaissance, a combat engineer company, and a support battalion that includes the service support units. Brigades may be tailored for their intended missions, and an air defense battery or aviation company or battalion could be assigned as well. A separate brigade is a formidable combat force, and some nations use the separate brigade as their primary combat organization.

A *division* (Fig. 3) is a combined arms organization with 7,000–22,000 military personnel commanded by a major general. It includes three combat brigades as maneuver elements, an artillery brigade of three to five artillery battalions, a cavalry squadron with three or four cavalry troops (some of which may be air cavalry), a separate air defense battalion, a separate signal battalion, a support command with three or four service support battalions, and frequently an aviation battalion. The division artillery brigade commonly consists of a direct support battalion with light or medium (105mm, 152mm, or 155mm) howitzers for each brigade and one or two other battalions, including heavy (203mm or 240mm) howitzers or multiple-launch rocket launchers for general support of the division. Each of the nine basic functions of land combat is represented explicitly in a combat division.

In many armies, including the U.S. Army, the brigades organic to a division are tactical headquarters to which infantry and tank battalions are attached for a particular battle or campaign, while the rest of the brigade units—artillery battalion, engineer company, and combat service support elements—remain assigned to their own divisional units and placed in support of the brigade. This organizational concept allows a division commander to tailor his subordinate brigades to the combat situation and his mission. Other nations (Soviet Union, U.K.), treat the major subordinate elements of a division as regiments, or relatively fixed organizations. Whether a division is flexible or fixed in theory, division commanders tend to organize their divisions for combat as they perceive necessary to accomplish their missions.

There are many different types of combat divisions, depending on the nature and mix of the included infantry and tank maneuver battalions. Infantry divisions have from seven to ten foot-infantry battalions and one or two tank or mechanized infantry battalions. Light infantry divisions include nine or ten light infantry battalions designed for rapid strategic movement and trained for low-intensity conflict. Airborne infantry divisions are designed to conduct parachute assaults, so the nine infantry battalions and other division units (including sometimes a light tank battalion) are designed for this role, and all division personnel are qualified parachutists. The U.S. Army has an air assault division with nine light infantry battalions manned by soldiers specially trained in helicopter operations. Armored divisions and mechanized infantry divisions are composed of a mix of 10 to 12 tank battalions and mechanized infantry battalions equipped with armored personnel carriers or infantry fighting vehicles. Tank battalions outnumber mechanized infantry battalions in armored divisions, while the converse is true in mechanized infantry divisions. In each of these divisions, the reconnaissance, artillery, engineer, and other units of the division base are equipped and trained to be compatible with the maneuver battalions. In an armored division, the artillery is all self-propelled on tracked vehicles, and the engineers ride in armored engineer vehicles. In a light infantry division, the artillery is light and towed by light vehicles, and the engineers have light trucks.

An *army corps* is the largest combined arms organization currently used as a standard army formation. It has a strength of 50,000 to 300,000 troops and is commanded by a lieutenant general. An army corps may consist of two to seven divisions and supporting units. A generic army corps is shown in Figure 4. It includes three divisions (two infantry and one armored), a separate combat brigade for augmenting a division or accomplishing a tactical mission, a corps artillery brigade with ten to fifteen artillery battalions organized into three or four artillery groups, an armored or air cavalry regiment with three or four cavalry squadrons, a corps support command with several area or functional commands, and brigades for the engineer, signal, air defense, and aviation functions.

The headquarters staffs for both division and corps are organized into more staff sections than are found at the division or brigade headquarters. In addition to staff sections for personnel, intelligence, operations, and logistics, there may be separate staff sections for planning, civil-military affairs, communications, and other special activities deemed important enough to warrant an additional principal staff officer.

Army echelons above corps are organized for specific theaters and situations, but all include common elements for specific collateral functions of land combat. Field armies, consisting of two or more corps with an array of supporting organizations, and commanded by a full general, exist in the armies of the larger nations, but usually they are tailored for a specific mission. In the 1991 Gulf War, Third U.S. Army Headquarters commanded VII Corps and XVIII Airborne Corps as the army component of the unified theater command for the Persian Gulf. (The U.S. Army also maintains several "CONUS Armies," which are administrative headquarters responsible for specific regions of the United States and are not intended to serve as field armies.) The Soviet Union used the term *army* to mean a corps, and *front* to mean field army. In World War II the Allies, Germans, and Soviets formed army groups consisting of several field armies.

The collateral functions of land combat that are provided for in the echelons above corps include intelligence, military police, chemical, logistics, personnel replacement, and special operations. Intelligence units exist at

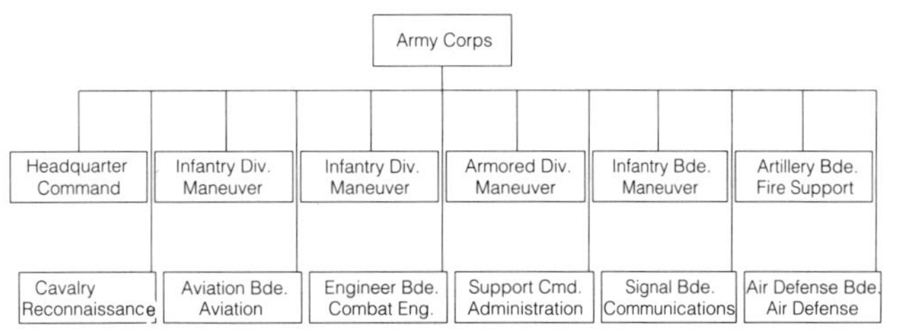

Figure 4. Organization of an army corps.

battalion and higher levels in the form of staff sections. There are also intelligence units devoted to the collection and interpretation of intelligence. Some of these units exist at the division and corps level, but often they are organized into a single theater-wide intelligence command. The military police function also exists in the divisions and corps; there is a military police company in each U.S. division and one or more battalions in an army corps to provide law and order, area security, and battlefield circulation control. That part of the military police function involved with prisoners of war and criminal investigation often is organized into a single command under the army commander for a theater. Chemical units also are provided at every level, and there is a chemical company for each division, but the control of chemical assets, including smoke generator units, often is held at the theater or theater army level. The personnel replacement function normally is performed by a replacement command under the theater army commander.

Special operations forces include special forces, rangers, special operations aviation, civil affairs, and psychological operations units. These special operations forces usually are formed into a single command for theater-wide operations under the theater commander. In the war with Iraq, the United States assigned or attached civil affairs units to the corps and divisions, retained control of psychological operations at the theater level while placing units in support of the corps and divisions, and conducted special forces and ranger operations under a special operations command for the theater.

Finally, the echelons above corps include logistical commands to operate ports, railways, pipelines, highway transportation systems, supply depots, maintenance facilities, and other activities to support the operations of the corps. These logistical commands are organized either on an area basis with units of different functions or on a single-function basis for the entire theater. The exact variety and organization of the units operating at the echelons above corps depends on circumstances and national doctrine.

The organization of armies as national institutions tends to vary widely, but some common elements exist. The army headquarters is headed by a senior military officer who usually reports to a civilian minister of war or defense. The army is usually part of a unified military organization with the naval and air forces. The staffs at army headquarters are concerned with the normal staff functions for the army in the field, and in addition have to deal with budgeting, public relations, and political issues. Armies commonly have major commands for the following functions: centralized personnel management, development and procurement of weapons and equipment, wholesale logistics (supply and maintenance), training and education, doctrinal development, and health care. In addition, there may be organizations devoted to computers and electronics, munitions, industrial production, political affairs and propaganda, and testing of weapons and equipment. The exact organization and delineation of responsibilities varies widely according to national preference and the size of the army.

Armies are usually separated into two or more components according to readiness standards. The active component consists of units with equipment manned by full-time personnel. There are a wide variety of reserve component schemes, but they all involve only a few full-time personnel augmented in some cases by part-time reservists who train regularly and in other cases by reservists who will report to their units only upon mobilization. Most armies keep some of their units in a reserve component with the same organizational tables, tactical doctrine, and training standards as the active component, although with reduced readiness and cost.

It is likely that the historical trend toward greater complexity and specialization in army organization will continue. Once considered a low-tech organization compared with air forces and navies, armies are now using large amounts of sophisticated high-technology equipment and will use more in the future. Consequently, the proportion of the strength of an army that engages directly in combat will continue to shrink. Since the earliest days, when every member of an army fought on the battlefield, the evolution of army organization has increased the proportion of support troops to combat troops, until now only a few riflemen, machine gunners, and tank crews actually operate on the front lines.

This increase in support, however, has also resulted in a greater increase in the overall combat power of armies, so these fewer combat soldiers can deliver greater amounts of lethal munitions faster and more accurately than ever before. Because of the need to counter this increased lethality, armies will continue to move toward greater dispersion in tactical formations. Air power and longer-range weapons mean that armies must disperse in depth as well as laterally. The combat area is getting deeper and more difficult to distinguish from the rear areas, if indeed there are any rear areas remaining.

Finally, as armies are becoming more technical, more specialized internally, and more lethal, they are becoming smaller. During World War II, the U.S. Army had 8 million military personnel, the German army numbered 4.5 million, and the Red Army about 7 million. Even during the height of the cold war, the two major opposing coalitions were planning armies with at most 4 or 5 million on each side. Currently, armies of the NATO nations are being reduced in size as the threat of a major conventional war diminishes. The trend among industrialized nations is for smaller armies that are well trained and equipped with modern, sophisticated weapons. The United States is planning an army of slightly more than 500,000 active and 600,000 selected reserve personnel for the mid-1990s. However, China, Vietnam, North Korea, India, and perhaps the Commonwealth of Independent States and Iraq are likely to have active armies over 1 million strong for the foreseeable future. Despite reductions in size and the introduction of modern weapons, the fundamentals of army organization will tend to remain very much the same as they have been since Napoleon and Wellington collaborated unwittingly to combine respectively shock and firepower with linear tactics during the early years of the nineteenth century.

JOHN R. BRINKERHOFF

SEE ALSO: Administration, Military; Force Structure; Manpower, Military; Military Police; Reserve Components; Staff; Task Force; Unit, Military.

Bibliography

International Institute for Strategic Studies. 1990. *The military balance, 1990–1991*. London: Brassey's.

Isby, D. C., and C. Kamps. 1985. *Armies of NATO's central front*. London: Jane's.

Keegan, J. 1983. *World armies*. Detroit, Mich.: Gale Research.

Scott, H. F., and W. F. Scott. 1984. *The armed forces of the USSR*. London: Arms and Armour Press.

Thomer, E. 1984. *Die Bundeswehr Heute*. Herford und Bonn: E. S. Mittler und Sohn.

U.S. Department of the Army. 1987. *Staff officers field manual 101-10-1/1: Organizational, technical, and logistical data*. Vols. 1 and 2. Washington, D.C.: Government Printing Office.

ORGANIZATION, MILITARY

There are many definitions of *organization*. For the purpose of this article, organization is the process that provides a military activity with a methodical structure and then transforms that structure into full working order. To do this, life must be added to the activity's various functions in the shape and substance of individual persons, groups of people, and their inter-relationships.

Organizational development entails identifying, specifying, and aligning the functions to be performed by each person or each group within an established system of formally regulated working relationships and procedures. It is then organization that binds these relationships and procedures together within the activity's structure, and links specific functions to the persons or groups charged with undertaking them. Organization is also the link between the activity's prescribed purpose and the method of executing or accomplishing that purpose.

Within the structure of military organization, the *unit* is the basic building block. Each unit has a specific combat or support role, and has an establishment (table of manpower and equipment) to enable it to carry out that role. The unit may be a battalion of infantry or a cavalry regiment, a formed column of horsedrawn wagons or a modern transport battalion, a supply depot or a maintenance workshop, a naval vessel or an aircraft wing, a joint headquarters or a communications center. Some units have a role only in war; they train in peacetime to remain operationally ready and fit for that role. Others have peacetime tasks that may change during transition to war. If a unit's organization changes in a crisis or in war, the amount of men and equipment it needs may change as well. There are also units that disband on the outbreak of war; their resources are transferred to other military purposes.

A *formation* is an operational grouping of combat and support units brought together permanently or temporarily for a specific mission. It may be a parachute brigade, an armored division, a logistic support group, or a joint task force comprising maritime, land, and air elements. It is, thus, an ordered arrangement or organization of army units composed of troops, vehicles, and equipments formed into a balanced and combined arms-services team; of ships in convoy or formed into a fleet; or of aircraft operating together. The term *formation* is also used to denote a tactical configuration of combat units, but this interpretation is outside the scope of this article.

Every unit and formation has a *commander* and a headquarters. On the one hand, a battalion commander has a small, mobile headquarters consisting of key officers and soldiers with well-defined operational or peacetime duties. The commander of a field formation, such as an armored division, has a larger, mobile headquarters comprising his general staff (operational planning staff), specialist support staff (artillery, supply, communications, intelligence, etc.), and a security and administrative element. The commander of an army, on the other hand, may well have a very large, static headquarters composed of his own personal and general staff, as well as others representing naval, air, or flanking forces.

The headquarters *staff* helps the commander to plan, direct, control, coordinate, supervise, monitor, and evaluate operations during an emergency or in war; the staff also assists with the regulation of peacetime training and domestic routine. Operational and administrative orders derive from the commander himself, although his staff may issue them on his behalf. The staff, collectively, and the chief of staff, individually, have no command authority over the units or formations in a military force; that is the sole preserve of the commander, who is the senior officer personally nominated and vested with that authority. A designated staff officer or another subordinate may be given powers, for example, to control the tactical movement of a unit or formation over an obstacle, or to control the release of operationally vital materiel in critical short supply. Nevertheless, these and other forms of control, which fall short of full delegated command, are always exercised directly on behalf of the commander.

A force structure that incorporates units and formations, commanders and staffs forms the foundations of military organization. The design, creation, and resources of that organization are its cornerstones and profoundly influence how well or how badly it functions, or whether or not it fulfills its mission. But it is people who actually make a chosen organization work and who principally determine its effectiveness.

History

A review of major organizational issues must start by outlining the evolutionary development of military structures during a long history of violent warfare, uneasy peace, and momentous change.

In prehistoric times, fighting men knew little, and needed to know little, about organization. Having found, made, or stolen their weapons, they roamed singly or in small groups, engaging or evading any threat that came their way. The most experienced and skillful—generally the elders of the group—made the decisions: where to go, when to leave and return to base, which route to use, and how to attack which prey. This required little organization.

This simplicity could not last. The groups of fighting men grew bigger and started to proliferate. Individuals had to be given additional duties: the young and fleet of foot reconnoitered and delivered messages, the less mobile and less aggressive pitched camp or found food for the combatants and others. Soon each fighting group needed several specialists to provide a variety of support, and the combatant troops themselves began to specialize as spearmen, bowmen, armed horsemen, and so forth.

Ancient and Medieval Military Organizations

Little detail is known of military organization before the rise of the Greek city-states in the early fifth century B.C. Earlier military structures, like those of Sumer, Akkad, Egypt, Assyria, and the Hittites, left little history, although some details of their equipment and tactics have come to light through archaeology.

Classical Greece and Macedon. The armies of the classical Greeks were built on a core of *hoplites*, armored spearmen who fought in close formation. Generally, the *hoplite* phalanx, usually eight men deep, and their supporting cavalry and light troops were organized in companies of 100 and "battalions" of 500 to 1,000. In the early fourth century B.C., for example, the Spartan army consisted of six or seven *morai*, each about 600 men strong. The organization of other Greek armies is less clear, but was probably broadly similar.

The Macedonian army of Philip II and his son Alexander III ("the Great") was organized differently. It was considerably larger than the Greek armies, and it relied to a greater degree on the offensive power of cavalry to achieve victory. The Macedonian *hoplites*, equipped with a pike (the *sarissa*) and a small shield, were called *pezetaeri* (foot companions) and were organized in *taxeis* (regiments) of about 1,500 men each, 16 men deep. The simple phalanx contained about 8,200 men. Alexander invaded Asia with four of these, leaving another three or four at home with the regent Antipater. The *pezetaeri* were supported by battalions, about 50 strong, of javelineers, archers, and *peltasts* (specially equipped light infantrymen). The final infantry force comprised the elite *hypaspists*, who were apparently trained to serve as either light troops or *pezetaeri*, as the occasion demanded; they wielded an 8- to 10-foot spear and often served as the hinge between the phalanx and the cavalry.

The Macedonian cavalry was grouped in units about 500 strong. The horse *companions* (the royal bodyguard), Macedonians and Thessalians, were heavy shock troops equipped with armor, shield, sword, and lance. There were also lighter horsemen for scouting, skirmishing, and pursuit duties, often recruited from less-civilized peoples. Some 5,000 of the 35,000 men in Alexander's army when he crossed the Hellespont in 334 B.C. were cavalry, about evenly divided between light and heavy types.

In the 150 years after Alexander's death, the Hellenic successor-kingdoms in Greece and the Near East retained the basic structure of the Alexandrian army, although they added elephants and significant numbers of native troops. Without Alexander's genius, however, these armies were outmatched when they met the legions of Rome in the second century B.C.

The Roman Army. Under the Monarchy and the early Republic, the Roman army was no more than a Graeco-Etruscan phalanx supported by skirmishers and noble cavalry. Under Servius Tullius in the late fifth century B.C., Roman manpower was classified on an economic basis, with the wealthier sections of the population serving as either cavalry or *hoplites* and poorer citizens serving as light troops and servants. Each class was organized into *centuries* of 100 men each.

The reforms of Marcus Camillus in the early fourth century B.C. and modifications made after the Roman defeat by the Samnites at the Caudine Forks (321 B.C) produced a much more flexible force. Legionary infantry was divided into four groups, separated by age and equipment. The youngest men were employed as light infantry or *velites*. The *hastati, principes*, and the oldest troops, the *triarii*, were arrayed in successive lines on the field. A legion of about 3,500 men had ten cohorts (regiments), each one containing one *maniple* (battalion) of each troop type. Each maniple contained two centuries (companies) of 60 to 80 men, except for the maniple of *triarii*, which had only one century. The cohorts were deployed for battle in three lines in a kind of checkerboard or *quincunx* formation, with intervals between the cohorts in one line covered by those in the line behind. Each cohort also had a *turma* (troop) of 30 cavalry, but these fought separately from the cohort in consolidated cavalry units on the legion's flanks. Normally, each Roman legion was paired with a legion (or legion-sized force) raised from Rome's Latin and Italian allies. Two such legionary pairs formed a consular army of about 15,000 men. This tactical system was more flexible than the Graeco-Macedonian phalanx, and was both stronger and more resilient in action. This organization carried the Roman army through the Punic Wars, persisting for over 200 years until Gaius Marius undertook his military reforms about 105 B.C.

The "Marian" reforms simplified Roman organization considerably. The division of legionary infantry into four troops types was abandoned, and maniples were abolished. Under Marius, the legion contained ten cohorts, each of six 80-man centuries. The centuries of the first cohort were double-sized, so an ordinary legion's field strength totaled about 5,280 men. Each legionary was equipped as a heavy infantryman with *pilum* (a javelin also usable as a short spear), *gladius* (a broad, short sword about 2 feet in length), and shield. Cavalry and light infantry were provided by the *auxilia*, organized in 500- and 1,000-man cohorts, which were assigned to individual legions as required. This organization persisted almost unchanged until Diocletian's reforms in the late third century A.D.

The army of the late Roman Empire contained two separate forces. The frontier troops, or *limitanei*, were a quasi-militia force manning frontier fortifications. The mobile field army, consisting of the *comitatenses* and the *palatini* (imperial bodyguards), contained a large cavalry element, both for increased mobility and because the fighting quality of Roman infantry had declined as the standards of discipline had lapsed. Further, the late Roman army became increasingly made up of barbarians. By the start of the fifth century A.D., nearly all the *limitanei* and most of the field troops were barbarians; the senior commander in the Western Empire, Stilicho, was a Vandal, and many other senior commanders were barbarians.

From tribes to feudal armies, A.D. *476–1300.* Although the barbarian tribes produced some cunning and capable warriors, their military sophistication came to them second-hand from the Romans. By the time the Western Empire collapsed in A.D. 476, most elements of Roman military organization had vanished from western Europe. In its place, the barbarian successor-kingdoms emplaced their own ruder military organization, based on clan, lineage, and personal loyalties rather than on formal units.

Germanic armies were led by chieftains, each of whom was accompanied into battle by a bank of warriors who had sworn to serve him. In exchange for their service and fealty, the chieftain undertook to provide sustenance for his followers. The economic aspects of this relationship were particularly important; the English word *lord* comes from the Anglo-Saxon *hlaford*, or loaf-giver, a person who provided sustenance to his followers. Chieftains in turn swore loyalty to higher-ranking chieftains, thereby providing a framework for controlling larger forces. This network of personal ties is the principal hallmark of feudalism, which dominated European social organization for nearly ten centuries after the fall of Rome.

As the social aspects of feudalism developed, many

chieftains (or feudal lords) adopted the practice of providing for their followers by granting them land that could provide for their material needs. This practice, known as *manorialism,* is often linked with feudalism but is properly a separate development. For instance, the central governments of both the Byzantine Empire, with its *pro noia* military fiefs, and the Ottoman Empire, with its Timariot fiefs, made grants of land in exchange for military service by the fiefholder.

Outside the Byzantine Empire and the centrally organized Muslim states, military organization in medieval Europe was decentralized and irregular. Armies like those of the Vikings and Magyars consisted of war bands gathered around individual war chiefs, who sometimes banded together for particular operations. In the more "civilized" areas of western and southern Europe, armies consisted of feudal contingents provided to an overlord on demand. These contingents were limited in size and duration of service by tradition and mutual consent. A lord could extend the service of his followers (or vassals, the contemporary legal term) beyond the usual period if he paid them, as their usual service period was unpaid.

By the twelfth century, it became increasingly common in France, England, and the surrounding areas to replace individual service (always a nuisance for the vassal) with a cash payment. The lord could then hire mercenaries for as long as he liked (or could afford) with the money so received. After 1050 or so, most European armies contained a significant portion of mercenaries.

Typically, a feudal army fought in three parts, called "battles." The vanguard, or forward battle, traditionally fought on the right wing; the main battle fought in the center of the line; and the rearguard or rear battle held the left. Each battle contained a variable number of separate contingents, most consisting of both infantry and cavalry. For purposes of combat, smaller groups of horse or foot soldiers were brigaded with other units of their type, but these groupings lasted only until the end of the battle. Mercenary forces often had a more permanent organization, and they were usually grouped in companies of 50 to 300 men. Larger organizations, as with the feudal troops, were strictly temporary.

Permanent armies: Muster and array, condottieri, and the Compagnies d'Ordonnance. By the beginning of the fourteenth century, most European states were making serious (if often unsuccessful) efforts to create permanent armies. The cost of such forces made the task difficult, but the English effort is especially noteworthy because it enabled a series of English monarchs to wage the Hundred Years' war against the vastly greater resources of France.

Under King Edward I, England undertook the conquest of Wales, a task that required not weeks but years. Feudal armies were unfit to perform such a task, and Edward introduced several reforms to enable him to keep an army in the field for months or years at a time. First, he issued "indentures" to individual lords, to provide specific numbers of troops with specified equipment, for a preset period of time. Second, he sent "commissioners of array" to the counties to muster the local militias and gather (or select) volunteers for service with the army. All these troops were paid and fed at royal expense, and were capable of serving abroad and for extended periods. This army, with foot soldiers armed with Welsh longbows, gave the English the military capacity to fight France (with five times' England's resources) for more than a century, twice nearly destroying the French kingdom.

Italy, because of the number of urban communities, had never developed the sort of feudalism present north of the Alps. Although Italian city-states at first depended on militia armies, they soon realized the costs and drawbacks associated with such forces. By the late thirteenth century, they began to employ mercenaries on a wide-scale basis, and by the mid-1300s the *condottieri* began to appear. These military entrepreneurs were a specific sort of mercenary; for a fee, a city could hire a general, who would in turn hire an army and conduct wars for the city-state. A written contract for such an agreement was called a *condotta,* whence the terms for the soldiers themselves. At first, the *condottieri* were free agents, switching their services from city to city as the situation dictated. By the 1420s and 1430s, however, they had lost much of their fiscal and political freedom and increasingly tended to spend their careers in the service of one state.

The armies of the *condottieri,* which often existed for long periods and indeed effectively became standing armies after 1440–50, were tightly organized. Troops were grouped in companies of several hundred men, generally armed and equipped similarly. Since most soldiers were long-term volunteer professionals, the sophistication of tactics and maneuver was considerable, and the ablest *condottieri,* like Francesco Sforze or John Hawkwood, were skillful generals indeed.

The effect of the *condottieri* was not limited to Italy alone. By the mid-fifteenth century, in the wake of the near-miraculous revival of French fortunes occasioned by the inspiration of Joan of Arc, the French undertook a major military reform. Until 1445, the French army consisted of numerous quasi-autonomous mercenary companies, many of them little more than bandits. In that year, King Charles VII (at the behest of his counselors) promulgated the *Grande Ordonnance,* which gave royal sanction and royal pay to some mercenary captains. Those mercenaries who did not gain official recognition were effectively outlawed. At one stroke, the French thereby created an army solely responsible to the crown, and at the same time cleared France of the bandit-mercenaries who had infested the country for decades.

Furthermore, this reform gave the French an army disciplined enough to drive the English from their shores, and effectively brought the Hundred Years' War to a close. This army consisted of a varying number of companies, each of between 30 and 100 "lances." Each lance contained a man-at-arms, his squire (counted as a soldier), two mounted archers, and two pages (both considered as noncombatants). The captain of the company was paid on the basis of the number of complete lances available in his unit, which was inspected regularly. As this army of the *Compagnies d'Ordonnance* (roughly translated as "legal companies") was also the first national standing army in Western Europe since the fall of the Roman empire, it also served as a transition from the medieval to the modern.

The Background to Modern Organization

Infantry on foot and cavalry on horseback received support from artillerymen, at first firing primitive cannon and later using weapons of ever-increasing sophistication and lethality. They were also supported by field engineers or pioneers who sapped at the walls of fortifications under siege and destroyed or built obstacles and bridges to make movement easier for their colleagues and more difficult for the enemy. As the means of mobility gradually improved, so the enhancement or obstruction of movement on and behind the battlefield became increasingly vital to operations.

Armed scouts were sent out to search for information and, when armed, found it easier to penetrate hostile areas, extricate themselves, and return to their leaders with the information gathered. Guides led mounted or dismounted troops through difficult terrain or to a special rendezvous. Signallers provided communications between groups and between leaders who shared a common cause; these were rudimentary systems initially, but as resourcefulness, ingenuity, and technology advanced, more reliable, secure communications became available and were used.

From earlier times, logisticians, accountants, paymasters, doctors, judges, police, and administrators of many types gave their services to those whose duty or vocation was to fight or provide direct support to the fighting. As fleets and armies grew in size, complexity, and power, the variety and amount of services needed to keep them at sea or on land in prime combat order multiplied.

Modern military organization comprising units, formations, and headquarters became discernible from the late sixteenth century onward in Europe. Armies had long consisted of cavalry, infantry (some armed with pike, some with hand guns), and artillery trains when, more than a century later, first Marlborough and then Frederick the Great took the field. However, the origin of the battalion or regiment as a basic military unit is a matter of some conjecture and dispute. There are those who claim the sixteenth-century Swiss and German mercenary *landsknechte* as the prototype, while others support the Italian *condottieri* as first.

Much of today's terminology was being developed at that time. The French word *bataillon* describes foot components of infantry or of artillery forming a subdivision of a regiment and itself comprising a number of companies. The French word *regiment* signifies a military component consisting of a number of battalions or cavalry squadrons commanded by a colonel. The term *formation,* also of French derivation, indicates a military organization composed of several diverse parts constituting a force, or a disposition of troops on the battlefield—for example, *formation dense* or *formation ouverte.*

The organization of European land forces was constructed from the bottom up: first the unit or battalion, then the regiment or brigade, later the division and larger formations. This continual, evolutionary process of development, experimentation, and refinement is well catalogued. As the scope of military strategies and commitments grew, as scientific discoveries and technological advances were made, so the structure and the capability of forces steadily expanded. In other parts of the world, forces were developed to match the prevailing local threat and conditions—terrorism, small wars, mountains, jungle, and desert. But it was mainly in Europe that most developments of modern force structure occurred and where the modern fighting formation became composed of a multiplicity of specialized, key units, many of them mutually supportive.

The organization of command and headquarters staff, on the other hand, was constructed from the top down: initially, a small group of senior officers and sometimes some civilians clustered around the commander, who was quite often the monarch. His force may have been relatively small, the number of his principal subordinates and levels of command within his force few, chains of command from top to bottom short, and the span of his command much narrower than in present-day forces. As the complexity of warfare and the size of forces grew, so the numbers on the staff of headquarters and their individual responsibilities grew. When a headquarters became too large to move frequently or to deploy far enough forward to observe and control the battle, the commander may have established a separate, small command group of himself and his principal tactical assistants. Then it became necessary to draw the distinction between the command group and the remainder of his staff. His headquarters and his staff there were instruments of command only when the commander was present with them or when he had formally delegated authority to another to act on his behalf.

During the late sixteenth and the seventeenth centuries, several important new senior staff appointments started to appear in the headquarters of European armies, among them a scoutmaster-general (reconnaissance), forage-master-general (procurement), proviantmaster-general (supply), wagonmaster-general (transportation), provost, and camp and judge marshals. The German province of Brandenburg added adjutants-general, quartermasters-general, a commissary-general, supply master-general, auditor-general, and a staff quartermaster, field paymaster, chaplain, apothecary, and surgeon. After the Thirty Years' War, the French introduced the appointment of a *Maréchal Général des Logis* with responsibility for providing quarters and lodgings. Small functional organizations were formed around the holders of these early posts; these later became the supporting services of the armies.

Napoleon's *état-major* operated in two echelons: main and rear headquarters, in modern parlance. His *maison*, or group of immediate assistants, comprised a writing staff (intelligence, orders preparation), a fighting staff (operations), and a riding staff (aides, communications). Some distance back, Imperial Headquarters prepared the orders for nontactical movement, supervised artillery and engineer support, provided military police, and supplied maps. The logistics of Napoleon's armies was by no means neglected, for he was always personally involved with the planning and execution of logistic support, but the mainly civilian staff responsible for these functions was not part of the emperor's field headquarters.

Meanwhile, Napoleon's opponent, the Duke of Wellington, had an adjutant-general who dealt with reports, correspondence, orders preparation, and discipline; his quartermaster-general was concerned with supply, transportation, and quartering. In addition, the duke employed five chiefs of special corps for cavalry, artillery, engineers, provost, and guides, and five heads of civilian departments for the commissariat, purveyors, storekeepers, surgeons, and paymasters.

The Prussian quartermaster-general was also responsible for quartering and a widening range of logistic support. There was, however, an important difference between the status of this appointment and its equivalent in the British army. The Prussians incorporated their quartermaster-general firmly within their General Staff—the tightly knit, cohesively organized, and smoothly functioning branch of their headquarters comprehensively responsible, under a single chief of staff, for all operational intelligence and for strategic, tactical, logistical, and administrative planning of operations. The *Generalstabs Officier* had to respond to all calls and emergencies across the complete range of operational staff duties. In short, as it was said at the time: "The General Staff is intended to convert the ideas of the General commanding into orders, not only conveying [orders] . . . to the troops [general staff officers also needed to be bold riders], but also working out all matters of detail, thus relieving the General from a great amount of trouble" (Schellendorf 1905).

In the British army, the quartermaster-general has never been part of the General Staff, but has always headed a separate military staff department reporting directly to a government minister but under the general coordination of the chief of the General Staff. Efforts were made in the latter part of the nineteenth century to correct this deficiency and indeed to introduce a proper General Staff, but these failed. It is not surprising, therefore, that, at the higher levels of British defense organization, logistics has tended to be viewed as a separate matter. The recent, partial introduction of a General Staff organization at lower, formation headquarters level in the British Army has helped to rectify the shortcoming, though no single chief of staff appointment in these headquarters is yet vested with universal responsibility for the direction and coordination of all operational planning on behalf of each formation commander.

Still more men and still more support were required when the railroad, telegraph, and telephone were invented and when new weapons, new surface and aerial vehicles, and other new battle equipments came into military use. Procuring, supplying, maintaining, and accounting for the impressive array of military materiel required much manpower and expertise, over and above the troops who used it all in battle. The framework for harnessing this manpower and equipment and for bringing the expertise together and to bear in war was provided by military organization. As armed forces developed over the centuries, a structure of units evolved. When standing forces were introduced, the difference between peace and war organization became even more important.

Organizational developments were slow and unenterprising in the British and French armies during the second half of the nineteenth century; this was certainly not the case as far as the Prussians were concerned. They introduced a series of significant structural and procedural improvements. By 1870, when the Franco-Prussian War started, the Prussian General Staff had fully earned its admirable reputation for meticulous planning and the efficient execution of its wide-ranging operational duties. It became a model for emulation and for export beyond the continent of Europe.

Prussian headquarters were divided into four parts at army, army corps, and divisional levels: the General Staff (which did all the operational planning), the Routine Staff or *Adjutantur* (which dealt with mainly administrative matters and the domestic running of the formation and its headquarters), the Intendance, and the Legal Departments. The Intendance included supply, transportation, quartering, medical, veterinary, and religious affairs. In addition, there were advisers for artillery, engineers, military police, and communications, which incorporated railways, postal facilities, and the telegraph. A registrar, directly responsible to the chief of staff, supervised the clerks and orderlies; seven to thirteen clerks were allowed in each army corps with a special dispensation for more in times of exceptional stress. The ratio of one general staff officer per approximately 5,000 troops deployed in the field was stringently economical, particularly as, at that time, the introduction of new weapons and communications must have significantly increased the amount of staff work.

The German general, the elder von Moltke, had devoted part of his immense energy and expertise to training the General Staff effectively and to supervising the planning and execution of the smooth, rapid mobilization, concentration, movement, and deployment of more than a million German officers and soldiers ready for operations against the French in 1870. In contrast, the *Corps d'Etat-Major* seemed a conservative outfit, isolated from the bulk of the French Army and lacking in efficiency.

Moltke had an advantage: he was chief of the General Staff and he was virtually commander-in-chief as well. However, at each formation level, there was also a chief of staff who supervised, coordinated, and generally ran the headquarters, freeing his own commander from overinvolvement with detailed planning, specialist support, and matters of routine. The concept and the practice of collegiality between commander and chief of staff had already begun, but was never present to the same extent in any other Western army. The issue of whether the general staff or any other staff department worked for the commander or the chief of staff was academic, for any difficulties were resolved by personalities and by thorough training, rather than by any contrived organizational adjustment.

From World War II to Today

The next major modification to staff organization happened during World War II, when General Eisenhower and others set up a unified command in the field for a campaign of indefinite length. The supreme Allied commander's naval, land, and air force subordinates had two roles: they helped Eisenhower develop plans, and they were then individually responsible to him for executing their respective parts of those plans, from the time of operations in the Mediterranean onward. Eisenhower consciously and conscientiously built up his Allied headquarters' organization from the bottom upward to avoid congestion at the top. He clearly appreciated and openly recognized the importance of integrated staffs through which the modern commander absorbs information and exercises his authority. He produced a fully interlocked, smoothly working mechanism and proceeded from the organizational and procedural assumption that all members of his staff belonged to a single nation, even though they were multinational.

In the latter stages of the campaign in northwest Europe, criticisms were raised that headquarters had become too large, unwieldy, and detached from the action, but the experience was of great value to the structure, functioning, and development of current, multinational, interservice staffs. The experience gained promoted similar initiatives within NATO that unfortunately have never been as successful, probably because what Eisenhower and his colleagues aimed to do was infinitely easier to achieve in wartime than in peacetime.

Issues in Modern Military Organization

The reader can find more specific details about modern military organizations in the separate articles on army, air force, and navy organization (keeping in mind that there are thousands of different military organizations contained within the armed services of the more than 150 countries that maintain modern military forces). There are, however, some central issues—some almost truisms—that are worth mentioning at the conclusion of this article.

Matching Organization to Requirement

Since World War II, some nations and their armed forces have tried to reconcile the different and often conflicting requirements of both general or total war and limited or small wars. The United States and the United Kingdom have found it necessary to develop separate forces for the North Atlantic Treaty Organization (NATO) and for their operations in other areas. The Soviet Union discovered that Afghanistan posed different requirements to those planned for its Warsaw Pact forces. On the other hand, in the case of the Federal Republic of Germany and the People's Republic of China, for example, armed forces have been tasked and organized for a single commitment, the defense of their own countries in a general war setting.

People Make the Difference

Given that a particular civilian enterprise or military organization is founded on a sound structure, why does it not function at least as well as some closely comparable equivalents? The answer in most cases is people. People make organizations work; they achieve the objectives set with the resources allotted them. Even casual observers may be able quite quickly to detect the basic difference between a really professional outfit and a far less professional counterpart. The two may be organized identically, but differences may stem from the caliber of people employed.

To the qualified military observer or inspector, the difference between two identically organized units, formations, or headquarters may also highlight variable standards of training, equipment, leadership, decision making, military judgment, experience, expertise, commitment, discipline, motivation, teamwork, comradeship, and morale. Furthermore, the units, formations, commanders, and headquarter staffs of different nations may be identically organized, yet their military bearing, behavior, capacity, and performance may markedly vary. Organizing allied forces in the same way will not produce similar results. The crucial part people play in the functioning of any military organization has been amply demonstrated in major wars and has been illustrated again in recent operations such as the 1991 Gulf War. The standardization of structure within allied forces is nevertheless of vital operational importance, for it helps forces "to fit together to fight together," and it gives them a common, familiar working basis for cooperation and training in peacetime.

The Relevance of Organizational Theory

Organizational theory (with its charts, diagrams, matrices, functional titles, job descriptions, and lines of reporting) is like a computer system, a tool to be used rather than an idol to be set up and worshipped. It is helpful as an aid but has to be kept in perspective: "Organisations do not consist of tidy lines on charts, but of men working together; and in the long run it is the personalities, skills and capacity for cooperation of the people that will produce efficient administration; not intellectually satisfying models that look good on paper." (Howard 1970).

Nevertheless, organizations can be complicated, bewildering interrelationships of functions, persons, and groups. Some way must be found to record the structure so that it can be understood, rationalized, and improved. Lessons must be learned so that, when a similar activity has to be organized from first principles, former mistakes and pitfalls are avoided. Therefore, some knowledge and application of organizational theory is important. The difficulty is that developing a military organization often relies more on personal idiosyncrasies, preconceived ideas, and the protection of vested interests than on clear, logical thought and precise calculation. The objective is to select a structure that maintains continuity and stability yet also dynamically pursues change when change is needed, gives scope for improvement, and facilitates cooperation with others.

To the theorist, another difficulty is that military forces like to be different. They like to be differently organized and their regiments like to wear and display different uniforms. They take some pride in doing things differently as a mark of their distinctiveness and prestige. They eagerly protect long-established traditions while striving to keep pace with technological and other changes. This perhaps partially explains why the organizational structures of the national components of NATO's so-called "integrated" operational commands have tended to become more dissimilar, rather than more similar, over time. This is despite the fact that they have faced basically the same perceived threat, in the same geographical area. Witness the protracted, failed endeavor to introduce a standard division with NATO, or the several unilaterally inspired experiments with unit and formation structures almost designed to obstruct allied integration and cooperation. Compare this with the structural standardization achieved within the now-defunct Warsaw Pact forces and the potential, important operational benefits that could have accrued. There are many pertinent lessons to be learned when new, future military organization is designed and constructed.

Lessons for the Future

One lesson is that an individual, a unit, a formation, a commander, a headquarters, or a national force may have to sacrifice what is considered the best organization for one that is commonly acceptable and attainable. Another lesson is that when change is necessary, the military inclination to remain the same must be overcome. Sometimes a fundamental reorganization is needed, yet the day is put off by tinkering with a comparatively small part of the structure. Expedient compromise and the selective application of this form of "spare-parts surgery" may do a great deal more damage to the organization and its collective purpose in the long run than if a fundamental, thorough reorganization had been courageously and effectively pursued from the outset.

Yet another lesson in designing efficient organizations is to eliminate the tendency in many nations to protect the military superstructures while cutting tactical forces. Often, those who wield the knife on these occasions are part of the monolithic, very expensive, over-large defense ministries, departments, or higher military headquarters that form part of the superstructure. Headquarters staffs sometimes lose sight of the fact that once the purpose of an activity is decided, most of the execution or accomplishment of that purpose is in the hands of the working organization. In the military context, this means that when reductions are necessary, the cuts should most often be made in strict priority: superstructures first and forces last. If the carefully considered and calculated disarmament process now underway leads to a decision to reduce forces by a certain percentage, this reduction should be at least counterbalanced in the reduction of national and multinational superstructures.

Those who design future military organizations will face unique challenges that are emerging with the approach of the 21st century. Weapons systems are becoming ever more capable, with expanding ranges, lethality, destructive power, and precision. The future warrior will be highly and expensively trained; skill and quality will likely continue to replace brawn and quantity. Fewer warriors will pit their systems and machines against opposing systems at lengthening distances. The organizations supporting these war machines will grow even more complex. Defining the requirements for future military forces and organizations may become increasingly difficult, due to imprecision in identifying the enemy and the threat. Driving all of this will be a world that changes more rapidly each year, and that becomes more and more integrated and interdependent as the revolution in information availability spreads and multiplies. To meet these challenges, military planners in the industrialized world will find themselves with dramatically reduced budgets as the tensions of the cold war dissipate. Both East and West have been reorganizing their military forces, and this trend will persist as the pace of change in politics and technology continues to quicken.

J. H. SKINNER

SEE ALSO: Administration, Military; Branches, Military; Cadre; Cavalry; Echelon; Formation; Hierarchy of Combat; Infantry; Logistics: A General Survey; Mercenary; Organization, Air Force; Organization, Army; Organization, Naval; Staff.

Bibliography

Barnett, C. 1970. *Britain and her army: 1509–1970.* London: Allen Lane.
Dupuy, T. N. 1977. *A genius for war: The German army and general staff: 1807–1945.* Englewood Cliffs, N.J.: Prentice-Hall.
Eisenhower, D. D. 1949. *Crusade in Europe.* London: Heineman.
Foster, H. 1913. *Organisation: How armies are formed in war.* London: Rees.
Hittle, J. D. 1944. *The military staff: Its history and development.* Harrisburg, Penn.: Military Service Publishing.
Howard, M. E. 1970. *The central organisation of defence.* London: Royal United Services Institute for Defense Studies.
Janowitz, M. 1964. *Changing patterns of organisation: The New Military.* Los Angeles: Russell Sage Foundation.
Schellendorf, B. von. 1905. *The duties of the general staff.* London: Her Majesty's Stationery Office.

ORGANIZATION, NAVAL

Countries establish navy organizations in order to perform prescribed military missions, usually related to the oceans, lakes, and waterways of the world. Navy organization can refer to how the service fits into the defense organization of the government, how the service is organized to perform its mission, or how navy units are organized to carry out their assigned tasks. This article addresses the subject from each of those three points of view.

Each navy of the world has its own unique relationship to the other armed forces of the country, and each also maintains its own special organization within units. Because all the world's navies cannot be included in detail here, those of the United States and the former Soviet Union have been selected to provide examples of different organizational structures.

Organization of the U.S. Navy

THE U.S. NAVY WITHIN THE U.S. GOVERNMENT

Two command lines extend from the U.S. president down to the individual units of the navy (which includes the U.S. Marine Corps). The first is the operational chain of command, within which all operations of units are controlled. Within this operational command, the navy's mission is specified by law: to be prepared to conduct prompt and sustained combat operations at sea. The second is the administrative chain of command, which is responsible for administrative functions such as training, maintenance and upkeep, overhaul, protocol and ceremonies, and a variety of inspections.

The operational chain of command (Fig. 1) extends from the U.S. National Command Authority (the president and the secretary of defense) through the Joint Chiefs of Staff and the Unified and Specified Commanders, to the Naval Component Commanders and the individual forces, groups, units, and elements.

Operationally, nearly all navy units fall under one of four geographically defined Unified Commanders in Chief (CINCs)—the commander in chief of the Atlantic, Pacific, European (while in the Mediterranean Sea), or Central (while in the Persian Gulf) command. Unified commands contain elements of all U.S. military services. Movement of a unit from one CINC's area to that of another requires a clearly defined change in operational control.

For administrative purposes a similar but separate chain of command is employed (Fig. 2). The unified commanders are not a part of this chain of command, but the secretary of the navy and the chief of naval operations (CNO) are in the chain of command that leads from the CNO

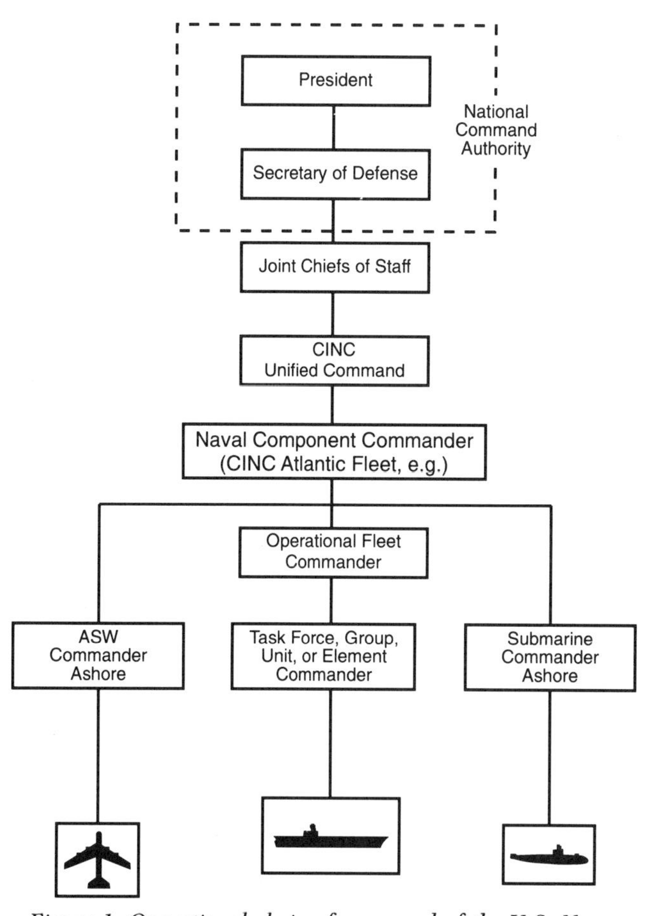

Figure 1. Operational chain of command of the U.S. Navy.

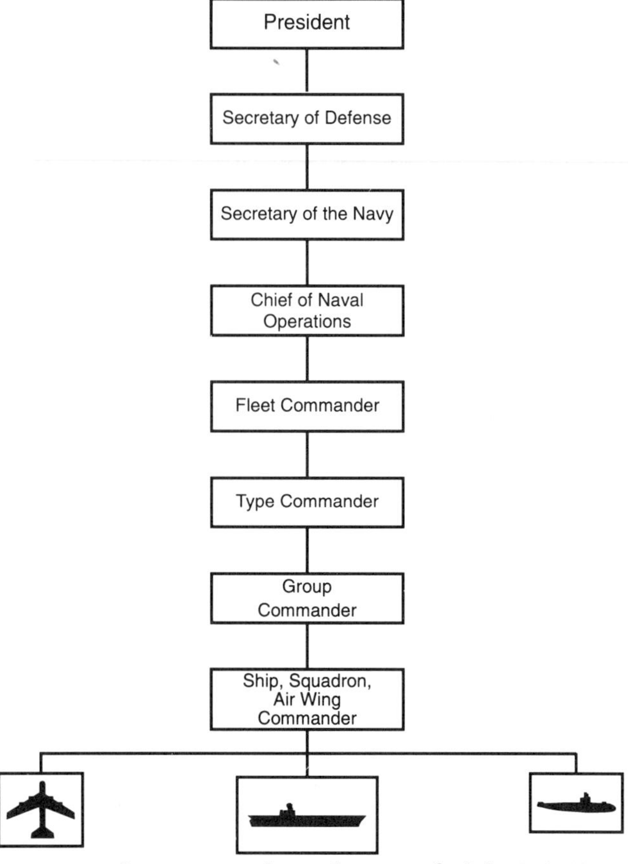

Figure 2. Administrative chain of command of the U.S. Navy.

through the fleet, type, group, squadron, and wing commander to the individual ships and aircraft.

THE INTERNAL ORGANIZATION OF THE U.S. NAVY

The U.S. Navy is also organized to carry out its three primary functions—sea control, power projection, and strategic sealift—along separate but interconnected operational and administrative lines. The U.S. Navy is divided, operationally and geographically, into four numbered fleets. In the Pacific Ocean area are the Third Fleet in the eastern Pacific and the Seventh Fleet in the western Pacific and the Indian Ocean. In the Atlantic Ocean area, the Second Fleet operates in the open Atlantic, and the Sixth Fleet in the Mediterranean Sea. The operational chain of command extends downward from the unified commander (CINCPAC for the Third and Seventh fleets, CINCLANT for the Second Fleet, and CINCEUR for the Sixth Fleet), then to task force, group, unit, or element commanders, and on to the ship, aircraft, or marine corps unit.

The administrative chain of command relies on type commanders to take care of training and administration for specific types of ships, aircraft, and other forces. Only CINCPAC and CINCLANT have type commanders assigned to them; the other area CINCs do not. Type commanders for the U.S. Pacific Fleet include: the Commanding General, Fleet Marine Force Pacific; Commander, Submarine Force, U.S. Pacific Fleet; Commander, Naval Logistics Command, Pacific Fleet; Commander, Naval Air Force, U.S. Pacific Fleet; Commander, Naval Surface Force, U.S. Pacific Fleet; and Commander, Training Command, U.S. Pacific Fleet.

INTERNAL ORGANIZATION OF U.S. NAVY UNITS

Depending on the kind of unit—air squadron or ship, for example—and the type—bomber or amphibious assault ship, for example—internal organization differs. In general, however, each unit has a commanding officer, executive officer, departments, and divisions. Exactly what departments and divisions are included in the organization depends on the kind and type of unit.

In some ways the internal organization mirrors the external organization—the commanding officer being responsible primarily for operational matters, and the executive officer bearing the brunt of the administrative duties. Ship and air organizations call for the execution of a variety of "bills" to regularize the activity of the crew. One example is the watch, quarter, and station bill, which details each man to a watch assignment and to battle and work stations.

Organization of the Soviet Navy

THE SOVIET NAVY WITHIN THE SOVIET GOVERNMENT

The Soviet organization was very different from that of the United States. Unlike the United States, which maintains the same organization in peace and war, the Soviet Union had separate organizations—or more accurately, evolving organizations—for wartime and peacetime. Figure 3 portrays the Soviet Navy high command organization.

This organization combined the operational and general administrative functions; with two exceptions—strategic aviation and airborne forces—operational and general administrative lines of control are identical. As a further indication of its pivotal position in the Soviet scheme, the general staff conducted the military planning for all the Soviet services, whereas in the United States that activity is performed at the level of the CINCs.

The Soviet Union maintained five military services: the strategic rocket forces, the national air defense troops, the ground forces, the air forces, and the navy. The Soviet equivalent of the U.S. Marine Corps, the Soviet Naval Infantry, was a small organization within the Soviet Navy.

The term *general administrative function* was employed above to distinguish it from *political administration*. The Soviet Navy was somewhat unique in that it maintained yet another chain of command, that of political organization and administration. This chain of command had responsibility for political education, discipline and political reliability of the crew, and for agitation and propaganda activities. Soviet naval units had political officers, or *zampolits*, who had an independent chain of reporting for political matters. Despite Soviet efforts to maintain the principle of one-man command or sole command respon-

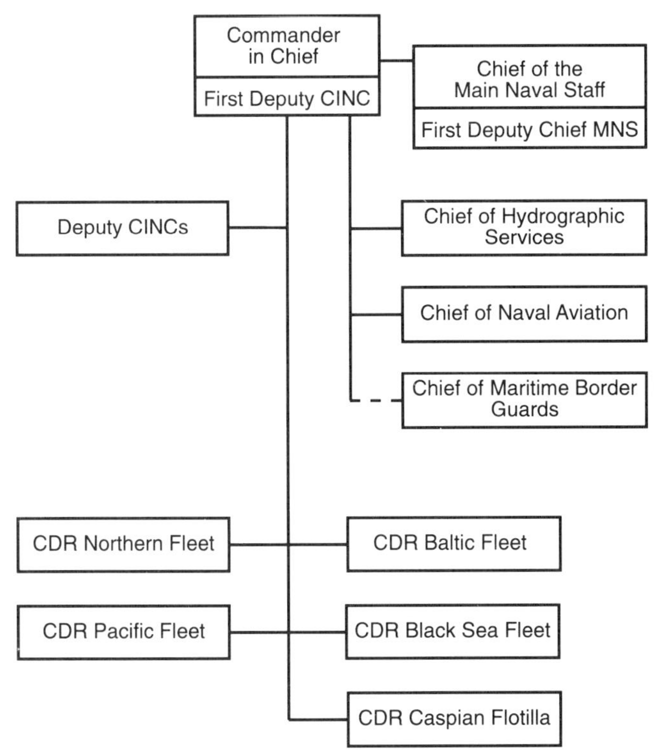

Figure 3. Soviet Navy high command organization. (SOURCE: U.S. Navy 1985)

sibility of the commanding officer, the very existence of the *zampolit* brought into question the ability of the unit commander to execute the command requirements in an independent manner.

THE INTERNAL ORGANIZATION OF THE SOVIET NAVY

The Soviet Navy combined the operational and administrative functions in a high command with line organization under the commander in chief. The line organization included a main navy staff, five deputy commanders in chief, and separate chiefs for hydrographic services, naval aviation, and maritime border guards. The chief of the main naval staff was responsible for the day-to-day operational direction of the fleet. The deputy CINCs performed administrative, technical, logistic, and training functions. One of the deputies led the political directorate and provided the separate line of reporting for the political officers in the operational units. Beneath this "headquarters" level, the Soviet Navy was organized geographically into four fleets and one flotilla. The fleets, widely separated geographically, and thus disadvantaged by an inability to provide mutual support to one another, were the Red Banner Northern Fleet, the Twice-Honored Red Banner Baltic Fleet, the Red Banner Black Sea Fleet, and the Red Banner Pacific Ocean Fleet. Among the four fleets, the Pacific Fleet had the largest number of ships in its inventory. The single flotilla was the Red Banner Caspian Flotilla.

The various fleets were organized somewhat in a mirror image of the manner in which main headquarters was organized.

Under the commander of ship brigades, flotillas and *eskadras* (Soviet squadrons) were organized into *diviziya*, *brigada*, *divizions*, and *detachments*. Flotillas performed in-area functions, whereas *eskadras* were for operations out of area. Divisions constituted the main tactical formation of the same kind of ship of the second, third, or fourth rank.

Within the Soviet command structure were wartime commands called *theaters of military operations* (TVDs) (Fig. 3). Five of these TVDs were continental, four were intercontinental, and four were oceanic, coinciding with the four fleet areas: the Black, Baltic, Northern, and Pacific. In wartime the navy would conduct its operations within a TVD and under the operational command of a TVD commander. Direction for navy units, therefore, would emanate from the State Committee of Defense through the general staff, not from main navy headquarters.

INTERNAL ORGANIZATION OF SOVIET NAVY UNITS

The Soviet Navy classified its ships into four ranks. The first rank included the largest surface ships (air-capable ships and cruisers) and nuclear-powered submarines. The second rank comprised diesel submarines and large missile and antisubmarine warfare (ASW) ships and destroyers. In the third rank were minesweepers; small escort, patrol, and missile ships; and some amphibious warfare ships. The lowest rank contained boats such as torpedo boats, landing craft, and small minesweepers. The rank of the ship determined, inter alia, the seniority of the commanding officer and the level of logistic support the ship deserved.

Ships of the Soviet Navy were organized into seven primary departments: navigation, missile-gunnery, underwater weapons, surveillance-communications, engineering, aviation (where present), and command and control. There were also suborganizations for electronics, finance, supply-logistics, and chemical warfare. How the departments were organized depended, in part, on the ship's rank. Fourth-rank ships, for example, did not have departments, but the departmental functions were carried out by "teams."

The political officer, and subordinates if assigned, had a place in the organization outside the line departments and reported directly to the commander. The executive officer, the second in command, performed many of the same functions that the executive officer in the U.S. Navy carries out.

The organization of a Soviet ship to perform the various evolutions that might be required was established, like its U.S. counterpart, by the watch quarter and station bill. The *primary* control station was the location of the commanding officer during combat, from which weapons and sensors were controlled and damage-control operations were coordinated. Control stations were the locations of those who had responsibility to coordinate or direct actions of others. Ships of the first, second, and third rank had primary control stations; fourth-rank ships had only control stations.

Concluding Observations

The ultimate test of a military organization is victory in battle. In peacetime the organization seeks to train forces so that they function most effectively should they be called upon to participate in combat. Historically, military organizations have demonstrated the complete range of effectiveness—from totally ineffective to highly effective. How armed forces are organized depends primarily on the political organization of the country and on its strategic culture. The purpose of this article has not been to evaluate the naval organizations of the United States and the Soviet Union; rather, it has been to describe those organizations from three points of view: how the service fits into the defense organization of the government, how the service is organized to perform its mission, and how units are organized to carry out their assigned tasks.

HIDEO SEKINO
SADAO SENO

SEE ALSO: Amphibious Forces; Fleet; Naval Forces; Navy; Reserve Forces, Naval.

Bibliography

U.S. Navy, Office of the Chief of Naval Operations. 1985. *Ship's organization and regulations manual.* OPNAV Instruction 3120.32 series. Philadelphia: Graceland Bros.

U.S. Navy, Office of the Chief of Naval Operations. 1985. *Understanding Soviet naval developments.* NAVSO P-3560. 5th ed. Washington, D.C.: Government Printing Office.

ORGANIZATION OF AFRICAN UNITY (OAU)

The Organization of African Unity (OAU) is a voluntary association of African states gathered to promote common economic, cultural, developmental, and defense goals. The OAU was founded in Addis Ababa, the capital of Ethiopia, on 25 May 1963 by the heads of state of 32 African nations. The creation of the OAU was in large part the result of efforts by the Nigerian, Ethiopian, and Guinean governments (Emperor Haile Selassie was a notable proponent), and followed on earlier unsuccessful efforts to create continental organizations.

History

Only months after it was founded, the OAU helped to end a border war between Algeria and Morocco. This conflict lasted from 13 October to 4 November, when the mediation of Emperor Haile Selassie of Ethiopia and President Modibo Keita of Mali was instrumental in arranging a cease-fire satisfactory to both sides. The OAU also provided valuable aid to Tanzania, providing African troops to replace the British forces that had quelled an army mutiny there in January 1964.

Barely a year after its creation, the OAU announced the denuclearization of Africa at a summit conference in Cairo on 21 July 1964. This declaration did not apply to either South Africa or Rhodesia, which were not members of the OAU at the time. Other OAU efforts were not as successful as those of the first year. The organization was ineffective in assisting the Democratic Republic of the Congo (now Zaïre) during the rebellion there in 1964–65, nor was it able to make progress toward peaceful resolution of the Nigerian-Biafran civil war (June 1967–January 1970).

On 22 July 1975, during the civil war in Angola that followed the departure of the Portuguese, the OAU appealed for a cease-fire. The OAU asked all parties to send representatives to Kampala, Uganda, site of the OAU's twelfth summit meeting. The appeal was ignored, and a later report prepared by a special commission chaired by President Idi Amin Dada of Uganda called for an OAU peacekeeping force to be sent to Angola. This idea was rejected by the de facto government of Angola, the Marxist Popular Movement for the Liberation of Angola (MPLA), which cited the presence of South African troops in the country as sufficient grounds for rejection. A subsequent emergency meeting of the OAU from 10 to 13 January 1976 ended in deadlock, and no action was taken.

Libyan intervention in the Chadian civil war (1979–81) also prompted OAU intervention. The success of the intervention was limited by chaotic conditions in Chad, and Libya has intervened twice more in Chadian affairs since the OAU compelled the withdrawal of Libyan forces in October 1981.

Current Membership

The OAU has 49 members, including those listed below.

Member States of the OAU

Algeria	Ethiopia	Nigeria
Angola	Gabon	Rwanda
Benin	The Gambia	São Tomé and Príncipe
Botswana	Ghana Guinea	Senegal
Burkina Faso	Guinea-Bissau	Seychelles
Burundi	Kenya	Sierra Leone
Cameroon	Lesotho	Somalia
Cape Verde	Liberia	Sudan
Central African Republic	Libya	Swaziland
Chad	Madagascar	Tanzania
Comoros	Malawi	Togo
Congo	Mali	Tunisia
Côte d'Ivoire	Mauritania	Uganda
Djibouti	Mauritius	Zaïre
Egypt	Mozambique	Zambia
Equatorial Guinea	Niger	Zimbabwe

Morocco is not currently a member of the OAU because of its opposition to OAU policy over the Western Sahara, a region that Morocco claims as its own. The OAU does not recognize Bophuthatswana, Ciskei, Transkei, and Venda, the nominally independent homelands created by South Africa, although these states are black-ruled.

Organization and Purposes

The charter of the OAU calls for noninterference in the internal affairs of states, observance of sovereignty and territorial integrity of members, peaceful resolution of disputes, condemnation of political assassination and subversive activities, nonalignment with power blocs, and the emancipation of white-ruled African territories. This last provision resulted in the formation of the OAU Liberation Committee, which supports various liberation movements directed against white regimes, now limited to South Africa.

The OAU has four organs: the assembly of the heads of state and government; the council of ministers; the general secretariat; and a commission of mediation, conciliation, and arbitration. The OAU's permanent headquarters is in Addis Ababa, and the unpopularity of the Ethiopian regime even among African states has hampered OAU activities since 1975. As of late 1991, the chairman was Yoweri Museveni of Uganda; the Secretary-General, Salim Ahmed Salim. The OAU conducts official business in Arabic, French, and English, all regarded as working languages.

For the most recent information on this organization, the reader may refer to the following annual publications:
The Military Balance. International Institute for Strategic Studies. London: Brassey's (UK).
The Statesman's Year-Book. New York: St. Martin's Press.
The World Factbook. Central Intelligence Agency. Washington, D.C.: Brassey's (US).

DAVID L. BONGARD
TREVOR N. DUPUY

SEE ALSO: North Africa; Sub-Saharan Africa.

Bibliography

Bukarambe, B. 1985. The role and impact of the OAU in the management of African conflicts. In *Southern Africa, regional security problems and prospects,* ed. R. Jaster. New York: St. Martin's Press.
Central Intelligence Agency. 1990. *The world factbook 1990.* Washington, D.C.: Government Printing Office.
Cervenka, Z. 1977. *The unfinished quest for unity: Africa and the OAU.* London: Julian Freidmann.
El-Ayouty, Y., ed. 1977. *The unfinished quest for unity: Africa and the OAU.* New York: Praeger.
Paxton, J., ed. 1989. *The statesman's year-book, 1989–90.* New York: St. Martin's Press.

ORGANIZATION OF AMERICAN STATES (OAS)

The Organization of American States is a voluntary association of North and South American countries dating to the Ninth International Conference of American States, held in Bogotá, Colombia, in the spring of 1948. The purpose of the OAS is to foster mutual understanding and cooperation among the nations of the Western Hemisphere.

Origin

Although the OAS was founded at the Bogotá Conference, held from 30 March to 2 May 1948, it was constructed on the basis of the eight previous International Conferences of American States, often referred to as the Pan-American Conferences. These were held in 1889–90 (Washington, D.C.), 1901–1902 (Mexico City), 1906 (Rio de Janeiro), 1910 (Buenos Aires), 1923 (Santiago), 1928 (Havana), 1933 (Montevideo), 1938 (Lima), and 1948 (Bogotá).

There was also an Inter-American Conference on the Maintenance of Peace (1936 in Buenos Aires), an Inter-American Conference on Problems of War and Peace (1945 in Chapultepec, Mexico), and an Inter-American Conference for the Maintenance of Continental Peace and Security (1947 in Quitandinha, near Petropolis, Brazil). These conferences, especially the six undertaken in the fifteen years from 1933 to 1948, laid a strong foundation for inter-American cooperation, particularly in light of more enlightened policies on the part of the United States, which began to treat its southern neighbors as equals under the Roosevelt administration's "Good Neighbor" policy. The 1947 conference at Quitandinha was particularly important because it resulted in the signing of the Treaty of Reciprocal Assistance, commonly known as the Rio Treaty. This treaty put into effect the principle that an attack on one American state was an attack on all, justified under article 51 of the United Nations Charter.

History

The conference at Bogotá resulted in the drafting and signing of the OAS charter, adopted on 30 April 1948. The charter stipulated the sovereign equality of the member states and banned interference in the affairs of one state by any other, except in the interests of peace and security. The structure of the OAS was also outlined, providing for the Inter-American Conference, the Meeting of Consultation of Foreign Ministers, and the Council of the OAS, which would meet permanently in Washington, D.C. This last council would execute tasks assigned to it by either of the other two bodies and supervise the secretariat of the OAS.

In response to developments in Cuba after Fidel Castro came to power in 1959, the OAS took steps to limit Cuban activities abroad, especially after Cuba repudiated the Rio Treaty in early 1961. Following the Cuban Missile Crisis in October–November 1962, the OAS imposed economic and diplomatic sanctions against Cuba in July 1964. Since that time, and especially since the mid-1970s, these sanctions have been applied relatively loosely, and some of the OAS states more sympathetic to Cuba (Mexico, for instance) make periodic efforts to lift the sanctions. Cuba is still officially an OAS member but has sent no representatives to meetings or conferences since 1962. The most recent political crisis was occasioned by the Argentine invasion of the Falkland Islands/Islas Malvinas and by the British expedition to recover them (2 April–14 June 1982). Argentina called for OAS and especially U.S. assistance to repel the invasion, but since this request followed unilateral Argentine aggressive action, it was generally ignored.

Over the decades, the OAS has been increasingly concerned with issues of economic development in Latin America. It provides specialized training for several thousand Latin Americans annually in a number of development-related fields and responds to specific requests from members.

Current Membership

All 34 independent states in the Western Hemisphere are members. Listed in alphabetical order, they are Antigua and Barbuda, Argentina, Bahamas, Barbados, Belize, Bolivia, Brazil, Canada, Chile, Colombia, Costa Rica, Cuba, Dominica, Dominican Republic, Ecuador, El Salvador, Grenada, Guatemala, Haiti, Honduras, Jamaica, Mexico, Nicaragua, Panama, Paraguay, Peru, St. Christopher (St. Kitts) and Nevis, St. Lucia, St. Vincent and the Grenadines, Suriname, Trinidad and Tobago, the United States, Uruguay, and Venezuela.

Current Issues and Activities

The charter, as amended, provides for the organization of the OAS. The General Assembly meets annually in various countries, and the Meeting of Consultation of Ministers of Foreign Affairs is held to consider urgent problems of common interest. There are three councils of equal rank: the Permanent Council (which replaces the old OAS Council), the Inter-American Economic and Social Council, and the Inter-American Council for Education, Science and Culture. These three bodies direct and coordinate work in their specific areas and have one representative from each member state.

The Inter-American Juridical Committee acts as an advisory body to the OAS on legal and juridical matters. Its eleven jurists are elected every four years by the General Assembly and represent all American states. The Inter-American Commission on Human Rights works to safeguard and enhance human rights. It is composed of seven members drawn from the member states.

The General Secretariat is the principal permanent central body of the OAS, handling most administrative and organizational tasks. Its offices are located in Washington, D.C. Besides these permanent organizations, the OAS periodically calls specialized conferences to deal with particular technical matters or developmental concerns. Likewise, the OAS contains several specialized organizations—intergovernmental groups formed by multilateral agreement to deal with particular issues, such as child welfare, Indian affairs, and health.

The OAS currently faces several major issues. Perhaps the most important is the problem of debt, and although this affects states other than those in Latin America, the debtor states of the OAS have taken a leading role in pressing for debt reform and an easing of the burdens posed by their obligations to foreign banks. Another major issue is that of U.S. involvement in Central America. Although the United States has made some effort to work with the governments in the area, for many Latin Americans the U.S. military presence in the region conjures up unpleasant memories of the Arbenz affair in Guatemala in 1954 and similar operations before and since. Despite these differences, the OAS is an important means for developing cooperation among the states of the Americas.

For the most recent information on this organization, the reader may refer to the following annual publications:
The Military Balance. International Institute for Strategic Studies. London: Brassey's (UK).
The Statesman's Year-Book. New York: St. Martin's Press.
The World Factbook. Central Intelligence Agency. Washington, D.C.: Brassey's (US).

DAVID L. BONGARD
TREVOR N. DUPUY

SEE ALSO: Central America and the Caribbean; North America; South America.

Bibliography

Hunter, B., ed. 1991. *The statesman's year-book 1991–92*. New York: St. Martin's Press.
OAS General Secretariat. 1977. *Organization of American States: A handbook*. Washington, D.C.: Organization of American States.
———. 1982. *The Americas in the 1980s: An agenda for the decade ahead*. Washington, D.C.: Organization of American States.

OSIPOV EQUATIONS

M. Osipov's work (1915) on how the strength of opposed sides influences their losses is a major contribution to the scientific study of combat. Osipov is largely unknown in the West, but from a historical and methodological viewpoint his brilliant work on the theory of combat is even more important than that of Lanchester (Lanchester 1914, 1916). In particular, Osipov tested the theory against historical data, while Lanchester did not, and so was the first to recognize that Lanchester's N-square law is in error.

Who Was Osipov?

Unhappily, we know nothing of M. Osipov, the author of this remarkable work. We do not even know his full first name; how old he was when he wrote these articles; whether he survived the foreign and domestic wars, social upheavals, and postrevolutionary attacks on intellectuals and "bourgeoisie" that racked Russia in the first half of this century; or what other materials he may have published. We do not know what his profession was. In his articles Osipov claims that he has no practical military experience—but he then displays a familiarity with various Russian Field Service Regulations and "planning factors" such as the percent of a unit's troops that would be committed in the assault echelon, the ratio of cannon to infantry, and the doctrinal spacing of troops in assault ranks. Similarly, while disclaiming any expertise in military history, he cites pertinent historical examples to illustrate his points and displays a general familiarity with military history. Osipov refers to an engineer's handbook for tables of hyperbolic functions and displays a solid mathematical and statistical analysis capability bespeaking what, for the time, would have been an advanced technical education. He also writes elegantly and with a large vocabulary, possibly indicating a scholarly background. Osipov complains of a lack of time to develop the subject and a hope to return to it "after peace is restored"—was he, perhaps, a young scholar-turned-officer hastily recording his work for posterity while training his unit and preparing to accompany it to the front? What else would explain his persistent complaints about the "press of events"? We would welcome further information regarding M. Osipov, the "Russian Lanchester," whose works are of immense historical significance and whose views on method remain of commanding importance today, 75 years after they first appeared.

The Question of Priority

The Soviets argue that Osipov was the first to discover both the differential equations commonly known as Lanchester's equations and the relation known as Lanchester's N-square law, and hence that these should instead be called the Osipov-Lanchester equations and the Osipov-Lanchester N-square law (Yusupov and Ivanov 1988). Regarding priority, we note that interest in a scientific theory of warfare was very much in the air during the nineteenth and early twentieth centuries. It appears that Chase (1902) was the first to state explicitly what are now called Lanchester equations. The first clear statement of a discrete version of these equations appeared in Fiske (1905) (see the summary in Robison and Robison 1942; Weiss 1962; and Engel 1963). Lanchester's work appeared much later in journal (Lanchester 1914) and book form (Lanchester 1916). Osipov's articles appeared in June through October of 1915. In them he derives, by a novel argument, the Lanchester differential equations and shows that the discrete version approaches them in the limit, thus anticipating Engel (1963). Apparently all arrived independently at their results.

Summary of Osipov's Series of Articles

In his preface Osipov poses the question "What are all of the principal causes or circumstances on which success in battle depends?" In response to it, he advances his main thesis—that losses are inversely related to strengths, which in modern mathematical notation can be expressed as

$$[\text{A's Losses/B's Losses}] = K[\text{B's Strength/A's Strength}]^p,$$

where K is a coefficient of proportionality and p is an empirically determined exponent.

Osipov's method is to compile for a large number of battles accurate data on numerical strengths, losses, artillery strengths, tactics, and so forth. Then, for example, to investigate the influence of tactics on losses, he would group the battles into two columns, one for use and the other for non-use of the tactic, and compute the total losses for each tactic. These totals, Osipov argues, depend principally upon the use or non-use of the tactic in question, for "Average tendencies, although masked in individual battles by random variations, in the aggregate stand out in high relief since they accumulate with increased numbers of battles and do not cancel one another out as do the random variations."

Osipov is quite explicit that his is a theory of averages, since ". . . it is not possible to demand of the theory that it agree with every individual battle. . . . it need be correct only for certain idealized [i.e., average] conditions." We must understand how the average or trend arises before we can explain the causes of individual departures from it. Osipov states, "For us the study of the average tendency is important rather than the random variations since it allows us to adjust our formulas to the conditions of the battle and to derive more accurate formulas for the determination of losses."

Osipov argues that, if Lanchester's N-square law is correct, then a, the losses to side A, can be written in terms of A and A', the initial and final strengths of side A, and the initial (B) and final (B') strengths of side B. His derivation of that relationship is as follows:

$$A^2 - A'^2 = B^2 - B'^2$$
$$(A - a)^2 = A^2 - B^2 + B'^2$$
$$a = A - (A^2 - B^2 + B'^2)^{1/2},$$

where he has used the relation $A' = A - a$. A test of the N-square law can be made as follows. For battle i, let v_i be the difference between the value of a in the historical account and its value computed by the above formula. Then v_i measures the degree to which the theory departs from the historical account for battle *i*. Osipov tested how well the theory agreed with history by examining the mean and standard deviation of the v_i's. If the mean is too far from zero in relation to the standard deviation, then the *N*-square law cannot be generally valid.

Osipov tested two theories in this manner. One theory (Lanchester's *N*-square law) uses the exponent 2. Another uses the exponent 3⁄2. From these tests, Osipov determined that Lanchester's *N*-square law is wrong. In particular, he found that the value $n = 3/2$ agreed much better with his historical data than the value $n = 2$. This result is "Osipov's Law."

Because Osipov worked with actual historical data, he realized that real battles seldom continue to the point where either side is annihilated. To explain this, he introduced a breakpoint hypothesis and estimated its value from historical data. He said, "Victory depends . . . principally on the ability to bear losses; therefore it is correct to reckon that battles last until the loss to one side has achieved some definite percent. That percent can be calculated as 20 percent, since the total losses to the victor in 38 battles . . . amounts to about 20 percent of the total numerical strengths." Later investigators have shown that this type of breakpoint hypothesis is untenable (Helmbold 1971; Taylor 1983), but it was quite an advance for Osipov's era.

Osipov assumed that the effects of qualitatively different weapons can be measured by an appropriately chosen weapons effectiveness index. His index is a conversion factor that measures the weapon's effectiveness in terms of the number of rifle equivalents. Lanchester (1916) mentions but does not carry out this approach. Osipov, using data from the battles of Borodino, Lutzen, and Waterloo, estimated that each cannon is worth between 60 and 150 rifles, the particular value depending upon whether an exponent of 2 (Lanchester's *N*-square law) or 3⁄2 (Osipov's Law) is used in the calculations. Osipov would have done the same for machine guns if he had had enough data to estimate the conversion factor value. However, he did give detailed mathematical equations for calculating attrition when forces composed of a mix of rifles, cannon, and machine guns oppose one another. These equations make essential use of the factors for converting other weapons into rifle equivalents.

Osipov recognized that the quantities in the differential equations refer to the troops actually engaged. However, he was also aware that the numbers in the historical accounts normally are for the total number of personnel present, or listed on the roster, rather than those actually engaged. Thus, using the historical values causes some degree of error. Osipov was sensitive to this issue and dealt with it in two ways. First, he estimated the size of the error involved and showed that it is not large enough to affect his principal conclusions. Second, he argued that his data are from pitched battles in which everyone had to take part "whether they wished to or not," so that again any errors from using the historical values should be negligible.

Osipov's Three Main Theses

Osipov summarized his principal points in three main theses. His first thesis is that "The side strongest in numbers bears the absolutely smaller losses, rather than the weaker side." The second: "If superiority in strength is on our side, then by increasing the number of our troops we gain time, diminish our losses, increase our enemy's losses, and stiffen our own troops' moral fiber." The third: "By the numerical strength of a side is meant the number of troops actively wielding military rifles, artillery, machine guns, sabers, etc.—but not the number on the unit roster nor the number of unengaged reserves."

Osipov also made the important point that his three theses do not depend on the exact nature of the attrition equations. Any law of attrition in which losses are inversely related to numerical strength would give qualitatively the same results. He says, "Deductions [on the value of concentration] could have been obtained not only from [the *N*-square law] but just as well from any theory that assumes simply that losses to the numerically strongest side will be less than those of the weaker, and would further decrease as the superiority of the stronger side increases." This is a considerable generalization of Lanchester's argument, and illustrates the depth of Osipov's thought on these issues.

R. L. HELMBOLD

SEE ALSO: Lanchester Equations.

Bibliography

Chase, J. V. 1902. Unpublished staff paper. In *The Navy as a fighting machine force*, Appendix C, ed. B. A. Fiske, 1988. Annapolis, Md.: U.S. Naval Institute Press.

Engel, J. H. 1963. Comments on a paper by H. K. Weiss. *Journal of the Operations Research Society of America* 11:147–50.

Fiske, B. A. 1905. American naval policy. *Proceedings of the U.S. Naval Institute* 113:1–80.

Helmbold, R. L. 1971. Decision in battle: Breakpoint hypotheses and engagement termination data. Rand R-772-PR. Santa Monica, Calif.: Rand Corp.

Lanchester, F. W. 1914. The principle of concentration. *Engineering*, 2 October.

———. 1914. The N-square law and its application. *Engineering*, 9 October.

———. 1916. *Aircraft in warfare: The dawn of the fourth arm.* London: Constable.

Osipov, M. 1915. The influence of the numerical strength of engaged sides on their losses. *Military Collection* (USSR). Part One, No. 6 (June), pp. 59–74; Part Two, No. 7 (July), pp. 25–36; Part Three, No. 8 (August), pp. 31–40; Part Four, No. 9 (September), pp. 25–37; Part Five (Addendum), No. 10 (October), pp. 93–96.

Robison, S. S., and M. L. Robison. 1942. *A history of naval tactics from 1530 to 1930.* Annapolis, Md.: U.S. Naval Institute Press.

Taylor, J. G. 1983. *Lanchester models of warfare.* Arlington, Va.:

Operations Research Society of America, Military Applications Section.

Yusupov, R. M., and V. P. Ivanov. 1988. Mathematical modelling of military engagements. *Military-Historical Journal* (USSR) 9:79–83.

Weiss, H. K. 1962. The Fiske model of warfare. *Journal of the Operations Research Society of America* 10:569–71.

OTTOMAN EMPIRE

The Ottoman Empire existed for more than 600 years. At its greatest extent, the empire stretched from the Persian Gulf to Morocco, from Yemen to the outskirts of Vienna. As a European, as well as a Middle Eastern, power, the Ottoman Empire played a significant role in European military and diplomatic history from the midfourteenth century to the second decade of the twentieth century.

The Growth of the Ottoman Empire, 1290–1566

The Ottoman (Osmanli) Turks first appeared in historical records as a small, obscure Turkic clan. Fleeing from the Mongol conquest of Khwaresm, the Ottoman Turks found refuge in the emirate of Sögüt—in northwestern Anatolia—as vassals of the Seljuk Sultanate of Rum. At the Battle of Köse Dagh (1243), the Mongol Il-Khan of Persia defeated the Seljuks. Thereafter, the Seljuks and their vassals became tributaries of the Il-Khanate of Persia.

The Mongol victory at Köse Dagh precipitated the disintegration of the Sultanate of Rum. Taking advantage of the breakdown of Seljuk authority, the emir of Sögüt, Osman (1290–1326)—in whose honor the Ottoman Turks named themselves—extended his authority northward over Brusa and Ephesus, at the expense of the Byzantine Empire.

Osman's successor, Orkhan (1326–62), added Pelekhanon, Nicaea, and Nicomedia to the Ottoman realm. The Ottomans first entered Europe in 1334, as allies of John Cantacuzene, a pretender to the Byzantine throne. The Turks entered Europe as Cantacuzene's ally again in 1352, against the Serbian king, Stephen Dushan. The Turks occupied Gallipoli in 1354 and began spreading out over Thrace.

Expansion into the Balkans

Ottoman expansionism followed a pattern of a westward thrust followed by an eastward thrust. Westward expansion took precedence over eastward expansion. As a result, the Turks were well entrenched in the Balkans long before they conquered eastern Anatolia, Syria, or Palestine.

The Turks took Adrianople in 1361, and the sultan, Murad I (1362–89), made it his capital in 1366. The primary objective of Murad's military expeditions was the conquest of Albania, Serbia, and Bosnia. Macedonia, Bulgaria, and the Byzantine emperor recognized Murad's overlordship in 1371, and Serbia submitted in 1386. However, in 1388, Bosnia, Serbia, and Bulgaria rebelled. After a series of rebel victories, Murad crushed a combined Bosnian and Serbian force at Kossovo (5 June 1389). Murad, however, was assassinated after the battle. In revenge, Bayazid, Murad's son and successor, executed Lazar of Serbia.

Bayazid I (1389–1402) continued his father's policy of expansion in the Balkans. In 1393, the Turks entered Bulgaria and, in April 1395, invaded Hungary. Bayazid crushed the Christian forces at Nicopolis on 25 September 1395.

Bayazid, having expanded Ottoman rule into Europe further than any of his predecessors, turned his attention to the conquest of eastern Anatolia. The sultan's actions in eastern Anatolia brought him into conflict with Tamerlane (Timur-i-lang), the most formidable conqueror since Genghis Khan. At the Battle of Ankara (28 July 1402), Tamerlane soundly defeated the Ottoman Turks and captured Bayazid. Confined in a cage, the once-proud sultan of the Ottoman Turks was put on display in town bazaars throughout Tamerlane's realm.

Bayazid's defeat and capture threw the Ottoman Empire into chaos, and ten years of civil war followed as his three sons fought each other for the throne. When Mohammed (Mehmed) I (1413–21) emerged victorious, the empire was on the verge of disintegration. Mohammed was able to reassert control over Anatolia by 1414 and, in 1417, was strong enough to commence military operations in Wallachia.

Sultan Murad II (1421–51) attempted to conquer Constantinople in 1424, without success. The sultan then renewed operations in the Balkans. He annexed Serbia in 1439 and besieged Belgrade in 1440. Turkish operations in Transylvania, however, were not successful. The Transylvanians and Hungarians, commanded by Janos Hunyadi, fought the Turks to a standstill. At Zlatica (1443), a Polish and Hungarian force defeated the Turks and retook Nish and Sofia. The Truce of Adrianople (2 June 1444) temporarily ended the fighting. The truce was soon broken by the "Varna Crusade" (mostly Hungarians and Wallachians), but on 10 November 1444, the Turks decisively defeated the crusaders. At the Second Battle of Kossovo (1448), the sultan defeated Hunyadi.

Mohammed (Mehmed) II, the Conqueror, 1451–81

Mohammed II is best known in the West for the conquest of Constantinople. Mohammed, however, was more than a conqueror; he was an administrative reformer and a statesman.

Mohammed reorganized the political structure of the Ottoman Empire, rationalizing the slipshod, jury-rigged administration of his polyglot empire. To administer the empire, Mohammed selected the brightest youths from the *devshirme*—a tribute consisting of young boys from the sultan's Christian subjects imposed every five years—and trained them in the Palace School. Palace School graduates were appointed to civilian and military posts throughout the empire. Together with the *janissaries*, who were also recruited from the *devshirme*, these administrators formed the *askeri* (soldier) class, the civil and military elite of the Ottoman Empire.

The conquest of Constantinople. Shortly after he became sultan, Mohammed began planning the conquest of Constantinople. The city was nearly all that remained of the once mighty Eastern Roman (Byzantine) Empire. Anatolia, Thrace, and most of the Balkans were already under Turkish rule. Morea (southern Greece), the Dalmatian Coast, and the Greek Isles were controlled by Venice. Though politically insignificant, Constantinople remained of great symbolic value to both Christian and Turk.

After two years of preparation, Mohammed launched his attack on 6 April 1453. For 50 days, Turkish artillery battered the walls of Constantinople, while assault after assault failed. On 29 May the Turks successfully stormed the Romanos Gate, and the city fell. Constantinople secured, Mohammed rebuilt the city and made it the capital of the Ottoman Empire. A tolerant and farsighted statesman, Mohammed incorporated the leaders of the Latin Church, the Greek Church, and the Jewish community into the administrative apparatus of the state.

Operations in the Balkans. Between 1455 and 1459, Mohammed conducted operations against the Serbians. The Turks besieged Belgrade in 1456 but the intervention of Hunyadi prevented the capture of the Serbian capital. In the southern Balkans, the Turks were more successful, and by 1460, Morea was under Ottoman control.

The Turkish-Venetian War, 1463–79. The Turkish occupation of Morea directly challenged Venice, then the dominant seapower in the eastern Mediterranean. To meet the Venetian threat, the Turks developed their own naval capability. Although a Venetian-papal fleet burned Smyrna in 1472 and threatened the Dardanelles, by the late 1470s, the Turks were winning the war at sea as well as on land. In 1477 the Turks raided the environs of Venice itself. In 1478 Kroia, Alessia, and Drivasto fell to the Turks. When the war ended in 1479, the Ottoman Empire was the dominant seapower in the eastern Mediterranean. The Second Turkish-Venetian War (1499–1503) resulted in the destruction of the Venetian fleet and the reduction of the Venetian trading empire to a few small islands.

The Conquest of Egypt, 1516–17

When Mohammed II died, the Ottoman Empire was the strongest Muslim state in the Middle East. During the reigns of Bayazid II (1481–1512) and Selim I the Grim (1512–20), the Turks came into conflict with two neighboring Muslim states: Egypt under the Mamelukes and Persia under the Saffirid Dynasty. The First Turkish-Egyptian War, fought over control of the Kingdom of Cilicia, lasted seven years and was inconclusive. The Second Turkish-Egyptian War ended in the destruction of the Mameluke state and the incorporation of Egypt into the Ottoman Empire.

The Persian War, 1514–15. The Persians, under the fanatical Shiite, Shah Ismail—first of the Saffirid Dynasty—were a threat to the Orthodox Sunni Muslim states of Central Asia as well as to the Ottomans. Selim I declared war on Persia in 1514, on the grounds that the Persians had been fomenting rebellion among the Taurus Mountain tribes. On 23 August 1514, at Chaldiran, Turkish cannon and firearms prevailed over Persian cavalry. By 1515, eastern Anatolia had been pacified and Kurdistan had been annexed.

The Egyptian War, 1516–17. Turkish victory in the Persian War brought the Turks again into conflict with Persia's ally, Egypt. At the Battle of Marj Dabik (24 August 1516), the Turks defeated the Mamelukes and killed Kansu, the Mameluke sultan. Following their victory, the Turks received the submission of Aleppo and Damascus. When Tuman Bey, the new Mameluke sultan, refused to recognize Ottoman suzerainty, the war was renewed. On 22 January 1517, the Turks occupied Cairo. Tuman Bey was executed, and a Turkish governor-general was appointed to administer Egypt. Soon after his conquest of Egypt, Selim I received the submission of Medina, Mecca, and the Arab tribes.

Suleiman I (the Magnificent), 1520–66

With Syria, Palestine, and Egypt under Ottoman rule, the sultan's attention once again turned northward, toward the Balkans and south-central Europe. In 1521, Suleiman I occupied Belgrade and prepared to invade Hungary.

Operations in Hungary. Suleiman invaded Hungary in 1526. At the First Battle of Mohacs, 29–30 August 1526, the Hungarians were routed and their king, Louis, slain. With Louis dead, two claimants to the Hungarian throne appeared: Ferdinand of Hapsburg, younger brother of Charles V, Holy Roman emperor (and king of Spain, under the designation Charles I); and John Zapolya, prince of Transylvania. Defeated by the Hapsburgs, Zapolya appealed to Suleiman for aid. In 1528, the Turks entered Hungary as allies of King John I Zapolya. From 26 September to 16 October 1526, the Turks besieged Vienna. Inclement weather, however, prevented them from properly deploying their artillery. Reluctantly, the sultan ordered their withdrawal, and in 1533, the Turks and Hapsburgs agreed to a truce. Hungary was divided unevenly between Zapolya and Ferdinand. For the small strip of Hungary awarded him, Ferdinand was required to pay annual tribute to Suleiman.

The Turkish-Venetian War, 1537–40. In March 1536 Francis I, king of France, and Sultan Suleiman I entered into a secret alliance against their common enemy, the Hapsburgs. In 1537, war again broke out between the Turks and the Venetians. The following year, the papal states, Venice, and Charles V entered into an anti-Turkish alliance, the Holy League. Following the Turkish naval victory at Prevesa (1540), Venice sued for peace. The Turks received Nauplion and a large indemnity from Venice in exchange for peace.

Operations in Hungary. King John I Zapolya died in 1540, whereupon Ferdinand invaded Hungary. Suleiman supported the claim of Zapolya's son, John Sigismund, to the Hungarian throne. By 1541, Hungary was under effective Turkish control, and both sides agreed to another truce in 1547.

Sultan Suleiman spent 1548 fighting the Persians. In 1551, however, the sultan was again at war with Ferdinand of Hapsburg. This round ended with a truce and a return to the *status quo ante.*

The conquest of Mesopotamia. The Persian capture of Erzurum in 1552 precipitated another Turkish-Persian war. During the fighting, the Turks conquered Mesopotamia. After peace was negotiated in 1555, the Ottoman Empire retained possession of Mesopotamia.

The Ottoman Military Machine

The early Ottoman army, in common with most other Turco-Mongolian armies, was composed almost exclusively of cavalry. In exchange for a grant of land (*timar*), the landholder provided a fixed number of cavalrymen (*sipahi*) under his own command. When mobilized, the *sipahi* marshaled under the overall command of their provincial governor (*sanjak-bey*).

Infantry units were gradually incorporated into the Ottoman forces. At first, infantry was made up of provincial irregulars or vassal contingents. During the reign of Murad I, a regular, standing infantry corps was established, the *janissaries.*

The Janissary Corps

The *janissaries* were originally recruited from among Christian captives. By the reign of Mohammed I, recruits were drawn from the *devshirme. Janissary* recruits were trained in both the profession of arms and Islam. Though technically slave-soldiers, the *janissaries* enjoyed many privileges, but were not allowed to marry until after retirement.

The *janissaries* soon became the elite unit of the Ottoman army. The size of the corps grew from approximately 12,000 men during the reign of Mohammed the Conqueror to 40,000 men during the reign of Suleiman the Magnificent. Initially organized as foot archers, the *janissaries* were later armed with firearms.

Artillery

The Ottoman Turks adopted both firearms and cannon from Western Europe. During the siege of Constantinople in 1453, the Turks used cannon cast by a Hungarian, Urban, and serviced, in part, by Italian mercenaries. The Turks used firearms and cannon to advantage against the Persians and the Mamelukes, as well as against European armies.

Naval Forces

The Turkish navy was late to develop. Although the Turks had used flotillas of small craft as early as the reign of Murad I, it was not until the war with Venice (1463–79) that the Turks developed a navy strong enough to defeat the Venetian fleet. While Bayazid II and Selim I were involved in wars with Persia and Egypt, however, the Turkish navy languished. When Suleiman I intervened on the behalf of John Zapolya, the Turks faced not only the army of the Austrian Hapsburgs, but also the naval might of Hapsburg Spain.

The creation of Suleiman's new Ottoman navy was the work of Khair-ed-Din, "Barbarossa" (1478–1546). Born Khizr, the fourth son of a retired *janissary,* Khair-ed-Din joined his older brother, Aruj (the original Barbarossa), in the life of a corsair. Between 1504 and 1512, the Barbarossa brothers were based in Tunis. In 1516, Aruj became the *Beylerbey* (ruler) of Algiers. When Aruj was killed in a battle with the Spaniards, Khair-ed-Din succeeded him as *Beylerbey.*

From 1519 to 1533, Khair-ed-Din Barbarossa raided the lands of the Hapsburgs in Spain and Italy. So successful was the *Beylerbey* of Algiers that, in August 1533, Suleiman I summoned him to Constantinople. The sultan charged Barbarossa with the reorganization of the Ottoman navy. Barbarossa's first task was to reorganize the Turkish shipyards and construct 61 new galleys.

In summer 1534 Barbarossa took part of his new fleet and raided the Kingdom of Naples. Italy was again subjected to massive Turkish raids between 1537 and 1540. During this period, Barbarossa and Andrea Doria, the celebrated admiral of Charles V, met at Prevesa. Barbarossa had 150 galleys under his command. Andrea Doria had 246 ships, including 50 galleons. Despite Doria's superiority in ships and firepower, Barbarossa outgeneraled and outsailed his adversary. Andrea Doria decided to withdraw rather than fight. Although the Christian forces had lost only seven galleys, the Venetians sued for peace.

In spring 1543 Barbarossa, the high admiral of the Ottoman navy, again raided southern Italy, with a fleet of 100 galleys. Barbarossa planned to inflict as much damage as possible on the Hapsburg lands in Italy. That summer, the Turkish fleet anchored in Toulon and, with the cooperation of his French allies, Barbarossa laid siege to Nice. After the surrender of Nice, the Turks returned to Toulon, while the French sacked and burned the city. Toward the end of summer, Barbarossa sent a flotilla to raid the coast of Catalonia.

The successes of Barbarossa and the Ottoman fleet in the central and western Mediterranean, and the success of the Ottoman army in Hungary, sent tremors of fear throughout Christian Europe.

The Decline of the Ottoman Empire

The reign of Suleiman the Magnificent was the golden age of the Ottoman Empire. The eastern Mediterranean was a Turkish lake, and, with the north African coast in Turkish hands, the Ottoman navy raided Hapsburg possessions at will. The Ottoman Empire was not only a great power, it was perhaps the greatest power of the sixteenth century. Yet, within 100 years of the death of Suleiman I, the empire was in decline.

The decline was gradual. Turkish forces, dominant in the midsixteenth century, suffered numerous reverses with only an occasional victory, from the midseventeenth century on.

Military Decline

Under the first ten sultans, the Ottoman Turks had been an aggressive military power, open to technological innovation and improvement. The *janissaries*, the elite of the Ottoman army, dominated the battlefield. Turkish generals were the equal of the best Austrian, Spanish, and French field commanders. The sultan himself commanded his armies in the field.

By 1650 Turkish weapons were outmoded. Within the *janissary* corps, corruption and nepotism were rife. Instead of seeking battle, the *janissaries* sought comfort, wealth, and political influence. Not only did they occasionally make and unmake sultans, they also blocked all attempts to reform and modernize the army. At the very time that Austrian and Russian military strength increased, Turkish military strength declined.

Military Defeats

The latter half of the seventeenth century was when the gradual Turkish retreat from the Balkans began. From 1682 to 1699, the Turks were at war with Austria and Poland. The failure of the Second Siege of Vienna (17 July–12 September 1683) was the first in a series of Ottoman defeats, broken only by the reoccupation of Belgrade in 1690. The Treaty of Karlowitz (26 January 1699) awarded Hungary, Transylvania, Croatia, and Slovenia to Austria; Podolia to Poland; Azov to Russia; and Morea and Dalmatia to Venice.

During the eighteenth century, the empire lost Little Wallachia, the Banat of Temesvar, Crimea, and northern Bosnia. The early nineteenth century was marked by increasing agitation for independence in Serbia, Wallachia, and Moldavia. Between 1821 and 1830, the Greeks of Morea fought for and won their independence. In 1832 Mohammed Ali Pasha, governor of Egypt, rebelled against the sultan. The success of the Egyptian forces further underscored the declining state of the Ottoman military.

Military Reforms

Faced with the constant threat of rebellion from within, and the constant threat of Austrian and Russian aggression, the Ottoman government attempted to reform and modernize its army. Previous attempts at military reform during the reign of Selim III (1789–1807) had been blocked by conservative factions within the government and by the *janissaries*. In 1826, Mahmud II (1808–39) disbanded both the *janissary* corps and the *sipahi* units and ordered the organization of a new army. In the 1830s, a Prussian military mission was active in Turkey, and, as a result, the new Turkish army had a definite Prussian look.

The Fall of the Ottoman Empire

The Ottoman Empire, on the verge of dissolution in 1833, enjoyed a brief period of renewed vigor. The outbreak of war with Russia in October 1853 found the Turks allied with the British and French in the Crimean War. At the Congress of Paris (25 February–30 March 1856) the Turks were accepted as members of the "Concert of Europe." On 15 April 1856, Great Britain, France, and Austria signed a treaty guaranteeing Turkish sovereignty. From 1856 to 1877, the empire enjoyed more than twenty years of relative tranquility.

The Young Turks

In 1877 the Ottoman Empire was once again at war with Russia. The war ended with Serbia, Montenegro, and Romania independent. In 1881, France seized Tunis, and in 1882, Britain occupied Egypt. During the last decades of the nineteenth century, rebellions flared up in Crete and Armenia. In the Balkans, the various ethnic groups fought each other when not fighting the Turks.

In 1896, company- and field-grade officers stationed in Macedonia formed a secret political organization, the Young Turks. The majority of these officers had been trained in foreign military schools or the Turkish military schools established in the 1870s with Prussian help. In 1906, officers of the Third Army, including Enver Pasha, staged a coup, which failed. On 5 July 1908, the Young Turks mounted another coup, which was successful. The Young Turks restored the Constitution of 1876 and called parliament. The reactionary sultan, Abdul Hamid, was later deposed, and his brother Mohammed V enthroned (1910).

The establishment of parliamentary government, and the attempted reform of the empire, proved futile. In 1908, Bulgaria declared itself independent. Rebellion in Albania, and Serbian and Bulgarian victories during the First Balkan War (1912), removed the last Balkan province from Turkish control. Mounting fears of Russia, the pro-German attitude of Enver Pasha, and the need for a European ally, drove the Young Turks closer to Germany. On 2 August 1914 Germany and the Ottoman Empire signed a secret military alliance. By 4 November 1914 the Turks were once again at war.

World War I

During the First World War, the Turks again proved their fighting prowess. At Gallipoli, Turkish tenacity and bravery won the day. In 1916, Turkish arms also proved victorious against the British in Mesopotamia. Despite the bravery of the Turkish soldier, however, Turkish forces were everywhere in retreat by early 1917. By 4 October 1918, the Turkish army was finished.

The Treaty of Sèvres (20 August 1919) was a humiliation for the Turks. The British, in effect, controlled Constantinople and the government. A large portion of eastern Anatolia had been incorporated into the Armenian Republic, and Greek troops occupied Smyrna and threatened all of western Anatolia, with the blessings of the British government. Gen. Mustafa Kemal, the hero of Gallipoli, broke with the Ottoman government and established a rival (Nationalist) government at Ankara. The Nationalists, led by Mustafa Kemal (Ataturk), eventually united the Turkish nation, drove out the Greek occupation forces, and won a revised peace treaty from the allies (Treaty of Lausanne, 1923). On 1 November 1922, the sultanate was abolished, and with it, the Ottoman Empire.

LAWRENCE D. HIGGINS

SEE ALSO: Byzantine Empire; Eugene, Prince of Savoy-Carignan; Genghis Khan; History, Early Modern Military; Kemal, Mustafa (Ataturk); Moghul Empire; Mongol Conquests; Peter the Great; Russia, Expansion of; Spanish Empire; Turkey; Turkic Empire; World War I.

Bibliography

Barber, N. 1973. *The sultans*. New York: Simon and Schuster.

Bradford, E. 1968. *The sultan's admiral: The life of Barbarossa*. New York: Harcourt, Brace and World.

Coles, P. 1968. *The Ottoman impact on Europe*. London: Thames and Hudson.

Davison, R. H. 1968. *Turkey*. Englewood Cliffs, N.J.: Prentice-Hall.

Langer, W. L., and K. R. Blake. 1932. The rise of the Ottoman Turks and its historical background. *American Historical Review* 37:468–505.

Riggs, C. T., trans. 1954. *Kritovoulos: History of Mehmed the Conqueror*. Princeton, N.J.: Princeton Univ. Press.

Merriman, R. B. 1944. *Suleiman the Magnificent*. Cambridge, Mass.: Harvard Univ. Press.

Miller, B. 1941. *The Palace School of Mohammed the Conqueror*. Cambridge, Mass.: Harvard Univ. Press.

Rustow, D. A. 1959. The army and the founding of the Turkish Republic. *World Politics* 11:513–52.

Shaw, S. J. 1965. The origins of Ottoman military reform. *Journal of Modern History* 37:291–306.

Vucinich, W. S. 1965. *The Ottoman Empire*. Princeton, N.J.: Princeton Univ. Press.

Wittek, P. 1938. *The rise of the Ottoman Empire*. London: Royal Asiatic Society.